An Introduction to
Social Psychology

An Introduction to
Social Psychology
Global Perspectives

James Alcock & Stan Sadava

Los Angeles | London | New Delhi
Singapore | Washington DC

Los Angeles | London | New Delhi
Singapore | Washington DC

SAGE Publications Ltd
1 Oliver's Yard
55 City Road
London EC1Y 1SP

SAGE Publications Inc.
2455 Teller Road
Thousand Oaks, California 91320

SAGE Publications India Pvt Ltd
B 1/I 1 Mohan Cooperative Industrial Area
Mathura Road
New Delhi 110 044

SAGE Publications Asia-Pacific Pte Ltd
3 Church Street
#10-04 Samsung Hub
Singapore 049483

Editor: Michael Carmichael
Development editor: Christopher Kingston
Editorial assistant: Keri Dickens
Production editor: Imogen Roome
Copyeditor: Bryan Campbell
Indexer: Martin Hargreaves
Marketing manager: Alison Borg
Cover design: Wendy Scott
Typeset by: C&M Digitals (P) Ltd, Chennai, India
Printed in India at Replika Press Pvt Ltd

Library of Congress Control Number: 2013956749

British Library Cataloguing in Publication data

A catalogue record for this book is available from
the British Library

ISBN 978-1-4462-5618-3
ISBN 978-1-4462-5619-0 (pbk)

Dedicated to the memory of
David William ('Bill') Carment
Friend ◊ Colleague ◊ Scholar

CONTENTS

Contents

Contents

PREFACE

Welcome to the first edition of *An Introduction to Social Psychology: Global Perspectives*. This textbook is directed to students taking a first course in social psychology. While the majority of our readers will have some background in general psychology and many of them will go on to major in psychology, others will be enrolled in other disciplines such as sociology, anthropology, communication studies, criminology and the health sciences, and even others will be taking social psychology as an elective, out of interest. We have written the book with all of you in mind.

Marshall McLuhan described our modern world as a 'global village'. We no longer live in a world of homogeneous nations kept separate by geography and language. We travel and work across borders, collaborate in business and research across borders, watch films from many countries, appreciate artists from all over the world and communicate globally through social media. We can text or email or Skype someone halfway around the world as quickly and as easily as someone just across the street. Multinational corporations have spawned a host of internationally recognized brand names, and whether in China or Peru, Lichtenstein or Scotland, consumers are drawn to many of the same leading global products. Many nations are becoming de facto multicultural; there is no longer one simple 'prototype' that describes a citizen of Britain or Canada or Australia, the Netherlands, USA, France or many other countries. With hundreds of television channels to choose from, programmes are now available from around the globe, in many different languages. Because of the immediacy of modern media, geography is no longer a barrier: Through television and the Internet we are transported in real time to the latest battle scene wherever it may be; to the struggles of rescuers to free survivors of an earthquake; to the United Nations to listen to a speech from a world leader; to a sporting event half way round the world; to a Royal wedding or a famous festival or the trial of a notorious crime boss. Indeed, McLuhan was right; we do live in a global village.

We have written this book from the perspective of this globalized world, and we have written it for students all over the world. The historical dominance of the United States in social psychological research and theorizing is undeniable, and we document this in the introduction. However, social psychology is now a thriving discipline in many areas of the world, including the United Kingdom and Europe, Japan, India, Australia and New Zealand, and Israel, and it has taken root almost everywhere around the globe. What does this mean for a textbook in social psychology? We have, of course, addressed mainstream social psychology reflecting the major currents in the discipline, much of this coming from the United States. But we also have sought to present social psychology as a dynamic international enterprise with relevance to people in every culture. Thus, we have included high quality research conducted by social psychologists in many countries, and we have paid close attention to the replication of major studies in different cultures. We also have taken pains to be up to date, and the reader will find many cutting-edge references from recent years, in addition of course to the classics which still are highly relevant.

We also discuss some new ideas in social psychology and the research that they have generated. For example, we acknowledge the growing importance of neuroscience as a means of expanding knowledge about social behaviour by referring to such research throughout the book. We address the growing influence of electronic communication and social networking on social relationships. We discuss studies of differences in values across cultures, and focus on both the explanatory power and the limits of a distinction between individualist and collectivist values as they bear on the results of classic research. We discuss the dual-process model of thinking developed by Nobel Laureate Daniel Kahneman, and show how it becomes relevant to the discussion of a number of topics throughout the book. We consider the perils of self-esteem that is too positive. We introduce topics from the so-called 'positive psychology approach', such as values and character, and forgiveness. Our discussion of social psychology in the courtroom takes heed of the considerable differences between nations and cultures. Hybrid mediation–arbitration models of conflict resolution are discussed, and we address current problems of terrorism. And we include two chapters not often found in social psychology textbooks – one devoted to the social psychology of language and communication, and the other to large-scale, collective behaviours.

We begin the book with an overall introduction to social psychology which will give the reader an idea of how social psychology has evolved to where it is today. Then we turn to a set of topics generally considered as fundamental and which relate primarily to the individual – how we think about, and make sense of, our social world, how we understand ourselves as 'social animals', how our attitudes and values are formed, and how they relate to our actions. Next, we discuss how the influence of others often leads to changes in our attitudes and our behaviours, and how we communicate with others, verbally, non-verbally and 'virtually' through social media. We explore how we become attracted to others and form relationships, and 'what is this thing called love?' Then we move to the study of conflict between people and groups of people, and to research about the psychological roots of both helping and harming one another.

The next series of chapters deal more closely with the 'social' side of social psychology. We will explore what happens in groups, how our identity is formed within the groups, and how groups find leaders and make decisions. We have included at this point an analysis of prejudice, for prejudices are very much tied to groups and the identities that groups generate. From relatively small numbers of people in groups, we turn to larger collections of people – masses, crowds – and their collective behaviours that at times seem irrational. Finally, the reader will see social psychologists emerge from the lab into the courtroom and the clinic, as we explore social psychology in action through a chapter on law and justice and another on health and well-being.

Social psychology is far from static; it shifts with changing circumstances and with new findings and developing theory. It encompasses both a basic research focus, seeking to understand the fundamental processes of human social behaviour, and an applied focus, undertaking to apply our knowledge for the betterment of people. We have intended our book to represent the dynamic nature of our discipline, from both of those perspectives, with the goal of serving the pedagogical needs of our colleagues while capturing the interest of students around the world.

ACKNOWLEDGEMENTS

First of all, we want to thank Michael Carmichael, Christopher Kingston, Amy Jarrold and Keri Dickens at SAGE Publications. We also wish to express our appreciation to Angela Book, Gordon Hodson, Danielle Sirianni Molnar and Mike Ashton for their helpful comments. In addition, we thank the reviewers, named below, for their thoughtful and constructive advice:

Dr Anat Bardi, Royal Holloway, University of London
Dr Alexander John Bridger, University of Huddersfield
Dr Gillian Bruce, University of the West of Scotland
Dr Kathy Carnelley, University of Southampton
Dr Alex Gillespie, The London School of Economics
Dr Lewis Goodings, Roehampton University
Professor Carolyn Hafer, Brock University
Dr Joe Hinds, Sheffield Hallam University
Dr Tim Hopthrow, University of Kent
Professor Cheuk Ng, Athabasca University
Professor Paddy O'Donnell, University of Glasgow
Dr Victoria Scaife, University of East Anglia
Dr Dan Shepperd, Aston University
Dr Fay Short, Bangor University
Dr Gavin Sullivan, Leeds Metropolitan University
Dr Alison Torn, Leeds Trinity University
Professor Kathleen Vohs, University of Minnesota
Dr Glenn Williams, Nottingham Trent University

And we express our gratitude to Karen Hanley and Maria Becker (our spouses), who in addition to providing much-appreciated advice, encouragement, and outright assistance, exhibited outstanding patience when family time was often redirected to book time.

James Alcock and Stan Sadava

GUIDED TOUR

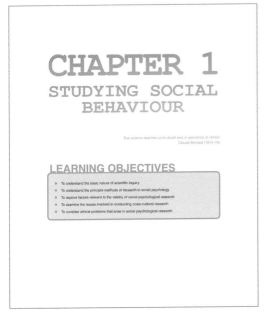

CHAPTER 1
STUDYING SOCIAL BEHAVIOUR

True science teaches us to doubt and, in ignorance, to refrain
Claude Bernard (1813–78)

LEARNING OBJECTIVES

- To understand the basic nature of scientific inquiry
- To understand the principle methods of research in social psychology
- To explore factors relevant to the validity of social psychological research
- To examine the issues involved in conducting cross-cultural research
- To consider ethical problems that arise in social psychological research

of antiquity, provided the foundation for medieval scholastic thought, and great importance was attached to the belief that pure reason could validate and illuminate what was already accepted as true on the basis of religious faith. Reason that contradicted dogma was presumed to be in error.

Modern science began when Copernicus (1473–1543) challenged the prevailing dogma about the earth and its place in the heavens. For many centuries, it had been accepted without question by Western scholars that the sun revolved about the earth, a belief consistent both with everyday experience and with the pronouncements of Aristotle and Judeo-Christian scripture. Even though astronomers had long recognized that the movement of the planets did not fit well with this geocentric belief, it was Copernicus who chose to trust data over dogma. In 1543, he published *De Revolutionibus Orbium Caelestium*, in which he proclaimed that not only is the Earth not the centre of the universe, but that it revolves around the sun. Even though other astronomers soon adopted his improved techniques for computing planetary positions, they nonetheless ignored and even ridiculed his heliocentric views. And later on, when Galileo (1564–1642) vigorously promoted Copernicus' theory, he was prosecuted by the Roman Catholic Church and forced to recant. In the long run, however, this nascent scientific notion survived because Copernican ideas accorded with observation, whereas dogma did not. The scientific revolution was born. Sadly, science continues to be vilified in some quarters by those still steeped in dogma. Think for example of fundamentalists of various religious orientations who continue to rail against the theory of evolution.

The scientific revolution was distinguished by the importance it placed both upon curiosity and hypothesizing on the one hand and upon testing hypothesis against data on the other (Boulding, 1980). Theory is essential to guide research, to organize its data into a coherent structure and to provide ideas for testing, for without theory, there is nothing to test. And without testing, there is no way to distinguish fact from fantasy.

Science is much more than laboratories and equipment and journals and books. It is first and foremost a *process*, a method of thinking about and exploring the world around us. Having developed across several centuries, it offers us the best method we have for finding fact and avoiding error. It involves not just observation, but *systematic* observation guided by consideration of possible sources of bias in data collection and interpretation. Notwithstanding some of the concerns raised by critics of experimental social psychology, as discussed in the introductory chapter, the scientific method is as vital in social psychological research as it is in physics or chemistry or biology, even though, as we shall see, it is not nearly so straightforward to apply to the study of social behaviour as it is to inanimate objects and biological processes.

> **KEY POINT:** While our senses generally serve us well, the patterns that we find can sometimes mislead us. Science is a systematic approach to understanding the world that aims to minimize bias in what we observe through data collection and interpretation.

MEASUREMENT

Before we can proceed very far in any scientific inquiry, we first need to be able to define just what it is that we are studying and then develop methods to measure it. We generally take measurement pretty much for granted. We have no difficulty measuring height or weight or how far an automobile can go on a litre of fuel. And whether we measure in inches or centimetres or pounds or kilogrammes, we trust our tape measures and scales to give us reliable information. But just what is 'measurement'? What does it mean to say that an object is three metres away from us? Or two feet? Or a furlong, or a league? What does a metre or a foot or a furlong or a league mean? Such units are not an inherent part of nature; they are socially defined. Thus, measurement is much more than just the assignment of numbers to various quantities of length or volume or weight; the units are based on a social accord, on agreements among people in a particular society or culture. You could of course invent your own system of measurements, but when you try to buy a *quarlog* of gasoline or a pair of size *muffigle* shoes, you will get nowhere. Measurement systems are the products of social agreement.

19

Learning objectives
Each chapter sets out clearly at its beginning what key information you should soon understand, so you can easily track your progress.

Key points
Throughout the chapters, Key Points offer markers of what important information you should take away from the previous section, and help you navigate quickly to the most important information.

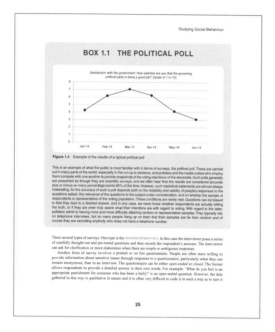

Boxes

The most interesting studies and debates in each chapter are presented in extended boxes to give you a deeper picture of some of the most important issues in social psychology.

Summary

Review the contents of each chapter by reading the Summary, a clearly laid out and easy-to-read reminder of the most important information you've read.

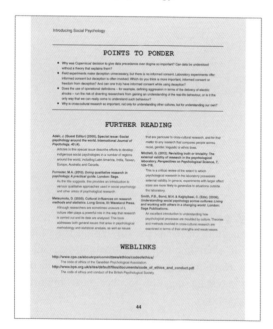

Points to ponder

These open-ended questions at the end of each chapter aim to inspire deeper reflection and could be starting points for your own essays or research.

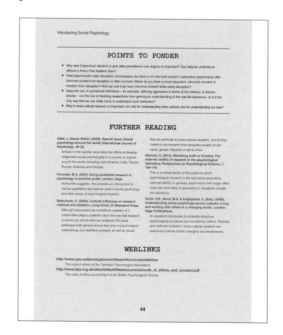

Weblinks

Useful websites are listed here, enabling you to go online and quickly check out important organizations or sources of information related to the chapter you've just read.

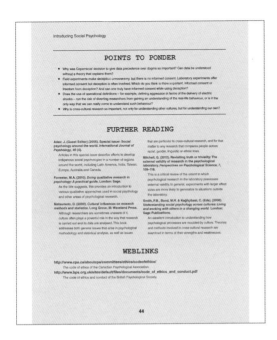

Further reading

If a chapter has inspired you to read more widely on that topic, the Further Reading section suggests some interesting and important books or articles you can look at.

Glossary

Definitions of key terms are collected at the back of the book, so if you're drowning in jargon or not sure of the meaning of a particular phrase, you can easily find an explanation here.

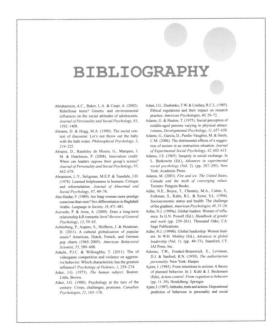

Bibliography

The extensive Bibliography offers you a library of further reading sources to deepen your understanding of seminal psychology literature or find sources for your own social psychology research project.

COMPANION WEBSITE

In addition to the wealth of information and activities contained in this book, further useful resources for both lecturers and students are available from the companion website. Simply head to study.sagepub.com/alcocksadava to discover the following resources:

For students

Quizzes for each chapter with both true-false and multiple-choice questions to test your understanding

Essay questions of the sort you might see on your exams, allowing you to practise or just think critically about important issues

Flashcards to help you learn the definitions of key terms

For instructors

An instructor's manual offering suggestions for activities, projects and multimedia that you can incorporate into your teaching

PowerPoint slides that can be used in lectures or edited to fit your needs

An extensive testbank of 100 multiple-choice questions for every chapter

PART I

INTRODUCING SOCIAL PSYCHOLOGY

INTRODUCING SOCIAL PSYCHOLOGY

… an individual who is unsocial naturally and not accidentally is either beneath our notice or more than human. … Anyone who either cannot lead the common life or is so self-sufficient as not to need to, and therefore does not partake of society, is either a beast or a god.

Aristotle, *Politics*

Our need to be with others has not changed across the 2300 years since Aristotle wrote those words; we are, as he maintained, social animals. We choose to live and work and play in the company of others; we seek diversion through the books, movies and songs created by others; we share our ideas and argue our opinions with others. We team up to erect buildings, build dams, fight fires, and defend ourselves from danger. And although we may enjoy short periods of being alone at times of our choosing, it is the rare person who prefers perpetual solitude. Indeed, forced solitude – solitary confinement – is the ultimate punishment for those who misbehave in prison.

Because we are social animals, we live our lives within a social fabric, and just as it has been said that 'fish don't know water exists till beached' (McLuhan, 1972, p.91), we are so inured to that social fabric that we are somewhat blind as to how much it shapes and regulates our lives. However, use your imagination and step outside that fabric for a few moments: You are marooned on a tiny desert island with no hope of early rescue. In many ways, things are perfect on the island: The climate is wonderful, food is abundant, the sea is warm and inviting and there are no wild animals to fear. Only one thing is missing: other people. Think about how your normal habits might change. Since there is no one around, do you bother anymore about your appearance? Do you still cover your mouth when you cough? Do you organize your life around three meals a day?

As time goes on and you contemplate your existence, you realize that even though you are alone, a great deal of your activity and thought continues to reflect the society that reared you. You think in words, in your mother tongue, even though language is no longer a means of communication because there is no one with whom to communicate. You brush your teeth with a homemade toothbrush, a habit you feel is worth continuing for the good of your teeth. You fashion a fork to use for eating, for you find it unpleasant to eat certain foods with your fingers, again reflecting the particular culture in which you grew up. You stand on a hill and sing to the sea, reciting the songs of the society that spawned you. You come to realize that you cannot escape, and do not want to escape the social forces that have shaped you; you have internalized them. In other words, the people in your life are still having a considerable influence on you, and you conform to the influence even though they are not there, and you may never see them again. Yet, you miss the treasured people in your life, and you cannot shake the feelings of loneliness. (Recall the 2000 movie, *Cast Away*, starring Tom Hanks, where he becomes marooned on a desert island and substitutes for human interaction by talking to a volleyball, 'Wilson', that he has decorated to look like a human face).

And then one day, a small raft washes up on the shore, carrying a survivor of a shipwreck. At first, it is wonderful to have the company of another human being. However, you gradually realize that this person's arrival is going to bring some changes to your life. While you like to play your makeshift bongos all night long and sleep until midday, the new arrival wants quiet after the sun goes down. For the first time, you begin to feel embarrassed about your small and cluttered hut as you watch your companion construct a much nicer and more comfortable dwelling. Gradually, you begin to resent the way this newcomer is 'taking over', and you cannot help but think that since you were here first, you should have a greater say over what happens on the island. Questions of power and privilege and social comparison start to bother you, just as they did back home. The need for rules, for a primitive social structure, becomes apparent in order to avoid conflicts that could make living together on such a small island very unpleasant. It becomes obvious that a social structure, some agreed-upon rules to coordinate and even govern behaviour, is essential to living in harmony. You will have to negotiate with that other person to bring this about.

And so, in every society, everywhere, across all time, a social fabric with its rules and roles and norms has developed to govern social interaction. And every individual in every society, everywhere and across all time, has grown up learning those rules and norms and generally living by them. And in every society, there is a distribution of power. Some are born into power and privilege; others work to acquire it; while still others seize it and hold onto it by force. And individuals everywhere and in every era have differentiated themselves into groups on the basis of common characteristics or beliefs or interests – families, circles of friends, gangs, ethnic conclaves, nations – in order to further and protect their interests. Groups, in turn, often fall into conflict with other groups, and such conflict leads to pressures within each group to ensure that its members work jointly to serve the group interest.

We are not the only species in which individuals form bonds and live in groups, but we are unique in the complexity and diversity of our social lives. Moreover, we often consider our relationships with others to be the central focus of our lives. This book explores these complexities – how we think, act and relate with respect to others.

WHAT SOCIAL PSYCHOLOGY IS AND IS NOT

In North America, social psychology has long had an individualistic orientation, focusing primarily on how the individual is influenced by other people. On the other hand, as will be discussed later, European social psychologists have taken a more group-oriented perspective. In the individualist approach, social psychology has traditionally been defined as the discipline that sets out *to understand how the thoughts, feelings and behaviours of individuals are influenced by the actual, imagined or implied presence of others* (Allport, 1935). What does this definition tell us? First, social psychologists study not only actual, observable behaviour, but also inferences about people's inner lives: how they feel; their attitudes, opinions and ideologies; how they form impressions and try to make sense of their world. Second, human experience is understood in terms of the influence of other people. Obviously, social influence is not the only kind – we may be affected by our physical health, the weather, what we have learned, brain and nervous system processes, psychotic and drug states, hormones, the state of the economy, and what we have eaten. However, social psychologists focus on the vital role of social influences and relationships. Finally, the definition tells us that people are influenced by other people, even those who are not present. We are aware of belonging to particular family, occupational and cultural groups and of liking, loving or feeling responsible towards certain people in our lives. These groups and individuals profoundly influence our thoughts and actions.

To better appreciate the range of phenomena social psychologists study, consider the following examples:

- In a competitive economy, a job interview can be decisive. Social psychologists have studied how *first impressions* are formed and how people act to influence or '*manage*' *the impression* that others have of them.
- Amnesty International has documented the routine use of torture (or 'enhanced interrogation') in many countries. For the most part, torturers are not unusually sadistic by nature, but simply *obedient* to the instructions of authority. A series of important experiments has been conducted on *obedience to authority*.
- A substantial proportion of all marriages in Western countries will eventually end in divorce. *Social attraction* and the dynamics of *intimate relationships* are areas of current research.
- Countries such as Canada, Belgium and India have more than one official language, while, in the age of globalization, millions of migrants have brought their languages into officially unilingual nations such as the United States and Germany, and business is now conducted globally in a multiplicity of languages. There has been extensive research on the social psychological aspects of *bilingualism*.
- It is not surprising that among the billions of inhabitants of our planet there are many disagreements about who can live where, what rules are to be followed, and how the earth's resources should be exploited or protected. How individuals and groups and nations can learn to constructively deal with *conflict* is another subject researched extensively by social psychologists.
- Many trials hinge on the credibility of a key witness. Social psychologists have studied *eyewitness testimony* and other aspects of the legal system.
- Genocide and terrorism continue to erupt in various parts of the world. The joint Canadian Psychological Association–American Psychological Association *Ethnopolitical Warfare Initiative* studies why people participate in genocide and terrorist attacks and why some people risk their lives to rescue others from genocide. The project also works to develop interventions to help prevent or de-escalate ethnic conflicts (Suedfeld, 2000).

As you can see, social psychologists study a wide range of social phenomena. Some of their concerns involve practical problems: Why don't patients do what their physicians recommend? What kinds of decisions do groups make and can the decisions be improved? Why do people persist in stereotyping males, females, professors, students and ethnic groups, regardless of the realities? Other equally important questions are more theoretical: What consistencies and inconsistencies are there between people's attitudes and their behaviour? What biases operate in the perception of cause and effect in interpersonal situations? How can we explain aggression in terms of social learning?

To clarify what social psychology is about, let us compare it with other areas of psychology and other related disciplines. Social psychology shares a focus on the individual with other areas of psychology. In particular, its interests overlap with the study of personality. However, the study of personality focuses primarily on factors operating within individuals and emphasizes *individual* differences in the ways that people think, feel and act. Social psychology, by contrast, looks at the situational factors that cause people in general to behave in certain ways. Thus, for example, personality psychologists study the *characteristics* of people who tend to behave aggressively; social psychologists focus more on the *situations* in which people are likely to behave aggressively. Of course, both personal and environmental factors determine behaviour, and students of social psychology must understand both types of variables.

Social psychology also shares many areas of interest with other social sciences, especially sociology (the study of society and social institutions) and anthropology (the study of human culture). Perhaps the major differences are found in each discipline's basic *unit of analysis* and *level of explanation*. The usual focus of study in these other social sciences is the large group, institution or custom (e.g., the school, the family, social norms and social class structure). The *rate* or typical pattern of behaviour in a population is also of concern. Sociologists and anthropologists are not interested in how one individual differs from another, but rather in how one *category* of individual differs from another (Macionis, Clarke & Gerber, 1994) and they seek to explain phenomena in terms of external characteristics such as social class mobility, customs of parental discipline, and the distribution of power in a society – for example, are people with postgraduate education less likely than others to endorse right-wing politicians? By contrast, social psychology generally focuses on the individual, or at most the small group. Social psychologists generally explain the behaviour of individuals in terms of specific situations as well as psychological processes such as attitudes, emotional states or perception of cause and effect. They also are interested in norms and class structure, of course, but the focus is on how they affect the individual, as in the vignette that opens this chapter.

SOCIAL PSYCHOLOGY YESTERDAY AND TODAY

While social psychology is relatively young as a discipline, its roots lie deep in the history of Western thought. Like all of psychology, social psychology emerged from the work of philosophers. Plato was deeply concerned with the nature of leadership and the most desirable form of government, while Aristotle thought and wrote about the nature of friendship. English empiricist philosophers such as John Stuart Mill and Thomas Hobbes attributed all social behaviour to the search for pleasure and avoidance of pain (hedonism) or to the need for power. The 19th-century French philosopher Gabriel Tarde wrote that 'society is imitation'. In other words, people have an innate tendency to imitate, which causes them to conform in order to live together. While all these themes continue to be of interest, social psychologists have turned from 'simple and sovereign theories' that explain social behaviour in terms of a single variable, such as power, pleasure or imitation, to more complex explanations.

Social psychology did not emerge dramatically through the declaration of a doctrine, a scientific breakthrough, or the influence of a personality such as Charles Darwin or Sigmund Freud. Rather, it evolved over several decades, marked by several key events. Interest in social psychological theory and research began to grow in the late 19th century. Its roots formed in several quarters: Philosopher William James, often referred to as the father of American psychology, identified the importance of the social self as well as other social psychological variables in his seminal work, *Principles of Psychology* (1890). Alfred Vierkandt's (1896) *Naturvölker und Kulturvölker: Ein Beitrag zur Sozialpsychologie (Natural People and Cultural People: A Contribution to Social Psychology)* was the first book dedicated to social psychology (Rudmin, 1985). Baldwin's (1897) *Social and Ethical Interpretations of Mental Development: A Study in Social Psychology*, Tarde's (1898) *Études de Psychologie Sociale*, and Ellwood's (1899) *Some Prolegomena to Social Psychology* were also among the earliest social psychology books (Rudmin, 1985). In Germany, a group of scholars based in philosophy identified themselves as 'folk psychologists', in the sense that they set out to study the 'collective mind', the rather vague but powerful concept that individuals think as members of a larger collective and that a general way of thinking characterizes whole groups or societies of people. Wilhelm Wundt, generally recognized as the founder of experimental psychology, was among them, and his ideas were summarized in his (1904) *Völkerpsychologie (Folk psychology)* (Danziger, 1983). The French scholar Gustave LeBon argued in *Psychologie des foules (Psychology of crowds)* (1895) that crowds often think and act as one, transcending the individual, a notion also addressed by English psychologist William McDougall in *The Group Mind* (1920).

While psychologists in Western Europe and the United States played fundamental roles in the formation of the new discipline, interest in social psychology was also taking root in various countries around the world. For example, a folk psychology focusing primarily on the analysis of language and social habits began developing in Russia from the mid-19th century, and in 1896, A.M. Bobrishchev-Pushkin published his empirical studies of juries and the psychological factors involved in their decision-making (Strickland, 1991). In 1906, Tokutani's *Social Psychology* brought the basic concepts of this new discipline to Japan (Hotta & Strickland, 1991).

Social psychological interest began to grow during the early 20th century – in Germany, as an outgrowth of Wilhelm Wundt's work; in France following the lead of Gabriel Tarde and others (Lubek, 1990); in Great Britain as an extension of evolutionary theory to social interaction (Collier, Minton & Reynolds, 1991); and in the United States, through the research of John Dewey and colleagues at the University of Chicago (Rudmin, 1985).

A pivotal event in the evolution of what became social psychology was the emergence of experimentation. Floyd Allport (1924) argued in his textbook that social psychology would not become a science until it began to conduct experiments. Norman Triplett (1898) is often credited (erroneously, as we shall see later) with the first experiment in social psychology. He was interested in bicycle racing, and set out to test the popular notion that cyclists ride faster when paced by other cyclists than when cycling alone. Triplett proposed that the presence of another cyclist aroused a 'competitive instinct' that aroused a 'nervous energy' (today called arousal) which led to faster cycling. In one of his experiments, children were given fishing rods to be used to turn silk bands around a drum. When competing with another child, some children were faster than those who were performing alone. However, some were slower in competition, and Triplett concluded that these children were overstimulated by the competition. In subsequent chapters, you will learn how limited this experiment was, but it was a valiant early attempt.

Note that while social psychology was rooted in Europe, it flowered in the United States, particularly as some prominent scholars fled from Germany and Austria during the era of Nazi rule. While social psychologists in the United States were, and still are to some extent, recognized as taking a leading role in the development of social psychology, partly as result of this, the discipline became rather unicultural and even ethnocentric, as though this one culture could represent all humanity and experimentation with samples of first-year American university students could be generalized to people everywhere. In recent years, many social psychologists have recognized these limitations, and have collaborated with and learned from colleagues in other countries. The American Psychological Association has an International Psychology division, with well in excess of one thousand members.

Given this widespread interest in social psychology, it appears somewhat ethnocentric that North American social psychology texts typically credit the beginnings of social psychology to two textbooks published in the United States in 1908: *An Introduction to Social Psychology* by William McDougall, a psychologist, and *Social Psychology: An Outline and Sourcebook* by E.A. Ross, a sociologist. That such credit should go to McDougall is especially curious, given that neither he nor those who reviewed his book considered it to be a treatise on social psychology, despite its title; it was actually dedicated to the discussion of instinct theories (Rudmin, 1985).

In 1924, Floyd Allport published the first textbook based on empirical research. This highly influential book presented a scientific social psychology that was psychological, as opposed to sociological (Parkovnick, 1992), established the individual as the basic unit of analysis and started social psychology on a scientific pathway (Minton, 1992). Allport viewed social psychology as a science of how behaviour is influenced by the presence and reactions of other people, and discussed such topics as conformity and how people recognize emotional states in others.

Since those early years, there have been several broad trends in the history of social psychology, all of which continue to the present. In the 1920s and 1930s, a dominant concern was the measurement and study of attitudes and related concepts, such as stereotypes. Later, work began on group-related phenomena – for example, Muzafer Sherif's studies of the influence of social norms on perception and action (Sherif, 1936), Kurt Lewin's work on the effects of styles of leadership on group functioning (Lewin, Lippitt & White, 1939), and the research of John Dollard, Leonard Doob and others into the effects of frustration on aggression (Dollard, Doob, et al., 1939). The Second World War generated research on topics relating to politics and combat – group morale, leadership and propaganda. By the 1950s, there was a renewed interest in attitudes, evident in research on persuasion by Carl Hovland and colleagues (Hovland et al., 1957) and on prejudice and personality (Adorno, Frenkel-Brunswick, Levinson & Sanford, 1950; Allport, F.H., 1954). Others studied the relationship between social behaviour and individual differences in the need for achievement and social approval and persuasibility.

The 1950s also marked the appearance of two seminal books that are still influential. Leon Festinger's (1957) *A Theory of Cognitive Dissonance* provided an explanation of how people deal with inconsistencies between attitude and behaviour. In the following year, Fritz Heider's (1958) *The Psychology of Interpersonal Relations* outlined a psychology based on how we infer what causes people to act as they do. In the same decade, the laboratory experiment became the predominant research method (Adair, 1980).

In the 1960s, social psychology expanded dramatically in scope. Social psychologists directed their attention to new areas of research – why we sometimes display excessive obedience to authority, how we make judgements about other people's behaviour, how we negotiate and resolve conflicts, how groups make decisions involving risk, how we attract and make friends, and why bystanders often fail to help in emergencies. In Canada, Wallace Lambert, Robert Gardner and others launched groundbreaking research into the social and psychological aspects of bilingualism. In that highly politicized decade, research also continued in areas of social concern, including aggression, prejudice and attitude change.

By the late 1960s, a distinctive social psychology, with its own areas of expertise, began to come of age in Europe. Recall Allport's (1924) definition of social psychology; it is focused on the individual. However, the North American focus on the individual as the basic unit of study and the reliance upon the laboratory as the mainstay research setting removed from consideration a range of social psychological phenomena associated with groups and their interaction, leading one American social psychologist to refer to 'the disappearance of the *social* from American social psychology' (Greenwood, 2004). European social psychologists have in general paid more attention to cultural and group phenomena, and social psychologists such as Serge Moscovici in France and Henri Tajfel in Great Britain worked to develop a discipline not steeped in the individualistic value system of the US (Moghaddam, 1987). Of course, Europe consists of a diverse set of nations, cultures and languages, and the cultural diversity that characterizes many of the formerly homogeneous European nations is reflected in a diversity of methods and approaches to social psychology (Smith, 2005). Perhaps as a reflection of such diversity, and as a European consciousness took shape that somewhat transcended national and ethnic boundaries, European social psychology extended its focus to international collaboration and the development of theory and research across nations and cultures. While social psychology in the United States and Canada has focused on the individual, particularly in terms of cognitions and attitudes, social psychology in Europe has studied processes within and between groups – how we derive our identity from our groups and cultures; how minorities can influence majorities; intergroup relations; social control; and the social psychological aspects of political economy and ideology (Taylor & Moghaddam, 1987). In short, Europeans by and large have advocated a more *social* social psychology, and their influence has been evident.

Several new directions have become evident over the past few decades. The first is an interest in social cognition (the study of how we 'make sense' of our social world), which has been influenced by fundamental research on cognitive processes such as memory, attention and problem-solving. The second is a growing interest in applying social psychology to areas of daily living. Social psychologists may now be found working in medicine, law, organizational management, the environment, education, sports and counselling. In the long run, these trends can only enrich social psychology and extend the validity of its theories and findings. And the emerging focus on brain research that has become so productive in other areas of psychology is also opening up new opportunities in social psychology – for example, for the study of neural correlates of social cognition and the neurobiology of social interaction (Forbes & Grafman, 2013; Pfeiffer, Timmermans et al., 2013).

CULTURE, GLOBALIZATION AND SOCIAL PSYCHOLOGY

Despite its European roots and the recent emergence of a vibrant empirical social psychology in Europe, researchers from the US have dominated social psychology throughout most of its history. Indeed, Moghaddam (1987, 1990) views the US as the first of three 'worlds' in which psychologists carry out research and practice: it is the major producer of psychological knowledge. The second world is made up of the other industrialized nations, including Canada, the United Kingdom, Australia, France, Germany, Japan and Russia. In some ways the second world is as productive as the first world, but its influence is greatest among its own constituents and upon the third world.

The third world comprises the developing nations, such as India, Pakistan, China, Egypt, Nigeria, Brazil and Cuba. Of course, this collection of nations and societies is far from monolithic, differing profoundly in dominant religions and philosophies, resources and level of economic development. Social psychology is beginning to take root in these countries as well. For instance, in India's rapidly evolving social environment, there is a focus among social psychologists on relationships among individuals, but at the same time, they also acknowledge the importance in Indian society of the concept of *dharma*, seen as an inherent force within people to act in a 'proper' manner, to do one's moral duty (Dalal & Misra, 2002). In Latin America, there is also an impetus that has emerged towards a 'liberation social psychology', with a focus on the realities of political oppression and widespread poverty (Burton & Kagan, 2009).

Psychologists in all three 'worlds' are becoming more sensitive both to the relevance and appropriateness of first- and second-world psychology for societies of the third world (Moghaddam, 1987), and to the importance of 'third world' psychology as a source of new insights and ideas in our expanding discipline. A body of cross-cultural research is developing, as a growing number of collaborative studies involve social psychological experiments carried out in a number of different cultures.

Of course, while we want to understand people in their own environments, we also hope to be able to identify and understand what is universal in human social thought, emotions and behaviour. Psychological universals, those fundamental mental and behavioural aspects that are shared by human beings all over the world, are elusive – how can we know that something found in one culture, or two, or many, is universal (Norenzayan & Heine, 2005)? For instance, we will see that people in Western cultures tend see other individuals as causing their own actions – people perceive that others smile because they want to, rather than because the situation causes them to smile. Do people in other cultures think in the same way in trying to understand each other? We shall see that it is not always so. Why is this important? In the final analysis, we want to understand human nature (see Norenzayan & Heine, 2005), and humans live in many different societies with many different norms and outlooks.

There are several good reasons to extend social psychology beyond a restricted time and place. One concerns sampling. To test a given hypothesis, we must have a representative sample or we must replicate our findings with different people at different times and places. For instance, in Milgram's famous studies of obedience to authority (discussed in detail later in this textbook), will people in general obey a command to shock an innocent victim or was this a peculiarity of the participants in the research – people who lived around Yale University in the United States in the 1960s? Further, if we were to find that people in one culture are more likely to behave obediently, what is it about that culture that might explain such a difference? What may be interpreted as an excessive obedience in one time and place may seem to others as a natural and normative deference to those in authority. Moreover, the cultural background of the social psychologist may greatly influence how such a phenomenon is defined and studied.

Globalization adds urgency to the need to extend the reach and application of social psychology (Berry, 2013). Defined broadly, globalization is a process of interaction and integration among people, businesses and governments of different nations (Chiu, Gries, Torelli & Cheng, 2011). At an economic level, business has become increasingly global, and increasingly integrated trading blocs such as Europe and the Americas are smashing barriers. Conflicts and crimes in one part of the world no longer are confined by geography. For example, reverberations of the ongoing conflict in Chechnya were felt at the 2013 Boston Marathon when two militant Chechen expatriates detonated bombs at the finish line. Sports teams now include talent from all over the world: hockey players from Russia, Sweden and Czech Republic play in North American professional leagues, Argentine athletes play for the Barcelona football team, and Africans play on English teams. In cinema, movies based in Hollywood involve actors and directors from all over the world, and Bollywood films have gained worldwide popularity. Societies which seemed in the past to be rather homogeneous are now increasingly diverse in their populations. Millions of people have migrated from their home society to another, sometimes out of necessity as refugees fleeing from persecution, sometimes to join other family already there, sometimes to seek better opportunities. As business becomes increasingly multinational, even global in scope, interactions with a broad range of people from and in various countries become part of our daily lives.

Indeed, social networks such as Facebook and Twitter can transform local or national happenings into international events, as shown in the revolution which overthrew the Mubarak regime in Egypt in 2011. Demonstrations of outrage erupted across the globe in 2012 when a young woman was brutally gang-raped and murdered while riding on a bus in India, and after a young girl was shot and almost fatally wounded in Pakistan by Islamic fundamentalists because she advocated publicly for education for women.

Globalization is having a profound psychological impact. Studies in China show that many people view globalization in terms of modernization and, to some extent, Westernization, and consider participation in globalization to be a signal of people's competence (Yang et al., 2011; see also Arnett, 2002). This does not mean that the world is becoming increasingly homogeneous and Americanized; for instance, popular music is becoming more diverse with regard to pop stars and styles from different countries (Achterberg et al., 2011). Consumers gravitate to well-known commercial brands from different parts of the world – although they may resist those which are perceived to be a threat to local culture (Torelli & Cheng, 2011).

In this book, we will frequently refer to cultural consistencies and variations in various areas of social psychology. To a large extent, these variations have focused on East–West differences in individualism–collectivism, the extent to which people want to see themselves as independent or interdependent. Indeed, this dimension of culture is often equated with geographical or national differences (see Chapter 4 for a discussion of national differences in values). While interesting, even impressive, findings are reported, one overview suggests that the cultures characterized as individualistic are not as clearly distinguishable from those characterized as collectivist as has been assumed (Oyserman, Coon & Kemmelmeier, 2002). Times change, history evolves and globalization itself begins to blur the boundaries between cultures.

We must also approach culture in a more sophisticated manner. If culture consists of shared schemas, social norms, and ways of looking at the world, then most if not all societies in our globalized world are essentially multicultural, and all of us share more than one set of cultural elements. For instance, your own parents may come from different cultural backgrounds and you may be further influenced by friends, travel and interest in different people. Further, we belong to several collectivities apart from our nationality, which, while sharing some commonalities, also have different and distinctive 'cultures'. Cohen (2009) argues that, in addition to our nationality and our ethnicity, religious involvement and affiliation, region of the country, and socioeconomic class all account for a substantial proportion of what is shared and transmitted in social norms, values, beliefs and predispositions to act. For instance, you may be from a Caucasian background, belong to a working-class family, identify yourself as an Anglican, and live in Queensland, Australia; all of this combines, along with your nationality, to form your cultural heritage. Any one of these elements may distinguish you from someone from a different class, regional or religious background in Australia. Someone from Barcelona may, at different times, identify himself or herself as Roman Catholic, working class, Catalan, Spanish or European. Moreover, your co-workers and your spouse may carry a different set of social categories, as ethnic, religious and cultural barriers continue to break down in our globalized world. Thus we cannot reduce our notion of culture to simple stereotypes based on narrow descriptions of what it means to come from some particular part of the world.

APPLIED SOCIAL PSYCHOLOGY

An early pioneer in social psychology, Kurt Lewin coined the term 'action research' to convey the notion of a constant two-way process of feedback between laboratory-based theory-driven research and applied interventions to solve real-life problems. Indeed, from its inception, social psychology has been vitally concerned with the problems of people and society. In its formative years, social psychologists worked to understand such phenomena as the economic depression, labour-management conflicts, racial prejudice and the rise of fascism in the 1930s (Fisher, Bell & Baum, 1984). During the Second World War, social psychologists applied their skills to the war effort (Wright, 1990; Bradley, Nicol et al., 2002). In more recent times, they have addressed such important societal concerns as the adaptation and acculturation of immigrants (Dompierre & Lavellée, 1990; Lalonde & Cameron, 1993), the effects of our multiculturalism policies (Berry & Kalin, 1995), the development of racial identity among Native children (Corenblum & Annis, 1993), and ways to encourage attitudinal and behavioural change to inhibit the spread of HIV/AIDS (Perlini &Ward, 2000). Social psychologists have also played prominent roles in the study of gender roles and discrimination against women (Marecek, 2001; Pyke, 2001; Stark, 2001).

Social psychological research has been applied to a wide variety of social concerns (Table I.1). In many cases, as you will discover, theories developed through 'pure research' have been applied to social issues; for example, attribution theory has been applied in understanding the experience of being physically ill, marital

Table 1.1 Examples of topics found in the *Journal of Social Issues*

- The intersection of psychology and globalization, 2012, 68(3)
- Same-sex marriage, 2011, 67(2)
- Immigration, 2011, 66(4)
- Stigmatization, 2011, 67(3)
- Post-apartheid intergroup relations in South Africa, 2010, 66(2)
- Collective action, 2009, 65(4)
- Animal welfare and animal rights, 2009, 65(3)
- Intergroup conflict and cooperation, 2009, 65(2)
- Multiracial identity, 2009, 65(1)
- Ethnic prejudice in Europe, 2008, 64(2)
- Intergenerational relations, 2007, 63(4)
- Homelessness, 2007, 63(3)
- Human behaviour and environmental sustainability, 2007, 63(1)
- Peace and psychology, 2006, 62(1)
- Intergenerational relations, 2007, 63(4)
- Ethnic prejudice and discrimination in Europe, 2008, 64(2)
- Treatment of animals, 2009, 65(3)
- How Latinos are transforming the United States, 2010, 66(1)
- Towards a psychology of globalization, 2011, 67(4)
- Sustainability in combining career and care, 2012, 68(4)
- After the genocide: Psychological perspectives, 2013, 69(1)

conflicts and addiction to cigarettes. In other cases, lacking applicable theory, social psychologists begin with the study of a real-life problem, for example, unprotected sex among young people in an age of liberal sexual mores and deadly sexually transmitted diseases.

The Canadian Space Agency has become interested in psychosocial research and has chosen to fund research in two areas where research by Canadian psychologists has been particularly prominent: the interactions among people from various multicultural groups and the effects of isolated and confined environments (Suedfeld, 2003). Both of these subjects will be of considerable importance to the planning of future space missions involving men and women from a variety of cultural, ethnic and linguistic backgrounds, living in confined quarters under stressful conditions for long periods of time.

Social psychological knowledge also has considerable application in clinical psychology, since social interaction both influences and is influenced by an individual's mental health (Alcock, 1997). Social psychology can further contribute to the betterment of society through evaluation research – the objective, data-based assessment of social programmes or changes.

This research actually can have practical benefits for people and societies (Rule & Adair, 1984). Pioneering research originating with Wallace Lambert's group in Montreal led to an internationally recognized model of bilingual education that combines language training with cultural integration (Gardner & Desrochers, 1981). Research on how northern Native peoples have adapted to cultural and economic changes, brought about in part by the opening of new mines and the building of huge hydroelectric projects has provided information that cannot be ignored by governments or by native groups in future policy decisions (Berry et al., 1982). Other research has contributed to multiculturalism policy, which encourages ethnic groups to maintain their cultural heritages while joining the societal mainstream (Berry, 2011).

As noted above, Lewin (1948) described this type of work as action research, in which the researcher obtains data about a problem or organization, feeds these data into the relevant system in order to influence change, measures the change and then repeats the process. Note that this model implies the social psychologist becomes an *agent* of change, a skilled advocate of policies, as well as a theoretician and researcher. While we are far from solving the most pressing social and human problems, social psychology carries with it the hope of beneficial, research-based change.

SCIENCE AND SOCIAL PSYCHOLOGY

Whenever we are confronted with important social issues, there is usually plenty of strong rhetoric and opinion – but little available data. In our everyday lives, we may trust our personal experience to provide the data upon which we base our opinions, but everyday experience is often a poor guide. Forty years ago, everyday experience would have seemed to confirm the then-common view that women could not drive buses or do construction work or serve as front-line police officers. Today, everyday experience leads to a different conclusion. History demonstrates the dangers of making judgements and decisions on the basis of authority, emotion, personal experience or 'common sense' alone. We need to look at 'data'. But data can be accurate or inaccurate, reliable or unreliable. Poor data, like poor common sense or misleading authority, are often worse than no data at all, for they lead us to believe we have a basis for understanding, when in fact we do not.

This is why scientific methods are important, for science concerns itself not only with the collection and analysis of data, but also with trying to protect researchers from error in interpreting those data. Of course, scientists make mistakes, but science tends to be self-correcting, and errors are ultimately weeded out, whereas opinions based only on authority or personal experience may never change, even when they are in error. Science is as important in social psychology as it is in physics or chemistry or biology. In this chapter, we shall explore why this is so.

What is 'science'? Science is a *method of studying nature*. And it is the method – not scientists, or the equipment used, or the facts proclaimed – that differentiates the scientific approach from other approaches to knowledge. Whether in astronomy, physics or psychology, what is fundamental is generating theory and testing it against observation. Theory is essential to guide research, to organize research results into a coherent structure and to provide ideas for testing. Without theory, there is nothing to test, and without testing, there is no way to evaluate which theories are correct. Indeed, as we shall see, the scientific approach is as valuable a tool for studying human social behaviour as for conducting research into chemical reactions and biological processes.

Science is fundamentally a rational process. In its simplest form, the rational model consists of four steps: (1) formulating a theoretical problem, which is then translated into testable hypotheses; (2) selecting the appropriate research method, and designing and carrying out the study; (3) analysing and interpreting the results; and (4) using the results to support, deny or modify the theory.

For most people, 'science' describes specific fields of study (physics, chemistry, geology, astronomy, biology), impressive laboratory technology and precise measurement. It may seem surprising that a field such as social psychology can be scientific. How can the study of smoking, violence, helping, leadership, bilingual communication, impression formation and attitudes be scientific in the same sense that research into the mysteries of the human cell, the atom and chemical compound reactions is scientific? Yet the scientific method is arguably even more important in a field where data are difficult to quantify, because such areas are most vulnerable to fuzzy and erroneous thinking.

However, it is not nearly as straightforward to apply the scientific method to social behaviour as it is to apply it to inanimate objects or biological processes. Because social psychology is a relatively young discipline, and because human social behaviour is so complex, no single, grand theory has yet emerged. Moreover, while social psychologists have excelled as experimenters and data collectors, they have tended to ignore the importance of theory development (Kruglanski, 2001). Indeed, much of what we loosely refer to as 'theory' in social psychology is not really theory in the sense the term is used in natural sciences. Our theories are more like theoretical models, usually built upon a loosely related set of assumptions about a limited range of phenomena, and the logical deduction process is typically informal in nature.

As we will see in subsequent chapters, various mini-theories or models have been developed to account for specific phenomena, such as leadership, attitude change or aggressive behaviour. While there is considerable variety among these theories, one theoretical orientation has dominated in North America, the cognitive-behaviourist, adapted from the mainstream of psychological theory and research.

Cognitive-behaviourist perspective

Behaviourism developed through the pioneering work of Ivan Pavlov on conditioned reflexes and of B.F. Skinner on operant conditioning. Its premise is that behaviour is governed by external reinforcement. In the past, 'radical behaviourists' such as Skinner argued that reinforcement is all we need to explain and predict behaviour. However, many theorists feel that the behaviourists exaggerated the degree to which we are passive recipients of external influences, arguing that we also act to interpret and change our environment. Cognitive psychologists argue that inner psychological processes, such as beliefs, feelings and motives, are influenced by external reinforcement and, in turn, influence behaviour. According to this view, it is also important to look within individuals, particularly at their *cognitive processes*, to understand behaviour. The cognitive perspective gained recognition with the early work on perception by the Gestalt psychologists, and was used early in the development of social psychology by Kurt Lewin (1951) in his field theory. Lewin argued that the 'environment' that influences human actions is not a set of physical characteristics and events per se, but the 'life space' of individuals – the environment in the context of what it means to them. People actively construct or make sense of the situations in which they find themselves. Lewin suggested an example from his own combat experience in the First World War: A physical landscape might consist of hills and valleys, trees, bushes and open spaces. However, this landscape would be a very different environment to soldiers in combat than to friends on a picnic, and would influence their behaviour in different ways.

Most social psychologists prefer the latter approach, in which both external events and psychological states must be studied. The cognitive-behaviourist perspective has led social psychologists to search for situational factors that influence behaviour. Cognitive and behaviourist influences are at the basis of a number of theories in social psychology, including the following, which are discussed in later chapters:

1. The reinforcement-affect model of attraction explains why we come to like someone by associating that person with some positive experience. (Chapter 8)
2. Researchers have explained the influence of film and television on aggression in terms of social learning theory. This theory states that we do not always need to be reinforced in order to learn new behaviours; we can learn simply by watching how other people act and observing the consequences of their actions. (Chapters 7 & 11)
3. Social exchange theory explains interactions and relationships in terms of the social reinforcements (e.g., affection, respect, power) that people provide for one another. (Chapter 8)
4. Social comparison theory explains how we often evaluate ourselves, our beliefs and our actions by comparing ourselves with others: Am I successful? Is my judgement accurate? Did I do a good job? (Chapters 3 & 6)
5. The theory of cognitive dissonance explains how we deal with situations in which there is inconsistency between our beliefs and our actions – when, for example, a smoker comes to believe that smoking causes cancer or when someone who has publicly supported a politician begins to doubt the politician's competency. (Chapter 5)
6. Attribution theories – and there are several of them – explain how people make inferences about the causes of another person's actions. (Chapter 2)

Other perspectives

This textbook focuses on experimental social psychology, with its deep cognitive and behavioural roots. Although it is clearly the dominant form of social psychology in the world today, it is important to be aware of other approaches to social psychology that have quite different historical roots and that largely reject as inappropriate the basic scientific methodology of experimental social psychology. Critics of the experimental approach argue that something very important is lost when we try to understand human beings and their behaviour by 'measuring' their responses to particular situations and then looking for general descriptions and laws that apply to everyone, while treating individual variation as 'noise' to be eliminated as much as possible. Can we really, the critic might ask, understand a person's 'attitude' towards something by having him or her respond to a number of yes–no questions on a questionnaire? Can we really measure 'aggressiveness' using as our yardstick the number of electric shocks one individual delivers to another in a very artificial situation? Can we really understand human beings through research that ignores what they may have to say about their experiences and overlooks historical and cultural factors that may play a powerful role?

Many of the alternative approaches to the study of human social behaviour share a common element: social constructionism. As Burr (1995) points out, social constructionism pushes us to question our assumptions about the world and to challenge the notion that empirical observation reveals the true nature of the world. For example, we divide people up into being either males or females and see this as a fundamental division of nature, but could we not have chosen to divide them into tall and short instead? Similarly we may distinguish between pop and classical music, but do such divisions, based on how we organize our perceptions, necessarily represent something fundamental about nature? Social constructionism challenges that notion. Furthermore, it also challenges the traditional scientific notion that we can discover objective knowledge about human beings that exists independently of the historical context (Gergen, 1985). Traditional psychology, it is argued, attributes behaviour to 'individual minds' that it then attempts to measure and classify in an objective manner, while excluding the influence and the biases of the researchers. However, social constructionism denies the possibility of true objectivity in the human sciences because the methodology has to rely upon 'one set of subjective humans' rating 'another set of subjective humans' (Owen, 1995).

The boundaries of what constitutes social constructionism are somewhat vague and there is no one particular form of psychology that could clearly be characterized as social constructionist (Potter, 1996). Indeed, there are at least two somewhat separate streams of social constructionist psychology, one concerned with issues of power and the subjectivity of knowledge, and the other focused more on discourse and related matters (Danziger, 1997).

Hermeneutics

One social constructionist perspective, the hermeneutic approach, has deep roots in European philosophy. One of the early contributors was Wilhelm Dilthey (1833–1911), a German historian, philosopher and psychologist who rejected the notion that the methods of the natural sciences could be applied to the 'human' sciences. He argued in *Der Aufbau der geschichtlichen Welt in den Geisteswissenschaften* (*The Formation of the Historical World in the Human Sciences)* (1910) that while the natural sciences focus on finding and understanding cause and effect in their pursuit of generalized laws, the goal of researchers in the human sciences is different; it is to understand human life and human history. Hermeneutics, he argued, provides a better approach. Hermeneutics is the art – and some of its proponents would say the science – of interpreting communication, whether verbal, non-verbal or textual. (It is said that the term 'hermeneutics' comes from the name of the Greek god, Hermes, who acted as a messenger for the gods, carrying and interpreting their messages to the human recipients (Virkler, 1995).) Dilthey was concerned with finding the meaning behind what people say, and such understanding, he argued, cannot come from the application of the scientific method borrowed from the natural sciences.

The hermeneutic tradition has evolved into a disciplined set of techniques guided by specific rules and procedures for the analysis of communications. Its proponents argue that it is the best route to gaining valid knowledge about human behaviour, and insist that one cannot understand a person's utterances or behaviours without understanding both the historical and cultural context in which they occur as well as the worldview of the individual who produces them.

Critical psychology

Critical psychology, sometimes referred to as radical psychology, began in Berlin, Germany, during the 1970s and now is centred in the United Kingdom, although the approach is taught in a few other universities in various parts the world. Critical psychology is based in the critical analysis of culture and society, and looks for societal causes of psychological problems. It reflects to some degree a Marxist analysis of society, and it draws on several influences, including hermeneutics and discursive psychology, which is discussed below. In *Grundlegung der psychologie* (*Foundations of psychology*) (1983), Klaus Holzkamp, one of the major contributors to this movement, presented an argument similar to the hermeneutic position just discussed, that is, that the traditional experimental psychological approach does not allow us to understand why humans act as they do, nor how the society and culture in which they live influence them to act as they do. Critical psychology considers all psychological approaches to be tied to some extent to their cultural and historical context, carrying with them particular ideological assumptions (Parker, 1999). Modern experimental psychology is viewed as being too focused on the individual and not allowing for the analysis of important group factors that, among other things, promote social change. As a result, it is argued, it facilitates inequality and even the oppression of marginalized groups (Fox, Prilleltensky & Austin, 2009).

Discursive psychology

Discursive psychology is also a part of the general critical psychology movement that has gradually developed in opposition to traditional experimental social psychology. It is building a following in a number of regions around the world including the United Kingdom, Australia, Canada, Scandinavia and South America (Billig, 2009). As the name suggests, its focus is on the study of discourse, and it seeks to establish new theoretical principles as well as to develop qualitative methodologies that stand in contrast to the quantitative laboratory approach that is dominant in experimental social psychology. It strongly opposes the approach to language taken by traditional cognitive psychologists: Discourse – communication using words – is generally viewed within mainstream social and cognitive psychology as a behaviour that reflects what is going on inside a person's head. On the other hand, the discursive approach, rather than viewing what a person says as reflecting some unobservable underlying process or mental state, focuses on the details of the utterances themselves, in terms of the social situation in which they occur (Billig, 2009). There are no experiments in discursive psychology, and there is no interest in finding cause–effect relationships. Furthermore, while experimental social psychologists try to minimize individual variability in their experiments as they seek general rules and laws of behaviour, individual variability is of great interest to discursive psychologists, for there is no interest in finding some generalized 'truth' about the 'average' individual.

All of these approaches are thoughtful and stimulating, although it is beyond the scope of this textbook to discuss them in detail. However, it is important to remember that experimental social psychology, despite the criticisms levelled against it, continues to provide a wealth of knowledge about human social behaviour, as the chapters in this textbook will attest.

AN OVERALL PERSPECTIVE

The early history of social psychology was marked by a euphoric optimism. For the first time, the methods of science were to be applied to human problems. Surely, it was believed, the same approach that had yielded spectacular advances in our understanding of medicine, atomic physics, chemistry and geology would help us to understand and eventually solve the problems of violence, crime, poverty and prejudice. Surely we could 'conquer' war as we had 'conquered' infectious diseases, and we could learn to live in harmony as we had learned to fly and to communicate instantaneously over long distances.

While the discipline has advanced significantly in the succeeding decades, those age-old social problems are still with us. Perhaps the fact that war, bigotry and poverty are rooted in culture and in the political, moral and economic realities of the times means that a purely psychological solution is unrealistic. It may also be true that, as critical psychology suggests, social problems are more complex than biological or physical phenomena and will not be solved so easily. We must also remember that social psychology is a young discipline.

In summary, social psychology is a dynamic field, continually evolving as new ideas, methods, research findings and theories emerge and affect one another: a theory can generate innovative research and controversy; research findings and new ideas can lead to an evolution in the theory; new areas of research can open up as a result of random events (e.g., a widely publicized incident of a murder in the presence of bystanders who failed to intervene stimulated research and theory on the problem). Some areas of research become hot topics almost overnight, generating cutting-edge ideas, while other areas may be slow to build, or even wane, for a while. A textbook can only provide a picture of the discipline at the time of writing – with some idea of where we have been and where we are going.

A NOTE ON THE TEXT

The best way to understand what social psychology is about is to get involved. The accompanying website provides exercises, mini-experiments and other information to stimulate your thinking about social psychology, but this involvement begins right here, in the chapter that follows, which introduces the fundamental principles of how research is conducted in social psychology. Then, a series of chapters explores how we come to understand our social world – how we perceive and understand other people and events and how we form values and attitudes. The next set of chapters deals with how people influence one another – how our attitudes change as we interact with others, how social influences lead us to conform, comply with and obey other people and how people communicate through language and non-verbal means. Then, a series of chapters examines how we interact with other people: what factors determine whether we are attracted to one another, the causes of aggressive and altruistic behaviour and how conflict develops and can be resolved. Next, we look at how the individual functions in a group and larger collectives. Finally, we consider some contemporary areas of practical concern including justice and law, and health and well-being.

SOURCES OF INFORMATION

At the end of each chapter are listed important, recent publications that provide further information on topics discussed in that chapter. A literature search through a computerized library database such as The American Psychological Association's PsycARTICLES, will provide specific references. The following list of basic reference works will serve as an introduction to most research areas in the field.

Some basic reference works

Zanna, M. P. & Olson, M. (Eds) (2010). *Advances in experimental social psychology.* New York: Academic Press.
   A review of cutting-edge social psychological research.
Berry, J.W., Poortinga, Y.H. & Pandey, J. (1997). *Handbook of cross-cultural psychology* (2nd ed.). Boston: Allyn and Bacon. In-depth information about progress pitfalls in carrying out psychological research across cultures.
Chiu, C.-Y. & Hong, Y.-Y. (2006). *Social psychology of culture.* Hove, East Sussex: Psychology Press.
   An excellent introduction to the influence of culture on social psychological behaviour.
Fiske, S.T, Gilbert, D.T. & Lindzey, G. (Eds). (2010). *The handbook of social psychology.* New York: Random House.
   An essential reference book for social psychologists.
Sadava, S.W. & McCreary, D.R. (Eds). (1997). *Applied social psychology.* Upper Saddle River, NJ: Prentice-Hall.
   An introduction to important applications of social psychological research to issues of social importance.

FURTHER READING

Collier, G., Minton, H.L. & Reynolds, G. (1991). *Currents of thought in American social psychology*. New York: Oxford University Press.
   A study of the people and intellectual currents – including British evolutionary theory, French social theory, and the ideas of Freud and Marx – that spawned social psychology in the United States.

Farr, R.M. (1996). *The roots of modern social psychology*. Malden: Blackwell Publishing.
   Traces the origin of both American and European streams of thought, both philosophical and experimental, which led to the emergence of contemporary social psychology.

Lubek, I., Minton, H.L. & Apfelbaum, E. (Eds). (1992). Social psychology and its history. *Canadian Psychology*, 33 (3). Special Issue.
   Important collection of papers by an international group of authors reflecting on the origins and development of social psychology.

CHAPTER 1
STUDYING SOCIAL BEHAVIOUR

True science teaches us to doubt and, in ignorance, to refrain.
Claude Bernard (1813–78)

LEARNING OBJECTIVES

* To understand the basic nature of scientific inquiry
* To understand the principle methods of research in social psychology
* To explore factors relevant to the validity of social psychological research
* To examine the issues involved in conducting cross-cultural research
* To consider ethical problems that arise in social psychological research

Figure 1.1 Image courtesy of Singapore Children Society's Bully-Free Campaign: www.bullyfreecampaign.sg

This anti-bullying advertisement from Singapore is intended to influence behaviour in a socially desirable direction. But do such advertisements work? And if so, what is it about them that leads people to change their behaviour? And what sorts of advertisements work best – those that aim to gently persuade, those that threaten, or those that appeal to a sense of justice? Think for a moment about some of the difficulties involved in trying to answer such questions. Has looking at this advertisement already affected *you* in some way? Can you be sure? Is it enough just to ask people whether an advertisement has influenced their behaviour? Or should we look for trends in rates of bullying to see if there is a change following an advertising campaign? And can we study the effects of such advertising in a laboratory setting?

Social psychologists have extensively studied how various forms of social influence – including advertising – affect attitudes and behaviour. In this chapter, we shall examine how such studies are carried out not just with regard to social influence, but in the study of social behaviour in general. We shall present the major research strategies used by social psychologists and explore both their strengths and their shortcomings.

FINDING PATTERNS IN NATURE

Pattern-finding is critical to survival, and humans are consummate pattern-finders. We find patterns everywhere: Out of the wild mixtures of wavelengths of light and frequencies of sound that impinge on our sensory receptors, we 'see' objects and landscapes and people, and we 'hear' melodies and harmonies and voices. We 'smell' jasmine, and its fragrance is quite distinct from the aromas of popcorn or lemonade. We readily discern temporal patterns as well: the sun rises in the east, moves across the sky and then disappears in the west; dark clouds form and soon we are pelted with rain; seeds planted in the ground begin to sprout. We also find patterns in people's behaviours: Martha must be a vegetarian, for I have never seen her eat meat; fat people are jolly; redheads have fiery tempers; crime rates are rising and criminals 'get off too easy'. And yet, although they often serve us well, our personal experiences can be very misleading, for we sometimes perceive patterns that do not correspond to reality. Our observations about redheads or overweight people may be in error because of personal or culturally shared prejudices, our beliefs about contemporary crime rates may be distorted because of anxiety, and our experiences with regard to the effects of punishment on behaviour may mislead us because we have such a narrow range of experience upon which to judge. This is where science is important. Scientific research strives to employ methods that minimize the risk that our beliefs and biases will distort our collection and interpretation of data.

For most of human history, whatever people could not directly apprehend about the workings of nature was explained either on the basis of 'revealed truth' as laid down in scriptures, or by the dogmatic pronouncements of scholars and kings. Until the scientific revolution of the 16th and 17th centuries, Western thought was dominated by such an appeal to authority: the biblical scriptures and the dictates of the ancient Greek philosophers were taken to be the wellsprings of infallible truth and knowledge. The works of Aristotle, the greatest philosopher of antiquity, provided the foundation for medieval scholastic thought, and great importance was attached to the belief that pure reason could validate and illuminate what was already accepted as true on the basis of religious faith. Reason that contradicted dogma was presumed to be in error.

Modern science began when Copernicus (1473–1543) challenged the prevailing dogma about the earth and its place in the heavens. For many centuries, it had been accepted without question by Western scholars that the sun revolved about the earth, a belief consistent both with everyday experience and with the pronouncements of Aristotle and Judeo-Christian scripture. Even though astronomers had long recognized that the movement of the planets did not fit well with this geocentric belief, it was Copernicus who chose to trust data over dogma. In 1543, he published *De Revolutionibus Orbium Caelestium*, in which he proclaimed that not only is the Earth not the centre of the universe, but that it revolves around the sun. Even though other astronomers soon adopted his improved techniques for computing planetary positions, they nonetheless ignored and even ridiculed his heliocentric views. And later on, when Galileo (1564–1642) vigorously promoted Copernicus' theory, he was prosecuted by the Roman Catholic Church and forced to recant. In the long run, however, this nascent scientific notion survived because Copernican ideas accorded with observation, whereas dogma did not. The scientific revolution was born. Sadly, science continues to be vilified in some quarters by those still steeped in dogma. Think for example of fundamentalists of various religious orientations who continue to rail against the theory of evolution.

The scientific revolution was distinguished by the importance it placed both upon curiosity and hypothesizing on the one hand and upon testing hypothesis against data on the other (Boulding, 1980). Theory is essential to guide research, to organize its data into a coherent structure and to provide ideas for testing, for without theory, there is nothing to test. And without testing, there is no way to distinguish fact from fantasy.

Science is much more than laboratories and equipment and journals and books. It is first and foremost a *process*, a method of thinking about and exploring the world around us. Having developed across several centuries, it offers us the best method we have for finding fact and avoiding error. It involves not just observation, but *systematic* observation guided by consideration of possible sources of bias in data collection and interpretation. Notwithstanding some of the concerns raised by critics of experimental social psychology, as discussed in the introductory chapter, the scientific method is as vital in social psychological research as it is in physics or chemistry or biology, even though, as we shall see, it is not nearly so straightforward to apply to the study of social behaviour as it is to inanimate objects and biological processes.

KEY POINT: While our senses generally serve us well, the patterns that we find can sometimes mislead us. Science is a systematic approach to understanding the world that aims to minimize bias in what we observe through data collection and interpretation.

MEASUREMENT

Before we can proceed very far in any scientific inquiry, we first need to be able to define just what it is that we are studying and then develop methods to measure it. We generally take measurement pretty much for granted. We have no difficulty measuring height or weight or how far an automobile can go on a litre of fuel. And whether we measure in inches or centimetres or pounds or kilogrammes, we trust our tape measures and scales to give us reliable information. But just what is 'measurement'? What does it mean to say that an object is three metres away from us? Or two feet? Or a furlong, or a league? What does a metre or a foot or a furlong or a league mean? Such units are not an inherent part of nature; they are socially defined. Thus, measurement is much more than just the assignment of numbers to various quantities of length or volume or weight; the units are based on a social accord, on agreements among people in a particular society or culture. You could of course invent your own system of measurements, but when you try to buy a *quarlog* of gasoline or a pair of size *muffigle* shoes, you will get nowhere. Measurement systems are the products of social agreement.

Figure 1.2   Is the scale accurate?

Source: Gts/Shutterstock.com

Measurement is as critical in social psychology as it is in any area of scientific research. But while scientists in other fields are usually able to agree upon unambiguous definitions of their measurement units, this is hardly the case in social psychology. Indeed, we have great difficulty even in defining the variables that we wish to study, let alone in measuring them precisely. This is because we cannot directly observe most of what we want to study, for our subject matter consists of *hypothetical constructs* – 'attitudes', 'prejudice', 'conflict', and so on. We need to take these words from everyday language and define them in such a way that they can be measured, but this is difficult because we can only infer their existence and their magnitudes on the basis of observed behaviour and self-report. Think about it: how can you determine if your friend is 'sexist'? First problem: What do we mean by 'sexist'? And if we can define the concept clearly enough, how then do we measure it? Self-report is not enough, for just because your friend denies being sexist does not mean that he or she is not. After all, a bigot never begins a racist comment with 'I am a bigot, but …' And even if we observe your friend's behaviour carefully and find no evidence of what we have defined as sexism, is it not possible that he or she is very socially aware and knows what to say and how to act to avoid appearing sexist, while at the same time harbouring strong sexist attitudes? So you can see the challenges that face social psychologists in dealing with their subject matter.

In general, we rely upon *operational definitions* to define and then measure our hypothetical constructs. That is, we define the variable in terms of the operation used to measure it. Consider aggression, for example. Researchers in one study may define it in terms of how many electrical shocks a research participant ostensibly administers to another participant. We can count the shocks and record their intensity in an unambiguous way. But have we really measured aggression? And if so, how does that sort of 'aggression' relate to the aggression that most of us are concerned about in everyday life? Bullying has been defined as 'repeated aggression in which there is a power differential' (Craig & Pepler, 2007). While we can all understand the aim of the definition, there remains ambiguity with regard to what constitutes both 'aggression' and 'power differential'. Thus, the researcher who studies bullying needs to carefully delineate just what actions are to be considered as aggressive and what criteria are to be used to determine the power differential.

Even when we can agree upon the definition of a variable and on how to measure it, we need to be concerned about the measure's **reliability** and **validity**. It is important that our measure be reliable: that is, if we measure more than once with the same instrument we should get the same result each time. For example, if you have a reliable scale, then if you weigh yourself three times in a row, the scale should give you the same weight each time. Beyond that, we also need to determine that the instrument provides a *valid* measurement, that is, that it measures what it is supposed to measure. If your scale tells you that you weigh 80 kilos, this measurement is valid only if you actually do weigh 80 kilos.

Apply this to psychological research: if we have developed a questionnaire to measure prejudice, then we want it to be 'reliable' – it produces similar scores when administered at different times to the same individuals – but we also need to show that the scores that it produces actually correspond to the degree of prejudice of the respondents.

Social psychologists are confronted by another concern not encountered by researchers in physics or chemistry or biology: reactivity. Human participants are more difficult to study in part because they react to the situation, that is, they may change their behaviour if they know that they are being studied. Hence, we need to try to find methods that minimize this reactivity. For example, in the study of bullying behaviour, the presence of a researcher with a video camera in the school yard during recess may well lead children to be on their best behaviour, so that no bullying is observed. However, observation with a hidden camera – ethical concerns aside for the moment – provides a nonreactive measure which is more likely to capture bullying behaviour if it occurs.

> **KEY POINT:** Developing reliable and valid measurement tools is challenging in social psychology both because we cannot usually observe our subject matter (e.g., attitudes) directly and because people may change their behaviour when they know that they are being observed.

RESEARCH METHODS

Social psychological research can be either *qualitative* or *quantitative* in nature, although the vast majority of published studies are of the latter type. With quantitative methods, we define our variables carefully in terms of how we can measure them, we collect data that is objective rather than subjective (that is, we rely on measurement rather than our feelings or what someone tells us), and we aggregate the data and rely on statistical analysis to help us draw conclusions (that is, we calculate means, and we focus on average outcomes for a condition or group rather than on individual outcomes). Quantitative psychological research strongly relies upon statistical analysis of its data and generally seeks 'statistically significant' effects – that is, outcomes that are unlikely to occur purely by chance. However, this can lead to over-interpretation of the data, for there is often a difference between what is statistically significant and what is psychologically significant. For example, anti-bullying advertisements might be shown to produce a statistically significant decrease in bullying behaviour, but if the actual decrease is only 0.5%, the observed effect is of virtually no significance psychologically; it is just too small to be important. Thus, we need to pay attention to the actual magnitude of the effect that the manipulation of the independent variable has produced, not just whether it is statistically significant.

Quantitative research typically focuses on gathering objective data about small bits of behaviour while ignoring the larger social context in which the behaviour typically occurs, and it deals with group averages, thus ignoring possibly important differences among individuals and without particular concern for why a given individual has behaved in a particular fashion. Moreover, because quantitative methods require that we be able to employ objective measures, we may miss out on important information that does not lend itself to ready measurement. How can we quantify grief or patriotism, for example?

In light of such concerns, there has been growing interest in recent years in qualitative methods as some researchers have made an effort to understand social phenomena that are very difficult to quantify (Rennie, 2002). Qualitative research does not rely on measurement and numbers and statistical analyses, which are the basis for quantitative research. Instead, it involves methods that are directed at trying to understand *how* people think and feel and *why* they behave as they do and how they interpret their own experiences. (Recall the discussion in the introductory chapter.) Interviews, open-ended questionnaires that allow participants to respond in their own words, diaries, direct participant observation and focus groups are among the methods used in the attempt to understand a particular social psychological phenomenon from the participant's perspective. The researcher typically interacts with the participant by posing direct questions and seeking clarification and amplification of the participant's comments. This is starkly different from what happens in quantitative research, where the researcher strives to remain as detached and objective as possible in the effort to avoid biasing the participant's responses.

There are several different qualitative approaches (Wertz et al., 2011). For example, researchers following the phenomenological approach are interested in how a particular individual in a particular situation comes to understand a particular experience – such as the birth of a child or the breakdown of a relationship; this is not something that would yield readily to quantitative methods. And, as discussed in the introductory chapter, the discursive approach is primarily directed at how people use language to construct meaning (Potter, 2012). It involves a detailed analysis of how individuals interpret and describe their social worlds, and the emphasis is on what people actually say and do rather than on an attempt to find psychological factors that account for their behaviour (Forrester, 2010).

Qualitative and quantitative approaches each have their strengths and weaknesses. The qualitative approach can yield a cornucopia of information about how individuals perceive a situation and why they react as they do, but because such data are subjective and descriptive in nature and there is little or no control over the variables being measured, it is usually more problematic to analyse the data and to generalize from the responses of particular individuals to the larger social context. On the other hand, while the quantitative approach offers much more precision, it does so at the cost of possibly missing out on what might be important personal information from the participants regarding their thoughts, feelings and actions. By using qualitative and quantitative methods in combination, we may come to a better understanding of complex social phenomena and be able to place the results of our quantitative approach into a meaningful human perspective (Madill & Gough, 2008; Trochim, 1999). However, in this textbook we shall present social psychology as it is today, and so more of our focus will be on quantitative research.

> **KEY POINT:** Social psychological research methods can be quantitative, involving analysis of objective data about narrowly defined behaviours and using group averages, or qualitative, focusing on subjective data concerning individuals' perceptions and feelings about a situation. Both approaches have strengths and weaknesses, and a combination of the two is likely to yield a fuller understanding of human social behaviour.

NON-EXPERIMENTAL METHODS

Non-experimental methods involve the collection of social psychological data without the manipulation of an independent variable. Qualitative research by its very nature is non-experimental, and some, but not all, of the non-experimental methods discussed below are essentially qualitative in nature. Each of the methods to be discussed has its strengths and weaknesses and the researcher needs to consider the trade-offs when selecting a particular research approach.

Direct observation

A very simple example of a non-experimental method is direct observation. Watching how people behave in a natural setting can yield valuable information about various social phenomena. However, researchers must go beyond the simple casual observations made by laypeople and employ *systematic* observation in order to try to control or eliminate influences that could bias their observations. Suppose, for example, that we are studying bullying with the assistance of a teacher. If the teacher stands in the schoolyard at noontime and makes notes about instances of bullying that take place, this would produce a number of methodological concerns. First of all, there is the problem of reactivity discussed earlier. But add to that the difficulty in deciding if a particular behaviour constitutes bullying. And is the teacher able to observe everything that goes on? Or is it more likely that her attention will be drawn to Billy and Martha, two students whom she already considers to be bullies at heart? To minimize the biases that such problems can produce, we would need to choose a better methodology – perhaps employing outside observers or a hidden video camera that captures all play activities, as well as a well-thought-out coding system that allows researchers who view the videos to make relatively unambiguous judgements about which behaviours involved bullying and which did not.

> **KEY POINT:** Direct observation can be misleading both because of difficulties in defining and recording behaviour and because the presence of the observer may influence the behaviour of the observed.

The case study

The **case study** is a qualitative research method. It involves an in-depth investigation of a particular instance of a phenomenon. This instance might involve a single person or group of people or a specific event. For example, if we are studying bullying, we might begin by carrying out a number of case studies of both victims and perpetrators, and these extensive interviews might shed light on important influences that might otherwise have been ignored.

This approach has several important advantages:

- It provides a comprehensive investigation of a specific instance of a phenomenon.
- Its data are useful as a basis for generating hypotheses for further research.
- If the case study continues for an extended time, it can provide information about changes in the phenomenon of interest over time.

Yet, as useful as the information may be for generating hypotheses, there are important limitations:

- Because the researcher is an active participant in the case study, he or she may inadvertently bias the data that is collected, either through the choice of questions asked or through responses made to the participant's comments.
- There is no way of knowing whether what the respondent says is true. The individual may be deceiving the researcher in order to put himself or herself in a good light. Such **evaluation apprehension** often motivates individuals to provide what they think to be socially desirable responses. Moreover, we do not always understand the reasons for our own behaviours, and so even when the respondents are being honest in their responses, their explanations may not be accurate.
- We cannot be sure that the individuals being studied are typical. If we are carrying out case studies of bullies or their victims, the people who are willing to be studied may be very different in some ways from others who have either escaped our notice or who are unwilling to participate in the research.
- Because the case study is a qualitative method, its data are often open to interpretation, and it is usually difficult to compare them with data from other case studies.
- While the approach is useful in providing information upon which to base future hypotheses, it cannot allow causal inferences.

KEY POINT: Case studies provide in-depth information about particular instances of behaviour, but are open to serious problems of bias, and are difficult to generalize.

The archival study

The **archival approach** involves using data that have already been collected and tabulated by others for other purposes. For example, as we pursue research into bullying, we may want to examine whether there have been changes in the rate of reported bullying over time or whether rates vary as a function of geographical location or ethnic group or age range. If such data exist, collected for example by a government department of statistics, then we can analyse them in terms of variables that are of interest to us. Or, suppose we wanted to study the effects on the population of London of the July 7, 2005 terrorist attack (Figure 1.3). Studying the data on hospital admissions

Figure 1.3 Remains of a bus after terrorist attack, London, July 7, 2005

Source: © Sion Touhig/Corbis

or the sales of antidepressant or antianxiety medication would be an example of an archival approach to the situation. Of course, we may not be able to address certain questions simply because the relevant data were never collected.

Archival studies offer several advantages:

- One can study large populations over a considerable range of time. For example, if the data exist, we can compare bullying rates in many different countries or regions.
- It allows for comparisons and assessments of trends across time. For example, in one such study, long-term trends in achievement motivation were assessed by examining themes in children's literature across many centuries (McClelland, 1967).
- The methodology is nonreactive; no one is being observed.
- Given that the data have already been collected and tabulated, the usual time and effort involved in data collection are eliminated.

However, there are limitations as well:

- Some of the data that we need may never have been collected or there may be missing data for some regions or for some years.
- We have to be very concerned about whether equivalent definitions of the relevant subject matter were employed in the various jurisdictions in which the data were collected. For example, in the study of bullying, behaviour considered to be bullying in one country may have been categorized as assault in another. Further, what is considered to be bullying at one time in a particular society may not be considered so at another.
- The biases of the researcher may, often without his or her awareness, influence the choice of data to be included, leading to a bias. For example, if there are data with regard to senior police officers bullying their juniors, one researcher may include these data as instances of bullying while another may exclude them, considering such behaviour to be 'normal' in a police or military setting.
- While the archival approach is useful for generating hypotheses, it cannot serve to verify them. Archival data do not allow us to draw conclusions about causal relationships between variables.

KEY POINT: Archival studies involve examining data that has already been gathered for other purposes. While such studies can provide information from different eras, different groups and different cultures, there are a number of problems associated with this approach.

The survey

Just as the term suggests, a survey involves asking people questions about some phenomenon of interest. We are all familiar with political polls, and they are a particular application of the survey technique (Box 1.1) technique. This approach is efficient because one can gather large amounts of data relatively quickly and inexpensively. For example, in the study of bullying, we might carry out surveys to find out how many people believe that they have been a victim, or even a perpetrator, of bullying. Yet, as you can well imagine, asking people about sensitive issues – bullying, for example – is often very problematic. Many people will simply refuse to answer, and those that do may be less than completely forthright in their answers. They may also differ in important ways from those who refused to participate

BOX 1.1   THE POLITICAL POLL

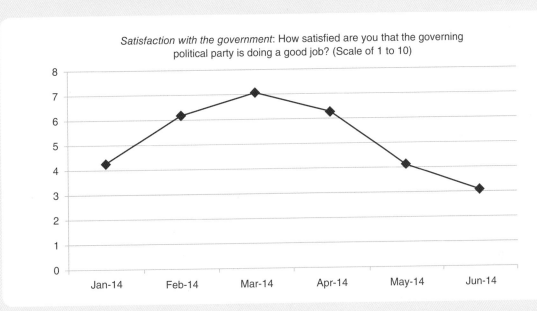

Figure 1.4   Example of the results of a typical political poll

This is an example of what the public is most familiar with in terms of surveys, the political poll. These are carried out in many parts of the world, especially in the run-up to elections, and pollsters and the media outlets who employ them compete with one another to provide snapshots of the voting intentions of the electorate. Such polls generally are presented as though they are scientific surveys, and we often hear that the results are considered accurate plus or minus so many percentage points 95% of the time. However, such statistical statements are almost always misleading, for the accuracy of such a poll depends both on the reliability and validity of people's responses to the questions asked, the relevance of the questions to the subject under consideration, and on whether the sample of respondents is representative of the voting population. These conditions are rarely met. Questions can be biased in that they lead to a desired answer, and in any case, we never know whether respondents are actually telling the truth, or if they are even truly aware what their intentions are with regard to voting. With regard to the latter, pollsters admit to having more and more difficulty attaining random or representative samples. They typically rely on telephone interviews, but so many people hang up on them that their samples are far from random and of course they are excluding anybody who does not have a telephone number.

There several types of surveys. One type is the **structured interview**. In this case the interviewer poses a series of carefully thought-out and pre-tested questions and then records the respondent's answers. The interviewer can ask for clarification or more elaboration when there are simple or ambiguous responses.

Another form of survey involves a printed or on line questionnaire. People are often more willing to provide information about sensitive issues through responses to a questionnaire, particularly when they can remain anonymous, than in an interview. The questionnaire can be either *open-ended* or *closed*. The former allows respondents to provide a detailed answer in their own words. For example: 'What do you feel is an appropriate punishment for someone who has been a bully?' is an open-ended question. However, the data gathered in this way is qualitative in nature and it is often very difficult to code it in such a way as to turn it

1a. Has anyone TEASED YOU or CALLED YOU NAMES recently?
     0 No (skip to 2a)
     1 YES

1b. How often?
     1 Most days
     2 About once a week
     3 Less than once a week

1c. How upsetting was it when you were teased?
     1 Not at all
     2 A bit
     3 I was quite upset

2a. Has anyone spread RUMOURS ABOUT YOU recently?
     0 No (skip to 3a)
     1 YES

2b. How often?
     1 Most days
     2 About once a week
     3 Less than once a week

2c. How upsetting were the rumours?
     1 Not at all
     2 A bit
     3 I was quite upset

Figure 1.5   Some items from a survey of bullying

Source: Bond et al., 2007

into a useful quantitative form. A closed questionnaire on the other hand limits responses to a small number of clearly defined options. For example, 'Children who bully: (a) should be expelled from school for ten days; (b) should be expelled from school for five days; or (c) should not be expelled at all. It is obviously much easier to score and analyse the results of closed questionnaires, but this must be weighed against the concern that respondents are forced to choose an answer that may not really reflect their position (Figure 1.5).

The World Wide Web and social media such as Twitter and Facebook offer new methods by which to carry out survey research in social psychology (Batanic & Göritz, 2009; Wilson, Gosling & Graham, 2012). Specialized websites, such as *SurveyMonkey* and *FluidSurveys,* make it relatively easy to conduct surveys over a much wider geographical area than was hitherto possible. However, the potential problems associated with surveys discussed above remain – whether the survey is carried out in a face-to-face interview, or through a questionnaire, or over the Internet.

In sum, there are important advantages to surveys:

* A wide range of information about beliefs, emotions and behaviours can be gathered which might be not be available through any other method.
* Compared to other methods, data collection is relatively easy and inexpensive.

Yet, while surveys can provide large amounts of data on almost any subject, they also pose significant methodological concerns:

* Unless the questions are unambiguous, they can produce meaningless data. In other cases, they can prompt the respondent to respond in a particular way. For example, consider the question '*Have you ever been thoughtlessly aggressive toward someone who is innocent, who is at a disadvantage, and who deserves to be treated with respect?*' Even if you had bullied others when you were younger, you might be less likely to answer such a damning question affirmatively than were the question simply: '*When you were younger, did*

you ever bully other children to the extent that you feel sorry for it now?' While neither of these are good questions, bullies would be more likely to reveal themselves through the second question than the first.

- The apparent meaning of an item can be altered by the content of the items that have gone before (Marsh & Yeung, 1999). Suppose that you were first presented with this question: *'Should bullying be treated as one of the very worst transgressions that a child can commit in a school setting?'* Then this question: *'Do you consider yourself to have been a bully at some time during your school years?'* If you had responded yes to the first question, you may now find it difficult to see your own behaviour as having been among the worst transgressions possible, and so you may respond 'no' to this question, even though, had this question been posed first, you may have answered in the affirmative.

- It is difficult for the interviewer to avoid introducing bias, even though he or she may be totally unaware of doing so. The way in which the question is posed, taking into account intonation, degree of eye contact and other non-verbal behaviours, can communicate the expectations or attitudes of the researcher and therefore influence the respondent. Consider the simple difference between 'Were you a bully?' compared to 'Were *you* a bully?' Similarly, the way in which the interviewer reacts to the respondent's responses can have a significant influence on subsequent responses. And there is always the possibility that the interviewer will misinterpret or misrecord an individual's responses. However, using a questionnaire in place of an interview overcomes most of these difficulties.

- Evaluation apprehension, which leads the individual to respond in what is perceived to be a socially desirable manner, is another potential source of bias.

- Because of faulty memory, the individual's responses may not be accurate.

- Some people typically tend to respond more frequently with 'yes' ('yea-sayers') or 'no' ('nay-sayers') regardless of the actual questions, while others may stick with answers that are 'middle-of-the-road' (Couch & Keniston, 1960; Arndt & Crane, 1975).

- Generally, researchers survey only a small portion of a population of interest. If the sample is not representative, then the results may be quite misleading. Thus, surveys carried out by inviting people to respond to Internet questionnaires or to mail their responses to a magazine questionnaire are doomed at the outset, for the pool of potential respondents is limited to those who visit that website or read that magazine and then take the time to respond. Those who do bother to respond are more likely to have strong feelings about the issue and may be quite unrepresentative of people at large.

- And once again, causal links between variables cannot be established.

KEY POINT: Surveys allow us to collect data from a large number of people relatively easily and quickly. However, participants' responses are subject to a number of biases that may distort the data, and moreover the representativeness of the sample of respondents is a major area of concern.

The field study

The field study is a qualitative approach in which people are directly observed in their natural setting. Field studies were famously employed by the anthropologists of the late 19th and early 20th centuries who travelled the world to live with and study people in various and diverse pre-technological societies. Records of the observations may be made manually, or in modern times by using audio or video recording equipment. When manual recordings are used, a predetermined method of coding behaviours is typically used to make the recording process simpler. Field studies can involve an observer who deliberately tries to remain aloof and separate from the people being studied, or it may involve participant observation – the traditional approach of anthropologists – in which the observer lives and interacts with the people being studied, often for substantial periods of time.

Field studies are relatively rare in experimental social psychology, although there are some important examples. In one such study, discussed in more detail in Chapter 5, social psychologists infiltrated a group that had gathered around Mrs Keech, a self-styled religious leader who claimed to have received a message from God indicating that the world was about to end (Festinger, Riecken & Schachter, 1956). By being part of this group, the psychologists were able to observe behaviour directly and gather information that otherwise would have been impossible to obtain.

The important strength of this approach is that it allows the researcher to observe spontaneous behaviours in a natural setting, thus providing us with a richness of information that is otherwise virtually impossible to obtain. However, there are a number of serious methodological concerns that need to be taken into account:

- The findings from the situation being studied may not be generalizable to other situations, and in such a case, the research will be of little value in terms of understanding social behaviour in general.
- The researchers, having ostensibly become part of the group being studied, may lose their objectivity.
- The people being studied may have changed their behaviour as a result of the presence of the researchers. This can occur even when it is not known that that newcomers are actually doing research. For example, imagine that a psychologist has joined a bully victim support group that involves people who had dropped out of high school because of bullying. The university-educated researcher, through his or her speech style and general behaviour, may inadvertently influence the behaviours of the people being studied.
- As with the approaches discussed earlier, this methodology does not allow for the determination of causal relationships.

KEY POINT: Field studies involve active participation by the researcher. This provides for the observation of spontaneous behaviour that might not otherwise be observable, but the presence of the researcher may change the behaviour that is being observed.

The correlational approach

Often, researchers are interested in how two or more variables co-vary with one another. For example, one may wish to see if there is a relationship between the incidence of bullying and the socioeconomic level of the family of the bully. Provided sufficient and appropriate data are available – through archival or survey data, for example – then one could calculate a correlation coefficient that would assist in evaluating the degree to which these two variables are related. If we found that the frequency of bullying increased as the socioeconomic status increased, then we would say that the two variables are *positively correlated*. And if we found the opposite, that greater levels of bullying were associated with lower levels of socioeconomic status, then we would say that the two variables are *negatively correlated*. This is the correlational approach.

Of course, while it may be tempting to interpret a strong correlation as implying causality, one cannot do so. Consider this example: With the widespread use of social networking, 'cyberbullying' has increased dramatically, and so have teen suicide rates (Hinduja & Patchin, 2010). Does this positive correlation mean that the bullying leads victims to commit suicide? While this may be so, we cannot base such a conclusion on the correlation alone. It may be that a third variable is involved and is responsible for the correlation. Suppose for example that children already suffering from depression and low self-esteem are more likely to become the targets of bullies. Perhaps – we cannot tell from the positive correlation between bullying rates and suicide rates – these depressed children would have killed themselves anyway and the bullying had nothing to do with it. One can plainly see that more information is needed beyond the simple correlation before we can conclude that bullying leads to suicide.

In recent years, social psychologists have been showing increased interest in what are known as *mediator* and *moderator* variables. A mediator variable is a third variable that apparently explains the relationship between two variables, whereas a moderator variable is a variable that influences the *strength* of the relationship between the two variables. For example, suppose that depression is a *mediator variable*, in that higher levels of depression lead both to poor academic performance and to a higher risk of being a bully. If that were the case, then when the effect of depression is removed, the relationship between academic performance and bullying would disappear.

Now, suppose we were to gather data relating to academic performance and bullying. Suppose further that we find a negative correlation – the lower the level of academic performance, the higher is the rate of bullying. Perhaps age is a moderator variable; for example in this case, we might find that the relationship between academic performance and bullying is more pronounced for older students than for those in the younger grades. In Figure 1.6 (note that this is artificial data), when all students are considered (purple line), it would appear that the bullying rate (defined as the number of reported bullying incidents during a three-month period) is negatively correlated with grade point average. However, if we look only at the younger students (red line), there is virtually no relationship, while this relationship is pronounced when we look at the older students. Thus, the relationship between bullying and academic performance is different depending on the age group; age is a moderator variable.

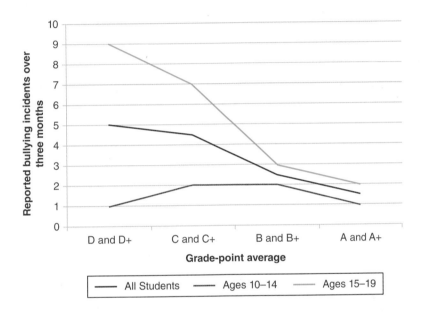

Figure 1.6 Bullying as a function of academic performance

Note: Example using artificial data

When more than two variables are of interest, then this correlational analysis can be extended so that the researcher can assess the influence of each of several variables upon a particular variable of interest. For example, one could use this approach to consider the relative effects of the family social economic level, position in the sibling line, and educational success upon rate of bullying. This process is termed *regression analysis*, and is an extension of the correlational analysis described above.

Advantages of the correlational approach include:

- A large number of variables and their interrelationships can be studied at the same time.
- Variables can be studied that cannot be manipulated in the laboratory – such as relationships among socioeconomic status, academic standing and birth order.
- Behavioural stability – the extent to which behaviour stays the same over time – can be assessed by looking at correlations between variables over an extended time interval.

Disadvantage:

- Causal inference is not possible.

[
KEY POINT: Correlational research provides an important source of information about which variables are associated with one another, but it cannot tell us about causality. Two variables that vary together may do so because each is related to a third variable, and not because there is a causal relationship between them.
]

EXPERIMENTAL METHODS

The non-experimental methods discussed above provide important ways of gaining information about social psychological variables of interest and are particularly useful in generating hypotheses to guide future research. However, when we want to determine what factors *cause* particular types of behaviour, we need to rely upon experimental methods.

The laboratory experiment

The laboratory experiment typically begins with a random sample of individuals from the population of interest and the experimenter assigns them randomly to two (or more) groups. When there are only two groups, a treatment variable (independent variable) is applied to one group, the *experimental* group, but not to the other, the *control* group. Given that there is no reason to expect differences between the two groups at the outset, any difference in what is being measured (dependent variable) following the application of the independent variable is presumed to have been caused by it. Though random assignment does not allow us to rule out absolutely the possibility of initial differences between the groups due to pure chance, it makes such differences less likely. Furthermore, when we apply statistical analysis to our results, that analysis will take into account the possibility that any differences that we observed could have arisen by chance at the time we assigned participants to groups.

For example, if one were interested in the possible relationship between the effects of personal failure and bullying behaviour, one might take two random samples of school-age teenagers and create a situation where the participants in one group each experienced some sort of failure, while those in the other group did not (independent variable). Subsequently, one could observe the extent to which individuals in the two groups act in a bullying manner (dependent variable) towards an ostensibly weaker individual. Any differences in bullying behaviour would presumably be due to the effects of the independent variable. Of course, it is essential to ensure that the experiences of the individuals in the two groups are as identical as can be with regard to everything except the independent variable. However, it is not always easy to recognize all the possible extraneous influences, and sometimes researchers conclude that their independent variable has caused a change in behaviour, only to find later that the change was due to an extraneous but unrecognized influence.

Another approach to minimizing initial differences between groups is to use matched pairs of participants, so that for every participant in the experimental group, there is a participant in the control group who is very similar in terms of all relevant variables. This approach deliberately attempts to eliminate any initial differences between the two groups in terms of factors considered important. It is more typically used in applied research. For example, Campbell and Campbell (1997) used this approach in evaluating the effectiveness of a faculty/student mentor programme on academic performance. Each undergraduate assigned to a mentor was paired with a non-mentored student on the basis of gender, ethnicity, grade-point average and other academic factors. As you can imagine, this approach is more time-consuming than random assignment, and it is not always easy to find a sufficient number of matched pairs. And while it does minimize differences based on variables deemed to be important, it does not rule out the possibility that the groups may differ initially in terms of some other variable upon which they were not matched, and which then has an unrecognized influence on the data.

Much of social psychological research is carried out in the laboratory. It is of course more convenient to do so, but convenience aside, there are important reasons for studying social behaviour in this setting. The laboratory offers us something that is difficult to obtain in the larger world outside: we are able to isolate important bits of behaviour and study them as a function of various influences while keeping out all the other influences that occur in a happenstance manner in everyday life. For example, in the study of bullying, we may want to assess how much the perceived weakness of a target is a catalyst for bullying behaviour, or how important it is that the target of bullying be someone who has already been devalued by the group. And what role does inability or unwillingness to defend oneself play? To study these various factors in the complex social context of everyday life would be extremely difficult, but the experimenter can examine each of them separately through carefully designed experiments, and can go on to explore how they interact with one another to produce bullying behaviour.

Of course, we have to ask whether behaviour produced in the laboratory has much to do with spontaneous behaviour in the 'real' world. In other words, are the findings of the laboratory research valid? Can we generalize our findings to the 'real-life' events in which we are interested? After all, the laboratory presents an artificial situation to the participant, and we must pay attention to the fact that participants may be acting differently than they might in a natural setting because of that artificiality, and because they know that they are being monitored. However, it is also important to remember that behaviour in the laboratory is also 'real' behaviour, albeit behaviour in a unique social psychological situation in which people assume the role of research participants being directed by an experimenter.

We need to be concerned about two types of validity: internal validity and external validity. Internal validity refers to the extent to which observed changes in the dependent variable are actually due to the independent variable rather than to some undetected extraneous variable. In other words, internal validity reflects the confidence that we have that the cause and effect conclusions we draw from our experiment are genuine (Wilson, Aronson & Carlsmith, 2010).

External validity, on the other hand, refers to the extent to which the findings from the laboratory are applicable to the world outside. Suppose that, for example, we find that the more an individual in a laboratory experiment is subjected to stress in the form of unpleasant noise, the more he or she engages in bullying behaviour. It may be that such stress has no such effect in the world outside of the laboratory simply because individuals can escape the stressful situation, in which case the external validity is low.

Given that the laboratory setting is quite different from the world of everyday life, how can we improve generalizability from the 'artificial' world of the laboratory to the 'real' world of everyday? Do we need to try to make the laboratory situation seem 'real' to the participants? Remember, no matter how much we might try to make it so, participants will still be aware that they are in an experiment, and nothing we can do is likely to change that fact.

We need to think about three different sorts of realism in an experiment. First of all, there is mundane realism; this refers to how much similarity there is between the experimental situation and situations that occur in 'real life'. For example, if we are studying cyberbullying over the Internet, a laboratory experiment in which participants actually use the Internet may be high in mundane realism, for the situation can be made to be very much like one of using the Internet at home. However, if participants were only able to communicate by passing notes to each other, this situation would be low in mundane realism.

Yet, while high mundane realism might seem to be desirable, it is not always important. Often, experiments are conducted in order to test a theory that hypothesizes certain causal relationships between two or more variables. The researcher may deliberately set up an experiment that is unlike any situation in the outside world in order to test the theory, and so long as that situation elicits reactions similar to those that come about in the outside world, then it will be possible to apply those findings to other situations where the same processes occur (Wilson, Aronson & Carlsmith, 2010). Indeed, what is most important is not mundane realism, but rather the *meaning* of what is happening to the research participants (Berkowitz & Donnerstein, 1982). For example, if a participant in a study of bullying believes that he or she is actually causing distress to another participant, the results of such a study should be applicable to other situations where the individual thinks that he or she is causing distress. This is experimental realism, the extent to which the participants become involved enough in the experimental situation that they take it seriously and react naturally to the situation rather than acting as they think is appropriate in the laboratory situation.

A third kind of realism is psychological realism (Aronson Wilson & Akert, 1994), which refers to the extent to which the *processes* that occur in the laboratory are similar to processes that occur in the outside world. Consider this study carried out by Gilbert and Hixon (1991). They wanted to explore the conditions under which a stereotype about a group comes to mind when you meet a person from that group. Participants in the study watched a video in which a woman held up a series of cards, each containing an incomplete word, for example POLI_E or S_Y. There were two groups of participants; for those in one group, the woman presenting the fragmented words was White, while for those in the second group, she was Asian. Participants were given 15 seconds to make as many different words as possible from each fragmented word. Participants who watched the Asian woman were more likely than those who saw the white woman to write down words consistent with a prevailing stereotype of Asian women – for example, POLITE and SHY. Note that this study was low in mundane realism, for the experimental situation was unlike any situation in everyday life, and it was also not very high in experimental realism, for it had very little impact on the participants. Yet, because it captured aspects of the non-conscious, automatic process of stereotyping that occurs in everyday life, it was high in psychological realism (Aronson, Wilson & Brewer, 1998).

Indeed, there is growing interest among social psychologists in automatic processes that occur without active thinking or planning, and in order to study such phenomena, one requires situations that actually are low in experimental realism, but high in psychological realism (Wilson, Aronson & Carlsmith, 2010). That is, to study automatic, intuitive processing, one needs a situation which does not involve the participant to the extent that he or she is so focused that such automatic processes are ineffectual. Another example: Langer, Blank & Chanowitz (1978) were interested in situations in which people are responding in a rather automatic way to the information that they receive. They delivered nonsensical memos that had the appearance of normal memos to a number of office secretaries. The memos stated either 'I would appreciate it if you would immediately return this memo to Room 238 through interoffice mail' or 'This paper is to be returned immediately to Room 238 through interoffice mail'. Nothing more was written on the memo. They predicted that the first message would be dealt with without much thought and then complied with, whereas the second, in the form of a command, would lead people to think about the message and ask themselves why, if the sender really wanted the memo back, it was sent in the first place. Sure enough, more memos – 90% – were returned in the first condition, compared to only 60% the other condition. Although low in experimental realism, for people do not actually send memos of that sort, psychological realism was high, and most people complied.

Every research method has its strengths and its weaknesses, and the laboratory experiment indeed does have a number of drawbacks. Although the procedure seems straightforward, it is actually complex; and so to avoid being misled by the results, we must take into account a number of important considerations.

Experimenter effects

The experimenter, having made certain predictions, can unwittingly influence the research participants in such a way that they produce the data that he or she is looking for (Rosenthal, 1966). Such influences are known as experimenter effects. For example, suppose in a study of bullying behaviour, both experimenter and a confederate of the experimenter are part of a five-person discussion group. There are two conditions. In one condition, but not in the other, the confederate bullies one of the participants. The hypothesis under study is that in the bullying condition, the non-targets will not come to the support of the target. If the experimenter inadvertently frowns when a participant begins to speak up in the target's defence, this might well inhibit the intervention, thus helping to support the experimenter's hypothesis. Because of this potential problem, double blind techniques are typically employed. That is, both the participants and the individual supervising the experiment are left unaware ('blind') about the hypothesis that is under study.

Participant effects

Participant effects are biases introduced into an experiment by the participants, and this can occur in at least two ways. First of all, if they make guesses about the goals of the research, then whether the guesses are right or wrong, their behaviour is likely to be affected by what they think is being studied. They are responding to the demand characteristics, a term coined by Orne (1962) to describe characteristics of the experimental situation that seem to cry out for, or 'demand', a certain response. Thus, a demand characteristic is any cue that gives the research participant an idea, whether correct or incorrect, about the hypothesis under investigation. Consequently, a helpful and compliant research participant, rather than responding spontaneously, may respond in a manner that supports the perceived hypothesis (Adair, 1973).

A second influence that can distort behaviour in the laboratory is evaluation apprehension, a problem that we also encountered with case studies and survey research. Because research participants do not want to appear foolish or unintelligent or weak or cruel in the eyes of the experimenter, they may react in what they think is a socially desirable fashion, thus departing from what might be their behaviour in similar situations outside the laboratory.

Advantages of the laboratory experiment:

- Complex social behaviours and situations can be broken down into smaller units.
- Extraneous variables can be minimized or eliminated.
- Causal relationships can be established.

Disadvantages:

- Experimenter effects, demand characteristics and evaluation apprehension may distort results.
- Not all social behaviours and situations can be examined in a laboratory setting.
- There is often difficulty in generalizing from laboratory results to the real world.
- The experiment by its very nature directs attention to the ways in which behaviour changes as a result of the independent variable, but overlooks behavioural stabilities – the ways in which behaviour stays the same.

KEY POINT: Laboratory experiments are of prime importance because they allow us to make inferences about causality, about what causes what. However, their results are not always directly generalizable to the larger world. Three types of realism – mundane, experimental, psychological – need to be considered. Furthermore, both the experimenter and the participants can unwittingly introduce bias.

The field experiment

Although laboratory experiments remain the primary source of knowledge in social psychology, we cannot rely on only one method in order to develop social psychological theory and to find solutions to social problems (Falk & Heckman, 2009). Once having found causal relationships in the laboratory, we need to go further in order to justify the application of our findings to the larger world. This is often best done through field experiments.

The field experiment, as the name suggests, is an experiment run in the 'real world'. It provides a way to increase external validity and mundane realism. Just as in the laboratory experiment, there is a control group and one or more experimental groups, and the experimenter manipulates an independent variable. However, in the field experiment, the participants are totally unaware that they are part of a study and that their behaviour is being monitored. Thus, reactivity is not an issue; there are no demand characteristics, and unlike both the laboratory experiment and the field study, evaluation apprehension does not occur.

But how can we assign participants to groups at random when they do not even know they are part of a study? Sometimes this is straightforward. For example, in a field experiment of bullying behaviour, children in a middle school in Italy were randomly allocated to one of four groups (Baldry, 2004). The children in each group watched one or the other of four brief videos set in a school setting. Those in one group watched a video depicting a single girl bully among a group of girls; those in the second group watched a similar video of one boy bully among a group of boys; those in the third group watched a video of several girl bullies among a group of girls; and those in the last group saw a video with several boy bullies among a group of boys. Subsequently, each student completed a questionnaire regarding their judgements of how much the bullying victim was at fault for what had happened to him or her, and how positively or negatively the bullies and the victims were viewed. It was found that, while in general the students reported positive feelings towards the victims and did not blame them, a bully acting alone was perceived to be braver and stronger than when several bullies were present in the same group.

At other times, randomization is based on 'choosing people at random' as they carry on with their daily lives. For example, in a study of whether pedestrians would be more likely to follow the lead of a well-dressed or a sloppily dressed confederate in crossing the street on a red light, the participants were people who happened to be at the intersection at the various times that either one or the other of the confederates would begin to cross (Lefkovitz, Blake & Mouton, 1955). However, one needs to consider the possibility that the particular intersection and the particular time of day will involve a group of participants who are not actually representative of a random selection from the general population.

Field experiments often provide participants with much more impact and involvement then do laboratory experiments, but they are limited to the study of only those variables present in the particular social situation under consideration. Yet, they can be useful in helping to extend laboratory findings to the larger world outside the laboratory. Thus, neither laboratory experiments nor field experiments are sufficient on their own; the integration of both laboratory and field experiments is essential for our progress in understanding social behaviour (Wilson et al., 2010).

Advantages of the field experiment:

- They are non-reactive, for the participants are not aware that they are in an experiment.
- They possess high external validity.
- They allow for the study of behaviour that is difficult or impossible to bring into the laboratory.
- Causal relationships can be established.

Disadvantages:

- It is often difficult to control or eliminate extraneous variables.
- It is often more difficult to measure the dependent variable in a natural setting.

KEY POINT: Field experiments provide high external validity, but often are more subject to interference from extraneous variables.

The quasi-experiment

As the name suggests, the quasi-experiment has some of the characteristics of a true experiment but does not completely come up to that standard of control that the experiment provides. In this case, while the researcher has no control over an independent variable, he or she takes advantage of significant changes that occur in the social world and treats these as representing a kind of 'quasi' independent variable.

For example, suppose that a school board is about to implement a new programme aimed at curbing bullying behaviour. The researcher may choose students at random and then measure their attitudes or observe their behaviours both before and after the new programme comes into effect. This would be what is known as the single group pre-test/post-test design. However, there is a drawback: while the researcher may observe significant changes in attitudes and behaviour, one cannot be certain that these were produced by the new programme. For example, perhaps at the same time that the study was being run, the children had watched an episode of a popular television programme that attacked bullying behaviour, and it was this programme and not the school programme that brought about the change.

Another variant of the quasi-experiment is the control group post-test design. As example in this case, two groups of schoolchildren would be chosen at random, one from a school with the new anti-bullying initiative and another from a similar school without that initiative. Each group would be observed and measured only once after the event of interest has taken place, in this case the introduction of the anti-bullying initiative in the one school. If there are other extraneous events, such as the television programme referred to above, then each group should be affected similarly. Thus, this approach provides us with a kind of control group. However, even if we find differences between the groups after the anti-bullying initiative has been introduced for one of them, we cannot be certain that these differences are not due to pre-existing differences between the two groups of students.

Advantages of the quasi-experiment:

- It allows us to study the effects of powerful manipulations (such as the introduction of anti-bullying pro-gramme) that the researcher could not independently produce.

Disadvantages:

- One cannot establish causal relationships because other factors could be responsible for the observed results.

KEY POINT: Quasi-experiments allow us to study real-life behaviour in natural settings, but lack the degree of control provided by experiments.

Neuroimaging research

Neuroimaging methodology is now being used to extend the reach of social psychology into the brain itself, and the methods that have been developed in cognitive neuroscience are now making important contributions to social psychological theory. Activation of neurons in a particular region of the brain brings more blood flow to that region, and these changes in blood flow can be detected through functional magnetic resonance imaging (fMRI), carried out while a research participant is fully awake. Through this procedure, researchers can now see which regions of the brain are activated when a participant is engaged in particular mental activities (Figure 1.7).

As a result, a door has been opened through which we can begin to understand the relationship between social activity and neural activity. Social cognitive neuroscience is an interdisciplinary approach to social behaviour that examines interactions among social psychological factors, relevant cognitive factors, and neurological factors that influence cognitive and social processes (Todorov et al., 2011). For example, *social* cognition appears to involve specialized neural processes that are distinct from those involved in cog-

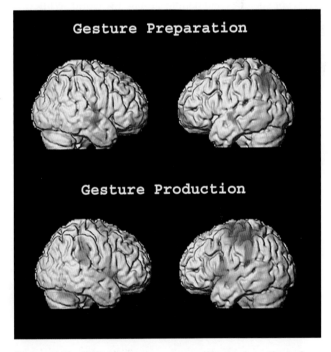

Figure 1.7 fMRI illustrating areas of the brain activated when thinking about making a gesture and when making it
Source: © Visuals Unlimited/Corbis

nition that does not involve social situations, and moreover these specialized regions of the brain appear to be unusually active even at times when individuals are at rest, suggesting that we may have a particular propensity for social thinking (Jenkins & Mitchell, 2011).

Social psychologists are applying neuroimaging techniques more and more widely – for example, studying the neural correlates of social categorization, the process by which we place people into categories (Van Bavel & Cunningham, 2010), and dehumanization, the process of coming to view certain groups of people as sub-human (Harris & Fiske, 2009). (These topics are discussed in later chapters). As an example of this kind of research, the brains of participants were scanned while they were playing a computer game (Gallagher et al., 2002). Participants in one experimental condition believed that they were playing against another person, while those in a second condition believed that they were playing against a computer; in each case the opponent was actually the computer. The results were fascinating, for it was found that only when the participants believed that they were playing against another human being was a particular set of brain regions activated, those associated with social cognition (anterior paracingulate nucleus).

KEY POINT: Neuroscience is opening new doors for social psychologists, allowing us to gain insight into what is going on in the brain when individuals are engaged in social activities.

CROSS-CULTURAL RESEARCH

Marshall McLuhan (McLuhan & Powers, 1989) described the modern world as being well on its way to becoming a *global village*, in which a worldwide collective identity, fostered by instantaneous electronic communication, gradually replaces the fragmentation brought about by the long-standing individualistic identities of societies and nations around the world. While we are not there yet, globalization is now a major force that affects just about everyone on the planet. But as globalization marches on, does our understanding of psychological processes keep pace? Does our psychological knowledge apply outside the relatively small number of technologically advanced societies in which psychological theory and research have thrived? Are there general psychological processes that are independent of culture or society or ethnic group? Cross-cultural psychology is focused on these very questions.

Cross-cultural psychology takes many forms. For example, there is what is known as international psychology. As described by the *International Psychology Division* of the American Psychological Association, international psychology 'seeks to develop a psychological science and practice that is contextually informed, culturally inclusive, serves the public interest, and promotes global perspectives'. The *International Union of Psychological Sciences* (IUPsyS) promotes exchanges of information among the more than 70 nations that are members and has a special interest in the development of psychology in developing countries. The *International Association of Cross-Cultural Psychology* is affiliated with the IUPsyS, and its goal is to facilitate communication among researchers focused on the intersection of culture and psychology. Other international psychological organizations include the *European Federation of Psychologists' Associations*, the *Sociedad Interamericana de Psicología*, and the *International Council of Psychologists*. However, while these organizations help coordinate and promote psychology throughout the world, with the exception of the International Association of Cross-Cultural Psychology, cross-cultural research is not their primary focus.

Cross-cultural psychology, on the other hand, is directed at understanding how cultural factors influence mental processes and behaviour, including social behaviour. In this perspective, the ultimate goal of social psychology is both to seek an understanding of human social behaviour that is universal and that applies across groups

Figure 1.8 How can we be sure that social psychological knowledge gained in one culture applies to another?

and societies and eras, and to understand how cultural factors moderate those social psychological processes. For example, prejudice may develop through the same processes in every culture, but the expression of prejudice may vary greatly as a result of differences in social norms: What is considered acceptable in one society may be considered impolite or illegal in another in light of their different cultures and social histories.

The rapid growth of globalization is spurring increased interest in cross-cultural research and promoting consideration of non-Western concepts and theories (Berry, 2013). However, at the moment, the reality remains that the vast majority of social psychological studies continue to be carried out in North America, primarily in the United States. Failure to take possible cross-cultural variations into account leads to the assumption that social psychological principles are universal. For example, in a later chapter we will discuss the well-established *fundamental attribution error* – the tendency to attribute the cause of other people's behaviour to their dispositions while downplaying or ignoring the role of situational factors. By 'well-established', we are referring again to studies carried out with North American undergraduates. Social psychologists have in the past assumed this to be a universal phenomenon, but it turns out that while it may well apply to more individualistic cultures such as those in Canada and the United States, it does not generally occur in collectivist cultures such as those found in Asia (Morris & Peng, 1994).

One concern is that social psychological research typically puts individuals into artificial situations, and because of this, their responses cannot automatically be generalized to real-world settings across a range of cultures (Rai & Fiske, 2010). Another serious problem is that not only is the bulk of social psychological research carried out in North America – although more and more is being carried in Western Europe – but it also is conducted with undergraduate students in laboratory settings. Canadian and American and Western European undergraduate students are not even typical of people in their own societies, and they are actually quite unusual compared with people in the rest of the world (Endler & Speer, 1998). This is certainly evident with regard to such concepts as cooperation, moral reasoning, self-concept, motivation, and sense of fairness (Henrich, Heine & Norenzayan, 2010). Henrich et al. (2010a, b) characterize this population of mostly North American and Western European undergraduate research participants by the acronym 'WEIRD' – for they come from **W**estern, **E**ducated, **I**ndustrialized, **R**ich, and **D**emocratic societies. And it is not just the research participants who are WEIRD, for the social psychological researchers themselves come largely from this same WEIRD subpopulation, and since it is they who define the research questions and develop the theories and design the studies, this also poses a problem for the generalizability of the most current social psychological findings (Meadon & Spurrett, 2010).

The Internet offers potential as a valuable tool in helping to overcome this problem (LoSchiavo & Shatz, 2009). For example, in one on-line study, more than half a million participants completed a personality questionnaire, and 20% of respondents were from non-Western countries. And while two-thirds of the respondents were from the United States, only one third of those were of college age (Gosling et al., 2010). However, you will immediately realize that such an approach raises serious concerns over issues that we have already discussed, such as sampling, honesty of responses and so on.

In terms of actually conducting cross-cultural research, there are two approaches. The first is simply to repeat studies already carried out in nations such as the United States and Canada to see whether the findings can be replicated in other nations. However, such research is problematic (Berry, 1978). First of all, language is an issue, for it may be difficult to provide translations of verbal instructions or interview questions and questionnaires in such a way that they provide equivalent nuances, and of course any reference to idiomatic expressions or to people or events within the original society may be meaningless to people of other societies. And the research situations themselves may not be comparable. For example, while North American university students may be generally familiar with what it means to be in a psychology experiment, that situation might involve a much more unusual and even upsetting experience to someone in another culture where there is little opportunity to be involved in social psychological research. Even more problematic, experimental manipulations which are meaningful in Western societies may not carry the same meaning in other cultures. The highly individualistic values of North American society that have shaped most existing social psychological research (Sampson, 1977) has led to research problems being defined in a particular way. For example, North American social psychologists interested in group influence are likely to consider those factors that keep individuals from following their individual initiatives – obedience, conformity, persuasion, bystander inaction. However, in more communal cultures, in which conformity and group harmony are valued, the important research questions may concern why some people deviate from group norms and communal values. Or if one were to study the dynamics of the social group, Western researchers would be likely to identify the leader as a person who is either formally selected by the group, who speaks the most, or whose ideas are most accepted by the group. Yet, this notion of leader does not apply in all cultures. Thus, we must do more than simply carry theories and methods developed in North America to other cultures, for otherwise we may fail to notice and to study aspects of those societies and cultures that are distinctive and important (Arnett, 2009).

The second approach to cross-cultural study involves the development of indigenous psychologies in various parts of the world where the research questions being asked are pertinent to the culture in which they are being posed. For example, in light of India's long history of having been dominated by a foreign ruler, the (diminishing) power of its caste system, and the fact that it is composed of many different linguistic and cultural groups, Indian social psychologists may ask questions about social identification, leadership and obedience that would not arise in Western nations. The development of such indigenous psychologies reflecting the cultures in which they arise can help us develop a social psychology that is truly universal (Berry, 1978).

> **KEY POINT:** Cross-cultural research is important not only in terms of understanding how social behaviour may differ from culture to culture, but, more importantly, it is needed for the development of social psychological principles applying to human beings in general.

META-ANALYSIS

The scientific literature involves a growing number of meta-analyses of research studies. It is important for the student to understand the basic notions involved here. Suppose we are faced with a number of studies that examine the relationship between bullying behaviour and self-esteem. Suppose again that some of these studies have reported a statistically significant relationship while others have not. What should we make of this collection of studies? Meta-analysis is a statistical technique devised by Glass, McGaw and Smith (1981) that allows us to consider the whole set of studies as a single study, treating each individual study as a single observation in a collection of observations. Suppose that there are only 20 research reports published that relate to self-esteem and bullying, and that ten of the studies found a significant negative relationship between self-esteem and bullying behaviour, while the other ten studies found no significant effect. It might seem as though the two sets of studies simply cancel each other out. Yet, suppose that in six of the ten studies that failed to find a significant effect, the non-significant difference was in the direction predicted by the hypothesis. In such a case, the data in 16 of the 20 studies is in the direction predicted by the hypothesis, and this paints a different picture than does the simple statement that only ten studies found an effect.

Conclusions reached through meta-analysis are only as good as the studies upon which the analysis is based, and poor research will lead to invalid meta-analytic conclusions. As well, the so-called 'file drawer problem' presents a challenge in that many pertinent studies that failed to find a significant effect were filed away and never published, and so we can never really be sure whether the collection of studies that we were able to find really constitutes all the studies that were carried out. Without those unpublished studies, our analysis may be quite biased. Overall, while meta-analyses are useful, they can only summarize, and cannot substitute for original research.

> **KEY POINT:** Meta-analysis is a statistical technique that allows us to combine the results of many independent studies in order to reach a broader overall conclusion about the processes being studied.

RESEARCH ETHICS

While social psychological researchers do not intentionally set out to harm their participants, they may unwittingly risk doing so in their zeal to study social behaviour. For example, suppose without your knowledge you are a participant in a field experiment. Would you be upset if, while sitting at a sidewalk restaurant, you notice someone across the street observing your behaviour and making notes about it? Not being aware that you are in a social psychological experiment, the realization that you are being watched might cause significant psychological distress. Or, consider the situation where you have volunteered to participate in a laboratory study, and as a result of that participation, you have learned that you are willing to bully a weaker individual. Did the researchers have the right to expose you to this most likely unwelcome lesson about your own character without having first sought your permission?

Social psychologists have become increasingly aware of the opportunity for harm that can present itself in social psychological research if appropriate preventative measures are not taken. The problem is magnified by the fact that the researcher is typically in a position of authority relative to the participant, and this status is likely to create a relationship of trust in which the participants let their guard down, assuming that they will be neither harmed nor exploited. The best way for the psychology discipline to mitigate against such harm is to sensitize researchers in advance to problems that might arise, and to provide them with guidelines that, if followed, will shield participants from any undesirable consequences of their participation.

Psychological codes of ethics stress the importance of obtaining informed consent, maintaining confidentiality, doing no harm, staying within one's limits of competence, and being accountable. These apply equally to research and to clinical situations. Sinclair (2002) points out that such principles have roots that run very deep into history. How deep? In 1901, a black stone was discovered in the Middle East that was carved with what we now know as the Code of Hammurabi, who ruled the Babylonian Empire from 1795 to 1750 BCE. This is the earliest known set of laws informing a populace of their obligations and the punishments that would ensue for failure to live up to those obligations. Included were laws dictating the punishments for physicians who harmed their patients – in other words, a code of ethics.

In ancient Greece, the Hippocratic Oath, written several centuries BCE, not only echoed the 'do no harm' of the Hammurabi code, but included other principles contained in modern codes of ethics including this one with regard to confidentiality:

> I will not divulge anything that, in connection with my profession or otherwise, I might see or hear of in the lives of men which should not be divulged, in the belief that all such things shall be kept secret (Sinclair, 2002).

Modern codes of ethical conduct relating to research involving human participants, be this in psychology or medicine or other disciplines, trace their lineage to the *Nuremberg Code,* which was developed in reaction to the atrocities carried out by Nazi medical researchers during the Second World War. Not only does it emphasize the need for protection from harm, it was the first ethical code that stressed the need for informed consent (Sinclair, 1993). The World Medical Association's 1964 *Declaration of Helsinki,* a code of ethics for medical researchers, also derives from the Nuremberg Code.

It is now the norm in universities and granting agencies in a growing number of nations for all proposed research involving human participants to undergo the scrutiny of a research ethics committee whose responsibility it is to protect research participants from undue exploitation, unnecessary deception or potential harm. The *Code of Ethics* of the Canadian Psychological Association, the American Psychological Association's *Ethical Principles of Psychologists* and the *Code of Ethics and Conduct* published by the British Psychological Society all address research involving human research participants. Many other countries have their own codes of ethics. Leach & Harbin (2009) compared the psychological codes of ethics of 24 such countries and found considerable similarity; this is in part because many countries have modelled their ethical codes after the American Psychological Association's *Ethical Principles of Psychologists.* The codes in four countries, Australia, Canada, Israel, and South Africa, share 100% of those principles, and overall about 70% of the principles in the various countries surveyed were identical with those of the APA.

These codes revolve around four primary ethical principles (e.g., Sinclair, Poizner, Gilmour-Barrett & Randall, 1987): respect for the dignity of the person; responsibility to society; integrity in relationships; and responsible caring. Although the last of these is more pertinent to applied psychology, all four relate to how we should treat people who come under our influence, whether as clients, patients or research participants. Such principles are also reflected in the *Universal Declaration of Ethics Principles for Psychologists* adopted at the International Congress of Psychology in Berlin in 2008 after several years of research and international consultation.

Among the ethical concerns that specifically apply to research, those that have received the most attention are protection from harm; the need for informed consent; and the right to privacy. In addition, social psychologists have shown particular attention to the practice of deception and to the social responsibility of researchers. We shall review each of these in turn. It is important to note that these concerns relate to social psychological research in general and not just laboratory experiments.

Protection from harm

It should go without saying that researchers must never expose participants to harm. And yet, while it is relatively straightforward to foresee possible physical harm that is to be avoided, the potential for psychological harm or distress is often much more difficult to recognize. Recall the example of the bullying experiment where the participant joins in with the bullies rather than defends the victim. While some participants will be unaffected by this revelation, and others will benefit in that they become determined to change their behaviour in future, yet others may be distressed and begin to devalue themselves in a way that could lead to significant psychological difficulties. Appropriate debriefing, discussed below, can mitigate any enduring emotional damage, but the researcher needs to be sensitive to the possibility of such harm and not simply assume that debriefing will prevent any distress or emotional damage.

Informed consent

By informing research participants as fully as possible about what will happen to them during their participation (without destroying the effectiveness of the experiment manipulation), they can then freely choose whether to participate. Even when deception is necessary, so long as they are told that it is impossible to tell them in advance all the details of the experiment without influencing their behaviour, they are unlikely to be upset when subsequently informed that deception took place.

The issue of informed consent is often more problematic with research outside the laboratory. Consider the difficulty in obtaining informed consent when systematically observing the behaviour of pedestrians at an intersection, people who do not even know that they are being observed; or in a field study involving a participant observer who pretends to be one of the group; or even in an archival study using students' school records. Is it sufficient, or even always necessary, to obtain consent *after* the data is collected? These are complicated issues, and before approving such research, ethics committees need to consider the risk of harm to participants, the extent to which individuals are identifiable, and the potential importance of the research.

Right to privacy and confidentiality

Privacy issues have garnered considerable public attention, especially in this era of Internet communications, electronic medical records, credit card data and so forth. In modern democratic societies, people tend to take for granted that government authorities and others will work to ensure their privacy and maintain the confidentiality of personal information. How does this extend into the research domain? In field studies and field experiments, participants generally do not know that they are participants, and so how is it possible to observe their right to privacy? And even when participants have consented to an invasion of their privacy – as is the case in formal laboratory studies where informed consent is obtained – it is still incumbent upon the researchers to maintain the confidentiality of research participants' responses, unless explicit permission has been obtained to publicize them. Data records must be stored somewhere, and the ethical researcher needs to ensure that during data analysis, data reporting or data storage, confidentiality is safeguarded. For example, if we were carrying out a longitudinal study of the bullying behaviour of children, following them from kindergarten to high school graduation, we would need to be able to identify each child in order to compare his or her data from year to year. However, we would do so by assigning a code to each student, and we would keep the actual name that corresponds to each code under lock and key, so that no one working with the data would be able to relate them to any individual child.

Deception

If research participants know the purpose of the study, it is unlikely that they will act as they normally would in a similar situation. This is one of the appeals of field experiments, for in this case research participants act naturally, since they do not know that they are participants. (But where is the informed consent?) However, the real aim of the laboratory experiment must often be disguised so that research participants may react almost as though they were in a real-life situation.

It is interesting to note that in the 1920s and 1930s, deception was rarely used in social psychology research, and it was not even all that common in the 1940s and 1950s. However, it became very prevalent during the 1960s and 1970s (Adair, Dushenko & Lindsay, 1985; Nicks, Korn & Mainieri, 1997). It continues to be used frequently. At the same time, social psychologists are now much more concerned about the ethics of deception and the moral problem that it presents. After all, deception means 'trickery', 'deceit' or 'lying', and this raises the question of whether this is something that psychological researchers should be involved with.

Deception in social psychological research became very controversial after the publication of Milgram's (1963) study of obedience (see Chapter 6), in which research participants were told they were participating in a study of learning that involved their administration of progressively stronger electric shocks to a 'learner'. Milgram was accused (e.g., Baumrind, 1964) of having exposed his research participants to potentially disturbing emotional reactions once they were informed of the true nature of the experiment and then evaluated their own behaviour in that context. Milgram (1964) argued that through his debriefing of the research participants, any possible emotional damage had been prevented, since they learned that no one had actually been hurt and that their behaviour had been reasonable given the circumstances. Psychiatric interviews of the research participants one year after the experiment found no enduring effects of the deception. Yet, many psychologists were not satisfied that all harm had been prevented.

In the light of concerns raised by Milgram's study, ethical research guidelines have become stricter over the years and now deception is viewed as something to be used as a last resort, when no other effective alternatives are available, and when its use is unlikely to harm the participants in any way. But what is the actual practice? Although, as noted above, the use of deception has dropped off since the 1960s and 1970s, it is still widely used. For example, in a survey of all the studies published in two of the world's preeminent social psychological journals, the *Journal of Experimental Social Psychology* (2002) and the *Journal of Personality and Social Psychology* (1996), 42% and 50% of their articles respectively involved deception (Hertwig & Ortmann, 2008).

On the other hand, social psychological knowledge is much richer because of the Milgram research. If we rule out deception, we make much social psychological research all but impossible. Do we stop our research? In so doing, may we not one day be judged guilty of a greater sin, that of failing to use the powerful methodology of science to understand human social behaviour so that we can learn to reduce aggression, diminish prejudice and enhance quality of life?

And in any case, do psychologists worry too much at times about the effects of deception? No one has actually demonstrated that there are any long-term negative consequences of deception in a social psychological experiment. We all agree that it is important to protect the research participant's self-worth, and this can be done even if they are 'tricked' as long as they are treated with respect (Weiss, 2001). It has even been argued that deception is at times not only ethically acceptable, but preferable to non-deceptive procedures (Kimmel, 2011). Indeed, most deception in social psychology experiments is so benign that few would fault it seriously, except on the general principle that we have no right to deceive. After all, if a research participant is led to believe that she is participating in a study of attitudes, but the real aim of the study is to see under what conditions research participants are most likely to help the experimenter pick up a stack of books that is 'accidentally' dropped on the floor, how likely is it that research participants will be upset emotionally as a result? Empirical studies of the reactions of participants in experiments using deception indicate that they do not appear to share psychologists' distaste for deception. Rather, they are more likely to view the deception as a necessary withholding of information or a necessary ruse or misrepresentation (Christensen, 1988; Smith, 1983); in other words, they are not surprised, for they expect it.

Alternatives to deception

If we were to give up deception, how could we study participants' behaviour when they know what it is that is being studied? In the past, it was suggested that participants could role-play (Kelman, 1967). That is, having been told what the research is about, research participants would be asked to act in the way that they think other people would act in such a situation. However, the problem is that participants can only really guess at the kind of responses people would make, and, in all likelihood the researcher's speculations, backed by an understanding of the psychological literature, would provide a better guide. Thus, such role-play has had very limited appeal to researchers.

Simulation, whereby research participants are immersed in a situation that closely mimics a real-life situation of interest, can be more useful, even though no deception is involved. A notable example of such research is the Stanford Prison study (see Chapter 14). Participants lived in a mock prison for several days. Some were given the role of prisoners and others the role of guards, and their interactions were observed to see whether these 'guards' would take on any of the negative attributes sometimes reported with regard to real-life prison guards. Even though the participants knew that the situation was make-believe, the behaviours produced were so powerful that the study had to be prematurely ended. However, even though simulations such as this can present relatively high experimental and mundane realism and provoke powerful emotions and dramatic behaviours, they have their own problems. Despite the advantage of avoiding deception, is it ethical to expose participants to such emotionally powerful situations that might leave them suitably stressed? Furthermore, can we really generalize the findings from such simulations to real-life situations, or are we likely instead to be misled?

Thus, we do not have any good alternatives to deception in social psychology. Of course, many studies do not require deception, but many others do. Although informed consent and debriefing help to minimize the risk of emotional harm, the experimenter must take all reasonable precautions to ensure such a risk is minimal, and that even this minimal risk is justified by the importance of what might be learned from the experiment.

Debriefing

When it has been determined that deception is justified and that the risk is minimal, it is nonetheless essential that the participants are substantively informed of the true nature of the experiment through the process of debriefing. Debriefing has two important components. First of all, there is dehoaxing: the deception is explained and justified in terms of the purpose of the experiment. Just as important is desensitization, which is aimed at helping the research participants to understand their own behaviour in the context of the research situation, and to minimize the likelihood that they will be upset with their own behaviour or suffer any other emotional distress.

Social responsibility of researchers

What obligations do researchers have to the society in which they live? While most psychology research is unlikely to harm society or its various subgroups, some research carries a great potential for such harm. For example, if careless or biased researchers were to carry out research that seemed to suggest that one group or race or gender was in some way inferior to others (and this has happened on occasion), such research could bring extreme harm to individuals and the community. Thus, research ethics committees must be particularly vigilant to ensure that research related to socially sensitive issues is carried out with appropriate concern for possible misinterpretation or misuse of the ultimate research findings.

[**KEY POINT:** Researchers must be cognizant of potential sources of harm to their research participants and discharge their ethical responsibility to take effective measures to guard against any such harm.]

A FINAL NOTE

For our understanding of human social behaviour to advance, we must be particularly careful about how we gather our data. As has been detailed in this chapter, there are many pitfalls and biases that can lead us astray, but by being aware of them and by being diligent in the application of good research methodology, we can build and test theories that truly do advance our knowledge. It is such careful research that distinguishes social psychology from the pop psychology literature of the bookshop and magazine stand.

SUMMARY

1. Science is an effective method of gaining knowledge and understanding. It consists of formulating hypotheses, testing them through systematic observation and building theories from these findings.

2. Precise measurement is the basic tool of science. In social psychology it is often difficult to translate a hypothetical construct (such as 'attitude') into an operational definition (i.e., a measure). Measurement problems include the following:

   (a) reliability – does the measure yield consistent readings?

   (b) validity – does it measure what it is intended to measure?

   (c) reactivity – does the measure affect the very thing that is being measured? and

   (d) sampling – are the data obtained representative of a population of interest?

3. In social psychology, research can be either quantitative or qualitative, although the majority of studies are quantitative in nature. Both experimental and nonexperimental methods of research are used. All methods have both advantages and disadvantages.

4. Nonexperimental research methods include systematic direct observation, archival methods, case studies, survey interviews or questionnaires, field studies, in which behaviour is observed systematically in a natural setting, and correlational research.

5. In experimental research, research participants are assigned randomly to experimental and control groups so that we assume the groups are identical before the experiment. An independent variable is manipulated so that its effects can be observed by comparison between the two groups. Other confounding variables that may influence results are controlled. Experimental research methods include: (a) laboratory experiments; (b) field experiments; and (c) quasi-experiments.

6. The outcomes of both nonexperimental and experimental research can be biased by the expectations and unintentional actions of experimenters, as well as by the actions of participants who act as they believe the experimenter wants them to act (demand characteristics) or who try to create a 'good' impression of themselves (evaluation apprehension).

7. Generalizations drawn from experiments are limited by: (a) external validity, that is, how comparable the experimental situation is to a real-life situation; and (b) internal validity, the extent to which the results were due to manipulation of the independent variable rather than to artefact.

8. Correlational methods, while limited with regard to cause and effect relationships, provide a powerful tool for examining how variables interrelate, and for analysing both behavioural stability and longitudinal change.

9. Neuroscience offers a new methodology for studying social behaviour and its correlates at the neurological level.

10. Cross-cultural research is very important, but care must be taken to avoid pitfalls that plague research into cultural differences. The growth of indigenous social psychologies reflecting the cultures in which they arise can lead to a social psychology that is truly universal. Ethical concerns in social psychological research include protection from harm; the right to privacy; the use of deception in experiments; the need for debriefing and informed consent; and the responsibility of researchers to the society in which they live.

POINTS TO PONDER

- Why was Copernicus' decision to give data precedence over dogma so important? Can data be understood without a theory that explains them?
- Field experiments make deception unnecessary, but there is no informed consent. Laboratory experiments offer informed consent but deception is often involved. Which do you think is more important, informed consent or freedom from deception? And can one truly have informed consent while using deception?
- Does the use of operational definitions – for example, defining aggression in terms of the delivery of electric shocks – run the risk of diverting researchers from gaining an understanding of the real-life behaviour, or is it the only way that we can really come to understand such behaviour?
- Why is cross-cultural research so important, not only for understanding other cultures, but for understanding our own?

FURTHER READING

Adair, J. (Guest Editor) (2005). Special issue: Social psychology around the world. *International Journal of Psychology, 40* (4).

Articles in this special issue describe efforts to develop indigenous social psychologies in a number of regions around the world, including Latin America, India, Taiwan, Europe, Australia and Canada.

Forrester, M.A. (2010). *Doing qualitative research in psychology: A practical guide.* London: Sage.

As the title suggests, this provides an introduction to various qualitative approaches used in social psychology and other areas of psychological research.

Matsumoto, D. (2000). *Cultural influences on research methods and statistics.* Long Grove, Ill: Waveland Press.

Although researchers are sometimes unaware of it, culture often plays a powerful role in the way that research is carried out and its data are analysed. This book addresses both general issues that arise in psychological methodology and statistical analysis, as well as issues

that are particular to cross-cultural research, and for that matter to any research that compares people across racial, gender, linguistic or ethnic lines.

Mitchell, G. (2012). Revisiting truth or triviality: The external validity of research in the psychological laboratory. *Perspectives on Psychological Science, 7,* 109–118.

This is a critical review of the extent to which psychological research in the laboratory possesses external validity. In general, experiments with larger effect sizes are more likely to generalize to situations outside the laboratory.

Smith, P.B., Bond, M.H. & Kağitçibasi, C. (Eds). (2006). *Understanding social psychology across cultures: Living and working with others in a changing world.* London: Sage Publications.

An excellent introduction to understanding how psychological processes are moulded by culture. Theories and methods involved in cross-cultural research are examined in terms of their strengths and weaknesses.

WEBLINKS

http://www.cpa.ca/aboutcpa/committees/ethics/codeofethics/
The code of ethics of the Canadian Psychological Association.
http://www.bps.org.uk/sites/default/files/documents/code_of_ethics_and_conduct.pdf
The code of ethics and conduct of the British Psychological Society.

PART II

UNDERSTANDING YOUR SOCIAL WORLD

CHAPTER 2
SOCIAL PERCEPTION AND COGNITION

There is nothing either good or bad but thinking makes it so.
William Shakespeare

LEARNING OBJECTIVES

* To understand the dual-systems model of thinking (rapid versus slower and deliberative) and how it applies to thinking in the social context

* To understand how we form first impressions of people

* To learn how we arrive at conclusions about cause and effect in our social world

* To explore how we tend to think rapidly with very little conscious deliberation, using categories about people and events (schemas), and applying implicit rules of thumb (heuristics)

* To understand how we process information about people and events, involving attention, memory, thinking in more or less concrete or abstract ways (construal) and thinking of what might have been

* To examine the biases that influence our thinking about our social world

Figure 2.1 Film star Humphrey Bogart
Source: © John Springer Collection/Corbis

While learning to drive a car, you are attentive to the many details of this complex task: get in the car, adjust the seat, adjust the mirrors, start the ignition, check the mirrors and rear window, shift into reverse gear, back into traffic when it's safe, shift into drive or first gear, drive in traffic, continually check the sides and rear as well as what's in front of you, brake well before a red light, move your foot from the brake to the gas pedal when the green light appears … it's all a conscious, focused performance. Contrast this with the experienced driver. All of this becomes automatic, and your mind may well be on the day ahead, what your partner said last night, or the music on your sound system. Fully focused attention is galvanized only when the unexpected happens – the car in front of you stops suddenly, the weather turns nasty, the fuel gauge hovers around 'empty'. Notice how your way of thinking about driving has shifted.

Think of old movies where smoking was portrayed as normal for certain characters, even glamorous, for example, those of Humphrey Bogart. Contrast this with most movies today in most cultures, where smoking is rarely portrayed. Note how smoking several generations ago was seen as normative, nothing to draw our attention, while today it is more unusual, drawing conscious attention.

This reflects the **dual-systems model** of thinking (Evans, 2008; Kahneman, 2011). We think in a manner that is rapid, automatic and unconscious (System 1), and we also think in a manner that is slow, deliberative and conscious (System 2). Thus, we may gradually and logically form an impression of someone if, for instance, we are interviewing the person for a job, or if this is a first date with a prospective romantic partner (System 2). More often, we form our impression rapidly, automatically and without conscious thought (System 1). Note that System 1 operates largely out of conscious awareness, although it is not the Freudian model of unconscious repressed feelings. Rather, it allows us to handle the routine tasks of daily life on 'automatic pilot'. As Fiske & Taylor (1991) suggest, we are cognitive misers, unwilling to expend any more effort into thinking than is necessary. Indeed, the rapid, non-conscious mode has evolved to serve us well where we have to appraise the situation based on immediate cues and react. On the other hand, conscious awareness and thinking things out have obvious advantages. Indeed, Langer (1989) presents vigorous arguments for a more 'mindful' way of living.

Social psychologists have made some intriguing discoveries in this area. This chapter begins with a discussion of how we form overall impressions of people based on traits such as friendliness, honesty, sneakiness or self-discipline. The discussion then turns to the study of attributions, how people draw conclusions about why other people act as they do. Finally, the chapter outlines more subtle processes of social cognition by which we 'construct' our own view of reality and the many shortcuts we take to get there. Much of the material in this chapter is fundamental to many areas of social psychology and will be elaborated upon in succeeding chapters.

> **KEY POINT:** We think in two different ways, a conscious, deliberative manner and an implicit, automatic system using the least possible effort. The latter system characterizes our routine daily manner of living.

FORMING IMPRESSIONS OF PEOPLE

Research on social perception began with how we form initial impressions of other people, how we decide that a person is friendly, arrogant, honest or interesting. In general, participants in those early studies were provided with a photo or a brief description of a person, in which one or a small number of characteristics or actions were varied, and then the participants were asked to rate the target person in terms of a set of traits. One of the key findings that emerged from those studies concerned the existence of central traits, certain characteristics that affect other judgements about that person. For instance, when participants were led to believe that a guest lecturer in a class was 'warm' as opposed to 'cold', they tended to make more positive judgements about that individual in terms of being popular, wise and imaginative (Asch, 1946; Kelley, 1950). When informed that the target person was a smoker, that person was rated by participants as less 'considerate', 'calm', 'honest', 'healthy', 'well-mannered', 'happy', less self-controlled, less imaginative, and less mature (Dermer & Jacobsen, 1986; Dion, Dion, Coambs & Kozlowski, 1990; Polivy, Hackett & Bycio, 1979).

Figure 2.2 What is your impression of this person? Why? Does knowing he is Leonard Cohen, poet, songwriter and singer, affect your impression?

Source: © Rune Hellestad/Corbis

Of course, we notice many different traits in the same person. We may first notice that a person is attractive, and then discover that this person also appears arrogant. How do we combine these observations about the person to arrive at an overall evaluation? Imagine that we have some kind of mental rating scale for each characteristic. The evidence indicates that we follow an implicit weighted averaging model in combining such information about the person (Anderson, 1965, 1978). That is, we keep a rough 'running' average of our trait ratings in our heads. For example, if we find someone to be highly intelligent (rating the person as 8 on a scale of 1 to 10) but only somewhat attractive (4 on that scale), our overall rating of that person would fall somewhere around 6 on that 10-point scale. However, if attractiveness were more important to us than intelligence as a basis for judging people, then the overall weighted average would be less than 6 because attractiveness is more important to us.

Clearly, we don't consciously think about others in such a mathematical way, but we implicitly combine impressions about people as if we were doing so. It is important to understand that people arrive at judgements about traits rather quickly and often with minimal information, System 1 in cognitive terms (Carlston & Skowronski, 1994). For instance, participants confidently provide the same trait ratings to photographs of people (Figure 2.2), whether they are exposed to those pictures for one-tenth of a second or a full second (Willis & Todorov, 2006).

Are these first impressions lasting? Intuitively, it would seem that as we get to know someone better over time, our impressions should change and become more accurate. This hypothesis has been tested in a longitudinal study, in which participants met in groups once a week for seven weeks. Before the first meeting, each participant completed self-rating forms, and after weeks 1, 4 and 7, they rated all of the other persons in their group on the same scales. As predicted, over time, their ratings of the other people more closely matched how people rated themselves (Paulhus & Bruce, 1992). Thus, first impressions are important but not immutable.

Biases in impression formation

Most people, at least in Western cultures, tend to form impressions of others that are positive rather than negative; this is known as a positivity bias, also known as the Pollyanna principle (Matlin & Stang, 1978).

49

Figure 2.3 A scene from the movie *Rashomon* in which different people remember and interpret the same criminal event in very different ways

Source: © John Springer Collection/Corbis

Consider, for example, student evaluations of their professors. At one university, students rated 97% of their professors as 'above average', a mathematical impossibility (Sears, 1983). Along with the positivity bias, our overall impression of a person tends be influenced more by negative information than by positive information (Fiske, 1980; Skowronski & Carlston, 1989; Anderson, 1965; Hamilton & Zanna, 1972). Of course, we may be influenced by both the positivity bias and negativity effect at the same time in forming our overall impression (Klein, 1991).

Eye of the beholder

Of course, perception of a person, event or object is subjective. We all have our own ways of interpreting people and events, consistent with our own experience and assumptions. The classic 1952 movie *Rashomon* vividly shows how different people report the same crime in startlingly different ways (Figure 2.3).

In forming impressions of others, people bring their own personal way of looking at the world. For instance, we have our own implicit personality theories – a set of unstated assumptions about human nature and people in general (Bruner & Tagiuri, 1954; Anderson & Sedikides, 1990; Sedikides & Anderson, 1994). We may believe people are, in general, trustworthy or untrustworthy, rational or irrational, altruistic or selfish. Implicit personality theories also concern our beliefs about what characteristics go together. For instance, many people believe that friendly people are also people to be trusted, which can be a dangerous delusion (Anderson, Lepper & Ross, 1980).

Cognitive neuroscience has contributed to our understanding of social perception. In particular, it has emerged that there are areas of brain activity specific to forming impressions of people, as opposed to impressions of inanimate objects. In one study (Mitchell, Macrae & Banaji, 2006), participants read a series of statements about personality traits such as extraversion, and were asked to pair these trait descriptions with one of a set of facial photos. In one experimental condition, participants were instructed to memorize the order in which the information was given, while in another condition, participants were asked to form an impression of what each person was like based on the picture and the information. While engaged in this task, brain activity was recorded by means of fMRI (functional magnetic resonance imaging) scans. Different brain areas were involved in the non-social task (e.g. superior frontal gyrus, caudate nucleus) and the social, impression-formation task (dorsomedial prefrontal cortex). This study and others suggest that distinct areas of the brain are involved in social cognition.

There are also cultural differences. For instance, when people in Western cultures are asked to describe the artistic type of person, they will use adjectives such as creative, temperamental and unconventional. A Chinese person would be mystified by this request, because the 'artistic type' is not a concept in that culture. On the other hand, in Chinese culture, people describe a type of person who is worldly, socially skilled and devoted to family (*shi gu*) (Hoffman, Lau & Johnson, 1986). Western participants tend to focus on objects in their perceptual field while East Asians focus more on the contexts and background of the scene (Ames & Fiske, 2010). When Chinese and American participants were asked to judge various pictures of target objects against a background, their fMRI responses showed that, compared to the Chinese, the Americans activated more neural regions involved in the processing of objects (e.g. middle temporal gyrus) (Gutchess, Welsh, Boduroğlu & Park, 2006). No consistent differences between the two participant groups were found when they were instructed to focus on background images. Thus, cultural differences in how people process visual information (such as other people) are reflected in selective activation of cortical areas.

ATTRIBUTIONS OF CAUSALITY

Zinedine Zidane is considered to have been one of the greatest football (soccer) players of his era. Of Algerian descent, his parents emigrated to France when he was a child, where his talents soon became evident. He eventually played as a midfielder for the Real Madrid and Juventus teams, and for the French national team, which won the World Cup in 1998. In the World Cup tournament of 2006, he was named as the outstanding player prior to the final match, which pitted France against Italy. At a crucial point in the second half of that match, he deliberately head-butted Italian player Marco Materazzi, for which he was sent from the field of play. The match ended in a draw, and, without Zidane, France lost in the penalty shootout. It was later determined that Materazzi had insulted Zidane's mother, which precipitated Zidane's angry response. How would you explain his action, which quite plausibly cost his nation's team the World Cup? Was it caused by Zidane's inability to control his temper, to his cultural sensitivities, to Materazzi's provocative actions, to the heightened tensions of the World Cup final? In this section, we explore how people explain the social and personal events in their lives, in short, how they make attributions (Heider, 1958).

Figure 2.4 Italy's Marco Materazzi falls on the pitch after being head-butted by France's Zinedine Zidane (right) during their World Cup 2006 Final match in Berlin, Germany. To what would you attribute Zidane's actions?

Source: © HO/Reuters/Corbis

Let us begin with several fundamental principles. According to the **discounting principle** (Kelley, 1972), people tend to accept the most likely cause and set aside or 'discount' other possibilities. For example, consider a boss who closely supervises a hard-working employee. Since the supervisor has a plausible explanation for that worker's productivity (close supervision), an alternative attribution for that worker's productivity – that she was motivated to do a good job – will be discounted (Strickland, 1958). In several studies, it has been shown that politicians are rated as having more integrity and strength when they oppose the position of their own party or when they speak before a hostile audience (Eagly, Wood & Chaiken, 1978; Pancer, Brown, Gregor & Claxton-Oldfield, 1992). If they follow the party line, we attribute their position to political pressure and conformity, and discount the possibility that they really mean it. Similarly, when we are told our success in a task indicates that we are competent, we discount other possible explanations, such as being lucky (Braun & Wicklund, 1989).

According to the **covariation principle**, when two events repeatedly occur together, people often see cause and effect between them. For example, suppose a person becomes very angry every time a certain topic of conversation comes up, but is rarely angry otherwise. We would probably attribute the anger to the topic of conversation. Of course, two events may coincide without one causing the other. There may be a correlation between the congestion on commuter trains and traffic on a bridge, but we cannot assume that the train congestion brings the cars or vice versa; (both happen to occur at rush hour). Such an obvious example aside, in general there is a bias, particularly in Western cultures, to assume causality where it may or may not exist.

ATTRIBUTION THEORIES

Several theories have been developed to explain how people form situational or dispositional causal attributions. The following discussion focuses on three theories: Jones and Davis's model of correspondent inferences, Kelley's covariation model, and Weiner's model of achievement attributions.

Theory of correspondent inferences

When a person tells you how attractive you are, does he or she really mean it? Can we use someone's behaviour as a guide to how that person is feeling, or what that person intends, particularly when we have only that one event to guide us? At first glance, one might surmise that 'actions speak louder than words'. However, at least two important factors complicate the picture. First, a person may seek to mislead others about her true feelings: the poker player with a straight flush, the salesperson who knows the real bottom-line price, the daughter who assures her mother that 'everything is fine'. Second, actions often stem from situational causes. Politicians are expected to make promises, students are expected to take useful notes in lectures, and the salesperson is instructed to act cheerfully.

Figure 2.5   A problem in perception: Does this poker player have a winning hand? How do his opponents decide?

Source: Beto Chagas/Shutterstock.com

The **theory of correspondent inferences** (Jones & Davis, 1965) concerns how we use certain cues to infer that an action corresponds to a personal disposition. What do we look for? First, we focus upon freely chosen behaviours and ignore those that are expected, required or coerced. We may know that the excessively friendly salesperson is probably following the manager's orders, and a correspondent inference (that she or he is friendly) is unlikely. Second, behaviours that produce uncommon effects – those that seem unique or out of role – are noticed. If your best friend expresses concern that you look tired, you may attribute that behaviour to the role, 'That's what friends are for'. However, if a salesperson says the same thing, a correspondent inference to to his or her disposition (that he or see is sympathetic) is much more likely. A third important cue is social desirability, adherence to social norms. We learn more about a people's taste in clothing if they wear pyjamas to class than if they wear jeans and a t-shirt.

These inferences seem to be logical 'best guesses' when we don't have much information. There are also two non-logical biases. People tend to make more confident correspondent inferences of someone's intent when the action has a strong consequence for themselves, rather than for someone else (hedonic relevance), and when they believe that the actor *intended* to benefit or harm them (personalism). When you are the target of an insult, you are less likely to make allowance for the person having a bad day (a situational attribution) than were that person insulting someone else. A series of experiments has supported the model of correspondent inferences (Jones & Harris, 1976; Jones, Davis & Gergen, 1961).

KEY POINT: Attributions involve the perception of the causes of people's actions and their consequences, and the attributions may be dispositional or situational. If we can judge a particular cause as plausible, we tend to discount other possible causes, and we tend to assume cause and effect between people and events that happen at the same time. We infer that a person's action corresponds to a disposition to act in that way when the act was freely chosen, the consequences are unexpected or are counter to social norms, when the action seemed directed at the us and when the consequences are significant.

As noted, the theory of correspondent inferences concerns a single act, and how we decide whether that act 'corresponds' to a disposition. However, we often make attributions about the actions of people whom we have observed over time. In these cases, the attributions that we make about their behaviour follow somewhat different principles. The covariation model was developed to apply to such cases.

Covariation model

Imagine that you are a reporter for a newspaper who has been assigned to interview a celebrated musician visiting your city. The musician praises you for conducting a great interview. Why did the visiting celebrity pay you that compliment? Kelley (1972) argues that people behave as 'naive scientists' in the sense that they sift through various clues, past and present, to arrive at a 'best guess' or hypothesis about the 'real cause' of someone's action. He developed an attributional model of covariation which accounts for how people put together information about the actor (the person performing the behaviour), the entity (the person to whom the behaviour is directed), and the situation (the social context in which the action takes place). In the case of the reporter and the celebrity, there are three sources of information that we would consider:

Distinctiveness of the entity
Is the celebrity generally known for charm and generosity to members of the press? If so, then there is nothing distinctive about the behaviour shown towards you (the entity) as a reporter. On the other hand, if the person's behaviour towards you is distinctive, different from how he or she treated other members of the press, then it must be something about you that caused him or her to praise you (an entity attribution).

Consensus across actors
Do most of your interview subjects praise you for your interviewing techniques? If so, it says something about you as a reporter (entity). If not, it indicates something about this particular individual (the actor is a nice person) or perhaps about celebrity interviews in general (perhaps all celebrities praise their interviewers).

Consistency across situations
Does the celebrity behave in this way towards you in different situations? If consistency is high, we would attribute behaviour to the actor or the entity – either she is generous with her praise, or you are a great reporter. However, low consistency would lead to a situational attribution.

Of course, wherever possible, we would use all three sources of information together. However, research shows that we use consensus information about how others act towards the entity less often (Nisbett & Borgida, 1975), and so we are less likely to consider how other interview subjects have reacted to our interviews.

Note the difference between the theories of correspondent inferences and covariation (Figure 2.6). Kelley has provided us with a useful model of how we use covariation information to make social attributions. However, it presupposes that we have sufficient consensus, consistency and distinctiveness information. The theory of correspondent inferences explains how attributions are made when we do not have such information (Higgins & Bryant, 1982).

Attributions about success and failure

Many of our actions have consequences, sometimes defined in concrete feedback: a mark on an examination, getting a job or promotion, making a lot of money, winning (or losing) that tennis match or being elected to office.

	Distinctiveness	Consensus	Consistency
Actor Attribution: Internal causes (attitudes, personal traits) made the person act in this way	Low	Low	High
Entity Attribution: External causes (your physical appearance, your behaviour) made the person act in this way	High	High	High

Figure 2.6 The theory of covariation – how we attribute social behaviour to internal or external causes
Source: Kelley, 1972

	Stable		Unstable	
	Internal	External	Internal	External
Controllable	typical effort	professor dislikes student	unusual effort	unusual disruption by other student
Not controllable	lack of ability	task difficulty	mood	luck

Figure 2.7 Weiner's model of achievement attributions

Source: Weiner, 1979

Beyond these milestones, success and failure can be experienced in more subtle ways: being well-liked, having a child who is admired, being respected by co-workers, being 'unlucky at love'. Many who experience divorce must deal with feelings of having failed in the relationship (Weiss, 1975), and attributions regarding success and failure are crucial in dealing with loneliness, as we shall see in Chapter 8 (Peplau & Perlman, 1982).

Weiner (1974, 1980) suggests that achievement attributions involve three choices. First, we decide whether the success or failure was caused by something about the actor (internal) or something about the situation (external). We also decide whether the internal or external cause was stable or unstable in nature. That is, the outcome may be attributed to a stable internal cause (ability of the actor), an unstable internal cause (effort of the actor, which can vary from time to time), a stable external cause (task difficulty) or an unstable external cause (luck). Finally, we must decide whether the occurrence was controllable by the actor, for instance by making efforts to improve his or her ability (Figure 2.7).

Earlier research found that males and females tended to attribute male success to internal factors and female success (particularly in a 'male task') to luck (Deaux, 1984). As this study was reported almost three decades ago, we could question whether the same results would be obtained today. In a later study to explore whether society had really changed in this regard (Beyer, 1998), students were asked to imagine that they had received either an 'A' or an 'F' in a course that was required for them to graduate. Then they were asked to rank the various possible causes for their grade. Among those who were to imagine the excellent mark, males tended to attribute their success to their own ability while females emphasized effort, such as studying and paying attention in class. On the other hand, males dealing with failure blamed it on a lack of effort, while females attributed their own failure to a lack of ability.

Weiner's model has also been tested with attributional data from the sports pages (Lau & Russell, 1980). Content analyses were performed on reports of games in which causal explanations for winning and losing were recorded. In general, unexpected outcomes ('upsets') generated a greater number of attributions – there seemed to be more to explain. Winning was generally attributed to internal factors ('We all had a great day; everyone gave 150%'), and losing to unstable/external factors ('It just wasn't our day'; 'The referee made some bad calls'). Other research indicates that winners tend to make attributions to more stable and controllable causes (effort) than do losers (Grove, Hanrahan & McInman, 1991). When we make attributions about a failure, we may be more prone to attribute it to unstable and external causes (Weiner, Figueroa-Munoz & Kakihara, 1991). In either case, the person has avoided self-blame.

> **KEY POINT:** The covariation model predicts whether we will attribute the cause of a person's behaviour to him or her personally (the actor), to the person to whom the act was directed (the entity) or to the situation. This attribution depends on information about whether the actor behaves in the same way to other people, whether others behave consistently in that manner to the entity and whether others behave in this way only in that specific situation but not in others. The theory of achievement attributions concerns how we make judgements about success and failure. It considers whether we make attributions to the actor or to the situation, whether we see that cause as stable (ability, task difficulty) or unstable (effort, luck) and whether we consider the outcome to have been controllable by the actor.

ATTRIBUTIONAL BIASES

Recall the metaphor of the 'naive scientist' who searches systematically for relevant information and uses it logically to explain behaviour. These attribution theories suggest that if people have the information, they will use it in a rational manner. However, research has also identified several attributional biases.

Correspondence bias: Overestimating dispositional causes

We tend to believe that people do what they intend to do. This correspondence bias, assuming that people's actions correspond to dispositional or personal factors, has been called the fundamental attribution error (Ross, 1977) because it is so pervasive in Western societies. In one experiment, people attributed what someone wrote or said to their 'true beliefs' even when they were told that the person had been instructed to argue a certain position (Jones & Harris, 1976). In another experiment (Ross, Amabile & Steinmetz,1977), a simulated quiz game was set up, in which some participants served as the quizmaster, others as contestants and other as simple observers. The questioners were invited to make up questions which would demonstrate their own wealth of knowledge. Examples: Where are the clearest waters for scuba diving? What is the fifth book of the Old Testament? Who won the football World Cup in 1962? Clearly the questioner has the advantage over the contestant because of the situation: they choose the questions. However, both the contestants and the observers rated the questioners as more knowledgeable in general than the contestants, because they underestimated the power of the situation.

The correspondent bias may reflect 'dispositionalism' (Krull, 2001), an underlying belief that people act as they do because of their own personal characteristics and intentions, and therefore the situation is just not all that important. For instance, one might easily explain the unrestrained actions of people at a rock concert as being due to the music and the crowded atmosphere. And yet, a dispositional bias may lead us to attribute their behaviour to what they are like as people who often attend such concerts (Sabini, Siepman & Stein, 2001). The effects of the correspondence bias are strongest where both consensus and distinctiveness are low (Van Overwalle, 1997).

Does the correspondence bias vary with age or income or education? With a nationally representative sample of adults in the United States, a consistent correspondence bias was found across a variety of demographic characteristics such as age, education level attained and income. However, it was far from universal; overall, only 53% of participants showed evidence of the bias (Bauman & Skitka, 2010).

BOX 2.1   TAKE ANOTHER LOOK

ATTRIBUTIONS ABOUT EVIL AND THE CORRESPONDENCE BIAS

In recent years, social psychologists have studied the vexing problem of evil (Baumeister, 1997; Waller, 2002; Newman & Erber, 2002; *Personality and Social Psychology Review* 1999, 3(3)). Evil is generally considered as the deliberate harming of human beings by other human beings, involving violence that is indiscriminate and often extremely cruel. While the Holocaust is generally recognized as the prototype, the modern history of evil includes atrocities in the Balkan states, Rwanda, Cambodia, Syria and Sudan, terrorism against innocent civilians in many parts of the world and the widespread use of torture as documented annually by Amnesty International. The term also may be invoked to describe horrendous crimes directed at specific individuals, such as those committed against children. In general, we consider actions as evil, rather than simply morally wrong, when they are excessive and incomprehensible even in terms of the goal of the action (Darley, 1999). While people act

Figure 2.8 To what extent would you attribute this terrorist act in Bali in 2005 to the person or to the situation? Does the correspondence bias apply here?

Source: © xPACIFICA/Corbis

in despicable ways for understandable goals – patriotism, fear, power, wealth – some actions cannot be explained simply as means to such ends.

How do people try to explain such actions? Reflecting the correspondence bias, we tend to ignore the situation and attribute evil actions to the perpetrators. One simple form of this dispositional explanation is simply that evil is committed by evil people, a process that Darley (1999) refers to as demonization. This, of course, constitutes circular reasoning: Evil acts are caused by evil people, who are evil because of the acts that they commit. It is a pseudo-explanation, which may seem genuine since it contains the word 'because'. It explains nothing.

Perhaps a more useful dispositional explanation posits that there is something unique in the personality of people who commit evil acts, perhaps a form of psychiatric disorder. Again, notice the circular reasoning: when we reason, post hoc, that they 'must be sick' to do what they did, we explain nothing. Indeed, psychological tests, along with in-depth clinical interviews, were administered to Nazi war criminals, both those in leadership roles who were tried and convicted in the war crimes trials in Nuremburg, and those in rank and file roles as killers. These tests have recently been reanalysed in terms of more contemporary methods, and compared to test protocols from the general population (Zillmer, Harrower, Ritzler & Archer, 1995). The analyses indicated that these Nazi mass murderers, on the whole, did not show any consistent pattern of psychopathology (see also Browning, 1992). Indeed, Nazi physicians who had earned international reputations for their legitimate medial research prior to the Nazi era subsequently conducted unspeakable 'experiments' on prisoners in the concentration camps (Lifton, 1986).

Social philosopher Hannah Arendt (1963) was assigned by a US magazine to cover the trial in Jerusalem of Adolf Eichmann, a German bureaucrat who had directed the logistical planning of the Holocaust, which involved organizing the transport of millions of people to the death camps, their murders and the disposal of their corpses. Based on both her own observations and psychological investigations, she described Eichmann as representing the 'banality of evil', an ordinary, ambitious civil servant who seized an opportunity to advance his career. It is a disturbing insight indeed, that ordinary people are capable of extraordinary evil. Needless to say, ordinary people are also capable of extraordinary kindness, altruism and heroism in certain circumstances, as we shall see in Chapter 9.

If we cannot attribute evil actions solely to the personal characteristics of people who commit them, then we must look to the situation. Baumeister (1997) suggests that in addition to possible sadistic personality characteristics, there are some conditions that may promote evil. These include an idealism in which the end justifies any means in promoting one's own group or nation, and threatened egotism in which members of the out-group are seen as a threat or challenge. In line with Arendt's report, Baumeister argues strongly that sadism is the least important of these three roots of evil.

In succeeding chapters we will explore theories and research concerning aggression and violence, as well as apparently blind obedience to an authority who directs a participant to torture another person with electric shock. (These famous experiments of Stanley Milgram are discussed fully in Chapter 6). The lesson, however, is clear. We must strive to avoid the correspondence bias and recognize that evil can be caused or at least promoted by the social situation. This is not a justification or excuse. We may explain evil actions, in part, by the situation, but we do not excuse the perpetrators.

While we are more likely to attribute the actions of others to stable trait dispositions, we tend to attribute our own behaviour to situational factors. This is known as the actor/observer bias. (Note that, as was the case earlier in this chapter, 'actor' refers to the person performing the action, not someone playing a role.) A good illustration is found in letters to newspaper and Internet advice columns. Writers of these letters tend to attribute their own difficulties to the situation (e.g., 'We're having marital problems because she refuses to have sex with me'). However, the person giving the advice (the observer) often tends to attribute the same marital problems to characteristics of the letter-writer ('You should bathe more often') (Schoeneman & Rubanowitz, 1985; Fischer, Schoeneman & Rubanowitz, 1987).

Several studies illustrate the actor/observer bias. In a simple experiment (Hansen, Kimble & Biers 2001), participants were randomly assigned to behave in either a friendly or unfriendly way towards a confederate, who had also been instructed to act friendly or unfriendly. Participants attributed the unfriendly behaviour of the other person to dispositional reasons ('unfriendliness'), while they attributed their own unfriendly behaviour to the instructions of the experimenter. In other research, when asked to explain why students chose their university majors and their romantic partners, participants tended to attribute their own decisions to external reasons (e.g., 'it is interesting'), but their friend's decisions to dispositions (e.g., 'he's insecure') (Nisbett, Caputo, Legant & Maracek, 1973). In a study conducted in a Canadian prison, inmates tended to attribute their criminal actions to situational factors, while their social workers blamed the criminal, even though their professional training stressed the social causes (Saulnier & Perlman, 1981).

Why do the attributions of actors and observers differ? One reason is that they have different perspectives on the same event. The actor's behaviour captures the attention of observers (Heider, 1958). In contrast, as actors, we generally cannot directly observe ourselves, and so are more aware of the situation. Indeed, if people are shown a videotaped replay of themselves, they are more likely to attribute their actions to their own characteristics (Storms, 1973). Also, as actors and observers, we have access to different information. We remember how different situations influenced our actions. Lacking this information about others, observers resort to a correspondent inference: friendly people do friendly things.

Of course, there are times when we know that our behaviour was caused by our own intentions, and the behaviour of someone else was caused by the situation. When external causes for a behaviour are clearly evident, both actor and observer make external attributions (Monson & Hesley, 1982). For example, most of us vividly recall television images of terrified people in the streets of New York, London, Mumbai and Madrid after terrorist attacks, and we attributed their understandable fear to the situation. Moreover, we are more likely to be able to take on the perspective of a person we know well, because we can empathize with them (Regan & Totten, 1975). This empathy grows over time: While in the earlier stage of a relationship, two people will focus on themselves in defining themselves to their partners, later, the focus shifts outward to the other person (Fiedler, Semin, Finkenauer & Berkel, 1995).

Does the correspondence bias reflect the individualism that characterizes Western cultures? In more collectivistic or communitarian societies in which the group is more highly valued, such as China, Korea, Japan and India, situational attributions are more frequent (Morris & Pang, 1994; Choi & Nisbett, 1998; Krull, Loy, Lin, Wang, Chen & Zhao, 1999), based on a belief that personal dispositions are more malleable or changeable in response to the situation (Choi, Nisbett & Norenzayan, 1999). When research participants from India and the United States were asked to describe the causes of various positive and negative events, situational causes were more frequently cited by Indian participants (Miller, 1984). One item described an accident in which a motorcycle driver is injured by an automobile driver; the car driver took the injured person to the hospital and then left him there in order to attend to his work. While Americans simply condemned the driver as irresponsible, the Indians considered the stress of professional work demands on the driver, the possibility that he was confused by the situation, and the possibility that the person did not seem to be seriously injured.

Westerners often ignore what is going on around the actor and focus only on his or her actions, whereas Asians are more likely to pay attention to what is happening in the background as well. For instance, in a study carried out at an aquarium, when Westerners observe fish in a tank, they tend to focus on the fish while Asians focus on both the fish in the foreground *and* the background setting (Norenzayan & Nisbett, 2000).

Yet, in our increasingly global world, people are capable of adopting more than one approach, depending on the cues (Oyserman & Lee, 2008). For example, in another study, students born in China and studying in the USA focused on the person after having been first exposed to US symbols (e.g. flag of the USA) and on the situation or background after having been first exposed to Chinese symbols (e.g. the flag of China).

Further information comes from studies of how news is reported. Morris & Peng (1994) carried out content analyses of newspaper articles that had appeared in Chinese- and English-language newspapers; for example, reports about multiple murders committed by a postal worker in Michigan and about murders by a Chinese graduate student living in the United States. Journalists writing in English about these crimes focused on the perpetrator (e.g. disturbed men) while those writing in Chinese emphasized situational factors (e.g. the postal worker not getting along with the supervisor). And in a study of real-life reporting in Japanese and American newspapers, an incident of illegal trading practices was attributed by the American newspapers simply to the trader, but by the Japanese newspapers to a lack of organizational controls (Menon, Morris, Chiu & Hong, 1999).

One caution about the covariation bias: consider the case of someone such as a banker who dresses very conservatively. Would attributing the choice of clothing to the banker be in error? Clearly the job requires such attire and may attract people who enjoy wearing such attire (Gilbert & Malone, 1995). While we are influenced by the situation, we also choose our situations.

Self-serving bias

People tend to attribute their own success to internal factors and their failure to external factors in order to protect their self-esteem. For example, students receiving good grades in an examination attributed those grades to ability or effort, but those with mediocre grades tended to attribute those results to task difficulty or just bad luck (Bernstein, Stephan & Davis, 1979). Taking credit for success but denying responsibility for failure is most likely to occur when the person has chosen to engage in the activity and is highly involved in the activity, and when the performance and its results are public rather than private (Bradley, 1978). This bias is not limited to Western countries; people in Japan and Latin America are also likely to attribute success to their own ability (Chandler, Shama, Wolf & Planchard, 1981).

There are limits to the self-serving bias. While people going through divorce generally have little trouble in finding fault with their former partners, they may attribute the failure of their marriages to themselves, particularly when they are still emotionally attached to their ex-partner (Lussier & Alain, 1986). In a field experiment by Taylor and Riess (1989), the experience of success or failure was manipulated experimentally in a realistic setting of competitive skiing. The participants were competitive skiers in a giant slalom race. Each competitor had two slalom runs, which were timed electronically, and the times were announced after each run. For half the racers, assigned to the 'success group', 0.7 seconds were subtracted from their real times before the announcement, while in the 'failure group', 0.7 seconds were added to their times (in competitive skiing, these are significant differences in time). Subsequent questioning showed that those in each group perceived their performance as a success or failure as expected. Then participants filled out questionnaires that assessed their attributions for their performances. The self-serving bias did not prevail in this case. Participants tended to attribute both success and failure to effort and ability.

When people are depressed, they tend to be relatively accurate in judging the extent to which they are personally responsible for their success or failure (Sweeney, Anderson & Bailey, 1986; Alloy & Abramson, 1979). This may be a mixed blessing, in that some degree of a self-serving bias, even if an illusion, may actually contribute to people's comfort by protecting their self-esteem (Taylor & Brown, 1988).

Are self-serving attributions used to protect our self-image or to polish the image we present to others? Riess, Rosenfeld, Melburg & Tedeschi (1981) tested these competing hypotheses in a rather ingenious way. Participants were told that they had succeeded or failed in a test of word associations. They were asked to attribute their success or failure to ability, effort, task difficulty or luck. To measure attributions, half the participants completed the usual questionnaire. The other half were hooked up to electrodes and told that this was a new, improved, extremely powerful lie detector that would indicate how they really felt; (no such machine exists). Then they were asked to respond to attributional questions in the way that they expected would be shown by the machine. The results were mixed: participants who believed that they were hooked up to a machine that would reveal their true feelings still showed a self-serving bias, but not as strong a bias as those who completed questionnaires. It appears that both protecting our self-esteem and protecting the image we create for others are important in this attributional bias.

[**KEY POINT:** Several attributional biases have been identified, including the correspondence bias, the actor versus observer bias and the self-serving bias. Other cues in the situation can override the bias, and cultural differences have been found.]

Attribution of responsibility and defensiveness

Other attributions are influenced by a need to feel secure. This is shown in a classic experiment by Walster (1966), in which participants were given a report about an accident. The driver, Lennie, left his car parked at the top of the hill. The parking brake cable came loose, and the car rolled down the hill. In one version, extensive damage was caused and someone was injured, while in the other, the damage was minimal. Participants were asked to indicate the extent to which they attributed responsibility to Lennie for the accident. Lennie was held more responsible when there was severe damage and injury than when the damage was minimal, even though there is no logic in making this distinction. This effect also has been found in other studies (Burger, 1981).

Why would severity of consequences affect the attribution of responsibility for the same action? Walster (1966) has suggested that people act in a defensive manner, avoiding thinking about the possibility of a threatening event. They often attribute responsibility for a serious crime or accident to the victim, because to interpret it as an outcome of bad luck would be to admit the possibility that it could happen to them. Of course, this defensiveness would be more likely to occur when the situation is similar to one that they might find themselves in, or when the victim is similar to themselves – they could imagine themselves 'in that person's shoes'. Students attributed greater responsibility to the driver for a severe-consequences accident when the protagonist was described as a student than a middle-aged business executive (Burger, 1981).

Now consider how we perceive people afflicted with HIV/AIDS or lung cancer. Of course, engaging in unprotected sexual activity or smoking can put anyone's health at risk, so to some extent we consider those who engage in such activities as 'responsible' for their illness (Mantler, Schellenberg & Page, 2003). However, we do not seem to 'blame' them, indicating that we distinguish between responsibility and blame.

Turning to historical events, research shows that we are more likely to attribute responsibility for a negative event to another group or nation than to our own group or nation (Doosje & Branscombe, 2003). Similarly, in reporting hate crimes such as a gang murder of a gay person, attributions in the media are represented in ways consistent with political orientations. That is, more conservative media, who are less sympathetic to gay and lesbian people, often find more situational attributions for such crimes (Quist & Wiegand, 2002).

[**KEY POINT:** We are more likely to make a defensive attribution and blame the victim when the situation is one in which we could find ourselves and when the victim is similar to ourselves. We tend to attribute responsibility to others for their behaviour, particularly when consequences are severe and negative.]

The illusion of control

We tend to pay attention to the effects of our actions, and to make the connection between our actions and events that follow them (Thompson, Armstrong & Thomas, 1998). Much of what happens in life is beyond our control. Perhaps in response, people cling to an illusion of control, an exaggerated belief in their own capacity to determine what happens to them in life (Langer, 1975). For instance, people often prefer to select their own lottery ticket, under the illusion that they can increase their chances of winning. In an experimental demonstration of this effect (Wortman, 1975), participants were presented with two coloured marbles in a can, each representing a different prize. Some were told which marble represented the desirable prize, while others were not. Then participants either chose a marble from the can, blindly, or were given one. In all cases, the participants had absolutely no control over the outcome. However, they attributed more outcome control to themselves when they blindly selected their marble. Lerner (1977) has identified an important implication of the illusion of control: an exaggerated **belief in a just world**, a belief that we get what we deserve in life. This is discussed fully in Chapter 15.

Indeed, when people experience a traumatic event that shatters their view of the world as just and predictable, they may respond to being victimized with self-blame. In examining the research on people who have been victimized, Miller and Porter (1983) present the following, rather unexpected, findings: (1) victims often exaggerate their own responsibility for the event and its consequences; and (2) the degree of self-blame is often positively related to how successfully the person will cope. Self-blame may enable the person to maintain the illusion of control in life, which can be channelled into constructive coping strategies.

Victor Frankl (1963), a psychoanalyst and survivor of the Nazi death camps, maintained that a search for meaning in life is an essential component of human experience. People who have emerged paralysed from an accident often struggle with the question, 'Why me?' Their success in finding a satisfactory answer, even if that answer is in their own ostensible failure, enables them to cope more effectively with their circumstances (Bulman & Wortman, 1977). Finding meaning may, to some extent, include attributing some responsibility to oneself, providing us with a sense of control that such misfortune will not happen again. In some forms of victimization, the search for meaning is more difficult. Silver, Boon and Stones (1983) interviewed 77 adult women who had been victimized in childhood by familial incest. Although an average of 20 years had elapsed since the last episode, more than 80% were still searching for meaning. Indeed, those who attributed some of the responsibility for their victimization to themselves adjusted more effectively in the future.

KEY POINT: We tend to hold an exaggerated belief in our own capacity to determine what happens to us in life. This is related to a belief that the world is just, that people get what they deserve and deserve what they get.

Society and attributional biases

As noted earlier, the correspondence bias is more strongly evident in Western cultures than in Asian cultures. The research reviewed in this chapter points to factors within the person as the causes of attributional choices, such as a need to protect self-esteem or a sense of control, or the attempt by cognitive misers to 'minimize effort'. This strictly 'psychological' orientation to attributions has been challenged by social psychologists, who argue that we have ignored the role of social factors in determining how we make sense of our world (Crittenden, 1983; Hewstone & Jaspars, 1984). For example, in the realm of politics, people are sometimes blamed for social problems which affect them, such as poverty, unemployment or underemployment, delinquency and drug abuse, while the role of the social system is ignored (Guimond & Dubé, 1989; Shapiro & Stelcner, 1987). This may also reflect a self-serving bias, where those afflicted by poverty are reluctant to blame themselves, and those who are doing well are willing to give themselves credit (Guimond, Bégin & Palmer, 1989).

AN EVALUATION OF ATTRIBUTION THEORIES

In the decades following the publication of Heider's (1958) seminal book, attributions became a major focus of attention in social psychology. Three critiques emerged concerning attribution theory: (1) that attribution theory is peculiar to a particular culture and does not describe human nature per se; (2) that much of what people do is pretty mindless – they usually do not ask why of themselves or others; and (3) that since people are not usually aware of why they behave in a given way, they are forced to come up with some answer when the researcher asks them. Each of these criticisms has some validity.

The cultural critique begins with the fact that both the theorists and the research participants have come almost entirely from the United States. Sampson (1977) characterizes this culture as being based upon the ideal of the self-contained individual, and so the correspondence error would reflect this ideal. Indeed, attribution studies in other cultures reveal differences. As noted earlier, comparative research shows clearly that Americans are highly subject to the fundamental attribution error, while people from Asian cultures give considerably more weight to situational factors in explaining why people do what they do (Nisbett, 2003).

As for the second critique, can it be assumed that people generally are aware of causes? Nisbett and Wilson (1977) reported a series of classic studies that indicate people are often unaware and unconcerned that something is 'causing' them to act in a certain way (System 1 thinking). Some of the experiments are rather ingenious. In one, shoppers were asked to evaluate the quality of four totally identical nightgowns or nylon hose. Participants showed a strong bias towards preferring the article placed on the right-hand side – although in later questioning the majority were unaware of this tendency and denied that they were influenced by it. In another experiment, participants were asked to memorize a list of word pairs. Some pairs were designed to influence later responses by association. For example, those who had memorized the pair 'ocean–moon' were twice as likely as controls to name Tide (a popular brand) when asked for a laundry detergent. However, rarely did participants make this connection when asked to explain their choice. Rather, they responded with apparently 'top of the head' remarks, attributing their response to the brand their mothers used. Nisbett & Wilson (1977) conclude that people generally do not make attributions in their daily activities unless asked to do so, such as when in an experiment.

Even when people think spontaneously about causal explanations (Weiner, 1985), it appears that much of what people do happens in a state of 'mindlessness'. Imagine participants being approached by an experimental confederate, as they were about to use a photocopy machine. Some were asked to let the person use the machine before them, but were given no reason. Others were presented with a similar request along with a meaningful reason: 'I'm in a rush'. And others were given the same request with a meaningless 'placebo' reason: 'May I use the machine first because I have to make some copies?' When the delay would be minimal to the participants, they complied when presented with what sounded like a reason, even when it was no reason at all. They simply responded automatically (System 1 thinking) according to a script: when someone asks a small favour and offers a reason or excuse for it, you will usually comply (Langer, Blank & Chanowitz, 1978).

Thus, the question now seems to be: when does attributional thinking occur? The evidence suggests three types of situations in which we tend to ask why someone acted as they did, or, indeed why we ourselves did something: (1) when something unexpected happens, such as when the underdog unexpectedly wins the game, the mark we obtained on an examination is much better or worse than expected, or when a person in obvious distress is not helped by bystanders (Bohner, Bless, Schwarz & Strack, 1988); (2) when an event is personally relevant, when the good mark or the unexpected defeat happens to us rather than to someone else (recall the theory of correspondent inferences); and (3) when someone feels a desire to find some meaning in an important event, such as a sudden loss of someone close to you, being the victim of major crime, illness or injury, perhaps falling in love. As an example of this, attributional thinking in marriage has been found to occur most often in the early 'honeymoon' stage and during times of conflict (Holtzworth-Munroe & Jacobson, 1985).

> **KEY POINT:** Attribution theory is built on the premise that we ask 'why' in certain circumstances: when we are asked to do so, when the situation is unusual or when it has a high impact on us.

SOCIAL COGNITION

In assessing what is known about impression formation and attributional processes, two facts stand out. First, as noted earlier in the dual-process model, people form impressions and make judgements about others quite rapidly, often on the basis of limited information. Second, people are active in processing information. Social psychologists have become increasingly interested in these automatic processes, and have linked their work to research in basic cognitive psychology. There are two fundamental concepts. First, our information about our world is organized or 'coded' in terms of meaningful categories (schemata). Second, in making decisions and judgements, we often use cognitive shortcuts or heuristics.

CATEGORICAL THINKING: SCHEMATA

Of course, we know that every person and event are unique. Yet, if we were to approach every person, place or event as totally unique, we would soon be overwhelmed by uncertainties. In fact, there are similarities among certain types of people or events. Thus, we tend to organize our view of the world in terms of categories. People are generally categorized in terms of easily observable characteristics, such as gender, ethnic group, occupation or age. We can also categorize people in terms of inferred characteristics, such as people who are friendly, honest, sarcastic or pessimistic. Similarly, we construct categories of events (parties, classes), activities (camping, reading), objects and even ideas. Then we build a collection of beliefs, assumptions, images and memories around these categories – schemata.

Social schemata

A cognitive schema (plural schemata, derived from the Greek word for plan or structure) enables us to organize and simplify information, memories and impressions. These are sets of interconnected beliefs, information, images, memories and examples about social objects: all that we 'know' about something. For example, our schema of automobiles might include our knowledge of how they work and how to drive them, our impressions of various brands and models of cars, perhaps memories of cars that we have owned or rented, trips we have taken, accidents, repair bills or pleasant events involving cars. Of course, it may also include our images of types and examples of automobiles, such as the one we drive or the one we would wish to have. Schemata help us to organize and simplify information that we have received, help us to interpret new information more rapidly, and determine what we will encode and remember.

There are various types of schemata. A **person schema** refers to specific people such as a famous star, a public figure, your parent, a professor. For example, suppose we have a schema of the current political leader as being honest, somewhat obese, hardworking, decisive (or indecisive?), concerned with people in distress, wanting to resolve conflicts. If he or she were to appear on TV with an eloquent request that all of us work hard and sacrifice for the good of the nation, we would interpret this speech in terms of our schema. However, if our schema were of a conniving, self-serving politician with a winning smile, we would interpret the same speech quite differently.

Another interesting type of schema relates to events. For example, we may have an **event schema** referring to a group of friends going to the game or match. Event schemata include mental images of the stadium or arena where the event occurs, which teams participate and what happens – the 'script'. It begins with purchasing the ticket, presenting it to a ticket-taker and finding our seats. We may buy a programme and begin to identify players as they warm up. We recognize the uniforms of the two teams, and the physical set-up of the field. We stand for the national anthem, then sit and shout encouragement during the opening, purchasing snacks and liquid refreshments. We have standard reactions to a score by our team, and we know how to express disapproval of the referee or opposition players. Think of other event schemata: a university examination, a date for the movies, supper in a restaurant, a trip to the beach, a day at work, air travel, being online. Of course, an important reason for building these schemata is that they enable us to experience the events as predictable, understandable and comfortable. Thus, for instance, we can go to a restaurant anywhere in the world and, with some variations, apply our schema for eating out.

Finally, we have schemata about social roles – organized mental structures about people who belong to social categories. We may have **role schemata** about physicians, rock singers, professors, students, smokers, non-smokers, friends, lovers, butchers, mothers. Role schemata are generally restricted to role-relevant situations, although not for every role. Priests and rabbis, for example, may often find themselves still being treated as priests and rabbis in a social situation. A role schema may be idealized, even unrealistic: few people can live up to a culturally shared schema of 'lover' as being always devoted, understanding, affectionate, passionate, and never selfish, unreasonable or tired.

Several characteristics are common to these types of schemata. First, schemata tend to be organized hierarchically, from the general to the more specific. For example, we may have a general schema for the concept 'party', and more specific schemata for each of an informal, loud-music party in someone's basement, a child's birthday party, a religious occasion, a wine-and-cheese party and an art gallery opening. Second, people or groups of people may differ in specific schemata. For example, university students think of 'intelligent people' primarily in relation to academic and intellectual matters, while people interviewed in supermarkets tend to see intelligence in terms of practical problem-solving and not 'acting foolishly' in social situations (Sternberg, Conway, Ketron & Bernstein, 1981).

Much research has been devoted to the study of the self-schema: the set of images, memories, beliefs and evaluations that people have concerning themselves. We will explore this topic further in the next chapter.

Prototypes

Cantor and Mischel (1979) suggest that we often use prototypes, mental images of a typical example of that category, as one component of a schema. For example, you may picture your own cocker spaniel as a prototype of the category dog, with four legs, fur, a tail, characteristic sounds of barking, whining and growling, licking your hand. If you were to see an unfamiliar dog of another breed, you would decide whether it was a dog by comparing the characteristics of that rottweiler or schnauzer to your prototype.

The extent to which a particular person (or animal) resembles the prototype, and the extent to which you allow for variations, will determine how readily you identify the person with the category. For example, Brewer, Dull & Lui (1981) presented participants with photos and verbal labels of people in certain categories, such as grandmother. Then they provided more information about the person. This information was included more frequently in the subject's impression of the person when it was consistent with the prototype (e.g., 'kindly' for a grandmother) than when it was not consistent (e.g., 'aggressive' for a grandmother).

A stereotype refers to a particular kind of shared prototype for members of a social group shared within a culture and applied to pre-judge an individual member of that category (Taylor, 1981). Since stereotypes are intrinsic to prejudice, we will discuss them fully in that context (see Chapter 13).

Social representations

Where do these schemata come from? While it is reasonable to suggest that schemata are learned, they do not depend entirely on direct experience. For example, people may have schemata about people that they have never met, or about life in countries that they have not visited. Similarly we may have a schema about being ill with cancer although we have not been afflicted personally; we may have observed someone else in that situation or we may have learned from on-line sources. Certainly much of the learning that shapes our schemata is vicarious in nature, coming from movies, television, books and the experience or imagination of others.

Many of our schemata are both acquired from other people and communicated among people, a process that requires shared meanings and symbols held by members of a culture, community or group. In other words, while cognition is necessarily located in the mind of an individual, the essence of social cognition is that it is shared collectively in a culture. These considerations support the notion of socially constructed schemata, or social representations (Moscovici, 1981). Thus, for example, a Canadian's event schema of an ice hockey game has evolved in Canadian culture. Russians, Swedes or people in the United States might hold a quite different event schema of a hockey game; the players are different, the styles of play may differ, the décor of the arena may differ. A schema about a prominent politician shared by many people in the country may change over time as individuals communicate with each other directly and through the mass media.

Moscovici (1981) identifies two processes by which social representations emerge and evolve: anchoring and objectification. Anchoring refers to integrating an unfamiliar event, person or idea into some existing structure of knowledge, so that we can compare a new object, person or experience in terms of what is familiar to us. Often we classify or categorize the new image or event, imagine it and think of it in terms of our own cultural worldview. Objectification refers to a process by which an abstract idea becomes concrete, perceived as part of common-sense experience. For instance, the abstraction of 'elections' becomes objectified in our minds through politicians, speeches to cheering throngs, lawn signs, TV advertisements and the reporting of results. Of course, elections in one culture or country may be distinct from those in another. Still, Canadians, Australians, Israelis, Dutch and Swedes share enough about the experience of elections to be able to understand each other. Personification is a common example of objectification (Moscovici & Hewstone, 1983). For example, while most people have only some vague ideas about psychoanalysis, they probably know the name Freud and the image of the analyst's couch. Similarly, while few understand the theory of relativity, most remember the name Einstein, perhaps news reports of the discovery of the boson, a subatomic particle, and connect it to the mysteries of the atom. Often the policies of a government or a country become personified in terms of the prime minister, premier or president. Much of the research in this area is descriptive; for example, some studies explore the social representation of mental illness in different historical periods and among people of different age groups (De Rosa, 1986).

> **KEY POINT:** Social schemata are organized cognitive structures of characteristics, memories, typical examples (prototypes) about certain kinds of people, events and social roles. They are derived from our social representations learned from our culture, which enable us to anchor a specific instance to what we already know and to objectify an abstract idea into concrete examples, memories and events.

PROCESSING SOCIAL INFORMATION

Why do we have schemata? While we can rarely know everything about everything, schemata help to fill in the gaps by providing us with a 'best guess' about what is true. They can help us to be prepared for the future by providing us with expectations (Fiske & Taylor, 1991). In particular, our schemata guide us, telling us what to pay attention to, and influencing what and how we remember.

Attention

Selective attention is one important effect of schematic thinking. In an environment in which we would be overloaded with sensory information, the schema guides us as to what to notice and process. For instance, at a tennis match, we will attend to the match itself and less so to what the spectators are wearing (unless the game is boring). In a negative schema about members of an out-group, people may attend to instances of negative characteristics and ignore the positives.

Memory

Many people assume that memory is akin to a bank or a hard disk; material is deposited and can be withdrawn later, as needed (Lamal, 1979). Occasionally one of these deposits is lost, and we say that we've 'forgotten'.

To the contrary, current research suggests that memories are encoded while they are being stored, in forms dictated by people's assumptions and schemata. For instance, you do not simply store what you read in this textbook, but you interpret what you read in terms of what you have already learned, how it relates to your personal life, what associations you make of the material. Remembering is much more than retrieval of a file on your hard disk: Rather, it is an active or 'constructive' process in which these assumptions and schemata influence the memory that is retrieved. Remember this as you study!

Think of someone who you would consider to be a 'memorable' person. A memory of a person will include specific things that the person has said or done, and more abstract memories of 'what the person is like', such as personality traits, prominent attitudes and dispositions (Srull & Wyer, 1989). Indeed, we often form clear overall impressions of a person, but cannot explain in any detail why we feel that way. This is explained in terms of dual representation (specific details and general impressions). For example, if we see a person do something very thoughtful for someone else, we will store in memory both the specific behaviour and our evaluation of the person as being thoughtful and kind. Over time, as we get to know the person better and observe many more such actions, we may forget the specific behavioural details. However, these behaviours will have an enduring impact on our overall evaluation.

Schemata may guide our memory of a person, enabling us to remember or ignore specific details about that person. For example, in an experiment (Zuroff, 1989), participants were induced by means of a brief description of a woman to think of her as 'traditional' or 'liberated' (feminist) in her beliefs and goals. Subsequently they were presented with a long list of adjectives that various people had ostensibly used to describe that woman. Although all participants had the same list, they tended to remember information consistent with the 'traditional' or 'liberated' schema they had been given. If they had been induced to think of her as 'traditional', they would be more likely to remember an adjective such as 'kind' than 'independent'. This particular effect of schemata, priming, will be explored later in this chapter.

What are your memories about high school? Do you look to your past through 'rose-coloured glasses'? We may recall our high school years as happier than they were because we now have a 'good old days' schema of that period of our lives (Ross, McFarland, Conway & Zanna, 1983). Of course, couples who separate often remember the conflicts and difficulties that led them to break up, not the good times and attractiveness of their partner that brought them together.

Our memory of past events can also be influenced by our expectation or 'theory' about what should have happened (Ross, 1989). In a study of students enrolled in an extravagantly advertised study-skills programme, participants first completed an initial questionnaire in which they evaluated their own study skills. Then they were assigned randomly to the programme or to a waiting list. After going through the study skills programme, all participants were re-interviewed. A follow-up showed that the programme had no significant effect on their grades. However, participants believed that they had improved despite their dismal marks. When asked to recall how they had rated their skills previously, participants who completed the programme now recalled that, before going through the programme, their skills were worse than it had seemed to them at the time before the programme. They applied the schema of self-improvement to distort their memory of the past in order to feel that they had, indeed, improved (Ross & Conway, 1985).

Thus, our memories of the past can be reconstructed to be consistent with our current thinking. Consider that people tend to assume that memory and activity level will decline as they grow older. Older adults remember themselves as having been more capable in these ways earlier in life than a matched group of younger adults. As a result, we may feel our memory has declined because we recall, perhaps in an exaggerated form, our prowess of earlier years and we assume decline with aging (McFarland, Ross & Giltrow, 1992).

Our memories of the past can also be influenced by our mood at the time of recall. A series of studies by McFarland and Buehler (1998) indicate that when people are induced to reflect on their feelings and what they might do to feel better, they tend to remember happy events. On the other hand, when people are simply instructed to dwell on how they are feeling, they tend to have unpleasant memories of the past. People may also remember having said something to someone if it sounds like something they might have said (Buehler & Ross, 1993).

A final note on memory: dual-process models suggest two distinct processes by which we remember. One system involves learning through experience, the gradual encoding and processing of ideas, experiences and prototypes which lead to the development of cognitive schemas. For instance, we encode a collection of experiences in restaurants which build the event schema of 'going out to eat'. This system builds gradually, with experience in different restaurants. The second system is rapid encoding and storage of a novel experience or object, where the novelty cues memory without much in the way of conscious effort (Smith & DeCoster, 2000). There is also evidence that people vary in their capacity to remember specifically threatening information (Peters, Hock & Krohne, 2012).

Related to this would be memory of implicit social cognitions, thoughts that are not in conscious awareness. Based on cognitive neuroscience research, there appear to be different memory systems involved in learning and unlearning of unconscious material (Amodio & Ratner, 2011). And, we can generally more readily remember material (such as words or paintings) that others in our social group, people similar to us, have also experienced. This shared experience makes the material more prominent in memory, and easier to recall (Shteynberg, 2010). For example, if talking to your friends about a movie they have also seen, you may recall more detail than if talking with people who have not seen it. This is also true of memory for music, which involves a system independent of verbal memory and which is specific to remembering music of our own culture (Demorest, Morrison, Stambaugh, Beken, Richards & Johnson, 2010).

KEY POINT: In sum, schemata enable us to process information efficiently. They guide our attention to, and interpretation, of what we perceive. Social representations of such material enable us to understand and become comfortable with novel ideas (anchoring) and people, and to understand them in a more concrete form (objectification). Memory is constructive, whereby the storage and retrieval of memories are guided and even altered by our schemata and our assumptions about the present.

CONSTRUAL-LEVEL THEORY AND COUNTERFACTUAL THINKING

When we think about persons, events or other objects, we perceive them spontaneously in terms of their con-strual level, that is, along a continuum from psychologically distant to psychologically close. Obviously the person sitting next to you is psychologically closer to you than if that person were to sit across the room, across the street or across your city. Receiving a personal email is psychologically closer than receiving the same message copied to numerous recipients. The object or event may be perceived as personally relevant or relevant to someone else – someone close to you, a stranger across the room or a hypothetical other person, all of whom are incrementally more distant in psychological terms. Thus, psychological distance, whether spatial, temporal, hypothetical or social, is anchored in the present, here-and-now reality.

According to construal-level theory (Trope & Liberman, 2010), the more remote or distant an object, person or event is from our own present reality, the more we 'construe' or think about that object or event in an abstract manner. For instance, if you are at your dentist's right now, that reality is quite concrete and immediate: the chair, the dentist plunging an implement into your mouth, the sound of the drill, the pain. This contrasts with how we construe a dental appointment scheduled in a few months, or the vague feeling that you really should have your teeth checked out sometime, somewhere. Some research even indicates that thinking about things at a psychological distance may increase creativity (Jia, Hirt & Karpen, 2009). Other research indicates that when you think about a past event while primed to think in concrete terms, you tend to recall more details about the event – although not necessarily with greater accuracy. Experimenters can induce an abstract or concrete mindset by instructing the participants to think about 'why an event occurred' (abstract) versus 'how an event occurred' (concrete) (Kyung, Menon & Trope, 2010).

Thinking of what might have been

One way in which we mentally transcend our present reality is by thinking of what might have been, counter-factual thinking (Figure 2.9). We can think about how an outcome could have been different (Roese, 1997). For instance, imagine that you have won an Olympic silver medal. This may well stimulate counterfactual thinking about how you might have acted differently and won the gold medal. However, if you were to win a bronze medal, it may well stimulate thinking about having acted in a way that could have caused you to miss winning a medal at all. Researchers used video clips in which participants rated the emotional state of competitors at the moment the medal placements were announced. Indeed, surprisingly, bronze medalists were observed to be happier than silver medalists (Medvec, Madey & Gilovich, 2002): 'I could have missed winning a medal.' Counterfactual thinking can lead to many outcomes. If you fail to purchase something on sale at 50% off, you are less likely to take the opportunity to purchase that same item at 25% off, because your counterfactual thinking centres on the much better bargain that you have missed (Tykocinski & Pittman, 1998).

When we reflect on what might have been, we may imagine an outcome that would have been better (upward counterfactual thinking) or worse than what really happened (downward counterfactual thinking) (Roese

& Olson, 1997). For instance, if you receive a 'B' in a course, you may imagine that it might have been an 'A+' or a 'C−'. Each kind of counterfactual thinking can serve a different purpose for us. Downward counterfactual thinking, imagining how it could have been worse, can give us some relief and acceptance of reality. If we have an accident that causes extensive damage, imagining that someone could have been injured can put things into perspective. On the other hand, upward counterfactuals can galvanize us into action to improve the results in the future. Imagining the 'A+' that might have been may lead us to making some improvements. However, counterfactual thinking can lead to feelings of regret, even if we were to imagine a worse outcome (Walchli & Landman, 2003). In one study of women with silicone breast implants, counterfactual thinking about how the operation might have yielded better results was related to a poor post-operative adjustment (Parker, Middleton & Kulik, 2002).

Figure 2.9 Counterfactual thinking: What if your horse had won the race?

Source: Dennis Donohue/Shutterstock.com

While upward counterfactual thinking can motivate positive change, we sometimes have illusions about self-improvement. Why do people persist in attempting to change themselves in some way despite repeated failure and frustration? For instance, we may persist in trying to lose weight despite repeatedly unsuccessful attempts with various diets. This pattern of unrealistic expectations about eventual success after repeated failure is called the false hope syndrome (Polivy & Herman, 2000, 2002). Failure leads us to conclude that just a few minor modifications in our strategy will enable us to control our drinking or smoking, lose that weight and keep it off, achieve that 'A' average or win a tournament. The pattern repeats itself.

Clearly some kinds of self-change are realistic or at least possible, as well as desirable. However, we must learn from experience and distinguish between realistic and unrealistic self-change goals. For instance, we tend to underestimate how long it will take us to complete a task (Buehler, Griffin & Ross, 1995). While hope and optimism are necessary for change, false hope will be a barrier to the kinds of change that can succeed over time.

> **KEY POINT:** We can think beyond present realities to other possibilities. We think in terms of psychological distance, the more immediate in more concrete terms, and the more distant, more abstractly. We can also think in terms of what might have been. Upward counterfactual thinking evokes how things might be better and can motivate self-improvement. Downward counterfactual thinking provides us with relief by imagining how things could have been worse.

RAPID REASONING

Let us return now to notions of rapid thinking. We must often make judgements where it would be unrealistic to try to think things through. As we have seen, we are 'cognitive misers' and tend to avoid expending more time and effort. We will never collect all relevant information about courses, cars or jobs before making our decisions. We have seen how we invoke certain biases in making attributions, and how we invoke a schema to perceive and interpret what we see and hear. Now we turn to how we take other cognitive shortcuts.

We often follow certain unstated 'rules' or heuristics – assumptions and biases that guide our decisions about uncertain events. One such 'rule of thumb' involves medical diagnoses: physicians are taught to consider the common illness before the rare and exotic disease; when you hear hoof beats, look for horses before you look for zebras. In everyday experience, we learn similar rules, without being taught what they are.

Research over the past decades has identified a number of these heuristics (Tversky & Kahneman, 1974). Here are a few of them.

The representativeness heuristic

Imagine that you are visiting a casino, and you record the outcome of 12 spins of the roulette wheel. Which of the following sequences are you more likely to observe (R = red; B = black)?

| 1 | RBR BRB RBR BRB |
| 2 | RRR RRR BBB BBB |

Mathematically, both sequences are equally likely to occur. However, most people would choose the first sequence, in which the two colours alternate, because it seems 'representative' of what 12 random spins of the wheel should look like (Tversky & Kahneman, 1974). The representativeness heuristic involves judging the likelihood of an event by how much it seems to resemble the typical case. While this seems reasonable, over-reliance on representativeness as one's rule of thumb leads you to ignore other important factors, such as luck, base rate information, and the independence of events. This can lead to the fallacious thinking of the compulsive gambler. These unfortunate people believe that they can make money even if others cannot, and that persistence will pay off. So, if you are losing at the roulette table, persist and the law of averages will catch up for you; if you are winning, also persist because you are on a 'hot streak'. In fact, each roll of the dice is an independent event.

Now, consider the following description: 'Steve is very shy and withdrawn, invariably helpful, but has little interest in people or in the world of reality. A meek and tidy soul, he has a need for order and structure and a passion for detail.' Would you guess that Steve is a farmer, a trapeze artist, a librarian or a surgeon?

If you actually had a set of personality test scores of representative samples of people from each profession, you could calculate the probability that Steve is a meek surgeon, a shy trapeze artist, a farmer with a passion for detail, and so forth. However, this would demand the kind of information that would usually not be accessible. The representativeness heuristic provides us with a quick and easy solution; we simply estimate the extent to which Steve is representative of the typical person (prototype) in each occupation. We would probably conclude that Steve most closely resembles a librarian. Now, imagine that you were told that Steve's name had been drawn from a list of 100 men, only 10 of whom were librarians. Most people would ignore this objective 'base rate' information that there is only a 10% chance that he is a librarian. They would still assume that Steve was a librarian (Tversky & Kahneman, 1973).

In a dramatic demonstration of this principle, participants watched a videotape of a psychologist interviewing a prison guard. For half the participants, the guard expressed very hostile attitudes towards prisoners while the other half saw a guard expressing more optimistic, humane attitudes towards prisoners. Some of each group were told that this guard was quite typical of prison guards, others that the guard was quite atypical, and still others were told neither. Participants then answered a questionnaire about prison guards in general. Those who had viewed an interview with a humane guard expressed significantly more positive attitudes towards prison guards in general, even when the guard was presented as atypical (Hamill, Wilson & Nisbett, 1980). They ignored base rate information and relied on the one example that they were provided with.

Finally, consider the case in which two different objects are exemplars of the same value, such as coins or banknotes of the same value. Several studies of participants in the United States show that they attached greater value to a $1 banknote than to the recently introduced $1 coins, and they overestimated how much money they had when it was in banknotes (Tessari, Rubaltelli, Tomelleri, Zorzi & Pietroni, 2011). Clearly, at least in this case, the two types of currency of equal objective value represent different entities to the consumers – a dollar bill really represents a genuine dollar to them!

The availability heuristic

Which is more common in the English language, words that begin with the letter K, or those that have K as the third letter? In fact, in the English language, there are more than twice as many words with K as the third letter (e.g., awkward, like, bake) as with K as the first letter (e.g., king, know, keep). However, most people incorrectly estimate that more words begin with the letter 'K', simply because it is easier to think of such examples (Tversky & Kahneman, 1982). For various reasons, we are accustomed to think of words in terms of their first letter. This is a demonstration of the **availability heuristic**, one of the most important cognitive 'rules' (Tversky & Kahneman, 1974). It is deceptively simple: if something comes readily to mind, we tend to assume that it's probably true and use it to judge the likelihood of an event.

Consider when people are depressed and tend to see life in negative terms. When asked to anticipate future events in their lives, they would be more likely to imagine negative events happening to them because these events would be more cognitively available to them (Vaughn & Weary, 2002). Another instance of the availability heuristic is our tendency to be excessively influenced by extreme examples, again because they come readily to mind. For instance, fame influences our judgements of people (McKelvie, 2000). Clinicians asked to offer a diagnosis based on a case history are influenced by cases that they have encountered recently (Schwartz, 1994), and teachers use available memories of similar students in predicting the performance of a current student (Jussim, Madon & Chatman, 1994).

The availability heuristic also influences business decisions. For example, Kliger & Kudryavtsev (2010) examined the effects on stock market activity of analysts' recommendations to buy or sell. They found that investors gave too much importance to whether a stock price was currently rising or falling (the most readily available information) while giving less weight to other information in the analysts' reports, such as their actual recommendations to buy or sell and their estimates of financial risk. The wild fluctuations in world markets in recent years no doubt reflect to some degree the effects of the availability heuristic in market investment decisions.

Priming and availability Triggering cognitive availability is called **priming**. Suppose that we have just watched a tearful movie involving marriage conflict and rampant infidelity. Then we meet the new couple who moved in next door. Are we more likely, as a result of having watched that movie, to notice signs of tension between them, or to interpret their tension as a marital problem rather than fatigue from moving? Research evidence suggests that this is often the case. A schema about marriage problems has been activated or 'primed' for us, which we may then use to interpret events. On the other hand, if we had just seen a movie showing passionate married love, we might notice, interpret and remember very different information about our new neighbours.

In an elaborate experiment (Srull & Wyer, 1980), male and female participants were instructed to construct sentences from four-word sets. Some of the word sets contained hostile content or suggestion (e.g., leg, break, arm, his), while others contained neutral content only (e.g., her, found, know, I). For one group of participants, 15 of the 50 sets suggested hostility, while for the other, 35 of the sets had hostile connotations. The object was to prime a memory category – 'hostility' – in the subject group using 35 sets of words conveying hostility. Then the effects of this priming were shown as participants read a paragraph that described the behaviour of a stranger in neutral terms with respect to hostility. The participants were asked to rate the stranger on a number of characteristics, one of which was hostility. Some participants were given the information about the person immediately after priming, some 24 hours later, and some a week later. The interval between receiving the information and rating the stranger also varied for different participants: no delay, 24 hours delay or one week. So, for example, some participants received the information immediately after priming and rated the person 24 hours later, and some received the information 24 hours after priming and rated the stranger one week later.

The results confirmed two predictions, and contained a surprise. As expected, the same stranger was perceived as more hostile after participants were primed with 35 items rather than with 15, thus confirming the effect of priming on category availability. Also as expected, the priming effect was greater when the information was received immediately than when there was delay. However, here is the surprise: the effects of priming were greatest when there was a rather long interval between receiving information (the paragraph about the target person) and making judgements about the stranger. Once the category of hostility had been primed and made available, participants formed their initial impression of the person, and then later remembered that person as being even more hostile than he or she had appeared earlier.

Table 2.1 Heuristic reasoning in society

Research on cognitive heuristics has extended beyond the lab into some real-life situations and applications. Here are a few examples:

REPRESENTATIVENESS

- In genetic counselling, parents who have had one abnormal child overestimate the probability of the having another (Shiloh, 1994).
- Psychiatrists and clinical psychologists tend to make clinical diagnoses on the basis of a prototype for a disorder rather than using established diagnostic criteria (Garb, 1994).
- In sentencing, judges tend to match the defendant before them with prototypical criminals (Lurigo, Carroll & Stalan, 1994).

AVAILABILITY

- People make judgements about how likely they are to die of various causes based on how often that cause has recently been mentioned in the media – which may or may not correspond to the real risks. For instance, many more people die in automobiles than in airplanes, but most people consider air travel as riskier (Lichtenstein, Slovic et al., 1978).
- People may judge illnesses based on one salient symptom (e.g. a lump), and ignore health problems that do not present recognizable symptoms such as high blood pressure (Chapter 16).
- Physicians are influenced by cases they have encountered recently and arrive at the diagnosis that comes to mind at that time (Schwartz, 1994). More in Chapter 16.
- Teachers use memories of similar students or siblings in predicting the performance of a specific student (Jussim, Madon & Chatman, 1994).

ILLUSORY CORRELATION

- It is commonly assumed that there is a relationship between women's emotional states and their menstrual cycles. While this may be true in specific cases, the assumption that all or most women suffer from PMS is illusory. For instance, when women were asked to keep daily diaries, irritability and depression typically did not increase during the premenstrual or menstrual phases, but when asked to recall later, they reported that they suffered menstrually related mood swings (McFarland, Ross & De Courville, 1989; Nisbett, 1980).
- We see this effect in prejudice. For instance, being treated rudely by one waiter can cause a tourist to condemn all waiters in that city, or even the entire nation (Spellman & Holyoak, 1992). See Chapter 13 for more details.

Simulation heuristic

How readily can we imagine various scenarios in order to guess what to expect (Kahneman & Tversky, 1982)? For example, imagine that Mr Crane and Mr Tees were scheduled to leave the same airport at the same time but on different flights. Both are caught in the same traffic jam on the way to the airport and arrive 30 minutes after the scheduled departure of their flights. Mr Crane is told that his flight left on time, while Mr Tees is told that his flight had been delayed and left five minutes before he arrived. Who is more upset? Most people would respond that Mr Tees is more upset, because we cannot imagine that Mr Crane could have made his flight, while Mr Tees might well have made it. The simulation heuristic enables us to imagine 'if only' conditions, which explains much about our reactions to near misses, second-guessing and other frustrations. Of course, you have correctly associated this principle with our earlier discussion of counterfactual thinking, haven't you?

The illusory correlation

As noted in our earlier discussion of causal attributions, we tend to notice covarying events, those that happen at the same time in our social world, and to assume that they belong together. However, the illusory correlation is evident when we tend to exaggerate the apparent correlations between things that 'go together'. For example, in an experiment, participants were shown pairs of words, and later asked to estimate how often each pair had occurred. Although all word pairs were shown the same number of times, participants tended to overestimate the frequency of word pairs that seemed to belong together, such as bacon–eggs and tiger–lion (Chapman & Chapman, 1969).

The implicit assumption that people from an out-group are 'all alike' is a vivid example of the illusory correlation heuristic, and is fundamental to the idea of a stereotype (Barkowitz & Brigham, 1982; Hamilton

& Gifford, 2000). Think of how the media can contribute to prejudice through an illusory correlation. For instance, if a mentally ill person kills a famous person (e.g. John Lennon) or if a small group who adhere to certain religious beliefs commit a terrorist act, many may leap to the illusory conclusion that mental illness or religious beliefs correlate with violent actions. Of course, such beliefs involve ignoring the low base rates for violence in such groups. We will return to this topic in Chapter 13.

The false consensus effect

In the **false consensus effect**, we tend to see our own attitudes and behaviour as typical, and thus we tend to assume that other people similar to us would hold the same attitudes, make the same decisions and act as we do. For example, in an experiment (Ross, Greene & House, 1977), students were asked to walk around campus for 30 minutes wearing a large sandwich board carrying a crudely lettered message, 'Eat at Joe's'. Some agreed, and some refused, but both groups later estimated that more than two-thirds of the other students on campus would have made the same decision they did. Other studies have shown that participants overestimate the extent to which others have the same smoking habits and hold the same political attitudes they do (Sherman, Chassin, Presson & Agostinelli, 1984; Fields & Schuman, 1976). Of course, there are limits to this heuristic. We may want to see ourselves as unique on certain very positive attributes, and would thus underestimate the number of people who share those desirable attributes (Campbell, 1986). For instance, some people who value taking good care of themselves, working out, eating healthy foods, etc., underestimate the actual number of people in their society who act in similar manner (Sul, Wan & Sanders, 1988).

BOX 2.2   INSIGHTS FROM RESEARCH

PSYCHOLOGY, BUSINESS AND ECONOMICS

Classic economics is based on utility theory, the premise that people, businesses and governments are rational, making choices that will maximize their gains and/or minimize their losses. Of course, this implies System 2 thinking, the system of conscious rational awareness. The assumption that people are rational actors in their own enlightened self-interest has been challenged by other economists and by social psychologists. Indeed, behavioural economics is based on the premise that people often make decisions contrary to their own best interests (Lambert, 2012). For instance, our personal economic decisions may involve paying our workers fairly, limiting how much we work so as to spend more time with our families, and buying the more expensive brand of car.

Daniel Kahneman (2011), a social/cognitive psychologist, was awarded a Nobel Prize in economics for his seminal work on 'rapid thinking' and cognitive heuristics in behavioural economics. He recalled an early experience in Israel where recruits in the Israeli defence forces were assigned to units and duties based on a 15-minute informal interview. This system was shown to have failed miserably, but persisted, because of an 'illusion of validity' held by those invested in it. We all have faith in what we have purportedly learned from our own experience, and confidently make judgements based on it.

Consider, for instance, an heuristic called the endowment effect. Parting with familiar objects, such as discarding a worn pair of jeans, giving away a favoured toy, selling one's home, can be emotionally difficult. Research clearly shows that people place a higher value on things that they own than on things that they do not own, even those lacking any sentimental value. For instance, if they are given a coffee mug and later offered to exchange it for a chocolate bar of relatively equal value, they will tend to refuse; similarly, if they had been given the chocolate bar, they will be reluctant to exchange it for the coffee mug. If we value the coffee mug more because it is ours, then we experience the exchange as a loss of our coffee mug, rather than a gain of a chocolate bar (Kahneman, Knetsch & Thaler, 1990). This aversion to loss which outweighs the pleasure of acquisition has been shown in a wide variety of contexts, including exchanging bottles of equal value wines (Van Dijk & Van Knippenberg, 1998). However, lest we leap to conclusions about human nature, consider the results of a series of studies (Maddux, Yang, et al., 2010) in which participants with a Western background (Canada, USA) showed the endowment effect to a greater extent than did those from a Chinese background.

Do entrepreneurs, particularly the successful ones, think differently than other persons? In order to seize the moment, the entrepreneur must work rapidly in situations that are often novel, unpredictable and complex. In this chapter, we see that people deal with such situations by resorting to cognitive heuristics, enabling rapid decision-making – but with the potential for unfortunate biases. For instance, entrepreneurs tend to be very confident, perhaps overconfident, in their own judgement. They also tend to make use of the representativeness heuristic – generalizing from small, non-random samples (Busenitz & Barney, 1997). Because they tend to be overconfident and optimistic, they are less likely to engage in counterfactual thinking – imagining what might have been (Baron, 2000). Baron (2000) points out that this is a mixed blessing. On one hand, counterfactual thinking may generate negative feelings, which may interfere with the ability to focus and function. On the other hand, counterfactual thinking enables one to understand why negative outcomes occurred, and to learn from one's mistakes.

Who becomes a successful entrepreneur? Much of the research provides a laundry list of characteristics: vision and drive, ability to raise capital, financial and management skills, ambition, self-efficacy, optimism, self-confidence, willingness to take calculated risks, ability to delay gratification and, of course, the willingness to work hard (VandenBos & Bulatao, 2000). Baron (1998, 2000) summarizes the set of skills as constituting social competence, the ability to get along with others, to interact effectively and persuasively.

Bounded rationality It is important to understand that we are neither rational beings in all circumstances, nor non-rational 'cognitive misers' always taking the easy shortcut to a decision. Rather, we seek to find the best alternative, given the limits of our minds to process information and the existing conditions: how much information do we have available, how much time do we have? In other words, rather than seeing the use of heuristic rules as laziness, we can see them as rational, having evolved to meet the demands of our environment and our lives. Rather than cognitive misers, Gigerenzer (2010) argues that we are cognitive optimizers.

Consider, for example, how physicians make decisions about diagnosis and treatment (Gigerenzer & Gray, 2008). Consider a situation where a patient appears in the emergency service with chest pains and is admitted to hospital, possibly having suffered a heart attack. Researchers compiled a list of 50 test results, signs and symptoms that would indicate a heart attack and supplied the emergency physicians with this list along with a calculator to apply a formula that combined this information. Armed with this formula, physicians admitted significantly fewer patients were admitted unnecessarily to the Intensive Care Unit. Later, when the physicians had returned to their clinics, without the calculators, the same improvement was evident. The physicians had not memorized the complex formula involving the 50 indicators. Rather, they learned what their experience showed them to be the most important criteria – in most cases it was just three – and ignored the rest. In other words, the physicians learned to apply their own 'fast-and-frugal' decision-making formula, and it worked.

Consider one more example. Which city in the United States has a greater population: Detroit or Milwaukee? Students in the United States and Germany were asked this question, and neither group of students had a sterling record of success (the correct answer is Detroit). However, a greater percentage of the German students were successful (Gigerenzer & Brighton, 2008). Why? Most students in the United States had some familiarity with both cities, but very few of the German students had heard of Milwaukee; hence they relied on the city that they knew of, at least by reputation. In short, they applied a heuristic rule, the recognition heuristic, which implies that, in a situation of uncertainty involving a choice between two of more objects, rely on the recognized object as being more important in some way. Of course, advertisers recognize the importance of brand-name recognition.

> **KEY POINT:** In rapid thinking, we evoke unstated rules or heuristics as cognitive shortcuts. We may judge the likelihood of something by how it seems to represent the typical case, and ignore base rate information. We tend to use what comes readily to mind although that may be something extreme or unusual. This is especially true when the event is primed beforehand. If we can imagine or simulate an event or object, it has greater impact on us. We are influenced by an illusory correlation between objects or events that occur at the same time. We tend to assume a false consensus between our actions and what we would expect of others. We may be best described as cognitive optimizers, rater than cognitive misers, using the best information that we have in the circumstances to make decisions.

INTEGRATIVE COMPLEXITY IN THINKING

Individuals also differ in their cognitive styles, in how they make sense of their social world. An important difference in cognitive style between people is the integrative complexity of the individual's information processing. People high in integrative complexity tend to be open-ended, flexible, able to integrate different perspectives. On the other hand, individuals low in complexity tend to be rather rigid and close-minded, and are incapable of integrating different perspectives. For example, the high-complexity person can see positive and negative in the same person, and so might see that the person is an admirable musician and obnoxious with other people. The low-complexity person would tend to see someone simply as good or bad, a friend or an enemy.

Do people have low integrative complexity because they are unable to think in more complex ways, or because they prefer to think in a less complex manner? In a series of studies, people were encouraged to broaden their thinking about problems, such as reconciling one's religious beliefs with the death of a child. Suggestions included seeking compromise rather than simply choosing one alternative or the other, looking for alternative approaches to solving a problem and looking for an overall philosophy that might underlie different approaches. In general, participants were able to increase the integrative complexity of their thinking when encouraged to do so (Hunsberger, Lea, et al., 1992). Religious fundamentalism seems to be related to a lack of integrative complexity on existential issues (e.g., reconciling a belief in God with a human tragedy), but this did not generalize to other issues, such as jobs versus environment (Hunsberger, Pratt & Pancer, 1994; Pancer, Jackson, et al., 1995). Thus, to a considerable extent, integrative complexity appears to represent a choice or a style in thinking.

Peter Suedfeld has explored this dimension of information processing, using non-experimental evidence in intriguing ways. In one study, the writings of a number of revolutionary leaders were coded for complexity, comparing them before and after the revolution had occurred (Suedfeld & Rank, 1976). It was hypothesized that, during a revolutionary struggle, the leader must be relatively categorical and single-minded towards the one goal of revolutionary change, whereas after a successful revolution, the leader of the new government must be more complex in both understanding and communicating. The results were striking: leaders who remained powerful after the revolution (e.g., Lenin, Stalin, Castro, Jefferson) showed this shift towards greater complexity after the revolution as compared to those who lost their influence (e.g., Trotsky, Che Guevara). In another archival study, researchers coded integrative complexity in the speeches of leaders in the US Civil War, the Second World War and the first Persian Gulf War of 1990. They found that, in all cases, low levels of complexity tended to be related to a decision to go to war (Conway, Suedfeld & Tetlock, 2001).

Other archival studies have examined integrative complexity of people at different stages of life (Suedfeld & Bluck, 1993). In one, the integrative complexity in letters of famous people was studied in relation to significant life events, both positive (e.g., marriage, coronation, major book published, election or appointment) and negative (death of spouse, political defeat). In this study, integrative complexity increased in response to negative life experiences, but not in response to positive events. In another study (Suedfeld & Piedrahita,1984), researchers coded the published correspondence of a number of eminent men and women over the last 10 years of their lives (e.g., Lewis Carroll, D.H. Lawrence, Freud, Liszt, Proust, Queen Victoria). Those who died at a ripe old age after a long illness showed a gradual decline in integrative complexity over their last four years. However, those who died unexpectedly showed a steep decline in integrative complexity in their last year, regardless of their actual age. Suedfeld & Piedrahita (1984) suggest that a decline in integrative complexity may occur naturally as an 'intimation of mortality' in the period preceding death. Of course, more evidence would be needed to support this intriguing interpretation.

[**KEY POINT:** People vary in integrative complexity, the extent to which their thinking is open-ended and flexible. Archival data shows that situational factors can have a strong effect on integrative complexity.]

A FINAL NOTE

Consider the following paradox. It is important for people to understand and make sense of the people, events and situations in their lives. Of course, the best way to understand anything is to gather as much information as possible and think about it carefully and logically. However, because there is simply too much information to process and too little time to do it, we rarely act in the optimal manner. We must figure out what is happening, decide what to do, and then act. While cognitive shortcuts can lead to error, they can in fact be seen as a source of strength and creativity in human functioning (Bargh & Chartrand, 1999; Wegner & Wheatley, 1999). They allow us to go beyond the available information and to fill in the gaps and make inferences, guesses, hunches. Unlike computers, which are compelled to follow precisely defined rules (algorithms), people make inferential leaps based on incomplete information. Indeed, in the field of artificial intelligence, computers are 'taught' to reason by means of the same cognitive shortcuts that characterize human intelligence (Newell & Simon, 1972).

SUMMARY

1. The dual-process model of thought processes states that we may think rapidly and automatically or consciously and deliberately. In general, people are cognitive misers, seeking the easier, more rapid way of thinking unless compelled or cued by the situation.

2. We form first impressions of people using a rough average of our impressions of individual characteristics, weighted by those characteristics most important to us.

3. Our impressions are biased by an orientation to think positively about others, but we are more influenced by negative information in forming an overall impression.

4. We bring our own individual and cultural assumptions about human nature to our perceptions of others.

5. We often look for explanations (attributions) about why people act as they do and why certain outcomes occur. When we find one explanation that fits, we tend to discount other possibilities and we tend to see cause and effect in events that occur together.

6. In making attributions, we choose between seeing the person or the situation as causing the action.

7. In a single event, we conclude that the act corresponds to a disposition to act that way when the person acted freely, the effects are uncommon or not according to usual social norms. Where we have more information about how the person acted in other situations and towards other people and how others acted to that person, we take this into account.

8. In our attributions about success and failure, we decide whether the success or failure was caused by something about the actor (internal) or something about the situation (external), whether the cause was stable or variable over time, and whether the occurrence was controllable by the actor.

9. Our attributions are subject to several biases, particularly that of overestimating the person's role in causing the action while ignoring the influence of the situation (correspondence bias). Culture plays an important role in moderating this bias. We may also explain

actions and outcomes in a self-serving manner, giving ourselves credit for success and blaming others for failure.

10. We tend to believe that our own environment is controllable and that life is generally fair or 'just', which leads us to search for meaning where uncontrollable events happen, and to blame victims for their fate.

11. Attribution theory is limited by a cultural bias to think in terms of cause and effect.

12. To reduce cognitive effort, we think in terms of categories, or schemata, about people, events and ourselves. Schemata are often represented in our minds by prototypical examples, and may become rigid stereotypes. Schemata guide what we pay attention to, how we interpret new information, and what and how we remember.

13. Construal-level theory states that how we think of people and events in terms of concrete or abstract formats depends on their psychological distance from us, in time, space and relatedness. One type of abstraction is counterfactual thinking, which enables us to contemplate alternative possibilities.

14. In order to facilitate rapid thinking, we apply an implicit rule, or 'heuristic' – a cognitive shortcut. In making judgements, we often ignore information about base rates and take the 'typical' as the rule, exaggerate the relationship between events (illusory correlation), overestimate how much others agree with us (false consensus effect) and use what readily comes to mind at the time. We also tend to value what we possess more than alternatives of the same or even greater value (endowment effect).

15. People vary in the extent to which they think in relatively simple or complex ways.

POINTS TO PONDER

- What is the dual-process model of social cognition? How would you apply this model to how we perceive and think about other people?
- Our capacity to process information about our social world is strongly influenced by biases that we bring to this task. How do these biases influence how we think about the causes of people's actions?
- We are described as 'cognitive misers' expending as little time and effort as possible in trying to understand the people and events of our lives. In what ways does our miserly nature show up, and when do we become more 'mindful' about our thinking?

FURTHER READING

Fiske, S.T. & Taylor, S.E. (2008). *Social cognition: From brains to culture*. Boston, MA: McGraw-Hill.

An updated and well-written overview of this burgeoning field, linking social cognition, social neuroscience and the role of culture. This book is indispensable as an introduction to this subject.

Forgas, J., Williams, K.D. & Wheeler, L. (2001). *The social mind. Cognitive and motivational aspects of interpersonal behavior*. New York: Cambridge University Press.

An interesting integration of the research on how our strategies in dealing with others are influenced by how we interpret and explain the social world. Dated in some ways, but still useful.

Gilovich, T., Griffin, D.W. & Kahneman, D. (2002). *Heuristics and biases. The psychology of intuitive judgments*. New York: Cambridge University Press.

The definitive review of this topic. It is filled with all kinds of practical implications (Note: author Daniel Kahneman won a Nobel Prize for his work in this area).

Kahneman, D. (2011). *Thinking, fast and slow*. New York: Farrar, Straus and Giroux.

An important and groundbreaking overview and recollection of various heuristics and biases that constitute our cognitive shortcuts, written in an amiable, accessible style. A scholarly book that made the best-seller list in several countries.

Kunda, Z. (1999). *Social cognition: Making sense of people*. Cambridge: MIT Press.

A comprehensive review of research and theory, accessible to students. Includes basic processes, applications to problems such as knowing yourself and forming prejudice, along with some cross-cultural perspectives.

Roese, N.J. (2005). *If only. How to turn regret into opportunity*. New York: Broadway Press.

A lively and entertaining treatment of counterfactual thinking, its advantages and its perils, with suggestions for personal change. The author is a pioneer researcher on this topic.

Spencer, S.J., Fein, S., Zanna, M.P. & Olson, J.M. (2003). Motivated social perception. The Ontario Symposium (Vol. 9). Mahwah, NJ: Erlbaum.

Set of advanced papers on how our motives, goals and need to maintain self-esteem impact on how we make sense of our world. Together, these chapters provide insight into the premise that we see what we want to see.

Personality and Social Psychology Review (1999) 3(3).

This issue of this journal is devoted to the psychological study of evil.

WEBLINKS

http://www.socialcognition.eu

A useful compendium of European resources in this area.

http://www.princeton.edu/~kahneman/multimedia.htm

A very useful collection of articles and lectures by Daniel Kahneman.

CHAPTER 3
THE SOCIAL SELF

This above all: to thine own self be true.
(Act I, Scene III) *Hamlet*
William Shakespeare

LEARNING OBJECTIVES

* To understand how we come to know ourselves by private introspection and by comparing ourselves to others

* To understand what it means to identify ourselves as male or female

* To understand the processes and the limitations of self-control

* To learn how we evaluate ourselves in terms of how we would or should be and the implications of high and low self-esteem

* To understand how culture influences how we evaluate ourselves

* To understand how we create and manage the impression that others have of us

* To address the question as to whether we seek high self-esteem or a realistic impression of ourselves

In his autobiography, Nelson Mandela (1994) traces how he came to an understanding of himself and his identity. Throughout his life, he was pulled by the opposite poles of traditional African society and the white European society. Rolihlahla, his name at birth, literally means 'pulling the branch of a tree' in the Xhosa language, but has the colloquial meaning of 'troublemaker', foreshadowing the many storms in his life. From an aristocratic background in traditional African society, he was sent to a Western school, where he excelled. At the age of sixteen, he underwent a traditional Xhosa initiation into manhood, marked by circumcision rituals. Subsequently he attended a Christian college, run by whites and dedicated to the higher education of an African elite within the racist apartheid system of the time.

In his final year at college, he heard a lecture by a great Xhosa poet, Krune Mqhayi, whom he describes as a 'comet streaking across the night sky'. From that experience, he developed an intense pride in his own black South African culture. After completing law school, he began a clerkship at a prominent white law firm in Johannesburg, an unusual opportunity for a black person at that time and place. While his legal training progressed rapidly, he encountered many incidents of racist insults and demeaning treatment. His anger was directed into political commitment to the cause of black liberation, even while he worked successfully as a lawyer within the white-dominated system. He describes his life as having run on two separate tracks – his work in the liberation struggle and earning his professional livelihood as a lawyer.

Ultimately, his political activity led to a dramatic trial, in which he was convicted of treason and imprisoned for more than 27 years by the regime. Mandela's commitment did not wane during this long period of imprisonment, and he became an enduring symbol of the liberation movement. Finally, the white leadership of the country, sensing the imperatives of history, economics and justice, arranged his release. Mandela and his associates subsequently negotiated a new constitution, which ended the racist apartheid system and empowered the black majority of his nation. He was elected president, and advocated not revenge but reconciliation and the building of a new, multiracial cooperative society. In 1993, he was awarded the Nobel Peace Prize. In 1999, after serving a full term as president, and overseeing the free election of his successor, Mandela stepped down and became a revered retired statesman until his death on December 5, 2013.

In struggling for peace and the freedom of his people, Mandela was compelled to sacrifice his chosen career, his family life, and 27 years of his life. How can we describe him? He is a member of a prominent Xhosa family, educated in the European traditions, a lawyer, a husband and father, a freedom fighter, a prisoner, a political leader, a revered retired statesman. While all of these roles are part of who he was, circumstances caused some roles to become more salient at various stages of his life.

The previous chapter addressed how people make sense of their social world – how they form impressions of people, infer why people act as they do (attribution), construct schemata and apply heuristic rules of thumb that influence their interactions with others. This chapter focuses on how similar social cognitive processes are applied to one very important object in our lives: ourselves. While the idea of 'self' is one that we commonly use, it is surprisingly difficult to define. How would we define ourselves? Clearly it includes our physical body, our beliefs and feelings and our experiences, as well as our social identity: our name, memberships in various groups, social roles. It implies something central to us, the core of what makes us unique as individuals. We may express who we are by our relationships with others, what we do and even what we possess (Haggard & Williams, 1992). For example, attending symphony concerts may have as much to do with our self-concept of being cultured and affiliating with like-minded friends as it does with our enjoyment of the music.

Figure 3.1 Nelson Mandela of South Africa
Source: @ Renata Sedmakova/Shutterstock.com

Imagine that someone asked, 'Who are you?' How would you complete the sentence 'I am _____'. Because you are a complicated person living in a complex world, you could answer that question in many ways (try it!). The sum total of your answers could define your own unique self-concept. However, while the specific content of your self-concept is unique, the overall organization of the self-concept is similar for most people. When Rentsch & Heffner (1994) asked the 'Who are you?' question of university students, they found there were eight categories by which the participants defined themselves. Some of these categories concerned personal attributes, such as interpersonal characteristics ('I am a student', or 'I date a lot'), interests ('I'm into psychology' or 'I enjoy ballet'), personal beliefs ('I am opposed to abortion' or 'I always vote for the more conservative party'), and self-awareness ('I am a good person' or 'I am easily hurt'). Others referred to how we are defined in our social environment, such as ascribed characteristics ('I am a woman' or 'I am a Chinese citizen of Singapore'), or social differentiation, how we differ from others ('I'm from another country'). The point here is that 'who am I?' has many meanings to us.

In this chapter, we first discuss the concept of the 'self' as a schema, and explore how we can come to 'know ourselves', both through thinking about ourselves and comparing ourselves to others. We will pay particular attention to how we know ourselves as women or men. Then we turn to the related question of how we evaluate ourselves, and to the pivotal issue of self-esteem. Next, we discuss how we regulate ourselves, exhibit self-control. We look at the role of culture in this area, and examine how we present ourselves to others in order to 'manage' the impression that others have of us. Finally, we address an apparent paradox: we want to know ourselves honestly (and for others to accept us as we are, both the positive and the negative), but we also want to feel good about ourselves. Note that social psychologists have been at the forefront in studying how our experience of ourselves is influenced by others (Olson & Hafer, 1990).

SELF-SCHEMATA AND THEIR EFFECTS

As discussed in Chapter 2, a schema is an organized sets of beliefs and feelings about people and events that guide the processing of information. Your schema about yourself includes everything that you know, think or feel about yourself, the images and memories you have of yourself, even the possibilities that you can imagine for yourself in the future. These self-schemata of individuals differ in a number of ways, such as in clarity, complexity and consistency over time (Campbell et al., 1996).

The self-schema acts as a guide, enabling you to process relevant information (Markus, 1977). What is important to understand is that simply measuring how you rate yourself on a characteristic is not sufficient. For instance, you might interpret a mark of 75% in social psychology as an achievement or as a mediocre outcome, depending on whether you see yourself as a budding psychologist and on how important high grades are to you. People respond differently to information depending on its relevance to the self-schema (Markus, Hamill & Sentis, 1987).

Like other schemata, the self-schema organizes information, beliefs, memories and impressions. Your self-schema includes not only how you might evaluate yourself on various characteristics, but also which characteristics you consider to be important to you. What are the characteristics about yourself that you would use to describe yourself? For example, John and Joan both consider themselves intelligent and persuasive. For John, intelligence is central, and he describes himself in those terms. When asked, he will also admit to being persuasive, but this is not fundamental to how he defines himself. On the other hand, Joan is a leader, and being persuasive is central to how she defines herself. If asked, she would rate herself highly on intelligence as well, but when asked to describe herself, she will mention persuasiveness but not intelligence. John is schematic with respect to intelligence and aschematic (without schema) with regard to persuasiveness, while Joan is schematic with respect to persuasiveness and aschematic with regard to intelligence.

In a study, people were asked to rate themselves along a dimension going from independence to dependence, and to indicate how important the trait was to them (Markus, 1977). Several weeks later, participants in the study were shown slides containing various words, and asked to push a button labelled 'Me' if it applied to them or 'Not Me' if it didn't. Those participants whose self-schema included independence–dependence made decisions more quickly about words related to that dimension (e.g., 'conform'). Thus, self-schemata helped them process information more rapidly. Men whose self-schemata stress masculinity think more of activities such as weightlifting or watching professional sports than gender-neutral activities such as eating an apple or playing recorded music (Markus, Smith & Moreland, 1985).

Self-schemata can also affect memory (Rogers, Kuiper & Kirker, 1977). We associate new self-relevant information with a rich store of prior encoded information, and thus our self-schemata provide us with more retrieval cues. When older participants were cued to positive stereotypes of aging (e.g., wisdom) rather than negative stereotypes (e.g., incompetence, dementia), they actually performed better on tests of memory (Levy, 1996).

The **self-reference effect** (Kihlstrom et al., 1988) refers to the fact that individuals remember information better when they can relate it to themselves. For instance, you will remember movie dialogue better if you identify with the character, and you will remember best the sections of a course in social psychology that you can relate to your own experience. The reasoning is that you have an extensive and complex set of knowledge, experience, images and beliefs about yourself, any of which can be associated with this information. Indeed, people attribute more traits to themselves than they do to other people, and they may even attribute to themselves traits that are apparently opposite, such as 'serious' and 'carefree', or 'intense' and 'calm' (Sande, 1990). It appears that chronically lonely people have a negative self-schema that causes them to pay selective attention to negative information consistent with this self-schema, and to remember it (Frankel & Prentice-Dunn, 1990).

Recall from the last chapter that a schema can be activated by priming. Certain conditions may arouse self-awareness: seeing oneself in a mirror, having one's picture taken or giving a talk in front of an audience (Duval and Wicklund, 1972). This focus on the self leads to self-evaluation, often with unpleasant emotional consequences. People may respond by leaving the situation – looking away from the mirror, avoiding the audience – or by changing their behaviour to reduce discomfort over negative self-evaluation (Gibbons & Wicklund, 1976). An interesting aside: one effect of alcohol is to reduce self-awareness and the processing of self-relevant information. This may well explain the so-called disinhibiting effect of alcohol, if drinkers are unable to process their own behaviour when drunk (Steele, Southwick & Critchlow, 1981).

Contemporary social neuroscience is beginning to establish some connections concerning how the self is represented in brain functions. At the clinical level, severe brain trauma from injury or illness can transform the self concept dramatically (Feinberg & Keenan, 2005). Using brain techniques such as fMRI, researchers report that brain activity of normal participants when processing self-relevant information occurs in specific brain centres that are distinct from those aroused when the processing concerns information that is not relevant to the self (e.g. Platek & Krill, 2009; Northoff & Panskepp, 2008).

> **KEY POINT:** A self-schema is an organized set of beliefs, evaluations, images, memories, and hopes about the self. It includes not only how people evaluate themselves on various characteristics, but also which characteristics are important to them in describing themselves. The self-schema guides how self-relevant information is processed, and how it is stored and retrieved in memory. The self-reference effect refers to how people remember information more effectively when they can relate it to themselves.

Comparing ourselves to others

Mandela, as a black South African, was uncertain as to how he fitted into a white-dominated society at that time. The white authorities certainly knew what his 'place' should be, but his own experience was different. He was inspired by a nationalistic black poet and by his own experience to seek his identity in his own cultural roots. An important source of information about ourselves is **social comparison**: comparing ourselves to others (Festinger, 1954). Indeed, we often cannot make sense of our own actions and feelings without looking outward to the actions and reactions of others. When we feel any uncertainty about who we are or how well we are doing, we seek comparative information. For instance, if you consider being generous to be an important part of who you are, then observing how others behave in similar situations provides feedback as to how generous you really are. Consider that evaluating oneself can be a challenging task, involving much cognitive effort. As the cognitive misers that we are (recall Chapter 2), social comparison offers us a relatively easy way to evaluate ourselves, acting as a heuristic rule-of-thumb in this process of self-evaluation (Corcoran & Mussweiler, 2010).

Even apparently objective feedback is influenced by social comparison. A grade of 75% in algebra may seem like objective information and may support your conception of yourself as mathematically competent, if not brilliant. However, if many of your classmates attained marks over 80%, that same mark would be a blow to your self-esteem. Conversely if most students obtained marks in the 60s or below, that mark of 75% would be a notable boost.

Social comparison theory is based on three premises:

1. Humans have a drive to evaluate their own opinions, feelings, abilities and actions.
2. In the absence of objective cues such as marks or profits, individuals will evaluate themselves in comparison with others.
3. People tend to compare themselves with someone similar to them in opinions, background or ability.

Now consider the case in which a close friend has performed better than you did on some task. On one hand, you may feel good about yourself for having such a smart, competent friend. However, your friend's superior performance may, in comparison, lower your own self-evaluation. It depends on how relevant the task performance is to your self-schema. If you identify yourself as a good golfer, then your friend's championship performance will threaten your self-esteem. However, if golf is not central to your self-schema, you can simply bask in reflected glory and actually feel better about yourself for having such an outstanding player as a friend (Tesser, 1988). Further, social comparison can evoke different aspects of the self-schema in different situations. For instance, a female chemist may well think of herself primarily in terms of her occupation when in the company of other women who are not chemists, but in terms of her gender when in the company of male chemists (McGuire & McGuire, 1988).

As a general rule, we compare ourselves to others who are similar to us on characteristics that are schematic to us (Wood, 1989). For instance, students will compare themselves to other students in intelligence, a trait important to them. However, at times we engage in upward or downward comparison. Downward comparison, with someone less able, less attractive or less powerful than ourselves, can boost our self-esteem (Wills, 1981). On the other hand, we may at times compare ourselves to someone better than us to inspire us to greater heights. Upward comparison can be either ego-deflating or ego-enhancing (Collins, 1996). If a recreational tennis player plays with a professional and manages to win one of three sets, the recreational player will feel better about himself or herself, even after being defeated.

In general, we compare ourselves to someone equal when the goal is to evaluate ourselves, to someone better (upward) when the goal is to improve ourselves, and to someone inferior to ourselves (downward comparison) when we want to feel better about ourselves (Wood, 1989). Consider that when we focus on ourselves as we are, then upward comparison can generate hope and optimism that we can be better (Lockwood & Kunda,1997, 1999). However, downward comparison will not always make you feel better, if, for example, you can see yourself vulnerable to what happened to the unfortunate comparison person (Lockwood, 2002). For instance, as an aspiring musician, you may feel that, if you don't have enough time to practise and perform, you could become as inept as that person. 'This could happen to me' is a powerful brake on downward comparison. One interesting variation on downward comparison is with yourself as you were in the past (Ross & Wilson, 2002). For instance, you may compare yourself as a musician with how you

Figure 3.2 The way we were: Family photo, Vienna 1885
Source: LiliGraphie/Shutterstock.com

were last year or even in high school. You may also compare your physical appearance at various stages of your life (Figure 3.2).

Envy and scorn We have discussed how upward and downward comparison relates to how we feel about ourselves. Fiske (2010) argues cogently that there may be adverse effects in how we relate to others. That is, upward comparisons may well be accompanied by envy, and downward comparisons by scorn. For example, if you are in the middle class in economic terms, then you may react to rich people with envy, and poor people with scorn. Envy humiliates and angers people and can even lead us to the experience of *schadenfreude*, a malicious joy in the misfortune of others (van Dijk, Ouwerkerk, et al., 2011). Meanwhile, scorn desensitizes people to the needs of those who are the objects of their scorn.

Sometimes in order to avoid distress at the misfortune of others, we simply don't process such information. In a neuroscience research study, participants were shown pictures of people from disadvantaged out-groups, such as homeless people, as well as pictures of people from their own socioeconomic level. The researchers found that the diminished affective reactions to disadvantaged out-groups were consistent with diminished activity in the prefrontal cortex. Such diminished neural activity was not found in these brain centres when the participants were shown pictures of people of their own socioeconomic status (Fiske, 2010).

In short, social comparison provides us with useful information about ourselves. Of course, we must take into account the context of our comparisons. Consider, for instance, students in academically elite classes and those in classes of mixed ability. Those in the latter situation would have a less impressive group of students for comparison and would likely feel better about their own abilities: the 'big-fish-little-pond' effect. Indeed, this effect has been shown to generalize across cultures and across nations at different levels of economic development (Seaton, Marsh & Craven, 2009)

Social comparison may occur in difficult circumstances. Imagine that you have been ill and are trying to understand your situation. Of course, with the abundance of information through the Internet, patients can more readily evaluate their illness and their prospects. When the situation is uncertain, as often may be the case, then we often compare ourselves with others. Cancer patients, for example, may benefit from both upward and downward comparisons (Wood & Vanderzee, 1997; Buunk et al., 1990). They may compare themselves with other people who have recovered from their illness (upward comparison) and thus serve as models for hope and self-improvement. They may also compare themselves with those who are more seriously ill (downward comparison), providing them with a sense that they are not so badly off, for 'things could be worse'. Indeed, in one study of cancer patients, the vast majority of these patients compared themselves to those who were more seriously ill (Wood, Taylor & Lichtman, 1985). Thus, through social comparisons, individuals can evaluate how seriously ill they are, how hopeful they can be about their outcome and how they are behaving as patients. This may also influence their choices of treatment and lifestyle changes.

Analogous social comparison processes may occur with caregivers and members of helping professions. People in such circumstances may experience a syndrome of burnout, a state of emotional exhaustion, of feeling dissatisfied with their accomplishments and detached from their work or from the recipients of their efforts (Maslach & Jackson, 1982). In a longitudinal study of nurses (Buunk, Zurriaga & Peiro, 2010), it was found that nurses who made upward comparisons with other nurses and felt positive about those comparisons were less likely to experience burnout than those who responded with negative feelings to such upward comparisons. They concluded that the feelings produced by upward comparisons may predict burnout.

Culture and social comparison Is social comparison a universal tendency or one specific to certain cultures? In an interesting study (Lee, Oyserman & Bond, 2010), bilingual Chinese students were first primed to think in terms of an individualistic or collectivistic mindset; this was done simply by administering the experimental procedure in English or in Chinese. When first induced to think in terms of an individualistic mindset typical of English-speaking cultures, the students distanced themselves psychologically from others who were outperforming them and made no comparisons with them. However, when primed to think within their home culture by administering the procedure in Chinese, this distancing tendency was significantly less pronounced. In a study of European Canadians (individualistic) and Asian Canadians (more collectivistic),

White & Lehman (2005) report that, again, the Asian Canadians made more frequent social comparisons, perhaps reflecting a greater motivation for self-improvement or perhaps just being more socially oriented. In another study comparing these same cultural groups of Canadians, Lockwood, Marshall & Sadler (2005) observed that, when given a description of another student of their own cultural background involving a positive academic record, European Canadian students responded with a stated intent to work harder. However, when the description of the target person was negative (a disastrous academic first year), it was the Asian Canadians who stated that they intended to work harder. Upward comparison led European Canadians to greater motivation to succeed, while downward comparison motivated Asian Canadians to avoid failure.

KEY POINT: Given that we seek self-knowledge, and 'objective' criteria are often lacking, we compare ourselves to others. While we usually compare ourselves to similar others, we sometimes compare ourselves to someone better (upward) or worse (downward). Upward comparison can lead to envy, and downward comparison to scorn, both of which impact relationships. Culture affects social comparison, and people from collectivist cultures tend to compare themselves to others more often, which motivates self-improvement.

Self-knowledge through observing ourselves

As discussed in the previous chapter, people tend to attribute the actions of others to stable dispositions or traits – honest people are those who behave honestly. Bem (1972) suggests that we observe ourselves as we observe others. Just as we form impressions of others by what they say or do, we form an impression of ourselves by what we say, think and do. If you observe yourself acting generously, generosity becomes part of your self-concept.

The notion of self-perception extends back to Schachter's (1964) work on emotion, suggesting that we infer our own emotional state from a sense of internal arousal, coupled with our interpretation of external cues. Thus, for example, you may decide that a joke is funny because you laughed uproariously when the joke was told. However, if you are led to believe that some external factor caused you to laugh (such as the 'canned laughter' on television sit-coms), then you may decide that you weren't really so amused after all (Olson, 1990). We will see in Chapter 8 how the same reasoning may be applied to the phenomenon of falling in love.

Imagine that as a volunteer in an experiment you are looking at pictures of attractive nude people. Electrodes have been attached to record your heart rate, and your heart rate is amplified and played back through a loudspeaker. Not surprisingly, you would tend to conclude that you are more attracted to those for whom your heart rate increased. However, in the actual experiment, the heart rate feedback was false, using previously recorded heart rates that were increasing, decreasing or steady. People who believed their heart rate had increased when looking at a picture were subsequently more strongly attracted to that particular nude picture (Valins, 1966).

We tend to be more favourable towards anything that we connect, explicitly or implicitly, to ourselves, including our names. For instance, if your name begins with the letter 'S', then 'S' may become a favourite letter, an effect shown in 12 different European languages (Nuttin, 1987). People are more likely than one would expect by statistical chance to have homes, jobs, even places of residence that contain the letters of their names (Pelham, Mirenberg & Jones, 2002). So, for instance, George is more likely to live in Georgia than would be predicted by chance, Laura to be a lawyer, and Sydney to live in Australia. By similar reasoning, it would be probable at a bit above the chance level for James to drink Jamieson Irish whisky, and Stan to read a newspaper called *The Standard*. The effect sizes are quite small but statistically significant, which is remarkable. Understand that we do not seek these associations out consciously, but an implicit connection with the self may influence our choices when other factors do not override them.

Further, we value things that we associate with the self. Recall, from the previous chapter the endowment effect, where we are reluctant to exchange something that we possess for something of equal or even greater value. We may value objects of little financial value because they represent something about ourselves, past or present: a diploma, an article of clothing, a brand of beer. For instance, it has been shown in an experiment that we value lottery tickets that we chose ourselves more than if they are handed to us. But of course, our chances of winning are exactly the same in either case (Langer, 1975).

The notion of self-knowledge through self-perception has an important message. Rather than introspecting about what you really believe in, and then acting on those beliefs, you first act and then discover your beliefs and values from your actions. You know that you are a fan of a certain team because you attend all their games and cheer for them. In later chapters, we will pursue this theme of how actions can lead to attitude changes.

KEY POINT: We can seek self-knowledge by observing what we do and concluding that this represents something about ourselves. This is especially true if we can connect what we observe to what we believe about ourselves.

BOX 3.1   INSIGHTS FROM THE LAB

DO WE CHOOSE OCCUPATIONS THAT MATCH OUR SELF-IMAGE?

Figure 3.3   Physicians? Nurses? Patients? Who is which? (There are four physicians and one patient)

Source: Andresr/Shutterstock.com

It's a familiar script: when we meet someone, the question soon arises, 'What do you do?' We usually are not referring to their hobbies, sports or sexual predilections but to their job or occupation or their career aspirations. To a considerable extent, our occupation defines us. It follows that the stereotypes that exist in society about various occupations also become part of our social selves (Vroom, 1964) and reflect our personal values (Rosenberg, 1957). Indeed, in a study of recent graduates of a programme in tourism and hospitality management, career choice was determined both by their perception of a fit between their self-image and the job requirements, and by their general sense of self-efficacy (Song & Chon, 2012).

Research by Maclean and Kalin (1994) supports the model that self-image drives occupational choice. First, they set out to establish what the stereotypes were in three traditionally male-dominated occupations (engineering, law, medicine) and three female-dominated occupations (nursing, rehabilitation therapy, teaching). Participants were asked to rate typical members of each profession on two characteristics: affiliation (wanting to be with others) and dominance (wanting to control others). Engineers and lawyers were rated as high in dominance and low in affiliation, a stereotypically male pattern, while the mirror-image pattern of high affiliation and low dominance characterized ratings of nurses, teachers and rehabilitation therapists.

Subsequently, they studied students in academic programmes leading to these six occupations and found that their self-images were congruent with the stereotypes of their chosen occupation. The self-images of law students, for example, tended to be high in dominance and low in affiliation, while the self-images of student nurses consisted of low dominance and high affiliation.

The interesting exception was medicine. While traditional participation rates have been considerably higher for men, the dominance-affiliation profile was closer to that of the 'female' professions. Medicine, of course, clearly involves both helping and technical competence, and women have entered the profession in substantial numbers in the past decades.

Men and women try to match their self-images to an image of compatible occupations. Of course, seeing oneself as competent in a field such as information technology would be a vital component in entering that field (Johnson, Stone & Nichole, 2008). If the person's self-image includes being helpful (or communal, associated with femininity, as discussed earlier), then the helping professions such as medicine, social work and teaching would be particularly attractive (Super, 1980). Similarly, a person whose self-image includes being good at solving technical problems will be attracted to more technical occupations. This may explain in part why, despite some significant progress, gender segregation in occupations remains a fact of life in Western nations. That is, men are overrepresented in some occupations, particularly those of a technical nature, while women predominate in clerical and service occupations, perhaps because these choices are consistent with how they view themselves, in accord with existing stereotypes. Another important factor is a willingness to enter what is perceived as a competitive occupation, such as entrepreneurship, where self-confidence must play an important role, and where being female may be a psychological barrier (Kamas & Preston, 2012; Thebaud, 2010). Indeed, those who enter male-dominated occupations tend to have more 'masculine' and less 'feminine' self-concepts (Gianakos & Subich, 1988).

Gender and self

Perhaps most central to our social identity is gender. Note that while the terms sex and gender are often used interchangeably, sex generally refers to biological characteristics and gender refers to the roles, preferences and behaviours observed or assumed to be typical of men and women. So when psychologists try to explain differences between the sexes, they tend to refer to them as gender differences when these explanations have to do with the roles of men and women in their society. Beginning in childhood, we learn what male and female mean and to identify role behaviour appropriate to our own gender identity in our own particular culture.

Traditional psychological tests measured masculinity and femininity as polar opposites, in which one selected the 'male' or 'female' response to each item. Later research has challenged this one-dimensional view (Bem, 1974; Spence, 1985). Rather than forcing participants to choose between 'male' and 'female' responses, these studies use separate scales measuring masculinity and femininity. It would therefore be possible to score high or low on each of the two scales, giving us four possible patterns: high-F and low-M, low-F and low-M, high-F and high-M, low-F and high-M. A high-low pattern of sex-role self-typing would be indicative of a schema as traditionally masculine or feminine, while those who are either psychologically androgynous (high in both masculinity traits and femininity traits), or undifferentiated (low in both) would be called aschematic; that is, without sex-typed schemata. People characterized by traditional sex-typed thinking tend to think of their social world primarily in terms of 'male' and 'female', while androgynous men and women tend to view people and events in terms of a greater variety of categories. Androgynous men and women also appear to be better liked, more adaptable to situational demands, more satisfied in their relationships and to have higher self-esteem than those who are strongly gender-typed (Rosenzweig & Daley, 1989).

These four types of individuals, both male and female, were compared in an experiment (Frable & Bem, 1985) in which they listened individually to a taped conversation among six people, while photographs were shown of each speaker as he or she spoke. For half the participants, the conversation group that they observed consisted of three males and three females. For the control participants, the group consisted of three whites and three blacks, all of the same sex as the participant. Then, participants were presented with a list of 72 quotations from the conversation and asked to identify the speaker for each one.

The pattern of errors by each group of participants was revealing. In the race-difference condition, no clear pattern of results was evident; that is, sex-typed or androgynous self-schemas did not predict accuracy. But with the sex-difference group, the sex-typed participants (high M, low F or high F, low M) made most of their errors by confusing who said what among the opposite-sex conversationalists. That is, for instance, a 'masculine' participant was less accurate in identifying which female conversationalist said what, as compared to a psychologically androgynous male participant. In short, a sex-typed self-schema caused participants to see members of the opposite sex as somehow less as individuals and more as 'all alike'.

The research consistently indicates that women are more likely to have an interdependent view of themselves, focusing on their relationships, while male self-concepts tend to be constructed around ideas of independence (Cross & Madson, 1997). For instance, recall the 'Who Am I?' test described earlier. Women will tend to complete it in terms of roles and relationships (I am a friend) or social characteristics (I am sociable), while men more typically use individual characteristics (I am honest. I am competitive). Similar differences are found across different cultures (Watkins, Adair et al., 1998; Watkins, Akande et al., 1998; Kitayama & Markus, 1994). However, other research suggests a more nuanced interpretation, wherein both men and women seek both independence and interdependence but in different ways; women are oriented more toward close relationships and men to larger groups and collectivities (Baumeister & Sommer, 1997).

What images, associations, memories, ideas and beliefs come to mind when you think of the words *man* and *woman*? Clearly, people in various cultures have a richly elaborated and complex network of cognitive associations concerning the concepts of male and female. Indeed, gender may be invoked as a way of categorizing people, even where it is irrelevant to the situation (Bem, 1985). However, the content of gender identity – what it means to identify one's self as male or female – differs markedly from one individual to another. Indeed, having to live up to rigid formulas of 'masculinity' or 'femininity' can be stressful (McCreary & Sadava, 1995).

Apart from the obvious biological characteristics, what is referred to as masculinity, as measured in traditional scales, has been described as instrumentality or agency, a concern with achieving goals and being active in the world, while femininity is described as expressiveness or communion, focused on other people and concerned with interpersonal relationships (Bakan, 1966; McCreary, 1990). Of course, to most people, a satisfying life would include both achieving in their environment and having satisfying close relationships – in other words, having both masculine and feminine psychological characteristics. Indeed, an excessively strong or unmitigated sense of agency would be destructive to the individual and society, suggesting one who acts regardless of the consequences to others (Spence & Helmreich, 1979). Similarly, an individual who is excessively communal, concerned only with the welfare of others, would not be able to function effectively in the external world. Thus, a balance between achievement and caring for others is necessary, avoiding either extreme (McCreary & Korabik, 1994).

Psychological androgyny represents the desire to be both competent and social, and signifies flexibility – a capacity to act in ways appropriate to the situation without its impinging on one's identity as male or female. Thus, it is important that women be assertive and concerned with achievement where this is appropriate. It is equally important that men be relationship-oriented and caring where the situation calls for this type of behaviour. In an era of rapid and transformational changes in the roles of 'female' and 'male' in many societies, the advantages of psychological androgyny are increasingly evident.

One more implication of gender concerns how we evaluate our competence. For instance, women may not consider themselves to be competent in math or science because of their gender. Many women who succeed in courses in social psychology as part of a major in psychology expect to have difficulty in coping with the math-oriented courses in research methods and statistics, which are often required courses. Do these perceived difficulties reflect something fundamentally different about the 'male brain' as contrasted with the 'female brain' or are they consequences of what we have learned about gender-role stereotypes? Although the research is not entirely consistent, it suggests that the latter outweighs the former in influence.

Indeed, in one study (Nosek et al., 2002), women who associated mathematical ability with being male rated themselves lower on mathematical ability, even where they had selected a math-intensive major. In another study, female participants scored as well as males on a test of scientific reasoning (Ehrlinger & Dunning, 2003). However, in their self-ratings of various abilities, the women rated their ability to reason about science more negatively than the men. Further, when invited to participate in a science jeopardy contest with attractive prizes, women were less likely to sign up or express interest in entering. Clearly, we have enduring views about our strengths and weaknesses that are influenced by gender stereotypes.

> **KEY POINT:** An important aspect of our self-concept is ourselves as male or female. Traditional conceptions represent masculinity and femininity as opposite polarities on a single dimension, while contemporary conceptions posit the two as having a degree of interdependence. That is, some people score high on measures of both masculinity and femininity (psychological androgyny) or low on both (undifferentiated, aschematic with regard to gender). Another feature of gender roles pertains to agency (actively engaged in the environment) and communion (focused on relationships). Psychologically androgynous people can be both, flexible in response to situational demands. Even in relatively egalitarian cultures, gender-linked perceptions of competence persist, for instance in regard to mathematics.

SELF-EVALUATION

Feeling positive about oneself has been identified as an important component of effective and happy living. Indeed, chronic low self-esteem has been linked empirically to various maladaptive behaviours. A considerable amount of research has been directed towards identifying the effects of low self-esteem. Much is based on the assumption that low self-esteem leaves people vulnerable to all sorts of personal difficulties and social pressures. Notions of self are derived in large measure from experiences and the reactions of others. Some people have relatively secure and consistent self-esteem, while others have self-esteem that fluctuates with the ups and downs of life, depending on the feedback they obtain from others (Baldwin & Sinclair, 1996).

Measuring self-evaluation   There are a number of direct or explicit measures of self-esteem, such as questionnaires that ask people how they evaluate themselves; for example, the widely used scale by Rosenberg (1965). These measures have shown good validity and have been used in a wide variety of studies (Table 3.1). However, as we have seen and will see later in this chapter, people also want to present themselves to

Table 3.1   Rosenberg Self-Esteem Scale (Rosenberg, 1965)

Instructions: Below is a list of statements dealing with your general feelings about yourself. If you strongly agree, circle **SA**. If you agree with the statement, circle **A**. If you disagree, circle **D**. If you strongly disagree, circle **SD**.

1. On the whole, I am satisfied with myself.
    SA   A   D   SD

*2. At times, I think I am no good at all.
    SA   A   D   SD

3. I feel that I have a number of good qualities.
    SA   A   D   SD

4. I am able to do things as well as most other people.
*5. I feel I do not have much to be proud of.
*6. I certainly feel useless at times.
7. I feel that I'm a person of worth, at least on an equal plane with others.
*8. I wish I could have more respect for myself.
*9. All in all, I am inclined to feel that I am a failure.
10. I take a positive attitude toward myself.

Scoring: SA = 3, A = 2, D = 1, SD = 0. Items with an asterisk are reverse scored, that is, SA = 0, A = 1, D = 2, SD = 3. Sum the scores for the 10 items. The higher the score, the higher the self esteem.

Figure 3.4 What would this portrait convey to you?

Source: © Christie's Images/Corbis

others in a good light, and also want to see themselves favourably, and so these measures can be susceptible to response bias (see Chapter 1). Therefore researchers have turned to more subtle, implicit measures of self-esteem, aspects of which the person may not be consciously aware (Asendorpf, Banse & Muecke, 2002; Greenwald, Banaji, et al., 2002). For instance, recall the discussion of people's tendency to feel more positive about the letter of the alphabet that is the first letter of their name. This provides a subtle approach to measuring self-esteem. When people are asked to indicate their liking for each letter of the alphabet, and for each number between 1 and 33, research indicates that people with higher self-evaluations show greater liking for the letters in their names and the numbers in their birthday. The idea is that these particular letters and numbers are self-relevant, and therefore will be preferred, more so by people who evaluate themselves more positively. Of course, people are not aware of the self-relevance of these letters and numbers in the rating task (Koole, Dijksterhuis & van Knippenberg, 2001).

Another innovative technique involves photography. Imagine that as a participant in a research study you are presented with the following assignment: We would like you to describe how you see yourself. To do this, we would like you to take, or instruct someone else to take, 12 photos that tell who you are. These photographs can be of anything, just as long as they tell something about who you are (Dollinger & Clancy, 1993). How would you complete this assignment? Would the photos show you dressed in formal attire or in jeans, would you be alone or with other people, would you be smiling or frowning, would some photos portray you working, studying or engaging in recreation? What might they indicate about how you feel about yourself? To use such photographs in systematic research, a technique called content analysis is employed in which the photos are coded in terms of clearly defined categories. For instance, photos may be coded as portraying self with others, self with children, self with adults, self in a group, self with a significant other, self alone (Dollinger, Preston, O'Brien & DiLalla, 1996).

Of course one must be cautious in interpreting these photos. For instance, we are conditioned to smile when the photographer says 'cheese!' While a smile generally indicates positive emotions, smiles may also be a way in which we create an impression of ourselves for others. For instance, in a study, participants were asked to imagine themselves applying for a job and having a photo taken of themselves to accompany the application. They were more likely to smile when the job was relatively lower in status, and women smiled more often when the job involved social contacts (Vrugt & Van Eechoud, 2002). In this case, impression management would be the dominant concern (Chapter 2).

Consequences of low self-esteem People who are chronically low in self-esteem face disadvantages in life. They are plagued with self-doubts about their abilities, they refrain from seeking advancement in their careers, they are less likely to cope well when faced with difficult circumstances and they are more vulnerable to depression. However, not everyone with low self-esteem suffers in this way, and cultural differences, still an area that needs more research, are no doubt important too.

It has often been assumed that low self-esteem renders individuals more gullible to persuasion. But is that so? The reality is that individuals with low self-esteem tend to have difficulties in understanding persuasive messages, perhaps due to anxiety or an inability to pay attention (Rhodes & Wood, 1992). Therefore, while high self-esteem individuals resist persuasion because of their self-confidence, low self-esteem individuals are not easily persuaded because they don't get the message. Those with intermediate scores on measures of self-esteem are the ones who are more easily persuaded. This is called a curvilinear relationship (Figure 3.5).

It has been assumed that women suffer more from lower overall self-esteem than do men, and that this difference originates in adolescence. However, recent evidence does not point to a sharp drop in self-esteem among adolescent women (Kling, Hyde & Buswell, 1999). Indeed, a recent meta-analysis of studies, most of them conducted in Western nations, indicates that only a modest difference exists between men and women (Kling, Hyde & Buswell, 1999). Does this effect cross-cultural boundaries? We don't really know.

One proposed explanation for the gender differ-

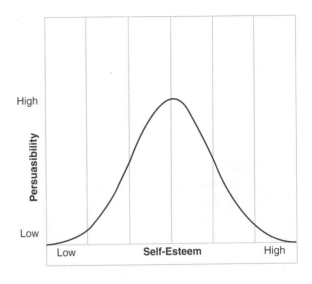

Figure 3.5 A curvilinear relation between self-esteem and persuasion

ence in self-esteem is that disadvantaged groups such as women are stigmatized as being of less value and therefore evaluate themselves less favourably (Crocker & Major, 1989). Members of such groups, including women, protect their self-concept in several ways: by attributing failure or other unwanted outcomes to prejudice against themselves, by making social comparisons with members of their own group rather than with the advantaged group and by placing more value on success in areas where their own group tends to do well. For instance, while women tend to earn less than men in equivalent occupations, they may protect their self-esteem by comparing their earnings to those of other women or to others in occupations where women predominate.

The dark side of high self-esteem Can self-esteem be inappropriate or too high? There is no consistent evidence that low self-esteem leads to violent behaviour or other social ills (Bushman & Baumeister, 2002). (This is discussed further in Chapter 11.) Members of groups that tend to be lower in self-esteem, such as women, people suffering from depression and disadvantaged minority groups, do not tend to be more aggressive than other people, but on the other hand, perpetrators of violent acts such as murder, rape, spousal and child abuse, political terrorism and genocide are often described as arrogant and confident, high in self-esteem (Baumeister, Smart & Boden, 1996; Baumeister, Bushman & Campbell, 2000). In other words, high self-esteem is not always a good thing. Yet, people in Western nations continue to believe that elevating yourself and convincing yourself as well as others that you are a 'winner' will make you a winner. This is sometimes reflected in formal education when personal development and raising self-esteem are given more importance than achievement and skills training.

Research by Baumeister and his colleagues challenges the simplistic view that high self-esteem is necessary and desirable in itself (Baumeister, Campbell, Krueger & Vohs, 2003). While self-esteem literally refers to how much people value themselves, it does not imply accuracy – we may think more of ourselves than the facts warrant. Indeed, high self-esteem may represent an honest and accurate appraisal of our strengths and weaknesses, or it may represent a narcissistic self-absorption, a defensive reaction or even conceit or arrogance. Obviously, while realistic self-esteem will help us to perform well, performing well can also boost our self-esteem. Similarly, while a person with high self-esteem may behave in a manner that leads to becoming a leader, being a leader may also boost self-esteem. Baumeister et al. (2003) review abundant evidence that efforts to boost self-esteem, such as through therapeutic interventions, does not improve performance in school or elsewhere – and, in general, low self-esteem people perform as well as those high in self-esteem.

Ancient Greek mythology tells the story of Narcissus, a hunter famous for his exceptional beauty. He was so impressed with himself that he disdained any of the nymphs and girls unfortunate enough to love him. Another goddess, the well-named Nemesis, lured him to a pool of water where he saw his reflection. Mirrors being an invention of the future, poor Narcissus fell in love with his own reflection. Unable to consummate his love or to part from the object of his love, he died at poolside, the victim of fatal self-absorption. Early pioneers in psychology, including Ellis and Freud, incorporated the concept of narcissism into psychology, particularly in clinical applications. The basic notion of narcissism is an excessive self-absorption, a sense of entitlement for the rewards that life brings, and often a willingness to exploit others. This is reflected in unrealistically high self-esteem.

Is narcissism a downside of the culture of individualism? In 1979, historian Christopher Lasch observed a malaise in contemporary American society, a loss of confidence in the future. This description seems just as applicable today. He attributes this malaise to the extremes of competitive individualism, 'which, in its decadence, has carried the logic of individualism to the extreme of a war of all against all, the pursuit of happiness to the dead end of a narcissistic preoccupation with the self' (p. 21). Think of advertising as an instructive example. In the past few decades, advertising has shifted its focus from the characteristics of the product to those of the consumer. The message is that people need a certain product to define themselves as individuals and attain their goals in life – being rich, popular or successful. Researchers refer to the 'commodified self-concept', in which one defines oneself in terms of wearing the right clothes, driving the right car, using the right cosmetics (Murphy & Miller, 1997).

An interesting recent study highlights the rise of rampant individualism in American society (Twenge, Campbell & Gentile, 2012). The researchers counted the use of various pronouns in books published in the United States from 1960 to 2008, using an Internet database of 766,513 books. They tested two hypotheses, that first person plural pronouns (e.g., we, us) would decrease in use and that first-person singular pronouns (I, me) would increase. The results supported both hypotheses, suggesting that the culture in general had changed in the direction of greater individualism. While individualism cannot be equated with narcissism, the shift to a more extreme egotism is certainly consistent with what Lasch (1979) described. Indeed, other research suggests a parallel increase in narcissistic traits among successive birth cohorts in the US (Twenge & Foster, 2010).

Baumeister et al.'s (1996) discussion of the 'dark side' of self-esteem carries echoes of Lasch's trenchant critique. Indeed, we might consider whether much of psychology conveys a 'sanction for selfishness', a message that we should be most concerned about ourselves rather than others or our society (Wallach & Wallach, 1983). Perhaps not coincidentally, the society that is most committed to the desirability of raising self-esteem, the United States, is also one of the world's more violent societies. Perhaps some of this commitment should be redirected towards instilling virtues such as modesty, humility and self-improvement (Baumeister, Smart & Boden, 1996).

> **KEY POINT:** Self-esteem is not always consistent over time, but chronic low self-esteem can be maladaptive, although results are variable and cultural factors come into play. Measures include self-reports, implicit measures and having participants construct photo-autobiographies. Attempts to inflate low self-esteem artificially are counter-productive, and unrealistically high self-esteem (narcissism) can be maladaptive. Cultural factors, particularly excessive individualism, can engender narcissism in the individual and in society.

Self-esteem and self-guides

It is important to understand that we are not limited to the here-and-now when we evaluate ourselves. We are not limited to images of the present or memories of the past, for we may also extend our thoughts about ourselves into the future. Imagine what you will be like in 10 years, 20 years or 40 years. You can imagine yourself as being quite different from the way you are now, in both positive and negative ways, what Markus and Nurius (1986) have called 'possible selves'. We all have visions of the self that we hope to become or dream of becoming, such as being rich, successful or thin. We also have visions of the self that we fear to become, such as being sick, unemployed or lonely.

These possibilities can have powerful effects in the present. If you can imagine yourself as successful in business, or as an artist or a world traveller, you are more likely to act in order to achieve that goal. On the other hand, if you tend to imagine yourself as being poor or chronically ill, you may act to prevent this possibility from occurring, or you may act fatalistically on the assumption that it will happen. The so-called mid-life crisis has much to

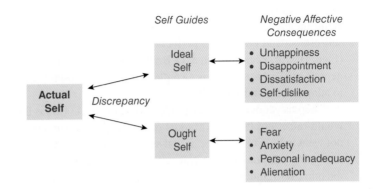

Figure 3.6 Self-discrepancy theory

Source: Higgins (1996)

do with people evaluating themselves in terms of where they expected or hoped to be.

The fact that you can imagine yourself in other possible ways also provides you with a frame of reference for self-evaluation. If you can imagine yourself as being very rich or poor, generous or stingy, happy or sad, then you can evaluate yourself as you are now in relation to these possibilities. Self-discrepancy theory provides a formal framework for this idea.

We have discussed low self-esteem, but what does the term really mean? Self-discrepancy theory defines self-esteem in terms of the discrepancy between actual and possible selves, and this gap, if large, can lead to emotional difficulty (Higgins, 1987). People compare their self-concept – themselves as they are at present – to 'self-guides', the standards that they strive to attain. One of these self-guides is the ideal self embodying their hopes and aspirations: myself as I wish I were. Another self-guide is the ought self, the obligations we place on ourselves, our own sense of duty and responsibility: myself as I should be. For instance, you might see yourself as a moderately successful student, wish you were at the top of your class (ideal), and feel that you ought to be able to raise all of your marks to at least a B level (ought). You might consider yourself generous, which is how you ought to be, but wish you could be even more generous. In other words, the actual self is monitored in comparison with some desired end-state (Higgins, 1996). It is interesting that even in video gaming, participants have been shown to perceive their avatars in terms of their ideal and ought selves (Jin, 2011).

As the poet Robert Browning wrote, 'Ah, but a man's reach should exceed his grasp, or what's a heaven for?' However, if the reach is too far, if the self-discrepancies are excessive, we may experience emotional distress, and the theory predicts the type of distress associated with each discrepancy. If we see ourselves as much inferior to what we think we should be (that is, a discrepancy with the 'ought' self), we tend to experience guilt, shame and possibly anxiety. On the other hand, if we see ourselves as much inferior to what we would wish to be (a discrepancy with the ideal), then we experience disappointment, frustration and perhaps debilitating depression. These self-discrepancies can be measured reliably (Watson, Bryan & Thrash, 2010) and tend to be relatively stable over time (Strauman, 1996). Moreover, such discrepancies can predict our reactions to major life events. For example, expectant parents who manifested large self-ideal discrepancies before the birth of their child experienced greater sadness after the birth (Alexander & Higgins, 1993).

While most research concerns people's global self-concepts and self-guides, we can also study how they vary in specific areas of life. For instance, how much time do you spend online, and how much would you ideally wish to spend? One such study found that self-ideal discrepancies in Internet activity often reflected more generalized self-ideal discrepancies (Tzeng, 2010). Another study reports that self-discrepancies among young women were related to seeking cosmetic medical procedures (Pentian, Taylor & Voelker, 2009).

When do we experience a self-discrepancy? It may represent an honest and reasonably accurate self-appraisal, or it may reflect an unrealistic appraisal. A self-discrepancy may be caused by an excessively low self-evaluation or unrealistically high self-guides, or both. For instance, Jennifer may see herself as a poor computer programmer because she doesn't realize her own abilities (low self-evaluation) or because she cannot attain the highest possible level in her profession (unrealistic self guide). A large discrepancy between one's self-esteem and unrealistic, perfectionistic standards of what one 'ought' to be has been related to depression (Flett, Hewitt, Blankenstein & O'Brien, 1991 and see Box 3.2). Does self-discrepancy cause people to become depressed? Perhaps, but it is also plausible that depression causes people to evaluate themselves negatively or to adopt unrealistic self-guides.

There is yet one more self-guide: the feared self. This is the kind of person you worry about becoming and would rather not become (Markus & Nurius, 1986). Imagine yourself now in a possible future as you would not want to be. For instance, if you see yourself as hardworking and ambitious and hope to be even more so in the future, can you imagine yourself as a failure, languishing without having achieved anything? In contrast to the other self-guides, this represents a discrepancy between your actual self and feared self that leaves much to be desired; the farther you see yourself from this dire possibility, the better you feel. Indeed, research finds that as your feared self corresponds to your actual self-concept, feelings of anxiety and guilt are aroused (Carver, Lawrence & Scheier, 1999).

KEY POINT: Our self-concept includes not only our self as it is, but possible selves, alternatives which can motivate and direct efforts to change. Self-discrepancy theory postulates two self-guides, the ideal self (myself as I wish I were) and the ought self (myself as I should be) and looks at discrepancies between the actual self-concept and these self-guides. A discrepancy may represent an honest and reasonably accurate appraisal of oneself, or an unrealistically low actual self-appraisal or unrealistically high self guides (ideal, ought). A discrepancy between the actual and ought self can lead to feelings of guilt, shame, anxiety, while a discrepancy between actual and ideal self can lead to feelings of disappointment and depression. A third proposed self-guide is a feared self, myself as I would not want to become, reflecting a prevention regulatory focus.

BOX 3.2   ANOTHER LOOK

PERFECTIONISM AND THE SELF

As noted, our self-evaluation is grounded on how we ought to be, or on how we would wish to be. Self-guides that are unrealistic, impossible to attain, can affect us profoundly. Perfectionism represents unrealistically high self-guides (Flett & Hewitt, 2002). While seeking to perform and achieve at a high level has obvious rewards and value, a preoccupation with excessively high standards can clearly be self-defeating. Indeed, perfectionism implies a focus, even an obsession, with attaining the ideal self and/or the ought self (Flett, Hewitt, Blankenstein & Mosher, 1991).

Three dimensions of perfectionism have been identified and scales have been developed to measure each of them:

Self-oriented perfectionism in which compulsive striving for high standards emanates from within; sample item: 'When I am working on something, I cannot relax until it is perfect'.

Social-prescribed perfectionism in which the individual perceives that others have unrealistically high expectations for oneself; sample item: 'The people around me expect me to succeed at everything'.

Other-oriented perfectionism in which the expectations for unrealistic perfection are directed outwards to others; sample item: 'If I ask someone to do something, I expect it to be done flawlessly'.

Most of the research reports that self-oriented perfectionism may be adaptive in some circumstances while socially prescribed perfectionism, trying to meet the exaggerated expectations of others, is generally maladaptive. In other words, people can deal with self-imposed pressure more readily than pressures from others. Indeed, attempting to meet what the person perceives as the excessive expectations of others can be damaging to one's health (Molnar, Sadava, Flett & Colautti, 2012) and even necessitate therapeutic intervention (Flett & Hewitt, 2002). However, it is also suggested that the consequences of perfectionism are influenced by other factors, such as the culture in which they occur. For instance, meeting even unrealistically high expectations from others can be seen as quite normative and adaptive in more collectivist cultures such as Japan (Sumi & Kanda, 2002) and China (Xie, Leong & Feng, 2008).

Consider another way to look at perfectionism, one which distinguishes between achievement concerns and evaluative concerns (Frost, Marten, Lahart & Rosenblate, 1990). Achievement concerns refer to setting the bar very high, striving to achieve very high standards for oneself. Evaluative concerns are generally shown as self-criticism when the person falls short of these standards. Looking at perfectionism in this way, comparative studies of Asian-Americans, African-Americans and Caucasian-Americans show relatively higher levels of evaluative concerns, that is, self-criticism, among Asian-Americans and somewhat lower levels in this dimension among African-Americans. While individualism/collectivism may account for some of these differences, a more convincing

Figure 3.7 Pursuit of perfection in ballet
Source: ayakovlevcom/Shutterstock.com

explanation lies in reported higher levels of parental criticism experienced by the Asian-American participants (DiBartolo & Rendon, 2011). Indeed, Asian-American high scores on perfectionism reflect this experience of parental criticism and self-criticism (DiBartolo & Rendon, 2012; Powers, Koestner, et al., 2011). Perfectionist expectations seem to act as a self-guide, to which the person compares his or her actual performance. A highly perfectionist person will set impossibly high levels for his or her ideal self. Certainly the perfectionistic is generally doomed to failure in meeting impossible standards and would therefore be expected to evaluate the self in a less than positive manner, thereby suffering low self-esteem (Zeigler-Hill & Terry, 2007; Trumpeter, Watson & O'Leary, 2006).

As discussed later in this chapter, we act in a way to create a favourable impression of ourselves in the eyes of others. With regard to perfectionism, some people need to appear perfect to others, even if it does not match what they expect of their own performance (Hewitt, Flett, et al., 2003). Perfectionistic self-presentation includes actively proclaiming one's successes and accomplishments to others (e.g. 'I try always to present a picture of perfection'), and concealing or not disclosing any weaknesses or mistakes (e.g. 'I should solve my own problems rather than admit them to others', 'I do not want people to see me do something unless I am very good at it'). Several studies show a link between perfectionistic self-presentation and symptoms of eating disorders such as bulimic behaviours and compulsive dieting, particularly where people were strongly dissatisfied with their body image (McGee, Hewitt et al., 2005).

Perfectionism is clearly driven by social expectations. On one hand, we are socialized into striving to achieve and rewarded for attaining high standards, whether in meeting the expectations of one's parents or employers, professional recognition, victory in sports or high academic marks. On the other hand, when we internalize these expectations into an obsession, this can become maladaptive. If one's sense of self and one's basis for self-evaluation rest on virtually impossible self-standards, then the person's 'ought self' and 'ideal self' will surely lead to disappointment and distress.

Coping with insecurity

While success generally enhances one's self-esteem, none of us is immune from anxiety and insecurity about our own abilities. Can we do well in school? Can we create the right impression in that job interview? Are we good enough to win that crucial game? Self-doubts can certainly generate renewed effort to improve and overcome. They can also cause people to behave in self-defeating ways. People who are upset are at greater liability to pursue unrealistic risks: to take wild guesses on exams, or gamble their money, all in the hope of getting out of that blue mood. Usually the risk will not pay off, which gives the person something else to feel bad about and perpetuates a downward cycle (Leith & Baumeister, 1996).

Figure 3.8   Self-handicapping with alcohol?

Source: thaumatr0pe/Shutterstock.com

Some people deal with such self-doubt in a way that actually reduces the chances for success. In a strategy called self-handicapping, people arrange in advance for impediments to a successful performance. These self-imposed impediments serve to protect their self-esteem from the aftermath of failure. For example, if Carole is anxious about an upcoming exam and considers good grades an important aspect of who she is, she may decide to party instead of studying the night before. She can attribute failure to the self-imposed handicap (not studying), rather than to effort or ability. Of course, an unlikely success despite that handicap would enhance self-esteem even more. You can't lose for losing! Note that people are generally unaware of what they are doing, but are acting in ways that are rewarding in a sense.

Various self-handicapping patterns of behaviour have been identified. Some involve actual changes in behaviour (e.g., not exerting enough effort, getting drunk), while others involve claims of illness or unfair task demands (Arkin & Baumgardner, 1985). Studies indicate that men tend to self-handicap more than women (Harris, Snyder, Higgins & Schrag, 1986) and that men tend to use alcohol and drugs for this purpose, while women are more likely to claim physical illness or stress (Hirt, Deppe & Gordon, 1991). Note that we're not talking here about finding excuses after the fact, but about acting in advance to create an excuse for failure.

> **KEY POINT:** People may cope with a low self-evaluation by renewed effort, by taking unrealistic risks or by self-handicapping. The latter involves arranging in advance for impediments to success (don't study, drink excessively etc.), so as to provide a convenient external situational attribution for failure. This is not a deliberate strategy, but one that has proven effective for the person in the past.

SELF-REGULATION

The capacity for self-regulation, being able to control our thoughts, feelings and actions to our own benefit or to accord with existing social norms, is crucial to how we function in our work, our leisure and our relationships. For instance, as a student qualified to attend university, you may well have exhibited your capacity to delay immediate gratification for a more substantial reward in the future. Carver & Scheier (1998, 2011) argue that self-awareness is necessary for self-regulation; in other words, we ask ourselves whether what we are doing or how we are reacting will serve our own needs and desires. They developed a feedback loop model known by the acronym TOTE: test, operate, test and exit. According to this model, we ask first whether our actions will meet the standards that exist or that we set for ourselves (test); then we act or react (operate), then we test again to see what the consequences of our actions were (test), then we either use that feedback to change our reaction or we can exit, knowing that our reactions were appropriate. For instance, imagine that you are driving on a freeway, looking for your appropriate turnoff. You can schematize the process in the following:

- Test – is this the turnoff that you're looking for? – No
- Operate – keep driving
- Test – is this the correct turnoff? – No
- Operate – keep driving
- Test – is this the turnoff? – Yes
- Exit

In short, self-regulation involves monitoring our actions and reactions in terms of their anticipated and actual consequences, and then changing in order to better achieve what we want to achieve.

Self-regulation also involves a conscious or unconscious decision to focus on certain aspects of the situation, and to ignore or delay attention to other aspects. In Higgins' (1996, 2011) research on regulatory focus, participants were cognitively primed to focus on how they wished they were, or on how they felt they should be. Higgins (1996) notes that people may adopt either a *promotion* or *prevention* regulatory focus, concentrating on what to do to achieve positive outcomes, or on what to do or not to do in order to prevent negative outcomes such as losing face. As would be expected, people from East Asian cultures such as Japan tend to focus on prevention forms of self-regulation, attempting to avoid negative reactions from others (Hamamura & Heine, 2008).

Given that the capacity for self-regulation has crucial implications for how well we function, especially as social beings who must relate to others, it would likely follow that our brains have evolved in a way to make this possible. Heatherton (2011) identifies important psychological components that serve to enable us to remain socially connected, and that are consistent with the TOTE model. First, we must have some kind of awareness of what we are doing, at least to be able to evaluate it. Second, we must also be able to understand that others are reacting or will react to our actions and reactions so as to be able to form some kind of expectancies of others' reactions. This represents a person's 'theory of mind', the capacity to understand that others have thoughts and feelings, a capacity that develops in childhood. Third, we must be able to detect any kind of threat to our well-being, such as people reacting negatively to us and rejecting or ignoring us. Finally, we must be able to do something constructive to rectify the situation, such as establishing or re-establishing good relations to the others affected by our actions. This means being able to control our impulses, restrain acting on how we may be feeling, and even avoid thinking nasty thoughts, none of which are easy at times.

Using tools such a functional magnetic resonance imaging procedure (fMRI) to localize activity in relevant brain centres, researchers have reported evidence of specialized activity related to aspects of self-regulation. For instance, the dorsal prefrontal cortex has been shown to be aroused when we process self-relevant information and when we apply our 'theory of mind', to figure out how and why others react to our actions. On the other hand, the amygdala is activated in detecting social threats (Vul, Harris, Winkielman & Pashier, 2009).

Of course, being human, we all have limits to our ability to self-regulate, and there are times when we give in to temptation or the heat of the moment. While the feedback loop model of self-control has proven to be useful, it has also been argued that self-control, willpower, or self-regulation is an exhaustible capacity, a resource that we can use up. If so, then when we exhibit extended self-control through this process of feedback, we may experience ego depletion in which our self-regulation is impaired for some time (Baumeister, Hetherton & Tice, 1994; Baumeister, Vohs & Tice, 2007). So, if you are following a diet and restraining your eating, day after day after day, limiting how much you eat and what you do not eat, eventually your self-control may well break down and that large slice of cake with ice cream will win for now. Or you may lose self-control in a different situation, as for example, not bothering to do your studying this evening.

Ego depletion has been demonstrated in experimental studies (Baumeister, Bratslavsky, Muraven & Tice, 1998). In one such study, participants were first food-deprived, then seated at a table on which there were two bowls, one filled with chocolate chip cookies and candies, the other with radishes. In one experimental condition, participants were instructed to sample both the cookies and the radishes, and in another they were told that they could eat only the radishes. The experimenter left the room and then observed each participant surreptitiously. The participant was then taken to another room and assigned a very difficult task involving tracing geometric figures without raising the pencil from the paper. Those who had first been in the radish-eating condition, in which they had to refrain from eating the forbidden cookies and candies – a task of self-control – tended to give up more easily on the frustrating task. Wanting candies but having to eat radishes reduced their capacity for self-control. This ego depletion effect has been replicated in numerous studies. Providing participants with glucose, a source of energy linked to self-control, can attenuate this effect (Muraven & Baumeister, 2000; Hagger, Wood, Stiff & Chatzisarantis, 2010).

> **KEY POINT:** The capacity for self-regulation involves control of our own thoughts, feelings and actions to gain a desired objective. First we must be aware of what we are doing and ask whether our actions will get us where we want to be (test), then we act (operate), then we observe the consequences (test), and finally we change or exit the situation. People vary in their regulatory focus on how actions will lead to positive results (promotion), or avoid failure (prevention), with differing consequences. Our capacity for self-control can be exhausted by previous efforts (ego depletion).

CULTURE AND THE SELF

Individualism and collectivism

The ways in which people perceive and define themselves are influenced by the culture to which they belong. Nelson Mandela sought to reconcile his sense of who he was, both as a successful lawyer in a white-dominated society and as a black African from a distinctive culture. In Western societies, social norms focus on the individual rather than on the group or community. Indeed, the American ideal is described as the self-contained individual, someone whose identity and sense of self is complete in and of himself or herself (Sampson, 1977). Canadian ideals are fairly similar, although leaning towards a lesser degree of individualism (Adams, 2003).

Not all cultures have such individualistic concepts (Triandis, 1989). Consider, for example, that we all have two (or more) names, our first name, which has been given to us by our parents, uniquely our own, and our family name, which we share with those closest to us. What comes first – what is uniquely us or what we share with the significant others in our lives? In Western culture, what is uniquely ours is our 'first name', but in Chinese culture, the first name is the shared family name, followed by the given name. This could suggest that in Chinese culture what is most valued is one's family connection in one's identity, not the uniqueness of the individual.

That is, in societies such as India, China or Japan, self-concepts are described as more relational or communal or collectivist (Markus & Kitayama, 1991; Kitayama & Markus, 1994). In studies of how people describe themselves, Korean respondents describe themselves, first and foremost, in terms of their family, while US respondents describe themselves as individuals with unique characteristics (Maday & Szalay, 1976). Chinese participants were more likely than US participants to describe themselves in terms of social roles (e.g., 'I am a daughter') and to qualify social roles as friends or partners (Ip & Bond, 1995). These studies reflect how different cultures reconcile independence and interdependence (Markus & Kitayama, 1991). That is, while we all seek to understand ourselves as distinct individuals, we also need to establish meaningful relationships with others. In Western cultures, we define ourselves primarily in terms of internal attributes, such as motives, abilities, values and personalities, while in many other cultures, people define themselves primarily in terms of their interdependent relationships with other people, groups and institutions (Draguns, 1988). It is also interesting to note that, on average, people from Eastern cultures are less clear and consistent in their self-concept than are people in Western cultures (Campbell et al., 1996).

However, even in individualist cultures, while we stress our uniqueness, we also define ourselves in terms of relevant roles and statuses in society. As noted earlier, it has been suggested that men are more likely to see themselves in terms of individual characteristics and activities, whereas women tend to express a 'connected self', embedded in a matrix of relationships (Gilligan, 1982). Apart from gender differences, people with a more connected, as opposed to individuated, self-concept tend to have a more sophisticated, complex self-concept (Pratt, Pancer, Hunsberger & Manchester, 1990).

Self-esteem and culture

As noted earlier, self-esteem is widely considered to be essential to happiness, mental health and a productive life. Yet, clearly the apparent need for high self-esteem that pervades Western cultures is not a universal need (Heine, Lehman, Markus & Kitayama, 1999). It is interesting that Asian immigrants who have lived in Western nations such as Canada for a longer time tend to have higher self-esteem than do those who are more recent immigrants, and that self-esteem increased over seven months among Japanese exchange students at the University of British Columbia (Heine & Lehman, 1995). It is apparent that, in the Japanese and other Eastern cultures, individuals are less concerned with protecting a high self-regard than with self-criticism, seeking to identify and improve what is lacking in themselves. They tend to view themselves habitually as incomplete and feel unsatisfied with their performance. In other words, their reactions are driven by self-guides (ideal, ought), not simply by self-protection.

While this would seem to be distressing to Westerners, in many Eastern cultures such a habit is seen as healthy, leading to self-improvement. The authors cite the example of a baseball player who, in North American societies, would be assumed to have a certain level of natural ability, brought to fruition by good coaching and hard work. In Japanese culture, there is no assumption of a limit to accomplishment set by natural ability. Consistent self-criticism motivates the person to improve, rather than discouraging the person.

In a study by Kitayama et al. (1997), a set of situations was described to participants. Some of the scenarios involved successes, such as serving an ace in tennis, passing exams, looking good or handsome, while others involved failures, such as breaking something valuable due to carelessness, doing unexpectedly poorly on a test or not being invited to a social event. Participants were asked to indicate the extent to which their own self-esteem would increase or decrease in that situation. American participants indicated that they would expect strong increases in self-esteem in the success situations and lesser levels or decreases in the failure situations. Conversely, Japanese participants responded more strongly to the failure situations. Kitayama et al. (1997) attribute their responses to a tendency among the Japanese participants to focus on what can be gained by failure, learning from it.

Thus far, we have discussed how individuals view themselves and how these views influence their behaviour and are influenced by the social environment – the looking-glass self based on what is reflected back to us about ourselves by others. People are not, however, simply passive recipients of others' views but also act to influence how others perceive them. Indeed, here again, we find cultural differences (Kim, Cohen & Au, 2010). Eastern cultures can be described in terms of face culture, wherein self-respect is derived from your position in society and how others perceive you. Indeed, in its more traditional form, it is meaningless to define yourself apart from how others see you in a face culture, and your own self-assessment is not particularly relevant to your self-esteem. In contrast, the term dignity culture applies to most Western cultures. One views oneself as a unique person, not entirely free from what others think of one but primarily evaluated in terms of one's own self-judgement and one's own actions. Note that face culture is not synonymous with collectivism, and dignity culture is not synonymous with individualism.

For instance, recall the experiment described in the previous chapter where participants judged a person asking questions as being more knowledgeable than those who had to answer the questions. They judged people by their behaviour in exhibiting knowledge and ignored the situation. Kim, Cohen & Au (2010) replicated the experiment in two settings, a public condition in which participants performed or observed the quiz face-to-face, and a private condition in which they worked in separate booths, receiving the questions and answers in written form. The participants were students at universities in China and the United States, representing face and dignity cultures respectively. The results showed that the participants from the dignity culture rated themselves lower than their partners when they were in the contestant role having to answer the questions, regardless of whether they performed in public or private. In contrast, the face culture participants gave themselves lower self-ratings when they looked stupid in public, but not when they would have felt stupid in private. In short, face cultures tend to give priority to 'knowing oneself from the outside', from the reactions of others, whereas dignity cultures tend to give priority to 'knowing the self from the inside' and resist allowing the self to be defined by others.

PRESENTING OURSELVES TO OTHERS

To be an effective political leader in a heterogeneous nation, Nelson Mandela must have been perceived by others as a leader of his people, one who was highly educated, wise and inspiring. Indeed, as an effective leader, Mandela clearly acted in ways to enhance this impression. All of us care what others think of us and thus we seek to create or maintain a positive image of ourselves. Self-presentation consists of any behaviour that is intended to convey information about the actor or an image of what that person is like. We talk about impression management to convey this sense of intention about how we are perceived by others.

Figure 3.9   The job interview. Fertile ground for impression management

Source: Zurijeta/Shutterstock.com

We can compare social interaction to a theatrical performance, in which each of us assumes certain roles or social identities. Indeed, the metaphor of a theatrical performance has become part of our everyday thinking, particularly in the sense of playing a role. Goffman (1959) argues that when circumstances threaten our ability to regulate the impression we create of ourselves, we are compelled to act to save face. We may even use props to help create the right impression. When we dress in a certain style, drive a certain car, serve the right wine or add those special personal touches to our homes, we are providing information to others about ourselves.

However, Goffman did not claim that creating a favourable image is the only motive underlying social interaction. While we want people to think favourably of us, we also want people to understand and accept us as we are, and so we want both to manage the impression that others have of us and to be open and spontaneous with others. At times, these two motivations are in conflict.

It is also important to understand that self-presentation is not always conscious and deliberate and indeed may often become automatic (Baumeister, Hutton & Tice, 1989). For example, someone who is usually serious and hardworking on the job may self-present as fun-loving off the job with friends. This does not necessarily imply something artificial in that person's behaviour, only that the person is capable of behaving in ways appropriate to various situations.

Think of impression management in the social media. The very nature of social websites dictates that people can easily present themselves in what they expect would be a favourable manner, even fraudulently, since one cannot verify what is claimed. Of course, business enterprises can present themselves in a similar manner in order to create a favourable impression of their enterprise or, indeed, to stimulate interest and demand in the goods and services for sale (Hooghiemstra, 2000). While research is at an early stage, the topic is currently being studied intensively (Brody, David, et al. & Cunningham, 2012).

Strategies for managing the impressions we create

Several impression management strategies are available, depending of course on what is appropriate in the situation (Jones & Pittman, 1982). One is ingratiation, making oneself likeable to another, such as by agreeing with the other person, praising the person or doing favours for him or her. Of course, a degree of subtlety is necessary – people don't respond warmly if they believe they are being manipulated. Another strategy is **self-promotion,** an attempt to be seen as competent or outstanding. For instance, a job applicant may even admit to a weakness in order to stress achievement in another, more important area: 'I'm not very strong in accounting, but I'm great at sales!' You might supplicate or beg for sympathy. Intimidation is also possible by attempting to convince the person that you are dangerous in some way. Of course, the other party can always call your bluff. Finally, in more collectivist, less individualistic cultures, people will self-present with appropriate modesty, not wanting to draw undue attention to themselves. People in Western cultures often have no such constraints, although when among friends they generally act with more modesty (Tice, Butler, Muravan & Stillwell, 1995). After all, our close friends already know our flaws.

Impression management may seem manipulative and phony. However, it is also appropriate to present those aspects of yourself that best suit your goals in the situation. Your inexhaustible supply of risqué jokes may create a favourable impression at a party but not in a job interview. It is reasonable to want others to be aware of your special qualities and to appreciate them. People can and do develop particular social skills to influence others to like, respect, admire and perhaps even fear them.

Finally, how do we present ourselves in comparison with others? Feltovich, Harbaugh & To (2002) argue that average people will express these comparisons clearly and in detail, while those who are outstanding or great in some way tend to say little or nothing to compare themselves to others. Thus, for instance, minor bureaucrats will prove their status by displays of their power and authority, while those who are truly powerful will downplay their power, perhaps by showing generosity. Mediocre students may answer the easier questions in class while the best students hold back, embarrassed to prove their knowledge in this way. Acquaintances show their good intentions by ignoring our flaws, while close friends show their intimacy by telling us about our faults, perhaps in a teasing manner. In short, modesty and reticence are ways of self-presentation. When you've 'got it', there is no need to flaunt it.

Relative deprivation in self-presentation

Consider how people express resentment or dissatisfaction about lacking something that others may have. This sense of relative deprivation stems from social comparison with others. However, the expression of resentment will be governed by the situation as well as the extent of perceived deprivation. For example, unions may exaggerate their dissatisfactions in negotiations to elicit greater generosity from management. On the other hand, people may minimize their statements of dissatisfaction in order to appear reasonable or likeable in a marriage or with a colleague at work.

In other words, our expressions of dissatisfaction may be governed by self-presentation motives. Two studies are instructive. In one, participants role-played an interaction in which they expressed their resentment about a mark in a course. Some were instructed to express their feelings honestly; others were told to act in such a way as to be 'taken seriously' by their partner; and a third group was instructed to ingratiate themselves to their partner. Those in the third group, whose goal was simply to be liked, tended to understate their resentment, while those instructed to intimidate their partner (to be 'taken seriously') tended to overstate their resentment (Olson, Hafer, Couzens, Kramins & Taylor, 1997).

In a second study, working adults were invited to express their feelings, either publicly or privately and anonymously, about the lack of day-care facilities in their city. Before they responded, the experimenter told them that she herself was either satisfied or dissatisfied with local day-care availability. When the participants' answers were public, their reports of how much they resented the lack of day care was influenced by the experimenter's alleged resentment or contentment, while their private responses were unaffected by the experimenter's expressed feelings. Thus, while we may feel resentment about relative deprivation, how we express it is influenced by how we want others to perceive us (Olson, Hafer, et al., 1997).

Personality and self-presentation

People vary in their conscious need to present themselves in socially desirable ways (Paulhus, 1990). It is important to distinguish between self-deception, giving biased self-reports that one honestly believes to be true, and impression management – deliberately giving favourable self-descriptions to others (Paulhus & Reid, 1991). This suggests a conscious process, that we are deliberately acting in ways to impress others. Self-deception enables us to deceive others, by avoiding the cues that would cause us to be aware that we are trying to deceive them (Von Hippel & Trivers, 2011). That is, in many cases when we practise deception of others, we are unaware of what we are doing, because we literally 'buy into' our own deception.

An interesting debate has arisen concerning a possible evolutionary basis to impression-management (e.g. Pinker, 2011a). Von Hippel & Trivers (2011) argue that the issue is not about feeling good about oneself, but about leading others to see us favourably. In this view, self-deception and self-enhancement are only by-products of the need to present ourselves to others in favourable ways. After all, when others see us favourably, the benefits are substantial, universal across cultures, and obvious: we become 'leaders, sexual partners and winners' (Von Hippel & Trivers, 2011, p. 5). From this perspective, the need to deceive others has evolved and is universal. On the other hand, Heine (2011) argues that we cannot assume that self-deception and self-enhancement have evolved in humans because there are significant variations amongst cultures. That is, as we have seen, self-enhancement is uncommon in Asian cultures, and so deceptive self-presentation and self-delusion would be unnecessary in such cultures.

People vary in how effective they are at self-presentation. Snyder (1979) has described how individuals vary in self-monitoring, adjusting one's self-presentation in response to subtle cues from others. His scale measures people's concern with the appropriateness of their self-presentation, whether they look to others for cues about how to act appropriately and whether they can use these cues to modify their behaviour. As we would expect, high self-monitors tend to be more friendly, conformist, adaptive and less shy. For example, in one study, low self-monitors tended to like an individual acting in an agreeable manner in a video, even if they were told that the person had been paid to be ingratiating; they relied solely on the individual's behaviour and ignored the social context. High self-monitors, on the other hand, differentiated between someone paid to be agreeable and someone being agreeable without being paid to be so (Jones & Baumeister, 1976). Note below in Table 3.2 that the widely used revision of the self-monitoring measure (Lennox & Wolfe, 1984) consists of two subscales; the capacity to modify one's self-presentation to suit the situation, and sensitivity to how other people are reacting to you.

Table 3.2 Examples of items in the Revised Self-Monitoring Scale

Ability to modify self-presentation

1. In social situations, I have the ability to alter my behaviour if I feel that something else is called for.
3. I have the ability to control the way I come across to people, depending on the impression I wish to give them.
7. When I feel that the image I am portraying isn't working, I can readily change it to something that does.
9. I have trouble changing my behaviour to suit different people and different situations.
10. I have found that I can adjust my behaviour to meet the requirements of any situation I find myself in.
12. Even when it might be to my advantage, I have difficulty putting up a good front.
13. Once I know what the situation calls for, it's easy for me to regulate my actions accordingly.

Sensitivity to expressive behaviour of others

2. I am often able to read people's true emotions correctly through their eyes.
4. In conversations, I am sensitive to even the slightest change in the facial expression of the person I'm conversing with.
5. My powers of intuition are quite good when it comes to understanding others' emotions and motives.
6. I can usually tell when others consider a joke to be in bad taste, even though they may laugh convincingly.
8. I can usually tell when I've said something inappropriate by reading it in the listener's eyes.

Source: Lennox & Wolfe, 1984

KNOWING YOURSELF, OR FEELING GOOD ABOUT YOURSELF?

Much of the preceding discussion reflects an important controversy in the research concerning the self. Two schools of thought contend: self-enhancement and self-verification. The self-enhancement position is based on the argument that we seek feedback that increases, or at least maintains, our feelings of self-worth. Recall the discussion in Chapter 2 on how the self-serving bias and defensive attributions enable self-enhancement. Of course, most people want to feel good about themselves, at least most of the time. Indeed, mild self-deception appears to contribute to a general state of well being, and even good health (Paulhus & Reid, 1991; Taylor & Brown, 1988). Older people are less likely to engage in self-deception when thinking about the future, not because their expectations are rosier but because they have learned through experience what to expect (Robinson & Ryff, 1999). The other position is self-verification, the premise being that we want feedback that seems accurate, that reflects what we know about ourselves. Moreover, we want to feel that people accept us as we really are.

As discussed earlier, through impression management we want both to create a good impression and to be authentic. Swann (1992) proposes that we present ourselves in ways that will verify or confirm our self-concept. That is, we want to feel that we know ourselves. For example, if you believe that you are not athletic, you may find it disturbing to be praised for playing a sport brilliantly because the comment challenges a long-standing aspect of your self-concept. Indeed, in an experiment, participants with negative self-opinions tended to choose partners who also appraised them accurately, even if unfavourably (Swann, Stein-Seroussi & Giesler, 1992).

Could this self-enhancing bias be peculiar to some cultures but not to others? As noted earlier, self-esteem seems to be more a need bordering on obsession in Western cultures than in Eastern cultures. Research suggests the self-enhancing bias may be culture-specific, particularly when comparing North Americans to people from Eastern cultures such as the Japanese (Markus & Kitayama, 1991). As noted earlier, protecting self-esteem is often less important than a self-critical stance – seeking to learn from experience. Indeed, Japanese tend to hold relatively negative views of themselves, a phenomenon called self-effacement (Chen, Bond, Chan, Tang and Buchtel, 2009). This is found to be a genuine reaction, not an attempt to conceal a more positive self-image in order to appear modest (Heine, Takata & Lehman, 2000). And, interestingly, Asians seem to hold more balanced views of themselves than Westerners, being able to accept both positive and negative self-relevant information, even contradictory information. This is interpreted as reflecting the yin/yang principle of the reconciliation of opposites. That is, they can describe themselves as both 'talkative' and 'quiet', depending on the situation and the role that they are thinking about (Boucher, 2010).

Indeed, studies suggest that the Japanese are not simply saying that they view themselves in a less positive manner: they truly believe it. In a study, students from Ritsumeikan University in Kyoto, Japan, were compared with those from the University of British Columbia in Vancouver (Heine & Lehman, 1999). All participants were asked to rate a series of descriptive adjectives in terms of how well it described them (e.g., I am extremely attractive) and then in describing the type of person they would ideally like to be (e.g., I would like to be extremely attractive). The differences between the two sets of ratings provided a measure of a self-ideal discrepancy as described earlier in this chapter. In comparison with both groups of North Americans, the self-ideal discrepancies were greater among the Japanese students. However, self-ideal discrepancy did not predict higher scores on a commonly used measure of depression among the Japanese as it did among Canadian students. In other words, the Japanese were more dissatisfied with themselves, but these self-critical orientations were less distressing to them. As noted earlier, Japanese tend to be more self-critical so as to promote self-improvement and better fit in with their groups (Kitayama, Markus, Matsumoto & Norasakkunkit, 1997). Even in Western societies, people can be realistic about themselves and may have a difficult time accepting unrealistic praise or even unexpected success.

According to the self-verification theory (Swann, 1990), there are two reasons why we might maintain a negative view of ourselves, or at least a balanced view. First, if we were to change our opinion of ourselves every time someone told us something different, even if it were more positive, it would be unsettling and confusing, and so we seek to maintain some kind of coherence and consistency in our self-concept. In fact, we will see in a succeeding chapter on attitudes that we appreciate a sense of consistency in what we believe and do. Second, it can be embarrassing when people have unrealistic expectations about us that we cannot hope to fulfill, so we feel we'd better let them know our limitations as soon as possible. Of course, we also crave acceptance as we are, and usually feel uncomfortable when someone has an idealized view of us. The pedestal is an uncomfortable place to be.

In short, we want to feel good about ourselves and to know ourselves. These two competing motives are illustrated in the following classic experiment (Deutsch & Soloman, 1959). Participants worked in four-member teams solving problems. At the end, they received feedback indicating that they had scored the highest (success) or lowest (failure) of their team on this test of 'flexible thinking'. Following the feedback, participants received a note, ostensibly from a teammate. In one condition, the note praised the subject's performance and desirability as a teammate; in the other, the note was very negative. Not surprisingly, those with positive self-evaluations reacted very positively to someone who confirmed their positive self-image and negatively to those who gave unfavourable evaluations. The interesting results came in the condition where the feedback indicated that they had failed. When people were told that they had poor ability in 'flexible thinking', they responded favourably to the writer of the positive note but just as favourably to the writer of the rather nasty note. Thus, the study provides some evidence both for a person's need for self-enhancement through creating a positive impression and for self-consistency, confirmation of one's own self-concept.

KEY POINT: We want to know ourselves and evaluate ourselves accurately. We want to feel good about ourselves. These two competing motives, self-verification and self-enhancement, are influenced by both culture and individual factors.

A FINAL NOTE

So, how do we answer the eternal question: who am I? We have presented a pair of dilemmas that we all face in our lives. First, we want to receive feedback from others that, at once, enhances how we feel about ourselves and verifies what we know or believe about ourselves, even when it is negative. That is, we want the truth about ourselves but in a manner that makes us feel good. Second, we want others to have a positive impression of us, but we want people to know us and accept us as we are. How we find the balance depends on who we are and on the norms of our culture. Social identity theory, described in detail in Chapter 12, posits a continuum of identity anchored by the personal at one end and the social at the other polarity. The personal identity pole pertains to who you are as an individual, what you think of yourself as someone who is fascinated with psychology, a fan of Manchester United, a romantic partner, a good swimmer. The social identity pole refers to how you think of yourself as a member of a group or social category, how you see yourself as a woman or man, a son or daughter, a student at your university, a citizen of Australia, the Netherlands, Singapore, or Israel, a resident of Capetown, Cambridge or Calcutta, or a member of a group or region within a country: Catalan, Hispano-American, Québecois, Scottish, or ethnic Chinese or Malay in Singapore. Of course, being on a continuum, there are situations in which we experience a mix of the personal and the social; being a fan of a team can mean, at the same time, something that makes you unique among your friends, and something that affiliates you with a group of like-minded fans. In short, our personal identity and our social identity are inextricably bound.

SUMMARY

1. The self is organized as a schema, which organizes information and impressions about the individual and defines what is important in terms of defining his or her self. As do other schemata, the self-schema guides attention and processing of self-relevant information.

2. People develop their sense of self primarily from their experience with others rather than through private introspection.

3. Self-knowledge derives from self-perception, gender-role socialization and comparison with other people. Social comparison is usually with similar others, but may be upward or downward in certain circumstances.

4. People adopt identities that are traditionally masculine or feminine, although many manifest features of both genders (psychological androgyny).

5. Self-evaluation has important consequences, but may not be as crucial as is commonly assumed.

6. Self-discrepancy theory is based on the premise that we compare our self-concept to self-guides, the ideal self and the ought self. Substantial discrepancy between self-concept and self-guides can lead to emotional difficulties.

7. To protect self-esteem, people may act to handicap themselves in advance, and then attribute failure to this self-imposed handicap.

8. In order to exercise self-regulation, we must be aware of what we are doing, and understand how others react to our actions, we must recognize threats to our well-being, and we must be able to act constructively to rectify the situation. When people exercise self-control in a given situation, they may subsequently show less capacity for self-control (ego-depletion).

9. Cultures that vary along the dimension of individualism–collectivism also vary in the extent to which self is tied to personal accomplishments and uniqueness or to social roles and relationships.

10. Individuals seek to manage the impression that others have of them, using tactics such as ingratiation, supplication, and intimidation.

11. People have conflicting motives, wanting both to have others see them in a positive light, and to have others accept them as they are.

POINTS TO PONDER

- 'Know thyself', we are instructed. How can we know ourselves completely, given our need to protect ourselves?
- How is our self-schema influenced by the culture in which we live?
- Given what you have learned in this chapter, is it really possible to be genuine and spontaneous with others, even those with whom we are closest?
- The chapter describes two concepts, self-esteem and narcissism. How can we distinguish between them? Does your society encourage narcissism?
- Relate notions of a self-concept or self-schema to the dual-processing model of social cognition.

FURTHER READING

Antaki, C. & Widdicombe, S. (Eds) (1998). *Identities in talk*. London: Sage.

An interesting set of papers on how social identity theory has developed and been applied to areas as disparate as business, divorce and being a gun owner.

Baumeister, R. (1999). *Self in social psychology. Key readings*. New York: Psychology Press.

A set of classic articles on topics such as self-knowledge, self-esteem, self-regulation, self-presentation, and the self and culture. While the collection is rather dated, the articles themselves are generally still influential.

Baumeister, R.F., Vohs, K.D. & Tice, D.M. (2007). The strength model of self-control. *Current Directions In Psychological Science*, 16(6), 351–355.

The ground-breaking paper on self-control as a capacity that can be developed and strengthened. It challenges some existing paradigms and assumptions.

Crocker, J. & Park, L.E. (2004). The costly pursuit of self-esteem. *Psychological Bulletin, 130*(3), 392–414.

A concise scholarly review of research and theory on the futility of trying to feel better about yourself. This paper also highlights the challenges of doing rigorous research in this area.

Leary, M. & Tagney, J. (2010). *Handbook of self and identity.* **(2nd Edn). New York: Guilford.**

A set of chapters by recognized experts on topics in this vital area, including how people develop self-awareness and a sense of identity. Includes both the latest developments in theory and some practical implications for understanding various psychological problems and disorders.

Vohs, K.D. & Baumeister, R.F. (Eds) (2011). *Handbook of self-regulation: Research, theory, and applications* **(2nd Edn). New York: Guilford.**

A broad scholarly set of reviews of research and thinking on the topic of self-control. It contains chapters by experts on the various topics concerning self-control.

Vohs, K.D. & Baumeister, R.F. (Eds) (2012). *The self and identity,* **volumes I–V. Thousand Oaks, CA: Sage.**

A current encyclopaedic overview of the social psychology of the self, with chapters by experts. Anyone with a deep interest on this topic, and anyone planning to do research in this area, will consult this indispensable book.

WEBLINKS

http://www.issiweb.org
International Society for Self and Identity.
http://www.self-esteem-nase.org
National Association for Self-Esteem.

CHAPTER 4
ATTITUDES, IDEOLOGIES AND VALUES

The meaning of things lies not in the things themselves, but in our attitude towards them.

Antoine de Saint-Exupery

LEARNING OBJECTIVES

* To learn what an attitude is, and what it means to say that attitude is a hypothetical construct

* To learn how attitudes are measured and to understand the concepts of explicit and implicit attitudes

* To understand the concept of values, and of sacred values, and how our values relate to each other and to our attitudes

* To understand trade-off reasoning and how it relates to values and attitudes

* To understand why we hold attitudes, what purposes they serve for us

* To learn what is an ideology, and how liberal/left and conservative/right ideologies differ

* To investigate how and why our actions often are not consistent with our attitudes, and the factors that can narrow the gap between attitude and behaviour

Figure 4.1 Still photo on the set of *Schindler's List*, a movie based on a true story about the Holocaust

Source: © David James/Sygma/Corbis

It is an enduring mystery why some people cling to certain attitudes despite clear and convincing evidence to the contrary (Sherman, 1997). Consider that some people in the United States are hostile to President Obama, believing that he is a secret Muslim. Consider that some people have negative attitudes towards the theory of evolution, even though many other people who practise various religions have no problem with evolution. Consider that some people with anti-Semitic attitudes maintain that the Holocaust, the deliberate murder of six million Jews by the Nazis, is a hoax. Conspiracy theories abound about political assassinations, terrorist attacks and the AIDS epidemic. Look online for many examples.

Clearly attitudes are established, maintained and changed for multiple reasons. In this case, we are talking about attitudes that contradict logic and evidence, not simply attitudes that depart from the mainstream. There may be legitimate disputes about some historical events, and resistance to new ideas is not uncommon in public affairs and even in science. Galileo persisted in his beliefs about the nature of our solar system despite the common beliefs of the time that the earth was the centre of the universe. In recent years, biomedical researchers have uncovered evidence that gastric ulcers are primarily caused by H. pylori bacteria despite the previous prevailing opinion that stress or spicy foods were the cause.

Attitudes have long been a core topic in social psychology. However, until recently social psychologists did not devote a great deal of attention to the study of values, higher-order general principles such as freedom or kindness. Braithwaite and Scott (1991) suggest psychologists may have neglected values because they have seemed so vague and imprecise that adequate measurement and experimentation was impossible. Recently, however, there has been increased interest in values within social psychology. This mirrors concerns about important value issues that are being debated in many societies, for example, concerning end-of-life: To what extent should people suffering from incurable illnesses and severe unrelenting pain be offered effective pain relief with powerful narcotics, notwithstanding possible addiction or even overdose? Should they be assisted in ending their own lives if that is their choice? What values may be implicated in such decisions?

Some physicians have acted on this issue, even where it violates existing laws. Some countries, such as the Netherlands, permit physician-assisted suicide in specific circumstances: the patient makes an informed and free request, and the patient is experiencing unbearable suffering – physical or psychological – that cannot be relieved. The attending physician then consults with a second, independent colleague, who must agree with the decision, and the physician must report the facts of the case to the coroner afterwards. In a highly public case in Canada, Sue Rodriguez, who was afflicted with painful amyotrophic lateral sclerosis (Lou Gehrig's disease), unsuccessfully petitioned the Supreme Court of Canada for permission to die with the assistance of a physician. While her case in court was unsuccessful, she died in 1995 by what was alleged to have been an assisted suicide. Similar cases have been reported in the UK, US and other countries.

The issue of assisted suicide invokes values and attitudes concerning the sanctity of life, religious convictions, the alleviation of suffering, as well as the role of physicians. Consider that the Hippocratic oath formulated in ancient Greece states that physicians should 'neither give a deadly drug to anyone if asked for it nor make a suggestion to this effect'. A distinction is drawn between refusing or withdrawing treatment, and administering or taking a drug at a lethal dose. While both will bring on death, can we distinguish between actively causing death and declining to preserve life? The ethical dilemma for physicians and hospitals is fundamental. On the one hand, they are dedicated to preserving life, and, on the other, to the relief of pain and suffering. What is the point, for example, of maintaining a patient with irrevocable brain damage on a life-support system, as was salient in the Terri Schaivo case in Florida some years ago? Should quality of life not be taken into consideration? What if the person wants to end his or her life, not because of pain but because of a concern about being a 'burden' to the family, fear of loss of control, feeling depressed or just not wanting to delay the inevitable? Or does the value of a human life surpass all others.

These are ethical issues, which cannot be resolved in a textbook of social psychology. What concerns us in this chapter is how people attempt to deal with issues such as these. This chapter examines the nature of attitudes and values. We then ask why people have attitudes and how values are important in relation to their attitudes. We explore how attitudes are structured, discuss the complex set of attitudes that constitute an ideology and, finally, address the puzzling problem of why our attitudes often do not match our actions. In the next chapter, we focus on how attitudes can change.

THE NATURE OF ATTITUDES

In the 1930s, Gordon Allport (1935), a pioneer in attitude research, defined an attitude as a mental and neural state of readiness, organized through experience, exerting a directive or dynamic influence upon the individual's response to all people, objects and situations with which it is related. This definition emphasizes certain important characteristics of the construct of attitude. First, an attitude implies an inner state that, given the situation, may ultimately result in some sort of behaviour. The definition also implies that an attitude is learned through experience and that our actions are related to it. This latter characteristic is important because it gives us the basis for deciding whether or not a given attitude exists, that is, whether a label can be attached to an individual (e.g., conservative, pro-choice, anti-religious, socialist) with some degree of confidence. Finally, it is important to understand that we can only infer an attitude from a behaviour, such as responses on a questionnaire. That is, an attitude is a hypothetical construct (Chapter 1), a concept used to organize and make sense of what we can observe.

Another point to note in Allport's definition in that attitudes may or may not be consciously held. Psychology has always recognized that there are thoughts, feelings and attitudes that are not always accessible to conscious awareness. It may be that the person is unwilling to report how he or she is thinking or feeling. Or, the person may simply not be aware of all of those thoughts and feelings. Recall in Chapter 3 that introspection may not be the best or only route to self-knowledge. Attitudes that are not fully in consciousness are called implicit attitudes and are subject to a great deal of research.

Social neuroscience provides some evidence linking activity in specific brain centres to aspects of implicit attitudes (see the review by Damian, Phelps & Banaji, 2008). Specifically, the amygdala, an identified centre for emotional experience, is related to the spontaneous evaluation of an attitude object. As well, the anterior cingulate, which plays a role in decision-making, is involved in bringing implicit attitudes into some kind of awareness, and the dorsolateral prefrontal cortex is involved with the emotional regulation of these implicit attitudes through its larger role in organization and planning. Perhaps most interesting, in some cases, activity in these centres relates to implicit attitudes but not to explicit self-reports.

This raises the question: which is the 'real' attitude? Taking all this into account, the core of an attitude is one's judgement of some target along a dimension of good to bad, positive to negative. Think of how we ask what a person's 'position' is on some issue – we are referring to their attitude toward the issue along this positive–negative continuum. Our evaluation may be explicit, in that we are aware of it, or implicit, an evaluation that is not accessible to our conscious awareness. Most readers will have had the experience of suddenly realizing that they like or dislike someone or something. Perhaps you had simply changed your mind. Or perhaps your evaluation was there beforehand, but only later did you become aware of it.

Of course, this conception of attitude as an implicit or explicit evaluation places it within the dual-process frame of reference which characterizes the field of social cognition (Chapter 2). Attitudes probably are best thought of as cognitive structures or internal states that reside in long-term memory (Tourangeau & Rasinski, 1988; Eagly & Chaiken, 1998). These states may be activated when a person is presented with a relevant stimulus, such as the

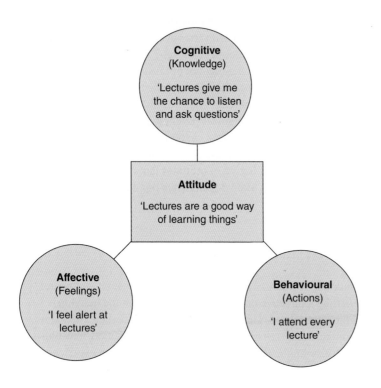

Figure 4.2   Tripartite model of attitudes

Source: Adapted from McGuire (1969)

question 'What do you think about the new smartphone?' Depending on the response, the individual can then be identified as having a pro or anti new smartphone attitude.

Models of attitudes

While the core of an attitude is an evaluation, attitudes are traditionally conceived as multidimensional and consist of a relatively enduring organization of three components: a cognitive component, an affective component and a behavioural component (Chaiken & Stangor, 1987; Zanna & Rempel, 1988), as shown in Figure 4.2. The cognitive component refers to the particular beliefs or ideas held about the object or situation; the affective component, to the associated emotions; and the behavioural component, to the associated action or actions, or at least predispositions to act. For instance, a person may believe that university students are arrogant (cognitive), may feel uncomfortable in the presence of a university student (affective), and may refuse to pick up a student who is hitch-hiking to classes (behavioural). It is important to add, however, that attitudes are not always directly expressed in action. This issue will be discussed in detail later.

This **tripartite model of attitudes** suggests something important about human nature. Many traditional theories and philosophies have grappled with the question of whether the essence of being human lies in thinking (rationality) or in emotions. Indeed, some schools of psychotherapy seek to minimize thinking so that we can get in touch with our 'real' feelings. On the other hand, some people may admonish us not to act on our feelings but to think things out, rationally. These notions imply that our thoughts and feelings are somehow independent. However, the concept of attitude implies that our thoughts, feelings and actions are integrated in some way and that we usually think, feel and act in a coordinated fashion.

Nevertheless, it is possible to distinguish among cognition, affect and behaviour. Breckler (1984) was interested in the extent to which these three components give similar estimates of the direction and strength of attitudes. He used a variety of measures of each component. For example, he monitored changes in heart rate and had participants rate their mood in the presence of snakes (affective), measured their beliefs about the dangers and benefits of snakes and had them list their thoughts about them (cognitive), and had the participants indicate how they would react to a snake, and observed how closely they were actually willing to approach a snake (behavioural). His analysis showed clearly that beliefs, feelings and behaviour were moderately but not highly interrelated and that each provided distinctive contributions to the hypothetical construct called 'attitude'. He argues that we should not assess someone's attitudes only by asking about feelings or beliefs, or only by observing behaviour.

Other researchers have discarded the behavioural component of attitudes and consider attitude to be a two-dimensional construct made up of cognition and affect, beliefs and feelings (e.g., Zajonc & Markus, 1982). Moreover, some (e.g., Fishbein & Ajzen, 1975), maintain a unitary view, regarding an attitude as only an affective orientation towards an object. As yet, there has been no definitive resolution among these competing models. Zanna & Rempel (1988) have outlined a model that takes into consideration all these conceptions of attitudes. They begin by defining attitude as a categorization of a stimulus object along an evaluative dimension (for example, abortion: evaluated along a dimension from favourable to unfavourable). They then propose that this evaluation can be based on three sources of information: cognitive information or beliefs about abortion, feelings about abortion including religious proscriptions and information or recollections of past behaviour. The evaluation can be based on any one source of information or any combination of sources. In other words, an attitude may, for example, be derived from cognitions alone, from cognitions and affect, or from all three.

It also is the case that individuals differ in the degree to which their attitudes are based on beliefs or on affect, or on both. Haddock & Zanna (1998) showed that participants whom they described as 'thinkers' based their attitudes on belief whereas those described as 'feelers' were more likely to use emotions as the basis. Similarly, Kempf (1999) found that some attitude objects elicit attitudes based on beliefs, while attitudes towards other objects are more likely to be derived from affect. For example, he asked participants to evaluate two different computer programs, a computer game and a grammar-checking program. Attitudes towards the computer game were found to be related to feelings (e.g. having fun), whereas attitudes regarding the grammar-checker were determined by beliefs (will it help me write a better essay?).

Attitude strength

Not only do we typically describe a person's attitude as an evaluation, pro or con (valence), we also estimate the intensity or strength of the attitude, from extremely positive to moderately positive, or moderately negative to extremely negative. Think of a food that you don't mind eating, one that you enjoy and one that you might consider as one of your favourites. You are evaluating all three foods positively, but differ in the strength of that positive evaluation.

Strong attitudes have a number of characteristics and consequences, in contrast with weaker or more moderate attitudes. They are durable – that is, they do not change over time and they resist persuasion, as will be shown in the next chapter. Strong attitudes also have a greater effect on people's behaviour, particularly as they are expressed more emphatically. In addition, strong attitudes are more likely to influence how we process information about the attitude objects, for instance by selecting what we attend to (Krosnick & Petty, 1995; Pomerantz, Chaiken & Tordesillas, 1995; Eagly & Chaiken, 1998).

Attitude ambivalence

While attitudes have traditionally been viewed as unidimensional – pro or con – the Zanna and Rempel (1988) and Haddock and Zanna (1998) model implies that attitudes can be considerably more complex. For example, MacDonald and Zanna (1998) found that male undergraduates assigned ambivalent ratings to 'feminists'. They rated them positively on 'admiration' but negatively on 'affection'.

Two conditions are necessary for the occurrence of ambivalence (Thompson, Zanna & Griffin, 1995). First, the positive and negative elements must be roughly similar in strength, and second, both positive and negative must be at least of moderate intensity. If you are in favour of organic eggs from free-range chickens, you will likely buy and eat them, and if you do not favour them positively, you will not likely buy them, but what if you are ambivalent: you like the taste and dislike the price? Ambivalence will not be experienced if one side of the issue clearly outweighs the other or if the issue is perceived as being relatively trivial or unimportant. You will probably behave less consistently, depending on what comes to mind – better taste or financial sacrifice.

BOX 4.1   ANOTHER LOOK

GENES AND POLITICS: ARE ATTITUDES INHERITED?

'I often think it's comical how nature always does contrive
That every boy and every gal that's born into the world alive
Is either a little Liberal or else a little Conservative'

W.S. Gilbert wrote these words in 1882, and Arthur Sullivan set them to music in the comic opera *Iolanthe*. Did Gilbert and Sullivan anticipate research that occurred more than a century later?

It has long been established that attitudes tend to be passed on from one generation to the next (e.g. Hatemi, Funk, et al., 2009). There are obvious exceptions: generations may differ in their attitudes toward historical changes such as in post-war Germany, post-apartheid South Africa, or post-9/11 USA. Young people may have had educational or economic opportunities that can influence their political orientations, and the nature of various political parties may change over time. Nonetheless, it is generally accepted that we are all influenced by the attitudes of our parents and siblings.

In addition, there is also some evidence that genes are involved (e.g. Hatemi, Hibbing et al., 2009). For instance, evidence is available from twin studies in which we compare monozygotic twins (fully shared genetics) with dizygotic twins and their extended families. As well, researchers can compare adopted and non-adopted people and their biological and adoptive parents, representing the extent to which the pairs share a common set of genes. The similarity in attitudes of monozygotic twins is greater than that of either dizygotic twins or ordinary siblings. It is also greater than that found between adopted children and either their biological parents (shared genes) or their adaptive parents (shared environments). Of course, with the advances in molecular biology, more precise research will enable us to specify which genes may be involved.

In several studies in large databases, people's political attitudes were compared with those of their siblings, spouses, parents and other family members (Eaves & Hatemi, 2008; Olson, Vernon, et al., 2001). While the data clearly show that the environment accounts for the lion's share of the variance in attitudes, these studies indicate that there also appears to be a significant heritable component (Hatemi, Medland, et al., 2007).

Does heritability depend on what the attitude is about? Note that the study by Olson et al. (2001) which included attitudes toward a range of matters such as reading books, enjoying roller-coaster rides and welcoming more immigrants into the country, showed that the genetic influence was specific to political attitudes. Abrahamson, Baker & Caspi (2002) questioned adopted young people annually for four years about their attitudes about religion and politics. Their attitudes, and changes in these attitudes, were compared to those of their two sets of parents (adoptive and biological). Politically conservative attitudes changed slightly in the direction of their biological parents, suggesting a genetic influence. It is interesting that, in this study, genetic influence appeared earlier in life than previously reported, and that this effect did not appear for religious attitudes.

Now the question becomes how genetics can lead to attitudes. It is not claimed that there is a direct link, a specific gene that would influence specific attitudes as it would influence eye colour. However, other characteristics of people that have demonstrable genetic links may well influence attitudes. Consider, for instance, a person who is athletically gifted. Such a person would have positive experiences in athletic competition, which would lead to highly favourable attitudes toward sports. Similarly, some personality dispositions appear to have genetic components, and such personality characteristics may predispose the person to certain attitudes or certain orientations, such as a preference for social rules and order (Smith, Oxley et al., 2011).

One example attracting some research interest concerns the genetic basis of a particular personality characteristic, novelty-seeking or sensation-seeking, a disposition to seek out new ideas and new experiences. This characteristic is linked to a particular receptor of dopamine, one of the major neurotransmitters. People who score low on measures of novelty-seeking tend to be more cognitively rigid and loyal, prefer the familiar and safe, and 'follow the rules' (Golimbet, Alfimova, Gritsenko & Ebstein, 2007). Using data from an extensive US national survey, Settle, Dawes, Christakis & Fowler (2010) found that people with the genetic predisposition to seek out new experiences did tend to be more liberal in their political orientation – but only if they had a group of friends with a variety of political attitudes. Of course, consider the possibility that people with this personality disposition will seek out and befriend a variety of people, including those with compatible political attitudes. That is, to argue that environment causes attitudes does not imply a passive unidirectional influence: we also select and act on our environments. Thus genetically disposed novelty-seeking leads to relationships with certain kinds of people who may have certain attitudes that buttress one's own attitudes.

In sum, there are strong indications from research spanning several nations that genetics influences attitudes, particularly but not exclusively in the political area. This influence is modest, and certainly cannot be said to override the influence of environment: the family, the peer group, the society and culture, as well as historical forces. Our best guess as to the mechanism of genetic influence is that it acts on broad ideological preferences such as the distinction between left and right, conservatism and liberalism, and that it acts through broad personality dispositions such as sensation/novelty-seeking predispositions. From this perspective, the findings should not be surprising: certain kinds of people have certain personal characteristics that predispose them to favour certain ways in which society should be ordered, and to seek out like-minded friends and partners.

Now one may ask whether genetics influence our attitudes toward non-political matters. What about attitudes towards a specific team or a specific sport? What about attitudes towards different styles of music; is there a gene that predisposes a person to prefer hip hop, classical or jazz (or all of them or none of them)? How about attitudes in the area of consumer preferences – your choice of beverage, for example? Evidence has been uncovered linking sensitivity to the bitter taste of 6-n-propylthiouracil (PROP) to inherited predispositions, and these taste preferences are likely to lead to food and beverage preferences, such as different brands of beer, green tea and citrus products (Drewnowski, Henderson & Barratt-Fornell, 2001). How is a genetic predisposition linked to the evaluative response that is the core of an attitude, and how would a genetic predisposition interact with the immediate personal environment, the culture and a moment in history? We are merely at the beginning of this process of discovery and understanding.

Attitude complexity

Some attitudes are rather simple and straightforward, while others are complex. For instance, a person may be asked, 'What do you think of medically assisted suicide?' and respond, 'I think it's very humane', but if pressed, be unable to present more detail. On the other hand, another person in response to the same query might reply, 'I'm generally in favour of it, but we have to worry about the possibility of it being misused'. Whether an attitude is simple or complex may be a function of the characteristics of the person, or it may be a function of the particular topic. Some issues by their nature do not allow for much mental intricacy. Thus, people's attitudes about brushing teeth after meals would likely be considerably simpler than their attitudes towards the question of the economic or political union of Canada and the US, or Australia and New Zealand, or the nations of the European Union.

Attitudes also have more or less complex associations with other attitudes. For example, you might believe that agricultural cooperatives are economically beneficial and should be fostered, but this attitude may exist in isolation and may not be related to other attitudes concerning, for instance, relations with your nations's trading partners, your beliefs about capitalism and free enterprise, your attitudes towards preserving the family farm. In other cases, very complicated networks of interconnected attitudes may occur. Thus, an individual's attitude towards immigration may be connected with many other attitudes concerning economics, unemployment, multiculturalism, prejudice, national security and urban planning.

> **KEY POINT** Attitude is a hypothetical construct defined as a readiness to react in a certain way to some object, with evaluation of that object as its core. It consists of cognitions (beliefs), affect (emotions) and behavioural tendencies. Attitudes may be conscious or implicit, may be simple, complex or ambivalent, and vary in strength or intensity.

MEASURING ATTITUDES

As first noted in Chapter 1, we must be able to measure something in order to study it scientifically. In that chapter, we introduced the concept of measurement and its characteristics of reliability and validity. Now we turn specifically to the measurement of attitudes. Attitude measurement is an important aspect of our lives. For instance, decisions that affect us, in marketing, government policies, health care, education etc., are, at least in part, based on the measurement of the attitudes of those affected by these decisions. The technological sophistication of attitude measurement has grown dramatically in the past decades.

There are two basic approaches to attitude measurement, direct or self-report, and indirect or implicit. The direct way is to ask the people, using various scaling techniques. The indirect way is to infer participants' attitudes from their responses to various stimuli, where the participant is not aware that a specific attitude is being assessed.

Direct measurement (self-report)

The Likert summated ratings is the mainstay of this approach. Participants are presented with a series of statements about the attitudinal object. A 5- or 7-point scale accompanies each statement. For instance, here are two such statements from a hypothetical measure of attitudes toward physician-assisted suicide:

1. People who are dying or suffering pain without relief have the right to end their lives with the assistance of their physician.
   Strongly agree   agree   not sure   disagree   strongly disagree
2. All life is sacred and physicians must not be allowed to end a life, even if requested by their patient.
   Strongly agree   agree   not sure   disagree   strongly disagree

The participant's choice for each item is assigned a numerical value. The scores for all items are added up (summated) to give a total score. Note that the assignment of the values for the second item must be reversed because a person who agrees with the first item logically should disagree with the second item. Thus, if 'strongly agree' is assigned the value 1 for the first item, it must be assigned the value 5 for the second item.

This is the most widely used method today, because it is easy for participants to understand, it is efficient to administer and it yields data that can be analysed by sophisticated statistical techniques. Other techniques such as interviews and the semantic differential (Osgood, Suci & Tannenbaum, 1957) are also used occasionally.

While self-report instruments are generally well-validated, they are subject to a number of biases, particularly the tendency for participants to respond in a socially desirable manner in order to create a favourable impression or to maintain a favourable self-concept. It also is the case that the respondent often can see through the scale and realize what attitude is being measured. To overcome such problems, a number of indirect attitude measures have been developed in which the connection between what is measured and the attitude is not evident.

Measuring implicit attitudes

Recall that attitudes are evaluative responses, which may be conscious and deliberative or may be automatic, spontaneous and beyond conscious awareness. In the latter case, it would not be useful to ask people for self-reports, as they are not aware of what they are being asked to report. The most commonly used current technique to get at such attitudes is the Implicit Association Test or IAT (Greenwald, McGhee & Schwartz, 1998). The test is rather complicated, involving a set of sorting tasks, usually presented on computer, in which the participant's reaction time or speed of response is taken as the measure of implicit attitude. It is important that the participant does these tasks rapidly, that is, spontaneously. For instance, you are first presented images of black and white faces, where you are to sort them into categories representing 'good' words, for example, good, honest, beautiful. Most people would do this rapidly. Now you are asked to sort the same set of faces into categories representing 'bad' words, for example, bad, dishonest, ugly. Each response is timed. It is reasoned that associations that come easily to the person will be reflected in more rapid responses. Thus, a black person who dislikes white people is expected to respond more rapidly when a white face is paired with a negative word. Check out the IAT website, and try one for yourself: (https://implicit.harvard.edu/implicit/demo/).

The IAT has been used in many studies in many different nations and cultures (Greenwald & Banaji, 1995). Note that these implicit attitudes are not necessarily strongly correlated with self-reported explicit responses. What do these implicit responses predict? Greenwald, Poehlman, Uhlmann & Banaji (2009) in reviewing the literature concede that this measure is generally less predictive of actual behaviour than are explicit, self-report measures – although it may be better when the topic is very sensitive.

Other indirect measures

- We can infer attitudes from behaviour towards the attitudinal object. For example, Cook & Selltiz (1964) had a confederate present himself as a representative of a publishing company and ask white participants whether they would be willing to pose for textbook photographs. If so, the participant was shown a series of line drawings of the proposed photos, including some in which he or she would pose with a white or black confederate. Those who were more prejudiced were less willing to allow themselves to pose with a black person, particularly in a more personal setting.
- We can infer attitudes from responses to apparently fact-based questions. For instance, asking people to estimate the level of neighbourhood crime would indicate their attitudes towards crime, particularly when they overestimate the level.

- **Bogus pipeline** ('to the soul'). A set of electrodes are attached to the person, leading to an impressive-looking but bogus electronic recording machine. The participants are told that their 'true' reactions will be measured by the machine and that the task at hand is to guess as accurately as possible what the machine will reveal about their reactions. Framed as a task of how well the participants know themselves, the participants are presumed to be motivated to provide honest and truthful responses.

Lest we go overboard in our enthusiasm for implicit and indirect measures as a corrective for self-report measures, several assumptions must be challenged (Gawronski, 2009). We cannot assume that implicit measures are an accurate window to the unconscious without convincing evidence. These measures do not necessarily overcome the problem of socially desirable responses, or indeed the problem of faking responses that plagues self-report measures. Indeed, these implicit measures cannot be used as 'lie detectors' (the issue of lie detection is discussed in Chapter 15). By similar reasoning, implicit measures of self-concept cannot be assumed to reflect one's 'true self'. While the research thus far is promising, we are not at the stage that such an assumption can be made comfortably.

> **KEY POINT:** Attitude measures include self-reports, most commonly the Likert scale. They also include indirect or implicit measures in which the nature of the attitude is inferred. These include the Implicit Association Test (IAT), responses to apparent fact-based questions, behaviours toward the attitude object and a purported (bogus) pipeline to the soul.

IDEOLOGY

An **ideology** is a more or less integrated or coherent set of attitudes, a worldview. While one can conceive of an ideology with regard to various areas such as science or religion, ideology is a concept usually associated with politics, such as liberalism, conservatism, socialism, fascism (Jost, Federico & Napier, 2009). Ideologies are shared cognitive frameworks for interpreting the environment or society, how it should be, and how the group or collective can get there. In other words, an ideology defines both a set of goals for society and ways to attain these goals. And so, for example, a socialist ideology would include a Marxist-based interpretation of how the economy works and how power is attained, what the desired or ideal structure of a society would be and, in some cases, would advocate revolution to overthrow the existing order and build a new one. A conservative ideology would include notions of more-or-less limited government, strengthening of existing traditional norms regarding certain behaviours, capitalist/free enterprise economics and tough policies on crime and national security. Note that while many may favour or oppose individual issues, it is the configuration of attitudes together that constitutes an ideology.

Beginning after the French Revolution, supporters of the status quo sat on the right side of the French Assembly, and opponents who advocated drastic change sat on the left side. Since then, political parties and their ideologies are usually defined in terms of this left–right dimension. Of course, in different countries and different historical periods, left and right have been associated with different labels: conservativism, individualism, capitalism, free enterprise, order, fascism, libertarianism, and protest, change, socialism, communism, radicalism, social democratic, solidarity. Further, the meaning of terms such as 'liberal' and 'conservative' can vary between societies and even within a society from one time to the next. In a meta-analysis of 88 studies conducted in 12 countries over 40 years, conservatism was associated with a persistent fear or anxiety about instability and about death itself, along with intolerance of ambiguity and need for order. Conversely, liberalism was associated with openness to new experiences, cognitive complexity and tolerance of uncertainty (Jost, Glaser, Kruglanski & Sulloway, 2003).

Is the left–right distinction the only one that we can make in political ideology? Some suggest that the important distinction is between moderate and extremist ideologies; liberals, social democrats and conservatives share democratic values and moderate positions on various issues, while extreme leftists (communists)

113

Figure 4.3 Political ideologies of left and right

Source: EvrenKalinbacak/Shutterstock.com and oconnelll/Shutterstock.com

and rightists (military dictatorships, fascists) share an authoritarian orientation to power. Others argue that there are social, religious and economic dimensions within both the left and the right which do not necessarily cohere. For instance, it is quite possible to be an economic conservative (capitalism, balanced budgets) and yet liberal in attitudes toward the rights of homosexuals, women and ethnic minorities. One can advocate very little government control of business and economic matters, and yet also advocate extensive government powers to control the drug use and sexual behaviour of individuals. As an example of this, a study utilizing data from a sample of 190 candidates running for election to the Canadian Parliament found only moderate correlations between social and political aspects of left–right ideology (Choma, Ashton & Hafer, 2010).

Further, it has been suggested that the left–right dimension exists because people vary in the extent to which they need to reduce uncertainty and threat. Conservatism generally supports the status quo and order, while liberalism implies change and acceptance of diversity. Finally, Ashton, Danso, et al. (2005) point to two other dimensions of political attitudes: moral regulation versus individual freedom (e.g. legalized abortion, physician-assisted suicide, legalized marijuana, casino gambling) and compassion versus competition (e.g. capital punishment, publicly funded day care, welfare policy). These two dimensions were found in data from samples in Canada, the United States, Wales and Hong Kong, but not in Ghana, suggesting that this structure may be widespread but not universal.

Of course, all manner of personality, social and economic differences between rightists and leftists have been studied. Consider, for example, whether liberals and conservatives differ in how they experience and act in their lives. Graham, Haidt & Nosek (2009) found in several studies in the US that liberals make moral judgements and decisions primarily on individual bases, reflecting concern with justice/fairness and caring and protecting others from harm. Conservatives (measured differently in different studies, and some research included analyses of sermons delivered in relatively liberal and conservative churches in the USA) make the same moral judgements based on factors such as in-group loyalty, respect for authority and sanctity. In other words, liberals and conservatives, at least in that society, have different understandings about human nature and the world.

Is political ideology associated with happiness? Choma, Busseri & Sadava (2009) administered measures of liberal and conservative ideologies, along with Diener's (1984) model of subjective well-being, which

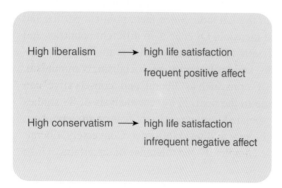

Figure 4.4 Are liberals or conservatives happier?

consists of three measures of positive affect, negative affect and life satisfaction (see Chapter 16). Among a sample of Canadian students, life satisfaction was related to strong ideologies, whether right or left. This suggests that both liberals and conservatives are happy – but in their own ways. Stronger liberalism was related to higher levels of positive affect, while stronger conservatism was related to lower levels of negative affect. In other words, liberals experience more positive feelings while conservatives avoid negative feelings.

KEY POINT: An ideology is a relatively integrated set of attitudes, most commonly political. They vary in terms of advocating or rejecting social change and accepting or rejecting inequalities among people and groups. Some argue that the ideology distinctions reside between centrist/moderate views and those on both radical extremes. Other ideological dimensions include moral regulation versus free choice, and compassion versus competition. Ideology terms such as left, right, conservative and moderate vary between societies and within societies over time.

PERSONAL AND SOCIAL VALUES

Values represent a person's judgements as to what is desirable, ideal or important in life. While attitudes are associated with specific objects, events or issues, values are global, abstract principles. For example, a person may hold attitudes against racial discrimination, favour equal treatment for members of different religions, and be in favour of equal pay to men and women for work of equal value. All of these may reflect a value for equality. Often, when we have intensely felt attitudes about controversial issues, we describe our attitude in terms of a value, such as the so-called pro-life and pro-choice positions on abortion, contraception and the ethics of cloning. In describing our positions this way, we use the value to define, from our own perspective, what the issue is really all about. Thus, values can be defined as 'desirable, trans-situational goals, varying in importance, that serve as guiding principles in people's lives' (Schwartz, 1996, p. 2).

Some social psychologists have attempted to catalogue a set of basic values on which individuals differ. For instance, Allport and Vernon (1931), building on the writings of the German philosopher Spranger, developed a measure for six values: theoretical (the discovery of truth), economic (what is useful), social (love of people), aesthetic (beauty in form and harmony), political (power) and religious (unity or transcendence). While it is probably futile to try to catalogue the exact number of values, it is clear that people have many attitudes and relatively few values. In general, the interest here was to develop typologies of people based on what was truly important to them.

In later research (Rokeach, 1968, 1979), a distinction is drawn between terminal values and instrumental values. Terminal values are preferences for certain end-states in life, such as salvation, a comfortable life, freedom, inner harmony and equality, while instrumental values describe people's preferred modes of conduct, such as being ambitious, obedient or imaginative. In other words, what do you value as goals of life, and what do you value as a way of getting to these goals? For instance, you may value a comfortable life, and may value being ambitious as a way of attaining this end state.

Rokeach developed a method to study individual values. Participants are asked to rank order a set of 18 terminal and 18 instrumental values in terms of their relative importance. In this way, the value priorities of an individual can be determined. For example, while most people would feel that a comfortable life is a good thing, they would vary tremendously on its relative importance to them.

Using this method, researchers have reported some interesting findings (Rokeach, 1979). Not surprisingly, people who attached high importance to salvation as a value were more likely to attend church regularly, while those who valued a world of beauty were likely to be concerned with environmental issues. Habitual cigarette smokers tended to rank the terminal values of an exciting life, freedom, happiness, mature love and pleasure more highly than non-smokers, who valued a sense of accomplishment, a world of beauty, family security, salvation and self-respect. Among the instrumental values, smokers felt it important to be broad-minded, capable, imaginative and independent, while non-smokers preferred to be cheerful, obedient, helpful, polite and self-controlled (Grube, Weir, Getzlaf & Rokeach, 1984). People who took care of themselves by exercising regularly, using alcohol moderately, eating a balanced diet and wearing a car seat belt, placed a high value upon pleasure, an exciting life and happiness.

Does Rokeach accurately convey the scope of human value? Health in itself can be considered a value, a desired end-state in life. Ware and Young (1979) included health in Rokeach's list of terminal values, and found that while the majority rated it first, about one-third of the participants did not include it among their five highest values. In general, those who value health highly tend to behave in ways to protect their health (Lau, Hartman & Ware, 1986). When Bond (1988) compared the Rokeach Value Survey (developed in the US) and the Chinese Value Survey (developed in Hong Kong), he identified a value using the Chinese Value Survey that is not measured by the Rokeach instrument. This value reflects the importance that the Chinese place on tradition and harmonious interpersonal relations, orientations that are 'invisible' in the United States, where people are strongly individualistic.

Figure 4.5 Who chooses natural foods?

Source: lola1960/Shutterstock.com

Differences in values have been shown to be related to many attitudes and behaviours. These include choice of occupation, cigarette smoking, cheating in exams, political attitudes and voting, as well as choice of friends (Homer & Kahle, 1988). Similarly, Kristiansen and Matheson (1990) found that values predict attitudes towards nuclear weapons. The values–attitudes–behaviour hierarchy is nicely demonstrated by a study of shopping preferences (Homer & Kahle, 1988). These investigators hypothesized that natural-food shoppers would attach more importance to internal values than people who did not choose natural foods, who would emphasize external or social values. Examples of internal values are a sense of accomplishment, self-respect and enjoyment of life. External values are exemplified by a sense of belonging, being well respected and security. By means of a statistical method called structural equation modelling, researchers were able to show that whether or not people purchased natural foods was based on their attitudes, and that these attitudes in turn were based on whether the participants held internal or external values.

The Rokeach model has been criticized for lacking a clear theoretical foundation (Rohan, 2000). For instance, is the distinction between terminal and instrumental values clear and useful? One may value freedom as an end state (terminal) or as a means to encourage creativity (instrumental). Nevertheless, Rokeach provided an impetus for renewed interest in values and a starting point for much subsequent research. For example, Schwartz's (1992, 1996) discomfort with the intuitive approach of Rokeach led him to empirically identify two value dimensions. One dimension he named 'openness to change versus conservation' and the second 'self-enhancement versus self-transcendence'. The first dimension underlines the conflict between a desire to take chances and pursue personal interests and a desire to maintain the status quo. The second dimension reflects the extent to which a person is concerned with the effects of actions on him or herself rather than the effects on others in a broader social context. Arising out of these dimensions Schwartz (1992, 1996) identified different combinations of values as a typology of people.

CHARACTER AND VALUES

Another approach to the study of personal values has emerged in the framework of positive psychology, the study of character strengths or virtues (Peterson, 2006). These combine the instrumental and terminal values and are seen as keys to living a life that is, at once, personally fulfilling and morally sound. By means of

Table 4.1 Character values

1. wisdom and knowledge: creative, love of learning, curiosity, open-minded
2. courage: authenticity, bravery, persistence, zest (approaching life with excitement and energy)
3. humanity: kindness, love, social intelligence (empathy)
4. justice: fairness, leadership, teamwork
5. temperance (protect us from excesses): forgiveness, humility, prudence, self-regulation
6. transcendence (connect to the larger, find meaning in life): appreciate beauty and excellence, gratitude, hope, religiosity/ spirituality

surveys of people and of various philosophical and religious traditions, a set of 24 character strengths were identified, grouped into six categories (Table 4.1).

A web-based study of more than 117,000 participants from 54 nations completed the Values in Action (VIA) survey (Park, Peterson & Seligman, 2004). The data showed remarkable consistency in character priorities across people, both within the USA and in other nations. The most commonly endorsed self-described character strengths are, in order, kindness, fairness, honesty, gratitude, and judgement, and the lowest in order from the bottom are prudence, modesty and self-regulation. In another study (Peterson & Seligman, 2003), participants completed the online VIA survey, some before the terrorist attacks on New York, on September 11, 2001, and some in the months after the attacks. Significant increases were reported in transcendence (hope, religiosity/spirituality) and humanity, particularly love, perhaps because they sought to reaffirm these values in the light of what had just happened.

Comparing national and cultural values

You will recall (Chapter 3) that views of the self can differ depending on the culture in which the individual lives. It is also the case that values, which of course are a fundamental aspect of our self-image, can vary between cultures and nations. Social scientists have long searched for a way to describe the unique character of a nation. Of course, we must understand that within any nation there will not be uniformity but considerable variation in values among individuals. The question is whether we can uncover patterns of the typical, or modal, values that characterize a nation.

Indeed, it has been demonstrated that we can describe and compare people of different nations by examining their aggregate values. For example, a study of values by a Dutch psychologist (Hofstede, 1983, 2001) involved a very large number of participants (116,000) in 40 different countries, at two different times. Through statistical analyses of these data, he identified four underlying value dimensions on which inhabitants of various nations could be compared: power distance, avoidance of uncertainty, individualism and masculinity-femininity. Let us examine them, particularly as a way of studying national character. Note that you can see how your own nation scores on each of these, alone or in comparison with another nation (geert-hofstede.com/countries.html).

1. *Power distance* The dimension of power distance refers to differences in the extent to which people can control one another's behaviour. In nations scoring high on this value (e.g., Mexico, India), individuals expect and accept autocratic leaders and employers, and parents expect obedient children. By contrast, in countries low in power distance (e.g., Canada, US), children are trained to be independent, and managers tend to consult with subordinates.
2. *Avoidance of uncertainty* This refers to the feeling of being threatened by ambiguity and acting to avoid it. In cultures where this value is strong (e.g., Greece), it is reflected in a concern with security, low risk-taking, written rules and the presence of a dominant state religion.
3. *Masculinity-femininity* The third value dimension is called masculinity-femininity. It refers to the extent to which members of a society value success (including, of course, money), as opposed to caring for others

and for the quality of life. On this dimension, Canada scores moderately masculine and the Netherlands highly feminine. In line with this, one study of conflict resolution showed that Dutch participants preferred harmony-enhancing procedures more and confrontation procedures less than did Canadian participants (Leung, Bond, et al., 1990). Success-oriented societies such as Canada and Japan have more differentiation between sex roles and more stress and competition in schools and jobs. Note: designating these values in terms of gender reflects the time at which the study was first designed and of course do not reflect the cultural changes in gender roles.

4. *Individualism-collectivism* We have already encountered this dimension in discussing comparative studies of social cognition and the self (Chapters 2 and 3). It refers to the extent to which people are expected to look after themselves and make decisions based on their own interests, rather than making decisions collectively and expecting society to act in the common interest. Many of the Western nations (e.g., Canada, Australia, US) score high on individualism, while collectivist-oriented cultures include otherwise capitalist states such as Hong Kong, Taiwan, Singapore, Peru, Venezuela and Chile. In collectivist cultures, there is less occupational mobility but greater group decision-making, while individualist cultures stress achievement and initiative (Triandis, 1987). We will encounter other distinctions between people of individualistic and collectivistic cultures throughout this textbook.

While the individualism/collectivism dimension has occasioned the most research, recent research indicates that individualism and collectivism may not be polar opposites. One can accept collective values without implying oppression by society. In addition, it seems that there are different types of collectivism. For example, the value of collectivism in the Japanese culture is probably not the same as the collectivism within the traditional Israeli kibbutz (Gelfand, Triandis & Chan, 1996). A review of research in which societies (in this case, the US and Japan) have been studied over time show a mixed pattern: individualism has risen in the past decades as both societies have become more affluent, but the two societies also retained much of their cultural heritage, particularly in terms of social relationships (Hamamura, 2012).

Of course, we have described the extremes, or polarities – most nations and cultures fall somewhere in the middle of each of the four value dimensions. We have to be cautious, too, about generalizing survey results to whole nations. Obviously, as noted earlier, there will be considerable variation in values within the population, permeating virtually all aspects of life, from child-rearing to work and even driving (Hofstede, 1983). For instance, there are variations within regions of many countries such as Canada (Québec, Alberta), Spain (Andalusia, Catalonia, Basque region), the United Kingdom (Scotland, Wales), as well as various regions of India, Israel, China, United States, etc. There may also be differences within a nation or region on the basis of age, gender and ethnicity. With the rise of globalization, migration and multiculturalism within formerly more homogeneous societies, one cannot characterize the 'national character' of most nations.

Schwartz (1994) begins with an approach grounded in the realities faced by societies. He defines three issues, from which value dimensions are derived. The first issue faced by all societies is to define the relationship between the individual and the society. At one extreme, that relationship is one of the autonomy of the person, while at the other, the issue is to preserve the culture of the group: conservatism. The second issue is to promote the kinds of behaviour that preserve the social fabric by considering the welfare of others. One polarity uses the power differences between people and their roles; their value is defined as hierarchical. The other is to recognize each other as equal in rights and needs, and thus to induce cooperation between people: egalitarianism. The third basic issue that confronts societies is the relation of people to their natural and social environment. One such value would be mastery, to assert control in our world and exploit it to achieve our interests. The other opposing value would be harmony, to accept the world as it is rather than trying to master it. These three value dimensions, autonomy versus conservatism, hierarchy versus egalitarianism, and mastery versus harmony, were studied in samples of urban school teachers, selected as representative of the predominant values of their society and assigned to transmit them to the next generation (Schwartz, 1992; Bardi & Goodwin 2011). The patterns of modal scores provide a basis for comparing different societies and cultures.

KEY POINT: Values refer to global abstract principles about what is desirable or ideal. According to Rokeach, they include both terminal values (desirable end-states) and instrument values (desirable modes of conduct). Values have also been studied in relation to character, strengths or virtues in areas including wisdom, courage, humanity, justice, temperance and transcendence. National differences have also been studied, particularly relating to four fundamental value configurations; power distance within society, avoidance of uncertainty, masculinity (personal success versus caring for others) and individualism–collectivism. Schwartz offers an alternative for social values based on the underlying needs of a society. He defines three value dimensions: autonomy versus conservatism, hierarchy versus egalitarianism, and mastery versus harmony.

Value conflict and change

In certain cases, placing a high priority on one value may cause conflict with another value. For example, it may be difficult to reconcile the values of freedom and equality, when freedom implies the right to earn as much money as you want, while equality implies the duty of the state to tax some of your wealth and redistribute it to people with less wealth. In one study, Rokeach (1968) performed a content analysis of the writings of well-known authors representing different political points of view. He found that moderate liberals or social democrats valued both freedom and equality highly, conservatives valued freedom more highly than equality, leftists valued equality above freedom, and an extreme right-wing writer (Hitler) did not consider either freedom or equality to be important. Several other studies of the speeches of US senators and British members of parliament show similar values in relation to liberal or conservative ideology (Tetlock, 1986).

Not surprisingly, when issues are framed in terms of a conflict in values, people find it more difficult to perceive common ground (Kouzakova, Ellemers, Harinck & Scheepers, 2012). This illustrates how fundamental values are to us. Using content analysis of historical documents from the period in American history prior to the abolition of slavery, researchers found that those who took compromise positions on permitting slavery in some states showed greater complexity in thinking than did either those who advocated for continued slavery and those who advocated abolition. Thus, complex reasoning cannot be equated with greater morality!

Rokeach (1968) also found that while those who were active in US civil rights organizations ranked both freedom and equality quite highly, those who were uninvolved or unsympathetic to that cause ranked freedom as much more important than equality. Rokeach then devised a procedure – value confrontation – in which participants were made aware of the discrepancies in their rankings of freedom and equality. It was suggested to them that people who consider freedom so much more important than equality may be concerned only with their own freedom, and not that of others. (In a control group, there was no such intervention.) Three months later, all the participants received a letter from a well-known US civil rights organization, inviting them to join. The rate of favourable responses – joining the organization – was more than twice as high among the group who had been prompted into self-awareness.

To test value confrontation with a mass audience, Ball-Rokeach, Rokeach and Grube (1984) produced a television show that featured two well-known US actors of the day (Edward Asner and Sandy Hill) talking about the values of a world of beauty, and of freedom versus equality. Follow-up studies showed that those who had watched the show were more likely to support or become involved in organizations concerned with sexism, racism and environmental pollution than those who had missed the show. Of course, there is an element of self-selection in who chose to watch the show. Nonetheless, these studies suggest that even though values are fundamental to individuals, they are susceptible to change.

Value pluralism and trade-off reasoning

How can we hold values that are in conflict? For instance, consider people who value both freedom and equality, and find that there are situations in which acting on their value for equality of all people will compromise their freedom, because, for example, of the need to raise taxes to enhance social welfare for people in need. If they oppose such taxation programmes, they are enhancing their freedom to spend their money as they see fit, but at the expense of the equality of opportunity for all people. Such value conflicts can be quite uncomfortable, and people will act to resolve the conflict.

Often, people resort to trade-off reasoning. Consider, for example, the competing demands of protecting the environment and developing profitable natural resources such as oil. Most people will value both a cleaner environment and cheap, abundant energy. Protecting the environment by limiting such development will be costly to the economy, including the loss of jobs, while unrestrained resource development can have serious environmental consequences. Finding the right balance can be difficult and will involve trade-offs of competing demands and competing values. Tetlock (2000) performed content analyses of political speeches, and found that politicians in office, faced with the reality of competing values, demonstrated trade-offs in their speeches, but once the campaign for re-election began, they reverted to simplistic arguments, promising all things to all people.

Value conflicts are reflected in political attitudes (Tetlock, 1986). In one US study, participants were asked to indicate their attitudes about some controversial issues involving conflicting values, such as higher taxes to help the poor (equality versus a comfortable life), whether the US Central Intelligence Agency should be allowed to open the mail of citizens (national security versus individual freedom), and whether physicians should be restrained from setting fees that some people could not afford (equality versus freedom). Then they were asked to write their thoughts about each issue and to rank-order the Rokeach values (see page 115).

When an issue did not involve a value conflict, participants responded as expected on the attitude scales. For example, those who ranked equality high and a comfortable life low were quite willing to pay more taxes to assist the poor. Of course, those who ranked a comfortable life high and equality low opposed raising taxes for that purpose. However, if both values were ranked high, the conflict in values was shown in their ambivalent attitudes about the issue. When participants were faced with an issue that involved competing values (value pluralism), they thought more about the issue.

This model of trade-off reasoning indicates that if the values are not of similar strength, the weaker value will be set aside and the stronger one bolstered. There will be no compromise. One value only will be selected. However, if the values are of roughly equal strength, the question then is whether trade-offs are possible. A trade-off approach may be risky because others may perceive trade-offs as 'selling-out' and thereby compromising principles. If the person is concerned about this possibility, she may try to conceal the trade-off or to mislead other people. However, if negative consequences are unlikely, the next question that arises is whether others would be concerned that the person is trying to avoid blame. If this is not a problem, the next stage takes other characteristics of the audience into consideration. If the audience is apathetic or ill informed, they probably will respond to 'demagoguery', which includes tactics such as anger arousal and fomenting agitation. If, however, the audience is more sophisticated and critical, the strategy must be more complex. In this case the person will, for example, make well-thought-out value comparisons such as 'How much extraction of oil am I willing to advocate for how much unemployment?' and try to come to grips with the diversity of values within the audience. In short, trade-off reasoning demands complex thinking, requiring much of one's attention.

Value pluralism has also been studied in relation to political ideologies (Tetlock, 1984). We have already seen that liberal/social democrats, conservatives, fascists and communists differ in their value priorities for equality and freedom. It has also been found that people with liberal/social democratic political attitudes are higher in integrative complexity than others. Many political issues, such as social programmes, antidiscrimination laws and government intervention in the economy involve conflicts between freedom and equality. Because liberal/social democrats rank both values highly, they must be able to think flexibly and in more complex ways to resolve the conflicts. On the other hand, people whose political ideologies dictate a clear priority of one value over the other can resolve the issues more easily.

We must be cautious in our conclusions about these studies. It is not possible to infer cause and effect, whether liberals show more integrative complexity because of the equality-freedom conflict, or whether people who think in this way tend as a result to value freedom and equality highly and to adopt social democratic political attitudes. Another issue concerns the culture being studied. Tetlock's research has been conducted entirely in economically developed democracies. Arguably, the realities of poverty, dictatorships and economic underdevelopment in the Third World would make such a trade-off more difficult, if not unrealistic, and could result in a different relationship between values and political ideology. The study of successful revolutionary leaders described in Chapter 2 suggests that more extreme political ideologies are not necessarily lacking in integrative complexity.

Some forms of trade-off reasoning are more demanding and troubling, particularly those involving values that are 'sacred' to the person. We turn to these values now.

Sacred values

Sacred values involve fundamental religious beliefs, core ideas of national and ethnic identities and moral norms. For instance, religions have their sacred objects or ideas that are experienced as transcendental and irreplaceable: a faith, moral values, religious rituals, a prayer book, a rosary, a Torah, an image of the Buddha, the Adi Granth, the Vedas, the Qur'an. Secular objects and ideas can acquire an analogous sacred quality. Suppose your place of residence was engulfed in a fire, and you only have time to take out three things before the place burns down. What would you take? While many people would grab their laptop or external hard drive, there would be a tremendous variety of responses with regard to what is chosen next.

What is impressive is that the monetary value of the object would not often be the determining factor. You may well leave your expensive flat-screen TV or your jewellery and grab a photo or video of a loved one, a love letter from long ago (or yesterday), a treasured piece of clothing. Of course, this can simply represent the endowment effect (Chapter 2), in which we value something simply because it is ours. However, when the endowment effect becomes one of much greater emotional and symbolic value, it has acquired, to us, the critical quality of 'sacredness', not necessarily tied to religion but something of inestimable personal value. At the time of writing, a major international dispute rages over Iran's acquisition of nuclear energy and, at least potentially, nuclear weapons. Research indicates that, to a significant proportion of Iranians, acquiring nuclear energy had become a sacred value, one tied to their sense of national pride and assertion and not open to compromise (Dehghani, Atran, et al., 2010).

In an experiment, participants were asked to sign a statement contradicting one of their core personal values (Berns, Bell, et al., 2012). The researchers used functional magnetic resonance imaging (fMRI) to record brain responses of participants. In the first phase, participants were shown statements ranging from the mundane, such as 'You are a tea drinker', to hot-button issues such 'You support gay marriage' and 'You are Pro-Life'. At the end of the experiment, participants were given the option of auctioning their personal statements, disavowing their previous choices for actual money. The participants could earn as much as $100 per statement by simply agreeing to sign a document stating the opposite of what they believed. They could choose to opt out of the auction for statements they valued highly. The brain imaging data showed a strong correlation between sacred values and activation of neural systems associated with evaluating rights and wrongs (the left temporo-parietal junction) but not with systems associated with rewards. Clearly some issues are processed in ways that involve personal values but not costs and rewards.

As discussed earlier, one can imagine several situations in which trade-off reasoning and compromise become less possible (Tetlock, 2003). The 'taboo trade-off' situation pits a sacred value against a non-sacred value, for instance, honour against money. Most of us will choose the former in at least most situations. However, some situations can become 'tragic', in the sense that one sacred value is pitted against another, and such decisions are much more difficult and emotional (Hanselmann & Tanner, 2008). Consider, for instance, Tetlock's *taboo choice* scenario in which a hospital administrator is faced with a decision to save one child's life (sacred) or save the hospital $1million. Participants asked to evaluate the administrator were more negative toward an administrator who took a long time to decide; even having to take time to think about violating the value of a human life was repellent. However, in the *tragic choice* situation, in which the administrator had to choose either between saving the life of one boy or that of another boy, participants were more positive toward the administrator who took a long time to decide. In this case, contemplation was perceived as signifying the gravity of the situation.

Consider the unpleasant reality that there is an international underground market for the buying and selling of human body organs for transplant, generally from destitute people in developing countries for well-off people in the developed world. Many people would find this to be repellent, but when the situation is qualified as the only way to save a life, some participants are more willing to consider the practice (Tetlock, 2003).

KEY POINT: Value conflicts, between two desired values, often include freedom versus equality, which have been related to political ideologies. Where such conflicts exist, people may decide to place one value as the priority or may engage in trade-off reasoning. There are also sacred values, desirable beyond material worth, including religious or transcendent values and values with important personal meaning.

FUNCTIONS OF ATTITUDES

We have described values as the global abstractions on which we base our attitudes. Can we infer people's values from their attitudes towards certain objects or issues? Can we predict people's attitudes towards capital punishment, the welfare state or rock videos if we know their values? To understand, we must turn to a more fundamental question: Why do we have attitudes? Several functions of attitudes have been identified and studied (Eagly & Chaiken, 1992; Olson & Zanna, 1993).

First, attitudes may serve a utilitarian or instrumental function, leading to greater rewards and fewer costs. In particular, holding specific attitudes may help us gain approval and acceptance from others and to be in harmony with our own group or people. This may be particularly important in the more collectivist societies in which community is greatly valued.

Second, attitudes can serve a knowledge function, enabling us to make sense of our world, avoid uncertainty, to cope with everyday decisions, and to feel that we do understand the world in which we live (Fazio, Blascovich & Driscoll, 1992). Attitudes assist people in selecting, from the myriad objects that enter their visual field, those stimuli that will receive attention (Roskos-Ewoldsen & Fazio, 1992a). That is, attitudes serve as schemata, helping us to avoid the uncomfortable feelings of uncertainty and ambiguity, guiding our reactions and interpretations of events.

Note also that implicit attitudes enable us to respond spontaneously with an evaluation, without expending cognitive effort. Indeed, attitudes can enable us to avoid thinking. Fazio and his associates have investigated how quickly participants respond to various objects by pushing buttons labelled good or bad (Fazio, Sanbonmatsu, Powell & Kardes, 1986). They demonstrate that some implicit attitudes are activated spontaneously or automatically from memory and do not require thinking (e.g., 'cockroaches are disgusting'), while other attitudes require more time and thought to be expressed.

Figure 4.6   Volunteers clearing up an oil spill, Staten Island, New York. A value-expressive behaviour
Source: © J A Giordano/Corbis

Third, attitudes may also serve an ego-defensive function, protecting people from becoming aware of harsh, uncomfortable truths about themselves or their world. As will be discussed in Chapter 13, prejudiced attitudes often serve ego-defensive functions. For instance, the bigot may express prejudice toward members of some out-group in order to feel more important and powerful than he or she really is. If people feel bad about themselves, it is comforting and protective to believe that others are worse.

Fourth, attitudes can serve a value-expressive function. Value-expressive attitudes demonstrate our uniqueness and what is important to us. They may take an apparently trivial form, as in the case of those who express positive opinions about certain styles in music, clothing and cars that represent certain values, or they may be much more important. For example, members of a religion may adhere to certain salient attitudes that indicate their devotion to their faith. Recall the review above of Tetlock's work on value conflicts and how these are manifest in attitudes.

It is important to understand that we cannot infer attitudes from values, or values from attitudes. Indeed, people with different attitudes towards the same issue often relate their positions to entirely different values, rather than to differences in the importance of a particular value. For example, both people who favour extensive government involvement in health care and those who oppose it may place high importance on the values of freedom and equality. However, those in favour may base their position on the value of equality and those opposed may refer to the value of freedom. A selective appeal to values may enable them to support and justify their attitudes (Eiser & van der Pligt, 1984; Eiser, 1987).

This **value justification effect** has been demonstrated by Kristiansen and Zanna (1988). Participants in an experiment were asked to indicate their attitudes towards two controversial issues of that place and time: access to abortion on demand and the deployment of nuclear weapons in Canada. Then they were asked to rank the eighteen Rokeach terminal values in terms of how relevant each was to the abortion and nuclear weapons issues. Proponents and opponents of each issue differed significantly in terms of which values were ranked as most relevant. For example, pro-abortion participants rated freedom, happiness and a comfortable life as more relevant to the issue than did anti-abortion participants. Interestingly, both sides rated equality, self-respect and inner harmony as equally relevant. On the nuclear weapons issue, national security was more relevant to those in favour, and wisdom and salvation to those opposed. We begin to see why people on opposite sides of some controversies cannot communicate. In terms of fundamental values, neither side understands or agrees with the other.

A final note concerning attitude functions pertains to dual attitudes, in which one's implicit and explicit attitude towards the same object are different. For instance, attitudes toward minority groups may well be expressed differently at explicit and implicit levels (Wilson, Lindsey & Schooler, 2000). Explicit attitudes may be expressed as being polite to members of the out-group while implicit attitudes may be expressed as avoiding them. This will be discussed in the chapter on prejudice.

> **KEY POINT:** Functions of attitudes can be utilitarian or instrumental, knowledge-oriented (avoid uncertainty), value-expressive or ego-defensive. Attitudes and values may be related in both directions: values may lead to attitudes derived from them, or values may justify existing attitudes.

THE RELATIONSHIP BETWEEN ATTITUDES AND BEHAVIOUR

One of the major reasons for measuring a particular psychological variable is to make some reasonably precise statement about how it affects behaviour. There is no question that attitudes have a powerful influence on how we act. Clearly Mandela's attitudes and actions were highly consistent, and he paid the price of 27 years of incarceration for acting on his beliefs. Yet, attempts to demonstrate that behaviour can be attributed to an underlying attitude have frequently been unsuccessful. In an early study, LaPiere (1934) observed a young Chinese couple as they toured the US, visiting more than 250 hotels and restaurants. Lapiere took careful notes of how they were treated and noted that they were refused service only once. Later, when LaPiere wrote to the same establishments asking whether they were willing to serve Chinese patrons, a startling 92% of those who responded said that they would refuse. The study has been criticized on several grounds. For instance, only 50% of the establishments responded and there is no way to ascertain whether the person who responded to LaPiere's letter was the same person who had offered service. However, it did suggest a substantial gap between what people say (attitudes) and what they do (behaviour).

A similar study (Kutner, Wilkins & Yarrow, 1952) conducted in the northern US, when racial segregation still existed, revealed that although blacks were served satisfactorily in a number of restaurants, the same restaurants would later refuse to make reservations for a social event which included blacks. As with the LaPiere study, different constraints were operating under different conditions. It is much more difficult to discriminate face-to-face than by letter or telephone, and there was no guarantee that the person handling reservations was the same person who originally had served the blacks. Yet despite their flaws, both these studies were important in alerting researchers to the problem of attitude–behaviour discrepancies. In a better controlled situation, Bickman (1972) found that although 94% of 500 individuals questioned said they felt personally responsible for the disposal of litter, only 2% actually picked up a piece of litter planted by the experimenter.

Of course, inconsistency between attitudes and behaviour should not be surprising. All of us fail to act on our attitudes from time to time, often for good reason (Wicker, 1969). It has been argued that these and other such studies fail to show the expected relationships between attitude and behaviour because they rely too much on a single behavioural act (Weigel & Newman, 1976). In an experiment, participants first filled out a questionnaire that measured their concerns about the environment, including various aspects of pollution and conservation. Then, at different times over the next few months, the participants were contacted for 14 environment-relevant actions, such as circulating a petition, agreeing to pick up litter, recruiting a friend and recycling bottles. The researchers found that the correlations between attitudes and single behaviours were quite modest (average of 0.29). However, when all 14 behaviours were combined into one index, a strong multiple correlation of 0.62 was obtained. Notice that in this study, attitudes were predicting observable behaviour in the real world rather than self-reported behaviour or laboratory behaviour.

Thus, there is some compelling evidence that attitudes are, to some extent, linked to actions. When and why do attitudes predict behaviour?

Variables influencing the attitude–behaviour relationship

The literature has revealed a set of intervening variables that explain why many studies have been unable to demonstrate a relationship between attitude and action. Characteristics of both the person and the situation can determine whether people will act according to their attitudes.

A number of personal factors can be involved:

- The person may hold other relevant attitudes. People may eat to control their weight, not out of concern for health consequences but because they believe that controlling their weight helps them to look better.
- The person may be motivated to satisfy other needs. For example, people may shop in a given clothing store despite its unfashionable attire because the prices are attractive.
- The person may not see how an action would be relevant to a particular attitude. For example, voters who oppose a certain political party may not realize the party stands for policies that they favour. Or they may feel that their one vote will not matter, and so not bother to vote at all.
- The cost of the behaviour to the person may be excessive (Campbell, 1963; Kaiser, Byrka & Hartig, 2010). A person may want to get in shape but find the costs of gym membership to be excessive.

Situational factors may also prevent people from acting in accordance with their attitudes:

- The real or implied presence of others may influence behaviours. For example, a person holding an unpopular attitude may feel too ashamed or pressured to express it in public.
- Social norms may conflict with certain attitudes. Thus, the prejudiced hotel keeper may feel that it is inappropriate to turn away actual, paying customers of whatever race, creed or national origin.
- People may act in a certain way regardless of attitudes because they have no acceptable alternatives. For example, they may subscribe to a mediocre newspaper with a repugnant editorial policy because it is the only newspaper in town.
- Unforeseen extraneous events can drastically change behaviour, regardless of attitudes. People who are opposed to welfare may suddenly become unemployed or disabled and thus compelled to seek public assistance.

It has also been shown that attitudes may be poor predictors of behaviour if the behaviour is socially proscribed or illegal. Hessing, Elffers & Weigel (1988) interviewed a large number of Dutch taxpayers who were known through prior questionnaires to be either tax evaders or non-evaders. They asked all participants whether they had underreported their income or had reported illegal deductions – in other words, whether or not they had cheated on their tax returns. The data indicate that the attitudes and self-reports of these respondents were uncorrelated with their actual behaviour. In other words, many taxpayers who had tried either successfully or unsuccessfully to dupe the tax authorities expressed attitudes against this sort of behaviour.

In short, behaviour is affected by previous experience, habit, social norms and the anticipated consequences of that situation as well as by attitudes. Kraus (1995) conducted a meta-analysis of 88 attitude–behaviour studies, and concluded that there is a substantial but limited relationship between attitudes and behaviour. He points out that the correlation is enhanced when factors such as attitude certainty, self-monitoring and the type of attitude measurement are taken into account. Interestingly, he also noted that attitudes predicted behaviour better for non-students than for students!

The attitude–behaviour problem has generated several influential theories. These will be discussed below.

KEY POINT: Attitude is a significant but not very strong predictor of behaviour. The reasons include personal factors such as other relevant attitudes involved, motivations to satisfy other needs and the costs of the behaviour relative to the rewards. Situational factors include the presence of others which may facilitate or suppress the behaviour, social norms and the absence of an appropriate alternative behaviour in the situation.

Theory of Reasoned Action

Ajzen and Fishbein (1980) tackled the attitude–behaviour problem directly. They began with the premise that people usually consider the implications of their actions and then act consciously and deliberately. In short, we eventually do what we intend to do and the best single predictor of a behaviour is an intention to act in that way. Of course, intentions vary in strength and we may intend to do a number of different things. Anna may intend to study tonight unless she is invited to a party – an invitation she intends to accept, despite her intention to study. Thus, we must specify what determines how strongly Anna intends to study.

According to Ajzen and Fishbein, the strength of an intention to act in a certain way is determined by two factors: attitude towards that action and subjective norms. That is, our intention to vote for candidate X is determined by our attitude towards voting in that way (not attitude towards the candidate but towards voting for that candidate) and our perception that the action is encouraged or approved by other people. Ajzen and Fishbein suggest the two factors are not necessarily equal in importance and that one may be weighted more than the other by different people and in different situations. For example, while two people may be equally determined to vote for candidate X, one may be influenced primarily by feeling positive about voting in that way (attitude) and the other by how family and friends intend to vote (subjective norm). In one study of weight loss among women, the subjective norm component (close friends) far outweighed the attitude component in predicting eventual success (Fishbein & Ajzen, 1975).

The Ajzen–Fishbein theory also specifies what determines attitudes and subjective norms. Attitudes towards a given action are: (1) determined by beliefs that the action will lead to certain outcomes; and (2) weighted by evaluations of these outcomes (Figure 4.7). For example, you will have a positive attitude towards voting for candidate X if you believe that this action will lead to relatively favourable outcomes (honest government, full employment) and you place a relatively high value on such outcomes. If you believe that voting in this way is unlikely to bring about such outcomes, or you really don't care whether such outcomes occur, your attitude will be less positive. Anna will attend the party if she doesn't see adverse consequences for her grades from this decision. Subjective norms (i.e., perception of social pressure to act) consist of the following: (1) beliefs that certain people or groups expect the action of you; and (2) your motivation to comply with these expectancies. Thus, you will feel encouraged or pressured to vote for candidate X if you believe that your friends want you

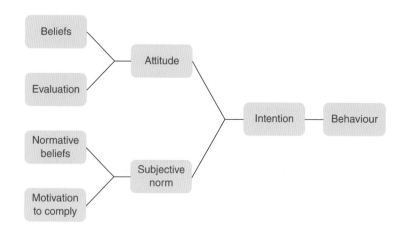

Figure 4.7   The Theory of Reasoned Action

Source: Fishbein & Ajzen (1975)

to vote that way and if you want to do what they expect of you. Anna will go to the party if she believes that her friends want her there, and she wants to make them happy.

Putting it all together, behaviour can be predicted by intentions. Intentions to behave in a given way are determined by some combination of attitudes towards acting that way and the subjective norms surrounding the behaviour. Expected consequences and evaluations of those consequences determine attitudes, while subjective norms are determined by beliefs about what others expect the motives to comply with these expectations. Thus, if you expect to enjoy a certain movie and would really like to enjoy it, and if you perceive that your friends want you to go with them to the movie and you want to please them, you are likely to intend to go.

The Theory of Reasoned Action (TRA) has been supported in many studies of socially significant behaviours such as family planning, consumer behaviour (buying particular brands), voting in elections in various countries, choice of occupation, changes regarding smoking and drinking and losing weight (Ajzen & Fishbein, 1980). While much of the research on attitudes has been criticized for focusing on relatively insignificant, short-term, laboratory-generated attitudes, this model has been tested with real-life behaviours and attitudes. For example, in the Ajzen & Fishbein (1980) study, participants were asked to indicate their intentions to perform various purchasing behaviours with regard to five brand names in each of three classes of products (e.g., intention to buy a brand of car or beer). For each behaviour, attitudes were assessed by rating bipolar choices (e.g., buying X beer for my own use in the next week would have good consequences/bad consequences). Subjective norms were assessed by having participants rate the extent to which they believed their families and friends thought that they should/should not buy X beer, etc. When the attitudes and subjective norms corresponded exactly to the behaviour, these two factors were highly predictive of behavioural intention. In another study, attitudes and subjective norms of married women regarding the use of birth control pills (but not birth control in general) predicted their use of birth control pills two years later (Davidson & Morrison, 1983). The Theory of Reasoned Action has also been useful in AIDS prevention (Gallois et al., 1994), with research focusing on safe sexual practices, especially the intention to use a condom. In general, these investigations offer considerable support for the theory, setting the stage for advertising and information campaigns.

As we noted earlier, attitudes vary in complexity. Yet the research generated by the Ajzen and Fishbein model usually measures attitudes in terms of simple positive or negative evaluations. As people become more involved and more experienced in an activity, they develop a more complex set of expectancies about various consequences than would be represented in this model. For example, in a survey of attitudes towards marijuana among high school students (Schlegel, D'Avernas, et al., 1992), a pattern of scores concerning attitudes on various aspects of marijuana use (e.g., frequency of marijuana use, expected pleasant and unpleasant effects, health consequences) predicted the extent of use more accurately than did a single score, pro- or anti-marijuana smoking, derived from the Theory of Reasoned Action.

The Theory of Reasoned Action has also been criticized on several other grounds (Liska, 1984). First, according to the model, our attitudes influence our intention to act in a certain way but do not influence our behaviour directly. However, it has been shown in several field studies using sophisticated statistical analysis (structural equation modelling) that attitudes influence behaviour even after accounting for intentions (Bentler & Speckart, 1981). In bypassing intentions, the theory of a direct attitude–behaviour link seems to challenge

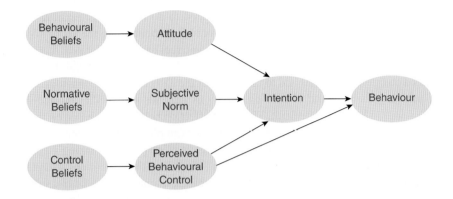

Figure 4.8 The Theory of Planned Behaviour

Source: Reprinted from http://people.umass.edu/aizen/tpb.diag.html. Copyright 2006 by Icek Ajzen. Reprinted by permission

the logic of a sequence of reasoned actions: 'I am favourable towards doing it, so I decide to do it' (intention) and then act'. It suggests a more spontaneous view of some behaviour.

The theory also seems to confuse normative beliefs (how we expect others to react) and beliefs about behavioural outcomes. The reactions of others are the most significant outcomes of many of our actions. Moreover, the theory neglects a number of other important variables such as other relevant attitudes. Finally, in this theory, attitudes are conceived as a cause and behaviour as the ultimate effect. As the next chapter will show, cause and effect can flow both ways: behaviour is often a cause of subsequent attitude change. Finally, the theory works particularly well when we look at the consistency within each participant to which attitudes and subjective norms predict behaviour (Trafimow & Finlay, 2001).

Ajzen (1985, 1987) has pointed out that the predictive utility of the theory can be improved if volitional control is also taken into consideration. For example, whether a high school student intends to continue on to university will depend not only on the original factors in the model but also on whether the student perceives that he or she has the required ability and financial resources – that is, perceived control. This led Ajzen to modify the Theory of Reasoned Action to take this factor into account, and he labelled it the Theory of Planned Behaviour (Figure 4.8).

The Theory of Reasoned Action is built on the premise that behaviour is, in the end, volitional: you can do something only if you want to do it and thus form an intention to do it. However, there are many situations in which intentions built on desires are not sufficient. Can you think of any? For instance, you may really want to purchase that luxury car, and intend to buy it someday, but that will depend on whether you can accumulate the necessary funds. You may intend to skip the final exams … if you perceive that you can get away with it. You may intend to study unceasingly between now and the exams – but is the road to hell paved with good intentions?

Ajzen (1991) built on the earlier reasoned action theory, essentially supplanting it. As in the TRA, the most direct determinant of what a person will do is the intention to do it. Intentions encapsulate how motivated the person is to act in a certain way. Intentions, in turn, are determined by three factors: attitudes, subjective norms and perceived behavioural control. Recall that attitudes concern a person's negative or positive evaluation of performing the act; for example, I would find recycling to be a pleasant and useful (or unpleasant/useless) thing to do. Subjective norms concern what others expect of the person with regard to the behaviour; for example, my friends would expect me to recycle. The third, added factor in predicting intentions is perceived behavioural control, that is, the extent to which the person believes that he or she has control over doing the act; for example, recycling would be something that I would be able to do. Interestingly, perceived behavioural control has been shown to predict behaviour directly, in addition to predicting intentions.

Of the three predictors of intentions, subjective norms have consistently turned out to be weakest in predicting intentions (Armitage & Conner, 2001). Thus researchers have made a distinction between the kind of norm that demands conforming to others' expectations, and moral norms – the individual's perception that recycling is the right thing to do, that one is morally obligated to do it (Rivis, Sheeran & Armitage, 2009). Perhaps related to this is the anticipated affect, how one would feel about doing the act or not doing it. If you would anticipate that recycling (or not recycling) would make you feel happy, exhilarated, regretful or angry, this will influence your intentions to actually do it (Rivis, Sheeran & Armitage, 2009). Thus, both subjective moral norms and anticipated emotional reactions add to the power of the TPB to predict behaviour, beyond attitudes.

The effect of perceived behavioural control on intentions depends on whether the individual perceives engaging in the behaviour to be easy or difficult. The direct effect on behaviour is based on the extent to which the person perceives the behaviour to be under his control. For example, Madden, Ellen & Ajzen (1992) found that participants reported less control over getting a good night's sleep than over taking vitamin supplements. If the behaviour is considered to be under high control (e.g., vitamins), then intentions will play the dominant role in predicting action. However, as perceived control decreases, intentions become less influential.

The Theories of Reasoned Action and Planned Behaviour have an elegant simplicity and have generated much research, perhaps more than any other theory in social psychology (Trafimow, 2009). The evidence indicates that the models perform well (Notani, 1998) and an extensive review of the literature revealed that the models predicted intention with an accuracy of between 40% and 50% of the variance, and behaviour between 19% and 38% (Sutton, 1998). Madden, Ellen & Ajzen (1992) compared the predictive value of the two theories (TRA and TPB) for 10 behaviours. They found that the inclusion of the behavioural control factor improved prediction significantly. They conclude that while the Theory of Reasoned Action applies when the target behaviour is under volitional control (people have the ability and resources to do it), the Theory of Planned Behaviour is superior when perceived volitional control is reduced. A study of problem drinkers (Schlegel, D'Avernas, Zanna, DeCourville & Manske, 1992) provides further support for this differentiation. It was found for non-problem drinkers that perceived control predicted intention to drink but that for problem drinkers it predicted behaviour (frequency of getting drunk). Presumably problem drinkers perceive less control over their drinking than do non-problem drinkers.

In a meta-analysis of research predicting physical activity and exercise, both models again performed well, but the Theory of Planned Behaviour predicted more of the variance. Interestingly, high scores on a measure of self-efficacy, the sense that one can actually do something, added to prediction after accounting for these models, and past behaviour was also a strong predictor of continued behaviour in the future (Hagger, Chatzisarantis & Biddle, 2002). Clearly, research will continue and new approaches will emerge, which will contribute to a better understanding of this fascinating and important problem.

KEY POINT: The Theory of Reasoned Action (TRA) postulates that the best predictor of an action is an intention to do it. Intentions are determined by attitudes toward the act (a belief that the act will lead to certain consequences and how the individual values those consequences) and subjective norms (beliefs about whether others expect the person to do it and the motivation to comply). Attitudes to the act and subjective norms are not necessarily equally weighted. The theory has been applied successfully to many behaviours by many populations, particularly consumer choices and health behaviours. However, it assumes that the person perceives that he or she has the necessary ability and resources to follow through on intentions. As this is often not the case, the Theory of Planned Behaviour (TPB) was formulated, extending the TRA to include a third component, perceived behavioural control, and which may directly predict behaviour as well as intentions. Subjective norms are generally the weakest of the three factors in predicting intentions, and thus we must differentiate between norms that generate conformity to the expectations of others and moral norms, involving doing the right thing.

Discourse analysis: an alternative approach

A radically different approach to the attitude–behaviour problem has emerged, particularly among some British social psychologists (Potter & Wetherell, 1987). Rather than conceiving of attitudes and behaviour as separate entities, the focus is on 'discourse', the analysis of what is said or written in the context of where it occurs. Consider, for instance, the issue of a 'right to die' raised earlier in this chapter. Through a content analysis of what is said, one may encounter several quite distinct frames of reference for a position. For instance, one may talk about this issue in terms of religious ideology and the sacredness of life. From a medical perspective, the frame may be the necessity to alleviate suffering, or may be a purely practical concern about hospitals overcrowded with patients who cannot be cured. People may take an individualistic approach by stressing one's personal freedom to live or die. Finally, during the Nazi era, ideology argued the right to euthanize those characterized by 'life unworthy of life', such as those with physical or mental disabilities or those deemed to be racially inferior. Note that one may take a position on this issue on either side from a very different frame of reference. It is argued that we must examine the entire 'discourse', what is said, how it is said, by whom and for what objectives, in order to understand the associated attitudes and the resulting behaviour (Billig, 1987). Thus the method of choice in this case is a content analysis of audio and video recordings of actual interpersonal interactions in naturalistic settings, eschewing questionnaires and experiments.

This type of qualitative analysis has been employed for a variety of purposes, including a study of how British people view their royal family (Billig, 1996). It has proven to be useful in uncovering hidden prejudices (Chapter 11) and other hidden agendas. In its basic form, discourse analysis rejects the notion of attitudes, behaviour and cognitions in a causal relationship because they all are represented in discourse, and so are not separable. Therefore, from this perspective, most of contemporary social psychology would be replaced by this alternative. As one would expect, this argument has been strongly criticized as a rather extreme, although provocative, challenge (Abrams & Hogg, 1990).

KEY POINT: Discourse analysis denies the separability of attitudes and behaviours in a linear causal relationship, and treats spoken or written discourse or conversation as the unit of analysis. It treats expressed attitudes and actions in their particular context.

A FINAL NOTE

From the beginning, the study of attitudes has been at the core of social psychology. Much of the early research was devoted to developing reliable and valid measures of attitudes, largely because it was believed that attitudes are accurate indicators of important social behaviour. However, as the evidence accumulated that attitudes are not as closely linked to behaviour as was expected, social psychologists began to wonder what the fuss was all about. Many turned to other problems and some even predicted that attitude research would soon be a thing of the past. Meanwhile advertisers and political tacticians spent vast amounts of money and time in tracking attitudes.

Indeed, attitude research has progressed through three distinct phases or generations in which different problems have been explored. The first generation asked, 'Is attitude related to behaviour?' The second asked, 'When are attitudes related to behaviour?' The third generation of research concentrates on how attitudes influence behaviour and, indeed, how behaviour influences attitude. Attitude research has thus become integrated with work on social cognition.

In the next chapter, we turn to the important issue of attitude change. Later, we focus on the specific attitudes that characterize prejudice. In the final chapter of this book, we will explore how attitudes are measured and changed in relation to health-relevant behaviours. It will become clear that the concept of attitude is alive and flourishing in social psychology.

SUMMARY

1. An attitude is a hypothetical construct representing an evaluative response to some object or issue. It involves cognitive (belief-related) and affective (emotional) components, and behavioural tendencies, and can vary in intensity and complexity. It may be explicit or it can be implicit, outside immediate awareness.

2. An ideology is a more or less coherent set of attitudes, usually a political world view. Ideology can be described in terms of the liberal/left vs conservative/right continuum, and some describe it in terms of the distinction between moderate/democratic and extreme/autocratic dimensions. Conservatism is associated with anxiety about instability and intolerance of ambiguity, moral judgements based on authority, and need for order. Liberalism is related to openness to new experiences, cognitive complexity, moral judgements based on fairness, and tolerance of uncertainty. While liberals and conservatives are equally happy, liberals experience more positive affect, while conservatives experience less negative affect.

3. A value is a higher-order abstraction of what individuals consider to be ideal, as an end-state objective in life or as a mode of conduct. Values can also be represented as character strengths. Values may also become 'sacred', impeding compromise or accommodation.

4. Where values are in conflict, change in a value, attitude or behaviour may result. Value pluralism can lead to trade-off reasoning.

5. Nations and cultures can be described in terms of several value dimensions, including power distance, avoidance of uncertainty, masculinity–femininity, and in particular, individualism–collectivism. Research indicates that tradition and interpersonal harmony are important values in Eastern cultures.

6. Attitudes serve a number of functions or purposes to the individual: instrumental or adaptive, providing a sense of knowledge or understanding of one's world, ego-defensive and value-expressive.

7. Attitudes are not robust predictors of specific behaviours, but can predict patterns of multiple behaviours. A variety of personal and social factors moderate the attitude–behaviour linkage, such as social norms, presence of others, free choice and personal relevance.

8. The Theory of Reasoned Action states that one's attitude toward a certain action (expected desired consequences) and the expectations of others predict intention to act in a certain way. Intention to act predicts action. The Theory of Planned Behaviour adds considerations of personal control to this equation.

POINTS TO PONDER

- Why is there so often such a gulf between attitudes and actions? How could this be narrowed, so that people would act directly on their attitudes and their values?
- How do our attitudes, ideologies and values reflect … or represent … our character and our individuality? How do they reflect the society and culture in which we live?
- Long ago, Allport suggested that the number of functions or purposes served by attitudes makes that concept indispensable in social psychology. Can you argue in favour of this proposition? Can you argue that social psychology could continue to progress without the concept of attitudes?
- How can we determine that an attitude expresses the individual's personal values rather than expectations of reward?
- How might you apply the Theory of Planned Behaviour to convince people not to drive while intoxicated?

FURTHER READING

Albarracin, D., Johnson, B.T. & Zanna, M.P. (Eds) (2005). *The handbook of attitudes*. New York: Psychology Press.

A comprehensive set of scholarly papers on all aspects of attitudes. It includes theoretical frameworks, detailed research and applications in a variety of areas. Useful for this chapter and the next one.

Fishbein, M. & Ajzen, I. (2009) *Predicting and changing behavior: The reasoned action approach.* New York: Psychology Press.

The major review and overview of this influential approach to the attitude–behaviour problem. It includes much research on how the theory has been applied.

Haidt, J. (2012). *The righteous mind: Why good people are divided by politics and religion.* New York: Pantheon Press.

A provocative, controversial take on the moral bases and biases in liberalism and conservatism (American style). Haidt begins with a notion of moral intuition, a rapid cognitive process of seeing things, people and ideas as right or wrong, from which ideology flows.

Hofstede, G. (2003) *Culture's consequences: Comparing values, behaviors, institutions and organizations.* London, UK: Sage.

The classic study of values across national boundaries. A useful resource for trying to understand how nations and cultures differ in how they see the world.

Jost, J.T., Kay, A. & Thorisdottir, H. (2009). *Social and psychological bases of ideology and system justification*. New York: Oxford University Press.

The key ideas and research on this emerging area of research and thinking. Most of the work centres on the cognitive and motivational distinctions between conservative and liberal ideologies, with some attention to religious ideologies as well.

Peterson, C. & Seligman, M.E.P. (2004). *Character strengths and virtues: A handbook and classification*. New York: Oxford University Press.

An influential overview of the VIA system outlined in this chapter. This is a basic resource in positive psychology today.

Petty, R.E., Fazio, R.H. & Briñol, P. (Eds) (2008). *Attitudes: Insights from the new implicit measures*. New York: Psychology Press.

An overview of this currently hot topic.

Upmeyer, A. (Ed.) (2012). *Attitudes and behavioural decisions*. New York: Springer.

An update of an earlier book; a good overview of research and thinking on the relationship between attitudes and behaviours.

WEBLINKS

http://implicit.harvard.edu/implicit/
> How to measure implicit attitudes.

http://www.positivepsychology.org
> Positive Psychology webpage.

http://www.viacharacter.org/surveys.aspx
> Values in Action (VIA) inventory of character strengths.

PART III

INFLUENCING OTHERS

CHAPTER 5
ATTITUDE CHANGE

Advertising can be described as the science of arresting human intelligence
long enough to get money from it.
Stephen Leacock

LEARNING OBJECTIVES

* To understand how both internal mental processes and external influences can lead to attitude change

* To understand how and when behaviour that is inconsistent with existing attitudes can cause subsequent attitude change

* To understand what factors in the source, audience and message contribute to the persuasion situation

* To understand the processes of persuasion within the dual theory of cognition, and how people may change by thinking about the message or by distraction

* To understand how people can resist attempts to persuade them

Figure 5.1 Steve Jobs in selling mode

Source: © ROBERT GALBRAITH/Reuters/Corbis

In the late years of the 20th century and into the new century, one of the most influential people in the world was not a politician, a rock star, an athlete or a warrior. He was a computer engineer, a person of aesthetic sensibility and a corporate CEO. Perhaps most interesting for students of social psychology, he was a supremely effective, charismatic marketer of his company's products. His name was Steve Jobs, co-founder, chairman, and chief executive officer of Apple Inc. He was born in 1955, and died of pancreatic cancer in 2011 at a tragically young age.

Jobs was not an inventor. Indeed, the personal computer for home use, computing with a graphic interface using a 'mouse', the MP3 digital music player, the tablet computing device, online 'stores' that sell computers, applications, music, movies, books, the 'smartphone' that provides Internet access and a host of applications … none of them were invented by Jobs or by Apple Corporation. But he saw the marketing potential of all of them, realized the importance of a 'user-friendly' interface, and realized the importance of design that was both effective and pleasing. Then he convinced the world of their value.

Jobs went his own way in persuading people to buy his products and his vision. Rather than always using advertising to advise people of upcoming products, he insisted on secrecy, thus arousing intense interest in what was next. When announcing new products, he would end his presentation, thank his audience, begin to walk off stage, stop suddenly and exclaim, 'Oh, one more thing!' That one more thing was invariably the big news, the new, exciting innovation. Everyone waited for that 'one more thing'; they came to be persuaded.

Other strategies were equally effective, if unusual. When the original MacIntosh computer appeared in 1984, it was introduced by a commercial which ran once, during the Super Bowl (US football championship game) (http://www.youtube.com/watch?v=HhsWzJo2sN4). It shows images related to Orwell's classic novel *1984*, which envisioned a future of blind conformity to the wishes of a dictator, 'Big Brother'. It then announces the appearance on the market of the MacIntosh computer, and promises that 1984 (the actual year) will not be '1984', the image of blind, bland conformity. When the PC market was dominated by IBM corporation, which had as a slogan, one word, 'Think', Apple countered with their own slogan, 'Think different'. This commercial praised the 'round pegs in the square hole', the rebels, the misfits: cue images of Albert Einstein, Thomas Edison, Mohammed Ali, Martin Luther King and John Lennon. Through the iTunes store, he even convinced millions of people to pay for music downloads that they might otherwise steal on file-sharing web sites.

Jobs saw himself as a visionary of innovative products. Success came from the design of the products themselves, functional and aesthetic, easy for the non-geek majority among us. Clearly much of the appeal for these devices came from Steve Jobs himself, a credible source of persuasive communications. His story is one example of supremely successful mass persuasion (Isaacson, 2011).

In modern societies, large sums of money are spent on attempts to change our buying practices. Corporations and political parties devote massive resources to advertising in the various media. Of course, persuasion also occurs frequently at a personal level when we try to influence our families and friends. We can conclude that attitude change is both a global priority and a basic component of interpersonal relationships.

At the same time, attempts to change attitudes often fail. At a personal level, we may fail to persuade each other on some issue and may simply agree to disagree. Opinions on controversial issues such as marijuana decriminalization, gay marriage, taxation and immigration policy may shift dramatically or remain consistent over time. Similarly, lavishly financed advertising campaigns may often fail; one such failure with regard to a new formula for Coca-Cola is remembered as a major marketing fiasco. And while money is vital to contemporary political campaigns, it is not always the candidate with the most money who wins the day,

Our study of attitude change is organized around two basic principles: cognitive consistency and external influence. In effect, we will look at how attitudes change 'from the inside out' and 'from the outside in'. The cognitive consistency principle explains why you might become more committed to your position after you vote than you were beforehand. The study of external influences on attitudes is the study of persuasion and we will examine two very different approaches to this problem.

FROM THE INSIDE OUT: COGNITIVE CONSISTENCY AND ATTITUDE CHANGE

Imagine that you see yourself as a creative, independent thinker. You are using a model of computer which is widely popular at that time. Then a supremely gifted salesperson tells you that most creative, independent thinkers use a different computer, his brand. How would you feel about the computer that you are now using? You may well have feelings of discomfort because we all need to feel that we are consistent in what we believe and how we are acting. And when we feel inconsistent, we are impelled to look for change, to restore consistency. The theory of cognitive dissonance is based on this need to feel consistent.

How can this be understood? Originally conceived by Leon Festinger in 1957 and subsequently modified and expanded (Brehm & Cohen, 1962; Aronson & Carlsmith, 1968; Wicklund & Brehm, 1976), the theory of cognitive dissonance is disarmingly simple, yet provocative, and has led to a number of interesting and unexpected predictions. It may well have been the most influential theory ever devised in social psychology, and its influence continues to be felt over a half century later. We will outline the basics of the theory and review some of the inventive research it has generated. Then we shall consider some criticisms of the original theory and some later developments that reflect how dissonance theory has evolved.

It is important to understand what was happening in psychology at the time that this theory emerged. Learning theory was paramount, captured by the image of the rat maze and the Skinner box. While there were differences, learning theorists such as Skinner, Tolman and Hull agreed about the importance of reward and reinforcement in driving behaviour. The larger the reward, the larger will be the behaviour change: it made sense. Then Festinger and his group of graduate students turned psychology on its ear, by showing that smaller rewards can drive greater change in attitude and behaviour. Moreover, the more people suffer to obtain something, the more they like what they suffered to obtain (Cooper, 2011). Above all, while the previous chapter discussed the premise that attitudes cause behaviour, cognitive dissonance theory showed that change in behaviour caused attitude change. We will see how these unexpected findings set social psychology on a new tack.

Basic principles

The theory of cognitive dissonance explains how cognitive elements – ideas, beliefs, preferences regarding behaviour – stand in relation to each other. If two elements are judged to be consistent (Festinger referred to this as being 'consonant'), you feel quite comfortable. So, if you believe that smoking is harmful to your health, and you have quit smoking, you enjoy a comfortable state. Dissonance exists when one cognitive element is opposed to another cognitive element in some way. For example, if you believe that smoking is injurious to your health, and you still smoke, this results in cognitive dissonance.

Cognitive dissonance is a state of psychological tension – the uncomfortable feeling people get when they become aware of inconsistencies in their thoughts and actions. Since cognitive dissonance is unpleasant, the person will try to reduce the dissonance. Of course, not just any inconsistency will cause cognitive dissonance. We all live comfortably with inconsistencies in our lives. You may eat mashed potatoes if they are served, even though you don't like mashed potatoes, and yet not feel any discomfort at all. Other inconsistencies can, however, cause dissonance and make us very uncomfortable. When inconsistency becomes uncomfortable is an important question that we will address later.

Two factors determine the overall level of discomfort or cognitive dissonance. The first is the ratio of dissonant cognitions to consonant cognitions. Thus, you may not experience dissonance about not owning the computer deemed to be the choice of independent thinkers if your present computer is reliable, a best-seller and inexpensive. The second factor in determining dissonance is the relative importance of the various elements to the person involved. While the current computer may be practical and economical – the importance of your self-image may outweigh the consonant elements.

Reducing dissonance

What will a person do to reduce dissonance when it is aroused? Consider a person who drives after consuming six alcoholic beverages. Driving in this intoxicated state is dangerous and illegal, and the person knows this well. A number of solutions are possible:

- Modify one of the cognitions to restore a sense of consistency. For instance, the person may decide that he or she is such a skilled driver that driving now would not be dangerous.
- Change the perceived importance of a cognition. For example, the driver may decide that the danger is not an important consideration because home is only a few kilometres away.
- Rationalize that the two cognitions are not really relevant to each other. Thus, the driver may simply deny that driving while somewhat intoxicated is all that dangerous; 'I've done it dozens of times'.
- Bolster the case for driving after having had a few drinks by adding new, consonant cognitions: 'people who drive while texting are more dangerous'.

Dissonance in action

Now let us turn to the situations where we are most likely to experience cognitive dissonance. Research in cognitive dissonance has concentrated on four areas: the discomfort often experienced after a difficult decision; the effects of exposure to new, dissonant information; seeking support from others; and the dissonance experienced after we act in ways contrary to our beliefs.

Post-decision dissonance Imagine that you are about to purchase a new car and must choose between two of equal value. Before the decision, you may experience a state of conflict that produces discomfort. While the conflict is resolved by making a choice, you may still feel twinges of regret about not having chosen the other car. This twinge is called post-decision dissonance. To reduce this discomfort, the chosen car becomes more attractive and the other automobile becomes less attractive to you than before you made the decision. The magnitude of post-decision dissonance will depend on the following:

1. The importance of the decision – for example, choosing a brand of laundry detergent would not be as important to most people as choosing an automobile;
2. The extent to which the choices were equally desirable – for example, if you are a great admirer of both cars, a choice between two desirable cars would arouse more dissonance than a choice between one of them and a less-desired car;
3. The extent to which you perceive that you made your choice freely rather than being compelled to make a particular decision (Linder, Cooper & Jones, 1967); and
4. Commitment to the decision (Kiesler, 1968). Note that immediately after the decision, you may first react with regret (Walster, 1964). However, you will then reduce the post-decision dissonance by over-valuing your choice.

Laboratory experiments have usually supported predictions of post-decision dissonance (Festinger, 1964). Furthermore, the phenomenon has been demonstrated outside the laboratory. For example, at a racetrack in Vancouver, Canada, bettors were asked to estimate the chance of their horse winning (Knox & Inkster, 1968). Some of these bettors were interviewed just before they placed their bets, others immediately after they had placed their bets. Those in the second group showed significantly higher confidence that their horse would win the race. According to cognitive dissonance theory, the act of placing the bet seemed to create post-decision dissonance (Figure 5.2), which the bettors then reduced by increasing their confidence in their choice. These results were replicated in a similar study of wagering in a game of chance (Younger, Walker & Arrowood, 1977).

The effect of post-decision dissonance extends beyond automobile dealers and gambling. In a study of voters in Canadian elections, those who had just cast their ballots were more inclined to think their candidate was the best than were voters just entering the polling station (Frenkel & Doob, 1976). Extensive public opinion polling before and after six presidential elections in the United States showed that voters who supported the winning candidate tended to express greater support for their candidate after the election than before. On the other hand, those who supported the losing candidate tended to express less support for that candidate and more for the winner (Beasley & Joslyn, 2001).

Figure 5.2 Will this shopper experience post-decision dissonance?

Source: vita khorzhevska/Shutterstock.com

The same phenomenon has been reported in making life-altering decisions to marry and to have children. People reminded of their wedding vows tend to be less open to the possibility of divorce (Stalder, 2012). Evidently having been reminded of their vows aroused post-decision dissonance regarding their decision to marry and caused them to value their marriage commitment more highly in order to reduce dissonance. Post-decision dissonance may also pertain to the challenges of parenting, and the costs of raising children. Research indicates that when these costs are made salient to parents, they tend to reduce dissonance by idealizing parenthood. They report having derived greater enjoyment from their children and express an intention to spend more time with them (Eibach & Mock, 2011).

Post-decision dissonance may occur in courts of law. Of course, juries must make decisions, and often do so based on a 'dominant hypothesis' that they develop about the case during the course of the trial. When later evidence appears that seems to contradict their 'hypothesis', dissonance may be aroused. In a set of experiments involving mock juries, dissonance was indeed aroused when the testimony by a witness contradicted their hypothesis about the case, although not when incontrovertible DNA evidence was presented (Ask, Reinhard, Marksteiner & Granhag, 2010).

Does post-decision dissonance occur in other cultures? One important factor appears to be for whom you are making the decision; are you deciding for yourself or deciding for a family member or friend? In a set of experiments, European-Canadian and Japanese-Canadian participants were asked to select their favourite dishes from an extensive list of a restaurant menu, all for a free lunch (Hoshino-Browne, Zanna, et al., 2005). Now, here's the innovation: half of each ethnic group of participants were asked to choose for themselves, while the other half of participants were asked to imagine a close friend, and to choose on behalf of that friend. For the Euro-Canadians, post-decision dissonance occurred when they selected for themselves (overvaluing what they just chose). However, when selecting menu items for a friend, it was the Japanese-Canadian participants who showed evidence of post-decision dissonance by devaluing the low-ranked dishes. Clearly, in more collective or communitarian cultures, people are expected to decide on the basis of the welfare of their own group members, and so making a difficult choice for someone else is a psychologically significant task.

So far, we have discussed post-decision dissonance that occurs after making a choice between attractive alternatives. But what if we have to choose between two undesirable alternatives, the lesser of two evils? Some research indicates that when we choose between undesirable alternatives, the decision leads to an increase in positive evaluation of the alternative that we chose (Schultz, Léveillé & Lepper, 1999).

Selective exposure to information It has long been hypothesized that people seek out and remember messages that are 'congenial' with their existing attitudes (Eagly, 1996). After purchasing a new car, you may read only those ads extolling the virtues of that car and avoid ads that depict other cars you had considered and rejected. Dissonance theory predicts that people will seek out information that decreases dissonance and avoid information that increases it (e.g., Ehrlich, Guttman, et al., 1957). However, the selective exposure effect appears to be unreliable (Eagly, 1996). Some research suggests that people may well seek out consonant information rather than simply avoiding dissonant information (Frey, 1986). In a revised statement of cognitive dissonance theory, Festinger (1964) argued that dissonant information is not always avoided and may even be preferred in some circumstances. When we expect that dissonant information can be easily refuted, we may actually seek out such a message in order to bolster our confidence and reduce dissonance.

Outside the laboratory, researchers have studied how people respond to new information that disconfirms previously held beliefs (Silverman, 1971; MacDonald & Majunder, 1973; Bishop, 1975). These studies concerned changes in attitudes towards US political figures after the resignation of President Richard Nixon over the Watergate scandal, 1972–1974. In general, dissonance theory was supported in the studies, although some individuals appeared to tolerate more inconsistency than others in the context of public affairs issues.

One interesting situation concerns information regarding events over which we have no control such as the outcome of an election. If we expect that a candidate other than the one we support is likely to win, we will not experience distress at that outcome. This is particularly the case when we feel a strong sense of personal involvement (Kay, Jimenez & Jost, 2002). Now consider the effects of political pundits and polls during election campaigns. If our preferred candidate appears to be losing favour, dissonance theory suggests that we may even change our vote because the likely winner has become more attractive.

Seeking social support As discussed in the previous chapter, our attitudes are more likely to lead to action if we also perceive that others would support the action (recall the Theory of Reasoned Action in Chapter 4). Festinger also argued that dissonance may be aroused by others voicing disagreement with us, especially if the topic is important and the opponents are credible. The two cognitions are dissonant: 'I am right' vs 'They say I'm wrong'. People may join a compatible group to obtain support for their beliefs. Festinger, Riecken & Schachter (1956) studied the role of social support by joining a doomsday cult (you may recall this study described in Chapter 1). The members of this cult believed they would escape a worldwide flood by being taken on a spaceship to a distant planet. Eventually, after several false alarms when the spaceship did not show up as predicted by their leader, the members realized that neither the flood nor their rescuers were coming: prophecy had indeed failed. One would expect that this hitherto secretive group would quietly disband and that members would go about their own lives. Indeed, this is often what happens (Hardyck & Braden, 1962; Thompson & Oskamp, 1974). In this case, however, instead of giving up their beliefs, some of the members began to proselytize actively, recruiting others to their cause. It felt more comfortable to claim that the flood was being cancelled because of their virtues and good deeds, thereby avoiding the conclusion that they had been foolish in their actions. Dissonance was thereby resolved.

Counter-attitudinal behaviour and insufficient justification
Perhaps the most important application of cognitive dissonance theory has been to the relationship between attitude and behaviour. We would suppose that people act on their attitudes – their attitudes come first and their behaviours follow as a consequence. Now, consider the proposition that people may act first and then change their attitudes to be consistent with what they just did. This counter-intuitive suggestion, that we may act first and then change an attitude, has generated some interesting and inventive research. Consider the basic

principle, derived from cognitive dissonance theory: *if we do something contrary to our attitude, and we lack sufficient justification for that action, then we may change our attitude to be consonant with our action.* The absence of *sufficient justification for a counter-attitudinal action* is key to the process of attitude change.

In a pioneering experiment (Festinger & Carlsmith, 1959), participants were brought individually to a laboratory and seated in front of a board containing a large number of pegs in holes. Their task was to turn each peg a one-quarter turn in sequence and to continue turning for 20 minutes, a tedious task indeed. At the end of the 'experimental session', the experimenter informed the participants that the experiment was designed to test the effect of prior instructions on motivation, and that because they were in the control group, they had not been given such instruction. The experimenter then stated that the next participant was waiting and was to be told that the task was interesting and enjoyable, but the assistant who was supposed to pass on this information had not yet shown up. Each individual then was asked to take the assistant's place. Half of the participants were offered $1 for their help; the other half were offered $20 – a substantial sum in 1958 dollars (more than US$150 today). The majority of the participants agreed to help, whether they were offered $1 or $20.

The participants then proceeded to tell the waiting 'subject' (actually a confederate of the experimenter) that the task, which they knew to be boring, was quite interesting and enjoyable. Then during a post-experimental interview, participants were asked as part of the debriefing to rate how boring or interesting they had found the experimental task. The question was: 'Would a counter-attitudinal behaviour (lying to the confederate) lead to an attitude change that represented a more positive evaluation of the task?'

Attitude change did occur, but it depended on the magnitude of the incentive to lie. It is important to understand that two important theories predict opposite results. Learning theory based on the notion of reinforcement would predict that the greater the reward, the more positive people would feel about the experience, even for a boring task. On the other hand, dissonance theory predicted that those paid only $1 to lie about the task would show greater attitude change because they would have insufficient external justification (only $1) for their action. They would reduce this discomfort by deciding that the task was 'sort of interesting' and that they had not, in fact, lied. Participants paid $20 could justify their actions by this payment, in the belief that anyone would do this for that amount of money, whereas few people would feel comfortable 'selling out' for one paltry US dollar.

The results supported dissonance theory (Table 5.1). Participants bribed with only one dollar rated the task as more enjoyable and of greater scientific importance, and expressed greater willingness to participate in another similar experiment than did those in the $20 group. That is, attitude change was greater among those paid $1 than for those paid $20. This experiment generated much debate and was followed by a series of other experiments in which the amount of the incentive was varied. In general the principle has been strongly supported: when attitude-discrepant behaviour is not accompanied by circumstances that justify that behaviour to the individual, he or she tends to experience cognitive dissonance and may then experience a change in attitude to be consistent with the action taken. Other experiments varied a threat of punishment and found similar results; when the threat of punishment was mild and thus insufficient to justify the behaviour, attitudes changed (Aronson & Carlsmith, 1963; Freedman, 1965; Lepper, Zanna & Abelson, 1970; Wan & Chiou, 2010).

In short, behaviour that is contrary to attitudes may arouse cognitive dissonance and lead to subsequent attitude change. This is particularly likely if the person is offered a small reward or threatened with a mild

Table 5.1 Average ratings on interview questions for each condition

Question on Interview	Experimental Condition		
	Control	One dollar	Twenty dollars
How enjoyable (–5 to +5)	–.45	+1.35	–.05
How much they learned (0 to 10)	3.08	2.80	3.15
Scientific importance (0 to 10)	5.60	6.45	5.18
Would you participate again? (–5 to +5)	–.62	1.20	–.25

Source: Festinger & Carlsmith (1959)

punishment and is therefore unable to justify the act in terms of expected reward or punishment. For dissonance to occur, the individual must believe that the act was freely chosen and that a public commitment has been expressed by the action. Careful analysis and research has led to an understanding of the conditions in which cognitive dissonance occurs.

[
KEY POINT: The theory of cognitive dissonance posits a state of psychological discomfort when there is inconsistency, leading to change in attitudes. Dissonance has been studied in the aftermath of a difficult decision between alternatives, selective exposure to information, seeking social support for one's attitudes, and induced attitude-discrepant behaviour. In the case of attitude-discrepant behaviour, dissonance is aroused when the act was freely chosen and the incentive is felt as insufficient to justify the behaviour.
]

THE EVOLUTION OF COGNITIVE DISSONANCE THEORY

Cognitive dissonance theory was perhaps unique in the history of social psychology in stimulating both so much research and so much controversy. Although the basic research was done over a half-century ago, it still resonates today. We have come to realize that we can change people's 'heart and minds' by first changing their behaviours. The following discussion highlights some of the issues raised in the decades that followed Festinger's (1957) original publication of the theory. They concern questions of what cognitive dissonance really is, and when it occurs.

Is dissonance reduction a matter of self-justification?

It has been argued that inconsistency is uncomfortable and motivating only when it threatens our own sense of self-worth (Greenwald & Ronis, 1978; Steele & Liu, 1983). Indeed Aronson (1984) and Thibodeau and Aronson (1992), early pioneers in dissonance research, argue that the effects of cognitive dissonance really amount to self-justification. Making people aware of their own inconsistencies is a powerful means of arousing dissonance (McGregor, Newby-Clark & Zanna, 1999). In short, they feel foolish or guilty about what they have done.

Feeling guilty or stupid is evident in several experiments, where participants were required to give a speech contradicting their own attitudes. When someone has written an essay opposed to providing services to disabled students at the university, and is then given feedback that cues his or her self-image as a compassionate person, this will likely lead to attitude change. However, if the feedback is about the person's own creativity, which is irrelevant to the essay, the individual is less likely to experience dissonance, and attitude change is unlikely (Stone, 2003). The cognitive dissonance effect was evident when participants believed that they were addressing an impressionable audience of children who might be persuaded to use drugs (Nel, Helmreich & Aronson, 1969); when participants were led to believe that they had actually persuaded someone that a boring task was interesting, but not if the person seemed unconvinced (Cooper & Worchel, 1970); and when participants were induced to lie to someone they liked, but not when they lied to someone they disliked (Cooper, Zanna & Goethals, 1974).

Recall the doomsday cult: If dissonance had been aroused in even one member of the group when prophecy failed, then others in that close-knit group might also have experienced the same dissonance-based discomfort vicariously through identifying with that fellow member (Cooper & Hogg, 2007). Results of a study (Norton et al., 2003) showed that observing a fellow in-group member behave in a counter-attitudinal manner caused the participant to change his or her attitude in the direction advocated by the speaker. In the absence of this strong in-group affinity, observing the counter-attitudinal behaviour did not result in attitude change.

Is cognitive dissonance about hypocrisy? A dean of admissions at a highly prestigious university in the United States was known for her harsh policies in rejecting applicants who were not entirely truthful or accurate on their résumés. As it later was revealed, she had embellished her own résumé to the point of claiming degrees that she had not obtained. This became known as the 'pot calling the kettle black' phenomenon (Barkan, Ayal, Gino & Ariely, 2012). It is argued that she resolved her own dissonance about a serious professional misconduct by judging the behaviour of others more harshly. She thereby could see herself as upholding the moral integrity of the institution by punishing others.

Most of us are guilty at some time of espousing a certain attitude and then not acting on what we have said. We tell others that wearing a seat belt can be life saving and then we neglect to buckle up on a short trip. We say that we need to exercise and then find excuses to avoid it. We may even tell someone that we like them and then act in a way that betrays our real feelings. When we are aware that our actions are not consistent with our professed attitudes, we may experience feelings that we identify as hypocrisy. Of course, this is a form of cognitive dissonance (Kenworthy, Miller, Collins, Rea & Earleywine, 2011).

Problems of the environment offer fertile ground for the experience of hypocrisy. We all know that conservation, recycling, and not littering are beneficial to all of us and we say so, but our actions may often fail to live up to our stated beliefs. We may need a direct prod to recognize the inconsistency. In experiments, participants were induced to state an attitude in favour of water conservation (Dickerson, Thibodeau, Aronson & Miller, 1992) or recycling (Fried & Aronson, 1995) and were then made aware of their wasteful behaviour or their failure to recycle. When both conditions were met (awareness of their stated attitude and their behaviour), their subsequent behaviour changed in environmentally beneficial ways. In other words, when dissonance is aroused in a manner to make us feel like hypocrites and we have an opportunity to correct our actions, we tend to do so.

However, we may find another way out. In an experiment conducted by Stone, Aronson et al. (1994) in the ostensible context of an AIDS prevention research programme, participants were made to feel hypocritical about their condom use. They were asked to prepare a video in which they advocated the use of condoms to prevent transmission of sexually transmitted diseases and then they were then asked to think about times in the past when they had not used condoms, and their reasons for not having done so. Then they were asked to think about reasons why men in general sometimes fail to use condoms (normative reasons). It was predicted that arousal of feelings of hypocrisy would be greatest after thinking of personal reasons. Then they were given a choice of purchasing condoms at a reduced price (direct dissonance reduction) or making a donation to a charitable agency (indirect reduction). The results were clear: when they were asked to focus on personal reasons for failing to engage in safe sex, most participants purchased the condoms, while when they focused on people in general, they chose the indirect method of making a donation. That altruistic donation enabled them to feel better about themselves without having to face their own condom issue.

Finally, consider the instance of what Batson, Kobrynowics et al. (1997) refer to as moral hypocrisy, when we are motivated to appear to be doing the right thing and at the same time act in our own self-interest. For instance in a set of experiments, participants were given a choice between two tasks, one of which was presented as both interesting and with possible financial gain, and the other as dull and boring with no rewards. Participants were told that they were to decide between themselves and another person who would do which task. Most participants acted in pure self-interest, choosing the attractive alternative for themselves. What is interesting is that, even where participants were told that there was a fair way to decide, such as by flipping a coin, only about half agreed to toss the coin.

Thus, we are particularly prone to cognitive dissonance when it's about ourselves. However, this misses the question of whether it's just a matter of protecting our self-esteem. Do we actually experience a state of uncomfortable arousal?

Is cognitive dissonance a state of arousal?

Is cognitive dissonance an unpleasant state of arousal, which a person is motivated to reduce or relieve in some way (Kiesler & Pallak, 1976)? Indeed, negative feelings from attitude-discrepant behaviour are aroused in some people even where there are no personal consequences to the individual (Harmon-Jones, 2000; Williams & Aaker, 2002). However, being inconsistent in our attitudes and actions is not always a problem to all people in all such situations. Consider that if we rationalized each decision and action solely to reduce cognitive dissonance, we would find it difficult to learn from our mistakes (Schultz & Lepper, 1996). A questionnaire measure has been developed to tap individual differences in a preference for consistency (Guadagno & Cialdini, 2010). Interestingly, when dissonance is aroused, it helps people perform a task better when the task is relatively simple, but when it is more complex, such as one involving remembering material one has read, dissonance arousal seems to interfere with task performance (Martinie, Olive & Milland, 2010). Recall the discussion of social facilitation: arousal improves simple tasks and hinders difficult ones. Thus, this certainly supports the notion that cognitive dissonance involves physiological arousal.

However, if there is arousal, then it can be measured physiologically. Gerard (1967) created different magnitudes of dissonance by offering to give some participants a painting chosen from two that they had ranked third and fourth choices in a group of 12 paintings, and other participants a choice between a highly desired (third choice) and less desired (eighth choice) painting. Presumably the former participants, facing a more difficult choice, would experience more post-decision dissonance than the latter participants. Arousal was assessed by means of an instrument that measures blood volume in the finger tips. Constriction of the blood vessels in the fingers is associated with arousal, and it was found that after they made their decision, the blood volume of participants in the higher dissonance condition was reduced significantly more than that of participants in the low dissonce condition. This is consistent with the view that dissonance produces physiological arousal.

Another approach to investigating the biological processes underlying dissonance involves fMRI studies of blood flow in different brain areas. It is known, for example, that the dorsal anterior cingulate cortex is activated when a person is detecting conflict of some kind. Indeed, this area was activated when a person argued that being ensconced in an uncomfortable fMRI machine is a pleasant experience, something that contrasted with the experience itself and thus would be expected to produce cognitive dissonance (van Veen, Krug, Schooler & Carter, 2009). Indeed, this led to brain activation in that region, and, even more interesting, the extent of such activity proved to be a good predictor of subsequent attitude change.

While we can be reasonably confident that arousal does occur under dissonant conditions, is arousal *necessary* for attitude change to take place? If it is the arousal associated with dissonance that leads to attitude change, then by reducing arousal by other means, attitude change should be reduced or eliminated as well. In one study (Steele, Southwick & Critchlow, 1981), participants were asked to write a counter-attitudinal essay, producing dissonance, presumably. Afterwards, some participants were induced to drink alcohol, which reduces arousal, under the guise of rating the taste of various beverages. When tested later, those who drank alcohol showed less attitude change.

What happens if an individual does not attribute the arousal to the cognitive dissonance? Several studies address this question in ingenious ways (Cooper, Zanna & Taves, 1978; Wright, et al., 1992; McGregor, Newby-Clark & Zanna, 1999). In some of the experiments, people were to behave in a counter-attitudinal manner but were not given a sufficient justification for their behaviour. While participants might then be expected to feel discomfort and therefore arousal after doing something contrary to their attitudes, some of them were provided with another basis for attributing the arousal that they might feel. Some were, with their knowledge, given a stimulant drug that produces arousal and others were told that the new lighting arrangements in the room might make them feel nervous and edgy. Participants in these conditions did not show the same attitude change as did those who had no other explanation for their discomfort, which again supports the notion that arousal attributed to cognitive dissonance drives attitude change.

So what is cognitive dissonance?

Festinger (1957) described cognitive dissonance as the result of a logical inconsistency in our thinking: we hold two cognitions, A and B, but B is inconsistent with A. For example, he suggested that if a person were to observe someone standing in the rain and not getting wet, these two cognitions would be dissonant. However, subsequent research indicates that this is not an example in which a person would actually experience cognitive dissonance. People might be amused, amazed, curious or concerned about their own sanity, but would not experience the psychological discomfort that leads to attitude change. Inconsistency is a normal part of life and much of the time does not bother us (Bem, 1970). It is important to distinguish between conflicting beliefs (e.g., taxes are good for the country but not for me, personally) and an emotional discomfort about this conflict (Newby-Clark, McGregor & Zanna, 2002). It is the latter that constitutes cognitive dissonance.

Is the need to be consistent peculiar to Western individualistic cultures? People in Eastern cultures with a more interdependent notion of the self also react to dissonance arousal, but in different situations: those involving behaviours discrepant with their relationships rather than with self-affirmation (Hoshino-Browne, 2012; Steele & Liu, 1983). Indeed, in a choice situation, Japanese participants justified their choice (dissonance reduction) when first primed by the notion that their choice was public, while those from the United States showed dissonance more when the choice was private, thus pertaining to their own self-image (Imada & Kitayama, 2010). In cultures described as interdependent, dissonance will be aroused when the identity of the group is threatened, when people are impelled to think, 'this is who we are' (Hoshino, 2012). It appears that the experience of cognitive dissonance is universal but when and where it is experienced will vary with the cultural context of the people involved.

A REVISED MODEL OF COGNITIVE DISSONANCE

We have seen from the above discussion that cognitive dissonance involves a state of physiological arousal, and that dissonance is aroused only in certain cases of inconsistency among personally relevant cognitions. Accordingly, Cooper and Fazio (1984) have outlined a revised model of cognitive dissonance (see Figure 5.3). They reason that when we act contrary to our beliefs, we take note of the consequences of our actions. Only if our act is perceived to have actual or potential negative consequences do we search for an explanation. If

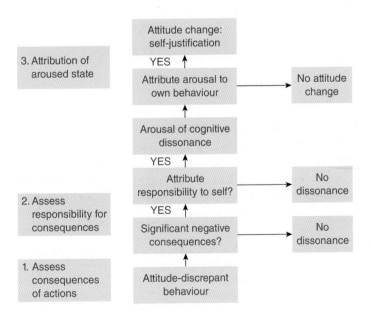

Figure 5.3 Cooper & Fazio's revised model of cognitive dissonance

it is clear that we had a free choice to act and that the consequences could have been foreseen, we attribute responsibility to ourselves. At this point, dissonance is aroused and we experience psychological discomfort. If we attribute this feeling of discomfort to our reaction to how we acted rather than to an external source (e.g., a drug or the situation itself), then we are motivated to reduce dissonance.

Thus, four steps are necessary for cognitive dissonance effects to occur:

1. The attitude-discrepant behaviour must produce significant negative consequences. If our actions somehow produce positive results, we may enjoy it but not feel uncomfortable.
2. We must feel personally responsible for these consequences; that is, we must believe that the choice was made freely and the consequences were foreseeable.
3. We then experience a state of arousal, a feeling of tension, discomfort, something that we want to reduce.
4. We attribute this arousal or discomfort to our own behaviour. In other words, it is not sufficient to feel a sense of arousal, but we must make the connection between the behaviour and that arousal.

Note the exits from cognitive dissonance along the way (Figure 5.3). We may decide that no harm was done by our actions. We may decide that we really had no choice but to lie, the money was too good or the boss ordered us to do it. If we do experience arousal, we may ignore or minimize it, attribute it to the weather, indigestion or nervousness in a psychology experiment. In short, the cognitive dissonance process involves both dissonance arousal and motivation to reduce dissonance, and both processes involve complex sets of attributions.

Of course, it is important to understand that this is not generally a conscious deliberative process but more along the lines of heuristic-driven 'fast thinking' regarding inconsistency. Zentall (2010) reports on experiments in which pigeons were induced to show greater preference for a food if they had exerted greater effort to get it by pecking, analogous in the bird world to the insufficient justification effect. Given that pigeons are unlikely to engage in serious conscious deliberation, the experience of cognitive dissonance may simply amount to the application of a 'fast thinking' heuristic.

The Cooper and Fazio model is useful in that it can predict when the insufficient justification effect will occur. Several studies demonstrate, for example, that when people feel personally responsible for the undesirable consequences of their behaviour, then dissonance is aroused and leads to subsequent changes in their attitudes, even when they have not acted in ways discrepant with their attitudes (Scher & Cooper, 1989; Johnson, Kelly & LeBlanc, 1995). On the other hand, dissonance has also been demonstrated in the absence of aversive consequences (Harmon-Jones et. al., 1996).

SUMMING UP

In the previous chapter, we questioned whether attitudes cause behaviour. The answer, as we saw, was a resounding 'maybe' depending on a set of factors. In this chapter, we have looked at the obverse question: can behaviour cause attitudes? We have seen that the answer, again, is a resounding maybe … but that inducing people to act in a way contrary to their attitudes can well lead to subsequent change in those attitudes. This is the contribution of cognitive dissonance theory, one that is nonobvious and insightful.

KEY POINT: The core issue of cognitive dissonance theory concerns attitude-discrepant behaviour. The impact occurs when an attitude-discrepant act threatens one's sense of self-worth and leads to feeling guilty or stupid. Hypocrisy, when our actions are not in accord with our expressed attitudes, is viewed as a special case of cognitive dissonance. Cognitive dissonance has been shown to involve a state of physiological arousal. The Cooper and Fazio revised model of cognitive dissonance limits a state of dissonance to attitude-discrepant behaviour with significant consequences for which the actor feels personally responsible, leading to a state of arousal and then to some change in order to reduce arousal.

ATTITUDE CHANGE FROM THE OUTSIDE IN:PERSUASION AND ATTITUDE CHANGE

The previous discussion centred on how inducing people to act can lead to subsequent attitude change, we now turn to direct attempts to change attitudes. Persuasion involves a deliberate attempt by someone to change another person's attitude. In the following sections, the topic is discussed in terms of two basic questions. The first question, which drove the earlier research, is what determines whether a person or people in general will be persuaded by a message. As we will see, this approach generated much research and some important insights. However, it was limited to the structure of the situation and did not go into the actual process by which persuasion can occur. This was the objective of the second approach to persuasion, one which is based on the fast thinking/slow thinking framework of cognition as presented in Chapter 2.

BOX 5.1   PERSUASION OR PROPAGANDA?

In 1622, the Vatican established the *Sacra Congregatio de propaganda fide*, translated as the 'sacred congregation for propagating the faith of the Church'. As this involved changing attitudes and behaviours, the word **propaganda** soon carried the notion of an intent to convince people of something by whatever means necessary (Jowett & O'Donnell, 1992). Propaganda may be designed to agitate, to incite rebellion or discontent, or to promote acceptance and support for an existing government or institution (Ellul, 2006).

Consider three historical examples of propagandists: Joseph Goebbels, Minister of Propaganda for Germany during the Nazi regime (Figure 5.4), George Lincoln Rockwell (US Nazi, assassinated in 1967) and Meir Kahane (US/Israeli, subsequently assassinated, who founded the Kach movement, later outlawed in Israel, which advocated expulsion of all Arabs from Israel). Finlay (2007) notes several features in common in their rhetoric. First was an effort to foster in-group consciousness, subordinating the individual to the group. The in-group or nation was portrayed as the victim, in which the threats by the chosen enemy justified any responses (Renz, 2010). Members of one's own group who do not buy into its worldview are portrayed as self-hating people who lack pride in their own identity. In analyses of Goebbel's diaries, some other principles of propaganda are evident (Doob, 1950). It is stated that the agency of propaganda, usually a government, must speak with one voice (Chomsky & Herman, 1988), and that all decisions must be considered for their propaganda implications. Note that the framing of an issue carries implications for propaganda; for instance, consider the use of the word 'terrorism' to describe killings by opposition groups, but not by groups or governments in one's favour (Silverstein, 1987).

Figure 5.4 Anti-Goebbels propaganda poster 1939–1945

Source: © Swim Ink 2, LLC/Corbis

Of course, one can substitute the word 'persuasion' for the word 'propaganda': are they equivalent? In an influential book on the topic (Pratkanis & Aronson, 1991), the authors suggest that propaganda is a type of persuasion, in which important information is withheld, facts are presented selectively and strategies are invoked to elicit 'rapid thinking' (Kahneman, 2011).

Does propaganda exist in a more subtle form in democratic societies?
Consider the following:

- Some present day cults indoctrinate their members under conditions of social, and even sensory, isolation, group pressure, endless repetition of the message and other elements of Goebbels' formula. Somewhat similar techniques are used to initiate recruits into some religious orders and elite military units (Pfeifer, 1992).
- Education is often concerned with shaping the attitudes and behaviours of students to fit into society. For instance, the teaching of history focuses on the accomplishments of the home country, including the prevalent economic system.
- Democratic governments and other institutions using public relations invariably seek to control their message, when and how information is revealed and interpreted. The term 'spin' conveys the notion that the interpretation of an event or issue is controlled by manipulation, often deception.
- A study of ubiquitous TV crime shows reveals a consistent pattern: the police solve the crime and the correct culprit is identified, arrested and convicted. Do these programmes represent wishful-thinking propaganda on behalf of the criminal justice system (Haney & Manzolatti, 1981)?
- Advertising has successfully created a need that did not exist. For instance, throughout most of human history and most cultures, while cosmetics existed in various forms, the vast array of cosmetic products now available did not exist. Potential consumers were sold on the notion that they needed these products. Can advertising be considered as propaganda?
- Propaganda material is also readily available on the Internet, including social media, and can be quite effective. In experiments, student participants in the USA were given excerpts from either a Holocaust denial document, a factual document about the Auschwitz death camp, or an unrelated document (Yelland & Stone, 1996). Those exposed to the Holocaust denial document scored lower on a measure of belief that the Holocaust actually happened.

KEY POINT: Persuasion is a deliberate attempt to change the attitude of someone else. Propaganda is a special case of persuasion, involving attempts to change or maintain acceptance of attitudes by the selective presentation of facts and deliberate withholding of important information, often promoting in-group consciousness and a sense of victimhood. While propaganda is characteristic of authoritarian regimes, it is also evident in the democratic context.

WHAT PREDICTS PERSUASION?

Who says what to whom, and how?

In his philosophical treatise, *On Rhetoric*, Aristotle argued that there are three modes of persuasion: *ethos*, an appeal to the authority or character of the speaker, *pathos*, an appeal to the emotions of the audience, and *logos*, an appeal based on the logic of the arguments themselves. The foundations for this direction in research on persuasive communication were established in the 1950s by researchers in the Yale University Communications Research Program (Hovland, Janis & Kelley, 1953). They examined the components of a persuasion situation, and boiled it down to the following four questions: Who presents the message? What is the content of the message? To whom is the message directed? And what is the channel – that is, by what means is the message sent and received, and how is it presented? By delineating the determinants of persuasion as variables relevant to the source of the message, the content of the message, the characteristics of the audience for that message, and the medium and context of the message, we can define specific variables of interest. This approach set the research agenda for decades.

The source of the message

In political campaigns, the credibility of political leaders is always an important factor. We generally consider the source of a message to be credible if we assume she is sincere and knows what she is talking about. Trustworthiness is especially enhanced if the audience believes the communicator has nothing personal to gain from his or her efforts. It is no accident that toothpaste is promoted by individuals in lab coats (an image of expertise) and that detergents are recommended by ordinary people who do the washing. In addition, if people perceive that the communicator is trying to impress others, credibility will be undermined (Saucier & Webster, 2010). Interestingly, credibility is effective only if the audience is aware of it before the message is presented, rather than after (Mills & Harvey, 1972). If we don't consider the communicator to be credible, we are unlikely to pay attention to the message.

In most cases, the expertise of the source must be compatible with the topic. A nuclear physicist is not especially persuasive when talking about sports or detergents. However, at times, high-status or attractive sources may be influential even outside their sphere of knowledge (Aronson & Golden, 1962; Roskos-Ewoldsen & Fazio, 1992a, 1992b). For instance, sports stars may be used in selling sports equipment, and also everything from beverages to rental cars. On the other hand, consider this: a beautiful woman could convincingly sell shampoo, but could she sell beer? Indeed, several studies show that source attractiveness affects persuasion even where the message has nothing to do with physical attractiveness, such as selling beer or automobiles (Praxmarer, 2011).

Figure 5.5 Which of these ads would be an effective ad for a vacation? Why?
Source: athikan/Shutterstock.com

Sleeper effect Consider the common occurrence in which we somehow recognize a name or face but can't remember where we met the person (Jacoby, Kelley, Brown & Jasechko, 1989). In one experiment, participants were read a list of names including 'Simon Weisdorf' and were informed that no one on the list people was famous. Afterwards, participants read a list of names, including 'Simon Weisdorf', some relatively famous people of that era (Roger Bannister, Minnie Pearl) and some who were not famous (Valerie Marsh, Adrian Marr) and were asked to rate the fame of each person on the list. Participants shown the second list immediately after the first did not rate Weisdorf as being famous, but those shown the list 24 hours later did. Further investigation revealed that the participants were, in fact, unable to recollect the source of that name.

The implications for persuasion are clear: the effect of the message may increase over time, often even when people cannot remember the source. This has been called the sleeper effect. In a pioneering experiment (Hovland, Lumsdaine & Sheffield, 1949), one group of soldiers viewed a US army propaganda film and another group did not. Attitudes towards the topic of the film were measured five days, and then nine weeks, later. Surprisingly, differences between the two groups were somewhat greater at nine weeks than at five days. The most popular explanation for this effect is the discounting cue hypothesis (recall Chapter 2), which states that the source of the film's message (i.e., the US army) was perceived as untrustworthy. This led the soldiers to discount the message initially, thus reducing its immediate effect. But as time elapsed, the connection between the source and the message was forgotten or weakened, while the message itself was remembered.

However, research has indicated that the sleeper effect is reliably produced only when the discounting cue is presented after the message. In an experiment (Pratkanis, Greenwald, Leippe & Baumgardner, 1988), participants were presented with a message arguing against a four-day work week and a discounting cue: a note from the editor stating that this conclusion was probably wrong. When participants were given the message only, the initial attitude change was significant, but it dissipated over the following six weeks. When the discounting cue was given before the message, little attitude change was obtained; the participants had been forewarned to expect a wrong conclusion. But when the discounting cue was given after the message, the immediate attitude change was low, but attitude change increased six weeks later.

Message factors

Of course, the content of a message can have obvious effects. Whether the message is highly discrepant from the audience's attitudes, whether humour is used, whether the message is relatively simple or very complicated, all can influence persuasion outcomes. We will consider the content of the message later in this chapter. Here we will examine a few other factors.

When trying to convince someone, should you recognize both sides of the argument or just present your one-sided case? Hovland, Harvey & Sherif (1957) conducted the initial studies on this topic. Among several findings was the discovery that, especially with intelligent audiences, it is best to present both the positive and negative sides of the argument and then to refute the negative evidence. However, when the audience has a firm position on an issue (e.g., a speech to delegates at a political convention, an admonition by a parent to a child), a two-sided presentation is usually not effective (Figure 5.6). Of course, if it seems likely that the audience will hear the other side from someone else, it is usually more effective for you to present both sides yourself (Karlins & Abelson, 1970).

With the increasing influence of the Internet, researchers are directing attention to this medium in advertising. A study compared the effects of sponsored content, in which the product is embedded in the message, and banner ads, in which an advertising message floats above or through the content of the website (Tutaj & van Reijmersdal, 2012). Participants found the sponsored content format to be less irritating and more informative, likely because they expressed more scepticism about the more intrusive banner ad.

What about negative political advertising, messages that attack the political record or personal characteristics of the opposing candidate? While the intent is obvious, the public may react with a 'backlash' against the source of the attack or with sympathy towards the victim of the attack. In a debate, insulting the other candidates or their families can result in negative reactions (Roese & Sande, 1993). In the Canadian federal election of 1993, two advertisements were aired by the Progressive Conservative Party that played up a distorted facial expression of Liberal leader, Jean Chrétien (Chrétien had contracted Bell's palsy as a child). In a quasi-experimental study of attitudes towards the five political party leaders of the time (Haddock & Zanna, 1997), the attitudes of some participants were assessed before, and some after, the airing of these advertisements (which were subsequently withdrawn). Those who were assessed after viewing the offensive ad showed significantly more negative feelings towards Conservative leader Kim Campbell and more positive feelings towards Jean Chrétien than those tested before seeing the advertisements.

One technique of advertising is to establish an association between the product and other desirable objects or ideas. For instance, ads for beer and for certain brands of cars may instil an association of the product with young, attractive people. A laundry detergent may be associated with fresh flowers, smiling babies, a sunny day. In two experiments, Dempsey & Mitchell (2010) told people about two fictitious brands of pens. The descriptions clearly indicated that one brand was superior to the other. But then participants in a seemingly unrelated experiment watched pictures flash by on a computer monitor. Some of these pictures portrayed the inferior pen with positive items. These participants then tended to choose the inferior pen, even when they were given as much time as they needed to make their choice and even when they were encouraged to choose the better one.

Figure 5.6 Do political debaters present one-sided messages?

Source: © Amy Sussman/Corbis

These results suggest that effective persuasion in advertising and elsewhere often is not based on making a rational argument but on making people feel good about their decision. It also suggests that advertising can influence us powerfully although we are not attending to the content. A theory to be discussed later (elaboration likelihood) will deal with this phenomenon.

Primacy – recency

If both sides of an argument are presented, which is likely to have the advantage, the side presented first (primacy) or the side presented last (recency)? Think of a political debate in which the candidates present their positions in turn: who has the advantage, the first or the last presenter? Most of the early experiments (e.g., Lund, 1925; Asch, 1946) indicated that the message presented first was more influential: the **primacy effect**. However, Hovland, Harvey & Sherif (1957) and others (Luchins, 1957; Anderson, 1959) showed that the passage of time is a critical factor. If one set of arguments immediately follows the other, the first set is likely to have the most impact (primacy). However, if a considerable period of time elapses between the presentation of the two arguments, recency becomes more influential (Miller & Campbell, 1959; Insko, 1964; Wilson & Miller, 1968).

Should messages arouse emotions or appeal to reason?

Recall in Chapter 4 that attitudes consist of both affective (emotional) and cognitive (belief) components. Some persuasive messages focus on changing the beliefs of the audience, while others attempt to change emotions in the listeners. Can persuasive messages have a selective effect on attitudes so that emotional messages change feelings but not beliefs, while cognitive messages have the opposite effect? Edwards (1990) studied this question by having some participants first taste a beverage (affective) and then read information about its ostensible health benefits (cognitive), while other participants first read the information and then did the tasting. She predicted that affective or cognitive changes would be influenced by the order of presentation, and that there would be a primary effect. That is what was found: when participants tasted first, their feelings about the beverage changed, but when the health benefits message preceded the tasting, their beliefs changed.

Figure 5.7 AIDS prevention poster, Philippines

Source: © Philippe Lissac /Godong/Corbis

Fabrigar and Petty (1999) conducted a pair of similar experiments, matching emotion or belief messages. In one, participants were told that they were in a marketing study and the first product was a new beverage. Some of them read the information about the product, while others tasted it. Then the cognitive and affective attitude components were measured. Affect was measured by having participants rate the extent to which 16 different emotions described how the beverage made them feel (e.g., happy, excited, tense, angry). Cognitions or beliefs were measured by having them indicate the extent to which 14 different characteristics described the beverage (e.g., useful, safe, harmful, worthless). Again as predicted, those who had tasted the beverage showed more positive attitudes on the affective measure, while those exposed to the informative message were more positive on the beliefs measure.

Do fear tactics work? Suppose you are in charge of public relations for a government department of highways and want to encourage citizens to obey mandatory seat-belt legislation. What would be your best advertising strategy? For instance, should television ads show the actual gory, fatal aftermath of automobile accidents? Or should statistics be presented about survival from automobile crashes?

The research on fear messages began with an experiment by Janis and Feshbach (1953), who were interested in finding out how various appeals affected people's dental habits. The researchers created three levels of fear arousal. The most extreme employed colour pictures of diseased mouths, gums and teeth and the least extreme used only X-rays and showed pictures of healthy mouths. They found that the most threatening appeal had the least effect and that the most change followed the mild appeal. The results seemed to show that the instigation of high fear leads to avoidance of the message and interferes with learning. It is also possible, since the high-fear condition was so unpleasant, that the association decreased the credibility of the source of the message and led to the message being discounted. In some studies (e.g., Higbee, 1969; McGuire, 1969; Leventhal, 1970), attitude change increased as fear increased. However, in general, it seems that low to moderate levels of fear will be positively related to attitude change, but high levels will make attitude change less likely (McGuire, 1968) (see Figure 5.7).

In general, people respond to fear messages, both to avert the danger mentioned in the message and to cope with the immediate unpleasant feelings engendered by the message (Sutton, 1982). Further, fear arousal must be accompanied by specific, credible recommendations on how to reduce the fear (Rogers, 1975). For instance, people may believe that driving too fast is dangerous and that accidents could happen to them personally, yet not believe that they can change their habits behind the wheel. Unless driving more slowly and cautiously seems plausible and desirable, people tend to respond defensively and change is unlikely (Janis & Feshbach, 1953). Since fear messages are so important in encouraging people to take care of themselves, they are used frequently in health promotion. This work is discussed further in Chapter 16.

The target: Audience factors

Are some people more easily persuaded than others? Much research has been devoted to the question of whether persuasibility is a general trait (Hovland et al., 1953; Janis & Hovland, 1959). The findings indicate that individual differences in persuasibility do exist, but that the effect is quite small relative to other variables such as source and message characteristics. For example, it would appear reasonable to assume that people with low self-esteem are more readily persuaded (recall Chapter 3). However, the research indicates that the effects of self-esteem on persuasibility depend on the message. Uncomplicated messages with poorly supported arguments are more likely to produce attitude change in people with low self-esteem than in people with high self-esteem. On the other hand, intricate, well-supported messages are more effective with people with high self-esteem than with people with low self-esteem (Nisbett & Gordon, 1967).

McGuire (1968) argues that it would inevitably be difficult to show a direct relationship between a personality trait of persuasibility and being persuaded, because the same characteristic can affect both the individual's attention to and comprehension of the message (reception) and the probability of actual attitude change in the direction of the message (yielding). For example, people with high self-esteem tend to be more receptive to a persuasive message (reception). At the same time, however, the likelihood of such individuals yielding to the persuasive arguments is lower. Indeed, low self-esteem people have difficulty receiving the message and so cannot be persuaded by it, high self-esteem people tend not to yield, but moderate self-esteem people are most readily persuaded because they can both receive and yield to the message (Rhodes & Wood, 1992).

Gender and attitude change For many years, it was assumed in social psychology that women were more susceptible to influence, were more easily persuaded and conformed more than men. The reasoning behind this assumption was that females in many societies had typically been socialized to be passive and yielding (Middlebrook, 1974). Subsequently, Eagly (1978) thoroughly reviewed the literature dealing with sex differences in persuasibility and concluded that there was little support for this contention, at least in US samples where most of the research was conducted. She noted, for example, that some of the reported differences between the sexes resulted from the researchers' use of experimental materials that were biased against the interests and abilities of women. They may be more likely to be persuaded by a message about power tools than about cooking, assuming that they know more about the latter than the former. She also suggests that women may indeed have a tendency to comply but that this compliance may indicate a concern for group harmony rather than genuine persuasibility.

Age may also be important in considering gender differences. One study examined reactions to image-oriented advertisements for tobacco and alcohol (e.g., personal attractiveness and lifestyle), as opposed to advertisements that focused on the qualities of the products. While female adolescents showed a stronger tendency to attend to image-oriented advertisements, the same gender difference was not obtained with adults (Covell, Dion & Dion, 1994).

The channel of communication

Does it make any difference whether a persuasive message is presented face-to-face via TV, through an email, on Twitter, radio or in a written document? The data on this question are not consistent (Williams, 1975; Worchel, Andreoli & Eason, 1975). Chaiken & Eagly (1976) suggest that these inconsistent findings might be explained by how comprehensible the message was. There is evidence that complex messages are better understood when written than when presented by video or audiotape (Eagly, 1974). An experiment that took several factors into account (Chaiken & Eagly, 1976) provided participants with two types of persuasive messages: those that were easy or difficult to understand, and those written or recorded in audio or video format. The difficult messages were more effective when written, while the easy messages were most effective on videotape and least effective in writing.

HOW THESE FACTORS COMBINE

Of course, in real life we cannot hold three of the four sets of variables constant while varying one of them. Source, message, audience and channel effects interact, and we must consider them together in various combinations. Several experiments illustrate this problem.

In one experiment (Wiegman, 1985), two interviews were taped with each of two Dutch politicians, both of them confederates of the experimenter, and representing the two main political parties. Neither party had taken a position on the issue of that time, whether an airport should be built in a particular location. In one interview, the politician advocated the proposal in a cool, sober, rational manner, while in the other, the same politician spoke in a strongly emotional, committed, dynamic manner. The four interviews were shown to different groups of delegates at meetings of the two parties. When attitudes were subsequently measured, the data indicated that a rational presentation resulted in a higher rating for the speaker but not in greater attitude change, while the more emotional presentation resulted in greater attitude change. Not surprisingly, attitude change was greater when the source and the audience belonged to the same political party. Thus we can see that source, message and target interact in complex ways.

Is the effect of the source of a persuasive message, or the message itself, influenced by the medium, be it TV, an Internet banner, radio or magazine? An experiment shows how the medium (channel) affects perception of the source and the message (Chaiken & Eagly, 1983). The likability of a speaker as perceived by students was varied by having the speaker praise or derogate the students and faculty and the general quality of their institution. Then they were presented with either a video, audio or written message from that speaker advocating change to a trimester system (that is, full courses to be completed in about 10-week terms). It was found that attitude change was greater when participants liked the speaker, but only when the speaker was seen or heard. Liking was not a factor in the written transcript condition.

A third study shows how a message can be tailored to the audience (Snyder & DeBono, 1985). Participants were first administered a scale of self-monitoring, which refers to the extent to which people gauge their behaviour in terms of how other people react. They were presented with advertisements using 'hard sell' or 'soft sell' techniques. 'Hard sell' methods stressed the quality, value and usefulness of the product while 'soft sell' techniques stressed the image of the product (colour, texture) or of the consumer who buys it (smart, affluent, sexy, discriminating). It was reasoned that since high self-monitors tend to adapt their behaviour to fit the social situation, they would be more concerned with how others perceive them and would thus be more sensitive to the 'soft sell' emphasis on images. On the other hand, since low self-monitors are guided more by inner feelings, dispositions and beliefs, they would be more receptive to messages about the product itself via the hard sell. In three studies, the data supported these hypotheses, showing these combinations of message and audience characteristics to be most effective in increasing the willingness of subjects to try the product and the amount they would be willing to pay for it.

A radically different approach is suggested by social neuroscience. It begins by addressing the question: what does it mean to 'feel persuaded'? Using fMRI assessment measures, American and Korean participants were exposed to messages, either by text or in a video format (Falk, Rameson, Berkman, et al., 2010). In all cases, there was a substantial relationship between feeling persuaded (in terms of rating the message) and activation in the posterior superior temporal sulcus and the dorsomedial prefrontal cortex, both of which have been associated in earlier research with conscious deliberative thinking. Of course, this study is about a conscious process of thought rather than the 'fast thinking' involving cognitive heuristics and other strategies. And indeed, can we equate rating how persuasive a message is to actually being persuaded? One can easily admire the crafting of an advertising message without being convinced, let alone buying the product.

While the research reviewed thus far provides us with information about the various factors that influence persuasion, it does not explain how people change their attitudes. Drawing on insights from research in social cognition (Chapter 2), contemporary research on attitude change has shifted its focus to the processes by which our attitudes change. Our discussion now turns to this work.

KEY POINT: The Yale model of persuasive communication posits four classes of variables: the source, the audience, the content of the message and the medium in which the message is presented. Factors studied include source credibility, whether the message is one-sided or two-sided, the primacy versus recency of when the argument is presented, individual and gender differences in persuasibility, appeals to reason versus emotion, and how such factors combine to determine persuasion. Neuroscience has linked rating a message as persuasive to activation in brain centres.

PERSUASION AND COGNITION: A DUAL-PROCESS APPROACH

What does it mean to be 'persuaded' of something? You may think of persuasion as 'changing someone's mind'. If you are in the supermarket to buy laundry detergent and you see a particular brand, you may recognize the brand or recall a catchy commercial tune, and you grab it. Were you really convinced that it was the best choice? Perhaps you may be convinced when you purchase a car or a house. These are major investments for most people and so you may gather evidence and think about what you want to buy and for how much. But for most purchases, we are influenced by other factors such as the attractiveness of the source, the familiarity of the brand name, an association with pleasant experiences, or where a product is placed on the supermarket shelves. We may not really be 'convinced', but our attitude changes enough for us to buy the product.

The basic question then becomes how we process the information that is contained in a persuasive message. To respond to this question, first recall our discussion in Chapter 2 on the notion of dual-process thinking: We think in a manner that is rapid, automatic and unconscious, and we also think in a manner that is slow, deliberative and conscious. We are cognitive misers, looking for the easier, more rapid way of thinking unless something cues us to think things out.

Now consider being on the receiving end of a message designed to persuade us to prepare assigned readings for class, vote for a candidate, or buy a particular brand of soap. The research has identified two distinct ways in which we deal with the contents of a message. One, known as systematic or central route persuasion, involves thinking through the arguments and evidence that is presented. Of course, this way involves time and effort, and as we have seen in discussing how we form impressions and make judgements about other people, we usually do not expend this time and effort. That is, we usually resort to the second approach called heuristic or peripheral route persuasion, because we use mental shortcuts (e.g., trust the experts, feel attracted to the young woman selling beer), and so the factors that cause our attitudes to change are peripheral to the quality of the arguments.

Thus, persuasion operates within the dual-process framework, slow thinking, which involves active deliberation about the message, and rapid thinking, which involves schemas and heuristics. Let us examine this peripheral, more superficial type of persuasion more closely, and then turn to the question of when we actually engage in 'central processing' – thinking about arguments and arriving consciously at a conclusion: that is, becoming convinced.

Peripheral route persuasion

Consider, again, the influence of source characteristics and why they influence us. As discussed earlier, people often use simple schemata and heuristic processing (Chaikin, 1980, 1987). For example, they may rely on the rule 'Trust the experts' in accepting a persuasive argument presented by someone perceived as expert. Similarly, they may rely on an activated rule of thumb that 'we agree with people that we like' and thus accept a persuasive communication from someone whom they like.

Distraction can operate to divert people from thinking about the arguments presented. In an experiment by Norman (1976), female students were asked to read a statement arguing that people should sleep less each night than they customarily do. The communication was presented as either a single statement or as a statement accompanied by several reasoned arguments. The second communication was expected to elicit more elaboration and to be more convincing. However, the students were presented with a photo and some information about the background of the communicator. Half the participants saw a distracting picture of a young, extremely attractive male, and the other half, a photo of an unattractive middle-aged male whose background suggested expertise on the topic of sleep hygiene. With the unattractive photo, attitude change was greater when several arguments were presented than with just a single argument. However, with the photo of the attractive person, attitude change was substantial, regardless of the arguments presented (Petty, Wells and Brock, 1976).

155

In this approach, a contrast is drawn between instances that involve active thought (elaboration), such as weighing the arguments for and against something, and instances in which the person simply invokes a rule of thumb, such as believing an attractive person or trusting an expert (Petty, Ostrom & Brock, 1981; Eagly & Chaikin, 1984). Let us now examine an influential theory dealing with this dual-process framework.

ELABORATION LIKELIHOOD MODEL

'People are motivated to hold correct attitudes, but have neither the resources to process carefully every persuasive argument, nor the luxury – nor apparently, the inclination – of being able to ignore them all' (Cacioppo, Petty, Kao & Rodriguez, 1986, p. 1032). As a contemporary dual-process theory of persuasion, the elaboration likelihood model (ELM) takes into consideration the fact that people can respond to persuasive messages either by active cognitive scrutiny of the content of the message (cognitive elaboration) or by taking more reactive and less effortful shortcuts (Petty & Cacioppo, 1981; Petty & Briñol, 2012; Petty, Wegener & Fabrigar, 1997). This theory concerns when people will actively process the message, that is, when elaboration is likely. In short: central route processing occurs when the individual is motivated to think things through, for example, when the consequences are real and personal, and when the individual has the opportunity to process the message.

Central route processes tend to lead to relatively enduring and real attitude change. Indeed, we tend to become more committed to our attitudes as we think more about the attitudinal object (Tesser, 1978). While peripheral route changes generally occur more readily because they demand less effort, these changes tend to be rather transitory because we have not really been convinced by the arguments. In this case, attitude change will persist only as long as the relevant cues are salient. For example, we may purchase a particular brand of beer until a more attractive association with another commercial appears.

One would think that the stronger the persuasive argument, the more likely it would persuade the audience. How a message is worded may stimulate people to think about an issue in a certain way (Eiser & Ross, 1977; Eiser & Pancer, 1979). One study measured activity in different brain centres while participants processed persuasive messages. Interestingly, a logical central-route persuasive message implicates activity in different brain centres than does one involving peripheral or heuristic influences, such as source characteristics, use of humour or a perception that 'everyone else' believes it (Cook, Warren, et al., 2011).

Perhaps both processes are involved. Indeed, it is important to understand that the metaphor of central and peripheral 'routes' does not imply mutually exclusive processes. For instance, in some research on high-involvement exposure to advertisements on the Internet (implying central processing), the peripheral cues, such as how the Web pages are actually presented (e.g. as serious or amusing, colourful or sedate), can enhance the effect of the actual content of the message (San Jose-Cabezudo, Gutierrez-Arranz & Gutierrez-Cillán, 2009). And people are more persuaded by information coming from multiple sources than by the same information presented by only one source (Harkins & Petty, 1987). The ELM explains this multiple-source effect; people must do more elaboration or thinking about the message because each new source cues the person to think about it. As well, the context in which the message is presented can influence the impact of the message, including the peripheral or heuristic cues. For instance, if you want to persuade someone to buy your product, would you place your advertisement in a frightening TV show, or in one that is romantic? Research indicates that if you appeal to a heuristic of doing what is popular, a romantic show will be an effective venue. On the other hand, if you want to implant the notion that your product is scarce, a 'limited edition', a frightening show will be more effective (Griskevicius, Goldstein, et al., 2009).

Therefore, there are distinct influences on persuasion. First, there are the arguments, pieces of information or logic that may induce attitude change under conditions of cognitive elaboration. Second, peripheral cues affect attitudes through invoking heuristic 'rules of thumb'. Finally, there are the conditions that promote cognitive elaboration. Let us consider now how people may be influenced to think about the issue at hand.

Conditions under which cognitive elaboration is likely

We have neither the time nor the energy to think through everything that may be involved in our attitudes. Cognitive elaboration, and thus enduring attitude change, is more likely to occur under two conditions: (1) when the person has the opportunity (such as time to think); and (2) when the person is motivated to carefully consider the arguments in the message. For instance, research suggests that a message framed in terms of a self-guide, how you wish you were or feel that you ought to be (recall Chapter 3), tends to stimulate more central processing of the arguments (Evans & Petty, 2003). Motivation to think about the message is also stronger when the issue is novel, unexpected or personally relevant (Zuwerink & Devine, 1996). Personal involvement may be manipulated, for example, by telling student participants that students would be required to pass a comprehensive examination in their major. Some were informed that this would take effect in the coming year (high involvement) or in 10 years (low involvement). As predicted by the ELM, under high involvement, strong arguments led to much more attitude change than did weak arguments. However, under low involvement, the source credibility (a peripheral cue) had a stronger effect on persuasion than did the actual arguments. These participants simply invoked a heuristic rule, 'Experts know best', to decide on the validity of the arguments (Petty, Cacioppo & Goldman, 1981).

Other research has obtained similar results by inducing personal involvement, and thus high motivation (Hutton & Baumeister, 1992). However, if the involvement is too high, people become less open to persuasion, perhaps because they are unable to elaborate or think open-mindedly about the message under such conditions (Sherif & Cantril, 1947; Johnson & Eagly, 1989).

The framing of the message can also have important effects. In a study (Smith & Petty, 1996), messages stressed either the benefits of increased recycling or the costs of not doing it. Strong and weak versions of both arguments were presented to different groups of experimental participants. Negatively framed messages were processed more carefully than positively framed messages in that the strength of the argument in a negatively framed message affected attitude change more. Messages are also processed carefully when the message is framed in an unexpected way. That is, if a patient expects dire warnings from the physician, the patient is more likely to elaborate on the message, and thus a strong argument would produce more attitude change.

Opportunity to engage in cognitive elaboration has been manipulated by varying time pressure and the comprehensibility of the message in the courtroom (Hafer, Reynolds & Obertynski, 1996). Prior attitude measures indicated that most people were opposed to plea bargaining, the practice of offering a reduced sentence to the accused in return for a plea of guilty. Participants listened to a speech advocating plea bargaining in which the following conditions were varied: (1) whether the speech was ostensibly given by a high-status or low-status person (a peripheral cue); (2) whether the speech had strong or weak arguments (related to central processing); and (3) whether the speech used complex language (such as legal jargon, infrequently used words and complex grammatical structure) or simple everyday speech. When the arguments were easily comprehensible, strong arguments produced more favourable attitudes towards plea-bargaining than did weak arguments. However, when the message was difficult to comprehend, the strength of the argument did not affect persuasion. In these conditions, persuasion was influenced by the status of the source: whether an eminent judge or a law student.

Finally, consider the possibility that certain peripheral cues may cause the person to attend more to the message itself. We have seen that certain source characteristics such as the attractiveness or expertise of the source influence persuasion. What if the source is presented as inconsistent, such as unattractive but expert, or very attractive but knowing nothing about the issue? Experiments show that in these cases the actual content of the message has a greater impact on attitude change (Ziegler, Diehl & Ruther, 2002).

Individual differences in elaboration likelihood: Need for cognition

Some people are more likely than others to engage in cognitive elaboration. Individuals differ in a **need for cognition**, a propensity to analyse the situation, search for clues and information and work on solving difficult problems (Thompson & Zanna, 1995). This need can be measured by a scale that includes the following items:

'I find satisfaction in deliberating hard and for long hours'; 'I like tasks that require little thought once I've learned them'; 'I would prefer complex to simple problems'; 'Thinking is not my idea of fun'. Note that while intelligent people may enjoy using their intelligence, they will not necessarily do so.

People who are high in a need for cognition will be more resistant to persuasion and more likely to be persuasive in a debate. For instance, Shestowsky, Wegener & Fabrigar (1992) presented participants with a description of a legal case. They were paired up on the basis of scores on need for cognition and asked to discuss the case and come up with a verdict. Those scoring high on need for cognition were more likely than their low-scoring partners to argue their points effectively and to come up with better counter-arguments to their partners' statements. Indeed, they were more likely to convince their partners in this joint decision. In another study, participants viewed a video of an interrogation of a defendant by both police and the defence lawyer. Those with a high need for cognition tended to adopt the perspective of whoever first questioned the suspect (primacy effect) while those with a low need for cognition agreed with whoever had the last word on the subject (recency effect) (Kassin, Reddy & Tulloch, 1990).

People with a high need for cognition are more likely to be influenced by the quality of the arguments, while those low on this variable tend to be more influenced by peripheral route factors (Haugtvedt & Petty, 1992). While people vary in their need to think things through, they also will differ in the degree of confidence that they have in their own thinking about the issue in the message. Petty, Briñol & Tormala (2002) have shown that confidence increases thinking about issues, that is, central processing. Attitude change among high-need-for-cognition people tends to persist over time (Verplanken, 1991).

Emotional state and cognitive elaboration

One's mood will also influence the likelihood of elaboration. People in a good mood tend to react favourably to weak arguments and to peripheral appeals. Indeed, it has long been known that when people are happy, they are generally more receptive to persuasion (e.g., Biggers & Pryor, 1982; Petty et al., 1993). When people are in a bad mood, they tend to think critically about arguments and to be more persuaded by the quality of the argument than by peripheral cues (Sinclair & Mark, 1992; Sinclair, Mark & Clore, 1994).

An overview on persuasion

We have seen two different theoretical approaches to persuasion that generate different research questions. The Yale model sets out the components of a persuasion situation: who says what to whom, and how. This led to programmes of research directed toward what characteristics of the source of the message predict persuasion, what kinds of messages are more persuasive in what situation, through what medium of communication, and how characteristics of the recipient of the message influence persuasion. Of course, these components invariably work in combination.

The ELM suggests real attitude change by means of persuasion is difficult and uncommon. For central route persuasion to occur, the recipient must have both the ability and the motivation to process the information – and, of course, the arguments must be logical or otherwise convincing. As noted in Chapter 2, we often act as 'cognitive misers', taking shortcuts and acting automatically. Thus, in our society of the 20-second commercial and the 'news bite', it is not surprising that peripheral route change is so common.

Looking at the two models together, it would seem apparent that the central route involves, in the main, characteristics of the message while peripheral route persuasion involves source and contextual characteristics. However, integration of the two models would prove more complicated than this. For instance, as we saw earlier, a message which is excessively complicated and full of legalese may reduce motivation to process the argument and direct attention to peripheral factors. Conversely, characteristics of the source, such as the expertise of the person delivering the message, may invoke a simple heuristic rule – trust the expert – but also may motivate the recipient to pay attention to the message and to process the argument.

As noted earlier, peripheral route processing does not mean that central route cognitive elaboration is impossible; both can occur simultaneously. Indeed, the theory specifies that the two routes form two ends of a continuum bounded at one end by an absence of thought about the issue and at the other by complete elaboration of all issue-relevant information and arguments (Petty, Wegener & Fabrigar, 1997). Further, even superficial attitude change can lead to immediate behavioural change consistent with it. At this point, cognitive processes are set in motion that may lead to enduring attitude change. Thus the ELM and cognitive dissonance theory meet.

> **KEY POINT:** Persuasion is conceived within the dual-process framework of cognition: slow thinking, which involves central route processing of the argument, and fast thinking, which involves peripheral route and distractions. According to the elaboration likelihood model, central route persuasion is more likely when the individual is motivated to think through the arguments, when the consequences are significant and personal, and when the opportunity for central route processing is present. Peripheral route processing leads more readily to persuasion, but it is transitory, while central route processing leads to more lasting attitude change. Individual differences in central route processing have been studied through a need for cognition, and a good mood has been shown to lead more readily to peripheral route change.

LIMITS TO PERSUASION

It is easy to be impressed by the extensive repertoire of persuasion techniques. Whether on a one-to-one basis or as members of a mass audience, we are subjected to an ever-increasing barrage of persuasive messages. Yet it is important to realize the limits of persuasion. Businesses with lavish advertising budgets, using the latest in expertise, may well fail to sell their product and may even fail to survive. Many politicians lose elections, many used cars are not sold, and most of us remain unconvinced by a great deal of what we see and hear. In the age of mass communications, people seem to have adapted rather well.

BOX 5.2   ATTITUDE CHANGE AND AGING

What is the effect of a person's age on openness to attitude change? Of course attitudes can change as interests and tastes change. For instance, as people in Western countries age, their preferences for wine grow, as compared with beer and spirits (Melo, Colin, Delahunty, Forde & Cox, 2010). What about their attitudes towards politics and other issues? There are two perspectives, both of which assert that people are most open to attitude change when they are young and then become less open to change as they age.

According to the *impressionable-years hypothesis*, people become socialized into adulthood during adolescence, and thus the events and historical environment of that time will have a profound influence on their attitudes for the rest of their lives. For example, people who came of age during the 1960s, a relatively liberal era of political protest and social change in the West, would be expected to remain relatively liberal during their lives, while those who came of age in the more conservative 1980s would remain relatively conservative thereafter. According to the *increasing-persistence hypothesis*, people may be relatively flexible and open to change when they are young, but as they age, their flexibility gradually decreases and they become 'set in their ways'. Perhaps people's capacity for information processing gradually declines with age or perhaps their accumulated store of knowledge and experience causes their attitudes to become more stable as they grow older. Note that both hypotheses assume that attitude change is greater earlier in life than later; the former focuses on the impressionable early years, while the latter presupposes a rigidity of thinking as characteristic of aging. Of course, a third possibility is that people who are highly flexible and open to change in opinions earlier in life remain so throughout their life cycle (Sears, 1983).

In a classic longitudinal study of this issue, a cohort of female students was followed before, during and after their years at Bennington College in the US (Newcomb, 1943; Newcomb, Koenig, Flacks & Warwick, 1967; Alwin, Cohen & Newcomb, 1991). These women, having been raised in socioeconomically advantaged and conservative families, were confronted by a liberal milieu at the college. During their years at the college, the students, particularly those who identified with the college and were involved in its activities, moved gradually towards the liberal end of the political spectrum. When they were re-interviewed 25 years later and again about 40 years after graduation, their liberal attitudes were shown to have remained quite stable despite important life changes during that period. These findings demonstrate the impact of influences on attitudes during the years at college or university, supporting the impressionable-years hypothesis.

Krosnick and Alwin (1989) examined the data from two longitudinal studies of political attitudes in the US in order to compare the extent to which attitudes change over time in different age groups. In the first study, a national cross-sectional sample of 1132 adults was interviewed at the time of the 1956 presidential elections, again in 1958, and again at the time of the 1960 presidential elections. In the second study, a sample of 769 adults was interviewed on three occasions during the year of the 1980 presidential election campaign – in January, June and October. In both studies, the participants were divided into seven age groupings (at the time of the first interview) ranging from age 18–25 for the youngest group, to 66–83 for the oldest. Significantly, both changes during an election campaign and changes between election campaigns followed the same pattern. Attitude changes were greatest in the youngest group, and susceptibility to change dropped off afterwards, supporting the impressionable-years hypothesis. Contrary to the increasing-persistence hypothesis, there was no evidence that attitudes became increasingly stable for the groups after the age of 33. Thus, it appears that while young people may be most responsive to shifts in the social and political climate of the times, aging does not inevitably lead to a hardening of attitudes.

In fact, other evidence indicates that commitment to one's attitudes increases during middle adulthood and then declines in late adulthood, so that older people may be more susceptible or open to changes (Visser & Krosnick, 1999; Eaton, Visser, Krosnick & Anand, 2009). Midlife adults may be more resistant to change because they attach more importance to their attitudes, or because of their network of supportive friends (Boninger, Krosnick, Berent & Fabrigar, 1995). As people move from young adulthood to midlife, they increasingly discuss important issues with a wide range of people outside their immediate families. However, older adults have fewer people with whom they discuss concerns that they share (Marsden, 1987). Therefore, they become more susceptible to changes in attitudes.

A final note

Older people in our societies have lived through decades of rapid and fundamental changes. Ancient enemies have become friends or at least allies, ancient prejudices have diminished or disappeared, religions have declined in influence in many countries, the Internet has changed the way they communicate with others, sexual mores and tastes in popular culture have been transformed. Attitudes have changed as the status quo has shifted.

How do people resist persuasion? A number of strategies have been studied (Cameron, Jacks & O'Brien, 2002):

Forewarning

If people know that they are about to be the target of persuasion, does this enable them to resist the attempt? It is important to distinguish between two types of forewarning. First, individuals may simply be warned ahead of time of persuasive intent, and second, they also may be informed of message content. In both instances, the likelihood of persuasion will be reduced, but the process differs. Of course, people cannot think about counter-arguments when they are warned simply of intent. The increased resistance observed under this condition is attributed to reactance (Hass & Grady, 1975). In other words, people *react* to protect their threatened freedom by clinging to their attitudes. In the second case, it appears that individuals are stimulated by the warning to rehearse their own position and to generate anticipatory counter-arguments (McGuire & Papageorgis, 1962). Petty and Cacioppo (1977) provide particularly strong evidence that participants forewarned of message content review their own arguments.

Inoculation effect

Usually the more strongly people feel about an issue, the less likely they will be to change their minds about it. Paradoxically, however, cultural truisms – the unquestioned attitudes held by a large majority of the population – are particularly vulnerable to change through persuasion (McGuire & Papageorgis, 1961). Examples include the following: 'You should brush your teeth after every meal'; 'Democracy is the best form of government'; and 'Penicillin is a boon to humankind'. Can you think of another truism from your own culture, one which is just assumed by the mass of people to be true?

McGuire used a medical analogy, pointing out that an individual is susceptible to infection when the body's defences are weak, and that in order to build up these defences, inoculations are administered. These injections of the microbe in weakened form lead the body to build up its defensive system and resist infection. Similarly, because the truism is so generally accepted, the individual may never have heard an opposing point of view. He or she must, therefore, be inoculated by being confronted with persuasive arguments against the truism and then having them effectively refuted. The person will then be able to use these counter-arguments to ward off any attempts at persuasion in the future.

There is some disagreement about whether the refutation should be passive or active. McGuire felt that active refutation (e.g., writing a counter-attitudinal essay) would not be effective because it would be distracting and because people are not very good at thinking up counter-arguments on demand. He preferred the passive strategy, such as having the person read a well-reasoned essay. His data support this contention as do other studies (Bernard, Maio & Olson, 2003).

In the decades since the early work, a substantial literature of research studies has accumulated. In a review of this research by Banas & Rains (2010), the inoculation procedure has been found to be effective, enabling people to resist persuasion by subsequent strong attacks on their positions. Recall that McCuire & Papageorgis (1961) argued that this effect would be most pronounced in cases of 'cultural truism', beliefs that are so widely shared in the participants' own environment that they would have been unlikely to have encountered attacks on them. However, later research showed that the inoculation procedure could work quite effectively in more controversial topics such as banning handguns, legalized prostitution and animal testing (Wood, 2007, Pfau, Semmler, et al., 2009; Nabi, 2003).

The attitude congeniality hypothesis

It has been hypothesized that attitudes bias memory in favour of attitudinally agreeable information – that we tend to remember information consistent with our attitudes and forget about the information that conflicts with our attitudes (Eagly & Chaiken 1998). In order to defend our attitudes against material that challenges them, we may not attend to that information, distort it or otherwise not store it in memory. Of course this is consistent with a cognitive dissonance interpretation.

In a meta-analysis of 70 relevant experiments, Eagly, Chen, Chaiken and Shaw-Barnes (1999) found that the results were inconsistent. And so the researchers designed a simple experiment in which attitudes towards an issue were premeasured, and then two weeks later participants were exposed to an audiotape in which a speaker took a pro or con position on the issue. Various versions of the experiment were run concerning attitudes towards abortion, gays in the military or the death penalty and then participants' memories were assessed. The results were clear and consistent: congenial and uncongenial information was remembered equally well, regardless of the issues, regardless of the participants' commitment to their attitudes, and regardless of whether memory was assessed soon after the message or two weeks later. Indeed, regardless of the message, it was remembered better if the participant was active in some way on that issue, had stronger attitudes and if memory was assessed immediately after.

The researchers concluded that participants hearing an uncongenial (or dissonant) message were more likely to process that message centrally and carefully, thinking of counter-arguments, and this enabled them to remember that message. Those receiving a congenial message remembered it as associated with their existing attitudes. In short, central processing overcame defensive dissonant reactions. In another study, it was found that providing a strong narrative story with compelling characters successfully overcame resistance to persuasion, particularly reducing reactance and counter-arguing (Moyer-Gusé & Nabj, 2010).

In sum: Can we instil resistance to persuasion? Programmes have been developed to assist adolescents to resist peer group pressure. Instilling resistance to persuasion can be successful particularly when they focus on the ulterior motives of the source and the vulnerability of the target to persuasion (Sagarin, Cialdini, Rice & Serna, 2002). That is, it is important that one dispels the illusion of invulnerability to persuasion: it happens to the best of us. Consider that if we successfully resist a strong attempt to change our attitudes, we subsequently become more confident and committed to our original position (Tormala & Petty, 2002). Of course, the opposite extreme is equally untenable; it is not a bad thing to be open to persuasion when the arguments are compelling and the source is credible.

> **KEY POINT:** Persuasive messages often fail to persuade – why? Forewarning of a persuasive attempt can cause people to review their own positions. The inoculation effect shows that when people are exposed to a relatively weak attack on their attitudes, particularly cultural truisms that are never challenged, they subsequently become more resistant to strong persuasive attempts. People tend to remember messages that are 'congenial' with their own attitudes. And causing people to focus on the purported ulterior motives of the source can increase resistance to persuasion.

IS ATTITUDE CHANGE 'REAL'?

Most estimates of attitude change depend on an individual's self-report, although some recent work uses implicit attitude measures. It is therefore important to consider whether these statements reflect actual changes in the underlying attitude and, second, whether persuasion is lasting.

The first question emphasizes the need to distinguish between compliance and attitude change. Kelman (1958, 1961) defines compliance as publicly yielding to a persuasive communication, going along with it without private acceptance. It usually occurs because the communicator is perceived as having the power to reward and punish us, or because we want approval and affection. In the absence of power figures, the target person would likely revert to his or her original opinion. Kelman goes on to point out that more basic changes can occur if the recipient identifies with the communicator or is able to internalize the message. Identification enhances persuasion because the individual is attracted to and wishes to be like the communicator. Internalization takes place when the new position is in line with the person's value system and is judged as being useful or valuable. While an attractive source would probably lead to identification, a credible source would more probably lead to internalization (Mills & Harvey, 1972). These characteristics of the communicator are not necessarily exclusive. For example, a parent may be simultaneously powerful, attractive and credible.

It must be noted that, during laboratory investigations, attitude change is usually measured only immediately after the administration of the persuasive message. Thus, the permanence of induced change is not known. Investigations into how attitudes change over time have generally found that most of the reversion to the original attitude occurs relatively quickly and then tapers off. For example, McGuire (1969), summarizing the results of a number of experiments, concluded that attitude change has a 'half-life' of about six months. In other words, on average, about 50% of the initial change is still present six months later. Remember, these data are based on a single administration of a persuasive message. Re-administration of the communication such as with an incessantly repeated advertisement is more likely to maintain change.

A FINAL NOTE

What, in the end, causes us to change our attitudes or, indeed, to resist attempts to change our attitudes? Clearly in our world today, we are bombarded with messages designed to persuade us, and in some instances they succeed. In some cases, our discomfort with inconsistencies and challenges to our sense of self-worth will cause our attitudes to change even in the absence of attempts to persuade us. In other words, our attitudes do not exist in some kind of cognitive vacuum but are embedded in our relationships with others and with our understanding of our world and ourselves.

SUMMARY

1. Attitude change can be viewed in terms of internal processes which generate change, and external communication which influences change.

2. The theory of cognitive dissonance states that when two related cognitions are not consistent, the individual is motivated to reduce discomfort by changing or reducing the importance of a dissonant cognition or adding consonant cognitions.

3. Four important areas of study in cognitive dissonance theory are post-decision dissonance, social support, selective information seeking, and dissonance after attitude-discrepant behaviour.

4. The magnitude of dissonance experienced after attitude-discrepant behaviour is a function of insufficient external justification for performing that action. This effect occurs when the action involves public commitment and free choice.

5. Cognitive dissonance is a state of arousal, which can be reduced when the arousal itself is reduced or when alternative attributions are made for the resulting uncomfortable state.

6. Dissonance occurs not in response to logical inconsistency but in response to an inconsistency within the self-concept.

7. Cooper and Fazio have developed a 'new look' attributional model that explains when cognitive dissonance occurs in response to attitude-discrepant behaviour: significant consequences, personal responsibility, arousal and attributing the arousal to the action's consequences.

8. Factors involved in persuasion include the source, audience, message and channel. Source credibility is generally determined by judging the source's trustworthiness and expertise.

9. Message effectiveness is influenced by the presentation's primacy or recency. Fear arousal up to a moderate level can increase persuasion.

10. The elaboration likelihood model of persuasion differentiates between central routes (understanding the arguments, thinking about the issue) and peripheral routes (focusing on characteristics of the source or distractions in the message, using heuristics). While changes are more likely to occur through the peripheral route, they are less likely to persist in the absence of salient cues; central route changes have more staying power. Central route processing is more likely when the person is motivated, has the opportunity to think, and has a strong need for cognition.

11. A written communication tends to cause the audience to focus more on the argument than on the source; in oral or visual presentations, the audience typically focuses more on the source.

12. The effect of persuasion is reduced by forewarning the audience of an attempt to persuade, and by inoculation, confronting the audience with mild counter-arguments.

13. In determining whether an individual has been persuaded, it is necessary to distinguish changes represented by behavioural compliance from changes associated with identification with the source or internalization of the message.

POINTS TO PONDER

- Perhaps the key take-home message of cognitive dissonance is that changing behaviour can lead to subsequent attitude change. How could you apply this to alleviate the problem of obesity in your society?
- How might you apply the principles of this chapter, both cognitive dissonance and persuasion, to design a political campaign for your favoured candidate?
- Much of what we see in this chapter suggests that attitude changes are superficial but often sufficient to influence what we buy, how we vote and how we act towards each other. How would you induce more central route processing, causing people to think more about their attitudes and their actions?
- Playwright Oscar Wilde wrote, 'Consistency is the last refuge of the unimaginative'. When and where, and why, do we need to be consistent?
- Why is the Elaboration Likelihood Model (ELM) a step forward in our understanding of persuasion? Where might we go from here?

FURTHER READING

Cialdini, R.B. (2007). Influence: *The psychology of* *persuasion.* **New York: Harper Business.**

An excellent discussion by an eminent social psychologist of the variety of means by which people influence people, with many examples from advertising and marketing, public relations, cults, fund-raising and politics. The writing style is clear, non-technical and even witty.

Cooper, J. (2007). *Cognitive dissonance: Fifty years of a* *classic theory.* **London: Sage Publications.**

A brief, well-written overview of a theory that has stood the test of time. Anyone interested in cognitive dissonance would want to read this.

Dickinson, A. (2011). *Persuasion.* **Toronto: Collins Canada.**

An entertaining presentation of how an entrepreneur used social psychology and her own talents to persuade, both in the boardroom with business executives and in marketing. This is not a book on social psychology, but social psychology provides the framework for understanding.

Eagly, A.H. & Chaiken, S. (1993). *The psychology* *of attitudes.* **Fort Worth: Harcourt Brace Jovanovich.**

An encyclopaedic coverage of attitude theory and research – thorough, analytical and integrative. It has become an indispensable source on this topic, even if dated.

Forgas, J.P., Cooper, J. & Crano, W. (Eds). (2010). *The* *psychology of attitudes and attitude change.* **New York: Psychology Press.**

A set of scholarly papers by social psychologists on various important topics in attitudes, including cognitive dissonance and other cognitive approaches, and persuasion.

O'Reilly, T. & Tennant, M. (2010). *The age of persuasion:* *how marketing ate our culture.* **Toronto: Vintage Canada.**

A well-informed and witty account by a very successful advertising expert on how successful – and not-so-successful – advertising campaigns have actually been conceived and applied.

Perloff, Richard M. (2003). *Dynamics of persuasion:* *Communication and attitudes in the 21st century.* **Mahwah, NJ: Erlbaum.**

A useful and updated overview of what we know about persuasion, looking at both attitude theory and theories about media. Some applied focus on specific attitudes regarding prejudice, politics and health.

WEBLINKS

http://www.influenceatwork.com/

Influence at work: proven science for business success, applying the social psychology of persuasion.

http://www.marketingpower.com/Pages/default.aspx

Website of the American Marketing Association.

http://www.youtube.com/watch?v=korGK0yGIDo

Zimbardo walks us through the classic experiment in cognitive dissonance.

CHAPTER 6
SOCIAL
INFLUENCE

To be yourself in a world that is constantly trying to make you something else is the greatest accomplishment.
Ralph Waldo Emerson

LEARNING OBJECTIVES

* To explain how behaviour is influenced by the mere presence of others

* To understand the effects of social modelling

* To examine factors underlying conformity to group norms

* To consider particular tactics used to promote acquiescence to requests

* To explore the influences that lead to obedience or disobedience to direct orders

Figure 6.1   The emperor's new clothes
Source: © Bettmann/Corbis

In Hans Christian Andersen's *The Emperor's New Clothes*, a vain and pretentious emperor is taken in by two 'scoundrels' who assure him that they can tailor for him the finest suit of clothes made from a special material that is invisible to anyone who is either too incompetent or stupid to appreciate its splendour. The scoundrels eventually pretend to dress the emperor in the invisible regal outfit, and although neither the emperor nor his ministers can see any fabric, no one speaks up for fear of being judged incompetent or stupid. The emperor then parades through the streets to show off his finery, and while everyone in the crowd sees only a naked emperor, they all express admiration for his new clothes, again for fear of looking stupid or incompetent. Each individual conforms to the behaviour of the group, not wanting to 'stand out from the crowd'. Finally, a small child, too young to be aware of group conformity pressures, announces that the emperor is naked.

We are social beings. Because of that, we are sensitive to how other people react to us, and most people experience some anxiety in situations in which they inadvertently stand out from everyone else – such as arriving at a social event wearing jeans and sneakers only to find that everyone else is dressed up, or being singled out to make a presentation in front of a group. As we grow up, we learn that although standing out from the crowd can sometimes bring positive attention – being the football hero, or the person with the latest smartphone, or the one who can make everybody laugh – standing out also carries risk, such as the possibility of being laughed at, of being bullied, or of being blamed. We can lessen such risk by blending in with the group and not drawing attention to ourselves. And so, if everybody is expressing admiration for the emperor's new clothes, we minimize risk by admiring them as well.

In Chapter 5, we examined the effects of social influence on attitudes. In this chapter the focus will be on changes in behaviour brought about by the influence of others. We shall begin the discussion by focusing on how we influence others without consciously intending to do so (and often without the awareness of the person being influenced). These influences include social facilitation, social loafing, the effects of mirror neuron activity, and social modelling. Then, we shall turn to direct efforts to influence behaviour, including pressures to conform to group norms. And finally, we shall explore obedience and disobedience.

UNINTENDED SOCIAL INFLUENCE

Social facilitation

Early psychological researchers explored the effects of the simple presence of another person on an individual's behaviour. For example, Charles Féré (1887) used a dynamometer, a device that measures the pressure applied to a handgrip, to study how the presence of others influences the muscular pressure that an individual applies in an experimental task. He reported that individuals applied twice as much pressure on average when in the company of another person engaged in the same activity compared to when acting alone (Crary, 2001; Stroebe, 2012). Why should that be? he wondered. A few years later, psychologist Norman Triplett, who was a bicycling enthusiast, noted that cyclists being paced by another cyclist on a faster machine travelled faster than those who cycled alone, and this led him to wonder how such behaviour could be influenced by the presence of another person, given the absence of any direct interaction or communication. Triplett (1898) then conducted one of the first ever social psychological experiments (although textbooks often incorrectly credit him with having carried out the very *first* such experiment (Stroebe, 2012)). Forty boys and girls aged nine to fifteen years worked at a task either alone or in competition with another child. Two fishing reels were attached to a wooden frame, and a silk cord ran from each fishing reel and looped around a wheel two metres away, creating a closed loop of four metres in length. A small flag was attached to the silk cord, and the child's task was to turn the reel so as to bring the flag around the complete four-metre circuit a total of four times for each trial (Stroebe, 2012). The time

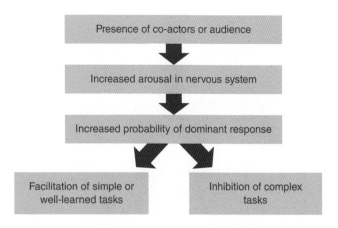

Figure 6.2 Zajonc's arousal theory

taken to complete this task constituted the dependant measure. Each child carried out six trials, three alone and three in competition with another child.

Twenty of the children performed better when in competition than when working alone, ten others did more poorly, and the performance of the other ten did not change at all. In those early days, statistical techniques that we take for granted today had not yet been developed, and so on the basis of simply looking at his data, Triplett concluded that the presence of another person somehow liberated latent energy that served to facilitate behaviour leading to increased performance, a phenomenon that subsequently came to be known as social facilitation (Crawford, 1939). However, a recent statistical analysis has revealed that Triplett's results did not actually depart significantly from chance (Strube, 2005); nonetheless, his work set the stage for numerous other studies.

Subsequent social psychological research branched in two directions: the study of audience effects that occur in the presence of one or more passive observers, and the study of coaction effects that occur when participants work simultaneously but independently on a common task. Early studies of simple audience effects (e.g., Meumann, 1904; Travis, 1925) found that performance generally improves in the presence of passive observers, and similar effects are found for coacting individuals (Allport, 1924).

Yet, other research found that the presence of others actually impaired individual performance (e.g. Dashiell, 1935). In light of such contradictory evidence, researchers concluded that either the phenomenon is not a robust one, or that the increases or decreases in performance reflect personality differences among the participants. As a result, interest waned to the point that by the end of the 1930s research into social facilitation had all but ceased.

However, Zajonc (1965) brought renewed interest when he reviewed the extant literature and detected a pattern: it appeared that people perform a simple or well-learned task better in the presence of others, but that the effect is negative when the task is complicated or still being learned. He hypothesized that the mere presence of another person increases arousal in the autonomic nervous system, which can either facilitate performance or interfere with it, depending on the situation (Figure 6.2).

Zajonc made sense of it in this way: When we are learning something new, we not only have to acquire the correct response but we have to get rid of incorrect responses – for example, hitting the wrong keys on the piano. Ordinarily these incorrect responses gradually disappear as learning progresses. However, the arousal induced by the presence of another person increases the strength of *both* the correct and the incorrect responses, which will lead to more mistakes. On the other hand, when only the correct response is available – that is, when an activity has been mastered and the incorrect responses have dropped out of the repertoire – then only the correct response can be facilitated, producing an enhancement in performance. If the task is a very simple one, the presence of others should only facilitate performance because no learning is required.

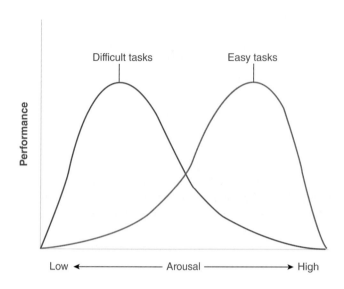

Figure 6.3 The effects of arousal produced by the presence of others

This is summarized in Figure 6.3: difficult tasks suffer in performance due to the arousal produced by the presence of others, while the performance of 'easy' (simple or well-learned) tasks improves.

Evaluation apprehension Zajonc considered physiological arousal due to the presence of others to be inborn. Cottrell (1972), on the other hand, argued that it results from learned **evaluation apprehension**. That is, beginning in early childhood, we learn that people watching our behaviour may be pleased or displeased by it, and their reactions teach us to be sensitive to evaluation whenever others are present. Cottrell carried out an experiment that supported this interpretation (Cottrell et al., 1968). Participants performed a simple task either alone, in the presence of two spectators watching from six feet away, or in the 'mere presence' of two people who were blindfolded (ostensibly to prepare for a later experiment). Clearly, if mere presence were critical, both types of audience should enhance performance equally, but if evaluation apprehension were the key factor, then only the observing audience should facilitate task performance. Evaluation apprehension was supported: There was no difference between the 'alone' and 'mere presence' conditions, but performance increased significantly in the presence of actual observers.

What is important is not the physical presence of others, but the awareness that one is being observed. Thompson et al. (2009) studied how long it took participants in a web-based programme designed to teach them how to locate information on a university library website to master the task. Some were informed that their training activities were being tracked (experimental condition), while others were not given this information (control condition). Heart rate was also measured. Participants in the control condition performed significantly better than the others, both during the training and subsequently. Moreover, a measure of heart rate variability that is correlated with mental workload was higher for participants in the experimental condition.

Yet, evaluation apprehension does not provide a full explanation for social facilitation either; while it can on its own produce social facilitation, it is not a *necessary* condition (Bond & Titus, 1983). Mere presence alone, without evaluation apprehension, is usually *sufficient* to produce social facilitation, but evaluation apprehension can further heighten arousal and thereby further facilitate dominant responses (Schmitt et al., 1986).

Distraction While audience and coaction effects are attributed to arousal (Platania & Moran, 2001), the reasons for the aroused state continue to be debated. As noted, Zajonc attributed the arousal and automatic biological response to the presence of others, while Cottrell attributed it to learned evaluation apprehension. A third interpretation is provided by **distraction-conflict theory** (Baron, 1986; Sanders, 1983), which views the arousal as the result of a state of 'attentional conflict' created by the distraction of comparing one's performance with that of a co-actor working on the same task. This results in 'information overload'; participants have more sensory input than they can handle efficiently; in order to cope, they concentrate on the task and shut out the distracting cues resulting from another person's presence. This increased attention improves simple task performance, but the performance of complex or novel tasks suffers because such tasks require less focused and intense concentration. Research by Muller & Butera (2007) suggests that this focusing effect is most likely to occur when the presence of a co-actor represents

168

a threat or potential threat to one's evaluation of one's own efforts – in other words, a social comparison process again.

This social comparison influence was neatly demonstrated in an experiment in which co-acting participants worked on either the same or on different digit-copying tasks (Sanders et al., 1978). A second factor was task complexity. Presumably, participants working on the same task would compare themselves to the other person, leading to distraction and social facilitation, while social comparison would be less important when the tasks were different, in which case social facilitation should be nonexistent or greatly reduced. That is exactly what occurred with regard to the simple task: the output was greater when the tasks were the same. However, there was no significant effect for the complex task.

Impression management Another perspective on social facilitation is provided by Bond (1982), who argued that it arises from impression management (recall the discussion in Chapter 3), as the individual deliberately strives to create a good impression – something that is most possible when working on an easy task where failure is unlikely. The errors that are likely to occur in a complex task cause embarrassment, which leads to task impairment. In a similar vein, Carver and Scheier (1981) suggest that the presence of an audience leads to increased 'self-attention', which in turn leads to concern about the behaviours that would create a good impression, resulting in enhanced performance. They account for performance decrements in difficult tasks by postulating that self-attention makes participants periodically interrupt their activity in order to assess their own progress.

An interesting example of the importance of good impressions is provided by a literature review of research into the effects of the presence of others on how much food people consume (Herman et al., 2003). The data show that when people eat in groups, they are likely to consume more than when eating on their own, which is a form of social facilitation. On the other hand, when in the presence of a model who eats either a lot or only a little, people are influenced by the model's behaviour and consume either a lot or a little respectively. Yet, when people eat in the presence of others who they think are evaluating them, they eat less than when alone – a clear instance of impression management.

Social loafing

While research shows that people tend to work harder and perform better on simple or well-learned tasks when in the presence of others than when alone, it is important to note that such research always involves some observation of the participants' efforts, even if just by the researcher. Would we observe such effects in everyday life when no one can measure a person's efforts?

Have you ever had to push a car that was stuck in the mud or a snow bank? And if others joined in, did you continue to put in as much effort? If you slacked off a bit, then you were exhibiting social loafing, defined as a decrease in individual effort when working in a task involving group effort (Murphy et al., 2003). This effect was first studied over a century ago when Max Ringelmann, a French agricultural engineer, discovered that individuals working together in a task typically become *less* individually productive as the size of the group increases (Ringelmann, 1913). He measured the efforts of individuals instructed to pull on a rope, and found that they contributed less and less as more people joined the task. Why should this be so? As more people join in, each individual tends to rely on the others to provide the necessary effort, and loss of motivation leads to reduced participation (Latané, Williams and Harkins, 1979). What is perhaps more interesting is that the individuals themselves are not always aware that their efforts have decreased (Karau & Williams, 1993).

Social loafing can occur in the cognitive domain as well. For example, Weldon and Gargano (1988) involved participants in a complex judgement task and found that those working in a group, but not held accountable for outcomes either individually or as a group, produced less complex responses than did those working alone.

If you are pushing a car out of the mud, it is not easy to know whether another person is pushing with maximum effort. This lack of knowledge is important, for research indicates that social loafing occurs only when the participants' outputs cannot be evaluated by others (Szymanski & Harkins, 1987). It does not occur when individual contributions can be identified, and the effect is also reduced when participants believe that the overall production of their group will be compared with that of other groups (Harkins & Szymanski, 1989). Thus, just as with social facilitation, evaluation plays a key role (Harkins, 1987).

However, people are less inclined to 'loaf' when working with people whom they like (Karau & Hart, 1998). And in some situations, the so-called Köhler motivation gain effect (Köhler, 1926; Kerr & Hertel, 2011) is observed. This occurs when less capable members of a group perform better when they are performing with others, compared to when performing the same task on their own. This is of particular interest in the sporting world, where team success relies upon motivating all team members to do their best. The largest effect is found when the overall performance of the group depends on the weakest member's performance, but it has also been found in tasks where a group's performance is defined as the sum of the group members' performances; (think for example of a relay race). There is more involved here than simple social facilitation; an important part of the motivation relates to the *indispensability of one's effort* for group success (Kerr et al., 2007). A second motivating factor is *upward social comparison* (Kerr & Hertel, 2011), that is, individuals may increase their performance goals when working with a more capable partner. This was demonstrated in a recent study (Osborn et al., 2012). The participants were swimmers competing in four-person relay teams, and a championship was at stake. The swimmers swam faster as part of a relay team than they did when they performed individually, but the increase in team performance was primarily due to the increased speeds of the 'inferior' members, those with the slowest individual performance times.

Social modelling

Another form of social influence occurs when we observe and then imitate someone else's behaviour, sometimes without realizing it, whether to achieve some goal (e.g., mastering a dance step), to fit in with others (e.g, dressing like others in one's group) or to be like someone we admire (e.g., the son imitating his father shaving). This reflects the direct influence of others on our behaviour, even though those others may be unaware of that influence. Social modelling influences are particularly important for health-related behaviours, for models have a powerful influence on our choice of lifestyle habits that can be either positive or negative for our health.

Social learning theory (Bandura, 1977) provides a comprehensive analysis of such social modelling and observational learning. For example, someone using a ski lift for the first time will likely watch others to see how they get on and off, and then try to copy their behaviour. The model need not be a live person for social learning to occur. We can watch a movie or read a book, or peruse an instruction manual (e.g., *Teach yourself golf*) and then imitate the model as best we can.

Of course, for modelling to occur, the observer must also be *motivated* to learn. If you have no interest in ever becoming involved in cricket or basketball, you are unlikely to be motivated to learn very much through observation. Then, the observer must *atte*nd to what the model is doing, and *remember* what has been observed, either as an image or in words. As we saw in Chapter 2, schemata can strongly influence both attention and memory and so our pre-existing schemata will influence our recall. We all have a schema for sitting down on a chair, but will that help or hinder learning how to get onto a chairlift by watching others? Next, in order to duplicate the behaviour that has been observed, the person must have the physical capacity to perform it. (For example, you cannot copy a ballet dancer doing the splits if you are physically incapable of that action). Such observational learning also provides information about consequences of a particular behaviour. If you watch someone get onto a chairlift in a particular manner and then immediately fall off, you are unlikely to try to copy that approach.

Modelling may also have *inhibiting* or *disinhibiting* effects on behaviours that have *already* been acquired. For example, if you see someone at a rally throw a brick through a window, will you follow suit? You know how to throw a brick, but what happens to that first individual may encourage or dampen your enthusiasm to do the same.

Bandura also considered reciprocal determinism to play an important role in social learning. That is, while the environment in which we live and function determines our behaviour to some degree because of the reinforcements that it provides for particular behaviours, we also 'reciprocate', that is, we determine our environment to some extent, and thereby increase or decrease the likelihood that certain behaviours will be reinforced. By choosing to join a biker gang rather than a glee club, an individual goes a long way towards determining both the models and the pattern of available reinforcements that will influence his or her behaviour.

Mirror neurons

Modern neuroscience offers an intriguing new avenue of unintentional social influence. Research shows that even though we are not aware of it, we often automatically imitate some of the movements other people make as we interact with them. Accumulating evidence (Iacoboni, 2009; Heyes, 2011) suggests that this automatic imitation is mediated by the mirror neuron system (discussed in both Chapters 9 and 14). These neurons fire not only when we initiate a particular activity, but also when we observe someone else performing that same activity. For example, observing an individual moving the right index finger produces increased specific muscle activation in the observer's right index finger (Catmur, Walsh & Heyes, 2007; Catmur, Gillmeister et al., 2008). Such behavioural mimicry suggests a biological preparedness to imitate the behaviour of those around us. However, there is significant controversy about the role that mirror neurons play in human behaviour, and there is some evidence suggesting that rather than being innate their function develops through our experience with others (Heyes, 2010). If this is so, not only do they play a part in social interaction, but they are also a product of it.

KEY POINT: The presence of others produces arousal, which in turn influences our behaviour. Whether our performance is enhanced or hindered depends on the type of task and whether, when acting in the group, our individual efforts can be identified. Social loafing occurs only when individual efforts cannot be identified. In team situations where an important goal is at stake and one's efforts are obvious, the performances of weaker team members are likely to show the most enhancement. Our behaviour is often influenced by the behaviour of others as we imitate their actions to achieve specific goals.

CONFORMITY

We now turn to conformity behaviour, when someone acts in a manner that avoids standing out from the group, even if that means ignoring his or her own judgement. Why do people conform? It generally makes life easier for one thing; groups typically reward conforming members with social approval, and this provides a feeling of connectedness. On the other hand, an individual who contradicts or ignores important social norms may experience unpleasant responses, including the threat of ostracism.

And because groups often function better when their members conform, there is even some speculation that natural selection may have shaped our neurological apparatus in such a way as to make conformity more likely. For example, Stallen et al. (2012) suggest that a particular brain chemical, oxytocin, might facilitate conformity behaviour. In their study, participants received either oxytocin or a placebo and were then asked to rate a number of visual stimuli after having been shown the ratings of those same stimuli ostensibly made earlier by other participants. Participants who had received oxytocin demonstrated more conformity with the earlier ratings, but there was no such effect among those who had received the placebo. However, this research is new and much more research is required before we can really understand the significance of such findings.

There are at least two motivations to conform, as described by the dual-processing model (Deutsch & Gerrard, 1955). The first of these processes is informational influence – in this case, we conform because the actions of the group appear to provide information that we need. To the extent that we trust the information to be accurate, we are likely to change our private beliefs and so there will ultimately be no inconsistency between what we believe and what we say or do. The second process is normative influence, where we act in a manner consistent with the norms of the group, even when this is contrary to our personal beliefs.

Informational influence

Imagine that you are a stranger in town with a couple of hours to kill. You decide to go down to the river to fish. As you stand alone fishing from the bridge, you notice a number of other people fishing from the riverbank. Since it seems likely that they must know what they are doing, you move to the riverbank and fish from there. Your conformity in this case is based on the assumption that those other people know something that you do not about where is the best place to fish. But what if everyone were 'new in town', everyone looking to each other for information? During the 1930s, Muzafer Sherif sought to answer that question. He employed the autokinetic effect. This effect was discovered during the Second World War when pilots flying on a dark night followed one another in a line, guiding themselves by the small light at the rear of the aircraft in front. However, officers on the ground were puzzled by their reports that these tail lights were observed to move around wildly, leading a pilot to think that the airplane ahead was moving erratically, which sometimes resulted in tragic collisions. This led to the discovery that when we observe a point of light against a dark background, with no frame of reference, the constant and automatic movement of our retinas leads our brains to conclude that it is the light, rather than our eyes, that is moving. The effect is nullified if the light is blinking, for our visual systems re-establish the position of the light and space with each new blink – hence the blinking lights on modern aircraft.

Now, imagine yourself in a room that is completely dark apart from a pinpoint of light some distance in front of you. Although the light actually remains stationary, it appears to move and, for some people, it seems to traverse a considerable distance. Since the effect is an illusory one, and people are perceiving movement that is not there, this provides an interesting social influence situation: How are people's assessments of movement influenced by those of others when there is no actual movement? Sherif (1936, 1937) placed groups of participants in this situation, and for each of a number of trials asked each participant to call out an estimate of how far the light had moved. Although the participants began with quite different distance estimates, their estimates gradually became more and more similar until there was very little variability among them. Sherif proposed this as a model of social conformity in which, without any direct pressure, individuals ultimately arrive at a common form of behaviour – a *social norm*, which subsequently exhibits very little variation. In other words, conformity in this case is the outcome of informational social influence and is accompanied by a reduction in the variability of the behaviour in question.

Such conformity behaviour can occur even when other group members are not physically present. For example, Wiener, Carpenter and Carpenter (1957) first asked participants to select labels for some ambiguous designs, after which they were shown fictitious percentages said to represent the choices of other participants, people they had not met and would not meet. When asked to choose again, the labels chosen by the participants shifted in the direction of the 'popular' choices. The assumption that 'if everybody is doing it, it must be right' is sometimes referred to as the bandwagon effect. In real life, the bandwagon effect can escalate rapidly once a majority is seen to be acting in a common manner.

Many aspects of our social world can be somewhat ambiguous at times. Being wrong can be uncomfortable, and being different is often perceived as being wrong. In situations of ambiguity, we frequently rely on the collective judgement of the majority for information about what is appropriate, and the result is increased conformity.

Normative influence

While it is of obvious benefit to be influenced by the group norm when one is deficient in information, conformity also frequently occurs simply because one does not want to stand out from the group. Peer pressure can be powerful, especially for children, but it is the rare adult who can escape it completely. The fear of being rejected by an important group is often enough to pull an individual's behaviour back into line with the group norm. Yet, even when there is no fear of rejection, most people feel discomfort if they are alone in deviating from the group norm.

Solomon Asch explored what happens when an individual deviates from the rest of the group. He used artificial groups of strangers, and so fear of rejection was not an issue, but he reasoned that as we grow up we all learn that it is often unwise, and we come to feel uncomfortable, if our behaviour or opinion diverges from that of the other members of the group.

One of his experiments (Asch, 1951) illustrates what might occur when a lone individual deviates from the group. This study used one real participant and a number of confederates of the experimenter. Their task was to choose which of three comparison lines matched a standard line in length (Figure 6.4 shows an example).

This was an easy task, and when the participants in a control group made individual judgements on their own, there were very few errors.

However, in the experimental group, there was only one actual participant, who was placed next to last in a group of confederates, all of whom made the same incorrect response on 12 of the 18 trials. Imagine yourself in that participant's situation: What would *you* do if, while looking at the lines in Figure 6.4, all of the people who answered before you chose line 3, even though it appears that it is clearly shorter than the standard line, and that line 2 is the correct answer? (This is like the situation faced by those who saw the naked emperor in his 'new clothes'). Would you trust your eyes or would you rely upon the judgements of the others? Or, trusting your own judgement, would you give the wrong answer in order not to stand out from the group? (And, of course, you may wonder if you have misunderstood something, if they know something that you do not.) Indeed, 76% of the participants went along with incorrect group choice at least once.

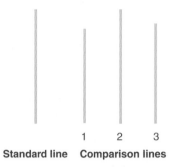

Figure 6.4 Example of the lines used in the Asch experiment

Crutchfield (1955) extended the Asch research by using a setup that did not require confederates. In this case, each participant worked alone in a booth facing a panel with lights that ostensibly communicated the responses of the other participants. This allowed the experimenter to present any desired pattern of the 'other participants' responses'. Crutchfield was able to reproduce Asch's work with a variety of stimuli. For instance, 79% of his participants agreed with an erroneous 'group judgement' that one of two (actually identical) circles was larger.

Not everyone succumbed to group influence in these studies, and only a few participants completely succumbed to group influence, while some others resisted it completely. However, it is clear that the effect was powerful and that few individuals could maintain complete independence. It is also important to recall, as was noted in Chapter 5, that the kind of behaviour change observed in the experiments described above does not necessarily mean that the respondents *believed* what they said when they gave the wrong answer. In that vein, it is interesting to note that when Asch had his participants write down rather than verbalize their decisions, thereby giving them some anonymity, the number of conforming responses was dramatically reduced.

We also must be careful to take the cultural and historical context into account before assuming that these findings apply to everyone everywhere. Remember that Asch's research was carried out in the United States during the 1950s when the political and social climate overtly encouraged conformity. (Consider the example of the anti-communist crusade led by Senator Joe McCarthy that resulted in the blacklisting of left-wing politicians and media figures. Deviance in political belief was risky.) By the 1970s, the political situation had changed; the 1960s had produced a strong willingness to express political dissent in the United States. When Larsen (1974) repeated the Asch study in the US, the rate of conformity was only about one-half of that reported by Asch. This finding was echoed by a meta-analysis of Asch-type research between 1952 and 1994 that reported a steady decline in levels of conformity among US subjects over time (Bond & Smith, 1996).

How would people in other countries respond to such conformity pressure? When Perrin and Spencer (1981) placed students in the United Kingdom into the Asch-type situation, they found very little conformity. And there were differences in the reasons that participants in the two countries gave for their conformity and nonconformity: When Asch had asked his American participants why they went along with the majority, they responded that they did not want to 'stick out like a sore thumb', or to have others think that there was something wrong with them. On the other hand, the students in the UK reported that they did *not* go along with the majority because they felt that to conform to an erroneous majority would make them look 'weak, ridiculous and stupid'. Of course we need to remember that studies were carried out in different eras and so the differences may reflect not only culture but the era as well.

There is evidence – for example, from a meta-analysis of conformity studies carried out in 17 nations that used the Asch-type judgement task (Bond and Smith, 1996) – that people in collectivist cultures tend to conform more than people in individualist cultures, presumably because people in collectivist cultures place a higher value on harmony in person-to-person relations, and harmony is promoted in part through conformity.

BOX 6.1   CONFORMITY PRESSURE AND THE COMMON GOOD

When everyone is acting in the same way, their actions do not provide any information about how each individual feels about his or her behaviour. Yet, when someone deliberately stands out from the crowd, either in terms of verbal or physical behaviour, we tend to consider such actions as more indicative of what the person is really like. This notion is the basis of deviance regulation theory (Blanton & Christie, 2003), which proposes that people govern their behaviour more on the basis of what they perceive as the possible negative social consequences of deviating from the norm than on the basis of possible positive social consequences of conforming to the norm. Thus, from this viewpoint, although standing out from the crowd in positive ways, such as being the most stylish dresser or the best athlete, may be welcome, it is not as important a motivating factor as are attempts to avoid being viewed negatively by the group.

Attempts to influence others will benefit from keeping this in mind. Consider this example (Goldstein & Cialdini, 2007): Suppose you are in charge of designing a poster campaign to encourage students to cover their mouths when they cough. What kind of message should you choose? It depends on what is the norm. If most people do cover their mouths – that is the norm – then according to deviance regulation theory, the message should stress the negative characteristics, such as irresponsibility, of those people who deviate from the norm. Since most people do not want to be seen as irresponsible, this will motivate greater adherence to the norm. On the other hand, if most people do not already cover their mouths when they cough – that is the norm – then the message needs to encourage *deviance* from the norm by stressing the positive characteristics of people who deviate, for example describing them as being thoughtful about the welfare of others.

This notion was put to the test in a study by Blanton et al. (2001). University students who had been surveyed two weeks earlier and asked to estimate the prevalence of condom use on their campus were now asked to read (fake) accounts ostensibly written by other students that either described condom users as intelligent and mature, or nonusers as lacking intelligence and being immature. Results showed that the more individuals considered condom use to be normative on the campus, the more they were influenced by the negative descriptions of non-users, and, conversely, the less that individuals believed condom use to be normative, the more they were affected by the positive descriptions of condom users.

As you can see, conformity behaviour is not always a bad thing. It can often be harnessed for the greater social good.

Although deviation from group norms is generally discouraged by the group, high-status group members are usually allowed more leeway than are low-status members. This may occur because high-status members have earned **idiosyncrasy credit** (Hollander, 1958; Homans, 1974) by contributing more than others to the effectiveness of the group. Each unit of such *good* behaviour is rewarded with an idiosyncrasy credit allowing high-status members, for example, to wear clothes that don't conform to the group's dress code. Of course, no one actually 'awards' such credits; it is simply that these implied credits mean that the individual is allowed more deviation from group norms without incurring negative reaction. However, once credits have been used in this way, more credits must be earned before further deviation will be allowed. Ostracism for deviant behaviour is, of course, the final threat. Keep in mind that groups pressure their members to toe the line only with regard to behaviours that are relevant to the group's well-being and efficiency. A work group concerned with behind-the-scenes television production would probably tolerate wide variations in dress; a motorcycle gang probably would not.

The effects of group size

Does the influence of a group become stronger as a group size increases? Latané's (1981) **social impact theory** posits that there are three factors that determine the likelihood that people will be affected by the social influence of others. First is the *strength*, or importance, of the influence. You can well imagine that if you are the only adult among a group of 12-year-olds, and they all dash out of the room after hearing a loud noise, you are less likely to follow them than you would be if they were all adults. Second is the *immediacy* of the influence; that is, the influence will be greater when the group providing the influence is in your close proximity than at some distance. If you see people a block away running from the sidewalk into the street, you are less likely to do likewise than were people in your direct vicinity doing so. Finally – and this brings us to the question of group size – it is predicted that the greater the *number* of people in the group, the greater will be the group's influence.

Effects of strength and immediacy would seem to be self-evident, but what about the effects of group size? A number of studies have examined this question. Among many variations on his basic theme, Asch (1951) tested whether increasing the size of the group would lead to more conformity. The conformity rate was 3% when there was only one confederate with the participant, but this increased to 13% when there were two confederates, and topped out at 32% with three confederates. Larger groups had no additional impact. However, other investigators have reported that the optimum number of confederates is actually between four and six. Wilder (1977) suggested that the reason that the effect of group size may be limited beyond a certain number may be that when the group size grows, the participant no longer perceives the various individuals as though they are separate entities. That is, when all the members express identical judgements, the participant is likely to treat them as encompassing a single point of view. She carried out an experiment in which she demonstrated that the judgements of a number of people divided into two groups had a greater influence on the participant than the judgements of the same number of people who were all part of single group.

Campbell and Fairly (1989) argue that the effects of group size depend on whether the situation brings *normative* or *informational* mechanisms into play. People trying to decide whether their judgement is correct will usually rely on information obtained from others in the same situation. The first source of information is likely to have the largest effect, and each additional source is less useful because the information is likely to be redundant. However, in situations where an individual conforms to the group judgement to avoid the possible social penalties associated with disagreeing with the majority, larger majorities should lead to more conformity.

Conformity and gender

For several decades, social psychologists described women as being more susceptible than men to social influences and pressures. This characterization, assumed to be factual and supported by early studies, was consistent with the stereotype of women as meek, submissive and easily swayed by emotion rather than reason. However, careful reviews of the literature and later research punctured this myth (Eagly, 1978; Eagly & Wood, 1985).

The vast majority of persuasion studies, in which participants are presented with a counter-argument and then asked to indicate their attitudes on a questionnaire (see Chapter 5), show no gender differences. However, one-third of the published studies show that females are likely to yield to group pressures. Let us consider why. One possible reason is bias in the actual studies. Typically, questions are asked for which there is a 'right answer' – lengths of lines, geometric shapes or information on geography, politics or science. It has been argued that at the time that those studies being carried out, men were likely to be more familiar with these topics and would therefore be more likely to resist social pressure to conform. A study by Sistrunk and McDavid (1971) set out to correct this bias. A panel of participants judged questions as being 'typically masculine' (sports cars, mathematics, politics), 'typically feminine' (cosmetics, cooking, sewing) or neutral. The questionnaire was then administered to male and female subjects. To induce conformity pressures, participants were told beside each question how a majority of students had supposedly responded. Results showed that women conformed more on 'masculine' items, but men conformed more than women on 'feminine' items. Overall, there was no difference in conformity levels of men and women.

There is some evidence that greater female conformity is found when the experiment is conducted by a male (Eagly & Carli, 1981). There is no reason to believe that male social psychologists are all male chauvinists who deliberately set out to prove a female stereotype. However, they may unintentionally design conformity situations in which males feel more comfortable. On the other hand female social psychologists, aware of the stereotype of female submissiveness, may design experiments in which females feel more comfortable and confident. In any case, the conflict reveals the sensitivity of research in social psychology to subtle influences.

It has also been argued that women and men are socialized differently in how to respond to social pressures and influence. For example, many traditional tests of sex-role identification link 'femininity' with such traits as nurturance, warmth and expressiveness and 'masculinity' with dominance, mastery and task-related competence. Yet, what may be labelled negatively as 'submissive' and 'passive' can also be seen in a positive light, as enhancing interdependence rather than independence (Greenglass, 1982) or as reflecting women's commitment to preserving social harmony and encouraging positive feelings within a group (Eagly & Wood, 1985). In this sense, expressing agreement may be a way of showing concern and support for others, which may be more important in many situations than giving the right answer. Another clue is that men resist conforming only when others are watching in order to convey an image as a nonconformist. Without surveillance, there are no differences in conformity between males and females (Eagly, Wood & Fishbaugh, 1981).

In short, we cannot support a generalization that women are more easily influenced than men. The effect as measured in the laboratory is small, inconsistent and limited to certain situations. It also seems to be related to another factor: women are usually in lower-status positions than men. Indeed, there is evidence that women are expected to conform more because of their low-status positions and that these expectations disappear when women are in higher-status roles (Eagly & Wood, 1982; Conway, Pizzamiglio & Mount, 1996). Stereotypes can become self-fulfilling prophecies and women may conform because of these expectations. As stereotypes change and better opportunities for women emerge in the workplace, even this small difference may disappear. Of course, keep in mind the role of culture, and the fact that gender roles, expectations, and stereotypes vary widely, while the research discussed above has been carried out for the most part in North America.

> **KEY POINT:** People conform at times because they lack information and at other times because they do not want to risk rejection by an important group. Conformity to group behaviour in laboratory experiments does not continue to increase as group size increases. Maximum conformity is reached in small groups of somewhere between three and six people. Gender on its own does not play a significant role in conformity.

DIRECT INFLUENCE

In the kinds of experimental groups described above, there were no actual sanctions applied to nonconforming individuals. Real-life groups, on the other hand, may not be so benign. Schachter (1951) set out to study discussion groups that were much more like those of real life. Several groups of male university students, 8 to 10 members each, were asked to discuss the case of Johnny Rocco, an apparently incorrigible delinquent. After reading his case history, each group member voiced his opinion as to how Johnny should be treated. Their opinions could range, on a five-point scale, from extreme kindness to extreme harshness. After group discussion, each participant again publicly voiced an opinion. However, three members of the group, all confederates of Schachter, had been coached to act in specific ways before and during the discussion. One, the 'deviate', took an initial position opposed to the majority and maintained it throughout the session. Another, the 'slider', began by acting like a deviate but as the session progressed gradually changed his opinion towards the majority view. A third confederate, the 'mode', expressed the majority view from beginning to end. (The initial opinions of real participants were nearly always lenient (i.e., 1, 2 or 3 on the five-point scale), and thus the confederates could be reasonably certain beforehand what position they would have to support or oppose).

Schachter observed two processes of interest: (1) the amount of communication directed to each type of confederate; and (2) how each confederate was treated at the end of the discussion session. Figure 6.5 illustrates the direction of communication. Notice that the 'mode' received very few communications, suggesting that people feel that there is little merit in preaching to the converted. The group paid almost as much attention to the slider as to the deviate in the early stages of the discussion, but as it became clear that the slider's position

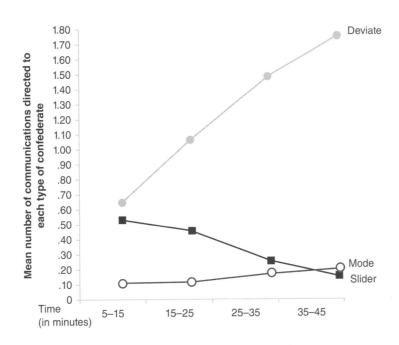

Figure 6.5 Participants' communication to the 'deviate', the 'mode', and the 'slider'

Source: Based on data from Schachter, 1961

was changing to that of the group, the group directed less attention to the slider and more attention to the trying to influence the position of the unchanging deviate.

At the conclusion of each discussion session, Schachter administered two measures of interpersonal attraction. One required the participants to submit nominations for memberships in one of three committees: executive, steering or correspondence. The deviates were invariably nominated for the least desirable (and least important) job – correspondence. In addition, participants were asked to rank the others in terms of their desirability as fellow group members. The instructions emphasized congeniality and compatibility. You will not be surprised to learn that the deviate was ranked as a much less desirable group member than either the mode or the slider. Moreover, the slider's case illustrates that the group does not penalize an individual for being different initially as long as he or she ultimately accepts the group norm.

One final point emerges from Schachter's research. Among those individuals who were ultimately the most rejecting of the deviate (giving him the lowest rankings), communication to the deviate initially increased as the session progressed, but when it became apparent that the deviate wasn't going to modify his opinion, communication rapidly declined. Not only did these individuals come to dislike the deviate; they eventually chose to ignore him. This sort of ostracism – or being 'sent to Coventry', as it is called in England – is well-documented in industry where work groups may pressure fellow workers to conform to output norms. A 'rate buster' who overproduces or a 'chiseller' who under-produces may be subjected not only to verbal pressure (or abuse) but to physical harassment as well.

Obviously, it is not easy to be a deviate. Given the pressures and sanctions the majority bring to bear, it is little wonder that most people simply choose to conform. The deviate, however, is not completely without influence, for under some conditions, a minority can actually have a significant effect on the majority.

KEY POINT: A person who deviates from the group is likely to come under pressure to come back into line, and continued deviation may result in rejection.

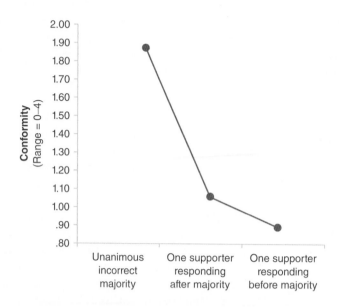

Figure 6.6 The effect of social support on judgement in a conformity situation
Source: Morris & Miller (1975)

THE ADAMANT MINORITY

Asch (1951) discovered that just having one other (confederate) person correctly judge the length of lines was sufficient to radically reduce, and in some cases entirely remove, erroneous conforming responses. This observation was later confirmed by Morris and Miller (1975), who also showed that a supporter (i.e., a person making a correct judgement) who precedes the incorrect responses of the majority reduces conformity to a greater extent than does one who responds after the majority (see Figure 6.6). Moreover, the quality of the support is not critical; any support is better than none. For example, Allen and Levine (1971) provided some participants who were being asked to make visual judgements with a supporter who wore glasses so thick as to raise serious doubts about his ability to see anything clearly. Other participants had a supporter with normal vision. When there was no supporter, participants conformed 97% of the time. With the addition of a 'competent' supporter, conformity declined to only 36%, but even when the supporter was 'incompetent' – that is, he apparently couldn't see well – conformity was still reduced to 64%. Thus, support in and of itself, quite apart from whether we have confidence in the opinion of the supporter, is enough to reduce conformity. Presumably, this is because when there is a supporter, the nonconforming participant is not left standing alone against the group.

Moscovici and colleagues (Moscovici et al., 1985; Papastamou, 1983) examined how a persistent minority can affect the majority. In one of their experiments, groups of six women, two of whom were confederates of the experimenter, were asked to look at slides and report what colour they saw. All the slides were actually blue and varied only in terms of intensity, but the two confederates consistently said that they saw green. Moscovici found that about 8% of participant responses were 'green' and that 32% of the participants said 'green' at least once. In a control group without confederates, almost none of the responses were 'green'. The impact of the minority became even more impressive when participants were individually given 16 discs ranging in colour from very definitely blue to very definitely green and were asked to label each disc as either green or blue on their own. Participants who had been in the experimental group were much more likely to call a disc green than were those who had been in the control group. The tendency to say 'green' was even observed in participants who had not said 'green' in the group situation.

It would seem that the minority had influenced all the participants even though some of them had not been willing to reveal it publicly in the group discussion.

Another experiment by Moscovici's group showed that it is important that the minority be consistent in its view. When the confederates were coached to respond in a more variable and inconsistent manner, the effects outlined above almost entirely disappeared. A consistent minority may be perceived as courageous, thereby fostering respect and thus possibly increasing its influence. Also, consistency implies confidence, and confidence gives the impression that there is indeed something in the minority position that is worth considering (Nemeth & Chiles, 1988). Yet, Papastamou and Mugny (1985) showed that the consistency of the minority is most effective if it is flexible rather than rigid. That is, the consistency should not be carried to extremes. While being consistent on important points, the minority should moderate or negotiate less important issues.

Overall, the research indicates that the outcome of majority pressure is usually confined to behaviour, while minorities can produce actual attitude change (Maass & Clarke, 1984; Moscovici, 1980; Personnaz & Personnaz, 1994). More in-depth analysis is stimulated by the minority view, whereas the majority view leads to relatively superficial thinking. Although the minority position is often quickly rejected, it can, if stated with consistency and confidence, lead others to consider many alternative and unique viewpoints. This divergent thinking results in decision-making that is therefore more reasoned, complex and stable (Nemeth, C.J., 1986; Nemeth & Kwan, 1987; Martin & Hewstone, 1999).

> **KEY POINT:** A persistent, but flexible minority can influence the majority, and when it does, this tends to produce not just behaviour change, but attitude change as well.

Justifying conformity

What happens when you submit to the opinion of the majority? In our daily lives, we often have to weigh the opinions of others and to decide whether to accept or reject them. How we then interpret our decision can have important implications. One possibility is to simply admit that to having 'given in' to their opinions. Another possibility is to decide – rationalize – that conformity was brought about by the facts, and not by perceived social pressure. Research (e.g., Griffin & Buehler, 1993; Buehler & Griffin, 1994) shows that most people take the latter route, rewriting history to justify their acquiescence. This process is automatic and immediate. And those who withstand the majority pressure and continue to dissent also engage in the same cognitive process, viewing their judgement as being based on the facts.

For example, in one study (Buehler & Griffin, 1994), participants were presented with newspaper, eyewitness and police accounts of an incident in which a black teenager driving a stolen car was shot and killed by a white police officer, and his passenger was arrested. The reports included accusations of police wrongdoing and racism. The participants then answered ten questions on a 'construal' scale designed to reveal how they construed the situation – whether the victims or the police were responsible for what happened. For example, one item asked, 'According to your image of the situation, what does it mean to say that the vehicle headed directly at both officers?' The choices ranged from 'would have hit both officers' (indicating victim responsibility) to 'same general direction' (indicating police responsibility). Participants then reread the reports and were asked, 'Do you agree?: The police officers are more than 75% responsible for the victim's death'. Then came the conformity manipulation: The participants were in groups of four and while waiting to respond, each 'inadvertently' learned that the other three in the group had agreed that the police were 75% responsible. Participants now had a choice either to agree with the majority or to dissent. After they had made their choice, they again completed the construal scale. This provided the researchers with two pieces of information: whether a participant agreed or disagreed with the unanimous majority, and whether his or her interpretation of the incident changed pre- and post-decision. The results can be seen in Figure 6.7. Not surprisingly, those who agreed with the 'group standard' of 75% police responsibility had begun with a more negative view of the role of the police than had those who dissented. However, in all cases, their interpretation of the roles of the victims and the police became more extreme – in the direction that supported their decision to conform or dissent.

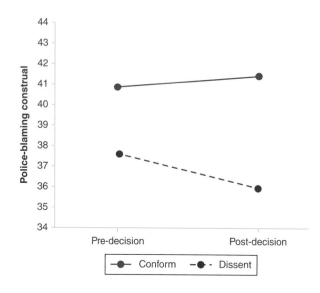

Figure 6.7 Pre-decision and post-decision construals by conformity decision
Source: Buehler & Griffin (1994)

Buehler and Griffin (1994) concluded that 'when faced with the choice between admitting that one has arbitrarily conformed to a group standard and proving that agreement with the standard was forced by the facts, almost everyone gets busy reconstructing the facts' (p. 993).

KEY POINT: When an individual conforms to the group, he or she is likely to justify that decision by rationalizing that the decision was based on reasoning.

NONCONFORMITY AND INNOVATION

Of course, if everyone were always to conform to group norms, little would ever change in life. Innovation feeds the forward march of civilizations. Innovation does not simply involve doing something in a new way. Thus, it could be questioned whether the Wright Brothers were true innovators, since they simply improved on available knowledge and techniques. On the other hand, Henry Ford's contribution to modern industry – the assembly line – completely revolutionized the manufacturing process. This ability to break out of the lock-step pattern of conformity is critical. Not only must innovators be able to resist normative pressures, they must also be willing to tolerate the risk of failure as well as potential public ridicule or scorn: Recall how Charles Darwin faced outrage from church and citizen alike (and continues to be vilified even today in some quarters), and Galileo was forced to recant his then-outlandish view that the earth was not the centre of the solar system. If an innovation goes too far beyond existing norms and expectations, it is unlikely to be accepted. For example, brewers who put 'diet beer' on the market in the 1970s made a similar error. It didn't sell. When it was reintroduced some years later as 'light beer', it captured a substantial proportion of beer sales because by that time the public had become considerably more health conscious.

While we shall discuss group decision-making in more detail in Chapter 12, a particular group technique, **brainstorming**, has been advocated as one way to foster innovative ideas. In this group situation, participants must feel free of any restrictions on the type of ideas they put forth. All notions, no matter how bizarre, are welcome. Yet, despite what advocates of brainstorming tell us, individuals working separately actually generate many more ideas, and more creative ideas (as rated by judges), than do groups (McGrath, 1984). So why does the illusion of group creativity persist? What seems to happen is that group members often believe that the brainstorming was effective because they overestimate the number of ideas that occurred to them during the group session, and they also have difficulty in differentiating their own ideas from those of the others in the group and give themselves credit for more ideas in the group situation than they actually produced (Stroebe, Diehl & Abakoumkin, 1992; Paulus et al., 1993).

Research into how new ideas and products spread throughout a society was spurred by E.M. Rogers' (1962/2003) book, *Diffusion of Innovations*, which even today provides the foundation in the marketing world for understanding how innovations are accepted and spread. His distribution curve of innovation adoption indicates that the innovators (inventors, designers and so on) make up about 2.5% of the overall population while the early adopters, quick to apply the idea or try the product, account for another 13.5%. These people then influence other people, the early majority, who are followed by the late majority, and those last to join in, the laggards. This process is

Figure 6.8 Think of important technological developments that have taken place during your lifetime: at what stage did you and the people you know adopt them?

Source: Canadapanda/Shutterstock.com

so important to marketers, especially those with very innovative products, that they often initially deliberately target those whom they assume to be early adopters. Of course, advertising also plays an important role, and many people are initially influenced directly by the media and then consult others only when the activities or products being advocated involve significant time, resources or risk.

The early adopters are risk-takers – the idea may not work; the product may be disappointing. They are motivated both by pride of being first and the status that conveys and by curiosity about a novel product or idea. For example, Chau & Hui (1998) studied early adopters of the Windows 98 operating system and discovered that those who had adopted the operating system early on were opinion leaders among their acquaintances with regard to computing, but they were also novelty-seekers, looking for new advances, and they had a great deal of experience working with computers.

> **KEY POINT:** Innovators need to go beyond existing norms, but if they go too far their innovations may not be accepted. Although brainstorming may assist in finding innovative solutions to problems, individuals working on their own typically generate more and better ideas than do groups. Innovation is usually embraced by a small number of early adopters who then serve as opinion leaders, influencing others to join in.

INTENTIONAL INFLUENCE

Obviously, people's lives extend beyond their memberships in groups, and frequently we stand alone. And when we are alone, attempts will be made to influence our behaviour – to get us to buy some product, to vote for a certain politician or to donate to a certain charity. Some of the techniques are sophisticated, employed in a deliberate manner, successful and undetectable by the individual involved. Five of these procedures are reviewed below.

The foot-in-the-door technique

The foot-in-the-door technique is based on the notion that if you can get someone to agree to a small request – you have a foot in the door – that person is subsequently more likely to agree to carry out a larger request. This means that if you want someone to do something and are not sure whether he or she will acquiesce, you should first make a request you are reasonably certain will be honoured. In this vein, Freedman and Fraser (1966) carried out a study of whether housewives (*homemakers* in today's preferred parlance) would agree to allow a survey team of five or six men to enter their homes and itemize all their household products. Obviously, this is a rather large request. However, while half of the participants had no prior contact with the researchers (one contact condition), the other half had been subjected to the foot-in-the-door technique – that is, they had been contacted by telephone nine days earlier with a simple request to answer a few questions about their favourite brand of soap. Of those who received this telephone call, only half of them were then actually asked the questions about the soap brand (performance condition) while for the others (agreement condition) the questions were not presented. This allowed the investigators to determine whether simple agreement to the first request was sufficient (that is, agreeing to answer questions) or whether the act actually had to be carried out (that is, actually answering the questions). As a further control to rule out the effects of the initial contact (that is, does simply having been contacted in advance by itself lead to more acquiescence to the large request?) participants in a fourth condition (familiarization condition) were contacted and informed of the nature of the survey but were neither asked any questions nor later asked to agree to the product inventory. The results are shown in Table 6.1. It is clear from these data that acquiescence to the first request considerably increased the likelihood of the larger request being accepted (52.8%). Merely agreeing helped a bit (33.3%), but the most effective inducement was having the person actually carry out the small request.

In a second experiment, Freedman and Fraser (1966) examined whether the person making the second, larger request needs to be the same person who made the earlier, smaller request, and whether the requests need to be similar in nature. (In the experiment described above, both requests had something to do with product brands.) The procedure was the same, but the small request was for participants either to put up a small sign on their lawn (promoting safe driving or keeping California beautiful) or to sign a petition (again, promoting safe driving or keeping California beautiful). In all cases, the second request was for participants to allow a large sign that said 'Drive carefully' to be placed on their lawn. The persons who made the first and second request were always different. One result of this experiment can be found in Table 6.2. The baseline for comparison here is the one-contact group; in this case, only 16.7% agreed to the large request. Clearly, all the other treatments improved on this outcome, but the most marked improvement occurred when, in the first instance, both the issue (safe driving) and the task (putting up a sign) were similar to the large request.

There is some evidence that the timing of the second request may also be important. Chartrand, Pinckert and Burger (1999) presented participants who had already agreed to a small request with a larger request either immediately or two days later, and either by the same requester or someone else. Compared to control subjects,

Table 6.1 Percentage of participants complying with large request

Condition	Percentage agreeing
Performance	52.8
Agree only	33.3
Familiarization	27.8
One contact	22.2

Source: Freedman & Fraser, 1966

Table 6.2 Percentage of participants complying with large request

Issue	Task	
	Similar (first request lawn sign; second request, lawn sign)	Different (first request, petition; second request, lawn sign)
Similar (both requests related to safe driving)	76.0%	47.8%
Different (first request related to beautiful California environment; second request to safe driving)	47.6%	47.4%

Source: Freedman & Fraser (1966)

the participants were more likely to agree to the larger request *except* when the same requester made the larger request immediately. In that case, there was *less* agreement to the larger request than in the control condition; one might imagine the individual may feel manipulated in such a case. Similar results have been obtained by Girandola (2002) in a study concerned with agreement to become a potential organ donor. As the researchers concluded, this means that the foot-in-the-door can backfire if the timing is not right.

Why does agreement to a small request facilitate agreement to a larger one? It has been suggested (Freedman & Fraser,1966; Dejong, 1979) that the small request changes the 'self-perception' of the participants who agree to it. Having agreed to the request, they conclude that they have been cooperative and helpful, and because they want to maintain this image, they then agree to the second request. This suggests a preference for consistency, and, in line with this interpretation, other research has found that individuals with a strong preference for consistency – that is, who experience significant cognitive dissonance when their actions are inconsistent – are more likely than others to agree to the second request (Cialdini, Trost & Newsom, 1995; Guadagno et al., 2001).

The door-in-the-face technique

The **door-in-the-face technique** is a variation of the foot-in-the-door procedure, one that many of us have either deliberately or inadvertently used at one time or another. In this case, the first request made is so extreme that the target is almost certain to refuse. The second request is considerably smaller and more reasonable. Cialdini et al. (1975) have shown this strategy to be an effective means of inducing agreement to the second request. For example, they accosted university students on the street and asked them if they would act as unpaid counsellors for two hours a week over the course of two years. Everyone refused the researchers. After being refused, they then asked the students to accompany a group of juvenile delinquents on a trip to the zoo. Fifty percent of the students were now willing to help compared to only 16.7% from another group who were asked only to go on the zoo trip.

Two explanations have been offered for the effectiveness of this procedure. One is based on the concept of *reciprocal concessions*. When the person making the large request reduces it to a smaller one, the other person then feels obligated to make a matching concession. The second explanation involves *self-presentation*. Most people prefer to present themselves to others in a positive light. By acceding to the second request, the students demonstrated that they were not really as bad as might originally have been implied by their initial refusal. In line with this, Pendleton and Batson (1979) observed that those who refused a moderate request later indicated that they thought that they would be perceived as 'less helpful, less friendly and less concerned' than if they had refused an extremely large request, something that any reasonable person might refuse.

The low-ball technique

To enhance the likelihood of a sale and to maximize the selling price, automobile and other salespeople, frequently use the **low-ball technique**, also sometimes referred to as the lure procedure (Guéguen, Joule & Marchand, 2013). Low-balling involves a 'bait and switch' and is based on the proposition that once an individual has agreed to carry out an act, he or she will carry it out even though the act is subsequently made more

Table 6.3 Percentage of participants making appointment and complying

	Condition	
	Control	Low-ball
Made appointment	31%	56%
Actually appeared	24%	53%

Source: Cialdini et al., 1978

costly. Cialdini et al. (1978) asked students to participate in an experiment scheduled at 7:00 in the morning. Participants in the low-ball condition were first asked whether they would participate in the experiment, and if they agreed, they were then told that the experiment would take place at 7:00 a.m. Those in the control condition were told about the study and the 7:00 a.m. start before being asked to agree. Two measures were obtained – the percentage of participants in each condition who agreed to participate and the percentage that actually showed up at the scheduled time. The results of the study, shown in Table 6.3, indicate that a much higher percentage of the students who were 'low-balled' both agreed to participate and actually showed up for the appointment.

In another experiment (Joule, Gouilloux & Weber, 1989), students were first invited to watch some interesting film clips, but after agreeing, they were then informed that there was no film to watch, and they were asked instead to memorize a list of numbers. Forty-seven per cent of them agreed to participate in the memory task compared to only 15% of students in a control group who had only been asked to do the memory task, without an initial (and subsequently withdrawn) invitation to watch a film. Again, low-balling worked.

Why does it work? It is important to note that it works only when the individual feels that he or she has made a free choice when making the first decision. Then, once the individual has committed to that decision, there is reluctance to change it (Cialdini et al., 1978). Consider how this is applied in the world of automobile sales. The salesperson gets the customer to make an active decision – for example, to accept an offer of an extremely low price on a car that interests the customer. Once this is done and the necessary forms are filled out, the salesperson says that since the price is so low, she must check with her supervisor. She then leaves for a few minutes and returns to report that the supervisor would not agree to the deal because they would be losing money on it. Now the purchase price goes up, and if the technique works, the customer will still enter into the agreement in spite of the increased cost. The initial decision persists.

Improving the deal: The 'that's-not-all' technique

The **'that's-not-all' technique** consists of offering a product to a person at a high price, preventing the person from responding for a few seconds, and then enhancing the deal either by adding another product or decreasing the price. For example, Burger (1986) ran a field experiment in which two experimenters sat at a table in various locations, selling cupcakes and cookies. The cupcakes were visible but the cookies were not. Some of those who approached the table were told that the price for the cupcakes was 75 cents each (which was a high price in 1986). Just then, the second experimenter tapped the first experimenter on the shoulder, and after a brief exchange, the first experimenter turned to the customer and said that the price included two cookies along with a cupcake. In the control group, the participants were told about the two cookies as soon as they asked the price of the cupcakes. It was found that 73% of those in the 'that's-not-all' condition bought the cupcakes (and cookies) compared to only 40% of those in the control condition.

Why does this technique work? Burger (1986) suggests two possible explanations: the norm of reciprocity and the effect of different anchoring points in attitudinal judgements. The norm of reciprocity indicates that people feel under some obligation to reciprocate gifts, favours and concessions. In the case of the 'that's-not-all' procedure, the seller improves the offer (adds the product or lowers the price) and the buyer then feels obliged to purchase the product as a reciprocal action. In terms of anchoring, the salesperson first offers the

Table 6.4 Number of participants complying

	Condition	
	Lie	Non-lie
Comply	20%	11%
Not Comply	11%	20%

Source: Freedman, Wellington & Bless (1967)

cupcake for one dollar, establishing an anchor point, allows a few seconds for the customer to process this, and then reduces the price to 75 cents. Against the anchor point of one dollar, the 75-cent price looks better than it would if initially stated as the price. Burger (1986) also presented data that suggests that this technique is more effective than the door-in-the-face method of inducing compliance.

Guilt

Feelings of guilt have powerful and pervasive influences on behaviour. Parents, for example, can be experts at creating feelings of guilt in their offspring when some particular action is desired. 'After all I've done for you …' In investigations of the power of guilt in the laboratory, participants are usually led to transgress in some way; then a request is made of them. For instance, Freedman, Wallington & Bless (1967) induced participants to lie and then requested their volunteer participation in an additional study. Their data are reproduced in Table 6.4. In comparison with a control group, almost twice as many participants who had lied complied. Darlington & Macker (1966) used a similar procedure to increase the likelihood of individuals donating blood.

This effect is not confined to helping those against whom the participant transgressed. Regan, Williams & Sparling (1972) had a male confederate ask female shoppers to take a picture of him with his camera. When they tried, the camera wouldn't work. Some of the participants were made to feel that it was their fault while others were assured they were not to blame. A second confederate then appeared carrying a torn bag of groceries with the contents falling out. Fifty-five per cent of the participants in the 'guilt' condition and only 15% in the control condition informed the confederate of the leaky bag. Although there was no direct request for assistance, it does suggest that individuals who have been made to feel guilty are then motivated to expiate the guilt through offering help, and that their helping act is not necessarily directed at the injured party.

KEY POINT: There are several procedures that have been shown to increase acquiescence to a request. Sometimes we use these techniques without awareness – guilt induction, for example – while at other times, salespeople in particular may deliberately use them to enhance sales.

OBEDIENCE

Obey the law. Obey your god. Obey your parents, your teacher, your superior officer, the referee, the police officer … Throughout our lives we are exhorted to obey, and to some extent this is a good thing, for without some obedience, societies would soon fall into chaos. If drivers ignore police officers at will; if students disobey their teachers; if children pay no heed to parents; if citizens violate the law at their pleasure; if soldiers make up their own minds about how to behave in battle; if hockey players ignore their coach; yes, there will be chaos.

But what happens when people taught the virtues of obedience are given orders to do bad things: to keep secret the malfeasance of a politician? To cover up research showing that a pharmaceutical product can be dangerous? To torture presumed enemies of the state? To exterminate an entire people? This question came into focus as the Second World War drew to a close and the world began to realize the full horror of the

BOX 6.2   TAKE ANOTHER LOOK: THE POWER TO PERSUADE

Who deliberately employs persuasion techniques? Salespeople, of course. Political parties, often. Social activists, sometimes. And police officers? You may be surprised, but yes, police officers often use deliberate persuasion techniques in the attempt to wrest confessions from those they assume to be guilty. But where is the harm? you might ask. Short of using torture, surely no one can persuade someone to confess to murder if they are innocent. And because of this presumption, judges and juries assume with great confidence that someone who has confessed to a crime is surely guilty. Yet significant numbers of innocent people – later exonerated through DNA evidence – have confessed and been convicted of heinous crimes elicited through interrogations using formal persuasion techniques.

Psychologist Timothy Moore is a noted critic of the Reid technique, a powerful interrogation procedure widely used by police across North America that can persuade some people to confess to crimes they have not committed (Moore & Fitzsimmons, 2011). It works with those who have waived the right to have a lawyer present, a situation that is much more likely to happen when a suspect is innocent and believes that asking for a lawyer would suggest guilt. The technique alternates between *confrontation* and *minimization* so that the interrogator is in a sense both 'good cop' and 'bad cop' rolled into one. Confrontation involves direct accusations of guilt and deliberate interruptions of the suspect whenever he or she tries to deny it. Often the accused is told that the police possess hard evidence that confirms his or her guilt (whether they have such evidence or not). Then through minimization, the interrogator appears to be understanding, and even sympathetic, and suggests that confession is the first step towards dealing with the problem, often implying that by confessing the suspect will be treated more leniently by the courts. The interrogation can be lengthy, and the suspect's isolation, anxiety and fatigue increase vulnerability to persuasion. The interrogator effectively creates a situation where confession may seem to be the only reasonable way to reduce the aversive nature of the interaction. At times, the persuasion has been so successful that the suspect has come to believe, at least in the moment, that he or she might actually be guilty – for how else could the police have the solid evidence that they claim to have – and such self-delusion is fostered when the interrogator presents pseudo-technical explanations as to how the suspect could have committed a crime without being consciously aware of it.

But the Reid technique pales in comparison to the Mr Big technique used by undercover police officers in Canada and sporadically in Australia. It is used when police are convinced that someone has committed a major crime, but without a confession will escape justice because of lack of evidence.

This is what the Mr Big persuasion scenario looks like (based on Moore, Copeland & Schuller, 2009):

Suppose that you are the only suspect in the murder of your close friend. Although innocent, the police are convinced of your guilt, but have no evidence that would lead to conviction. A special group of undercover officers is provided with substantial financial resources to set up a persuasion situation with the goal of eliciting your confession – a situation that may take months to construct. Members of the undercover group begin to make your acquaintance – for example, a stranger strikes up a conversation with you in your favourite billiards parlour. Over time, you 'happen' to encounter that person again, until at some point you share a beer or a cup of coffee as your acquaintanceship grows. Let us assume that you are a petty criminal, so that when the acquaintance lets slip that he (or she) is part of a gang that is making a lot of money illegally, your interest is piqued. Gradually, as a friendship grows, you are invited to participate in some minor crimes – perhaps serving as a lookout during a robbery – although unbeknownst to you, the crimes are all faked by the police. Gradually, you meet more and more members of the gang; you go drinking together; you play baseball with them; they become your buddies. And you become intrigued to learn that big money is to be made by members of the gang, and you are subtly encouraged to become a member. By now, this appeals to you, but you are told that before you can be accepted into the gang, you need the approval of the big boss (Mr Big). And to increase the gravity of the situation, before you actually get to meet him, you 'inadvertently' witness what happens to someone who crossed him – you see the person being beaten up or murdered or buried (all faked of course). By the time you finally meet Mr Big – of course, he is also an undercover police officer – you have been informed that he knows about the crime of which you are accused because some of his gang members have infiltrated the justice system. Mr Big does not care that you are a murderer, but he does not want the risk of further investigation if you become a gang member. In order to have his insiders expunge everything from the record to make sure that the police will no longer pursue you, he vehemently pressures you to confess so that he can clean up the mess. You appear to have nothing to lose by confessing, even though you are innocent, and at some point it appears that 'confession' is the only way to end the pressure and to be accepted into the gang. And so you confess, and suddenly the scene changes; the theatre is over and you learn that these people who have befriended you for months and months are all police officers whose only goal is to see you convicted of murder. On go the handcuffs, and now you face the near impossible task of persuading a judge and jury that you have confessed to a murder of which you are innocent. You have succumbed to overwhelming social influence and persuasion. Fortunately, some judges are beginning to question and even reject confessions obtained through Mr Big.

Holocaust. How to make sense of the fact that large numbers of Germans, many devoted Christians among them, had participated in the genocidal slaughter of millions of innocent Jews and the systematic extermination of other 'undesirables' including the Roma, homosexuals and the mentally disabled? Nazi leaders brought to judgement at the Nuremberg War Crimes trials provided no insight into this question, for their common defence was that they were 'only following orders'. Were their terrible acts the simple product of blind, destructive obedience to orders from the poisoned minds of Nazi leaders?

Psychologist Stanley Milgram recognized that not all obedience is directed towards violence, but it was the 'destructive obedience' underlying the Holocaust that interested him. Was it something peculiar to the German psyche, or the rigorous code of obedience of the German Officers' Corps (Snow, 1961)? He wondered if ordinary American adults would follow orders from a legitimate authority if those orders involved harming other people, and he set about to try to do what no one had ever done before, to study obedience in the laboratory (Milgram, 1963, 1965, 1974). His discovery of the apparent ease with which ordinary people could be led to obey orders and to inflict harm on an innocent and protesting victim stunned the psychological world, and the shock reached far beyond the confines of academe. Milgram's research has become the most widely known social science research in history (Reicher & Haslam, 2011a).

He set about to see whether the simple authority of an experimenter in a laboratory would be enough to produce destructive obedience in ordinary people. For his study, he recruited 40 male participants from the general public through a newspaper advertisement inviting them to participate in research at Yale University. The procedure was as follows: Two participants reported to the laboratory at the scheduled time, but one of them was a confederate of the experimenter. They were met by the experimenter, dressed in a white lab coat, and it was explained to them that they were to participate in a study of how punishment might facilitate learning. The participant and the confederate then were assigned, supposedly at random, the roles of learner and teacher, but the selection was rigged so that the real participant was always designated as the teacher. The learner was then taken to a separate room, and, in full view of the teacher, strapped into a kind of 'electric chair' which would deliver an electric shock to his arm. At this time, the 'learner' casually mentioned that he had a heart condition. (In fact, of course, the learner never actually received any shocks.) The teacher then was given a sample shock, which involved a significant jolt.

The teacher and experimenter then returned to the main room, and the teacher sat down in front of a 'shock machine'. Although this was actually a fake apparatus, it looked to be very real, and had 30 settings running from 15 to 450 volts inscribed with labels varying from 'Slight Shock' to 'Danger: Severe Shock'.

The experimenter then instructed the teacher to read a list of paired associates to the learner over an intercom. Next, the teacher read the first word of each pair and the learner was required to respond with the correct partner to that word from a list of four possible choices. The teacher was told to administer a shock whenever the learner was unable to respond with the correct word, and the shock intensity was to be increased by one level on each additional trial on which an error was made.

Public Announcement

WE WILL PAY YOU $4.00 FOR
ONE HOUR OF YOUR TIME

Persons Needed for a Study of Memory

*We will pay five hundred New Haven men to help us complete a scientific study of memory and learning. The study is being done at Yale University.

*Each person who participates will be paid $4.00 (plus 50c carfare) for approximately 1 hour's time. We need you for only one hour: there are no further obligations. You may choose the time you would like to come (evenings, weekdays, or weekends).

*No special training, education, or experience is needed. We want:

Factory workers	Businessmen	Construction workers
City employees	Clerks	Salespeople
Laborers	Professional people	White-collar workers
Barbers	Telephone workers	Others

All persons must be between the ages of 20 and 50. High school and college students cannot be used.

*If you meet these qualifications, fill out the coupon below and mail it now to Professor Stanley Milgram, Department of Psychology, Yale University, New Haven. You will be notified later of the specific time and place of the study. We reserve the right to decline any application.

*You will be paid $4.00 (plus 50c carfare) as soon as you arrive at the laboratory.

TO:
PROF. STANLEY MILGRAM, DEPARTMENT OF PSYCHOLOGY, YALE UNIVERSITY, NEW HAVEN, CONN. I want to take part in this study of memory and learning. I am between the ages of 20 and 50. I will be paid $4.00 (plus 50c carfare) if I participate.

NAME (Please Print). . . . .

ADDRESS . . . .

TELEPHONE NO. . . . . Best time to call you . . . .

AGE . . . . OCCUPATION. . . . . SEX . . . . . .
CAN YOU COME:

WEEKDAYS . . . . EVENINGS . . . . . . WEEKENDS . . . .

Figure 6.9 The original advertisement to recruit participants in the Milgram Experiment
Source: Wikimedia Commons

In fact, the verbal responses from the 'learner' were standardized: they were pre-recorded and presented by means of a tape recorder at specific times, depending on shock level. For example, at 75 volts the learner would be heard to grunt and moan, at 150 volts he demanded to be released, at 180 volts he cried out that he could no longer stand the pain. If the teacher continued to the 300 level, the learner refused to provide any more answers. The experimenter then instructed the teacher to treat silence as a wrong answer and to continue with the series of increasing shocks. When the teacher showed any hesitation, the experimenter (remember, dressed in a white laboratory coat, looking like a scientist) responded with, one of an escalating number of prods: The first hesitation elicited the prod 'Please continue'. The next hesitation was met with, 'The experiment requires that you continue'. The final two prods were: 'It is absolutely essential that you continue' and 'You have no other choice, you must go on'. (Note that only this final prod is actually an explicit order.)

Milgram's dependent variable was the highest level of electric shock administered by the teacher before he refused to continue on. And how far did the participants go? Although they typically became agitated and tense and frequently indicated that they wanted to stop the experiment, all participants continued to the 300-volt level, and twenty-six of the forty participants – almost two-thirds – continued all the way to the maximum shock, despite the protests and ultimately the silence of the learner (Milgram, 1963)! These results astounded not only the psychological community but the world at large, for they seemed to demonstrate that decent, ordinary people are capable of committing terrible harm to others simply out of blind obedience to an authority – even when the authority is only a man dressed in a laboratory gown.

Were the participants blindly and unemotionally complying with the experimenter's dictates? No, they were not. Make no mistake; while two-thirds of them did indeed continue to the highest shock level, they did not do so as cold-hearted functionaries. Rather, they showed significant signs of anxiety and emotional distress and even anger, and every participant hesitated at some point and questioned the experimenter out of concern for what was happening to the learner.

Milgram conducted a number of variations of this procedure, changing one aspect of the situation at a time, and he found that, depending on the conditions, participants' average obedience varied tremendously, from 100% to close to zero (Figure 6.10). An earlier pilot study that when the learner gave no feedback at all, all of the participants delivered the maximum voltage. In other studies, he examined the possibility that the obedience had occurred because the learner was physically isolated from the victim, and he found that as the victim and the participant were situated physically closer to one another, the level of obedience was reduced. Yet, when in the closest condition, the participant was required to hold the victim's hand on the shock-plate while administering the shock, 30% of the participants still administered the highest level of shock!

Milgram also found that obedience decreased even further (to 20.5%) when the experimenter was physically absent from the laboratory and instead delivered his orders over the telephone. In yet another variation, the teacher was given free choice in choosing shock levels, in which case most people chose only low voltage shocks and fewer than 3% of them continued to the maximum level.

In yet another variation, Milgram held the experiment in an office away from the university in order to eliminate any effect of the prestige of university setting. The level of obedience declined somewhat, but about half the participants still continued to the maximum shock level.

Ethical firestorm

As you might well anticipate, Milgram's research raised a number of ethical concerns, primarily with regard to placing participants in a situation that clearly produced pronounced psychological distress. For his film, *Obedience*, which documents his research, provides clear evidence that the experience was very upsetting for at least some of the participants. Although Milgram argued that his careful debriefings provided assurance enough that participants had not suffered any long-term effects, many psychologists believed that was insufficient and that this kind of experiment should not be carried out (e.g., Baumrind, 1964). Modern ethical guidelines for psychological research require, among other things, that participants be informed that they can discontinue an experiment whenever they wish, and that the experimenter must comply, whereas the experimenter in the Milgram experiments explicitly challenged the participants' requests to stop and told them that they had no choice but to continue. As discussed in Chapter 2, these ethical considerations fostered the creation of university ethics panels, and not long after Milgram published his book *Obedience to authority: An experimental view* (Milgram, 1974), the first set of ethical principles governing research with human participants was published by the American Psychological Association, and new federal regulations regarding research with humans came into effect in the United States, all which made it virtually impossible to do further research of this sort in that country (Blass, 2012).

International research

However, while obedience research came to a sudden halt in the United States in the mid-70s, it continued to be carried out in other countries. Studies in Jordan (Shanab & Yahya, 1977), Spain (Miranda et al., 1981), Germany (Mantell, 1971), and Australia (Kilham & Mann, 1974) all produced results very similar to those of Milgram, with between 50% and 85% of participants administrating the highest shock level. Blass (2012) reviewed Milgram-type obedience studies, including both published articles and doctoral dissertations that had been conducted in several other countries – India, Austria, Italy, South Africa, Puerto Rico, Scotland, Holland and Canada – and reported that the average obedience scores were approximately the same as those found by Milgram in United States, suggesting that this phenomenon is a general one.

Modern studies

While much attention has been paid to the violent aspects of Milgram's research, obedience can readily occur in many less dramatic situations where there is no physical punishment involved – for example, in responding to administrative orders in a company setting. Meeus and Raaijmakers (1986) conducted a study of such administrative obedience in Holland. Their research involved having a participant administer an employment test to an ostensibly unemployed person (actually a confederate of the experimenter) who was applying for a job. The participant was told that the 'applicant' had been invited to the laboratory to take a selection test that, if passed, would guarantee a job. Participants administered the test orally to the applicants, but they were directed to disturb the applicant during the test by making denigrating remarks about his or her test achievement and personality. They were provided with a set of 15 remarks that they could make, and these were scripted to become increasingly distressing as time passed. If the participant proceeded all the way to the most upsetting comments, the applicant (confederate) responded by appearing to be unable to cope, thereby failing the test and forfeiting the job. Would the participants administer the most severe comments?

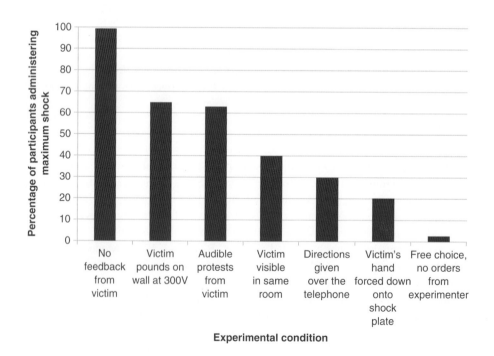

Figure 6.10   Effect of experimenter actions on the percentage of participants in the Milgram study who administered the maximum shock level of 450V

Source: Data from Brown, 1986

In fact, 91.7% of the participants made all 15 remarks, thereby ensuring that the applicant would not get the job. This outcome represents a considerably higher level of obedience than was observed by Milgram and others and suggests that this type of psychological harm is easier to perpetrate than physical violence.

Bocchiaro & Zimbardo (2010), using a modified version of the procedure employed above, carried out a study using undergraduates in an Italian university as participants. Thirty per cent of their participants obeyed fully and delivered all of the 15 levels of increasingly hostile feedback, while the other 70% refused at some point to continue. They concluded that their findings mirrored those of Milgram for comparable conditions, despite cultural differences between the United States and Italy.

It is one thing to study administrative obedience, as described above, but what would happen if the Milgram studies, complete with shock apparatus, were to be repeated today? But how could social psychologists conduct such research in an ethically responsible manner? Virtual reality may provide an avenue in the future, for it has been reported that when a 'virtual' rather than a real human participant is used in the Milgram procedure, participants respond to the learner's protests with the same subjective, behavioural and physiological responses as if the virtual participant were real (Slater et al., 2006). In the meantime, what if one were to use the traditional Milgram procedure but discontinued the experiment at a point before the participant is likely to become distressed, and yet where conclusions could still be drawn about how likely it is they would have delivered the maximum shock had they been allowed to continue? As it turns out, a meta-analysis of Milgram's experiments (Packer, 2008) reveals that the most common point at which participants stopped and refused to continue was at the 150-volt level (although in Milgram's original experiment, described earlier, everyone continued to at least the 300-volt level). The 150-volt level is the point when the learner first announces that he wants to be released, crying out, '*Ugh! Experimenter! That is all. Get me out of here. I told you I had heart trouble. My heart started to bother me now. Get me out of here please. My heart started to bother me. I refuse to go on. Let me out*' (Milgram, 1974, p. 56). Participants who continued past this point were likely to continue all the way to the 450-volt maximum. Packer (2008) interpreted this as indicating that the participants who refused to continue past that point did so because they considered the learner's right to stop the experiment superseded the experimenter's orders to continue. However, it is also noteworthy, as Packer observed, that for those who continued, the learner's escalating expressions of pain did not trigger any subsequent disobedience.

So, if those who are willing to proceed beyond the 150-volt level typically continue all the way to the end, then once the participant has indicated willingness to beyond 150 volts, why not stop the procedure at that point, where there is as yet little reason for distress on the participant's part? One could then assume those who are willing to go on would have proceeded to the maximum voltage. This is how Burger (2009) proceeded in his experiment. His procedure and shock apparatus mirrored that of Milgram, with the key difference being that that participants were stopped once they delivered a shock at the 150-volt level and had agreed to continue beyond that point. His results showed only slightly lower obedience rates than those found by Milgram half a century earlier, and this despite the fact that Burger's participants had been psychologically screened in order to eliminate those people with personality characteristics that might put them at greater risk of being negatively affected by this experimental situation.

Modelling effects

Burger (2009) also carried out a 'modelled refusal' condition. In this case two confederates were used, one as the learner and the other as a second teacher. The two 'teachers' sat side-by-side in front of the shock machine, but when the shock level reached 90 volts, the confederate-teacher refused to participate any further. Unexpectedly, this refusal to continue had no significant effect on the behaviour of the participant. This is contrary to what Milgram (1974) found in another of his experiments in which there were three teachers, two of whom were confederates. One confederate teacher refused to go on after the 150-volt level was reached, and the second refused to continue beyond the 210-volt level. Even though the experimenter instructed the real participant to continue on alone, only 10% of them continued all the way to the maximum voltage level.

Culture and gender effects

Blass's (2012) cross-cultural review of studies of obedience found that the average obedience rates in replications carried out in South Africa, Germany, Australia, Jordan, Spain, India, Austria and Italy to be very similar to those reported by Milgram in the United States. Furthermore, there were no differences between males and females in the majority of studies, the two exceptions being studies carried out in Australia and India where, in each case, females were found to be less obedient than males. However, given the near-exclusive use of male participants in obedience research, the extent to which women obey orders has not been thoroughly investigated. Milgram employed female participants in only one of his experimental conditions – but even then, the learner was a male – and there was no gender difference. Burger (2009) also found no significant gender difference in his research.

Obedience across the decades

A very significant shift in child-rearing philosophy has gradually taken place in industrialized Western nations over the course of the past half-century. While obedience had long been considered the most desirable quality to be encouraged in children, and disobedience to be the most serious behavioural problem (Benjamin & Simpson, 2009), in modern times the typical parental focus has become the encouragement of independence and self-esteem. This was borne out in the European Values Survey carried out in nine countries in the European Community in 1981: Compared with people born in 1936 or before, people born after 1936 indicated a much stronger preference for encouraging independence and imagination in children, and less preference for instilling social conformity and obedience (Lesthaeghe & Meekers, 1986). A similar trend has been found in the United States (Alwin, 1996). Typically, children are now taught not to act like sheep, to think for themselves and to do what they think is right. (This modern emphasis on assertiveness and independence has arguably been *too* successful: not only are modern children more likely to possess greater independence and higher self-esteem, there has been a corresponding upsurge in narcissism (Twenge, 2009). Recall the discussion in Chapter 3.)

However, Burger (2009) reported that there was no statistical difference between the rate of obedience in his research and that of Milgram carried out half a century earlier. And when Blass (2012) carried out his review of research using a Milgram-type procedure (discussed earlier), he found no indications of changes in obedience over time. So why has there not been a greater decline? It may well be that we are making the fundamental attribution error here: we tend to attribute behaviour to individual dispositions while ignoring the powerful influence of the situation, and this leads us to erroneously expect that because child-rearing now place more emphasis on individuality and non-conformity, we should observe less obedience in a Milgram-type experiment (Burger, 2009).

The power of the situation

What is it about the situation that seems to promote obedience? To understand better what is going on, imagine yourself to be the participant. You have agreed to participate in scientific research, you have arrived at the laboratory in the university, the experimenter seems to be a decent chap, and you are looking forward to taking part in a psychological experiment. You are introduced to another participant, and you are chosen to be the teacher while the other person is to be the learner in a study into the effects of punishment as a stimulus to learning. So far, it is all very interesting. However, when you find that part of your task is to deliver electric shocks to the learner who is hooked up to a shock apparatus in another room, you start to feel a little uneasy, and your unease grows a little when the learner mentions a cardiac condition. As the experiment progresses, your unease magnifies when the learner starts to yell out in pain. However, something is a little odd: the experimenter appears unfazed by the learner's distress, and he pressures you not only to continue with the experiment but also to keep increasing the shock level, even though the labels on the shock machine indicate that your shocks are approaching a dangerous level. This is troubling to you. Surely this university scientist cannot be so corrupt of spirit that he is unconcerned by the learner's suffering – to the extent that he encourages you to deliver more harm? Are you missing something? How to make sense of this? Are you going to risk ruining the experiment by refusing to continue? Or is there some reasonable explanation for what is going on?

As you can see, the Milgram situation is not as straightforward as it might have seemed when you first read about it. Consider these questions:

1. *Who has the authority?* As a demonstration of the power of the trappings of authority, Bushman (1988) carried out a field experiment in which a female confederate was dressed either in neat attire, or in a sloppy outfit, or in a uniform. While the experimenter pretended to search for change while standing next to an expired traffic meter, she stood nearby and stopped pedestrians and ordered, 'This fellow is over-parked at the meter and doesn't have any change. Give him a nickel!' When wearing a uniform, 72% of the pedestrians supplied a nickel, whereas in the neat and sloppy attire conditions only about 50% obeyed. In addition, no one questioned the confederate when she was in uniform, while 23% questioned her when she was neatly dressed and 29% when she was sloppily dressed.

   Back to the Milgram experiment: The researcher looks like a scientist; he is dressed in a lab coat and is employed at a university. Why should you not do as he asks?

2. *Who has the responsibility?* Who is responsible if the learner suffers harm? The participant might well conclude that it is the experimenter who must bear responsibility for any harm that occurs. This is in line with Milgram's (1974) analysis: He interpreted the obedience that he had observed in terms of the participants having moved into an **agentic state**, ceasing to act according to their own values and interests but instead becoming agents of the authority, and thereby following orders out of a desire to fulfil their duties as a participant in the experiment.

   Yet, can people switch from acting as an individual at one moment to acting as an agent the next? If they had become mere agents, one would expect them simply to focus on carrying out the instructions of the experimenter, and not to react with the obvious hesitation and confusion and distress that was observed.

3. *Whose team are you on?* Although Milgram interpreted his data in terms of obedience to authority, he also considered the possibility that the development of a shared social identity over the course of the experiment might play an important role (Milgram, 1965). With the participant separated from the learner and in the same room with the experimenter, it may be that that the participant feels part of an in-group with the experimenter (Reicher & Haslam, 2011a). In line with this possibility, Milgram found in one of his experiments that obedience decreased when all three were together in the same room. (We shall return to this theme later in this chapter, with regard to disobedience.)

   There is another interesting point to be made here: Remember the experimenter's four prods to continue? It is only the fourth one, '*You have no choice, you must go on*', that actually takes the form of a direct order. In the Burger (2009) study, on every occasion when the experimenter issued the fourth prod, the participant refused to go any further, which argues against Milgram's interpretation that people were just following orders, for if so, why would they stop at that point? Reicher and Haslam (2011a) suggest that this prod, the first actual 'order', may have broken the participant's sense of being part of an in-group with the experimenter. As a result, if the participant and experimenter are no longer on the same team, the participant can now resolve the conflict between the experimenter's demand to continue and the learner's demand to stop. That is, there is now justification to do what the learner has been asking and stop the experiment (Haslam & Reicher, 2012).

4. *What is going on here anyway?* Burger (2009) reminds us that these participants were in a very strange setting, one that they never experienced before, and their only source of information was the experimenter. Since the experimenter did not seem to show any reaction to the learner's agitated protestations, that would suggest that all was proceeding normally and that nothing harmful was actually occurring. Obedience in Milgram's experiments fell from 65% to 40% when participant and victim were both in the same room, and to 30% when the participant had to hold the learner's hand to the metal shock plate in order to administer the shock. One could interpret this as providing more information about what is really going on, and that, as information increases, obedience decreases.

5. *When does it get serious?* Is there anything about Milgram's procedure that reminds you of the earlier discussion of influence in Chapter 6? Think about the graduated approach to harm: Each time the participant delivered a shock, it was only slightly higher in intensity (15 volts) than the previous shock. We are dealing with a variation of the foot-in-the-door technique: the experimenter directs a participant to deliver small

shocks at first, and then larger shocks as time goes on. We might expect to see much less obedience if the shock levels were to increase by 100 or 200 volts at a time. When Milgram initially contemplated carrying out his research, he wondered whether obedience would be greater if the participant were first informed of the highest shock level that he or she might be asked to administer, or whether obedience would be more likely when compliance was extracted piecemeal, step-by-step (Russell, 2011). In this vein, military training also involves gradual escalations in violence, and wartime itself can provide a piecemeal slippery slope to the carrying out of greater and greater violence and atrocity.

6. *Was this actually 'obedience'?* Milgram's research was undertaken in the attempt to understand the obedience of German soldiers, police officers and execution squads who rounded up and killed millions of innocent people. As history has made all too evident, the orders to kill were generally carried out with Teutonic efficiency. However, to promote that efficiency and to protect the apparatus of genocide from any weakness by the faint of heart, the Nazis operated according to a 'terror-justice' principle – anyone who refused orders, including orders to massacre innocent civilians, would either be executed or interred in a concentration camp, and there was a risk of harm to one's family members as well. This terror-justice principle was widely believed among those who were ordered to do the killings (Kitterman, 1991).

Contrast that obedience situation to the Milgram research where no participant faced any personal danger, and the only risk associated with refusing to continue was the possible discomfort involved in confronting the experimenter and backing out of the experiment. Was their 'obedience' really a matter of 'following orders' in the way that the Nazi executioners did? Or were the participants obviously aware that they were participants in a psychological research study, and were simply confused about what was going on? Gibson (2011) provides a fascinating alternative interpretation of Milgram's obedience studies using the perspective of a form of discursive psychology (discussed in Chapter 1). He undertook a detailed analysis of Milgram's tape recordings of the interactions between experimenter and participants and pointed out that the interaction between the experimenter and the participant really boils down to a situation in which the experimenter, through the use of the prompts, is essentially arguing the case for why the experiment should continue, and the participant is presenting counterarguments as to why it should not go on. In other words, Gibson suggests that Milgram's research really had little to do with obedience as we normally think of the word, and that the experimenter's prompts to participants who expressed an unwillingness to continue should not be viewed as orders intended to elicit obedience, but rather as arguments meant to convince and persuade the participant that the experiment should continue. Gibson goes on to conclude that the experimenter elicits what appears to be obedience when using prompts that are indirect, but when direct orders actually are issued (recall prompt number 4 – 'You have no other choice, you *must* go on') – disobedience, rather than obedience, is the typical result.

And even this analysis may still be leaving out important information, for Gibson points out that Milgram (1974) indicated that on many occasions the defiance of the participants was communicated not just in words but by moving away from the table at which they were sitting. Since detailed records of such behaviour were not kept, there is no way of analysing non-verbal manifestations of reluctance or disobedience.

Who has the authority, who takes responsibility, how do participants make sense of the situation, how do they negotiate with the experimenter? All these questions point to the fact that the behaviour elicited in the Milgram paradigm is much more complex than it at first seems. Perhaps Milgram focused too much on looking for obedience and overlooked something even more important: disobedience.

DISOBEDIENCE

Why do some people disobey orders while others comply, especially when disobedience outside of laboratory studies may involve a significant personal risk? While Milgram was motivated to understand the obedience of Nazi executioners, Kitterman (1988) reports that there are least 100 documented cases of German soldiers and police officers who refused to follow orders to kill Jews or other unarmed civilians or prisoners of war during the Nazi era. He examined 85 separate cases of such refusals by army generals, police commanders, Waffen SS officers and even members of the *Einsatzgruppen*, a specialized execution unit. In each case, these individuals disobeyed orders to kill, even though they reported that they had been certain that they would be shot or sent to concentration camp because of their refusal. (However, surprisingly, in actual fact none of them was executed, and in almost two-thirds of the cases there were no consequences at all. Some of these individuals were even subsequently promoted, for reasons unrelated to their refusal.) Kitterman concluded that 'in every case of documented refusal to obey orders to exterminate people, the coercive powers of the Nazi system proved to be impotent or ineffective (p. 252)'.

Considerable disobedience occurred in the Milgram studies as well. Recall that in Milgram's first published study (Milgram, 1974), while 26 of the 40 participants continued to the end, administering 450 volts to the learner, 14 others disobeyed at some point and refused to go on. Across all of his experiments, 60% of Milgram's participants refused at some point to continue, leading Miller (2009) to argue that this militates against the usual interpretation of the Milgram experiments as demonstrations of an inherent evil in our human nature. And as we have seen, the physically closer the learner was to the teacher and the more realistic the suffering, the greater was the disobedience.

Yet, why did some participants refuse to continue while others did not? Was this to do with their personalities? Were those who disobeyed more independent-minded, more self-assured, more empathic, more conscientious, or more easily disturbed by another person's suffering? It seems not, for researchers have failed to find persuasive evidence of personality differences between those who obeyed and those who did not (Packer, 2008; Burger, 2009; Bocchiaro & Zimbardo, 2010). So how can we explain this?

Let us take a step back for a moment and look at the larger picture: Ultimately we want to understand how it is that large numbers of soldiers in various parts of the world – be it Syria or Libya or Rwanda or Vietnam or in Western Europe during the Holocaust – have followed orders to kill innocent civilians. Milgram's research was prompted by the atrocities of the Holocaust, but as historian Ian Kershaw has pointed out, the murderous efficiency of the Nazi state did not stem from blind, or even reluctant, obedience to orders, but rather from the fact that the Nazi leaders *did not have to* issue orders to followers because followers did what they did because they believed that it was the right thing to do (Kershaw, 1998). Indeed, modern analysis of the protests of Nazi officers at Nuremberg that they were 'just following orders' interprets this only as an attempt to excuse their actions in front of the court (Reicher & Haslam, 2012).

Just as those who followed the orders of their Nazi superiors apparently doing what they thought was the right thing to do, Reicher and Haslam (2012) suggest that Milgram's obedient participants were not being obedient, but instead were doing what they thought was the right thing to do, what was required of them in a scientific experiment. But why would someone possibly conclude that continuing to deliver shock to a protesting – and ultimately silent – victim is the 'right thing to do'? The answer may lie in social identity theory (discussed in detail in Chapter 12). Reicher, Haslam & Smith (2012) suggest that participants in Milgram's studies could identify either with the experimenter, and by extension with the scientific community at large, or with the learner, and that this identification would ultimately determine whether they complied with the experimenter's instruction to continue or the learner's demands to stop. Which identification was chosen was likely determined by situational factors. Thus, physically separating the 'teacher' from the 'learner' favoured identification with the experimenter, and indeed more shocks were given in that situation than when teacher and learner were physically close by. And conducting the research in a prestigious university setting 'where science is done' also favoured identification with the experimenter, and again, compliance with the experimenter's demands was greater than when the study was conducted in a commercial building away from the university. Once participants had identified with the experimenter, that individual essentially became their leader, and then, Reicher, Haslam & Smith (2012) argue, those who continued to deliver shock up to the maximum level did not do so out of obedience; rather, having become committed followers of their leader, they consciously did whatever was needed to achieve the goals that their leader had set out.

Keeping this in mind, although Milgram's research has revealed a psychological phenomenon of obvious importance to the world, his disturbing notion of blind obedience has distracted us from an even more serious implication of his data: the possibility that many participants in his experiments were willing to harm other people and ignore their protests either because they sought a way out of the conflict between the experimenter's demands and the learner's protestations, or because they had identified with the experimenter rather than the learner and so it seemed to be the right thing to do.

> **KEY POINT:** Research consistently shows that significant numbers of individuals of both sexes, sampled across a wide range of cultures and across decades, will comply with orders to administer electric shocks to a protesting victim in a laboratory study. However, the situation in which these people find themselves is more complicated than it first appears, and treating this compliance as 'obedience' is misleading. Participants are caught up in a confusing situation, and their verbal discourse suggests that they attempt to find an appropriate way to resolve the conflict between the demands of the experimenter and the demands of the learner/victim. An explanation based in social identity theory suggests that participants who continued to deliver shocks had identified with the experimenter and, rather than following orders, were voluntarily working towards that goal set out by their 'leader'.

A FINAL NOTE

We all influence one another, sometimes simply by our mere presence, at other times as part of groups, and in still others through deliberate efforts to change someone's opinion or behaviour. At its extreme, social influence involves pressure to obey. However, blind obedience to authority is not so pervasive as Milgram's research appears to suggest. Perhaps the most important lesson from the Milgram studies is the warning offered by Reicher & Haslam (2011b): the larger danger to society comes not from blind obedience by people who do not know or care that what they are doing is wrong, but instead from zealous followers of ignoble causes who believe that what they are doing is right.

SUMMARY

1. Individuals influence one another in a variety of ways. The most primitive form of social influence arises from the mere presence of an audience or co-actors, which facilitates the performance of simple or well-learned tasks and impedes performance of complex or novel tasks.

2. Zajonc postulated that arousal induced by the presence of others is innate, while other researchers have argued that the presence of others leads to arousal due to social comparison and learned evaluation apprehension.

3. Distraction-conflict theory posits that the arousal is due to conflict arising from the need to attend, to both the others present and the task. To cope, distracting cues are shut out resulting in increased attention, which improves simple task performance, but inhibits the performance of complex or novel tasks that require less focused concentration.

4. Social loafing refers to the reduction in the effort of individuals in group situations.

5. Conformity is the modification of one's behaviour in order to be consistent with social norms and group pressures.

6. Most conformity arises in response to majorities, but consistent and confident minorities can affect majorities.

7. Innovation requires open-minded individuals to think in non-normative ways. Innovations are diffused through both opinion leaders and the media.

8. Tactics employed to enhance compliance include the foot-in-the-door; the door-in-the-face; low-balling; improving the offer; and guilt inducement.

9. Obedience is a response to a demand or a command of someone who is perceived as having some form of authority. Situational influences appear to be more powerful than characteristics of the individual in determining whether obedience or disobedience will occur.

10. The Milgram paradigm is actually a very complex one, and new interpretations focus on the participants'

attempts to negotiate with the experimenter an appropriate way out of a confusing situation.

11. An explanation of the Milgram paradigm based on social identity theory suggests that those participants who continued to deliver shocks had identified with the experimenter, rather than with the learner/victim, and were acting, not out of obedience, but in an attempt to achieve goals set out by their new 'leader'.

POINTS TO PONDER

- What kind of society would you envisage if most people were to strive to be nonconformists and try their best to avoid yielding to group pressures? Would this be a good society in which to live?
- How might people in individualistic and collectivist cultures view conformity differently?
- Advertising is a powerful and successful form of social influence, and it often works best when it does not seem to be advertising – as, for example, in product placement in movies. How should society respond to such manipulative tactics? Ban them? Educate people about them? Do nothing?
- We train our soldiers to obey orders without question. We punish civic officials who do not follow the rules. How can we find the balance between the need for obedience and the importance of defying laws or commands that are unjust or harmful?
- What about whistleblowers? Should we laud or should we punish those who break the rules of the government or the companies they work for in order to publicize otherwise secret information that they have, on their own, deemed to be in the public interest? (Think of Wikileaks.)

FURTHER READING

Claidière, N. & Whiten, A. (2012). Integrating the study of conformity and culture in humans and nonhuman animals. *Psychological Bulletin*, *138*, 126–145.

This fascinating article discusses the concept of conformity behaviour in animals and how it may be evolutionarily related to human behaviour.

Martin, R. & Hewstone, M. (2012). Minority influence: Revisiting Moscovici's blue-green afterimage studies. In J.R. Smith & S.A. Haslam (Eds), *Social psychology: Revisiting the classic studies*. London: Sage Publications. (pp. 91–105).

A discussion of the contribution made by these well-known after-image studies and how they shaped the development of minority influence research.

Plaut, V.C. & Bartlett, R.P. (2012). Blind consent? A social psychological investigation of non-readership of click-through agreements. *Law and Human Behavior*, *36*, 293–311.

This article focuses on an interesting form of (almost) inadvertent social influence that occurs whenever – without having read the details – you click 'I agree' after installing a piece of software or downloading a file, or you sign a mortgage document or a car-rental agreement or an application for an insurance policy.

Prislin, R. & Crano, W.D. (2012) A history of social influence research. In A.W. Kruglanski & W. Stroebe (Eds), *Handbook of the history of social psychology*. East Essex: Taylor & Francis. (pp. 321–340).

This chapter provides a fascinating history of research into social influence, from the early days of experimental psychology to the present.

Smith, J.R., Louis, W.R. & Schultz, P.W. (Eds) (2011). Special issue: Social influence in action. *Group Processes & Intergroup Relations*, *14*(5).

This special issue of this journal comprises eleven empirical articles that represent the spectrum of modern research into social influence.

WEBLINKS

http://www.influenceatwork.com

This is psychologist Robert Cialdini's website, and a number of informative interviews with Dr Cialdini dealing with various aspects of social influence are included.

http://www.stanleymilgram.com

This website was created by psychologist Thomas Blass as a compendium of accurate information both about Milgram's research and about Stanley Milgram himself.

http://www.online-persuasion.com

A website managed by several psychologists and dedicated to the discussion of techniques to promote persuasion through the Internet.

CHAPTER 7
LANGUAGE AND COMMUNICATION

Electric communication will never be a substitute for the face of someone
who with their soul encourages another person to be brave and true.
Charles Dickens

LEARNING OBJECTIVES

* To understand the roles of language and paralanguage in communication

* To examine the influence of language in communicating and maintaining status, and in the definition of group boundaries

* To explore second-language acquisition and its social psychological consequences

* To consider possible gender differences in communication

* To learn about the various channels of non-verbal communication and how they combine with speech to provide a double-coded communication system

Figure 7.1   No man is an island

Source: Anton Brand/Shutterstock.com

Think back to the opening chapter: Still stranded alone on a desert island, but this time no one comes to join you. Beset by loneliness, you put a note in a bottle and toss it into the water in the faint hope that it will reach some other shore, and that someone will find it and come to the rescue. Not communication at its finest, but an attempt to communicate nonetheless. Your behaviour is understandable, for, with few exceptions, people do not like endless solitude. And when we are with other people, communication of one form or another allows the sharing of thoughts and emotions and the coordination of actions, and through it we encourage, discourage, threaten, command, cajole, agree, disagree and express love or hatred or ambivalence.

Attempts to understand the various factors involved in communication go back at least as far as Aristotle, who focused on the chain of elements involving the *speaker*, the *content* of the message, the *occasion* on which the message is delivered, the *audience*, and the *effect* of the speech on the audience. This ancient model is paralleled by the Shannon-Weaver model (Shannon & Weaver, 1949) that was developed to describe the transmission of information over the telephone, involving an information source, a transmitter that codes the message into a signal, a channel that carries the signal, a decoder to decode the message, and a receiver. A similar psychosocial model (Lasswell, 1948) can be summarized in terms of *who* says *what* to *whom* by which *channel* and with what *effect*. The model pushes researchers to examine the effectiveness of communication as a function of characteristics of the speaker, qualities of the message, effects of the particular medium (speech, radio, television), and characteristics of the audience.

Let's apply this to the message in a bottle. First, the *who*: Will the effect of the message be any different if you identify yourself as a teenager, or an escaped convict, or a 'lady in distress'? And what aspects of the message itself might increase the likelihood that someone will respond? What personal characteristics of the finder will influence the likelihood that he or she will act to bring about a rescue? And how likely is it that this particular channel – a bottle floating in the ocean – will lead to successful message transmission?

Communication has undergone profound change as a result of the World Wide Web, and social media such as Twitter and Facebook have had transformative effects around the world. Even in developing nations, where poverty remains a major issue for many people, the use of cellular telephones is widespread, and in modern industrialized nations it is unusual for individuals not to have either an Internet-connected mobile telephone or computer, or both. Not only do millions of individuals communicate in this way on a regular basis with friends and family and business sources, but such media have changed the way that people meet new friends, find lovers, coordinate civil disobedience, and even organize protests against dictators. The series of revolutionary protests in 2012 known as the Arab Spring were in part made possible by social media.

[KEY POINT: Communication is essential to social interaction. Characteristics of the source, the message, the medium and the receiver all influence the extent to which the communication is effective. **]**

And what is the essential element of communication? While language comes quickly to mind, we also communicate with gestures, facial expressions, body movements and non-linguistic vocalizations such as whistles, grunts and groans. In fact, non-verbal communication is a vital part of every direct social interaction, and it has been estimated that about two-thirds of every communication consists of non-verbal signals (Chung, 2011). A raise of the eyebrows, a pucker of the lips or a clenching of the fist can often communicate more about our motives or feelings than would a dozen words. Subtle non-verbal cues also communicate information about our attitudes and beliefs, and about which ideas or behaviours we favour and which we do not (Weisbuch & Ambady, 2009). Yet, while a substantial part of our formal education is devoted to learning the formal rules of language, there is never any formal instruction to teach us non-verbal communication. This we must learn on our own, through observation and imitation.

Communication, both verbal and non-verbal, is shaped by the culture in which it develops, and particular words and phrases and gestures reflect the communication needs of the people who use it. While you could develop a language of your own (as did J.R. Tolkien for the inhabitants of his fictional *Middle Earth*), and you could come up with a personal system of gestures and secret handshakes, all would be useless for communication unless at least one other person shared your 'code' (Box 7.1).

BOX 7.1 TAKE ANOTHER LOOK: THE MEDIUM AND THE MESSAGE

f U R intRStd n how wrds R communicated – or for those not familiar with texting lingo, *if you are interested in how words are communicated* – then think about the many different ways that words and their meanings can be communicated to others. While we can generally put our thoughts into words – *our* words in *our* language – it is very difficult and sometimes impossible to communicate those thoughts to others who do not understand our language or who are unable to hear us speak or see what we have written. True communication only takes place if others understand our code, if they can 'read' our symbolic representations.

Some languages share enough similarity that we can make out the meaning of some of the words even if we do not know the language. For example, we can easily guess that this Finnish word, *Sosiaalipsykologia*, means *social psychology*.

But many languages have no similarity to English either in their spoken or written form. If we do not know the particular language involved, or the script that is used to express it, how would we ever guess that each string of symbols below also means *social psychology*?

社会心理学	علم النفس الاجتماعي	социальная психология
Japanese	Arabic	Russian

We typically think of language in terms of spoken words or groups of letters printed on a page. However, words can be transmitted in many different ways using visual and auditory and tactile faculties. What does this series of dots and dashes mean to you?

```
...  ---  -.-.  ..  .-  .-..      .--.  ...  -.--  -.-.  ....  --
-  .-..  ---  --.  -.--
```

Most likely nothing. But to the telegraph operator of fifty years ago, its meaning would be clear – *social psychology* again – and the operator would probably understand even more quickly if this were presented as an auditory sequence of short and long sounds.

And if you ran your fingers across this series of raised dots?

To the blind Braille reader, it is *social psychology* once again. And to the deaf individual who knows American Sign Language, this is how one says *social psychology*:

And finally, here is how the Boy Scout and the Army Signal Corpsman of old would have transmitted *social psychology* in semaphore:

Because a particular sound or movement or facial expression means little to those who do not share the same code, it is not surprising that those who grow up learning a common language feel connected with one another, and feel apart from others whose languages they do not understand. As a result, shared language in particular – since language is so much more extensively codified and so much more central to social interaction than is non-verbal behaviour – is an important determinant of social identity and group boundaries. It binds people together. On the other hand, differences in language often cleave people apart, and such differences can be the well-spring of prejudice, discrimination and aggression.

WHAT IS SAID: THE WORDS

One cannot do justice to the study of human social activity if language is ignored, for it is central to almost all areas of social psychology, and it is difficult to imagine social interactions that are completely language-free (Maynard & Peräkylä, 2003). Yet, while exchanging words is usually easy enough, words do not always capture our ideas and feelings. People often miscommunicate, sometimes even deliberately, and the misunderstanding that follows can lead to serious conflicts among individuals, groups and even nations. The risks of dysfunctional communication become even greater when the communicators are from different cultural or linguistic backgrounds.

Social psychological interest in language began with pioneers such as Wallace Lambert at McGill University in Canada, who devoted most of his career to the study of bilingualism (Taylor, 2011; Vaid et al., 2010), and Howard Giles and Peter Robinson in England, who succeeded in creating a viable sub-field of language research within social psychology (Taylor & Usborne, 2007). As a result, social psychological language research has been growing rapidly over the past 25 years (Kroger & Wood, 1992), and there are now specialized journals as well as a seminal handbook dedicated to the subject (Robinson & Giles, 2001). Social psychologists are paying increasing attention to the central role that language plays in many important social phenomena, such as causal attribution, social identity, status, intimacy and interpersonal relations (Krauss & Pardo, 2006). And as pointed out in the introductory chapter, discursive psychology is based on an analysis of language.

It is not easy to study the social psychological aspects of language, for spontaneous speech is affected by a host of factors, and it is difficult to capture the influence of these variables in a natural social environment. While much social psychological language research has been carried out in laboratory settings, one needs to be particularly cautious when extending the findings of such research to interactive talking in natural settings (Hughes & Reed, 2011).

Before delving into the social psychology of language, first consider just how truly complex a language is, and how readily we speak our native tongue despite the complexity. All spoken language is based on a phonetic system, in which short, meaningless sounds, phonemes, are combined into units of meaning, morphemes. By using a relatively small number of these sounds (up to 45, depending on the language) and by combining them two, three or more at a time, different human languages have generated as many as 100,000 morphemes (Argyle, 1969).

It was quite a step for our ancestors to go from speech to writing, and initially a different symbol was used for each word (e.g., a hieroglyphic). Such a system necessitated a very large number of symbols. In most languages, a few letters reflecting the spoken phonetic code rather than syllables or words eventually came to be used in place of thousands of symbols. However, the Chinese evolved a set of 10,000 characters, each one representing a different word element in the language, and these characters are still in use today, a situation that has posed problems with regard to literacy, for in order to read a newspaper, the reader needs to know at least several thousand characters. However, it is somewhat ironic that Chinese is actually better suited to microblogs, such as Twitter, that restrict messages to a maximum of 140 symbols. *Sina Weibo*, a Chinese message service similar to Twitter, serves over 300 million bloggers in China, but because of the considerable amount of information packed into each character, few messages ever reach that 140-symbol limit.

Language provides more than a means of communication. Our thinking is enriched by the powerful symbolic abilities it affords us, for it allows us to construct a model of the world inside our heads, a model that we can use in order to contemplate long sequences of future actions and consider their consequences without actually taking those actions (Holland, 1992). Language also allows us to draw on the immense pools of knowledge and thought that have been laid down in writing or in sound and video recordings by millions of other people, living and dead. We can explore Aristotle's philosophy, Martin Luther's theology and Einstein's scientific reasoning. We can be inspired by Shakespeare, stimulated by McLuhan, horrified by de Sade and brought to tears by Dostoevsky. We can listen and read and hear about the opinions of politicians, scientists and entertainers. Language allows social groups to transfer their knowledge, beliefs and values from generation to generation, and without it modern culture as we know it could never have developed.

All children learn language automatically, for so long as there is language in their environment, they will acquire it. As Pinker (1994) points out, children acquire complex grammatical rules very quickly even before being exposed to formal instruction, and they grow up able to produce novel sentences 'never before uttered in the history of the universe' (p. 9), as well being able to understand novel sentence constructions that they encounter for the first time.

Language does not necessarily involve speech. Sign languages such as American Sign Language all possess the formal qualities of language – nouns, verbs, grammar – even though no sounds are made. And the motivation to communicate is so powerful that when deaf children are not given the opportunity to learn a formal sign language, they invent their own non-verbal ways to communicate with one another. Consider, for example, what is happening in the village of Al-Sayyid in Israel (Kreiner, 2011). As a result of a shared genetic condition, there are many congenitally deaf people in the village, and over the past three generations they have been gradually and informally developing their own sign language, *Al-Sayyid Bedouin Sign Language* (ABSL). It began with very simple signs, but over time grammatical rules have developed and the language now contains some of the universal features found in all languages, such as a preferred word order: ABSL has a subject-object-verb word order (e.g. *I the cow milked*). This has been a purely spontaneous development, for that word order does not occur in any of the languages spoken in the region, although it is found in certain other languages such as Japanese.

[
KEY POINT: Language is ubiquitous in human societies; if not taught a language, people will ultimately develop one of their own. It serves not just to communicate but helps us to think, to plan, and to transmit knowledge from generation to generation.
]

HOW IT IS SAID: PARALANGUAGE

While we use words and sentences to communicate with each other, the actual communication goes far beyond the words themselves. Spoken communications are actually double-coded in the sense that meaning is conferred both by *what* is said and by *how* it is said. This 'extra-linguistic' information can both change the meaning of the words and tell us much about the speaker as well. And beyond that, other non-verbal behaviour – a smile, a frown, a stare and so on – can also significantly modify the meaning of the words, as is discussed later in this chapter.

We judge a person's intentions and motives as much or more by how something is said as by the words themselves. Saying, 'You pig!' to a friend dipping into a box of chocolates can communicate either friendly teasing or admonition, depending on tone of voice. We automatically, without having to think about it, modify the meaning of the words according to how they are delivered.

Paralanguage refers to the 'how' of speaking, the non-verbal aspects of speech; it includes such characteristics as timing, pitch, loudness, stress, pauses and even non-linguistic sounds including throat-clearing, grunts and sighs. The first three of these, timing, pitch and loudness, are referred to as the prosodic features of language and are critically important in oral communication. They are used to give emphasis to certain points, to indicate doubt, to suggest what we are thinking and to communicate emotion. Children acquire the ability to use these prosodic elements early in their language development. Indeed, our ability to express and perceive the emotional 'tone' in speech is vital to communication, and a deficit in either ability can have profound consequences for social relationships (Bachorowski, 1999). For example, how do we know when someone is 'talking down' to us? Or ordering us? Or beseeching us? It is primarily through prosody. Certain prosodic patterns communicate specific emotions: aggression or dominance tend to be signalled by a low pitch while happiness and lack of aggressiveness usually involve a higher pitch, and there is very little evidence of variation in this behaviour either among individuals in a given culture or across cultures (Frick, 1985).

People are capable of separating the two aspects of the communication and interpreting each one individually when they are inconsistent. For example, in one study (Solomon & Yaeger, 1969) students listened to a teacher talking about a student's work. When the emotion that was communicated prosodically was at odds with the verbal content of the message, the students tended to interpret the verbal communication as indicative of how the teacher felt about the student's work, and the prosodic information as indicative of how the teacher felt about the student. In fact, research has shown that paralanguage can actually impair one's memory for the specific meaning of the words that are uttered (Hertel & Navarez, 1986): in recalling a videotaped conversation, participants confused what was said with how it was said. Thus, if someone says something critical, but in a friendly and jocular way, we may later remember the words as having been less harsh than they actually were.

For successful social communication to occur, the recipient has to be able to recognize and integrate paralinguistic and other non-verbal signals of emotion with information communicated verbally. When spoken words are transcribed into print, punctuation must be added to try to compensate for the missing non-verbal information, but, even then, some of the message may be lost (Argyle, 1975). This is of course a problem with modern electronic communication – email, texting and social media – and can sometimes result in significant miscommunication. Millions of people around the world spend many hours at their computers each day communicating with strangers they will never meet. How does this form of communication, stripped of all non-verbal cues that might provide important information about emotional states, affect the communicators, the development of their understanding and even the relationships between them? As more and more people routinely use the Internet, social psychologists are becoming very interested in how such communication differs from face-to-face communication and how computer networks influence the structure of both work and social groups.

However, people generally fail to appreciate the problems caused by the absence of non-verbal cues when texting or emailing, and assume that because they can themselves understand the emotional context of their comments, so will the recipient. This overconfidence in success of their communication seems to reflect a kind of narcissistic focus, a failure to see the message from the recipient's perspective (Kruger, Eply, Parker & Ng, 2005). In a study conducted in China (Shuang-shuang, 2010), it was found that impolite communication was more frequent in computer-mediated interactions than in face-to-face conversations. Other research (Ickes, Park & Robinson, 2012) points to rudeness towards strangers being employed as a tool in computer-mediated interactions in the quest to obtain power and status in interpersonal struggles for recognition and acceptance.

However, just as punctuation evolved to bring some of the aspects of prosody into written communications, so too text-based cues can be used to signal emotion in computer mediated communications (Whalen & Pexman, 2009). The use of the 'smiley' emoticon **:-)** reflects an attempt to make up for lack of non-verbal cues (Provine, Spencer & Mandell, 2007). In a study comparing text-based communication over a computer network with face-to-face communication (Walther, Loh & Granka, 2005), it was observed that participants in the text-based condition were as successful in communicating emotional tone as were those in the face-to-face condition. They spontaneously substituted for non-verbal indicators of affect by using text-based cues – such as offering personal information, or giving praise when suggesting an alternative to what had been proposed, or being indirect when in disagreement. Thus, the use of a text-based, computer-mediated communication channel need not be a barrier to the communication of emotional feelings, so long as the communicators are motivated to communicate them.

KEY POINT: Paralanguage is a vital component of communication. It provides a separate source of information that modifies the meaning of a verbal utterance.

WHO SAID IT: LANGUAGE AND IMPRESSIONS OF THE SPEAKER

Differences in how people speak serve as markers of their social status and their membership in various social and cultural categories, and on this basis we make inferences not only about people's age, gender, social class, ethnicity or education but even about their personalities, competence and intelligence (Bradac et al., 1977; Giles & Powesland, 1975; Seligman, Tucker & Lambert, 1972). For instance, when talking with a stranger on the telephone, one would usually have no difficulty on the basis of voice alone in distinguishing a poorly educated female English teenager from a well-educated male Indian adult. And surprising as it may be, research shows that people are even able to estimate a speaker's height and weight from a two-sentence voice sample, and they are almost as accurate as when looking at a full-length photograph (Krauss, Freyberg and Morsella, 2002)! In addition to the qualities of the voice itself, the choice of words, the use or misuse of grammar, and errors in pronunciation also help the listener to make judgements about the speaker. Even minor aspects of language can have a major effect on how one is viewed by the listener. For example, a speaker who consistently drops the g's – '*I was runnin' to the store when I saw a bus speedin' by …*' – creates a different impression than when the g's are all carefully enunciated (Box 7.2).

BOX 7.2   THE POWER OF A WORD

Ideas, provided that they can be communicated to others, can be much more dangerous than any armament; the pen, so it has been often said, is mightier than the sword. However, words sometimes have power that is almost independent of their meaning. Consider a made-up word, *fac*. One can safely pronounce that monosyllable without fear that anyone will react with any more than a puzzled look, perhaps thinking that one meant to say *fact*. Now change the word slightly to another monosyllable, *fuck*. Seeing the word in print, particularly in a respectable textbook, might be enough to arouse negative emotion in many people, and in the not-so-distant past – a mere 40 or so years ago – would have prevented the book from being published, for it was considered a terrible

Figure 7.2 A French Connection store in London, branded with the FCUK logo

Source: Justinc, Wikimedia Commons

obscenity. While the origin of the word is lost in history (and is not, as some urban legends suggest, connected to acronyms such as that derived from 'For Undue Carnal Knowledge'), that little monosyllable and some of its sexually related relatives have been taboo words for centuries, even though some people, almost always male, have always used them regularly, but out of earshot of 'decent' women and 'respectable' society. The word did not appear in *any* English language dictionary between 1795 and 1965! Recall (in Chapter 5) that reading a list including words such as 'fuck' constituted a 'severe' initiation for undergraduate research participants in 1959!

In recent years, *fuck* has come into its own and is now used as a common expletive, or simply to add a bit of emphasis, by both men and women, and indeed by boys and girls, teenagers particularly. It is used in all sorts of ways that have nothing to do with its original sexual meaning, and it is used in more ways – as a noun, or a verb or in an adjectival form – and to mean more things, than almost any other word in the English language (e.g., 'You are a stupid fuck', 'Fuck what the government says', 'All fucked up', 'I don't give a fuck', 'Why the fuck did you do that?').

According to White (2002), there are in excess of 2.5 million web pages with the word *fuck* indexed, and: 'Fuck is a ubiquitous word, heard everywhere and used in an amazing variety of ways, by young and old alike. From schoolyards to television, street cafes to radio station, its usage is, today, commonplace' (p. 21).

How did such a once-taboo word come to be so commonly used today? And how did such a word originally associated with sex come to take on such an angry edge? What does that reflect about the evolution of our society?

The power of this word to produce autonomic arousal has not totally diminished despite its common employment. Students may use the word frequently but still feel a sense of shock if a physician or a university lecturer were to refer to *fucking* instead of *intercourse* or *love-making* when discussing sexuality. A series of advertisements bore the letters FCUK (acronym for French Connection, United Kingdom, a clothing retailer) with the obvious intention of using the shock value that derives from a word resembling *fuck* (Figure 7.2).

Moreover, the use of this word sometimes still elicits a strong reaction from authority and, since it is more likely to be used by people in some sub-cultures than in others, it can lead to discrimination. White (2002) points out that in Australia, aboriginal youth are often the victims of the selective use of laws against offensive language. He argues that Australian laws dealing with offensive language are a key mechanism in the social control of young indigenous people by the police, and that the application of such laws serves to reinforce popular stereotypes of 'indigenous deviancy'.

Among contemporary youth, *fuck* has become so common that the word is often used without any intent to offend others and without realization of the deep offence that the word is still capable of causing. To the degree that older people do find the word offensive, it serves as a means of social identification and rejection of authority. Indeed as Drury (2003) has noted, adults, particularly those in positions of authority, typically view adolescents as lacking in communication ability, and the frequent use of swear words reinforces this perception. Adolescents, on the other hand, typically view the problems in communicating with adults as stemming from issues of power and lack of respect for them.

Accents and dialects

As we grow up, we are reinforced for speaking in the 'accepted' manner of those around us. And we do not change very much, for the way that people express themselves verbally is quite consistent across time and situations (Pennebaker & King, 1999). We spot strangers in our midst often by how their way of speaking is different from ours, even when speaking the same language.

The way a language is spoken can vary considerably. A dialect refers to a form of a language spoken by people either in a particular geographic region (regional dialect) or social class (social dialect). Regional dialects tell others where we are from, and social dialects tell others about our social status (Grondelaers, van Hout & Steegs, 2010). Dialects differ from one another both in regard to accent and to variations in vocabulary and grammar. An accent refers specifically to pronunciation, and relates to intonation and how consonants and vowels are pronounced. Thus, if an English person, an Irish person and a Scot were to read the same sentence aloud, the grammar and vocabulary would be identical, but the obvious variations in pronunciation would reflect their different accents. However, the spontaneous speech of the three may differ in more than just accent; because of variations in vocabulary and grammar, they may speak somewhat different dialects.

Although people in a given geographical region typically speak with a particular dialect, there are also likely to be variations within that region associated with social class, ethnicity and age group. These social dialects generally make it easy in any society to distinguish, for example, the speech of an uneducated labourer from that of a more highly educated individual such as a lawyer or teacher. Similarly, within a given dialect, a teenage girl is likely to speak distinctly differently from a middle-age woman. Some such distinctiveness is so general that it is maintained even when one is provided only with written transcripts.

Consider these two transcripts of spontaneous speech (Tagliamonte, 2006):

> I don't know, it's jus' stuff that really annoys me. And I jus' like stare at him and jus' go ... like, 'huh'.

> It was sort-of just grass steps down and where I dare say it had been flower beds and goodness-knows-what ...

We would not have any difficulty in deciding which of these two sentences was spoken by a young person and which by an older person, for they reflect different social dialects. And you may be able to guess the speakers' gender as well. The first was spoken by an eighteen-year old woman, and the second by a seventy-nine-year-old woman. The use of phrases such as 'I dare say' and 'goodness knows what', may even suggest more to you about that speaker and where she is from.

In the United Kingdom, before television and other electronic media brought their influence to bear on the way language is spoken, some linguists were able to accurately determine the region of a person's origin – and social class – by listening to his or her speech. (Recall the words from *My Fair Lady*: 'An Englishman's way of speaking absolutely classifies him. The moment he talks he makes some other Englishman despise him.') The opportunity for socioeconomic advancement used to be seriously affected by accent, and educated people with the 'wrong' accent (Cockney, in Great Britain, for example) sometimes took elocution lessons to 'correct' their speech style.

In the United States, speech is also an important source of information about social status, and geographical distinctions are also possible: for example, the Brooklyn accent would never be confused with the upper-class Boston accent or the Texas drawl! However, it is more complicated than that, for the group context also plays a role. For example, not pronouncing the *r* in words such as *bear* and *court* reflects membership in an aristocratic, high-status group of older European-American speakers in Charleston, South Carolina, while the same pattern of dropping the *r* is associated with working-class, low-status groups in New York City (Wolfram, 2004).

Just about every language has its different accents and dialects. Hindi, the most common of India's 18 official languages, has at least ten major dialects. In Australia, linguists have identified three varieties of Australian English – Cultivated, Broad and General (Edwards & Jacobsen, 1987). There is very little accent or dialect diversity among English speakers in Canada (Lavov, Ash & Boberg, 2006), although the traditional Newfoundland accent is usually easy to discern. However, there are a number of different dialects among Canadian francophones; for example, the Acadian dialect is different from the Québecois.

Not all varieties of a particular language are viewed as being equal within a given society. The prestige form of a language, called by linguists the 'standard' accent or dialect, is the one spoken by the educated or upper or 'noble' classes. Research around the world has demonstrated that from childhood through adulthood, use of the standard speech style communicates status and competence (Wiemann & Giles, 1988; Stewart, Ryan & Giles, 1985). In Australia, for example, speakers of the prestige Cultivated accent are rated not only as highest in competence, but also highest with regard to social attractiveness (Edwards & Jacobsen, 1987). Those who speak in this more 'refined' manner usually view other variants of the spoken language as 'vulgar' or 'low class', and even the speakers of the nonstandard dialect typically share the view that their dialect is inferior (Niedzielski and Preston 2000).

But how is the 'standard' chosen? Is the so-called *British Received Pronunciation* (BRP) better in some way, or more agreeable to the ear? Did the *Île-de-France* dialect – 'Parisian French' as most of us know it – become the standard for similar reasons? Certainly many of us would agree that those forms of those two languages strike us as eloquent, clear, and refined. Moreover, when we learn a second language through formal courses, we are usually taught the prestige form, and thus tend to view other forms as substandard. Yet, if Cockney English or Acadian French sounds less pleasant to some than BRP or Parisian French, is it because they actually *are* less pleasant? Or did the standard varieties only become standard because they were spoken by the people who historically ruled those nations, and they now seem more pleasant to our ears because we have learned to respect them? That very interesting question has been addressed by asking people with no familiarity with a particular language to listen to samples of both standard and non-standard varieties of the language and then to rate them in terms of how pleasant they are to the ear. If Parisian French is rated as more pleasant than Acadian French to a non-French speaker, then this would suggest that there is some inherent aspect of the dialect that has led it to become the prestige form.

Giles, Bourhis and Davies (1977) articulated two possibilities:

- The **inherent value hypothesis**. The standard dialect becomes the prestige form of the language because it is the aesthetically ideal form of that language.
- The **imposed norm hypothesis**. Standard and non-standard dialects are equally aesthetically pleasing, but the non-standard form is viewed negatively because of social norms that are biased against it.

They asked Welsh students who knew no French to listen to tape recordings of the same text spoken by the same person in three different French accents: Parisian ('standard') French, educated Canadian French and working-class Canadian French. Participants then rated the speech in terms of pleasantness and aesthetic appeal and they also rated the speaker in terms of status, intelligence, likability, ambition and toughness. No significant differences were found, supporting the imposed-norm hypothesis. Further, the participants were unable to identify which is the prestige from of the language. The imposed-norm hypothesis received further validation in a similar study in which British undergraduates who knew no Greek were exposed to both the Cretan and the more prestigious Athenian dialects; again, they were unable to pick out the prestige form of the language (Giles et al., 1974).

In sum, the standard form of a language becomes so not because it is more aesthetically pleasing, even though it may seem so to speakers of the language. Its prestige reflects historical social stratification and its association with the upper echelons of the society. This is obvious in some instances. For example, it is not by chance that the so-called *Received Pronunciation* in Britain used to be referred to as the Queen's English. And following the French Revolution, the Parisian bourgeoisie who took control of the country chose their own variety of French (*Île-de-France*) to be the national standard, and the use of any other accent or dialect was banned in schools (Bourhis, 1982).

Even though each society has its standard accent or dialect spoken by the educated classes, there is also, on an international level, an overarching accent or dialect of a given language which, even if not spoken locally, nonetheless is viewed as the most prestigious. Again, Parisian French is an example. And the British Received Pronunciation is also the prestige form in other English-speaking countries such as Canada, the United States and Australia, and is rated very highly in terms of a standard–non-standard continuum by English speakers worldwide (Milroy & Milroy, 1999). Its prestige beyond Great Britain is reflected in a study that was carried out at a university in the southwestern United States (Morales, Scott & Yorkston, 2012). Participants listened to a 45 second advertisement in which the speaker spoke with either the BRP accent or the Southern American English (SAE) accent, the most widely spoken 'nonstandard' accent in the United States. (Neither accent was a local accent for the participants, and the experimenters reported that Southerners and the British alike would be viewed as out-groups.) Participants not only rated the BRP accent as the more favourable of the two, but they also separately rated the advertised product more favourably when the speaker spoke with the BRP accent. The prestige of the Queen's English is alive and well, at least in some parts of the world.

> **KEY POINT:** The prestige dialect of a language is not an aesthetically superior form; it is the dialect of the powerful who have historically dominated the society.

Speech registers

There are other aspects of speech that carry information beyond the words themselves. Even within a particular combination of regional and social dialects, a given individual's speech varies from situation to situation in terms of speech register (Romaine, 2000). Speech registers are varieties of a language that are used in particular situations. They reflect one's emotional state, and we can quickly judge whether a person is angry or happy or unfriendly just by listening to a tape recording of the voice. Choice of speech register also reflects the relationship between the individuals who are conversing, as well as factors such as the speaker's perceived relative status, and the speaker's judgement about the listener's own typical speech register. Do you speak any differently to your mechanic than you would to your physician or professor? Our choice of register can tell people a great deal about how we view them. Speech registers also vary with the context: Think of a professor intoning a lecture with authority and eloquence. If you were to overhear that same person speaking in the same manner to a companion over dinner in a restaurant, he or she would likely strike you as pretentious and over-bearing – all because the speech register is inappropriate in that setting. We adjust our speech to the situation, and as we go through our daily lives, we change registers frequently as we encounter a variety of situations.

Because the use of certain speech registers reflects a speaker's power relative to the listener, the choice of speech register can have debilitating effects. In some situations, this is because it reminds listeners of their relative lack of power and independence. For example, one speech register that we all are familiar with is what linguists refer to as baby talk or BT. This refers not to the way that babies speak but to the way that adults talk to two- to five-year-olds. It is recognizable by its high pitch and exaggerated intonations (Caporael, Lukaszewski & Culbertson, 1983), and it is a feature of all languages (Ferguson, 1977, 2011). Of more interest to the social psychologist is secondary baby talk, which is the use of the BT register in contexts other than when talking to babies. Most of us would resent being spoken to in such a manner and would consider it belittling. However, such talk appears to be rather common in institutions for the elderly, and it may promote helplessness and dependency. It has been noted that elderly people often 'instantly age' – that is, they appear to move, talk and think more slowly – when interacting with people who speak to them in baby talk, compared to when talking with people who address them as adults (Giles, Fox & Smith, 1993).

As an example, a field study conducted in a private nursing home in California found that nearly a quarter of the communications by nurse's aides to elderly patients were in baby talk (Caporael, 1981). While college students who subsequently listened to recordings judged the baby talk to be more positive than non-baby talk because of its 'nurturant' quality, only those elderly people who actually had lower functional ability tended to prefer it; higher functioning individuals felt it to be condescending and were insulted by it. Another study found that German nurses also used secondary baby talk in addressing some elderly residents (Sachweh, 1998); the typical recipient of such talk was female, physically frail, and was either not well-liked or was very well-liked by the staff. Nonetheless, that study also concluded that some of the recipients react very positively to this manner of speaking. Even onlookers are influenced by the use of a condescending speech style: participants in a study (LaTourette & Meeks, 2000) observed elderly women in a nursing home being spoken to by nurses in either a patronizing style or a non-patronizing style. The onlookers judged the women who were spoken to in a patronizing style to be less competent. The onlookers were in effect 'blaming the victim': if you are spoken to as though you are incompetent, then you must be incompetent. Indeed in the institutional setting, BT may reflect a process of establishing social control (Ryan et al., 1986).

What about speech registers used when speaking to people from other countries who speak your language with some difficulty or to intellectually challenged adults? To answer this question, a study was conducted in which undergraduate women were asked to teach a block-design task either to a six-year-old child, an intellectually challenged adult, a peer who spoke English as a second language or a peer who was an unimpaired native speaker of English (DePaulo & Coleman, 1986). It was found that the speech addressed to children was clearer and simpler, used more techniques to maintain attention and included longer pauses. Speech addressed to intellectually challenged adults was similar but even more babyish in some ways (e.g., repetitiveness). On the other hand speech addressed to non-native speakers, apart from being more repetitive, was not different from that spoken to native speakers'.

The way we talk to people tells them a great deal about how we view them. Talking to the elderly or to those with learning difficulties as though they are children may well reinforce feelings of incompetence and helplessness and discourage them from operating at their fullest potential.

Direct and indirect speech

As if it is not already complicated enough, there is another feature of speech to be considered: Communication sometimes involves direct speech, in which the meaning of the sentence is consistent with the speaker's meaning, and indirect speech, which lacks this consistency (Searle, 1969, 1975; Sbisà, 2009). The choice of direct or indirect speech is often influenced by the relative status of the speaker compared to the listener. Through the use of indirect speech, we can avoid direct challenges to authority or to high-status individuals. Suppose you disagree with a pronouncement by your professor. You might start by saying something like 'I am not quite sure that I follow you. I don't understand how classical conditioning can account for …' The professor, on the other hand, would be more likely to use direct speech: 'Classical conditioning leads to… .'

Research has demonstrated that indirect speech is also used in an effort to maintain 'face' in potentially face-threatening situations (Holtgraves, 1986). Suppose, for example, that you have finished an essay and you want your friend's opinion. Asking directly 'What do you think of my essay?' signals that you want an indication of its quality, and yet there is a danger that an honest reply might be a threat to your self-esteem. On the other hand, if you hand it to your friend while saying rather unenthusiastically, 'I finally finished it', you are *indirectly* asking for an opinion, while at the same time implying that maybe it was not your best effort, so that you will not lose face if your friend criticizes it. And not only do we often try to save face ourselves, in our daily interactions with others we often try to help people 'save face' as well. In the case of your essay, if your friend thinks that it is rather weak, an indirect response, such as, 'Well, as least you finished it on time', can shift the focus from quality to timeliness, thus helping you save face, while still indirectly communicating a low opinion of the quality.

[
KEY POINT: We use different speech registers throughout each day, and the choice of register, along with the choice of direct or indirect speech, reflects our perception of our status relative to the listener.
]

LANGUAGE AND GENDER: DO WOMEN AND MEN SPEAK DIFFERENTLY?

We can almost always identify the sex of an individual by hearing his or her voice. For one thing, men's voices are typically lower in pitch than are women's. Yet, while there is on average a male–female difference in pitch due to different physiology, social factors also play a very significant role. For example, adult Polish men have higher pitched voices than American men (Romaine, 2000) and this has nothing to do with physiology. We can teach ourselves to speak with a pitch that does not correspond directly to the size and shape of our larynx.

Because we tend to associate low pitch with power, so-called feminine speech qualities – such as higher pitch, softer volume, more variability and a more relaxing pleasant tone of voice – typically lead listeners to attribute lower social power as well as lower intellectual ability and greater interpersonal warmth to the speaker (Montepare & Vega, 1988).

So, if someone wants to sound powerful and authoritative, what should she do? Consider former United Kingdom Prime Minister Margaret Thatcher, whose 'female' voice did not correspond to the tough image that she wanted to project. Through voice lessons, she learned to speak with a lower, 'more powerful' pitch (Fromkin, Rodman & Hyams, 2011). And it was not just Margaret Thatcher who wanted to sound more powerful. When women first began to read the news they were not taken as seriously as male newscasters, and as a consequence were encouraged to lower their pitch. Compared to the few women in the field a generation ago, the pitch of contemporary female newsreaders has dropped considerably, not only in the English-speaking world but in other countries such as Japan as well (Karpf, 2006). And not just newsreaders. A comparison of recordings of 18–25-year-old Australian women made in the mid-1940s with those of similar women made in the 1990s shows that the average pitch of women in general in that country has dropped significantly (Hewlett & Beck, 2006; Pemberton, McCormack & Russell, 1998).

Many people believe that men and women have typical and distinctive styles of speaking beyond simple voice pitch. Women are typically said to be more verbally skilled than men, more polite than men, more emotional, more talkative, more positive and supportive in how they evaluate people, more tentative ('It's cold, isn't it?'; 'I may be wrong, but …'), and more indirect. They are said to talk more than men because communication is more important to them; and it is also said that they talk more about relationships and feelings, while men talk more about things and facts. Moreover, women's communication is said to be more cooperative while men's is competitive and focused on status. On the other hand, men are believed to use more slang and profanity, to argue, criticize, lecture and command more, and to be more likely to talk about business, politics and sports (Lakoff, 1975; Tannen, 1990). It has also been reported that women tend to be less competitive in conversations, less domineering, and more likely to look for compromises and spare other people's feelings. This can extend even to the professional level. For example, Hall and colleagues (1994) studied the interactions of male and female physicians with male and female patients. They reported that the female physicians on average spent more time with the patient and were more talkative than their male counterparts; they smiled and nodded more; and they gathered more medical information from their patients. This was interpreted as evidence that female physicians tend to be more nurturant and expressive and more focused on interpersonal rapport than are their male colleagues. Women have even been found to be more expressive in the email messages that they send (Fox et al., 2007).

A number of studies conducted in a number of different countries have found that women are more likely to use a higher status form of a language than are men (e.g. Coates, 1993; Gordon, 1997; Romaine, 2000). This difference has been found in such widely separated countries as England (Trudgill, 1974), Iraq (Abu-Haidar, 1989), New Zealand (Gordon, 1997), Jordan (Malkawi, 2011), and China (Wang & Ladegaard, 2008). Why is this so? Various explanations have been offered. Romaine (2000) suggests that for English-speakers, this may trace back to Victorian days when 'speaking properly' was a requirement of being a 'lady'. Trudgill (1974) suggested that this is because women are more concerned with politeness and that nonstandard forms of speech are associated with masculine impoliteness. The greater use of the prestige language form by women has also been attributed to greater sensitivity to social norms because of an insecure social position. Three decades ago, it was reported that women in a German-Hungarian community in Austria were using the prestige language form as a result of modernization in the society (Gal, 1978); they were said to be more aware of the potential economic benefits of 'speaking well' than were men.

This notion that men and women communicate in fundamentally different ways has spawned a number of best-selling popular books such as *Men are from Mars and Women are from Venus* (Gray, 1992), all of which inform the public that men and women not only speak differently but think differently as well. Yet, Cameron (2007) reviewed 30 years of language research and concluded that it is a myth that men and women communicate in fundamentally different ways. Further evidence of this myth comes from Leaper & Robnett (2011), who conducted a meta-analysis of studies that examined gender differences in the use of tentative language, that is, language that seems to communicate indecisiveness. They concluded that tentative language is neither male nor female, but is part of both men's and women's language. Very little research into languages other than English has been conducted in this regard. However, as one example, randomly selected English and Persian family-oriented films were examined with respect to whether males and females differed in their use of tentative and indirect language (Nemati & Bayer, 2007). No such differences were found in either language group.

It is not gender that is the determinant key in the use of tentative speech; it is lack of social power. While some studies have found that women tend to address men using a powerless speech, this reflects the fact that, even in contemporary society, women are often relegated to less powerful positions than are men. (We shall discuss power further in Chapter 10.) Both sexes, however, tend to adapt their speech to the sex of the listener. One study found that when a woman was in discussion with a man, she actually had more influence when she spoke in a tentative way than when she was assertive, although the opposite was true when she was in discussion with a woman. The conversational style of men had no effect on how influential they were with either men or women (Carli, 1990).

Times change; child-rearing practices change; social norms change; cultural beliefs change. As gender-based differences in child-rearing, societal expectations and social norms disappear, language differences unrelated to physiology are likely to gradually disappear as well.

KEY POINT: Because of the historical dominance of males in just about every society, characteristics of the male voice and typical male patterns of speaking are associated with power. We 'read' this power into messages virtually without awareness.

LANGUAGE AND DISCRIMINATION

Within a given society, language provides an efficient vehicle for communicating prejudices and promoting discrimination (Sachdev, 2007; Ng, 2007). A child sitting at the breakfast table who listens to his parents denigrating members of other races, or telling jokes about disabled individuals, or making fun of other peoples' accents, learns a great deal about their parents' values with respect to such people. Racist and sexist epithets teach racism and sexism and overhearing one's parents refer to a homeless person as a 'bum' or 'freeloader' is likely to have a strong influence on how the children come to perceive those individuals. Derogatory labels (e.g. *fag*) appear to elicit different and more negative automatic associations than do simple category labels (e.g. *gay*) referring to the same group of people (Carnaghi & Maass, 2007). Many languages have built-in sexism, reflecting the patriarchal nature of the societies in which they evolved. Because there is no gender-free first-person pronoun in English, *he* and *his* have been used to indicate the generic case – for example, *the student put the books in their knapsack*. This standard usage subtly conditions us to think of physicians as typically being male. A similar bias is found with many other English words such as *mankind, man-made, fireman,* and *chairman.* The past few decades have witnessed a concerted effort, especially within universities, to eliminate this bias: *mankind* becomes *humankind, chairman* becomes *chair* and the generic *his* is replaced either by the awkward *his or her,* or by the (ungrammatical) *their,* as in *the doctor examined their patient.* We shall return to the study of sexist bias in Chapters 12 and 13.

Language also provides a vehicle for prejudice in general. In every language, some words stand out in that they reflect a society's negative views of particular minorities, of the disadvantaged, or of the enemy. We all recognize the destructive power of such words as *nigger, wop* and *faggot.* However, language can foster discrimination in many ways that go beyond simple pejorative labelling. Consider racist or sexist jokes, for example.

Language contributes in another way to prejudice and discrimination. In order to discriminate, one must be able to identify members of the target group. Of course, physical features such as skin colour, gender or signs of intellectual disability provide a ready basis for identifying people who are different from the majority. However, just as powerfully, the language we speak and the way we speak it also provide powerful identifiers of group membership. And just as the stirring words of leaders can inspire people to work together – think of Churchill's '*blood, sweat and tears*' and Martin Luther's '*I have a dream*' – they can also whip up cyclones of hatred – think also of Adolf Hitler's anti-Semitic tirades. The use of language that targets and denigrates a particular group is common especially in wartime and creates what Donohue (2012) refers to as an *identity trap*, assigning everyone to the categories of *friend or foe;* you are either with us or against us. By employing various linguistic conventions – for example, using themes relating primarily to power while making no reference to themes referring to commonalities and affiliation between the majority group in the minority group – the speaker bolsters the identity of his or her group, while at the same time belittling the target group. This provides so powerful a rationale for discrimination towards the target group that it sometimes leads to genocide.

> **KEY POINT:** Language is an important vehicle of prejudice and discrimination. In addition, the language we speak and the way we speak it provide a powerful method for identifying group membership, making identification of a target group easier for those who wish to discriminate.

LANGUAGE ACCOMMODATION AND GROUP BOUNDARIES

If you are at a party chatting with a well-educated individual one minute and the next minute find yourself alone with another person whose manner of talking suggests a poor education, does your speech change? People often shift, or *converge*, towards the speaking style of the other person (Giles, 1973). Convergence may be upward – trying to speak in the style of a speaker from a more prestigious group – or it may be downward when, for example, an employer from a high-status group tries to be 'one of the boys' in interactions with workers. Even one-year-old children show convergence – to the pitch patterns of their parents. They lower the basic frequency of their babbling in the presence of the father and raise it in the presence of the mother (Giles & Smith, 1979). Adults, in return, use simplified vocabulary and grammar in talking to children.

However, there are times when we are most careful not to converge, and we may even on occasion diverge – that is, emphasize the features of our speech style or register that accentuate the difference between 'us and them'. Why do people shift their speech style or register in some instances and not in others? According to communication accommodation theory (Giles & Wadleigh, 1999), we modify our speech style to be more like the other person's in order to be liked or to fit in. However, too much convergence may appear as an attempt at ingratiation or even ridicule. Imagine how visitors from another country would feel if we tried to mimic their accent, speech rate and verbal expressions all at once! In each interaction, some optimal level of convergence is needed to gain favourable responses from the listener, but beyond that there is a risk of it appearing to be mockery (Giles & Smith, 1979).

Communication accommodation theory incorporates ideas from four different areas of social psychology: similarity-attraction, social-exchange, intergroup distinctiveness and causal attribution.

* Similarity-attraction theory (to be discussed in Chapter 8) suggests that the more similar we are to others in terms of attitudes and beliefs, the more likely it is that we will be attractive to them. Convergence is one way to increase our similarity to other people.
* Social exchange theory (to be discussed in Chapters 8 and 10) reminds us that convergence may carry with it certain costs as well as rewards. We must evaluate whether we will be perceived as having lost integrity or whether our group identity will be compromised. If the potential costs exceed the rewards, then social exchange theory predicts that convergence would not occur (Giles & Smith, 1979).

- Maintaining intergroup distinctiveness (to be discussed in Chapter 12) is an important motivation for groups who feel that their language and culture are threatened. We are likely to see divergence when members of a minority group are interacting with people from a majority group that threatens to assimilate them.
- According to attribution theory (discussed in Chapter 2), whether or not we react positively to another's convergence would depend upon what we took to be the motives behind it – is it a friendly gesture or an attempt to manipulate us?

Not only does language play an important role in social interactions between individuals, but it also helps groups mark boundaries and define identities. For example, adolescents' language, while often the bane of their parents, serves first of all to maintain distinctive group boundaries, helping to differentiate themselves from adults and from other groups of adolescents (Eckert, 2003) and, secondly, to strengthen their individual social identities and promote acceptance within their own group (Fortman, 2003). Sometimes, in order to highlight one's group identity, divergence, rather than convergence, occurs and individuals deliberately emphasize the differences between their speech style and that of another person. The Canadian who emphasizes the 'zed' pronunciation of z when talking to Americans, who pronounce it 'zee'; the Cockney who goes out of his or her way to accentuate the Cockney speech style when in conversation with someone of the 'upper classes'; someone from Normandy who refuses to converge to the Parisian accent when in Paris, but instead accentuates the Norman accent … these are all ways of defending group identity and, as well at times implicitly rejecting any suggestion of inferiority.

In terms of national group identity, consider a study of New Zealand speakers responding to an Australian speaker (Babel, 2010): the New Zealanders generally accommodated to the speech style of the Australian, and this occurred both in conditions where the Australian had either flattered them or insulted them. However, it was found that the degree of accommodation was predicted by their scores on tests that measured the extent to which they were pro-Australian. Those with the pro-Australian bias were more likely to accommodate to the Australian speech style. Another study (Drager, Hay & Walker, 2010) found that convergence or divergence can occur automatically even in the absence of another person! They asked New Zealand participants to read aloud a list of words that involved vowels whose pronunciation differs between New Zealand and Australian English. One group of participants was first presented with 'good' facts about Australia (e.g. the Australian government's donation of $1 billion dollars to the Japanese tsunami relief effort was the biggest made by any country), while those in another group were presented with 'bad' facts about Australia (e.g. as of 2005, Australia was the world's largest per capita emitter of greenhouse gases), and a third was given only neutral facts. Simply being exposed to positive or negative statements about Australia led to pronunciations that were respectively more or less similar to Australian pronunciations.

There are times when an inability to converge to another's speech register can contribute to communication breakdown. An important everyday example is provided by patients who feel unable to communicate with their physicians. Most people view physicians as successful, intelligent and high in status and power, and indeed, they exercise a high degree of power in all medical encounters with patients (Watson & Gallois, 2002). When a physician asks someone to undress, the person rarely asks, 'Why?' If the physician tells the patient to take two of the little green pills and one of the large red pills each day, few people seek understanding of what the pills really do, what their side effects might be and so forth. They not only trust; they often dare not ask. Thus, it should come as no surprise that physicians' speech styles reflect power in their interactions with their patients. Bourhis, Roth and MacQueen (1989) examined how medical practitioners speak to their patients. The patients and physicians in their study all agreed that it is important for physicians to converge to the patient's speech register rather than vice-versa. Indeed, physicians believed that while they spoke medical language to other health professionals, they converged to the everyday language of their patients when addressing them. Patients reported that they actually tried to converge to medical language when speaking to physicians. However, patients perceived little convergence by physicians, an opinion that squared with the observations of student nurses. This not only reflects the imbalance in social power but also often leaves the patient feeling as though he or she has not obtained all the information that was desired from a visit to the doctor. Perhaps this contributes to the serious problem of noncompliance with 'doctor's orders' (see Chapter 16).

Interestingly, similar problems can arise between general practitioners and specialists, the former often being unfamiliar with the terminology spoken by the latter (Barcia, 1985). Physicians enjoy higher status and power than patients, and medical specialists have even more status. It is not surprising to find that the less powerful try to converge to the speech register of the more powerful.

What determines the kind of accommodation that occurs when bilingual individuals of different native tongues interact? A native speaker of the minority language may converge to the dominant language not only out of a desire to communicate efficiently, but this could also reflect a conscious or unconscious effort to socially integrate with a more powerful social group (Bourhis, 1990). Of course, linguistic skill plays an important role; if one person is fluently bilingual while the other has some difficulty in the second language, they will tend to use the language that is easier for both. And in some cases, norms governing the particular situation apply. A salesperson, for example, quickly uses the client's language. Willingness to communicate in a second language is also in part determined by **ethnolinguistic vitality** (Clément, Baker & MacIntyre, 2003). This term refers to the relative status and strength of a language in a particular social structure (Giles, Bourhis & Taylor, 1977; Harwood & Vincze, 2012); it reflects the proportion of the population that belongs to the particular language group, their socioeconomic status and the extent of institutional support for the language (such as schools and newspapers). The ethnolinguistic vitality of German is high in Zürich, but relatively low in Geneva where French is the dominant language. Thus when a bilingual but mother-tongue German speaker from Zürich converses with a bilingual but mother-tongue French speaker from Geneva, they are likely to speak German with each other when in Zürich and French when in Geneva.

> **KEY POINT:** Whether we converge or diverge in a conversation depends on whether our goal is to facilitate communication, to try to 'fit in' with the listener, or to accentuate the differences between our group and that of the listener.

WHO BECOMES BILINGUAL?

Because of increasing globalization, more and more people are interacting with people from other cultural and linguistic backgrounds. As a result, even though English has become the de facto language of international science and commerce, there is an increasing need for some people to become fluent in languages other than their own. It may be surprising to learn that most people in the world are already bilingual (Tucker, 1981). Bilingualism is common in many European and Asian nations, and both the formation of the European Community and the North American Free Trade Agreement are fostering second-language learning. In North America, the 86,000,000 Spanish speakers in Mexico and the 7,000,000 French speakers in Canada may turn the North American common market into a trilingual marketplace (Bourhis, 1994).

This raises some important social psychological questions about how we can communicate effectively across language barriers, about who chooses and who succeeds in becoming bilingual, and about how bilingualism, and even multilingualism, can be promoted. Some children are fortunate enough to grow up in a bilingual environment and become proficient in two languages as they grow. For most people, however, learning a second language requires a good deal of formal effort. Motivation to learn a second language is greatly dependent upon social context including attitudes in the home and in society in general (Gardner, 1985).

Becoming bilingual involves more than just learning a second language; it also requires mastering a new set of social norms. We must learn to recognize when and how the intent of a communication in the second language is different from the meaning of the words spoken. Skill at using a language in a social context is referred to variously as **sociolinguistic competence** (Holmes & Brown, 1977) or **communicative competence** (Romaine, 2000), something that is difficult to teach formally since often even the native speaker of the language cannot verbalize the rules. For example, how does someone just learning English know that when we invite a person to 'drop in anytime', this is not, in fact, an invitation to drop in anytime? Or that asking

'Would you mind running to the store for me?' is not actually a question, but a polite request, and does not involve actual running. In French, particularly in France, 'Merci' spoken in response to being offered something usually means 'No, thank you', not just 'Thank you'. In English, 'Thanks' in that context means 'Yes, thank you'.

Thus, the process of becoming bilingual is more of a socialization process than the student usually expects. Moreover, exposure to speakers of another language in their own language can sometimes produce unexpected social psychological consequences. The learner may become aware of stereotypes held by members of a new linguistic group about his or her own group. These new insights may even undermine the learner's sense of identity. For example, what happens once you become fluent enough to share jokes or criticisms with speakers of the new language about your own maternal language group? If you laugh at the jokes, you may feel uneasy or even guilty; if you respond defensively, you may be excluded from the group. Within your own language group, you may find yourself defending the other group from criticisms, leading to feelings of estrangement. A person in this situation may become marginalized – no longer a typical member of his or her own group but never fully one of the new group. To avoid being placed in this position of psychological inconsistency, some people may withdraw from second-language learning, and they may support this attitude with clichés such as 'I'm too old to learn a new language' and by avoiding cross-cultural interaction that might remind them of the need to acquire the second language (Lambert, 1981; Taylor & Simard, 1975).

Why do some people persevere even when their social situation does not demand it? Why do some students go on to become fluently bilingual, while others, despite years of instruction, remain essentially unilingual? Several factors that facilitate language learning have been identified (Gardner, 1985; Lalonde & Gardner, 1984):

- *Intelligence.* Intelligence obviously facilitates any kind of learning. Thus, intellectually superior individuals should normally find language learning an easier task than it might be for someone less capable.
- *Specific aptitude for learning language.* Some people are simply better at learning languages than others (Bylund, Abrahamsson & Hyltenstam, 2010). Verbal skills that lead to high ability in one's native language are also likely to facilitate learning a second language.
- *Motivation.* Someone who *wants* to become bilingual is more likely to succeed. Motivation has been found repeatedly to be a crucial determinant of second-language success (Gardner, 1984; Pae, 2008). Individuals whose motivation is primarily instrumental (e.g., improving their chances of a good job) do not do as well as people who want to become involved in the culture of the other language community: to go to plays, see movies, talk to friends, meet members of the opposite sex. For example, a Hungarian study (Csizér & Kormos, 2009) found that students who were studying English were motivated by the perceived importance of being able to interact with people from outside the country. Interestingly, direct contact with English speakers was not related to motivation; it was only contact through the media – watching foreign films, for example – that played an important role. In another study, carried out in Santiago, Chile, the motivation of students studying English as a second language was related to their view of English as an international language and a desire to be able to communicate internationally (Kormos, Kiddle & Csizér, 2011).
- Motivation also depends in part on ethnolinguistic vitality within the community. An anglophone living in Paris will be more likely to want to learn French than an anglophone in New Delhi. And when one of two linguistic groups living side by side is lower in ethnolinguistic vitality (usually the minority group), its members are likely to be motivated to learn the majority language since proficiency brings material and psychological benefits. Yet, when the minority language group fears acculturation, group identity may lead to opposition to learning the majority language (Clément, 1987). Such an opposing motivation has been openly expressed in Québec by those who fear that francophone language and culture will be swallowed up in the huge North American anglophone milieu. The net motivation to learn the majority language will depend on which of these basic motivations is stronger.
- This relates to what Lambert (1978; Lambert & Taylor, 1984) termed additive and subtractive bilingualism. When anglophones in South Africa learn Afrikaans, Israelis learn Arabic or English, or anglophone Canadians learn French, they are not threatening the continued existence of their sociolinguistic group. The individuals have simply acquired another socially useful skill. However, when minority groups are

struggling to maintain their identity, learning the language of the majority can be considered subtractive in that it threatens the continued importance of the native language in that society. Bilingualism is likely to be encouraged, or at worst ignored, when it is additive for a given group. It may be actively discouraged when it is subtractive.

- *Anxiety and self-confidence.* When two linguistic groups both possess high ethnolinguistic vitality, then a personal factor, self-confidence in one's ability to use the second language becomes an important determinant of who does or does not become bilingual (Clément, 1987). Anxiety is a major obstacle in second-language learning (Bailey, Onwuegbuzie & Daley, 2000), and self-confident individuals will have less anxiety about learning the new language and more success at mastering it (Gardner, 1985; Young & Gardner, 1990).

Notwithstanding the risk of coming to feel marginalized, as discussed above, acquiring competence in a second language has important social psychological consequences such as engendering more positive attitudes towards the target language group. Indeed, when students have the opportunity both to become bilingual and to mix with members of both linguistic groups, barriers do appear to come down. Guimond and Palmer (1993) examined the attitudes of francophone and anglophone students studying each other's language and found that the greater the degree of bilingualism, the less the favouritism displayed towards the native-tongue group. Other research has shown that acquiring competence in a second language promotes greater positive feeling towards out-groups in general and a greater willingness to intervene when the rights of others are unfairly threatened (Rubenfeld et al., 2007). On the other hand, lack of linguistic skill in a second language can generate anxiety, and a non-fluent speaker may misattribute this anxiety to the other person and react negatively to the individual, to the language or to speakers of it in general.

KEY POINT: Bilingualism also involves sociolinguistic competence, the ability to use and understand social nuances. Success in learning a second language is facilitated by intelligence, specific aptitude for languages, motivation to be involved in that language community, and self-confidence.

NON-VERBAL COMMUNICATION

The meaning of words is modified not only by non-verbal aspects of speech itself, the paralanguage discussed above, it is also changed by other non-verbal behaviours such as smiles, gestures, and body position. It has often been reported that women are somewhat better than men at both sending and picking up non-verbal cues across a wide range of situations (Brown, 1986; Eagly, 1987), probably as a result of child-rearing practices that encourage girls to be emotionally expressive and attentive to others. Since we are rarely fully aware of information received non-verbally, it is easy to understand on this basis the persistent and popular belief in women's intuition: women may pick up non-verbal cues that men miss and, being unable to specify which cues led them to a certain inference, describe the inference in terms of a 'feeling'.

To understand fully how we communicate, we need to study these non-verbal influences, but this is not easy, for even brief interactions involve many quick and spontaneous exchanges that are difficult to record. It has been estimated that we can produce 700,000 different physical gestures and movements (Pei, 1965) 20,000 different facial expressions (Birdwhistle, 1970) and 1000 different postures (Hewes, 1957). Imagine the difficulty in trying to make records of so many possible non-verbal cues. Early research was severely hampered by lack of agreement on how to describe so many different movements, but coding systems were eventually developed. They are based on the analysis of changes in a large number of different parts of the face and body over a series of short intervals (Ekman & Friesen, 1978; Frey et al., 1983). By feeding all this information – gathered with regard to the entire body – into a computer, very detailed analyses of movements can be carried out, allowing researchers much greater precision in measuring and quantifying changes in body position or facial expression.

217

Non-verbal signalling begins at a very young age, and body movements and facial expressions provide substantial communication long before we learn to communicate verbally. While non-verbal behaviour does vary from culture to culture, there also seems to be some universality in the early development of gesturing. Blake et al. (2005) systematically observed the development of gestures in infants from a number of different cultural backgrounds and found that the children showed similar changes in the use of gestures over time. For example, the gestures of Italian-Canadian infants were as similar to those of Japanese infants as they were to English-Canadians, whose cultural environment was much more similar to their own. As children grow, they learn the cultural display rules of their particular society – rules about appropriate facial expressions, postures, gaze, how much distance to keep between oneself and others, how to orient one's body during interactions and when to engage in touch (Maass, 2009; Masumoto, 2006).

The coding and decoding of non-verbal signals can be a quite complex matter at times, for a particular non-verbal signal can take on different meanings depending on the relative status of the individuals, their genders, and the particular social environment. To make things even more difficult, sometimes conflicting non-verbal messages are included in the same communication. We are not usually aware of the non-verbal signals that we send, but we are usually automatically responsive to the social environment, and our non-verbal behaviour reflects the social norms that apply in the particular situation. For instance, if you roll your eyes towards the ceiling while listening to a professor who is criticizing your essay plan, this gesture would likely be considered as disrespectful, thus causing interpersonal tension. However, if the professor asked how you were enjoying your part-time job, the same eye roll could be employed quite appropriately and would probably convey your feelings about the job more succinctly than a verbal reply.

The cultural specificity of non-verbal cues can create problems when interacting with people of other cultures. Consider for example the so-called 'head bobble,' involving movement of the head from side to side in a manner similar to a bobble-head doll, that is common among East Indians. The movement is sort of a cross between a head nod and a head shake, and with subtle variations it can mean anything from 'yes' to 'no' to 'I understand'. While its meaning is clear to most other Indians, it is a source of considerable confusion to visitors to that country.

Researchers first assumed that non-verbal communication acts as a separate communication channel that serves to add additional information – emphasis and subtlety – to what is being communicated through the verbal system. However, we now know that verbal and non-verbal communications do not involve separate channels, but instead are intimately intertwined and represent different manifestations of a common process in the brain. Even though we use many gestures and facial expressions in a deliberate effort to communicate, the greater part of non-verbal behaviour occurs without our intent or even awareness. Indeed, research has shown that when two people in a social interaction cannot see each other, they continue to produce non-verbal behaviour at almost the same level as when they have visual contact (Rimé, 1983). This is readily apparent when you see someone gesturing while using the telephone; the gestures are not communicating anything in such a case. Such gestures are so closely tied up with communication that even speakers who have been blind since birth gesture when talking to listeners who are also blind (Iverson & Goldin-Meadow, 1998).

Non-verbal and verbal responses are normally highly correlated, unless we make a deliberate effort to try to hide what we are thinking or feeling. Verbal communication ability actually develops on top of non-verbal motor activity, and thus non-verbal behaviour, rather than being an independently generated set of responses, is a fundamental part of the process of translating thoughts into words (Rimé, 1983). Consequently, gesturing serves to help the speaker as well as the listener. Given that non-verbal and verbal communication are so intertwined, and given that non-verbal signals vary from one linguistic group to another, what happens when young children are brought up learning two different languages? In a longitudinal Canadian study (Mayberry & Nicoladis, 2000), the development of gesturing in children being reared in a bilingual English-French environment was observed as they made progress in learning each of the two languages. Again, in line with the view that non-verbal behaviour is an integral part of communication and not something separate from it, the children did not gesture less as they learned to talk, but instead gestured more frequently, and their use of gestures in speaking each of the two languages was tied to the level of development of that language. For example, a child whose French-speaking ability was advanced relative to his or her English-speaking ability also used more complex and frequent gestures when speaking in French than in English, and the opposite was the case for children who were more advanced in speaking English.

Functions of non-verbal behaviour

While verbal communication is built upon a substrate of non-verbal communication, and some non-verbal behaviour assists the speaker when communicating verbally, non-verbal communication also has important functions in its own right (Argyle, 1975; Patterson, 1982, 1983):

1. Non-verbal signals provide a superior means of communication in some situations. For instance, our vocabulary for shapes is limited, and it is easier to describe a complex shape with hand movements than to name it (Holler & Stevens, 2007), or while describing a bird, the speaker may point to show the listener where the bird is sitting.
2. As indicators of emotion, non-verbal signals are more spontaneous and less easily controlled and therefore more likely to convey genuine information. For example, gazing into someone's eyes can often express intimacy more readily than words. We can choose our words to project a certain emotional state, but our non-verbal behaviour may be more likely to portray what we honestly feel. And people are quite good at perceiving emotional states on the basis of non-verbal information, although, for some reason, this ability appears to decline across the lifespan (Lambrecht, Kreifelts & Wildgruber, 2012).
3. Non-verbal signals can quickly establish dominance or promote social control (e.g., threatening gestures or ingratiating smiles).
4. Non-verbal signals provide a basis for judging qualities of the speaker. Gestures, facial expressions and other non-verbal cues can strongly influence our perception of an individual's attractiveness (Morrison et al., 2007), social identity (Munhall & Buchan, 2004), and personality (Levesque & Kenny, 1993).
5. Non-verbal signals provide a second communication channel that allows us to coordinate the flow of verbal communication during a conversation. In every linguistic group, there are norms covering not only who speaks next but also virtually every aspect of the verbal exchange from beginning to end. This occurs automatically, usually without awareness, and is based in non-verbal behaviour including the paralanguage discussed earlier. Without such conversation control, conversations would turn into verbal traffic jams. Some of the 'turn-yielding' signals we use were described by Argyle (1988):

   - Coming to the end of a sentence.
   - Prolonged intonation – for example, raising or lowering the voice: 'Do you like this?'
   - Paralinguistic drawl – the final syllable is drawn out: 'And then I came ho-o-m-me'.
   - Body motion – if the speaker was using hand gestures, they cease; if the speaker's hands have appeared tense, they now relax. The speaker's eyes tend to open wider with the last note of a question, to indicate that the listener can begin to answer; if a question is being asked, the speaker tends to lift his or her head on the final syllable. In television interviews, it has been observed that people tend to look directly at the interviewer only when ready to finish making a point.
   - Verbal cues – at the end of phrases: 'I was going to go to the movies tonight, but, uh ...'

There is more to conversation control: Sometimes we try to butt in while someone else is speaking, and then the speaker who wants to continue puts out **attempt-suppressing signals**: the voice maintains the same pitch; the head remains straight; the eyes remain unchanged; the hands maintain the same gesture; the speaker may speak slightly louder or faster and may keep a hand in mid-gesture at the end of sentences (Argyle, 1975).

How does the speaker know that the listener is paying attention? Listeners regularly do this by **back-channel communication**: that is, the listener nods from time to time, or says 'mm-hmm' or 'okay'. In Japan, back-channel communication occurs at a higher rate than in North America (White, 1989). Thus, a Japanese person talking to a Canadian or American by telephone may frequently ask, 'Are you still there?' because the North American emits back-channel signals at too slow a pace for the speaker. Back-channel communication does more than tell the speaker that we are listening. Bavelas, Coates & Johnson (2000) carried out a study that examined its role as a narrator tells a story. They found that listeners were in a sense co-narrators, in that their responses to the narration – in terms of nodding, making verbalizations such as 'mhm', wincing and so on – not only helped illustrate the story but affected the narrator's performance. When listeners were distracted so that they did not provide the same feedback, narrators told their stories less well.

Finally, how do we signal that we wish to terminate a conversation altogether? More non-verbal signals. When speaking face-to-face, we tend to move slightly away and to look away. (Looking at our watch is also a powerful signal!) When using the telephone, we may allow for a longer interval before responding to the speaker.

[
KEY POINT: Non-verbal behaviour is fundamentally tied to verbal communication; it serves to modify its meaning and to regulate conversation. It provides information about the speaker's emotional state and motives and can be used to establish and maintain social control.
]

CATEGORIES OF NON-VERBAL BEHAVIOUR

Researchers divide non-verbal behaviours into a number of categories (Anderson, 2008) including: kinesics, the 'body language' of popular literature, which includes all bodily movements except those that involve direct contact with someone; oculesics, eye movement and gaze; haptics, the use of touch as communication; proxemics, the use and structuring of space as communication; chronemics, the use of pauses and silences; and artefacts, the use of clothing and tattoos and piercing and hairstyles and so forth to signal something about ourselves. We shall examine each of these areas in turn.

Kinesics

One need only observe a mime artist to recognize the power of the eyes and face and indeed the whole body in communicating feelings and thoughts. Although less so than the face, the body is a source of non-verbal messages and a number of popular books have promised to teach readers how to understand and exploit 'body language'. For example, it has been claimed that someone sitting with arms crossed while talking to someone else is unknowingly revealing a protective emotional stance. However, such books rarely back up their claims with empirical evidence and should be approached warily. Still, there is evidence that others often perceive certain particular postures as reflecting specific feelings, whether or not they actually do so. For example, leaning towards another person or standing or sitting in close proximity is generally interpreted as demonstrating a positive feeling towards that person.

Gestures
Gestures are also a form of kinesics, and we have already discussed how these develop in early childhood, beginning even before production of speech. Gestures vary somewhat society to society and from culture to culture. It is trouble enough when one is unaware of the meaning of a gesture, but it is more problematic when the same gesture means something different in different cultures. Consider the common gesture involving the touching of forefinger to thumb. In North America and the British Isles, this gesture communicates a positive sentiment, 'A-OK' or 'well-done!' Yet in some European countries, it communicates a 'zero', and is thus interpreted as an insult – 'you are worth nothing'. Even more serious – in some other countries, including Germany and Brazil, this gesture is taken to be a reference to the anus, and therefore an obvious insult. Imagine

the unknowing tourist who, having enjoyed a great meal in a restaurant, salutes the German waiter in this fashion! And while a sidewise shake of the head means *no* in Canada, in Turkey, no is signalled by moving the head backwards and rolling the eyes upward (Rubin, 1976). There are many other such examples: The Japanese are surprised when we point to our chest in referring to ourselves; they do so by putting a finger to the nose (DeVos & Hippler, 1969). Drawing one's finger across one's throat means 'I've had it' in Canada; in Swaziland it means, 'I love you'. (Even stick figures can communicate emotions as in Figure 7.3.)

Figure 7.3   Stick figures and their emotions
Source: Hannah Ensor/Shutterstock.com

Mimicry   There is considerable research showing that head and eye movements, facial expressions, and gestures, as well as non-verbal aspects of speech itself, become somewhat coordinated during a conversation so that speaker and listener tend to be producing similar non-verbal cues. (Recall the discussion of mimicry and mirror neurons in Chapter 6.) A non-verbal cue produced by one individual is predictive of a symmetric response on the part of the other (Boker & Rotondo, 2002), producing a kind of 'dynamic coupling'. Because of this, non-verbal cues can influence the development of conversation, affecting not just how you move, but also guiding the verbal exchange so that they influence what you say as well. Most such mimicry occurs quite unconsciously, and it has been found that it generally leads to increased positive feelings in terms of empathy and interconnectedness on each side of the conversation, although this does not happen with people who are generally more competitive than cooperative (Stel, Rispens, Leliveld & Lokhorst, 2011).

Facial expression   Facial expression is a particularly important form of kinesics, and it plays so major a role in communication that when words and expression are contradictory, the face is often taken to be a more accurate guide to the meaning of what was said (Bugental, Kaswan & Love, 1970). In our everyday lives, we often rely upon other people's facial expressions as the best guide to their true feelings. And while we have to take turns with verbal utterances during a conversation, facial expression provides an ongoing stream of information related to the person's emotional reactions during a conversation, as well as his or her degree of attentiveness (Parkinson, 2005).

Smiles convey a virtually universal connotation of happiness, absence of anger, positive feeling towards the other individual and so forth. Indeed, our faces are like little advertising billboards, allowing us to present ourselves to the world. Self-presentation comes to the forefront when we select a photograph of ourselves to be published alongside our name, whether in a company brochure, a local newspaper, a student yearbook or a Facebook page. A number of studies, both longitudinal and in different cultures, have focused on the photographs that students have chosen to put into their yearbooks. A persistent gender effect has been found: women are more likely than men to smile in their photographs, at least in the United States (DeSantis and Sierra, 2000) and France (Guéguen, 2010). The gender effect is likely widespread. For example, in a Japanese study (Kawamura, Komori & Miyamoto, 2008), participants rated the degree of masculinity of 48 male faces and the degree of femininity of 48 female faces. Half of the faces presented a neutral expression and the other half showed a smile. It was found that smiling significantly reduced the average masculinity ratings of men's faces, particularly for male raters, while there was no effect of smiling on the femininity ratings for female faces, suggesting that people tend to associate smiling with women. Another study (DeSantis, Mohan & Steinhorst, 2005) examined photographs of children, older teenagers, and adults. The gender effect in terms of smiling was age-dependent. There is no such effect in the photographs of children of preschool and grade school age, but such an effect was evident in the pictures of teenagers and adults, where females were again more likely than males to show a smile. The tendency to smile is a rather stable one: When the same researchers examined pictures of well-known personalities taken at various periods during their adult lives, it was found that there was very little change over time in

Figure 7.4 Smiles and frowns are powerful images

Source: sarininka/Shutterstock.com

a given individual's tendency to smile or not smile in photographs.

Researchers have devoted considerable attention in attempting to demonstrate that facial displays, including smiles, are innately linked to emotion and are therefore universal. This is the emotion-expression model and it has until recently been the dominant model for the social psychological understanding of the connection between emotion and facial display. This idea goes back to Charles Darwin, who suggested in 1872 that human emotional behaviour evolved from that of the lower animals, and so we should expect all human beings to be similar in their way of expressing emotion – that is, the physical expression of emotion is to some degree innate. In support of this view, there is evidence of an underlying correspondence between some facial expressions related to emotion and specific activity in the brain and autonomic nervous system (Levenson, Ekman & Friesen, 1990). In addition, research has demonstrated the similarity of facial expressions of emotion across a wide range of cultures; for example, in cultures as disparate as those of native-born Americans and the Minangkabau of West Sumatra (Levenson, Ekman, Heider & Friesen, 1992). A meta-analytic study reported that emotions are universally recognized from photographs at better than chance levels, although this ability is better when judging someone of the same national ethnic or regional group analysis (Elfenbein & Ambady, 2002). While facial expressions appear to be most useful in revealing the survival emotions – anger, disgust, fear, happiness and sadness – body movements appear superior in communicating social status emotions such as embarrassment, guilt, pride and shame, and touch appears to be best at communicating intimate emotions such as love and sympathy (App, McIntosh, Rees & Hertenstein, 2011).

However, such research is plagued with methodological problems. For one thing, much of this research has assessed the participant's ability to judge emotions from photographs. However, the portrayed emotions were posed – that is, people were deliberately attempting to convey a particular emotion for the photograph. It turns out that posed and spontaneous displays of emotion are generated differently, using two separate neural pathways that carry signals from the brain to the facial muscles. One pathway is employed for deliberate expression and the other for spontaneous expression. This is clearly demonstrated by the existence of two particular neurological disorders: in one, a patient told a joke will produce a spontaneous smile but will not be able to smile when asked; in the other, a patient will smile when asked but will show no facial reaction when told the joke (Ekman, 1982).

What happens when researchers employ photographs involving spontaneous expressions of emotion gathered by covertly photographing people's faces as they are exposed to some stimulus? In this case, only happiness is easily recognized, although anger and disgust can also be detected at an above-chance rate (Wagner, MacDonald & Manstead, 1986).

What about showing participants videos rather than still photographs? In one such study (Hejmadi, Davidson & Rozin, 2000), American and Indian participants watched videotapes portraying ten classic emotions that are described in Hindu texts: anger, disgust, fear, heroism, amusement, love, peace, sadness, wonder and *lajya* (which translates as shame/shyness/embarrassment but is viewed as a positive emotion in India). The participants viewed both facial and bodily signals. On average, each group of participants was accurate in their judgement of these emotional portrayals approximately two-thirds of the time. It is particularly notable that even 'indigenous' Indian emotions (peace, heroism and *lajya*) were reliably recognized by the American participants, although the Indians were a little more accurate in identifying them. This is very interesting for it indicates that individuals can identify emotional states that they were not even aware of, provided that they are given an idea of what it means to be in that particular state.

However, consider this: As persuasive as the evidence might seem to be that people from various societies are able to 'read' emotions in the faces of individuals from other quite different societies, the effect is actually not very strong, except possibly with regard to happiness, and the research does not rule out the possibility that individuals are making inferences that are based on information that the face provides about intended action, liking, attention and so forth, rather than emotion per se (Parkinson, 2005). In fact, researchers have found that facial displays reflecting emotion are more consistent among members of the same subculture or group than between members coming from different cultures or groups, which contradicts the notion of universality. Further, the presence of an audience is important, and the emotion-expression model cannot account for the fact that even strong emotions are not always accompanied by what is assumed to be the corresponding facial expression, unless an audience is present (Fernandez-Dols & Ruiz-Belda, 1995).

So, while almost no researcher would argue that there is not some genetic component underlying facial displays, until there is clear evidence that the presence of emotion directly and automatically produces a particular facial movement, one must withhold judgement with regard to the emotion-expression model (Parkinson, 2005). The question is whether those displays relate directly to emotions, or instead to other factors correlated with the emotion, such as social motives. This leads us to the motive-communication model, which posits that facial displays are deliberately used to communicate particular social motives to the individuals being addressed (Fridlund, 1994). In this view, facial displays reflect intentions, and not emotion that has 'leaked out' into the social world.

In any case, whether biological factors play much of a role in facial displays of emotion, social and cultural factors certainly do (Matsumoto, 2006). In Western societies, social norms typically dictate that we should suppress tears when we are disappointed, but may show them at funerals; and that we may demonstrate happiness at parties but should suppress any sign of it if we have just humiliated an opponent on the squash court. Cultural differences can be dramatic. For example, people in Japan are taught to use laughter or smiles to conceal anger or grief (Argyle, 1988). When university students from Canada, the United States and Japan were asked to judge the appropriateness of the expression of each of seven basic emotions in a number of different situations, it was found that not only was the expression of powerful negative emotions such as anger, contempt and disgust, considered less acceptable in Japan, but the Japanese participants were also less likely than the North Americans to endorse as appropriate the expression of positive emotions such as happiness and surprise (Safdar et al., 2009).

It may be that such differences may be related to the extent to which a society is individualistic or collectivist. Masuda et al. (2008) presented evidence suggesting that the North American emphasis on individuality leads individuals to focus on personal, freely chosen actions while considering the wishes and expectations of others as less important in terms of making a decision. On the other hand, they point out that in East Asian cultures in general and Japan in particular, proper behaviour is defined in terms of the expectations and wishes of other important people in one's life, with less concern devoted to personal needs and goals. In order to see whether such differences are reflected in terms of the judgement of emotions based on facial expressions, university students in the United States and Japan were shown cartoon images in which a central character was expressing a clear emotion – happy, sad, angry or neutral – while other characters in the background were also expressing a clear emotion, either the same or different from that of the central character. For the Japanese participants, background characters influenced the judgement of the emotion being shown by the central character, but this did not occur with the American participants. In a second study, the researchers actually tracked eye movements of the participants and found that the Japanese looked at the background characters more often than did the Americans. They concluded that for Americans emotion is viewed as something associated only with the individual, whereas for the Japanese the individual's emotions are viewed as inseparable from those of the group.

Similarly, in a study involving more than 5000 university students from 32 countries – Australia, Canada, Israel, Japan, New Zealand, United States and Zimbabwe among them – participants were asked how they should react when experiencing each of seven emotions – anger, contempt, disgust, fear, happiness, sadness, and surprise – in response to various people, for example, father, male friend, female professor, and in various situations, some of them private and some of them public. As was expected, participants from individualistic

Figure 7.5   Each one of us can communicate many facial expressions
Source: tommaso lizzul/Shutterstock.com

societies were generally more prone to express their emotions, and this was particularly true of positive emotions (Matsumoto et al., 2008). Matsumoto, Hwang & Yamada (2012) replicated the finding that Asians, in this case Japanese and South Koreans, are influenced more by contextual influences than are Americans. Their data suggested that these differences were related to differences in personality traits such as neuroticism and extroversion rather than to the individualistic or collectivist nature of the society. Interestingly, they suggested that in cultures where people are typically higher in neuroticism and lower in extroversion, individuals have less confidence that people's facial expressions are consistent with their emotions, whereas in cultures in which people are relatively higher in extroversion and lower in neuroticism, there is a more open expression of emotion and therefore individuals can rely more upon people's facial expressions as reflecting their feelings.

Research continues in this fascinating domain, but it is now quite clear that there is *not* a strong link between specific facial patterns and specific emotions. Yet, most people believe that there is one. Why should this be so? Carroll and Russell (1997) suggest that this is due to cognitive schema formation (see Chapter 3): As we grow up, we form schemata associated with various emotional states. Of course, children must learn how to interpret facial presentations and what facial display corresponds to which emotion. The growing child may observe various facial actions in association with, for example, anger: one day it may be furrowed brows; another day, the 'Arnold Schwarzenegger look' with downturned lips, and so on. Gradually, a schema forms that is a composite of all these facial displays, which rarely appear all together. Then if the child is asked to mime anger, this composite image is presented. Indeed, Carroll and Russell (1997) suggest this is what mimes and actors, especially amateur actors, also do when presenting a given emotion. Observing these mimes and actors reinforces the child's erroneous schema. These facial expressions of emotion, despite their inaccuracy, live on as cognitive schemata in our minds – and in the theatre.

Reading faces

Yet, however we learn to do it, most of us obviously have some ability to correctly make inferences about people based on their facial display. Our confidence in such judgements can lead to very significant social consequences – perhaps even influencing our voting choices! For example, Japanese and American researchers carried out a series of cross-cultural studies in which participants from both countries rated the faces of political candidates from both the United States and Japan in terms of five personality traits: competence, dominance, maturity, likability, and trustworthiness (Rule et al., 2010). The respondents showed high agreement in their ratings regardless of their own culture or that of the politicians. More interesting, their judgements were predictive of the percentage of votes each candidate received in the actual election, but this only held true with regard to candidates of their own culture.

Imagine that you will now sail from Troy to Ithaca. Who would you choose to be the captian of your boat. Circle your choice.

The person on the left   The person on the right

Figure 7.6   An example of a pair of faces used
Source: Antonakis & Dalgas (2009)

In other research carried out in the United States, participants rated the competence, trust and likability of candidates in congressional elections on the basis of only a one-second exposure to photographs of their faces. They were presented with pairs of photographs of the faces of winners and runners-up, and their ratings of competence predicted the winners at a substantially better than chance rate – for example, the candidate perceived as more competent was elected 68.8% of the time in the 2004 Senate races (Todorov et al., 2005). Yet, their inferences about trust and likability based on the pictures were not predictive of the election outcome. Extending this to the larger population, the researchers concluded that such a very rapid inference based on a photograph, with no time for contemplation, can have a significant effect on actual voting choices, choices which we would like to believe are based primarily on rational deliberation.

In another study (Antonakis & Dalgas, 2009), adults in Switzerland were shown pairs of faces and asked to rate the competence of each individual; they had no knowledge of whom the individuals were. The pictures were actually pairs of winners and runners-up in the run-off stages of the 2002 French parliamentary election. The person picked as appearing the most competent turned out to have been the winner 72% of the time, much higher than one would expect by chance (Figure 7.6). Children aged 5 to 13 years were then shown the same pairs of pictures, this time in a computer game involving a simulated voyage from Troy to Ithaca. They were asked to choose the person from each pair of pictures who they thought would be best-suited to be the captain of the boat, and they too chose the face of the election winner – 71% of the time! Thus children and adults alike were able to pick election winners at a rate significantly better than chance, simply based on their judgements of competence based on photographs.

Just think about that for a moment. What is going on if children can, by picking the captain of an imaginary boat, point to the election winner 71% of the time?! In the earlier study with adults, it was the estimates of competence, not trustworthiness or likability, that predicted the winners, but we have no information to suggest that the winners were actually any more competent than the losers. The larger question is this: If these photos of politicians have such an influence in laboratory studies, did they sway the voters as well? Did the winners win for the same reason that they were chosen by children to captain an imaginary boat? That question must wait further research.

Insensitivity to facial cues   What happens to people who do not learn how to recognize facial emotions? Much still needs to be learned in this regard, but there is some suggestive evidence. For example, criminal psychopaths appear to be deficient in being able to recognize disgust on the basis of facial cues (Kosson et al., 2002) and, perhaps because of this they fail to show a startle response when viewing scenes of mutilation (Levenson et al., 2000). And in a study of helping behaviour, it was found that participants' ability to recognize fear in a facial display was a better predictor of whether the individual would provide assistance to the individual than were other factors such as the participant's gender, mood at the time, or score on an empathy scale (Marsh, Kozak & Ambady, 2007). The individual who cannot make correct inferences about another person's emotional state is unlikely to develop sensitivity to other people's pain.

KEY POINT: Gestures, mimicry and facial expressions provide powerful means of communication. Facial expressions often communicate emotion better than verbal communications.

Oculesics

Eye movement and gaze provide powerful communication signals, so powerful in fact that if we see someone staring intently in a certain direction, we usually feel an impulse to do the same (Parkinson, 2005). While facial expression can be easily captured by a photograph, a gaze (looking in the direction of another person's face and eyes) and eye contact (mutual gaze) cannot. Gaze is obviously an important non-verbal cue. For example, Dutch researchers found that when an individual observes another person gazing at an object, this actually increases the desirability of that object (van der Weiden, Veling & Aarts, 2010). In a study of British six- and nine-year-olds, it was found that even at age six, children use interpersonal gaze behaviour as a cue about an individual's motivation (Einav & Hood, 2008), and adults and children alike have been observed to interpret gaze aversion as a cue that an individual is lying.

There is considerable evidence that there are some innate aspects to eye contact. Within a few days of birth, the infant will make eye contact with a caregiver, and the distance at which the infant focuses most readily turns out to be the distance between infant and mother when breastfeeding (Burgoon, Buller & Woodall, 1989). The gaze of others is arousing to human infants just as it is to other primates – horses, dogs and cats – and neuroimaging studies show that there is actually a neural basis for the emotional impact that we feel when someone makes eye contact with us (Kawashima et al., 1999). Making eye contact with a wild animal can provoke attack; visitors to the Rocky Mountains are specifically warned against making eye contact should they encounter a grizzly bear. And no doubt we have all had the experience of locking eyes with a stranger and then having some difficulty in letting go and looking away.

Norms vary among cultures with regard to eye contact during conversations. Understanding the 'non-verbal language of the eyes' helps us in understanding other people and their emotional states, and this facilitates our day-to-day social interactions (MacRae et al., 2002). Among most North Americans and Europeans, a person who wants to initiate interaction with another will often look directly at the other's eyes. If the other person looks back, this usually signals a willingness to engage in the interaction. However, by avoiding the gaze, by not letting someone 'catch one's eye', an individual can avoid the obligation to interact (Argyle, 1988). Gazing generally increases as a function of positive attraction, and people who maintain considerable eye contact with each other are generally judged by observers to like each other more. 'Making eyes' at someone is a means of indicating sexual or affectionate interest. However, a

Figure 7.7 Looking 'shifty eyed' affects how people perceive you

Source: doglikehorse/Shutterstock.com

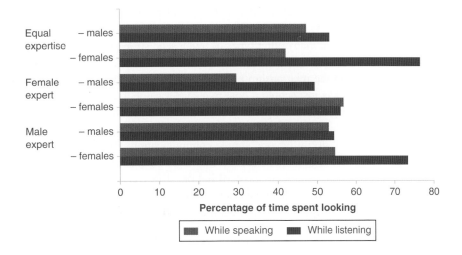

Figure 7.8   Time spent while speaking and listening

Source: Dovidio et al. (1988)

high degree of eye contact does not always indicate affection. There may be times when you deliberately glare at someone to indicate anger or disapproval.

Yet in many cultures, eye contact is considered disrespectful except under particular circumstances. (Think of 'dissing' someone – showing disrespect by making eye contact.) This can sometimes lead to much misunderstanding in intercultural interactions. Most North American children learn to look someone straight in the eye to show that they are paying attention, and not looking someone in the eye can be taken to signal guilt or dishonesty. A visitor to a society where eye contact is avoided may be viewed as showing disrespect when making what for him or her is normal eye contact. In turn, the visitor may interpret the disinclination to make eye contact as indicative of deceit or being 'shifty eyed' (Figure 7.7).

In general within any given human society, visual behaviour is very important in establishing and maintaining dominance just as it is with primates (Ellyson & Dovidio, 1985). Although we are rarely aware of it, the way we look at others can reflect our perception of our relative social power. For example, in a study of pairs of participants in the United States, it was found that a participant of high status or power spent as much or more time looking at the other while talking as while listening (Figure 7.8), while low-power participants looked at the other significantly more while listening than while speaking (showing that they are 'paying attention') (Dovidio & Ellyson, 1985). This effect has been demonstrated with regard to a number of power variables such as educational level, expert power and military rank. This unconscious manifestation of differences in perceived power can cause difficulties in interpersonal and intergroup conflicts that go unrecognized.

KEY POINT: Gaze and eye contact are particularly important in establishing and maintaining dominance.

Haptics

Of our five senses, it is touch that provides infants with their most important contact with the external world (Knapp & Hall, 1992). By exploring the environment through touch, and through being hugged and cuddled by adult caretakers, the child begins to develop both cognitively and emotionally. Being coddled and caressed is important for normal psychosocial development in childhood, but being gently held by someone who cares about you is important in adulthood as well, particularly in times of great stress.

We both send and receive signals via touch. A firm handshake, a flaccid grip, a poke in the ribs, a pat on the back, a kiss on the lips – these and many other types of touch send strong signals and can arouse powerful emotions. Where and when one person touches another also sends a message; the interpretation of the touch reflects both the social context and the relationship between the two individuals. For example, a slap on the back means one thing if someone has just scored a goal in a soccer game, but quite another if the person has just transgressed. And of course the significance of one person touching another differs according to whether the other is an intimate partner, a stranger, a patient or a casual acquaintance.

Touching has consequences that go far beyond simple communication. For example, research shows that touching another person can have a significant effect on that individual's compliance with various requests, can influence one's attitudes, and can foster feelings of affiliation. However, much remains to be learned about the cognitive and neurological mechanisms that underlie this behavioural influence (Gallace & Spence, 2010).

The amount of touching varies considerably from culture to culture (Schut et al., 2011), to the extent that some anthropologists divide cultures into 'contact' and 'noncontact' groups. People in Latin America, Greece, Turkey, the Arab countries and several African countries tend to touch each other a great deal, while relatively little touching occurs among North Americans, Northern Europeans and Asians (Argyle, 1988).

Gender is clearly an important factor in touching. Men have been observed to touch women more often than women touch men, and people are much more likely to touch members of the opposite sex than members of their own sex, although this difference is not found in older adults (Henley, 1973; Hall & Veccia, 1990). Research in the United States (Derlega, Catanzaro & Lewis, 2001) found that heterosexual men and women (but not gay or bisexual individuals) viewed touching between men as incompatible with the traditional male role, while touching between two women or between a man and a woman is acceptable so long as it does not violate traditional gender norms.

Just how much can we communicate by touch? It may be surprising to learn that in an experiment (Hertenstein et al., 2009) in which two strangers could not see each other but could touch each other through a hole in the wall between them, they were actually able to communicate a number of emotions – anger, fear, disgust, love, gratitude, sympathy, happiness and sadness – at an above chance rate simply through varying the nature of the touch. Further research is necessary to determine just how reliably we can code and decode on the basis of touch alone.

> **KEY POINT:** Communication through touch reflects much about the relationship between two people. There are significant cross-cultural differences in the frequency of touching.

Proxemics

How comfortable would you feel while sitting alone at a table in the library if a stranger came and sat down in the chair beside you rather than across from you or at the other end of the table? And when you are at a party, how do you decide just how far away or how close you should stand from the people to whom you are talking? These examples reflect the fact that we have a certain spatial comfort zone around us at which we feel comfortable in social interactions, depending on whom we are with and what we are doing. This has been referred to as personal space (Sommer, 1969), and the study of how we use space as a non-verbal signal in the regulation of our social interactions is called proxemics. Research indicates that inappropriate invasions of personal space are generally anxiety-arousing and produce observable blood pressure and heart rate changes that are correlated with anxiety (Sawada, 2003).

Personal space also has a communicative function. For example, we can communicate feelings of intimacy by allowing someone to draw physically closer to us in a conversation, or we can send the opposite message by increasing distance. Hall (1966) described four distances or 'zones' at which people feel comfortable in interactions, at least in the US where the research was conducted (Figure 7.9).

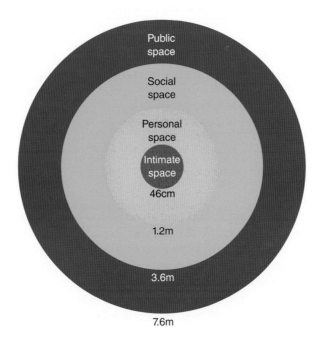

Figure 7.9 Personal and other space

Research in North America has found that about two-thirds of everyday interactions with others occur at a distance between 46 cm and 60 cm (Altman & Vinsel, 1977). Not surprisingly, friends stand closer than strangers (Ashton, Shaw & Worsham, 1980), and people who are sexually attracted to one another stand even closer (Allegeier & Byrne, 1973). This sense of personal space develops early in life; research with nursery school children indicates that it begins to develop at around age four (Gifford & Price, 1979). We, of course, acquire our notions of personal space from the society in which we grow up, and there are considerable variations from culture to culture. North Americans, Britons and Swedes prefer the largest personal space during a conversation, while Southern Europeans stand closer and Latin Americans and Arabs stand the closest (Hall, 1966; Sussman & Rosenfeld, 1982). Asian preference falls somewhere in the middle (Beaulieu, 2004). There are even differences among northern Europeans: In a study of naturally occurring dyads in France, England and the Netherlands (Remland, Jones & Brinkman, 1991) it was found that Dutch dyads maintained greater distance from each other than the French, who in turn maintained a larger distance than the English (see Figure 7.10).

These differences can fuel serious misunderstandings. For example, imagine an English Canadian and a Latin American in conversation at a party. They have different spatial preferences; the English Canadian feels most comfortable at a distance that would seem large and stand offish to a Latin American. Unaware of their cultural differences, the two unconsciously engage in a dance across the room, the Latin American advancing and the English Canadian retreating. When they part, the Latin American is likely to feel that the English Canadian was cold and unfriendly while the English Canadian may feel that the Latin American was pushy and overly intimate.

Personal space even enters the world of 'virtual' human beings: Research participants in three-dimensional virtual rooms maintained a greater distance from virtual humans when approaching them from the front rather than the back, and they also maintained a greater distance when the virtual human made virtual eye contact (Bailenson et al., 2003)!

Culture	M-DHI
Dutch	25.96
MM	22.82
FF	28.69
MF	25.60
English	17.80
MM	17.27
FF	18.73
MF	17.16
French	23.66
MM	15.00
FF	25.17
MF	23.57

Figure 7.10 Mean distance between heads, for male–male (MM), female–female (FF) and male–female (MF) dyads

Source: Remland, Jones & Brinkman (1991)

Finally, it is interesting in the context of discussing personal space that we very often use spatial language to communicate information about our feelings and our relationships. We describe ourselves as feeling 'close' to someone, or being ready to 'stand by their side' if needed, or sensing a growing emotional 'distancing' in a relationship. Even social psychologists employ spatial references in using the term *social distance* to describe how comfortable one group is in terms of interacting with another (Matthews & Matlock, 2011).

[**KEY POINT:** Personal space varies from culture to culture, and unwanted invasion of one's personal space typically leads to the arousal of anxiety.]

Chronemics

Chronemics are time-related cues that are an important aspect of non-verbal communication (Jaworski, 1999). Pauses in conversations can produce tension and the manipulative speaker can use them to pressure the other person to say something. When the rhythm of conversation is not smooth, when it does not seem to 'flow', this may be taken by the listener to indicate a lack of interest or perhaps even evasiveness on the part of the other individual. The use of pauses and silences can also have a powerful effect on the interpretation of message. For example, 'Would you like to see this movie with me?' '… (pause) … Sure, let's go.') The hesitation in the response is likely to suggest a lack of enthusiasm. Pauses are often used to great effect in public speaking, where the dramatic pause adds special emphasis to the point that was just made, as the speaker seems to wait for the audience to assimilate it fully. Longer pauses can have a significant effect during negotiations, even to the extent that one side may state a position and then walk away from a conversation altogether, thereby putting pressure on the other to yield somewhat.

Again, there are cross-cultural differences. For example, while North Americans expect other people to respond to their statements right away, people in some cultures are taught to leave a gap before responding. As a result, while North Americans tend to be uncomfortable when there are periods of silence during a conversation, people in cultures for whom scattered silences are normal may perceive North Americans to be overly talkative, and even thoughtless or disrespectful.

It is interesting to note that pauses and silences – delays in responding – play an even more important role in computer-mediated communication such as social media and emails than they do in face-to-face communication (Kalman & Rafaeli, 2011). Because of the absence of other forms of the non-verbal cues provided by facial expression, body language, tone of voice and so forth, the response time to a communication stands out as an important indicator of whether the respondent is interested in the exchange or not. Of course, response time can mislead. A delay in responding may be because the respondent is taking time to consider your message carefully, or perhaps the delay is due to some technical problem in the communication system.

[**KEY POINT:** The use of pauses and silences adds important information to a communication. The way in which chronemics are used varies from culture to culture.]

Figure 7.11 What do this man's clothing and posture communicate?
Source: Cory Thoman/Shutterstock.com

Artefacts

Clothing, tattoos, piercing, makeup, hairstyles and colour, shape of eyeglasses, type of wristwatch and other 'artefacts' are also means of non-verbally communicating to others information about ourselves and the groups to which we belong. Wearing a hat turned sideways, or covering one's head with a hoodie, or exposing considerable flesh are all means of telling others something about who we are. Teenagers, with their great concern about being accepted, often choose such artefacts carefully in order to fit in with others with whom they wish to associate.

Of course, the use of artefacts goes beyond lipstick and designer sunglasses and the latest fashions and gang insignia; think of status symbols such as fancy cars, or expensive watches, or cutting-edge gadgets – and, even beyond that, breast augmentation and Botox injections (Giles & LePoire, 2006). These are all in one way or another part of our communication to the people around us.

> **KEY POINT:** The way we dress, the cars we drive and many other artefacts provide information about us, the groups that we belong to, and the impressions that we want to communicate.

A FINAL NOTE

We express ourselves through language and non-verbal behaviour, but the way we do so communicates much about us and the groups to which we belong. Subtle and often unintended signals – of power or prejudice, competence or incompetence, friendliness or coldness – may both change the meaning of our message and lead to judgements about our character.

SUMMARY

1. Language is central to human social interaction and children acquire it even without formal instruction.

2. Differences in speech style are used as markers of social status, as guides for forming impressions of others and as markers of group boundaries.

3. The prestige or standard form of a language develops from the speech style of those who are in a position of power, rather than reflecting an aesthetically ideal form of the language.

4. Communication accommodation theory suggests that because people usually want to be liked and approved of by others, they modify their speech style to make it similar to the speech heard around them (convergence). However, if group identity is threatened, individuals may accentuate the distinctiveness of their speech style (divergence).

5. Gender differences in speech, apart from pitch, largely reflect differences in social power rather than gender itself.

6. Factors involved in successful second-language learning include intelligence, specific language learning ability, motivation and self-confidence. Motivation to master a second language is influenced by the relative status and ethnolinguistic vitality of the second language, compared with the learner's own language.

7. Becoming bilingual involves more than learning another language; we must also acquire relevant sociolinguistic skills.

8. Bilingualism is likely to be encouraged when it provides a socially useful skill without threatening the existence of the speaker's own language, but discouraged when it contributes to assimilation into the majority linguistic group.

9. Language often serves to bind groups together but it also provides a basis for discrimination towards members of minority groups by the majority group.

10. Paralanguage is the non-verbal component of speech; the prosodic features of paralanguage (timing, pitch and loudness) appear to have a biological component in terms of their involvement in emotional reactions.

11. Non-verbal behaviour is used to provide information about feelings and intentions, to regulate verbal and other interactions, to express intimacy, to promote social control and to facilitate goal attainment.

12. Non-verbal behaviours include kinesics, oculesics, haptics, proxemics, chronemics and artefacts.

13. Facial displays of emotion share some universal features, although social conditioning modifies whatever biological basis there is for this similarity. Eye contact, 'body language' and gestures, along with facial displays, provide powerful non-verbal channels of communication.

POINTS TO PONDER

- Consider a deaf individual who reads lips. While he or she is able to decode the words and to observe non-verbal behaviour, how might communication be made difficult in the absence of paralinguistic cues?
- Suppose that you speak a second language, but imperfectly. You visit the country where that language is predominant, but whenever you begin to speak in that language, people respond in a heavily accented version of your native language. How do you interpret their behaviour? Are they telling you that you do not speak well enough for them to carry on the conversation and so they will switch to your language? Are they simply being polite? Or are they converging as a way of being friendly and showing that they like you?
- How would you design a course in order to help immigrants or business people from various nations to understand and use the non-verbal behaviour of your society?

FURTHER READING

Agnihotri, R.K., Khanna, A.L. & Sachdev, I. (1998). *Social psychological perspectives on second language learning.* **London: Sage.**

This book is based on research carried out in a number of multilingual and multicultural countries. It provides in-depth discussion of various issues relating to bilingualism and multilingualism, and the kinds of pressures felt by people in a minority language group as they try to become proficient in the language of the majority in their society.

Axtell, R.E. (1997). *Gestures: The do's and taboos of body language around the world.* **New York: Wiley**

An easy-to-read guide to the pitfalls of intercultural non-verbal communication. A country-by country analysis of the meanings of various gestures and movements, and how the same non-verbal signals can mean something quite different in different cultural contexts.

Guerro, L.L. & Hecht, M.L. (Eds). (2007). *The non-verbal communication reader: Classic and contemporary readings* **(3rd ed.). Prospect Heights, IL: Waveland Press.**

As the title suggests, this is a comprehensive collection of important research articles about how partners in a communication are affected by non-verbal information

of which they are often not even aware. An interesting survey of various approaches to the study of non-verbal communication.

Hager, M. (2011). *Culture, psychology and language learning.* **Oxford: Peter Lang.**

Because language is interwoven with the culture in which it is spoken, this book argues that language and culture should be taught simultaneously and from the outset when someone sets out to learn a second language. There is also an interesting discussion on what happens as one becomes bilingual and bicultural. Attention is also paid to the role of cognitive processing, emotion and motivation in learning a second language.

Reynolds, W.E. & Lambert, W.E. (1991). *Bilingualism, multiculturalism, and second language learning: The McGill Conference in honour of Wallace E. Lambert.* **London: Routledge.**

A collection of chapters, each written by an internationally renowned researcher, paying tribute to Professor Lambert's contributions to the social psychology of language and bilingualism. Excellent review of the field in general and stimulating suggestions for future research.

WEBLINKS

Center for Nonverbal Studies http://center-for-nonverbal-studies.org/1501.html

This website provides a wealth of information about non-verbal signals, including facial expressions, gestures, and body movements.

Language Portal of Canada http://www.noslangues-ourlanguages.gc.ca/index-eng.php

This site is an excellent source for information about Canadian expertise in the area of language, including information about languages used in Canada, language standardization, and links to other websites related to the various languages, including aboriginal, currently spoken in Canada.

Goethe Institut, Language http://www.goethe.de/ges/spa/enindex.htm

An interesting source of information about language and social identity, multilingualism, and dialects – from a German perspective.

PART IV

FRIENDS AND FOES

CHAPTER 8

INTERPERSONAL ATTRACTION AND CLOSE RELATIONSHIPS

The pleasure of love lasts only a moment.
The pain of love lasts a lifetime.
From poem by Jean de Florian (1755–1794); music by Berlioz

LEARNING OBJECTIVES

* When do we want to be with others, and when with a particular other person?

* Why are perceived similarity and physical attractiveness so important in initial attraction?

* We like people who reward us – when and what are limits to this proposition?

* How do social psychologists study love and what have they found out?

* What is involved in interpersonal intimacy?

* How and why do relationships end?

Figure 8.1 The Duke and Duchess of Cambridge on their wedding day

Source: Featureflash/Shutterstock.com

She was born and raised in a village in Berkshire, to middle-class parents, who had established a successful business selling party supplies through mail order. Her paternal family had some aristocratic and political links, while her maternal family were labourers. He was born and raised in London, of a very prominent family. After his parents' marriage ended acrimoniously, his mother died tragically while he was still young, and he was subsequently raised by his father and grandparents. They met as students in university and dated for some years. The couple broke up for a time, and he stated that he was not ready for a committed relationship. Soon, the relationship was rekindled, and in time an engagement was announced.

The courtship and wedding of Prince William and Catherine Middleton, and the birth of Prince George two years later, were followed breathlessly by millions in the United Kingdom and around the world. They were young, attractive celebrities in love. Indeed, the course of true love captures our interest. The tragic tale of Romeo and Juliet endures in Shakespeare's play, and in film, opera, ballet and music. Innumerable novels, plays, movies, soap operas and songs deal with the theme. The romantic problems of the famous and powerful fascinate millions of ordinary people.

Why is there so much interest in love and close relationships? Humans are, as Aristotle observed, social animals, and so we all seek the company of others, form friendships with a few and find happiness and despair in our most intimate relationships. However, it is only in recent years that scientific methods have been applied to the study of attraction and close relationships.

In this chapter, we will review the theories and research about attraction and close relationships. First, we will see where and why we have a need to be with others, affiliation, and with special others, attachment. Then we examine the factors that lead us to become initially attracted to someone, to like someone. Then we turn to the study of close relationships, intimacy, friendship and love. Finally, we will turn to the study of relationship problems: the process of breaking up and loneliness.

AFFILIATION AND ATTACHMENT

People need people. This need is expressed in two forms. People need to feel a sense of belonging, a need to be with other people in general; this is called the need for affiliation. Second, even as infants, people have a need to form close bonds with special others, a process referred to as attachment. Later in this chapter, we will discuss loneliness and review the serious consequences of when our needs for affiliation and attachment are not fulfilled.

Affiliation

Clearly, affiliation, being with others, is a defining characteristic of being human. Research participants agreed to carry communication devices or 'beepers' for several weeks (Csikszentmihalyi & Figurski, 1982). At random times during their waking hours, they were 'beeped', a signal to fill out a brief questionnaire on what they were doing at that time. The study showed that these adults spent 71% of their time in situations involving other people.

Laboratory research has identified some of the factors that tend to increase or decrease affiliation need. A classic experiment by Schachter (1959) tested the hypothesis that, under some conditions, people affiliate to reduce fear. Female research participants were informed by an experimenter either that they would be subjected to electric shocks that would be painful (high fear condition) or that they would be subjected to shocks that would involve only a tingle (low fear condition). Those with high fear showed a strong preference to be with others rather than alone.

The key to understanding this experiment is the process of **social comparison** (Chapter 3). In an unusual situation, we turn to others as a source of information, to compare our feelings with people in the same boat. To demonstrate this premise, another experiment (Schachter, 1959) aroused fear in different groups of research participants. They were given three choices: to wait alone, to be with other participants in the same experiment or to be with students waiting for interviews with faculty advisors. As social comparison theory predicts, fearful research participants preferred to be with others in the same fearful situation rather than with people who were in a different situation. Misery loves miserable company.

However, in a field study (Kulik & Mahler, 1989b), patients about to undergo major surgery (coronary bypass) were interviewed about their preferences for room-mates. The patients expressed a strong preference for a room-mate who was already recovering from the surgery, rather than someone waiting, as they were. These results suggest that people may prefer to be with someone who can draw on their immediate experience and possibly provide reassurance rather than someone who might be reacting emotionally in a similar way.

Attachment

In George Bernard Shaw's play *Pygmalion*, upon which the musical *My Fair Lady* was based (Figure 8.2), Eliza Doolittle and her mentor, Professor Higgins, have decided to part. They later discover that there is a bond between them, not one of lovers but something close and significant. Higgins admits, 'I shall miss you, Eliza. I have learnt something from your idiotic notions: I confess that humbly and gratefully. And I have grown accustomed to your voice and appearance. I like them, rather.' And Eliza explains why she has returned to him: 'I did it because we were pleasant together and I come – came – to care for you; not to want you to make love to me, and not forgetting the difference between us, but more friendly like.' As both characters in this remarkable play recognize, this is not romantic love, but something quite powerful.

What is driving the wishes of Eliza and Henry Higgins is not romantic love but attachment. Social attachment begins in early infancy when the child learns to distinguish familiar people, usually the mother at first, and to respond in a special way to them. The infant smiles and vocalizes to the attachment figures, shows distress when they leave and is obviously comforted by them. Bowlby (1969), the pioneer of attachment theory, argued that there is a biological basis for attachment, a survival mechanism for the helpless infant. On the other hand, social learning theorists explain attachment behaviours in terms of children associating caretakers such as their mother with rewards such as food, comfort and physical closeness. In any case, attachment is our first experience of selectively affiliating with another person.

Why do we as adults form attachments to certain people? According to attachment theory derived from Bowlby's formulations, an attachment figure represents a safe haven in response to threat, and a secure base from which we can explore and engage with our world. The theory

Figure 8.2 *My Fair Lady*, 1963
Source: © Sunset Boulevard/Corbis

also posits the affect regulation hypothesis. According to this principle, securely attached people can deal with strong emotions such as fear or anger through their attachment to another person, even in that person's absence (Maunder & Hunter, 2001).

It is generally established that attachment orientations in adulthood are based on early experience, but can be modified by later experience (Mikulincer & Shaver, 2007; Fraley, 2002). Bowlby referred to attachments as mental 'working models' of how we see ourselves in the eyes of others as worthy of love, and how we see certain other people as reliable safe havens. People vary in their mental working models or attachment style. The majority are secure, finding interpersonal closeness to be relatively easy, reliable and comfortable. Others may be avoidant in their attachment orientation, feeling uncomfortable when too close or intimate with someone, or anxious/ambivalent, feeling that others are not as close as they would wish, sometimes clinging to partners to the extent that it may drive them away. Bartholomew and Horowitz (1991) pointed out that there are actually two types of avoidant attachment: fearful avoidant (people who desire intimacy with others but are afraid of being hurt) and dismissive avoidant (people who feel that they do not need or want intimacy). These secure, avoidant and anxious attachment orientations have been identified and measured in adulthood (Hazan & Shaver, 1987) and found in many cultures (Schmitt et al., 2004). While a secure attachment orientation is normative in most samples, the preoccupied (anxious) orientation is particularly prevalent in East Asian cultures. However, attachment avoidance has been found to be more strongly related to dissatisfaction with relationships in individualistic cultures than in collectivist cultures such as Hong Kong and Mexico (Friedman, Rholes, Simpson, Bond, Diaz-Loving & Chan, 2010).

We can consider attachment style as reflecting one's schema about relationships (Baldwin, 1992), which will guide people's actions and reactions in their relationships. For instance, people with a secure attachment style might want to spend more time with their partners, tell them how deeply they feel about them and welcome expressions of intimacy. People with an avoidant orientation might not be able or willing to respond in the same manner (Baldwin, Fehr, Keedian, Seidel & Thomson, 1993). Like other schemata, your attachment orientations may be cued by the other person or situation: you may feel securely attached in one relationship, anxious in another, avoidant in yet another (Baldwin, Keelan, et al., 1996).

A secure attachment style has been related to a host of variables in relationship interactions, including general marital adjustment and self-esteem (Murray, Rose, et al., 2002; Gallo & Smith, 2001). Interestingly, in one study of newlyweds during the first three years of marriage, attachment security increased over time despite the fact that marital satisfaction declined during that post-honeymoon period (Davila, Karney & Bradbury, 1999). Nonsecurely attached people (avoidant or anxious) are more fearful of a break-up (Sprecher, Felmlee, Metts, Fehr & Vanni, 1998), and their constant concern with rejection influences how they interact with their partners (Murray, Bellavia, Rose & Griffin, 2003). People with secure attachment styles react in a more supportive and trusting way to their partners (Simpson, Rholes & Nelligan, 1992; Keelan, Dion & Dion, 1994). An avoidant or anxious attachment style may be expressed by anger and is associated in men with spousal abuse (Dutton, Starzomski, Saunders & Bartholomew, 1994).

Sensitivity to rejection in anxiously attached people interferes with their ability to perceive their partners accurately. They may believe that they have communicated romantic interest to someone even though, in reality, their romantic interest has not been clearly communicated. They assume that the other person can and should take into account their anxieties and recognize how they really feel: a 'signal amplification bias' (Vorauer, Cameron, Holmes & Pearce, 2003). That is, they expect the other person to pick up on small cues to their feelings, and then be able to translate these into an awareness of the deeper feelings that lie behind those cues. Failing to understand that the other person did not get the message becomes a self-fulfilling prophecy that leads to rejection.

We must note one caveat to this impressive body of research and thought. Attachment style is typically measured by one's orientation to one's romantic partner. If not at present involved in a romantic relationship, one is asked to recall a past relationship or to imagine one in the future. Think of the people whom you consider to be both a safe haven from threat and a secure base for engagement with the world. A close friend, a sibling, an older child, a mentor, coach or teacher, or colleague may well become attachment figures. Moreover, as noted earlier, our style of attachment may not be consistent; one may feel anxious in attachment to a romantic partner but secure with one's best friend. Measures of adult attachment orientation need to reflect the multiplicity of our attachment experiences.

INTERPERSONAL ATTRACTION

While all of us need people, we are also selective. Much of the research in this area has been devoted to interpersonal attraction: the reasons why one person will like another. It has been shown that, with certain qualifications, we tend to like people who are similar to us, who reward us, who like us, who are conveniently nearby, who are physically attractive and who are pleasant, agreeable, competent and otherwise good and desirable people.

Of course, there are many kinds of attraction. We may enjoy a casual conversation with the person seated beside us on a flight and leave it at that. We may be attracted to a person as a friend but not as a lover, as a tennis partner but not as a close friend, as a colleague at work but not as a social companion. What determines liking of a stranger will not necessarily determine attraction in an intimate relationship, as a friend or lover. We turn first to the study of that initial attraction.

Propinquity

Before attraction develops, there has to be an opportunity for the first contact. People are more likely to meet and develop relationships if they are in physical proximity (the propinquity effect). This was shown dramatically in a classic study by Festinger, Schachter and Back (1950) and later replicated by Athanasiou and Yashioka (1973). They selected apartment buildings which contained two storeys, 10 apartments and a number of stairways. The experimenters asked all the residents to complete a 'sociometric test' identifying their three closest friends in the apartment complex. Friends were most likely to be next-door neighbours and the probability of friendship decreased as apartments became more distant. It was also found that people in the central apartments were reported as friends more often than were the residents of all the other apartments, probably because people had to pass by and thus they had the greatest opportunity to notice and interact with each other.

Why are people attracted to those near them? The most important factor is the mere exposure effect. Contrary to the old saying, 'Familiarity breeds contempt', an important body of research shows that familiarity with a novel stimulus usually leads to greater attraction (Suedfeld, Rank & Borrie, 1975; Zajonc, 1970). In one experiment, research participants shown a photograph of the same person each week for four weeks expressed greater liking for that person (whom they had never met) compared with research participants shown a different photograph each week (Moreland & Zajonc, 1982). In another study, pre-schoolers who watched *Sesame Street* episodes involving Japanese Canadians and North American Indians were more likely to indicate a desire to play with such children than were children not exposed to these episodes (Goldberg & Gorn, 1979).

A final note: psychologists have noted the effects of the architecture and design of buildings on human interactions (Baum & Valins, 1977; Baum, Aiello & Calesnick, 1978; Wollin & Montagne, 1981; Russell & Mehrabian, 1978). In consequence, architects and psychologists are beginning to work together to design university classrooms and residences, psychiatric and medical hospitals, shopping centres and work environments that are better suited to their inhabitants and their interactions.

THE POWER OF PHYSICAL ATTRACTIVENESS

Common sense tells us that 'beauty is only skin deep' and 'you can't judge a book by its cover'. And so, people tend to underestimate the impact of attractiveness (Hadjistavropoulos & Genest, 1994). Moreover, it is not enough to say simply that beauty is in the eye of the beholder. Within a given culture and age group, research participants who are asked to make independent ratings of the physical attractiveness of various target

Figure 8.3 Would the attractiveness of Sarah MacLachlan influence our appreciation of her music?

Source: s_bukley/Shutterstock.com

persons tend to show high levels of agreement in these ratings (Berscheid & Walster, 1974a). The average ratings of attractiveness by independent judges will predict how much other people will like the target persons (Curran & Lippold, 1975). We also make judgements of attractiveness almost instantaneously. In one experiment, when faces were flashed on a screen for 150 ms, the ratings for beauty were identical to those given when participants had a much longer interval to inspect the photograph (Goldstein & Papageorge, 1980).

When someone is highly attractive, others desire to interact with them, but may fear rejection (Shanteau & Nagy, 1979). Rather than risk the humiliation of being rejected, many people are satisfied to form relationships with those they feel similar to in attractiveness. Highly attractive individuals may find themselves admired from a distance (Shanteau & Nagy, 1979), while average-looking people more often seek out those more in line with their perception of their own attractiveness (Kalick & Hamilton, 1988). Thus, it is not surprising that pairs of friends and romantic partners tend to be roughly similar in physical attractiveness (Cash & Darlega, 1978; Murstein, 1972; Feingold, 1988).

While men and women are obviously attentive to each other's sexual attractiveness, we should keep in mind that attractiveness is also important to other kinds of relationships. Even children as young as three years old prefer attractive children (Dion, 1972; Cavior & Dorecki, 1969). In addition, adults treat attractive and unattractive children differently. For example, Clifford and Walster (1973) showed fifth-grade teachers a report card about a hypothetical student that included a photograph of an attractive or unattractive boy or girl. Although the report cards were identical, the attractive child was assessed by the teachers as having a higher IQ and was expected to achieve more in the future.

Together these studies suggest that the power of physical attractiveness cannot be ignored. Note that the evidence indicates that standards of beauty are fairly consistent across cultures (Ritter, Casey & Langlois, 1991). Indeed, Langlois et al. (2000) suggest that this effect may have roots in evolutionary theory. Let us examine this interpretation.

Beauty, attraction and evolution Consider a basic premise derived from Darwin's theory of evolution: the impulse toward reproductive success, which means perpetuating our genes into the next generation. To do so, we are attracted to a partner who is 'fit' to reproduce, capable of having healthy babies who will carry the parents' genes into the following generation. Consider that attractive people are perceived to be healthier (Kalick, Zebrowitz, Langlois & Johnson, 1996; Hadjistavropoulos, McMurtry & Craig, 1996). Thus, it is argued, we are attracted to people who are physically attractive because of their potential for reproduction.

What do women value in a man? According to evolutionary psychologists, since women are limited in how many children they can produce to perpetuate their genes, they are hypothesized to have a greater investment in their children than do men, who can sire many offspring. A woman will seek a mate who can sire healthy offspring and protect them. Therefore, she will value characteristics in men, such as size and strength, as well as financial resources. A man who can continue to provide resources for his family is one who is dependable and stable, intelligent and in good health. What do men value in women? Again, the driving force is reproductive success. Therefore, they will tend to be attracted to women who are young and attractive, both of which are assumed to imply good health and fertility.

Therefore attractiveness represents fitness to have or sire children in order to perpetuate one's own genes. What characteristics are attractive to us in terms of reproductive fitness? Evidence ranging from Stone Age art to contemporary beauty contests indicates that men are attracted to women whose waists are 30% narrower than their hips, a shape associated with fertility (Singh & Young, 1995). Other evidence suggests that both men and women are attracted by symmetry in which facial features, hands, ankles and so forth are equal on the left and right sides (Thornhill & Gangestad, 1993). This preference for symmetry is interpreted as an indicator of health, which implies reproductive fitness.

Is the preference for symmetrical features rooted in biology? In one rather startling study, 41 men were each assigned a T-shirt to wear for two nights while sleeping. The extent to which various physical features (ear length, fingers, wrists, arms, ankles, feet) were symmetrical was also measured for each man. Then, women sniffed each shirt and estimated the attractiveness of the man who had worn it. The women did not see or know any of the men. Of course, other olfactory cues were controlled such as having the men not wear aftershave, sleep in sheets washed in unscented detergent and not eat foods such as garlic, pepperoni or cabbage. The women preferred the scent of the men whose features were symmetrical, but only during the times that they were ovulating, hence most fertile. At other times of the month, no such preference was observed (Gangestad & Thornhill, 1998). The authors speculated that symmetry is reflected in olfactory cues because these cues are indicative of good health, hence reproductive fitness.

If you were to describe someone as 'average' in physical appearance, it would not seem to be a compliment. However, a set of studies suggests that we are attracted to persons who appear close to the average in terms of specific facial and physical features (Grammar & Thornhill, 1994). Computers allow us to input thousands of points on the face of each individual. From the photos that result, an image can be generated of a hypothetical person who will be the 'average' of all the people whose photos were entered: average size and shape of nose, average mouth, average size and distance between eyes, etc. This composite is typically judged as more attractive than photos of individual faces (Langlois & Roggman, 1990).

Research such as this provides some indirect support for an evolutionary interpretation. However, these findings do not rule out alternative interpretations. Certainly 'averageness' in physical appearance would be an indicator of what we usually see, and, as noted above, mere exposure and familiarity do lead to attraction. Using the same methodology described above, research has found a positive relationship between 'averageness' and perceived attractiveness in rating dogs, birds and wristwatches, and we do not perpetuate our genes in dogs, birds, or wristwatches (Halberstadt & Rhodes, 2000). Consider as well that we continue to seek sexual partners who are healthy and attractive, indicating reproductive fitness, even while taking precautions to avoid pregnancy (Etcoff, 1999). While it is difficult to test the theory of evolution as applied to our profound intimate lives, the work in this area represents an exciting challenge to social psychology.

Note that evolutionary theory differs sharply from mainstream social science, in which it is argued that the notion of beauty as a universal standard is largely a 'myth' engendered by cultural conditioning and stereotypes about the 'beautiful people' (Wolf, 1991). While there may be some commonalities across cultures such as symmetry and 'averageness', there is far from a uniform standard of beauty among cultures, and even within a culture over time (Apicella, Little & Marlowe, 2007; Tovée, Swami, Furnham & Mangalparsad, 2006).

Indeed, some evidence indicates that physical attractiveness produces better outcomes in life in individualistic cultures than in those which focus on interdependence (Anderson, Adams & Plaut, 2008). Men also appear to be more concerned about the physical attractiveness of women than women are about men (Miller & Rivenbark, 1970; Krebs & Adinolfi, 1975). Consider the following: a cross-cultural study of folk tales in a variety of cultures around the world indicated that these stories provide much more detail for female attractiveness than for male attractiveness (Gottschall et al., 2008). The authors interpret this as support for an evolutionary interpretation, because men would value female attractiveness as an indicator of their fertility. Male fertility is not as variable as female fertility and is more difficult to detect from appearance except in the very young, the very old and the very sick. Thus people and their societies would value female physical attractiveness more than male attractiveness. However, it is equally plausible that most of the people who transmitted these stories were males, most of whom would be more interested in female pulchritude. A study of works of visual art shows that while long legs in women are usually seen as attractive they actually varied significantly in length in such works over time (Sorokowski, 2010).

Given these inconsistencies, let us turn to an alternative interpretation of the effects of physical attractiveness, one that does not involve evolutionary assumptions.

What is beautiful is good 'What a strange illusion it is to suppose that beauty is goodness', observed Tolstoy. In fairy tales and movies, the hero is handsome, the heroine beautiful and the villains ugly (e.g., Cinderella and Prince Charming versus the ugly stepsisters and the wicked stepmother). Thus, it is not surprising that when people are described or presented as physically attractive they are rated as having more desirable personality characteristics, a higher occupational status, more likely to be happily married, pleasant and of higher status (Dion, Berscheid & Walster, 1972; Adams & Huston, 1975). This has been found to be true in courtroom decisions: attractive defendants were judged less guilty and received less severe punishment than less attractive defendants (Effran, 1974). In short, beauty is assumed to signify goodness in our impressions of people.

However, in some situations, physical attractiveness may lead to negative outcomes. For example, other research found that attractive female defendants were more likely to be convicted if they had apparently used their physical assets to accomplish the crime (Sigall & Ostrove, 1975; Izzett & Fishman, 1976). In addition, those who believe in a just world – beliefs that people get what they deserve and deserve what they get in life (Chapter 2) – rate physically attractive males as having more socially desirable characteristics than did those without strong just-world beliefs (Dion & Dion, 1987).

Again, remember that the attractiveness effect is not limited to sexuality. Effran and Patterson (1974) had judges rate the appearance in photos of 79 candidates in the 1972 Canadian federal election. A comparison then revealed that the unattractive candidates averaged fewer votes than did the attractive ones.

However, in a meta-analysis of these studies, Eagly, Ashmore, Makhijani and Longo (1991) found that the effects of physical attractiveness on positive stereotyping were not as strong as had been believed. It appears that we do stereotype attractive people as socially competent (popular, likeable, sociable) and, to a lesser extent, as intellectually competent. However, physical attractiveness does not affect our judgements of integrity (honesty, faithfulness) or adjustment (high self-esteem, happiness, maturity). Further, people from less individualistic cultures, such as the Chinese, base their judgements more on group-related attributes such as position in the community or family background than on individual characteristics such as physical attractiveness (Dion, Pak & Dion, 1990). In the final analysis, the stereotype about the power of physical attractiveness has limited validity (Ashmore & Longo, 1995).

Now consider the following. A number of animal studies have identified certain brain centres as involved in the perception of reward (e.g. Schultz, 2000), including the nucleus accumbens and the orbito-frontal cortex. Other fMRI studies show that these same brain centres are activated when human participants are expecting or receiving a reward such as money (Elliott, Newman, Longe & Deakin, 2004). Some studies report that this same neural circuitry is activated when men view women whom they rate as attractive (Cloutier, Heatherton, Whalen & Kelley, 2008). Indeed, the higher they rate the woman in attractiveness, the greater is the neural activity. However, when women view attractive men, the same activation is not reported. Thus, physical attractiveness is more important to men than to women in mate selection.

SIMILARITY AND ATTRACTION

We like people similar to ourselves in attitudes, values and interests. In a classic study, transfer students to a US university were offered free housing in exchange for their participation in research (Newcomb, 1961). None of the students knew any of the others before arriving on campus. At intervals throughout the semester, they were asked to fill out a questionnaire assessing: (1) their values and attitudes regarding religion, politics and other matters; (2) their perception of each other's attitudes; and (3) how much they liked each other. The findings showed a strong relationship between friendship and perceived similarity in attitudes and values. Interestingly, people did not first learn about their similarities with others and then become friends. Rather, friendships formed quite rapidly and friends tended to assume from the beginning that they were more similar than they really were. As they came to know each other over time, friendships shifted so that actual attitude similarity was significantly related to attraction in the final weeks of the study. In other words, rather than change values and attitudes, the students changed friends (Newcomb, 1961).

In a series of well-controlled experiments, Byrne (1971) applied the similarity-attraction principle in the laboratory. Each subject filled out a brief attitude questionnaire. The experimenter then surreptitiously filled out a questionnaire with views similar or dissimilar, in varying degrees, to the participant's and asked the participant to rate the attractiveness or likability of the person who had made these responses. With factors such as physical appearance, status or personality excluded, attraction to the stranger increased as the proportion of similar attitudes increased. This has become known as **Byrne's law**: attraction to a stranger is a function of the proportion of similar attitudes.

Outside the laboratory, Byrne's law holds up well. Dating partners tend to be similar in age, religion, education and physical attractiveness (matching), and even height (Hill, Rubin & Peplau, 1976; Shanteau & Nagy, 1979). Both similarity and physical attractiveness predict satisfaction with one's room-mate at university (Carli, Ganley & Pierce-Otay, 1991). In one study, males and females were paired on the basis of similar or dissimilar responses to an attitude questionnaire (Byrne, Ervin & Lamberth, 1970). Each couple was introduced and sent away on a brief 'Coke date' nearby. (Note: in those days, 'Coke' only referred to the soft drink!) When they returned, couples with highly similar attitudes rated each other more favourably, indicated greater feelings of attraction, and even stood closer to one another.

Limits to the association between similarity and attraction

However, it may be the type of similarity that counts. In a study of adolescent friendship dyads, it was found that best friends tended to be highly similar in attitudes towards drug use and in certain characteristics such as age, school grade and ethnic group. However, best friends did not share similar attitudes towards teachers and parents (Kandel, 1978a, 1978b). Hill and Stull (1981) found that among female room-mates at university, but not among male room-mates, similarity in values was very high among those who chose to room together or to stay together. Finally, a longitudinal study of married couples showed that partners did not become more similar in attitudes and values over 20 years of marriage; rather, their initial similarities remained remarkably constant over that period of time (Caspi, Herbener & Ozer, 1992).

Recall that people scoring high in self-monitoring tend to be guided primarily by cues in the situation, particularly the reactions of others, while those scoring low in self-monitoring tend to be guided primarily by their own feelings and beliefs (Chapter 2). High self-monitors tend to choose romantic partners on the basis of physical attractiveness and friends on the basis of similar recreational preferences. Low self-monitors tend to be guided more by similarities in personality traits and attitudes (Glick, DeMorest & Hotze, 1988; Jamieson, Lydon & Zanna, 1987). Thus, while perceived similarities influence attraction, high and low self-monitors appear to consider different kinds of information in assessing similarity.

Finally, in certain circumstances, similarity may not be rewarding. In one study (Novak & Lerner, 1968), some research participants were led to believe that the other person had recently suffered a nervous breakdown, had been hospitalized and was still seeing a psychiatrist. In this case, similarity in other characteristics actually decreased liking, evidently because the participants did not want to see themselves as similar to this stigmatized person.

Reasons for the similarity–attraction relationship

Why are similarity and attraction so strongly related? Several explanations are plausible. First, it is *rewarding* to have someone agree with your opinions, for it bolsters your confidence in your own ideas. Similar values and interests provide opportunities for doing things together such as playing tennis, working for a cause or going to a particular movie.

Another explanation is derived from the *consistency principle*, which we encountered in relation to changing attitudes (Chapter 5). According to Heider's (1958) interpersonal balance model, liking someone while disagreeing with that person about something important is psychologically uncomfortable. Thus if you and your friend hold strong but differing views about abortion, your feelings towards that person may be influenced by her views on the subject. Of course, agreement may not always signify liking. If John and Brian agree about the attractiveness of Susan, the result may be bitter competition.

While the balance model predicts change if there is imbalance between orientations towards persons and attitudes, the model cannot predict which of the components will change in order to restore balance. For example, if you like basketball and you like someone who hates it, will you change your orientation towards the person, your orientation towards basketball, or your perception of the other person's attitude? The answer may depend on your commitment to the attitude or the relationship, or your love of basketball. If you have already purchased expensive season tickets, you may be more likely to change your orientation towards the other person. But if you are in love with the other person, you may change your attitude towards basketball, or you may decide that basketball is not an important issue between the two of you.

A third interpretation challenges the proposition that we are attracted to someone as a consequence of perceived similarity. Since our everyday experience is to like people who agree with us, we expect that the people we like are like us. When participants in an experiment were first instructed to think of a recent positive event involving a friendship, thus cuing satisfaction with the relationship, they were later found to perceive themselves as more similar to that friend than were participants who thought of a negative event involving that friendship (Morry, 2005). In fact, typically, people assume that others share their attitudes and even personality characteristics and thus tend to like other people in the absence of contrary information (Byrne, Clore & Smeaton, 1986; Murstein, 1972). Note, however, that a study of friendships among undergraduate students shows that the length of time that they have known each other relates to more accurate perceptions that are less reflective of assumed similarity (Biesanz, West & Millevoi, 2007).

The repulsion hypothesis

Finally, it has been argued that similarity itself has little effect on attraction, but people are repelled by those who are dissimilar (Rosenbaum, 1986). In one study, research participants were presented with photos of people and were told that the person's attitudes were similar or dissimilar to their own. Consistent with the repulsion hypothesis, attraction did not differ between the similar-attitude and no-information groups, but was significantly lower in the dissimilar-attitude condition. But in other studies when the number of dissimilar attitudes was held constant, attraction increased as the number of similar attitudes increased (Smeaton, Byrne & Murnen, 1989). It appears that while attraction is increased by feedback suggesting that the other person has similar attitudes, people may be more affected by dissimilar than by similar attitudes, an example of the negativity effect (see Chapter 2). For some reason, younger children respond more to dissimilarity-rejection and adolescents to similarity-attraction (Tan & Singh, 1995).

While both similarity and dissimilarity in attitudes influence attraction, the evidence shows that we tend to dislike people who are dissimilar to ourselves more than we like people who are similar to ourselves. For instance, in judging politicians, we may claim that we wish that they would be consistent and speak their minds openly, but in fact we reject those who do not share our views (McCaul, Ployart, Hinsz & McCaul, 1995) or our experience (Singh & Ho, 2000).

REINFORCEMENT, RECIPROCITY AND ATTRACTION

Thus far, we have seen that we tend to like people who are in close proximity to us, who are attractive and who are similar to us in some way. Not surprisingly, we will evaluate someone more positively who makes us feel great through a compliment, as compared to someone who deflates us with an insult. This will include non-verbal signals – smiling and eye contact will arouse positive emotions in your conversational partner, while yawning and avoiding eye contact will arouse negative emotions and lead to negative evaluations.

Now, imagine meeting someone at a pleasant party after a good meal to celebrate success in your exams. The reinforcement-affect model predicts that people will be attracted to someone whom they associate with good feelings even if the person is not the cause (Byrne & Clore, 1970). For example, research participants were given false feedback on a personality test they had completed earlier. Half were informed that the test showed many strong, positive characteristics, while the other half were told that the test revealed many personal problems and inadequacies. Then each participant encountered a stranger in the waiting room. Those who had received the positive feedback subsequently indicated greater attraction to this person.

Perhaps the most powerful reward that others can give us is to like us (Backman & Secord, 1959). This is the principle of reciprocity in attraction – we like people who like us. Indeed, one study by Berscheid & Walster (1978) showed that people liked someone more when they said eight nice things about them than when they said seven nice things and one critical comment. In another study, a female confederate showed liking of male participants by maintaining eye contact, leaning towards them and listening intently to what they said. In this condition, the men expressed great attraction towards her despite the fact that they had been informed that she disagreed with them on some issues that were important to them (Gold, Ryckman & Mosley, 1984). In short, the perception of similarity was trumped by a cue for liking. Finally, after being informed in advance that their partner in an experiment disliked them, participants were instructed to have a conversation with that partner (Curtis & Miller, 1986). When participants believed that their partners disliked them, they disclosed less about themselves and behaved in a colder and less friendly manner than when they believed that their partner liked them. Thus the reciprocity in liking effect can become a self-fulfilling prophecy.

Limits to the reinforcement-attraction effect

There is also evidence that because individuals who have everything going for them remind us of our own inadequacies, they may not be liked as much as someone who appears to have at least some human failings. An experiment by Aronson, Willerman and Floyd (1966) dramatically illustrates this phenomenon. On audio-tape, some research participants heard a student correctly answer 92% of a very difficult series of questions, while other research participants heard the same student correctly answer only 30%. Half the research participants in each of these conditions then rated how much they liked the person. The superior student received a higher average attractiveness rating than the less able student. For the remaining research participants, the tape continued and they heard the student exclaim, 'Oh, my goodness, I've spilled coffee all over my new suit.' Compared to the ratings of those other participants, their ratings of attractiveness were considerably higher for the superior student, while they were significantly lower for the less able student. In other words, the competent individual's rating *increased* after demonstrating at least some inadequacy. Other research has indicated that this 'blunder' effect occurs for people of average self-esteem. Both those who are high and low in self-esteem decrease their liking of a person after a blunder, the former because they identify with highly competent people and the latter because they look up to them (Helmreich, Aronson & LeFan, 1970).

By the same reasoning, when we perceive that someone has come to like us more over time, this is a more potent source of reward than is constant praise. In an experiment involving a complicated series of scenarios, research participants heard themselves being evaluated by a confederate on seven different occasions. In one condition, the confederate was consistently positive about the subject while in another the confederate was consistently negative. In the third condition, the confederate was initially negative but gradually became more positive about the subject ('gain' condition). A fourth group of research participants heard the confederate begin with a positive evaluation and gradually become negative about the subject ('loss' condition). Subsequently, the research participants were asked to indicate their degree of attraction to the confederate. Needless to say, research participants liked the person who praised them and disliked the person who evaluated them negatively. More important, the confederate was liked more in the gain condition than in the constant positive condition and disliked more in the loss condition than in the constant negative condition. This is known as the gain/ loss effect. Subsequent research suggests that the gain effect tends to be stronger than the loss effect (Clore, Wiggins & Itkin, 1975).

Another limit to the reinforcement effect is represented by the principle of equity, or fairness, in our social relations (Walster, Walster & Berscheid, 1978). While we want rewarding relationships, we also want to feel that we are neither exploiting someone else, nor being exploited ourselves. Indeed, people sometimes react quite negatively to generosity from others, particularly if they are unable to reciprocate or if it implies dependency or helplessness on their part (Gergen, Ellsworth, Maslach & Seipel, 1975). This may explain in part why people who receive welfare and nations that receive aid may not always respond with gratitude and good feelings. This is discussed further in Chapter 9.

INTIMACY AND CLOSE RELATIONSHIPS

Levinger and Snoek (1972) describe a stage in which two persons in a relationship have become interdependent, and each assumes some responsibility for the well-being of the other. To a considerable degree, the individuals share an understanding, often unspoken, of the 'rules' of the relationship, a sense of 'we' and 'us' as contrasted with 'you' and 'I'. Self-disclosure is fundamental to this kind of a relationship.

Importance of self-disclosure

The development of a relationship involves getting to know the other person, which obviously depends on the willingness of the other person to be known. Although the processes of self-disclosure have been researched extensively, many questions remain. Do we reveal more to people we like or do we come to like people to whom we have disclosed ourselves? Must self-disclosure be reciprocal, or can we accept someone knowing more about us than we know about that person? Can we reveal too much too soon?

It is clear that people will reveal more about themselves to people they like than to people they dislike (Chaiken & Derlega, 1974). However, imagine that someone whom you have just met begins to tell you personal details about their family, their hopes and fears, their sexual needs. Strangers may be repelled if we are overly intimate. In such cases, intermediate levels of disclosure create a more favourable impression (Cozby, 1973). Research (e.g., Rubin (1975) indicates that if too much is revealed, the other person is likely to become less rather than more open. The reciprocity norm is powerful in human affairs: we try to keep the 'books balanced', whether in sending greeting cards or in revealing personal information (Altman, 1973; Chaiken & Derlega, 1974).

Self-disclosure is also influenced by gender roles. In one study, male and female experimental assistants approached male and female travellers in an airport departure lounge (Rubin, 1974). Half the travellers were asked to participate in a study of handwriting analysis and the other half in a study of self-disclosure. Many refused and the pattern of refusals was interesting. Regardless of the topic, females were twice as likely to refuse a male as a female assistant. Males were more likely to refuse to participate in the self-disclosure study when asked by a male confederate than by a female. In general as one might expect, self-disclosure tends to be more reserved among males (Dindia, 2000).

Finally, note that verbal self-disclosure and intimate communication are supplemented by non-verbal communication (discussed in Chapter 7). Vocal inflections or dynamics can reveal or conceal our feelings. Facial expressions, interpersonal distance, eye contact and body orientation may all communicate intimacy. The social context or the physical environment may also play a role. The same words in different contexts may be spoken as a profession of love, a description of the weather or a political opinion. Taking a sip of wine may communicate the sipper's feelings about the wine or about their companion – depending on the quality and vintage (of the wine and the companion).

Among couples that experience serious marital problems, breadth of communication decreases. As the relationship deteriorates, the partners restrict the number of topics that they are willing to talk about, but tend to 'bare it all' about these topics. Perhaps they are willing to risk more to save the relationship or perhaps they simply feel that they have nothing to lose by being open (Tolstedt & Stokes, 1984).

Equity exchange and relationships

Equity, the perception of fairness, is important to any relationship. Even when it entails sacrifice, we are motivated to maintain a sense of fairness between our friends and ourselves. According to the principle of social exchange (discussed in detail in Chapter 10), we try to maximize rewards and minimize costs in our relationships. This is most likely to apply between strangers and casual acquaintances and in the earliest stages of a relationship. As the bonds become more firmly established and mutuality develops, immediate exchange and even fairness figure less and less. As intimate partners, we have more to gain and more to give and we become increasingly concerned with building the relationship. Interestingly, while feelings of inequity do not predict later dissatisfaction in a relationship, the reverse is true: when people are dissatisfied, they are more likely over time to perceive inequity (Sprecher, 2001a).

Foa (1971) proposes six interpersonal resources that can be exchanged: love, status, information, money, goods and services. When we examine these, we can understand that the value of some resources depends on the person who gives them (particularism). For example, money is valuable regardless of who gives it, a supper probably tastes better when cooked by a special person (service), and love is a value that depends almost entirely on who offers the loving. Social exchange is also complicated by an egocentric bias: people tend to overestimate their own contributions. In one study of married couples, spouses rated independently how much responsibility they took for 20 relevant activities (e.g., cleaning house, planning recreational activities, childcare). On a 150-point scale, responsibility ratings by husband and wife ought to total 150. For example, if he rated himself as 80/150 responsible for childcare, she would rate her responsibility as 70/150. In fact, the average total for 73% of the couples came to more than 150 (Ross & Sicoly, 1979). Generally, more satisfied couples tend to agree about the contribution of each partner to the relationship (Christensen, Sullaway & King, 1983; Sprecher, 2001b).

Exchange versus communal relationships

Intimacy involves a transformation from exchange relationships to communal relationships (Clark & Mills, 1993). As noted, in exchange relationships, people seek to maximize benefits and minimize costs. Equity is established by reciprocity: you do this for me and I do that for you. Communal relationships are dramatically different. The goal is not reciprocity but providing a benefit for the other and continuing the relationship. If the relationship is secure and mutually satisfying (i.e. equitable), both participants can forgo immediate reciprocation and will not need to 'keep score' of rewards and costs. Concerns with equity, in a relationship are less important when people 'include the other in the self', that is, think in terms of 'we', the relationship, rather than 'you' and 'I' (Medvene, Teal & Slavich, 2000).

Not surprisingly, a study of people who were divorced and remarried showed that they expressed a sense of inequity or deprivation in their former marriage but equity in the current marriage. Perhaps more surprisingly, satisfaction for women in the present marriage was strongly associated with feelings of equity, whereas satisfaction for men was related to feeling that they received more than they contributed (Buunk & Mutsaers, 1999). Perhaps they were trying to 'balance the books' with their past deprivations.

Illusion and reality in close relationships

The poets tell us that 'love is blind', suggesting that illusions about the partner are part of our schema of romantic love. Indeed, loving relationships are shown in a body of research on various perceptual judgements to be an interesting mélange of reality and illusion, which includes idealization of the loved partner ... and with our feet firmly planted in reality (Fletcher & Kerr, 2010). Of course, while love may be blind, we also want the other to 'love us as we are'.

Research into this dilemma informs us in several ways. In a longitudinal study of dating couples, participants were asked to indicate their predictions about the future of their relationship as well as their general feelings about romantic love and about their current partners. Although the dating couples had been together less than six months, fully one-third expected to remain together for a lifetime – a level of optimism far above what was shown in the follow-up study. Outside observers to the relationship, who had seen the matched questionnaires, were somewhat more pessimistic (Buehler, Griffin & Ross, 1995).

Do people show similar positive illusions about their partners? Participant couples in a study (Murray, Holmes & Griffin, 1996) rated themselves and their partners on a number of characteristics (e.g., kind and affectionate, critical and judgemental, distant, emotional, understanding). Then they rated what they would consider to be the 'typical partner' and 'ideal partner' on the same dimensions. Overall, the results showed evidence that they idealized their partners, rating them as closer to their own ideal than the partners rated themselves. Perhaps more important, those who saw their partners in a positive light – even an illusory positive light – were most satisfied with their relationships

Rusbult (e.g., Rusbult et al., 2005) offers another interesting perspective, one that she calls the Michelangelo phenomenon. The great painter and sculptor evidently did not seek to shape a piece of marble to his specifications, but rather chipped away at the stone in order to allow an idealized form to emerge. The notion is that intimate partners in a long-term relationships influence each other's personality characteristics, interests, and aspirations. In this way, they affirm each other, and yet shape each other towards an ideal that they have about their partner (Rusbult, Finkel & Kumashiro, 2009; Rusbult, Kubacka, Kumashiro & Finkel, 2009). Research evidence indicates that this process depends on the extent to which our partner affirms that ideal that we have for ourselves (Drigotas, Rusbult, Wieselquist & Whitton, 1999). In the most satisfying relationships, both people act so as to bring out the best in each other, reaching towards some implicit ideal that they implicitly share.

One other point of illusion and reality: it is generally assumed that the ideal for a satisfying relationship is the maximum degree of closeness in which we confide fully to each other, and research generally supports that assumption. Is that always true? When you see your partner dressed to the nines, does he or she really want an honest appraisal or encouraging approval? And do we always seek greater closeness in a relationship? Mashek, Le, Israel & Aron (2011) asked US undergraduate participants to describe what they thought is meant by 'wanting less closeness' with a romantic partner. Responses included needing time alone, needing space, wanting to spend less time together, wanting other interests and goals, and, for 17% of them, 'feeling suffocated'. Then in an experiment, participants were given a word puzzle which included words such as 'need space', 'feel trapped' and 'suffocated'; other participants were cued with neutral words. Those primed with the 'less closeness' words indeed viewed their relationship as somewhat less close. Having been led to think about 'less closeness' and what that means, they had apparently found signs of being less close in their own relationships. It is important to keep in mind that while we generally think of having greater intimacy as being a desirable goal, sometimes, for some people in some relationships, this may be too much of a good thing, resulting in a desire at least by one partner for greater distance and less intimacy.

Commitment and investment

After we have been in a relationship for some time, we often feel that we have a stake in continuing the relationship. In other words, we have an investment in the close relationship, defined in terms of both tangible things (possessions) and the intangibles, the time and emotional energy that we estimate that we have spent in sustaining the relationship (Rusbult, 1983). When we are conscious of such an investment, we may remain committed to a relationship although not necessarily satisfied with it. A recent meta-analysis of 52 studies and over 11,000 participants provides impressive support for the importance of this notion (Le & Agnew, 2003).

Adversity can indeed bring people together or drive them apart. It depends on two factors: the level of adversity that they face and their level of commitment to the relationship – this is the commitment calibration hypothesis (Lydon, 1999; Lydon, Meana, Sepinwall, Richards & Mayman, 1999; Lydon, Fitzsimons & Naidoo, 2003). If the self-reported level of adversity is lower than the level of commitment, the relationship will not be threatened and no action is required. Now consider the case where the level of adversity is significantly greater than commitment. There will be little incentive to persist and try to save the relationship. We act in adversity to save the relationship when adversity and commitment are more-or-less equivalent. Interestingly, when we forgive our partner for some kind of transgression, the other person's trust in us and in the relationship grows, and both partners typically go on to feel a stronger sense of investment in the relationship (Wieselquist, 2009).

A common modern form of relationship is cohabitation, a committed relationship involving living together without marriage. Cohabitation offers a way to blend two opposing needs: independence and relatedness. That is, while many people are striving for independence and individual validation, they still want and need an intimate, supportive relationship (Newcomb, Huba & Bentler, 1986). A study of a sample of Swedish and Norwegian participants supports this contention; in comparison with married respondents, cohabitors were less satisfied with their relationship and more likely to consider ending it. However, if they responded affirmatively to a question of whether they intended to marry within the next two years, their satisfaction and stability did not differ from married partners (Wiik, Bernhardt & Noack, 2009).

Intimacy and cyber-relationships

Imagine a robot built with human features, including skin that feels almost human and the ability to talk and express emotions. And suppose that the robot is always loyal and attentive to you. Could you have a friendship or loving relationship with him or her? Before you scoff at what seems to be impossible, consider Turkel's (2011) description of the use of robots to provide 'human' companionship in seniors' residences, and contrast it with the loss of personal contact in our daily lives, substituted by 'friending' and 140-character personal messages. Now, would you accept a robot as a partner in a personal relationship? Turkel (2011) describes many of all ages who do.

Of course, the Internet offers people a new and powerful means of communicating with others over great distances, and new forms of relationships have emerged particularly through social networking sites. And it must be understood that people have different and multiple purposes in using Internet communication: to socialize with relatives and friends over distances, to meet new partners, to interact with people with the same interests, and to gain information (Fogel et al., 2002).

Some evidence suggests that loneliness is related to frequent Internet use. The lonely individual begins with the goal of alleviating loneliness but perhaps instead actually increases it, given that he or she is isolated from real social interactions. Internet relationships can be described as 'impersonal intimacy' because the interaction is limited to one channel, which enables each partner to have complete control over the breadth, depth and even accuracy of self-disclosure. The individuals are, in most cases, completely disconnected from each other's network of family, friends and other relationships. Moreover, cues for detecting deception (Chapter 2) are, for the most part, lacking, and so people can present themselves as they wish.

One can readily understand the allure of such relationships to those who are shy, unattractive or have limited mobility. It is also possible to explore new roles: in one case, an apparently disabled woman turned out to be an able-bodied male psychiatrist who wanted to see what it felt like to be perceived as female and experience the intimacy of female friendships (Van Gelder, 1996). In the absence of physical cues (age, gender, attractiveness, non-verbal cues) that are so salient in face-to-face interactions, the networks offer a shortcut to intimate self-disclosure and mutual support.

But does interpersonal communication over the Internet actually reduce social involvement? A longitudinal study (Kraut, Patterson, et al., 1998) assessed participants before and then again one to two years after they had begun using the Internet; it revealed that greater use of the Internet was indeed associated with declines in the participants' communication with others in their households, as well as decreases in the number of people with whom they socialized at least once a month. Perhaps more alarmingly, those who spent the most time online showed increased levels of loneliness and depression over that time. Similarly, Cacioppo & Patrick (2008) report strong evidence that lonely people experience a greater proportion of their interactions online, and considerably fewer in face-to-face interactions. Thus, Internet relationships may have become an unsatisfactory substitute for genuine strong ties with others (Kraut et al., 1998).

The idea that those who are frequent users of the Internet tend to be lonely, unattached people who lack the necessary social skills to find friends and lovers through the usual social activities has been referred to as the social compensation hypothesis (see Fehr, 2008; Amichai-Hamburger & Ben-Artzi, 2003; Fogel, Albert, et al., 2002;). However, the 'rich get richer' hypothesis contends that people who have strong social skills can use and benefit from them in the context of social websites. One study of high school students found support for the social compensation hypothesis among boys; those who were socially anxious tended to have better friendship quality when they engaged in online chatting. However, the 'rich get richer' hypothesis was supported among girls, and those who engaged in online chatting showed no evidence of social anxiety (Desjarlais & Willoughby, 2010).

Can intimate relationships be formed exclusively online or must they then lead eventually to face-to-face interaction? In a study of participants from 48 countries on a music social network, it was found that people interacted frequently with others in terms of their shared passion for music. However, the relationships did not progress beyond that shared interest unless they communicated in a more personal way, such as face-to-face, texting, email or telephone (Baym & Ledbetter, 2009). Indeed, relationships formed online frequently do move to other means of communication (Fehr, 2008).

What happens when an online relationship moves from the screen to face-to-face? McKenna & Bargh (2000) found that two people are actually more likely to like each upon meeting if they had earlier met online. Those who can disclose their 'true' or inner self to others online will be more likely than others to move these friendships to a face-to-face situation (McKenna, 2002).

BOX 8.1   A PRACTICAL QUESTION
THE POWER AND PERILS OF ONLINE DATING SERVICES

Online dating sites have become a global phenomenon and a profitable business. An extensive review of research by Finkel, Eastwick, et al. (2012) focused on two questions that we can ask about online dating. Does online dating differ in fundamental ways from other ways of meeting and dating? And does online dating really lead to better outcomes for the people involved than do the traditional, face-to-face meetings in which people become acquainted and attracted?

With regard to the first question, the researchers looked at three services that online dating sites offer: access to a wider variety of potential partners, opportunity to communicate in a meaningful way, and using a formula from prior questionnaires to match people with their dream dates. With all of these, the online format really has altered the landscape of dating and mating. For instance, if you meet someone in a pub, you will typically learn a few things and gain a first impression from casual encounters, while online dating offers a broad range of facts and impressions about the person before you meet him or her. Rather than relying on the advice of friends and relatives, you will be matched with someone who, according to the matching formula, will be especially compatible.

As to the second question, is online dating superior? Levine (2000) suggests several ways in which 'virtual attraction' is unique in terms of what we understand about social attraction. Self-presentation is more fluid and spontaneous and under personal control (e.g., sending or exchanging sound or picture files). Self-disclosure and intimate communication often take place more quickly online than in the face-to-face situation, perhaps because there is less risk. Indeed, participants sometimes express amazement at the companionship, warmth and intimacy that may develop in these relationships (Lea & Spears, 1995). However, Finkel, Eastwick et al. (2012) found that the answer to the question of whether online dating leads to better outcomes is 'no'. They did not find evidence that the matching algorithms were successful in producing good match-ups, and they found that while online communication can facilitate intimacy, it can also lead to unrealistic expectations that are deflated upon meeting. They also reported a tendency to commoditize relationships, resulting in a reduced willingness to commit to any one person.

Friendship

Same-sex friendships Studies within Western cultures consistently show that men's same-sex friendships tend to be less intimate and supportive than female friendships. That is, female friends talk about difficulties and feelings, while men engage in activities together (Bank & Hansford, 2000). It has been suggested that this is because men lack parental models for more intimate friendships, or because of a more competitive orientation among men.

Fehr (1996) discusses the confusion that still exists about this topic. One interesting suggestion is that men may seem to be less intimate in their friendships only because intimacy is defined in a 'female' manner. That is, if intimacy is defined in terms of verbal self-disclosure and support and women engage in more of this type of behaviour, then female friends are more intimate. However, if we define intimacy more broadly in terms of an emotional bond, a feeling of closeness or 'we-ness', then perhaps it can be attained either through self-disclosure (the 'female path') or through shared interests and activities (the male path). Clearly there is more to friendship than emotionally based self-disclosure (Wellman, 1992). On the other hand, research suggests considerable overlap between male and female patterns, particularly since both men and women specify self-disclosure as part of their definition of intimacy (Monsour, 1992).

Opposite-sex friendships From an evolutionary perspective, Bleske-Recheck & Buss (2001) hypothesize that while both men and women may form friendships with the other sex to acquire a possible mate, men also seek (or hope for) sexual access while women seek protection. Questionnaire data from two studies supported these hypotheses. However, the literature on this topic reveals a more complicated picture. O'Meara (1989, 1994) suggests a number of challenges to opposite-sex friendships. The two people must define their emotional bond in a way that is comfortable to both of them, such as in how intimately they will disclose to each other. Since friendship implies equality, then issues of gender equality must be considered. Further, it seems that individuals in cross-gender friendships sometimes must deal with societal disapproval (or at least suspicion), having to 'explain' their friendship to others. In some occupational settings and cultures, gender segregation persists.

The 'platonic' friendship Can former lovers still be friends? Busboom Collins, Givertz & Levin (2002) interviewed students about their current relationships with former dating partners. Consistent with social exchange theory, those who received more resources from their former lovers (help, support, etc.) were more likely to remain friends. However, involvement in a new romantic relationship and disapproval by friends were barriers to such friendships.

A perspective: From attraction to intimacy

As we have seen, the factors that lead to initial attraction are not those that lead to committed, intimate relationships. After studying factors that predicted the longevity of dating relationships, Kerckhoff and Davis (1962) proposed a sequential filter model. Individuals first compare themselves on social and demographic characteristics (religion, socioeconomic status). Then they look for what they have in common in attitudes and values. If the relationship survives, long-term commitment will be based on the extent to which their needs are complementary (Winch, 1954, 1958).

How then can we describe an intimate relationship? A number of criteria for intimacy have been proposed: (1) two people interact with each other more than with others; (2) they seek to restore proximity when they are apart; (3) they engage in self-disclosure; (4) they communicate about what is unique about their relationship; and (5) they anticipate the reactions of the other person (Burgess & Huston, 1979). In order to maintain a close and satisfying relationship over time, those involved 'mind' their relationship (Harvey & Omarzu, 1997) in a five-step process:

1. Continuing behaviours aimed at understanding one's partner, including listening, observing and questioning.
2. Making attributions both about one's partner and about things that happen, indicating one cares about the partner and the relationship. (For instance, we may give our partner the benefit of the doubt when things go wrong.)
3. Accepting what one has learned about the partner through self-disclosure and attempting to soothe and neutralize tensions and anger.
4. Reciprocating the thoughts, feelings and actions of the partner.
5. Continuing this process over time.

LOVE

While philosophers, poets, songwriters and artists have always been fascinated with the topic of love, it may be considered daring – perhaps presumptuous – for social psychologists to study it scientifically. Indeed, some have argued that science is misplaced in this area. One of the pioneers in social psychological research on love described her experience as a researcher in this area as analogous to 'stepping on land mines' (Berscheid, 2003).

Sternberg and Grajek (1984, p. 312) observe that 'people have been known to lie, cheat, steal and even kill in its name, yet no one knows quite what it is'. Think of the adjectives and synonyms that we used to describe love: infatuation, puppy love, desperate love, obsessive love, eros, romantic love, being 'in love'. While love would seem to be a universal human experience, about 10% of adults believe they have never been in love and others have decided that love is too painful and thus intend to avoid it in the future (Tennov, 1979). For different people, romantic love may represent a passionate emotional and physical involvement, an interpersonal 'game' of manipulation, or a relaxed, down-to-earth friendship. In a study of prototypes for love (see Chapter 2), Fehr (1988) asked participants to list words that they considered to be features of love, and other participants to rate each word on how central it was to representing love. Some characteristics were consistently rated as central to what love is about (e.g. trust, caring), while others were more peripheral (e.g. butterflies in the stomach, uncertainty).

Indeed, love can become a compulsive pattern of thought and action that some have argued is indistinguishable from gambling or substance addictions, all linked to opioid, oxytocin and dopaminergic systems in the brain (Reynaud, Karila, Blecha & Benyamina, 2010). Diamond & Dickerson (2012) review evidence that love and sexual desire are associated with some distinct patterns of activation in the brain, although there are also some overlaps (e.g. caudate nucleus, anterior cingulate cortex). Indeed, pair bonding in animal studies and love relationships in humans have both been linked to dopamine reward systems in the brain, the activation of which is observed both when a mother views photos of her child and lovers view photos of each other (Young, 2009). In addition, men with a variant of a particular human gene (AVPRIA) are twice as likely as men without that genetic variant to remain unmarried or experience crises in their marriages (Young, 2009). While none of this provides conclusive evidence of the neural substrate of love, these findings and others are tantalizing. Can the promise of a love potion be eventually fulfilled?

Our proposition is simple: since we have much to learn about love, and since love is intrinsic to the human experience, perhaps the scientific method, which has proved so successful elsewhere, can be useful here as well (Thompson & Borrello, 1992). The idea of a science of love is not new (Reis & Aron, 2008). Darwin proposed that reproductive success underlies evolution, and it was a natural progression to study mate selection and attachment. Freud highlighted the role of eros in human existence and the role of motives that we may not be aware of. Let us see what social psychology has to offer.

BOX 8.2   LOVE

CAN WE MEASURE IT?

If we are to study love as a scientific phenomenon, we must be able to measure it. Of course, we must first define what it is that we intend to measure. Then we must validate it, for example by showing that it correlates with other relevant variables (see Chapter 1). The history of attempts to measure love has been marked by two different approaches (Graham, 2011; Hatfield, Bensman & Rapson, 2012). One of them is to define a set of categories or types of love and to measure them, such as the initial phase of romantic love, love of a friend, love of a companion. The other is to home in on a type of love, usually romantic or passionate love, and to measure the intensity of love. Here are a few examples.

1. One of the first attempts to measure love was developed by Rubin (1970a, 1973), with a focus on distinguishing between liking and loving. After gathering an assortment of descriptions of love by novelists, poets, clinicians and scientists, he compiled two scales, measuring each of the two constructs. Loving included items such as 'If I were lonely, my first thought would be to seek out X', 'I would do almost anything for X', and 'I feel very possessive about X'. Liking was measured by items such as 'Most people would react favourably to X after a brief acquaintance', 'I have great confidence in X's good judgement' and 'In my opinion, X is an unusually mature person'.

   These scales were administered to 182 dating couples. Each person filled them out with relation to his or her partner and best friend. Scores on the liking and loving scales were correlated positively, but only moderately so. While liking and loving are related, people, especially females, can like someone very much without loving that person and they can even love someone without liking him or her. In a laboratory investigation, couples who scored high on the love scale spent more time gazing into each other's eyes during a conversation. In a follow-up six months later, those who had scored high on the love scale reported that their relationship had become more intense. Another study (Dermer & Pyszczynski, 1978) showed that people who have been erotically aroused produced significantly higher love scores (for their partners), but not liking scores. However, Sternberg and Grajek (1984) report that scores on the liking scale were the single most powerful predictor of the long-term success of a love relationship.

2. Attitudes toward love. Lee (1973) proposed that we may think of love in different ways, as possessive and dependent (mania), or as passionate (eros), or in terms of a logical 'shopping list' of desirable traits in the person (pragma), or as friendship and companionship (storge), or as game-playing manipulation (ludus) or as selfless giving to the other person (agape). Hendrick & Hendrick (1986) developed scales to measure these different attitudes about love. Notice that we can define a person by the highest score or by a pattern of high and low scores.

3. Passionate love scale. This measure was developed to measure love as defined as 'intense longing for union with another regardless of whether that longing is reciprocated …' (Hatfield & Sprecher, 1986). It includes cognitive components (e.g. preoccupation with the partner, desire to know him or her) emotional components (e.g. attraction, particularly sexual attraction, negative feelings when things go wrong, physiological arousal) and behavioural components (e.g. trying to understand the other person, doing nice things for the other). This measure has been used in a wide range of countries and has been correlated with fMRI response patterns particularly evident in the reward centres of the brain (Hatfield & Rapson, 2009), and with other measures of love and sexuality.

4. Triangular theory of love scale. Sternberg's (1986) triangular theory of love (to be discussed in detail later) has been operationalized into three scales: passion (including physical attraction), intimacy (feeling close and connected to the other person) and commitment (a decision to maintain the relationship into the future). Graham (2011) compiled data from 103 samples of participants and conducted a meta-analysis to see if there were some underlying dimensions or factors of romantic love. She found three such factors: 1. general romantic love, which generally included the types of factors mentioned above; 2. romantic obsession, including items such as 'If my partner ignores me for a while, I do stupid things to get his/her attention', and 'I get so exited about being in love with my partner that I cannot sleep'. The third dimension of love which extends across the various measures is labelled as 'practical friendship', which includes the pragma and storge types outlined above, and which may approximate the notion of companionate love.

In sum, we have learned from this research that liking and loving are related but not identical.

What is his thing called love? In reviewing the research, Berscheid (1985) suggests several ways in which liking and loving differ: Liking is relatively stable over time, whereas romantic love tends to be more fragile

Figure 8.4 *Before Sunrise*: a young couple meet and fall in love during a brief encounter in Paris. The relationship unfolds over the years of two subsequent movies. What can we learn from them about love?

Source: Corbis

Figure 8.5 Scene from *Fiddler on the Roof*. These parents wonder whether love follows from an arranged marriage

Source: © Robbie Jack/Corbis

and volatile. Liking is strongly influenced by an actual exchange of rewards, whereas romantic love is influenced more by what we anticipate for the future. Liking is influenced in a logical way by rewards (we like people more who reward us more), whereas romantic love is often unrelated or even intensified by frustration or rejection.

Of course, romantic love also implies sexuality, and the relationship between love and sex is a topic of enduring interest (Hendrick & Hendrick, 2002). Thompson and Borrello (1992) argue that the predominant characteristic of romantic love is obsessive and often sexual thought about the loved one. The evidence from research is that, over time, the obsessive thinking tends to fade away unless one is dissatisfied with the relationship. However, deep involvement with one's partner can and often does persist over time (Acevedo & Aron, 2009). Moreover, in longitudinal research, it was found that falling in love was accompanied by increases in feelings of self-worth (Aron, Paris & Aron, 1995).

People make a clear and sharp distinction between loving someone and being 'in love' with someone (Berscheid & Meyers, 1996). In Western cultures, we tend to 'fall in love' (a revealing expression!) and then marry. Note that in the medieval period of Western civilization, romantic love was called 'courtly love', usually secret, very passionate, and sometimes but not always physically consummated. In many cultures (India, for example), parents traditionally arrange marriages, and the couple may not even meet until the time of the wedding. The movie *Monsoon Wedding* portrays a modern couple in India encountering the traditional expectations of a marriage arranged by the family. After some bumps in the road, including the revelation that she was having an affair with a married man, love wins out in the changing yet traditional context. In the musical *Fiddler on the Roof*, which takes place in a Jewish shtetl in 19th-century Russia, the husband, Tevye, asks his wife, 'Do you love me?' She responds with how they have shared a life, their marital bed and parenting, but he persists: 'Do you love me?' Finally, in exasperation, she exclaims, 'I'm your wife!' Then he gets it; in that culture, love is not a motive for marriage but an expected outcome of the union.

How would you respond to the following question: If you were to meet someone who has all the qualities that you could desire, would you marry that person if you were not in love with her/him? People in 11 countries were asked this question. Those in Western countries (United States, England, Australia) clearly considered love as the most important prerequisite for marriage while those in less-developed, collectivist countries (India, Thailand, Pakistan) were much more willing to consider marriage, in that circumstance (Levine, Sato, Hashimoto & Verma, 1995; Schmitt, Youn, et al., 2009). The latter cultures certainly do not deny the existence of passionate love (Jankowiak, 1995) but may consider it as a thin reed upon which to base a marriage.

A number of theories of love have been developed within social psychology (Berscheid, 2010; Hendrick & Hendrick, 2000).

A triangular model of love

Sternberg (1986) has proposed a triangular model of love representing the varieties of love. All love experiences have three components, represented as points on a triangle (see Figure 8.6). These components are as follows:

Intimacy   The closeness or bond between the two people including communication, self-disclosure and a desire to care for the loved one.

Passion   The emotional and physical arousal in the love relationship. While physical attraction and sexuality may be prominent, especially in the early phases of the relationship, other intense feelings may also contribute to the experience of passion. Note that the emotions associated with feeling 'madly in love' may be elicited by memories of special times involving the partners or by special songs (Mashek, Aron & Fisher, 2000). Interestingly in a study of Chinese participants, relationship satisfaction was related to the intimacy and commitment components of Sternberg's model but not to passion (Ting Kin & Cheng, 2010).

Commitment   Labelling one's feelings towards one's partner as love, and extending this decision over time.

Varieties of love experiences can be described in terms of the relative importance of the three components (indicated by the solid and dotted lines in Figure 8.6). For instance, liking in a friendship involves intimacy and commitment in the absence of passion. Infatuation consists of passion without intimacy or commitment. Romantic love involves a combination of intimacy and passion without commitment; with the addition of commitment, this turns into ideal love. Companionate love involves intimacy and commitment in which the passion, at least in a physical sense, has subsided. Sternberg also describes the stagnant love relationship ('empty shell') in which commitment persists without intimacy or passion, and the ideal, consummate love represented by an equilateral triangle in which intimacy, passion and commitment are combined in full measure.

Sternberg's framework pulls together many previous research findings and concepts. For example, Fehr (1993) describes a prototype – what people consider a typical example – of love. Three fundamental features of this prototype have been identified (Aron & Westbay, 1996): coincident with Sternberg's model, they are passion, intimacy and commitment. Thus, our behaviour and experience in love can be described as schema-driven, the schema of love (Fehr & Russell, 1991).

Another interesting question concerns change over time. For instance, passion is gen-

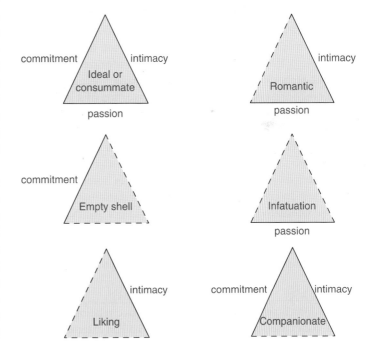

Figure 8.6   Sternberg's triangular theory of love

erally recognized as high in the early 'honeymoon' phase of a relationship, while intimacy builds more gradually as the relationship is sustained over time. However, does passion diminish as a consequence of increasing feelings of intimacy or closeness in a relationship? While there is some evidence that passion does increase as people feel more intimacy with each other, further research is needed to establish the conditions under which passion may wax or wane over time (Baumeister & Bratslavsky, 1999).

A useful perspective on this question of change is the distinction between passionate love and companionate love (Walster & Walster, 1978). Passionate love is an overwhelming, ecstatic condition, while companionate love is a low-key but deeply felt involvement and commitment. It would seem reasonable to assume that passionate love characterizes the earlier stages of the relationship and that, when the honeymoon ends, passion is inevitably replaced by companionate love. Yet women studied after an average of 33 years of marriage exhibited both companionate love and considerable passion for their mates (Traupmann & Hatfield, 1981).

Is romantic love a universal experience or one peculiar to Western cultures? Evidence from anthropology suggest that romantic love is, indeed, found in most human cultures and societies (Jankowiak, 1995). However, cultures vary widely in how the prototype of romantic love is expressed and, indeed, how widely it is accepted. The prototype outlined above applies to individualist cultures such as those of Canada and the United States. As noted above, in collectivist societies such as India, China and Japan, romantic love is less likely to be valued as a basis for marriage, and personal fulfilment and intimacy characterize family relationships as well as romantic dyads (Dion & Dion, 1996). However, in this era of Western-dominated mass media, younger people in societies with collectivist traditions often adopt Western, individualist values.

Gender differences in love

At least in Western cultures, men and women differ with respect to romantic love (Dion & Dion, 1985; Hendrick & Hendrick, 1986; Peplau & Gordon, 1985). Surprisingly, men tend to have a *more* romantic view, believing more often than women that 'true romantic' love comes once and lasts forever, conquers all barriers and social customs, is essentially strange and incomprehensible and must be basic to marriage. On the other hand, women are more likely to be pragmatic: they believe they can be in love many times, that it may not last, that it may inevitably fade into disillusionment when the honeymoon ends, and that economic security and friendship are more important as bases for marriage.

However, women's actual experiences do not always reflect this pragmatism. While men report that they tend to fall in love earlier, and women report that they have been in love more frequently and more intensely, women also tend more to like and even idealize their partners; they more often report emotional experiences and euphoric 'symptoms' such as 'floating on air' or having trouble concentrating (Brehm, 1985). Perhaps women are more pragmatic in their selection of a love partner and in defining what love means, and yet more able to experience love as an intense emotional experience. Or perhaps women are simply more willing or able than are men to report intimate, intense experiences. Evidently, women more than men feel that they cannot waste too much time with the wrong partner (Hill, Rubin & Peplau, 1976).

One fascinating study revealing sex differences was conducted by Dion and Dion (1976). Couples were recruited in the Ontario Science Centre in Toronto. Each was asked to observe the other walking through an 'Ames room', a trapezoidal perceptual distortion apparatus in which objects look unusually large at one end and unusually small at the other as the floor and the ceiling partially converge. For males, the distortion effect was evident in observing both their partners and a stranger in the Ames room. However, for women, distortion of their partner's appearance was significantly less than that of the stranger. Love seemed to modify women's perception of their partners – in the direction of reality.

Love and cognition

Both men and women believe that a love relationship should be intrinsic, based on concerns about the relationship itself and the partner, rather than on external rewards. To study this belief, Seligman, Fazio and Zanna (1980) recruited dating couples and then manipulated their cognitive set by having each subject complete open-ended sentences. Half were sentences containing the phrase 'because I', while the others contained the phrase 'in order to' (e.g., I date my boyfriend because I … or I date my boyfriend in order to …). Previous research had shown that repeated exposure to the phrase 'because I' induced an intrinsic cognitive set while 'in order to' led to an extrinsic set, doing something as a means to an end. Students given an extrinsic cognitive set then scored lower on Rubin's love scale than those with the intrinsic set. When the research participants became conscious of possible extrinsic reasons, their feelings of love actually waned.

The experiment does not suggest that thinking in itself diminishes love. Indeed the more you think about an issue, the more polarized your attitude will be on that issue (Tesser, 1978). Dating students were asked about their love for their partner and how often they thought about their partner (Tesser & Paulhus, 1976). The data from two testing sessions two weeks apart showed that loving and thinking did influence each other: the more you love her, the more you think about her, and vice versa.

Can passionate love be a misattribution?

According to an influential attributional model of romantic love, three conditions are necessary for someone to 'fall in love' (Berscheid and Walster, 1974b). First, the person must be raised in a culture that believes in the idea of romantic love. Second, the person must feel a state of emotional arousal that is interpreted as love, an attribution for their feelings (Chapter 2). Third, an appropriate love object must be present. Crucial to this model is how people interpret symptoms of their own physiological arousal such as a faltering voice, faintness, inability to concentrate, blushing, heart palpitations, muscle tremors. That is, a person experiences a state of arousal and, in the presence of certain cues, attributes those feelings to romantic love.

Both experimental and field studies have supported the model. In one study, couples were asked to report on aspects of their relationship at two different times, six to 10 months apart (Driscoll, Davis & Lipetz, 1972). Examining changes over time, the researchers noted a Romeo and Juliet effect among unmarried couples: romantic love increased as parental interference increased. Couples reattributed at least some of their arousal produced by being upset with their parents as associated with the love they felt for their partner. In another study, after male participants had walked across the shaky Capilano suspension bridge, which crosses a deep gorge in North Vancouver (Dutton & Aron, 1974), they encountered an attractive female experimental assistant. These men later expressed more sexual imagery and were more likely to telephone the assistant later on than were men who had met the same young woman after crossing a solid concrete bridge. Somehow the arousal caused by fear while wobbling in space was subsequently misattributed to attraction to the woman.

However, this interpretation of the Capilano bridge experiment was challenged. Kenrick and Cialdini (1977) argued that at the moment research participants met the young woman, they were feeling relief at having reached solid ground rather than arousal due to fear. Thus, they associated the woman with this feeling of relief. Yet, other research has linked arousal with attraction even when the arousal was caused by exercise (Allen, Kenrick, Linder & McCall, 1989). Given the presence of an appropriate person, a diffuse state of arousal may well be attributed to romantic love.

Figure 8.7 The Capilano suspension bridge, Vancouver, Canada

Source: Lissandra Melo/Shutterstock.com

Gay and lesbian relationships: Are they different?

Over time, societies have come to recognize and accept, to varying degrees, the reality of same-sex relationships. Indeed, in increasing numbers of jurisdictions, gay marriages have gained legal acceptance. While the

Figure 8.8   A gay wedding

Source: Lisa F. Young/Shutterstock.com

social psychology of same-sex relationships would be expected to be similar to that of heterosexual relationships concerning intimacy, communication, commitment and love as outlined in this chapter, there are several complicating factors to consider: the still-controversial societal norms surrounding same-sex relationships, the impact of homophobic prejudices, differences in norms within the subculture of the gay/lesbian community, and the role of transgendered and bisexual orientations (Huston & Schwartz, 1995; Herek, 2000; Lewis, Derlega, Berndt, Morris & Rose, 2001).

Some findings from longitudinal research indicate that the same set of factors predict relationship persistence over time, whether same sex or opposite sex (Kurdek, 2000). On the other hand, it cannot be assumed that relationships between lesbian women are similar in all respects to those between gay men. Indeed, Peplau (2003) documents evidence of four important gender differences in sexuality, all of which characterize both heterosexuals and homosexuals: men tend to show greater sexual desire than women; women place greater emphasis than do men on commitment as an important component of a sexual relationship; aggression is more strongly linked to sexuality among men than among women; and women's sexuality tends to be more open to change over time. Of course, note that these all represent average tendencies and cannot predict the individual behaviours of men and women of same-sex or opposite-sex orientations.

One finding is that what constitutes a 'successful' relationship may differ in same-sex as compared to opposite-sex relationships. Issues of communication and power, in which we have seen gender differences, become different where power may be defined in male terms as 'getting your way', but in female terms as creating consensus and rapport. Male partners tend to be more tolerant than female partners to sexual infidelity, although monogamy is a growing trend due in part to the ever-present threat of HIV/AIDS. Interesting gender differences are evident here: gay men more than lesbian women find their partners' emotional infidelity (involvement with another person) as most upsetting (Dijltstra, P., Groothof et al., 2001).

Perhaps with increasing social acceptance, same-sex relationship norms and dynamics will converge with those governing heterosexual relationships. Clearly, 'coming out' about one's same-sex orientation and one's sexual partner is a major consideration. This may have implications, for example, about how the individuals are perceived at work and the extent to which they experience stress or support in their job (Griffith & Hebl, 2002).

RELATIONSHIP PROBLEMS

Social psychology has turned recently to the study of relationship problems, an area formerly the preserve of clinical disciplines. Theories and methods applicable to the study of close relationships can help us understand relationship disruption and loneliness.

Dissolution of relationships

After some years of apparent contentment, the birth of two princes and an increasingly glamorous image reflected by the new Princess of Wales, tensions between Prince Charles and Princess Diana began to appear in public, amplified by the incessant interest of the tabloids. The marriage finally ended in 1996, 15 years after the storybook wedding. Later, Diana died tragically in Paris.

While we cannot diagnose this relationship at a distance, marital failures are generally explained in terms of the following factors (Kurdek, 1993): (1) social factors such as socioeconomic class differences, differences in religious affiliation or financial difficulties; (2) personality traits that may predispose a person to distort the relationship; (3) an absence of interdependence perhaps because one or both partners has available alternatives; and (4) large discrepancies between the partners such as incompatible personality traits or conflicts in values, attitudes or interests. In this case, and many others, we can add the pressures of external circumstances to the toxic mix. However, we still have much to learn.

The antecedents and process of ending a relationship

Can we predict which marriages will survive and which will eventually break up? Several longitudinal studies provide insights. Bentler and Newcomb (1978) compared characteristics of couples who later did separate with those who remained together. Those who were destined to separate were less similar in age, attractiveness, personality and interest in art. The men described themselves as more extroverted and orderly and the women described themselves as less clothes-conscious and less congenial. In another study, it was found that both men and women who remain married are more conventional, less neurotic (over-reactive to stressful events) and less impulsive (Kelly & Conley, 1987).

Consider the process of breaking up described as a 'cascading' effect, in which couples at risk of subsequent separation communicate in a manner characterized by more conflict, anger, withdrawal and whining and less affection and interest in their partner (Gottman and Levenson, 1992). These couples also experience less marital satisfaction (not surprisingly) and poorer health, all of which lead to more stubbornness and withdrawal from interaction and to active consideration of separation. Can we compare the breakup of marital partners to the breaking up of friendships? Interestingly, while couples tend to act directly to terminate the relationship, friends are more likely to use more passive strategies such as avoidance or withdrawal, simply letting the friendship 'fade away' over time (Fehr, 1996).

To understand the process of ending an intimate relationship, Hill, Rubin and Peplau (1976) compared 103 dating couples who had broken up with 117 who were still together. Women initiated the majority of the break-ups. Whether the couples had engaged in sexual relations early or late in the relationship or abstained from sexual involvement did not predict whether the couple remained together or broke up. A longitudinal study of dating couples found that, among those who broke up, the quality of the relationships was lower and an alternative partner was often available (Simpson, 1987). In addition among those who had broken up, emotional distress was related to how close they still felt towards the former partner. Finally, an interview study of dating couples by Felmlee (1995) found that, in some cases, the same qualities that first attracted one to the other such as being 'unusual', 'exciting', 'unpredictable' were then cited as reasons for the breakup.

Of course, relationships tend to fluctuate rather than simply grow in one direction. Even in a successful marriage, the partners feel very close at some times, more distant and casual at others (Altman, Vinsel & Brown, 1981). In an ongoing process, people balance their need for closeness and intimacy with a need to maintain a sense of self and privacy. As a relationship deteriorates, this balance tilts towards the privacy polarity.

Figure 8.9 Are this couple on the verge of a break-up? (Painting by Pablo Picasso)

Source: © The Gallery Collection/Corbis

Why do people remain in unsatisfying relationships?

Levinger (1979) argues that in deciding to remain in or leave a marriage, people consider both the rewards and costs of staying and the rewards and costs of leaving. (This is discussed further in Chapter 10.) Rewards such as an alternative relationship or the freedom of being single again will tend to lead the person to dissolve the relationship, while anything that makes separation more costly will tend to maintain the relationship. A person may stay in an unsatisfactory marriage because of a concern about the children, a fear that friendships and social networks will be disrupted or a realization that a break-up will entail major financial sacrifices. This is the 'empty shell marriage', where the marriage itself is unsatisfactory but formidable barriers to leaving remain. As noted earlier, when people feel that they have invested a great deal of time and effort in a relationship, they tend to persist (Rusbult, 1983). Longitudinal research shows that couples who will break up tend to be less dependent on the marriage and on each other and also that one partner is less dependent than the other on the relationship (Drigotas & Rusbult, 1992; Kurdek, 1993).

Abuse and breaking up. Why do people who have been physically abused by their partners sometimes choose to stay in the relationship? While some have tried to explain such behaviour in terms of personal dispositions such as low self-esteem or masochism, such explanations ignore the crucial role of the situation. Rusbult and Martz (1995) interviewed women at a shelter and reported that their commitment to remaining in the relationship was determined by three important variables: (1) satisfaction with the relationship despite the abuse; (2) the absence of external alternatives, including education and employment opportunities; and (3) their investment in the relationship, including the duration of the marriage, shared children and material possessions, and, a sense of interdependence with the partner. This investment model (discussed earlier in the chapter) has been successful in predicting the course of various types of close relationships and it is striking indeed to find that abusive relationships follow similar patterns (Truman-Schram, Cann, Calhoun & Vanwallendael, 2000). That is, people remain with an abusive partner in part because they have invested so much in the relationship, both in effort and in years.

The impact of dissolving a relationship

There is abundant research evidence linking marital separation to a wide variety of stress-related disorders (Bloom, Asher & White, 1978; Burman & Margolin, 1992). In comparison with both now-married and never-married persons, separated and divorced persons are more prone to automobile accidents, psychiatric disorders, alcoholism, suicide, and death from tuberculosis, cirrhosis of the liver and certain forms of cancer and coronary diseases. Obviously, stressful factors in divorce – financial difficulties, sexual problems, feelings of shame, guilt or failure, problems with children and sheer loneliness – play a role. Compounding these burdens may be a profound feeling of conflict or ambivalence, and each partner can have both intense negative and positive feelings towards the other. Weiss (1975) observes that a strong attachment often persists after love has disappeared.

Some evidence also suggests that men often suffer more adverse effects of divorce than women (Chiriboga, Roberts & Stein, 1978). Perhaps a partial explanation may be found in evidence discussed earlier concerning gender differences in friendships. Wright (1982) describes friendships between females as 'face-to-face' and those between males as 'side-by-side'. In Western cultures, males are generally reluctant to be intimate with other males (Rand & Levinger, 1979) and tend to be more dependent on marital relationships than are women. Thus, lacking the intimacy and support of their former relationship, men often do not fare well.

Fischer and Phillips (1982) found that when a man marries, he tends to give up friendships but to keep in touch with casual acquaintances. Women tend to do the opposite; their circle of casual acquaintances diminishes, but intimate friendships are not affected. Thus even with a greater social network, the male who loses the romantic relationship may be emotionally isolated. This may explain why divorced women report that the most stressful period was before the separation, while divorced men consider the period after the separation to have been the most difficult (Hagestad & Smyer, 1982).

LONELINESS

Most people have experienced situations in which they feel lonely – visiting a new country or location, being temporarily separated from a loved one. However, some people suffer from chronic or dispositional loneliness. During their first year of university, 75% of students questioned experienced some degree of loneliness (Cutrona, 1982). By the end of the year, only 25% were still lonely. These individuals tend to be more self-focused, and also tend to be inappropriate in their style of self-disclosure (Solano, Batten & Parish, 1982): Either they pour their hearts out to a total stranger or they are unusually closed, revealing little of themselves even to someone they know well. Chronically lonely persons also tend to be less effective in non-verbal communication, such as when expressing and judging emotions (Gerson & Perlman, 1979). They are also more anxious about their perceived deficiencies in social skills (Solano & Koester, 1989).

What is loneliness? Perlman and Peplau (1981) identify three characteristics:

* It results from the individual's perception of deficiencies in relationships.
* It is distressing and unpleasant.
* It is subjective rather than objective – we can feel intensely lonely in a crowd and not at all lonely when alone. (It is said that in order to portray loneliness, an artist must portray a person with others.)

Peplau, Russell and Heim (1979) outline an attributional model of loneliness based upon Weiner's (1974) model of achievement attributions (see Chapter 2). Weiner observes that we explain our successes and failures in terms of internal or external causes and stable or unstable causes. Peplau et al. (1979) argue that the experience of loneliness depends on how we explain the time or circumstance in which we find ourselves alone or relatively isolated, and whether the person blames himself or herself.

Not surprisingly, married people in general are less lonely particularly in comparison with the divorced or widowed (Perlman & Peplau, 1981). Among people who are separated, divorced, widowed or who have never married, men tend to experience greater loneliness than women (Peplau, Bikson, Rook & Goodchilds, 1982; Rubenstein & Shaver, 1982). However, Sadava & Matejcic (1987) found surprising levels of loneliness in those who had been recently married. Loneliness reflected the quality of the relationship rather than simply its presence or absence. Since the research participants were recently married, some of them may have been chronically lonely persons who chose mates unwisely or who lacked the social skills to make their marriages function more satisfactorily. However, a comparative study of Chinese, Anglo and Italian Canadians showed that loneliness was not highly related to lower satisfaction with life among Chinese participants, perhaps reflecting the social cohesion in Chinese culture (Goodwin, Cook & Yung, 2001).

What about the elderly? It is often believed that, as we age and our generation begins to die off, our lives become more isolated and lonely. However, research indicates that loneliness among older people is not typical (Pinquart & Sorensen, 2001).

Weiss (1973) distinguished between *social* loneliness, or a lack of a network of friends, acquaintances and colleagues, and *emotional* loneliness, a lack of intimate relationships. People may feel lonely because they lack romantic involvement, friendships, family bonds or ties in the larger community (Sermat, 1978). The research suggests that a lack in one area does not necessarily mean a lack in other areas; nor can one kind of relationship compensate for deficiencies in another.

There also seems to be a generalized underlying disposition or trait of loneliness, and several scales have been developed to measure it (Rubenstein & Shaver, 1982; Russell, Peplau & Cutrona, 1980) (Table 8.1). People who score high on global measures of loneliness tend to manifest introversion, self-consciousness, a lack of assertiveness, low self-esteem, anxiety, and depression (Peplau & Perlman, 1982). There is also some evidence that lonely people, particularly males, are more likely to be hostile or aggressive especially towards women (Check, Perlman & Malamuth, 1985) and that lonely people who drink excessively are more vulnerable to alcohol problems (Sadava & Thompson, 1986). Of course, any of these personal characteristics may be both

TABLE 8.1 UCLA loneliness scale

INSTRUCTIONS: Indicate how often each of the statements below is descriptive of you.

O indicates 'I often feel this way'; S indicates 'I sometimes feel this way'; R indicates 'I rarely feel this way'; N indicates 'I never feel this way'

1. I am unhappy doing so many things alone

    O   S   R   N

2. I have nobody to talk to
3. I cannot tolerate being so alone
4. I lack companionship
5. I feel as if nobody really understands me
6. I find myself waiting for people to call or write
7. There is no one I can turn to
8. I am no longer close to anyone
9. My interests and ideas are not shared by those around me
10. I feel left out
11. I feel completely alone
12. I am unable to reach out and communicate with those around me
13. My social relationships are superficial
14. I feel starved for company
15. No one really knows me well
16. I feel isolated from others
17. I am unhappy being so withdrawn
18. It is difficult for me to make friends
19. I feel shut out and excluded by others
20. People are around me but not with me

Scoring:

Make all O's = 3, all S's = 2, all R's = 1, and all N's = 0. Keep scoring continuous.

Source: Russell, Peplau & Cutrona (1980)

a cause and a consequence of loneliness. For example, hostile or depressed people may experience failures in relationships, thereby increasing their loneliness and their anger or depression. Cacioppo (2008) reports evidence that chronically lonely people have higher levels of the neurotransmitter epinephrine, linked to stress. The perception that we are lonely is in itself a source of great distress (Hawkley & Cacioppo, 2010) and is related to increased blood pressure (Hawkley, Thisted, Masi & Cacioppo, 2010). Indeed, in a large epidemiological study of a large sample in California, chronic loneliness was found to be a predictor of earlier mortality (Patterson & Veenstra, 2010; Hawkley & Cacioppo, 2003). Clearly loneliness must be seen as a significant health issue.

A final note: loneliness is not synonymous with being alone. Indeed, it is not uncommon to feel lonely among many people. On the other hand, solitude is not necessarily a negative experience, and indeed most people in Western societies spend up to 30% of their waking time alone (Larson, Csikszentmihalyi & Graef, 1982). Indeed, consider the paradox: while we have strong, biologically based needs for attachment, affiliation, social interaction and love, we all seek to have time to ourselves in solitude. Long & Averill (2003) outline several important benefits of solitude. As a state of disengagement from the expectations and demands of other people, it can be liberating, not only freeing the individual from the constraints of others but freeing her or him to engage in desired activities, including contemplation and doing nothing. Freedom is a prerequisite for creativity, and thus, while much creativity is in collaboration with others, the writer alone in a cabin in the woods, the scientist alone in the lab, the painter alone in the studio are all familiar images. Many people experience feelings of intimacy and connection with another even while alone. Finally, the spiritual experiences of mystics and prophets often occur in solitude. In our modern life of being constantly 'connected' by the media, are we losing this important component of our social lives?

SUMMARY

1. The need to affiliate with others begins at the stage of infant attachment and persists throughout life. Certain factors such as intense fear or stress increase affiliation needs while others, such as social anxiety, decrease affiliation.

2. Attachment is an emotional bond to someone who represents a safe haven from threat and a secure base from which we can explore our environment. Attachment orientations relate to behaviour in relationships and to health and well-being.

3. We tend to be attracted to people in close physical proximity and to those who are physically attractive. To an extent, we are influenced by a stereotype that equates attractiveness with goodness and we are motivated to choose others who are roughly equal to ourselves in attractiveness.

4. When people are first getting to know each other, attraction is related to the perception that people are similar and that the interaction is rewarding. We are attracted to people with similar attitudes because it is rewarding to be with them, because we seek consistency in our attitudes and relationships and because we expect people we like to be similar to us.

5. If we have no choice about interacting in a situation, our liking of neutral or even negative persons may be enhanced.

6. Mutuality involves the perception of interdependence and intimacy. Reciprocity in self-disclosure is crucial to intimacy. Self-disclosure increases in depth and breadth as intimacy increases, but is limited by a need to preserve privacy and by the use of non-verbal as well as verbal communication.

7. Equity or perceived fairness is important to social relations, including exchanges in love, status, information, money, goods and services. In intimate relationships, exchange becomes more particularistic, more flexible and less egocentric.

8. In intimate relationships, the principle of complementarity becomes more important. The sequential filter model suggests that similar values are more important in the earlier stage of a relationship and that complementarity needs assume more prominence at a later stage.

9. Romantic love consists of varying degrees of passion, commitment and intimacy. An attributional model suggests that if a culture propagates the notion of romantic love, a state of arousal may, in the presence of certain cognitive cues, lead to an attribution of 'being in love'.

10. According to the evolutionary perspective, we are attracted to potential partners by their 'reproductive fitness', which may be represented by their beauty.

11. The dissolution of a relationship may depend on the anticipated costs and rewards of leaving it and on the anticipated costs and rewards of staying within it.

12. Loneliness arises from a perception of deficiencies in one's relationships. This may be social or emotional in nature and may have nothing to do with being alone.

POINTS TO PONDER

- We argue in this chapter that people have a basic need to be with others and to form attachments with a few of them. However, we also have a need to be alone at times. How can we reconcile these two needs? Can you formulate a testable hypothesis?
- We like people who are physically attractive, and it's not all about sexual attraction. Think of examples where we favour physically attractive people for reasons that are not romantic or sexual. Why is physical attractiveness so important to us in such situations?
- Can we study love scientifically? Critically examine the research on this topic that is reviewed in this chapter.
- Some have argued that our society makes us feel lonely. Think of arguments for and against this hypothesis. How might we test such a hypothesis?
- Suggest three explanations for the similarity-attraction relationship. Can you think of exceptions to this rule?

FURTHER READING

Berscheid, E. (2010). Love in the fourth dimension. *Annual Review of Psychology, 61*, 1–25.

A thought-provoking and masterly overview of psychological thinking on love by a pioneer researcher in this area of research, isolating some of the key issues and puzzles.

Hendrick, C. & Hendrick, S.S. (Eds). (2002). *Close relationships: A sourcebook.* Thousand Oaks, CA: Sage Publications.

A useful set of reviews of theoretical thinking and research in this rapidly expanding area of social psychology.

Marche, S. (2012). Is Facebook making us lonely? *Atlantic Magazine,* May 2012.

A popular press article grounded in psychological research that makes the case that we are more networked than ever, yet more lonely.

Mikulincer, M. & Shaver, P.R. (2007). *Attachment in adulthood: Structure, dynamics and change.* New York: Guilford Press.

An indispensable overview of the research, theory and thinking about how attachment theory can be applied to the study of adults.

Reis, H.T. & Aron, A. (2008). Love. What is it, why does it matter and how does it operate? *Perspectives on Psychological Science,* 3, 80–86.

A lively and scholarly overview of love from the perspective of psychological science, a convincing argument for the relevance of science in understanding love.

Rhodes, G. & Zebrowitz, L.A. (Eds). (2002). Facial attractiveness: Evolutionary, cognitive and social perspectives. *Advances in visual cognition, Vol. 1.* Westport, CT.: Ablex Publishing.

What's in a pretty face? A set of papers look at facial attractiveness from the perspectives of biological and evolutionary theory, social status and cross-cultural research. The notion that beauty is simply in the eye of the beholder is challenged.

WEBLINKS

http://www.sexscience.org/

A useful site about research on sexuality.

Note: there are many websites on related topics, including love, computer matchmaking, sexuality, enhancing your attractiveness, divorce. *Caveat emptor!*

CHAPTER 9
PROSOCIAL BEHAVIOUR

The quality of mercy is not strained; It droppeth as the gentle rain from heaven upon the place beneath. It is twice blessed – it blesseth him that gives and him that takes.
William Shakespeare

LEARNING OBJECTIVES

* To understand the meaning of *prosocial behaviour* and its relationship to altruism

* To examine the role of empathy

* To explore the effects of personal, social and situational variables

* To consider various forms of prosocial behaviour, including direct help, gratitude, forgiveness, volunteerism and promotion of a sustainable environment

* To investigate situational factors that inhibit intervention in emergency situations

* To appraise the nature of heroism and the traits of heroes

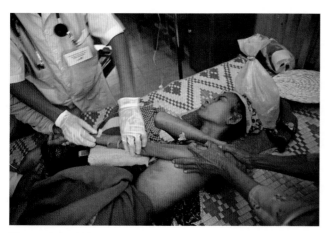

Figure 9.1 Médecins Sans Frontières doctors treating a sick child in Cambodia

Source: © Karen Kasmauski/Corbis

In 1999, *Médecins sans Frontières* was awarded the Nobel Peace Prize for its medical and humanitarian assistance to people caught in crisis in nearly 70 nations around the world – victims of war, civil strife or natural disaster. Its many volunteers provide life-saving intervention despite the risk of political kidnapping, epidemic disease, or death from bombs and bullets.

In June 2012, the life of 68-year-old Karen Klein, a school bus monitor in a town in New York State, took a sharp turn. A group of grade seven boys in the back of the bus began to verbally attack her, calling her 'ugly', 'bitch', 'fat ass', and other nasty things. As tears ran down her cheeks, others joined in the cruel jeering. A student captured this on video and posted it on the Internet where it quickly went viral. Having seen that video, a 25-year-old Toronto man – who had never met Mrs Klein – was moved to set up an online fundraising campaign with a goal of raising enough money to send her on a 'dream vacation'. Within a few days, this campaign raised more than $700,000.00 for this now not-so-unfortunate woman!

How do we explain such willingness of strangers to offer help? Why do some physicians leave their comfortable practices in their home countries to bring medical assistance to strangers in distant battlefields? And why would thousands of individuals donate money to someone they do not know and are unlikely ever to meet? And on the other hand, why do people sometimes fail to provide help in emergencies, not even when calling for an ambulance or the police involves no risk to themselves? In this chapter, we explore both helping and the failure to help.

EXPLORING THE MEANING OF PROSOCIAL BEHAVIOUR

Prosocial behaviour refers to actions carried out to assist other people without being motivated by external incentives (reward, or fear of negative consequences for not helping). The term is often used interchangeably with **altruism**, a term coined by philosopher Auguste Comte in 1832 to describe acts of selfless assistance to others. However, altruism has traditionally been considered by theologians and philosophers to be behaviour intended to help others not only without *external* incentives, but without *self*-reward as well. Self-reward might take the form of increased self-esteem – feeling good for having helped someone else – or avoidance of the guilt and shame that might come from not helping. Yet, is it ever possible to eliminate completely the anticipation of self-reward? We shall return to this question later in this chapter. In any case, should we care whether a person feels good after helping someone, so long as help is provided?

Prosocial behaviour can take many forms: direct help, intervention in emergencies, volunteer work, cooperating with others, working to save the environment (Kollmuss & Agyeman, 2002), employee 'whistle-blowing' (Gundlach, Douglas & Martinko, 2003), political activities aimed at bringing about positive social change, assisting people to develop skills, or standing up for others who are being bullied (Bergin, Talley & Hamer, 2003). And as we shall see, gratitude and forgiveness are also forms of prosocial behaviour. But how do we decide that someone has acted prosocially? Did an individual help out of kindness, or out of the desire to win favour from others? What is or is not judged to be prosocial behaviour is ultimately in the eye of the beholder, for one must make attributions about what has motivated an individual's actions. Of course, motives are often difficult or impossible to assess, and, in addition, we sometimes make faulty attributions. When a campaigning politician helps an elderly person across a busy street, we might attribute this to the desire to 'look good' to win votes, but how can we be sure that he or she was not motivated solely by concern for the elder's safety? A policewoman helping a lost child is also unlikely to be viewed as acting prosocially, for we might conclude that she is only doing her job. But what if she risks her life to plunge into a raging river to save a child? Is this prosocial behaviour, or is this still just 'doing her job?' One cannot answer this question, for even this rescuer cannot know for sure whether she would have acted in the same way were she not a police officer.

KEY POINT: Prosocial behaviour refers to actions intended to help others, carried out without external incentives. Whether an act is viewed as prosocial depends on the attributions we make about the motivation behind it.

THE ROOTS OF PROSOCIAL BEHAVIOUR

Prosocial behaviour stems from a number of different influences, including emotional, social, personal and cultural factors as well as possible genetic factors.

Possible evolutionary roots

Are we born altruists or do we acquire prosocial behaviours as we develop? This has long been a matter of debate. It is clear that young children, even as young as 14 months, spontaneously demonstrate both prosocial behaviour and a concern for other's welfare in the absence of any external reward (Hepach et al., 2012). During their second year, children begin to respond emotionally to the suffering of others and make efforts to comfort or help a distressed individual (Kärtner, Keller & Chaudhary, 2010). In light of such evidence, it has been argued that we begin life as 'indiscriminate altruists' and that as we grow up socialization leads us to become more selective in terms of whom and when we help (Warneken & Yomsello, 2009).

Evolutionary psychology assumes that this early childhood prosocial behaviour reflects a natural disposition, and that there are evolved biological factors underlying at least some social and moral behaviours. According to evolutionary psychologists, each organism is engaged in a struggle to send as many of its genes as possible into the gene pool of the next generation; any behaviour promoting this end is itself likely to be 'selected' and reproduced from generation to generation. Of course, this notion of a struggle is only a metaphor; it is not that genes themselves are motivated to do anything, but rather that a variant of a gene that gives an organism a reproductive advantage will as a result be reproduced more frequently.

Suppose, the argument goes, that a mutation produces a gene – let us call it a prosocial gene – that somehow motivates an individual to provide assistance to others. Such assistance is likely to increase the likelihood that those others who have been helped will survive and reproduce. As a result, their genes are now as likely as the helper's to make it into the next gene pool, and that will not create any reproductive advantage for the helper. But suppose that the helper is selective about who is helped. Given that we share some genes with our close relatives, we could improve the likelihood that our own genes will be better represented in the gene pool of the next generation by preferentially giving help to our relatives, enabling them to survive at least long enough to reproduce. In this way, even if behaviour is not directly beneficial to the individual and his or her ability to reproduce, it could be 'selected' by the processes of evolution, provided that it benefits other closely related individuals.

This hypothesized motivation to provide help primarily to close relatives is what evolutionary psychologists refer to as the **kinship principle**. This principle also leads to other predictions: Since males can sire countless children, but females must depend on only a relatively small number of offspring to carry their genes into the next generation, each individual child is more valuable as a gene propagator to a woman. Thus, the kinship principle suggests that mothers should behave more prosocially towards their children than do fathers. The same reasoning suggests that parents will act more prosocially towards male children than towards female children, given that males carry a greater potential for transporting each parent's genes forward.

This evolutionary theory is difficult to test, and as fascinating as its hypotheses may be, it is wise to view it with caution until solid evidence is forthcoming (Panksepp & Panksepp, 2000, 2001). Its support comes largely from archival data (for example, statistics on child abuse) and from examples in the animal kingdom. No 'prosocial' genes or combinations of genes have ever been identified, and, moreover, the failure of the theory to give much importance to learning and social influences is a significant shortcoming. It is also important to note that while evolutionary psychology proposes that prosocial behaviour will be preferentially biased towards kin, in reality this is not what is observed in human groups (Warneken & Tomasello, 2009). While most people are likely to help family members first, this includes adopted children as well as one's biological children; and we are more likely to help close friends than strangers. This suggests that factors other than genetic ones must contribute to helping behaviour.

However, reserving judgement on evolutionary theory is not to say that there are no genetic influences on prosocial behaviour, for that is unlikely to be the case. For one thing, there are genetic influences that affect the development of personality, and personality certainly plays a role in prosocial behaviour, as is discussed later in this chapter. Personality traits associated with helpfulness may be favoured by natural selection, as is posited by **gene-culture co-evolution theory** (Richerson & Boyd, 2005). This theory suggests that as ideas, knowledge, and skills are transmitted via social learning across generations within a society, some aspects of this cultural heritage are more likely to promote survival of the group than others and therefore will be subject to the pressures of natural selection in a similar manner to the way that genes are. That is, those behaviours that contribute to survival and reproduction of the group are more likely to be taught to the next generation than are those that do not. One such cultural aspect is self-sacrifice for the good of others in a group, and societies that encourage this behaviour are likely to out-compete and out-survive and out-reproduce groups that are less pro-socially oriented. Gradually, as a result of this process, stronger group norms favouring prosocial behaviour may develop over time. Richerson & Boyd (2005) argue that individuals who best serve the welfare of the group – in this case by their helpfulness to others in the group – may well become the preferred mating partners and as a result become the most reproductively successful. In consequence, whatever genetic characteristics that contribute to their helpfulness – perhaps genes that relate to anxiety-proneness or the propensity to experience emotions such as guilt and shame – would be more likely to be reproduced in the next generation's gene pool. In this way, genes and cultural variables interact to favour cross-generational transport of prosocial behaviours.

> **KEY POINT:** Arguments suggesting that prosocial behaviour has an evolutionary basis lack strong evidence. However, heritable traits that influence such behaviour, such as those involved in personality, may be favoured by natural selection.

Emotional roots

Empathy with the suffering of others plays a major role in prosocial behaviour (Litvack-Miller, McDougall & Romney, 1997). Empathy is an emotional reaction that is very similar in quality to the perceived emotional state of the suffering individual (Eisenberg & Fabes, 1990). That is, we really *feel*, at least to some degree, the other's pain or sorrow or distress. Empathic arousal appears to be a universal human response, which is present to a degree even in one- and two-day-old infants, although it is modified by experience (Hoffman, 1981). Despite its importance, however, it has not yet been shown to be a *necessary* condition for prosocial behaviour.

Physiological arousal is involved in empathy, and because people vary in their physiological responsiveness, different people are likely to experience different degrees of empathic response in a given situation (Liew et al., 2003). The degree of arousal is important. Relatively low arousal is likely to lead not to empathy, but **sympathy**, which is much more of a cognitive response, a heightened awareness of another person's suffering combined with the desire to eliminate it. On the other hand, intense arousal may be so distressing that the individual may become focused on his or her own anxiety and discomfort, rather than on the needs of the other person (Eisenberg et al., 1996).

Empathy and cognition Both cognition and emotion contribute to prosocial behaviour; there is usually a two-stage decision process (Dickert, Sagara & Slovic, 2011). The cognitive appraisal that comes with sympathy – thinking about what another person must be feeling – often leads to emotional arousal, while the decision about how much help to give is tied to how much empathy one feels for the person needing help (Levenson & Ruef, 1992).

What about 'empathy at a distance' elicited by people who are suffering and in need, but are not actually present for us to see? Research shows that the magnitude of the empathic response is generally greater when a potential donor considers helping a single, identifiable victim rather than a multitude. This greater willingness to provide assistance to a single sufferer has been referred to as the identifiable victim effect (Slovic, 2007), and it appears to explain the relative indifference often shown by potential donors when large masses of people are victims of starvation or other disasters. Slovic argues that this occurs because while we can relatively easily process information about a single individual in need and feel empathy for that person, it is difficult to experience an empathic response to large numbers of unidentifiable people. At its worst, this leads to genocide neglect, when the world watches and does nothing as mass slaughters result in the deaths of hundreds of thousands or even millions of people.

The identifiable victim effect was demonstrated in the following study (Small, Loewenstein & Slovic, 2007): As participants left a psychological experiment, they were given the opportunity to donate up to five dollars to a charity, *Save the Children*, to help victims of a severe food crisis in Africa. There were three conditions. In the first ('identifiable life'), they were told that the money would be earmarked for a specific victim, Rokia, a seven-year-old girl in Mali who was facing starvation. In the second condition ('statistical life'), no specific victim was mentioned and participants were provided only with statistical information informing them that millions of people in that part of Africa, many of them children, were in desperate need of food. In the third condition ('identifiable life with statistics'), they were provided with the statistical information but were also told about Rokia, and informed that any donation on their part would be specifically earmarked for her. The results are summarized in Figure 9.2. Clearly, people were much more generous when a single individual was identified than when faced with only statistical information about mass suffering. And note that adding statistical information to information about Rokia actually *reduced* the contributions! It is as though being faced with large-scale suffering dilutes our empathic response.

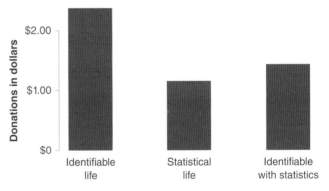

Figure 9.2 Mean donations

Source: Small et al. (2007)

> **KEY POINT:** Cognitive and emotional reactions combine when making decisions about helping others.

Empathy and neuroscience Empathy sometimes occurs prior to or in the absence of cognitive appraisal, and appears to involve an automatic emotional mimicking of the perceived emotions of the person in distress. Usually when we think of mimicry, we think of behaviour, and behavioural mimicry is common in the animal kingdom, although some species are much more proficient mimickers than others (recall the discussions in Chapters 6 and 7). Think of the parrot's ability to imitate human sounds, or the ape's proclivity to mimic a human's actions – to the extent that we describe someone who is deliberately imitating another person as 'aping' the behaviour. Recall the discussion in Chapter 6: Behavioural mimicry comes naturally to humans, and accumulating evidence suggests that this automatic imitation is mediated by the mirror neuron system (Iacoboni, 2009; Heyes, 2011). When people passively observe another person's bodily movements, particular motor neurons respond in such a way as to selectively activate the particular muscles that are involved in the observed behaviour. For example, observing an individual moving the index finger of the right hand produces increased specific muscle activation in the observer's right index finger (Catmur, Walsh & Heyes, 2007). Behavioural mimicry may play an indirect role in prosocial behaviour, for it has been found to increase feelings of trust (Bailenson & Yee, 2005) and affiliation (Hove & Risen, 2009), as well as a sense of interconnectedness between the mimicker and the individual being mimicked. This can promote greater empathy and prosocial behaviour, and the effect appears to extend even to others than the mimicked individual (Stel, Van Baaren. & Vonk, 2007; Stel & Harinck, 2011). But there is more: Mirror neurons also appear to lead to *emotional* mimicry as well, automatically leading the individual to experience directly to some degree the emotional state of another person. This suggests that we may actually be 'wired' for empathy (Iacoboni, 2009).

Social neuroscience has made a strong contribution to the study of empathy that goes far beyond mirror neurons. For example, the hormone oxytocin appears to play an important role in the development of trust and social attachment (e.g., Kosfeld et al., 2005) and has a positive influence on generosity (Zak et al., 2007). And while, as noted earlier, no 'prosocial' genes have ever been discovered, there is growing evidence that genetic factors influence children's susceptibility to parental influence. Knafo, Israel & Ebstein (2011) studied prosocial behaviour in 168 twin pairs (average age 44 months) and reported that genetic effects accounted for between 34% and 53% of the variance in prosocial behaviour. What appeared to account for this was the presence or absence of a particular dopamine receptor D4; this is genetically determined. Thus, depending on the gene, a child may be more or less responsive to parental encouragement of various behaviours including prosocial behaviour.

> **KEY POINT:** Accumulating evidence points to neurological and genetic factors that influence the development of empathy.

Empathy–altruism hypothesis Research into the role that empathy plays in prosocial behaviour has rekindled the debate about whether true selfless altruism exists. Some researchers (e.g., Buck, 2002) continue to argue that there is indeed empirical evidence for genuine altruism and that it has a genetic basis. Batson and others (e.g., Batson & Powell, 2003) have presented data in support of the **empathy–altruism hypothesis**, which posits that pure altruism is elicited as a result of empathy induced by witnessing a person in distress. While helping another person may bring both external reward such as praise and respect and self-reward in terms of heightened self-esteem and so on, and while it may also avoid negative outcomes such as guilt for not helping, or distress at another's suffering, the empathy–altruism hypothesis posits that the ultimate goal is to remove the other person's suffering that produced the empathy in the first place (Batson, 2011). This brings us full circle to the philosophical debates of old. Batson and colleagues have run numerous experiments that they argue support this hypothesis. Yet, how can we be sure that by helping to reduce another person's distress, one is not being reinforced by relief from one's own empathic distress? And how can we be sure that feelings of pride or satisfaction or avoidance of guilt are not key motivators? Moreover, some have argued that the experimental conditions used by Batson and his colleagues produce feelings of *self–other overlap* – that is, feelings of a sense of 'we-ness' with the other person, where we would use 'we' to describe the relationship (Cialdini at al., 1997; Neuberg et al., 1997). Such we-ness is not the same as empathic distress for it reflects *self*-interest. For example, if your sister were to drown, you would suffer a serious personal loss, and so rescuing her is to some degree self-serving as well. Such we-ness can develop even with strangers in some circumstances.

However, Batson (2011) contends that these alternative explanations cannot account for his evidence, leaving only the empathy–altruism hypothesis as a viable explanation. This issue has not yet been resolved.

> **KEY POINT:** There continues to be debate about the existence of true altruism, but it is wise to approach claims for its existence with caution.

Mood   There is evidence that being in a positive mood facilitates individual acts of charity or helping (Kayser et al., 2010), while negative moods more often impede such behaviour (Forgas, 1998). For example, when children in one study were asked to reminisce about happy experiences, they subsequently gave more to charity than did children who were asked to reminisce about sad experiences, or than children who were not asked to reminisce at all (Rosenhan, 1972). In another study, participants who had just viewed sad movies donated less money to charity than other participants who had watched neutral movies (Underwood et al., 1977). Since success in some activity or venture usually produces a positive mood, then prosocial behaviour should be more evident when someone has experienced the warm glow of success (Isen, 1970), compared to when the outcome has been failure. On the other hand, the image-repair hypothesis suggests that those who have failed in some way are also more likely to help, but only those who know of their failure. This is a form of impression management (see Chapter 3). Indeed, various studies have found that making a mistake or committing a *faux pas* in public actually influences people to be more helpful to others. Other experiments have shown that a person who has harmed or hindered another often resorts to reparative altruism (Baumeister, Stillwell & Heatherton, 1994). Through prosocial behaviour, the individual tries to reduce guilt and compensate for the harm done, although these efforts are not always directed at the person who was harmed.

> **KEY POINT:** People are not equally generous or willing to help at all times. Variations in mood, often caused by situational circumstances, can lead to a greater or lesser response to other's needs.

Social roots

Although cooperative behaviours do occur in other species such as apes, dolphins and elephants, only humans show widespread prosocial behaviour and cooperation, and much of this is the result of our ability to establish and enforce social norms (Buckholtz & Marois, 2012). As we saw in Chapter 6, social norms exert considerable and often unrecognized control over behaviour. Essentially, they prescribe which actions should be carried out and which should not. We should not blow our noses on our sleeve; we should say 'thank you' when someone serves us coffee; we should not steal; we should help someone who needs our help. We begin learning social norms early in life as we are being shaped by our parents and others to fit into our social world, and even preschoolers know and enforce social norms among their peers (Schmidt & Tomasello, 2012).

Several norms are of specific relevance to prosocial behaviour:

The norm of reciprocity pushes us to help people who have helped us in the past; in other words, we reciprocate their assistance (Warnekin & Tomasello, 2009). This norm has been found to operate in all cultures (Gouldner, 1960), although with some variations. For example, research has found that while people in both China and Canada feel an obligation to reciprocate a gift given by a close friend, Canadians are less likely to feel the need to reciprocate after receiving a gift from a casual acquaintance. Chinese on the other hand are more likely to *refuse* a gift from a casual acquaintance in circumstances where they would be unable to reciprocate in future (Shen, Wan & Wyer, 2011). Thus, culture influences the way in which the norm of reciprocity is applied.

The norm of social responsibility requires that we help people who are in need regardless of what they have done for us in the past or might do for us in the future (Berkowitz & Daniels, 1963).

The norm of equity specifies that fairness should serve as a criterion for the way we treat others (Walster, Walster & Berscheid, 1978). Equity is defined in terms of equal ratios of inputs to outcomes. If another person has put in as much effort as we have, whether at some specific task or in life in general, but has not been as fortunate in terms of outcome, this would be inequitable, and this norm would push us to share some of our good fortune with that individual because 'it is only fair'. If, however, we perceive that the individual brought on his or her misfortune, then, according to this norm, we need not help, because the inputs have not been the same. Thus, equity considerations are likely to motivate us to help an individual who has 'lost everything' in a fire, but not an individual who 'lost everything' in a gambling game.

In a series of studies carried out with university students in the United Kingdom (Zagefka et al., 2011), participants were presented with accounts of disasters that were either natural in origin – such as the Japanese tsunami of 2004 – or caused by people– such as the humanitarian crisis resulting from ethnic strife in Darfur, Sudan. Participants were found to be more reluctant to make donations to victims of people-caused disasters compared to victims of natural disasters. The former were seen as more blameworthy and less proactive in helping themselves. These perceptions came about in the absence of any actual information about the victims' blameworthiness. Nonetheless, this fits with the norm of equity: victims of natural disasters, being viewed as blameless, are seen to deserve more help than victims of humanitarian disasters, who are seen to share some of the blame for their plight.

How much of an effect do these norms have? The research literature generally indicates that people's behaviour often departs from what is prescribed normatively, and that a large number of situational variables influence whether normative behaviour will be forthcoming (Krebs & Miller, 1985). Moreover, while social norms may appear useful for describing behaviour after the fact, they sometimes may mislead or confuse us when we must make a decision about what to do. They offer only vague direction (e.g., 'We should help those less fortunate than ourselves') and they can conflict with one another (e.g., we are taught to 'keep our nose out of other people's affairs', but also to help others when they need help). In order for these norms to trigger prosocial behaviour, it is argued that one must be aware of and feel personally responsible for the adverse consequences that would follow from not acting, and one must recognize one's own ability to provide relief (Steg & de Groot, 2010).

> **KEY POINT:** While norms at times can play an important role in prosocial behaviour, that role is often limited because they generally offer only vague direction and sometimes are in conflict with one another.

Social learning As was discussed above, prosocial behaviour is observed early in life. However, according to the social learning perspective (recall Chapter 6), such behaviour is learned in the same way that any other behaviour is learned – through reinforcement, self-attributions and modelling. Parental discipline is assumed to play a key role.

Reinforcement Prosocial behaviour is acquired and maintained, at least to some degree, through consequences deriving from the behaviour. Social learning theorists have pointed out that a rigid view of reinforcement suggesting that humans are like automatons responding on the basis of external reinforcement is misleading; in part, people regulate their actions by *self*-produced consequences (Bandura, 1974). That is, they anticipate a desired consequence for behaving in a certain way. Thus, a child may learn to share toys or to help a sibling because he or she anticipates reward in the form of parental praise – if praise has been given for similar behaviour the past. As children develop, self-reward (feeling good about oneself in some way) and self-punishment (e.g., feeling guilty) take on more importance in prosocial behaviour. In other words, the child is motivated to help others because he or she anticipates feeling good about having done so, or, if no action is taken, feeling guilty for not having helped.

Self-attributions Self-reward involves making attributions about ourselves, that is, identifying a cause for our own behaviour. Children are more likely to behave well if they attribute their behaviour to internal causes (their own personal morality) rather than to external causes such as threats of punishment or hopes of reward (Walters & Grusec, 1977). For example, a child who is tempted to steal and who attributes feelings of anxiety to moral self-judgement is more likely to avoid antisocial behaviour than a child who interprets the anxiety as fear of the teacher coming back into the room. And a child who attributes his or her acts of charity to a personal concern with the welfare of others may be more likely to repeat such prosocial behaviour than the child who interprets such generosity as the result of pressure from a parent.

Modelling Several studies have demonstrated that children's responses to charitable models are durable and can be generalized. For example, in one early study, witnessing an adult donate to a charity positively influenced the children's own donations 10 days later, even when the donations were elicited in a different setting by a different experimenter (Midlarsky & Bryan, 1972). Other research has shown that direct suggestions and instructions about the importance of prosocial behaviour can have both an immediate

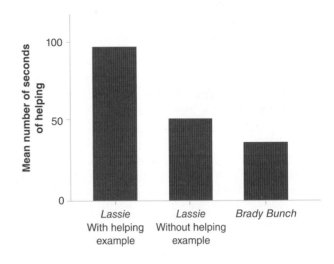

Figure 9.3 Duration of children's helping behaviour after watching television

Source: Sprafkin, Liebert & Poulos (1975)

influence on children's prosocial behaviour and produce enduring long-term results (Eisenberg & Mussen, 1997). However, when models say one thing and do another, as many parents sometimes do, the typical outcome is that the child imitates the inconsistency of the model: The child's actions are influenced by the model's actions and the child's words are influenced by the model's words (Radke-Yarrow & Zahn-Waxler, 1984).

What about prosocial models on television? A number of relevant studies were carried out in the 1970s. In a classic study (Sprafkin, Liebert & Poulos, 1975), 30 first-grade children watched one of three half-hour programmes popular with children at that time: an episode from the *Brady Bunch* (a situation comedy), an episode from *Lassie* in which a boy risks his life by hanging over the edge of a mining shaft to rescue a trapped puppy, and an episode from *Lassie* that did not portray helping behaviour. The children then played a game in which each child at some point had to choose between continuing to play the game (which led to prizes for points accumulated) or helping a puppy in distress. Those who had seen the *Lassie* programme with the helping scene helped significantly more than did the children from the other two groups (Figure 9.3).

Other studies have produced similar findings. A meta-analysis of some 34 studies of the effects of prosocial television involving more than 5000 children provided further evidence that such programming does indeed positively influence children's prosocial behaviour (Mares & Woodard, 2005).

Of course, many children, adolescents and young adults pass more time these days playing video games than in front of a television set. Can prosocial video games lead to increases in prosocial behaviour? Gentile et al. (2009) reported results of research carried out in three countries: correlational research conducted with middle school students in Singapore indicated that those who played more prosocial video games also acted more prosocially; longitudinal research involving Japanese children and adolescents found that prosocial gameplay predicted subsequent increases in prosocial behaviour; and laboratory experiments with university undergraduates in the United States found that playing prosocial video games fostered prosocial behaviour. Research in Germany (Greitemeyer, Osswald & Brauer, 2010) suggests that such games lead to increased empathy for others in distress: University students played either a prosocial video game, *Lemmings*, or a neutral game, *Tetris*. They were then asked to read a vignette in which a famous individual had suffered an unfortunate experience, following which they filled out measures of empathy and *schadenfreude* (pleasure at another's misfortune) with regard to that individual. It was found that the prosocial game, but not the neutral game, led to increased empathy for the victim, along with decreased *schadenfreude*.

On the other hand, research with both children and young adults shows that playing *violent* video games leads to *decreases* in prosocial behaviour, along with increases in aggressive thoughts, feelings and actions (Anderson & Bushman, 2001; Anderson, Shibuya et al., 2010).

The role of parents The parent–child relationship plays a unique role in childhood socialization (Maccoby, 1992). Parents play several roles in terms of promoting the development of empathy and prosocial behaviour in children. First of all, they are the major source of reinforcement that shapes their children's behaviour. Of course, they also serve as models, and if they do not behave in a prosocial manner, it is much less likely that their children will grow to do so. Parents also guide children in the development of a personal set of values and attitudes that motivate them to provide assistance to others in certain situations. In addition, one of the most important determinants of the development of prosocial behaviour is the emotional atmosphere of the home and the degree to which the parent displays a nurturing, affectionate attitude towards the child (Eisenberg, 2002). In a meta-analysis of five studies involving a total of 150 families with young children, children's prosocial behaviours were found to be positively related to how much the parents responded to the child's own emotional distress in a tolerant and non-punishing manner (Roberts, 1999). By being guided and controlled through affectionate means, the child is likely to develop an internalized code of conduct involving a positive regard for others and sensitivity to other people's needs and feelings. In this regard, Soenens et al. (2007) carried out a study with tenth- and twelfth-grade students in Belgium. Students first rated their mothers in terms of such affectionate guidance and support and then completed measures of empathy and perspective-taking (i.e., the ability to 'put oneself in another person's shoes'). Scores on these measures were positively correlated with ratings of maternal support (as rated by both mothers and the students).

Does the prosocial disposition that grows through childhood and adolescence endure? Apparently so. A longitudinal study examined the relationship between prosocial behaviour in childhood (as documented by reports and observations of prosocial behaviour in preschool) with prosocial characteristics when the participants were in their twenties (as reported by the participants themselves and by their friends). It was found that prosocial dispositions in adulthood were related both to demonstrations of empathy/sympathy and to prosocial behaviour in early childhood (Eisenberg, Guthrie et al., 2002).

KEY POINT: Much prosocial behaviour acquired through social learning is a result of direct reinforcement, modelling and self-attributions. Parents play a key role in shaping such behaviour in their children.

Cultural roots

Of course, there is a strong cultural influence upon how children are reared (Kärtner, Keller & Chaudhary, 2010). Very significant differences in prosocial behaviour are found from culture to culture (Henrich et al., 2005). For example, Levine et al. (2001) measured helping behaviour in large cities in 23 different countries: Would a pedestrian provide help when a researcher 'accidentally' and apparently without noticing dropped his pen on the sidewalk, or when a researcher wearing a large leg brace and walking with a pronounced limp 'accidentally' dropped a pile of magazines, or when an apparently blind researcher, wearing dark glasses and walking with a white cane, was about to cross a street? There were very pronounced differences from country to country. For example, the average percentage of people offering help in Rio de Janeiro across those three situations was 93%, and people in cities such as Calcutta and Vienna were also found to be among the most helpful. On the other hand, the helping rate was only 45% in New York City and 40% in Kuala Lumpur. The authors of that study found no relationship between the rate of helping and the degree to which a country is individualistic or collectivist.

Knafo, Schwartz & Levine (2009) reanalysed the Levine et al. (2001) data and found a strong negative correlation ($r = -.43$) between embeddedness and the offer of help to strangers. That is, the greater the embeddedness, the less the likelihood that help would be offered to strangers. Embeddedness refers to the extent to which a society emphasizes the shared goals of the family or in-group as a key social unit, with little concern for others outside that unit. This of course makes sense, for the more that people are taught to focus their attention on their own family and in-groups, while ignoring the plight of others, the less likely they will be to offer help to strangers.

KEY POINT: Cultural factors influence prosocial behaviour. This reflects both childrearing practices as well as a general cultural orientation regarding the limits of one's responsibility, whether to the family unit or in-group, or to people at large.

The neighbourhood Some research has shown that willingness to help strangers varies even between neighbourhoods within a given city. For example, Holland, Silva & Mace (2012) used the lost letter technique to compare helping rates in 20 different London, UK, neighbourhoods that varied considerably in average income levels. The lost letter technique involves dropping on the sidewalk a sealed and stamped letter addressed to the researcher. The dependent variable is simply how many letters are put in the mailbox and therefore returned to the researcher. In that study, 87% of the letters dropped in the richest neighbourhoods were returned compared to only 37% in the poorest neighbourhoods. The authors were unable to specify what accounts for these differences, although they point out that income is correlated with many other factors. For example, education level in low-income neighbourhoods may be lower on average than in high-income areas.

Is a person from the countryside generally more inclined than a person from the city to help others? Some studies indicate that people in large cities are less likely to mail a lost letter that was stamped and addressed (Korte & Kerr, 1975), or to assist someone who reached them by dialing a wrong number (Milgram, 1970). And in a review of 67 pertinent empirical studies, Steblay (1987) found that people in rural areas did indeed show significantly more willingness than did city-dwellers to help others in distress.

Is it that city people are somehow different from rural people, or is it the difference in the situation that leads to the findings noted above? Milgram (1970) argued that it is the latter – that people in the city, surrounded as they are by so many other people, out of necessity have to limit their social interactions. The urban person cannot afford to help every person who is in need and must be selective to survive in the urban culture. And of course city-dwellers encounter many more strangers than do residents of small towns.

Moreover, specific aspects of the social climate of cities, such as a concern with crime, would inhibit helping (House & Wolf, 1978). In addition, while rural people are considerably affected by rare emergencies such as fires, the city-dweller becomes blasé about them, assuming that authorities will deal with the situation. When the city-dweller encounters an emergency, he or she is more likely to be in the company of other witnesses or to assume that there are other witnesses, and, as we shall see, this could lead to less helping behaviour (Latané & Darley, 1969). Moreover, since the city person must compete for service (taxis, etc.), norms develop (privacy, aloofness, etc.) to protect people from constant interaction with others. It has been suggested that the intensity of urban stimuli (noise, pollution) may also decrease prosocial behaviour. People living in cities have been found to be less trusting than people living in towns (Merrens, 1973; Milgram, 1970). Fischer (1976) suggests another reason why the city environment may discourage prosocial behaviour: a large city usually provides a great diversity of people; thus, there is a greater chance that the stranger in need of assistance will appear to be a member of an unfamiliar group, producing fear in the onlooker and resulting in less willingness for the onlooker to 'get involved'.

An Australian study (Amato, 1983) also found that small population size was a strong and consistent predictor of helping. However, the results also suggested that urban lack of helpfulness was primarily limited to individuals suddenly faced with the need to provide help to a stranger, a situation that may be perceived as being more potentially dangerous by the city-dweller than by the rural inhabitant. Likewise, in a study of 36 US cities, Levine, Martinez, Brase & Soreson (1994) found a negative correlation between population size and many forms of helping behaviour. Yet, the propensity to help a blind person cross the street was almost unaffected by population density. Presumably, city-dwellers may learn to be wary of requests for help, but remain willing to assist those they assume to pose no threat.

Religion How does religion influence prosocial behaviour? After all, Christianity, Judaism, Islam, Hinduism and Buddhism all promote helping others to some degree, and all view selflessness as a virtue. Yet there are differences from religion to religion in the way that helping is seen as an obligation (Jha, Yadav & Kumari, 1997; Kanekar, 2001).

The 2007 report of the Centre for Global Prosperity concludes that religious people are generally more charitable than non-religious people, regardless of demographic variables such as income or social class, and this applies not only to donations to their congregations but to secular donations and informal giving as well (Myers, 2012). A Gallup World Poll carried out in more than 140 countries between 2006 and 2008 (Figure 9.4) reported that 'highly religious' people (who indicated that religion is important in their everyday life and that they had attended a religious service in the past week) were more likely to report having made recent charitable donations.

However, research also suggests that, while individuals who believe that helping others is their religious duty are more likely to volunteer help (e.g., Sappington & Baker, 1995), simply being 'religious' in itself does not correlate well with helping behaviour or compassion for those in need (Batson & Gray, 1981). Perhaps *how* one is religious is more important. For example, some religious people (sometimes referred to as being intrinsically oriented) view religion as an end in itself; that is, they see their whole duty in life as ultimately to serve their God. Others (who are extrinsically oriented) view being religious as a means to an end, a way of achieving other goals, such as gaining power and influence in their community. And there are other religious people who view their religion as an open-ended quest for meaning and understanding and ultimate values (Batson & Ventis, 1982).

Research (e.g., Batson et al., 1989; Chau et al., 1990) has shown that it is intrinsic – but not extrinsic – religious orientation that is linked to prosocial behaviour. But why do intrinsically religious people act more prosocially? Batson & Gray (1981) examined the willingness of religious people to help a woman either in a situation where she expressed a desire for such help or in a situation where she expressly indicated that she did *not* want help. Intrinsically oriented religious people offered help whether or not the woman in need desired it, while individuals who viewed their religiousness as a quest for meaning offered help only when it was wanted. Intrinsically oriented religious people then may see providing help to others either as a duty or as a way of helping themselves achieve grace or a reward in an afterlife.

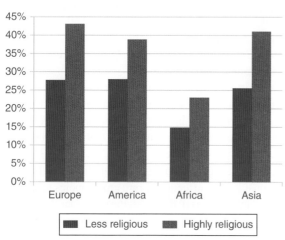

Figure 9.4 Percentages of respondents to the Gallup World Poll who indicated that they had donated money to a charity in the past month.

Source: Pelham & Crabtree (2008) © 2008 Gallup, Inc. All rights reserved. The content is used with permission; however, Gallup retains all rights of republication

Personal roots

Personality Naturally, social psychologists have attempted to find personality correlates of prosocial behaviour. However, there is little evidence of a generalized 'altruistic' personality, and some researchers (e.g.,

Gergen, Gergen & Meter, 1972) have argued that it is futile to seek general personality predictors of helping behaviour. Nonetheless, people who help have been found to be more socially oriented and more 'internal' in terms of locus of control – the extent to which people believe that the events in their lives are caused by their own actions (internal), or by luck, higher forces, or other powerful people (external) – than those who do not help (Ubbink & Sadava, 1974). It has also been found that people with a high need for approval are more generous in their donations, particularly when the donations are made publicly (Deutsch & Lamberti, 1986). This makes intuitive sense; by being publicly charitable, they can court the approval and admiration of others.

> **KEY POINT:** While it is likely that personality factors such as locus of control and need for approval influence the propensity for prosocial behaviour, evidence is lacking in support of a generalized 'altruistic personality'.

Gender   As we have seen, empathy plays an important role in prosocial behaviour. While it is not clear whether gender differences in empathy exist, females often describe themselves as being more empathic than do males, but this may reflect more the image that is expected of them than some predisposition (Eisenberg & Lennon, 1983). Moreover, one might speculate that since traditional child-rearing has allowed and encouraged females to be sensitive to distress, they may recognize their own anxiety or distress and therefore are more touched by the plight of others in a similar situation. Males, who have been discouraged from such sensitivity, may try to deny or minimize personal anxiety and therefore downplay its effects when they witness others undergoing it.

Males and females are also subject to somewhat different norms regarding helping (Eagly & Crowley, 1986; Eagly, 1987). Men are expected both to rescue others who are in difficulty and to demonstrate courtesy and protectiveness towards subordinates, both in close relationships and among strangers. Women, on the other hand, are expected to help through caring and nurturing other people, especially those within a close relationship. Women in the past have been discouraged from associating with strangers; this most likely also discourages women from giving help to strangers.

It must also be noted that social psychological research has typically focused on short-term interactions with strangers and has therefore largely ignored the very behaviours prescribed for the traditional female gender role – behaviours manifested primarily in close, long-term relationships (Eagly & Crowley, 1986). The 'masculine' roles and the skills that are acquired in them may better prepare men to assist others in distress. That being said, there is no clear evidence of gender differences in the willingness to help others. For example, no gender differences were found in the Levine et al. (2001) 23-country study described earlier.

> **KEY POINT:** Clear evidence of gender differences in prosocial behaviour is lacking, and it may be that it is social roles, and not gender itself, that are most important.

PROSOCIAL REACTIONS TO HELP AND HARM

How do we react when people do something good for us, or when they harm us? Prosocial behaviour involves responding with gratitude to the former and with forgiveness to the latter.

Gratitude

Gratitude involves more than just recognizing that one has been the beneficiary of someone's assistance. It also reflects a motivation to respond in a prosocial manner to the benefactor. (Think back to the norm of reciprocity). There is evidence that suggests that a disposition to be grateful for others' good deeds is a stable personality trait and that it is associated with prosocial motivation and behaviour on one's own part

(McCullough, Emmons & Tsang, 2002). That is, people who tend to act prosocially are also usually grateful when treated prosocially.

Gratitude is reinforcing in that it encourages benefactors to act prosocially again in the future (McCullough et al., 2001). But what is the reinforcement? It is more than just a matter of the helper feeling pleased at having been thanked; what is important is that gratitude leaves the helper feeling more socially valued by others (Grant & Gino, 2010). That is, when someone thanks you for your assistance, this signals that you have some value to the other person.

Gratitude plays an important role in our everyday relationships. In a series of studies of people in romantic relationships, Gordon et al. (2012) found that gratitude contributes to the maintenance of intimate bonds. When people feel more appreciated by their partners as a result of gratitude, they express more appreciation of their partners, are more responsive to the partner's needs, and become more committed to the relationship.

> **KEY POINT:** Gratitude is reflected in prosocial behaviour that serves to reinforce the actions of people who have been helpful, and also contributes to emotional bonding in relationships.

Forgiveness

Forgiveness is the one form of prosocial response that can only occur when one has been the recipient of malice or harm, rather than kindness or help. Various cultural and religious traditions tell us that forgiveness is a 'good thing', a noble virtue. English poet Alexander Pope penned the famous phrase, 'to err is human; to forgive, divine'. Mahatma Gandhi taught that forgiveness is an attribute of the strong and that it is only the weak who can never forgive.

Forgiveness is crucial to the functioning of groups, for it allows people to recover from strains in inter-personal interactions and to continue in cooperative relationships (Van Vugt & Van Lange, 2006). Research suggests that those who are disposed to forgive transgressors are more emotionally stable than those who are not, and factors such as empathy, religious inclination and situational attributions appear to foster forgiveness (McCullough, 2001).

Research also shows a number of clear benefits of forgiveness: It aids in psychological healing and improves physical and mental health – indeed, a forgiving personality has been found to be a significant predictor of longevity (Toussaint, Owen & Cheadle, 2012). This is perhaps because of a reduction in unresolved anger, which has also been found to typify the 'type-A' coronary-prone personality (see Chapter 15). It also restores a victim's sense of empowerment, helps bring about reconciliation between offender and victims, and promotes hope that other conflicts can be resolved.

Recall from Chapter 4 how Nelson Mandela, freed from years of incarceration and made president of South Africa, did not seek vengeance for the crimes of the apartheid regime, but instead insisted on forgiveness. He told his nation, that 'Men of peace must not think about retribution or recriminations. Courageous people do not fear forgiving, for the sake of peace.' A Truth and Reconciliation Commission was established in which victims were invited to testify, and those who committed crimes and violations of human rights under that regime were encouraged to come forward and take public responsibility for their actions, after which they were generally forgiven or at least granted a legal amnesty. They were encouraged to seek reconciliation with their victims. Similar bodies have been set up in Argentina (National Commission for Forced Disappearances), Canada (Indian Residential Schools Truth and Reconciliation Commission), Rwanda and others. Germany has acknowledged the crimes of the Nazi era and has paid reparations to the families of victims, and today Germany and Israel have close relations. Forgiveness under defined conditions thus sometimes becomes a matter of national policy.

But what does it actually mean to forgive someone? There is no clear consensus among researchers. In general, forgiveness is defined as a positive or prosocial change in your orientation toward someone who offended you. Some see it as 'letting go of past hurt and bitterness' (Berecz, 2001, p. 255). Others define it in terms of motivations: less retaliation, more seeking reconciliation (McCullough, Worthington & Rachal, 1997). Exline and Baumeister (2000) view forgiveness as debt cancellation; just as we speak about forgiveness of a debt in literal terms, this is an extension to more metaphorical 'debts'.

Research has shown that forgiveness can be either induced or discouraged by the situation. Certainly, the severity of the transgression will make a difference; we are more likely to forgive someone for forgetting our birthday than for sexual infidelity, or for violence against us. As well, the perpetrator would usually be expected to acknowledge responsibility for the transgression and to ask for forgiveness; indeed, accepting responsibility is very important (Wenzel, Woodyatt & Hendrick, 2012). In a romantic relationship, we are more likely to forgive someone to whom we are deeply committed than someone who is a casual partner (Fincham, Jackson & Beach, 2005). Of course, perpetrators may also have reasons to seek forgiveness for their own actions – for example, in order to repair their own sense of self-worth, to restore justice, to repair the relationship, or for impression management.

Some people are more likely to forgive than are others (Fehr, Gelfand & Nag, 2010): People with a tendency to forgive tend to score lower on measures of neuroticism (anxiety) and anger, and higher on measures of agreeableness and empathy. There is also a substantial correlation between forgiveness as a trait and involvement with organized religions, but this should be viewed with caution. Almost all such studies are with Christian samples in the USA, and so cannot be generalized to other religions and other cultures. Further, such findings typically reflect a willingness to agree that, in hypothetical situations, one would forgive, and this is not the same as actual forgiveness. Indeed, religiosity is more strongly related to attitudes about forgiveness than about actual forgiving; (see Chapter 4 regarding the gulf between attitudes and behaviour).

Finally, the brain and the culture both play a role in forgiveness. As noted earlier, neuroscientists have identified a set of cognitive mechanisms, linked to brain mechanisms, that regulate our behaviour and our attitudes towards our goals. When a serious transgression occurs, people may have a difficult time in forgiving that person, even though they would actually like to forgive and remain in the relationship. A set of studies reveal that people with a high level of executive functioning are more able and willing to forgive (Pronk et al., 2010). The key mechanism here is rumination, thinking obsessively about what has happened. In order for forgiveness to happen, the person must be able to let go of negative thoughts. Executive functioning enables the person to focus on the positive and to eliminate the negative.

Research has compared forgiveness in collectivist and individualistic societies (Ho & Fung, 2011; Hook et al., 2009). In individualistic societies, forgiveness is generally seen in interpersonal terms relating to personal goals (e.g. preserving a relationship or partnership), and forgiveness is seen primarily as a change from negative to positive emotions towards the transgressor. In collectivist societies, people are more concerned with social well-being and interpersonal harmony, and forgiveness is seen more as a conscious decision rather than an emotional reaction. However, a comparison of how people in Western Europe and Latin America conceive of forgiveness reveals more similarities than dissimilarities, with people in both samples agreeing, for instance, that forgiveness can be extended even to people who have died. Perhaps we can talk of a 'forgiveness schema' which extends across cultures, in which the perceived intent of the person to cause harm, the severity of harm produced by the act and the apology by the perpetrator all can influence forgiveness (Azar & Mullet, 2001).

[**KEY POINT:** Forgiveness is a prosocial behaviour that can bring many benefits both to the forgiving individual and to the forgiven.]

TAKING PROSOCIAL ACTION: VOLUNTEERISM

December 5 of each year has been designated as International Volunteer Day by the United Nations, a day of recognition of the volunteer work of millions of people around the world. Volunteerism is defined as freely chosen helping activities that extend over time and are often performed through organizations on behalf of needy people or important causes (Snyder & Omoto, 2008; Mannino, Snyder & Omoto, 2011). It is an important form of prosocial behaviour and is alive and well. For example, in 2010, 47% of the Canadian population aged 15 and over volunteered their time – 2.1 billion hours in total – to assist charitable non-profit organizations (Statistics Canada, 2011). Thousands of people in the UK volunteered their services to assist with the 2012 Olympic Games. Every April, on a day designated as Global Youth Service Day, millions of young people in 120 countries around the world celebrate their participation in the volunteer youth movement.

Why do people volunteer to spend long hours working for some cause that usually provides no direct benefit to themselves or even to people whom they know? Of course, there is usually a strong motivation to help others – for example, find a cure for a disease or help underprivileged children. Ellemers & Boezeman (2010) studied members of Dutch volunteer organizations (e.g., an organization devoted to raising funds for diabetes research) and identified two factors that predict volunteer satisfaction and willingness to continue working with the organization: (1) pride in being involved with the organization based on a strong belief that the volunteer work is of importance; and (2) a feeling of being respected as a result of task support provided by the volunteer organization to the individual. This is in line with Omato and Snyder's (1995) **volunteer process model**. According to this model: (1) dispositional factors such as personal motives, social needs and current circumstances influence the initial decision to volunteer; and (2) whether an individual continues to serve as a volunteer or volunteers again depends on whether one develops a positive evaluation of the volunteer setting and the experience. When Omato and Snyder tested this model by studying volunteers helping AIDS victims, they found that satisfaction with and positive feelings about the organization were directly related to the length of time that the volunteers served, and it was self-centred motives rather than prosocial motives that correlated with length of service. On the other hand, a later study of AIDS volunteers (Penner & Finkelstein, 1998) found that the only motive associated with length of service was a prosocial one, a desire to help; similar findings emerged from the study of AIDS volunteers in Spain (Fuertes & Jiménez, 2000). Thus, these studies point both to self-rewards (pride, respect) and prosocial goals as important motivators.

We saw that there is evidence for a religious influence on prosocial behaviour in general, but does this extend to volunteering? Myers (2012) cites evidence from a poll carried out in the United States indicating that 34% of religiously active respondents also indicated that they were active in volunteer organizations, compared to only 15% of non-religious people. He further cites a Gallup World Poll that reports that highly religious people (who state that religion is important in their lives and who had attended a religious service in the past week) are also more likely to report having been involved in a volunteer organization (Figure 9.5).

Again, while we could question whether some or all of the motivation is self-serving in terms of feeling better about oneself in living up to religious ideals, whether the involvement is extrinsically or intrinsically motivated generally matters little to the people being helped.

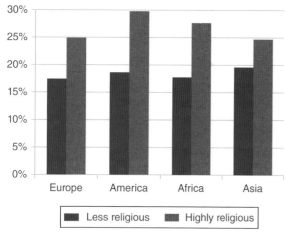

Figure 9.5 Percentages of respondents to the Gallup World Poll who indicated that they had volunteered time to an organization in the past month

KEY POINT: Volunteers are motivated both by prosocial goals and by self-rewards such as pride and respect. Actively religious people have been found to be more active than other people in terms of volunteering.

THE BYSTANDER EFFECT

Of all the forms of prosocial behaviour, intervention is the most dramatic. Intervention is the act of an individual voluntarily giving assistance in an emergency, often at personal risk. For example, in 2013, when a clothing factory in Bangladesh collapsed killing many hundreds of workers, ordinary civilians rushed in to help authorities with the dangerous work of trying to rescue those trapped in the wreckage.

Emergencies share several elements that make them somewhat unique (Darley & Latané, 1970):

1. They typically involve threat or harm to a victim. The person who intervenes can at best prevent further damage or possibly return the situation to the way it was before the emergency occurred.
2. The possible costs, including legal action or even death or injury, are often high.
3. They are rare, so few people have experience in dealing with them.
4. They are unpredictable, occurring suddenly and without warning, and immediate action is required. Thus people usually cannot plan for emergencies or consult with others about how to respond.
5. They vary widely in their form and in terms of what response is appropriate, making it impossible to prepare people by teaching them a short list of rules on dealing with emergencies.

And while we may celebrate those who risk their own well-being to intervene for the good of others, all around the world there are disturbing instances where passers-by take no action, not even simply telephoning emergency responders, when they observe another human being in extreme distress. Are they heartless? Are they emotionally stunted? Do they fear getting involved? Consider these stories:

Figure 9.6 Collapsed clothing factory, Bangladesh
Source: © Anwar Shamim/Demotix/Corbis

- January 2012, Rotorua, New Zealand: A 24-year-old woman is attacked by a female stranger while in a shop on one of the busiest streets of the city. She is dragged from the shop by the angry woman, who accuses her of 'sleeping with her man' and is viciously beaten in front of at least 20 people who are waiting for a bus. No one does anything to help, not even call the police.
- October 2011, Foshan, China: a two-year-old child is struck by a minivan while crossing the street. Surveillance camera footage shows that the driver stops, looks out at the child, and drives on, running over her again with the back wheel. She is then hit by another vehicle. At least a dozen people, including a woman walking nearby with a child, ignore her. Finally, a woman garbage collector pulls her from the street and calls for an ambulance. She dies in hospital eight days later.

This phenomenon of not offering help in an emergency is known as the bystander effect: when people witness an emergency, the probability of any particular person helping decreases with the number of other people present. Interest into bystander inaction was catalysed by a sensational murder in March of 1964 in New York City (Box 9.1), and because of it, social psychologists began the study of bystander inaction in the laboratory.

BOX 9.1   THE MURDER OF KITTY GENOVESE

According to the way the story is typically told in psychology textbooks, a man attacked Catherine ('Kitty') Genovese with a knife as she was walking home at night in New York City. Her screams brought her neighbours to their windows, and the sudden glow of their bedroom lights and the sounds of their voices temporarily drove the attacker away. However, when he saw that no one had responded to her cries for help, he attacked her again. She managed to get away from her attacker a second time, but again, despite her shouts for help, no one responded. The man returned to attack her yet again – this time killing her. Half an hour had elapsed between the first attack and the killing. As the typical account continues, even though at least 38 people watched from the windows of their apartments and houses as he attacked and repeatedly stabbed the young woman, no one even telephoned the police. When asked later why they had not called the police, most of the witnesses said they had been afraid to get involved, but seemed unable to furnish a basis for this fear. Various social scientists proposed a variety of ad hoc explanations for their inaction (Latané & Darley, 1970): alienation and apathy resulting from 'depersonalization'; confusion of fantasy and reality brought about by a steady diet of television violence; even the vicarious gratification of sadistic impulses.

However, the witnesses were not apathetic. They did not turn away and ignore what was going on in the street below: 'Caught, fascinated, distressed, unwilling to act but unable to turn away, their behaviour was neither helpful nor heroic; but it was not indifferent or apathetic ...' (Darley & Latané, 1970). It has been reported that even 15 years after the Genovese murder, a number of these witnesses reported that they still felt responsible for her death (Walster, Walster & Berscheid, 1978).

Manning, Levine & Collins (2007) argue that this tragic story, distorted as it is, has become a social psychological parable, a parable that unfortunately suggests that groups and crowds are associated with negative behaviours. (See the discussion of crowds in Chapter 11.) Yet, this story strays significantly from the details of the actual event, as described by the available trial evidence. There were rather fewer than 38 eyewitnesses, and none of them were in a position to watch the attack for the full 30 minutes because Ms Genovese and her attacker were visible to them for only a few minutes. None of them actually saw the stabbing. In addition, calls were made to the police, although in those days this was a more difficult task because there was no 911 line.

However, the point remains: at times, despite the presence of many people, victims are ignored. And sometimes the helper can become the victim. In New York City in April 2010, Hugo Alfredo Tale-Yax intervened when he saw a woman being threatened by men with a knife, and he was then stabbed and left bleeding on the sidewalk for over an hour. By the time an ambulance arrived, he was dead. Subsequent analysis of surveillance video revealed that at least 25 people had walked by. One used his cellular telephone to take a picture and another person rolled his body over, revealing the bleeding wounds. No one did anything to help.

What accounts for the bystander effect, the inhibitory effect of the presence of others? If people are not apathetic, if their behaviour is not callous, what is it that holds them back from helping a person in distress? It is usually not for lack of concern: Several studies have found that when people witness another person being harmed, they show marked signs of emotional upheaval such as gasping, running aimlessly around, having sweating or trembling hands and experiencing an increase in physiological responses associated with anxiety (Walster, Walster & Berscheid, 1978).

The failure of people to help others is sometimes taken to suggest an alarming breakdown in the power of social norms to regulate social behaviour. However, as we saw earlier, while there are social norms involved in prosocial behaviour, their role is limited. In an emergency, norms are not very useful guides, partly because they are too vague about what to do and partly because they are conflicting (Darley & Latané, 1970). Suppose that you are walking down Lovers' Lane on a wintry night and you see a couple sitting motionless in a parked car with the engine running. One norm tells you to try to help others who need your help: if they are dying of carbon monoxide poisoning, you should do something. Yet another norm teaches you to respect people's privacy. After all, they are in Lovers' Lane: if they are just making out or communing with nature, you should not butt in. The bystander effect does not seem to reflect a breakdown of social norms – only the inadequacy of such norms in specific situations.

The inhibiting presence of others

Many emergency situations are ambiguous and it is often surprisingly difficult to decide whether an emergency is actually occurring. If new neighbours in your apartment building seem to be having a squabble and you hear screams through the walls, do you intervene directly or call the police? It is difficult to decide whether someone is in trouble in such a situation and usually people (especially men) do not want to look foolish by intervening if there is no emergency (Siem & Spence, 1986).

In the face of ambiguity, how do we judge whether something is an emergency? If we are alone, we may intervene despite the ambiguity because, if help is needed, there is no one else available to provide it. On the other hand, if we are among others, we may rely on their reactions as a guide to whether intervention is required. However, if each person is uncertain about what is going on and looking to the reactions of others as a guide, everyone may hesitate to react and, through their lack of reaction, people may reassure each other that no reaction is needed, that there is not an emergency. Of course, this will be less likely to occur among acquaintances, since they are likely to discuss the circumstances before coming to judgement.

The influence of the presence of others was evident in one of the earliest experimental studies of the bystander effect (Latané & Rodin, 1969). Participants who thought they were participating in a market research study heard a woman, who had just left them to go into an adjoining room, ostensibly climb up on a chair to get something and then fall down and cry for help. Participants could go directly into her office (the two rooms were separated only by a curtain), could go out into the hallway to seek help or could call to her to find out what they could do to help. In one condition, each participant was alone, and 70% of them intervened. When there were two participants, strangers to each other, the intervention rate fell to 40%. When one of the two participants was a passive confederate, only 7% of participants intervened, suggesting that the participant considered the passivity of the confederate as an indication that there was no emergency.

In order to separate the effects of ambiguity from effects simply due to the presence of others, Latané and Darley (1968) conducted an experiment in which participants were requested to fill out a questionnaire. They worked either alone, with two 'passive' confederates or with two other naive participants. Several minutes after the person in charge left the room, smoke was introduced into the room via a small wall vent. By the end of four minutes, the room was filled with acrid smoke to the extent that it obscured vision. Only 75% of the participants in the alone condition left the room to report the smoke to someone. When three naive participants worked together, in only 38% of the groups did someone intervene. The others toughed it out, working on their questionnaires despite the cloud of smoke! And when a participant was in the company of two passive confederates, only one of 10 participants reported the smoke. Those who remained coughed, rubbed their eyes and even opened the window but did not leave the room.

These results support the interpretation that, independent of ambiguity, the passivity of others contributes to the ambiguity of the situation. In other words, we use the reactions of others to help decide whether there is an emergency and what action is appropriate.

However, might it be that the hesitancy to act is due to a fear of looking foolish by doing 'the wrong thing?' To address that question, Ross and Braband (1973) carried out a study that used either an apparently blind or a sighted confederate in each of two emergency conditions. In the 'internal' emergency condition, the participant and the blind confederate worked in a room that filled with odourless smoke;

283

since the 'blind' man could not see the smoke, he could not serve as a source of information about what reaction would be appropriate. In the 'external' condition, the emergency was signalled by a scream from outside the room; in this case, the blind man would be aware of the emergency and his reaction could serve as a guide to appropriate behaviour. In fact, the participants in the internal condition responded to the emergency just as quickly as did participants in a control condition who worked alone. It could be argued, however, that these participants were not concerned about acting inappropriately since the blind man could not see them. Yet this explanation is not tenable, for in the external condition in which the blind man's reaction could be used as a guide, the participants were inhibited to the same extent as when they were with a sighted confederate. This experiment lends strong support to the notion that the inaction of non-responding others inhibits a person's response because their inaction helps to define the situation as a non-emergency, and thus makes intervention seem inappropriate.

One more classic study merits discussion (Latané & Darley, 1970): What happens when a person knows that others are aware of an emergency situation, but cannot see whether or not they are reacting? In this experiment, the participant sat alone but was led to believe that he or she was participating in a discussion, carried on over an intercom system, of adjustment problems among university students. Participants had been told that the experimenter would not be listening to the initial discussion and that a mechanical switching device would automatically give each participant in turn about two minutes to talk while all other microphones were switched off. In fact, unknown to the real participant, the other 'participants' were simply recordings. In any case, the participant heard the first person report having an epileptic condition, which was particularly problematic when under stress. Later in the conversation, when it was that person's turn again, he became increasingly loud and incoherent and in a stuttering voice asked for help. Amid choking sounds, he stammered that he was going to die, called again for help and then was silent. When the 'seizure' occurred, it appeared to the real participant that all participants could hear the seizure but that only the microphone of the seizure victim was switched on.

The major independent variable in this study was the apparent size of the group of participants, while the dependent variable was the time it took the participant to go and report the emergency to the experimenter. The belief that other people were listening had a strong effect on both the rate and the speed of participants' intervention (see Table 9.1). The larger the group, the less likely it was that the participant would respond, and the longer it took those who did.

Table 9.1 Effect of group size on likelihood and speed of response

Group size	Percentage responding by end of seizure	Percentage responding within six minutes	Average time in seconds
2 (participant & victim)	85	100	52
3 (participant, victim & one other)	62	85	93
6 (participant, victim & four others)	31	62	166

Source: Latiné & Darley (1970)

Thus, it appears that a person is less likely to offer help if others are present or presumed to be present even in the absence of ambiguity produced by the passivity of others. Participants in this study who did not report the emergency did not show signs of apathy or indifference. In fact, when the experimenter finally entered the room to end the study, they appeared to be considerably emotionally upset and concerned for the victim. They found themselves in a conflict situation, worried about the victim and about the guilt they would feel if he was not helped, yet concerned about looking foolish, overreacting or ruining the experiment by leaving the room. When others seemed to be present (even in this case, via intercom), the participant had less responsibility in the matter. In other words, a diffusion of responsibility occurred: 'Other people are listening and so it is not up to me alone to take action; someone has probably already done something about it.'

However, other research has clearly demonstrated that it is not just how many people are present in an emergency that determines whether help will be given, but how those people relate to each other. Increasing the number of bystanders produces more inhibition of helping in some instances – for example when the bystanders are strangers to one another – and yet promotes helping in other instances – such as when the bystanders are all friends (Levine & Crowther, 2008).

> **KEY POINT:** The presence of other people often inhibits bystander intervention, both as a result of ambiguity in the situation that occurs when no one else is responding with help, and diffusion of responsibility, since each individual is less personally responsible than he or she would be if alone with the victim.

Rewards and costs of bystander helping

Not all research has found a bystander effect. A classic field experiment carried out in New York – a city with no outstanding reputation for altruism – found no bystander effect when a confederate of the experimenter collapsed on a moving subway car. The experiment also examined the effects of certain characteristics of a victim (whether he appeared drunk or ill, whether he was black or white) on the amount of help given. It was expected that an apparently 'drunk' confederate (who carried a bottle in a paper bag and who smelled of alcohol) would elicit less aid than an ill one (carrying a cane) since it was assumed people might anticipate the drunk becoming disgusting, embarrassing or violent. The most surprising outcome was that there was a generally high rate of help given in all conditions. In fact, the 'ill' person received help on 95% of the trials, and even the 'drunk' was helped on half the trials. Moreover on 60% of those occasions when help was given, more than one person helped. Since the ill person was not thought to be ill by choice, while the drunk was clearly in need of help as a result of his own actions, people may have been less willing to help the drunk because he 'deserved' his suffering (Piliavin, Rodin & Piliavin, 1969). (Note, however, that in this study, there was no apparent risk of becoming a victim oneself.)

Piliavin and colleagues developed the arousal: cost–reward model of helping (Piliavin et al., 1981; Dovidio, Piliavin et al., 1991), which assumes that we experience unpleasant arousal when we encounter someone in distress and that we are naturally motivated to reduce that arousal. We can choose among helping or fleeing (both of which will reduce anxiety) or doing nothing. The model predicts the following: (1) as arousal increases, the probability of one or more observers taking action of some kind increases; (2) for a given level of arousal, as cost for helping increases, the probability of helping directly decreases, and the probability of giving help indirectly or of leaving increases; and (3) as cost for not helping increases for a given level of arousal, the probability of helping increases. Thus, the potential helper faces an avoidance-avoidance conflict. The potential costs for both not helping (guilt, possible public criticism) and for helping (possible embarrassment, possible bungling of the effort, involvement with police if victim dies) are high.

The analysis of rewards and costs will be influenced by a number of factors:

1. *The number of other people present* – If we are alone, we may face more guilt if we do nothing, but also more potential harm if we intervene.
2. *The reactions of other bystanders* – The more they appear to be upset, the more aroused we become; the more passive they are, the less our arousal.
3. *The characteristics of the person in distress* – We may be more upset to see a child in distress than we would an adult, and we may be more upset to see someone collapse because of a heart attack than we would if he or she were simply drunk.
4. *The degree of closeness in the relationship between the person in distress and ourselves* – We are likely to experience more arousal when a friend or relative is in distress than when the victim is a stranger. Similarly, we may experience more arousal when the victim is from our group or subgroup than when the victim is from some other group.

Table 9.2 Number of people helping or refusing to help

	Bad knee		Bad heart	
	Help	No help	Help	No help
Easy escape	2	12	5	7
Difficult escape	9	7	14	2

Source: Staub (1974)

Why was so much inaction observed in the Darley and Latané laboratory research but not in the Piliavin field experiment? Why was there less diffusion of responsibility on the subway? There were important differences between the two sets of studies. First, the victim was in full view in the Piliavin study; thus the need for help was less ambiguous. Second, the natural groups were considerably larger than the laboratory groups. Thus, any diffusion of responsibility that might have occurred may have been more than offset by the increased probability of someone actually helping in a large group. In other words, the larger number of bystanders in the subway study may have increased the probability of getting a prosocial response from someone (Piliavin & Piliavin, 1972). Moreover, it was much more difficult for the participants in the Piliavin study to leave the area – it was several minutes until the next stop – than it was for participants in the Latané and Darley studies to avoid the victim.

Ease of escape bears more examination. Whether a person helps another may depend on how easily he or she can avoid the helping situation. In an experiment designed to examine this hypothesis (Staub, 1974), a confederate collapsed, holding either his chest or his knees (to vary the apparent seriousness of his condition), either in the pathway of a pedestrian (difficult escape) or across the street (easy escape). As can be seen in Table 9.2, many more people helped when escape from the situation was difficult than when it was easy. In fact, the person with the apparent heart attack was almost always approached in the difficult escape condition. (This suggests as well that the perceived degree of need for help also influences helping.) Interestingly, a fat confederate who clutched his chest was more likely to receive aid than was a non-obese confederate; this may be because participants were more likely to think that an obese person was having a heart attack.

KEY POINT: When faced with emergency situations, there are both rewards and costs associated either with helping or not helping. How readily one can get away from the emergency also can play an important role in many situations.

Dangerous intervention

Previous research was carried out primarily in situations where there was no personal danger to an intervener. More recent research (Fischer et al., 2006) has focused on the effects of danger in an emergency situation. What would you expect to happen when a bystander is faced with serious personal risk? It might seem likely that this would reduce the likelihood of intervention. However, these authors predicted that bystander effect would *not* be observed in situations of real danger, first of all because there is likely to be much less ambiguity, and secondly because the costs of not helping are higher. In their experiment, participants were led to believe that they were watching, via a television screen, a live interaction between a man and woman in another room, although in reality they were only watching a prepared video. As the participant watched, either alone or with a passive confederate, the man began to make sexual advances toward the woman, and when she protested, he shoved her across the room and then blocked her way as she tried to leave the room, and all the while she was shouting out for help. In the high-danger condition, the man was 'strong built, thug-like', whereas in the low-danger condition, he was 'a skinny man of small stature'. As predicted, when the danger associated with intervening was low, the bystander effect was observed and more help was given when the participant was alone, but when the potential danger was high, the participant was equally likely to help the victim whether alone or with the other person.

Other researchers have produced similar results: In a meta-analysis of bystander intervention research conducted between 1960 and 2010, Fischer et al. (2011) concluded that the bystander effect is reduced or absent in situations that are clearly dangerous – such as an assault in which an intervener might face some personal risk – compared to those that are non-dangerous, such as a medical emergency. Indeed, they found that intervention in dangerous situations usually *increases* as the number of bystanders increases. They interpreted these findings through the arousal: cost–reward model discussed above. Because dangerous emergency situations are less ambiguous, they are recognized more quickly and cause increased physiological arousal in the bystander because of the distress of the victim. Moreover, if there is actual risk involved if the bystander intervenes, this leads to even more arousal. The arousal can be reduced by providing help to the victim. In addition, if the bystander is not alone when there is personal danger, the other bystanders represent potential physical support should the intervener be attacked. Indeed, some situations might be so dangerous that one person alone is not enough to reasonaly intervene, and the coordination of several people's efforts is required to provide the necessary help.

[**KEY POINT:** Research shows that the bystander effect is absent or reduced in dangerous situations, and intervention actually increases with the number of bystanders present.]

HEROISM

- In June 1944, 27-year-old Pilot Officer Andrew Charles Mynarski of Winnipeg was flying an RCAF Lancaster bomber in an attack on German positions when the airplane was hit and set afire. The crew parachuted to safety except for the tail-gunner, Pat Brophy, who was trapped in his tiny rear compartment by a damaged door, and Mynarski, who instead of saving himself, lurched back through the flames to attempt to free Brophy. Covered with blazing hydraulic fluid, he worked barehanded to try to get the door open. Finally, driven back by the fire, he stood and saluted Brophy before bailing out. He had no chance of survival: his parachute was on fire. He was posthumously awarded the Victoria Cross on the evidence of the tail-gunner who, ironically, survived the crash of the bomb-laden airplane when he was thrown free upon impact (Franklin, 1977).

Stories of such heroic action are a step up from the kind of emergency interventions that we have discussed so far. Such heroism is greatly admired in all societies. But what is the stuff of heroism? While it is difficult to define because it is based on perception and attribution, heroism is usually considered to involve intervention in the face of extraordinary personal risk. Franco, Blau & Zimbardo (2011) divide heroism into three general categories: (1) martial, involving extreme physical risk in the line of duty – including police, firefighters and paramedics and military personnel; (2) civil, also involving extreme risks, but not associated with an individual's normal activities or training; and (3) social, which usually does not involve physical danger, but does run the risk of serious consequences in terms of financial losses, social ostracism, or possible long-term health problems.

The Carnegie Hero Fund Commission was founded in the United States in 1904 to award medals for 'outstanding acts of selfless heroism performed in the United States and Canada' by civilians who risk their

Figure 9.7 UK Carnegie Hero Medal

lives to an extraordinary degree while saving or attempting to save the lives of others. The award cannot be given to parents or emergency personnel, to anyone for whom there is an obvious personal incentive to carry out the rescue. As of 2012, the organization has recognized close to 9539 people; almost all of whom acted alone. The Carnegie Hero Fund Trust in Britain was established in 1908 and has since recognized some 6000 heroes (see Figure 9.7). Nine similar Carnegie Funds have been set up on the European continent.

Heroism and gender Given the literature on bystander intervention, we should not be at all surprised that heroes generally act alone. But most of these designated heroes are men; almost all the Carnegie Hero Medals' recipients have been male. How can we explain this? Of course, men may be more inclined than women to intervene in emergencies given that they are generally larger and stronger. Yet, that is not the major reason. It is not that women are not given to heroism, but rather that the concept of heroism has been defined (by men) in stereotypically male terms (Polster, 1992). For example, since the Carnegie Hero Commission excludes from consideration people who rescue family members except if the rescuer dies or is severely injured, women (who according to the traditional female gender role should be particularly concerned with the welfare of their children) are not considered heroic if they risk their lives in saving their own children! As society becomes more egalitarian and as male and female gender roles become less differentiated and less rigid, the tendency to view women as less heroic will no doubt change.

The Scarlet Pimpernel: Rescuing strangers from tyranny *The Scarlet Pimpernel* is the name of a book and a fictional character created by Baroness Orczy and set during the French Revolution. The book concerns a British nobleman who could have remained in the comfort and safety of his own homeland, but instead risked his life to smuggle French aristocrats out of Paris and out of the country, saving them from the certain fate of the guillotine.

This fictional tale of heroism was replayed for real again and again during the days of the Third Reich when an estimated 50,000 to 500,000 individuals repeatedly risked their lives and often those of their families to help Jews escape from the Nazis (Oliner & Oliner, 1992). Many of them perished as a result of their efforts; the vast majority have never been identified, and only a very few became famous for their courage.

It was during the trial of Adolph Eichmann in 1960 that interest began to focus on such rescue efforts. Eichmann was charged with crimes against the Jewish people and against humanity arising from his zealous implementation of the Nazi genocidal policy. During the trial, reference was made to Christians who had rescued Jews from concentration camps. Subsequently, social psychologists and others began to track down as many of these rescuers as possible to determine whether there were any common factors in their personalities or family backgrounds.

Yad Vashem is an Israeli organization dedicated to commemorating and documenting the Holocaust. It has undertaken a worldwide project to honour those who risked their lives to save Jews during the Holocaust, and to date has named 24,811 people as the Righteous among the Nations. Most of these have been ordinary people whose exploits remain relatively unknown. Others, perhaps because of their social status, are more widely celebrated. Raoul Wallenberg, a wealthy Swedish diplomat, is credited with saving nearly 100,000 Hungarian Jews by issuing them false Swedish documents (Henry, 1985/1986). German industrialist Oskar Schindler (whose story was chronicled in the film *Schindler's List*) saved more than 1200 Jews after persuading Nazi authorities that they were needed to run his factories, which were vital to the war effort. And then there was Albert Goering, the younger brother of senior Nazi leader Hermann Goering. He apparently despised the Nazis and risked his life to save hundreds of Jews, sometimes obtaining exit permits to extract them from concentration camps, and at other times smuggling them across borders to safety; he is currently under consideration for *Yad Vashem*'s Righteous among the Nations Award. (And recall from Chapter 6 the discussion of disobedient Nazis.)

What is it that leads people to risk their lives for strangers? Social psychologists have sought to answer this question. An early study located 27 rescuers and 42 rescued people (London, 1970), but then had to be terminated because of a lack of funds. In a subsequent and much more extensive study, the Altruistic Personality Project, 406 rescuers whose actions had been documented by *Yad Vashem*, as well as 150 rescued survivors, were interviewed (Oliner & Oliner, 1992). The rescuers were compared with 126 non-rescuers – people who had been in situations in which they *could* have become rescuers but had chosen not to do so. The researchers wanted to know what had motivated their heroic acts, but could not identify any one common motive. Some had deliberately chosen to rescue Jews. Others became involved without thinking about it, or even by mistake: one person reluctantly agreed to let his secretary's Jewish husband stay in his office over the weekend to hide from the Nazis. Once involved, however, he was drawn in more deeply and developed considerable compassion for those he helped, eventually rescuing about 200 people at great personal risk and cost. Some of the rescuers were very religious, while others were atheist and some were even anti-Semitic!

There were at least three different motivations involved (Oliner & Oliner, 1992): (1) Some rescuers were motivated by empathy for the suffering of the Jews. In some cases this empathy was based primarily on emotional attachment to specific victims, which led to a sense of responsibility and caring; (2) Others were motivated by the social norms of groups to which they were strongly attached such as church congregations (e.g., 'Do good unto others'); and (3) for a small minority it was dedication to a moral code based on justice and social responsibility that motivated them to risk their lives. Morally motivated rescuers rescued people whether they liked the victims or disliked them and whether or not they had known the victims previously (Fogelman & Weiner, 1985; Fogelman, 1994).

Characteristics of the rescuers What personal characteristics did the rescuers share? In his early study, London (1970), while cautioning about the possible non-representativeness of their upbringing, noted that many rescuers reported that their parents had stressed – both in words and by behaviour – the importance of helping others and the importance of accepting that differences in group, race or culture do not make a person superior or inferior. The typical rescuer in London's study was raised in a close family relationship in which parents acted in a loving manner towards their children and communicated caring values. The parents set high standards with respect to caring for other people, and children were encouraged to develop qualities such as dependability, self-reliance and responsibility – qualities associated with caring. Parental discipline experienced by rescuers rarely involved physical punishment, and there was almost never any gratuitous aggression. Discipline involved a great deal of reasoning, and efforts were made to explain to the children why some behaviours are inappropriate and what their consequences are for other people (see, for comparison, the discussion of child rearing and aggression in Chapter 11).

Incidentally, not all rescuers had such strong moral values. For example, Oskar Schindler apparently acted at first out of self-interest, to obtain cheap factory labour (Rappoport & Kren, 1993), but became more prosocially motivated as time went on.

These studies of rescuers recall to mind the earlier discussion of the effects of models and upbringing on prosocial behaviour in general. Identification with a prosocially oriented parent, a parent who both teaches and practises the importance of caring for and helping others, appears to be of outstanding importance in inculcating selflessness in individuals. Most of those brave people who rescued Jews from the Nazis had been taught by their parents to believe in justice that applies to all, and not merely to members of one's own group or class or nation (Reykowski, 2002). Similarly, strong identification with a moralistic parent was also found to be an important characteristic of 'fully committed' American civil rights workers in the late 1950s and early 1960s. These activists had been taught by their parents not only to believe in certain principles but to act upon them (Rosenhan, 1970).

KEY POINT: Heroism is in the eye of the beholder, but those who act in ways that result in their being considered as heroes often were raised to believe in principles of justice and in the importance of helping others.

Encouraging bystander intervention

How might we encourage individuals to render assistance to others in emergencies – even in the presence of non-reacting others? In other words, how can we prepare people to deal with the bystander effect? There are several courses of action that are likely to prove beneficial:

Encouraging emergency intervention in the schools We teach children to obey and to conform. We are much more careful to teach them what they are *not* to do than to teach them how to act prosocially. Children in emergencies are often torn between the wish to help and the desire to act appropriately; the absence of permission to intervene is often as powerful an inhibitor as is a direct prohibition (Staub, 1974). This influence may endure into adulthood. It may be beneficial to teach children that it is all right to break rules when others appear to need help.

Encouraging emergency intervention in the home By regularly assigning children the responsibility of caring for or helping others (often automatic in large families), we may foster the development of a feeling of personal responsibility for the welfare of others. We might teach children that intervention behaviour is desirable; we could even have children rehearse such behaviour and then reward them for it. However, emergencies are difficult to plan for and the problem of defining a situation as an emergency is bound to arise.

Promoting leadership roles Most bystanders in an emergency are very willing to help once someone takes control of the situation and begins to issue orders: 'You, go call an ambulance!'; 'You, keep the crowd back!'; 'You, get some blankets!' One problem in these situations is that often no one will assume leadership.

Laboratory research (Baumeister et al., 1988) has found that participants designated as group leaders in an experimental situation (for example, a discussion group) are likely to continue to act as leaders in an unexpected emergency even when intervention involves violating the experimental instructions. While subordinate group members generally fail to intervene, diffusion of responsibility seems not to occur to individuals already placed in a role of responsibility and leadership.

Not everyone can be a leader, but by giving children practice at being leaders in different situations and by teaching them the importance of leadership in an emergency, we encourage them to consider it appropriate to 'take charge' and accept responsibility in such crises.

Increasing public awareness of the bystander effect Disseminating information about the effects of group size on bystander intervention may help increase intervention as people realize why they are hesitating to help. Most people do not know about the bystander effect and that it occurs frequently. It seems to contradict the proper etiquette of 'responsible behaviour'. There is much educational work to be done towards reducing the effect. You, the reader, now are familiar with it. The next time a relevant situation presents itself will you stand by, or will you remember this effect and take action?

THE BENEFICIARY

Before leaving the subject of prosocial behaviour, there is one more important aspect to discuss, the beneficiary. We have been focused on the helpers and on the situations where help is needed. Not only are some people more likely to provide help than others, but some people in need are more likely than others to *be* helped. Are 'good Samaritans' (Figure 9.8) willing to help everyone equally? Think about it for a moment. You might be willing to assist a well-dressed senior citizen change a tyre but not if he or she appears to be drunk. The degree to which a person is dependent on another also generally plays an important part in determining how much help will be given. Several studies have found a positive relationship between the potential beneficiary's level of dependence and the amount of help given, but this relationship may apply only when the cost for the helper is low (Krebs, 1970; Gruder, 1974).

When the cost of helping is great, we may resent the burden that the requester's needs place upon us (Berkowitz, 1973). The greater the person's dependency upon us, the greater is both our felt obligation to help and our 'reactance', that is, our desire to re-establish our independence and freedom (Brehm, 1966). We may gladly help a person in and out of a wheelchair unless we feel that we are obliged to do so. Perhaps a felt obligation robs us of the good feelings we would normally experience if we voluntarily helped the person.

Attributions may play an important role in determining who will or will not be helped. As noted earlier, if another person's need appears to be controllable – that is, the person seems responsible for the plight he or she is in – we may be less willing to help than if we perceive the person's need as owing to circumstances beyond control (Weiner, 1980).

Other factors that affect the probability of receiving help are physical attractiveness (West & Brown, 1975); degree of apparent need (Staub & Baer, 1974); and perceived similarity between the requester and the helper (Sole, Marton & Hornstein, 1975). Thus, you are more likely to help someone who is physically attractive to you, who is in great need of help and who is part of your in-group (race, social status).

Before leaving the question of who gets helped, consider an important perspective that has been largely ignored in social psychology: the relative powerlessness of some groups in our society. Think back to the Kitty Genovese murder. Cherry (1995) argues that rather than understanding such attacks simply in individual behavioural terms, social psychologists must turn their attention to the long history of non-intervention when violence is visited upon powerless groups. Women have long been special targets for violence, as have children, the aged and members of racial minorities. Would someone have intervened had Genovese been a well-dressed man?

And what about racism? In a US study, Kunstman & Plant (2008) created a laboratory situation in which each participant saw and heard through closed-circuit television another same-sex participant – who was ostensibly the participant's partner for an upcoming task, but actually a confederate – in an emergency situation: the confederate, who was in another room, leaned back in a chair and then fell over backwards. In a 'low emergency' condition, the confederate expressed pain but was able to get up again, although apparently hurt and still shaking because of pain. In the 'high emergency' condition, the confederate tried to get up, but slumped back to the floor and remained there, moaning in apparent pain. What was of interest to the researchers was how the race of the participant and that of the apparent victim would affect how much time it took for the participant to offer assistance. In the first study, all the participants were white and the confederate

Figure 9.8 'The Good Samaritan' (after Delacroix) by Vincent Van Gogh

Source: © Todd Gipstein/Corbis

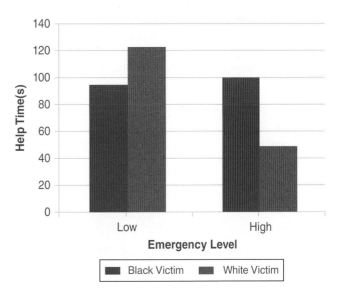

Figure 9.9 Helping speed as a function of victim race and emergency condition

Source: Kunstman & Plant (2008)

was either white or black. While there was no significant difference in the speed of assistance given to black and white victims in the low emergency condition (Figure 9.9), the response to white victims was much faster when the emergency was high than when it was low, but this was not the case for black victims.

In a second study, both black and white participants were involved, and again race played a significant role. There was no significant difference in how long it took for black participants to come to the assistance of the victim regardless of the victim's race. However, white participants took much longer to respond to black victims. The researchers reported that the white participants evaluated the seriousness of the high emergency as being less severe, and themselves as less responsible for providing assistance, when the victim was black than when the victim was white. This interpretation allowed the white participants to justify their tardiness and defuse any risk of appearing prejudiced.

Reactions of the beneficiary

Recall the discussion of gratitude. It is important to understand that not all helping behaviour leads to gratitude, and this is because the act of providing help not only clearly distinguishes between helper and beneficiary, but also defines a power hierarchy (Worchel, 1984). If the person who is helped cannot repay the help in any way, then – at least in Western society – accepting help places the person in a position of inferiority. There may even be a loss of face (Fisher, 1983). If you are desperately short of money and someone gives you money but refuses to accept repayment, you may feel some discomfort – unless, of course, the benefactor is in a role that might justify munificence (e.g., your father or mother). In general, the greater the threat to self-esteem, the more likely it is that the recipient will feel negatively towards the helper (Fisher, Nadler & Whitcher-Alagna, 1982; Fisher, Nadler & DePaulo, 1983).

Experimental studies with participants from the United States, Sweden and Japan have found that participants give more positive evaluations to donors who oblige them to repay the donation than to those who ask nothing in return (Gergen et al., 1975). Such a reaction might be more expected when the donor is a close friend than when he or she is a stranger (Nadler and Fisher, 1984), for it is more important to avoid feelings of inferiority with a friend. In fact, most people needlessly worry about 'losing face'. There is actually little evidence to support the claim that donors perceive beneficiaries as inferior (Rosen et al., 1986).

Negative evaluation of donors who do not want reciprocation may occur at the international level as well. Developing nations may feel less gratitude for aid from developed nations if they have no way of reciprocating, for such aid underlines the beneficiary's position of dependency (Andreas, 1969). Indeed, help from a developed nation to an undeveloped one – or for that matter from a dominant, high-status group within a society to a low-status group – can actually serve to encourage continuing dependency and preserve an existing system of social inequality (Halabi & Nadler, 2010).

> **KEY POINT:** Not everyone is equally likely to receive help when needed, and potential helpers are influenced by a number of factors in making a decision whether to help. Moreover, beneficiaries who are unable to reciprocate sometimes react negatively to the help that they need.

BOX 9.2 SUSTAINABILITY

HELPING SAVE THE WORLD

Prosocial behaviour is not only directed towards specific individuals or groups; it is also manifested through unselfish efforts to aid and protect the environment, upon which we all ultimately depend. In order for our species to survive in the world threatened by resource depletion, global warming, extinction of species, and air, water and soil pollution, this kind of prosocial behaviour is vitally needed. Social psychologists are particularly interested in finding ways to persuade people to change their behaviours in an environmentally friendly direction (Alcock, 2006). Consider the following two examples of such applied research.

Cialdini et al. (2006) argue that persuasive appeals aimed at encouraging the public to protect the environment can be either effective or ineffective depending on whether the messages focus on what people should do or what they should not do. In a study carried out in Petrified Forest National Park in Arizona, researchers examined the effects of messages urging visitors not to steal petrified wood. Some of the messages involved *descriptive* norms (referring to other people's behaviour) that were either; (1) weakly (that is, positively) worded: 'The vast majority of past visitors have left the petrified wood in the park, preserving the natural state of the Petrified Forest'; or (2) strongly (that is, negatively) worded: 'Many past visitors have removed the petrified wood from the park, changing the state of the Petrified Forest.' Other messages carried *injunctive* norms, telling people what to do or not do. Again they were either: (1) weak (positive), 'Please leave petrified wood in the park'; or (2), strong (negative), 'Please don't remove the petrified wood from the park.' As can be seen in Figure 9.10, the study found that the strongly worded injunctive message led to the least theft, while the strongly worded descriptive message was associated with the most!

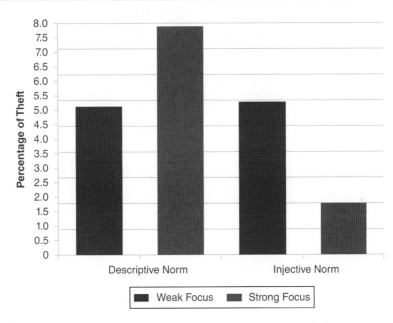

Figure 9.10 Percentage of theft as a function of norm and strength of normative focus

Source: Cialdini et al. (2006)

Another example: most large hotel chains now invite their guests to reuse their towels from day to day as a way of helping save the environment by reducing the amount of water and detergent needed for towel laundry. Goldstein et al. (2008) conducted two field experiments to determine how best to motivate guests to comply. In the first, they monitored guests who stayed for at least two nights in 190 rooms in a mid-priced hotel belonging to a national chain in the southwest United States. Rooms were randomly assigned to one of two conditions. The signs in one condition ('standard environmental message') simply invited guests to help save the environment by reusing their towels. In the second condition ('descriptive norm message') guests were invited to 'join your fellow guests in helping to save the environment'. It was further stated that 'Almost 75% of guests who are asked to participate … do so by using their towels more than once'. A significantly higher towel reuse rate (44.1%) was found with the descriptive norm condition than in the environmental protection condition (35.1%), indicating that the hotel guests were more motivated to reuse towels when informed that most others have chosen to do so (Figure 9.11).

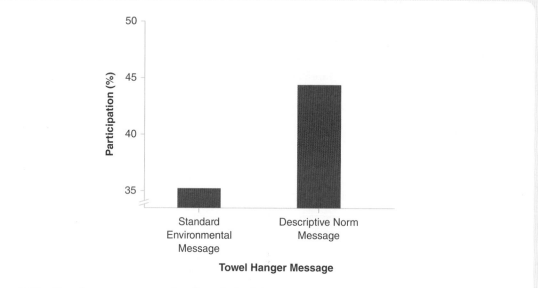

Figure 9.11 Towel reuse rates as a function of sign in room

Source: Goldstein et al. (2008)

A FINAL NOTE

Prosocial behaviour is an important contributor to a well-functioning society, whether it be provided through direct help to individuals, through charity work, or through helping to save the environment (Box 9.2). However, as we have seen in this chapter, there are a number of important factors that determine who is helped and when help is given, and, just as importantly, when help is *not* forthcoming.

SUMMARY

1. Psychologists prefer the term 'prosocial behaviour' to 'altruism' because it does not involve judgements about internal self-reward.

2. There is some evidence in support of a genetic basis for prosocial behaviour, mediated by empathy, but the issue of the role of heredity and evolution has yet to be fully resolved.

3. Empathy plays a significant role in many forms of prosocial behaviour.

4. Prosocial behaviour may be influenced by one's emotional state and may involve attempts to repair self-image.

5. Norms of reciprocity, social responsibility and equity can influence prosocial behaviour, but their role is usually a minor one.

6. Social learning theory emphasizes the acquisition of prosocial motivation and behaviour through processes of reinforcement, self-attribution, modelling and parental discipline.

7. Prosocial behaviour is influenced by a number of factors including culture, religion, and setting (urban or rural).

8. Personality factors and gender are also involved in determining when and how assistance is provided to others.

9. Gratitude and forgiveness are two forms of prosocial behaviour that do not involve directly extending assistance to others. Gratitude leads the helper to feel socially valued. Forgiveness is important for group functioning because it allows people to recover from interpersonal hurts and continue in cooperative relationships.

10. Volunteerism involves freely chosen helping activities that extend over time and that are often performed through organizations on behalf of needy people or important causes.

11. Emergency situations involve threat or harm to the victim, are rare and unpredictable, vary widely in form and appropriate response and may involve risk or costs to the benefactor.

12. The bystander effect occurs when each bystander feels that he or she is less responsible for the victim's welfare because there are other people present who could take action ('diffusion of responsibility') and because the inaction of others makes the situation more ambiguous to each bystander with regard to whether help is needed and what response is appropriate.

13. The arousal: cost–reward model explains that bystander behaviour is also influenced by the anticipated rewards and costs of helping or not helping.

14. People who repeatedly act heroically to assist others have typically been reared in close-knit, loving families where discipline was not physical and where parents taught the importance of caring for others.

15. Bystander intervention can be encouraged by increasing public awareness of the bystander effect, by teaching children to 'break the rules' of social convention when necessary, by training children to take responsibility for helping others and by encouraging leadership roles.

16. People are less likely to receive help if they are perceived as being overly dependent or if their need for help appears to be controllable or brought on by their own actions.

17. Recipients of help who cannot reciprocate sometimes react with resentment.

POINTS TO PONDER

- Recall the identifiable victim effect. Charities often use pictures of individual sufferers to persuade people to offer assistance. Is there a risk that this practice may encourage a focus on a few 'celebrity victims' while inadvertently leading to less concern for the plights of masses of unnamed sufferers?
- Are there limits to our social and moral responsibility? If while visiting a foreign country you are confronted by children begging on the streets, is it heartless to pass them by? And if you do help, and dozens of other needy children rush to your side, where should your help end?
- What role does heroism play in society? Is it simply the recognition of people who have acted in a brave and selfless fashion, or is there more to it than that? Do we actually need heroes to inspire us and to make us feel good about our society or group?
- Does the maxim 'it is better to give than to receive', while encouraging charity, indirectly reflect a negative attitude towards those who are in need?

FURTHER READING

Batson, C.D. (2011). *Altruism in humans*. New York: Oxford University Press.
An in-depth exploration of the empathy–altruism hypothesis and the data that support it.

Fischer, P., Greitemeyer, T., Pollozek, F. & Frey, D. (2006). The unresponsive bystander: are bystanders more responsive in dangerous emergencies? *European*

Journal of Social Psychology, 36, 267–278.

This research explores effects of danger on bystander intervention.

Franko, Z.E., Blau, K. & Zimbardo, P.G. (2011). Heroism: A conceptual analysis and differentiation between heroic action and altruism. *Review of General Psychology, 15*, 99–113.

A treatment of various kinds of heroism and their relationship to altruism.

Stout, L. (2011). *Cultivating conscience*. Princeton, NJ: Princeton University Press.

A thoughtful discussion of various factors that trigger conscientiousness and lead to unselfish assistance to others.

Stürmer, S. & Snyder, M. (Eds) (2010). *The psychology of prosocial behaviour*. Chichester, UK: Blackwell.

An overview of current directions in theorizing and research with regard to prosocial behaviour.

WEBLINKS

Public apathy toward genocide: http://www.youtube.com/watch?v=E0MmAg6wo0g

In this video, psychologist Paul Slovic discusses his research into factors that contribute to public apathy with regard to genocide.

Empathy and helping behaviour in rats: http://www.youtube.com/watch?v=3jkOwYKBJEI

This video presents evidence suggesting that empathically motivated helping behaviour has a strong biological basis.

CHAPTER 10
COOPERATION AND CONFLICT

*Let everyone sweep in front of his own door, and the
whole world will be clean.*
Johann Wolfgang von Goethe

LEARNING OBJECTIVES

* To understand the nature of conflict from a social psychological perspective

* To explore social exchange theory and how it applies to relationship conflict

* To examine the use of experimental games in illuminating conflict processes

* To learn about collective dilemmas and how they can affect us all

* To gain insight into predispositional variables that influence the course of conflict

* To understand the role of threats, promises, communication and power in situations of conflict

* To consider the role of third-party interveners in conflict situations

Figure 10.1 United States destroyer intercepting Soviet freighter, November 12, 1962
Source: © Bettmann/Corbis

Figure 10.2 Raising a barn in Lansing, Ontario, in the early 20th century

Over a half century ago, in the fall of 1962, our planet came as close as it has ever been to nuclear Armageddon. Following the deployment by the United States of long-range nuclear weapons to Turkey and Italy, and in light of a failed American invasion of Cuba, the Soviet Union was intent on installing nuclear-tipped missiles in Cuba, its ally. Soviet ships carrying the missiles were on their way to Cuba when, because of the threat this posed to the United States, the Americans set up a naval blockade (Figure 10.1), threatening to sink any ship that tried to cross it. When several Soviet ships attempted to run the blockade, orders were sent to US ships to fire warning shots and then, if the ships did not turn back, to open fire – an action that might trigger a full-scale nuclear war. Neither side appeared willing to back down, and the world held its breath. Finally, with the assistance of United Nations Secretary-General U Thant, negotiations were successful in averting disaster: The Soviets agreed to turn their ships back, and the Americans promised not to attempt another invasion of Cuba and to remove their long-range missiles from Turkey and Italy. Crisis resolved, and because of that peaceful resolution, you are here to read this today.

We all experience many conflicts throughout our lives. Most of them are minor and are quickly resolved. Some are serious and are difficult to manage. And not only individuals, but groups as well, must deal with conflicts, sometimes within the group itself – for example, when one faction wants to reduce membership fees while another faction does not – and sometimes with other groups, for example when an animal rights group wants to end an annual hunt and a hunters' organization wants to preserve it. Indeed, conflict exists at every level of society. It is important to understand that the fundamentals are basically the same in all conflicts, whether it is between you and your friend or between two warring nations, although the latter situation is obviously more complex.

In this chapter, we shall begin with a discussion of interpersonal conflict – conflict between two individuals – and then extend the focus to collections of individuals where each person acts out of self-interest. Subsequently, the discussion will move to conflicts between groups, and finally we shall address methods that are helpful in the resolution of such conflicts.

Sometimes we interact as individuals, and sometimes as part of groups represented by our leaders. Some of our interactions involve cooperation in reaching shared goals: all must cooperate if we want to enjoy a dinner out together, just as mountaineers tied together as they ascend a treacherous peak must cooperate to get to the top. Others involve competition and even aggression: there is little opportunity for cooperation in a chess game or on a battlefield, although, even there, the adversaries must cooperate at least to the extent of observing some basic rules and conventions. Most interactions are 'mixed motive' in that both cooperation and competition are involved. Hockey players, ballerinas and politicians all must cooperate with others of their team in order to reach their desired goal, and yet most will also find themselves in competition with their team members in terms of who scores the most goals, or who is chosen to be prima ballerina, or who becomes a cabinet minister. And even in the midst of the Cuban Missile Crisis, the United States and the Soviet Union, while locked into a desperate conflict where neither side seemed willing to back down, ultimately chose to cooperate in order to avoid mutual destruction.

Why do people ever cooperate? Why not, if one of you has the power to do so, just take what you want? Part of the reason for cooperating is that it often brings positive benefits for the individual.

A person can hardly build a barn on one's own, and, as the saying goes, many hands make light work (Figure 10.2). But is it only because of personal benefit that we cooperate with others?

Figure 10.3 Demonstration against government austerity cuts, London, England, 2012
Source: © Mike Kemp/In Pictures/Corbis

Cooperative behaviour is a form of prosocial behaviour, but it involves more than just helping others in need. Paying taxes, participating in Neighbourhood Watch, recycling and even voting are all examples of cooperative behaviour on a large scale, and without the cooperation of many individuals, society would collapse (Henrich & Henrich, 2007). Yet, if most people cooperate in such activities, others can enjoy the benefits whether they cooperate or not, and so why bother?

Just as with prosocial behaviour in general, cooperation among humans is likely the result of gene-culture co-evolution (recall the discussion in Chapter 9), through which both genetic influences and cultural needs have favoured the development and cultural transmission of cooperative behaviours (Henrich & Henrich, 2007). Cooperation comes so naturally that cognitive neuroscience research suggests that – even in the context of the relatively simple experimental games that will be discussed later in this chapter – it is linked to activation in regions of the brain associated with reward and pleasure (Decety et al., 2004; Tabibnia & Lieberman, 2007). Thus, it appears that we may have a built-in propensity to cooperate, although this propensity is of course modified by personality factors, our own social learning history, and social norms.

The word conflict is commonly used as a synonym for warfare or aggression, but there is an important distinction to be made between conflict and aggression. While aggression refers to behaviour directed towards hurting others, conflict, at least in its social psychological sense, refers to a situation in which the interests or aspirations of two or more interdependent parties are perceived as mutually incompatible. You want to go with your partner to the movies this evening, but your partner wants to go with you to a hockey game. There is a conflict. Management wants to cut wages, while the union wants a wage increase. There is a conflict. The United Kingdom and Argentina both claim ownership of the Falklands/Malvinas. There is a conflict. In such situations, neither side can have what it wants without denying the other side what it wants. Yet, depending on the particular antagonists, the conflict may end with an amicable resolution, or it may end badly – in divorce, a labour strike or war.

However, even though some conflicts result in deadly violence, conflicts are not bad or undesirable in and of themselves. They are often the product of changing circumstances, as the needs and goals of individuals or groups evolve (Figure 10.3). For example, as children grow into adolescence, they chafe under parental rules that were acceptable in earlier years; something has to change. As a marriage matures, the partners' individual needs and goals may evolve in somewhat different directions; something has to change. When economic circumstances lead workers to demand more pay, or companies to insist on lower wages, something has to change. Peaceful and constructive resolution of conflict allows people to accommodate to changing circumstances so that children do not become estranged from parents, marriages do not end in divorce, corporations are not closed down, and workers are not deprived of their livelihoods.

Of course, sometimes the antagonists have quite inaccurate perceptions of the situation. For example, a married couple may believe that their basic problem is due to 'incompatibility', whereas the real issue may be that, because of cognitive biases or poor communication, neither really understands the other's needs. Other conflicts may involve misattributions in which the disputants wrongly blame each other for their difficulties. For example, during a period of financial restraint at universities, students may criticize professors for not providing enough individual attention, while professors in turn criticize students for demanding too much of their time. Both students and professors actually have a common cause against the agency (e.g., government) that controls the budget. Yet other conflicts may be based on false premises, as for example when a union acts upon the erroneous belief that management has much more money available than it really does and then goes out on strike.

Constructive conflict resolution occurs when two parties cooperate and find a mutually acceptable alternative to their incompatible goals. What happens if they cannot find a mutually acceptable resolution? One possible outcome is simply to end the interaction: nations sometimes break off diplomatic relations; factories sometimes are permanently closed; couples sometimes divorce. Yet, at other times, the conflict in a relationship will continue, unresolved, and this is especially likely when there is no better alternate relationship to take its place. If separation is likely to cause two marital partners even more distress than staying together, if closing the factory will cause the owners to incur greater losses than by keeping it running, or if going on strike is unbearable for workers in terms of potential lost wages, if breaking diplomatic relations will lead to unacceptable losses in terms of trade in such circumstances, it may be preferable to continue in the relationship despite the unresolved conflict. Of course, it is often tempting for one party, especially if it has more power than the other, to attempt to impose its preferred solution through the use of force – physical, economic, political or military. While this may seem to succeed in the short run, this is actually *destructive* conflict resolution. The underlying conflict continues to simmer, and because of the use of force it ultimately becomes even more difficult to resolve.

KEY POINT: Conflict occurs when two or more parties have incompatible objectives. It can be constructively resolved by finding some mutually acceptable alternative, it can be destructively (and temporarily) overcome through the use of force, or it can be ended by the two parties breaking off their relationship.

SOCIAL EXCHANGE THEORY

Many conflicts can be thought of in terms of a social exchange that takes place between two parties. The exchange may involve money and benefits in a union–management dispute; trade issues or territorial claims or environmental concerns in the case of the two nations; or affection, money, housework, baby-sitting, and emotional support in the case of a couple. The exchange may be positive on some levels (e.g., one nation needs to buy oil, the other needs the money; a couple enjoy each other's company both on the tennis court and on the dance floor), but very poor on others (e.g., there is an ongoing territorial dispute between the two nations, or an ongoing dispute about finances in the couple).

Social exchange theory (Homans, 1958; Thibaut & Kelley, 1959) concerns factors that determine which course of action – leave the relationship or stay despite the difficulties – is likely to be chosen. It furnishes a useful framework for understanding a wide range of social conflict situations, including, for example, the quality of marital relationships (Tallman, Burke & Gecas, 1998), family reactions to the alcoholism of a family member (Ruben, 1998), adolescents' romantic relationships (Laursen & Jensen-Campbell, 1999), and the provision of care for elderly family members (Keefe & Fancey, 2002). While social exchange theory has petered out as a research focus, it continues to offer insight into many conflict situations that we encounter throughout our lives.

According to this approach, all social interaction can be viewed as a kind of economic interaction in which an individual (or group) obtains certain benefits but only at certain costs. The outcome or 'profit' is the difference between benefits and costs, and an individual will presumably be unhappy with an unprofitable interaction.

Outcome = benefits − costs

Let's apply this to a domestic situation, but remember that a similar analysis can be applied to any sort of interaction, whether between individuals, groups or nations. Suppose that John and Martha have been living together for the past year. At first, they were very happy and felt very compatible. John spent a lot of time at home with Martha, and he always enjoyed her company, even though this meant that he no longer had much time to be with his friends. His outcome was positive because the benefits of being with Martha clearly outweighed the cost of giving up time with his buddies. Martha, too, enjoyed a positive outcome, for despite the costs in terms of additional time and work involved in keeping the apartment neat (in light of John being a messy person), the pleasure she felt when in John's presence far outweighed this cost. They were a happy couple.

But then, something changes. John joins a squash club, and a strain begins to develop in the relationship. Martha has no interest in squash, but now John is spending three nights a week with his buddies at the squash club. She is beginning to resent this and she feels ignored, and so the costs of being in the relationship have increased. And when she complains to John about this, he reacts negatively and accuses her of trying to control his life. Her costs go up as a result, to the point that her outcome is now a negative one. And because of what he characterizes as her 'nagging', his costs in the relationship have gone up as well. However, his benefits from the relationship still outweigh his costs, and so his outcome remains positive.

Will Martha leave the relationship because she feels so neglected? Will John become irritated to the point that his costs exceed benefits and he leaves? Social exchange theory suggests that it is not just the outcomes that will determine whether the relationship will continue or dissolve; there are two other important considerations as well. First, *satisfaction* in a relationship depends not just on the 'outcome', but also on one's expectations in the relationship. It is determined by the difference between the current outcome and what one considers that one should receive – the **comparison level** (CL). Thus, Martha might compare her current outcome with what she perceives to be the outcomes that her girlfriends are obtaining in their relationships, or with her outcomes in past relationships. Her satisfaction can be summarized thus:

Satisfaction = Outcome − Comparison Level (CL)

When she thinks about it, she recalls that her previous boyfriend had an alcohol problem; John doesn't. Her two best girlfriends are involved in abusive relationships; she is not. She views her parents' relationship as a very good one, but her father is often away from home on business. So, in light of all this, her relationship with John, while not ideal, does not seem so bad. On the other hand, John's past partners have all been very submissive and have never complained about his time spent with his friends, and his buddies' partners don't seem to mind their absences, and so when he compares his current outcome with his CL, his level of satisfaction has become negative.

But even a negative level of satisfaction is not enough on its own to lead someone to leave a relationship. This is where a second consideration comes into play. How *dependent* is the individual on this relationship to satisfy his or her needs? Is it 'the only game in town'? That depends on what alternatives are available and if they are any better. If there is a better alternative available – Thibaut & Kelley (1959) referred to this as the **comparison level for alternatives** (CLalt) – then the individual is not as dependent on the current relationship and may be strongly tempted to leave.

Dependence = Outcome − Comparison Level for Alternatives (CLalt)

Even then, were John to opt for an alternative relationship (or even living alone) he would need to consider not just the positive benefits that a new relationship or situation may provide, but also the costs associated with leaving Martha – possible economic loss; difficulties in dealing with Martha's reaction; embarrassment or shame in facing friends and relatives; and if there are children, the effects on their lives. All these potential costs factor into that comparison level for alternatives.

Dependence is equal to the difference between the current outcome and the comparison level for alternatives. So, individuals in a difficult relationship may nonetheless choose to stay together, unsatisfying though the relationship is, if there is no better alternative. But when John subsequently meets Betty at the squash club and they strike up a friendship, he comes to see that she can satisfy his emotional needs better than can Martha and so he decides to break up with Martha. The potential positive benefits of being with Betty now outweigh the costs of leaving Martha. Thus, only if a person's outcome from the relationship is greater than his or her CLalt will the relationship continue (Figure 10.4).

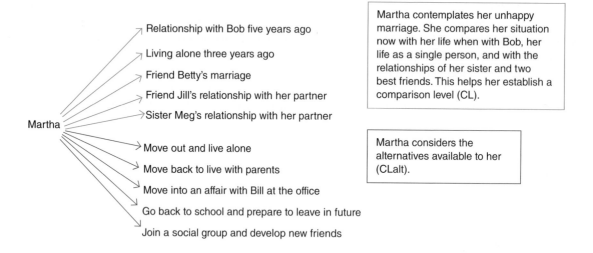

Figure 10.4   Martha's consideration of her CL and CLalt

Of course, parties involved in a social interaction often try to influence the other side's perceptions of both the benefits of staying in the relationship and the costs of leaving it. A weaker partner sometimes may try to solidify the relationship by actually increasing his or her dependence on the stronger party in order to make the costs associated with leaving the relationship higher (in terms of guilt or social conscience). For example, an unhappy but dependent spouse might contrive to be fired from work, and now if the partner 'deserts', he or she will feel greater guilt and risk even greater social disapproval. On the other hand, a stronger partner may try to dissuade the other from leaving by offering more in the exchange, such as promising more money or affection.

KEY POINT: Considering conflicts in terms of a social exchange provides important insights that help predict whether a relationship will continue or will break down.

SOCIAL CONFLICT AS A 'GAME'

In 1944, Von Neumann and Morgenstern published their classic *Theory of Games and Economic Behaviour*, which provided a new model of conflict that influenced not only political science and economic theory, but social psychology as well. In common with social exchange theory, the **game theory** model treats all conflicts as though they involve exchanges of a variety of resources such as material goods, services or affection. Each party to the conflict is viewed as 'rational', that is, capable of ordering his or her preferences for various outcomes (e.g., prefers romantic love to friendship; prefers friendship to enmity) and capable of choosing actions that minimize personal losses and maximize personal gain. Simply put, it is assumed that in social exchanges people are economic rationalists who try to get the most for themselves. In the 1960s and 1970s, many social psychologists used experimental games to study the degree to which participants did indeed act in this economically rational manner, and to examine the effects of a wide range of psychological variables on the interaction. However, it turns out that this kind of rationality does not always – or even usually – present itself in conflicts either in the laboratory or in real-life contexts.

A 'game' in its broadest sense is virtually any kind of situation in which two or more interdependent parties (or 'players') make decisions that affect one another according to rules. The outcomes of these decisions depend on the joint actions of the players. There are two major classes of games. In **zero-sum games**, one party's gain is exactly matched by the opponent's loss – gains and losses always add up to zero and no cooperation is possible (e.g., a two-handed poker game). In **non-zero-sum games**, some of the outcomes are mutually preferable to some of the others. More about such games later.

Sometimes it is difficult to assess the value of gains and losses for the parties, for money or other resources may vary in importance for different people; a dollar means much more to a pauper than it does to a millionaire. In light of this, game theory requires that utilities rather than objective measures of value be used. **Utility** refers to the importance or value that a given outcome has for an individual. It is assumed that people can rank a number of different possible outcomes with regard to utility. For example, a new smartphone probably has more utility than a glass of water – unless you are in the middle of a desert. Rational players act to obtain the greatest possible utility.

However, this fundamental assumption of rationality does not mean that purely selfish ends always motivate people, for it is the utility and not the objective value of an outcome that is involved, and sometimes the other person's satisfaction has utility for us. If an adult plays a game of cards with a child, the maximum utility for the adult may be associated not with winning, but allowing the child to win. And individuals who pride themselves as being kind and generous may attach considerable utility to finding a 'fair' division of resources rather than one that brings lopsided personal gains.

The Prisoner's Dilemma

Some conflicts are very difficult to resolve because actions that are rational on an individual level can lead to collectively irrational or mutually destructive outcomes. The prototype of this problem is the so-called **Prisoner's Dilemma Game** (PDG), which has been a workhorse in laboratory studies of conflict, and although not used nearly so often now as in the past, it is still a valuable tool (e.g., Balliet, Li & Joireman, 2011; Dijk et al., 2011). It is a special type of non-zero-sum game and it takes its name from the following dilemma:

Imagine that you are a villain, and that you and your villainous partner have carried out a daring heist and have absconded with a huge sum of money, but in the process, the robbery victim was very seriously injured. Based on a tip, but lacking solid evidence, you have both been arrested and charged with robbery and aggravated assault. You are held in separate cells, unable to communicate with one another.

The police are quite certain that you two are guilty, but lack the necessary evidence to convict you. A clever prosecutor decides to suggest a little plea-bargaining and visits you both separately. She tells each of you that she cannot hope to convict either of you without a confession, but she promises that if *you* confess, and then testify against your partner, she will reduce your charge to one of being an accessory. As a result of your testimony, your partner will be convicted and then sent to prison for fifteen years, while you will get off with only a six-month sentence for being an accessory. However, she continues, if you *both* confess, she cannot extend such generous

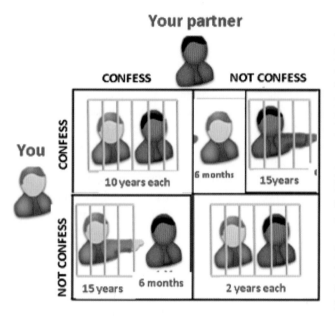

Your partner

CONFESS   NOT CONFESS

You   CONFESS

10 years each   6 months   15 years

NOT CONFESS

15 years   6 months   2 years each

Figure 10.5   Your prisoner's dilemma

leniency to you both, but will recommend leniency to the judge, and you will each go to prison for only ten years instead of fifteen. She also confides that if neither of you confess, the best she can do is to pursue convictions for vagrancy and resisting arrest, which would lead to two years in prison for each of you. She then leaves you to think about her offer, but she tells you that she is going to make the same offer to your partner.

You are left to ponder whether to remain loyal to your partner or to confess. As it turns out, each of you have some knowledge of game theory and so you each scratch out a 'payoff matrix' (Figure 10.5) on the wall of your cell.

If you do confess, you won't have to worry about being confronted by the partner for the next fifteen years! But that would be very selfish, and so you think some more about the matrix. You mull it over, and tell yourself that, 'Whatever my partner does, I am better off to confess, in terms of my own sentence. First, what happens if he confesses? My best choice is to confess, for in that case, I will get ten years, but if I do not confess, I will end up in jail for 15 years. On the other hand, what happens if he does not confess? By confessing, I'll get only six months, but if I don't confess, I will be in the pen for two years. So, confession is my best strategy whatever my partner does: ten years instead of fifteen and six months instead of two years.' But then you think yourself, 'Hold on, how I can rat out on my partner like that? On the other hand, I wonder what my partner is thinking. Even if I put my self-interest aside and choose not to confess, how can I be sure that my partner won't confess? After all, my partner by not confessing must be prepared to accept two years instead of six months, but he must also trust that I won't confess, or two years will turn into 15 years.'

Added to the problem is that you and your partner don't know each other all that well, and so there is no real basis for trust, and, more than that, you are both violent thieves. Because you cannot communicate, and because of insufficient trust, you each choose what is rationally your best outcome – you confess. You each minimize your losses in this way, whatever the other does. And as a result, the prosecutor is happy to have two confessions, and you both end up in prison for ten years. Two individually rational choices have led to a collectively irrational one, for had you both refused to confess, then both would be out of prison after only two years.

You may find this 'normative' (i.e., theoretical) outcome of mutual confession a little unsatisfying. Surely, you might ask, two people would not act collectively in such an irrational way, would they? That is a good empirical question. Research using a matrix equivalent to the dilemma (where outcomes are points or money instead of prison terms) and involving pairs of players playing the same game many times in succession has demonstrated that real players typically do not cooperate (the equivalent of not confessing in the earlier example) very much. The percentage of mutually cooperative responses is typically quite low (around 30 to 40%).

However, in real-life situations similar to the Prisoner's Dilemma, factors such as trust and suspicion and the emotional relationship between the two people are also important. Consider the Prisoner's Dilemma story again, but this time suppose that the suspects are a pair of lovers, Henry and Marie. For these two, the prospect for either one of going free after six months while the other languishes in jail for 15 years is much more unpleasant than it would be for two ordinary criminals. That is, the utility of their outcomes involves not only their own freedom but their lover's freedom as well and their ability to be together. Furthermore, each lover 'knows' (i.e., trusts) that the other feels likewise. For these players, the only two outcomes worth thinking about are of either both of them confessing or of neither confessing. Since each strongly believes that the other will react the same way, neither confesses and they go free after two years in prison. Trust promotes cooperation in all types of conflict situations because it reduces fear of exploitation and increases the importance of fairness (De Cremer, 1999).

Now, suppose the prosecutor has persuaded both Henry and Marie that the other is emotionally involved with a third person. In such a case, they would presumably modify their judgement of the other's utility structure and would also likely modify their own. Judging the other person's ordering of utilities is obviously crucial, for if one party misjudges – for example, if Marie believes that Henry has another girlfriend or assumes that Henry puts a higher value on being free than on her freedom or being with her – then the action that is chosen will reflect that misjudgement. In real-life negotiation situations of all sorts, people often try to misrepresent their real utility preferences as well as to modify the other person's utility (e.g., 'I am really very attached to this car, so unless I get a very good offer, I won't sell it' or 'This suit really makes you look very dashing').

One constraint typically placed on the behaviour observed in the Prisoner's Dilemma Game is the absence of communication. Although communication channels by themselves do not always lead to more cooperation, the opportunity to communicate in a situation as simple as the PDG would at least allow the parties a chance to inform each other of their intentions, whether the other person believes them or not. After all, the non-cooperative response in the PDG might be a defensive rather than an offensive move because of the assumption that the other will act only out of self-interest. In fact when players in a PDG have been allowed to communicate, it has usually had a positive effect on the level of cooperation. For example, in a repeated Prisoner's Dilemma (Miettinen & Suetens, 2008), cooperation was highest when the two players could communicate and had agreed beforehand to cooperate. However, as in real life, communication in the PDG is sometimes used only to try to manipulate the other party rather than to coordinate actions toward a mutually beneficial outcome.

Many everyday situations have a Prisoner's Dilemma type structure. Think for example of doping among professional athletes (Schneier, 2012). Suppose that you are a professional cyclist in training for a major race, and you are contemplating whether to take performance-enhancing drugs, despite the risk of being caught and then banned from competition (or perhaps losing all your medals sometime in the future – think of Lance Armstrong, who was stripped of seven Tour de France titles in 2012 because of evidence of doping). Let us assume that you consider the risks of being caught to be very low, and the benefits of winning as extraordinary. To make the analysis straightforward let us suppose that you have only one opponent. You are of about equal ability, and so it is hard to know just who will win the all-important race. The 'payoff matrix' is shown in Figure 10.6; the entries below the diagonal lines represent your payoffs for each combination of choices, while your opponent's payoffs are shown above the diagonals.

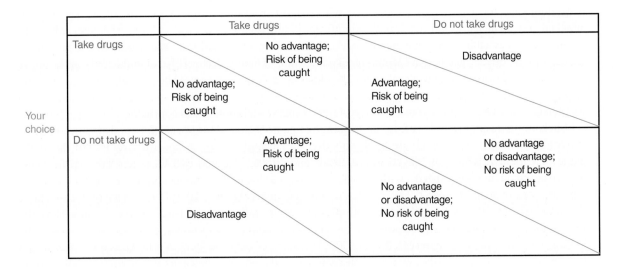

Figure 10.6 Doping as a PDG

Of course, if neither 'dopes up', neither has an advantage over the other and neither risks being identified as a doper (lower right cell). If you take the drug and your opponent does not, then you will be at an advantage that will probably allow you to win (lower half of the upper right cell in Figure 10.5), although there is now the risk of being caught. However, you suspect that your opponent may take the drug, and in that case you will be at a disadvantage if you do not, and will be almost certain to lose (lower half of lower left cell). And if you both dope up (upper left cell), any advantage from the drug for either of you will cancel out, and you will both be left only with the risk of detection – clearly an undesirable outcome. What to do? Just as the prisoners did in their dilemma, you reason that if your opponent takes the drug, you are much better off doing the same, for otherwise you will be at a considerable disadvantage. Further, if your opponent does not take the drug, it would still be best to take it because that would give you the advantage that you seek. Thus (again assuming that the likelihood of being caught is low), regardless of what your opponent does, your best strategy is to dope up. Your opponent goes through the same reasoning and comes to the same conclusion, and so the two of you end up with the worst possible outcome, with neither having an advantage and both now at some risk of detection. This outcome is clearly much less desirable than had neither doped (lower right quadrant). Again, individually rational decisions have led to a collectively irrational outcome.

> **KEY POINT:** Experimental games such as the Prisoners Dilemma have allowed researchers to study basic aspects of conflict situations, particularly in situations where individually rational choices lead to collective irrationality.

Dangerous games

Recall the opening vignette: Soviet ships challenging a blockade; Americans threatening to sink the ships; our planet teetering on the brink of nuclear catastrophe. If neither side backs down, mutual disaster will result. When the Soviet ships eventually turned back, United States Secretary of State Dean Rusk commented, 'We're eyeball to eyeball, and I think the other fellow just blinked.'

Forward to 2012: Despite warnings from many countries around the world, in particular the United States and Israel, Iran is reported to be building nuclear weapons. Israel, fearing what might happen if Iran, a hostile nation, openly opposed to Israel's very existence, possesses such weapons, implicitly threatens a preemptive strike to end the programme before these weapons can be fully developed. Iran vows to continue its nuclear programme and threatens massive retaliation with support from other Middle Eastern nations should it be attacked. Yet, an attack would cost Iran the significant destruction of its nuclear industry. If neither side backs down, war is inevitable. If Iran unilaterally backs down, its leaders would lose face, would lose credibility in terms of future threats, and perhaps would invoke the wrath of their citizens. If Israel unilaterally backs down, it is left exposed to a potential nuclear attack. The most desirable outcome would be for both to back down – for Israel to call off its threat to attack and for Iran to provide convincing assurance that it is not building nuclear weapons. You can easily draw yourself a payoff matrix that would capture this conflict.

Such conflicts are examples of, in the language of game theory, dangerous games, dangerous because if neither side backs down, both are likely to suffer catastrophic losses. A real-life example of this is the game of Chicken, which, as played in the 1950s and 1960s, involved two teenagers driving their cars towards each other at high speeds, with the one who swerves losing face and becoming the 'chicken'. In the laboratory equivalent, this can be represented as a payoff matrix (Figure 10.7; Player A's payoffs are above the diagonals, and Player B's below). If both players choose to back down (i.e., swerve), both lose a little face in the eyes of onlookers (−10 points in the matrix). If neither backs down, each suffers a catastrophic loss, a powerful collision represented by −1000. However, if only one person 'chickens out', that person loses a great deal of face (−100), while the one who 'stays the course' wins a great deal of approbation from onlookers (+100).

Dangerous games are non-negotiable. Unless both sides simultaneously back down, there can be only one winner; the other must lose – although both can lose disastrously. For example, in Chicken played with automobiles, no cooperation is possible and any conciliatory move by one player – deviating a little from the straight path – will only encourage the other to press on. However, in some circumstances, the resolution of a dangerous game can be helped by agreements over future actions unrelated to the game at hand. For example, in the Cuban mis-

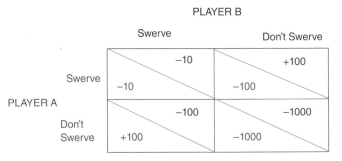

Figure 10.7 The game of Chicken

sile crisis, the Soviets 'lost'; they backed down and turned their ships back as the Americans had demanded. However, they were able to save some face, not within the context of that 'dangerous game' itself, but in terms of promises that the Americans made with regard to the future – no more attempts to invade Cuba, and withdrawing missiles from Eastern Europe.

Sometimes in such a situation, an antagonist may try to force the opponent to back down by appearing to be more ready to accept mutual loss than he or she actually is (i.e., deceiving the other about one's utility structure). For example, although it is hard to imagine this ever happening, suppose one of the teenagers were to throw the steering wheel out the window. In such a case, it is only the other driver who can now avoid catastrophe and must back down in order to do so. This kind of action occurred during the Cold War of the 1960s: the leaders of the Soviet Union sought to put the United States at a disadvantage by stating that they were quite prepared to accept the loss of 60% of their citizens in an all-out nuclear war – the equivalent of throwing the steering wheel out the window. If the leaders of a government can appear hardened or demented enough not to care about such losses, they can then 'pre-empt' the confrontation, forcing the other side to back down in order to avoid what appears to be certain mutual catastrophe.

The study of decision-making through gaming has had very significant appeal to military planners. The war in Vietnam was the most heavily 'gamed' war in history, and the kinds of games considered above were used in the development of military strategy. And some game theorists have interpreted the 2003 invasion of Iraq as having been the pursuit of a 'chicken' strategy by the United States (Roddy, 2003).

While you may wonder about the limits of what gaming research can teach us about how people deal with interpersonal conflicts in everyday life, research has shown that when faced with decisions where the outcome depends not just on one's own choice of action but also on that of another person, we tend to conceptualize such situations in terms of a sort of mental payoff matrix, and these various matrices correspond to the payoff matrices associated with experimental games such as Chicken or the Prisoner's Dilemma (Halevy, Chou & Murnighan, 2012). We do not need a formally constructed payoff matrix to represent our choices, but once we have conceptualized the conflict in such a way, that conceptualization then determines our behaviour.

> **KEY POINT:** Dangerous games involve the risk of a mutually destructive outcome that can only be avoided by one side backing down. If played out in real life, the consequences can be horrific.

Collective dilemmas

After thousands of studies using the Prisoner's Dilemma Game and related games, their use gradually waned, and although these games still are used in some modern studies, much of the interest has shifted to collective dilemmas (Dawes, 1980), sometimes referred to as social dilemmas. A collective dilemma more closely reflects many real-life conflict situations, and is an extended form of the Prisoner's Dilemma that involves many participants. This dilemma occurs whenever the *individually* rational actions of a number

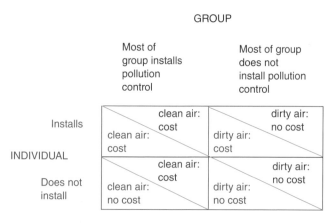

Figure 10.8 Collective dilemma and air pollution

of interacting parties produce an outcome that is *collectively* undesirable. In other words, people must choose between behaving out of self-interest (to maximize their own outcomes) and behaving cooperatively (to maximize group outcomes). As in the Prisoner's Dilemma Game, the dilemma arises because if everyone acts selfishly, *everyone* will be worse off than if they had been cooperative. As an example, suppose that air quality is being seriously degraded by pollution from gasoline engines, and the public is informed about alternative engines that run on non-polluting energy sources such as electricity or hydrogen. Yet, switching to a new form of energy involves some cost. What should the 'rational' person do? What would you do? The 'rational' choice, defined as what is best for one's own self-interest, is, at least for the short term, to do nothing. How can this be rational when the air we all breathe is becoming more and more polluted? The simple truth is that if the majority of people opt for cleaner engines, the air quality will improve even if you do nothing, and in this case your switching to cleaner energy, at some cost to you, will have no measurable additional effect. On the other hand, if only a few people switch to cleaner energy, your investment would be a waste of time, since the air quality will not improve anyway, even if you make the investment (Figure 10.8). The dilemma arises because the effect of whatever you do as an individual is minimal, while the outcome depends on what a lot of other people do.

Thus, in a situation where the actions of a number of people are involved, the contribution of any given individual usually has only a minor effect on the outcome, and the individual receives virtually the same benefit whether contributing or not. As a result, individual self-interest militates against the collective interest, and ultimately the individual suffers as well. This did not escape the Greek historian Thucydides almost 2500 years ago, who wrote that people:

'... devote a very small fraction of the time to the consideration of any public object, most of it to the prosecution of their own objects. Meanwhile each fancies that no harm will come of his neglect, that it is the business of somebody else to look after this or that for him; and so, by the same notion being entertained by all separately, the common cause imperceptibly decays' (Thucydides, *The history of the Peloponnesian war Book 1*, cited by Lipp (2001), p. 92).

Population growth often involves the same kind of dilemma. Why would poor peasants in a nation struggling with burgeoning overpopulation choose to limit their families to only one or two children, even if that is what their government urges? Given that they will need to depend on their children to support them in their elder years – there are no old age pensions – the more children they have, the better off they are likely to be, despite the fact that, in the long run, their society as a whole may suffer.

In reality, some people view collective dilemmas as an opportunity to exploit others – for example, letting other people pay to clean up pollution – while others see them as occasions in which they should try to build cooperation (e.g., Brann & Foddy, 1987). And in some instances, people may hesitate to cooperate, not because they do not want to contribute to the group goal but because they suspect or misinterpret the motivations of others (Alcock & Mansell, 1977).

Collective dilemmas occur in two essential forms: the resource dilemma and the provision of public goods dilemma.

The resource dilemma The resource dilemma involves a collective good that already exists, which the group members can use at will. Individuals have to decide how much of the public resource each should take for personal use, and overuse will lead to a loss for all. The resource dilemma is often referred to in the literature as the **commons problem**, in reference to the 'tragedy of the commons'. As Hardin (1968) tells it, it happened like this: In England in the 1800s, there were public pastures set aside for common use. However, as individual farmers increased the size of their cattle herds, the commons eventually were so overgrazed that the herds were threatened by lack of food. This overgrazing led to an enclosure movement that eventually involved fencing off the commons, resulting in the loss of pasture for many people. The heart of the problem was this: for each herdsman, the positive utility associated with enlarging his herd was much greater than the negative utility derived from overgrazing. The short-term gains were more enticing than the possibility of losses in the long term. Thus, each enlarged his herd to the point where all the formers suffered.

However, this story of the English Commons is not historically accurate. In fact, most commons pastures were never open to the public, but only to certain people who had inherited the right to use them, and their usage was subject to regulation. Further, overgrazing was not the reason for the enclosure movement and the decline of the commons system (Cox, 1975). However, the story nonetheless captures the essence of many modern-day resource dilemmas. For example, as fishing boats from around the world increased their take of cod from the Grand Banks off Newfoundland, over-fishing threatened the continued existence of the cod fishery, necessitating a complete ban on cod fishing. That collective dilemma evolved gradually, beginning long before there was any obvious danger to the fishery. Note that the resource dilemma typically has an important temporal component; it is essentially a dilemma with delayed consequences. The collectively negative outcomes only occur later in time, while the rewards of pursuing self-interest and the costs of acting cooperatively are immediate. Collective dilemmas involving such a time lag are also sometimes referred to as social traps (Platt, 1973), for obvious reasons.

The provision of public goods dilemma While the resource dilemma involves individuals drawing from a common resource, the provision of public goods dilemma relates to contributions by individuals to the collective or public good that benefit everyone – contributors and non-contributors alike (for example, donating blood, supporting public television, or installing municipal pollution controls). As long as most people act in line with the common good, the individual who does not contribute will benefit as much from the efforts of the majority as does the person who contributes. Since an individual does not have to contribute in order to benefit, the economically 'rational' action is to not contribute. Yet if everyone does this, there will be no public good. For example, there would be no need to collect tickets on a commuter train if everyone were honest about paying the fare. Such a system, however, would most likely break down because free riders would exploit the situation. (Thus, the provision of public goods dilemma is sometimes referred to as the **free rider** problem.)

Both this dilemma and the resource dilemma are identical in terms of the decision facing the individual. He or she must decide whether to act according to individual self-interest (refrain from contributing), thereby risking a negative outcome if most others do the same, or to act according to the collective interest while incurring some personal cost, with the knowledge that unless most others also act this way, nothing positive will come from it. It is important to emphasize this point: the problem in each dilemma arises when each individual's behaviour has a relatively minor influence on the group outcome, while the overall group behaviour has a strong effect on each individual's outcome.

Enhancing cooperation in a collective dilemma

How should people deal with collective dilemmas? To philosopher Immanuel Kant, people should follow this imperative: 'Act only according to that maxim which you can at the same time will to be a universal law' (Joad, 1957, p. 393). Thus, you should keep using pesticides in your garden only if you are content to have everyone do likewise. You will drop your gum wrapper on the sidewalk only if you are content to allow everyone else to do the same. You will continue to drive your gas-guzzling SUV only if you are willing to accept that everyone can do so as well. If we all acted according to the Kantian imperative, then we would be acting in the common interest because it would be the same as our self-interest, and collective dilemmas would vanish. However, people do not, by and large, follow Kant's dictum because it is against their individual short-term interests to do so. How then can cooperation be encouraged?

Of course, positive incentives can enhance cooperation. Think about water conservation. If the government offers rewards to people who reduce their consumption of water, many will be happy to comply. On the other hand, coercion can also be effective. Sometimes, coercion in the form of social pressure – for example immediate expressions of disapproval when someone openly litters – is sufficient to prevent individuals from ignoring the common good and from acting only from self-interest (Samuelson, Messick, Rutte & Wilke, 1984; Allison & Messick, 1985). Hardin (1968) suggested that mutual coercion, mutually agreed upon, is the only way out of the commons dilemma. This course of action is already common in some circumstances: We all agree through our elected representatives to pay taxes and to punish those who do not. And many cities have banned the use of pesticides for garden maintenance. Other cities facing water shortages impose fines for overconsumption. Indeed, there is considerable empirical evidence that the imposition of costs on free riders – public shaming, fines and even incarceration – can successfully maintain cooperation (Kiyonari & Barclay, 2008).

Given that both positive incentives and coercion can lead to collectively desired outcomes, is one approach more effective than the other? A meta-analysis of collective dilemma studies (Balliet, Mulder & Van Lange, 2011) found that coercion and positive incentives are equally able to enhance cooperation. Thus, to encourage people to car-share during rush hours, we can either pass a law forbidding single-driver vehicles on major roads during rush hour and fine people who fail to comply, or we can set up an incentive system, such as a High Occupancy Lane, that rewards only those who act in the cooperative manner by providing them with speedier trips. Often, the combination of incentive and coercion is chosen.

Moreover, a single individual acting cooperatively can often influence others to do the same. Recall the discussion of conformity behaviour in Chapter 6: When even one person failed to conform, that was enough to lead some other participants to act according to their individual judgements. Consider the implication of that finding in the context of groups and organizations. Groups need their members to cooperate in working towards a common goal, but it is all too easy for at least some individuals to have a free ride. What to do? Weber & Murnighan (2008) suggest a solution. In their research, they found that in the context of a social dilemma, if one individual consistently contributes to the group cause, this leads others to contribute more and to cooperate more, and this typically leads to gains for the consistent contributor as well. This influence appears to come about because the consistent contribution on the part of the one individual leads to changes in the assessment that other members of the group make about group norms and about the importance of cooperation.

But all is not roses for the consistent contributor, for it turns out that while he or she may foster cooperation in the group, there is also a risk of being rejected by the group. In one study (Parks & Stone, 2010), it was found that not only did selfish members of a group who contributed little to the public good face expulsion, but so too did unselfish members who contributed substantially to the public good. Why would that be so? Those who favoured such expulsion saw the unselfish individual either as establishing an undesirably high standard for behaviour in the group or as breaking group norms.

The social psychological study of conflict has shifted away in recent years from a focus on experimental games that exclude communication to games that involve actual negotiation (Pruitt, 2012), including comparisons between face-to-face and computer-mediated negotiations (Thompson, Wang & Gunia, 2010). Nonetheless, the kinds of games discussed above have taught us important lessons about conflict in its simplest forms, lessons that help us to understand the nature of conflict in real-world settings.

> **KEY POINT:** Many everyday problems in society take the form of collective dilemmas. Because an individual's contribution is small relative to the collective contribution of others, and because the individual shares the collective outcome whether contributing or not, the individually 'rational', self-serving choice, if chosen by most or all, leads to a very undesirable collective outcome.

FACTORS AFFECTING THE COURSE OF CONFLICT

Of course, real-life situations are much more complex than any matrix game. Whether or not antagonists in a conflict will seek to resolve matters peacefully or by force depends greatly on three classes of variables: (1) predispositional variables, which refer to personal characteristics of the antagonists, their cultural framework and their past history of interaction; (2) structural variables, which are directly related to the nature of the conflict situation (e.g., whether the situation is purely cooperative or if cooperation is even possible; whether promises or threats can be made; whether communication is possible; whether the antagonists have equal power); and (3) strategic variables (e.g., whether one or more of the antagonists adopts a conciliatory stance).

Predispositional variables

The study of predispositional variables focuses on both the previous history of interactions between the antagonists and the personal characteristics of the antagonists, and whether the conflict is between individuals acting in their own interest, or between leaders representing groups. In a later chapter, we shall address the question of how personal characteristics relate to leadership, but it is obvious that if you had to negotiate with a Hitler instead of a Gandhi, or a Churchill instead of a Stalin, the course of the negotiations is likely to be quite different. The way different people deal with conflicts is influenced by personality variables, cultural background, age and gender, and beliefs about each other. We shall examine each of these in turn.

Personality When you stop to think about it, you probably know some people who seem to lean towards cooperation and consideration for others in their interpersonal interactions, and others who seem motivated primarily by self-interest. The same has been observed in experimental games: some people appear more predisposed towards cooperation than others, even though they are still likely to react competitively if interacting with other competitive people (Alcock & Mansell, 1977; Kelley & Stahelski, 1970). Not only are some people more cooperative in general, they are also more likely to elicit cooperation from at least some others. Then, because of such experience, they learn that some people are cooperative while some others are not, and they adjust their actions according to the behaviour of the other party.

On the other hand, competitively oriented individuals are typically competitive just about all the time, regardless of the behaviour of their adversaries. Because this orientation is likely to elicit competitiveness from everyone with whom they interact, such people are likely to view their own competitiveness as reasonable and normal, given that everyone else seems to be competitive too. This is borne out in research, which has found that while cooperators view cooperation as the intelligent and socially appropriate way to act, competitive individuals tend to view cooperation by others as an indication of weakness, and view their own competitiveness as an indicator of strength (Komorita & Parks, 1995).

Such cooperative and competitive orientations have been formalized in terms of different types of social value orientation (Emonds et al., 2011). A cooperative predisposition is referred to as 'prosocial', while a competitive disposition is referred to as 'proself'. As the label suggests, proself individuals are generally more self-centred and approach a social exchange situation in a very calculating manner, choosing the strategy that best suits their self-interest. On the other hand, prosocials generally seek a mutually beneficial outcome. They exhibit a greater sense of social responsibility and are more likely to reciprocate their partner's actions than are proselfs (De Cremer & Van Langge, 2011). These two different social value orientations are so fundamental that they are associated with observable differences in neural activation during interactions in experimental conflict situations (Emonds et al., 2011). Neuroscience research has explored neural mechanisms associated with important factors involved in social conflict situations – such as trust, conformity to social norms, the ability to delay gratification, and emotion regulation. Given that social judgement is obviously involved, it is not surprising to find that the prefrontal cortex plays an important role in such situations (Rilling & Sanfey, 2011).

Trust As was clear in the story of the two prisoners being offered a deal by the prosecutor, trust plays a crucial role in social conflict situations. If you are going to invest money to install pollution control equipment, this investment will only have a significant effect on the environment if many others do the same. Even if you are of good will, if you cannot trust them to do so, then you may be unlikely to make such an investment.

Trust depends both on one's own tendency to trust or distrust others and on one's prior history with the people involved. By virtue of their personalities, some individuals are willing to trust others unless and until they prove themselves untrustworthy, while other people are more hesitant about trusting until there is enough evidence to justify their trust. Of course trust, while often difficult to build up, is very easily destroyed. It would be difficult ever to trust again a friend of many years who steals your wallet.

The degree to which trust influences conflict behaviour appears to be related to social value orientation. In one study (Boone, Declerck & Kiyonari, 2010), it was found that people with a prosocial value orientation were significantly affected by how much they could trust others in the group, and were less influenced by incentives. On the other hand, individuals with a proself value orientation were strongly influenced by incentives, and not much affected by trust. Again this makes sense. Incentives appeal to the proself individual's self-interest and there is less need to trust others if one has no intention of cooperating with them in working towards a common goal. Prosocial individuals, on the other hand, because they are concerned about collective goals, would be expected to downplay the importance of incentives that are related to personal advancement.

Cultural factors We should not be surprised to find that culture plays an important role in determining how individuals approach a conflict situation. There are indeed important differences, particularly between people who are brought up in non-Western cultures and those who have grown up in the West (Pruitt, 2012). As has been addressed earlier in this textbook, people in Western nations tend to be much more individualistic and focused on maximizing their own benefits, while people in non-Western societies tend to be more collectivist, with more focus on the well-being of the group rather than the individual.

In line with this, conflict in China has typically been approached differently than in the West. Because of the enduring influence of Confucian ideals, people consider their differences and disagreements from a perspective in which harmony is the predominant guiding principle (Leung et al., 2011). The goal of maintaining harmony when faced with conflict reflects the importance with which people view maintaining and improving the quality of their interpersonal relationships (Leung, 1997). Of course, the pursuit of harmony at an individual level does not mean that all interpersonal conflicts are resolved harmoniously, nor does it suggest that intergroup conflicts or political disputes are tackled with harmony foremost in mind. Moreover, the rapid social change that is occurring in China, bringing increasing competitiveness and commercialism, is likely to weaken adherence to the traditional harmonious ideal of times past.

India, too, is different. Given the long history of rigid status and power differences imposed by the caste system, it is not surprising that, at least until recent times, considerations based on status and power have played a significant role in conflict management. This can even be observed in the context of experimental games. For example, in a study carried out some years ago (Alcock, 1975), pairs of university students in Canada and India played against each other in a bargaining game. In one condition, they were on an equal footing in terms of potential payoffs, whereas in a second condition each player ostensibly had an advantage over the other (i.e., each seem to be 'top dog'), and in a third condition each player was ostensibly at a disadvantage ('underdog'). When the members of pairs of Canadian players each thought they were top dogs, they became more cooperative, as though they were more willing to share the available payoffs. On the other hand, when each was apparently an underdog, they dug in their heels and became more competitive in their bargaining. The opposite was found in India: when each player appeared to be at an advantage, they both became very competitive, but when each appeared to be an underdog, they became conciliatory and very cooperative. This strong cross-cultural difference appeared to mirror the sharp difference in the social structures of the two countries. In Western countries in general, people are encouraged to do their best and not give in when they are at a disadvantage, whereas in the rigid status hierarchy that characterized India at the time, people born with natural advantages in the social structure learned to expect to dominate those with less advantage, and conversely people born at a social disadvantage learned to yield without complaint to those above them on a higher social echelon.

These are but two examples of the strong influences that culture brings to bear on how conflicts are interpreted and managed.

Age and gender It seems that competitiveness increases as a child grows through adolescence to adulthood (McClintock & Nuttin, 1969; Leventhal & Lane, 1970). As for gender, in years gone by it appeared that males in Western societies were typically more competitive than females, and this difference showed up in many published studies. Cooperativeness on the part of females was taken to be a reflection of their gender role which included sensitivity to other's needs. However, most likely as a result of the significant changes that have taken place in gender roles in Western society over the past 40 years – girls are now allowed and encouraged to be as competitive and goal-oriented as boys – such gender differences are no longer so obvious. Indeed, in a recent meta-analysis of gender differences of cooperation in social dilemmas (Balliet et al., 2011), no difference was found between men and women in terms of cooperation overall. (However, the study did find women to be more cooperative than men in mixed-sex interactions.)

Prior relationship and beliefs about one another The prior relationship of parties to conflict is often of vital importance. Two people trying to save themselves from drowning by climbing onto a piece of flotsam barely large enough for one are much less likely to cooperate if they are strangers than if they are family members or lovers. And how people have interacted with one another in the past will not be forgotten. As the old saying goes, 'Fool me once, shame on you; fool me twice, shame on me.' We learn from the actions of others whether we can trust them to act in an unselfish way or whether they are purely self-interested, and perhaps even deceptive and manipulative. Moreover, reciprocity is a factor as well. If someone has been helpful to you in the past, you are more likely to want to reciprocate and be helpful in return. Thus, be it between individuals or groups or nations, their past history of interaction and what each antagonist has come to believe about the other will have a very significant influence on how they act during a contemporary conflict.

KEY POINT: A number of factors relating to the individuals involved in a conflict, including aspects of personality, age, gender, culture and the nature of prior relationship, influence the course of conflict.

Structural factors

As important as such predispositional factors can be, the evidence from game studies suggests that they are generally overridden by the effects of situational variables. That is, even to people who view themselves as being cooperative and who have a history of cooperative interaction are likely to become competitive in certain situations. Some situations are more likely to encourage competition than others, and it is easy to understand why: Think again about the two people trying to climb onto a piece of flotsam. If they are strangers to one another, they are much more likely to be willing to help each other if the flotsam is large enough to easily accommodate them both than if it will barely accommodate one of them. And the conflict that occurs when a partner finds that his mate has eaten up the entire box of chocolates that she gave him for his birthday is much easier to resolve than one in which a partner catches her mate in bed with someone else. In these examples, aspects of the situation are likely to be more important than the predispositional variables in determining whether the individuals cooperate or compete as they deal with the conflict.

There are a number of particular situational aspects that are of key importance in a conflict situation, including communication, the use of promises and threats, and power.

Communication While participants in experimental games often are not allowed to communicate, it is rare in real-life conflicts for there to be no communication between antagonists, although there are times when one side or the other does not want to listen. Communication can certainly help when dealing with a conflict; a meta-analysis of research in social dilemma situations found that communication generally enhances cooperation (Balliet, 2010). But this is not always the case: even when communication does occur, there is no guarantee that it will be understood or believed, and if it is misinterpreted or untrusted, it can not only fail to help but may instead fan the flames of antagonism, thus exacerbating the conflict. The kind of communication is also important; respectful communication signalling that the recipient is viewed as both worthy and competent can promote cooperation, while demeaning communication will not (Andersen, Saribay & Thorpe, 2008). Communication can also assist by clarifying each person's perception of the other's intentions and by providing the opportunity to make promises (Orbell, Van-de-Kragt & Dawes, 1989). As long as the promises are kept, cooperation will be fostered.

Communication across cultural lines has its own special considerations. For example, in one study (Brew at al., 2011), Chinese students attending an Australian university were compared with Australians of European background in terms of how they evaluated a number of conflict scenarios involving different communication styles, including 'constructive controversy', 'constructive diplomacy', 'smoothing' (seeking harmony) and 'destructive confrontation'. It was concluded that the Chinese participants were more concerned with the *appropriateness* of communication – that is, whether the disputants' communication style was in line with the social norms that apply to such conflicts – while the Australians were more focused on *effectiveness*, that is, which communication style was most effective in producing a solution to the problem. This is consistent with the view discussed earlier that people in China, and collectivist societies in general, tend to be more concerned with harmony – maintaining and building the relationship – while those from individualistic societies are more likely to want to achieve results quickly by articulating the issues and openly 'talking things through'. As a result, as Brew et al. (2011) point out, when in a conflict with people from collectivist societies, individualists face frustration because of the perceived ineffectiveness of the 'smoothing' approach, while collectivists when dealing with individualists are often irritated by what to them is the inappropriate tactic of immediately presenting arguments and opinions, something that may threaten the equilibrium of the relationship.

Promises and threats Sometimes, promises are made in the attempt to resolve a conflict. Consider a father who wants his child to clean her room and a child who instead wants to play. The father may try to influence the outcome of this basic conflict of interest by making a promise – 'If you clean up your room, we will go to play in the park', or more generally, 'If you do A, I will bring about B (some desirable consequence).'

A threat is like a promise except that the outcome, B, is undesirable. For example, 'If you do A (fail to clean your room), I will cause B (you will not be able to watch your favourite show on TV tonight).' Research shows that, at least in the laboratory, threats can often prove very successful in eliciting concessions during a negotiation (Sinaceur et al., 2011). However, there may be long-term negative consequences, and we will discuss this later in the chapter. In any case, for a promise or threat to be successful, it must first be credible. Credibility depends on three factors:

a) Past record – If the father has generally kept his promises and threats in the past, the child is likely to believe that B will indeed follow if she does A. On the other hand, if the person making the promise or threat has in the past failed to carry it out, credibility will be low, and the promise or threat will lose its power. And what if there is no history upon which to base credibility? One way to establish credibility in such a circumstance is to persuade the other person that you have little choice but to adhere to the promise or threat. For example, if you promise someone a financial reward if he or she carries out a particular action, you can make the promise highly credible by giving the money to a neutral third party who is instructed to pay it out once the desired behaviour has occurred. Or if a union leader threatens a walkout and persuades management that the union will vote to replace him or her as leader if the threat is not carried out, the threat is more credible.

b) Reasonableness – the threat or promise must fall within the realm of reason. A parent who promises her child that he will not have to go to school ever again as long as he cleans his room is unlikely to be believed. And a threat must not carry too high a cost to either party, or it is likely to suffer in terms of credibility. Loving parents who threaten to send their child to an orphanage if the child misbehaves are unlikely to be believed; both parents and child would suffer too much if the threat were carried out.

c) Contingency – there must be reason to believe that the promised or threatened B is actually contingent on A. If parents promise a trip abroad if their child obtains good grades and if the child has overheard her

314

parents saying that the whole family is going to take that trip abroad in any case, the promise is robbed of potential effectiveness. And with regard to threat, the threatened action must also have some negative consequences for the threatener as well, in order to assure the threatened party that the threat will not be carried out whether there is compliance or not. For example, if a father tells a child who is hiding under the bed that he will spank him if he does not come out right away, the threat will be ineffective if the child believes that he will be spanked in any case. The child needs to believe that the father does not enjoy delivering a spanking and will not do so if the child acts as demanded. And while promises achieve their goal only if they bring about a behaviour that warrants them being carried out, threats serve their purpose only if they do not have to be carried out. Spanking a disobedient child who ignored the threat adds credibility to future threats, but means that the current threat has actually failed.

However, unlike promises (unless they are not kept), threats by their very nature have negative effects on the process of conflict resolution, often turning what might have been a constructive process into a destructive one. Despite the fact that they can often be effective, threats usually poison the relationship somewhat so that future conflicts may be increasingly difficult to resolve. Unfortunately, the presence of threat capability very often leads to its use, for it is just so tempting to use a threat as a short cut to try to bring the conflict to a quick end. However, once the threat is issued, the nature of the conflict changes and what comes to the forefront is the perceived intimidation. Yielding to threats or coercion leads to a loss of face in many cultures (Goffman, 1955), and saving face often becomes the primary goal for an individual who has received a threat. This leads to increased determination to 'hold one's ground', and the threatened individual may respond with a counter-threat or even with an aggressive act. Unless someone backs down, this triggers a series of escalating threats, a **threat–counter-threat spiral.**

Relationship counsellors frequently encounter such threat–counter-threat spirals: A couple disagrees on something as relatively trivial as where to go on an evening out, and, in order to press the point, one of them makes a threat ('Maybe I should just stay home'), leading the other to respond with a counter-threat ('Fine – if you don't want to come, I'll go alone and I'll have a good time without you'). The dispute has now quickly morphed from a minor conflict about where to spend the evening into a challenge as to who is going to back down first. On and on – parry, thrust; thrust, parry – the dispute builds. The threat about staying home may escalate to a threat to end the marriage, even though that outcome is not at all desired by either. At this point, it becomes very difficult to resolve the conflict because the actual issue has been lost in the struggle to win the face-saving battle. Unfortunately, such threat escalation tends to be self-sustaining: When a certain level of threat is successful, the person who 'won' is likely to resort to it again in future, and when it fails, it usually promotes a hardening of resolve and even more serious threats.

It should not be surprising that face-saving is important to most people, for not only is it tied up with self-esteem but it also can be critical with regard to future interactions, for yielding to threat now may encourage more threats in the future. Such future consideration is important not only for individuals but for groups and institutions as well. For example, if a government gives in to terrorists' demands now, other terrorists may be encouraged to make more such demands in future.

Let's go back to the opening vignette: The Cuban missile crisis occurred in the context of the Cold War that was ongoing between the world's only two superpowers, the Soviet Union and the United States. Those two countries were engaged in an arms race at the time, each fearing the other, each building its military arsenals to defend against the other, and each viewing the other's arsenal-building as an indication of planning for an attack. Such an arms race is an example of a threat–counter-threat spiral, and arms races usually escalate quickly. Adding to one's arsenal, even motivated by self-defence, is threatening to the other, producing a response that is interpreted as being threatening rather than defensive, thus requiring even more buildup of armaments.

Power   Of course, power is essential in carrying out a threat. A parent who threatens to spank a 17-year-old high school boxing champion probably lacks the power to carry out the threat. What happens when a powerful individual, or group, or nation is in conflict with a considerably weaker adversary? Certainly, at times, power determines all: the Nazis did not hesitate to use their overwhelming power to dominate not only individual citizens but neighbouring nations as well. Fortunately, power is not wielded with such vigour in most conflict situations, and there is evidence (Pruitt, 1976) that parties involved in a conflict may be more likely to take coercive measures when they have only moderate, rather than great or small, power relative to their adversary. This may at first appear counter-intuitive, but it becomes clearer when one realizes that having only little power relative to the other is often viewed as ineffective, while wielding great power can lead to destructive results and ruin the opportunity for a positive relationship with the adversary in future. In more everyday terms, if you are guarding the cookie jar and your only coercive response is to say, 'Bad, bad, when the child takes a cookie without permission, the measure may have no effect on the child – so why bother to use it? Similarly if your only means of coercive power is to use a whip, you are unlikely to employ it to protect the cookie jar from marauding toddlers.

> **KEY POINT:** Characteristics of the structure of the conflict situation often are more influential in determining the course of a conflict than the characteristics of the individuals involved. The use of threat is often tempting, but it changes the nature of the conflict and may lead to a threat–counter-threat spiral.

Strategy

Whether at chess or at war, or at the car dealer's or the bargaining table, many people try to work out in advance a plan, or strategy. A formal strategy is simply a plan that contains instructions about what to do in every imaginable contingency. In theory, any 'game' can be reduced to a series of choices. For example in a game of tic-tac-toe, you could plan the following: 'If she chooses a corner on the first move, I'll choose the centre. If she chooses another corner on the second move but not the corner directly opposite, I'll choose the middle position between the two corners. However, if she instead chooses …' This interior monologue could continue until the game ends. There are many different possible strategies, but once you have chosen one, there is nothing left to decide. However, in a game of chess, there is such a large number of possible strategies available that an individual could never hope to specify them all. (Thus a chess-playing computer has a great advantage in this regard.)

However, in the typical 2 x 2 matrix game employed in experimental studies, it is relatively easy to construct strategies because of the limited number of possible response patterns. The effects of following a particular strategy are examined either by having a confederate follow a pre-selected strategy, or by presenting (in a laboratory situation where participants respond via computer terminals) a computer-generated response as the 'other player'. Many strategic factors can be studied. For example, does an opponent who cooperates only 10% of the time have greater or less influence on the participant than one who cooperates 90% of the time? In fact, such fixed strategies have been found to have very little success in influencing participants (Vinacke, 1969). Unconditionally cooperative or unconditionally 'tough' strategies fail to produce cooperative responses from the opposition (Solomon, 1960).

More effective are dynamic strategies responsive to the other participant's behaviours. One of these is the so-called tit-for-tat (or 'delayed matching') strategy whereby the confederate begins with a cooperative response and then on the next trial, trial n + 1, makes the same response that the participant made on trial n. (In other words, in a series of interactions, each time a participant is cooperative, the confederate or the computer produces a cooperative response the next time.) This strategy responds in a positive way to the other person's cooperativeness, but does not reinforce non-cooperative moves by the other player. There is a wealth of empirical evidence that shows that this approach is the best way to induce cooperative responding in others (Wing-Tung & Komorita, 2002).

Research (Axelrod & Dion, 1988) has found that there are three important things that need to occur for the tit-for-tat strategy to lead to stable cooperation: (1) niceness – the interaction must begin with a cooperative move by the person using this strategy; (2) provocability – at the first non-cooperative move by the other player, there must be retaliation, that is, a non-cooperative response on the next trial; and (3) forgiveness – after appropriate retaliation, it is necessary to return to cooperative responding. In other words, the tit-for-tat strategy leads to the perception that the other person is 'fair but firm' (Komorita, Hilty & Parks, 1991; Van Lange & Visser, 1999). Indeed, this is the 'strategy' often recommended for parents – enforce 'consequences' for behaviours. When the child misbehaves, follow this with an appropriate punishment, be it admonishment, short-term deprivation of a favourite toy, or whatever, and when the child behaves as desired, follow that with a positive response, such as praise.

Strategy studies have also been used in negotiation games, such as buyer-seller games in which two players negotiate over the 'sale' of some item. In this context, a tough strategy (extreme opening offer and infrequent concessions) has been found to be the most successful in terms of obtaining the larger share of the joint payoff (Chertkoff & Conley, 1967). Pacifist strategies, on the other hand, typically result in exploitation. Overall, the bulk of the evidence indicates that in a conflict or bargaining situation, neither an overly generous nor an overly tough position is effective in bringing about mutual cooperation. The most effective strategy is one of firm resistance to exploitation coupled with reciprocation of the other's cooperative behaviour.

> **KEY POINT:** In general, the most productive strategy in dealing with conflict in experimental games or in negotiations is to resist exploitation but reciprocate cooperative behaviour.

INTERGROUP CONFLICT

In a later chapter (Chapter 12), we shall examine groups and their leadership and how in-groups and out-groups relate to one another. In this chapter, the focus is on whether people behave differently in a conflict situation when they are acting as individuals or when they are part of a group. There are a number of pressures and social influences that an individual, and especially a leader, experiences as part of a collectivity. While the individual needs to consider only his or her own interests if acting alone, when one is part of a group, there are pressures from group members to conform to group-endorsed methods and to seek group-endorsed goals, and failure to do so is likely to result in significant backlash. As individuals yield to group pressures and suppress any reservations about excessive competitiveness, the result is that the group as a whole typically becomes much more competitive and less cooperative than one would expect based on the motivations of the particular individuals involved. This is such a common finding that it is referred to as the interindividual–intergroup discontinuity effect (Wolf et al., 2008). Consider this example: You have joined a newly formed union and are participating in a meeting dedicated to choosing the bargaining stance to be taken in dealing with management. Even if you begin with a very cooperative orientation, it is not difficult to imagine that conciliatory opinions advocating compromise may be drowned out by calls for strong action as people identify themselves with the union and its collective goals.

Not only are groups that are involved in a conflict generally more competitive and more focused on self-interest than are individuals in dealing with one another, but groups are also more likely to exploit cooperative behaviour forthcoming from their adversaries (Wildschut, Insko & Pinter, 2007). This comes about as individuals and especially their leaders feel the pressure to do what they can to bring benefits to the group. This effect has been found not only in individualistic societies, but also in more collectivist, interdependent societies as well – for example, in Japan (Takemura & Yuki, 2007).

Prior history was listed as an important predispositional variable when discussing interindividual conflict earlier this chapter. Prior history is just as important when groups are in conflict as well. Intergroup conflict, sometimes resulting in violence, is often based in age-old disputes tied to ethnic, religious or national group identity. According to United Nations estimates, there are more than 5000 ethnic minorities in the world and ethnic groups continue to be involved in scores of protracted conflicts around the globe. There have been more than 250 wars since 1945

Figure 10.9   Northern Ireland street mural
Source: © Richard Baker/In Pictures/Corbis

in which at least 30 million people have been killed, 10 million of them children. Think about such awful violence as that associated with the Protestant-Catholic conflict in Northern Ireland, the Arab-Israeli conflict, the events of September 11, 2001, and the civil strife in Rwanda in which 500,000 civilians, mainly members of the Tutsi tribe, died in 1994. There is much more involved in these conflicts than just disagreements over sharing of resources. Groups and societies have long collective memories that can transcend centuries, and many intergroup and inter-nation conflicts have much to do with enduring historical intergroup enmity and the collective beliefs that accompany it. The intergroup bias that grows from remembering such history, the 'us versus them' orientation, is a potent breeding ground for destructive conflict (Hewstone, Rubin and Willis, 2002).

Consider these examples:

- Every Irish schoolchild learns about the importance of the year 1690. The Protestant King William III, head of the Dutch Royal House of Orange, had been invited by powerful Protestant political figures in England to seize the throne from his father-in-law King James II, a devout convert to Roman Catholicism. James fled to France but later, with the help of Irish soldiers, began an attempt to retake the throne. The attempt failed in a decisive battle on the banks of the Boyne River. Irish Catholics have never forgotten their defeat at the Battle of the Boyne. Irish Protestants have not forgotten either, and every year members of the Protestant Orange Order in Northern Ireland lead a ceremonial march on July 12 to honour that historic Protestant victory, a practice which raises the ire of the Roman Catholics. To add fuel to the fire, until peace was brought about in recent times, the Orangemen insisted on marching through Catholic neighbourhoods.
- In 1999, Christian Serbs in Kosovo carried out 'ethnic cleansing' that resulted in the brutal deaths of many thousands of their Muslim compatriots. The simmering conflict that underlay this despicable crime has its roots in the terrible Battle of Kosovo Polje fought on June 28, 1389 between some 80,000 Serbian knights – defenders of the Christian faith – and an army of invading Muslim warriors from the Ottoman Empire. The Serbs were defeated and surrendered their land, and as a result, by the late 20th century, ethnic Albanian Muslims made up 90% of Kosovo's population. However, Serbs never forgot the Battle of Kosovo Polje. For example, on June 28, 1989, the 600th anniversary of the battle, over one million Serbs (about 10% of the Serbian population) made a pilgrimage to the battle site to honour their Serbian heroes who fell so long ago.

Eidelson and Eidelson (2003) have identified five types of core collective beliefs that are particularly important in such intergroup conflicts, beliefs that often provide a basis for defining the group and making it cohesive:

1. Superiority – the belief that members of one's own group are superior in important ways to members of another group. This is sometimes driven by theology, when a group views its religion as the only true religion and all others are seen to be pagan or even diabolical. At other times – as in Nazi Germany with its concept of the Aryan master race – ethnic origin may be the distinguishing factor. Sometimes both sides hold identical, mirror-image views of one another, each seeing the other as inferior and threatening for the same reasons. During the Cold War between the United States and the Soviet Union, Americans commonly believed that communism was an evil system greatly inferior to capitalism, and that the communist Soviets were intent on world domination and the destruction of the United States. However, Soviet citizens held a mirror-image belief of Americans, viewing capitalism as an evil system, and the capitalist American society as bent on aggression towards and domination of the Soviet Union (Bronfenbrenner, 1961).

2. Injustice – the belief that one's own group has been significantly wronged by another group and that there has been an injustice that needs avenging. The persecution of the Muslims of Kosovo reflects such a belief on the part of the Serbs.
3. Vulnerability – the belief that one's group is very vulnerable to harm from the opposing group. For example, Israelis and Palestinians alike feel themselves to be particularly vulnerable to harm from each other, leading to a situation where disputes over resources and territory are viewed as issues of basic survival.
4. Distrust – the belief that leaders and members of the opposing group are untrustworthy and out to deceive. Such belief is often held on both sides, making constructive conflict resolution extremely difficult to achieve.
5. Helplessness – a belief in collective helplessness can inhibit a group from defending itself against an oppressor. Black South Africans shared such a belief under apartheid, which dampened any enthusiasm for a movement aimed at rebelling against the white masters. This belief, while promoting the status quo, also militates against any action that will resolve the underlying conflict between the subjugators and the subjugated.

This helps us to understand the seeming intractability of conflicts such as those in the Middle East, and the repeated failure of mediators and leaders of good will to bring about a stable peace. When people on both sides of a conflict grow up believing that members of the other group or nation or religion are inferior, or untrustworthy, or threatening, or have done one's group or nation major wrong, sooner or later there is likely to be hostile behaviour that serves to reinforce these beliefs. Collective beliefs handed down across the generations continue to pose a towering challenge to those who seek peace in the world.

KEY POINT: Groups are more competitive and less cooperative than are the particular individuals in the group. Prior history of interaction and collective beliefs about another group can feed conflict that endures from generation to generation.

BOX 10.1   TERRORISM

When conflicts between groups or nations elude peaceful resolution, the result is sometimes violence as each side tries to obtain its goal by force. Gang wars, forcible suppression of workers and union violence, unruly demonstrations and police action, civil wars and battles between nations all reflect the attempt to use violent means to advance towards a desired end. Sometimes the struggle reaches epic proportions as it did in the First and Second World Wars. At other times, a lesser power succumbs to a greater power, as when the Soviet military invaded Hungary in 1956.

And what happens when a mightier force subdues a lesser one? In some cases, domination is so complete that resistance is futile. However, resistance movements often develop that, although weak in terms of armaments and personnel, employ sabotage and terrorism to thwart the enemy to some extent.

Just who is labelled a terrorist depends on who is doing the labelling. To the Europeans who conquered the Americas, aboriginal resistors could have, in today's parlance, been considered to be terrorists. To the Nazi occupiers, members of *La Résistance française* no doubt were viewed as terrorists when they blew up bridges or munitions dumps, or assassinated Nazi officers and their collaborators. Yet these same saboteurs and assassins were seen as courageous and heroic figures in the eyes of their own people. Similarly in 2012, during the civil hostilities in Syria, Syrian president Bashar Al-Assad, at the same time that his forces were bombing his own cities, killing many civilians, labelled all those who were rebelling against his government as 'terrorists'.

However, there is a difference between armed resistance and terrorism. Terrorism, as the name suggests, is meant to bring terror to a population by directly and randomly attacking civilian targets. A bomb in a bus station, an incendiary device thrown into a restaurant – the idea is to make citizenry so frightened that it will pressure its government to yield to the terrorists' demands. Suicidal terrorism poses a special threat because it is so difficult to deter. People usually can be deterred by the threat of physical force, and when a police officer points a gun at someone, this is likely to produce compliance because of the threat that otherwise one may be shot and even killed. Even the threat of being captured and incarcerated may deter many from terrorist acts. However, that deterrent power is nullified when the individual is quite willing to die in the process.

Terrorism works best when the target is a democratic society, for autocratic regimes willing to engage in wanton violence themselves can at least to some extent deter terrorism, even suicidal terrorism, by massive retaliation against the terrorist's family and community. Consider this horrifying example: On May 27, 1942, Free Czech agents killed SS Obergruppenführer Reinhard Heydrich in Prague. In retaliation, the Nazis executed anybody they thought connected to this assassination, more than 1000 in all. To drive home the message, the small Czech village of Lidice, accused of having been complicit in the Heydrich killing, was liquidated: All males over age 16 were shot to death, and all the women and children were sent to concentration camps. It did not stop there: the town was levelled, its name was removed from all German maps, and a grain field planted over where it had once stood. Terrorism is unlikely to succeed against an enemy with such total disregard for humanity. Nonetheless, in the long term, such massive retaliation leads to increased sympathy for the terrorists.

Suicidal terrorist attacks have become common in recent years (see Figure 10.10).

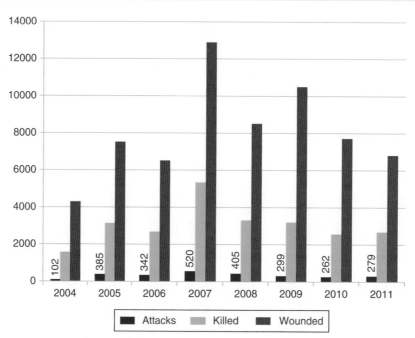

Figure 10.10   Global suicide attacks, 2004–2011. Figures from Worldwide Incidents Tracking System, National Counterterrorism Center, US Government

Source: Jeffrey Lewis (2013) The human use of human beings: a brief history of suicide bombing, *Origins*, 6(7)

Suicidal terrorism is typically a weapon of the weak, for if other means were available through which one could achieve the same desired goals, then the notion of killing oneself in order to kill and terrorize others would quickly lose appeal. But then there is also state-sponsored terrorism: in some cases, countries have harnessed the power of suicidal terrorism to sew terror among its enemies without formally taking the risks of going to war.

Suicidal terrorism in modern times began in the early 1980s, and almost all the attacks since that time have been carried out by groups that follow a militant Islamic ideology; the one exception being the Tamil Tigers in Sri Lanka (Merari, 2010). The vast majority of the attackers have been male, and most of them single and under age 30. Most of these attacks – 90% – have occurred in five countries, Afghanistan, Iraq, Israel, Pakistan and Sri Lanka, but there have been attacks in 37 different countries in total (Merari, 2010), including the attack on the twin towers in New York City. Such attacks, along with non-suicidal terrorist acts, such as the bombing of a train in Madrid in 2004, the 2005 bombings of trains on the Underground and a double-decker bus in London, the coordinated bombing and shooting attack on the Taj hotel in Mumbai in 2008, and the bombs set off at the finish line of the 2013 Boston Marathon, clearly show that no nation is invulnerable to terrorism.

When tragedy unfolds as the suicide bomber detonates his or her explosives, we tend to focus on the person, the bomber, and as we do so, it is easy to neglect the power of the situation. It is easy to assume that the terrorists must be mentally deranged, or must have been brainwashed by their leaders, or are motivated by promises of martyrdom in Paradise. Yet, we would be wrong to do so. Pape (2006) examined all 315 terrorist attacks that occurred around the world between 1980 and 2003. There were 462 attackers in all, and it was concluded that these attacks could not be explained either by mental illness, social alienation, or fanatical religious belief. None of the attackers had significant criminal histories or were otherwise deviant within their society, or were they depressed and despairing. Indeed, they came typically from working or middle-class families, and only a few of them were actually poor or unemployed. It is interesting to discover that most of them were people who could have expected to do well for themselves; they were generally educated and capable individuals. Their minds had not been twisted by propaganda; very few of them had been being subjected to anything other than mild indoctrination, and most of them chose to volunteer on their own and had received very little training before they carried out their deadly attacks.

Why should social psychologists be interested in these individual acts of terrorism? It is because terrorism is best understood as a group phenomenon, reflecting shared beliefs and values. Suicide terrorists carry out their acts in a social context that leads them to believe that they will be remembered and respected as heroes and martyrs for their actions. It is a necessary condition for the deployment of suicidal terrorism that their community believes that such violence is justified and effective, and that other options, peaceful or otherwise, are unavailable or have failed. If their community and society were to consider such acts to be cowardly or heinous or stupid, then no one would be likely to carry out the act (Merari, 2010). Many are motivated by the desire to improve the lot of their people, whom they see as being unjustly treated and humiliated; others may seek hero status as their legacy. And some seek revenge: The Black Widows of Chechnya, a notorious suicidal terrorist group, is a good example of this. Many of their members have sought to avenge the killing of loved ones by the Russian military (Pape, 2006). And finally, it is true that some terrorists may be motivated in part by heavenly reward promised by their religion. Yet, based on interviews of suicide bombers apprehended when their bombs failed to detonate (Merari, 2010), even when there was a firm belief that their deaths would lead to martyrdom and paradise, this was not the primary reason for wanting to carry out the attack.

On the other hand, as Bloom (2007) points out, whatever the individual motivation, the organizations that train and arm these terrorists are very calculating and carefully wield terror in a manner aimed at achieving a specific goal, such as political independence or ending foreign occupation.

Terrorism represents the tragic failure to resolve conflict constructively, whether the conflict is between a dictator clinging to power and a citizenry determined to be free; or between people who believe that their nation has been exploited or humiliated and the stronger power that they blame for it; or whether it is an attempt to right what are perceived as old and festering wrongs.

RESOLUTION OF CONFLICT

How can we promote constructive conflict resolution? Suppose someone wants to play music loudly while a neighbour wants quiet. The offended neighbour might call the police to complain, and if there is a municipal ordinance against excessive noise, the neighbour may be forced to turn down the volume. Or short of involving the police, one of the antagonists could simply give in. Or through negotiation, the parties might arrive at a mutually acceptable compromise such as an agreement that loud music is acceptable but only at certain times. Another possibility is that one of the parties may 'leave the field', for instance by moving to another part of town. Instead, however, people often end up in a stalemate.

We shall now explore a number of factors that can facilitate conflict resolution, including identification with one's group, the introduction of superordinate goals and third-party intervention.

Group identity One way to be successful in reducing conflict and fostering cooperation *within* a group is to make the identity of the group more salient to each individual (Croson & Marks, 1998). Group identity – the extent to which we see ourselves as part of a particular group – plays a very important role in our lives, as will be discussed at length in a later chapter. Where conflict is concerned, if you identify with a particular group, and are reminded about this, you are more likely to act in a manner that is likely to help the group as a whole. If the person with the loud music and the irritated neighbour both perceive themselves as belonging to a common group, 'we are neighbours', then they are more likely to be able to sort out the problems than if one person sees the other as a young and thoughtless punk, and the other views the first as a nosy old crank.

Consider this actual example: During a serious water crisis brought on by drought in California in 1991, it was found that the extent to which individual citizens cooperated by restricting their use of water was related to the extent to which they felt themselves to be a part of their community. Moreover, those who felt a strong identification with the community also expressed a greater belief that the civil authorities were acting fairly and appropriately in the imposition of penalties for high water consumption (Tyler & Degoey, 1995).

Superordinate goals Given the importance of group identity as discussed above, two groups engaged in conflict may be able to manage that conflict much better if they can find commonalities between them so that, in a sense, they can identify with a larger collectivity, the two groups combined. As we shall see, jointly shared goals can help bring this about.

When two groups are locked in ongoing friction such that minor situations turn into significant conflicts, negotiation alone may be insufficient to bring about a harmonious relationship. Sometimes, when two fractious groups are able to focus on a superordinate goal that is important to both, this may bring about a new positive relationship between them. This was demonstrated in a classic study carried out by Sherif (1958). He recruited 11-year-old boys, all strangers to one another, to attend a summer camp (in Robbers' Cave State Park in Oaklahoma). At the camp, the boys were randomly divided into two groups, which were isolated from each other during the first week. Then, throughout the second week, the two groups interacted in athletic contests for group prizes. This produced friction and fighting between the two groups, and the members of each group began to describe the members of the other group as the 'enemy' and to build up stereotypes about them. More than 90% chose only members of their own group as friends.

During the third and final week of camp, Sherif and his colleagues attempted to reduce the conflict that their manipulation had generated. First, they tried simple intergroup contact: the two groups ate together, watched movies together and shared common activities. This failed to reduce conflict. Then they created common goals, for example by surreptitiously damaging the camp's water supply so that the boys had to work together to repair it, and by allowing the boys to cooperate on raising money for a film to be shown at the camp. Working together towards these superordinate goals led to a gradual reduction in hostility and, by the end of the third week, boys from both groups were chumming around together.

The results of this study indicate that simple contact between hostile groups is not enough to reduce conflict, but cooperative interaction in working towards common goals can successfully reduce hostility. Remember, however, that the two groups of boys had no basic underlying conflict in the first place.

Although the findings of the study have been supported by numerous short-term, small-scale studies, there has never been a replication on the scale of this original study (Campbell, 1986), and given the ethical sensitivities of the modern research era, it is unlikely that such a study could ever be carried out again. In any case, there is considerable empirical evidence that members of opposing groups typically overestimate their differences on important issues, with each side believing that they alone are guided by fact and objectivity (Robinson et al., 1995), but through working together for some common goal they can develop better understanding of each other and develop more positive interactions.

Third-party intervention It has been shown that a conflict is generally more likely to be resolved when another person is present, even if that person is not actively involved in the negotiations (Meeker & Shure, 1969).

As discussed earlier, conflicts are often accompanied by significant distortions or misperceptions of each party's motives and values, resulting in even greater hostility. In order to resolve conflicts constructively, it is vital for both sides to view the situation and each other realistically and accurately. If you think that your romantic partner is upset with you because you do not earn enough income to allow the two of you to buy a house, you will have a difficult time smoothing things out if your partner is actually upset because he or she thinks that you value your work more than your relationship. A third party may be able to help the two of you clear up the misperceptions and identify the basic conflict (Carnevale & Pruitt, 1992; Fisher, 1989).

A third party may be able to accomplish more than that: even with accurate perceptions of each other's motives and goals, conflicts over resources, status and power still exist. As we have seen, once threats or coercion are employed, saving face may become more important than the resolution of the original conflict. Obviously, then, to reduce conflict, this third party must find a way to allow the parties to find a compromise without losing face. Such consideration applies as much to a relationship dispute as to an international 'incident', as couples counsellors and international arbitrators are keenly aware. The third party has a number of procedures from which to choose. Sometimes the approach will be selected by mutual agreement of the disputants, while at other times (e.g., in labour disputes) the procedure might be determined by law. Two common procedures are mediation and arbitration.

Mediation Mediation typically involves assisting the process of negotiation, rather than actually suggesting any direct resolution of the problem. In other words, the mediator may provide a channel of communication for the two sides (thus allowing them to avoid face-to-face confrontation). Mediators may also teach the disputants proper bargaining techniques or try to change their motivational orientation – for example, by redirecting them from competitive concerns to problem-solving. Recall the opening vignette: the United Nations Secretary-General played an important role in mediating the dispute between the United States and the Soviet Union.

A variation of mediation has been developed by Fisher and his colleagues (Fisher, 1998; Keashly & Fisher, 1996; Keashly, Fisher & Grant, 1993). In this case, the third-party consultation is concerned with improving the overall relationship, in addition to resolving the current conflict. Unlike traditional mediation, which often keeps the participants separated, skilled mediators help the parties analyse the conflict and search for mutually acceptable solutions. (Recall the discussion of how working towards superordinate goals can help bring people together.)

Arbitration Arbitration differs from mediation in that the intervener in this case reaches a decision about what is a fair resolution of the conflict, and this decision is usually binding. That is, the disputants must agree in advance to accept the arbitrator's decision. Arbitration usually involves content interventions; rather than simply facilitating the process as the mediator does, the arbitrator directly considers the actual content of the dispute. Solutions are suggested and imposed if necessary.

There are two main types of arbitration: *conventional* and *final-offer*. In conventional arbitration, the arbitrator listens to each side of the issue, evaluates the arguments and makes a decision. If the parties know that the usual outcome of conventional arbitration is to split the difference, it is to their advantage to exaggerate their claims in order to offset the effects of such a decision.

In **final-offer arbitration**, each side presents the arbitrator with its final position and the arbitrator then selects one or the other – that which appears to be the fairer of the two – so that there is no compromise. Notz and Starke (1987) examined these types of arbitration to see whether the two procedures would lead to different outcomes even when the elements of the conflict were the same. Under conventional arbitration, the decision was most likely to be based on 'splitting the difference' (equality). Final-offer decisions were more likely to be based on equity, with the arbitrator considering inputs such as productivity and ability to pay comparable salaries, and comparing such factors with labour's demand and management's offer. However, final-offer arbitration involves more risks to each side and thus increases the likelihood of concession and compromise before the final offers are made.

More recently, hybrid procedures combining both mediation and arbitration have been studied. It has been found that antagonists in a dispute who first go through an arbitration procedure where they learn how arbitration works, and then go into mediation, are more frequently able to reach settlement during mediation – and to reach settlements that are more beneficial to each party. Antagonists who first attempt to reach settlement through mediation and then, after that fails, go into arbitration are less successful (Conlon, Moon & Ng, 2002). It may be that experiencing the arbitration procedure first encourages the antagonists to resolve the conflict themselves, for they know what the arbitrator will do if they do not (Ross & Conlon, 2000).

KEY POINTS: When people are in conflict, interaction alone is unlikely to reduce the conflict, but interaction involving working together towards a common goal can reduce feelings of antagonism and lead to greater cooperation towards finding solutions to the conflict. Third-party intervention can also facilitate conflict resolution by improving each parties' understanding and perception of the other's position, by fostering better communication, and by suggesting alternative outcomes. When mediation fails, arbitration can be used to allow an outside party to determine how the conflict is resolved.

A FINAL NOTE

Social psychology has much to offer in terms of understanding and managing conflict. The concepts discussed in this chapter, combined with knowledge of the many other topics discussed in this textbook, provide important insights that can help in reducing or resolving conflict. Think for a moment about a counsellor trying to assist a couple with relationship issues. The counsellor's clinical-counselling ability will be greatly aided by social psychological knowledge – for example, how people build schemata of each other and themselves; how social perceptions and misperceptions develop; how attitudes and beliefs are held or changed; and how communication is often double-coded, so that each person may be 'saying the right things', but through paralanguage or gestures communicating quite a different message. Each of us, by keeping in mind these important considerations, stands better equipped to deal with the many conflicts that present themselves in our everyday lives.

SUMMARY

1. A conflict occurs when the interests or aspirations of two or more independent parties are perceived as irreconcilable.

2. Social exchange theory concerns the perception by each person of the relative value of rewards and costs in a relationship, evaluated in terms of the comparison level (CL) of others in that situation and the comparison level for alternatives to that relationship (CLalt).

3. A 'game' is a situation in which two or more interdependent parties make decisions that affect each other according to rules. Games are either zero-sum, in which one party's gains match the opponent's losses, or non-zero-sum (mixed motive), in which some outcomes are mutually preferable to others.

4. Games such as the Prisoner's Dilemma are based on the assumption that people act rationally to maximize utility.

5. A game that is non-negotiable (only one winner), in which the goal-directed behaviour is threatening, and in which both players can lose disastrously, is called a dangerous game.

6. A collective dilemma occurs when rational behaviour by individuals produces an outcome that is collectively undesirable (e.g., the commons problem and the provision of public goods problem).

7. A threat is more credible when the threatener has behaved consistently in the past, the threatened action has negative consequences for the threatener as well as for the party threatened, and the threatened consequences are not excessive in the situation.

8. Threat often intensifies conflict because of people's need to 'save face'; a spiralling series of threats and counter-threats can develop.

9. Communication sometimes reduces conflict by clarifying the intentions of either side, but it can also be used to manipulate and deceive.

10. The most effective strategy in bargaining combines firm resistance to exploitation with reciprocation of the other party's cooperative behaviour.

11. Mediation and arbitration are third-party interventions designed to reduce conflict.

POINTS TO PONDER

- What would a world be like without conflict? Would change and progress be possible? Would life in a conflict-free world lead to widespread happiness, or would boredom become the dominant emotion?
- Imagine that you work in an office where the coffee room operates on an honour system. You and the other employees share the costs of coffee and morning muffins by leaving the appropriate amount in the moneybox each time you take refreshment. However, it becomes clear that at least one person is eating and drinking without paying. How would you deal with this if no one admits to being the free rider and the situation does not change?
- Can you recall a time when you have become caught up in a threat–counter-threat spiral in the context of a close relationship? If so, what should you do the next time such a situation arises to try to prevent the spiral? Can this be done without looking weak or appearing to accept undue blame?
- Many science fiction writers have explored the theme of a threat to the earth from extraterrestrial armies, suggesting that such external threat would quickly lead all earthlings to forget their differences and unite against a common enemy. Given what has been discussed in this chapter, how likely is it that an external threat would reduce intergroup conflict, and for how long?

FURTHER READING

Carpenter, J. & Cardenas, J.C. (2011). An intercultural examination of cooperation in the commons. *Journal of Conflict Resolution*, 55, 632–651.

A fascinating exploration of the effects of cultural setting on the commons dilemma.

Klapwijk, A. & Van Lange, P.A.M. (2009). Promoting cooperation and trust in 'noisy' situations: The power of generosity. *Journal of Personality and Social Psychology*, 96, 83–103.

An interesting exploration of the effectiveness of generosity as a strategy in conflict situations.

Platt, J. (1973). Social traps. *American Psychologist, 28,* 641–651.

A classic paper describing how we can so readily become trapped and patterns of behaviour that are collectively irrational.

Pruitt, D.G. (2012). A history of social conflict and negotiation research. In A.W. Kruglanski & W. Stroebe (Eds), *Handbook of the history of social psychology*. New York: Psychology Press. (pp. 431–452).

This provides the reader with a thorough exploration of social psychological research into social conflict and bargaining.

Thompson, L.L., Wang, J. & Gunia, B.C. (2010). Negotiation. *Annual Review of Psychology, 61*, 491–515.

A review of recent social psychological and organizational psychological research into negotiation processes.

WEBLINKS

Society for the Study of Peace, Conflict and Violence: http://www.peacepsych.org

A website of the Division of Peace Psychology of the American Psychological Association. Its goal is to encourage psychological research and training in regard to nonviolent conflict resolution and the causes, consequences and prevention of destructive conflict.

CHAPTER 11
AGGRESSION

How many does it take to metamorphose wickedness into righteousness?
One man must not kill. If he does, it is murder ... But a state or nation
may kill as many as they please, and it is
not murder. It is just, necessary, commendable, and right.
Only get people enough to agree to it, and the butchery of myriads of
human beings is perfectly innocent. But how many does it take?
Adin Ballou, *The Non-Resistant*, February 5, 1845

LEARNING OBJECTIVES

* ✳ To understand difficulties involved in defining the concept of aggression

* ✳ To explore the relevance of biological factors in human aggression

* ✳ To examine the effects of social learning on aggressive behaviour

* ✳ To examine the effects of media violence on violence in real life

* ✳ To learn about factors contributing to violence towards women

* ✳ To consider ways to reduce aggression

Oslo, Norway, July 22, 2011: A bomb hidden in the back of a car explodes in front of the building that houses the office of the prime minister. Eight people are killed and 209 others are injured. Two hours later, a heavily armed man dressed as a policeman opens fire at a youth summer camp on the Norwegian island of Utoya. Sixty-nine people are killed and more than a hundred others are injured. Anders Breivik, a 32-year-old right-wing extremist, is arrested and convicted for both attacks.

Kingston, Ontario, June 30, 2009: A car carrying three teenage sisters and an adult woman, members of an Afghani family that had immigrated to Canada two years earlier, plunges into a canal; all aboard are drowned. This was no accident, and the teenagers' parents and brother are subsequently convicted of their murders – honour killings triggered by the teenagers' dating behaviour.

Indeed, it often seems that the world is awash in violence. Headlines announce terrorist attacks, genocides, violent suppressions of dissident groups, gang violence … According to the *Global Study on Homicide* (United Nations Office on Drugs and Crime, 2011) based on data from 207 countries, 468,000 people were murdered around the world in 2010. And then there is war: News reports are filled with stories of ongoing warfare somewhere on the globe – but that is nothing new: in the 40 years following the end of the Second World War, there were about 150 wars, and in all that time there were only 26 days when war was not being waged somewhere in the world (Sluka, 1992).

Yet, most violence – sexual assaults, spousal and child abuse, 'road rage', aggression by schoolyard bullies – in other words, the violence of everyday life, does not make the headlines. Some violence is impulsive, involving sudden deadly outbursts, some is calculated and cold-blooded, and some, especially that which occurs in the home, is chronic, continuing day after day.

Despite such sad commentary on the human condition, the news is not all bad, for it appears that we are gradually making progress as a species and that we have become significantly less violent over time. Pinker (2011b) adduces a wealth of evidence that shows that violence of all sorts – wars, genocides, murders, tortures, rapes and even child-spanking – has been in decline over the past several millennia, leading him to assert that we are living in the most peaceful era of our species' existence. However, that is small comfort to the legions of people around the world who are the contemporary victims of violence.

Why is it that humans so often resort to violence? What led Breivik to the slaughter of innocent strangers? And how could any father or mother or brother murder their own kin, no matter how 'dishonoured' they may feel? And why, on the other hand, do so many humans never become violent? Social psychologists strive to find answers to these questions.

In this chapter, we will first consider the difficulties involved in defining and measuring aggression. Then we will examine the extent to which evolution and biology may predispose us towards aggressive behaviour. Next, we shall discuss how social learning leads to greater or lesser aggressiveness in individuals and how aggressive models in the media influence this process. And given that violence within relationships, and violence towards women in particular, is of great concern in contemporary society, we shall review what social psychology teaches us in that domain. Finally, cultural and personality factors relating to aggressiveness will be considered.

EXPLORING THE MEANING OF AGGRESSION

We all know aggression when we see it, right? A moment's reflection shows that this is not so, for we use the term 'aggression' to describe a variety of behaviours that vary greatly in terms of the actions involved as well as the emotions and motivations associated with them. A neighbourhood bully who trips a child; a hockey player who delivers a body check to an adversary; a mother who yells at her children; a child who hits another child in order to retrieve a favourite toy; a boxer who pummels an adversary in the ring to the delight of the crowd; an air force bombardier who drops tons of bombs on unseen targets miles below; a rapist who overpowers a woman on her way home from work; a back alley scrapper who lets blows fly over a perceived slight – all of these people would be described as having acted aggressively, despite the huge variation in the behaviours, emotions and motives that are involved.

Indeed, aggression is essentially in the eye of the beholder, for a behaviour can be viewed as either aggressive or non-aggressive depending on the social context in which it occurs. Is punching someone in the abdomen aggressive? That depends on whether the punch was intended to hurt an adversary or to dislodge food from the throat of a choking dinner companion. What then are the defining features of aggression? It has to involve more than just a deliberate action that produces pain or distress, for otherwise a physician who administers a painful injection to a struggling, protesting child would be considered aggressive. An intention to hurt or harm is surely central to the concept of aggression – but is it necessary that someone actually be hurt or is the attempt to do harm sufficient? Is emotional involvement (anger) necessary? And must aggression be directed towards people, or is kicking the wall or pounding the desk also 'aggressive'?

Taking these considerations into account, social psychologists typically define aggression as *behaviour that is intended to harm or destroy another person*. Thus, someone who fires a gun intending to hit another person would be considered to have committed an aggressive act even if

Figure 11.1   Gossip as indirect aggression
Source: auremar/Shutterstock.com

the shot misses its mark. And aggression can be indirect – poison pen letters, gossip (Figure 11.1), giving someone the 'cold shoulder', verbal attacks, or starting a malicious rumour aimed at ruining another person's marriage (Hamilton & Tafoya, 2012). The term violence is generally applied to the more extreme forms of aggressive behaviour.

And, of course, some aggression seems cold-blooded and calculated while other aggression involves angry outbursts. Surely there must be a difference between the bully who deliberately seeks you out in order to hurt you or humiliate you and the bully who reacts with anger and aggression after you accidentally knock his cup of hot coffee into his lap. Because of such differences in cognitions and emotions, psychologists distinguish between proactive aggression, which is a premeditated means to some desired end and not accompanied by anger, and reactive aggression, which is accompanied by anger and has as its primary goal the infliction of harm (Anderson & Bushman, 2002; Richetin & Richardson, 2008). More about this later. However, we need to pay attention not only to factors that lead to aggression, but also to those that serve to inhibit it (Box 11.1).

BOX 11.1   TAKE ANOTHER LOOK

INHIBITION

Notable social activists such as Mahatma Gandhi and Martin Luther King did not lash out in anger despite much provocation do so. Instead, they were pacifists, working diligently to change the abhorrent aspects of their society through peaceful means. Are some people biologically predisposed towards pacifism, or is this something that is learned? Not surprisingly, once again both physiological and environmental factors play a role.

Research suggests that some individuals may be genetically predisposed to difficulty in inhibiting their reactions to insults and other emotionally arousing stimuli. For example, as a result of conditioning during childhood, the word 'no' becomes capable of preventing or stopping behaviour in most individuals. However, Nelly et al. (2009) discovered that while individuals with one variant of a particular gene respond to 'no' with activation in the frontal lobes, associated with judgement and anger control, individuals with another variant of the gene show *decreased* frontal lobe activation along with increased activation in the limbic system, which is associated with arousal. The latter arousal pattern suggests anger activation with diminished anger control, and thus a vulnerability to aggressive responding.

Perhaps this goes some way towards explaining why some people are often unsuccessful in keeping themselves from sudden outbursts of anger and aggression that are completely out of proportion to the situation, even though they may later realize that there was little or no provocation or justification for such a reaction. The psychiatric diagnosis of intermittent explosive disorder is applied to people for whom this is a chronic problem. Such aggression is typically linked to increased autonomic arousal, and there is also evidence that two neurotransmitters, serotonin and dopamine, play a major role: There is decreased secretion of serotonin in the frontal lobes, which presumably undermines the ability of the prefrontal cortex to exercise control, and this is accompanied by an increased secretion of dopamine, which has an energizing effect. This combination appears to render the individual quick to react with anger and yet with a diminished ability to control it, and this may result in aggression if the individual is under sufficient stress (Seo, Patrick & Kennealy, 2008). However, although impulsive aggression often appears to be uncontrollable and irrational, it is important to remember that, even in this case, an attribution process is usually involved. For example, a comment that is interpreted as an insult will lead to arousal in the limbic system, while the same comment interpreted as an innocent remark will have no such effect (Bandura, 1983).

Of course, inhibition is also a product of social learning. As we grow up, we learn that aggression in certain situations leads to negative outcomes and so we develop the ability to inhibit an aggressive response, and this inhibition becomes almost automatic in most situations. In addition, such inhibition is sometimes the result of deliberate reasoning: 'Hold on, stay cool, anger is not going to solve anything.' And at other times, it is an emotional response that serves an inhibitory function. For example, imagine that as you feel your temper rising and you clench your fist toward someone who has insulted you, that person breaks into tears. If the tears elicit compassion, your temper is likely to quickly dissolve. And of course we all recognize that another emotion, fear, can certainly serve to inhibit an aggressive response. A person who yells and pushes an adversary of equal or smaller stature is likely to quickly inhibit such aggressiveness when the adversary's larger and stronger friend joins the scene.

The degree to which we are able to inhibit aggressive tendencies no doubt varies from individual to individual in light of individual differences at the neural level, in learning history, in the propensity to think about consequences before acting, and in emotional responsiveness. And our inhibitory ability can change over time or across situations. Most of us are aware of how some otherwise mild-mannered individuals can become quite aggressive under the influence of alcohol, and changes in the brain with advanced old age can reduce inhibitory ability, leading to more impulsive aggression. And, of course, we cannot forget that as we grow up, most of us learn to use language instead of fists to deal with conflict, to cooperate rather than compete when sharing food, and to look for ways of resolving conflicts without resorting to violence.

KEY POINT: Aggression involves intention to harm another person; violence refers to the more serious forms of aggression. Aggression can be proactive – deliberately carried out with the goal of obtaining a particular outcome; or reactive – governed primarily by emotion with the goal of inflicting harm.

RESEARCHING AGGRESSION

How can we study aggression? We cannot simply rely on direct observation, for knowing that one is being observed is likely to influence the very behaviour of interest, and it is in any case difficult to be in the right place at the right time in order to observe aggression when it occurs naturally. What about using hidden cameras? They can be useful in some situations. For example, Pepler and Craig (1995) employed unobtrusive video cameras and wireless microphones to observe school children's interactions wherever they were at play on the school ground, without their being aware that they were under constant observation. Because they were children, only their parents' consent was needed. But this would not work if we wish to study adult aggression: How could we ever obtain consent from adults without making it obvious that they are going to be under observation?

What about studying aggression in the laboratory? Although aggression is defined in terms of intention to harm, it is very difficult to assess intention, and so most laboratory studies ignore it altogether and instead operationally define aggression in terms of specific actions. For example, a frequently used operational definition has been the number and intensity of shocks delivered in a Milgram teacher–learner paradigm (see Chapter 6). Yet, ignoring intent in this way produces ambiguity about the nature of the response. Is shock administered only

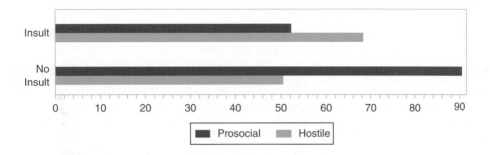

Figure 11.2 Average intensity of shocks delivered as a function of the confederate's insult and the perceived value of the shock

Source: Rule & Nesdale (1974)

in order to hurt, or might participants sometimes do so in the belief that they are actually being helpful? Rule and Nesdale (1974) compared the behaviour of participants who were told that increasing the shock intensity would help the learner to that of participants who were told that this would hinder learning. In addition, half the participants in each group were insulted by the learner (a confederate of the experimenter) during the learning sequence. Participants who were told that the shocks would help the learner delivered, on average, the *highest* intensity of shocks, *provided that they had not been insulted by the learner* (Figure 11.2). Even though they believed that they were causing pain to the learner, they apparently also believed that the victim's own interests justified the pain. However, when they had been insulted, they delivered *less intense* shocks, which suggests that as a result of the insult they were being less helpful. On the other hand, participants who were told that shocks interfered with learning delivered less intense shocks when they had not been insulted compared to those who had been told that the shocks were helpful, but more intense shocks when there had been an insult. Clearly in this instance, the administration of intense shock could be viewed as either a helpful act or a harmful one, depending on what the participants had been led to believe. This must serve as a caveat when we consider studies that treat shock administration as synonymous with aggression.

> **KEY POINT:** It is difficult to study aggression, both in real-life settings and in the laboratory, because intention to harm is necessary for an action to be considered aggressive, and the researcher can only ever make inferences about intentions.

THE ROOTS OF AGGRESSION

How might we explain the violence that humans visit on one another? Is it, as Freud suggested, that we cannot help it, that violence is in our genes? Or could it be that we are like Rousseau's 'noble savage', born good and gentle but corrupted over time by the societies that rear us?

Instinctual roots

We often talk about someone being 'fired up and angry' about something, and about the need to 'blow off steam'. Instinct theories of aggression assume that there is a build-up of 'aggressive' energy, held in check by various inhibiting forces, which eventually must be discharged either through aggression or through activities that are somehow related to aggression (e.g., contact sports). Freud referred to such discharge as catharsis (Freud, 1933). He believed that aggression in some form or another is inevitable and that we can only strive to channel and control it. According to Freud, through 'displacing' one's anger by hitting a punching bag, or even by simply witnessing a boxing match, some degree of catharsis will occur, leaving the individual less aggressively inclined. As we shall see below, the data have proved him wrong. Freud's was not the only instinct theory, but instinct theories in general are too simplistic, and, simply put, there is no empirical evidence for either an aggressive instinct or an aggressive 'energy' in humans.

Catharsis Instinct theory aside, is there something of value in the catharsis notion? The idea has been around for a very long time. Aristotle described catharsis as the purging of feelings of pity and fear that are aroused in an audience when watching a dramatic tragedy: the viewer identifies with the hero, and by feeling the hero's pain, those emotions are expressed and drained away. On the other hand, Plato believed that witnessing emotional discharges actually increases rather than subdues emotional feelings.

It turns out that Aristotle was wrong; modern research supports Plato, and the evidence against the catharsis hypothesis is compelling. Such activities as watching or participating in aggressive sports, directing aggression towards objects, watching film violence or lashing out verbally at other people are not effective means of reducing hostile arousal, and instead are more likely to increase aggressive thoughts and feelings and promote aggressive behaviour (e.g. Bushman, Baumeister & Stack, 1999; Verona & Sullivan, 2008). For example, in one study, it was found that the blood pressure of insulted or irritated individuals, along with their reported feelings of hostility, decreased more rapidly when they were simply left alone, rather than when given the opportunity to face their antagonist and verbalize their annoyance, as the catharsis notion has suggested (Vantress & Williams, 1972).

> **KEY POINT:** Despite popular belief to the contrary, we do not have aggressive instincts or energies, and participating in or witnessing aggressive activities actually increases aggressiveness rather than reducing it.

Frustration as a root of aggression

No one is angry or aggressive all of the time. An early focus was on the effects of frustration within a situation, and it was speculated that there may be an inborn tendency to aggress following frustration of some kind. This frustration–aggression hypothesis as originally proposed by Dollard et al. (1939) posited that every instance of frustration, defined as interference with behaviour directed towards a goal, produces some tendency towards aggression, and that every instance of aggression is preceded by some sort of frustration. It was assumed that both learning and environmental cues would determine the particular form that aggressiveness would take and what its target would be. However, research has shown that this view, like Freud's approach discussed earlier, is untenable, and that while frustration may lead to aggression, it may lead to other behaviours as well, such as passive withdrawal. Moreover, aggression is not always preceded by frustration.

However, most people know that when they are in pain or distress – after hitting one's thumb with a hammer, for example – they feel more irritable and perhaps more ready to lash out at others, even with little provocation. Taking this into account, Berkowitz (1983, 2012a, 2012b) developed a cognitive neo-associationist model (which simply means a new – 'neo' – form of a model based on 'associations' between two stimuli). The model begins with an aversive stimulus (pain, excessive heat, frightening news, etc.) that produces negative emotion (fear, anxiety, anger) associated with arousal in the autonomic nervous system (the so-called 'fight or flight' response'), which in turn produces either the tendency to escape or the tendency to attack. Thus, according to this model, aversive stimulation can trigger anger, fear or anxiety directly.

The emotion associated with this reaction will also elicit various thoughts and memories that have been associated with that emotion or that situation in the past. Some thoughts (e.g., 'No one does this to me and gets away with it') may lead the individual to react with aggression, while others (e.g., 'I'm going to get hurt') are more likely to lead to flight, and others still (e.g., 'I've got to stay calm and manage the situation') bring about a reduction in autonomic arousal. Yet, if the arousal is too high, people may react ('in a blind rage') before there has been enough time for cognitive influences to have any effect. The aggressor may subsequently claim with sincerity, 'I didn't mean to hurt anybody.' The model thus predicts that aggressive behaviour can at times occur without any deliberation having taken place, leaving the aggressors ignorant of their own motivations (Berkowitz, 1994).

Excessive heat is an instance of aversive stimulation, and according to Berkowitz it can lead directly to anger and aggression. Does this explain why city violence often seems more prevalent during long, hot summers? Although the data in this regard are not uniform, there is fairly consistent support for the notion that aggression becomes more likely when temperatures rise, at least up to a point, and then becomes less likely again when the temperature is very high, perhaps because in really hot weather people feel sapped of energy (Bell, 2005). It is assumed that the increased aggression is the result of increased hostility and aggressive cognitions brought about by the discomfort caused by the heat. Research in the United States (Rotton & Cohn, 2000) supports this; correlating ambient temperature to police reports of aggravated assaults, it was found that during the daylight hours in the spring months, there is less aggression reported to the police when the temperature is either very high or very low, while at other times aggression increases as temperature increases.

Consider another notion that emerges from the Berkowitz model: the weapons effect. It is posited that through repeated pairings of guns with aggressive behaviour in movies and on television, the presence of a gun can elicit classically conditioned arousal and aggressive thoughts that may in turn promote aggressive behaviour in some situations. A number of studies have demonstrated this effect, which is most likely to occur when participants are angry or frustrated (Carlson, Marcus-Newhall & Miller, 1990). This will be discussed in more detail later in this chapter.

KEY POINT: Aversive stimuli may increase autonomic arousal and then thoughts triggered by the situation, combined with situational cues that have been seen associated with aggression in the past, may make aggressive behaviour more likely.

Evolutionary roots

Evolutionary psychology (discussed earlier in Chapters 8 and 9) is a relatively new and still somewhat controversial approach to the study of human social behaviour. While all agree that both genetic and environmental factors influence behaviour, it is *how* genes provide their influence that is at issue. Evolutionary psychologists assume that just as physical adaptations to environmental circumstances have evolved – for example, walking erect – at least some traits and behaviour tendencies that helped humans to survive and reproduce, such as aggression, are subject to the same evolutionary processes (Confer et al., 2010; Salmon & Crawford, 2008). And just as all normal human beings now walk erect, it is expected that these evolved traits and behaviour tendencies are now also universal, although their expression may be influenced both by social factors and by the normal genetic variations that distinguish us from one another in so many different ways.

Survival of the fittest has often depended on being 'red in tooth and claw', that is, on being physically able to defeat the predators out to eat you, to overcome the competitors out to dominate you, and to scare off those who are trying to steal away your mate. As a result, aggressive responses are virtually 'built in' in many species, and evolutionary psychologists suggest that, like other mammals, humans too have evolved with a tendency to become aggressive towards one another in specific situations (Buss & Shackelford, 1997). It is hypothesized that there are also specific genes or combinations of genes in humans that are responsible for an aggressive tendency, and that these genes were favoured by natural selection – at least in males, because more aggressive men had better success at mating and thus reproduced more frequently, resulting in their aggression-related genes being more prevalent in the gene pools of successive generations (Buss, 1994). It is similarly posited that genetically based male sexual jealousy was favoured by natural selection because, by controlling one's mate, males could ensure that their own genes and not those of another male were passed to the next generation. This evolving male aggressiveness and the consequent power differential between males and females is said to account for gender-based hierarchies in modern societies.

Such reasoning has led to some specific hypotheses, based on the notion that any organism is motivated to get as many of its genes into the next generation as possible. For example, recall the kinship principle (Chapter 9): It is argued that because an individual shares many of his or her genes with close relatives, the propagation of at least some of one's genes also occurs when those relatives reproduce. Deadly aggression towards those relatives would work against such propagation, and so it is claimed that male aggressiveness is inhibited when interacting with close relatives. This implies that aggression among modern males will be more perilous when the individuals involved are distantly rather than closely related (Daly & Wilson, 1988). The fact that the murder rate of step-children by step-parents is significantly higher than the murder rate for parents' biological children is offered as support for this claim, although you may be able to think of an alternative, non-biological, explanation for that fact.

Evolutionary psychology has both strong proponents (e.g. Confer et al., 2010; Machery & Barrett, 2006) and strong critics (e.g., Buller, 2005; Gannon, 2002). A common criticism is that its claims are not testable, that they 'explain' behaviour in a way that cannot be falsified. For example, regarding the differential murder rates of children and step-children, there is no direct genetic evidence available to support the claim, and critics point to other likely explanations, such as (is this the explanation you came up with?) while biological children are with the parents from birth, this is not usually the case with adopted children, which may lead to less opportunity for the development of emotional closeness during infancy. As a result, in some cases the emotional bond between step-parents and step-children may not be as strong as that between natural parents and their children. Whether or not this accounts for the difference in murder rates, the essential point is that one must consider that there are other differences apart from genetic ones that may make comparisons between adopted and biological children more complex.

And what about male domination of females, patriarchal societies, and sexual jealousy? Critics accuse evolutionary psychologists of largely disregarding the rich body of historical and anthropological evidence that bears on kinship and mating patterns (McKinnon, 2005). Wood & Eagly (2002) maintain that status differences have emerged between the sexes *not* because of greater genetically based male aggressiveness, but because males and females are biologically specialized in such a way that they are more efficient at performing some activities than others. For example, only females can bear and nurse children, and this has had a significant effect on the division of labour and the social organization within a group, to the extent that males, unencumbered by pregnancy and nursing of children, have been in a better position to hunt for food, to acquire resources, and even to acquire and practise new skills useful for increasing status and power. As a result, a sex-typed division of labour became institutionalized, and over time parents began to rear their children with sex-typed roles and stereotypes.

In sum, although the debate over evolutionary psychology continues, because of its problems of testability, its tendency to ignore evidence that does not fit with the genetic model, and the small effect sizes it claims relative to the much larger effects due to psychosocial variables, it is wise at present to remain cautious with regard to its claims. Nonetheless, we must not forget that despite the controversy about some of the particular claims put forward by evolutionary psychologists, we are indeed the products of evolution. As is discussed below, genetically determined brain mechanisms are likely to influence at least some of our aggressive tendencies, even though, because of genetic variation, the propensity for such behaviour is likely to vary from individual to individual.

KEY POINT: Although evolutionary processes have shaped our brains and nervous systems, arguments that human aggression has evolved through natural selection remain at best controversial.

Genetic roots

Regardless of whether there are genes that relate directly to aggression, the interaction between genes and environment certainly plays a significant role in whether children grow up to be more or less aggressive. Even at birth, there are clear differences in temperament, which is defined in terms of how excitable an infant is, combined with the ability to calm down (Jong et al., 2010; Rothbart, Ahadi & Evans, 2000). Bang some cymbals together in a hospital nursery and all the children will cry, but some will soon stop and others will cry for what seems to be ages. This reaction presumably reflects inborn differences in their autonomic nervous systems, and these differences, in interaction with environmental factors, can lead to quite different reactions to threat or provocation later on in life.

Some particular genes appear especially important to an understanding of aggressive and antisocial behaviour. For example, Caspi et al. (2002) followed a sample of male children from birth to adulthood in the attempt to understand why some children who are maltreated during childhood develop antisocial behaviour and others do not. Although parental maltreatment often leads to aggressive and antisocial behaviour in children, they found evidence that children with a particular genotype (related to the gene MAOA, which encodes an enzyme that makes some particular neurotransmitters inactive) were less likely to develop such problems despite parental maltreatment. They concluded that particular genotypes can render children less sensitive to the effects of harsh treatment.

Other research has found that certain versions of three particular genes appear to influence an individual to react more aggressively when in a stressful situation (Simons et al., 2012). Yet, the effect is indirect, for what is inherited is not a propensity for aggression per se, but a greater sensitivity to stimulation in the social environment, which those researchers explained through the differential susceptibility model: As a result of genetic variation, some brains are more 'plastic' than others, and the greater the plasticity, the more the development of the brain will be affected by environmental factors as the person is growing up. Thus, when people with such susceptibility suffer harsh treatment from parents or grow up in a neighbourhood rife with violence, the development of their brains is likely to be more affected by those circumstances than the brains of those of people lacking this susceptibility. In turn, because of both this sensitivity and a negative social environment, such people are at greater risk of coming to view the social world as hostile and threatening, and they may develop toughness and aggressiveness in order to deal with it.

> **KEY POINT:** Genes play a primary role in the development of brain structure, but their effects on aggressiveness are likely to be indirect.

Neural roots

Let us leave genes aside and look at how brain function may relate to aggressiveness. In light of the explosion in neuroscience research over the past few years, there has been renewed attention to the role that particular brain structures and neurotransmitters play in aggressive behaviour. But not all aggressive behaviour is cut from the same cloth: Recall the distinction between proactive and reactive aggression. Not surprisingly, reactive aggression is more closely linked to the limbic system where emotionality is based; whereas, given that it involves more thought and less emotion, proactive aggression appears to be largely regulated by higher-order cortical functions, especially those of the prefrontal cortex, a region that is important in cognitive appraisal and judgement. What happens when that region is damaged or not fully developed? Frontal lobe damage is sometimes accompanied by increases in aggressive behaviour, and a number of brain imaging studies of antisocial, psychopathic and violent individuals have reported impairments in the prefrontal regions of their brains (Yang, Glenn & Raine, 2008; Yang & Raine, 2009).

[
KEY POINT: Proactive aggression appears to be associated with the prefrontal cortex, while reactive aggression is more closely linked to the limbic system. Impairment in these areas can have significant influence on the manifestation of aggressive tendencies.
]

Hormonal roots

There are substantial sex differences in aggressiveness found in many species: often, males fight readily while females do not, except in defence of their young (Archer, 1976). These differences do not seem to be the result of learning, and so it makes one wonder about the role played by the so-called sex hormones. Castration eliminates one important sex hormone – testosterone – and when stallions, bulls and other animals are castrated, they become more docile and rarely fight. The administration of testosterone restores 'normal' aggressiveness, suggesting that testosterone plays an important role in animal aggression. Castration also appears to reduce aggressiveness in human males (Johnson, 1972), and when testosterone is administered to normal adult human females, their physical activity and their general aggressiveness often increase to levels typical of males (Bardwick, 1971). There is also evidence that differential exposure to testosterone during prenatal development plays a role in aggressiveness (Collaer & Hines, 1995). McAndrew (2009) argues that as a result of natural selection, testosterone levels in males rise in situations involving competition or challenges to status, and that such a rise in testosterone level is an essential ingredient in any aggression that follows. He goes on to note that male-to-male aggression is most intense in adolescence and early adulthood, a period when both testosterone levels and competition for status and sexual partners are highest.

However, it should not be assumed that the relationship between testosterone and aggression is directly causal. For example, androgens also enhance musculature and increase available energy, and how this increased physique and energy are employed depends on socialization (Eagly & Steffen, 1986). (This muscle-building and energizing feature of testosterone made it the hormone of choice for some athletes before drug regulations and drug-testing policies were introduced.) Moreover, testosterone level is actually influenced by social factors, including the perception and interpretation of a situation; research suggests that cues related to aggression may trigger a higher testosterone level, which in turn may make an aggressive response more likely. For example, in one experiment (Klinesmith, Kasser & McAndrew, 2006), male participants who handled a gun experienced a greater increase in testosterone levels than did those in a control condition. Thus, whatever relationship there is between testosterone and aggression, it is undoubtedly a complex one involving not only biological but also social and cultural factors as well.

[
KEY POINT: Testosterone appears to play a significant role in some aggressive behaviours, but does not on its own explain human aggression.
]

Social roots

While genes, brain structure and hormones play a role, they can only partially account for why some individuals manifest much more aggression than do others, and attempts to explain aggression only in terms of biological factors overlook the very powerful influences of both social learning and social structure within a society.

Social learning theory According to social learning theory, it is through both direct reinforcement of their behaviour and imitation of others that children learn how to aggress, when to aggress, and against whom to aggress (Bandura, 1973). Most research has shown that early life is a particularly critical time for learning about aggression (Olweus, 1972). The learning process probably proceeds in the following manner (Sawrey & Telford, 1975): the newborn infant responds to a limited range of stimuli – a loud noise, a sensation of falling, a cold draft, a hampering of body movement – with a single, diffuse emotional response pattern (related to sympathetic nervous system arousal) that might be labelled 'excitement' or 'fright'. Through classical conditioning, other stimuli can come to evoke the same response. The 'startle' reaction in infants is accompanied by internal physiological changes as well as behavioural changes. There is first a stiffening of the body followed by tantrum-like behaviour involving squirming, uncoordinated thrashing about of the arms and legs and crying. It is through reducing this discomfort that the infant learns to 'aggress' or 'withdraw' when frightened. If the child's outbursts are effective in removing the aversive stimulus, the diffuse outburst may be perpetuated. However, it is more likely that certain features of this reaction pattern are more effective in specific situa-

Figure 11.3 Do water guns ignite aggression or do they just get kids wet?

tions than others. Waving the arms, for example, may stop the advances of an overly friendly cat, but crying may be totally ineffective in that situation.

Eventually, language enables the child to gain some control over behaviour. While pushing or hitting may reduce or eliminate pain or frustration, the child also learns that in certain situations, aggression is met with counter-aggression. Overt aggression may then be replaced by verbal or symbolic aggression. Moreover, the child who communicates through language learns to use verbal means (e.g., flattery and persuasion) to obtain goals that were previously obtained through the use of force. Children who have difficulty in language acquisition may never fully learn to substitute words for fists.

What young children learn about aggression and how acceptable it is exerts a very strong influence on their social behaviour as they grow up (Huesmann & Guerra, 1997) (Figure 11.3). Children in some societies and in some families, boys in particular, are encouraged to be aggressive and to 'stand up for themselves', while others are taught to be more pacifistic and to try to resolve conflicts in an unaggressive manner. However, the child's physical abilities interact with the environment to produce a particular set of experiences that may themselves promote or discourage the learning of aggressive responses. For instance, children who are small for their age are not likely to be successful at throwing their weight around, while larger children may soon learn that aggression is useful in achieving certain goals. (One such goal may be simply the attention that aggression brings.) On the other hand, small individuals may tire of having sand kicked in their faces and ultimately take measures to become more powerful, possibly becoming a bully, while the larger child may be left alone, never developing the need to develop aggression-related physical skills.

Although direct reinforcement is important in the development and maintenance of aggressive behaviour, children are also capable of acquiring aggressive behaviour simply by watching someone else who is acting aggressively. What happens to the aggressive model that helps inform the child about the reinforcement contingencies that are in effect? If the model is rewarded by achieving a particular goal, or at least is not punished, children may imitate such behaviour when they find themselves in a similar situation. Bandura and his colleagues (Bandura, Ross & Ross, 1963a, b) performed a series of classic experiments that demonstrate this. For example, children were shown a television film of a boy who refused to share his toys with a second boy. The latter reacted by attacking the first boy and throwing darts at his toy cars. In one version of the film, the aggressor ends up with all the toys, and the film finishes by showing him taking them all away. The second version ends differently, with the aggressor being subjected to a punishing counter-attack by the first boy. While most of the children said that they disapproved of the aggression, those who saw the unopposed-aggression ending were subsequently observed to behave more aggressively in a play situation than those who saw the other ending, or those who saw no film at all. These findings are supported by a naturalistic study carried out in an urban daycare centre. Goldstein et al. (2001) found that children were more likely to behave aggressively if they witnessed a child's aggressive act that resulted in a positive outcome for that child than if it resulted in an aversive one.

The influence of models and the observation of what happens to them continues to affect us throughout our lives. For example, when a spectator at a football game observes someone throw a beer can at the referee and there are no negative consequences, the spectator may be prompted to throw things as well. The model's aggressive behaviour can also serve to heighten emotional arousal, which in turn can facilitate an aggressive response, given the appropriate situational cues.

Repeated experience in childhood, either personal or through observing models, leads to the development of cognitive scripts (Huesmann, 1988). These are like the event schemata discussed in Chapter 2 that tell us what is likely to occur in a given situation, how we should respond, and what is the likely outcome. These scripts are shaped not just by personal experience and its consequences, but also through observing what happens to others in everyday life and by portrayals in the media. For example, preferring to watch television programmes that portray police officers as dishonest ruffians probably both reflects and reinforces a negative script about the police. These scripts become automatic and then influence our cognitive appraisal of a situation, our choice of action and our interpretation of the outcome, all virtually without our awareness (Huesmann, 2007; Huesmann & Kirwil, 2007). They often contribute to self-fulfilling prophecies. For example, a script involving notions such as 'you cannot trust the police, they are out to get you' is more likely to lead to negative interactions with the police, along with outcomes that will reinforce the script.

KEY POINT: Social learning plays a very significant role in determining behaviour, including aggressive behaviour. Reinforcement, modelling and the learning of cognitive scripts are all important in determining the extent to which an individual will tend towards aggression.

Parental influences Parents are the child's first models. From the social learning perspective, the behaviour of parents – who largely control the young child's world – play a critical role in determining whether a child grows up to be aggressive. They also teach the child how to interpret the social environment; they manage the child's behaviour, they set standards of conduct and enforce rules; and they serve as teachers, directly supplying knowledge, imparting values and encouraging particular attitudes and manners (Klama, 1988).

As you can imagine, it is not easy to study the relationship between parents' characters and behaviours, their child-rearing style, and the subsequent aggressiveness of their children. The researcher cannot manipulate independent variables or exclude all extraneous variables, and so the typical study instead examines the correlation between aspects of the parenting style and aspects of the child's behaviour or personality. Often, such studies rely on parental ratings of the child's behaviour as well as the child's self-report, but these sources of information can be very misleading.

However, despite such difficulties, a body of research relating to the effects of parental characteristics and parenting styles on children's aggression has gradually emerged (Coie & Dodge, 1997). Parents who frequently use physical punishment or threats to discipline their children serve as aggressive models and indirectly teach children that aggression 'works' when one is in a position of power. Moreover, physically punitive parents are more likely to reinforce or condone aggression by their children when they are in disputes with other children. And when aggression is used to resolve conflicts within the family, the child not only learns about its effectiveness, but is deprived of the opportunity to learn non-violent problem-solving strategies, and this may be the most important influence (G.R. Patterson, 1982), leading to an increased risk that individuals will respond with aggressive behaviour when conflicts arise later in life (Moore et al., 1989). And keep in mind that, as mentioned earlier, biological factors appear to make some children more susceptible to the effects of parental discipline than others.

And remember the discussion of proactive and reactive aggression. Research suggests that they often spring from different experiences in childhood – proactive aggression is more likely to develop in an environment that directly or indirectly reinforces aggressive behaviour, and reactive aggression in a threatening and harsh environment such as that produced by cold and abusive parents (Brendgen et al., 2006). Then when the child enters school, he or she is exposed to a whole set of new peer relationships, and these serve to encourage or discourage particular behaviours. Children who are reactively aggressive are often rejected or mistreated by their peers as well as being reprimanded by adults, while on the other hand, proactively aggressive children, even when they are bullies, tend to be tolerated more and their behaviour reinforced more by other children, especially by similarly aggressive children with whom they become friends (Poulin & Boivin, 2000) (Box 11.2).

BOX 11.2   TAKE ANOTHER LOOK
BULLYING

Being reared in a home characterized by a punitive parental style, family conflict and poor conflict resolution strategies often leads to 'externalizing behaviour' in children, including defiance, theft, vandalism, fighting and bullying (Brubacher et al., 2009). Some bullies outgrow their bullying, but others continue to have problems in their social interactions as they grow up, and what was considered bullying in the school context may become relationship violence later in life (Pepler et al., 2002). While it is often assumed that boys are more likely to engage in bullying behaviour than girls, recent research indicates that gender does not seem to be a significant predictor (Hong & Espelage, 2012), although girls are clearly more at risk of becoming victims of *sexual* bullying, much of which is verbal in nature.

Only a few children grow into bullies, but many others are their victims. While once accepted as 'part of growing up', leading parents to encourage their children, especially their boys, to stand up for themselves when bullied, bullying is now being recognized as a pervasive form of violence that brings misery to the lives of many children at a time in their development when they lack the resources to respond appropriately. Some suffer severe and long-term emotional effects as a result. And in this electronic age, bullying has taken on a new and modern form – *cyberbullying*. Through emails or Facebook or other social media, a child can be hounded and humiliated by an anonymous bully.

Bullies harass those who are least likely to be able to defend themselves, and children with developmental difficulties may be especially vulnerable to being singled out as targets (Marini, Fairbairn & Zuber, 2001). Moreover, research in both the UK (Rivers, 2001) and the United States (Birkett, Espelage & Koenig, 2009) reveals that students who are identified as lesbian, gay, or bisexual are many times more likely than other students to be bullied both verbally and physically. Similarly, straight boys who do not seem 'masculine' enough may become targets. A British study of 11- to 14-year-old boys in 12 London schools (Phoenix, Frosh & Pattman, 2003) reported that a common feeling among these boys was that they had to present themselves as properly masculine to avoid being bullied by other boys and labelled as 'gay'.

Bullying is a worldwide problem. A questionnaire study carried out in Spain, Italy and the United Kingdom involving almost 6000 adolescents reported that between 3% and 7% of the respondents, depending on the country, reported having been bullied, with cyberbullying playing a significant role (Ortega et al., 2012). In face-to-face interviews of a large representative sample of the Czech population of age 12 or higher, approximately 10% of Internet users reported that they had been victims of cyberbullying (Ševčíková & Šmahel, 2009). In these studies, the bullying, whether direct or cyber, was found to have a damaging emotional impact on the majority of its victims, leading to academic and psychosocial difficulties, low self-esteem, depression and in some cases externalized hostility. On the other hand, some victims indicated that they had not been affected at all, pointing to the need to understand what it is that makes some victims more resilient than others.

While bullying is usually considered in terms of the characteristics of the bully, there is often a group-level process involved that rewards the bully and encourages further bullying, to the extent that the bullying takes on the qualities of a social role within the peer group (Salmivalli, 2010). Others in the group may not directly bully the target themselves, but their reaction – laughter, for example – both encourages the bully and further humiliates the target. Some children will imitate the bully's behaviour in order to win favour with the bully or with others in the group, and the bully's usually dominant status inhibits those who might otherwise come to the target's defence lest they too become targets.

Bullying does not stop when children leave school. Adults, too, often experience serious and destructive consequences when they are bullied. Bullying is widespread in the workplace, in the armed forces, in prisons, and in many other social institutions (Monks et al., 2009). For example, a Japanese study (Giorgi et al., 2012) reported a prevalence rate of workplace bullying of 15%. And in the study of Internet bullying in the Czech Republic mentioned earlier (Ševčíková & Šmahel, 2009), it was found that some people 50 years of age and older also reported being victims of cyberbullying.

Effects of domestic violence While we like to think of parents as striving to do their best to rear their children in a safe and healthy manner, domestic violence accounts for the majority of violent acts within any given society (Tolan, Gorman-Smith & Henry, 2006), and much of this violence is directed at children. Child abuse is a worldwide problem (Newton & Vandeven, 2010), and abused children are at risk for developing serious problems of psychological and behavioural adjustment. Physical abuse in the home is a significant predictor of aggressive behaviour both for boys and girls (Muller & Diamond, 1999), and there is accumulating evidence that such abuse can inhibit the development of a sense of self-efficacy and self-mastery in children, which can extend into adulthood and produce not only emotional difficulties but even significant health problems that extend into old age (Sachs-Ericsson et al., 2011). However, societies vary in terms of what is considered to be child abuse. What is considered unacceptably harsh in one society may be viewed as appropriate discipline in another. For example, spanking a child is considered to be abusive in Sweden, while it is viewed as normal, harmless punishment in many other countries.

Parental verbal and physical aggression directed at adolescents is significantly correlated with verbal and physical aggression in these adolescents' romantic relationships when they become young adults (Cui et al., 2010). Furthermore, longitudinal research has also shown that harsh child-rearing tends to perpetuate itself with each new generation of parents as they repeat the same child-rearing techniques that they themselves experienced. This effect has been observed across three generations (Huesmann, Eron & Yarmel, 1987; Bailey et al., 2009).

Even if one is not directly abused, simply witnessing family violence (e.g., seeing one's mother being battered) may produce as much psychological damage in children as being directly abused (Jaffe et al.,1986). Sadly, many children are regularly exposed to scenes of spousal violence. Studies of children as young as 12 months of age have found that children who are exposed to anger, even when it is not directed at them, react in a distressed manner that sometimes includes aggressive behaviour (Emery, 1989). And some children who grow up witnessing violence between their parents go on later in life to treat their partners in a similar manner (Moore et al., 1989; Emery, 2010; Smith et al., 2011).

However, the link between child abuse and adult violence is not straightforward. We must be careful not to assume that every child who has been abused or who grew up watching family violence will become a harsh and abusive parent. While the empirical evidence reveals that there is a greater likelihood of child abuse if the parents had been abused as children, most child abusers were never themselves abused, most delinquents were not abused as children, and most abused children do not turn into delinquents (Glasser et al., 2001; Widom, 1989; World Health Organization, 2007). Nor do aggressive children necessarily grow to be aggressive adults. In a 15-year longitudinal study of more than 1000 boys in Montreal, it was found that only one in eight boys who had been particularly aggressive in kindergarten maintained their aggressiveness into the high school years (Nagin & Tremblay, 1999). Does this mean that the effects of child abuse are not nearly so serious as has been feared? No. But although the reasons are not yet understood, while some abused or neglected children become more aggressive, others instead become depressed, withdrawn and even self-destructive, and still others appear to be relatively unaffected. Some children simply seem to be more resilient than others. Various psychological characteristics of the child, as well as aspects of family life apart from violence, all play some role in determining the impact of violence on the child; the child's appraisal and cognitive processing of the violence in the home is most likely an important factor (Rutter, 1987; Werner, 1989). Some children may be able to distance themselves emotionally from family violence, and may be less likely to blame the situation on some shortcoming in themselves (Moore & Pepler, 1989). The presence of one adult who plays a significant role in the child's life and who provides a warm and secure relationship may, for some children, have a very significant effect in preventing the development of psychological maladjustment and aggression (Gonzales et al., 2012).

Before leaving this topic, it is important to point out that in addition to child abuse and witnessing domestic violence, child neglect also has negative consequences, and such neglect is even more common than physical abuse (Éthier, Palacio-Quintin & Jourdan-Ionescu, 1992). Neglected children sometimes show even higher rates of aggressiveness in adulthood than do children who have been physically abused (Widom, 1989).

> **KEY POINT:** Parents establish and control most of the child's environment and reinforcement contingencies and therefore play a primary role in establishing what the child learns about the effectiveness and the desirability of aggressive behaviour.

Media influences

Advertisers certainly believe that television influences attitudes and behaviour, for they spend billions on it. And it is certainly possible that, given the powerful influence of models, and given that most children spend a good deal of time watching television or videos or playing video games, the way that violence is presented in the media may significantly influence their own behaviour.

Traditional members of the Cree community of Norway House on Lake Winnipeg in Manitoba, Canada, refer to television by the Cree word *koosapachigan*, which means 'shaking tent', a place where the shamans of the past conjured up spirits of the living and spirits of the dead. Some of these spirits were not very friendly. Indeed, much of what is shown on television is not very friendly, and there has long been a debate about whether media violence – be it at the cinema, on television, or on the Internet – leads people, especially children, towards greater aggression. And modern youth-oriented music and video games often have violent themes, some that make targets of women, racial minorities and unpopular authority figures such as the police. Given that children are exposed to both aggressive and non-aggressive models in the media, it is likely that the more a child is similar to and identifies with the model, the more that modelling will occur (Eron, 1980).

But how significant is the effect? While adults also are influenced by models, most studies of the effects of media violence have been carried out with children because they are assumed to be more vulnerable given that their beliefs, values and attitudes are actively developing. The research evidence has been somewhat mixed, but in recent years more and more evidence is accumulating that supports a significant positive link between media violence and real-life aggression by those who watch it (Bushman and Anderson, 2001). Even pre-school age siblings have been found to become more aggressive towards one another after being exposed to violent television programming (Miller et al., 2012). Yet, these findings generally refer to relatively mild aggressive behaviour, such as that observed among children at play or among participants in a laboratory study. On the other hand, the influence of media violence, including violent interactive video games, appears to be minimal in terms of any relationship to criminal acts (Ferguson, 2013; Ferguson & Kilburn, 2009). It is important to keep this in mind in the discussion that follows.

Social psychological studies of the effects of watching violent television have taken several forms:

- Laboratory studies: Participants are exposed to either a violent or a non-violent film and then observed when presented with the opportunity to aggress.
- Field studies: Children in natural (usually residential) settings are randomly assigned to a television diet either high or low in violence, then observed and measured for aggressiveness.
- Correlational studies: In these studies, some of them longitudinal, measures of the amount of violent television watched are correlated with measures of aggressiveness.

While laboratory studies are useful in examining relationships among variables that are important in the real world, and while such studies have clearly demonstrated that the viewing of television or film violence in the laboratory leads to increased aggression – in the laboratory, we must hesitate when extending these results elsewhere. It is not clear, for instance, that the measures of aggression in the laboratory (e.g., pushing a button to deliver shock to another person) have much to do with real-life aggression. More importantly, the demand characteristics of the laboratory situation would suggest that the experimenter approves of or permits the aggressive behaviours the participant is given the choice to perform. It is also important to note that in reality no one is exposed to a single violent film; television violence is more likely to be viewed on a regular basis over a period of years. Furthermore, TV violence will be interrupted with a good deal of non-violent programming, which is likely to influence the net effect.

Longitudinal studies generally find a positive correlation between watching violent television and aggressiveness. Yet, rather than violent television causing aggression, could it be that a tendency towards aggressiveness leads aggressive people to choose violent television? Huesmann, Lagerspetz & Eron (1984) carried out a longitudinal study of 758 children in the United States and 220 children in Finland over a period ranging from Grade 1 to Grade 5. They found that the viewing of television violence was indeed significantly related both to present and future aggressiveness. However, they concluded that while the simple observation of media violence does have some effect on aggressiveness, the effect may be related to changes in attitude brought about by seeing the apparent effectiveness of aggression in problem-solving. There was no evidence that children who appeared to be predisposed to aggression or children of aggressive parents were more influenced by TV violence than were any other children.

Another longitudinal study, this one carried out in Germany (Krahé, Busching & Möller, 2012), examined the relationship between adolescents' consumption of media violence and both self-reported and teacher-rated aggression over a period of two years. Media violence consumption predicted both self-reported and teacher-rated aggression over time. Participants whose consumption of such programming dropped across the course of the study also manifested a corresponding drop in aggressiveness.

Violent video games are becoming more and more popular, especially with young males, and there is growing concern that such games lead their players to deal with real-life conflicts by means of physical aggression. Anderson and Bushman (2001) conducted a meta-analysis of 35 studies of the effects of violent video games and concluded that playing such games is definitely associated with heightened aggressive behaviour. They indicated that the strength of the relationship between playing violent video games and aggression is as strong as the relationship between condom use and lowered risk of HIV infection! Of course, while a causal link between condom use and lowered HIV transmission makes intuitive sense, it is still not clear just what is the causal link, if there is one, between violent video games and aggression. However, one possibility is suggested in another study by Bushman and Anderson (2002): Participants in their study played either a violent or a non-violent video game and then read ambiguous introductions to stories involving potential interpersonal conflicts. They were then asked to guess at what the main character would do or say or think as the story progresses. Compared to those who had played the nonviolent games, those who had played the violent games suggested that the main character would feel more angry and have more aggressive thoughts and act more aggressively. The authors concluded that the violent games produced a 'hostile expectation bias', the tendency to expect others to react aggressively to conflicts.

Other research has found that effects of playing violent video games can continue long past the game itself. Bushman & Gibson (2011) had participants play either a violent or nonviolent game for 20 minutes, and afterwards half of each group was asked to ruminate about the game – that is, to think about violent aspects of the game. A full day later, those who had played the violent game were more aggressive than those who had played the nonviolent game, but only if they had been led to ruminate about the violence in the game (Figure 11.4). The authors conclude that the rumination keeps aggressive thoughts, feelings and tendencies in mind. It is interesting to note that these effects were found for men but not for women. This is possibly because men enjoy the physiological arousal associated with these games. It was found in one study that when playing violent video games accompanied by a loud soundtrack, male players' heart rates increased, reflecting arousal, while female players' blood pressure increased, indicative of stress (Tafalla, 2007). Perhaps that is one of the reasons that women are less likely to be attracted to such games than men (Hartmann & Klimmt, 2006); they may tend to avoid violent games because the games produce a stress reaction.

The aggression-promoting effects of video game violence have been found in a number of different cultures. Anderson et al. (2010) conducted a cross-cultural meta-analysis of studies of the effects of violent video games on aggressive behaviour both in Japan and in Western countries. Their results strongly suggest that exposure to violent video games is a causal risk factor in terms of increased aggressive thoughts, feelings and behaviour as well as decreased empathy and prosocial behaviour. Other research (Huesmann & Rowell, 2010) has supported this finding for both males and females.

Yet, despite such studies, researchers remain divided on the question of whether media violence *actually* causes an increase in aggressive behaviour (Ferguson, 2013). Why such hesitation? Some researchers (e.g., Ferguson & Kilburn, 2010)

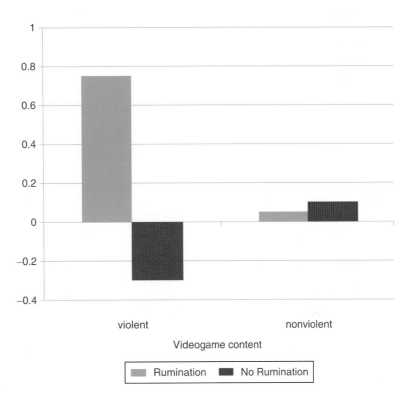

Figure 11.4 Aggressive behaviour in males as a function of game type and rumination (standardized scores)

Source: Based on information from Bushman & Gibson, 2011

point to methodological flaws in some of the research relating media violence to aggression, and argue that the reported relationship is a weak one that is not supported by statistics regarding youth violence in the real world. Another concern is that media violence is generally confounded with excitement – violent television programmes or movies or video games are generally more exciting and enervating to observers and players than more neutral programmes. Therefore, when studying changes in behaviour after participants have watched a violent television programme or have played a violent videogame, one cannot be sure that any increase in observed aggressiveness is not due simply to the excitement rather than the violence. And there is another possible confounding factor: video games, violent or not, generally involve competition. When Adachi & Willoughby (2011) compared aggressive behaviour in participants who had played either a violent or nonviolent video game, they found that more competitive games subsequently led to greater aggressive behaviour regardless of whether violence was part of the game.

Thus, controversy continues not only about the strength of the effects of media violence and aggression, but even about their very existence. This debate has raged for several decades now and it will no doubt continue to rage for years to come. In December 2011, the *International Society for Research on Aggression* set up a special committee of internationally recognized researchers in the field of media violence to examine the link between media violence and aggression. Its report (Report of the Media Violence Commission, 2012) concluded that:

> … exposure to media violence can increase not only aggressive behaviour in a variety of forms, but also aggressive thoughts, aggressive feelings, physiological arousal, and decrease prosocial behaviour. The effects of media violence can be different for different people, and can be very subtle, especially when examined over the course of a person's lifetime. Media violence effects have been found in all types of media examined (TV, movies, video games, music, cartoons, etc.) (p. 335).

The report goes on to say:

> Some commentators have argued that violent media, especially violent video games, are the primary cause of school shootings. Other commentators have argued that there is no good evidence of any harmful effects of violent media, usually based on the results of one or two studies. Neither extreme is supported by the vast body of research in this domain. What is clear is that exposure to media violence is one risk factor for increased aggression in both the short run and the long run.

And that is really the best we can say about media violence at this time – it is one risk factor for increased aggression, but it certainly does not inevitably lead to aggression. It is likely that most readers of this textbook have watched a considerable amount of television or movie violence and yet have not grown up to be overly aggressive individuals.

Apart from the direct effects of media violence, it can produce a number of indirect effects:

Imitation When the media shower attention on perpetrators of violence, some attention-seekers may try to emulate the violence with the hope of acquiring celebrity status. Such copycat aggression is common; even in the 19th century, the news of Jack the Ripper's exploits provoked a series of female mutilations in the English countryside (Berkowitz, 1971). A flurry of assassination attempts around the world followed US President Kennedy's assassination in 1963 (Weisz & Taylor, 1969), and both that assassination and other well-publicized murders have been followed by an unusual increase in violent crimes in the United States (Berkowitz & Macaulay, 1971). In a study of violent youth offenders, a quarter of them indicated that they had themselves attempted copycat crimes (Surette, 2002). In addition, television and cinema dramas – especially those that have been carefully researched and present criminal activities with considerable attention to detail – may actually teach people how to commit particular crimes.

Stimulus pairing Recall the weapons effect. Berkowitz (1984) speculated that when violence is repeatedly associated with weapons on television, such 'stimulus pairing' may give weapons the power to prime aggressive thoughts and elicit aggressive behaviour in situations of anger or fear. In a seminal study more than 30 years ago, Berkowitz and LePage (1967) demonstrated that the mere presence of a gun produced a greater level of retaliatory aggression in a laboratory experiment than did the presence of badminton rackets. As noted earlier, this has been successfully replicated in different contexts by a number of different researchers. The actual weapon itself is not necessary: A picture of a weapon or even the name of a weapon produced a similar effect (Anderson, Benjamin & Bartholow, 1998).

However, while the importance of aggression-related cues has been amply demonstrated (Carlson, Marcus-Newhall & Miller, 1990), other research suggests that the effects of such cues may depend on the extent to which an individual has characteristically used violence in the past (Josephson, 1987).

Desensitization Research has demonstrated that habitual exposure to media violence can lead to desensitization, that is, a reduction in emotional responding. It has been argued that the desensitized individual is less likely to notice the cues that would normally initiate a moral evaluation situation and therefore be less likely to respond to them (Funk 2005; Huesmann, 2007; Huesmann & Kirwil, 2007). As a result, aggressive behaviour may be tolerated or initiated without any consideration of moral implications, and the opportunity to intervene in a prosocial manner may be ignored (Bushman & Anderson, 2009). For example, one study (Krahé et al., 2011) reported that individuals with a history of habitual media violence exposure responded with lower levels of galvanic skin conductance (which typically increases when a person is excited, anxious or frightened) when watching a violent film clip, but not when watching a sad or funny film, suggesting less arousal, and thus a desensitization effect, specific only to violent content. In another study (Strenziok et al., 2011), participants repeatedly watched videos with varying degrees of violence while their brain activity was monitored by means of a functional MRI (fMRI). While these videos initially produced arousal in the expected regions of the brain, repeated exposure to the more aggressive videos led to a decrease in this arousal, supporting the view that repeated viewing of

344

aggressive content can blunt an individual's emotional response. Other research has found clear evidence that playing violent video games can produce a reduction in physiological arousal when subsequently faced with depictions of real violence (Arriaga, Monteiro & Esteves, 2011; Bailey, West & Anderson, 2011). In one study (Carnagey, Anderson & Bushman, 2007), participants played a violent video game for only 20 minutes, and then watched a film involving real violence. Compared with participants who had not played such a game, their heart rates and galvanic skin responses were lower, indicating actual physiological desensitization.

But does such desensitization actually result in increased aggression? Certainly some laboratory research appears to indicate that it does (Englehartd et al., 2011). But is desensitization produced by violent video games enduring or does it evaporate soon after the game is over? In an experiment (Mullin & Linz, 1995), male university students were shown a series of violent films, with two days separation between films. Both self-reported emotional response and measures of physiological arousal diminished over the series of films. Moreover, three days after viewing the last film in the series, the participants showed considerably less sympathy towards victims of domestic violence than did a control group of participants. Yet, five days after the final film, their level of sympathy towards domestic violence victims had returned to the same level as that of the control group. This study demonstrates that people whose sensitivity to violence is diminished as a result of watching violence can rather quickly resensitize. But will a viewer who chooses a steady diet of such violent films fail to resensitize? Researchers have not yet provided an answer to that question.

Effects on values and attitudes It is possible that a steady diet of violent media will lead to changes in values and attitudes, such that violence becomes more acceptable. Violent television programming suggests that, at least in the television world, violence is generally a successful means of obtaining personal goals: it is usually not punished and law enforcement agencies whose job is to reduce violence often use violence to do so. It is not difficult to manipulate the emotions of viewers so that they welcome violence in a film even if they do not normally enjoy watching violence. Stories that lead us to sympathize with victimized individuals or groups, eventually forced to 'stand up and fight' for their rights and vanquishing their tormentors in the process, can produce positive feelings even when violence and law-breaking are the means used, and these can contribute to the development of cognitive scripts that serve to justify aggressive behaviour, as discussed earlier.

Increased apprehension The rate of violent crime in most Western nations has been declining year by year over the past two decades (Tseloni et al., 2010) and yet media violence cultivates a perception of the social world as a dangerous place where people must constantly be on guard. Television and movies perpetuate stereotypes about criminals and their crimes that have little to do with reality. For example, while most murders in television dramas are committed by strangers to the victim, more than 80% of murders in Canada are carried out by people who know the victim (Gartner, 1995).

Sexual violence in the media While the large majority of research studies examining the effects of media violence have focused on non-sexual themes, some researchers have been particularly concerned about whether erotic depictions, especially those involving violent sexual activity, promote sexual violence. Not so many years ago, media depictions of sexual acts, or even simple nudity, were illegal just about everywhere in the world. Times have changed, and as erotica has come to be publicly available in many countries over the past two decades, there has been a sea change in terms of community standards. In most Western countries, now almost 'anything goes' in terms of sex and violence in movies, with the exception of child pornography. Because today's children, adolescents and young adults in such countries have grown up in a world with easy access to erotica, their attitudes and reactions are obviously going to be different from those of most of their parents and grandparents. And whether parents become aware of it or not, the ubiquitous presence of X-rated material on the Internet gives many children and adolescents the opportunity to watch uncensored sexual content, sometimes violent, sometimes degrading, regardless of their age.

Of course, erotica varies tremendously in the message it conveys. Check (1985) drew important distinctions among erotica (sexually explicit materials emphasizing sharing of sexual pleasure rather than only the satisfaction of male needs and fantasies), nonviolent dehumanizing pornography (which portrays women as the playthings of men, enjoying sexual degradation) and violent pornography (in which women are forced into painful or dangerous sexual acts). It would seem obvious that if such media actually do result in increased violence, is more likely that violent pornography would present the major concern. Yet, dehumanizing pornography that portrays women as enjoying being sexually victimized promotes rape myths, and it is possible that the adolescent male viewer may come to believe that women 'need to be forced' to have sex and that they will ultimately come to enjoy it. Thus, non-violent dehumanizing pornography can lead to sexual callousness towards women and decreased concern about the effects of rape (Check & Guloien, 1989).

In any case, it is still not clear just what are the effects of sexually oriented media on adolescent attitudes and behaviours (Braun-Courville & Rojas, 2009; Escobar-Chaves et al., 2005), and the data have been somewhat contradictory. For example, a longitudinal study (Ybarra et al., 2011) reported that exposure to X-rated material is strongly associated with subsequent sexual aggression later in the life, and that this is particularly so for violent X-rated material. Yet, on the other hand, a review of available data in the United States appears to have ruled out any causal relationship between pornography consumption and rape (Ferguson & Hartley, 2009). But, then again, a large meta-analysis of studies comparing adolescent sex offenders to non-offenders (Seto & Lalumière, 2010) concluded that adolescent sex offenders were more likely to have experienced sexual violence, child abuse or neglect, social isolation – and early exposure to pornography. However, such data do not tell us whether pornography actually contributed to their becoming sexual offenders, or whether it simply reflected antisocial tendencies that lead both to consumption of pornography and to sexual offences.

Perhaps the most reasonable response to whatever problems pornography may pose is to develop programmes to educate males, especially teenage males, about the reactions of women to coercive sex and to counter the development of potential harmful attitudes towards women (Donnerstein, Linz & Penrod, 1987). Even a little information can go a long way: Sinclair, Lee and Johnson (1995) examined the effect of a single 'social comparison cue' on reactions of male university students to erotic films, violent sexual films and violent non-sexual films. The cue consisted of a male confederate saying aloud, just before the film clip ended, 'This is really disgusting. It's incredibly degrading towards women.' This cue was enough to lead the male participants to evaluate the portrayal of women as being more negative in both the erotic and the violent non-sexual film clips. Further, when these participants participated in an ostensibly unrelated subsequent experiment in which they had the opportunity to deliver electric shocks to a female confederate in a Milgram-type learning paradigm, they delivered shocks of lower intensity. This suggests that the presentation of appropriate social-comparison information to men might lead to a reduction in male violence towards women, although it is not clear just how one might make such social-comparison cues available and relevant.

And what about the emergence of tough and domineering female figures in video games and films? Ferguson (2012) conducted a study in which young adults watched either neutral media or sexually violent media, and each with either strong or subordinate female characters. When the female characters were subordinate, female participants who watched the sexually violent video reported greater anxiety than did females in the neutral condition, and males reported more sexist beliefs and negative attitudes towards women than those in the neutral condition. On the other hand, when the video involved strong female characters, there were no effects on either anxiety or attitudes for either sex. Ferguson refers to this as the *Buffy effect* in reference to strong female characters as found in *Buffy the Vampire Slayer.* However, since the conclusions of this study were based on self-reports of a sample of university students, they should be treated as preliminary.

Excitation transfer Another concern about the admixture of erotica and violence is the possibility of excitation transfer. This notion was captured in David Cronenberg's 1996 film *Crash* (Figure 11.5)

Figure 11.5 A scene from David Cronenberg's *Crash* (1996)

Source: © Ronald Siemoneit/Sygma/Corbis

in which people amplified their feelings of sexual excitement through the physiological arousal produced by being involved in car crashes. Sexual arousal and aggressive arousal along with other kinds of arousal reflect the same underlying sympathetic nervous system activation. The excitation brought about by anger or physical pain is no different from the excitation that underlies sexual desire and activity, and an individual cannot differentiate excitation as 'sexual' or 'aggressive' on the basis of nervous system activity alone (Zillmann, 1984). Thus, residues of excitation following sexual arousal can intensify subsequent emotional states, such as those associated with aggression, just as residues following aggression can intensify subsequent sexual reactions. This explains the reported passion involved in 'make-up sex' following a lover's quarrel: the residue of the nervous system arousal associated with anger, now that the anger seems over, is interpreted as additional sexual arousal, thereby intensifying this enjoyable emotional state.

> **KEY POINT:** Violence in film and video games may contribute to increased aggression, but the data are far from clear. Effects of such media in terms of desensitization and using aggression as a problem-solving technique are also of concern. Mixing violence and erotica complicates the picture even further.

Cultural influences

In addition to cultural differences that relate to intimate partner violence, there are also very dramatic differences in homicide rates in general from country to country around the world. Consider these 2004 homicide rates (per 100,000) (United Nations Office on Drugs and Crime, 2004): Iceland, 1.0; England and Wales, 1.6; Canada, 1.75; United States, 5.8; Haiti, 35; Columbia, 53. (See Figure 11.6 for a summary of 2010 homicide rates around the world). How can we explain such dramatic differences?

Obviously, this is not due to some evolutionary process, nor to neural structures or sex hormones. These differences are related to culture, and cultures differ greatly in the value placed on aggression. Some encourage it – think of the notion of the *macho* man in some societies – and yet there are cultures in which violence of any kind has been actively discouraged. For example, the Pygmies of the Congo, the Zuni Indians of the southwest United States, the Lepchas of Sikkim, and the Inuit in Canada have historically been peace-loving societies. While the influence of Western culture is modifying the values and the behaviour of people in many such societies, the fact that groups can still be found who prefer and practise a non-aggressive existence illustrates that violence is not an inevitable aspect of social life. The Jains of India also believe strongly in nonviolence, and take vows to avoid harming others. The Amish and the Hutterites renounce all kinds of force, and crime is practically unknown among them. In such cultures, aggressive behaviour goes unrewarded or discouraged while pacifism is stressed as a lifestyle. And even though these children experience severe pressure in the course of being socialized (which should lead to frustration), they are virtually free of interpersonal aggression (Bandura & Walters, 1963).

Thus while conflicts will always occur from time to time among individuals and groups, our culture plays a large role in determining how we deal with conflict, whether by negotiation, a flurry of fists or a knife in the side. Children in Western nations are most often taught the importance of winning, and aggression is often a means to that end. In contrast, children in Japan have been traditionally discouraged from quarrelling. They learn that yielding is more honourable and more desirable than being assertive in the quest for personal goals. Traditional Japanese mothers tell their children, '*Makeru ga kachi*', when they start to argue or fight,

Homicide rates
- 0.00 - 2.99
- 3.00 - 4.99
- 5.00 - 9.99
- 10.00 - 19.99
- 20.00 - 24.99
- 25.00 - 34.99
- >=35
- No data available

Note: The boundaries and names shown and the designations used on this map do not imply official endorsement or acceptance by the United Nations.

Figure 11.6 2010 homicide rates by country

Source: http://www.unodc.org/documents/data-and-analysis/statistics/Homicide/Globa_study_on_homicide_2011_web.pdf

which means literally 'to lose is to win'. The child who gives in, who contains his or her assertiveness in order to promote group peace and harmony, receives reinforcement from the mother and is viewed as more mature (Azuma, 1984).

Some cultures maintain a code of honour that insists on violent retribution for actions perceived to bring dishonour to the individual or the family (Osterman & Brown, 2011). Thus, in some very traditional societies such as Afghanistan, women who break the rules set up by the patriarchal culture, especially those rules associated with interactions with men, are sometimes killed by their own fathers and brothers, such murder being the only acceptable way to cleanse the family of dishonour. Vestiges of codes of honour persist even in some modern Western countries.

> **KEY POINT:** Cultures vary in the degree to which aggression and violence are glorified or discouraged, and this reflects again the importance of social learning and gender roles for an understanding of aggression.

Neighbourhood influences

As a child grows, peer influence becomes more and more important, and group pressures push the child to conform (recall Chapter 6). A child who grows up in a neighbourhood rife with violence is more likely to be tempted to view aggression as a means of solving problems, and toughness as a defence against aggression, and this may be encouraged both by peer pressure and by the presence of aggressive adult models. (Recall the earlier discussion of a gene that influences the child's susceptibility to the influence of the social environment.) Social capital refers to aspects of community involvement that promote cooperation among residents. This includes social networks (e.g., churches, neighbourhood associations), shared trust, and strong norms of reciprocity – all of which give individuals the ability to seek and receive help from others (Coleman, 1990). Neighbourhoods that are low in social capital are more prone to violence and crime; such violence and crime serve as a mirror of the social environment (Kawachi, Kennedy & Wilkinson, 1999). Using American data, Kawachi et al. (1999) found that measures of social capital are actually the strongest correlates of violent crime (homicide, assault, robbery) across communities. Dysfunctional communities with low social capital are often the result of economic deprivation, and other research has found that homicide and other crime rates are positively correlated with economic inequality, both across regions within a country, and between countries (Fajnzylber, Lederman. & Loayza, 2002).

> **KEY POINT:** People who grow up in disadvantaged and economically deprived neighbourhoods are at greater risk of resorting to aggression, at least in part because of peer influence and the presence of aggressive models.

Personal roots

Of course, personal factors, including gender and personality, have important influences on all behaviour, including aggression.

Gender Gender seems to have an important relationship with aggression. Historically, it has been men, not women, who have marched off to battle; men, not women, who have duelled to the death to avenge wounded pride; men, not women, who have relied upon physical force to dominate others (Figure 11.7). But to what extent is aggression primarily a male behaviour?

Developmental psychologists report that gender differences in aggression appear early in life: For example, at 27 months of age boys are much more likely than girls to grab another child's toy (Campbell, Shirley

& Caygill, 2002). Although physical aggression typically peaks and begins to decline by four years of age as conflicts begin to be resolved more and more by nonphysical means, about 10% of children, most of them boys, maintain a relatively high level of aggression even at age 11, and the gender gap in aggression continues into adulthood (Archer, 2004). In a study of 1400 children aged 7 to 10 years in a number of countries – including China, Colombia, Jordan, Italy, Kenya, Philippines, Sweden, Thailand and the United States – boys in each of these countries reported more physically aggressive behaviours than did girls (Lansford et al., 2012). What's more, research also indicates that of the approximately one-third of children who show minimal aggression during childhood, the majority are girls (Archer & Côté, 2005).

As children reach their late teen years, a few go on to commit violent crimes, a trend that peaks in early

Figure 11.7 Duke of Wellington's duel with George Finch-Hatton, March 21, 1829

Source: © Lebrecht Music & Arts/Corbis

adulthood. But what is notable about these violent crimes is that both the aggressor and the victim are overwhelmingly male (Archer, 2004, 2009). In Canada and the United States, 80% of the people arrested for violent crimes are male (Statistics Canada, 2012; United States Department of Justice, 2010), and around the world, men account for approximately 80% of violent perpetrators (United Nations Office on Drugs and Crime, 2011).

How can we account for this apparently overwhelming gender effect? There are several considerations:

Physiological We have already considered as being very controversial the claims of evolutionary psychologists that natural selection has made males more aggressive and more controlling of their sexual partners, and we also discussed the effects of testosterone, noting that while it appears to play some role in male aggressiveness, it cannot by itself explain such aggressiveness.

Risk avoidance Some researchers have suggested that the gender difference comes about not simply because of greater aggressiveness on the part of males, but because women avoid getting into fights for fear of getting hurt and instead rely upon indirect aggression. Indeed, females from a wide variety of cultural backgrounds, in nations as diverse as Poland, Finland, Italy, Israel, Australia, Argentina, Canada and the United States, have been found to prefer indirect aggression (Vaillancourt, 2005). When indirect forms of aggression are taken into account, women are as likely to aggress as are men (Archer & Coyne, 2005).

Moreover, laboratory studies carried out in North America – where participants have no fear of any retaliation outside the laboratory – do not show a strong gender effect with regard to aggressiveness, and although some studies have reported greater physical aggression by males, the differences are relatively small and are greatly diminished if one takes provocation into account (Eagly & Steffen, 1986; Loeber & Hay, 1997). When sufficiently provoked, females are as likely as males to respond with aggressive behaviour (Bettencourt & Miller, 1996).

Cultural roles and stereotypes In virtually all cultures, masculinity is associated with qualities of strength, courage, risk-taking, and, the willingness to fight when necessary (Weinstein, Smith & Wiesenthal, 1995; Garbarino, 1999), and, as a result, boys are often strongly discouraged from showing emotional 'weakness'. It follows that for men to back down in the face of a threat has traditionally been considered 'sissyish' or 'effeminate'. Parents often openly encourage boys to grow up to 'be a man', while girls traditionally have been encouraged to be non-aggressive and more concerned with maintaining interpersonal harmony. Perhaps as a result, women have typically experienced more guilt and anxiety about aggression and are more concerned with the harm that comes to victims and with the risks to themselves if they are aggressive (Eagly, 1987).

However, contemporary media – television, music videos and video games – are more and more frequently presenting aggressive female characters (Snethen & Van Puymbroeck, 2008), thus providing the kinds of aggressive models for growing girls that have always been available for boys.

Power   Most aggression is perpetrated by the stronger against the weaker. Men are on average larger and stronger than women, and, combined with that size and strength advantage, men have wielded social power through the patriarchal structure of almost all societies. As a result, women have traditionally been 'kept in their place' and strongly discouraged from acting aggressively. In much of the world, women still find themselves at a huge disadvantage in terms of the power distribution. In some nations, they are unable to vote, or to drive a vehicle, or even to go out of the home without a male family escort.

However, there has been a sustained effort over the past several decades to diminish the patriarchal nature of Western societies and to remove the social power differential favouring men. Perhaps as a result, it has become clear in recent years that females are also quite capable of acting aggressively, and this tendency appears to be on the rise. Consider, for example, these Canadian data: Violence among adolescent girls is the only area consistently showing an increase in reported rates of violent offending, even though, relative to male adolescent violence, the rate still remains low (Leschied et al., 2001). Moreover, between 1991 and 2011, the adult violent crime rate declined significantly for men while the rate for women increased 34%, although males still accounted for 80% or more of people accused of violent crime (Statistics Canada, 2012). In the USA, arrests for physical aggression are also increasing for girls while decreasing for boys (although it is not yet clear whether the greater number of female arrests may reflect a change in law enforcement policies, with the result that police now may be less likely to turn a blind eye to female aggression).

Sexual violence towards women

Some male violence is directed specifically at women, and sexual assault including rape is a tragically serious problem everywhere in the world. For example, statistics show that one woman in seven in the Netherlands reports having been sexually abused and that one woman in six has been a victim of rape or attempted rape in the United States (Bohner et al., 2002). For many rapists, much of the gratification comes from domination and control (Malamuth et al., 1995), and, shamefully, rape has all too often been used as a terrifying tool of domination in war. The systematic rape of civilian women was employed as a tactic by Japanese troops in Korea, China and the Philippines during the Second World War; in Bangladesh during its war of independence; in recent civil wars in Africa and in the Balkans; and in the 1992–95 conflict in Bosnia-Herzegovina where it is estimated that somewhere between 20,000 and 50,000 Muslim women were systematically raped by Serb soldiers (Watts & Zimmerman, 2002).

Social psychological factors often make it difficult for women to obtain justice after being sexually assaulted, and this is particularly so in societies where women have little power. When women are totally dependent upon their husbands and their husbands' families, both physical and sexual aggression directed towards them is not only more common, but often viewed as acceptable (Archer, 2000a, b). Belief in a just world (see Chapter 2) can lead to a shift of some or all of the blame from the rapist to the victim: 'She should not have been wearing a low-cut blouse when walking alone at night.' And various 'rape myths' also serve to minimize the seriousness of the offence – for example, 'If a woman does not physically fight back, you cannot say it was rape' (Payne, Lonsway & Fitzgerald, 1999) or 'A woman who goes to a man's apartment on their first date implies that she is willing to have sex' (Burt, 1980). Such myths not only provide perpetrators with partial justification for their actions, but can influence the reactions of medical professionals and the justice system as well.

Intimate partner violence

However, most violence directed towards women by men is not sexual but physical, and is not directed at strangers but at intimate partners. Intimate partner violence is a worldwide problem (World Health Organization, 2005) and the figures are staggering: The *Global Study on Homicide* (United Nations Office on Drugs and Crime, 2011), mentioned earlier, indicates that the vast majority of the almost half million homicide victims around the world were women murdered by their past or present male partners. Such violence victimizes somewhere between 30 to 60% of women worldwide, depending on the region (Morse et al., 2012). According to the Parliamentary Assembly of the Council of Europe (2000), one European woman in five is a victim of violence every day, and women aged 15 to 44 years suffer as much death and ill health from violence as from cancer (Venis & Horton, 2002). Researchers in China report that close to 20% of Chinese wives suffer abuse by their husbands at some time during their lives, with emotional abuse being most common, followed by physical and sexual violence (Tang & Lai, 2008). Empirical estimates of a woman's lifetime likelihood of intimate partner violence in Middle Eastern countries range from 32 to 43% (Morse et al., 2012). Moradian (2009) reported that 68% of married women in Iran suffer from domestic violence committed either by their husbands or their in-laws during the first year of their marriage. In North America, too, domestic violence is the most common form of violence (Widom, 1989). In Canada in 2008, 51% of women who had been physically assaulted were assaulted by their current or former spouse or boyfriend. By comparison, only 12% of men who had been assaulted were assaulted by a former spouse or girlfriend. Similar findings were reported in the United States (Vaillancourt, 2010). There is growing evidence that violence occurs frequently in dating relationships at the teenage level as well (Pedersen & Thomas, 1992; Princz, 1992). Alcohol consumption often catalyses such violence (Moore et al., 2011).

Jealousy (discussed in Chapter 8) is one of the major triggers of such violence (Puente and Cohen, 2003) and jealousy-based violence is seen as being justified in many cultures. In addition, as noted earlier, strong codes of honour in some societies not only allow but encourage male family members to punish and even kill female family members who have brought 'disgrace' by breaking the strict social conventions that govern their romantic and sexual behaviours. Such was the case with the family described at the beginning of this chapter.

Yet, despite all that has been said about gender and aggression, research also shows that when it comes to intimate partner violence, females in developed Western countries are just as likely to be aggressive towards their heterosexual partners as are males (Archer, 2000a,b; Kwong, Bartholomew & Dutton, 1999; Cross & Campbell, 2011). What accounts for the difference between the data based on police reports indicating that most victims of intimate partner violence are women, and the research reported above? A meta-analysis (Archer, 2004) of studies conducted in the United States provides a clue. It was found that women were actually slightly *more* likely to be physically aggressive than men, but men were more likely to inflict a significant injury, and of those who were injured by a partner, 62% were women. Because of the typical difference in physical size, male victims of female aggression are less likely to become police statistics. Another possible bias in police statistics is the likely reluctance of many men to admit that they were injured by a woman.

While it is true that in developed Western societies males and females are more or less equal with regard to physical aggression towards their partners, this is definitely not the case in many other countries. Archer (2006) meta-analysed studies of intimate partner violence carried out in sixteen widely dispersed nations around the world and found that where there was greater gender equality and individualism, there was decreased female victimization and increased male victimization. A second analysis of data from 52 countries produced similar results (Archer, 2006). This suggests that as women gain in emancipation, they also gain power, and it appears that it is relative power that underlies much of intimate partner violence.

KEY POINT: While physiological factors cannot be ignored, social and cultural factors, including gender roles and the distribution of power between males and females, play a larger role in producing gender differences in aggression.

Personality Some personality theorists view personality as a collection of response patterns or traits. Is there a trait of aggressiveness? Can we characterize people as being more or less aggressive? While, as mentioned earlier, there is evidence that certain personality characteristics have a genetic component (Miles & Carey, 1997), any inborn tendencies interact with the environment to produce response patterns in children.

Such tendencies are likely to influence a child's interaction with his or her parents, and this in turn will change the social environment.

However, there is no single cluster of traits that describe the aggressive person. The same behaviour may be judged as aggressive or non-aggressive, depending on such variables as age or sex. Moreover, research shows that situational factors generally have more impact on aggression than do personality factors. For example, automobile drivers are more likely to experience aggressiveness and stress when driving in highly congested traffic conditions than when there is little congestion (Hennessy & Wiesenthal, 1999; 2002). However, while there is no good basis for talking about a trait of aggressiveness per se, there are a number of individual characteristics that have some influence on aggressiveness:

Intelligence In a 22-year longitudinal study of intellectual competence and its relationship to aggression (Eron et al., 1987), it was found that aggressiveness of most toddlers decreases as they grow and learn other coping strategies, many of them verbal. However, the lower the child's IQ, the more difficult it may be to learn coping and verbal conflict resolution skills. In fact, success at any endeavour may be more difficult for children of lower intelligence, leading to increased anger and more aggression. In turn, aggressive children may be avoided by teachers and peers, thereby limiting their learning opportunities.

Self-esteem and narcissism As was discussed in Chapter 3, self-esteem is a central personality variable. However, the relationship between self-esteem and aggression is not yet fully understood (Ostrowsky, 2010). It has been assumed that poor self-esteem is a major factor in aggressive behaviour and that threat to self-esteem, such as criticism or insult, often produces anger and aggression (daGloria, 1984). Indeed, bullies who throw their weight around sometimes are insecure individuals trying to bolster their image by being tough. However, accumulating evidence indicates that it is not so much low self-esteem but rather *inflated* self-esteem associated with narcissism (recall Chapter 3) that typically gives rise to a tendency towards aggression. People with inflated but unstable self-esteem (narcissists) are more likely to view the feedback that they receive from the world around them as very inadequate in light of their perceived self-importance, and then are prone to react with anger and aggression both to this apparent injustice and to anything else that challenges and threatens their high self-image (Baumeister, Smart & Boden, 1996; Bushman & Baumeister, 1998; Kernis et al., 1989).

Social rejection, real or imagined, is certainly a threat to one's self-image, and narcissists have been found to be more likely to react with anger and aggression to rejection. In one study (Twenge and Campbell, 2003), after filling out a measure of narcissism (the Narcissistic Personality Inventory), participants mingled with one another and then each was led to a separate room. Half the participants were led to believe that they had been well-received by the others and half were informed that no one wanted any further interaction with them. At this point, a measure of anger was administered. As can be

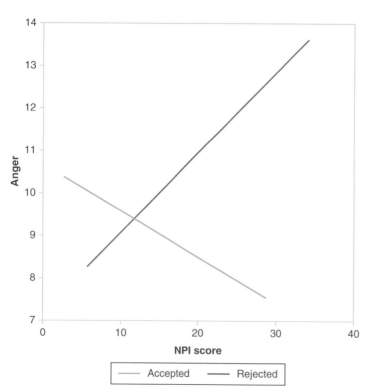

Figure 11.8 Anger following social acceptance or rejection as a function of Narcissistic Personality Inventory score

Source: Twenge & Campbell (2003)

seen in Figure 11.8, for those who had been told that they had been accepted, anger scores decreased with increasing narcissism, presumably reflecting a higher need for acceptance and greater satisfaction at being accepted, by those higher in narcissism. On the other hand, among those who had ostensibly been rejected, anger increased dramatically as narcissism scores increased.

Each participant then played a number of trials of a computer video game, ostensibly against one other person. The participant was told that he or she could set in advance the noise level of a sound that would be played into the earphones of the other player each time that player lost on a trial. The higher the level, the more unpleasant it would be for the other player, and thus the noise level was the operational definition of aggression. The results showed that those who were high in narcissism were more aggressive after they had experienced social rejection, but there was no such effect following social acceptance (Figure 11.9). This effect was found whether the other player was ostensibly either a stranger or a member of the original group. This suggests that narcissism combined with social rejection is a powerful predictor of aggression.

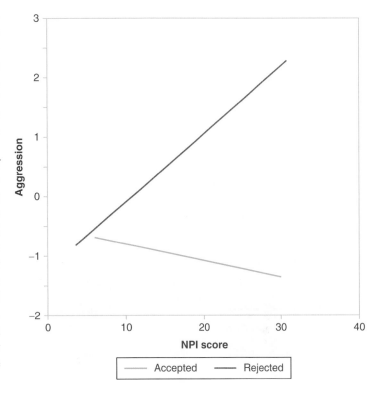

Figure 11.9 Aggression towards an innocent third party following social acceptance or rejection as a function of scores on the Narcissistic Personality Inventory

Source: Twenge & Campbell (2003)

Other research (Ferriday, Vartanian & Mandel, 2011) has highlighted the importance of the public nature of the threat to the narcissist's ego. It was found that narcissism predicted subsequent aggression only when an insult was presented publicly to the individual, but not when delivered privately. That makes some sense, for one's ego takes much more of a beating when others are aware of the criticism directed at you. There is no inconsistency with the previous study, for although in that case the negative information was delivered in a private manner, a report that nobody wants anything more to do with you has the markings of a public rebuke.

Authoritarianism Authoritarianism is a personality syndrome characterized by cognitive rigidity, prejudice and an excessive concern for power (see Chapter 13). Higher authoritarianism in males is also associated with a higher likelihood of sexual harassment of females (Begany & Milburn, 2002), and may also be accompanied by authoritarian aggression – a general aggressiveness perceived as sanctioned by authority figures (Altemeyer, 1988: 782).

Self-control The ability to control aggressive impulses varies from person to person. Weak controls lead to obvious problems of aggressiveness. The individual angers quickly and responds to frustration or provocation with physical aggression. Recall the discussion of neural factors in this regard. On the other hand, too much control sometimes poses the larger hazard (Megargee, 1966). Such a person operates under rigid inhibitions and, even when frustrated or provoked, 'keeps the lid on' with regard to expressing anger. There is empirical evidence that some people – those with 'over-controlled' personalities – are more prone to erupt in severe anger. This is because people with such personalities experience more pressure and more challenge to their self-esteem in stressful situations (Neighbors, Vietor & Knee, 2002).

The Dark Triad Most narcissistic individuals do not turn into criminals. However, in recent years some researchers have focused on the 'Dark Triad' of personality traits that often seem to occur together – narcissism, psychopathy, and Machiavellianism (Paulhus & Williams, 2002; Lee & Ashton, 2005). It is been suggested that successful dictators such as Saddam Hussein and Moammar Gaddafi, who were eccentric but not insane, are likely candidates for this category, as are heartless terrorists such as Anders Breveik, discussed at the beginning of this chapter, and Osama Bin Laden (Furnham, Richards. & Paulhus, 2013). We have already discussed the influence of narcissism. *Machiavellianism* refers to a pattern of manipulativeness and deceit, while psychopathy refers to a particular cluster of personality traits that has a strong connection with antisocial behaviour. Psychopaths typically lack empathy, remorse or guilt, have little concern for the feelings and well-being of others, exhibit weak self-control, extreme selfishness, impulsiveness and thrill-seeking, show little fear of punishment and often fail to learn from the negative consequences of their behaviour. Some people with psychopathic personalities manage to function relatively well in society, but psychopaths receive more convictions for violent crimes and once in prison behave more violently than do other prisoners (Hare & McPherson, 1984). A study of convicted murderers in Canadian penitentiaries found psychopaths' crimes to be typically 'cold-blooded' and lacking in terms of a clear motive, although revenge was sometimes a factor. These individuals were found to have poorly developed emotions and weak inhibitions against aggression (Williamson, Hare & Wong, 1987). Unfortunately, treatment programmes designed to reduce their dangerousness sometimes actually serve to increase it (Rice, 1997).

These three traits, while overlapping to some extent, are sufficiently different to warrant being treated separately (O'Boyle et al., 2012). It is interesting to note that some contemporary heroes of popular culture – think of James Bond (Figure 11.10), Dr Gregory House or Batman – certainly possess Dark Triad traits (Jonason et al., 2012). Does this suggest that in some circumstances the public perceives positive benefits to those characteristics?

Figure 11.10 Daniel Craig, the current James Bond.

Photo credit: Piotr Zajac/Shutterstock.com

IS VIOLENCE SICK?

Most aggression can be understood in terms of psychological and social factors. We have discussed the many different influences that contribute to whether a given person in a given situation reacts aggressively. And we saw in Chapter 10 that war and terrorism can be realistically viewed as calculated attempts to resolve conflict.

But there is another type of violence that often seems as incomprehensible as it is pointless, violence in which the aggressor targets strangers, usually as many as possible, and sometimes ends up taking his own life as well. Consider these infamous examples from around the world: in 2011, 32-year-old Anders Breivik, discussed at the beginning this chapter, killed 77 people and injured hundreds of others in Norway; in 2013, the Tsarnaev brothers, ages 19 and 25 years, stood accused of the Boston marathon bombings that killed three people and injured 264; in 1989, 25-year-old Marc Lépine, while claiming to be 'fighting feminism', killed 14 women and four men at the École Polytechnique in Montréal in under 20 minutes before killing himself; in 2012, 20-year-old Adam Lanza, after killing his mother, stalked the hallways of Sandy Hook Elementary School in Newton, Connecticut, killing twenty young children and six adult staff members before killing himself; in 2012, 24-year-old former graduate student James Eagan Holmes entered a cinema in Aurora, Colorado, during the opening night of the Batman movie *The Dark Knight Rises* and began shooting, killing 12 people and injuring 15 others; in 2007, 23-year-old Seung-Hui Cho, a senior level university student from Korea, killed 32 people and wounded 17 others in attacks at two university campuses in Virginia, before killing himself; in 2008, 22-year-old Matti Juhani Saari opened fire on fellow students at Seinäjoki University in Finland, killing 10 people before killing himself; in 2007, 18-year-old Pekka-Eric Auvinen shot and killed eight people in his high school in Tuusula, Finland; in 2002, 19-year-old Robert Steinhaeuser, after having been expelled from school is Erfurt, Germany, killed 13 teachers, two former classmates and a police officer and then killed himself; in 1996, 29-year-old Martin Bryant murdered 35 people at a seaside resort in Tasmania, Australia, and is now serving a life sentence in a psychiatric wing of a prison; in 1996, 43-year-old Thomas Hamilton shot and killed 16 kindergarten children and their teacher in Dunblane, Scotland, before killing himself; in 2009, 29-year-old Farda Gadyrov opened fire on fellow students at the State Oil Academy in Azerbaijan, killing 12 people before killing himself … The list goes on.

All of these killers were males, almost all of them in their teens or 20s, many of them well-educated, and none of them the product of despair brought about by poverty. Some were driven by political, religious or their own idiosyncratic ideology: for example, Breivik and Lépine were motivated at least in part by their warped ideologies – in Breivik's case, militant right-wing and in Lépine's, anti-feminism. But many people have such aberrant viewpoints without becoming mass murderers.

Were they mentally ill? Before his trial, Breivik was diagnosed with Narcissistic Personality Disorder, part of the Dark Triad discussed earlier, but this is a dysfunctional personality, not 'craziness'. Cho's abnormal behaviour along with his writings, which carried violent themes, had on several occasions raised some concerns before his murderous rampage, but, again, such characteristics do not lead directly to becoming a mass murderer. People with mental illnesses only rarely become violent, and most mass murders are committed by people who are not mentally ill. Moreover, many people have violent fantasies without going on killing sprees. The point is that mass murderers are not necessarily 'crazy' or psychotic, and may even be 'normal', albeit unhappy. These are generally not crimes of the moment carried out in the context of a passing emotional frenzy. In fact, several of these murderers, including Breivik and Lépine, had planned their acts well in advance.

It is very difficult to find a pattern, if there is one, that would help explain mass murderers, in part because this behaviour is of extremely low frequency (Meloy et al., 2004). However, there are some data that bear on this: In a study carried out in the United States, Meloy et al. (2001) studied 34 adolescent mass murderers and reported that there was a documented psychiatric history for approximately one-quarter of them, but only 6% of them were considered to be psychotic at the time of the murders. (Much more common were depressive symptomatology and a history of antisocial behaviour.) Most of them were 'loners' who abused drugs or alcohol and were preoccupied with violent fantasy, and almost half of them had been bullied by others. In most cases, there was a precipitating event such as romantic rejection or failure in school. Based on this sample, the authors noted that the adolescent mass murderer is usually 'predatory' rather than emotional in his violence, and therefore typically does not present highly emotional warning signs in advance of the crime.

These 34 adolescents were subsequently compared with 30 adult mass murderers (Meloy et al., 2004). Just as were the adolescents, some of the adults were found to be suffering from various psychiatric problems and dysfunctional personality traits, but again psychosis did not provide an explanation. A 'warrior mentality' was a predisposing factor among most of the adults, and, as with the adolescents, most had experienced a major rejection or loss in the hours or days prior to the mass murder.

In another study in the United States, Kennedy-Kollar & Charles (2012) examined the backgrounds of 28 men who committed mass murders. No particular psychological profile could be found that would distinguish them from other kinds of murderers or from nonviolent people, but the majority were suffering from financial, social, romantic or psychological stress at the time of the crimes. The authors concluded that these stressors threatened their masculine identity, and that they engaged in violence in the attempt to bolster their sense of masculinity.

What can we conclude from all this? Only that mass murderers are influenced by a complex set of intertwining factors, some relating to personality, some to family background, and some to current stress, but there is no pattern that allows us to predict under what circumstances and in which type of individuals the motivation to engage in mass murder will emerge.

[
KEY POINT: A number of personality attributes have a positive relationship with the tendency towards aggression. These include self-esteem, narcissism, psychopathy, Machiavellianism, authoritarianism and self-control, as well as general intelligence. There is no particular personality profile associated with mass murderers.
]

THE GENERAL AGGRESSION MODEL

Often, the approaches that researchers have brought to the study of aggression have focused on only one or a few factors that influence the onset of aggressive behaviour. Some concentrate only on the individual's learning history, while others look closely at emotional arousal or cognitive processes. The General Aggression Model is a recent and comprehensive theory that is intended to explain variations in aggressiveness among individuals in various circumstances (DeWall, Anderson & Bushman, 2011; Gilbert & Daffern, 2011). Why are some people aggressive in some situations and not others? Why are some people generally more aggressive than others over a range of situations? Therefore, it integrates many influences – including the effects of biological factors, personality, social processes, basic cognitive processes and decision-making processes. Further, it attempts to combine a number of mini-theories of aggression, such as social learning and cognitive scripts, into a single overarching theory that provides a framework through which aggression can be conceptualized and understood.

This theory stresses the importance of specific psychological constructs that influence whether an individual is likely to react aggressively, including aggression-related knowledge structures, maladaptive cognitions, and anger (Gilbert & Daffern, 2011). According to this theory, aggression generally occurs only when a number of factors, including personal characteristics, anger and situational factors, converge. Those personal characteristics that contribute to aggressive behaviour build up over an extended period of time, and so aggressive behaviour is to a considerable degree dependent on a history of experiences that have shaped the individual to behave aggressively in specific types of situations. This learning history produces a set of aggressive cognitive scripts that are triggered in certain situations. Research is accumulating in support of the idea that individuals who are more typically aggressive than others have built up a set of cognitive scripts tied to aggression (Collie, Vess & Murdoch, 2007).

When the individual acts in an aggressive manner, this can lead others to react aggressively or to back down, and if an individual is non-aggressive, this may lead the others to react similarly or may encourage them to press their advantage and become more aggressive. Thus, a feedback loop can lead to increased or decreased propensity to aggress, sometimes resulting in an escalation of violence (DeWall & Anderson, 2011).

The main features of the General Aggression Model are summarized in Figure 11.11. First of all, the particular individual with his or her tendency towards aggression or non-aggression interacts with a specific situation. For example, Harry who is quick to

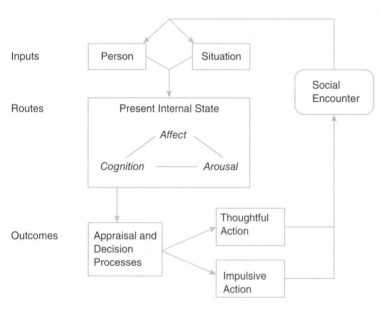

Figure 11.11 The General Aggression Model

Source: Anderson & Bushman (2002)

anger, and Martha, who is not, find themselves turned away from a restaurant, being told that there is no room, even though they have a dinner reservation. This leads to both cognitive and emotional reactions. Harry experiences considerable autonomic arousal, along with a cognitive script that says that 'you can't let people take advantage of you'. Martha does not react with much autonomic arousal, and her script says that 'people make mistakes and it is nothing personal'. Harry's thoughts and emotions lead him to appraise the situation as one demanding immediate action (appraisal and decision process) and he rushes back inside (impulsive action) and begins to harangue the manager (social encounter). On the other hand, Martha decides that she will let this go, but will write a letter of complaint to the restaurant. Harry's action creates a scene, leading the manager to threaten to call the police, and Harry leaves feeling even more angry. Thus, an individual's personal characteristics in a particular situation lead to cognitive and emotional consequences that then determine outcome. The nature of this outcome feeds back to affect how the individual views such situations in future.

Although not without its critics (e.g., Ferguson & Dyck, 2012), who argue that the model has outlived its usefulness), this integrative model has received considerable empirical support, and its authors argue that it can help us to understand a whole range of aggressive acts, including interpersonal violence perpetrated by strangers, spousal and family violence, and intergroup violence, as well as explaining the lack of aggressiveness in certain people and in certain situations.

KEY POINT: The General Aggression Model integrates a wide range of influences on aggression including the effects of biological factors, personality, social learning, cognitive scripts and basic cognitive processes into a single theory. Although it has received considerable support, some researchers believe that it has outlived its usefulness.

THE REDUCTION OF AGGRESSION

It is unlikely that aggression will ever be eliminated entirely from our society. For one thing, it is often a symptom of social inequality and injustice: When a group is disadvantaged economically and socially relative to others, violence often can appeal, for it appears to be the surest and quickest way to force the majority group to recognize minority needs and to correct injustice. Similarly at an individual level, television, with its display of lifestyles far beyond the reach of the socially disadvantaged, may raise expectations and increase feelings of powerlessness, possibly leading to violent responses (Lore & Schultz, 1993).

However, consider these suggestions about how to reduce violence, which flow from the social psychological literature:

- *Reduce and de-glorify media violence.* As long as violence is presented as an efficient and often as an honourable masculine manner of solving problems and obtaining justice, it will continue to be used, and to be viewed by some in a positive light. By teaching children to become more analytical and critical about what they watch, the impact of violent media can be reduced (Nathanson, 2003).
- *Educate parents.* Parent education is crucial if aggression is to be reduced. Many parents are unprepared for the extremely difficult task of training, educating and socializing their children and do not think or know about child-rearing styles that reduce aggressiveness. As has been discussed, child-rearing practices involving an excessive use of physical punishment are likely to encourage aggressive behaviour rather than discourage it. While a child's aggressive act does need to be stopped quickly, discussion and explanation are also needed to effectively change future behaviour especially over the long term (Singer & Singer, 1986). Increasing sensitivity to the products of violence – suffering, increased hostility – has been shown to reduce anger and aggression.
- *Interventions with at-risk children.* Programmes directed at children who appear to be at risk for developing aggressive behaviour can have a significant effect in overcoming that tendency. For example, one project

(Metropolitan Area Child Study Research Group, 2007) targeted aggressive behaviour, fantasy and beliefs in early elementary school-age children who were of higher than average aggressivity. Such intervention, which involves modifying not only a child's behaviour but also his or her cognitions can successfully decrease the tendency towards aggression.

A FINAL NOTE

Although interpersonal and intergroup aggression continues to be a major problem around the world, we should not be discouraged, for it takes a long time to change values, to teach people to teach their children peaceful methods of conflict resolution and to correct social injustices. Remember that slavery was once normative, as was cigarette smoking. Change is possible. As we come to better understand the roots of aggression, the better equipped we will be to work towards its reduction.

SUMMARY

1. Aggression is defined as behaviour that is intended to harm or destroy.

2. Aggression can be proactive – used to achieve a desired goal; or reactive – instigated by anger and directed at harming another person.

3. Instinct theories assume that aggressive energy held in check must eventually be released either directly or indirectly (catharsis). However, research evidence does not support catharsis as a means of reducing aggressive behaviour.

4. The frustration–aggression hypothesis does not hold up empirically, although aggression may be due to frustration under certain circumstances. Berkowitz' cognitive neo-association model posits that aversive stimulation produces negative emotions (anger or fear), which in turn lead to aggression or flight.

5. Genetic, neural and hormonal influences are indirect and may affect an individual's ability to control aggressive behaviour.

6. Social learning occurs through direct reinforcement and punishment and by observation of others. It teaches children how, when and against whom to aggress.

7. Cognitive scripts include information about what is likely to occur in a given situation, how we should respond and what is the likely outcome. These scripts are learned on the basis of experience and function automatically.

8. Certain child-rearing practices may enhance the aggressiveness of children. The socialization factor most strongly related to aggression is the use of physical punishment, especially within a rejecting atmosphere. However,

neglected children may actually show higher rates of violence in adulthood than do children who have been physically abused.

9. The long-term consequences of experiencing or observing violence in the home on a recurrent basis may place a child at risk to perpetuate violence or child abuse in adulthood.

10. Bullying and its modern manifestation of cyberbullying have damaging emotional impact on the majority of victims. This impact can include academic and psychosocial difficulties, low self-esteem, depression and in some cases externalized hostility.

11. There has been considerable research on the effects, especially on children, of violence in the media. The consensus is that viewing violence and aggressive behaviour does increase the likelihood of violence in children and has long-lasting effects. However, not all children react in the same way, and characteristics of the family setting play an important moderating role.

12. Pornography, whether violent or non-violent, may teach males negative attitudes towards women and may mislead them into believing that women enjoy coercive sex even when they resist it.

13. The prevalence of aggressive behaviour varies considerably among cultures. In some, aggression is actively encouraged while in others violence of any sort is frowned upon and rarely occurs.

14. Low social capital in a neighbourhood or nation is associated with higher violent crime rates.

15. The relationship between gender and aggression is not straightforward. Women are as aggressive as men in some circumstances. Learned gender roles, which encourage aggressiveness in males and discourage it in females, are an important factor.

16. Intimate partner violence is the most common form of violence, and men and women are equally likely to be aggressive, although women are much more likely to suffer harmful outcomes.

17. Certain personality types are associated with a greater tendency towards aggressiveness. No set of factors has been found that distinguishes mass murderers from other murderers or from nonviolent people.

18. The General Aggression Model is an overarching social-cognitive model that includes the influences of biological factors, personality development, social processes, basic cognitive processes and decision-making processes.

19. Violence in society may be reduced by reducing media violence and by teaching parents how to socialize their children, using appropriate forms of discipline.

POINTS TO PONDER

- When you think about your own upbringing, how do you think your tendency towards aggression or pacifism was influenced by parental discipline, by social norms among your friends, or by the media?
- Based on your own experience, does the categorization of women as the *gentler sex* continue to apply?
- What relationship can you see between the way that parents respond to childhood anger and aggression and the way that nations respond to provocation from their enemies?
- Children are sometimes taught that the best way to deal with the bully is to stand up and fight. What does such advice and the possible effects of following it teach children about aggression?

FURTHER READING

Borum, R., Fein, R. & Vossekuil, B. (2012). A dimensional approach to analyzing lone offender terrorism. *Aggression and Violent Behavior, 17,* 389–396.
A discussion of a particular form of violent offender, the single individual who opens fire in a classroom, workplace, cinema or other public venue, with the apparent aim of killing as many people as possible.

DeWall, C.N., Anderson, C.A. & Bushman, B.J. (2011). The general aggression model: Theoretical extensions to violence. *Psychology of Violence, 1,* 245–258.
An extensive treatment of the General Aggression Model.

Dutton, D.G. (1995). *The domestic assault of women: Psychological and criminal justice perspectives.* Vancouver: University of British Columbia Press.
An in-depth exploration of the social psychology of the wife assaulter, how such men differ from other men, the effects of such abuse on the victim and how wife abuse is dealt with by the criminal justice system.

Monks, C.P. & Coyne, I. (Eds) (2011). *Bullying in different contexts.* New York: Cambridge University Press.
International researchers discuss bullying in a wide range of settings including the home, the schoolyard, the workplace, cyberspace, and institutional settings.

Shaver, P.R. & Mikulincer, M. (Eds) (2011) *Human aggression and violence: causes, manifestations, and consequences.* Washington, DC: American Psychological Association.
International experts present the latest research in the psychology of aggression and violence.

WEBLINKS

World Health Organization: World Report on Violence and Health: http://www.who.int/violence_injury_prevention/violence/world_report/en/summary_en.pdf

A survey of violence and its effects in many regions of the world.

National Consortium for Violence Research: http://www.ncovr.heinz.cmu.edu/

A United States organization that promotes research, training and data resource sharing with regard to violence research.

PART V

PEOPLE IN GROUPS

CHAPTER 12
SOCIAL IDENTITY, GROUPS AND LEADERSHIP

No man is an Iland, intire of itselfe; every man is a peece of the Continent,
a part of the maine;
if a Clod bee washed away by the Sea, Europe is the lesse …
John Donne (1572–1631)

LEARNING OBJECTIVES

* To analyse the processes of social categorization, social identification and social comparison

* To examine how social belief structures foster or inhibit social change

* To explore the nature of small groups and the effects of group membership

* To understand different types of social power and the nature of leadership

* To consider the influence of culture and gender on leadership style and choice of leader

* To explore how decision-making occurs in groups

Figure 12.1 *Lord of the Flies* performance in London
Source: © Robbie Jack/Corbis

Nobel Prize winner William Golding's *Lord of the Flies* chronicles the lives of a group of well-educated British schoolboys marooned on an uninhabited island with little hope of a timely rescue. Most are strangers to one another; there is no group structure; there are no rules and there are no adults to supervise them. As they try to sort out how to organize and govern themselves, leaders emerge who enjoy their new-found power, emotionality overwhelms rationality, and gradually the children descend into savagery. A story with a moral: Take away the social fabric that overlays our lives and we sink into social chaos.

Almost no one lives alone in a cave these days; we live our lives in groups. Our beliefs, attitudes and behaviours are influenced by the groups to which we belong, just as we in turn influence those groups. The social fabric that helps define us is composed of many groups, each with its own leaders and followers. We take this social fabric for granted – unless catastrophe strikes and, as happened to Golding's schoolboys, it disintegrates around us.

This chapter is about groups, about how we 'group' people into categories, and about how our own identities are defined to a significant degree by group membership. Until now, our focus has been primarily on the individual. This *individualistic* approach to social behaviour can be traced back to Floyd Allport's textbook *Social Psychology* published in 1924. In Allport's view, group phenomena can be understood simply through understanding the behaviours and attitudes of the individuals who make up the groups. Thus, to understand how your family functions, we would only have to analyse the personalities, attitudes and behaviours of each of your family members. This 'bottom-up' approach, focusing on the individual constituents of the group in order to understand the group, all but ignores the powerful role that group membership, society and culture play in shaping the behaviours and attitudes of the individual in the group. Do you think for a moment that your attitudes, values and beliefs would be as they are now had you grown up in a different family or a different society?

On the other hand, the *systems* approach, which remains the basic approach of sociology and political science, focuses on how groups and classes of people interrelate and mutually influence each other. Thus, it approaches the study of human behaviour from a 'top-down' perspective – that is, the most important features of individual social interactions are seen as being largely determined by large-scale factors, such as cultural background, educational level or socioeconomic status. From this perspective, the study of the impact of cultural and socioeconomic factors on such matters as family size, parental involvement and family life can provide insight into the functioning of a specific family – yours, for example.

For many years, social psychologists pursued both approaches in the study of group phenomena. However, beginning in the 1960s, social psychologists in North America, much more so than their counterparts in Europe and Asia, shifted to the individualistic approach almost to the total exclusion of the systems perspective. This reflected the individualistic ideology that predominates in the United States (Sampson, 1977) (recall Chapter 4). As a result, systems concerns, such as those associated with intergroup and international conflict, have been left mainly to sociologists and political scientists (Brewer & Kramer, 1985).

There is a middle ground, the interactionist approach that takes into account both individual and group influences. This was championed early in social psychology by a small number of psychologists in the United States – for example, Solomon Asch, Muzafer Sherif and Kurt Lewin (see Chapter 6) – and over the past half century, it has flowered through the work of European psychologists such as Henri Tajfel, John Turner and Howard Giles in the United Kingdom, Serge Moscovici and Bernard Personnaz in France, and Willem Doise and Jean-Claude Deschamps in Switzerland. In this chapter, we shall explore behaviour in the group context from this perspective.

We begin by exploring both how we categorize people in terms of the groups to which they belong, and how belonging to groups helps to determine our own sense of identity. Later in the chapter, the focus will shift to small groups, in which individuals interact with each other directly, and we shall address how groups regulate themselves, how leaders emerge and how group decision-making occurs.

SOCIAL CATEGORIZATION, IDENTIFICATION AND COMPARISON

Interactions with others, especially people whom we do not know very well, would be much more difficult if we could not view them in context. Knowing that someone we have just met is a female violinist in a symphony orchestra, or a male professional football player, or a politician, or a high school teacher is likely to have a significant effect on our interaction with that individual, for such classifications provide us with a useful guide to what the individual's personality, interests and abilities are likely to be. We would be surprised if the violinist enjoys raunchy locker room jokes, just as we would be if the football player turns out to be an aficionado of modern art. Moreover, as we shall see, such classifications influence not only our views of others, but, when applied to us, our own sense of self as well.

Figure 12.2   Henri Tajfel (1919–1982)

However, classifying ourselves and others into groups can have a significant downside. It was Henri Tajfel (Figure 12.2) who laid the groundwork for much of our understanding about our automatic tendency to see ourselves and others as part of one group or another, and how this provides a basis for discrimination and prejudice. His preoccupation with such matters is easy to understand in terms of his own history: he was born a Polish Jew, and as a young man went to France to study chemistry. The Second World War broke out not long after he took up his studies, and he then joined the French army. He was taken prisoner by the Germans, who fortunately did not discover that he was Jewish. When the war ended and he returned home, he was shocked to find that all of his immediate family and most of his friends had perished in the Holocaust. As he struggled to cope with this terrible loss, he was drawn to the study of psychology. The focus of his studies, which he pursued in England, was on intergroup relations and prejudice as he strove to understand how group membership could lead to murderous hatred towards members of other groups.

Tajfel brought into focus the processes of social categorization, social identification and social comparison through which we construct cognitive patterns that not only allow us to identify ourselves and others within a social context, but also inform us about what to expect with regard to other people's attitudes and behaviours.

Social categorization

As we discussed in Chapter 2, the process of social categorization is automatic; we automatically classify people into categories, or schemata, that we already know something about (e.g., 'male, teenager, school drop-out'). Try to think of anyone you know without thinking of the social categories or groups to which the person belongs; this is very difficult to do. You will of course automatically identify some people as family members or relatives, others as classmates, and still others as professors, secretaries or bus drivers. Such quick categorization allows one to act 'appropriately' and to know roughly what to expect from each person, based on what we know about the categories or groups to which he or she belongs.

For each category or group, we have a prototype (also discussed in Chapter 2), a schema representing the feelings, attitudes and behaviours of the 'typical' individual in that group, characteristics that distinguish the group from other groups. When you think of the typical police officer or schoolteacher, you are coming up with prototypes. Prototypes reflect the meta-contrast principle (sometimes also referred to as social differentia-tion effect (Lemaine, Kastersztein & Personnaz, 1978) or the out-group homogeneity effect (Simon, 1992). That is, we accentuate similarities within the category and exaggerate differences between groups (Hogg, 2006). This reflects the well-known perceptual phenomenon of assimilation and contrast. For example, if we know little about motorcycle clubs, all motorcyclists may seem very different from us but very similar to each other in terms of style of dress, attitudes, and so on. Indeed, whatever the group we are looking at from the outside, we tend to view its members as though they are all more or less cut from the same cloth, while we readily recognize that there is a great deal of variation among the members of our own group. This effect occurs because we are more likely to relate to our own colleagues as individuals and to have more information about each of them, while lacking such knowledge of members of other groups.

Doise, Deschamps and Meyer (1978) demonstrated this effect in several experiments. In one, Swiss school-children were assigned to one of two conditions, with equal numbers of males and females in each condition. In one condition, the 'no-anticipation' condition, participants were told only that they would be required to describe members of their own social category, in this case, gender. They were then shown three photographs of children, all unknown to them, and asked which of 24 adjectives applied to each child. After these ratings were completed, they were then asked to repeat the procedure with three new photographs, this time of children of the opposite sex.

Participants in the second condition, the 'anticipation' condition, were informed that they would be describing people of both their own and the opposite sex. They were given all six photographs at once, but were instructed to begin by rating the three photos of the children of the same sex as themselves.

The children in the anticipation condition, who knew that they would be rating both boys and girls, produced data with greater inter-category (boy–girl) differences and smaller intra-category differences (differences within each gender group), compared to the no-anticipation group, demonstrating social differentiation (the meta-contrast principle). Simply knowing that one would be rating people of both genders made gender a salient variable, leading them to differentiate the two categories. Similar results were obtained in an experiment using language rather than gender as the salient dimension.

Cross-categorization

Depending on the context in which you meet someone, some social features of that person may be much more important to you than others. Moreover, the importance of each feature or dimension may change as the inter-action continues. Suppose that you are both a young woman and a classical pianist, and you consider male football players to be 'macho jerks', a belief that may or may not be based on past experience. You meet a man at a party, and when you learn that he is a fullback on the university football team, you are inclined to avoid him, taking for granted that he is likely to be 'macho'. But then he sits down at the piano and plays a touching rendition of the 'Moonlight Sonata'. Now how do you react? He clearly falls into two categories, one to which you respond negatively and the other to which you attach considerable value.

This dilemma occurs whenever we encounter someone who shares a group or category with us (i.e., an in-group member), but not others (i.e., belongs to out-groups). This is referred to as cross-categorization, and since we all belong to many overlapping groups and categories, such cross-categorization is likely to occur rather often, and all the more so in a multicultural society (Crisp, 2010; Crisp & Hewstone, 1999). Think of all the ways in which you may identify yourself, and all the groups or categories in which you belong. You may be a young female engineer of Chinese heritage living in Vancouver, a British musician of Jewish extraction working in Paris, a male Dutch student at a Scottish university who plays football for the university team. You may have parents of different ethnic backgrounds and feel quite at home with both families. Generally, these multiple identities are not mutually exclusive, and you may feel quite comfortable as a young female engineer (regardless of stereotypes).

You share one category with other engineers, another category with young people, yet another with other women, and, of course, a smaller common category with young women, whether or not they are engineers.

Cross-categorizations may help to break down stereotypes, although there can also be a downside: people with two out-group categorizations are in a 'double out-group' (e.g., female socialists in a highly conservative and misogynist society) and may face a double dose of rejection.

A number of studies have been carried out using a 'crossed-categorization paradigm'. Consider what happened when Deschamps and Doise (1978) asked one sample of teenage students (the 'simple' condition) to describe, by means of an adjective checklist, females, males, young

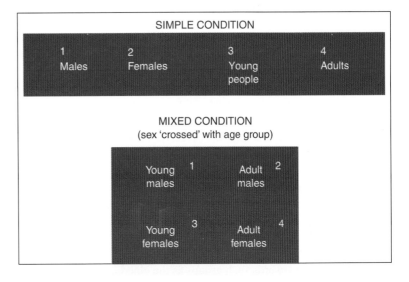

Figure 12.3 Simple and mixed conditions

Source: Deschamps & Dosie, 1978

people, and adults, and another sample of students (the 'mixed' condition) to describe 'crossed' categories: young females, young males, female adults and male adults (Figure 12.3).

The crossing of the categories led to a decrease in social differentiation. For example, the difference between males and females was rated to be much greater by participants in the simple condition than was the difference between young males and young females as rated by the participants in the mixed condition. Note that while each participant belonged to either the male or female category, all participants belonged to the 'young' category. When rating adult males and females, the perceived differences were also smaller than when rating males and females in general – again, while the participants were not adults, all were obviously male or female. Thus, when the participants characterized groups of people the perceived differences were smaller when two categories were involved, one of which they shared, than when comparisons were made on the basis of a single feature.

Deschamps & Doise (1978) also found that while a simple division of people into groups could produce a positive bias favouring the participants' own group, the introduction of a second, neutral characteristic (i.e., producing no bias of itself) could eliminate such discrimination. In this case, the participants were nine- and ten-year-old boys and girls. Half the participants were in the simple category (male versus female) condition. The rest were in the crossed category condition: half the boys and half the girls were assigned to a 'red' category and the remainder to a 'blue' category. The children worked individually on a series of pencil and paper games. Later, they were asked to estimate the number of games that each of the other children had correctly completed. Participants in the simple category condition rated the probable success of the other participants of their sex as significantly higher than that of opposite-sex participants. However, no such distinction was made in the crossed-category condition (e.g., red male versus red female), even though the red–blue split did not by itself produce any difference. Thus, simply adding a meaningless variable and crossing it with the gender variable eliminated gender discrimination. Similar findings have been observed in experiments aimed at fostering cooperation in social dilemmas (Wit and Kerr, 2002).

Coser (1967) anticipated the importance of cross categorization when he argued that intergroup conflict serves to bind the elements of society together. He reasoned that society is composed of many categories, often in conflict with each other, and yet, since each individual belongs to many different categories, it is highly unlikely that a given set of people will be on the same side in every conflict. Thus, a woman may oppose a man on an issue relating to gender equality, but agree with him on an environmental issue. Hence, society is knit together. It is easy to see how this binding process applies to nationhood. In Canada, French

Canadians and English Canadians, or natives and immigrants, or Easterners and Westerners may find themselves in conflict with each other with regard to various issues. Gun control and anti-gun control groups in the United States may dispute bitterly with each other. And in the European Community, Spanish, German and French citizens may clash with regard to economic and immigration issues. However, as long as there is not a clear division along linguistic, ethnic or geographic lines on every major issue, but instead if these categories are 'crossed' with other categories (e.g., males versus females, capitalists versus socialists, environmentalists versus 'exploiters'), the fabric of the whole society will hold together.

Finally, it seems that when a person is perceived to belong to two categories that are inconsistent in terms of prevailing stereotypes, the perceiver tries to resolve the inconsistency by paying more attention to the personal characteristics of that individual. Dealing with such inconsistent categories can promote tolerance of out-groups. Vasiljevic & Crisp (2013) argued that this kind of experience can have persisting effects that will generalize to other situations. In their study, participants were asked to generate their own novel social category combinations that were either consistent (e.g., male firefighter) or inconsistent (male midwife) with prevailing stereotypes. They predicted that the effort of producing such inconsistent category combinations would promote cognitive flexibility and produce greater tolerance towards out-groups. A series of laboratory studies supported their prediction: the effort of producing inconsistent category combinations led to a reduction in prejudice towards such groups as the elderly, disabled and HIV-positive individuals. Even more interesting was their field research carried out in the former Yugoslav Republic of Macedonia, which had been riven by ethnic violence; the inconsistent category task led to indications of greater tolerance and increased trust with regard to ethnic out-groups.

> **KEY POINT:** We automatically classify people into groups and categories that facilitate social interaction and help us to predict attitudes and behaviour based on that classification. We tend to see people in other groups as being more similar to one another than they are, and as being more different from us than they are. This effect is lessened when we see them as belonging to more than one category, one of which we share.

Social identification

In Chapter 3, we discussed how people come to 'know themselves'. Although we may not always be aware of it, we categorize ourselves just as we categorize others. While our self-schema includes our personal characteristics, expectations and experiences, another core element is derived from our social environment. Through social identification (Tajfel & Turner, 1979), we define ourselves in terms of the social categories and groups to which we belong. Tajfel (1972) defined social identity as those aspects of a person's self-image that relate to the knowledge that he or she belongs to certain social groups that have value and emotional importance for the individual.

A group is considered to exist when people view themselves as sharing attributes that distinguish them collectively from other people (Hogg, 2006). Thus, people who belong to a particular nationality or religion, or race or political party – for example, Canadians, Germans, Boy Scouts, environmentalists – can be viewed as constituting separate groups. (To forestall confusion later on in this chapter, you will see that 'group' is defined somewhat differently by researchers studying behaviour among small numbers of people who interact directly with one another.) Obviously, each of us belongs to many different social groups, probably many more than we realize: we are male or female, British, Canadian, Australian, American, black, white, tinker, tailor, soldier and so on. We also belong to groups based on religion, age, ethnicity, geographical origin and marital status. Although such categories may not always be meaningful to us, under certain circumstances they can become very important. For example, a newspaper article criticizing the selfishness of high school students may not bother you because you do not belong to that category. However, an article that criticizes the attitudes of university and college students may produce quite a different reaction: people are now talking about you.

Social identities serve two important functions. Recall from Chapter 3 that we both want to feel good about ourselves (self enhancement) and to know and understand ourselves (uncertainty reduction). In terms of self-enhancement, do you not feel some satisfaction that you are a university or college student? Or take some pride in the fact that your nation (at least in your eyes) is one of the better nations in the world in which to live? Or cheer for athletes who wear your nation's flag at the Olympic Games, even though all of them are strangers to you? As for uncertainty reduction, recall the discussion in Chapter 6 about the discomfort that people feel in situations where they do not 'fit in'. Our membership in particular groups and categories provides norms that guide our behaviour, allowing us to be 'one of the group' and thereby reducing or eliminating uncertainty.

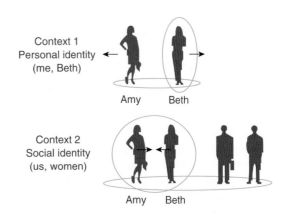

Figure 12.4 Personal and social identities

Tajfel (1974) viewed social behaviour as varying along an interpersonal–intergroup continuum. At the interpersonal end of this dimension, interactions between people are the result of their personal relationships with each other and their individual characteristics. On the other hand, at the intergroup extreme, their social group membership determines their behaviour toward one another.

Social identity is the key link between individual behaviour and group phenomena (Haslam, Reicher & Reynolds, 2012), for once we identify with a particular category or group, then the norms, attitudes and behaviours that distinguish that category or group from others will begin to exert a strong influence on our own attitudes and behaviours as a result of conformity (Turner, 1982, 1985). Of course, there can be a dark side to this: prejudice and discrimination against people in other groups and categories occur when individuals' self-concepts are primarily group-focused, that is, are tied most strongly to their social identities (Hogg & Williams, 2000).

But, members of groups are not clones of one another. Everyone possesses some uniqueness that goes beyond their social identity, that is, a self-schema. Thus, people also have a personal identity defined by personality factors and their particular histories of personal experience. Even then, group experience often plays a significant role in the development of personal identities (Figure 12.4).

> **KEY POINT:** The groups and categories to which we belong form the basis for our social identity. This social identity brings self-enhancement and reduction of uncertainty. We also have personal identities that reflect the individual aspects of our attitudes and behaviours.

In-group–out-group bias Social identification not only highlights the in-groups, those groups and categories to which we belong, but it also delineates out-groups, those groups and categories to which we do not belong. This often produces a competitive relationship between the members of different social categories. We want 'our' team, our age group, our sex, our neighbourhood, our city or our country to win, whether it is a spelling prize in elementary school, a sporting championship or an international medal. Indeed, most conflict around the world is based on group membership, whether the groups are defined in terms of race or religion, or ethnic origin or political persuasion. The emphasis placed on in-group versus out-group – the *we* versus *they* division – also inevitably leads people to view some groups or categories as superior in some respect, and others as inferior. This is the breeding ground for prejudice.

Recall that Tajfel began his studies of social identification and group membership in an effort to comprehend the hatred of the Nazis towards certain categories of people. He was not the first to try to understand the disturbing and toxic Nazi worldview. Psychologists in the United States also explored the roots of vile Nazi bigotry, but reflecting the strong individualism of that country, they focused not on the power of groups to generate and promote prejudice, but on the individual bigotry of the group members. Out of their efforts, concepts such as the authoritarian personality emerged. (We shall discuss prejudice at greater length in the next chapter.) However, Tajfel believed that there was something much more important to be understood about prejudice and discrimination than an analysis of individual personalities alone could provide. He believed that there was something fundamental about the division of people into in-groups and out-groups, *us* versus *them*, that lies at the root of prejudice.

Tajfel pursued this idea by creating *we*-versus-*they* situations that were completely artificial and meaningless. He and his colleagues conducted a number of experiments (e.g., Tajfel 1970; Tajfel & Turner, 1986) that demonstrated how arbitrary or even random assignments of individuals to minimal groups (artificial groups with no structure, no pre-existing norms, no history) lead to discrimination favouring the in-group. The reason for using minimal groups was to eliminate the influence of all other variables except for group membership itself. For instance, you might divide people on the basis of some meaningless criterion, such as whether they wear yellow or black T-shirts, or whether their birthdays are on odd- or even-numbered days. In one such study (Tajfel, 1970), participants were divided into groups on the ostensible basis of whether they had been 'over-estimators' or 'under-estimators' in a previously administered task where they made visual judgements. In reality, each individual worked alone and did not know the identities of the other group members. Each participant participated in several trials in which it was necessary to select one of several different ways to assign a number of points to two other people. These points were later to be exchanged for money, so that something of real value was involved. On some trials, the participant had to divide a number of points between two members of his or her own group, while on other trials, the division was between two members of the other group, and on yet other trials, it was between one member of his or her own group and one member of the other group.

When a participant had the opportunity to assign points either to two members of the in-group or to two members of the out-group, the division was more or less equal; each person received about an equal number of points. However, when points were to be divided between a member of the in-group and a member of the out-group, a large majority of participants awarded more points to members of their own group than to members of the other group. In doing so, they discriminated in favour of their own group: (1) even though they did not know who was in their group and who was in the other group; (2) even though the division into groups was based on a trivial criterion; and (3) even though they would in no way benefit personally as a result of their choices. Note that this discrimination occurred in the absence of any pre-existing antagonism, and indeed in the absence of any social interaction.

Why did the participants act in this manner? We all have had many years of experience in which in-group/out-group discrimination has been subtly or not so subtly encouraged; for example, as children, we have been encouraged to want our side to win, whether in a football game or a school debate. Tajfel (1970) thought this to be the likely reason that people discriminate more or less automatically against out-groups and favour their in-group, even when there is no direct personal benefit, and before any hostility or prejudice has formed. He referred to this common reaction as the generic norm of out-group discrimination. However, he later considered this explanation to be too vague and concluded instead that such in-group favouritism serves to add to the positive distinctiveness of the in-group (Tajfel, 1974). Our self-esteem is enhanced when we belong to a superior group, and as a result we have learned to want our group to do well. Therefore, we favour our in-group, even when the in-group is arbitrarily defined and meaningless.

In-group bias can sometimes lead to the infra-humanization of members of the out-group (Paladino & Vaes, 2009; Leyens et al., 2001). That is, people may attribute fewer uniquely human traits, such as rationality, morality, pride and regret, to members of an out-group, as though they are somewhat lacking in terms of these human qualities. This infra-humanization appears to occur in one direction only, from high status groups toward low status groups, for research suggests that individuals who belong to low status groups do not infra-humanize those of higher status (DasGupta, 2004). For example, Capozza et al. (2012) conducted research both with members of real groups – Northern and Southern Italians – and with artificial groups in which perceived socioeconomic status was manipulated. In each case, members of higher status groups perceived people in their in-group as having more of the 'human' traits than those in the out-group, and they also attributed more 'animality' – more of the basic emotions that we share with animals – to members of the low status group. However, the low status group did not differentiate between members of their in-group and the higher status group with regard to either humanity or animality.

In another study (Capozza, Boccato et al., 2009), Northern Italian participants were presented with a series of photographs that included a mixture of non-ambiguous faces (of both apes and humans) interspersed with ambiguous faces that could be either ape or human. They were asked to identify each photograph as human or ape. In one condition (the 'in-group condition'), the participants were told that the human faces were those of Northern Italians, while in the other condition (the 'out-group' condition) they were told that the human faces were of Southern Italians. Not surprisingly, participants in both conditions did not differ in their responses with regard to the non-ambiguous faces, for they could easily identify them as either ape or human. However, participants in the in-group condition were more likely to categorize the ambiguous faces as ape, while those in the out-group condition did not show that tendency. The authors interpret this as an avoidance of 'animal contamination' of their in-group, as though the participant is thinking: 'If this one does not look quite human, surely it cannot be one of us, and so it must be ape.' On the other hand, if told that the ambiguous faces are either ape or Southern Italian: 'It could be either; I had better look more carefully before deciding.'

Think of the parallel between what has been observed in these laboratory studies and what occurs in the context of racism and genocide. The transatlantic slave trade was made palatable in part by viewing Africans to be animalistic and not fully human. The Holocaust was facilitated by the Nazi declaration that Jews were *untermensch* – 'subhuman' – a term that they subsequently extended to Russians, Ukrainians and Poles as well. Dehumanization comes about all too easily, and its roots trace back to this virtually automatic in-group favouritism and the negative stereotyping of out-groups that grows from it. (We shall expand upon this theme in Chapter 13.)

BOX 12.1 TAKING ANOTHER LOOK

EVOLUTION AND IN-GROUP FAVOURITISM

Where does in-group favouritism come from? Given its apparent universality, could it be that we are born with an automatic tendency to discriminate against out-groups?

One way to approach this question is to study children young enough that they have little experience with social differentiation. Do they gradually acquire an in-group/out-group bias as they grow, or do they seem to be predisposed to such a bias? To study this, Dunham, Chen & Banaji (2013) presented pictures of racially ambiguous faces to Taiwanese toddlers (Figure 12.5), and asked the children to identify each as either Taiwanese or white. The children typically identified a smiling face as Taiwanese (part of their in-group) and the non-smiling, possibly threatening face as that of a white person (out-group). In contrast, three-year-old white American children shown the same ambiguous faces identified the smiling face to be that of a white person (their in-group). Given the young age of these children, these results support the possibility of an inborn in-group bias, given that there has been little time for them to learn such discrimination.

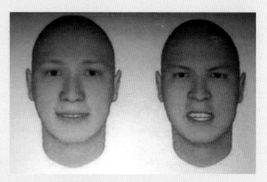

Figure 12.5 White or Taiwanese?
Source: Dunham, Chen & Banaji (2013)

KEY POINT: We see each other in large measure in terms of the groups to which we belong, and there is an automatic tendency towards out-group discrimination as we favour members of our own group. While much of the time this may be harmless, it is also the wellspring of prejudice and discrimination.

SOCIAL COMPARISON

Social identification leads inevitably to social comparison. You will recall from Chapter 3 that we often evaluate ourselves through comparisons with other people. Now we turn to how we compare the categories and groups to which we belong to other categories and groups perceived to be of higher or lower status and power. As noted above, group members generally strive to evaluate their group positively (Tajfel and Turner, 1979). While this sometimes is done by simply focusing on one's satisfaction with the group, it more often comes about by comparing one's group to some other relevant group; this is basically a competitive approach (Gagnon & Bourhis, 1996). Indeed, the positive aspects of social identity and the value that we place on membership in particular groups or categories *depend* upon comparisons with other groups. Do you feel good about being a university student? If so, is this not because of an implicit comparison with those who are *not* university students? If everyone were a university student, the fact that you are one would give no basis for pride.

When social comparison occurs at a national level, the consequences can be very serious. Research carried out in Canada and Australia (Amiot & Aubin, 2013) suggests that when social identity is primarily focused on the inherent satisfaction of being a member of the group, it is more likely to result in enhanced personal self-esteem and patriotism, but when the focus is on comparison with other groups, the resulting competitiveness is likely to lead to increased nationalism, which in the past has all too often proven to be destructive.

[**KEY POINT:** Social comparison is a competitive process that serves to enhance the importance of the groups to which we belong.]

SOCIAL IDENTITY THEORY AND SELF-CATEGORIZATION THEORY

These three processes, social categorization, social identification and social comparison, are at the heart of Social Identity Theory (Tajfel, 1972; Tajfel & Turner, 1979) and its extension, Self-Categorization Theory (Turner, 1985). These theories have jointly had a powerful impact on modern social psychology, particularly with regard to our understanding of large-scale social phenomena such as prejudice, stereotyping, ethnocentrism and intergroup conflict. While we have seen how Social Identity Theory focuses on how group and category memberships shape our social identities, we shall now explore how its derivative, Self-Categorization Theory, describes how individuals become unified into a psychological group (Turner, 1985; Turner & Oakes, 1986).

Turner (1985), partly in response to the growing interest in social cognition within American social psychology, focused attention on the importance of the categorization of oneself and others as being at the root of both social identity and the group and intergroup phenomena associated with it. According to Self-Categorization Theory, group behaviour would not be possible without the cognitive process of social identity (Turner, 1982; Hogg, 2006). A *shared* social identity leads to a shared social vision and social norms and provides the basis for cooperation and leadership. Because we identify ourselves as members of groups, we are influenced by the shared belief system of the group to the extent that it shapes our thoughts and values and behaviours. For example, if you are a volunteer member of an environmental group, your membership will further sensitize you to a number of serious environmental issues and will also provide a path of action to deal with them. Thus, we have many social identities, and the situation determines which is salient at a given moment. As Turner pointed out, our social identities are the critical pivot point between our lives as individuals and our lives as social beings (Turner, 1982; Haslam, Reicher & Reynolds, 2012).

But on what basis do we categorize ourselves at a given moment? That is, why is one social identity rather than another salient at a particular time? Do you think of yourself at this moment in terms of being male or female? You might do so if in the next sentence there is a comment that criticizes males or females in some way. Or maybe you think of yourself just now as a student, or as an American, or as a member of the football team, or as a fan of Manchester United or the Toronto Maple Leafs. Again, it depends on the social context. According to Self-Categorization Theory, categories take shape in such a way that the differences between categories are larger than the differences within. For example, if you are with a group of fellow Australians in a bar in Istanbul, and there is a group of Americans at the next table, being Australian may be the salient social group for you at the moment, for the differences between Americans and Australians are greater than the differences among Australians. However, suddenly, a commotion breaks out in the bar and people begin to shout in Turkish; neither you and your mates nor the Americans can understand what is going on. At this point, both the Australians and the Americans may feel themselves to be part of an English-speaking group, for the differences among them are smaller than the differences between them and all the others who are speaking Turkish. Again, the meta-contrast principle is at work, and you see yourself as having much more in common with the Americans than you did before the fracas developed. (Cross-categorization again.) As this demonstrates, whether people consider themselves to be similar to, or different from, others varies with the situation. Being part of a group with others is not based on interpersonal feelings of attraction and liking for the others, but rather on mutually perceived similarities that lead to a group identity.

To the extent that our social identity becomes the predominant influence on how we define ourselves, then depersonalization comes into play. This is essentially self-stereotyping: we come to see ourselves not as unique individuals, but as prototypical members of the groups and categories to which we belong. Some people become so identified with a particular group that the boundary between their social and personal identities all but disappears. This is referred to as identity fusion, which involves a 'visceral feeling of oneness' with the group (Swann et al., 2012). In such cases, individuals become willing to go to extreme lengths, even sometimes to the point of sacrificing their lives, for the sake of the group. Some extreme animal rights activists and anti-abortion activists fit this description. Note that this is not knee-jerk conformity to the demands of a leader, for the 'fused' individual would refuse to undertake actions, even if commanded to do so, that would bring harm to the group. Rather, his conformity is based on acceptance of the group's methods and goals.

> **KEY POINT:** Social Identity Theory describes how our social identities are shaped by the groups and categories to which we belong, whereas Self-Categorization Theory describes how individuals come together and feel part of a unified group.

Social belief structures

In some groups, shared group beliefs that distinguish members from non-members are central to how group members see themselves and how they are seen by others. For example, members of religious groups may share beliefs about morality, life after death, the authority of the Pope, or the need to eat only food that is kosher. Such group beliefs are so important that they often serve to draw the line between in-groups and out-groups, showing how other people are different from 'us' and even encouraging members to feel and act superior to others. (Recall the discussion in Chapter 10 – group beliefs can make conflict resolution extremely difficult.) Some group beliefs are related to the perceived status of the group relative to others. Group beliefs also serve as a filter through which members interpret new information (Bar-Tal, 1986). For example, members of the GLBT community (gay, lesbian, bisexual, or transgendered) are likely to share a number of common beliefs about how they are viewed by people outside their group, and these beliefs may shape their interpretation of information coming from outside the group.

Social Identity Theory considers such shared beliefs as constituting social belief structures that encompass understanding both about the relative status of one's in-group compared to other groups and about how *legitimate*, *stable* and *impermeable* the boundaries are between them (Tajfel, 1974).

Legitimacy is important, for if everyone accepts that the status structure is appropriate, there is not likely to be pressure for change. For example, for centuries, the caste system in India, tied to beliefs about cycles of rebirth, was viewed by all – high status and low alike – as legitimate; it was simply seen as reality. As a result there, was no revolutionary fervour among those at the bottom of the status ladder to overturn it. However, when disadvantaged groups view their disadvantage as illegitimate, then considerations of *stability* and *permeability* are likely to guide their actions (Hogg & Williams, 2000).

Stability refers to the degree to which the status structure is fixed and unlikely to change. For example, 150 years ago, almost no one imagined that women would one day be allowed to vote. And a century ago, virtually no one in the United Kingdom anticipated that its rigid class structure would soon begin to break down; Indians did not anticipate that their caste system would weaken to the extent that an 'untouchable' would become president in 1997; and neither South Africans nor Americans imagined that black men would become their presidents.

Permeability refers to how easy or difficult it is to move across a group or class boundary – for example, for a Cockney to become part of the upper classes in the United Kingdom, or for a low-caste Indian or a black American or a First Nations Canadian to move into the higher echelons of those societies.

Whether or not disadvantaged people try to change what is perceived as an unfair social structure depends on the permeability and the stability of that social structure (Hogg & Williams, 2000):

Impermeable and unstable If the shared belief is that group boundaries and status relationships are impermeable but unstable, members of low status groups are likely to enter into competition with higher status groups with the goal of changing or eliminating the group boundaries. South African blacks (and some sympathetic whites) were thus motivated to seek societal change, and this ultimately led to the end of apartheid.

Permeable and stable If the belief is that group boundaries and status relationships are permeable but stable, some individuals in the less-favoured group may try to pass into, and be assimilated by, the more favoured group. For example, this is what Gustav Mahler, the great Jewish composer, did when he converted to Roman Catholicism. As a Jew, he never could have obtained his highly desired appointment to the Vienna Court Opera that was awarded to him after his conversion. Nonetheless, he was never fully accepted as a Catholic.

Impermeable and stable If the belief is that group boundaries and status relationships are both impermeable, preventing movement from one to another, and stable, there is little motivation to try to change them. This was the viewpoint of many people, white and black, during apartheid in South Africa, where the dominant whites assumed that the boundary was a genetic one that was reflected in terms of skin colour. So how can a disadvantaged group enhance its self-esteem when the group boundaries are both impermeable and stable? In such case, people often compensate by finding a new basis of comparison that does not directly challenge the status and power of the more advantaged groups (Lemaine, Kastersztein & Personnaz, 1978). That is, they find a way to compensate for their apparent disadvantage by focusing on other characteristics in which they see themselves to be superior. Contemporary research has found that *morality, competence* and *sociability* are fundamental dimensions in in-group/out-group comparisons, and that when you belong to a low status group, you may concede higher competence to the higher status out-group, but claim greater morality and sociability for your in-group (Capozza et al., 2012). For example, Northern Italians are typically viewed as being more successful economically than Southern Italians, but while both groups view the Northerners as achievement-motivated, both also view Southerners as more emotionally expressive and more focused on maintaining interpersonal relationships (Jost et al., 2005; Capozza et al., 2012). Another example: In a study conducted some years ago, it was found that while East Indians in South Africa during the apartheid era considered themselves inferior to whites in the context of science and the economy, but saw themselves as superior in spiritual and social matters (Mann, 1963).

This compensation process was also demonstrated in a series of field studies carried out with children (Jamous & Lemaine, 1962; Lemaine, 1966; Lemaine & Kastersztein, 1972). In one experiment (Lemaine, 1974), two groups of boys competed for a prize, although they did not directly interact. Each group had to build a hut in the forest. One group – picked by the toss of a coin – was allowed to use string; the other was not. The 'handicapped' group, lacking string, was less efficient in organizing tasks; they were preoccupied with their disadvantage and considered withdrawing from the competition. They wasted a lot of time watching the other group before they finally buckled down to work themselves, and then only after 'closing their frontiers' and not allowing members of the advantaged group to observe what they were doing. At that point, they set about to compensating for their handicap by doing things differently from the other group. While the goal was to build a hut, the disadvantaged group redefined the situation by arguing that building a hut also involved making a garden, a table and a fireplace, items they had built and the other group had not. Similarly, Lalonde (1992) studied how the players on a last-place hockey team reacted to their inability to win. After each of eight games, he asked the players to rate how they perceived their team, the opposing team and themselves. He found that the inferior team was quite realistic concerning their lack of skill, but they chose to distinguish themselves in a positive manner from the other team by claiming that they had the moral high ground because their opponents played more 'dirty'.

> **KEY POINT:** Our beliefs about the stability and permeability of a group boundary will motivate people in the inferior status position either to try to change those boundaries, or to try to cross the boundary in order to become part of the more desirable group, or to accept the status quo and focus on finding ways of enhancing satisfaction in the group to which they belong.

Can groups change? Another important aspect of our social belief structure is the extent to which we believe that groups in general – and especially hostile and aggressive out-groups – are capable of positive change.

Consider a study carried out in the context of the ongoing and seemingly relentless Israeli–Palestinian conflict (Halperin et al., 2011): First of all, 500 Jewish-Israeli participants were assessed in terms of their beliefs about whether groups can change their ways, and they were also assessed with regard to their attitudes towards Palestinians. As predicted, the stronger the belief that groups never change, the more negative were their attitudes towards Palestinians. The study was then repeated with a new set of Jewish-Israeli participants sampled from across the political spectrum. This time, half the participants were asked to read an article that depicted aggressive groups as being able to change their ways and reduce their aggressiveness ('growth mindset'), while the other half read an article that suggested that such groups never really change ('fixed mindset'). There was no mention of Palestinians in either article. Later, in a totally different context, their attitudes towards Palestinians were assessed. It was found that those who had read the growth mindset article, in contrast to those who had read the fixed mindset article, now expressed more favourable attitudes towards Palestinians, as well as a substantially greater willingness to support compromises that would lead to peace. Thus, simply changing their beliefs about the changeability of groups, without saying anything about Palestinians at all, produced significant and positive changes in their attitudes towards Palestinians, along with an expressed willingness to compromise.

The researchers repeated the study with Palestinian-Israelis, and in this case, even for the most 'hawkish' participants, the growth mindset article led to more favourable attitudes towards Israelis along with a greater willingness to support major compromises. But, the researchers wondered, perhaps Palestinian-Israelis, given that they are living in Israel, are more susceptible to changing their views? The research was repeated again, this time with Palestinians living in the West Bank – a region where people often express pronounced hatred of Israel. Once again, those who read the growth mindset article expressed significantly more positive attitudes towards Jewish-Israelis and a greater willingness to support major compromises in the quest for peace than did those who read the fixed mindset article. Moreover, those who read the growth mindset article were much more likely to agree to participate in an interaction with Jewish-Israelis than were the other participants.

This research demonstrates that attitudes towards an out-group, even a hated out-group, can be positively influenced without ever mentioning the out-group itself, without attempting to increase understanding or empathy for the out-group, and without any actual or imagined interaction with the out-group. Simply by communicating the idea that groups are capable of change, that they need not be 'evil' or aggressive forever, can lead to such positive outcomes (Dweck, 2012).

SMALL GROUPS

We noted earlier in this chapter that the term 'group' is defined somewhat differently by social psychologists who focus on relatively small numbers of individuals interacting with one another directly. Recall that in Social Identity Theory and Self-Categorization Theory, the term 'group' refers essentially to a category – at a given moment you may categorize yourself as a student, a Canadian, a Roman Catholic and so forth. But in small-group research, being part of a group involves something more. It is defined by these criteria:

1. *Mutual awareness and influence*: First, there are two or more people involved in an interaction in which they are both *aware of* and *influence* each other. Without mutual influence, there is no group. When you are one of a number of people milling about the baggage carousel at an airport while waiting for your luggage, it is unlikely that you would think that you had just joined a group. Or, although when walking along the street, you may categorize people into 'drivers' and 'pedestrians', you would be unlikely to think of the drivers and pedestrians around you as constituting two distinct groups; they probably do not know one another, and their classifications are temporary, for pedestrians may later be drivers, and drivers become pedestrians the moment they get out of their cars.

2. *Enduring relationship*: Mutual awareness and influence alone, however, do not define a group. Consider a driver who splashes a pedestrian. They become aware of one another, and the driver's actions certainly influence the pedestrian and the pedestrian's reactions may have some influence on the driver. But the two do not constitute a group because their interaction lacks continuity. The driver and the pedestrian may never encounter each other again – at least not as driver and pedestrian. Groups involve enduring relationships within a relatively stable framework. A family, a poker club or a local charitable organization all involve continuing relationships, unwritten rules ('norms') that govern the members' interactions and enduring roles for the individuals in the group.

3. *Common purpose*: These preceding criteria remain incomplete, however. A prisoner and a guard in a penitentiary certainly have a mutual influence on each other and they may also have an enduring relationship within a very stable framework, but we would hardly view them as belonging to the same group. They stand in opposition to one another, whereas, to be part of a group, group members share a common sense of purpose or have a common goal.

4. *Feeling of belonging*: There is still something missing. Suppose that you share a bus shelter with the same set of people every morning. There is likely to be at least some mutual influence, and the relationship, minimal as it is, endures over time in a relatively stable way. Moreover, all of the individuals share a common goal – to get on the bus. Yet they are not likely to consider themselves part of a 'group'. In the final analysis – and this is similar to the Social Identity Theory perspective – a crucial characteristic of a group is the belief held by the individual members that they *belong to a group*, that they are part of a specific entity (Tajfel, 1978, 1982).

> **KEY POINT:** Social psychologists apply the term 'group' in two different but related ways. In the context of Social Identity Theory, a group comprises people who view themselves as sharing attributes that distinguish them from other people. On the other hand, social psychologists studying small groups define them in terms of relatively small numbers of people who are aware of each other, who both influence and are influenced by one another, who are engaged in an ongoing and relatively stable relationship, and who share common goals, as well as viewing themselves as belonging to a group.

There are, of course, various kinds of groups. While children cannot choose their families, and people called for jury duty cannot choose their fellow jurors, most groups involve voluntary membership. Why does an individual join one group and not another? People sometimes join groups to achieve specific objectives, and sometimes just to interact with others. Task-oriented groups are goal-focused; its members want to win the trophy, or stop global warming, or improve their photographic abilities. Others are social-oriented; their *raison d'être* is largely social – to play bridge, talk about books, play a hockey game. They provide companionship, entertainment and information, allowing people to interact with others who have common interests. Some groups are formal with a clearly specified structure and clearly delineated roles for members. Others are informal, such as a group of friends who go to the pub every Friday night.

Differentiation within the group

Roles and status   In most groups, and especially in task-oriented groups, different members have different duties to perform. Roles may be informal and evolve gradually, or they may be organizational with titles such as 'secretary' or 'chairperson'. Two important informal roles that are often found in most task-oriented groups are the 'task specialist' and the 'social-emotional specialist'. The person perceived as most competent to direct the group to its objective generally fills the first role. However, such a person may not be suited to the task of guiding the group through all the emotional upsets that arise as the group is being pushed towards its goal. That task is left to the social-emotional specialist, who tries to smooth out any interpersonal conflicts within the group.

Within any group, there tends to be a kind of 'pecking order'. High-status members tend to dominate group discussions, play a more important part in decision-making and have a greater influence on low-status members than low-status members have on them. High-status members are naturally more likely to assume leadership roles; leadership is discussed later in this chapter. High status can derive from a number of factors, such as providing significant help towards achieving the group's goals, or personal popularity, or a recognized and important role within the group (e.g., social convener).

Norms   As you will recall, norms are shared beliefs about what behaviours are and are not acceptable. They usually involve a certain amount of judgement on the part of group members. For example, if you are part of a factory work group, there is unlikely to be any clear rule about the limits of productivity, but if you consistently produce more than your fellow workers, you may draw their displeasure. When norms are not observed and when a transgression is considered serious, group members will usually take measures to draw the deviant member back into line. The ultimate threat, of course, is rejection from the group. To the extent that membership in a particular group is important, such a threat can push the member to conform to the norms. Recall the group rejection that occurred in Schachter's (1951) discussion groups when the 'deviate' was ultimately excluded from the group discussion (Chapter 6).

Group socialization   How is it that people become part of one group and not another? What is it about a group that attracts an individual, and what is it about an individual that leads the group to accept him or her as a member? The process of becoming part of the group, being accepted by it and learning to adapt to its norms and rules is referred to as **group socialization.** Three basic processes are involved (Moreland & Levine, 1982). First of all, there is an evaluation process. Here, the individual evaluates the group and the group evaluates the individual, each in terms of how much the other can contribute to mutual goals. As the individual becomes more and more involved with the group, each considers any discrepancies between what is expected of the other and what is actually occurring, and then usually tries to reduce them. For example, if you join a photography club, you may be disappointed first to discover that the members spend much more time chatting about irrelevant topics than they do in taking pictures, and if you are not totally disillusioned at this point, you may try to influence them to shift their focus back to photography. Or if you are perceived as talking too much, group members may attempt to influence you to calm your chatter.

The second process is commitment. At this point, depending on the outcome of the evaluation process, the individual and the group either move toward a committed relationship or drift away from one another. If there is commitment, then a third process, role transition, gradually occurs. This refers to changes in the new member's role within the group, reflecting positive outcomes in the evaluation process and perhaps involving increasing responsibility for helping the group to attain its goals.

This is but a brief description of the overall socialization process. Some researchers (e.g., Anderson, Riddle & Martin, 1999; Myers & Anderson, 2008) describe a more elaborate five-stage process in which communication plays a key role. Such a detailed approach is helpful in coming to understand why some groups are very successful while others become dysfunctional as the membership grows.

> **KEY POINT:** The process of becoming part of a group is more complex than might appear at first, as the individual and the group members evaluate each other. Once satisfactory evaluations are reached, socialization into the group continues, first through commitment and then through gradual role transition as a new member assumes more and more responsibility.

Mutual attraction within the group What holds a group together? The collective attractiveness that a group has for its members is referred to as cohesiveness. This is a difficult concept to define (and measure), but in general terms it refers to how much the members are committed to the group and to the group task (Cota et al., 1995). A cohesive group sticks together and displays feelings of harmony and solidarity. The more factors that there are that keep individuals in the group and the fewer the factors that tempt them to leave, the more cohesive will be the group.

Factors that contribute to cohesiveness include personal attraction among members, congruity between group goals and individual goals, and uniqueness of the group in being able to satisfy individual needs. For example, if you belong to a poker group, love playing poker and do not know any other poker players outside the group, leaving the group would involve a considerable loss. On the other hand, if various other groups were constantly trying to get you to play poker with them, your allegiance to your current group would have to be based on other factors, such as your attraction to the individual members or the quality of play. (Think back to Social Exchange Theory and CLalt, the comparison level for alternatives). Cohesiveness within groups usually increases when the importance of the group increases for its members – for instance, when it is in competition with other groups or when there is some kind of external threat.

Cohesiveness can both help and hinder the productivity of task-oriented groups. Members of highly cohesive groups are usually somewhat more influenced by group norms since group membership is so important to them (Berkowitz, 1954). Thus if the group norm calls for high productivity, cohesiveness will foster productivity, while if the norm calls for low productivity (as might be the case among workers in some industrial settings), cohesiveness will promote lower output (Mullen & Copper, 1994). Members of highly cohesive groups can also lose productivity if their attraction to one another leads them to spend too much time in social interaction, or to become so absorbed by the social interaction as to lose sight of the group goal (Langfred, 1998).

> **KEY POINT:** To the extent that a group remains attractive to its members, the group will be cohesive and stick together.

LEADERSHIP

To lead people, walk beside them … As for the best leaders, the people do not notice their existence. The next best, the people honour and praise. The next, the people fear; and the next, the people hate … When the best leader's work is done the people say, 'We did it ourselves!'

Lao-Tsu (6th century BCE)

While power and influence in a group are usually distributed across the membership, with some members having more and others less, there is often one person who is more influential than the others. This person, designated or not, is the leader, an individual who is both able to influence followers to work towards group goals and who is able to coordinate efforts towards the attainment of those goals (Van Vugt, Hogan & Kaiser, 2008).

And a group may have more than one leader at the same time; a member having the most knowledge or skill relative to achieving the group goal may serve as the task leader, while another member may play the key role of social-emotional leader, maintaining cohesiveness by helping sort out emotional situations that arise, and helping motivate the members to coordinate their efforts (Hamblin, 1958). Moreover, a person formally chosen to be the 'head' of a group sometimes does not automatically become the actual leader. Heads are often imposed from outside, while leaders emerge from within. If you are a soldier under the command of a weak sergeant who is belittled by others in your unit, it is likely that someone else whose competence is more respected – a corporal, for example – will emerge as the real leader. The sergeant may have legitimate power, but the corporal may be much more effective in managing the unit. Gradually, the sergeant may come to recognize this and actually yield to the implicit power of the corporal.

Social psychologists have long searched for the factors that determine who becomes the leader of the group, but have not yet found a totally satisfying answer as to what qualities a good leader needs to possess. Social Identity Theory provides a particular view

Figure 12.6 Lao-Tsu

of leadership and how it emerges (Hogg, 2001): Leadership is seen as the result of a group process whereby the most prototypical member of the group – that is, the one who most embodies the positive attributes associated with the group – becomes *de facto* leader, and he or she then wields the most influence by providing a model to which others strive to conform. This influence in turn generates status for the leader. Because of being seen as a prototype, followers take for granted that this individual is motivated by the same needs as they are and wants to achieve the same goals. Empirical research supports this view: In one study, it was found that leaders who were most similar to the group prototype were perceived the most favourably (Platow et al., 2006), and other research has shown that, within formal organizations, those individuals whose beliefs, attitudes and motivations best match those of the organization are most likely to emerge as leaders (Hains, Hogg & Duck, 1997).

If leaders represent the prototypical characteristics of group members, how can they lead members in new directions? That is, how do groups and organizations ever change? Successful leaders sometimes need to make decisions and find compromises with other leaders that fly in the face of their group's position. What happens then? Are they turfed out? In fact, groups do not always react to deviant leaders in the way that they react to deviant members. Recall from Chapter 6 the notion of idiosyncrasy credits. Hollander (1958) argued that successful leaders acquire idiosyncrasy credits that allow them a certain latitude in terms of departing from group norms. As a result, effective leaders are often viewed as 'positive' deviants (Abrams et al., 2008) and are respected for their efforts towards innovation and change.

> **KEY POINT:** Leaders tend to exemplify the positive attributes that a group associates with itself. Effective leaders are usually given more latitude to depart from group norms.

Social power

Leaders of course have power, and within any group, especially a task-oriented group, some followers also enjoy more power than others. Similarly, some groups have more power than others within a society. Power refers to the capacity to influence another person or group to act in a desired way (Pruitt, 1976). In its most primitive form, as exhibited by the schoolyard bully, power derives from physical might. However, power also derives from such things as social position, financial clout and political influence. Power has always interested and intrigued social scientists and philosophers, and some have even argued that it should be the primary focus of the social sciences. To quote the English philosopher Bertrand Russell (1962): 'I shall be concerned to prove that the fundamental concept in social science is Power, in the same sense in which Energy is the fundamental concept in physics' (Pollard, Mitchell et al., 1972, p. 9). Power has not so far attained such an important position in social psychology. (However, recall the mention in the introductory chapter of a relatively new branch of psychology that has developed in Europe, Critical Psychology. It considers mainstream psychology to have largely disregarded the effects of power differences among individuals and groups, and its research places strong emphasis on the role that power plays in human affairs.)

Notwithstanding the lack of attention to the concept, various theories of social power have been developed in mainstream social psychology. Six major sources or 'types' of power have been discussed in the literature (Stahelski & Frost, 1989; Hinkin & Shriesheim, 1989; Raven, Schwarzwald & Koslowsky, 1998).

Reward power   One can reward another (via money, approval, love, etc.) for complying with one's wishes or demands. A mother can lead her son to clean up his room by promising him some chocolate cake as a reward. If the boy wants the cake and has no other way of obtaining it, he will probably do what his mother has asked.

Coercive power   One can punish another for noncompliance. The same mother can threaten her child with a spanking if he does not clean up his room. Since she is bigger than he is, she can carry through on the threat.

Legitimate power   Society provides its authorities (e.g., teachers, police) with power to exercise their duties. Individuals usually comply with the demands of such people by accepting their authority. While such power is ultimately backed up by coercive power, no coercion is necessary if the individual has internalized respect for designated authorities.

Expert power   This is the power of people who have important and special knowledge to offer. We follow the orders of a physician not because of coercion but because we believe that the physician knows more than we do about how to maintain our health.

Informational power   'People in the know' (newspaper editors, governmental press secretaries, university professors) have the power to provide or withhold information (Pruitt, 1976).

Referent power   Such power derives from the respect and admiration that one has for a leader. If you are a member of a political party and you admire and respect the party leader, you will probably do as the leader says because you assume it is appropriate and because you want to act as the leader does.

More research still needs to be done to substantiate this classification of sources of power. The list is not necessarily exhaustive, and these forms of power are not mutually exclusive.

Does power corrupt?   Despite the power that people may wield in their personal relationships, only a few ever rise to positions of power within an institution, such as a company, or government or university. Do people change when they attain power? In fact, power is often viewed as having a corrupting influence: In the words of Lord Acton, 'Power tends to corrupt, and absolute power corrupts absolutely'. And indeed it is sometimes disappointing to see the changes that power brings to an individual's behaviour and personality. Being surrounded by flatterers and sycophants can lead an individual to magnify his or her own sense of importance. In addition, power often demands a changed perspective. Consider a company setting, for example. While an individual worker may be very considerate of others when still a regular employee, when he or she is promoted to manager, it may be necessary to step on some people's toes in order to carry out the job of managing the department, and this may be interpreted by others as a change in character. Such a perceived change is magnified if the new manager finds it easier to supervise others by maintaining a psychological distance from them and avoiding emotional involvement ('the loneliness of command'). This may further add to the perception by subordinates that the person who has assumed power has changed and lost interest in them. And sometimes the power-holder may begin to take more and more credit for the accomplishments of the 'underlings', thereby devaluing their efforts and abilities. Gradually, harmonious interpersonal relationships may become more and more difficult to maintain.

The effects of power on the relationship between the power holder and those subject to that power were demonstrated in an experiment carried out by Kipnis (1972). Each participant was given the role of a 'manager' in charge of some workers said to be in another room. In fact, there were no workers. The manager could speak to the workers, but was told that the workers would not be able to respond. The manager's task was to maximize the workers' output. Every three minutes, pre-programmed output records were brought from the (nonexistent) worker to the manager.

There were two conditions. In one condition, managers were given power to give rewards (extra pay), or punishments (deduction from pay) or to transfer the worker to a more boring job. In the second condition, no such power was available. As predicted, researchers found the following:

- Participants with power made more attempts to influence the workers than did those without it. Very few participants (16%) relied solely on persuasion: most used the power at their disposal. The presence of power seemed to bring about its use.
- Participants with power devalued the worth of their workers more than did participants without power, and they were more likely to attribute the workers' efforts to a motivation only to obtain pay. Only 28% of those with power, versus 72% of those without it, viewed the workers' performance as a self-motivated effort to do a good job.
- Psychological distance was greater among those with power: Seventy-nine per cent of those without power, but only 35% of those with power, expressed a desire to meet socially with the workers.

These findings support the view that power over others, at least in an institutionalized setting, leads both to devaluation of the efforts of those subject to the power and to increased psychological distance from them. More recent research has found when people have power over others, there is a tendency to objectify the subordinates and see them as a means to an end rather than as individual persons with their own particular qualities (Gruenfeld et al., 2008).

People who rise to power sometimes rely upon stereotypes that seem to justify their superior position in life (Fiske, 1993) – for example, think of city politicians who blame homelessness on the inherent laziness of people who live in the streets. Such stereotypes are maintained because those in power do not pay attention, and may not want to pay attention, to information about powerless individuals that runs contrary to the stereotype (Guinote & Phillips 2010).

Henry Kissinger once referred to power as 'the greatest aphrodisiac', and there is empirical evidence to suggest that he may be literally correct in some cases: In a series of experiments, Kunstman & Maner (2011) found that giving managers legitimate power over opposite-sex subordinates activated sexual themes, including expectations of sexual interest on the part of the subordinate, and the researchers suggest that this may be one reason that power sometimes leads to sexual harassment.

> **KEY POINT:** Power comes in many forms, and it often changes the relationship between the power-holder and subordinates, sometimes leading to the power-holder devaluing the abilities and efforts of the subordinates.

Leadership and culture

The world has become a much smaller place in recent years, functionally at least. As a result of sophisticated transportation and communication – and in particular the Internet – we now live in what Marshall McLuhan referred to as a 'global village', and multinational organizations can no longer assume that the leadership qualities admired at head office in the home country will be accepted and respected and successful in all cultures.

The values attached to leadership and power, and the way in which that power is expected to be used, vary greatly across cultures. In broad terms, we might expect that people in more individualistic societies are more likely to achieve high status through competition, by rising up the ladder and outperforming others. On the other hand, in more collectivist cultures – think of Eastern European countries before the fall of the Berlin Wall, or many Asian countries today – one's position on the social ladder may depend less on actual achievement and more on 'who you know', or on the family or class into which you were born.

Brodbeck et al. (2000) studied leadership prototypes in 22 European countries and found significant differences with regard to what are considered the characteristics of a good leader and what constitutes successful leadership. Smith, Dugan & Trompenaars (1996) examined data relating to the behavioural intentions and personal values of 10,000 employees and managers from across 43 different nations. Among other findings, they reported fundamental differences in the way power and leadership are viewed in various parts of the world, and even between the countries of Eastern and Western Europe. In some societies, people expect their leaders and managers to be efficient and task-oriented. In other societies, leadership and paternalism go hand in hand; leaders are expected to show an interest in the personal and professional lives of their subordinates, and subordinates respond to this with respect and loyalty (Gelfand, Erez & Aycan, 2007). Such paternalistic leadership is positively associated with job satisfaction in some countries, such as India, but not so in highly individualistic societies like the United States (Pellegrini, Scandura & Jayaraman, 2010).

For effective leadership, there needs to be a match between the leader's qualities and style on the one hand and the cultural expectations of leadership on the other. (This is in line with the contingency model of leadership, discussed later in this chapter, which specifies the need for a match between qualities of the leader and the demands of the situation (Muczyk & Holt, 2008).) Hofstede (Hofstede & Hofstede, 2005; de Mooij & Hofstede, 2010) identified five cultural dimensions that need to be taken into account when considering the leadership style that is most appropriate in a particular society: (1) *individualism–collectivism* – the extent to which a society tends to be individualistic or collectivist; (2) *avoidance of uncertainty* – how comfortable people in a given society are in dealing with ambiguous situations where there is little ability to predict future events; (3) *masculinity–femininity* – the extent to which so-called 'male' characteristics of aggressiveness, independence – and dominance are emphasized in a culture; (4) *power distance* – how willing people are to accept the existence of power and status differences in their society; and (5) *long-term/short-term orientation* – the importance that society places on longer-term objectives relative to objectives that can be obtained in the immediate future. This list is not necessarily complete, and other researchers (e.g., Javidan & House, 2001) have added additional dimensions to it.

KEY POINT: Cultural factors play an important role in terms of what is considered good leadership within a society.

CHARACTERISTICS OF THE LEADER

It has often been said that great leaders have shaped history. Indeed, we often think of historical eras in terms of their leading figures: Genghis Khan, Charlemagne, Joan of Arc, Napoleon, Catherine the Great, Churchill, Nehru, Mao, Mandela, to name but a few. What is it that made such leaders so remarkable? Was it their character that promoted their rise to greatness or was it the situation – did they just happen to be in the right place at the right time? These possibilities, referred to in the literature as the great person approach (or trait approach) and the situational approach, have been explored in considerable detail by social psychologists. A more recent view, the interactionist approach, holds that both traits and situation are important.

The great person approach

In the 19th century, Francis Galton investigated the hereditary background of 'great men' and attempted to explain leadership on the basis of inherited capability (Stogdill, 1974). Good leaders, he assumed, were born and not made. Can hereditary influences on personal characteristics determine leadership capability?

Although this question has been studied in detail, there has been little empirical evidence to support the great person view of leadership. Nonetheless, one study (Albright & Forziati, 1995) did find that those who were leaders in one situation with regard to one particular task were also likely to become the leaders in other situations with different tasks, and in addition that an individual who was a leader in one group of people also was likely to become a leader in other groups made up of different people. This suggests that there may be a set of traits associated with becoming a leader. Indeed, a number of such traits have been identified:

- *Intelligence*: This has a strong relationship with leadership, which is not surprising since leadership is achieved at least partly on the basis of the leader's ability to provide followers with something that they cannot provide for themselves. Yet, if the gap in intelligence between the leader and followers is too great, the followers may become dissatisfied since they cannot identify with the leader and may have difficulty following his or her reasoning (Gibb, 1969).
- *Physique*: There is also evidence of modest positive correlations between leadership and physical size, health and physical attractiveness. Are these correlations due to the visual impact of such traits on followers? Or do they have an early and indirect effect on personality by influencing the reactions of other people? A tall person, for example, may develop greater self-confidence as a result of being given more respect for physical prowess. Steadily maturing self-confidence, rather than height itself, might then be responsible for the leadership capacity. Indeed, leaders generally rate higher than followers in terms of self-confidence (Gibb, 1969).

BOX 12.2   LEADERSHIP AND THE PERCEPTION OF HEIGHT

People tend to overestimate the height of people in high-status positions (Keyes, 1980). The height of adults is fairly stable, although we may shrink a little as we get older. However, a study has shown that people adjust their estimates of tallness according to changes in the target's status and prestige (Carment, 1992; Higham & Carment, 1992). Respondents were asked before and after the 1988 Canadian federal election to judge the heights of political leaders Brian Mulroney, John Turner and Ed Broadbent. Before the election, Turner, the then prime minister, was judged to be taller than Mulroney, the leader of the opposition, and Broadbent, the third party leader, was seen as the shortest. However, after winning the election, Mulroney grew taller in respondents' perceptions while Turner shrank, now giving Mulroney the edge over Turner. Broadbent was judged to be shorter still. Moreover, the taller the candidate actually was, the more votes he obtained: Mulroney, 185 cm; Turner, 181.7 cm; and Broadbent, 180 cm, the exact order of the election results! Similarly, when researchers examined presidential election results in the United States from 1789 onwards, they found that the taller candidate won the election 58% of the time, and was ahead in the popular vote 67% of the time, again showing a height leadership advantage. Only seven presidents were shorter than the average male (Stulp, Buunk, Verhulst & Pollet, 2013). And while a great deal of research has shown that taller, more physically imposing individuals are more likely to attain positions of power, recent research has found that when asked to estimate their *own* height relative to a fixed pole, people who have been made to feel more powerful actually overestimate their stature (Duguid & Goncalo, 2012).

Other research in the United States has found that taller people earn more money, at the rate of about $1500.00 per inch (Landsberg, 2009). Also, the benefits of height appear early according to Persico et al.

(2004), who found that men shorter than their peers as adolescents earned less as adults even though they had subsequently grown taller.

Blaker et al. (2013) asked participants to rate the leadership qualities of a number of business leaders by looking at their pictures. Half the participants were shown a short version of each leader, and the other half a tall version. The taller versions of each leader were rated to be more leader-like, and this height advantage was even greater for male leaders than for female leaders. Further investigation determined that the participants took greater height to be related to both better health and to dominance. This is in line with speculation that we may be genetically predisposed towards a preference for taller leaders, given that along the course of evolution, groups led by strong and healthy leaders would have a survival advantage (Van Vugt, Hogan & Kaiser, 2008). What about short leaders? Napoleon comes to mind, for the British referred to him as the 'little corporal'. However, he was actually not so little for the times. In fact, he was the same height as the British hero Nelson, 172.7 cm or five foot eight, which was the average height of a Frenchman in those days. Calling him 'little' was a British put-down.

While there may be some evolutionary relationship between height and perceptions of leadership, we need to remember that even if there are hereditary factors involved, the environment plays a powerful role in shaping our behaviour. Charles de Gaulle, himself a man of imposing stature, once quipped that tall people can be trusted because, as children, they stood out from their peers and thus their transgressions were more likely to be noticed by adults. Of necessity, he claimed, they learned the importance of being honest and obeying rules.

- *Talkativeness*: This is another leadership characteristic that has been consistently identified, and the group member who talks the most is actually most likely to be chosen as leader (Mullen, Salas & Driskell, 1989), a phenomenon that has been observed in India as well as in the United States (Janowski & Malloy, 1992; Ruback & Dabbs, 1988). Why should talkativeness be associated with leadership? It may be that participation rate in conversations is perceived by others as a measure of how motivated the person is to be a member of the group and to assist the group in achieving its goals. Participation also allows individuals to demonstrate their relevant expertise and leadership characteristics. Perhaps this salience leads people to identify the high participator as the obvious choice for leader. Conversely, people who are shy and thus have a low rate of participation may not be perceived to have leadership qualities or may even be thought to be lower in intelligence.
- *Extraversion*: Of the Big Five personality traits (extraversion, agreeableness, conscientiousness, neuroticism and openness), it is extraversion that most highly relates to whether one is likely to become a leader, and to others' ratings of one's effectiveness as a leader. Talkativeness is associated with extraversion, but it appears that it is actually the extraversion expressed through talkativeness, rather than simple sociability, that is responsible for this relationship (Van Vugt, Hogan & Kaiser, 2008).
- *Dominance*: Individuals who are high in the need to dominate others have also been found to be more likely to emerge as leaders (Nyquist & Spence, 1986). In this regard, consider a study that followed Canadian Forces officer candidates over a four-year period (Bradley et al., 2002). It was found that dominance was the most significant predictor of who would be identified as a leader.

However, even though these traits have all shown some correlation with the emergence of leadership, their overall influence is not great, and the trait approach has not succeeded in providing a satisfactory explanation as to why some people emerge as leaders and others do not.

Could evolution play a role in determining who is likely to become leader? Because our ancestors evolved in group settings, sharing hunting, foraging, parenting and defence activities, evolutionary psychologists think it likely that specialized psychological adaptations that facilitated planning, communication, conflict management, coordination and group decision-making would have been chosen through natural selection to be passed down the evolutionary trail, resulting in the emergence of heritable features associated with leadership and followership (Kenrick, Li & Butner, 2003; Van Vugt, Hogan & Kaiser, 2008). This is not unique to humans, for simple leader–follower mechanisms for coordination and group activity are found in many species of insects and animals nonhuman primates included (Couzin et al., 2005). There is some emerging empirical evidence that inherited factors may indeed have some role to play in determining who becomes a leader. Of course, sometimes this influence is indirect. As noted in Box 12.1, height, which is obviously affected by genetic factors, is related to leadership potential, but this reflects an indirect genetic influence. However, DeNeve et al. (2013) report evidence that a specific genotype (rs4950) appears to be associated with a greater likelihood of becoming a leader. They used a large twin sample, studying the genotypes of 4000 individuals, along with information about their jobs and whether they occupied supervisory positions, and found a significant correlation between the presence of that genotype and leadership. Indeed, they estimated that about a quarter of the variation in leadership behaviour between pairs of twins can be explained in terms of genetic inheritance. Yet, while this genotype appears to have a significant influence in determining who becomes a leader, the researchers stress that it is still the development of leadership-related skills that is of prime importance in determining who becomes a leader, although the genotype may assist in the development of such skills.

The situational approach

Another approach to leadership is based on the idea that different situations call for different kinds of leaders and that the person who happens to have those traits and abilities needed at a particular time will emerge as leader. For example, Churchill was a great wartime leader but lost the election following the war. Postwar Britain, it seems, wanted a different kind of leader to rebuild the country. Leaders have more influence when a group is facing a crisis; however, the group is likely to look for a new leader if the old one cannot deal with the crisis (Hamblin, 1958). (And although it may surprise you, in modern times people are often more likely to turn to a woman leader in times of crisis, as is discussed later in this chapter.)

The interactionist approach

Not only do leaders influence followers, but followers also influence leaders, and to be a successful leader an individual needs to be in tune with the expectations and needs of the followers (Hollander, 1992; Sims & Manz, 1984), just as Social Identity Theory would suggest. Thus, successful leadership is a combination of 'right leader' and 'right situation' – in other words, an interaction between the characteristics of the leader and the characteristics of the situation. The situational approach, in contrast to the trait approach, does not assume that a person who is a good leader in one situation will be a good leader in other situations.

Early studies of leadership effectiveness focused on democratic and autocratic leadership styles in a variety of situations. Democratic leadership, which involves group members in decision-making rather than emphasizing clear-cut orders, produces greater satisfaction among followers (Shaw, 1981). But does it lead to greater productivity? Some research has indicated that it does (Kahn & Katz, 1953); other researchers have reported that autocratic leadership is more effective in this regard (Hare, 1962). Further research has found that the situation itself is a key factor. Autocratic leadership leads to greater productivity in stressful situations, while democratic leadership produces greater productivity in non-stressful circumstances (Rosenbaum & Rosenbaum, 1971). Thus, no one leadership style is likely to be effective in all situations.

Fiedler (1967, 1971, 1981) proposed a contingency theory of leadership, based on the ideas that there are two basic styles of leadership (task-oriented and socio-emotional) and that the leader's effectiveness is contingent upon appropriate matching of the leadership style to the situation. The task-oriented leader will not be overly concerned with the feelings and personal needs of the followers. The socio-emotional leader may strive for good interpersonal relationships even at the cost of efficiency in attaining group goals. Contingency theory proposes that the best way to measure leadership orientation is to assess the leader's attitude towards the 'least preferred co-worker' (LPC) in the group. The LPC is determined by asking the leader to indicate who, out of all the people he or she has ever encountered at work, was the most difficult to work with. Then the leader rates that person on a set of 18 pairs of bipolar adjectives (see Table 12.1, next page), such as 'boring–interesting', using an eight-point scale. If the leader rates the LPC in a negative way, he is a low-LPC leader; if the leader rates the LPC in a positive manner, he is a high-LPC leader. The high-LPC leader is assumed to be more people-oriented, while the low-LPC leader is assumed to be more task-oriented.

Table 12.1 Sample LPC items

Leaders are asked to select the person whom they least liked as a co-worker in their entire careers and then to evaluate that person on a series of scales such as the following:

Friendly	8 7 6 5 4 3 2 1	Unfriendly
Agreeable	8 7 6 5 4 3 2 1	Disagreeable
Pleasant	8 7 6 5 4 3 2 1	Unpleasant
Cooperative	8 7 6 5 4 3 2 1	Uncooperative
Helpful	8 7 6 5 4 3 2 1	Frustrating

By adding up the scale values, a total LPC score is derived. Rating the LPC in a negative direction scores a low score and an individual producing such a score is referred to as a *low-LPC leader*, while an individual who produces a high score is referred to as a *high-LPC leader*.

In Fiedler's model, style of leadership interacts with *situational control*, the amount of control the leader can exert over the members of the group. This depends on a combination of three factors: (1) the affective relationship between leader and followers; (2) how highly structured is the group's task; and (3) the leader's power to reward or punish. Power is the least important of the three. The theory suggests that both the productivity and the morale of members will be increased when the leadership style matches the situational control (Chemers, 1983).

According to contingency theory, a task-oriented leader should be most successful in situations that are either very favourable or very unfavourable for the leader. Under unfavourable leadership conditions (ambiguous task, poor leader–follower relations, low leader power), the group may be more receptive to a leader who can get them moving towards their goal; a person-oriented leader may spend too much time on trying to promote interpersonal harmony and not enough time on the group goal. When conditions are highly favourable (structured task, good leader–follower relations, high leader power), the task-oriented leader, content that the group is moving towards its goal, may become more attentive to the 'people' concerns. On the other hand, a people-oriented leader in a situation already characterized by interpersonal harmony may now try to demonstrate that she is *really* a leader by pursuing self-aggrandizing activities. In so doing, the leader may actually lose some esteem while not being concerned enough with the task (Fiedler, 1971). In intermediate conditions, friction between group members may become more serious and the person-oriented leader can do more to cope with the group's needs (Figure 12.7).

Think of a team and its coach in this framework. When a team is doing poorly, it generally needs a task-oriented (low-LPC) coach, and when it is doing very well, the coach should probably interfere as little as possible (again, probably low-LPC). However, a team at an intermediate level of achievement may need the encouragement and social support that is likely to come from a high-LPC coach

The contingency model has received considerable support from a large number of different studies (Strube & Garcia, 1981) and over time been viewed as one of the most useful approaches for ascertaining the effectiveness of leadership (Peters, Hartke & Pohlmann, 1985). However, its focus is on the quality of the relationship between leaders and members, and this neglects some important aspects of leadership success, not the least of which is how well the task is achieved. Of course, in the business world, what is most important is how well the leader manages to achieve the goals of the organization. Steve Jobs was certainly an exceptional leader, taking his Apple Corporation to the pinnacle of success in the corporate world, and yet, by all accounts, he was low LPC: abrasive, condescending, and difficult to get along with. His influence on those who worked for him did not come from being Mr Nice Guy. While he was probably an exception in the workplace, the emphasis that psychologists place on an individual's ability to influence others in the group to work towards, and achieve, group goals often ignores other important requirements for the leader to be successful. This is because psychologists typically focus on what Kaiser, McGinnis & Overfield (2012) refer to as the *how* of leadership: how does the leader move the group towards goal attainment? However, in real-world organizations,

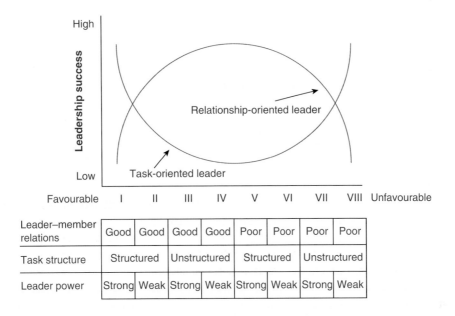

Figure 12.7 Contingency model of leadership and group performance

the *what* is also a vital importance: *what* does the leader do to set goals, to choose appropriate staff, to organize and allocate resources, to plan action, and to monitor performance? Based on ratings of hundreds of senior managers by thousands of their superiors, peers and subordinates, Kaiser et al. (2012) found that both interpersonal skills – the *how* – and organizational skills – the *what* – contribute about equally to the perceived effectiveness of these leaders.

> **KEY POINT:** Someone can be an excellent leader in one set of circumstances, and yet not in another. Great leaders are typically the 'right person' in the 'right situation' at the 'right time.'

Transformational leadership

Weber (1947) coined the term **charismatic leader** (now more often referred to as a transformational leader), whose **charisma** (Greek for 'divine gift') is an exceptional quality that enables him or her to gather a large number of disciples as a result of appearing to possess supernatural, providential or extraordinary powers. Martin Luther King, Winston Churchill, Pierre Trudeau, John F. Kennedy, Mahatma Gandhi, Nelson Mandela, and, yes, even Adolf Hitler, were all transformational leaders, and their political lives were distinguished to a considerable degree by charisma. Followers saw them as leaders who would uplift their lives and breathe new life and purpose into their nation – perhaps an impossible task for any person.

Charismatic leadership is characterized by an intensely personal relationship between the leader and followers. The followers are inspired to obedience, loyalty, commitment and devotion to their leaders (Howell & Frost, 1989), and in return the leaders push their followers to act in ways that go beyond personal self-interest and current needs. They inspire a vision of a better future, and provide 'transcendent' goals often expressed in moral rhetoric (Bass, 1990; Conger & Kanungo, 1998; Conger, Kanungo & Menon, 2000). Because the leader has high expectations of the followers as well as confidence in them, the self-esteem of the followers is enhanced, which further motivates them to achieve desired goals. Of course, charisma is not always directed towards the good of followers; many cult leaders have been highly charismatic, using their powerful influence to indoctrinate follow-ers into a highly authoritarian social structure that they alone control (Raubolt, 2003).

Frequently, the phrases that embody the charismatic leader's vision enter the language as enduring monu-ments. Consider Martin Luther King's '*I have a dream …*'; Churchill's '*We shall never surrender*'; Trudeau's call for a '*Just society*'; Gandhi's vision of an India free of British rule ('*Quit India!*'); Hitler's appeal to past and future German glory ('*Germany awake!*'); and John F. Kennedy's call to patriotism ('*Ask not what your country can do for you …*').

How do such leaders come to wield such power over their followers? How are they capable of appealing to their followers on a raw emotional level? House (1977) argues that the charismatic leader is typified by a specific set of characteristics:

1. An extremely high level of self-confidence.
2. An extremely high level of dominance. Such leaders seem to have a strong need to influence others, which drives them to acquire the persuasive skills they need to do so.
3. An apparently strong conviction in the moral righteousness of their beliefs. The charismatic leader often provides a role model and a value system for the followers that sometimes endure long after the leader's death. For example, Gandhi continues to be respected and admired, and his teachings are followed by mil-lions of Indians and non-Indians alike. However, some charismatic leaders may not have such convictions but are capable of acting as though they do. Certainly, there have been charismatic religious leaders who were later shown to be manipulators using their charisma for their own ends.

In addition, personal characteristics such as charm, originality and speech fluency are important attributes that encourage devotion from followers (Sashkin, 1977).

Yet, charisma does not reside solely in the leader; it depends on the relationship between a leader who pos-sesses charismatic qualities and a situation in which people are more likely to be influenced by charisma (Klein & House, 1998). The charismatic leader often emerges in a time of stress, and he or she usually epitomizes the deeply held feelings of the followers. As the situation changes, the charismatic leader may lose his or her appeal; once the stress is lifted, the public can quickly throw off its fascination for the leader.

> **KEY POINT:** Transformational leaders not only lead, but also inspire others to work towards what otherwise might seem to be impossible goals. High self-confidence, dominance and conviction are characteristics often associated with such leadership.

Gender and leadership

Until very recently, the rule of nations has with few exceptions been the prerogative of males. For sure, there have been some notable women rulers throughout history – think of Cleopatra, Catherine the Great, and Queen Elizabeth I and Queen Victoria – who ran their empires with vigour and skill, but their powers came to them through their bloodline. Until only very recently in human history, the top elected roles in national governments – president or prime minister – have been filled by men. The first woman in the world to become an elected national leader was Sirimavo Bandaranaike, who became the prime minister of Ceylon (now Sri Lanka) in 1960. Then in 1966, Indira Gandhi, daughter of Jawaharlal Nehru (India's first prime minister), became the first (and so far, only) female prime minister of that nation. In 1969, Golda Meir became the first (and so far, only) female prime minister of Israel. In 1979, Margaret Thatcher became the United Kingdom's first (and so far, only) female prime minister. In 1993, Kim Campbell became Canada's first (and so far, only) female prime minister (although her government survived only a few months). In 2006, Michelle Bachelet became the first female president of Chile.

However, by 2012, a record number of women were serving as elected national leaders, among them such notables as Angela Merkel of Germany and Dilma Rousseff of Brazil, although the number subsequently dipped slightly in 2013 (Table 12.2).

Table 12.2   Female national leaders, 2013

Country	Leader
Germany	Chancellor Angela Merkel
Liberia	President Ellen Johnson-Sirleaf
Argentina	President Cristina Fernandez de Kirchner
Bangladesh	Prime Minister Sheikh Hasina Wajed
Iceland	Prime Minister Jóhanna Sigurdardóttir
Lithuania	President Dalia Grybauskaite
Costa Rica	President Laura Chinchilla
Trinidad and Tobago	Prime Minster Kamla Persad-Bissessar
Slovakia	Prime Minister Iveta Radicová
Brazil	President Dilma Rousseff
Kosovo	President Atifete Jahjaga
Thailand	Prime Minister Yingluck Shinawatra
Denmark	Prime Minister Helle Thorning-Schmidt
Jamaica	Prime Minister Portia Simpson Miller
Malawi	President Joyce Banda
South Korea	President Park Geun-hye
Slovenia	Prime Minister Alenka Bratusek
Cyprus (North)	Prime Minister Sibel Siber

Yet, progress towards gender equality in the political domain remains slow, as the data in Table 12.3 attest.

Table 12.3   Percentage of women in national parliaments in 2012

Rank	Country	Total seats	Women	% Women
1	Rwanda	80	45	56.3
2	Andorra	28	14	50.0
3	Cuba	586	265	45.2
4	Sweden	349	156	44.7
11	Norway	169	67	39.6
24	Germany	620	204	32.9
27	New Zealand	121	39	32.2
34	Switzerland	200	57	28.5
37	Afghanistan	249	69	27.7
38	France	577	155	26.9
47	Australia	150	37	24.7
47	Canada	308	76	24.7
60	United Kingdom	650	145	2.3
66	China	2978	635	21.3
82	United States	430	73	17.0
110	India	545	60	11.0
123	Brazil	513	44	8.6
144	Yemen	301	1	0.3
145	Saudi Arabia	52	0	0.0

These are partial results of a 2012 survey of the percentage of women in 190 national bodies of government. Canada ranks 47th, while the United Kingdom comes in at 60th, and the United States at 82nd. Only in twenty-three countries do women hold more than one-third of the parliamentary seats, but this at least is an improvement over the results of a similar survey carried out by the Inter-Parliamentary Union in 2003, when the corresponding figure was only nine countries.

For historical reasons, women have had difficulty achieving positions of power (see Chapter 13), and the gender-role stereotypes that associate power uniquely with men may lead to women not being given the opportunity to exercise power, and even to them being perceived as having less power than they actually do (Ragins & Sundstrom, 1989). It also appears that men are more likely than are women to use expert and legitimate power, whereas women are more prone to use referent power, which relies on gaining admiration and respect from subordinates. This means that women often develop different strategies than men to influence others, and when they do employ reward or coercive power, something not typically expected from women, such approaches may not be effective (Carli, 1999). Some women may also feel that the exercise of legitimate power is incompatible with femininity and thus avoid situations and positions that involve such power.

Women continue to face a number of obstacles to becoming leaders in mixed-gender groups. In such situations, men are quicker to try to take over the leadership role, even when they are clearly less qualified than the women with whom they are working (Mezulis et al., 2004). Indeed, men and women alike are inclined to look towards males rather than females for leadership in mixed-gender groups (Eagly & Karau, 1991). This should not be too surprising given that most contemporary adults have grown up in patriarchal societies where the father has been invested with the traditional ultimate authority in the family. There is perhaps, above all else, the expectation held by many men and women that women are not 'suited' to leadership, and as a result we often hear about a glass ceiling that prevents women from rising up to the top of an organizational structure. Gender stereotypes describe men as capable of being tough, assertive, brave and commanding respect, while stereotypes of women emphasize not only gentleness but weakness, fickleness and submissiveness. And not only is it more difficult for women to assume leadership positions in mixed-sex groups; when they do, they are scrutinized more carefully. Ironically, female subordinates of female leaders in mixed-sex groups have been found to be more negative towards these leaders than are male subordinates of the same leaders (Eagly & Karau, 1991). In other words, the successful woman has to struggle against the negative attitudes of both sexes.

These gender stereotypes, combined with the socially inferior position of women in most societies around the world, present even more trouble for female leaders: they are not likely to receive the same treatment as male leaders from other people (both male and female) of equal or greater stature in the power hierarchy. Their viewpoints are less likely to be given attention in meetings and they are more likely to be interrupted when speaking, even by other women. Koenig et al. (2011) described this situation in terms of cultural mismatch between the perceived demands of the leadership role and the stereotypes of women. While assertiveness, competitiveness, and 'getting things done' are qualities more likely to be associated with men than with women, the 'female' qualities of compassion, maintaining social harmony and being nice to others are seen as being at odds with what is required in a good leader. Thus stereotypical male traits fit better with cultural perceptions of what is required in leadership than do stereotypical female traits. Indeed, the 'masculinity' of the cultural stereotype of leadership is a strong effect found across a wide range of social contexts (Koenig et al., 2011), and this makes it more difficult for women to move into leadership roles because they do not appear to have what it takes. Does this mean that women should try to take on a masculine leadership style – appearing tough, decisive, aggressive? The irony is that, when they do, the negative evaluation of their leadership is likely to be even greater (Eagly, Makhijani & Klonsky, 1992), and because they are now seen to be lacking in terms of the compassion and 'niceness' expected of women, they are often disliked by people they work with (Rudman & Glick, 1999, 2001). Thus, women are discouraged from presenting as either too masculine or feminine. Moreover, women who do succeed in leadership positions by assuming a masculine style may experience a conflict between that role and their 'femininity'. Men do not experience such conflicts.

Yet despite the history of discrimination, women are moving more and more into leadership roles in government and industry, and, as noted above, are becoming an increasingly significant force at the highest levels of world leadership (Adler, 1999a). Indeed, globalization of industry and communication networks may require leadership that differs significantly from other forms of leadership. Rather than leading a single group or society, the global leader has to deal with the differing goals, expectations and cultural values of many groups and societies. It has been argued that the 'feminine' qualities often associated with female leaders, such as greater interpersonal sensitivity and concern and a desire to compromise rather than dominate, are needed to meet many of the challenges posed by positions of global leadership (Adler, 1999b).

It is interesting to note that, in modern times, women are more likely to be made leaders during times of crisis in an organization. This phenomenon is referred to as a **glass cliff** (Bruckmüller & Branscombe, 2010) in contradistinction to the glass ceiling mentioned earlier. When promoted to leadership in such circumstances, the risks of failure, of falling over the cliff, are high because the organization is in trouble, and thus the leader is left vulnerable to blame for future difficulties should she not be able to right the ship. Ryan & Haslam (2005) report that their study of the top hundred companies on the London Stock Exchange revealed that women were more likely to be appointed to executive boards when the company had been performing consistently poorly during the preceding period. They followed up this analysis with laboratory research and found that when participants considered an organization that had been performing poorly, they recommended a female leader more often than when considering an organization that was performing well.

Why should women leadership candidates be evaluated more positively when there is a crisis than when things are going well? Experimental studies of the glass cliff suggest that this choice has as much or more to do with perceptions about men and leadership as it does about women and their leadership abilities. That is, women appear capable of bringing something to the leadership role – compassion, interpersonal sensitivity – that men, according to stereotype, lack, and since the 'male' approach is not working, the organization turns in desperation to a different, 'feminine' approach (Bruckmüller & Branscombe, 2010).

It appears that men and women may typically view a leadership role somewhat differently: Rink et al. (2012) conducted a study with 146 Dutch business students as participants. They were asked to imagine being employed by a large company that was going through a financial crisis, and further to imagine that they had been asked to take a top leadership position with the task of solving the crisis. There were three experimental conditions: In the control condition, participants were told that both social and financial resources were available: management had decided to provide additional funds and employees had approved the appointment. In the no-social-resources condition, it was indicated that while management would provide additional funds, employees disapproved of the appointment. In the no-financial-resources condition, it was stated that management would not provide additional funds, but that employees had approved the appointment. There was a strong gender difference; men evaluated the position lacking in financial resources as the most negative, while women evaluated the position without social resources as the most negative.

A second study provided insight into those findings. It was found that women were reluctant to take on a difficult leadership position without social resources because they anticipated difficulties in being accepted by the group, whereas men were reluctant to take a position with limited financial resources because of anticipation that they would not be able to succeed in the task. Women considered that in order to have any likelihood of succeeding in the task, it was important to be accepted as the leader, whereas men believed that acceptance by employees would come as they demonstrated their ability to carry out the assigned task.

But do men and women actually lead differently? After many years of research into the relationship of gender to leadership, all that can confidently be concluded is that the appearance of gender differences in leadership is determined by the situation in which the leadership occurs (Butterfield & Grinnell, 1999). For example, in one study (Gardiner & Tiggemann, 1999), women more often than men adopted an interpersonally oriented leadership style when working in female-dominated industries (childhood education, nursing, hairdressing), while no such differences between men and women were found in male-dominated industries (academia, information technology, automotive industry, forestry). Nonetheless, in male-dominated industries, women who adopted an interpersonal leadership style reported greater stress and poorer mental health than did those who did not. Conversely, in those same male-dominated industries, men who chose an interpersonal style actually reported better mental health than did males who did not. Thus, the effects of gender on leadership style and the ultimate consequences for the leader depend on situational variables – not just on gender. As a result, men are often more effective in positions defined in masculine terms (for example, in the armed forces) while women are more effective in situations that require a less autocratic, more participative style (for example, in education and social service organizations) (Eagly, Karau & Makhijani, 1995).

> **KEY POINT:** Leadership has been the prerogative of males in most cultures throughout history. Women are beginning to make great strides in terms of rising to top leadership positions. To some extent, the 'glass ceiling' which has stopped women from rising to top management positions is being replaced by a 'glass cliff' where women are promoted to top management at a time of crisis, which carries a high risk of failure.

e-leadership

We live in an age of globalization and instantaneous worldwide communication. More and more decision-making in business as well as in government is done over the Internet, through online discussions. People in such interactions become members of **virtual groups,** groups that exist only in that particular electronic environment. In some cases, the individuals will never meet face-to-face. However, just as with any group, goals and objectives and the means to obtain those goals are of great importance. Research has just begun to examine how being in a virtual group affects both activities and perceptions of leadership and followership. And yet, the essential tasks of leadership remain the same: Activities still need to be coordinated; individuals still need to be motivated; results need to be monitored. Leadership is just as vital as in any face-to-face interaction, and leaders need to be able to communicate effectively, persuade others to pursue common goals, arouse enthusiasm, build trust, mentor subordinates and monitor and control social loafing (DasGupta, 2011).

GROUP DECISION-MAKING

Most important decisions in society are made by groups of people, whether they are in business, government or juries. Groups are often faced with choices among actions that carry varying degrees of risk. In the late 1960s, group risk-taking became a major research area in North American social psychology, and participants were observed as they made decisions in hypothetical situations. Typically, a group of participants (usually four) would begin by individually filling out questionnaires, such as the Choice Dilemmas Questionnaire (Table 12.4).

Table 12.4   Sample item from the Choice Dilemmas Questionnaire

Mr E is the president of a light metals corporation in the United States. The corporation is quite prosperous and has strongly considered the possibilities of business expansion by building an additional plant in a new location. The choice is between building another plant in the US where there would be a moderate return on intial investment, or building a plant in a foreign country. Lower labour costs and easy access to raw materials in that country would mean a much higher return on the intial investment. On the other hand, there is a history of political instability and revolution in the foreign country under consideration. In fact, the leader of a small minority party is committed to nationalizing – that is, taking over all foreign investments.

Imagine that you are advising Mr E. Listed below are several probabilities or odds of continued political stability in the foreign country under consideration.

Please check the lowest probability that you would consider acceptable for Mr E's corporation to build a plant in that country.

____The chances are 1 in 10 that the foreign country will remain politically stable
____The chances are 3 in 10 that the foreign country will remain politically stable
____The chances are 5 in 10 that the foreign country will remain politically stable
____The chances are 7 in 10 that the foreign country will remain politically stable
____The chances are 9 in 10 that the foreign country will remain politically stable
____Place a check here if you think Mr E's corporation should not build a plant in the foreign country, no matter what the probabilities

In that questionnaire, each item describes a person forced to decide between pursuing an attractive but risky outcome, or a less attractive but more certain outcome, and each participant is asked to indicate the minimum probability of success required before he or she would recommend the riskier choice. The participants then discuss the situation, having been instructed to reach a unanimous group decision (consensus). Individual participants then fill out a new copy of the same questionnaire. The measures of interest are as follows: (1) the differences between individuals' initial choices and the consensus position of the group; and (2) the differences between individuals' initial and final choices.

Research showed that both the group decision and the average of the individuals' final decisions were more 'risky' than the individuals' initial decisions, and even when the experimental situations involved real monetary gain or loss for the participants, or when the participants were risking painful shocks, this 'risky shift' was still observed (Bem, Wallach & Kogan, 1965). However, both group discussion and the necessity to reach consensus were necessary in order to produce this effect; it was not found when groups voted on a decision without discussion, nor did it occur following discussion if there was not an onus to reach a collective decision.

Various explanations were offered for the risky shift, such as diffusion of responsibility (recall Chapter 9), for each member in a group setting may feel less personally responsible for the decision (Kogan & Wallach, 1967). It was also suggested that since risk-taking is valued in Western society, discussion will produce more arguments favouring risk than favouring prudence, because, not wanting to look stodgy and conservative, members will opt for the riskier proposals (Brown, 1986).

However, the shift towards risk turned out to be only a specific example of a much more general phenomenon: group-induced attitude polarization. In a wide variety of situations, group decisions are found to be more extreme than the initial decisions of the individuals involved and in the direction of the views of the majority – not necessarily in the direction of greater risk. Risky groups shift towards risk, and cautious groups shift towards caution (Turner, Wetherell & Hogg, 1989). The group polarization effect is also evident in such situations as group aggression, in which individual tendencies towards aggressiveness are magnified by the group, and in bystander intervention when helping is inhibited in group situations because individuals want to avoid looking foolish.

Sources of polarization

What accounts for group polarization? Why does the group shift away from the *average* attitude in the group? Research has focused on four possible explanations.

1. Social comparison: The social comparison interpretation of the polarization effect assumes that individuals try to see themselves and present themselves to others in as favourable a light as possible; this is referred to as a self-enhancement bias (Krueger, 1998). To that end, they carefully observe how others act or express themselves and tend to shift in the direction in which the group is perceived to be leaning.

2. Persuasive argumentation: Group discussion has been suggested as the source of the polarization effect. Individuals in a group discussion are exposed to arguments for and against a particular position and, according to this view, a group shift will occur only if members present persuasive arguments that are new to the other individuals. The direction of any group shift will depend upon the preponderance of persuasive and novel argumentation in one direction or the other (Isenberg, 1986). In line with this explanation, one study (Brauer, Judd & Gliner, 1995) found that repeated expression of opinions produced a reliable shift towards a more extreme position – that is, the more group members talked about an issue, the more polarization that occurred. This effect was increased when participants were instructed to use each other's arguments in their discussion, compared to a condition in which they were instructed to avoid doing so.

   However, it is interesting to note that members with extreme positions do not appear to have a particular influence on polarization. Van Swol (2009) studied three-person groups in discussion about possible decriminalization of marijuana. While it was found that participants with more extreme opinions talked more during the discussions, no difference in consensus was found between those groups in which there was someone with an extreme opinion and those where there was not.

3. Social identification: As discussed earlier, social identification is a process whereby individuals define themselves with respect to other people and conform to the norms and stereotypes associated with their

group. Thus, someone in a decision-making group may reason as follows: 'I am a police officer, I am part of a group and I don't want to lose status in it or be rejected by departing too far from the others; the others will take a risky stance because police are brave and take many risks all the time.' According to this explanation, individuals hold a stereotype of their group as more extreme than it actually is and are motivated to conform to the perceived extreme group norm.

4. Aggregation decision process (Zuber, Crott & Werner, 1992): According to this perspective, group polarization is the result of opinion change resulting from the application of an informal decision rule (such as 'majority rules'), leading individuals to shift their opinions towards that of the perceived majority.

There has been empirical support for all of these explanations (Isenberg, 1986; Mackie, 1986; Zuber et al., 1992). Which explanation is most accurate in a given situation probably depends on the particular situation and on the personalities of the individuals. For example, the persuasive argumentation explanation is more likely to apply when rational evaluation of input is probable. However, persuasion will be less effective when members are emotionally involved with the issue, in part because of the emotional importance and in part because, given that importance, they may already have examined and rejected divergent viewpoints.

Computer-mediated communication Social media provide an excellent opportunity for rapid and widespread commentary on just about any matter of interest. In light of the burgeoning importance of online discussions, some researchers have looked for group polarization effects in this context. While some studies suggest that individuals in online discussions shift even more towards extreme positions than is the case with face-to-face groups, other studies have failed to find such an effect (Taylor & MacDonald, 2002). Yardi & Boyd (2010) looked for evidence of such an effect in the Twittersphere, and examined 30,000 tweets related to the conversations of pro-life and pro-choice advocates in the United States immediately following the murder of an abortion physician in Kansas by an anti-abortion activist. They found little change in the extremity of opinions over a 24-hour interval.

> **KEY POINT:** Group decisions are typically more extreme than the average of the decisions made by the individuals in the group. This polarization can come about because individuals shift their opinions in the direction that they think others are leaning, because they are persuaded by the arguments of others, because of the stereotype that they hold of their group, or because of the attempt to satisfy a shared decision rule.

GROUPTHINK

When the United States, along with a few allies, invaded Iraq in 2003, President Bush characterized the invasion as a 'war on terror', claiming that Iraqi leader Saddam Hussein was behind the 9/11 attack on New York City and that the Iraqis possessed weapons of mass destruction. Both claims turned out to be false. Houghten (2008) attributes the misguided decision to invade Iraq partly to groupthink. Groupthink (Janis, 1972; McCauley, 1989) describes the tendency for members of a group, especially an elite group, to assume that they have arrived at the correct answer to a problem without fully considering all the possible alternatives. It is most likely to occur when the problem under consideration is complex and with no easy answer, and it is fostered by conditions of external threat, involving either crisis or time pressure. However, while few would deny that some conformity is necessary for the well-being of groups and of society in general, the conformity pressures involved in groupthink can lead to very destructive consequences.

In order for groupthink to occur, a number of factors need to be present: The group members typically have somewhat homogeneous social backgrounds and ideologies and tend to insulate themselves from consideration of opposing views; they share high confidence that the group is more effective than it actually is, and that the group decision will be correct; there is excessive optimism and willingness to take risks; and warnings about the risks associated with the preferred solution are discounted. As discussion proceeds, group members set aside any personal doubts, resulting in an illusion of unanimity. Finally, self-appointed mind guards shield the group from external information that might challenge group decisions, and contradictory information coming from outside the group is regarded as inaccurate and misleading. Another important trigger for groupthink is promotion by the leader of a favoured policy alternative early in the proceedings (Whyte, 1998). It was the result of such a process, Houghten (2008) argues, that most members of the Bush administration not only actually came to believe that Saddam Hussein possessed weapons of mass destruction, but they also clearly *wanted* to believe it. Anyone who dissented with that view was pressured to remain silent, and if they dissented further, they were considered to be off the team and gradually lost access to the president. Saddam Hussein was toppled, no weapons of mass destruction were found, Iraq continues to struggle for stability and democracy, and the United States is left with a trillion-dollar debt – an outcome, apart from deposing Hussein, that was unanticipated by the decision-makers.

The Iraq war is not an isolated example. Janis (1972, 1982) developed the initial conception of groupthink from an analysis of a number of what he called 'fiascos' resulting from decisions made by important policy-making committees in the United States. Although the recommendations of the committees had crucial national implications, the members of these groups were more concerned with maintaining group solidarity than with voicing unpopular views that, although possibly correct, would also be disruptive. Such decisions abound, including: the pursuit of the defeated North Korean Army beyond the 38th parallel during the Korean War, which brought in China; launching the Bay of Pigs invasion of Cuba; the Cuban missile crisis (when the US demanded that the USSR remove its missiles and blockaded Cuban ports); the Watergate cover-up (Raven, 1998); escalation of the involvement in the war in Vietnam; the decision to launch the space shuttle *Challenger* despite concerns for its safety (Badie, 2010; Moorhead, Ference & Neck, 1991); and the Iran-Contra affair (Whyte, 1989). International examples include major management decisions in the United Kingdom that had serious negative consequences for British Airways and Marks & Spencer (Eaton, 2001), and decisions that led to the financial collapse of Swissair (Hermann & Rammal, 2010).

Tetlock (1979) analysed the content of the statements actually made by important US decision-makers – Presidents Harry Truman, John F. Kennedy and Lyndon Johnson – during the crises originally examined by Janis, and his results strongly support Janis's model. Public statements by policy-makers during these crises were more simplistic and were more directed towards their own group. He also found evidence of mind guards who filtered information from outside so that the decision-making group learned little if anything about external, dissenting opinions.

The groupthink model provides a good basis for understanding these collective decision processes (Esser, 1998; Kramer, 1998). Yet it is clear that conformity under these conditions is both intellectually stultifying and dangerous, for it leaves no room for individualism or innovation. Indeed, Nemeth (1986, p. 31) contends that 'robust dissent is not only a manifestation of a democratic principle, but it is the mechanism by which better solutions are found and better decisions are made'. Groupthink steamrolls over such dissent.

> **KEY POINT:** When decision-makers with relatively common backgrounds and experience are faced with important decisions under time pressure or external threat, and when the leader proposes a favoured course of action, they sometimes close themselves off from contradictory information and converge with high confidence to support a course of action which later proves to be ill-considered and sometimes even disastrous.

A FINAL NOTE

We are not islands, entire unto ourselves. We spend much of our lives in a group context, subject to group pressures that can sometimes be invisible to us. And we are often unaware of the extent to which the groups and categories to which we belong determine both other people's perceptions and evaluations of us and our own perceptions and evaluations of ourselves. By understanding the nature of our social identities and the dynamics of groups, we can come to better understand ourselves.

SUMMARY

1. We construct our social world in terms of social categories and we govern our behaviour according to the salient category in a particular situation.

2. Individuals tend both to see members of a given group as more similar than they really are and to see the differences between members of different groups as greater than they really are (social differentiation).

3. Every individual belongs to different categories simultaneously, and this cross-categorization can reduce conflict and discrimination.

4. Just as we categorize others in terms of the groups to which they belong, we also categorize ourselves. This is called social identification.

5. Social identification leads to social comparison, which serves to enhance the importance of our group membership.

6. One basic distinction that we make is between the in-group, to which we belong, and other groups, the out-groups. In-group favouritism leads to discrimination against an out-group, even in the absence of any self-interest or of pre-existing hostility towards the out-group.

7. Social Identity Theory and Self-Categorization Theory respectively describe how group membership shapes our identities and how people come together to participate in a unified group.

8. Social belief structures reflect our views about group boundaries and about the relative status of our in-group compared to other groups.

9. The perception of being part of a group, along with mutual interaction and influence, ongoing and relatively stable relationships, and shared goals are among the defining characteristics of small groups.

10. Within a small group, members may assume various roles, and norms regulate their behaviour.

11. Leadership has been explained in terms of the traits of the leader, characteristics of the situation, and the interaction of leader and group characteristics.

12. Fiedler's contingency model of leadership effectiveness relates the characteristics of the group to task-oriented and relationship-oriented leadership styles.

13. Leaders described as transformational or 'charismatic' tend to be self-confident and dominant with strong convictions; they provide their followers with transcendent goals and a model for values.

14. Considerations of both gender and culture are very important to an understanding of leadership success.

15. Group decisions tend to be more polarized than do individual decisions. Four explanations have been suggested: social comparison, persuasive argumentation, social identification and following a decision rule such as 'the majority rules'.

POINTS TO PONDER

- Think about some of the groups to which you belong. To what extent do these groups help shape your character, and to what degree do they reflect your influence on them?
- Consider cross-categorization. In your own experience, can you think of two groups in conflict where a second level of categorization might reduce the conflict?
- Recall the discussion of persuasion and conformity pressure in Chapter 6. What might be the similarities and differences between the situation in Asch's conformity experiment and a top-level executive meeting where groupthink takes hold?
- What was so special about the leadership of Winston Churchill during the Second World War? Is he considered a great leader only in hindsight – because the Nazis were defeated – or were the Nazis defeated in part because he was a great leader?

FURTHER READING

Brown, R. & Capozza, D. (Eds) (2006). *Social identities: Motivational, emotional, cultural influences.* New York: Psychology Press.

> This book brings together contributions from leading social psychologists and provides an excellent exploration of the Social Identity Theory and its application in the study of intergroup behaviour including prejudicing conflict.

Conger, J.A. & Kanungo, R.N. (1998). *Charismatic leadership in organizations.* Thousand Oaks, CA: Sage Publications.

> Comparisons, with supporting evidence, of a number of theories of charismatic leadership. Includes examples of charismatic leaders.

Gelfand, M.J., Erez, M. & Aycan, Z. (2007) Cross-cultural organizational behavior. *Annual Review of Psychology, 58,* 479–514.

> A comprehensive review of cross-cultural research into organizational behaviour, including topics such as leadership, negotiation, and the difficulties of interpreting such research.

Mugny, G. & Perez, J.A. (2010). *The social psychology of minority influence.* Cambridge, UK: Cambridge University Press.

> A psychological examination of the importance of minority ideas to the development and dissemination of social innovation. The authors' research relating to minority influence, attitude change persuasion and intergroup conflict is reviewed.

WEBLINKS

Group Dynamics Resource Page: https://facultystaff.richmond.edu/~dforsyth/gd/

> This site provides a wealth of reference material relating to the social psychology of groups, power and leadership.

Groupthink: http://www.psysr.org/about/pubs_resources/groupthink%20overview.htm

> Dedicated to the analysis of examples of groupthink. An annotated bibliography of books, research articles is included.

CHAPTER 13
PREJUDICE

Prejudice is opinion without judgement
Voltaire (1694–1778)

LEARNING OBJECTIVES

* To understand prejudice in both its direct and more subtle forms

* To understand stereotypes as rigid, socially shared schemata about some group, which may or may not be somewhat accurate, and which may change over time

* To understand the emotional component of prejudice, including the role of hate

* To understand the range of behaviours against out-groups

* To evaluate the impact of personality and social factors on prejudice

* To understand how prejudice can affect the person to whom it is directed

* To understand how prejudice can be reduced, and particularly the effect of intergroup contact

* To understand sexism as a particular form of prejudice

Figure 13.1   The new Europe in a globalized world

Source: michaeljung/Shutterstock.com

A casual glance at the news provides ample evidence that prejudice persists as a problem for all societies and cultures. For instance:

- Immigration of culturally distinct groups has been a major issue in the United States, United Kingdom, Australia, Germany, France and other nations (Zick, Pettigrew & Wagner, 2008).
- In July 2011, an armed gunmen killed 76 Norwegians, none of them Muslims and many of them children, in order to 'save Europe' from 'Muslim colonization'.
- Discrimination and violence against Roma people is evident in Hungary, Czech Republic and elsewhere.
- The rights of gay and lesbian people have been the subject of vehement disagreement, and 'gay-bashing' persists. Countries such as Russia and Uganda have enacted restrictive laws.
- Resentment among Hindus, Sikhs, Tamils, Sinhalese and Muslims in India, Pakistan, Bangladesh and Sri Lanka has occasionally spilled over into violence.
- Anti-Semitic attitudes, including Holocaust denial, have resurfaced in the Middle East, Europe and North America, fuelled in part by selective disagreement with Israeli policies.
- Mass murder through terrorist attacks, driven by Muslim jihadist ideologies, occurred in New York, Madrid, Jerusalem, Bali, Mogadishu, Mumbai and London.
- While South Africa has emerged from a racist apartheid regime into a society of majority black rule, anti-black prejudice persists in many nations, often in disguised form, as we will see in this chapter.
- Aboriginal communities in Canada, United States, Latin America, Australia and elsewhere often suffer from poverty and discrimination.

On the other hand, enmities have declined or disappeared. In the United States, half a century after the country elected its first Roman Catholic president, an African-American was elected and re-elected to that position. Women have made significant progress towards full equality. After centuries of conflict and hatred, Europe is at peace, albeit with economic and intergroup challenges. In an age of globalization, harmonious intergroup contact is unprecedented. Prejudice is not incurable, as we shall see.

PREJUDICE

Prejudice has been defined as 'an individual-level attitude (whether positive or negative) towards groups and their members that creates or maintains hierarchical status relations between members' (Dovidio, Hewstone, Glick & Esses, 2010, p. 7). Note what follows from this definition. Prejudice can be either favourable or unfavourable, but psychologists use the term almost exclusively in the negative sense. While most people think of prejudice in terms of ethnic, national or religious groups, it also exists in attitudes towards members of other categories of people: prejudice toward people based on their age, their gender, sexual orientation, place of residence, occupation, musical preferences and their body shape.

To be prejudiced, then, means to 'prejudge' a person based on which group he or she is seen to belong to in terms of characteristics one associates with that group. Once persons have identified themselves as belonging to one group (the in-group) and others as belonging to another group (the out-group), regardless of the original reasons for this social categorization, they will expect to find intergroup differences and will go so far as to create them if necessary (Tajfel & Turner, 1979). Moreover, they will probably overestimate intragroup similarity (see Chapter 12).

Prejudice disguised

In many contemporary societies the overt expression of prejudice is not considered to be socially acceptable. In these situations, a more subtle form has emerged, one known by some as 'modern racism'. The notion is that many people are ambivalent; they want to see themselves as fair and unprejudiced, but they still harbour feelings of discomfort or worse towards certain groups (Dovidio, Kawakami, Smoak & Gaertner, 2008). In some instances, it becomes aversive; the prejudiced person will avoid situations in which his or her prejudice may become manifest.

As an instance of subtle prejudice, consider this study: Students in Britain were presented with a case study of a robbery in which the defendant was either black or white (Hodson, Hooper, Dovidio & Gaertner, 2005). When the evidence was strong and incontrovertible, participants judged the defendant as guilty, whether black or white. But when the evidence was ambiguous because one piece of incriminating information was ruled inadmissible by the judge, the black person was more likely to be convicted than was the white defendant. While participants knew that they were not supposed to consider the inadmissible evidence, they were more likely to grant the benefit of the doubt to the white defendant.

Social norms can also dictate the expression of sexism (Glick & Fiske, 2001). Consider that, as men and women, we need each other and relate intimately to each other. It is argued that women idealize men who are protective of them and their offspring, while men idealize women whom they love and who love them. At the same time, women may resent men for their power, and men may demean women who are assertive. Thus the two sexes can be hostile and benevolent towards each other at the same time. This model has been supported in research across many nations (Glick, Lameiras, et al., 2004) and will be discussed later in this chapter.

Note that to measure this kind of prejudice, more subtle means are necessary, measures of implicit attitudes (recall Chapter 4). Does a critical attitude towards Israel mask anti-Semitic attitudes? Sometimes, it does. Of course, it is possible and reasonable to be critical of any policies of any government. However, to demand a standard of conduct by one group or nation that we do not expect of any other, including ourselves, is another matter. Terror management theory postulates that, when one becomes consciously aware of one's own mortality, we seek to affirm our own worldview so as to supersede our own mortality. In a set of studies with US participants (Crandall & Eshleman, 2003), ethnocentric attitudes were elicited by causing participants to think of their own mortality by exposure to death-related words and images. Under this condition, participants expressed both more critical attitudes towards Israeli government policies and a more general anti-Semitism. Indeed the two attitudes were clearly linked, suggesting that prejudice towards Jews underlies at least some of the unreasonably critical attitudes towards Israel; for example, being critical of human rights violations by Israel but not by India or Russia. In general prejudices may often be suppressed by prevailing norms and values, but expressed when stereotypes or other events provide justification.

Another means by which bigoted people will attempt to disguise prejudice is by affirming their own lack of prejudice: 'I'm not prejudiced ... but ...'. Methods of discourse analysis have been employed to 'unpack' the meaning and context of such declarations (Potter & Wetherell, 1987; Wetherell & Potter, 1992). Western societies have developed ways of 'giving voice' to racist and other prejudiced attitudes while, at the same time, keeping faith with egalitarian values. An interesting example is provided by a TV debate between a CNN anchorperson and a guest over denials of racism on the one hand and accusations of using 'code words' about immigration to disguise racist intent on the other (Chiang, 2010). In a context in which overt expressions of prejudice are not considered acceptable, particularly in the public arena, people are motivated to present themselves as unprejudiced. They may also be concerned with affirming a self-image as unprejudiced. Qualitative methods can be valuable in teasing out the hidden meanings of words and phrases.

KEY POINT: Prejudice has been defined as an individual-level attitude towards groups and their members that creates or maintains hierarchical status relations between members. It may apply to groups defined in terms of ethnicity, age, gender, sexual preference, body shape, etc. It carries the notion of 'prejudging' an individual based on perceived group characteristics. In view of prevailing norms against overt expression of prejudice, it generally occurs in more implicit or disguised forms. Discourse analyses reveal some of the ways in which implicit prejudice is expressed.

THE NATURE OF PREJUDICE

As with other attitudes, prejudice can be conceived as comprising the following components: cognitive, affective and behavioural. Let us examine each in turn.

The cognitive component: Stereotypes

The beliefs that make up the cognitive component of prejudice are called stereotypes (see Chapter 2). The term is usually attributed to the United States journalist Walter Lippman (1922), who borrowed it from the lexicon of the printing industry of that era to describe 'pictures in the head' about members of a group. However, Rudmin (1989) points out that the English author James Morier was actually the first to use the word stereotype to describe human behaviour, in his book *The Adventures of Hajji Baba* (1824).

Stereotypes are cognitions concerning the members of a particular group. These cognitions are usually simple, often over-generalized and frequently inaccurate, although not necessarily incorrect or illogical (Taylor & Lalonde, 1987). In one sense, stereotypes serve a useful purpose in that they help us deal more efficiently with our environment. They can be thought of as cognitive 'energy-saving devices' (Macrae, Milne & Bodenhausen, 1994). For example, consider how complicated it would be if every new person you met would have to be considered as a separate entity instead of being included in some general category such as teenager, nun, construction worker or professor. By invoking your stereotype – placing the newcomer into some category – you can begin the interaction as though you already know quite a bit about the person.

Key characteristics (real or imagined) used to differentiate among groups are called *diagnostic attributes*. For example, identifying Scots as intelligent would not be very useful in terms of distinguishing Scots from others, since many ethnic or national groups are stereotyped in this manner. However, people may seize on what they perceive as different about a group, whether accurate or not, such as that Scots are parsimonious. This would be more useful because it would supposedly set the Scots apart from the English, Welsh, Americans and Canadians (Ford & Stangor, 1992). Stereotypes are more than abstractions about group categories. They can act as 'cognitive filters' through which we select what information to use, what to ignore and how to interpret it. Bodenhausen (1988) finds that people are better able to recall information about a person that is consistent with their stereotypes. In addition to stereotypes about specific attributes of the members of a group, we may also have more abstract, symbolic beliefs, which imply that a group threatens (or upholds) social values and norms (Esses, Haddock & Zanna, 1993; Donakowski & Esses, 1996).

Are stereotypes pervasive and persistent across different times and groups? Are they accurate? Let us examine the evidence.

Pervasiveness Do residents of London, Liverpool, Glasgow and Cardiff hold the same stereotype about a given out-group? A classic study conducted in the United States (Allport & Kramer, 1946) found that stereotypes about blacks and Jews in a part of South Dakota, where almost no blacks and Jews lived, were more negative than those in a state with substantial black and Jewish populations. Berry and Kalin (1993, 1995) asked respondents in Montreal, Toronto and Vancouver how comfortable they would feel being around individuals from a number of groups: first, if these individuals were immigrants to Canada, and second, if these individuals had been born and raised in Canada. The results varied considerably among the three cities, with Montreal being the least positive.

Persistence of stereotypes How stable are stereotypes? Do they change readily or do they last over long periods of time? As with attitudes in general, stereotypes are often modified over time. Obvious examples can be found in the characterization of the Japanese or Germans during the Second World War, and Arabs when terrorist incidents may occur. As might be expected, stereotypes about the out-group become more negative in the face of violence, but other less aggressive forms of conflict – economic and social – can have similar effects.

Not surprisingly, governments facing increasing unemployment usually curtail immigration. Indeed, if there is a perceived competition for resources such as jobs, attitudes towards immigration and immigrants may become more negative (Berry, Kalin & Taylor, 1977; Esses, Jackson & Armstrong, 1998). Palmer (1996) notes that surveys do not support the proposition that all opposition to immigration is based on racism. Indeed, the strongest opposition comes from younger people concerned with jobs and careers, although they are generally more tolerant as a group than older people.

Three classic US studies (Katz & Braly, 1933; Gilbert, 1951; Karlins, Coffman & Walters, 1969) are often referred to as the 'Princeton trilogy' because they were carried out at Princeton University using a common procedure but across a span of 36 years. Participants were asked to select from an extensive list of traits those that best described the members of each of 10 ethnic groups: Americans, Chinese, English, Germans, Irish, Italians, Japanese, Jews, Turks and blacks. The traits most frequently assigned to blacks by Katz and Braly's subjects in 1933 were 'superstitious', 'lazy', 'happy-go-lucky', 'ignorant' and 'musical'. Over the years, fewer people endorsed 'superstitious' and 'lazy', while more endorsed 'musical'. In a more recent replication by Madon, Guyll, et al. (2001), the data indicated that, while there was greater consensus among participants on attributing traits to the ten ethnic and national groups, the content of the stereotypes had changed, generally in a more favourable direction. For instance, whereas in the earlier studies African Americans were described as 'superstitious', 'lazy' and 'ignorant', the participants in the more recent study chose descriptions such as 'musical', 'very religious' and 'loyal to family ties'. Stereotypes as consensus judgements seem to persist, at least among American university students, but their content can change with the culture.

However, we must consider the limitations in this research. First, these data were obtained from university students who, as noted in Chapter 1, do not necessarily represent the general population. Second, we do not know whether other equally derogatory characteristics have taken the place of the old ones. Third, social desirability bias may have had some effect (see Chapter 1). Indeed, as noted above, aversive or 'modern' racism may not be reflected in responses to measures such as adjective checklists. Do the responses reflect the person's true feelings or were they responding as they thought was expected of them? To test this possibility, Sigall and Page (1971) replicated the Karlins et al. study but used a different procedure – they hooked up participants to a bogus lie detector that led half the subjects to believe any lies they told would be detected. Subjects who believed that lies would be detected gave considerably more negative evaluations.

A study by Devine and Elliot (1995) also suggests that certain stereotypes have not faded. They repeated the Princeton trilogy study with Caucasian students from the University of Wisconsin, adding an experimental condition. They asked participants not only to list the adjectives that 'make up the cultural stereotype of blacks' but also to list 'those adjectives you personally believe characterize blacks'. Their data led them to conclude that there continues to be a consistent and negative stereotype of blacks. Prejudiced individuals did not differ from those low in prejudice in their knowledge about the stereotype, but they differed greatly in their acceptance of the stereotype. There's an interesting footnote to this study: While all the participants were willing to complete the stereotype task, 21% refused to do the personal beliefs component.

For a variety of reasons such as social desirability or workplace harmony, negative stereotypes are frequently suppressed. On the face of it, this would seem to be a good thing. But we are left with an interesting question: Why do such negative stereotypes persist when they are inconsistent with many people's personal beliefs? It is clear that most people, the tolerant as well as the prejudiced, know the prevailing stereotypes.

Are stereotypes accurate? As Jussim, McCauley & Lee (1995) point out, most people believe that stereotypes are inaccurate and exaggerated, and consider that only racists, sexists and other varieties of bigots would be interested in promoting stereotypes. But might there be some truth in some stereotypes? Consider, for instance, that while it is demonstrably false to assert that all or most members of a given group are on social assistance, there are average differences in socioeconomic status between different groups in all societies. To say that Germans tend to be efficient or that librarians tend to be introverted may be factually correct in characterizing typical members of a group. However, holding a stereotype about a group may lead us to notice instances that confirm the stereotype, the introverted librarian or the efficient German. To assume that a given individual who is a member of a group is efficient or introverted is the essence of stereotyping and is a logical fallacy: to generalize from the group to the individual. It is the rigidity of stereotyping, the tendency to ignore individual differences within any group, that becomes a matter of prejudging an individual according to the stereotype ascribed to his or her group.

Yet, it has been argued that because stereotypes seem both persistent and pervasive, they must, at least to some extent, be true (the kernel-of-truth hypothesis). However, there are a number of grounds on which this notion can be refuted:

- The simultaneous existence of incompatible stereotypes concerning the same group of people ('Jews are pushy'; 'Jews stick to themselves').
- The labelling of the same behaviour in positive or negative terms, depending on which group exhibits it ('The Dutch are frugal and careful about their finances'; 'Scots are miserly and penny-pinching').
- Changes in the stereotype are often not accompanied by any change in the target group ('Immigrants are energetic, reliable workers'; 'Immigrants work excessively and take jobs away from people born here').
- The application of the stereotype to all members of the group without consideration of individual differences ('The Welsh are good singers' – no doubt some are mediocre singers).

Nevertheless, in some instances, it seems possible to verify the accuracy of stereotypes. People from Spain and Chile do tend to speak Spanish, and basketball players are usually tall and athletic. It must be understood that to attribute a characteristic to a group, or even to a typical member of a group, is not the same as to attribute a characteristic to an individual solely because he or she belongs to that group. When information about an individual is lacking or ambiguous, people indeed will rely on the stereotype (Nelson, Biernat & Manis, 1990).

Much has been made of differences between groups on scores in standardized intelligence tests, implying inherent differences in intelligence. Before we leap to such conclusions, we must examine the research carefully. Are these tests really standardized across different ethnic groups so that scores would be derived from a 'level playing field'? What is meant by 'intelligence'? For instance, can we assume that people who are high achievers in academia will show the same 'intelligence' in solving practical problems, in coaching a team or in repairing a car? Finally, what do group differences on an IQ test mean in inferring the 'intelligence' of an individual? Given that intelligence scores are distributed normally, a difference in mean scores between two groups still means that the two distributions overlap and many people from the disadvantaged group will score higher than many from the advantaged group. Suffice it to assert that, on the basis of a large body of research, inferring the intelligence of an individual from any group based solely on his or her group membership is unwarranted.

One of the difficulties in testing the accuracy of stereotypes is to find a reliable measure of the characteristic in question. For example, can a reasonably precise estimate be obtained of the extent to which a group is 'happy-go-lucky', or 'stingy' or 'smart'? Ashton & Esses (1999) tackled this problem by using academic performance as the target characteristic and having undergraduates estimate the academic performance of Toronto high school students from nine

Figure 13.2 Is this representative of Scottish people, or does it reflect a stereotype?

Source: © Richard T. Nowitz/Corbis

ethnic groups. Since these were actual students, their marks were available for comparison with the estimates. The results indicated that the estimates were on average actually quite accurate and that none of the ethnic groups was substantially over- or underestimated. Note, however, that 'academic performance' may not elicit as powerful a stereotype as might some more emotion-laden terms that have long been associated with racism.

Finally, stereotypes exist among and between members of occupational groups, and even subspecialties within occupations. For instance, football players may have stereotypes about goalkeepers, physicians about surgeons, psychology professors about mathematics professors. In the world of dance, those who participate in ballet and in modern dance have different stereotypical views of each other. In one study (Clabaugh & Morling, 2004), dancers from both specialties filled out a personality test for themselves and then were asked to predict how members of the other group would typically fill it out. Interestingly, in both groups, the participants accurately predicted how members of the other group would respond, but in an exaggerated manner. For instance, while ballet dancers showed a greater fear of negative evaluation, the modern dancers predicted that they would respond more strongly to such assessment than they actually did respond.

Stereotype Content Model (Cuddy, Fiske & Glick, 2008) In discussing the cognitive component of prejudice, research reviewed thus far is based on determining which adjectives from a list will be selected by participants as descriptive of a certain group. Are there fundamentals to how we describe members of a group? According to the stereotype content model, we see out-group members in terms of their status relative to our own group. Stereotypes vary along two dimensions: perceived warmth and perceived competence. Stereotypes about warmth are influenced by competitiveness – we see less competitive groups as warmer. Stereotypes about competence are influenced by the group's status in society – the higher the status, the more competent they are perceived to be.

Although these are dimensions along which groups (and individuals) may vary, the model is simplified by the use of 'high' and 'low' as descriptions. Recall from the previous chapter: Members of one group may be seen as high on both warmth and competence, often members of one's own group or a reference group. Members of another group may be perceived as low on both warmth and competence, such as people who are poor, homeless, on welfare, and some people may react with scorn or disgust to these people. Of course, members of some groups may be high on one and low on the other. The elderly may be stereotyped as high on warmth and low on competence, and people may react with pity. Other groups may be seen as high on competence and low on warmth, such as wealthy professionals, people of Jewish or Asian backgrounds, and others may react with envy. Fiske (2011) points out that the emotions that emanate from comparisons may 'corrupt the comparer' (Fiske, 2011, p. 698). Envy makes people feel angry at perceived injustice, which may cause their prejudices to intensify. Scorn can cause people to be insensitive to the needs of others. In the mixed groups (high in perceived warmth or perceived competence and low in the other), stereotypes will also be of a mixed character. We may perceive people as nice, but lazy and incompetent, and respond with paternalism, with overtones of compassion mixed with disrespect; we may feel warmly ourselves towards the elderly, but see them as needing care rather than support and respect. In contrast, when we see groups as competent but not warm (e.g. non-traditional women, Jews, Asians), they are admired for their work ethic but not respected for 'working too hard', and so envy ensues (Fiske, Cuddy, Glick & Xu, 2002). Note that a study of participants from seven European cultures characterized as individualistic and three collectivist Asian cultures replicated these findings (Cuddy, Fiske, et al., 2009). That is, people from groups high in status are perceived as competent but not necessarily warm, and those seen as most competitive are seen as lacking warmth. Stereotypes indeed are shown as emanating from the hierarchy of status in a society, and many of these stereotypes are ambivalent, that is, warm but not competent, or competent but not warm. Finally, Durante, Volpato & Fiske (2010), using archival data analysing the contents of an Italian Fascist magazine during that era, found that out-groups were stereotyped according to the competence and warmth dimensions. Interestingly, while envy was apparent towards some out-groups in the competent but not warm condition, no paternalistic reactions were observed, probably reflecting the fascist ideology of the time.

Illusory correlation and stereotypes It has been suggested (Hamilton & Sherman, 1989) that many instances of stereotyping arise and are maintained through the operation of illusory correlation, an information-processing bias whereby the association between characteristics or events is overestimated (see Chapter 2). Hamilton & Gifford (2000) postulated that one basis for illusory correlation is that observers tend to overestimate the frequency of co-occurrence of infrequent but distinctive events. An example of this might be a nurse noting on a couple of occasions that the maternity ward is particularly busy and that there also happens to be a full moon – leading to a common but incorrect belief that the two events are associated. In one of their studies, participants were told of two groups, Group A and Group B. A list of statements were then presented, each of which described a negative or a positive behaviour by a member of one of the groups; for instance, a member of Group A is not always honest about small amounts of money. Participants were advised that, in the real world, Group A has more members than Group B, and so there are more statements about Group A than about Group B. So, of the 39 statements, 26 were about Group A and 13 about Group B. At the same time, of the 39 statements, 27 were positive and 12 were negative. Overall, the statements that were presented were in the same ratio of positive to negative regarding each group; that is, for Group A, 18 were positive and 8 were negative, and for Group B, 9 were positive and 4 were negative (ratio of 9:4 for each group). You can see that there is no reason to see one group in a more positive light than the other. However, there was a significant bias. When presented with the list of 39 and asked to indicate which of the two groups was linked to the behaviour, participants overestimate the undesirable behaviours of the minority group (B), ignoring the relative size of the two groups.

Consider what this tells us about stereotyping. When one group of persons 'occurs' less frequently than another – that is, it is a minority – and when a certain type of behaviour occurs infrequently, the research indicates that observers are likely to overestimate the frequency of that type of behaviour being performed by members of that group. And so if we see a member of the minority group behaving in an obnoxious manner, we pay attention to that coincidence, and tend to generalize and stereotype the behaviour as typical of that group. Once such an association has been made, subsequent judgements will be biased in the same direction. Disconfirmations of the stereotype are learned more slowly or are forgotten more quickly than neutral or confirming information (Hamilton & Rose, 1980; Hilton & Von Hippel, 1996). In other words, 'Believing is seeing'.

Stereotypes and prejudice Will prejudice inevitably follow because of the existence of stereotypes? The inevitability argument ignores the distinction between awareness of a stereotype and acceptance of it. As mentioned earlier, there is no good evidence that simply knowing a stereotype goes hand in hand with prejudice (Devine, 1989; Taylor & Lalonde, 1987). To further complicate things, individuals may hold ambivalent beliefs about a group. Katz and Hass (1988) point out that US whites often perceive blacks as both deviant and disadvantaged. This duality leads to feelings of both aversion and sympathy. Blacks may be perceived as deserving help but at the same time as not doing enough to help themselves.

KEY POINT: Prejudice consists of cognitive, affective and behavioural components. The cognitive component is the stereotype, a rigid set of generally shared characteristics attributed to members of a group, that is, a schema about members of a group. Stereotypes are fairly pervasive within a society but not uniform, often change over time, and may have some accuracy, but not necessarily. The stereotype content model posits perceived warmth and perceived competence as basic dimensions, and reactions to groups are based on these dimensions. The overgeneralization of stereotypes represents an illusory correlation.

The activation of stereotypes While we are all aware of culturally shared negative stereotypes, they may not affect how we judge an individual from that group. This often happens, for example, in work situations or in team sports, where we may react favourably to a colleague even if she or he is from a certain stereotyped group. However, if a member of that group happens to act in an obnoxious manner, this may cause people to revert to the stereotype – he acted in that way because he belongs to that group, not because he happened to be in a bad mood. One racist comment by someone may activate the stereotype that white people hold about black people, and this comment may lead them to evaluate a black person's performance negatively (Greenberg & Pyszczynski, 1985).

Devine (1989) suggests that, under certain conditions, a stereotype may just pop into our mind, such as one that homosexual men are all effeminate. Usually, we can consciously suppress this stereotype perhaps by simply reminding ourselves that generalizing in this way about people is not fair, or by recalling the gay men that we know who do not act in an effeminate way. However, people who are highly prejudiced will act on this stereotype regardless of whether they are conscious of it (Fazio, Jackson, Dunton & Williams 1995).

Whether we may bring a stereotype to mind (activate it) or suppress our awareness of it may depend on motives such as self-enhancement (Sinclair & Kunda, 2000; Kunda & Spencer 2003). When a stereotyped reaction to another person will make an individual feel better about himself or herself, or when it enables us to understand and make sense of a situation, the stereotype will more readily come to mind and be used. Recall from Chapter 2 that stereotypes are cognitive structures and that they can be useful to us for self-enhancement or comprehension (Wheeler & Petty, 2001).

In one experiment, white male students answered a series of questions designed ostensibly to assess their interpersonal skills and then received a video feedback from a white or black 'manager'. Half the participants in each group received positive feedback, and the other half received a negative evaluation. Sinclair & Kunda (2000) predicted that those who received positive feedback from the black manager would suppress the negative stereotype about blacks, while that stereotype would be activated among those who had received a negative evaluation from a black confederate.

Their assessment of stereotype activation was rather ingenious. After this 'management evaluation' procedure, the participants were asked to participate in a supposedly unrelated study. They were presented with word fragments and asked to complete the word. In some cases, the word fragment could be seen as representing a racial word (e.g., __ __ ACK may be completed as 'black' or 'stack' or 'shack') or a word suggesting a negative stereotype about blacks (e.g., CR __ __ __ may be completed as 'crime' or 'crisp' or 'cream'). The results were as predicted. Those who had been praised by the black manager completed fewer racial/stereotypic words than even those in the control group who had been evaluated by a white confederate, indicating that the stereotype had been suppressed. On the other hand, those who had been poorly evaluated by the black manager completed more racially tinged words than any other participants, indicating that the stereotype had been activated.

In other work, Sinclair & Kunda (2000) found similar reactions in stereotypes about women. Male participants evaluated female instructors as less competent than their male instructors only when they had received a low grade in that course. When they had received a high grade, no differences were observed. Indeed their evaluations of male instructors were not influenced by their grades. This work shows that we can push the stereotype out of mind, or we can use it to salvage our self-esteem when it is threatened.

One additional factor that may activate a stereotype is our belief that members of the other group hold a stereotype about us. For instance, Vorauer, Main & O'Connell (1998) found that white students at the University of Manitoba believed that Native Canadians perceive whites as prejudiced, selfish, arrogant and materialistic. Not surprisingly, those who most strongly held these meta-stereotypes about natives were more likely to express more prejudice towards them.

KEY POINT: As is the case with any schema, a stereotype can be activated. As well, we may hold meta-stereotypes, an awareness of how we are stereotyped by others.

THE AFFECTIVE COMPONENT OF PREJUDICE

Stereotypes are accompanied by emotions, which are usually expressed in terms that can be distributed along a continuum ranging from the intensely negative (e.g., contempt, disgust, hate) to the very positive (e.g., admiration, liking, identification). Feelings may be accompanied by arousal of the sympathetic nervous system, and the increased physiological activity can be measured by galvanic skin response (GSR). Such responses can be used, at least for research purposes, to determine emotional reaction even when the participant is unable or unwilling to overtly express it. In this way, Porier and Lott (1967) demonstrated that individuals who scored high on ethnocentrism (belief in the superiority of one's own ethnic or cultural group) showed a stronger GSR in the presence of black, compared with white, research assistants, in contrast with those who scored low on the scale.

A study in the Netherlands (Dijker, 1987) illustrates the relationship between emotions and attitudes, in this case towards immigrants from Suriname (a former Dutch colony), and towards Turks and Moroccans. Analyses of the data showed that for all groups the expressed emotions fell into four categories: positive (e.g., admiration), irritation (e.g., annoyance), anxiety (e.g., fear), and concern (e.g., worry). Positive emotions were more predictive of attitudes towards Surinamers, who were generally perceived favourably by the Dutch, whereas attitudes towards those from Turkey and Morocco, who were not well received, were better predicted by the negative categories of irritation and concern.

Consider how anxiety may relate to prejudice. Clearly, intergroup contact in our globalized, multicultural world can be experienced as stressful (Crocker, Major & Steele, 1998), which has been reflected in measures of physiological arousal (Amodio, 2009). Discomfort about those who are perceived as 'different' in some way can itself contribute to negative prejudices about such people, negative stereotypes serving to affirm or validate the emotions felt by the individual. Further, as noted earlier, in many societies today, people do not want to see themselves as prejudiced, nor do they want to appear to be prejudiced to members of the out-group, and so such encounters will often be fraught with an undercurrent of anxiety (Trawalter, Adam, et al., 2012). The anxiety may also come from uncertainty, from what to expect and how to react to people who are, indeed, culturally different. Thus, the model of intergroup anxiety proposed by Stephan & Stephan (1985): intergroup anxiety discourages contact between members of the two groups and is associated with increased prejudice (Swart, Hewstone, Christ & Voci, 2011).

One particular topic of emotional reactivity towards the out-group pertains to feelings of disgust regarding purported deviant sexual practices (Adorno et al., 1950), and even a fear of sexual coercion or violation. Clearly, a desire to avoid violation by out-group members is related to prejudice towards that out-group. Moreover, in one study (Navarette, Fessler, Fleishman & Geyer, 2009), both a fear of violation and prejudice toward the other racial group by black and white women was found to be strongest during the time in the menstrual cycle at which they were most receptive to conception. This may be interpreted within an evolutionary framework in which women are predisposed to avoid persons and situations perceived as dangerous in terms of an unwanted pregnancy. Of course, this interpretation depends on the perception of danger, which is tied to socially transmitted stereotypes.

Fear and disgust, although generally well-disguised, may surface in an indirect manner in the expression of prejudice. Questionnaire instruments have been developed to measure disgust sensitivity in general and towards out-groups (e.g. 'I feel disgusted when people from other ethnic groups invade my personal space'). These variables were found to be related to scores on a measure of prejudicial attitudes towards Muslims (Choma, Hodson & Costello, 2012). In a second study by Choma, Hodson & Costello (2012), film clips that had previously been shown to arouse either fear, sadness or happiness were shown to different groups. When fear was aroused, the link between out-group disgust and negative attitudes towards Muslims was greater than in conditions where other emotions were aroused. Clearly emotions play a key role in the experience and expression of prejudice.

Mood can also affect the activation of stereotypes. In particular, studies carried out in Canada by Esses and Zanna (1995) found that individuals in a negative mood were more likely to assign unfavourable stereotypes to out-groups (especially Native Canadians, Pakistanis and Arabs) than were individuals in a neutral or positive mood. Such reactions are magnified when one identifies with a group felt to have been wronged. However, when we feel that our group has committed the wrong to another group, the sense of collective guilt can generate action to redress the wrong (Wohl, Branscombe & Klar, 2006). For example, the Canadian government accepted responsibility for having wrested Aboriginal (First Nations) children from their parental homes and placed them in residential schools, where many were mistreated.

BOX 13.1   ANOTHER LOOK

ON HATE AND HATE LAWS

Figure 13.3   Neo-Nazis demonstrate against 'gypsies' in Prague
Source: © Jim McDonald/Corbis

We tend to equate prejudice with hate, assuming that prejudice must flow from hatred. Indeed, it is widely believed that hate is the emotion common to all prejudice. Let us examine what hate means, and then see whether it is an inevitable component of prejudice.

Clearly, hate is an intense emotion (Allport,1954), with synonyms such as loathe, despise, 'be repulsed by', and 'be revolted by'. It is also generally observed that hate is not a temporary emotional state; you may be angry with someone at a certain time and circumstance, but hate tends to be relatively enduring. In this sense, hate has characteristics in common with love, and, indeed, some see love and hate as opposite ends of a continuum. Indeed, Sternberg & Sternberg (2008) have developed a 'duplex theory' of hate that corresponds to the tripartite

theory of love, consisting of passion, intimacy and commitment (Chapter 8). The model of hate consists of the following:

• Negation of intimacy – a distancing predisposition, repulsion, disgust;
• Passion, which means emotional arousal, experienced as anger, disgust and/or fear;
• Commitment, realizing that one hates a certain group and feels contempt for it often accompanied by an effort to influence others to share in the hatred.

The three components can exist in various combinations, a typology of hate. For instance, *cool* hate is characterized by feelings of disgust, wishing to have nothing to do with the targeted group. *Cold* hate is characterized by an evaluation of the targeted group as unworthy, perhaps less than fully human, and thus deserving of rejection or worse. In contrast, *hot* hate is predominantly about passion, involving an intense anger or fear. Finally, consider the example of *seething* hate, the feeling of revilement toward the target, that may explode into *burning* hate, consisting of all three components listed above, often along with a desire to annihilate the targeted group. Common to these conceptions of hate is a strong notion of 'us versus them', seeing the target as not just different but different in ways related to inferiority or moral deficiency that make them unworthy of being treated as 'us' (Staub, 2005).

Several criticisms have been advanced of this theory of hate. First, by emphasizing the parallels with love, the theory omits the group-level hate which is common; one can easily conceive of hatred shared between members of one group towards another, but it is hard to think of love in this way. Indeed, hate has been described as unique in the sense that it generally targets a group and is driven by a judgement that the group is intrinsically evil by nature (Halperin, 2008). As well, hatred can be seen as belonging to a subset of prejudices but not necessarily to all prejudice; for instance, sexism usually is not conceived as driven by a hatred of women but rather by a stereotype of what women are and should be.

Finally, as noted earlier in this chapter, much of the prejudice extant today assumes a more subtle form, such as implicit or aversive prejudice (Dovidio, Gaertner & Pearson, 2005). This prejudice in a latent form can well be transformed into a more virulent hatred by perceived threat and provocation, by ideologies that attempt to justify the disadvantaged status of the target group, and by group members coming to view themselves, the haters, as the real victims. Hate crimes committed against Muslims or those thought to be Muslims in North America and Europe in the wake of recent terrorist attacks illustrate the point (Esses, Dovidio & Hodson, 2002).

Hate crimes involve words or actions that are intended to harm or intimidate individuals simply because they are members of a particular group. These crimes can include physical attacks on members of a designated group, defacing cemeteries or religious institutions, burning crosses, Holocaust denial, and promises of divine punishment to people of a different sexual orientation (Herek, 2009). In some countries, there are laws against hate speech, along with penalties for inciting hatred against members of a minority group. Such laws are controversial to some, who argue that they infringe upon free speech, while others counter that free speech does not give anyone the right to cry 'Fire!' in a crowded room. Do such laws reduce or increase prejudice in a society? Some defend them, arguing that prejudice should be curbed when possible because society has clearly defined it as wrong. Others are concerned that such laws end up giving bigots a public forum for their views, which then seems to make those views a matter for legitimate debate. In one highly publicized case in Canada, the evidence suggested that convicting a person in a court of law for inciting hatred had little effect on public opinion towards the target group (Weimann & Winn, 1986).

KEY POINT: Prejudice generally is accompanied by emotional arousal, often intergroup anxiety. Sometimes the emotion is identified as disgust, often tied in to sexual concerns. Hate sometimes accompanies prejudice, a model of which consists of negation of intimacy, passion and commitment to one's prejudice.

Figure 13.4 Institutionalized discrimination during apartheid in South Africa

Source: © Alain Nogues/Sygma/Corbis

DISCRIMINATION: THE BEHAVIOURAL COMPONENT OF PREJUDICE

While prejudice is an attitude, discrimination refers to negative behaviour towards members of out-groups. This may range from avoidance to expressions of hostility, crude 'jokes', defacing property or physical attacks. In most Western nations and many others, discrimination has been legally outlawed or restricted. Minority group members can enter professions, vote, marry and otherwise participate in their society. As one example, in Canada, opposition was voiced in 1989 when the famed Royal Canadian Mounted Police agreed to allow Sikh officers to wear a turban rather the traditional Stetson. Within a short period of time, it ceased to be an issue. Certainly discrimination is difficult to eradicate, but it can be done.

It is interesting that the ideals of a multicultural society have sometimes come into collision with the dominant norms, raising the question of how minority groups should be expected to make 'reasonable accommodation' to the society in which they live. Should members of immigrant groups make reasonable accommodations to the cultural norms and values of the dominant society? Consider that different cultures have restrictive norms regarding the role of women, which may bring them in conflict with the government and predominant norms in Israel, United States, Europe and elsewhere.

Discrimination may occur at the level of interaction between individuals, as in these examples, or it may be institutionalized and supported by either implicit or explicit regulations. For instance, legislation in France, the Province of Québec in Canada, and elsewhere has been directed at limiting or restricting the wearing of overtly religious symbols in public institutions. And remember apartheid in South Africa from 1948–1994, a system of racial segregation based in white supremacy, a case of discrimination mandated by law. Examples of groups falling victim to state-sanctioned discrimination are also all too numerous even in democratic societies; Canadians and Americans of Japanese origin during the Second World War had all their possessions taken from them and were displaced from their homes. Similarly, treatment of aboriginal peoples has varied from condescending paternalism to outright racism (Backhouse, 1999). Where capital punishment is still practised, the likelihood of being executed has been much greater for people from minority out-groups (Avio, 1987; Hooker, 1988). It has been argued that the language laws enacted in Québec in the 1970s to promote French and restrict

Figure 13.5 Driving the last spike, 1885. Craigellachie, British Columbia, Canada. In one of the most famous historical photographs in Canada, the Hon. Donald A. Smith drives home the final iron spike completing the transcontinental railroad line, surrounded by dignitaries and businessmen. While more than 15,000 Chinese workers laboured to build this railroad, none of them was invited into this photograph

the use of English constituted legal support for discrimination, discrimination that many felt was justified in order to save the French language in a North American milieu (see Bourhis (1994) for a review of ethnic and language attitudes in Québec).

Does history repeat itself? After the terrorist attacks on the World Trade Center in New York and the Pentagon in Washington, several thousand people, most of them young Muslim men, were apprehended by United States forces in other countries. These men were held in detention on a US base without any rights whatsoever, not even the rights accorded to prisoners-of-war under the Geneva Convention. Similar imprisonment was imposed by the British government on Irish IRA prisoners during the 'troubles' in Northern Ireland.

Too often, discrimination is based on the belief that certain races are genetically inferior to others, with very disturbing consequences. The so-called 'medical experiments' conducted by the Nazis on concentration camp inmates were rationalized in this manner, and it is probably no accident that the first human trials of the contraceptive pill were carried out on women in Puerto Rico. This notion of genetic inferiority was developed in the United States in the early part of the century when intelligence tests were first administered to immigrants. Not unexpectedly, many immigrants, coming as they did from other cultures, were purported to be 'intellectually deficient'. On this basis, it was argued that certain ethnic groups were 'genetically inferior', and restrictive immigration quotas were applied for many years (Kamin, 1974).

Reverse discrimination As society becomes more sensitive to racial issues, many people will resist expressing prejudicial attitudes. In fact, some may go so far as to behave in a manner that implies they are more tolerant than they really are, acting in a more positive manner towards a particular outgroup than towards people in general. This is called reverse discrimination and has been demonstrated in a number of studies by Dutton and colleagues (Dutton, 1971, 1973; Dutton & Lake, 1973; Dutton & Lennox, 1974). In the first experiment, carried out in Vancouver and Toronto, either black or white couples entered a restaurant, and, in each case, the man was wearing a turtleneck sweater, in violation of the restaurant's dress code requiring ties for men. Only 30% of the white couples were seated, compared with 75% of the black couples. It is evident that the persons in charge went out of their way to appear non-discriminatory. Accordingly, Dutton (1973) hypothesized that minority groups perceived by the public as being most discriminated against would experience the most reverse discrimination. A survey had indicated that middle-class whites in Vancouver felt that blacks and Native peoples were the focus of considerable discrimination, but that Asians were not. Dutton then asked Natives, blacks and Asians to solicit donations for a charity and found, as hypothesized, that more money was given to the Natives and blacks than to the Asians.

It should be noted that this effect appears to be most common among educated middle- and upper-middle-class whites who are especially concerned not to appear intolerant. Dutton & Lake (1973) selected 80 students who had been identified as having a low degree of anti-black prejudice and who valued equality. Through means of false feedback, half the students were made to feel that they might be prejudiced; the rest of the students acted as controls. After the laboratory session, either a white or a black panhandler approached all the participants. Those subjects who had been led to doubt their tolerance towards blacks gave significantly more money to the black panhandler. The experimental manipulation had no effect on the amounts given to the white panhandler.

The behaviour described in these studies is relatively trivial. But a person who has demonstrated tolerance by such a token act may be less likely to exhibit reverse discrimination the next time. In a study by Dutton and Lennox (1974), three groups of students were made to doubt their tolerance towards blacks. Subsequently, one group was approached by a black panhandler, the second by a white panhandler, while the third was not panhandled. The next day they were all asked to give some of their time for an 'interracial brotherhood campaign'. Students who had been panhandled by the black volunteered less of their time than did those in the other two groups. Note that reverse discrimination tends to be restricted to relatively unimportant behaviours and may have the counterproductive effect of discouraging real and long-lasting tolerance.

We have explored the nature of prejudice through its cognitive, emotional and behavioural components. Now we turn to the origins of prejudice.

> **KEY POINT:** The behavioural component of prejudice is discrimination, ranging from avoidance, to verbal hostility, to acts of aggression. The behaviours may be individual or institutionalized in a society. In a globalized environment, the issue of 'reasonable accommodation' has become prominent. Reverse discrimination is an attempt to demonstrate that one is not prejudiced.

THE ORIGINS OF PREJUDICE

Innate or acquired?

Hebb and Thompson (1968) concluded that the higher animals – such as chimpanzees and human beings – have an inherent fear of the unfamiliar and unusual. If this is correct, it would be reasonable to argue that this tendency could form the basis for the development of prejudice, which is directed towards people perceived as being in some way different. It is generally agreed that people are anxious or fearful in situations that they do not understand. Perhaps the negative emotions directed at the members of an out-group have their roots in the spontaneous arousal generated by a novel stimulus. Infants as young as three months of age are able to distinguish between the face of their mother and that of a stranger. Although at this age their reactions to the unfamiliar stimulus do not show signs of avoidance or fear, by about the age of nine months, aversive reactions often do appear, frequently to the mother's embarrassment (when, for instance, the unfamiliar stimulus is the child's grandmother).

It is also possible that a finding first reported by Zajonc (1968) can be used to support Hebb's view of an inherent preference for the familiar. Zajonc demonstrated that frequent exposure to a stimulus makes it more attractive (recall Chapter 8). Initially, it was thought that this 'mere exposure' effect occurs regardless of the person's initial attitude, but later research (Perlman & Oskamp, 1971) indicates that only positive or neutral stimuli are enhanced. Evaluation of initially disliked stimuli are unlikely to improve.

Conflict between groups

In Chapter 10, we discussed the conflicts that arise and often persist between groups. Here, we address the question of whether such conflicts constitute an adequate explanation of prejudice. Clearly when groups are in conflict, prejudice and discrimination tend to increase. Indeed in some cases, conflict can be related to 'mirror image' stereotypes where, for instance, each group sees the other as threatening or as inferior in some way. Of course, the question then becomes one of causality – is prejudice the cause or the result of conflict?

According to realistic conflict theory, in cases where there are limited resources, groups may find themselves in conflict and prejudice can increase. Recall Sherif's Robbers Cave experiments (Chapter 10) where the conflict induced between the two groups of boys led to name-calling and prejudiced statements about the other group.

Similarly when unemployment is high and few jobs are available, negative attitudes towards immigration and immigrants increase (Palmer, 1996). Esses, Jackson & Armstrong (1998) set out to establish evidence on whether scarcity of jobs caused negative attitudes towards immigrants, or whether these negative attitudes might cause the perception that they were in conflict over scarce jobs. Participants read one of two statements about immigration in Canada. In one version, the statement focused on scarce jobs and the tendency of immigrants to take those jobs while the other did not mention employment problems. Then the participants read about a new group of immigrants who were arriving in Canada. This fictitious group, the Sandirians, were described in positive terms as ambitious, hard-working, smart,

Figure 13.6   Combatting racism in sports
Source: © Mark Leech/OFFSIDE/Corbis

family-oriented and religious. However, when the participants had first been primed to think about immigration in terms of 'realistic conflict' over jobs, they construed these characteristics in a negative manner. For instance, being 'family-oriented' was interpreted as being non-accepting of others. These participants also expressed more opposition than did the control group to allowing immigration in general and by this group in particular.

THE PREJUDICED PERSONALITY

Since there are wide differences among people with regard to their levels of prejudice, whether in societies that promote or suppress bigotry, research has focused on the personality characteristics in which prejudiced people differ from their peers. Some researchers have approached this issue in terms of basic personality dispositions such as the 'Big Five' personality traits: conscientiousness, openness to experience, extraversion, neuroticism and agreeableness. However, a meta-analysis reveals that the relationship between personality traits and prejudice is largely accounted for by two aspects of personality, right-wing authoritarianism and social dominance orientation (Sibley & Duckitt, 2008), and so we will turn to a consideration of these variables.

Authoritarianism   In the aftermath of the catastrophe of the Second World War, a group of psychologists undertook the task of identifying the psychological characteristics of the 'potential fascist' (Adorno, Frenkel-Brunswik, Levinson & Sanford, 1950). The researchers identified a syndrome of attitudes that was characteristic of the **authoritarian** personality, and this stimulated much research over the ensuing decades (Christie & Jahoda, 1954; Cherry & Byrne, 1977). It was found that individuals who can be characterized as authoritarian hold rigid views towards authority and perceive the world in categorical black/white, superior/inferior, us/them terms. The *F scale* was developed to tap into this syndrome of personality, and it has been used in numerous studies in the years that followed.

Authoritarians also are likely to be prejudiced. Adorno and his colleagues were initially interested in anti-Semitism, but later broadened their perspective to include ethnocentrism; that is, attitudes in which people who are 'different' in some way are rejected. For white Americans, this would have included people who are black, foreigners in general, homosexuals and people who live distinct lifestyles. As part of their study, they constructed a number of scales to measure anti-Semitic attitudes and generalized ethnocentrism. In general, people who rejected Jews also manifested prejudice against other out-groups as well.

The personality dynamics outlined by Adorno et al. (1950) were not consistently identified in subsequent research. Indeed, the powerful role of the situation and the culture had been underestimated (Pettigrew, 2001). More recently the core idea of an authoritarian set of attitudes has been revitalized by work on right-wing authoritarianism (RWA) by Altemeyer (1981, 1988), who has constructed a scale to measure this characteristic. Right-wing authoritarianism involves a high degree of submissiveness to authorities (who are perceived as having legitimate power), strong adherence to conventional social values, and hostility and punitiveness towards people who deviate from those values. (See Table 13.1 for sample items.) In addition to confirming that authoritarians are conventional, highly submissive to authority and aggressive towards those whom they believe to be inferior or 'different', Altemeyer (1988) found that they also feel themselves to be morally superior. Esses, Haddock & Zanna (1993) report that English Canadians who were identified by Altemeyer's scale as high authoritarians had more negative attitudes towards French Canadians, Native peoples, Pakistani immigrants and homosexuals than did low authoritarians. An Australian study corroborates the link between RWA and prejudice towards Asians and Australian Aboriginals (Heaven & St. Quintin, 2003). The evidence also indicates that prejudice and religious fundamentalism are positively correlated (Hunsberger, 1995, 1996; Altemeyer and Hunsberger, 1992).

One other manifestation of authoritarianism may be scapegoating, which occurs when individuals are frustrated by conditions or situations they cannot directly control or change, such as crime rates, the economic situation or the government. When the source of the frustration is vague and difficult to locate, tension and hostility may be aroused and displaced onto a convenient out-group. This out-group is then blamed for the discomfort and difficulties being experienced. The classic evidence of such scapegoating linked lynchings (extrajudicial murder) of blacks in the US South to economic difficulties as reflected by the world price of cotton (Hovland & Sears, 1940). When cotton prices were low, reflecting poor exonomic times in the cotton belt, the number of lynchings increased. However, we should be cautious about that finding, for in an attempt at replication, Green, Glaser & Rich (1998) failed to find a relationship between economic conditions (e.g. unemployment) and crimes against gay and lesbian people, Afro-Americans, Asian-Americans or Jewish-Americans.

Table 13.1 Sample items from the Right-Wing Authoritarianism Scale

---

- The way things are going in this country, it's going to take a lot of 'strong medicine' to straighten out the troublemakers, criminals and perverts.

- It would be best for everyone if the proper authorities censored magazines and movies to keep trashy material away from the youths.

- The real keys to the 'good life' are obedience, discipline and sticking to the straight and narrow.

An authoritarian would agree with the items above and disagree with items such as the following:

- There is nothing wrong with premarital intercourse.

- 'Free speech' means that people should even be allowed to make speeches and write books urging the overthrow of the government.

- There is absolutely nothing wrong with nudist camps.

Source: Altemeyer (1981)

Social dominance orientation People vary in the extent to which they both desire to see their own in-groups have dominance over other groups in society and are willing to endorse values and actions that suppress these other groups (social dominance orientation, or SDO). Research in various countries has indicated that out-group derogation and identification with one's own group are particularly strong among people who are high in social dominance orientation (e.g. Duckitt & Sibley, 2010; Sidanius, Levin, Federico & Pratto, 2001).

While there would appear to be an overlap between authoritarianism and SDO, several studies suggest that SDO and RWA together influence prejudice and are not redundant (Duckitt & Sibley, 2010). How do we integrate these findings regarding RWA and SDO in relation to prejudice? We can consider that the two seem to predict different forms or functions of prejudice. People higher in RWA fear people who are different, such as minority groups, while people higher in SDO value power and see the world as a competitive place, thus rejecting disadvantaged groups. There would seem to be considerable overlap between authoritarianism and social dominance, and indeed Jost, Glaser et al. (2003) argue that they represent different facets of political conservatism. Much remains to be done in research, particularly in non-Western cultures, where conservatism may represent a very different worldview.

Finally, is prejudice simply a matter of stupidity? In our everyday lives, we sometimes attribute prejudice to ignorance, implying either a lack of accurate knowledge or a disinterest in trying to understand group differences. Indeed, intelligence has been found to relate negatively to prejudice (Adorno, Frenkel-Brunswik, Levinson & Sanford, 1950; Deary, Batty & Gale, 2008). Hodson & Busseri (2012), using data from both British and US samples, found support for the view that low levels of intelligence can contribute to the development of right-wing authoritarianism, as well as to avoiding contact with members of out-groups, and this culminates in prejudice. Perhaps prejudice is more firmly rooted in ignorance than we have realized.

KEY POINT: The origins of prejudice are multifactorial. Some evidence suggests the presence of an inherited component, avoidance of that which is different. Group conflict over limited resources can galvanize or exacerbate prejudice. The prejudiced personality is represented by right-wing authoritarianism and by a social dominance orientation.

THE VICTIMS OF PREJUDICE

While much has been written on how prejudice develops and is maintained, less attention has been devoted to how the victims of prejudice and discrimination respond. How do they defend themselves? Over 40 years ago, Gordon Allport (1954) identified more than 15 possible consequences of being victimized. Among these are withdrawal and passivity, clowning, militancy, hostility against their own group and self-hate. In some cases, minority group members will be hostile towards their own group, whereas others will be loyal to their own group and aggressive towards other groups. Extending Allport's approach, Tajfel and Turner (1979) postulate three types of responses. The victims can simply accept their situation with passivity and resignation, although not without resentment; they can try as individuals to break free and 'make it' in society; or they can attempt collective action to improve the status of the group itself. Subsequent research has enhanced our understanding of the variety of individual and collective reactions to prejudice (Dion, 1989; Dion & Kawakami,1996). (Recall as well the discussion of this subject in Chapter 12.)

When people encounter failure or frustration because of the barriers caused by discrimination, they may attribute it to that discrimination, or they may blame it on the characteristics of their own group or they might well blame themselves in order to avoid blaming other members of the group (Ruggiero & Taylor, 1995, 1997). Dion (1989) points out that it is common for people to report more discrimination against their group than against themselves as individuals. For example, in one survey of university women, respondents consistently reported that they believed there was more discrimination directed at women in general than they had personally experienced (Taylor, Wright & Porter, 1994). Why would individual members of disadvantaged groups (such as women) minimize the experience of personal discrimination? One argument is that group members are reluctant to admit that their failures are due to discrimination because this would indicate that what happens to them is controlled by others. An unfortunate implication is that if individuals attribute failures to their own shortcomings, thereby ignoring discrimination based on their group membership, they are less likely to try to improve their status or that of their group through such efforts as protest or legal action. For instance, in one study, female students completed a test ostensibly measuring their future career success and were told that a high mark made them eligible for a $50 prize. They were told that a panel of male students would then evaluate them and that, in the various conditions, 100%, 75%, 50%, 25% or none of them were known to discriminate against women. Then all participants were told that they had failed the test. When asked to explain why they felt they had performed so poorly, those who had been told that they would be evaluated by a panel of male chauvinists attributed their failure to discrimination, as one would expect. However, the female participants in other groups tended to blame themselves – indeed those who were told that there was a 75% chance that they had been the victims of discrimination blamed themselves as much as did those told that there was only a 25% chance. That is, where there was any room for doubt, they tended to deny that they were personally the target of sexist discrimination. It seems that people can often accept that their group is the target of discrimination, but will often deny having been a direct victim of it themselves (Foster & Matheson, 1999).

Dion and his colleagues (Dion & Earn, 1975; Dion Earn & Yee, 1978) have experimentally studied other reactions when minority group members perceive that they have been the targets of prejudice. In these studies, a situation was created in which members of an out-group (e.g., Jews, Chinese and women) were asked to complete a task on which their success or failure depended on the action of in-group members (e.g., Christian, men). It was found that perceived prejudice led both Jews and women to strengthen their positive stereotypes of themselves. However, the Chinese subjects reacted more defensively, denying the negative stereotypes and attributing their own successes to themselves and their failures to external factors. Because our identity as individuals is influenced so powerfully by our identity as members of groups – religious, ethnic, national, sexual – we can also conceive of a group-serving bias in which we attribute successes to positive group characteristics and failures to external factors such as discrimination. In some cases, attributing failure and frustration to being a victim of prejudice can protect people from feeling depressed about the rejection (Major, Kaiser & McCoy, 2003).

Other factors may include self-esteem and amount of stress. Crocker and her colleagues (Crocker, 1999; Crocker & Lawrence, 1999; Crocker & Quinn, 1998) suggest that many individuals who are stigmatized, whether by ethnic membership or physical characteristics such as obesity, do not suffer from low self-esteem, because their self-esteem arises from different sources of information. Thus, African Americans who do not suffer from low self-esteem are less likely to be affected by devaluation and discrimination. In other words, they attribute these experiences to prejudice rather than to their own shortcomings. On the other hand, surprisingly perhaps, Asian Americans on average possess significantly lower self-esteem than do other groups. Crocker argues that this is because they base their self-esteem, as do whites, on the approval of others. Thus, for them, prejudice and discrimination are assumed to reflect, at least in part, actual personal defects.

Not surprisingly, however, the targets in these studies also experienced some degree of stress. For example, in the face of anti-Semitism, Jewish subjects reported feeling aggressive, sad and anxious. Clearly, discrimination is perceived as threatening, and under some circumstances those discriminated against may act overtly against the dominant group. For example, when prejudice and discrimination lead to deprivation and inequality in the distribution of employment or educational opportunities, militancy and violence may result. Caplan and Paige (1968) have reported that blacks who took part in the US race riots in the 1960s were more sensitive to perceived discrimination, reported that they more frequently experienced discrimination, and were less willing to accept the stereotype of black inferiority than were blacks who remained inactive.

Indeed, being the victim of prejudice can have severe consequences for one's physical and mental health. For instance, the stigma, prejudice, discrimination and even the threat of violence experienced by many gay, lesbian and bisexual persons create a social environment of chronic stress. Whether they react by internalizing homophobic attitudes or concealing their sexual orientation, or live with expectations of hostility and rejection by others, the evidence suggests a relatively high prevalence of psychiatric disorders among them, all related to stress reactions (Meyer, 2003).

Consider how stereotypes can become self-fulfilling prophecies. That is, people may come to accept the stereotype that has been imposed upon them and then act as expected. As an example, consider a study (Rosenthal & Jacobsen, 1968) in which teachers were led to believe that intelligence tests showed that some (randomly selected) children were performing well below their abilities. In light of this information, the teachers treated these children differently, working harder to bring out their supposed talents, and as a result those children actually performed better than matched peers a year later. As Shaw point out in Pygmalion, 'The difference between a lady and a flower girl is not how she behaves, but how she's treated.' The self-fulfilling prophecy can be a powerful influence not only on how people respond to positive attention, but on how people react to prejudice as well. Tell people long enough that they are inferior and make it difficult for them to succeed, and many will come to accept that they are indeed inferior and incapable of success.

Finally, some individuals will not accept and internalize the stereotype imposed on their group and may express anger about it (Dion, 2002). For instance, stereotypes about aging people may include positive attributes such as wisdom and experience, but also may include being slow, rigid, even cognitively incapable. However, many resist the stereotype by not identifying themselves as 'old' or 'elderly', finding positive information about themselves, and developing compensatory behaviour that staves off the self-fulfilling prophecy of the stereotype (Zebrowitz, 2003). However, the stereotype, when activated, can still influence the behaviour of others towards aging individuals.

Stereotype threat effect When members of a negatively stereotyped group are placed in a situation involving performance, they are at a disadvantage, having to struggle with the stereotype that they may have internalized and that they feel others will have accepted. The resultant apprehension and anxiety will undermine their performance. This is known as the stereotype threat effect (Steele, 1997).

Steele & Aronson (1995) demonstrated this effect in an experiment in which black or white students were led to anticipate that they would be taking a 'very difficult' test. The test was defined for them as being 'diagnostic of intellectual ability' or 'just a lab exercise'. The researchers reasoned that because the test was indeed difficult, all participants would struggle with it. However, if the test was framed as about intellectual ability, Afro-American participants would feel anxiety about the stereotype of black intellectual ability as well as about the test itself, and so their performance would be impaired. And that is what happened. Where the test was just about a 'lab exercise', black and white participants performed equally well. But when it was about intellectual ability, the performance of blacks was much lower than that of whites. Another study looked at gender differences in mathematical performance (Figure 13.7). Where participants were cued in advance about the stereotype that women cannot do math, female performance was impaired; where no such cue was provided, women and men performed equally well (Spencer, Steele & Quinn, 1999).

This effect has been demonstrated in a variety of cultures with a variety of extant stereotypes (Smith, 2004). These have included people with a history of mental illness, student athletes primed to think of themselves as athletes before taking a math test, older adults taking a memory test when primed to think of it as about memory rather than forming impressions about people, women in a driving simulation task, and lower socioeconomic status individuals when primed to think of a test as about intellectual ability. In all cases, there appears to be several psychological processes which can undermine performance (Schmader,

Figure 13.7 Women and math: Stereotype threat effect?
Source: © Peter M. Fisher/Corbis

Johns & Forbes, 2008; Steele, 1997). These include physiological arousal, which interferes with performance, causing people to become distracted as they try to suppress thoughts about stereotypes; feeling worried and trying to avoid failure rather than achieve success; and 'dis-identifying' from the domain, deciding that doing well in education or athletics or whatever else is involved, is no longer important or relevant to their self-esteem. Note that people not subjected to the negative stereotype (such as men doing math) may benefit from a stereotype *lift*, leading to an enhanced performance, after a negative stereotype of the 'inferior' group is made salient (Walton & Cohen, 2003).

KEY POINT: People who are the targets of prejudice may passively accept their situation, or try as individuals to break free, or attempt collective action to improve the status of the group itself. They often minimize the prejudice that they experience personally, while perceiving that it is directed against their group. The victims of prejudice often suffer diminished self-esteem, and their mental and physical health may suffer. A stereotype may produce a self-fulfilling prophecy. The stereotype threat effect causes people to experience additional stress, which hampers achievement.

CAN PREJUDICE BE REDUCED OR ELIMINATED?

Discrimination is a behaviour and can be controlled by laws, such as those mandating fair employment practices for women and minorities, voting rights, and hate speech. However, prejudiced attitudes obviously cannot be dealt with in the same way. We have seen in general how attitudes can be changed, by arousing cognitive dissonance or by persuasion (Chapter 5). Is it possible to reduce prejudice and make individuals more tolerant?

Research over many years in many societies has addressed the problem, and while we have learned a lot, the problem is not solved … yet. Some of the research (reviewed by Paluck & Green, 2009) is correlational, studying how different circumstances and interventions can have an impact, particularly in societies that are multicultural – a reality that is increasingly the norm in our globalized world. Others have focused on various ways of changing attitudes, using experimental, quasi-experimental and field-experimental procedures.

One interesting example is the 'jigsaw classroom', first proposed and tested by Blaney, Stephan et al. (1977). The classroom can be a competitive environment, particularly where the students compete for the 'right' answer and for the teacher's approval. In schools in Texas and California that had only recently been desegregated at that time, the researchers devised a new, more cooperative model of education. Students were assigned to small groups, each of which was racially mixed. The material to be mastered was divided into subtopics, and each student was assigned one of the pieces of the puzzle to learn (with help from the teacher if necessary) and to teach the others in the group. In short, this led to everyone having a particular area of competence, and the success of every member of the group depended on all other members of the group. The method worked well in terms of what was learned, and, equally important, the students were happier in school, had higher self esteem, and were less prejudiced towards the other race.

Think of these results in terms of categories and multiple identities outlined above. In terms of a common in-group identity model (Gaertner & Dovidio, 2009), the procedure first caused each member to pay less attention to which race they belonged to because of the demands of the situation, and to see members of the other group as individuals who could help them succeed academically. Then they refocused their conception of an in-group to the learning group they belonged to, rather than fixating on the racial divide. Experience that stresses the common in-group clearly can break down in-group/out-group biases. (Recall as well the discussion of cross-categorization in Chapter 12.)

Above all, this experiment involved placing members of the two groups in sustained contact, in defined conditions. In an open multicultural society, members of different groups – ethnic, religious, socioeconomic class, sexual preferences – come into contact under various conditions. The notion that such intergroup contact can have a significant impact has been the subject to a vast research literature. Let us see what has been discovered.

Intergroup contact

It is often assumed that increased interaction between the members of various groups will enhance mutual understanding and goodwill. Clearly it would seem that the nature of the contact is as important as frequency. Gordon Allport (1954) wrote the classic social psychological treatment of prejudice, in which he defined conditions under which intergroup contact will lead to prejudice reduction, all of which were substantiated by research (Amir, 1976; Pettigrew, 1998):

1. The members of each group must be of equal status (e.g., same income group or similar occupations), or the members of the minority group should be of a higher status than the majority of group members.
2. There must be a favourable climate for intergroup contact, one consistent with the laws or customs of the society at that time, and the contact must be rewarding and pleasant. Indeed, situations which will induce members of one group to take the perspective of the others, to see things as they see them, will contribute to the reduction of prejudice (Vescio, Sechrist & Paolucci, 2003).
3. The two groups should have mutual goals that require interdependent and cooperative action. Recall Sherif's Robbers Cave experiments described in Chapter 10 (Sherif et al., 1961).

Rarely are all these conditions likely to be present in actual interethnic situations. Tourism, for example, has been advocated as a means of improving national as well as international understanding, but given that the experience occurs largely through the windows of a bus or in a souvenir shop, it will meet none of these conditions.

And, yet, recent reviews of the literature point to a clear, simple conclusion: contact generally leads to reduced prejudice to some degree (Lolliot, Schmid, et al., 2013; Pettigrew & Tropp, 2011). While some circumstances such as those proposed by Allport (1954) can increase the impact of contact, or indeed reduce or minimize the effects of contact, the overall results are clear across a wide variety of research methods, cultures and ethnic groups involved. The reason for this is likely the mere exposure effect (Chapter 6). We tend to be more favourable towards people and objects that we are familiar with, that we encounter more frequently. It is evident that this applies as well to members of out-groups, and by extension to the out-group itself (see below).

If contact leads to friendships, prejudice is further reduced (Davies, Tropp, et al., 2011). This harkens back to Allport (1954), who argued for the benefits of genuine encounters among members of the different groups as opposed to the role-regulated relationship of the sales clerk and customer, the domestic and the employer. Indeed, cross-group friendships are most beneficial when they show evidence of real friendship, such as mutual self-disclosure and spending significant amounts of time together. The importance of close relationships is emphasized by Pettigrew (1997, 1998) and his colleagues, who conducted surveys in four European countries. They found that respondents who reported that they had out-group friends were more tolerant and had more positive feelings towards out-groups generally.

Indeed, we may not even need to have direct face-to-face exposure to members of the other group. We may encounter these individuals in social websites on the Internet, which can facilitate contact without provoking anxiety (Amichai-Hamburger & McKenna, 2006) in comfortable equal-status conditions. Such contact between Jewish and Arab students in Israel resulted in more positive attitudes to the other group. Turner, Crisp and Lambert (2007) took it a step beyond virtual contact by having people imagine that they were in a contact encounter with out-group members. Such an exercise in mental imagery resulted in improved attitudes to the out-group (Crisp & Turner, 2011), including changes in stereotypes (Brambilla, Ravenna & Hewstone, 2012). Finally, researchers have investigated the notion of 'extended contact', being aware that members of one's own group are friends with members of an out-group (Turner, Hewstone et al., 2007). Again, the research shows that direct personal contact is not necessary for reduced prejudice.

However, there is one serious gap in our knowledge. The mass of studies shows that the average levels of prejudice in general population, and student samples are reduced in the context of intergroup contact. That is, people who show moderate levels of prejudice will show reductions. But is intergroup contact effective with the individual whom one would most want to benefit from it: the highly prejudiced person? We saw in Chapter 5 that extreme, polarized attitudes are most resistant to change. Hodson (2011) reviews the limited evidence directly relevant to this issue, and concludes that if intergroup contact and intergroup friendships can occur, they do indeed work well among intolerant people, likely by reducing anxiety and threat, and perhaps by increasing empathy as well. But we still have much to learn about changing the bigot.

Finally, we must consider the issue of causality between contact and prejudice. Binder et al. (2009) conducted a longitudinal study, following students over time from ethnic majorities and minorities in Belgium, Germany and the United Kingdom. They found that contact did indeed reduce prejudice, but that prejudice also reduced subsequent contact. Indeed, the contact effects were negligible for the minority group members, while the prejudiced among them were led to avoid contact with the other group. The latter effect appears to be a result of anxiety about the consequences of contact. Thus, in the real world, contact may be desirable, but it will be helpful only if it happens.

Let us examine some of the research. To test the contact hypothesis in a Canadian setting, Clement, Gardner and Smythe (1977) studied 379 anglophone Grade 8 students from London, Ontario. About half the students (181) went on an excursion to Québec City while the control group (198) remained at home. All the students completed a battery of tests before and after the trip. Those who visited Québec were subsequently divided into two groups on the basis of the amount of interaction they reported having had with francophones while in the city. The high-contact group had more favourable attitudes, compared to either the low-contact or control groups, towards French Canadians and towards learning French as a second language. In fact, the low-contact group actually had a less favourable attitude towards learning French after the trip than before. And in a study of contact between German and Turkish students in Germany, only leisure-time contact was related to reduced prejudice and then only for the German students. The Turkish students were unaffected by contact whether it happened in the neighbourhood, the school or during leisure time (Wagner, Hewstone & Machleit, 1989).

A study by Henderson-King & Nisbett (1996) suggests that even a small amount of negative behaviour by a member of a minority group can have a significant impact. They found that the negative behaviour of one black person led white participants in their research to stereotype blacks more and subsequently to avoid a black person whom they encountered. In fact, simply overhearing a conversation in which a black person was alleged to have committed a crime was sufficient to increase negative stereotypes and in-group favouritism. Equally subtle and similarly powerful effects can arise from the labels used to identify groups. For example, Donakowski and Esses (1996) identified a group as either Aboriginal peoples, First Nations peoples, Native Canadians, Native Indians or Native peoples. They found that the attitudes of subjects were more negative when the labels 'Native Canadians' and 'First Nations peoples' were used. Donakowski and Esses suggest that this outcome may arise because the labels elicit symbolic beliefs of a political nature.

Figure 13.8 Intergroup contact at the Olympics. Are these the appropriate conditions for prejudice reduction?
Source: © Leo Mason/Corbis

Will intergroup contact generalize? If some positive modification of a stereotype does occur as a result of intergroup contact, how likely is it that the change will generalize to other members of the same group? Unfortunately, studies (Cook, 1984; Esses & Seligman, 1996) indicate that the new attitude may not extend beyond the situation or to other members of the group. This is so because the individuals involved in the contact may not be perceived as 'exemplars' of the larger category. Allport (1954) called this phenomenon 're-fencing'. When categories conflict with the evidence, special cases are excluded and the category is kept intact (Kunda & Oleson, 1995).

In the final analysis, the prescription for stereotype-disconfirming information is that it should be:

(1) linked to typical out-group exemplars; (2) presented to highly motivated perceivers; and (3) provided under conditions that do not induce intergroup anxiety (Hewstone, 1989). This of course is easier said than done. It also is evident that even when the opportunity for contact exists, many people will not take advantage of it.

Roadblocks to intergroup contact

There are a number of factors that militate against contact with members of negatively stereotyped outgroups. First of all, there is intergroup anxiety (Stephan & Stephan, 1985). That is, anxiety about being with the other group may cause people to avoid them and may also be a consequence of a fear of the unknown (Plant & Devine, 2003).

In addition, intergroup contact poses the risk of some negative psychological consequences for the individual. People often know very little about the values, norms, non-verbal behaviours and expectations of the members of other groups. This ignorance about the 'subjective culture' of the other group (Triandis, 1972) may lead to fear of embarrassment or of being made to appear incompetent in intergroup interactions. These fears can be quite realistic. For example, suppose that you are a Hindu. If an orthodox Hindu is present at a meal in your home, will it be offensive to that person if you serve beef to the other guests? Or when a European is introduced to someone from Japan, should the European bow and, if so, how low? There is also sometimes a fear of rejection, ridicule or disapproval by the out-group if contact is attempted (Wilder and Shapiro, 1989).

Yet, in light of our earlier discussion, it is likely that if we could somehow propel prejudiced individuals into the appropriate social milieu, some positive change might occur. Cook (1970) carried out extensive laboratory research in the United States that supports this contention. He employed a simulation game in which black and white women interacted over a one-month period. All the black women and half the white women were confederates of the experimenter. The real participants, all white, initially had very negative attitudes towards blacks. (Their attitudes had been measured in a different context so that there would be no apparent connection with the study.) The game required the participants to cooperate and to be in close contact in an equal-status situation. If they won, they shared the rewards. There were also breaks during each two-hour session during which the black confederate led the conversation to race-related issues. She also interjected personal comments that emphasized her individuality and distinguished her from the stereotype. In comparing the participants' attitudes before and after this experience, it was found that about 40% of these white participants compared with only 12% of those in the control group, became more tolerant towards blacks. Obviously, this sort of contact is effective – even though a majority of the white women did not change and, inexplicably, a small number became more prejudiced.

While it would be expensive and difficult to mount a project of this sort to reduce prejudice among the public at large, it would be quite feasible to create similar situations in schools where many opportunities exist for students to work together on cooperative educational projects. In this regard, think back to the jigsaw classroom discussed earlier.

An extensive project conducted by Six (1989) emphasizes the importance of using more than one educational approach to modify prejudice. The purpose of the study was to reduce prejudice of German students towards those of Turkish origin. To this end, two TV films were produced that showed both the positive and negative aspects of life for a Turkish girl and boy living in Germany. In addition, a teaching programme was developed with similar goals to those of the films – that is, to present new information, to teach different ways of social categorization, to inform about prejudice in general and to create positive emotional involvement. Students between the ages of 10 and 15 were assigned to five conditions: (1) films only; (2) soundtrack only; (3) teaching programme only; (4) a shorter teaching programme and the films; or (5) a no-treatment control group. Measures of prejudice were obtained over a 10-week period, beginning one week prior to treatment and then continuing immediately after treatment and three, six and nine weeks later. All treatments caused short-term changes but long-term change was significant only with the combined teaching and film programme. In addition the more prejudiced a student had been, the less the prejudice was reduced. In fact, the television conditions (video or audio only) had no effect on highly prejudiced students. It appears that pre-existing prejudice causes information to be devalued, distorted and misinterpreted. The teaching programme that prepared the students for the films reduced the negative influence of the pre-existing prejudice, and so the films became more effective.

Acculturation and multiculturalism

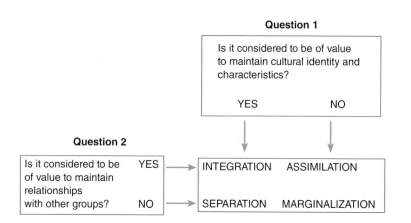

Figure 13.9 Types of relationships between cultural groups in a multicultural society

When a country has many ethnic groups, such as Canada, Australia, United States and, increasingly, Europe, intergroup contact is very likely. The amount of contact and the desire to interact should influence the extent of change that may occur in the values, attitudes and behaviour of each group. This is the process of acculturation, which takes place when 'two groups come into continuous firsthand contact with subsequent changes in the original culture pattern of either or both groups' (Redfield, 1955, p. 149).

As Berry (1986, 1992) points out, in pluralistic societies there are two important intergroup issues: the strength of the desire to maintain one's cultural distinctiveness and the strength of the propensity for interethnic contact. As described in Chapter 12, our identity is derived to a considerable extent from the groups with which we identify. These two orientations, maintaining cultural distinctiveness and contact with other groups, are not really compatible, and Berry (1984, 1999) has constructed a framework that distinguishes the potential outcomes of the four possible combinations of the two motives (Figure 13.9). These are as follows: assimilation, integration, separation (or segregation) and marginalization. Assimilation occurs when a group surrenders its cultural identity and is absorbed into the larger society (the 'melting pot' concept). Integration is the result when the group maintains its culture, but also interacts with other groups. In cases where intergroup contact is unwelcome and cultural integrity is maintained, the outcome will be either segregation (if the group is a weak minority) or separation (if the group is more powerful). The final possibility, marginalization, results when the traditional culture is lost and there is little contact with the larger society. Marginalization is usually accompanied by confusion, anxiety, hostility and feelings of alienation, a syndrome that has been termed *acculturative stress* (Berry, 1987).

In Canada, Israel and other countries, the relationship of second-language learning to attitudes has also received attention. The social psychological effects of bilingualism are discussed in detail in Chapter 7, but it should be mentioned here that individuals who have acquired a second language seem to have more positive attitudes towards other cultural groups than do monolinguals (Lambert et al., 1963), if their initial orientation was integrative (an interest in the culture) rather than instrumental (to improve job prospects). It has also been shown that anglophone parents with an integrative orientation have positive attitudes towards francophones even though they may not know any (Gardner & Lambert, 1959). The relationship of such attitudes and integrative motivation to competence in another language has been found to hold in locations as diverse as Maine, Louisiana, Connecticut and the Philippines (Gardner, Gliksman & Smythe, 1978).

[
KEY POINT: When two or more groups exist in substantial numbers in a society, they may assimilate, integrate, segregate from each other or become marginalized from the larger society. Individuals in multicultural societies often have multiple social identities. Education may promote intergroup acceptance and integration, including second-language learning in appropriate circumstances.
]

SEXISM

Among the many groups experiencing prejudice and discrimination, the largest by far comprises women. In many lands, women have struggled long and hard to achieve the status they have today. In many other parts of the world, progress has been minimal or nonexistent, and women continue to be relegated to the inferior roles they have occupied throughout history. Prejudice towards women includes the cognitive component, particularly stereotypes, and the behavioural component, discrimination, but is often not accompanied by the overt hostility that is frequently directed at other out-groups (other than in the all-too-frequent violence towards partners and spouses, as discussed in Chapter 11). Several decades of research in social psychology have been devoted to documenting the more subtle sexisms that have escaped the attention of most people, female and male (Swim & Hyers, 2009).

Sexism is unique among the various forms of prejudice for several reasons. First, gender stereotypes are often prescriptive rather than descriptive – they define how women and men should behave. Few people would argue that gay people should be artistic, Jews and Scots should be stingy, or old people should be forgetful, but many say that real men should be stoic and not emotionally expressive, and real women should be nurturing and not competitive. Another unique aspect of sexism as a prejudice is that there is no clearly separated out-group; men and women do interact as co-workers, friends, lovers and within families. Thus there is an ambivalent quality to sexism, derogating those whom we love and put on a pedestal. Glick & Fiske et al. (2001) describe this ambivalence as a hybrid sexism, combining hostile sexism, that is, negative attitudes towards women's abilities and their challenge to male power, and benevolent sexism, the affectionate and patronizing belief that women need the protection of men. Complimenting a woman for her physical attributes in a situation in which her job performance is being evaluated might be considered as an example of benevolent sexism.

In many of the societies of the world, to be female means to be perceived as less competent and to have lower status than men, while at the same time possessing other desirable characteristics such as warmth and expressiveness (Deaux, 1985). Among the many social stereotypes that are maintained about women (by both men and women) are those pertaining to role assignments. Certain occupations, such as nursing, secretarial positions and truck driving have been sex-typed, and those of the other sex who enter non-traditional occupations may be viewed as aberrant. Similarly, higher levels within occupations are often available to men and women on an unequal basis. We still find relatively few women in positions of power in industry or commerce (the 'glass ceiling'), even though women may be equally represented or over-represented in the lower ranks. Historically, they have simply been perceived as less competent than men (Broverman, Vogel et al., 1972; Deaux & Emswiller, 1974; Bechtold, Naccarato & Zanna,1986).

Kalin & Hodgins (1984) noted that sex-role congruence tends to be important only in an abstract situation where no other information is available. However, in reality, a person with hiring power has considerable information from interviews, letters and résumés about the background and personal characteristics of applicants. They outline a social cognition model of occupational suitability which begins with applicant-job schemata including the following: (1) associations between social categories such as sex and occupation (e.g., 'bank teller' is associated with a female and 'construction worker' with a male); (2) associations between social categories (sex, occupation) and personal characteristics (these are the stereotypes held by people about men, women, insurance agents, truck drivers, professors of psychology and so forth); and (3) associations among various personal characteristics (e.g., 'friendly' is associated with 'trustworthy' (implicit personality theory)). Thus, using information about social categories and personal characteristics, we base our evaluations on patterns of associations among them. When we know only the categories, we may use a simple congruency rule between sex and occupation (e.g., 'A suitable truck driver is male'). However, when we have information about personal characteristics, we rely more on these impressions and match them with occupational stereotypes. If the occupation is strongly sex-typed, then the occupational stereotype will include 'masculine' or 'feminine' characteristics.

Hodgins and Kalin (1985) tested this model in two experiments in which the subjects (university students) were asked to play the role of guidance counsellors. They were given brief descriptions of three male and three female high-school students and were asked to rate the students' suitability for each of four male-typed occupations (commercial traveller, surveyor, engineering technician, sales manager) and four female-typed occupations (social worker, nurse, librarian, occupational therapist). In this minimal information situation, subjects showed a strong tendency to match sex of person with sex-type of the job. However, in a second experiment, subjects were also provided with brief descriptions of personality consisting of traits previously rated by other subjects as 'masculine' (self-confident, strong, assertive, opportunistic), 'feminine' (affectionate, warm, sensitive, charming) or neutral (formal, calm, determined). In this case, subjects matched the sex-type of personality characteristics with the sex-type of the job, regardless of whether the actual client was male or female. In this study, the occupations selected as female-typed and male-typed were those that previous research has shown to be equivalent in status. However, although women have gained access to some of the high-status 'male' occupations, most still work in 'female' jobs, which tend to be lower in both status and pay (Greenglass, 1982).

As we have seen, stereotypes can cause the stereotyped person to underperform because of the stereotype threat effect. Consider fields such as mathematics and engineering, where women have been stereotypically expected to be disadvantaged relative to men. In an experiment (Logel, Walton et al., 2009), male engineering students first completed a measure of sexist attitudes and then interacted with a female confederate posing as another engineering student. Observations indicated that the male students who had scored high in sexism behaved in a more dominant and sexual manner to the woman than did the less sexist students. But did this affect how the female students performed? In a second study, male confederates were first trained to act in a dominant, sexually interested manner, just like the real students observed previously. The female participants then scored much more poorly on an engineering test. And, yet, they reported that they were more attracted to the 'sexist' confederate than to others who did not behave in this way. The researchers reasoned that the stereotype had been activated in these women, and this stereotype threat caused anxiety which interfered with engineering-related performance (Logel, Walton, et al., 2009). However, there is another possible interpretation: perhaps the women were distracted by being 'turned on' sexually by the sexist confederate, and this distracted them from the task at hand. Yet another experiment was devised and conducted. In this study, while some women were given a math test, others were given an English test (an area in which the stereotype would not apply). Performance was again hampered in the company of the sexist confederate, but only in the math test, and not in the English test. Clearly it is the stereotype activation, not sexual distraction, that brings about the stereotype threat response. Indeed, just having a confederate casually mention that the experimenter seems sexist has been shown to be sufficient to hamper performance by women on a task relevant to gender stereotype (Adams, Garcia, et al., 2006).

Along similar lines, it has been found (Conway, Pizzamiglio & Mount, 1996) that individuals perceived as being of lower status, whether male or female, are also perceived as more communal (a stereotypic female trait) and less agentic (a stereotypic male trait) than individuals of higher status. Similarly, men in low-status jobs are less assertive and less dominant (less agentic) than men in high-status jobs, and women in high-status jobs are less sensitive and more leadership-oriented (less communal) than women in low-status jobs. It seems that gender not only assigns status to occupations, but, conversely, the status of an occupation assigns male or female characteristics to those in the occupation irrespective of their gender. Fortunately, in addition to removing barriers to occupational choice and abolishing inequities in pay for the same occupation, society is becoming aware of inequities based on the sex-typing of occupations. Such awareness is manifest in the slogan 'Equal pay for work of equal value'.

Glick, Zion and Nelson (1988) point out that while an employer's stereotypes may be responsible for that employer hiring a male or female in the first place, once an occupation has been labelled as 'male' or 'female', discrimination is likely to continue even if stereotypes change. Krefting, Berger and Wallace (1978) found that the best prediction of the sex-type of a job was the percentage of men and women in the various occupations, and that the actual job content – that is, what the person was required to do – was not significant. This implies that the reduction or elimination of sex stereotypes may not have a large effect on employment practices at least in the short run.

Discrimination against women has not been confined to the workplace. For example in a well-publicized study at that time (Goldberg, 1968), identical essays were submitted to judges to be assigned a grade. In half the cases, the 'author' was identified as male; in the other half, as female. Essays ostensibly written by males received higher grades. However, some studies did not completely support Goldberg's (1968) contention that females are generally perceived as less competent than males (Pheterson, Kiesler and Goldberg, 1971). Swim, Borgida and Maruyama (1989) reviewed 123 studies and concluded that there was little evidence to support Goldberg's original conclusion. However, in a later review of 58 controlled experiments conducted over a period of 20 years, Swim & Sanna (1996) found results that were remarkably consistent: when a man was successful on a task, observers attributed his success to ability, but the success of a woman on a similar

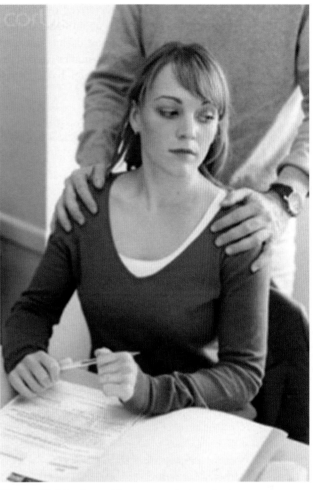

Figure 13.10 Sexual harassment at work
Source: © Burger/phanie/Phanie Sarl/Corbis

task tended to be attributed to hard work. Failure on a similar task was attributed by observers to bad luck or a lack of effort when the protagonist was male, but to lesser ability when the protagonist was female.

For example, Simpson, McCarrey and Edwards (1987) studied supervisors in a large organization and found that those with traditional attitudes towards women judged the women they supervised as less able than men to do the following: (1) autonomously direct their subordinates; (2) assist in the career development of subordinates; and (3) effectively monitor the day-to-day performance of their subordinates. Moreover, these supervisors were unwilling to assign technical, high-profile projects to women. Along the same lines, Dion (1987) and Dion and Schuller (1991) found that women who used the title Ms were stereotyped as being more achievement-oriented, socially assertive and dynamic than women who used Mrs or Miss – but also as less warm. And the stereotypes associated with the Ms label included those of a successful middle manager whereas those associated with the traditionally labelled person did not.

While overt instances of old-fashioned sexism may be decreasing in frequency, sex discrimination is far from dead, and gender stereotypes have persisted (Martin, 1986). Tougas and her colleagues (Tougas, Brown, Beaton & Joly, 1995) refer to a new form of gender attitudes, *neosexism*, defined as a 'manifestation of a conflict between egalitarian values and residual negative feelings towards women'. It is similar to modern racism. In this case, the public expression of gender-related beliefs is inhibited, but some underlying prejudice remains, which may be manifest in disguised forms of discrimination.

Traditional sexism was characterized by the support of traditional gender roles, differential treatment of men and women and stereotypes about lesser female competence. Modern sexism denies that discrimination continues. At the same time, the past decades have seen significant changes in sexist attitudes and practices in many societies. Many of the earlier studies cited above are snapshot portrayals of a time and place that may not apply today and in other cultures in a global environment.

KEY POINT: Sexism is the most universal form of prejudice, unique because the norms are prescriptive, and hostility is not usually a part of sexism. Evidence is reported from many studies of the subtle or implicit nature of much of sexism. Sex-role stereotypes vary with the culture and historical period.

SUMMARY

1. Prejudice is a positive or negative attitude towards perceived differences or characteristics that are unjustly generalized to all the members of a group. In modern times, the term is almost exclusively used in the negative sense. Like other attitudes, sexism has three components: cognitive, affective and behavioural.

2. Stereotypes are cognitions or beliefs about the members of other groups. They are usually overgeneralizations and are often inaccurate.

3. Stereotypes can change depending on changes in social conditions and changes in the relationships between members of different groups.

4. Those stereotypes that have some validity may arise from the operation of the 'self-fulfilling prophecy' and the situational pressure created by prejudice.

5. The behavioural component of prejudice is called discrimination, and, in its more extreme form, racism. While laws have been enacted making discrimination illegal, many subtle forms, such as biased hiring practices, still exist.

6. Innate fear of the unusual or the unfamiliar may be a primitive basis for prejudice. The acquisition of prejudice begins in the home when the child is about three years of age. Parents, teachers, peers and the media all contribute at various times to this process.

7. Some individuals develop authoritarian personalities. They are likely to be prejudiced and ethnocentric and may be hostile towards out-groups.

8. One manifestation of pent-up hostility is scapegoating, through which the individual blames out-groups for the frustration that he or she experiences.

9. Under the appropriate circumstances, prejudice can be reduced by intergroup contact. Unfortunately, intergroup anxiety often prevents people from interacting with members of other groups.

10. Acculturation refers to the changes in values, attitudes and behaviour that occur when groups come into direct contact.

11. The victims of prejudice may react with aggression, diminished self-esteem, changes in group allegiance or modification of the strength of positive or negative stereotypes held about their own group.

12. The stereotype threat can impair performance by members of stereotyped groups.

13. Sexism is usually directed at women and results, among other things, in differential treatment in employment.

POINTS TO PONDER

- What are some of the more subtle effects on the individual of being the target of prejudice?
- Can a stereotype be accurate, at least to some degree? Can we argue that stereotypes are useful in helping us fit into our environment?
- Is prejudice (including sexism) a product of our environment? Why are some people more prejudiced than others?

- Some have argued that international sports events such as the Olympics, the Davis Cup and the World Cup are ways of bringing people of different cultures and nations together in a peaceful and joyful competition. Others argue that such events can only exacerbate tensions and increase prejudice. Based on what you have learned about intergroup contact, what do you think?
- Researchers have observed that people have stereotypes about and are prejudiced toward people with different tastes in music or style of dress. Does it all boil down to in-group versus out-group?

FURTHER READING

Aboud, F. (1988). *Children and prejudice.* Oxford: Basil Blackwell.

An account of the developmental aspects of intolerance that culminates in a new social-cognitive theory of prejudice.

Allport, G.W. (1954). *The nature of prejudice.* Reading: Addison-Wesley.

This classic account of the development and maintenance of prejudice is still relevant today.

Anderson, K.J. (2010). *Benign bigotry: the psychology of subtle prejudice.* New York: Cambridge University Press.

This very readable, award-winning book outlines the results of a long-term research programme and discusses the role of parents, religion and education in the development of authoritarian attitudes.

Dovidio, J., Hewstone, M. & Esses, V. (2010). *The SAGE handbook of prejudice, stereotyping and discrimination.* London: Sage.

An encyclopaedic collection of papers by international experts on the various aspects of prejudice.

Backhouse, C. (1999). *Colour-coded: a legal history of racism in Canada, 1900–1950.* Toronto: The Osgoode Society for Canadian Legal History.

A disturbing examination of the effects of direct and indirect racism on the framing of laws and the administration of justice in Canada.

Eberhardt, J.L. & Fiske, S.T. (Eds). (1998). *Confronting racism: the problem and the response.* Thousand Oaks, CA: Sage Publications Inc.

A wide-ranging set of articles on the intrapersonal, interpersonal and intergroup processes that lead to racism.

Fiske, S. (1998). Prejudice, stereotyping and discrimination. In D.Gilbert, S. Fiske & G. Lindzey (Eds). *Handbook of social psychology* (4th ed.). Vol. 1. New York: McGraw-Hill.

An excellent overview on the topic, particularly the discussion of stereotyping.

Hodson, G. & Hewstone, M. (Eds). *Advances in intergroup contact.* New York, NY, US: Psychology Press.

An up-to-date set of papers on what we know, and new ideas about contact between groups.

Paluck, E.L. & Green, D.P. (2009). Prejudice reduction: What works? A review and assessment of research and practice. *Annual Review of Psychology*, 60, 339–367.

An up-to-date overview of what we know about the various ways to reduce prejudice.

Yueh-Ting Lee, Lee J. Jussim, and Clark R. McCauley (Eds). *Stereotype accuracy. Towards appreciating group differences.* Washington, DC: American Psychological Association.

A set of papers which review evidence that stereotypes are not always inaccurate, although they may be exaggerated, and that this may not be a bad thing.

Swim, J.K. & Stangor, C. (Eds). (1998). *Prejudice: The target's perspective.* San Diego, CA: Academic Press.

A summary of research focusing on the victims of prejudice.

WEBLINKS

Understanding prejudice: http://www.understandingprejudice.org/
A good set of educational resources.

Implicit association test: https://implicit.harvard.edu/implicit/
Try it yourself!

Anti-defamation League: www.adl.org
Founded in 1913, this American organization is an important and enduring civil rights/human relations agency fighting anti-Semitism, prejudice and bigotry.

CHAPTER 14

CROWDS AND COLLECTIVE BEHAVIOUR

Do you ask me what you should regard as especially to be avoided?
I say, crowds; for as yet you cannot trust yourself to them with safety
Seneca (4BCE–65CE)

LEARNING OBJECTIVES

* To explore the nature of behaviour in crowds

* To study contagion of behaviour and emotion

* To consider the causes of mass psychogenic illness

* To examine how rumours, urban legends and conspiracy theories spread and the needs they serve

* To understand the development and maintenance of social movements

In May 2001, New Delhi was gripped by reports of people being attacked in their sleep by a hairy 'Monkey Man' described as being four feet tall with a dark face, large eyes and metal claws, and having super powers including being able to jump to a height of six metres and to become invisible. The Monkey Man was blamed for injuries to 100 people, and 50 such attacks were reported on one night alone. An additional 1000 police officers were deployed to patrol the streets of New Delhi at night, and people began sleeping in groups for greater protection. According to news reports, fear held the city in its grip. However, the wave of reports died away after a committee of experts concluded that there was no Monkey Man and that the reports were the result of rumour-mongering and 'mass hysteria'.

From August 6 to 11, 2011, after a man was shot dead by police during a traffic stop, thousands of people in London, England, took to the streets, setting fires, looting, and battling the police. The disturbances – often referred to as the 'summer riots' – or the 'BlackBerry riots' because many people used their smart phones and social media to organize and draw others into the melee – soon spread to other towns and cities across England, ultimately resulting in five deaths and hundreds of millions of pounds' worth of property damage.

Such events cannot be readily explained in terms of interpersonal and intergroup processes, such as social facilitation, conformity, compliance and obedience, that we have discussed so far. These people did not behave as they did because of social pressure to do so; there was no pre-existing group structure generating pressure to conform; and there was no leadership demanding obedience. Instead, large numbers of people who had had very little to do with one another beforehand became active participants in a large-scale social event. One person who reports having seen a Monkey Man is not newsworthy and does not lead to widespread alarm. One person or even a handful of people throwing stones through store windows does not a riot make. However, when a Monkey Man has been reported by a number of people, or when several dozen people roam down a street smashing windows, others take notice, and the initial actions of a few people attract a great many others to react similarly. Be it sleeping in groups for protection or going on a rampage, when such spontaneous, uncoordinated and unplanned behaviour that is largely ungoverned by existing social norms spreads through a large collectivity of people, we refer to it as collective behaviour.

Figure 14.1   Summer riots, Clapham Junction, England, August 2011

Source: © mirrorimage photos/Demotix/Corbis

Such activity is on a continuum with other crowd phenomena in which there has been some planning and at least some minimal coordination. For example, in the spring and summer of 2012, thousands of students in Montréal withdrew from their classes and marched through the streets day after day to protest the provincial government's decision to raise tuition fees. While it was first assumed by observers that the protest would quickly die out, it did not. The protests continued and the numbers of participants increased – some demonstrations involved as many as 100,000 people – and similar protests developed in other regions of Québec (Figure 14.2). Night after night, citizens in sympathy with the demonstrators banged pots and pans to signal their support. This evolved into one of the largest protests in Canadian history, and its focus shifted from initial anger about tuition fees to a larger concern about educational quality and opportunity.

Sometimes, such collective behaviours grow into social movements (discussed later in this chapter), with formal spokespersons, specific demands and careful tactical and strategic planning. For example, in mid-December 2010, a wave of revolutionary protests that came to be known as the *Arab Spring* began in Tunisia after a 26-year-old street vendor, Mohamed Bouazizi, burned himself to death in protest of ongoing harassment by police and municipal authorities. The public reacted with outrage and came together in massive demonstrations that eventually forced Tunisia's president to resign after 23 years in office. The movement evolved far beyond a large group of people spontaneously shouting out slogans in public meeting places; leaders emerged, demands were formalized and strategies to maximize pressure on the authorities were developed.

The success of the Tunisian protest movement encouraged widespread protests in neighbouring countries, and the wave of generally peaceful rebellion soon spread through much of the Arab world: After two weeks of massive protests in Egypt following the police killing of a blogger, Khaled Said, whose Internet postings were critical of the authorities, Hosni Mubarak was forced to step down after 30 years as president. In Libya, protests against the rule of Moammar Gaddafi resulted in military attacks on the protesters, who fought back with substantial assistance from NATO warplanes. Gaddafi was eventually overthrown and later killed. The Yemenese leader was also forced from power, and an uprising was ignited in Syria that led to massive and enduring military action against the protesters. Other countries too felt the sting of a citizenry aroused. Not surprisingly given the significant number of young people involved, social media played an important role throughout the Arab Spring (Box 14.1).

Figure 14.2 Thousands of Québec students protest tuition increases, Montréal

Source: © Darren Ell/Demotix/Corbis

BOX 14.1 COLLECTIVE BEHAVIOUR AND THE VIRTUAL CROWD

The Internet is the most extensive social network that the world has ever known. It brings us the wonderful ability to communicate widely, to share ideas, to organize and participate in activities, to locate long-lost relatives and friends, and to access seemingly endless sources of information – not always accurate information, however. Consider these examples of how electronically interconnected individuals become 'virtual crowds', acting collectively for good or for ill.

Flashmobs: A flashmob is a group of people, organized by social media or a viral email initiative who suddenly come together in a public place and carry out some particular activity – it could be dancing, or singing, or some pointless but attention-grabbing activity – and then just as quickly disperse.

Cyberbullying: Bullying has taken on a new and ugly form as it has harnessed the power of the Internet. Although anyone could be a victim, it is a particular problem for teenagers and pre-teens, given that virtually everyone in those age groups uses electronic communication and most are active participants in social media. The bullying involves messages aimed at the individual that are embarrassing or insulting or demeaning, and when such messages are dispersed through social media, then in the child's eyes 'everyone knows about it'. Worse, the bully can hide behind a screen name so that the victim remains unaware of just who is the tormenter. Worse still, others may join in so that the bullying becomes something like sharks in a feeding frenzy, leading the child to feel isolated, scorned and humiliated by many or most of his or her peers. Unfortunately, not only does such bullying lead to huge distress, it sometimes results in suicide as well.

The Arab Spring: Social media such as Twitter, YouTube and Facebook have frequently been credited with spreading the flames of revolution during the Arab Spring – indeed some have even referred to the uprisings as the 'Facebook Revolution' (Howard et al., 2011; Moss, 2012). Indeed, social media appear to have played a crucial role. Despite years of the public dissatisfaction with their governments, it was not until emotionally distressing pictures and stories were circulated through social media that people became enraged and those revolutions were born. Communication is a key component in any uprising, both in terms of inflaming passions and organizing a collective response, and social media have the advantage that as long as they are in operation, authorities lose their ability to control the flow of information, and thus can no longer substitute propaganda for truth. Women in particular were front and centre in the Arab uprisings, emboldened by encouragement and coordination through social media to fight for social change (Radsch, 2012).

WHAT IS COLLECTIVE BEHAVIOUR?

The examples above illustrate three defining characteristics of collective behaviour (Milgram & Toch, 1969). It is:

1. A relatively rare phenomenon that emerges spontaneously in a collectivity of people (e.g., a crowd or an entire society).
2. Unplanned and relatively unorganized, initially without a formal governance and without the specific rules and norms that characterize formal groups.
3. Energized by inter-stimulation among the participants – that is, individuals are influenced by the actions of others, and their reactions in turn influence the very people who have affected them.

Sometimes collective behaviour involves an intensification of anticipated reactions. For example, while teenagers may go to a rock concert expecting to be excited, interaction among audience members can create a collective experience that is much more powerful than anticipated and more intense than anything the individual would experience alone or in a small group. Inter-stimulation is reinforcing to some extent; otherwise the behaviour would quickly die out. If one person throws a rock through a window and is admonished by others, it is unlikely that this behaviour will spread. However, if some in the crowd cheer, then a second person may also break a window, and a third, and the behaviour may spread quickly throughout the throng.

The study of collective behaviour is an important part of social psychology, not only in its own right, but also because there is hardly any aspect of social behaviour that does not occasionally find expression, sometimes even extreme expression, through some type of collective episode (Milgram & Toch, 1969). For example, prejudice is sometimes expressed through mob behaviour, which can involve aggression. Both attitude change and impression management are evident in fads and fashions; people adopt behaviours that would earlier have seemed frivolous ('high fives') or even repugnant (e.g. body piercing).

Yet, collective behaviour is very difficult to study. Laboratory research is all but impossible for both practical and ethical reasons. Could one design a laboratory experiment equivalent to a rock concert or a mob? Or simulate a fad or fashion or riot? Or create a social movement? Not likely! That being said, there have been sporadic attempts at such research in the days before ethical review committees were established. In one such study (Meier, Mennenga & Stoltz, 1941), researchers were apparently successful in convincing participants that a terrible crime had been committed, and the researchers' confederate then attempted to generate and lead a mob to seek out the perpetrators! Only about 12% of the participants were inclined to join the mob. In another study, French (1944) tried to simulate a panic by locking participants in a room, and then sounding a fire alarm while forcing smoke under the door and into the room. However, ethics aside, the study was a failure: One group of participants calmly discussed the possibility that they were being observed for their psychological reactions, while in a second group, the first person to notice the smoke immediately kicked the door open, knocking over the smoke machine. There have also been reports that Nazi researchers studied panic by putting prisoners in real-life panic situations (Farago, 1942).

Another difficulty in studying collective behaviour is that it occurs spontaneously and unpredictably, not allowing researchers time to prepare to study it. Furthermore, it is often all but impossible to isolate and measure all of the relevant variables that are at play, for even the participants are unlikely to be aware of all the important influences that are acting upon them. However, we should not just ignore these important social phenomena because they do not bend easily to our research methods. Instead, we should try to gain some understanding of the various factors involved, even if we lack the kinds of empirical control that we normally expect.

KEY POINT: Collective behaviour emerges spontaneously among large numbers of people, many who do not know each other, and involves unplanned and relatively unorganized activity. It spreads through inter-stimulation, and individual behaviour is reinforced by the responses of others.

Crowds

We have all heard about the 'madness' of crowds, and how a crowd seems to develop 'a mind of its own'. But just what is a **crowd**, anyway? It is a relatively large collection of people physically close enough to influence each other's behaviour although there is no particular relationship among them. It is *unorganized*, *anonymous*, *casual* and *temporary* (Milgram & Toch, 1969). Such a collectivity of people is ideal for the development of collective behaviour because of the lack of group structure and appropriate norms. However, being in a crowd is not the same thing as feeling crowded, and being in a crowded place such as a busy street or a shopping centre is not synonymous with being in a crowd. That is, there is a difference between a large number of people in close physical proximity in which each individual is focused on his or her own particular goals of the moment, and a crowd, in the psychological sense of the word, where a common focus has developed.

Crowding Crowding is the subjective feeling of discomfort when an individual perceives there to be 'too many people'. What feels 'crowded' to one person at a particular time may not seem crowded to someone else, and a given individual may enjoy feeling crowded in some circumstances and yet find it aversive in others. For example, you might enjoy being in a high-density situation at a concert or hockey game, but you might dislike it intensely when in a library or on a bus at rush hour. And as we all know, there are situations in which even 'three is a crowd'. So, our sense of feeling crowded depends on a number of factors, including social and cultural norms, our role at the time, our degree of control in the situation, and whether at that given moment we are seeking stimulation or privacy (Figure 14.3).

But what if we are living in overcrowded conditions and have no control? The **social pathology hypothesis** suggests that significant overcrowding leads to high rates of crime and mental illness. This notion grew out of an early study (Calhoun, 1962) that found that animal overcrowding was associated with physiological indicators of stress and resulted in abnormal behaviour, including aggression and social disorganization. However, results of studies in human crowding have been inconsistent, and it appears that people are generally able to cope with living in crowded circumstances (Ramsden, 2009). This does not mean that overcrowded living conditions are always healthy. Indeed, research conducted in

Figure 14.3 Crowded train, Lucknow, India
Source: © PAWAN KUMAR/Reuters/Corbis

Los Angeles found small but significant negative effects of residential crowding on children's well-being in terms of behavioural problems, mathematics and reading achievement, and physical health (Solari & Mare, 2012).

What is it about feeling crowded that is stressful? Four explanations have been proposed:

1. Sensory overload

Milgram (1970) argued that crowding produces stress because of **sensory overload**: too many people and too much activity overwhelm our senses. People then react by screening out much of the stimulation, minimizing social contact, and paying attention only to what seems important or unusual. Milgram based his analysis on observations made in New York City, a city with a very distinctive ambience, and we do not know whether symptoms of overload would be equally apparent in cities everywhere. Perhaps trust and cultural norms regarding social interaction are at least as important as stimulation levels in determining how well people relate to each other even in crowded cities.

2. Density–intensity

Figure 14.4 Tourists on St. Charles bridge, Prague, 2012. Would you be excited or overwhelmed by the crowd?

Freedman (1975) observed that high-density situations tend to be either extremely unpleasant and stressful or quite pleasant and exciting (Figure 14.4). High density appears to magnify our usual reactions to situations in the same way that turning up the volume of a stereo, within limits, magnifies our reaction to the music. The notion fits nicely with many of our experiences. If we enjoy parties, we enjoy a party more when there are many guests. In fact, a few guests in a huge room will usually congregate in one corner of the room to increase density. If we dislike riding a bus, then a crowded bus is even more unpleasant.

Laboratory research supports this **density–intensity hypothesis**. In one study (Freedman, 1975), groups of six to eight participants worked together in either a large room (low density) or a small room (high density) to solve word puzzles. Half the groups in each density condition were given relatively easy problems; they successfully solved most of them. The others were confronted with some extremely difficult problems and were able to solve only a few of them within the time limit. All participants were then asked to rate their experience. Those who had been successful while working in a small room rated this experience as being more interesting, lively and positive than did those who, although also successful, had been working in a large room. On the other hand, the groups who failed the task while working in the small room were more negative about their experience than were those who had failed in the large room. Thus, increasing the density magnified the effects of both success and failure. It is also of interest to note that, regardless of success or failure, participants in the crowded room were generally more positive in their ratings of each other.

3. Loss of control

With many people in a small space, each person is less able to move around freely and to avoid unwanted social or physical contact, and Baron & Rodin (1978) argue that this **loss of control** can make one feel helpless, vulnerable, and stressed. Thus, we do not feel crowded at a game or party because we expected to find a lot of people; we chose to be there and we know that we are free to leave. Research has backed this up: In one study (Sherrod, 1974), two groups of participants worked in high-density conditions, but while the participants in one group were given a button that they could use to signal the experimenter that they wanted to leave the experiment, those in the other group had no means of ending the experiment. As a result, those in the first group manifested considerably less stress, both in terms of their performance and their subjective reports, than did the participants who had no such control. Just knowing that one is free to leave a crowded situation will minimize stress.

4. Attribution theory and crowding

Although culture influences our reactions to crowding to some extent, within a given culture individuals react differently to crowded circumstances. To account for this, the **attributional theory of crowding** (Worchel & Teddlie, 1976; Schmidt & Keating, 1979) postulates that people who feel crowded first experience arousal because of violations of personal space and then attribute this arousal to the crowded situation. Thus, you will not feel crowded if you do not experience such arousal, but even if you are aroused, you will only feel crowded if you attribute the arousal to violations of personal space. Indeed, many high-density situations are experienced as enjoyable either because people do not feel that their space is being invaded or because they make a positive attribution, attributing the arousal to the excitement of the occasion.

KEY POINT: Being in a crowded situation can be pleasant or unpleasant depending on such factors as whether we feel overwhelmed by the sensory stimulation, whether we would normally find the situation pleasant or unpleasant even without the crowding, whether we feel that we are free to leave the situation, and how we interpret any arousal produced by the crowding.

The madding crowd ...

Let's go back to the alleged dangers of the 'madding crowd', the frenzied and irrational mob that reacts with animalistic emotion and wreaks havoc on everyone in its path. Is there any truth to this notion? Early social scientists certainly thought so. For example, in his seminal work *Psychologie des Foules* (Psychology of Crowds), (1895/1960) French sociologist Gustave Le Bon argued that the sheer number of people in a large gathering produces feelings of overwhelming power accompanied by a sense of anonymity and a reduction in individual responsibility. (This brings to mind Darley & Latané's (1968) model of bystander non-intervention, reviewed in Chapter 9.) He believed that an unconscious collective mind emerges, along with a kind of hypnotic influence that renders people very suggestible, leading them to set their own judgement aside. As a result, he argued, this leads to the liberation of 'savage, animalistic instincts' that are normally suppressed. Members of the crowd then imitate the behaviours of others around them and in turn stimulate others to act similarly, and so their behaviour cannot be predicted simply by studying their individual personalities and motivations.

Le Bon obviously saw danger in crowds and feared that if the unruly masses gained control of society, civilization would crumble and despotic barbarism would take its place. This was in all likelihood a reaction to the threat that the 'masses' seemed to pose to the existing social structure of the time. Because of the perceived threat, crowd behaviour was interpreted as being pathological, leading researchers to focus on its apparent mindlessness and hysteria, rather than on the relationships of crowd members to each other, or their reasons for acting together as a crowd (Apfelbaum & McGuire, 1986). Misguided though it was, Le Bon's work nonetheless stimulated modern psychological interest in crowds and collective behaviour. Yet, this interest was not always benign: Le Bon was credited by both Mussolini and Hitler as having provided the basis for their techniques of mass manipulation (Reicher, 1996).

Losing oneself in the crowd Although Le Bon's notion of a crowd in terms of animalistic instincts and a collective mind is now considered naive and erroneous, his basic ideas have been honed and repackaged as **deindividuation**, a term coined by Festinger, Pepitone and Newcomb (1952). Zimbardo (1970) described deindividuation as a complex process in which a series of antecedent social conditions leads to changes in self-perception; the person comes to see himself or herself more as a member of a group than as an individual. This leads in turn to a lowered threshold for normally restrained behaviour, and when conditions are right, can produce antisocial behaviour. Thus, this approach views collective behaviour as involving not so much the spread of emotionality throughout a crowd, but the loss of individuality, leading to the flouting of social norms in a situation of relative anonymity.

Deindividuation, according to Zimbardo (1970), develops as a result of five factors:

1. *Loss of identifiability*, occurring when a person is in a crowd of strangers or wearing a mask.
2. *Loss of responsibility*. If many people are engaging in violence, each person's share of the blame may seem diminished.
3. *Presence of group physical activity*. Such activity is arousing and sustaining. For example, when everyone is yelling and screaming at a rock concert, such stimulation may readily lead others to yell and scream.
4. *Limited temporal perspective*. The person 'lives for the moment' and ignores past obligations and future accountings.
5. *A novel or unstructured situation*. The absence of the cues that might otherwise restrain behaviour can result in lowered inhibitions. For example, police are an important thread in the fabric of restraint against violence. Their absence sometimes leads to outbreaks of vandalism and even rioting.

Various studies of participants' behaviour in conditions of anonymity have been cited in support of the deindividuation hypothesis. For example, when participants were asked to discuss their parents in a group setting, more negative comments were forthcoming when the participants were dressed in grey lab coats and seated in a dimly lit room than when they were readily identifiable (Festinger et al., 1952). In another study, Zimbardo (1969) compared the 'aggressive' behaviour (defined as the number and intensity of shocks given to a simulated victim) of college students in each of two conditions. In the first, participants sat in a darkened room and were dressed in shapeless overcoats and wore hoods over their faces, their outfits reminding one of the Ku Klux Klan, a notorious racist organization in the United States. No participant could see how much shock the other two participants were administering to a 'victim'. In the second condition, participants wore no hoods or overcoats, sat in a well-lit room and wore nametags. In keeping with the deindividuation hypothesis, the participants in the anonymous condition were much more 'aggressive' than those in the other condition.

However, while that study appeared to provide persuasive support for deindividuation, could it be that participants were actually responding to social norms? Johnson and Downing (1979) repeated the study with an interesting twist. In one condition, participants were rendered anonymous by means of the Ku Klux Klan-like garments and hoods. However, in a second study, although also anonymous, the participants wore nurses' uniforms. Compared to participants in a control condition, those dressed like the Ku Klux Klan delivered more shocks, while those dressed as nurses actually delivered fewer! That finding supports a normative explanation – suggesting that participants were affected by normative cues associated with the clothing they wore.

Zimbardo and colleagues (Haney, Banks and Zimbardo, 1973; Zimbardo et al., 1982) went on to carry out a now-famous simulation study, employing mock prisoners and mock prison guards, that was interpreted as supporting the deindividuation hypothesis (Box 14.2).

BOX 14.2   THE STANFORD PRISON EXPERIMENT

At times, the contrived situation of the psychological laboratory can become startlingly real. Researchers (Haney et al., 1973; Zimbardo et al., 1982; Zimbardo, 2007) set out to simulate what they considered to be the deindividuating conditions of a prison setting by creating a mock prison in the basement of the Stanford University psychology department. Voluntary participants were randomly assigned the roles of guards and prisoners. Those designated as 'guards' were given identical khaki uniforms, reflecting sunglasses, billy clubs, handcuffs, whistles and sets of keys. The 'prisoners' were picked up on the first day at their homes by police cars, taken to the police station where they were 'processed' and then taken blindfolded to the 'prison'. They were assigned numbers as identification and wore identical hospital-type gowns and stocking caps. The guards were instructed to maintain 'law and order', and events were allowed to unfold.

While participants initially approached their role-playing in a light-hearted fashion, the situation soon began to deteriorate. The guards became increasingly abusive and punitive towards the prisoners – to the extent of stripping them naked and forcing them to do push-ups, while the prisoners became passive, helpless and showed symptoms of stress such as crying, agitation, confusion and depression. At one point, the prisoners blockaded themselves in their cells, which led to a forceful response from the guards. Even the principal researcher, Zimbardo, found himself preoccupied with rumours of a 'prison break', forgetting his responsibilities as a scientist. At this point, after six days, an experiment planned to last two weeks was terminated. The roles had become reality to the participants.

The experiment has been criticized on several grounds (Banuazizi & Movahedi, 1975; Thayer & Saarni, 1975). Participants had signed consent forms in which they agreed to be paid to participate in a study in which some of their rights would be waived. Thus they might have felt a moral or legal obligation to continue and might have exaggerated their symptoms of distress in order to get out of their obligation. The 'guards' might have been acting according to their stereotypes of prison guards in order to succeed as 'good participants' because it was expected of them in order to make the study more realistic. (This would be in line with the SIDE model, discussed later in this chapter.) There were also some individual differences; some of the prisoners did not become apathetic or distressed, and some of the guards were not abusive.

In 2002, BBC television repeated the Stanford experiment under the supervision of two psychologists, Stephen Reicher and Alexander Haslam (Reicher & Haslam, 2006). Participants were screened to exclude anyone not emotionally healthy. In this case, the prisoners ultimately coalesced into a cohesive group and challenged the guards' authority. On the other hand, the guards did not identify with the role and therefore did not share a social identity. As a result, they were reluctant to assert their authority and respond coercively. Ultimately, prisoners and guards agreed to form an egalitarian commune. However, when they then could not agree on a set of rules for everyone, four individuals attempted to take over the commune and set up a strict and harsh regime under their control. The study was deliberately terminated before they could achieve that goal (Fagan, 2011). It was concluded that the movement toward tyranny by the few was not the outcome of uncontrolled or mindless group behaviour, but rather the result of the breakdown of groups and their inability to exert power. Had the groups succeeded in forming an egalitarian commune, the tyrants would have not had the opportunity to emerge. Reicher and Haslam (2006) concluded that it is when people fail in creating a social system with shared social identities that a greater willingness develops to accept extreme solutions proposed by others. In reinterpreting the Zimbardo Prison Study, they note that the prisoners in that study initially formed a shared identity and threatened to dominate the guards. This changed when they were told that they could not quit the study. At that point, they reacted with confusion and stopped supporting one another against the guards. Their collapse as a group allowed the guards to behave towards them in a tyrannical manner. Thus, while group solidarity is often viewed as giving rise to tyrannical actions, it is the failure to form or to maintain a shared social identity that is the real breeding ground for tyranny.

The concept of deindividuation is attractive for many people because it provides an appealing explanation for otherwise senseless behaviour in a crowd context: individuals were disconnected from their sense of personal responsibility. It has even been accepted as an extenuating factor in several murder trials in South Africa (Colman, 1991). In one case, during a night of singing, dancing and great emotion following the funeral of a popular leader, more than a thousand people pursued several vigilantes who had attacked the group. One of the vigilantes was killed and six people were arrested in connection with the death. After viewing a journalist's videotape of the events and hearing expert testimony from a psychologist who argued that the defendants were likely 'deindividuated' at the time of the killing, the court concluded that deindividuation had been an extenuating factor and gave the defendants only custodial sentences.

However, while the deindividuation hypothesis is superficially appealing, there is actually very little evidence to support it. A meta-analysis of 60 independent studies found little support for deindividuated, anti-normative behaviours or for the existence of a deindividuated state (Postmes & Spears, 1998). A more likely explanation for 'uncontrolled behaviour' is simply that people are less restrained from antisocial behaviour when anonymity makes punishment or social sanction unlikely (Freedman, 1982). And the reality is that, most of the time, crowds do not act inappropriately or irrationally. Indeed, people often deliberately seek out crowds for pleasure – such as when they congregate in large numbers at a festival or parade. Think about it for a second: you no doubt have been at times part of one crowd or another, be it at a sporting event, or watching a parade, or at a rally, or taking part in a political demonstration. Did you lose your individuality at such times? Did you hand over control of your thinking processes to some mindless collectivity? And have you ever awakened in bewilderment a day later, stunned by the memory of your behaviour after a crowd took over your thinking? Not likely.

Our personal experience of crowds is generally quite different from what we are often, even in modern times, told about crowds – and some social science textbooks must share the blame for this: Sociologists Schweingruber and Wohlstein (2005) reviewed 20 introductory sociology textbooks and found that all of them presented as fact a number of claims about crowds that actually lack any solid empirical support. These 'myths' include:

1. The *myth of spontaneity* – that groups form without any social norms to govern them, leading to spontaneous collective behaviour unfettered by the usual implicit social controls. There is no good evidence that people in crowds feel free from social controls.
2. The *myth of suggestibility* – that people in crowds become overly suggestible and readily fall under the influence of an emerging leader. Again, there is no good evidence to support this. And if crowds are so suggestible and so willing to follow leaders, why do they not disperse immediately when told to do so by authorities (Couch, 1968)? Obviously, crowds are not swayed by just any leader, and if people are protesting against the authorities, the orders of those authorities are unlikely to be respected.
3. The *myth of irrationality* – that crowds become irrational and this irrationality leads to violence. In reality, crowds are almost always peaceful, and most people in crowds want to avoid violence.
4. The *myth of emotionality* – that people in crowds react more emotionally than they would when away from the crowd. There is no evidence to support the notion that just because people are in a crowd, they automatically become more emotional. However, this is not to say that an individual's normal emotional reaction cannot be intensified by the presence of a crowd; after all, recall the density/intensity hypothesis discussed earlier.
5. The *myth of anonymity* – that individuals, because of anonymity offered by being in a crowd, are more likely to lose their inhibitions and their sense of responsibility and then act in ways that violate the social norms of the larger society. Again, there is no good evidence to support this. It is also important to remember that most individuals in crowds are actually not completely 'anonymous'; they are often there with friends or acquaintances and they remain with them until the crowd disperses.
6. The *myth of unanimity* – individuals coming together in a crowd act as single unit. Not true: In fact, crowds are usually made up of small groups of people who know each other and have more influence on each other than some emerging leader. It is very rare that a crowd acts as a single unit.
7. The *myth of destructiveness* – that crowds are often dangerous or violent. Not true. While it may be easy to bring to mind news reports of violent crowds, such as in the Summer Riots in England, this reflects the availability heuristic (Chapter 2). In reality, few crowds actually become violent, and, even in such crowds, most of the people are only onlookers. Only a minority are responsible for the violence, and there is no empirical basis for suggesting that their violent actions were shaped by the crowd. And when crowd violence does occur, it is typically related to over-consumption of alcohol or other stimulants, or occurs in a situation in which a very large crowd is physically restrained in such a way as to prevent people from freely moving about, thus taking away their sense of individual control (McPhail, 1991).

Yet, even though there is no good evidence that individuals become more suggestible or irrational in crowds, it is not surprising that this may seem to be the case to onlookers. For example, suppose that while swimming at the seaside, you observe someone else running out of the water, and so you do the same. When it subsequently turns out that the mass exit to the shore was triggered by someone having mistaken a beach ball for a shark, observers on the shore may conclude that people were overly suggestible and that they ran like panicked sheep. However, each individual's decision to join the flight to the shore was actually quite rational, for it is safer to assume that others are running out of the water for a reason than it is to wait for personal evidence of danger – a shark, for example – at which point, escape may no longer be possible.

Before leaving this topic, it is interesting to note that Reicher, Spears & Postmes (1995) suggest that just as Le Bon was reacting in his day to perceived threats to the social order and the risk of massive upheaval, so too was Zimbardo's deindividuation theory a reaction to the wave of urban protests that characterized big cities in the United States in the late 1960s. Indeed, Zimbardo himself wrote that his society was in the grip of 'Dionysiac forces' leading to 'motiveless murders, senseless destruction and uncontrolled mob violence' (1969, p. 248).

Crowd behaviour and Social Identity Theory Recall (Chapter 12) that Social Identity Theory describes a three-part process in which: (1) individuals first categorize themselves and others into distinct categories or groups; (2) the norms and stereotypes associated with the category or group become very salient; and (3) people conform to the norms and stereotypes associated with the group. The Social Identity Model of Deindividuation Effects (SIDE) (Reicher, Spears & Postmes, 1995) extends this to crowd situations, positing that in the absence of formal organization and leadership, people in the crowd look to other people close by – often strangers, but sometimes people they know – for cues as to what is the salient social group and social identity. The SIDE model predicts conformity to the norms associated with the specific group or social identity, rather than to the general norms of the larger society. Thus, what might be taken to be deindividuation resulting from anonymity is not uncontrolled behaviour, but instead reflects the effect of the group on enhancing a particular social identity and providing an opportunity for the members of the group to express it (Fagan, 2011). For example, if you are a student immersed in a large group that is protesting your university's policy on some issue, how should you behave? Both the behaviour of others around you and your own stereotype of what is appropriate protest behaviour may lead you to behave quite differently than you normally would.

In the same vein, experimental manipulations used in deindividuation studies may actually strengthen the salience of the newly formed collectivity (e.g., 'I'm playing the role of a prison guard and so are these other people, and we are different from those playing the role of prisoners'). This leads to conformity to norms associated with the specific social identity or stereotype associated with that group. Anonymity and dimly lit rooms, it is argued, may enhance the interchangeability of group members – there is no importance attached to individual identity – and thereby reinforce group, rather than individual, salience (Reicher, Spears & Postmes, 1995; Drury, Reicher & Stott, 2003).

Thus, suppose you are part of a student crowd that has occupied the university president's office to protest poor campus housing. In this case, your salient social identity is that of student protester and you have a certain stereotype of what student protesters are like and how they behave based on your own experience and past learning through books and television. The other protesters have a similar stereotype. When university authorities threaten to evict you, this sharpens the social identity in terms of 'us' versus 'them', and implicit pressure grows to act in the manner that the stereotype of being a student protester suggests – which is not to apologize and go home! Thus, members of the group may ultimately act in an antisocial manner quite out of keeping with general social norms and with their own usual patterns of behaviour. While it may seem to onlookers that the students have developed a collective madness of some sort, they are actually being governed by the social norms associated with their social identity of the moment.

Think again about Zimbardo's (1969) laboratory experiment with the overcoats and hoods: The supposed 'deindividuated' behaviour in the laboratory was actually anything but uncontrolled. The participants did not run amok. True, they administered more electric shocks when supposedly deindividuated, but they had been given permission to do so. There was actually no evidence that the participants became antisocial or were in a state of diminished self-control at the time (Freedman, 1982). And imagine yourself assigned the role of prison guard in the Zimbardo prison study. Is it not likely that all the movies that you have seen involving prison guards have left you with an aggressive stereotype that will influence your behaviour in this artificial situation?

Support for the SIDE model was provided by the meta-analysis mentioned earlier (Postmes & Spears, 1998) that failed to find support for the deindividuation hypothesis, and a number of other studies have also done so (e.g., Douglas & McGarty, 2002; Kugihara, 2001). Rather than being 'deindividuated', people are conforming to situation-specific norms. Further support for the SIDE model comes from research carried out on the Internet. The proliferation of email communication and Internet chat rooms allows for varying levels of anonymity in social interaction among people from all over the world, providing a natural testing ground for ideas about 'deindividuated' behaviour. As one example of such research, Taylor and MacDonald (2002) manipulated the degree of personal anonymity and strength of group identity in email discussion groups and then examined the content of communications, looking for the emergence of 'uninhibited' commentary – that is, commentary that departed from the social norms of the larger society. How much more were correspondents willing to communicate unpopular information when anonymity prevailed? In fact, the data offered no support for the deindividuation hypothesis, but did provide support for the SIDE perspective.

As we leave the discussion of deindividuation, it is important to note that it is unwise to try to explain a crowd's behaviour as though every individual is reacting in a similar fashion or is affected by circumstances in a similar way. Indeed, empirical observations of crowds indicate that they are rarely homogeneous. Some members of a rioting crowd may feel great hostility towards a target, while others may be simply enjoying the excitement, and still others may be trying to get away.

> **KEY POINT:** A crowd is a relatively large and unorganized collection of people temporarily gathered together with no particular relationship between them. There is no evidence to support claims that individuals lose their identity when in a crowd, or that crowds are typically inclined to act in an irrational or aggressive manner. Crowd behaviour is best explained in terms of the social identity that is most salient at the time. Participants in the crowd are influenced by stereotypes associated with that salient identity.

CONTAGION

Contagion is a social psychological metaphor referring to the rapid spreading of emotionality, beliefs and behaviour throughout a crowd or population, somewhat analogous to the spread of disease from person to person. However, rather than Le Bon's idea of a hypnotic influence and the development of a group mind, contagion is brought about by the observable inter-stimulation of crowd members by one another (Wright, 1978). For example, you notice someone standing on a corner looking up, and so you do the same in order to see what that person is looking at. That person in turn sees you looking at the sky, reinforcing his or her belief that there must be something to look at. Others come along and begin to join in, each person both influencing and being influenced by others.

While in this case people consciously chose to imitate the others' behaviour, in other cases, we may automatically mimic an observed behaviour even when we do not intend to do so (Heyes, 2011). Think of the children's game *Simon says*, in which participants have to mimic the actions of the leader, 'Simon', but only when Simon's action is preceded by the phrase 'Simon says do this'. Imitation in the absence of first hearing that phrase results in elimination from the game. However, it is difficult in such a context to avoid automatic imitation of Simon's actions regardless of presence or absence of that verbal instruction. While children playing *Simon says* are aware of their imitations even if they cannot always control them, there is an even more basic form of imitation, behavioural mimicry (recall discussions in Chapters 6, 7 and 9), which involves automatic and *non-conscious* imitation of another person's movements and gestures. For example, in one study (Chartrand & Bargh, 1999), hidden cameras recorded interactions between a participant and a confederate as they discussed a set of photographs. In one condition, the confederate repeatedly touched her face, while in the other, she frequently moved her foot. In the first condition, the participants touched their faces more often than they moved their feet, while the opposite was the case in the second condition, indicating mimicry of the motor response. However, the participants reported being unaware of this mimicry.

Indeed, there is accumulating neurological and developmental research indicating that we are born as great imitators. Within a few weeks of birth, babies imitate motion such as a moving finger, a mouth opening, or a tongue peeking through the lips. This behaviour is not simply the result of conditioning (Meltzoff & Moore, 1977). Although initially there is only simple imitation, by 18 months of age infants can begin to regulate their imitation – for example, when they watch as someone else imitates the experimenter's emotions and that imitation is followed by an angry response from the experimenter, they are less likely to imitate than when there has been a happy or neutral response (Repacholi & Meltzoff, 2007; Repacholi, Meltzoff & Olson, 2008). It appears that automatic imitation is mediated by the mirror neuron system (Heyes, 2011) that we have discussed in earlier chapters. Research into the influence of mirror neurons on social behaviour is ongoing, although a great deal more research is needed before that role is completely understood (Gallese et al., 2011).

But what does this have to do with the spread of emotion throughout a crowd? Remember that we never 'see' other people's emotions; we only observe their behaviour. We are certainly all familiar with the influence that *displays* of other people's emotions can have on us. We are more likely to laugh more in a cinema if others are laughing uproariously; this is the reason that so many television comedies carry laugh tracks in the background. Or if you unexpectedly wander into the midst of an angry crowd protesting a change in campus parking regulations, you may feel yourself becoming angrier too, especially if you share the concern about parking. There is accumulating evidence that such emotional contagion is a genuine phenomenon. For example, Neumann and Strack (2000) told participants that they were in a study of text comprehension, and then had the participants listen to a text being read either in a slightly sad or in a happy voice. The researchers then assessed the participants' moods by means of a questionnaire and concluded that the happy or sad voice did indeed induce a congruent mood state in the listeners. Of course, this should not be surprising for we know just how readily our moods can be changed by watching good actors emote even though we know that they are acting. (Think back to the discussion of empathy in Chapter 9.) While this research focused on reactions to the apparent mood of one other person, other research has studied the emotions of small groups of workers in their natural setting. For example, in one study, 65 community nurses in 13 teams made daily records of their moods and stresses for three weeks. It was found that there was a significant correlation between their moods and those of their team members, and this correlation was not due to sharing the same stresses (Totterdall et al., 1998).

It appears that the induction of a shared mood comes about in a non-conscious manner as a result of an involuntary mimicking of facial expressions. Research shows when people view a facial expression of emotion, a mimicked response in the corresponding facial muscles often automatically occurs within a second, even though the individual may be unaware of this reaction, and this simple motor mimicry then elicits an emotional reaction (Moody et al., 2007). That is, as a result of the automatically mimicked expression, facial feedback then elicits an emotional reaction similar to that of the person who is being mimicked. This is known as the facial feedback hypothesis (Hatfield, Cacioppo & Rapson, 1994; McIntosh, 1996): emotional experience is directly affected by the feedback our brains receive about our facial expressions. (Could this explain why it is often so difficult not to yawn and then feel drowsy when others around us yawn?) This idea actually goes back to Charles Darwin, and it continues to receive growing empirical support (Wild, Erb & Bartels, 2001; Soussignan, 2002). This suggests that if you smile a lot, this may actually lead you to experience a happier mood than if you frown. Perhaps this might explain some of the claims that psychotherapists have made about the supposed benefits of 'laughter therapy', where clients who are stressed, depressed or in chronic pain are encouraged to laugh even if they have to force it.

There are very significant social consequences to such mimicry. It has been found to be associated with increased feelings of trust (Bailenson & Yee, 2005) and affiliation (Hove & Risen, 2009), as increased feelings of interconnectedness develop between the mimicker and the individual being mimicked. These feelings then appear to be extended to others, thus promoting greater empathy and prosocial behaviour in general (Stel & Harinck, 2011). While people are more likely to cooperate with someone who mimics their behaviour, they are also more likely to mimic others with whom they would like to have a trusting relationship (Van Baaren et al., 2004). And we tend to mimic someone whom we like or is a member of our in-group more often than we do someone whom we dislike or who belongs to out-group (Stel & Harinck, 2011).

Stel & Harinck (2011) examined the influence of such mimicry on voting intentions in the Netherlands. It was reasoned that if mimicry leads to increased prosocial behaviour, it should lead people to lean towards left-wing political attitudes associated with increased concern for the welfare of others. The participants interacted with a confederate, who in one condition mimicked some of their behaviours, while in the other condition did not. In an ostensibly unrelated part of the experiment, participants were then asked which party they would vote for if the election were held at that time. The percentage of left-wing voters was significantly higher among participants who had just been mimicked as compared to those who had not.

> **KEY POINT:** Mimicry is a virtually automatic process, something that often occurs without awareness. Mimicked behaviours can trigger corresponding emotional reactions, and, as a result, both behaviour and emotion can be disseminated throughout a crowd.

Types of contagions

The contagion of emotion and behaviour has typically been categorized in terms of the predominant emotion or goal that is involved. We shall consider contagions of expression, enthusiasm, anxiety, fear and hostility in turn.

Contagions of expression Expressive contagions have no particular goal other than emotional release, whether they be motivated by joy, sorrow, frustration or guilt (Klapp, 1972). Although such behaviour may affect an entire society, it is often most apparent in crowd settings. An expressive crowd may gather to pay homage to a new Pope or cheer the return of a Stanley Cup champion hockey team. The emotionality that seems to spread though throngs of gasping teenagers that flock around a rock star provides another example. Such contagions are propelled in part by their own success: as the contagion grows, more people are drawn to see the Pope, or cheer the team, or surround the rock star, which lends increasing importance to the event, in turn drawing more people to join the crowd.

Such enthusiasm can at times lead to disaster. For example, in Mecca in 2006, as tens of thousands of Muslim pilgrims were rushing toward al-Jamarat, a series of three pillars that represent the devil and which the pilgrims strike with stones to purge their sins, some in the crowd tripped and fell, and as the people behind them surged ahead, at least 345 people were crushed to death. And on December 3, 1979, the popular band The Who was scheduled to perform at the Riverfront Coliseum in Cincinnati, Ohio. Seating was unreserved, and when the doors to the Coliseum opened, the large crowd outside began to push their way towards the entrance, and 25 people fell to the ground just a short distance from the entrance. Even though people around them tried to help them up or to shield them from the surging crowd, the surge continued and people were forced over those who had fallen. The pile-up was five people deep, but only a short distance back, people were unaware that people had fallen and continued to push ahead to try to get into the Coliseum. Eleven people died. This sad event was described in the media as a stampede fueled by mob psychology, but nothing could be further from the truth, for people who recognized that there was a problem did their best to help (Henein & White, 2009). Such front-to-back communication failure can occur in any situation where a large crowd is trying to move towards a particular point.

Contagions of enthusiasm Tulips were introduced into Western Europe from Turkey in the middle of the 16th century. Over the next 100 years, they became objects of such admiration, especially in Holland, that anyone of substance without a decent collection of bulbs was held in some contempt. In the period 1634–1636, the interest in tulips was so pronounced that it became known as the Great Tulip Mania, and it swept through Holland, England and France. The cost of bulbs soared so high that tracts of land and even small fortunes were sometimes traded for a single bulb. Special arrangements were made for the sale of rare tulip bulbs on the Amsterdam and Rotterdam stock exchanges. So greedy were the speculators, so anxious were rich and poor alike to profit from the rising market in bulbs that normal industry in Holland fell into serious neglect: the nation had gone tulip-mad. Finally, the market for bulbs, held artificially high by speculators, collapsed and many people suddenly realized they had given up most of what they owned for a collection of tulip bulbs that no one wanted anymore. The Great Tulip Mania is an example of a contagion of enthusiasm (Figure 14.5).

Such contagions involve the spread of an extra-ordinary hope or delusion, usually about becoming wealthy. Thus the Cariboo Gold Rush, which began in 1858, attracted many tens of thousands of people to British Columbia (at a time when the normal population of B.C. was only 7000), almost all of whom dreamed of striking it rich. Forty years later 'Klondike Fever', spiked by rumours of massive deposits of readily obtainable gold, led tens of thousands of people, most of whom had never mined before and knew nothing about survival in the north, to Yukon gold fields (Figure 14.6). Few made their fortune, and as with other contagions the bubble ultimately burst.

Contagions of anxiety A contagion of anxiety involves the rapid dissemination of exaggerated fears throughout a populace, often resulting in unrestrained emotionalism. The Monkey Man of Delhi mentioned at the beginning of this chapter is a good example. So was the Phantom Anaesthetist of Mattoon (Illinois), who in the 1940s was reported to be sneaking around the town with an agricultural spray can and spraying a noxious gas into people's windows at night (Johnson, 1945). Just as there was no Monkey Man, there was no Phantom Anaesthetist either.

This phenomenon is not new, and history offers many dramatic examples. For instance, in the 15th century, a nun in Germany developed a compulsion to bite other nuns who, in turn, began compulsively to bite yet others. Gradually, this bizarre mania spread to convents throughout Italy, Holland and Germany. In the 18th century, there was an epidemic of nuns meowing like cats. It began when a French nun began meowing, and before long other nuns in her convent begin to meow as well. Eventually, all the nuns in the convent were meowing at a certain time each day for several hours a time. This continued until complaints of neighbours brought in soldiers who threatened the nuns with punishment if they did not stop meowing, which brought the problem to an end (Bartholomew, 2001).

These seemingly strange forms of social behaviour present themselves in two different forms

Figure 14.5 The Great Tulip Mania

Figure 14.6 Goldminers crossing the Chilkoot Pass, 1898
Source: © Michael Nicholson/Corbis

(Bartholomew & Goode, 2000; Boss, 1997; Wessely, 1987), although symptoms from both types can occur together (Ali-Gombe, Guthrie & McDermott, 1996). The first and more common form is typically triggered by sudden stress and involves physical symptoms typically associated with anxiety such as hyperventilation, nausea, fainting, dizziness and headaches. Such symptoms usually resolve within a day or so. The second form involves motor behaviours – recall the biting and meowing described above – such as twitching, facial tics, excessive laughing, hysterical dancing, difficulty in communicating, pseudo-seizures, and symptoms of convulsions. In this case, the onset is usually gradual, but symptoms may last for an extended period.

Sometimes the anxiety is manifested as illness. In such cases, otherwise healthy people begin to feel very ill, in the absence of any actual physical disorder, and the apparent illness spreads rapidly to others. This is mass psychogenic illness (Colligan, Pennebaker & Murphy, 1982), also variously referred to as *epidemic hysteria* (Boss, 1997), *mass sociogenic illness* (Weir, 2005; Wessely, 2002), *contagious conversion disorder*, or *mass hysteria*. Anxiety is at the core. We know that when we are anxious, we may feel light-headed or have a queasy stomach, and the heart rate often increases and breathing becomes more rapid. What happens if instead of properly attributing these symptoms to anxiety, an individual interprets them as symptoms of physical illness? And witnessing symptoms of apparent illness in others who share that anxiety or stress can trigger similar symptoms in oneself (Wessely, 2002). Then, when several people begin to report physical symptoms, this becomes of interest to the media, and news reports serve to spread the symptoms. Modern communication, including texting and social media, can almost instantaneously fan the flames of spreading anxiety.

Consider these examples:

- In 1983, 900 people in the Israeli-occupied West Bank, most of them Arab schoolgirls, complained of head-aches, stomach aches, blue discolouration of the arms and legs and even blindness. Initially, Arab leaders charged that Israelis had deliberately caused the malady by spreading toxins, while Israeli leaders claimed the symptoms were being deliberately faked. However, the list of victims grew to include some Israeli military and police personnel. Ten days later, poisoning was ruled out, and authorities concluded that the symptoms were due to hysterical contagion (Hefez, 1985).
- In 1984–85 and again in 1987, two epidemics of *koro*, a rare hysterical disorder characterized by complaints of shrinkage of the penis and an overwhelming fear of impending death, swept through Guangdong, China, affecting thousands of men (Tseng et al., 1988).
- In 1990, fear of 'genital thieves' spread through Nigeria to the extent that after any accidental contact with a stranger in a crowd, a man would quickly grab his genitals to make sure that they were still there. Some-times, and the 'victim' would accost a supposed thief and accuse him publicly, then a crowd would gather, and the 'victim' would disrobe to show that the theft had occurred. Invariably the penis was still there, and people concluded that the thief had returned it after the alarm was raised. Victims often complained the penis had shrunk and so the 'thief' was beaten – occasionally to death – in the attempt to force him to return the organ to its normal size (Bartholomew & Goode, 2000).
- In April 1993, a wave of swooning swept through Egyptian schools, afflicting more than a thousand school-girls and leading to school closings and political debates. Physicians could find no physical basis for the fainting spells and nausea.
- In February 2005, a worker in the Virgin Blue terminal of Melbourne's Tullamarine Airport complained of feeling ill, and within a few hours 47 people reported respiratory problems, dizziness, nausea and vomiting. Forty people were taken to hospital by ambulance, the terminal was evacuated, 60 Virgin Blue flights were cancelled and 14,000 people were stranded. The reported symptoms resolved after short while, and a subsequent investigation could find no medical basis for the reported symptoms (Balaratnasingam & Janca, 2006).

Mass psychogenic illness typically occurs when generalized, diffuse anxiety builds up in a group of peo-ple who fail to recognize its actual causes. Some precipitating event then occurs to which the anxiety can be attributed, and now that the cause seems to have been identified, the 'disease' is born. Anxiety on its own can produce discomfort, sweating, palpitations, nausea, vomiting, terror and even fainting, and as one thinks that one has been poisoned or has caught some terrible illness, anxiety mounts and these symptoms are more likely to be manifested. Personality factors may also play a role in susceptibility to such hysteria: insecure people or those who are on the fringes of the social structure and thus less constrained by group norms may be more vulnerable, although research has failed to demonstrate that any particular personality feature makes one more susceptible to this kind of social influence. Cultural factors are also important, and outbreaks in more traditional societies are much more likely to involve physical acting out, as can be seen in some of the above examples (Bartholomew & Sirois, 1996).

Once a single individual begins to manifest symptoms, others experiencing the same stressors and anxiety who witness this individual's reaction, or who hear of it through word-of-mouth, or formal media reports, or social media, become even more anxious and then begin to interpret their own symptomatology in terms of the supposed illness. If motor behaviours are involved, non-conscious imitation often occurs. When the apparent outbreak of illness begins to spread, epidemiologists quickly try to find the cause, for it cannot be automatically assumed that there is no physical basis. However, once careful testing has been carried out and it has been determined that the afflicted individuals are actually in good health, that reassurance is usually enough to bring the 'epidemic' to an end.

Such events are not all that uncommon. There were 70 documented outbreaks of mass psychogenic illness around the world between 1973 and 1993, including 34 in the United States, seven in India, seven in Singapore, five in England, three in Malaysia, two in Canada and one in each of 12 other countries (Boss, 1997).

KEY POINT: Mass psychogenic illness involves the attribution of symptoms of anxiety to some external event that seems to explain the symptoms. Others who share the same anxiety develop the same symptoms through social influence.

Contagions of fear: Mass emergency behaviour Mass emergency behaviour includes all possible crowd behaviours, rational or irrational, that can occur in a mass emergency event. Such an event occurs when a large number of people face a severe threat, often of death, and have a possible but time-limited avenue of escape (Quarantelli, 2001). It is a popular notion that people in such situations 'panic' and react in a frenzied and non-rational manner as they try to flee. This belief is so widespread that authorities sometimes hesitate to give the alarm for fear of causing panic. For example, the alarm bells on the cruise ship *Andrea Doria*, which sunk at sea in 1956, were not rung for that reason, even though a collision with an approaching ship was unavoidable.

When panic flight does occur, it is because an avenue of escape is available but is closing quickly (Fritz & Marks, 1954). Consider the difference between what occurred on two doomed passenger ships: In 1914, while bound for Liverpool with 1500 persons aboard, the *Empress of Ireland* was rammed in heavy fog in the St Lawrence River. The ship quickly listed so much to one side that only three lifeboats could be launched. One thousand and twelve people had no means of escape and they perished. However, according to reports from those who survived, there was no 'panic'. On the other hand, panic ensued immediately on the *Noronic*, a cruise ship that caught fire in Toronto Harbour in 1949. In this case, escape was possible for all, but although help was close at hand and the fire department arrived quickly, 121 lives were lost in the ensuing scramble.

Consider the collective dilemma that develops when an escape route is perceived to be closing quickly; (recall the discussion in Chapter 10). Each person has two choices of action: to remain calm and proceed in turn, or to run and push one's way towards the exit. If you choose to remain calm, and so does everyone else, then perhaps all will escape. However, if others run, then there is likely to be crowding at the door and many may die; in such a case, by remaining calm you may not be able to escape. Reacting immediately by running and pushing may improve your chances. Thus, flight becomes 'non-social and non-rational' (Quarantelli, 1957) in that the individual thinks of his or her own physical survival and pays no attention to how this action may be detrimental to the collective welfare of the group. The individually 'rational' behaviour is collectively irrational, and many may die in situations where an orderly exit might allow everyone to escape. Organized groups such as military units are rarely participant to panic; because of their training, they respond to the orders of the leader. Only when the leadership structure breaks down is there a risk of panic flight.

Yet careful analysis of actual disasters in several different cultures shows that disorganized flight is actually relatively rare (Pastel, 2001). Most individuals manage to maintain a rational approach and react

The New York Times.

NEW YORK, MONDAY, OCTOBER 31, 1938.

Radio Listeners in Panic, Taking War Drama as Fact

Many Flee Homes to Escape 'Gas Raid From Mars'—Phone Calls Swamp Police at Broadcast of Wells Fantasy

A wave of mass hysteria seized thousands of radio listeners throughout the nation between 8:15 and 9:30 o'clock last night when a broadcast of a dramatization of H. G. Wells's fantasy, "The War of the Worlds," led thousands to believe that an interplanetary conflict had started with invading Martians spreading wide death and destruction in New Jersey and New York.

The broadcast, which disrupted households, interrupted religious services, created traffic jams and clogged communications systems, was made by Orson Welles, who as the radio character, "The Shadow," used to give "the creeps" to countless child listeners. This time at least a score of adults required medical treatment for shock and hysteria.

and radio stations here and in other cities of the United States and Canada seeking advice on protective measures against the raids.

The program was produced by Mr. Welles and the Mercury Theatre on the Air over station WABC and the Columbia Broadcasting System's coast-to-coast network, from 8 to 9 o'clock.

The radio play, as presented, was to simulate a regular radio program with a "break-in" for the material of the play. The radio listeners, apparently, missed or did not listen to the introduction, which was: "The Columbia Broadcasting System and its affiliated stations present Orson Welles and the Mercury Theatre on the Air in 'The War of the Worlds' by H. G. Wells."

Figure 14.7 *New York Times* headline – the Martians are coming

relatively calmly. Researchers who have studied disastrous high-rise hotel fires report that most people do not panic and that most of those who miss opportunities to escape do so because of errors in judgement rather than irrational behaviour (Keating & Loftus, 1981). So it was, following the attacks on the World Trade Center in New York City in September 2001: people in the building reacted in a relatively calm and rational manner. Despite the obvious danger from the intense fires, there was no stampede down the crowded stairwells, but instead people took their turns and helped those who needed help, and as a result the large majority of those people situated below the area where the airplanes struck managed to get out safely (Drury & Reicher, 2010). Thus, we cannot treat all mass behaviour during a mass emergency event as though it inevitably involves panic. Indeed, when an individual in an emergency situation identifies himself or herself as a part of the collection of people trying to escape danger, that sense of shared identity makes it more likely that he or she will act in a manner that reflects concern for the welfare of others. Support for this was found in a study of 21 survivors of 11 mass emergencies (Drury, Cocking & Reicher, 2009). Moreover, that study concluded that a shared identity can emerge even among strangers as a result of the simple fact that they are all sharing the same emergency experience. (Recall the discussion of self- categorization theory in Chapter 12.)

If mass panic is relatively uncommon, where do these notions of panicking crowds come from? The reality is that reports of crowd behaviour in the face of danger can be very misleading, and crowd behaviour in general is all too often 'pathologized' in media reports when in fact individuals were not actually behaving irrationally (Drury, 2002). Consider the example of apparent panic flight that occurred in 1939 when Orson Welles' *Mercury Theatre* radio programme carried a dramatization of H.G. Wells' *The War of the Worlds*, involving fake news reports of Martian landings. It is often stated that despite frequent warnings about the fictional nature of those newscasts, many hundreds of thousands of people ignored those cues, and thinking the invasion to be real, 'panicked' and did their best to flee. We are told that traffic became snarled as people fled, 'heading for the hills' and looking for a place to hide (Cantril, 1940). There is just one problem with this dramatic account: the panic flight never actually happened. Even if many were frightened by what they heard on the radio, there is very little evidence that they did anything more than try to call the police (Bartholomew, 2001; Campbell, 2010) (Figure 14.7).

Another common misperception is that once the immediate danger has passed, people sit around in a daze and are unable to cope. Yet, in reality, only a minority of disaster victims succumb to apathy and shock and then only for a short time. In general, people react immediately and logically to their situation. Looting in such situations is actually very rare, also contrary to popular belief. The myth of a 'disaster syndrome' may have arisen because people seem to run about aimlessly when in fact they are desperately looking for missing friends and relatives (Killian, 1952).

Collective inhibition Arousal in the autonomic nervous system underlies fear, but it also underlies feelings of excitement and pleasure. When something happens that produces intense autonomic arousal, and when this arousal is attributed to danger and there is an avenue to escape, flight may follow. The behaviours of others in the vicinity serve to increase or decrease the arousal level and to suggest an appropriate response, and, if the arousal is interpreted as excitement, there may be no effort to escape. If others stay calm, you may appraise the situation as manageable and then calm down and make a rational decision about what to do next. Taken to its extreme, such collective calmness can itself lead to tragedy. For example, in the early hours of January 1, 1980, a fire broke out during a New Year's Eve party in a social club in Chapais, Québec. Most of the 44 people who died could have escaped but they instead stood in a semicircle watching the fire blaze away. The euphoria of the crowd, the loud music, the alcohol and the wish to avoid looking foolish or cowardly – all these combined to inhibit escape behaviour. Only when it was too late did panic flight occur through a wall of flames, leaving many dead.

Contagions of hostility Aggressive crowds are instances of contagions of hostility – consider for example the Summer Riots mentioned at the beginning of this chapter. However, such contagions can operate over a much longer time frame than is typical of a crowd, and sometimes underlying frustration and hostility is expressed through violence towards scapegoats – individuals who provide safe and easy targets. The word scapegoat comes from the biblical account of the Hebrews ridding themselves of evil by loading their sins onto a goat that was allowed to escape into the wilderness while a companion goat was sacrificed to God. Today, scapegoats do not escape; they are the objects of hostility and violence; see Chapter 13.

In the Middle Ages, commonplace events – a poor crop, hail, a stillbirth – were attributed to the actions of witches; they became the scapegoats for everything bad that happened. Tens of thousands of people were convicted of witchcraft and burned at the stake in Europe between the 15th and 17th centuries. In 1692 in Salem, Massachusetts, a contagion of hostility towards supposed witches occurred on a much smaller scale. Some young girls who had dabbled in black magic developed hysterical illness, which involved convulsive behaviour. They blamed witches for their problems and readily pointed out the 'guilty' adults. The contagion spread beyond Salem to Boston. Twenty people, including a minister, as well as two dogs, were executed as witches.

Another ugly form of contagion of hostility is the baiting crowd (Mann, 1981). This is the kind of crowd that has been observed from time to time to gather around an individual who is threatening suicide by jumping from a high building. People in the crowd, rather than discouraging the individual or looking for ways to prevent the suicide, instead chant 'jump, jump …' Fortunately, baiting crowds are somewhat rare.

> **KEY POINT:** Anxiety, fear, and anger can all find expression through collective behaviours, and the inter-stimulation among people can both justify and reinforce behaviour.

RUMOUR

While collective behaviour is typically associated with crowds, they are not necessary for its appearance. It can occur as readily within a collectivity of people who are not in physical proximity. Indeed, some of the most dramatic instances of collective behaviour such as rumour transmission (which creates a collective belief or apprehension) and fads and fashions, usually occur in the absence of crowds.

A **rumour** is 'a specific … proposition or belief, passed along from person to person, usually by word of mouth, without secure standards of evidence being present' (Allport & Postman, 1947, p. ix). It plays an important role in many forms of collective behaviour, and it is often the mechanism through which a collective perception of a situation is formed within a crowd (Wright, 1978). We are all familiar with rumours – rumours that the prime minister is going to resign, that a leading public figure is having an affair, that the company we work for or the university we go to may be going broke. Some rumours have a basis in fact, but often they simply reflect uninformed fear or consist of bits of speculation and gossip woven into a coherent story.

To be the subject of a rumour can be an extremely trying experience, for rumours, once begun, are very difficult to stop. Denying the allegations carried by a rumour often makes the rumour even more believable to many, for one expects the guilty to protest. Rumours in the marketplace can also have a devastating effect, not only on sales but even on a company's survival. Would you ignore a rumour that a new candy product has been implicated in the deaths of several children, especially if you are a parent? Could you overlook the rumour that a huge international fast-food chain is owned by the Church of Satan? Or that a major brand of bubble gum

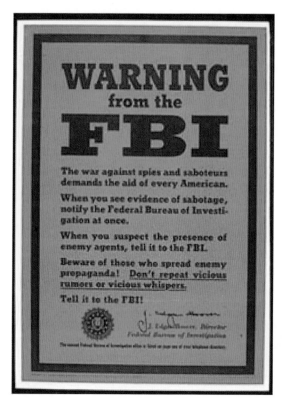

Figure 14.8   Fighting rumours in wartime USA

Figure 14.9   Fighting rumours in wartime Britain

contains spider eggs? These are all examples of actual rumours that have flourished and then died away (Koenig, 1985).

Rumours, even when based on fact, can bring serious harm. Indeed, during the Second World War, Allied nations were particularly concerned, and the United States government instituted a number of measures to try to counteract rumours that were likely to compromise national security or damage civilian morale (Figures 14.8; 14.9). Social psychologists were engaged to study and find ways to combat rumours, and a number of 'rumour clinics' were established to try to decrease their spread through public education (Faye, 2007).

Today, with virtually instantaneous global communication, rumours can bring about dramatic negative consequences very rapidly, both for individuals and for nations (Fine & Ellis, 2010). Stock markets can suffer huge losses following a rumour that a particular nation is about to devalue its currency, or that a large international bank is about to founder. A country that depends heavily on tourism can experience huge economic disruption by a rumour about some disease or other that puts tourists at risk.

It is natural then for marketers to have a considerable interest in the study of rumour transmission. Word-of-mouth appears to be the most effective communication route when consumers make choices about the products they will purchase (Allsop, Bassett & Hoskins, 2007), and, in light of this, word-of-mouth transmission of positive messages is a specific goal of many marketing campaigns (DuBois, Rucker & Tormala, 2011). Positive rumours can help sell a product, while negative rumours can totally destroy a brand.

Why do rumours form? Why are they often repeated so uncritically? Four variables influence their development and transmission (Rosnow, 1991): general uncertainty, credibility, outcome-relevant involvement, and personal anxiety.

General uncertainty General uncertainty refers to widely held doubt and apprehension within a collectivity of people – uncertainty about the identity of a stranger who has been 'hanging around town'; uncertainty about whether the fish plant will be closed and everyone laid off; uncertainty about why the mayor suddenly resigned; uncertainty about whether authorities are giving us the information about the risks of living next to a nuclear power station. In times of uncertainty, when sufficient information through formal channels is lacking, people, whether friends or strangers, rely on one another to fill the information gap (Shibutani, 1966).

The importance of uncertainty was demonstrated in a classic study in which a rumour was planted in a girls' school (Schachter & Burdeck, 1955). Six classes were used, with two classes assigned to each of the three experimental conditions: (1) the cognitive ambiguity condition in which a situation of ambiguity (uncertainty) was created; (2) the rumour condition in which a rumour was planted; and (3) the combined cognitive ambiguity-rumour condition. To create the cognitive ambiguity, the school principal went to the four classrooms in conditions (1) and (3) and did something unprecedented: she pointed to one of the girls, 'K', and instructed her to take her hat, coat and books and accompany her out of the room. Presumably, the students would seek an explanation for this curious event. Then a rumour was planted in the classes in conditions (2) and (3): a teacher asked two girls in each of the pertinent classes, 'Do you know anything about exams that were taken from the office?' Teachers were instructed to record all questions directed to them by the students and this information, plus that gathered from individual interviews of all the students at the end of the day, provided the basic data. As it turned out, practically every girl had heard the planted rumour and made inquiries to one or more teachers. Almost all the questions were of the form 'What happened to K?' or 'Why did the principal take K out of class?' And in classes in which the cognitive ambiguity had been generated, the rumour had the greatest impact. The girls in those classes reported having spent twice as much time discussing the rumour as did girls from the classes given the rumour without the ambiguity manipulation.

Rumour spreading was by no means confined to the planted rumour. The students generated a number of new rumours of their own. Figure 14.10 shows both the numbers of new rumours reported in each condition and the percentage of participants who reported hearing these new rumours. New rumours were most prevalent in the conditions involving cognitive ambiguity where there was presumably a greater need to make sense out of the ambiguity of the situation. Note in Figure 14.10 that cognitive ambiguity alone led to almost as many new rumours as did cognitive ambiguity combined with a planted rumour.

In this fast-moving modern world we are barraged by information from a multitude of news sources, some which we trust, some which we do not. As people strive to make sense of confusion of information, rumours can hardly be ignored, for they may be true or partially true. Those who generate rumours sometimes know what they are talking about, but in any case the rumour itself does not carry information about how much the people who circulate the rumour actually believe it. Sometimes rumours are deliberately spread in the hope that discussion with others will lead to their confirmation or denial (Fine & Ellis, 2010).

Initial uncertainty about the content of the rumour may diminish as it is passed from one person to another, and it often appears to become more and more factual over time. Thus, information clearly viewed as rumour at the beginning may gradually come to be seen as fact, as the uncertainty initially associated with it diminishes with repeated retelling. Conversely, factual information might over time come to be treated as rumour, as initial certainty associated with it diminishes with the retelling.

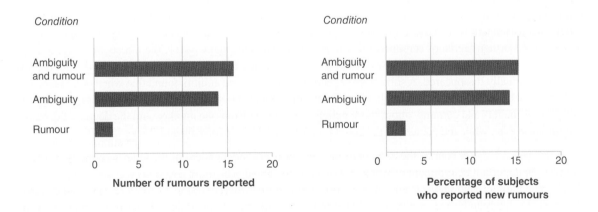

Figure 14.10 Number of new rumours and percentages of students reporting new rumours in the Schachter & Burdeck study

Source: Rosnow & Fine (1976)

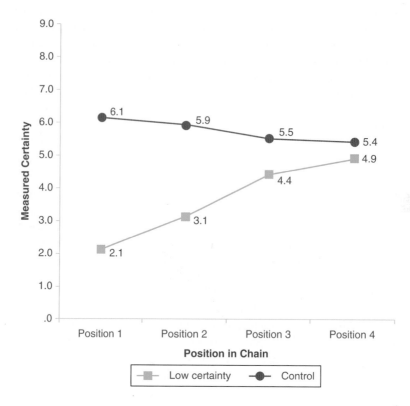

Figure 14.11   Differences as a function of certainty manipulation and position in chain

Source: DuBois, Rucker & Tormala (2011)

In an experiment (DuBois, Rucker & Tormala, 2011), four-person chains of participants took part in a message game. The first participant in each chain would be given a message – a 'negative rumour' – which he or she was instructed to communicate as accurately as possible to the second person in the chain five minutes later, and so on down the chain. There were two conditions. In the first condition, information that a particular restaurant was using worm meat in its hamburgers was communicated to the first individual, along with an indication of uncertainty about the truth of the information. In the control condition, there was no mention of uncertainty. After each participant received the message, he or she reported in writing the content of the message received as well as his or her degree of certainty about it. As can be seen in Figure 14.11, the effects of being told that one was not certain about the truth of the rumour diminished across retellings, so that by the fourth retelling, the effect had virtually disappeared. A subsequent experiment by the same authors found that whether a message is accompanied by a statement of certainty or uncertainty, the effects of both similarly diminish across retellings. In other words, beliefs and certainty about those beliefs are separate from one another, and the degree of certainty can diminish even while the content of the belief remains unchanged (Tormala and Rucker 2007).

Credibility   Of course, the content of the rumour itself, independent of the teller's certainty or uncertainty, is an important determinant of whether it is likely to spread. The more a rumour seems to offer a believable explanation for ambiguous events and the more any reported source for the rumour is considered credible, the more it is likely to be accepted as true, because it serves to reduce uncertainty. It has been observed, to no one's surprise, that believable rumours tend to be spread more often than unbelievable rumours and people often repeat a rumour in a way that increases its credibility by omitting the more dubious elements (Rosnow, Yost & Esposito, 1986). Because it seems so exceedingly unlikely, the rumour that Elvis is alive and well is ignored by most people, despite the many claims that Elvis has been sighted in various parts of the world.

Outcome-relevant involvement However, we do not respond equally to every rumour that reaches us. If the rumour contains information that is relevant to us, we are more likely to pay attention and to repeat it to others. If the fish plant is not relevant to us, we are not likely to pass on the rumour of its closing. However, the involvement does not have to be direct. We may become involved in rumours about a particular actor's marital problems or Rihanna's latest sexual preferences if we are interested in those people or enjoy being titillated by, or titillating others, with such gossipy tidbits.

Personal anxiety In this context, personal anxiety refers to anxiety – acute or chronic – produced by apprehension about an imminent and unwanted outcome (Rosnow, 1991). If you work for the fish plant and production is down, you may be legitimately worried about your job and eager to find out what is going on, making you more susceptible to rumours. Anxiety may in turn diminish the ability to tolerate uncertainty (Rosnow & Fine, 1976). Cognitive dissonance theory suggests that when people are anxious but without good reason, they will strive to find a reason in order to reduce the dissonance between the cognitions 'I am anxious' and 'I have no reason to be anxious'. Rumour may reduce this dissonance (e.g., 'I am anxious because civil war is imminent'). In a similar vein, hostility towards some group can be justified via the rumour 'I don't like the neighbours because they may be communist spies'.

Walker & Beckerle (1987) asked students to retake an examination that they had previously written, ostensibly to help the professor assess the validity of the test. Half the participants were assigned to a 'high-anxiety' condition: while waiting their turn, they witnessed a confederate of the experimenter fail the exam. The other participants were assigned to a 'low-anxiety' condition: they were not exposed to the failing confederate but instead simply reviewed easy sample questions. The confederate also planted a rumour relating to the 'real' reason for having the participant redo the examination. The high-anxiety participants were more likely than those in the low-anxiety condition to repeat the rumour.

> **KEY POINT:** Rumours develop as an attempt to explain unusual events or situations in the absence of clear information about causes. General uncertainty, source credibility, the importance of the rumour to the individual and personal anxiety all influence whether one will believe and/or repeat the rumour. Information relating to uncertainty about the accuracy of the rumour often is dropped as the rumour is repeated.

URBAN LEGENDS

Urban legends have much in common with rumours (Cornwell & Hobbs, 1992). These are accounts of surprising and implausible events that probably never happened but are told and retold as 'true' stories. The source is usually a 'friend of a friend'. For example, Brunvand (1981, 1986) describes accounts of the alligators that supposedly live in New York sewers (the supposed result of people having flushed baby alligators that had been given to children as pets down the toilet); the cement truck driver who catches his wife in bed with a stranger and fills the stranger's convertible with cement; the woman who dries her wet dog in the microwave oven; and the man who is visiting a large city and who wakes up to find himself naked in a bathtub filled with ice with a large incision on his body and a note telling him to call 911 immediately, because he has just undergone surgery and a kidney has been removed! Many such stories endure over time, becoming part of our folklore, and the content often evolves to reflect societal or technological changes. Some seem to be an expression of underlying generalized anxiety. For example, the story about drying the dog in the microwave began to circulate at a time when people were worried about the possible dangers of microwave energy leaking from ovens.

CONSPIRACY THEORIES

Sometimes rumours contribute to and are derived from an interconnected set of beliefs about some supposedly nefarious group that is plotting the destruction of the individual or the society. The attribution of the

Black Death in the Middle Ages to physicians or Jews is but one example. The enduring myth of the 'Jewish-Communist conspiracy' to weaken the Western banking system as a step towards world domination is another. Such a phenomenon has been labelled a conspiracy theory (Graumann & Moscovici, 1987): a collection of people come to share a common but irrational set of beliefs about a group of supposed conspirators and then they apply to these beliefs a very rational and very stubborn logic (Groh, 1987). If physicians are spreading the plague, then stone the physicians.

A conspiracy theory, like an individual rumour, is likely to be believed to the extent that it has some explanatory power for a group distressed by ambiguity and social uncertainty (Kruglanski, 1987). Extreme political movements are often disposed to develop conspiracy theories. The notion of a conspiracy can not only bind the group together emotionally and intellectually, but also explain why the group members seem incapable of obtaining their goals (Inglehart, 1987). A modern example is the 'birther' conspiracy theory in the United States. 'Birthers' consider Barack Obama's presidency to be illegitimate on the grounds that, they claim, he is not a natural-born citizen of the United States as the American Constitution requires. When Obama produced a birth certificate showing that he was indeed born in the USA, birthers viewed that document as a forgery. A Harris public opinion poll conducted in 2010 found that 25% overall of those polled (and 45% of Republicans) shared the belief that he was not born in the USA and therefore was not eligible to be president. Of course, if true, many people must be involved in order to have allowed him to have faked his birth certificate and to have achieved the presidency. How might we explain such a ridiculous point of view? A study involving university students in the United States (Hehman, Gaertner. & Dovidio, 2011) reported that these bizarre beliefs about Obama reflect racial prejudice. The authors suggest that because modern social norms, especially in university settings, dictate that racial prejudice is inappropriate, racially prejudiced individuals may feel the need to legitimize their negative feelings by focusing on something unrelated to race. To believe that his presidency is illegitimate because he is not a native-born American allows one to express negative feelings without appearing, perhaps even to oneself, as racist.

Disasters are often a breeding ground for conspiracy theories as the public tries to make sense of what has happened. Rumour formation typically follows a pattern of crisis management, then blame and then conspiracy (Fine & Ellis, 2010). Initially, people try to get a grip on things as they deal with confusion and anxiety. They try to gather information by talking with others, comparing their impressions in order to deal with the emergency, and prepare for whatever might be coming next. Once the situation has settled down somewhat and some stability has been re-established, the focus of rumours typically shifts to deciding who is at fault for the disaster, and the desire for appropriate justice and punishment grows. A conspiracy theory seems to explain in simple terms what led to the disaster, and identifies a group or groups of enemies. This serves to make vague anxieties more concrete and to increase cohesiveness within the in-group (Campion-Vincent, 2005). Conspiracy theories do not usually make enemies out of groups that in the past were viewed positively; instead it is more likely that they will be aimed at groups of people already held in some suspicion or disdain (Fine & Ellis, 2010).

Prior to the existence of the Internet, rumours, urban legends, conspiracy theories were spread largely by word-of-mouth. The Internet is now the engine for rapid and widespread dissemination of both: large numbers of people interact relatively anonymously with information being fed into the network without any screening for accuracy.

> **KEY POINT:** Urban legends involve attention-grabbing stories that are accepted uncritically; they sometimes reflect widespread underlying anxiety. Conspiracy theories are much more serious and often are based on underlying prejudice towards certain target groups. They claim to identify an otherwise hidden cause of a threatening situation, resulting in the assignment of blame to the target group.

FADS AND FASHIONS

In 14th century England, a passion for twirling a hoop made of wood or metal around the waist swept the country, involving children and adults alike. In 1957, a similar passion, originating in the United States, swept much of the world – this time with hoops made of plastic. Twenty million Hula Hoops were sold in six months. Yet, before long, the passion for Hula Hooping faded, although their use has not died out completely.

This is an example of a fad, one of the most common types of collective behaviour. A fad is a short-lived, extreme, frivolous bit of behaviour that is fun because 'everybody is doing it' (Klapp, 1972). Typically, fads take us by surprise and develop quickly, enjoy widespread popularity for a time and then vanish usually never to appear again. Some fads, such as the 'streaking' fad of the 1970s mentioned earlier, are actually the rebirth of fads that have come and gone decades before. Others, such as flagpole sitting, goldfish swallowing and telephone booth stuffing, have come and gone and, so far at least, have never returned.

Fad behaviour involves a great deal of anonymous interpersonal interaction. People do not directly com-

Figure 14.12   Kids and hula hoops
Source: © Bettmann/Corbis

municate about whether they should swallow a goldfish or run naked through crowds, but all know whether the behaviour is in keeping with the times. They can anticipate how others will react to them. No one can predict when a fad will appear or what its nature will be.

A fashion is more serious than a fad in that it begins with something perceived as necessary: we all need clothes. Many billions of dollars are spent around the world on clothing, and so fashion in clothing is of considerable consequence. A fashion is more likely than a fad to be cyclical, and bygone fashions often are brought into vogue again. Fashion plays an important role in self-definition and in interpersonal relationships. Choice of fashion often reflects one's group membership, or the tastes of a group to which one aspires to belong. New fashions are sometimes 'risky' in that they attack or violate existing social norms, and the early adopters undoubtedly enjoy the attention that their new fashion attracts. Yet, what is viewed as risqué today is likely to become blasé tomorrow. For example, when the brassiere first made its appearance, women who wore one were considered to be shameless because the undergarment accentuated the bust-line. Yet, when some women in the 1960s began going without brassieres, as their grandmothers and great-grandmothers had done, they were greeted with similar criticism. The low-cut jeans worn by young women in the early 2000s were also viewed as provocative by older generations. And fashion involves more than just clothing: Moustaches, definitely 'out' in the 1950s, were definitely 'in' in the 1970s and 1980s. Long hair, the virtual symbol of counterculture in the 1960s and early 1970s, became acceptable in the mainstream (and remains widespread among artists and musicians), but then the fashion moved in the direction of shorter hair. By the 2000s, earrings became almost *de rigueur* among teenage males. Yet piercing the ears for earrings is only part of a larger fashion, one that is much more startling to many older people: body piercing has gained popularity, with incisions for rings being made in virtually all parts of the body including eyebrows, lips and sexual organs.

Since fashion continues to change, it must serve some important function. While there is no good research on the subject, sociologists have suggested that being 'in fashion' serves both to mark a person's status – or at least status aspirations – and to relieve the banality of modern technological society (Klapp, 1972).

Status marking

Status marking through clothing serves to communicate the wearer's status (real or coveted). Even such fashions as piercing can serve to mark one's status within a particular group and can be used to differentiate oneself from more 'traditional' or conservative people. Yet, in recent years there has been an anti-status marking trend in some circles: Dressing as casually as possible for work was particularly embraced within new and creative 'dot.com' companies, and in itself became a kind of status symbol, showing perhaps that one was important enough not to have to follow arbitrary dress codes. And not that many years ago, physicians wore laboratory coats, nurses dressed in white and wore caps, nuns were easily recognized by their habits, university professors wore academic gowns, and academic staff dressed in business attire. All of this served to reflect particular social order; it was easy to know a person's status by how the person was dressed. Nowadays, one can no longer distinguish one professional from another simply on the basis of their attire.

Status marking is nothing new, of course. Historically, fashions, especially clothing fashions, have distinguished people of different social levels, making it easy to recognize an aristocrat or a peasant. However, for those who could afford it, there was always the temptation to emulate the dress of those a little higher in the hierarchy, which suggests a reason for the ever-changing fashions of the elite: they sought constantly to differentiate themselves from lower-status imitators. In fact, there have been occasions when the law itself has been used to prevent people from dressing above their social level. For example, the *sumptuary laws* of medieval England specified what type and colour of clothing, and with what trim, could be worn by people of various social ranks. By forbidding people to dress above their station, social confusion was to be avoided, while at the same time these laws discouraged both extravagant spending and the import of foreign textiles.

Today, of course, fashion is not determined only by an elite; almost any group may be the source of some new style. Consequently, fashion serves to communicate more than social class; it can also tell others about a person's attitudes, values and lifestyle. A professor who always wears a suit and tie is making a statement quite different from that of a professor who dresses in a sweatshirt and jeans. For some people, it is important to be 'up-to-date'; they derive attention and respect from being 'well dressed', which can lead to slavish adherence to fashion trends. There also seems to be a widely understood 'language' of clothes that allows people to 'read' other people or to tell others about themselves. (Recall the discussion in Chapter 7 of artefacts as communication.) For example, in a British study (Gibbins & Coney, 1981), teenage girls substantially agreed on characteristics of girls who wore various types of clothes, including whether the girls smoked or drank and how many boyfriends they were likely to have. This fashion sense is acquired early: Grade 4 and 6 children have been found to make personality inferences about others – including inferences about friendliness and popularity – on the basis of the brand of jeans worn (Solomon, 1986).

Banality Novelty appears to be a primary reinforcer of human behaviour (Berlyne, 1960); we seem predisposed to be curious and attracted to new stimuli. If all cars were grey, many people would prefer a red one or a yellow one, and if everyone is wearing a white shirt, someone may wear a blue shirt to be 'a little different'. Changing fashions, whether in clothing or cars, can alleviate boredom and assert our individuality.

How do fashions spread? While an element of contagion is involved, there is reason to believe that most people hesitate before risking ridicule or rejection by adopting some new fashion. Instead, there is a two-step flow of communication (Katz & Lazarsfeld, 1955; Rogers, 2003/1962): Local opinion leaders who are most knowledgeable about fashion trends are the first to don the new garb and their action indicates to others that such fashion is acceptable. (Recall the discussion of acceptance of innovation in Chapter 6.)

> **KEY POINT:** Fads are typically frivolous behaviours that spread rapidly throughout a society, and generally have no purpose apart from the pleasure produced both by novelty and by being part of a rapidly developing social trend. While in the past, clothing fashions served to delineate class boundaries, this is no longer the case, and one's choice of clothing serves to make a statement about oneself, as well as to counter boredom and banality.

SOCIAL MOVEMENTS

In September, 2011, the *Occupy Wall Street* movement took over Zuccotti Park in New York City's Wall Street area in an event initiated by *Adbusters*, a Canadian-based, pro-environment, anti-consumerist organization that publishes a respected international activist magazine of the same name. The protesters' slogan, *We are the 99%*, was intended to draw attention to the disparity between enormous wealth of the top-earning 1% and the relatively modest means of the rest the population. The goals were lofty – bank reform, equitable distribution of wealth, social equality and democratic renewal, but specific demands were not articulated, making it difficult for authorities to consider any form of compromise even if they were motivated to do so. Within only a few weeks, the idea quickly spread, and *Occupy* protests were soon occurring in cities around the world, from Armenia to Canada to Cyprus to Israel, New Zealand, Nigeria and Switzerland, 82 countries in all, and often involving tent communities in urban public spaces. Although helped by social media, why did the *Occupy* message resonate so loudly in so many different societies? Was it the beginning of a world-wide social movement? And why did it not endure?

A **social movement** is defined as 'a spontaneous large group constituted in support of a set of purposes that are shared by the members' (Milgram & Toch, 1969). The study of social movements overlaps with what we have already learned about crowd behaviour, for such movements involve rallies, protest marches, and occasionally they even spawn riots. Typically, a social movement is aimed at either promoting or resisting change in society, and it attracts people who feel that a problem exists, that something can be done about it, and who *want* to do something about it (Toch, 1965). Initially, there are no specific rules or norms or procedures that define people's interactions with one another. However, as people begin to coalesce, leaders gradually emerge, specific goals are articulated, tactics are chosen and recruitment efforts are made. Modern history has witnessed many social movements that have had dramatic and fundamental effects on the societies in which they occurred – for example, think of the women's suffrage movement, the civil rights movement in United States, the modern feminist movement, the gay rights movement, Ghandi's *Quit India* movement, Mandela's anti-apartheid movement, and the ill-fated student movement in China that led to deadly reprisals in Tiananmen Square. Such movements are considered to be a form of collective behaviour because their initial development and spread are more or less spontaneous and not under the control of those who are at the root of the movement. Whether the movement actually takes hold and becomes a major force for change in the society is beyond the power of any individual or group to decide.

Social movements usually begin very slowly. Some soon die out, while others grow and eventually evolve into a formal organization that continues to pursue the desired social change. Such groups can endure for years, decades and longer. Rohlinger & Snow (2003) identify four basic concepts involved in the formation of social movements: grievances, symbolization, emotion and identity:

- *Grievances*: If there were no widely shared grievances, social movements would never spring up. Think of the Arab Spring. There were good reasons for people to join the rallies; they were upset at dictatorial rule and inspired by the possibility of democracy.
- *Symbolization*: This refers to how people choose a particular target as a symbol of their grievances and then decide upon actions that they need to take to reduce or eliminate these grievances. Leaders emerge who are able to articulate their goals, stimulate people to action, and explain their goals to the larger public in order to draw more people into the movement. For example, during the uprisings of the Arab Spring, the president in each country became the symbol of all that was wrong, and the short-term goal was to force his resignation.
- *Emotion*: Emotion plays a significant role in the development of social movements, just as it does in most collective behaviours. Strong emotional feelings about an issue lead individuals to commit themselves to the movement, and to work hard for the movement so that it can be sustained over the long-term even in the face of disappointment in the short term.
- *Identity*: Those who participate in a social movement typically develop a strong identification with it and a sense of 'us against them'. This identification helps motivate people to stay with the movement and to work to achieve its goals.

But given that the world is awash in grievances, why is it that social movements emerge in some circumstances and not in others? It cannot simply be due to hunger or privation, or social and economic inequality, for these conditions have reigned in many parts of the world for centuries with no particular signs of the social unrest that could give birth to a social movement. It is usually not the actual degree, but the *relative* degree of privation that is important. (Recall the discussion of social comparison in Chapters 3 and 10.) When people compare themselves to other appropriate groups and find that the others are – seemingly unfairly – better off,

455

this leads to frustration and discontent and provides a basis for the social unrest that underlies the growth of social movements. Poor individuals in British Columbia, or New South Wales or New Delhi may be frustrated when they compare themselves to a neighbour who has a better home and a higher income, but if they do not see themselves as being part of a deprived group – that is, their comparison stays at the interpersonal level – collective action is unlikely to emerge. It is intergroup comparisons that feed social movements, and the comparison need not be in terms of housing, food or material wealth; it may reflect perceived differences in power or status within the larger society. But for a social movement to develop, members of the deprived group must also perceive their deprivation as unjust. If people believe those differences in power and wealth are divinely ordained or are due to their own inferiority, they are likely to accept their status with resignation. Of course, people only begin to agitate for change when they feel that there is some chance that change will occur. In totalitarian states, demands for change can produce massive reprisals, and social movements are quickly stifled, as for example in Tiananmen Square. (Recall the discussion of the *legitimacy*, *stability* and *impermeability* of group boundaries, Chapter 12.)

However, oftentimes those who lead and participate in social movements are not the poor, the disadvantaged, the 'huddled masses'. Social movements are more usually led by educated, highly principled and non-deprived individuals who take it upon themselves to fight for fairness towards those who are too weak or too disorganized or too politically unsophisticated to stand up for their own needs. The Mahatma Gandhis and Nelson Mandelas of the world did not inspire movements because of their own privations, but rather because of principled concern for their fellow human beings.

Finally, it is important to note that not all social movements spring from legitimate grievances on the part of the downtrodden. For example, think of the anti-immigrant social movements in some European countries, some of which have morphed into political parties. The right-wing Tea Party movement in the United States is another example; it drew on general anger towards the political establishment, promoted both tax reduction and reduced government spending, demanded freedom from government interference in people's lives, and rejected 'socialist' health-care policies.

Types of social movements The goals of social movements vary from very general (e.g., to gain equality for women or to fight for better working conditions in developing countries) to very specific (e.g., to prevent clear-cutting in British Columbia forests or to oppose the World Trade Organization). There is an important difference between reform movements and revolutionary movements. Reform movements accept the basic structure of society but seek to modify part of it (Blumer, 1969), while revolutionary movements seek to overthrow the existing social order. As a result, revolutionary movements are often driven underground while reform movements usually appear respectable and attempt to gain support through discussion and persuasion. Reform movements try to win the support of the middle class, while revolutionary movements typically appeal to those in the oppressed or distressed group.

The life of a social movement Although there are exceptions, social movements typically develop through a series of four stages (Blumer, 1969; Macionis & Gerber, 2011):

1. *Emergence*: At its inception, a social movement often reflects no more than social unrest, a restless dissatisfaction with contemporary society coupled with a dream about a new kind of society. At this stage, there are just grievances. The suffragist movement, the women's liberation movement and the gay liberation movement all began when various individuals expressed their dissatisfaction with their role in society. There are as yet no definite goals, and agitators are likely to play an important role as they try to make people aware of the shortcomings of contemporary society. Such 'consciousness-raising' is important, for unless others become aware of the problems that they apparently endure, they are unlikely to show interest in the movement.

2. *Coalescence*: Gradually, more definite ideas about the causes of their problems and about their goals emerge, and popular excitement develops. More and more individuals are drawn into the movement, some because they identify with the cause and others because the perceived potential benefits outweigh the costs (Simon et al., 1998). Challenges to the contemporary social order become more frequent and powerful. However, this often triggers a push back from those who wield the formal levers of power in the society.

3. *Bureaucratization*: As a social movement gathers impetus, it gradually takes on formalized organizational form with leaders, division of duties and an agenda (Blumer, 1951). Policies are formalized and a leader, likely to be a kind of statesperson, is chosen. An ideology or a collection of beliefs, myths and doctrines develops along with it. The ideology defines and defends the goals of the group, condemns the existing social order, outlines policies and tactics and contains the myths of the group. The intelligentsia of the group generally provide a highly respectable formal ideology that can be defended to certain members of the intelligentsia outside the movement. However, the ideology also takes on a popular form for the masses, composed of emotional symbols, stereotypes and so on.

4. *Decline*: Every social movement reaches a point where it begins to decline, either as a result of success or failure. Failure may come about for a number of reasons: splintering into competing factions because of internal disagreements; repression by authorities; or being abandoned by the leader. Success also leads to decline: As time goes by and the social movement gains more support within a society, radical demands gradually typically decline (Milgram & Toch, 1969). This makes the organization less threatening to society at large and leads to an institutionalization of the movement, whereby it evolves into a fixed organization with a formal structure and specific division of duties and becomes a part of regular society. Alternatively, the social movement may be absorbed, or 'co-opted', by an existing and more powerful social organization that has seen fit to take on its cause.

Social movements are an important engine of change that forces the society to respond to long-overlooked or changing needs. As yesterday's social movements become today's institutions, new movements, some large, some relatively small, grow up. Even in societies dominated by rigidity and totalitarianism, social movements sometimes take root despite powerful efforts to prevent them. Recall how Nelson Mandela, discussed in Chapter 3, spent many years in a South African prison, finally to emerge and become the president of the nation!

KEY POINT: Social movements are an engine for social change and continue to play an important role in societies around the world. Their development reflects widely shared grievances within a society and an effort to change society to eliminate the grievance.

A FINAL NOTE

Recall the words of John Donne, 'No man is an Iland, intire of itselfe; everyman is a peece of the Continent, a part of the maine.' As we learn more about our automatic tendency to imitate others, as we see how emotions and behaviours and beliefs can spread, sometimes rapidly, through a group or an entire society, Donne's words take on new significance. Our mutual influence upon one another, whether we are aware of it or not, is constant and powerful.

SUMMARY

1. Collective behaviour emerges spontaneously in a group of people. It is relatively unorganized and unplanned and is the product of inter-stimulation among participants.

2. The view that crowds take on a mind of their own and that the individual in the crowd gives up personal responsibility and rationality is mistaken, but is part of a widely held mythology.

3. Population density is not equivalent to crowding, which is an aversive psychological state. Four models of the effects of crowding have been proposed: sensory overload; density–intensity; loss of control; and an

attributional model. In general, one's sense of control appears to determine whether a situation of high population density will be experienced as crowding.

4. Collective behaviours may occur without interpersonal contact. These include fads, fashions and contagions of expression, enthusiasm, anxiety, fear and hostility.

5. Contagion refers to the rapid spread of beliefs, emotionality and behaviour throughout a crowd by means of suggestion, rumour and imitation.

6. One explanation for the contagion of antisocial behaviour is provided by deindividuation theory, which refers to a loss of a sense of personal identity leading to a lowering of normal restraints on behaviour. Conditions said to contribute to deindividuation include a loss of identifiable characteristics (e.g., wearing a mask), loss of responsibility, an arousing group activity, loss of temporal perspective and a novel situation without the usual restraining cues.

7. Deindividuation theory lacks good empirical support. A more recent theory, the Social Identity Model of Deindividuation Effects (SIDE), has received considerable

empirical support. It is based on Social Identity Theory and the norms associated with the salient social identity.

8. Mass psychogenic illness refers to the spread of a strong emotional reaction accompanied by physical symptoms with no physical cause. This is often triggered by some unusual event that occurs in the context of ongoing stress or anxiety, combined with the spreading of rumours.

9. Uncertainty, outcome relevance, personal anxiety and credibility all influence whether an individual is likely to be influenced by and repeat a rumour.

10. Fads and fashions are related to status marking, which is the desire of people to identify with certain groups and to differentiate themselves from other groups. Fads and fashions also provide relief from the banality of everyday life.

11. Social movements are large groups formed spontaneously in support of shared goals. They often develop through stages of social unrest, popular excitement, formalization and institutionalization.

POINTS TO PONDER

- Why it is so widely believed that crowds develop a mind of their own, when, as individuals, we do not see ourselves as having abandoned our rationality when in a crowd?
- When large-scale anti-social behaviour does occur, and when transgressors are interviewed and explain that they don't know what overcame them, that they were caught up in the action of the crowd, is their claim to be a matter of deliberate shirking of responsibility, or is it more likely that the transgressor is automatically making attributions that spare him or her personal guilt?
- If you wear a tattoo or a piercing, did you make a rational choice or were you trying to fit in with others who are important to you, while at the same time distinguishing yourself from many other segments of society?
- Undoubtedly, we have all contributed to rumour transmission. Is it wise not to pass on a rumour when something important seems to be going on in the absence of direct information?

FURTHER READING

Bartholomew, R.E. (2001). *Little green men, meowing nuns and head-hunting panics: A study of mass psychogenic illness and social delusion*. Jefferson, NC: McFarland.

An excellent study of collective behaviour across the ages. Using case histories from medieval times to the present, the author explores the psychology of mass hysteria and social delusions.

Fine, G.A. & Ellis, B. (2010). *The global grapevine: Why rumours of terrorism, immigration and trade matter*. New York: Oxford University Press.

The authors explore four major foci of contemporary rumours: immigration, terrorism, international trade and tourism. Such collective behaviours are analysed in terms of how they reflect the anxieties of the culture in which they spread.

Goodwin, J. & Jasper, J.M. (Eds) (2009). *The social movements reader: Cases and concepts.* New York: Wiley.

    A collection of articles relating to social movements around the world. New developments in theoretical and empirical approaches to the study of social movements are discussed.

Mackay, C. (1841/1932). *Extraordinary popular delusions and the madness of crowds.* New York: Farrar, Straus and Giroux.

    A classic mid-19th-century account of some of the great collective delusions throughout history. Collective behaviour, in keeping with the spirit of the time, is viewed as irrational and even pathological.

WEBLINKS

http://www.badfads.com/

    An entertaining website that presents numerous fads that have come and gone.

http://www.snopes.com/

    A highly respected website devoted to the vetting of urban legends, rumours, and myths.

http://www.prisonexp.org/

    Philip Zimbardo's website dedicated to the discussion and description of his Stanford Prison Study.

http://www.bbcprisonstudy.org/bbc-prison-study.php?p=17

    A website describing the BBC replication of the Stanford Prison Study.

PART VI

SOCIAL PSYCHOLOGY
IN ACTION

CHAPTER 15
APPLIED SOCIAL PSYCHOLOGY

There is nothing so practical as a good theory.
Kurt Lewin

LEARNING OBJECTIVES

* To understand the limitations of eyewitness testimony in judicial trials

* To understand the dynamics of a jury and how these are studied

* To understand the two types of justice, and how we judge whether a decision has been fair

* To learn the fundamental beliefs that people have about justice itself

* To understand the psychosocial influences on health, including socioeconomic status, stress, social support, perceived control and personality dispositions

* To understand how intimate relationships can protect health and how loneliness can be a health risk

* To explore the psychosocial processes underlying health-care treatment, including communication between patient and physician and the vexing issue of patient noncompliance

* To apply theoretical models of how people make decisions about health and act on them

* To understand well-being as more than an absence of symptoms

Social psychology is much more than an academic discipline; it also has a long history of real-world application of its theories and research findings in a wide range of settings – schools, hospitals, sports, labour-management negotiations, environmental planning, and international conflict resolution, to name but a few. Throughout the earlier chapters, we have seen a number of instances of how social psychology can be applied. Consider these examples: Research on language has brought about improvements in the methods of second-language acquisition; research on intimacy has been applied to enhancing relationships; and research on persuasion has led to more effective advertising techniques. And, of course, research into prejudice has played an important role in the societal battle against discrimination.

In this final chapter of this book, we focus on two important areas of contemporary application of social psychology: justice and the law, and health and well-being. What can social psychology tell us about instances in which people have been wrongfully convicted of a crime? Why is eyewitness testimony often unreliable and how might it be improved? What about the countless thousands of people who have died as a result of tobacco smoking? Can social psychology be used to influence present-day smokers to abandon self-destructive behaviour?

SOCIAL PSYCHOLOGY AND THE LAW

Figure 15.1 Courtroom scene
Source: Everett Collection/Shutterstock.com

Few events in contemporary life have the compelling drama of the criminal trial. Countless novels, movies and television programmes have been built around this familiar sequence of legal events. The intensely competitive atmosphere, the consequences for the accused, victim, families and lawyers, and the clash of different interpretations of the same evidence all contribute to a fascinating arena in which to observe human social behaviour. Thus, it is not surprising that psychologists have been interested in the legal system since the early days of the discipline (Munsterberg, 1908). Events in the courtroom constitute a social world in miniature in which everyday social psychological processes are magnified because the stakes are so high (Pennington & Hastie, 1990). Consider these questions:

- The police take reports of eyewitnesses. Do the eyewitnesses remember and report accurately?
- On the basis of eyewitness and other evidence, the police develop a hypothesis about the crime. How does this influence their investigation and their interpretation of evidence?
- A suspect is apprehended and identified from a police line-up. Could the witness have been subtly pressured by the police to make an identification or could the line-up itself have biased this identification?
- The case goes to trial. How do the persuasive abilities of the prosecuting and defence lawyers influence the jury? How could biases among the jurors influence the verdict?

THE TRIAL

The witness

While physical evidence, such as a fingerprint, a document or DNA, may be available, the most convincing and decisive evidence is often the testimony of an eyewitness, someone who can identify the perpetrator and describe what happened (Loftus, 1974, 1979; Lindsay, Wells & O'Connor, 1989).

Even though the eyewitness may be honestly attempting to be truthful and accurate, there are two issues to consider: (1) Is the testimony of an eyewitness usually accurate? and (2) Do the judge or jurors believe such testimony? Let us consider these questions in the light of research evidence.

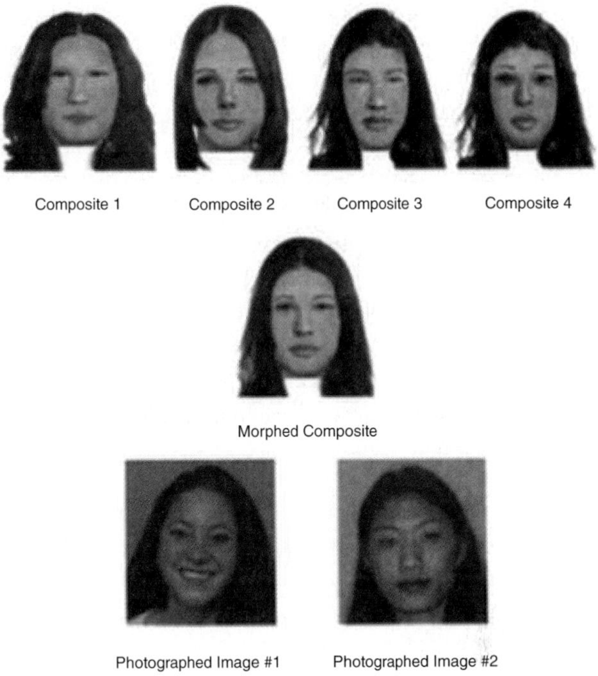

Eyewitness accuracy In days gone by, a sketch artist would sit with an eyewitness and develop a drawing that captures the details presented by an eyewitness. Nowadays, sophisticated software is used that provides many different categories of facial features (e.g., hair, chin, ears, eyes), and within each category, there are many choices, for instance, 33 goatees and 593 nose shapes. Once a feature is selected, it can be moved or sized according to the directions of the eyewitness. After each of several witnesses has developed a sketch of the target person, the software then combines the various images to create a composite, which generally is more accurate than each individual sketch alone (Figure 15.2).

Can we depend on the accuracy of eyewitnesses (Wells, 1978)? Consider the following fact: The most common cause of the wrongful conviction of an innocent person is a mistaken report of an eyewitness (Wells, Memon & Penrod, 2006). And, yet, jurors continue to overestimate the accuracy of eyewitnesses (Wells & Hasel, 2008).

Composite 1   Composite 2   Composite 3   Composite 4

Morphed Composite

Photographed Image #1   Photographed Image #2

Four individual composites, a morph of the four individual composites, and the comparison photographs.

Figure 15.2 A composite morphed image from the recall of several witnesses

Source: Hasel & Wells (2007)

Several decades ago, in 1972, the US Supreme Court suggested five criteria for evaluating the testimony of an eyewitness:

1. the opportunity of the witness to view the criminal clearly at the time and place of the crime;
2. the extent to which the witness was paying attention to the incident;
3. the accuracy of the witness's description of the criminal before seeing the accused;
4. the extent to which the witness is confident of what he or she saw;
5. the time elapsed between the crime and the identification.

Most people, as potential jurors, would accept these criteria as reasonable (Kassin & Barndollar, 1992), but the research does not give us reasons for confidence that any of them will protect us from eyewitness error (Wells & Murray, 1983; Krug, 2007). For instance, research shows that the level of illumination during the event (daylight, early twilight, night) will not necessarily predict greater accuracy. In addition, the relationship between confidence and accuracy is inconsistent (Wells, Olson & Charman, 2002).

Consider the following research (Buckhout, 1980). Television viewers in New York City were shown a 127-second tape of a simulated incident in which a mugger stole a woman's purse and then ran directly towards the camera. Viewers were then shown a six-person line-up that included the actual criminal and were invited to identify that person. Of the 2145 viewers who called the station, only 15.3% correctly identified the mugger, which is close to what would be expected by pure chance. In fact, 33% identified the white assailant as being black or Hispanic, and a few were even convinced that the same actor had also victimized them in the past! In other experiments, research participants showed large variations in their estimates of a perpetrator's height (average error of 20 cm), hair colour (83% in error) and age (average error of eight years) (Loftus, 1979).

In another experiment (Wells & Olson, 2002), participants were shown a video of what appeared to be a terrorist planting a bomb. At one point, the camera zoomed in to focus clearly on the perpetrator's face. Participants were then shown a photo line-up of six people who looked similar to the bomber, but none of the people in the photo was the bomber. Nonetheless, all participants identified one or another of the pictures as that of the perpetrator. After having made their choice, participants were then randomly assigned to several conditions. Some were told of evidence that seemed to corroborate their identification, others were informed of evidence that exonerated the individual that they had identified, and still others were given no feedback. Participants were then asked a series of questions about how confident they were in their choice. As expected, those told that the evidence confirmed their decision were more confident than those who were not. However, confidence did not mean accuracy: none of the alternatives was correct.

Other factors influence our ability to identify someone accurately. For example, we are usually more able to identify people of our own race than those of other races (Brigham & Malpass, 1985; Luce, 1974; Shepherd, Deregowski & Ellis, 1974). In part, this is because people tend to perceive people of other races as more similar to each other than they really are; 'they all look alike', and, as a result, more errors in identification are likely to occur (Barkowitz & Brigham, 1982).

In a meta-analysis of 128 relevant experiments involving 16,950 research participants, Shapiro and Penrod (1986) found that a number of variables influence accuracy in facial recognition. These included whether research participants made inferences about psychological traits or looked for distinctive features of the face; whether the target was seen as distinctive or unusual; whether the target's face had been changed in some way between the time of observation and identification (glasses, hairstyle or expression); and whether identification (that is, memory) was tested in the same context in which the target had been observed.

Memory distortion People who witness an event may later be exposed to new, often misleading information about that event, or 'leading questions' by investigating officers or lawyers. As a result, recollections of the event may become distorted (Loftus, 1992). In one research study, participants were shown a simulated traffic accident. Then they received a written report about the accident, which, in some cases, provided incorrect information. For example, when a stop sign was referred to as a yield sign, participants given this misinformation tended to report that they had seen a yield sign (Zaragoza & Mitchell, 1996).

The stress of witnessing actual or threatened violence may distort memory of the event (Yarmey & Jones, 1983a). Witnesses tend to fix their gaze on unusual or significant objects such as a weapon or an injured person (see Yarmey & Jones, 1983b; Christianson & Loftus, 1991), rather than the perpetrator. Research on the relationship between emotional stress and memory shows that eyewitnesses tend to be relatively accurate under these conditions in remembering central details but relatively inaccurate in remembering peripheral details (Christianson, 1992). However, in another experiment (Porter, Spencer & Birt, 2003), participants viewed a series of photographs that had been previously shown to arouse either positive emotions or disturbing emotions (e.g., a picture of a fatal accident) or to be neutral with regard to emotional arousal. Half of each group was then exposed to misleading questions such as the suggestion of a large animal in the picture. Later, all participants were asked to recall the scene and asked a series of questions including some about the nonexistent animal. As expected, having been exposed earlier to the misleading questions increased false memories about the picture, particularly where strong negative feelings had been aroused.

The police line-up In a police line-up, a witness is asked to identify the perpetrator from among a number of people similar in their physical characteristics. Witnesses are more likely to identify someone in a line-up as being the perpetrator – and they are often mistaken – than they are to positively identify a person presented as a single suspect (Gonzalez, Ellsworth & Pembroke, 1993; Brewer & Palmer, 2011). Why? It is argued that an evaluation of a single suspect requires an absolute judgement – ('This is the person that I saw') – while a line-up leads to a relative judgement as to which of the persons most resembles the witness's memory of the perpetrator. Moreover, confidence does not predict accuracy in that judgement (Sporer, Penrod, Read & Cutler, 1995).

Think of a line-up procedure as analogous to research procedures (see Chapter 1), in the sense that police officers test their 'hypothesis' regarding a suspect (Yarmey, 1979; Wells & Luus, 1990). The procedure can be subject to 'experimenter biases'; for instance, the suspect may be placed among a group of police officers (out of uniform) who tend to turn their eyes slightly towards the accused (Gilligan, 1977). In other cases, the line-up consists entirely of suspects in the case, which tends to increase the probability of misidentification perhaps because all of them show signs of nervousness (Wells & Turtle, 1986). Varying instructions, such as whether the subject is told that the perpetrator is in the line-up, can also influence responses (Kohnken & Maass, 1988). Showing witnesses mugshots may bias later identification in a line-up (Brigham and Cairns,1988). The critical feature of a line-up is not the absolute number of people but the functional number. For example, if the suspect is known to have been fat and there are only two fat people in the line-up, the functional number is only two, and there is a 50% likelihood of one of them being identified by pure chance.

Research suggests a number of changes in the procedures of line-ups that would enhance accuracy (Brigham & Pfeifer, 1994; Wells, Small, et al., 1998). First, the line-up must be large enough that the probability of selecting the wrong person by chance is relatively low (Wells, 1984). Even better would be a double-blind procedure similar to that used in drug research, in which neither the individual conducting the inquiry nor the others in the line-up would know who is suspected. Social scientists working with professionals in the law could develop standards for line-ups that would be scientifically defensible and consistent with the goals of justice (Brewer & Palmer, 2011).

KEY POINT: Eyewitness testimony, both in trials and police line-ups, is often inaccurate and distorted by the presentation and by leading questions. Confidence does not necessarily mean accuracy.

Testimony

What makes a credible witness? Many trials hinge on the credibility of witnesses. Witnesses are of two types: an eyewitness and an expert witness. Expert witnesses can assist juries in evaluating evidence that they might otherwise have difficulty in comprehending. Consider, for instance cases in which battered women have reacted violently against their violent partners. Simulated jurors rendered more lenient verdicts or accepted pleas of self-defence when expert witnesses explained the *battered woman syndrome* and the effects of stress, or the social situation of a woman in such circumstances (Schuller, 1992; Schuller & Hastings, 1996). They may also testify about the inaccuracy of common beliefs concerning abuse, such as, 'The woman is free to leave at any time' (Schuller, 1994; Schuller & Vidmar, 1992). Interestingly, those who are strong believers in a 'just world' where victims are held responsible for their own fate (recall Chapter 2) are less likely to accept expert testimony regarding this syndrome (Schuller, Smith & Olson, 1994).

Indeed, psychologists often serve as expert witnesses in both civil and criminal cases, testifying about psychological subjects such as eyewitness reliability, as well as providing information about clinical evaluation, cognitive and developmental factors and other relevant areas of psychological research (Cutler & Kovera, 2011; Loftus, 1983). However, some psychologists argue that such expert testimony is unwieldy, unnecessary and unlikely to have much of an impact on the jury (McCloskey & Egeth, 1983; Maass, Brigham & West, 1985). Moreover, mock jury studies indicate that expert witnesses are not always believed by jurors, and do not necessarily influence the outcomes (Neal, Christiansen, Bornstein & Robicheaux, 2012). However, jurors are more likely to accept such expert testimony when they are explicitly released from a strict application of the law and encouraged to use their own judgement (Schuller & Rzepa, 2002).

Leading questions Trials in many countries are based upon a system in which lawyers act as unreserved advocates for one side. Witnesses are called to present evidence supporting one side and can be cross-examined and challenged by the other side. The cross-examination may also capitalize on errors in peripheral details to discredit the witness. While juries may sometimes believe eyewitness testimony even when the witness is discredited (Loftus, 1974), most of the research supports the position that eyewitness testimony can actually be effectively discredited by leading questions (Kennedy & Haygood, 1992).

A series of experiments shows how testimony can be influenced by the phrasing of questions (Loftus, 1979). In one, research participants were shown a film of an automobile accident in which a green car drove past the scene of the accident. Immediately after viewing the film, research participants were questioned about what they had seen. Some were asked, 'Did the blue car that drove past the scene of the accident have a ski rack on the roof?' Others were asked the same question without the misleading word, 'blue'. Later, research participants were asked to identify the colour of the car from a set of colour strips. Most of the research participants who were asked about a 'green car' selected a shade of green that closely matched the actual colour of the car. However, those who were asked about a blue car selected a shade of blue consistent with what was suggested by the leading question. The effect occurred after an interval of 20 minutes and persisted over one week.

Of course, the astute lawyer knows how to use this technique of asking leading questions. The very nature of the adversarial process may create subtle biases. In an experiment by Sheppard and Vidmar (1980), research participants were shown a filmed fight. They were told that they were to testify at a mock trial about what they had seen and that they might be contacted by a lawyer before the trial. Other students not shown the fight were assigned roles as lawyers, some representing the plaintiff or defendant and others in a neutral role representing the court. The participants who witnessed the event were interviewed by 'lawyers' and then gave their testimony. A 'judge' and two observers rated the accuracy and bias of the testimony. Both the observers and the judge found little bias in the testimony of witnesses who had been interviewed by neutral lawyers. However, those who had been interviewed by a lawyer representing one side gave testimony in a way that favoured that side. When interviewed after the experiment, none of the research participants were aware of having been influenced by the lawyer's style of questioning.

Improving testimonial credibility Research indicates that the procedures for giving testimony might be improved (Wells & Olson, 2003). In one study (Marquis, Marshall & Oskamp, 1972), research participants viewed a film in which two young men witnessed a female pedestrian being knocked down by a car. A fight ensues between her male companion and the driver, and the onlookers subsequently become involved in the argument. Trained observers had previously identified 884 distinct facts regarding the people and events in the film. All research participants were first asked to give a report of what happened in as much detail as possible. Then they were questioned in one of four formats: (1) broad, general questions; (2) specific questions equivalent to direct examination; (3) forced-choice leading questions equivalent to an aggressive cross-examination; or (4) multiple-choice questions of the type known and loved by most students. The results show that each technique has advantages and disadvantages. Free recall provides greater accuracy but relatively few details. Under more direct questioning, accuracy is somewhat reduced, but the testimony becomes more complete. Perhaps witnesses should be allowed to narrate freely with as few interpretations as possible in the early stage of testimony. Then, subsequent questioning could elicit more detail.

KEY POINT: Eyewitness testimony can be distorted by leading questions, but accuracy can be increased by asking general open-ended questions before specific examination questions.

The jury

Countries such as Canada, the United States, the United Kingdom, Australia and New Zealand enshrine the principle of trial by 'jury of one's peers', assumed to be an 'impartial' group (Vidmar & Schuller, 2001). In France, Russia and Brazil, jury trials are reserved for the more serious crimes, while in India, the Netherlands and China, juries are not used, and guilt or innocence is determined by judges alone. In Japan and Germany, a mixed system of judges and jurors is used. Clearly the nature of the jury system varies with the nation, its history and its culture (Kaplan & Martin, 2006).

A jury is an interactive group. Indeed, research on how juries arrive at decisions can contribute both to the legal system and to our understanding of how groups function (Bornstein & Greene, 2011). However, designing appropriate research on these social psychological processes is challenging. It is not possible to intervene directly in a real trial, and in some jurisdictions it is not legal to interview jurors after the trial. Hence, researchers use jury simulations in which summaries of the evidence and arguments are presented briefly to participants in oral or written form, perhaps arguments by lawyers, perhaps instructions by a judge, perhaps witnesses acting roles in person or on videotape. In some cases, actors play the roles of lawyers, judges, witnesses and defendants. The group must then deliberate and reach a verdict (Bray & Kerr, 1982).

Do these simulations represent the reality of the courtroom? Real juries are exposed to a much richer array of information, including important non-verbal cues. In addition, real juries make decisions that can have serious consequences. In one simulation study, this was examined by telling some groups that the instructor would accept their verdict in the case of a student accused of cheating, while other groups were told that the case was hypothetical. Jurors in the apparently real case were more likely to judge the defendant as guilty, and less likely to be influenced by characteristics of the defendant (Wilson & Donnerstein, 1976). There is some evidence that mock juries composed of students are more likely to acquit than are groups selected from actual jury pools (Simon & Mahan, 1971), although MacCoun & Kerr (1988) found no difference between student and community samples after controlling for pre-discussion bias. However, mock juries can have considerable experimental realism (Chapter 1) and cannot be dismissed out of hand

Are juries impartial? The underlying notion of a jury system is the right to be tried by a group of 'one's peers', who are assumed to be impartial. But is this a reasonable expectation? Research suggests that potential biases in jurors can be induced in several ways – by the instructions given by judges; by information provided by the media; and, in experiments, by the instructions given by experimenters (Burke & Freedman, 1996; Pfeifer, 1999).

What about the influence of the media? Are there systematic biases in media shows involving law? If so, do such biases influence potential jurors? One such bias is the so-called CSI effect, named after a popular TV programme, *Crime Scene Investigation*, which portrays the use of science to solve cases (Kim, Barak & Shelton, 2009). Jurors who have watched this particular programme sometimes expect physical forensic evidence such as DNA to be provided, and if it is not, then assume that the case for guilt has not been made, thereby raising the standard for what constitutes 'proof' beyond a reasonable doubt (Hayes-Smith & Levett, 2011; Park, 2011).

The long-running *Law and Order* television series offers another example of a programme that may lead to bias in prospective jurors. Shniderman (2013) argues that the show and others like it present a message that undermines the presumption of innocence and glosses over the abuses to defendants' rights. One of the detectives in this particular series occasionally acts coercively and even violently toward a suspect during interrogation, violating that person's rights. Moreover, more faith in eyewitness accuracy is demonstrated in the programme than empirical research would justify.

Can we minimize jury bias by careful selection of the people who form juries? In the United States, social psychologists have been utilized as consultants in jury selection, although the usefulness of their contribution is in some doubt (Lieberman, 2011). To what extent can we predict how individual jurors will lean? Consider that jurors who are older, less educated and of lower socioeconomic levels are more likely to vote to convict (Nemeth, 1981). Male and female jurors show different patterns only in rape cases; women are more likely to convict and to favour harsh sentences (Nemeth, 1981). Overt prejudice may be relatively easy to detect in questioning potential jurors. However, more subtle forms of prejudice may influence their decisions. In a study (Pfeifer, 1999), research participants acting as jurors viewed an audio-visual presentation of a trial. The prosecuting lawyer, played by a male or female, was vigorously engaged in questioning a submissive male defendant. Male, but not female, research participants rated the defendant as less likely to be guilty when the prosecutor was female. Interestingly, the male jurors also rated the female prosecutor as more effective than did female jurors. Thus, the research participants expressed their sexism in an indirect or 'symbolic' manner, downgrading the female prosecutor who acted against stereotypic expectations by voting 'not guilty'.

Many jurors have been sequestered for extended periods during the trial. They often find the experience highly stressful, and often experience depression, feelings of hopelessness and helplessness, difficulty in concentration and memory, reduced self-confidence and loneliness: a 'sequestered syndrome' (Chopra, Dahl & Wrightsman, 1996). This does not promote unbiased and careful decision-making.

Of course, the judge can influence the jury through instructions on the law and on the admission of evidence. When mock juries considered a case in which the female defendant had killed her abusive spouse, judicial instructions to adopt an 'objective' standard – how an ordinary person would act in that situation – were more likely to convict than those instructed to adopt a 'subjective standard' – considering whether the defendant thought she was in danger (Terrance, Matheson & Spanos, 2000). Note that juries do not always heed the instructions of the judge, for instance to disregard a piece of evidence (Tanford & Penrod, 1984). And if the instructions are lengthy and technical, jurors may fail to understand them (Hafer, Reynolds & Obertynski, 1996).

> **KEY POINT:** Because it is not possible to study actual juries during their deliberation, most research uses mock juries given case summaries to discuss and decide. A number of potential biases may serve to sway jurors.

The verdict

What cognitive processes do jurors go through in arriving at a verdict? Pennington and Hastie (1992) observe that jurors construct a story, a narrative of what happened based on information presented at the trial. Causal relationships between events and intentions of the actors are crucial to the decision. Of course, the credibility of the witnesses and the arguments of lawyers will have a bearing on how the jurors put together pieces of information to construct a narrative that makes sense to them. Indeed, jurors and judges alike tend to dismiss purely statistical evidence and rely more on eyewitness accounts, which we know to be error-prone (Wells, 1992).

Finally, the sentence must be pronounced after the jury has voted to convict. The values of both the society and the individual will influence sentencing decisions (Lau, Tyson & Bond, 2009; McKee & Feather, 2008). According to Feather's (1999) model, we judge both the extent to which the accused was responsible and the seriousness of the offence. These two factors together lead us to conclude that the individual deserves a penalty and how harsh that sentence would be.

Deception and responsibility To determine that the accused is guilty, the judge and jurors must often make judgements regarding who is telling the truth and who is not, and must attribute responsibility to the defendant for the consequences of that action. But how do people detect deception and attribute responsibility? Some interesting research has addressed these problems (DePaulo, Lindsay et al., 2003).

It has been found that, in general, people can distinguish truth from lies only at slightly above a chance level (Miller & Burgoon, 1982; Zuckerman, DePaulo & Rosenthal, 1981). Surprisingly, those with training and experience do not seem to be much more effective. For instance, when law enforcement officers and students viewed videotapes of individuals interviewed about their attitudes, the trained officers did no better than the students at distinguishing truthful from untruthful responses (DePaulo & Pfeifer, 1986). In another study, mock customs inspections were conducted with real airline passengers, some of whom were smuggling various kinds of contraband. On viewing the videotapes, the trained customs officers did not perform better than a sample of laypeople (Kraut & Poe, 1980). However, another study found that research participants were less successful at hiding facts when they thought the target person was an expert (Fugita, Hogrebe & Wexley, 1980).

What are the cues for deception? In general when people are lying, their speech has a higher pitch, they are more nervous and less fluent and take long pauses, and they give less plausible and shorter answers with longer hesitations prior to responding (Kraut, 1978; Ekman & Friesen, 1969). While individuals make some effort to control facial expression when trying to deceive someone, they are less aware of the 'language' of the rest of the body (Ekman & Friesen, 1974). Observers are generally more accurate in detecting disguised emotions when viewing the body rather than the face, but when factual material is involved, for example, one is lying about smuggled goods, judgements based on the face are likely to be more accurate (Littlepage & Pineault, 1979). Note, however, that people may be too dependent on certain cues particularly when dealing with an experienced liar (Alcock, 1996). For instance, while those who are lying may show larger pupil size and higher voice, both indicative of nervousness, they may be nervous for all kinds of reasons apart from lying, such as a fear of being unjustly accused of lying.

In an interesting study (De Paulo & Rosenthal, 1979), male and female students were videotaped while they described several acquaintances that they liked, felt ambivalent about or disliked. They were then instructed to lie by pretending they liked some of the people they disliked and vice versa. Research participants watched the videotapes and attempted to identify deception. They were good at identifying the occurrence of deception but not at identifying the real underlying feelings. However, with practice, it is possible to improve one's skill at detecting deception (Zuckerman, Koestner & Alton, 1984). Indeed, other studies indicate that some professional law enforcement officers and clinical psychologists can dramatically increase their accuracy in detecting who is lying by taking specialized training workshops (Ekman, O'Sullivan & Frank, 1999).

BOX 15.1   INSIGHTS FROM THE LAB

LIE DETECTION AND THE POLYGRAPH

It is obvious that we cannot have justice in a criminal justice system unless we can determine the truth. In medieval Britain, the accused was required to swallow a 'trial slice' of bread and cheese. It was reasoned that an inability to swallow it would indicate a dry mouth, which might indicate lying. The high-tech descendant of this technique is the polygraph, a controversial device.

The polygraph technique measures physiological changes, particularly skin conductance (which indicates perspiration), as well as blood pressure and respiratory rate. In general, the polygraph can indicate changes in the level of physiological arousal as the person responds to various questions. Since we generally cannot control these reactions consciously, the polygrapher can compare our reactions under different circumstances. However, we cannot conclude that a person is lying if he or she shows increased arousal to critical questions ('Did you murder your wife?'), but not to neutral questions ('Did you eat ice cream in the past week?'). There are many possible reasons for arousal: grief over the murder, fear of being falsely accused, shame at being suspected by the police, anger at being asked such an outrageous question.

Thus, more sophisticated techniques are used. For example, reactions are compared while the person responds to critical, and neutral questions. It is reasoned that while the person may show increased arousal to any questions concerning an emotionally upsetting situation, a greater level of arousal would be shown if upset is combined with lying. Hence, reactions might be compared while the person responds to a general, control

Figure 15.3   Was Pinocchio's nose a better lie detector?

Source: Olivier Juneau/Shutterstock.com

question ('Did someone murder your wife?') and then to a specific question ('Did you murder your wife?'). Another technique is to ask about details that only the perpetrator and police would know. For example, if the victim was wearing a green sweater, one can ask a series of yes/no questions: Was the victim wearing a white sweater? A blue ski jacket? A green sweater? A grey parka? If the accused answers, 'I don't know', to all the questions, but shows arousal only to the green sweater then we may be on to something.

The research indicates accuracy of around 70% of the time, which may seem impressive, but is not foolproof or beyond a reasonable doubt (Lykken, 1974; Yarmey, 1979; Horvath, 1977, 1984). Moreover, as the research evidence accumulates, scepticism has grown among qualified researchers and professionals as to the validity of polygraph evidence and whether it should ever be admitted as evidence (Iacono & Lykken, 1997). Interestingly, the public is also sceptical. In a study, participants were provided with a vignette of a case. Three versions were presented to different participants, in which the defendant had 'passed' or 'failed' a polygraph test, or no polygraph had been administered. The results of the polygraph had no significant impact on guilt judgements, whether the defendant had passed or failed.

Recent work using more sophisticated physiological indicators, such as electrical evoked potentials (ERPs) in the brain and functional magnetic resonance imagery (fMRI), may be more effective. For instance, in a study, participants completed two procedures in which they were to identify the culprit in a police line-up. In one situation, they were instructed to try to identify the culprit accurately, while in the other, deceptive condition, they were asked to conceal their recognition of the culprit, to pretend that they did not know. When the participant was looking at the culprit as opposed to others, an ERP response (P300) was obtained, even when they were instructed to conceal their identification (Lefebvre, Marchand, Smith & Connolly, 2009).

However, certain types of people or those who have been coached beforehand can 'beat the machine' by using such techniques as mentally distracting themselves during critical questions or biting their tongues during neutral questions (Honts, Hodes & Raskin, 1985). There are also important ethical and legal issues that arise, such as invasion of privacy and self-incrimination. Perhaps, in the end, there is no substitute for competent and professional police work.

The concept of responsibility in law is crucial. The modern conception of legal responsibility is based on the intentions of the actor, not just the act: that is, an attribution (recall Chapter 2). Consequences of the act also play a role. Recall the study described in Chapter 2 (Walster, 1966), in which the driver of a car with a failed parking brake was deemed more responsible for the consequences when the runaway car hurt someone than when it caused minimal damage.

The law also accepts the attribution of diminished responsibility. In 1843, a young man named Daniel M'Naghten, while attempting to kill British Prime Minister Sir Robert Peel, killed the prime minister's private secretary instead. M'Naghten's lawyer presented a novel defence: M'Naghten could not be held legally responsible for his actions because he was under the insane delusion that he was being hounded by the prime minister. In the judge's historic judgement, known as the M'Naghten Rule, the defendant was acquitted because 'he did not know the nature and quality of the act he was doing or, if he did know it, he did not know he was doing wrong'. The principle of legal insanity persists despite some controversy (Stover & Nightingale, 1985).

[
KEY POINT: Processes of judgement in a trial are based on how people can recognize cues of deception, and how people may attribute responsibility to the defendant.
]

JUSTICE

Social scientists have long been concerned with the concept of justice in social behaviour (Homans, 1961, 1974; Lerner, 1977; Walster, Walster & Berscheid, 1978). One major concern of theorists and researchers in social psychology has been distributive justice, the conditions under which the allocation of a resource or the outcome of an event would be judged as just or unjust. Other researchers have been concerned with procedural justice, often referred to as fair play, the process of arriving at a decision or an outcome. In other words, social psychologists are concerned with both what has been decided and how it has been decided.

However, conceptions of justice differ between cultures. For example, consider the following two situations: (1) For selfish reasons, someone takes another person's train tickets from a coat pocket without permission; and (2) For selfish reasons, a person does not deliver the wedding rings to his best friend's wedding. The first violates someone's rights, while the latter violates interpersonal responsibilities or expectations. In a comparative study, it was found that research

Figure 15.4 Justice personified
Source: ER_09/Shutterstock.com

participants in the US gave priority to justice concerns, while those in India tended to see interpersonal responsibilities as moral issues that gave them precedence over matters of justice (Miller & Bersoff, 1992).

Distributive justice

We arrive at justice or fairness decisions, in court and in life, on the basis of distribution rules or norms that are an integral part of our value system. It appears that these rules are universal, although how and why they are applied may vary from one culture to another. Three major rules of distributive justice have been identified: equity, equality and need (Austin, 1979).

Equity Aristotle argued that distributive justice requires an equality of proportions; we measure our gains against what we view as our contributions and our worthiness. Thus, for instance, the notion of 'pay equity' implies not that everyone be paid the same amount, but that pay reflects the amount of responsibility, training and effort required to perform the job. Considerations of equity may involve the value of one's contributions to others (e.g. medicine), or the dangers of the work (e.g. police, mining). This concept has been developed as equity theory (Adams, 1965; Austin, 1979; Walster, Walster & Berscheid, 1978; see also Chapter 9). Equity theory is related to the theory of cognitive dissonance in the sense that fairness can be restored by changing behaviour or by changing perceptions. It proposes that a relationship between parties is a just one when the ratio of perceived outcomes to perceived inputs (assets and liabilities that lead to a deserved outcome) are equal (Austin, 1979). The principle of relative deprivation is important here, a comparison between our experience and our expectations (Walker & Smith, 2002).

Equality Sometimes resources are distributed equally even though the participants have not made equal contributions. When group stability and esprit de corps are of primary concern, it may be disruptive to allocate outcomes differentially to group members (Sampson, 1975). Research has shown that allocations are most likely to be equal if the participants are women and expect to meet again (Major & Deaux, 1982). These different orientations based on gender have been shown to be present in children as young as seven years of age (Vinacke & Gullickson, 1964). It has been suggested (Benton, 1971; Weinstein, DeVaughan & Wiley, 1969) that females are more concerned than males with the interpersonal aspects of the situation, and avoid actions that could disrupt the harmony of the group. At a national level, it is often considered to be sound policy to redistribute incomes and resources from the rich to the poor, in order to provide a decent level of food and shelter, health care and a minimal standard of living for all citizens.

Need Another rule of distributive justice is that those who need the most should get the most. Need is closely associated with the norm of social responsibility and, not surprisingly, affects such activities as charitable donations (see Chapter 9). Need also is taken into consideration at the interpersonal level in groups. For instance, an individual who has few resources (Leventhal, Weiss & Long, 1969) may be over-rewarded in a work situation (Taynor & Deaux, 1973), but only if the person is not considered responsible for his or her own misfortune.

Procedural justice

The interest of social psychologists in procedural justice (e.g., Thibaut & Walker, 1975; Tyler & Lind, 2001; Napier & Tyler, 2008) focuses on the relationship between the methods used to arrive at a decision and the perception that the decision was just. For example, research participants' ratings of politicians and teachers are strongly influenced by the perceived fairness of how the teachers grade papers, or how the politicians arrive at voting decisions independent of their actual decisions (Tyler & Caine, 1981).

As one would expect, the outcome can have a bearing on whether people feel that justice has been served. If people expect to win a legal case, they are less sensitive to issues of procedural justice (Heuer & Penrod, 1986; Conlon, Lind & Lissak, 1989). On the other hand, an unfair procedure may provide us with a credible explanation for unfavourable outcomes (van den Bos, Bruins, Wilke & Dronkert, 1999). For instance, students are certainly more likely to question the fairness of marking when their own mark was lower than they expected. When we are compelled to pay taxes that we perceive as excessive, our sense of procedural justice may be violated (Tyler, Rasinski & McGraw, 1985).

Of course, notions of justice vary with different cultures, and even at different times in history. Since research has been conducted largely in Western societies, we cannot automatically generalize to other societies with regard to how people construe procedural justice. Beyond understanding justice in its particular context, we must consider whether there are universal rules about procedural justice that extend beyond the particular society.

KEY POINT: The perception of justice rests on an evaluation that the participants have received a fair share of the rewards (distributive justice) and that the process by which the outcome was arrived at was fair (procedural justice).

The just world

Do you believe that we get what we deserve and we deserve what we get in life? People vary in their belief in a just world (BJW), and the consequences can be profound. Imagine that as a participant in a classic experiment by Lerner & Simmons (1966), you watch while someone you believe to be another volunteer receives what seem to be painful and severe electric shocks. After ten minutes of this ordeal, you are given a break before the next session of observing the shocking treatment of another, innocent person. Now you are asked to evaluate both the participants and the situation. Would you do as the participants in that study did? They blamed the victim for his or her suffering, rather than the experimenter! Lerner & Simmons (1966) reasoned that those who believed that the suffering was inevitable denigrated the victim, in order to justify what they had seen and what they were helpless to prevent. Note that the belief in a just world is considered to stem from a need to believe that we have some control over the cruel twists of fate (Hafer & Bégue, 2005).

Indeed, situations in which one observes an innocent person being victimized threaten such beliefs. Thus, people with strong just world beliefs tend, because they like to believe that the world is just and that people get what they deserve, to have negative attitudes about people with mental illness, for example (Bizer, Hart & Jekogian, 2012). Interestingly, some evidence indicates that some people may see the world as just or fair to others but not to themselves (Bégue & Bastounis, 2003).

It also is the case that people who strongly believe in a just world tend to react less strongly to situations that do not seem to be fair even to themselves. They manage somehow to rationalize that there has been fairness after all. For instance, in two experiments, Hafer and Olson (1989) found that believers in a just world who had received feedback that they had failed in a task did not feel as aggrieved as those who did not believe in a just world. Again, a set of studies indicates that believers in a just world do not experience the same sense of injustice, anger and resentment as do those with weaker just-world beliefs, both in a laboratory experiment and among working women faced with various types of job dissatisfaction (Hafer & Olson, 1993).

In the extreme case, just-world beliefs allow us to be indifferent to evil (Ellard, Miller, Baumle & Olson, 2002). In a comparative study, scores on a scale of just-world beliefs were higher among white South Africans (during the era of apartheid) than among white British participants (Furnham, 1985). Indeed, in the same vein, some have even argued that the six million Jewish victims of the Holocaust were acquiescent and therefore somehow responsible for their own fate, ignoring both the overwhelming, brutal force directed against them and the heroic revolts that did occur in ghettos and concentration camps (Davidowicz, 1975).

KEY POINT: People vary in the extent to which they believe that the world is just and that people get what they deserve in life. This has strong implications for how we judge victimization.

Perceiving that life can be unfair

When do people experience a sense of unfairness or injustice? Three factors have been identified (Mikula, 1994): (1) violation of entitlement, the extent to which people perceived that they have been deprived of what they had come to expect; (2) causation, the extent to which people attribute this violation of entitlement to some external agent (another person, the government, the court) rather than themselves; and (3) lack of justification for the decision or action. Thus for example, in court decisions, people on the losing side would feel a sense of injustice if they realistically expected to win the case and believed that they deserved to do so.

Feelings of injustice may not be predictable from the objective outcome alone. A sense of injustice often pertains to *relative* deprivation, a perceived discrepancy between one's own outcome and some point of reference (Olson & Hafer, 1996). We may be very fortunate in terms of having enough food and clean water, but if we compare ourselves to others who have better food, we may come to feel deprived. Further, as discussed in Chapter 13, people often report more deprivation for their group than for themselves (Taylor, Wright, Moghaddam & Lalonde, 1990) and sometimes may exaggerate the claimed injustice to which their group has been subjected in order to validate claims for more benefits (Olson & Hafer, 2001).

We must also consider the individual's scope of justice, the boundaries within which justice is perceived to be relevant (Hafer & Olson, 2003). There will be situations in which our judgements are not influenced by motivations to be just or fair. For instance, most people are willing to kill certain species of animals (e.g., mosquitoes, rats), but we differ on whether doing harm to animals that provide food or that serve in laboratory experiments falls within our scope of justice. Genocide and slavery may be seen as resulting from the exclusion of entire groups of people from the scope of justice, seeing the victimized people as less than human (Waller, 2002).

KEY POINT: Perceptions of injustice are influenced by comparisons with others, leading at times to feelings of relative deprivation. One's scope of justice determines to whom one extends considerations of fairness and justice.

Adversarial and inquisitorial models of a system of justice

Most of our discussion of trials has concerned the adversarial procedure, used in British, Canadian, Australian, New Zealand and US courts, in which the case is developed, argued and defended by the parties to the dispute or their lawyers, and presented to a neutral judge and jury. In the inquisitorial procedure as used in France and other European nations, a judge is assigned a role in supervising the collection of evidence and occasionally questioning witnesses (van Koppen & Penrod, 2003). The crucial psychological differences between the adversarial and inquisitorial trial procedures involve who controls the process of the trial (Houlden, Latour, Walker & Tibaut, 1978). In the adversarial system, the two parties control the gathering of evidence, the calling of witnesses and the presentation of arguments, while in the inquisitorial system the judge, at least in part, directs the gathering and presentation of evidence. Not surprisingly, people in the English-speaking democracies prefer the adversary system, which is familiar to them (Houlden, Latour, Walker & Thibaut, 1978; Lind, Kurtz, Musante, Walker & Thibaut, 1980). Interestingly, however, in France, many people also indicate that they would prefer the adversarial procedure (Lind, Erickson, Friedland & Dickenberger, 1978). Maximizing the sense of process control by the participants will tend to increase the perception of fairness; participants feel more confident that all important aspects of their case will be presented. In the inquisitional system, people may feel that something important was omitted or misinterpreted (Thibaut & Walker, 1975).

Bennett and Feldman (1980) suggest that in the adversarial system the side that tells the most coherent story, regardless of its actual truth, tends to win the case. In an experiment, research participants were presented with scenarios surrounding a homicide case involving a 52-year-old man who ended the life of his terminally ill 49-year-old wife. Three conditions were varied in the videotaped presentations: (1) whether death was caused by unplugging a respirator or by gunshots to the head; (2) whether the accused showed a state of sadness or lack of emotional arousal; and (3) whether the instructions to the jury allowed for 'jury nullification', a principle of law in which juries are free to disregard both the judge's instructions and the law itself if they see fit. Participants were less likely to convict when they were aware of the possibility of jury nullification. Jurors were also more accepting of euthanasia when the respirator was disconnected, representing a more passive action than gunshots to the head. Interestingly, the wishes of the patient do not always carry the day in public attitudes. In another study, only about half the participants recommended euthanasia even when the individual was in intractable pain and had requested death (Darley, Loeb & Hunter, 1996).

Specific issues of justice

Judging the victim: The case of rape In 2013 in New Delhi, four men were convicted of all charges in the rape and murder of a 23-year-old woman who was attacked when she boarded a bus. The case attracted wide attention in India and around the world, as did a similar case in Kenya, some weeks later. Trials concerning rape or sexual assault can be particularly troubling. Using mock juries and other methods, researchers have found that the victim is often judged harshly, unlike in most other crimes. Matters irrelevant to the case intrude, such as whether there was a history of previous sexual involvement between complainant and accused (Schuller & Hasting, 2002; Shotland & Goodstein, 1992), and the woman's marital status, sexual experience and profession often influence judgements about the case (Feldman-Summers & Lindner, 1976). It also seems that rape victims who do not express visible emotional distress are viewed as less believable (Calhoun, Selby & King, 1976). And if the victim was intoxicated at the time, again she is likely to attact more of the blame. When participants were given a description of a sexual assault case, the description included whether either or both or neither party was intoxicated. Harsher judgements were rendered when the victim was intoxicated, as she was apparently seen as more sexually disinhibited and thus less the victim (Wall & Schuller, 2000).

Clearly, there are a number of reasons why many crimes, including rape, are not reported to the authorities: fear of reprisal, feelings of helplessness and the belief that the police are powerless to arrest and punish (Kidd & Chayet, 1984; Yurchesyn, Keith & Renner, 1992).

BOX 15.2   EUTHANASIA

Acts of commission, such as assisted suicide, are often seen as unacceptable, while acts of omission, terminating treatment or intravenous feeding, are more acceptable (Wellman & Sugarman, 1996). As medical technology develops and the population ages, the issue of euthanasia becomes increasingly salient. Some people may spend years in a permanent vegetative state, Ariel Sharon, former prime minister of Israel suffered a stroke at the height of his political career and was in a coma for eight years until his death in 2014. Increasingly, patients in a terminal, painful condition are demanding the right to assisted suicide. In a few countries, this right has been recognized under certain conditions.

We must look closely at how euthanasia may be carried out. In some cases, the act may be active, such as when a physician prescribes a deliberate overdose of medication. In other cases, the euthanasia is passive, through discontinuation of treatment or feeding. Public attitudes are much more accepting of passive euthanasia (Ho & Penney, 1992). Recall the study discussed earlier in which the manipulation involved euthanasia by gunshots to the head or disconnecting the respirator. We must also distinguish between cases in which the individual expresses a wish to die and others in which the individual may be comatose and unable to respond.

Indeed, the public is more accepting of euthanasia when performed by a physician than when performed by others (Albright & Hazler, 1995). Attitudes towards euthanasia and acceptance of a 'right to die' are also influenced by factors, such as whether effective relief of pain and suffering is made available, concern that such an irrevocable decision may be made when an individual is seriously depressed, and the possibility that an individual may accept euthanasia to relieve the stress on others (Soifer, 1996).

KEY POINT: In the adversarial procedure the case is developed, argued and defended by the parties to the dispute or their lawyers, and presented to a neutral judge and jury. In the inquisitional procedure, as used in France and other European nations, a judge is assigned a role in supervising the collection of evidence and questioning. Each system has advantages and disadvantages.

HEALTH AND WELL-BEING

How do we die? By the mid-20th century, the threat of smallpox, tuberculosis, the bubonic plague and cholera had been virtually eliminated in the developed world. Public health measures such as ensuring a safe water supply, waste management, vaccinations, encouraging mothers to breast-feed their babies, and using mosquito netting have had dramatic health benefits across the world. The major causes of death in industrialized nations are the chronic diseases (coronary and circulatory, respiratory, diabetes, cancers) and accidents (Figure 15.5). Note the differences between countries based on median income.

Health care is a priority for citizens, and its future has been a major political issue in many countries. However, health policies that focus almost exclusively on the treatment of illness fail to address some major problems of public health. Note that many of the causes of mortality in Figure 15.5 are determined or influenced by personal behavioural choices, such as smoking, driving habits, diet and exercise, gun control and protection of the environment. The World Health Organization has identified three important goals or 'national challenges', which have guided public policy for decades (Health and Welfare Canada, 1987):

- to reduce the gross inequities in income and opportunity that adversely affect health;
- to increase efforts to prevent injuries, diseases and chronic disabilities by means such as immunizing school children against a wider range of diseases, measures to ensure safe water supplies, reducing drunk driving and smoking, encouraging exercise and promoting prenatal and neonatal care;
- to enhance people's capacity to cope with chronic conditions and disabilities, such as depression, respiratory ailments, hypertension and arthritis, as well as to assist seniors who may be partially incapacitated to live as freely and independently as possible.

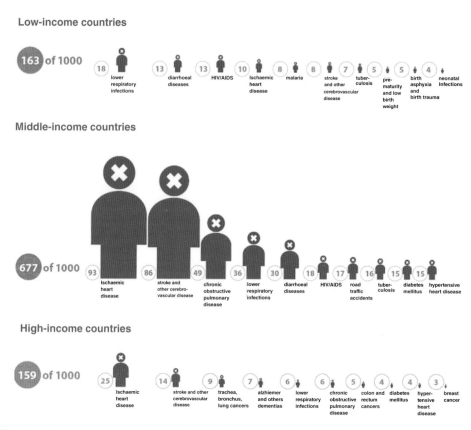

Figure 15.5   Leading causes of mortality, World Health Organization, 2012

You may wonder how social psychologists can contribute to solving the problems that would seem to be the domain of the medical sciences. Let us first examine some important health risks from the perspective of social psychology. Then we turn to research on the process of treatment and recovery from illness. We then discuss how social psychology contributes to public health and prevention. Finally, we turn to the perspectives of positive psychology regarding well-being, extending beyond an illness model.

PSYCHOSOCIAL HEALTH RISKS

The socioeconomic health gradient

Economically disadvantaged groups have relatively lower life expectancies and poorer health (Townsend & Davidson, 1982). However, the effects of socioeconomic status on health are not limited to the dire effects of living in poverty. As we move up the ladder of socioeconomic status, health improves, life expectancy increases and the incidence of many chronic and infectious diseases decreases. That is, those at the highest socioeconomic levels tend to be healthier than those who are somewhat less advantaged, who in turn are healthier than those still less advantaged. This is known as the socioeconomic gradient effect (SES) on health.

Research is trying to unravel this mystery of the SES gradient effect (Matthews & Gallo, 2011; Adler et al., 1994; Marmot, Ryff, et al., 1997). One hypothesis is that those who are successful in life, in socioeconomic terms at least, may have been endowed with better health from the onset. Gottfredson (2004) suggested a more controversial interpretation: that the socioeconomic gradient effect on health may be explained by differences in general intelligence. Those who are smarter not only succeed in life, but take better care of themselves. However, intelligence cannot be equated with wisdom, and very intelligent people are capable of making very unwise choices in life. For instance, high-status people are more likely to indulge in high-caloric food in some countries (McLaren, 2007). However, in general, people at the higher SES levels do tend to take better care of themselves in terms of diet, exercise, smoking and substance use (Pampel, Krueger & Denney, 2010), perhaps because of having more information about health and more access to healthy food, medical care and exercise.

While job-related stress can be found at all levels of the occupational ladder, work generally becomes more intrinsically rewarding and fulfilling at the higher levels. Indeed, young adults who see themselves as under-employed tend to report less favourable health, even after accounting for the effects of income and lifestyle on health (Sadava, O'Connor & McCreary, 2000).

> **KEY POINT:** The socioeconomic gradient effect reflects the association of higher socioeconomic levels with better health.

Health behaviour: Taking care of yourself

Consider all the behaviours that may affect our health: our dietary choices, smoking, excessive drinking and other substance use, exercise, wearing seatbelts and developing safe driving habits, using sunscreen and wearing clothing to protect against harmful exposure to the sun, getting flu shots, rejecting violence and abuse, expressing our sexuality safely, obtaining adequate sleep, brushing and flossing our teeth, taking medication as prescribed and coping effectively with stress. Are we consistent in taking care of ourselves?

And do people fall into patterns of health risk behaviours? Jessor and colleagues (Jessor & Jessor, 1977; Jessor, 1993) argue that, among adolescents, the use of alcohol and other drugs is part of a more general pattern of problem behaviour that includes lying and stealing and precocious and unprotected sexual involvement (Donovan, Jessor & Jessor, 1983; Jessor, Donovan & Widmer, 1980; Sadava & Forsyth, 1977a, 1977b). However, the assumption that there is a pattern or 'syndrome' of health-risk behaviours has received only mixed support (Willoughby et al., 2003). Indeed, while some people may exercise regularly, they will not necessarily eat well, or they may also smoke (Sadava, DeCourville & McCreary, 1996; Donovan, Jessor & Costa, 1993). Often we act without heed to the consequences of our actions to our health (Gibbons, Kingsbury & Gerrard, 2012).

Consider that a given health risk may be quite variable from one person to another. For instance, the risk of heavy drinking cannot be predicted accurately if we know only how much alcohol is consumed (Sadava, 1985; DeCourville & Sadava, 1997). Women who drink heavily are more vulnerable to adverse consequences than are heavily drinking men (Wilsnack, 1982) perhaps because of physiological differences, perhaps because of different gender role expectations. Heavy drinkers are more likely to suffer adverse consequences from their drinking if they also are highly lonely or under stressful life circumstances (Sadava & Thompson, 1986; McCreary & Sadava, 2000).

Modelling influences It has been shown (see Chapter 6) that our actions are often modelled after others (Bandura, 1977). Consider drinking as an example. It has been demonstrated through longitudinal research that when their parents drink heavily, adolescents tend to seek out friends who drink heavily and then drink in the same manner (Huba, Dent & Bentler, 1980). In a laboratory experiment (Caudill & Marlatt, 1975), research participants were asked to taste several wines and to rate each on flavour, aroma and other characteristics. The task involved allowing research participants to take any amount – from one small sip to an entire beaker if they wished – of each wine. A confederate posing as a research participant drank either a lot or a little of each wine. Research participants who participated along with a heavy-drinking model consumed significantly more than those with a light drinker. The experiment was repeated in a bar (Reid, 1978), where a model behaving in a warm friendly way to patrons was observed to be more likely to influence drinking than one who was cold and distant. Such modelling influences on drinking behaviour have also been observed in naturalistic studies in bars in which groups of drinkers were observed (Hennessy & Saltz, 1993). Note that larger groups tended to stay longer in the tavern (ordering rounds), and, thus, individuals in larger groups often consume more (Sykes, Rowley & Schaeffer, 1993).

Modelling effects have also been shown on our eating behaviour. For instance, one study found binge eating to be more common in some university residences than in others, and by the end of the academic year, a person's binge eating could be predicted from the binge eating of her friends (Crandall, 1988).

> **KEY POINT:** Behaviours relevant to health may form part of a general pattern of actions related to 'taking care of yourself', but the evidence is mixed. This may be because of other considerations that are involved, such as social norms. Health-relevant behaviours are also influenced by social modelling.

Stress

Beginning with the pioneering research of Hans Selye (1956), it has become commonly accepted that our state of health can be adversely affected by stress (Cohen & Williamson, 1988; Watson & Pennebaker, 1989). Indeed, stress tends to elicit the release of hormones that have negative effects on the immune system and thus leave the person more vulnerable to illness (Johansson, Collins & Collins, 1983; McClelland, Alexander & Marks, 1982). To begin, it is important to understand the two components of the stress system: the stressor, a challenge to the system (e.g. an interpersonal conflict, an impending exam), and the stress response, how the system deals with this challenge, first by vigilance and eventually by exhaustion.

One common way of measuring stressors is through life events, a checklist of major life changes that have recently occurred, weighted by their empirically determined impact (Holmes & Rahe, 1967). Examples of such events range from divorce, bereavement, serving time in prison, being fired or laid off work, trouble with the boss and sexual problems, as well as (usually) positive events such as getting married and pregnancy. Moreover the daily hassles of life also take their toll (Kanner, Coyne et al., 1981) such as concern about weight, health of family members, increased prices, home maintenance, too many things to do, misplacing things, crime, and one's physical appearance. These and several other studies suggest significant linkages with physical and emotional health (Stone & Neale, 1982; DeLongis, Coyne et al., 1982). A study over time showed that conflicts in intimate relationships are, by far, the most important sources of stress in daily life (Bolger, DeLongis et al., 1989).

Of course, as Selye (1956) pointed out, stress is intrinsic to life, and can also contribute to the development of health and strength. Many people experience very negative circumstances from which they emerge perhaps sadder but wiser. Indeed, researchers in this area are now studying post-traumatic growth, where aversive events are met by an impressive reserve of human resilience (Bonanno, 2004). It also appears that positive daily experiences can contribute positively to better health (Brown & Siegel, 1988).

BOX 15.3 TAKE ANOTHER LOOK

LINKING STRESS, SOCIAL SUPPORT AND THE COMMON COLD

While stress has been amply documented as a factor in illness, including the common cold, a series of experiments by Sheldon Cohen and his research group provides the missing direct causal link (Cohen, Tyrrell & Smith, 1993; Cohen, Frank, et al., 1998). After two days of preliminary screening to determine that all of their participants were healthy, nasal drops were administered, in some cases containing the cold virus. The participants then spent nine days in seclusion. During that time, nurses took their vital signs as well as mucous samples, and looked for signs of a cold, such as runny nose, watery eyes, and a sore throat.

At the end of that period, none of the placebo group had a cold, but 82% of those exposed to the virus became infected, and 46% manifested symptoms of a cold. Now the question becomes: is it possible to predict who will catch a cold among those exposed to the virus? Indeed, Cohen could. Among those reporting high stress (via questionnaire responses), 53% caught the cold, while only 40% in the low stress group became ill – not a huge difference but nonetheless statistically reliable. Those who had recently experienced stress over time, such as ongoing marital problems or unemployment, were much more likely to become ill than were

Figure 15.6 To be on the safe side, don't let anyone squirt a cold virus into your nose
Source: Creativa/Shutterstock.com

those who had experienced a single stressful event. In further research, Cohen and colleagues also found that, among those exposed to the virus, participants who were more sociable as measured in a questionnaire were more resistant to the virus: thus, the stress-buffering effect of social support. Socioeconomic status was also measured, and revealed a striking finding. While actual levels of income or education did not predict vulnerability, people who perceived themselves as economically disadvantaged were more vulnerable to catching a cold (Figure 15.6).

Thus it would appear that stress can weaken the immune system, which leaves people more vulnerable to the common cold (Kiecolt-Glaser, McGuire, Robles & Glaser, 2002). These effects of stress on the immune system may well be attenuated by protective factors, such as a supportive social environment and satisfaction with one's status in society.

KEY POINT: Stress can be understood in terms of a stressor, a challenge to the system, and a stress response, how the system reacts to the stressor. Stressors can include both major life-changing events and the hassles of everyday life.

Social support

How do soldiers cope with the conditions of war? Janis (1951, 1958) found that those who belonged to a cohesive combat unit were able to endure such severe stress, while those who did not belong to such a close-knit group often experienced psychological breakdown. This effect is equally true for health care workers such as nurses (Walters, Lenton, et al., 1996). Subsequent research shows that people who lack supportive bonds with others are more likely to become ill (Burman & Margolin, 1992; Cohen & Herbert, 1996).

Social support is also important in recuperation from serious illness (Lynch, 1977; Fontana, Kerns et al., 1989). After major surgery, married patients who received support from their spouses while they were in hospital subsequently took less medication and recovered more quickly than their less-supported fellow patients (Kulik & Mahler, 1989a). Interestingly, considerations of equity in a relationship become less important when one partner is seriously ill (Kuijer, Buunk, Ybema & Wobbes, 2002); what is important is feeling valued. A longitudinal study that followed patients who had undergone coronary bypass surgery found that patients who received feedback of being valued and respected by their partner experienced fewer uncomfortable symptoms (King, Reis, et al., 1993). Although most cancer patients report relatively high levels of support, some also join self-help groups of cancer patients (Taylor, Falke, et al., 1986), and the support that flows from participation in such groups has positive effects on outcomes (Spiegel, Bloom et al., 1989).

Another longitudinal study followed groups of teenage mothers through their pregnancies and after the birth of their babies (Unger & Wandersman, 1985). Social support from their families, friends, neighbours and the fathers contributed to the mothers' adjustment and effectiveness as parents, and even to the birth weight and the subsequent health of the child.

Why is social support related to health? According to one hypothesis, social support has a stress-buffering effect. Indeed, people are clearly better able to avoid illness when under stress and to recover from any illness that might develop if they interact with others rather than remaining isolated (Roy, Steptoe & Kirschbaum, 1998; Scrimshaw, 2002). Similar findings are reported in terms of coping with other sources of stress, including military duties (Britt & Bliese, 2003; Langholtz 1998) and other occupational stress (Bellman, Forster, Still & Cooper, 2003; Bradley & Cartwright, 2002).

Social support may also contribute to health indirectly. For instance, individuals with support from others may be more likely to comply with treatment, quit smoking or otherwise take better care of themselves. In societies where people move frequently and divorce almost as frequently, a lack of consistent social support is an increasingly apparent problem. In these circumstances, community services such as rape crisis centres, family services, support groups, child-care, hostels or services for senior citizens are vital (Pilisuk & Minkler, 1985).

Of course, culture plays a role. One might expect that people from collectivist cultures, those which emphasize interdependence, would be more likely to seek support from others than would members of individualistic cultures. Actually the reverse is true; people from East Asian cultures are less likely to seek social support, based on their concern for disrupting the harmony of their group (Taylor, Welch, Kim & Sherman, 2007). To be sure, members of Asian cultures certainly receive as much support as do those from the more individualistic cultures, and there is some evidence that they suffer less from stress-related illnesses (Cross & Vick, 2001). But they do not ask for the support directly in a way that would indicate that they are having problems (Kim, Sherman & Taylor, 2009).

Health, intimacy and loneliness

Beginning with a seminal paper by House, Landis, and Umberson (1988), evidence of the health-enhancing properties of close social relationships has accrued dramatically (Cohen, 1988; Ryff, Singer, Wing & Love, 2001). For instance, studies from many different countries show that married people, on average, enjoy better physical and mental health than those who are unmarried ((Burman & Margolin, 1992; Kiecolt-Glaser & Newton, 2001; Slatcher, 2010; Loving & Slatcher, 2013). This effect of intimacy on health cannot be attributed solely to overall integration into our society, nor to social support. We need those committed emotional bonds with another person for our health and well-being (Ryff et al., 2001).

Research has linked a non-secure attachment orientation (Chapter 8) to symptoms of poor health and more frequent visits to physicians and hospitals (Cooper, Shaver & Collins, 1998; Maunder & Hunter, 2001). On the other hand, a secure attachment style is associated with reduced stress, access to greater social support and more positive emotional states, all of which contribute to health (Maunder & Hunter, 2001; Sadava, Busseri et al., 2011).

Loneliness Another perspective is that a lack of social support itself may be a stressor. Loneliness, a pervasive feeling of distress about lack of satisfying relationships (Chapter 8), has been identified as a health risk. Recall that loneliness is defined as perceived deficiencies in the person's relationships, and that it is a subjective state. That is, solitude is not synonymous with loneliness; you can feel lonely in a crowd at times, and at times feel quite comfortable alone. Cacioppo (2008) suggests that there may be a 'genetic thermostat' for loneliness that is set at different levels for different people, rendering some individuals more vulnerable to feelings of loneliness. Lonely people have been found to be at more risk of impaired immune functioning, leaving them more open to viral infections (Dixon et al., 2001; Cacioppo, Hawkley, et al., 2002). A major longitudinal study in Chicago followed people over several years (Hawkley, Thisted & Cacioppo, 2009; Cacioppo,

Hawkley & Thisted, 2010) and found that an increase in loneliness predicts a subsequent decline in levels of physical exercise, as well as increased levels of depression. Indeed, chronically lonely individuals tend to have poor quality of sleep and appear to be at increased risk of developing high blood pressure (Cacioppo et al., 2002). All these findings indicate that loneliness should be seen as a health hazard.

One final comment: We have been discussing how a close relationship, because of the social support it provides, can positively affect the health of the people involved. Consider the impact of a serious illness on the course of the relationship. A study of couples in which one partner was coping with cancer (Manne & Badr, 2010) emphasized the importance of the partners being willing to disclose to each other their feelings and fears regarding the cancer and the often-debilitating treatment regimens. Where this was lacking, feelings of intimacy and closeness were diminished and distress was greater in both partners.

KEY POINT: People with strong committed emotional bonds and intimacy with another person experience better health. Social support buffers the effects of stress. Loneliness has been clearly identified as a health risk.

Personality and illness

Accumulating research shows personality to be related to risk for five diseases: asthma, chronic headaches, peptic ulcers, arthritis, and circulatory and heart disease (Scheier & Bridges, 1995; Angell, 1985; Friedman & Booth-Kewley, 1987). The three most consistently identified personality variables are anxiety, depression, and anger or hostility. For instance, depression has been linked to allergies and to deficiencies in the immune system (Herbert & Cohen, 1993, Levy & Heiden, 1990). As well, a so-called coronary-prone personality has been identified: competitive, achievement-oriented, rather impatient and somewhat hostile – the so-called Type A syndrome (Rosenman, Brand, et al., 1975; Nielson & Neufeld, 1986). However, a meta-analysis of numerous studies carried out in many different countries (Myrtek, 2001) shows that an unexpressed 'cynical hostility', in which people tend to expect the worst of others, is the specific predictor of both chronic high blood pressure (Raikkonen et al., 1999) and coronary illness (Booth-Kewley & Friedman, 1987; Weidner, Istvan & McKnight, 1989).

When people believe that they are not in control of their lives, this can have an impact on their health (Lachman & Andreoletti, 2006). Research has demonstrated that it is the perception of control that provides resistance to stress, whether or not that control is actually exercised (Glass & Singer, 1973; Cramer, Nickels and Gural, 1997). Lack of a sense of personal control may also influence health indirectly by influencing health-related behaviours (reviewed by Pampel, Krueger & Denney, 2010). However, a note of caution: there is some evidence that people in collectivist Asian cultures are less likely to feel stressed in the absence of personal control (Sastry & Ross, 1998). This is not surprising given the importance of family, group and community in such cultures.

Sometimes, even well-intended (but ultimately condescending) kindness can do unintended harm by diminishing one's sense of control. With the desire to help and protect, we sometimes treat our elders as though they need to be looked after just as children do, and this takes from them some degree of personal control. This is often a major problem for institutionalized elderly persons, who often live in situations where all decisions are made for them. In a classic field experiment, Langer and Rodin (1976) investigated the consequences of loss of control in a residential nursing home for seniors. The residents and staff were divided into two groups. Residents of one floor were told that they would be well cared for and that staff would assume all decisions and responsibilities, the usual situation in such institutions. The members of the other group were told that they were responsible for their own lives. For example, they would care for the plants in their rooms, select movies and decide on activities.

Three weeks later, those who had assumed more control over their daily lives were found to be feeling happier and healthier and were rated by nurses as being more active and having a more positive outlook. Eighteen months later, the differences were even more dramatic, in terms of activity, vigour and sociability (Rodin &

Langer, 1977). In addition, 30% of the control group had died during this period, while only 15% of the person-ally responsible group had died. These findings were replicated in another study of geriatric patients (Stirling & Reid, 1992). However, with regard to treatment, some patients desire to participate in decision-making, but others prefer to leave it to the experts (Mahler & Kulik, 1991; Cromwell, Butterfield, Brayfield & Curry, 1977). One size does not fit all.

KEY POINT: Personality plays a role in terms of being at risk for asthma, chronic headaches, peptic ulcers, arthritis, and circulatory and heart disease. Studies of the Type A personality, a competitive, time-regulated orientation, show a vulnerability to coronary disease through unexpressed hostility. A lack of perceived control hinders stress tolerance and creates vulnerability. This includes situations where the person is given the best of care, but without personal control.

TREATMENT AND RECOVERY

We now consider what is involved in being ill and seeking treatment. A successful health care interaction fol-lows a sequence of steps, an event schema (Chapter 2):

- The patient identifies symptoms that require medical attention.
- The patient presents the symptoms to the physician.
- The physician diagnoses the problem and selects a treatment.
- The physician presents the treatment, plans for referral to a specialist, or makes other recommendations to the patient.
- The patient adheres to the physician's recommendations.
- The patient improves or recovers.

Each of these steps involves the expectations, schemata and behaviour of both the physician and the patient (Ditto & Hilton, 1990; Jones, 1990). Thus, the characteristic actions of the person who is ill – how she com-municates with family or physician, whether she follows the physician's orders – and the reactions of family, friends and physicians to that person constitute an important set of social psychological phenomena.

Sickness as a social role

Just what does it mean to say that someone is sick? Physicians diagnose illnesses based on their interpretations of patients' symptoms, and test results and other observable cues from a physical examination. On the other hand, people in general will decide that they are sick when they 'don't feel well'. Remember that a headache may be symptomatic of a cold, influenza, a brain tumour, ill-prescribed glasses, stress, lack of caffeine or lack of sleep. Judgements of being sick are related to some combination of experienced symptoms and incapacity to perform usual activities (Blaxter, 1990).

Social psychological factors play a role in defining some illnesses, helping us to decide when we are 'sick'. Consider the syndrome of premenstrual distress (PMS). While it is generally accepted that many women experience symptoms such as tension or cramping late in their menstrual cycle (Hurt & Schnurr, 1992), social definitions complicate the picture. For instance, studies in which women keep daily diaries of their moods or perform cognitive tests show little evidence of fluctuations across the menstrual cycle, even among those who say that they suffer from PMS (Hardie, 1997; Sommer, 1992). Some scientists argue that PMS is largely a socially constructed disorder, although this view is controversial (Rodin, 1992).

Particularly in the case of long-term, disabling or life-threatening illnesses, the people involved can be viewed as behaving in accordance with a role schema for being sick (Alcock, 1986). The role also defines how others perceive and act towards the sick person. People who are sick are excused from their normal duties, whether at home or at work, but they are expected to behave in an appropriate manner. They should be doing their best to rest, and seek treatment when necessary. We do not expect someone who is sick at home with the flu to spend hours on the telephone talking and laughing with friends, or to be exercising on a treadmill. Such behaviour departs from the sick role. Imagine how neighbours, and even family members, would react to a labourer claiming to be unable to work because of a disability who nonetheless spends hours gardening at home. Now, it may be that gardening does not produce or increase pain, but that the tasks required in the course of daily work would do so. But people cannot see one's pain; they only have one's word for it, and working in the garden suggests that maybe the pain is not so limiting as is being claimed. Such reactions quickly teach the injured worker to avoid gardening and to behave in line with what is expected of an injured person. Thus, injured or sick people act accordingly; they avoid physical activity, look sad or distressed, and are reinforced for this sick behaviour. A self-fulfilling prophecy is set up that may, because of deconditioning and disuse-induced muscle atrophy, end in genuine disability.

On the other hand, people with serious illnesses often try to minimize their suffering for the sake of their families. Yet, this is often impossible, for the changes brought on by disease cannot be hidden. Consider a person who is suffering from life-threatening cancer (Dunkel-Schetter, Feinstein, et al., 1992). Changes in the person's appearance or demeanour become a constant reminder of the illness and the treatment regimen, and so become a source of anxiety to those around him or her (Dunkel-Schetter & Wortman, 1982). As well, people often feel somewhat anxious and confused about what to say or do in response. This can lead to a breakdown in communication. Interviews with women who had had radical mastectomies for breast cancer revealed that the vast majority had not discussed it in any detail with their husbands before or while in hospital and only 50% did so afterwards (Krantz & Johnson, 1978). Often, people choose to 'tell them what they want to hear', being as 'positive' as possible. Indeed, the model of the 'heroic' cancer patient implies that the person can overcome the illness by becoming more expressive, positive and courageous (Doan & Gray, 1992). The noted author Susan Sontag (1978) has written eloquently about the social role of the patient with a serious illness such as cancer or AIDS.

Pain Social psychological factors play an important role in the experience of pain and how we signal it to others (Alcock, 1986). We begin to learn about how to label pain and how to deal with it in early childhood. When a child falls down and begins to cry, parents often ask, 'Where does it hurt?', focusing on pain even though the child may be crying because of fear or surprise. Other parents simply reassure the child – 'You're fine – don't cry'. Through such responses, children learn about the importance of pain (something to be really upset about or something that we can bear), about how to describe it appropriately, and about what to expect from others (Craig, 1978). In some cases, children learn to feel anxious about pain. As a result, not only does pain bring physical discomfort of greater or lesser intensity, but it can also bring about rumination that often leads to magnification of its intensity and meaning, and to feeling helpless about it (Sullivan, Bishop & Pivik, 1995; Sullivan, Rodgers & Kirsch, 2001; Tennen et al., 1992). The tendency to catastrophize when in pain contributes to more intense pain experiences and increased emotional distress (Sullivan et al., 2001).

Given that children are brought up somewhat differently in different cultures, it is not surprising that reactions to pain also vary somewhat with culture. People in various ethnic groups tend to experience and report pain in distinctive ways (Lipton & Marbach, 1984; Peacock & Patel, 2008), and these can have important clinical implications (Tait & Chibnall, 2005). Strong cultural and ethnic differences have been found in pain threshold (i.e., the minimum level of intensity for a stimulus at which pain is detected) (Rahim-Williams, Riley, et al., 2012), in when people report to others that they are in pain, and in how others perceive that a person is in pain (Wandner, Scipio, et al., 2012). For instance, while Asian patients do not typically under-report symptoms, they tend to be less emotionally expressive about it (Lai & Linden, 1993). A study carried out in the United States (Zborowski, 1969) found that male patients from the New England states tended to suffer quietly on the assumption that crying or complaining would not help, while male Irish-American patients also suppressed complaints but only to protect a masculine self-image. Italian-American patients, in contrast, were very expressive in the expectation that they would gain sympathy and support from family and staff. However, it is important to note that as members of an immigrant ethnic group become more acculturated, succeeding generations gradually adopt the norms and behaviours of the dominant culture (Lai & Linden, 1993).

> **KEY POINT:** Being ill is seen as a social role with norms and prescribed behaviours, including the obligation to cooperate and get better. The role also defines how others perceive and act towards the sick person. The 'good patient' is obliged to be cheerful and optimistic, setting up communication barriers. People suffering pain may often react with denial or catastrophizing, which can make the situation worse. In all of this, cultural differences are evident.

Communication between physicians and patients

Communication is fundamental to the caregiver–patient relationship, as in any relationship, but there are some special features to consider. The average appointment with a family physician is usually brief and to the point (Nelson & McLemore, 1988). During that time, the physician may attempt to establish or renew feelings of trust and cooperation with the patient, gain information about medical history and current complaints, conduct the appropriate physical examination, order appropriate tests and procedures, and discuss alternatives for further diagnosis and treatment. Clearly, communication skills are necessary for effective medical practice. Indeed, social psychologists have designed programmes in medical schools to train physicians in more effective communication (Roter & Hall, 1992).

As noted, the sick role prescribes what it means to be a 'good patient'. Most people try to be cooperative with a medical authority and as cheerful as they can manage in the circumstances. Physicians come to like their patients more when they are in better physical and emotional health, and when patients are more satisfied with their care (Hall, Epstein, Deciantis & McNeil, 1993). Because of this, patients may be reluctant to disclose information that seems trivial (Taylor, 1979). The price patients may pay as a result is ignorance about their own health and treatment (Abramson, Seligman & Teasdale, 1978).

As we discussed in Chapter 7, much of interpersonal communication between physician and patient is non-verbal (Friedman.1982). In an experiment, physicians were instructed to act in differing ways to different patients. The same physicians were evaluated most favourably by the patients when they leaned forward without folding their arms and nodded their heads in response to patients' comments (Harrigan & Rosenthal, 1983). In a study of 25 family-practice physicians, a self-report measure of non-verbal expressiveness was administered. Over the subsequent six months, the more emotionally expressive physicians were more in demand (Friedman, Prince, Riggio & DiMatteo, 1980). It has been reported that female physicians conducted longer visits, asked more questions, made more back-channel non-verbal responses and smiled more at their patients. And patients, both male or female, revealed more relevant information to them (Hall et al., 1993)

What to tell the patient How much should the physician tell the patient, particularly about a life-threatening illness or a painful medical procedure? The question is troublesome from both sides of the relationship. On one hand, becoming a patient need not imply that one sacrifices the right to receive the information needed to make decisions about one's health. On the other hand, the physician bears the legal and ethical responsibility for the patient and may honestly believe that full disclosure would further damage the patient's health. Furthermore, being human, physicians do not like to deliver bad news (Saul & Kass, 1969; Tesser & Rosen, 1975), and patients who are seriously ill may honestly prefer to cling to illusions and hopes (Miller & Mangan, 1983), even while most say that they want to be informed (Blumenfeld, Levy & Kaufman, 1979).

If the physician must relay unpleasant news, communicating such news in a calm and reassuring manner will be better received and more accurately remembered by the patient (Shapiro, Boggs, Melamed & Graham-Pole, 1992). The same applies to preparing the patient for an unpleasant procedure (Johnson & Leventhal,

1994). When people must face major surgery, those who are moderately anxious about it actually fare best in post-operative recovery (Janis, 1958). These people tend to seek out information and to prepare themselves mentally for what is ahead – the 'work of worrying'.

> **KEY POINT:** Communication between patient and physician is important, both in providing important information to the physician and in boosting the morale of the patient. Non-verbal communication is also important in this process.

Patient noncompliance

Typically, a visit to the doctor's office concludes with one or more recommendations, such as to follow a restricted diet, or to fill and take a prescription as directed. However, research in various cultures shows that overall noncompliance with medical advice is only around 50% (Haynes, McKibbon & Kanani, 1996). For instance, many patients fail to comply with a regimen of using eye drops daily to counteract glaucoma, and noncompliance with this simple recommendation is a leading cause of blindness (Goldberg, 2000). Despite their best efforts, physicians are remarkably ineffectual in influencing patients to follow a treatment regimen such as monitoring blood sugar levels, adhering to dietary restrictions or taking medications as prescribed (see Werthemier & Santella, 2007; van Dulmen, Siuijs, et al., 2007). Adherence is higher among patients with acute illnesses such as cancer, somewhat less with diabetes and cardiovascular diseases, and lowest with hypertension (high blood pressure).

Hypertension is common, easily diagnosed and if untreated can lead to strokes, heart failure, renal failure, blindness and heart disease (Herd & Weiss, 1984). Many patients believe mistakenly that they can tell when their blood pressure is high, relying on unreliable cues such as an elevated pulse rate (Leventhal, Meyer & Nerenz, 1980). High blood pressure can be treated effectively, primarily by medication, weight control, a sodium-restricted diet or relaxation techniques. Yet between 70 and 90% of patients diagnosed as hypertensive fail to take their medication regularly or to comply with other recommendations (Leventhal & Hirschman, 1982).

Research shows that patients comply more often when they perceive their physician as friendly, caring and interested in them, as well as having sound knowledge (DiNicola & DiMatteo, 1984). Of course, in a multicultural world, familiarity with the language and the culture of the patient is crucial to obtaining compliance (Villagran, Hajek, Zhao, Peterson & Wittenberg-Lyles, 2011). Rodin and Janis (1979) also suggest that physicians can enhance the therapeutic relationship by encouraging disclosure by the patient,

Figure 15.7 Physician, patient and prescription
Source: iofoto/Shutterstock.com

giving positive feedback of acceptance, asking whether the patient understands the recommendations and implying that the patient has the ultimate control and responsibility. Patients are also more likely to comply with physicians who make definite follow-up appointments with their patients to track progress (DiMatteo et al., 1993).

However, the research evaluating attempts to increase compliance is rather discouraging. The effects are fairly weak and not lasting (Roter et al., 1998; Haynes, McKibbon & Kanani, 1996; van Dulmen et al., 2007). The costs of noncompliance, both to health care systems and to patients, are significant.

> **KEY POINT:** Patient noncompliance to the recommendations of health care providers is now recognized as a major problem.

Maintenance or relapse

While many people have begun exercise programmes and have shown significant improvements in fitness, relatively few remain active, even in cardiac rehabilitation programmes (Oldridge & Streiner, 1990). While a calorie-restricted diet may help, people collectively lose metric tons of fat each year, but few can keep it off beyond one year (Tinker & Tucker, 1997; Wilson, 1984). And while many alcoholics, heroin addicts and smokers successfully complete treatment programmes or quit by themselves, about two-thirds relapse within three months after withdrawal (Hunt, Barnett & Branch, 1971).

To understand why people lose control after a lapse, it is important to understand how people interpret the slip, a phenomenon called the abstinence violation effect (Marlatt & Gordon, 1979). The person experiences cognitive dissonance between the slip as a behaviour and their self-image as an ex-smoker, dieter or recovering alcoholic. Further, the person will tend to make a dispositional attribution, explaining the slip in terms of personal weakness and inadequacy, rather than viewing it as a momentary lapse in judgement. This produces discouragement and feelings of not being able to exercise control, and this feeds into a self-fulfilling prophecy. Lapse becomes relapse.

One startling instance of *non*-relapse was reported by Robins, Helzer & Davis (1975). Urine screening procedures revealed that a relatively high proportion of US soldiers in the Viet Nam War had become addicted to daily use of high-grade heroin. This stopped upon their return to the USA. Did they relapse? Almost 900 of them were interviewed two years later. While most of them reported that heroin was readily available to them, only about 12% were addicted although some of the others did report occasional use. Clearly the addictive pattern of heroin use was established in a specific environment, and in most cases did not generalize to their home environment.

> **KEY POINT:** Behavioural change towards more healthy behaviours often ends in relapse and failure. The abstinence violation effect consists of two social psychological processes: cognitive dissonance between the behavioural slip and one's self-image, and a dispositional attribution concerning the behaviour.

SOCIAL PSYCHOLOGY AND PUBLIC HEALTH

Thus far, we have seen that our behaviours have a strong impact on our health. If people act in ways to endanger their health, it is only sound public health policy to change these behaviours. Consider this question: why do people persist in acting in ways harmful to themselves even when they are aware of the risks? The key seems to be that they must be given a credible alternative. Keep this in mind as we examine two decision-making models.

Health beliefs model

What will lead us to change our behaviour in a way that is beneficial to our health? We can reason that there are two stages to this process of change. First, we must decide that we must 'do something' to protect our health;

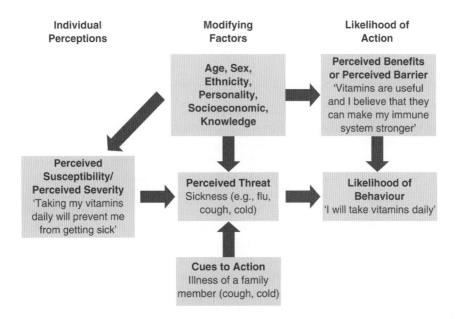

Figure 15.8 The health beliefs model

Source: Based on Becker 1974

lose some weight, get more exercise, stop smoking. Then we must decide what to do and how to achieve that goal. The health beliefs model (Figure 15.8) represents such a two-stage process (Becker, 1974).

Let's take the example of Roberto who works in an office, watches sports on TV and has a sedentary life-style. His physician has recommended some form of exercise to promote cardiovascular fitness and to reduce the risk of heart attack.

The process begins with a person's appraisal that something is wrong. Roberto has come to believe that he is *susceptible* to a health problem: he could have an early heart attack unless he acts. His friend Joanne is in hospital after a heart attack, which reminds him of the danger of heart disease, and he has been noticing that his heart races when he has to run to catch his commuter train.

If the perceived threat of possible illness is accompanied by cues to action, such as urging by his family, then he decides to 'do something'. Now he must decide what to do. The choice of action will depend upon the relative costs and benefits perceived for various alternatives. Roberto has been 'sold' aerobic exercise as an effective preventive action and also likes the prospect of losing weight and looking and feeling better. He considers joining his sister's health club. However, perceived barriers include the time required and the membership fees. After weighing the long-term benefits against the costs, Roberto decides that it is worth it and so he is likely to begin aerobic exercise. In short, he believes that coronary disease is a real and per-sonal threat and he perceives exercise as an effective way to reduce that threat without excessive personal sacrifice.

In general, the model has been helpful in showing how beliefs about health become translated into action (Janz & Becker, 1984; Harrison, Mullen & Green, 1992; Strecher, Champion & Rosenstock, 1997). For instance, it predicts compliance in wearing protective helmets by cyclists (Quine, Rutter & Arnold, 2000), increased caution regarding AIDS-related sexual behaviours (Lollis, Johnson & Antoni, 1997). The model also predicts adherence to a medical regimen for insulin-dependent diabetes among adolescents (Bond, Aiken & Somerville, 1992) and breast self-examination as a means of detecting early-stage breast cancer among women (Savage & Clarke, 1996).

Protection motivation model

In Chapter 5, we addressed the question of fear-arousing persuasive messages (Rogers, 1975, 1983). Briefly, protection motivation theory states that individuals engage in a health behaviour to the extent that they are motivated to protect themselves from a threat. It involves two processes of judgement or appraisal: threat appraisal and coping appraisal. Individuals first evaluate the threat – is it a severe threat? Are they personally susceptible to it? Then they appraise the suggested behavioural response to the threat – would the behaviour be effective? What are the obstacles to the behaviour? Note that the four appraisals – threat severity, personal vulnerability, behavioural effectiveness and self-efficacy relative to obstacles – are similar to those suggested in the health beliefs model.

However, these factors would not be sufficient to lead to action. The person must also believe that he or she has the capacity to perform the recommended action consistently, that is, possesses a sense of self-efficacy (Wulfert & Wan, 1993; Seydel, Taal & Wiegman, 1990). For example, self-efficacy beliefs predicted whether workers were likely to use protective devices when they were exposed to harmful noise levels (Melamed, Rabinowitz, et al., 1996). In another study, the theory predicting reactions to messages concerning the danger of cancer from smoking when the research participants felt personally capable of giving up smoking (Sturges & Rogers, 1996).

In sum, a fear message arouses two needs at once, two parallel processes (Witte, 1994; Maloney, Lapinski & Witte, 2011). One process involves the need to manage the danger contained in the message. Thus a decision to use condoms can address the danger of contracting a sexually transmitted disease. The other process involves managing the emotional state aroused by the message at that time. The individual may well focus on the experience of fear itself, and act to reduce that fear, such as through ignoring the message, distraction, humour or derogating the source (all in Chapter 5).

One final point regarding persuasion in health promotion: the approaches outlined above are all based on the assumption that we make rational decisions about actions that affect our health (Ronis, 1992). However, much of our health-relevant behaviour is not planned, and occurs spontaneously and 'thoughtlessly' (Gibbons, Kingsbury & Gerrard, 2012). Further, people may have reasons irrelevant to health for behaving in ways that enhance or impair their health. For instance, dieting will often reflect concerns about physical appearance rather than health. And describing osteoporosis in terms of being visibly disfiguring rather than a health problem enhances the probability that people at risk will exercise and take calcium supplements (Klohn & Rogers, 1991).

WELL-BEING: MORE THAN ABSENCE OF ILLNESS

In a series of studies conducted in a variety of nations, participants were simply asked to rate their current state of health, usually along a Likert-type scale: poor–excellent. These participants were then followed up, over periods of up to 27 years. The results were striking: their subjective ratings of their own health were a robust predictor of how often they would be ill and how long they would live (Idler & Binyamini, 1997). It is important to note that these predictions held after controlling for other factors which would predict health outcomes: current state of health and lab tests at the time of the questionnaire administration, personal medical history, family history of certain illnesses. A sense of well-being seems to be associated with better health outcomes.

What does having a sense of well-being mean to you? Would you see it in terms of your mood, happiness, or how satisfied you are with your life? Or would you look deeper, and find your sense of well-being in terms of what your life means to you, such as your relationships with others, making the most of your abilities, finding a purpose to your life? These two notions of well-being are not identical (Keyes, Shmotkin & Ryff, 2002).

The former is called hedonic well-being, defined in terms of your emotional states, positive and negative, and your satisfaction with life (Diener & Lucas, 2003). Note that these may combine in various ways. For instance, you may generally find yourself in a good mood, but be dissatisfied with your life as it is now (Busseri, Sadava & DeCourville, 2007; Busseri & Sadava, 2011). Indeed, you may be the type of person who experiences intense emotions, positive and negative, or you may be a person who keeps an even keel; positive emotions are not simply the obverse of negative emotions (Frederickson, 2001). In line with what has been discussed earlier, a substantial body of research links positive emotions to good heath and even longevity (Pressman & Cohen, 2005).

In contrast, the eudaimonic conception defines well-being in terms of living a life that is personally meaningful. Ryff (1989) suggests a model of psychological well-being (PWB) in terms of six dimensions: self-acceptance, positive relations with others, the ability to shape one's environment to meet one's needs, a sense of personal autonomy and self-determination, making the most of one's talents and abilities (personal growth) and finding meaning or purpose in life. Those who scored high on a composite score of eudaimonic well-being also showed lower levels of biological stress markers, lower cardiovascular risk and longer duration of sleep (Ryff, Singer & Love, 2004).

Kilpatrick and Cantril outlined a method of visualising your life as a ladder – where the top represents the best possible life for you, and the lowest rung represents the worst possible life for you.

Figure 15.9 Cantril Self-anchoring Ladder of Life Satisfaction

Source: Kilpatrick & Cantril (1960)

What factors contribute to a sense of well-being?

Certainly money matters, but less than one might think, at least when above the poverty level (Akin, Norton & Dunn, 2009; Fischer & Boer, 2011; Oshi & Schimmack, 2010). The country in which you live will certainly have consequences for your life: your job opportunities and income, your risk of becoming a victim of violence, your access to health care, and the pride that you feel for your country. In a survey of 132,516 respondents in 128 countries, life satisfaction was related to national satisfaction, as measured by the self-anchoring ladder technique (Figure 15.9), in which the bottom rung represents the worst possible life, and the top rung represents the best possible life (Morrison, Tay & Diener, 2011). However, this relationship between satisfaction with your life and with your nation was strongest in the poorest countries and for people who had lower incomes. The researchers also found a stronger relationship between life satisfaction and satisfaction with one's country in collectivist, non-Western nations.

KEY POINT: A personal sense of well-being has a strong relationship with health and mortality. The hedonic conception of subjective well-being consists of high levels of life satisfaction and positive emotions, and low levels of negative emotions. The eudaimonic conception of a meaningful life, a multidimensional mode of psychological well-being (PWB) consists of six dimensions of thriving: self-acceptance, positive relations with others, the ability to shape one's environment to meet one's needs, a sense of personal autonomy and self-determination, making the most of one's talents and abilities (personal growth) and finding meaning or purpose in life. A variety of factors contribute to well-being, including health, economic prosperity, the quality of interpersonal relationships and national differences. A common measure of well-being is the Cantril ladder of life satisfaction (Figure 15.9).

Social Psychology in Action

SUMMARY

1. The reliability of eyewitness testimony is questionable in a number of circumstances. It is influenced by police line-up procedures, stress, time elapsed between incident and recall, the nature of the protagonist, and biased questioning.
2. Findings from simulated jury studies indicate biases among jurors particularly related to authoritarianism.
3. Deception may occur by commission (telling a lie) or omission (concealing or omitting something). Individuals vary in their capacity to use verbal and non-verbal cues to detect deception.
4. Attributions of responsibility are influenced by the severity of consequences of the act.
5. The perception of justice concerns both what is fair (distributive justice) and how such decisions are arrived at (procedural justice), and is influenced by beliefs in a just world.
6. Distributive justice follows the rules of equity (a fair ratio of inputs to outputs in comparison with other people), equality (a uniform distribution of resources) or need (distribution of resources according to need).
7. Health care is a global concern, involving more than medical treatment of disease. Social psychological factors play a role.
8. The socioeconomic status gradient effect links health to relative status in society.
9. People may behave in health-risky or health-enhancing ways, and there does not seem to be a consistency across various behaviours. Social modelling is a major influence.
10. Stress may derive from both major life events and the hassles of daily life. Social support enhances health,

both by buffering the effects of stress and by alleviating loneliness.
11. Perceived lack of control can affect health. The Type A personality linked to a risk of heart attacks consists of high achievement orientation, impatience, and especially unexpressed cynical hostility towards others.
12. Close relationships with specific others can enhance health, and loneliness is an established health risk.
13. The health beliefs model begins with a perception that one is at risk of illness, leading to a readiness to act, which becomes translated into an action depending on the rewards and costs attributed to that action. Fear-arousing communications can be effective if an appropriate and realistic action is recommended to deal with the threat.
14. Being sick can be seen as involving a social role with a script for being sick.
15. Patient noncompliance with the recommendations of caregivers, including taking prescription drugs, is a widespread problem.
16. After beneficial change in behaviour, relapse is common. The abstinence violation effect, specific to addictive behaviours, converts a momentary slip into a full-blown relapse.
17. There are two models of well-being: subjective, or hedonic, well-being defined in terms of high positive affect, low negative affect and a positive life satisfaction; and psychological, or eudaimonic, well-being, living a life that is personally meaningful and including self-acceptance, positive relations with others, a sense of personal efficacy, and finding meaning in life.

POINTS TO PONDER

- The ideal to which a just system of justice strives is a fair trial. Given the evidence presented in this chapter, how would you change the trial system to ensure fairness?
- How do you think the media (movies, TV, Internet, novels) have influenced the ways in which we perceive trials and the justice system? Are these effects advantageous or disadvantageous?
- Think about some of the ways in which the basic processes of social cognition (Chapter 2) are reflected in how jurors form impressions and judgements about the defendant. Consider the extent to which each of the two processes of thinking, fast and slow, are involved.

492

- How do considerations of distribution and procedures influence our perceptions of justice? Do we live in a relatively 'just world'?
- What are the advantages and disadvantages of the adversarial and inquisitorial systems?
- It seems obvious that being with people, especially the people important to us, is good for us, and loneliness is unhealthy. But why?
- Why don't people take better care of themselves, to avoid being sick and to recover when they are sick?
- What does it mean to be healthy? To feel healthy? Is it more than 'not being sick'?

FURTHER READING

L. Bagnoli & G.B. Traverso (Eds) (2013). *Psychology and law in a changing world: New trends in theory, practice and research*. London: Routledge.

Articles on various aspects of social psychology and criminology, with a focus on consistencies and comparisons between nations, cultures and legal systems.

D.R. Bobocel, A.C. Kay, M.P. Zanna & J.M. Olson (Eds) (2011). *The psychology of justice and legitimacy: The Ontario symposium* (Vol. 11). New York: Psychology Press.

A set of excellent papers by established scholars in this emerging area.

Kaplan, M.F. & Martin, A.N. (2006). *Understanding world jury systems through social psychological research*. New York: Psychology Press.

A fascinating collection of papers in which various systems of trial justice, particularly juries, are examined.

Lampinen, J.M., Neuschatz, J.S. & Cling, A.D. (2012). *The psychology of eyewitness identification*. New York: The Psychology Press.

A comprehensive and updated review of what we have learned about the accuracy and reliability of eyewitness testimony from the perspective of basic psychology research.

Revenson, T.A., Kayser, K. & Bodenmann, G. (Eds) (2005). *Couples coping with stress: Emerging perspectives on dyadic coping*. Washington, D.C.: American Psychological Association.

An in-depth set of papers dealing with how couples cope with stress within and outside of the family, and stress caused by physical and mental illnesses.

WEBLINKS

Law and psychology website: http://www.apa.org/research/action/law.aspx

Access to Justice: www.acjnet.org

Very useful links to legislation, organizations, databases and discussions.

The health psychology network: http://www.healthpsychology.net/pages/290031/index.htm

Material on evidence-based treatment, research topics and how to obtain training in health psychology as a profession.

Health section, social psychology network: http://www.socialpsychology.org/health.htm#general

A wealth of resources related to social psychology and health.

BIBLIOGRAPHY

Abrahamson, A.C., Baker, L.A. & Caspi, A. (2002). Rebellious teens? Genetic and environmental influences on the social attitudes of adolescents. *Journal of Personality and Social Psychology, 83,* 1392–1408.

Abrams, D. & Hogg, M.A. (1990). The social context of discourse: Let's not throw out the baby with the bath water. *Philosophical Psychology, 3,* 219–225.

Abrams, D., Randsley de Moura, G., Marques, J. M. & Hutchison, P. (2008). Innovation credit: When can leaders oppose their group's norms? *Journal of Personality and Social Psychology, 95,* 662–678.

Abramson, L.Y., Seligman, M.E.P. & Teasdale, J.D. (1978). Learned helplessness in humans: Critique and reformulation. *Journal of Abnormal and Social Psychology, 87,* 49–74.

Abu-Haidar, F. (1989). Are Iraqi women more prestige conscious than men? Sex differentiation in Baghdadi Arabic. *Language in Society, 18,* 471–481.

Acevedo, P. & Aron, A. (2009). Does a long-term relationship kill romantic love? *Review of General Psychology, 13,* 59–65.

Achterberg, P., Aupers, S., Heilbron, J. & Houtman, D. (2011). A cultural globalization of popular music? American, Dutch, French, and German pop charts (1965–2005). *American Behavioral Scientist, 55,* 589–608.

Adachi, P.J.C. & Willoughby, T. (2011). The of videogame competition and violence on aggressive behavior: Which characteristic has the greatest influence? *Psychology of Violence, 1,* 259–274.

Adair, J.G. (1973). *The human subject.* Boston: Little, Brown.

Adair, J.G. (1980). Psychology at the turn of the century: Crises, challenges, promises. *Canadian Psychologist, 21,* 165–178.

Adair, J.G., Dushenko, T.W. & Lindsay, R.C.L. (1985). Ethical regulations and their impact on research practice. *American Psychologist, 40,* 59–72.

Adams, G. & Huston, T. (1975). Social perception of middle-aged persons varying in physical attractiveness. *Developmental Psychology, 11,* 657–658.

Adams, G., Garcia, D., Purdie-Vaughns, M. & Steele, C.M. (2006). The detrimental effects of a suggestion of sexism in an instruction situation. *Journal of Experimental Social Psychology, 42,* 602–615.

Adams, J.S. (1965). Inequity in social exchange. In L. Berkowitz (Ed.), *Advances in experimental social psychology* (Vol. 2). (pp. 267–295). New York: Academic Press.

Adams, M. (2003). *Fire and ice. The United States, Canada and the myth of converging values.* Toronto: Penguin Books.

Adler, N.E., Boyce, T., Chesney, M.A., Cohen, S., Folkman, S., Kahn, R.L. & Syme, S.L. (1994). Socioeconomic status and health: The challenge of the gradient. *American Psychologist, 49,* 15–24.

Adler, N.J. (1999a). Global leaders: Women of influence. In G.N. Powell (Ed.), *Handbook of gender and work* (pp. 239–261). Thousand Oaks, CA: Sage Publications.

Adler, N.J. (1999b). Global leadership: Women leaders. In W.H. Mobley (Ed.), *Advances in global leadership* (Vol. 1). (pp. 49–73). Stamford, CT: JAI Press, Inc.

Adorno, T.W., Frenkel-Brunswick, E., Levinson, D.J. & Sanford, R.N. (1950). *The authoritarian personality.* New York: Harper.

Ajzen, I. (1985). From intentions to actions: A theory of planned behavior. In J. Kuhl & J. Beckmann (Eds), *Action-control: From cognition to behavior* (pp. 11–39). Heidelberg: Springer.

Ajzen, I. (1987). Attitudes, traits and actions: Dispositional prediction of behaviour in personality and social psychology. In L. Berkowitz (Ed.), *Advances in experimental social psychology* (Vol. 20). (pp. 1–63). New York: Academic Press.

Ajzen, I. (1991). The theory of planned behavior. *Organizational Behavior and Human Decision Processes*, *50*, 179–211.

Ajzen, I. & Fishbein, M. (1980). *Understanding attitudes and predicting social behavior.* Englewood Cliffs, NJ: Prentice-Hall.

Akin, L.B., Norton, M. & Dunn, E.W. (2009). Wealth and well-being: Money matters but less than people think. *Journal of Positive Psychology*, *4*, 523–527.

Albright, D.E. & Hazler, R.J. (1995). A right to die? Ethical dilemmas of euthanasia. *Counselling and Values*, *39*, 177–189.

Albright, L. & Forziati, C. (1995). Cross-situational consistency and perceptual accuracy in leadership. *Personality and Social Psychology Bulletin*, *21*, 1269–1276.

Alcock, J.E. (1975). Motivation in an asymmetric bargaining situation: A cross-cultural study. *International Journal of Psychology, 10*, 69–81.

Alcock, J.E. (1986). Chronic pain and the injured worker. *Canadian Psychology*, *27*, 196–203.

Alcock, J.E. (1996). Training, experience and the detection of lying. *Legal Medical Quarterly*, *20*, 20–23.

Alcock, J.E. (1997). Social psychology and mental health. In S.W. Sadava & D.R. McCreary (Eds), *Applied Social Psychology* (pp. 113–135). Upper Saddle River, NJ: Prentice-Hall.

Alcock, J.E. (2006). Believe in survival. In E. Laszlo & P. Seidel (Eds), *Global survival* (pp. 85–100). New York: SelectBooks.

Alcock, J.E. & Mansell, D. (1977). Predisposition and behaviour in a collective dilemma. *Journal of Conflict Resolution*, *21*, 443–458.

Alexander, M.J. & Higgins, E.T. (1993). Emotional trade-off of becoming a parent: How social roles influence self-discrepancy effects. *Journal of Personality and Social Psychology*, *65*, 1259–1269.

Ali-Gombe, A., Guthrie, E. & McDermott, N. (1996). Mass hysteria: One syndrome or two? *British Journal of Psychiatry*, *168*, 633–635.

Allegeier, E.R. & Byrne, D. (1973). Attraction toward the opposite sex as a determinant of physical proximity. *Journal of Social Psychology*, *90*, 213–219.

Allen, J.B., Kenrick, D.T., Linder, D.E. & McCall, M.A. (1989). Arousal and attraction: A response-facilitation alternative to misattribution and negative-reinforcement models. *Journal of Personality and Social Psychology*, *57*, 261–270.

Allen, V.L. & Levine, J.M. (1971). Social support and conformity: The role of independent assessment of reality. *Journal of Experimental and Social Psychology*, *7*, 48–58.

Allison, S.T. & Messick, D.M. (1985). Effects of experience on performance in a replenishable resource trap. *Journal of Personality and Social Psychology*, *49*, 943–948.

Alloy, L.B. & Abramson, L.Y. (1979). Judgements of contingency in depressed and non-depressed students: Sadder but wiser. *Journal of Experimental Psychology: General*, *108*, 441–485.

Allport, F.H. (1924). *Social psychology.* Boston: Houghton-Mifflin.

Allport, G.W. (1935). Attitudes. In C.M. Murchison (Ed.), *Handbook of social psychology* (pp. 798–844). Worchester, MA: Clark University Press.

Allport, G.W. (1954). *The nature of prejudice.* Reading, MA: Addison-Wesley.

Allport, G.W. & Kramer, B.M. (1946). Some roots of prejudice. *Journal of Psychology*, *22*, 9–39.

Allport, G.W. & Postman, L.J. (1947). *The psychology of rumour.* New York: Holt, Rinehart & Winston.

Allport, G.W. & Vernon, P.E. (1931). *A study of values.* Boston: Houghton-Mifflin.

Allsop, D.T., Bassett, B.R. & Hoskins, J.A. (2007). Word-of-mouth research: Principles and applications, *Journal of Advertising Research*, *47*, 388–411.

Altemeyer, B. (1981). *Right-wing authoritarianism.* Winnipeg: University of Manitoba Press.

Altemeyer, B. (!988). *Enemies of freedom.* San Francisco: Jossey-Bass.

Altemeyer, B. & Hunsberger, B. (1992). Authoritarianism, religious fundamentalism, quest, and prejudice. *The International Journal for the Psychology of Religion*, *2*, 113–133.

Altemeyer, B. & Hunsberger, B. (1993). Religion and prejudice: Lessons not learned from the past: Reply to Gorsuch. *International Journal for the Psychology of Religion*, *3*, 33–37.

Altman, I. (1973). Reciprocity of interpersonal exchange. *Journal of the Theory of Social Behavior, 3*, 249–261.

Altman, I. & Vinsel, A.M. (1977). Personal space: An analysis of E.T. Hall's proxemics framework. In I. Altman & J.F. Wohlwill (Eds), *Human behavior and environment: Advances in theory and research* (pp. 181–259). New York: Plenum.

Altman, I., Vinsel, A. & Brown, B.A. (1981). Dialectic conceptions in social psychology: An application to social penetration and privacy regulation. In L. Berkowitz (Ed.), *Advances in experimental social psychology* (Vol. 14). (pp. 107–160). New York: Academic Press.

Alwin, D.F. (1996). From childbearing to child-rearing: The link between declines in fertility and changes in the socialization of children. *Population and Development Review, 22*, 176–196.

Alwin, D.F., Cohen, R.L. & Newcomb, T.M. (1991). *Political attitudes over the life span: The Bennington women after fifty years.* Madison: University of Wisconsin Press.

Amato, P.R. (1983). Helping behavior in urban and rural settings: Field studies based on a taxonomic organization of helping episodes. *Journal of Personality and Social Psychology, 45*, 571–586.

Ames, D.L. & Fiske, S.T. (2010). Cultural neuroscience. *Asian Journal of Social Psychology, 13*, 72–82.

Amichai-Hamburger, Y. & Ben-Artzi, E. (2003). Loneliness and Internet use. *Computers in Human Behavior, 19*, 71–80.

Amichai-Hamburger, Y. & McKenna, K.Y.A. (2006). The contact hypothesis reconsidered: Interacting via the Internet. *Journal of Computer-Mediated Communication, 11*, 825–843.

Amiot, C.E. & Aubin, R.M. (2013). Why and how are you attached to your social group? Investigating different forms of social identification. *British Journal of Social Psychology, 52*, 563–586.

Amir, Y. (1976). The role of intergroup contact in change of prejudice and ethnic relations. In P.A. Katz (Ed.), *Towards the elimination of racism* (pp. 245–308). Elmsford, NY: Pergamon Press.

Amodio, D.M. (2009). Intergroup anxiety effects on the control of racial stereotypes: A psychoneuroendocrine analysis. *Journal of Experimental Social Psychology, 45*, 60–67.

Amodio, D.M. & Ratner, K.G. (2011). A memory system model of implicit social cognition. *Current Directions in Psychological Science, 20*, 143–148.

Andersen, S.M., Saribay, S.A. & Thorpe, J.S. (2008). Simple kindness can go a long way: Relationships, social identity, and engagement. *Social Psychology, 39*, 59–69.

Anderson, C.A., Benjamin, A.J. Jr. & Bartholow, B.D. (1998). Does the gun pull the trigger? Automatic priming effects of weapon pictures and weapon names. *Psychological Science, 9*, 308–314.

Anderson, C.A. & Bushman, B.J. (2001). Effects of violent video games on aggressive behavior, aggressive cognition, aggressive affect, physiological arousal, and prosocial behavior: A meta-analytic review of the scientific literature. *Psychological Science, 12*, 353–359.

Anderson, C.A. & Bushman, B.J. (2002). Human aggression. *Annual Review of Psychology, 53*, 27–51.

Anderson, C.A., Lepper, M.R. & Ross, L. (1980). Perseverance of social theories: The role of explanation in the persistence of discredited information. *Journal of Personality and Social Psychology, 39*, 1037–1049.

Anderson, C.A. & Sedikides, C. (1990). Thinking about people. Contributions of a typological alternative to associationistic and dimensional models of person perception. *Journal of Personality and Social Psychology, 60*, 203–217.

Anderson, C.A., Shibuya, A., Ihori, N., Swing, E.L., Bushman, B.J., Sakamoto, A, Rothstein, H. R. & Saleem, M. (2010). Violent video game effects on aggression, empathy, and prosocial behavior in Eastern and Western countries: A meta-analytic review. *Psychological Bulletin, 136*, 151–173.

Anderson, C.M., Riddle, B.L. & Martin, M.M. (1999). Socialization processes in groups. In L.R. Frey, Gouran, D. & Poole, M.S. (Eds) *The Handbook of Group Communication Theory and Research.* (pp. 139–166). London: Sage.

Anderson, N.H. (1959). Test of a model of opinion change. *Journal of Abnormal and Social Psychology, 59*, 371–381.

Anderson, N.H. (1965). Adding versus averaging as a stimulus combination rule in impression formation. *Journal of Experimental Psychology, 70*, 394–400.

Anderson, N.H. (1978). Cognitive algebra: Integration theory applied to social attribution. In L. Berkowitz (Ed.), *Cognitive theories in social psychology*. New York: Academic Press.

Anderson, P. (2008). *Nonverbal communication: Forms and functions* (2nd Ed.). Long Grove, IL: Waveland Press.

Anderson, S.L., Adams, G. & Plaut, V.C. (2008). The cultural grounding of personal relationships: The importance of attractiveness in everyday life. *Journal of Personality and Social Psychology, 95,* 352–368.

Andreas, C.R. (1969). 'To receive from kings ...' An examination of government-to-government aid and its unintended consequences. *Journal of Social Issues, 25,* 167–180.

Angell, M. (1985). Disease as a reflection of the psyche. *New England Journal of Medicine, 312,* 1570–1572.

Antonakis, J. & Dalgas, O. (2009). Predicting elections: Child's play! *Science, 323,* 1183.

Apfelbaum, E. & McGuire, G.R. (1986). Models of suggestive influence and the disqualification of the social crowd. In C.F. Graumann & S. Moscovici (Eds), *Changing conceptions of crowd mind and behavior* (pp. 27–50). New York: Springer-Verlag.

Apicella, C.L., Little, A.C. & Marlowe, F.W. (2007). Changing perceptions of attractiveness as observers are exposed to a different culture. *Perception, 36,* 1813–1829.

App, B., McIntosh, D.N., Reed, C.L. & Hertenstein, M.J. (2011). Nonverbal channel use in communication of emotion: How may depend on why. *Emotion, 11,* 603–617.

Archer J. (2004). Sex differences in aggression in real-world settings: A meta-analytic review. *Review of General Psychology,* 8, 291–322.

Archer, J. (1976). Biological explanations of psychological sex differences. In B. Lloyd & J. Archer (Eds), *Exploring sex differences* (pp. 241–266). New York: Academic Press.

Archer, J. (2000a). Sex differences in aggression between heterosexual partners: A meta-analytic review. *Psychological Bulletin, 126,* 651–680.

Archer, J. (2000b). Sex differences in physical aggression to partners: A reply to Frieze (2000), Leaery (2000), and White, Smith, Koss and Figueredo (2000). *Psychological Bulletin, 126,* 697–702.

Archer, J. (2006). Cross-cultural differences in physical aggression between partners: A social-role analysis. *Personality and Social Psychology Review,* 10, 133–153.

Archer J. (2009). Does sexual selection explain human sex differences in aggression? *Behavioural and Brain Sciences, 32,* 249–311.

Archer, J. & Côté, S. (2005). Sex differences in aggressive behavior: A developmental and evolutionary perspective. In: R. Tremblay, W.W. Hartup & J. Archer (Eds), *Developmental origins of aggression*. New York: Guilford. pp. 425–443.

Archer, J. & Coyne, S.M. (2005). An integrated review of indirect, relational, and social aggression. *Personality and Social Psychology Review, 9,* 212–9,230.

Arendt, H. (1963). Eichmann in Jerusalem: A report on the banality of evil. New York: Viking.

Argyle, M. (1969). *Social interaction.* London: Tavistock.

Argyle, M. (1975). *Bodily communication.* London: Methuen & Co.

Argyle, M. & Dean, J. (1965). Eye-contact, distance and affiliation. *Sociometry, 28,* 289–304.

Arkin, R.M. & Baumgardner, A.H. (1985). Self-handicapping. In J.H. Harvey & G. Weary (Eds), *Attributions: Basic issues and applications* (pp. 169–202). New York: Academic Press.

Armitage, C.J. & Conner, M. (2001). Efficacy of the theory of planned behaviour: A meta-analytic review. *British Journal of Social Psychology, 40,* 471–499.

Arndt, J. & Crane, E. (1975). Response Bias, yea-saying, and the double negative. *Journal of Marketing Research, 12,* 218–220.

Arnett, J.J. (2002). The psychology of globalization. *American Psychologist, 57,* 774–783.

Arnett, J.J. (2009). The neglected 95%, a challenge to psychology's philosophy of science, *American Psychologist, 64,* 571–574. DOI: 10.1037/a0016723

Aron, A. & Westbay, L. (1996). Dimensions of the prototype of love. *Journal of Personality and Social Psychology, 70,* 535–551.

Aron, A., Paris, M. & Aron, E.N. (1995). Falling in love: Prospective studies of self-concept change. *Journal of Personality and Social Psychology, 69,* 1102–1112.

Aronson, E. (1984). *The social animal* (4th ed.). New York: W.H. Freeman.

Aronson, E. & Carlsmith, J.M. (1963). Effect of the severity of threat on the devaluation of forbidden behavior. *Journal of Abnormal and Social Psychology, 66,* 584–588.

Aronson, E. & Carlsmith, J.M. (1968). Experimentation in social psychology. In G. Lindzey & E. Aronson, (Eds), *Handbook of social psychology* (2nd ed.). (Vol. 2). (pp. 1–79). Reading, MA: Addison-Wesley.

Aronson, E. & Golden, B.W. (1962). The effect of relevant and irrelevant aspects of communicator credibility on attitude change. *Journal of Personality, 30*, 135–146.

Aronson, E., Willerman, B. & Floyd, J. (1966). The effect of a pratfall on increasing personal attractiveness. *Psychonomic Science, 4*, 157–158.

Aronson, E., Wilson, T.D. & Brewer, M.B. (1998). Experimentation in social psychology. In G. Lindzey, D. Gilbert & S.T. Fiske (Eds), *The handbook of social psychology, 4th edition, Volume 1.* (pp. 99–142). New York: Oxford University Press.

Aronson, E., Wilson, T.D. & Akert, R. (1994). *Social psychology: The heart and the mind.* New York: HarperCollins.

Arriaga, P., Monteiro, M.B. & Esteves, F. (2011). Effects of playing violent computer games on emotional desensitization and aggressive behavior. *Journal of Applied Social Psychology, 41*, 1900–1925.

Asch, S.E. (1946). Forming impressions of personality. *Journal of Abnormal and Social Psychology, 41*, 258–290.

Asch, S.E. (1951). Effects of group pressure upon the modification and distortion of judgements. In H. Guetzkow (Ed.), *Groups, leadership and men* (pp. 177–190). Pittsburgh: Carnegie Press.

Asendorpf, J.B., Banse, R. & Muecke, D. (2002). Double dissociation between implicit and explicit personality self-concept: The case of shy behavior. *Journal of Personality and Social Psychology, 83*, 380–393.

Ashmore, R.D. & Longo, L.C. (1995). Accuracy of stereotypes: What research on physical attractiveness can teach us. In Lee, Yueh-Ting (Ed.); Jussim, Lee J. (Ed.); McCauley, Clark R. (Ed.), (1995). *Stereotype accuracy: Toward appreciating group differences*, (pp. 63–86). Washington, DC, US: American Psychological Association.

Ashton, M.C. & Esses, V.M. (1999). Stereotype accuracy: Estimating the academic performance of ethnic groups. *Personality and Social Psychology Bulletin, 25*, 225–236.

Ashton, M.C., Danso, H.A., Maio, G.R., Esses, V.M., Bond, M.H., Keung, D.K.Y. (2005). Two dimensions of political attitudes and their individual difference correlates: A cross-cultural perspective. In R. M. Sorrentino, D. Cohen, J. Olson & M.P. Zanna, (Eds) *Cultural and social behavior: The Ontario Symposium*, Vol 10. (pp. 1–29). Hillsdale, NJ: Erlbaum.

Ashton, N.L., Shaw, M.E. & Worsham, A.P. (1980). Affective reactions to interpersonal distances by friends and strangers. *Bulletin of the Psychonomic Society, 15*, 306–308.

Ask, K., Reinhard, M., Marksteiner, T. & Granhag, P.A. (2010). Elasticity in evaluations of criminal evidence: Exploring the role of cognitive dissonance. *Legal and Criminological Psychology, 16*, 289–306.

Athanasiou, R. & Yashioka, G. (1973). The spatial character of friendship formation. *Environmental Behavior, 5*, 43–65.

Austin, W. (1979). Justice, freedom, and self-interest in intergroup conflict. In W.G. Austin & S. Worchel (Eds), *The social psychology of intergroup relations* (pp. 121–144). Monterey, CA: Brooks/Cole.

Avio, K.L. (1987). *The quality of mercy: Exercise of the Royal Prerogative in Canada.* Unpublished manuscript, Department of Economics, University of Victoria.

Axelrod, R. & Dion, D. (1988). The further evolution of cooperation. *Science, 242*, 1385–1390.

Azar, F. & Mullet, E. (2001). Interpersonal forgiveness among Lebanese: A six-confession study. *International Journal of Group Tensions, 30*, 161–181.

Azuma, H. (1984). Secondary control as a heterogeneous category. *American Psychologist, 9*, 970–971.

Bable, M. (2010). Dialect divergence and convergence in New Zealand English. *Language in Society, 39*, 437–456.

Bachorowski, J.-A. (1999). Vocal expression and perception of emotion. *Current Directions in Psychological Science, 8*, 53–57.

Backhouse, C. (1999). *Colour-coded: A legal history of racism in Canada, 1900–1950.* Toronto: The Osgoode Society for Legal Canadian History.

Backman, C.W. & Secord, P.F. (1959). The effect of perceived liking on interpersonal attraction. *Human Relations, 12*, 379–384.

Badie, D. (2010). Groupthink, Iraq, and the War on Terror: Explaining US policy shift toward Iraq. *Foreign Policy Analysis, 6*, 277–296.

Bailenson, J. N. & Yee, N. (2005). Digital chameleons: Automatic assimilation of nonverbal gestures in immersive virtual environments. *Psychological Science, 16*, 814–819.

Bailenson, J.N., Blascovich, J., Beall, A.C. & Loomis, J.M. (2003). Interpersonal distance in immersive virtual environments. *Personality and Social Psychology Bulletin, 29*, 819–833.

Bailey, J. A., Hill, K. G., Oesterle, S. & Hawkins, J. D. (2009). Parenting practices and problem behavior across three generations: Monitoring, harsh discipline, and drug use in the intergenerational transmission of externalizing behavior. *Developmental Psychology, 45*(5), 1214–1226. doi: 10.1037/a0016129

Bailey, K., West, R. & Anderson, C.A. (2011). The association between chronic exposure to video game violence and affective picture processing: An ERP study. *Cognitive, Affective, and Behavioral Neuroscience, 11*, 259–276.

Bailey, P., Onwuegbuzie, A.J. & Daley, C.E. (2000). Correlates of anxiety at three stages of the foreign language learning process. *Journal of Language and Social Psychology, 19*, 474–490.

Bakan, D. (1966). *The duality of human existence.* Chicago: Rand McNally.

Balaratnasingam, S. & Janca, A. (2006). Mass hysteria revisited. *Current Opinion in Psychiatry, 19*, 171–174.

Baldry, A.C. (2004). 'What about bullying?' An experimental field study to understand students' attitudes towards bullying and victimisation in Italian middle schools. *British Journal of Educational Psychology, 74*, 593–598.

Baldwin, M.W. (1992). Relational schemas and the processing of social information. *Psychological Bulletin, 112*, 461–468.

Baldwin, M.W., Fehr, B., Keedian, E., Seidel, M. & Thomson, D.W. (1993). An exploration of the relational schemata underlying attachment styles: Self-report and lexical decision approaches. *Personality and Social Psychology Bulletin, 19*, 746–754.

Baldwin, M.W., Keelan, J.P., Fehr, B., Enns, V. & Koh-Rangarajoo, E. (1996). Social-cognitive conceptualization of attachment working models: Availability and accessibility effects. *Journal of Personality and Social Psychology, 71*, 94–109.

Baldwin, M.W. & Sinclair, L. (1996). Self-esteem and 'if … then' contingencies of interpersonal acceptance. *Journal of Personality and Social Psychology, 71*, 1130–1141.

Balliet, D. (2010). Communication and cooperation in social dilemmas: A meta-analytic review. *Journal of Conflict Resolution, 54*, 39–57.

Balliet, D., Li, N.P., Macfarlan, S.J. & Van Vugt, M. (2011). Sex differences in cooperation: A meta-analytic review of social dilemmas. *Psychological Bulletin, 137*, 881–909.

Balliet, D., Li, P. & Joireman, J. (2011). Relating trait self-control and forgiveness within prosocials and proselfs: Compensatory versus synergistic models. *Journal of Personality and Social Psychology, 101*, 1090–1105.

Balliet, D., Mulder, L.B. & Van Lange, P.A.M. (2011). Reward, punishment, and cooperation: A meta-analysis. *Psychological Bulletin, 137*, 594–615.

Ball-Rokeach, S.J., Rokeach, M. & Grube, J.W. (1984). *The great American values test. Influencing behavior and belief through television.* New York: The Free Press.

Banas, J.A. & Rains, S.A. (2010). A meta-analysis of research on inoculation theory. *Communication Monographs, 77*, 281–311.

Bandura, A. (1973). *Aggression: A social learning analysis.* Englewood Cliffs, NJ: Prentice-Hall.

Bandura, A. (1974). Behavior theories and the models of man. *American Psychologist, 29,* 859–869.

Bandura, A. (1977). *Social learning theory.* Englewood Cliffs, NJ: Prentice-Hall.

Bandura, A. (1983). Psychological mechanisms of aggression. In R.G. Geen & E.I. Donnerstein, (Eds), *Aggression: Theoretical and empirical reviews* (Vol. 1). (pp. 1–40). New York: Academic Press.

Bandura, A., Ross, D. & Ross, S.A. (1963a). Vicarious reinforcement and imitative learning. *Journal of Abnormal and Social Psychology, 67*, 601–607.

Bandura, A., Ross, D. & Ross, S.A. (1963b). A comparative test of the status envy, social power, and secondary reinforcement theories of identificatory learning. *Journal of Abnormal and Social Psychology, 67*, 527–534.

Bandura, A. & Walters, R. (1963). *Social learning and personality development.* New York: Holt, Rinehart & Winston.

Bank, B.J. & Hansford, S.L. (2000). Gender and friendship: Why are men's same-sex friendships less intimate and supportive? *Personal Relationships*, *7*, 63–78.

Banuazizi, A. & Movahedi, S. (1975). Interpersonal dynamics in a simulated prison: A methodological analysis. *American Psychologist*, *30*, 152–160.

Barcia, D. (1985). Communication between psychiatrists and general practitioners. *Actas Luso-Espanolas Neurol. Psiquiat. Cienc. Afines*, *13*, 259. Cited by Bourhis, Roth & MacQueen, 1989.

Bardi, A. & Goodwin, R. (2011). The dual route to value change: Individual processes and cultural moderators. *Journal of Cross-Cultural Psychology*, *42*, 271–287.

Bardwick, J.M. (1971). *Psychology of women: A study of bio-cultural conflicts.* New York: Harper & Row.

Bargh, J.A. & Chartrand, T.L. (1999). The unbearable automaticity of being. *American Psychologist*, *54*, 462–479.

Barkan, R., Ayal, S., Gino, F. & Ariely, D. (2012). The pot calling the kettle black: Distancing response to ethical dissonance. *Journal of Experimental Psychology: General*, *141*, 757–773.

Barkowitz, P.B. & Brigham, J.C. (1982). Recognition of faces: Own-race bias, incentive and time delay. *Journal of Applied Social Psychology*, *12*, 255–268.

Baron, R.A. (1998). Cognitive mechanisms in entrepreneurship: Why and when entrepreneurs think differently than other people. *Journal of Business Venturing*, *13*, 275–294.

Baron, R.A. (2000). Counterfactual thinking and venture formation: The potential effects of thinking about 'what might have been'. *Journal of Business Venturing*, *15*, 79–92

Baron, R.M. & Rodin, J. (1978). Perceived control and crowding stress: Processes mediating the impact of spatial and social density. In A. Baum & Y. Epstein (Eds), *Human response to crowding.* Hillsdale, NJ: Erlbaum Associates.

Baron, R.S. (1986). Distraction – conflict theory: Progress and problems. In L. Berkowitz (Ed.), *Advances in experimental social psychology* (Vol. 19). (pp. 1–40). New York: Academic Press.

Bar-Tal, D. (1986, June). Group political beliefs. Annual Meeting, International Association of Political Psychology, Amsterdam.

Bartholomew, K. & Horowitz, L.M. (1991). Attachment style among young adults: A test

of a model. *Journal of Personality and Social Psychology*, *61*, 226–244.

Bartholomew, R. E. (2001). *Little green men, meowing nuns and head-hunting panics.* Jefferson, North Carolina: McFarland & Company.

Bartholomew, R.E. & Goode, E. (2000). Mass delusions and hysterias: Highlights the past millennium. *Skeptical Inquirer*, *24(3)*, 20–28.

Bartholomew, R.E. & Sirois, F. (1996). Epidemic hysteria in schools: An international and historical overview. *Educational Studies*, *22*, 285–311.

Bass, B.M. (1990). From transactional to transformational leadership: Learning to share the vision. *Organizational Dynamics*, *18*, 19–31.

Batanic, B. & Göritz, A.S. (2009). How does social psychology deal with new media? *Social Psychology*, *40*, 3–5.

Batson, C. D. (2011). *Altruism in humans.* New York: Oxford University Press.

Batson, C.D. & Gray, R.A. (1981). Religious orientation and helping behaviour: Responding to one's own or the victim's needs? *Journal of Personality and Social Psychology*, *40*, 511–520.

Batson, C.D. & Powell, A.A. (2003). Altruism and prosocial behaviour. In T. Millon & M. Lerner (Eds), *Handbook of psychology: Personality and social psychology (*Vol. 5). (pp. 463–484). New York: John Wiley & Sons, Inc.

Batson, C.D., Kobrynowics, D., Dinnerstein, J.L., Kampf, H.C. & Wilson, A.D. (1997). In a very different voice: Unmasking moral hypocrisy. *Journal of Personality and Social Psychology*, *72*, 1335–1348.

Batson, C.D., Oleson, K.C., Weeks, J.L., Healy, S.P., Reeves, P.J., Jennings, P. & Brown, T. (1989). Religious prosocial motivation: Is it altruistic or egoistic? *Journal of Personality and Social Psychology*, *57*, 873–884.

Batson, C.D. & Ventis, W.L. (1982). *The religious experience: A social psychological perspective.* New York: Oxford University Press.

Baum, A., Aiello, J.R. & Calesnick, L.E. (1978). Crowding and personal control: Social density and the development of learned helplessness. *Journal of Personality and Social Psychology*, *36*, 1000–1011.

Baum, A. & Valins, S. (1977). Architecture and social behavior. *Psychological studies and social density.* Hillsdale, NJ: Erlbaum.

Bauman, C.W. & Skitka, L.J. (2010). Making attributions for behaviors: The prevalence of correspondence bias in the general population. *Basic and Applied Social Psychology 32*, 269–277.

Baumeister, R.F. (1997). Evil. *Inside human cruelty and violence*. New York: W.H. Freeman and Company.

Baumeister, R.F. & Bratslavsky, E. (1999). Passion, intimacy and time: Passionate love as a function of change in intimacy. *Personality and Social Psychology Bulletin, 3*, 49–67.

Baumeister, R.F., Bratslavsky, E., Muraven, M. & Tice, D.M. (1998). Ego depletion: Is the active self a limited resource? *Journal of Personality and Social Psychology, 74*, 1252–1265.

Baumeister, R.F., Bushman, B.J. & Campbell, W. (2000). Self-esteem, narcissism, and aggression: Does violence result from low self-esteem or from threatened egotism? *Current Directions in Psychological Science, 9*, 26–29

Baumeister, R.F., Campbell, J.D., Krueger, J.I. & Vohs, K.D. (2003). Does high self-esteem cause better performance, interpersonal success, happiness or healthier lifestyles? *Psychological Science in the Public Interest, 4*, 1–44.

Baumeister, R.F., Chesner, S.P., Senders, P.S. & Tice, D.M. (1988). Who's in charge here? Group leaders do lend help in emergencies. *Personality and Social Psychology Bulletin, 14*, 17–22.

Baumeister, R.F., Heatherton, T.F. & Tice, D.M. (1994*). Losing control. How and why people fail at self-regulation.* San Diego, CA.: Academic Press.

Baumeister, R. F., Hutton, D. & Tice, D. (1989). Cognitive processing during deliberate self-presentation: How self-presenters alter and misinterpret the behavior of interaction partners. *Journal of Experimental Social Psychology, 25*, 59–78.

Baumeister, R.F., Smart, L. & Boden, J.M. (1996). Relation of threatened egoism to violence and aggression: The dark side of high self-esteem. *Psychological Review, 103*, 5–33.

Baumeister, R.F. & Sommer, K.L. (1997). What do men want? Gender differences and two spheres of belongingness: Comment on Cross and Madson. *Psychological Bulletin 122*, 38–44.

Baumeister, R.F., Stillwell, A.M. & Heatherton, T. F. (1994). Guilt: An interpersonal approach. *Psychological Bulletin, 115*, 243–267.

Baumeister, R., Vohs, K.D. & Tice, D.M. (2007). The strength model of self-control. *Current Directions in Psychological Science, 16*, 351–355.

Baumrind, D. (1964). Some thoughts on ethics of research: After reading Milgram's 'Behavioral study of obedience'. *American Psychologist, 19*, 421–423.

Bavelas, J.B., Coates, L. & Johnson, T. (2000). Listeners as co-narrators. *Journal of Personality and Social Psychology, 79*, 941–952.

Baym, N.K. & Ledbetter, A. (2009). Tunes that bind? Predicting friendship strength in a music-based social network. *Information Communication and Society, 12*, 408–427.

Beasley, R.K. & Joslyn, M.R. (2001). Cognitive dissonance and post-decision attitude change in six presidential elections. *Political Psychology, 22*, 521–540.

Beaulieu, M.J.C. (2004). Intercultural study of personal space: A Case Study. *Journal of Applied Social Psychology, 34*, 794–805.

Bechtold, A., Naccarato, M.E. & Zanna, M.P. (1986, June 19). Need for structure and the prejudice-discrimination link. Annual Meeting of the Canadian Psychological Association, Toronto.

Becker, M.H. (Ed.). (1974). The health belief model and personal health behavior. *Health Education Monographs, 2*, (whole no. 4).

Begany, J.J. & Milburn, M.A. (2002). Psychological predictors of sexual harassment: Authoritarianism, hostile sexism and rape myths. *Psychology of Men & Masculinity, 3*, 119–126.

Bègue, L. & Bastounis, M. (2003). Two spheres of belief in justice: Extensive support for the bidimensional model of belief in a just world. *Journal of Personality, 71*, 435–463.

Bell, B.E. & Loftus, E.F. (1989). Trivial persuasion in the courtroom: The power of (a few) minor details. *Journal of Personality and Social Psychology, 56*, 669–679.

Bell, P.A. (2005). Reanalysis and perspective in the heat–aggression debate. *Journal of Personality and Social Psychology, 89*, 71–73.

Bellman, S., Forster, N., Still, L. & Cooper, C.L. (2003). Gender differences in the use of social support as a moderator of occupational stress. *Stress & Health, 19*, 45–58.

Bem, D. J. (1970). *Beliefs, attitudes, and human affairs*. Stamford, CT: Brooks/Cole.

Bem, D.J. (1972). Self-perception theory. In L. Berkowitz (Ed.), *Advances in experimental social psychology* (Vol. 6). (pp. 1–62). New York: Academic Press.

Bem, D.J., Wallach, M.A. & Kogan, N. (1965). Group decision making under risk of aversive consequences. *Journal of Personality and Social Psychology, 1*, 453–560.

Bem, S.L. (1974). The measurement of psychological androgyny. *Journal of Consulting and Clinical Psychology, 42*, 155–162.

Bem, S.L. (1985). Androgyny and gender schema theory: A conceptual and empirical integration. In T.B. Sonderegger (Ed.), *Nebraska symposium on motivation: Psychology and gender* (pp. 179–226). Lincoln, NE: University of Nebraska Press.

Benjamin, L.T. & Simpson, J.A. (2009). The power of the situation: The impact of Milgram's obedience studies on personality and social psychology. *American Psychologist, 64*, 12–19.

Bennett, W.C. & Feldman, M.S. (1980). *Reconstructing reality in the courtroom: Justice and judgement in American culture.* New Brunswick, NJ: Rutgers University Press.

Bentler, P.M. & Newcomb, M.D. (1978). Longitudinal study of marital success and failure. *Journal of Consulting and Clinical Psychology, 40*, 1053–1070.

Bentler, P.M. & Speckart, G. (1981). Attitudes 'cause' behavior: A structural equation analysis. *Journal of Personality and Social Psychology, 40*, 226–238.

Benton, A.A. (1971). Productivity, distributive justice, and bargaining among children. *Journal of Personality and Social Psychology, 18*, 68–78.

Berecz, J. M. (2001). All that glitters is not gold: Bad forgiveness in counseling and preaching. *Pastoral Psychology, 49*, 253–275.

Bergin, L., Talley, S. & Hamer, L. (2003). Prosocial behaviors of young adolescents: A focus group study. *Journal of Adolescence, 26*, 13–32.

Berkowitz, L. (1954). Group standards, cohesiveness, and productivity. *Human Relations, 7*, 509–519.

Berkowitz, L. (1971). The contagion of violence: An S-R mediational analysis of some effects of observed aggression. *Nebraska Symposium on Motivation 1970.* Lincoln: University of Nebraska Press.

Berkowitz, L. (1973). Reactance and the unwillingness to help others. *Psychological Bulletin, 79*, 310–317.

Berkowitz, L. (1983). Aversively stimulated aggression: Some parallels and differences in research with animals and humans. *American Psychologist, 38*, 1135–1144.

Berkowitz, L. (1984). Some effects of thoughts of anti- and prosocial influences of media events: A cognitive-neoassociation analysis. *Psychological Bulletin, 95*, 410–427.

Berkowitz, L. (1994). Is something missing? Some observations prompted by the cognitive-neoassociationist view of anger and emotional aggression. In L.R. Huesmann (Ed.), *Aggressive behavior: Current perspectives* (pp. 35–57). New York: Plenum Press.

Berkowitz, L. (2012a). A cognitive-neoassociation theory of aggression. In P.A.M. van Lange, A.R. Kruglanski & E.T. Higgins (Eds), *Handbook of theories of social psychology (Vol. 2).* Thousand Oaks, CA: Sage Publications Ltd. pp. 99–117.

Berkowitz, L. (2012b). A different view of anger: The cognitive-neoassociation conception of the relation of anger to aggression. *Aggressive Behaviour, 38*, 322–333.

Berkowitz, L. & Daniels, L.R. (1963). Responsibility and dependency. *Journal of Abnormal and Social Psychology, 66*, 664–669.

Berkowitz, L. & Donnerstein, E. (1982). External validity is more than skin deep: Some answers to criticism of laboratory experiments. *American Psychologist, 37*, 245–257.

Berkowitz, L. & LePage, A. (1967). Weapons as aggression-eliciting stimuli. *Journal of Personality and Social Psychology, 7*, 202–207.

Berkowitz, L. & Macaulay, J. (1971). The contagion of criminal violence. *Sociometry, 34*, 238–260.

Berlyne, D.E. (1960). *Conflict, arousal and curiosity.* New York: McGraw-Hill.

Bernard, M.M., Maio, G.R. & Olson, J.M. (2003). The vulnerability of values to attacks: Inoculation of values and value-relevant attitudes. *Personality and Social Psychology Bulletin, 29*, 63–75.

Berns, G.S., Bell, E., Capra, M., Prietula, M., Moore, S., Anderson, B., Ginges, B. & Atran, S. (2012). The price of your soul: Neural evidence for the non-utilitarian representation of sacred values. *Philosophical Transactions of the Royal Society B, 367*, 754–762.

Bernstein, W.M., Stephan, W.G. & Davis, M.H. (1979). Explaining attributions for achievement. A path analytic approach. *Journal of Personality and Social Psychology, 37*, 1810–1821.

Berry, J.W. (1978). Social psychology: Comparative, societal and universal. *Canadian Psychological Review, 19*, 93–104.

Berry, J.W. (1984). Multicultural policy in Canada: A social psychological analysis. *Canadian Journal of Behavioural Science, 16*, 353–370.

Berry, J.W. (1986). Ethnic minorities and immigrants in a cross-cultural perspective. In L.H. Ekland (Ed.), *Selected papers from the regional IACCP conference: Ethnic minority and immigrant research.* Lisse: Swets and Zeitlinger.

Berry, J.W. (1987). Finding identity: Separation, integration, assimilation, or marginality. In L. Driedger (Ed.), *Ethnic Canada: Identities and inequalities.* Toronto: Copp-Clark-Pitman.

Berry, J.W. (1992). Acculturation and adaptation in a new society. *International Migration, 30*, 69–85.

Berry, J.W. (1999). Intercultural relations in plural societies. *Canadian Psychology, 40*, 12–21.

Berry, J.W. (2011). Integration and multiculturalism: Ways towards social solidarity. *Papers on Social Representations, 20*, 1–21.

Berry, J.W. (2013). Achieving a global psychology. *Canadian Psychology, 54*, 55–61.

Berry, J.W., Kalin, R. & Taylor, D. (1977). *Multiculturalism and ethnic attitudes in Canada.* Ottawa: Supply and Services Canada.

Berry, J.W. & Kalin, R. (1993, May). *Multicultural and ethnic attitudes in Canada: An overview of the 1991 national survey.* Canadian Psychological Association annual meeting, Montreal.

Berry, J.W. & Kalin, R. (1995). Multicultural and ethnic attitudes in Canada: An overview of the 1991 national survey. *Canadian Journal of Behavioural Science, 27*, 301–320.

Berry, J.W., Wintrob, R.M., Sindell, P.S. & Mawhinney, T.A. (1982). Psychological adaptations to cultural change among the James Bay Cree. *Naturaliste Canadien, 109*, 965–975.

Berscheid, E. (1985). Interpersonal attraction. In G. Lindzey & E. Aronson (Eds), *The handbook of social psychology* (3rd ed.). New York: Random House.

Berscheid, E. (2003). On stepping on land mines. In R.J. Sternberg (Ed.), *Psychologists defying the crowd: Stories of those who battled the establishment and won* (pp. 33–44). Washington, DC: American Psychological Association.

Berscheid, E. (2010). Love in the fourth dimension. *Annual Review of Psychology, 61*, 1–25.

Berscheid, E. & Meyers, S.A. (1996). A social categorical approach to a question about love. *Personal Relationships, 3*, 19–43.

Berscheid, E. & Walster, E. (1974a). Physical attractiveness. In L. Berkowitz (Ed.), *Advances in experimental social psychology* (Vol. 7). (pp. 152–215). New York Academic Press.

Berscheid, E. & Walster, E. (1974b). A little bit about love. In T.L. Huston (Ed.), *Foundations of interpersonal attraction.* (pp. 356–382). New York: Academic Press.

Berscheid, E. & Walster, E. (1978). *Interpersonal attraction.* Reading, MA: Addison-Wesley.

Bettencourt, B.A. & Miller, N. (1996). Gender differences in aggression as a function of provocation: A meta-analysis. *Psychological Bulletin, 119*, 422–447.

Beyer, S. (1998). Gender difference in self-perception and negative recall bias. *Sex Roles, 38*, 103–133.

Bickman, L. (1972). Environmental attitudes and actions. *Journal of Social Psychology, 87*, 323–324.

Biesanz, J.C., West, S.G. & Millevoi, A. (2007). What do you learn about someone over time? The relationship between length of acquaintance and consensus and self-other agreement in judgments of personality. *Journal of Personality and Social Psychology, 92*, 119–133.

Biggers, T. & Pryor, B. (1982). Attitude change as a function of the emotion-eliciting qualities of the environment. *Personality and Social Psychology Bulletin, 8*, 203–214.

Billig, M. (1987). *Arguing and Thinking.* Cambridge: Cambridge University Press.

Billig, M. (1991). *Ideology and opinions. Studies in rhetorical psychology.* London: Sage.

Billig, M. (1996). *Arguing and thinking. A rhetorical approach to social psychology.* Cambridge, UK: Cambridge University Press.

Billig, M. (2009). Discursive psychology, rhetoric and the issue of agency. *Semen, 27*, 157–184.

Binder, J., Zagefka, H., Funke, R., Kessler, F., Mummendey, T., Maquil, A., Demoulin, A. & Leyens, A. (2009). Does contact reduce prejudice or does prejudice reduce contact? A longitudinal test of the contact hypothesis among majority and minority groups in three European countries. *Journal of Personality and Social Psychology, 96*, 843–856.

Birdwhistle, R. (1970). *Kinesics and context: Essays on body movement communication.* Philadelphia: University of Pennsylvania Press.

Birkett, M., Espelage, D.L. & Koenig, B. (2009). LGB and questioning students in schools: The moderating effects of homophobic bullying and school climate on negative outcomes. *Journal of Youth and Adolescence, 38*, 989–1000.

Bishop, G.F. (1975). Resolution and tolerance of cognitive inconsistency in a field situation: Change in attitude and beliefs following the Watergate affair. *Psychological Reports, 36*, 747–753.

Bizer, G.Y., Hart, J. & Jekogian, A.M. (2012). Belief in a just world and social dominance orientation: Evidence for a meditational pathway predicting negative attitudes and discrimination against individuals with mental illness. *Personality and Individual Differences, 52*, 428–432.

Blake, J., Vitale, G., Osborne, P. & Olshansky, E. (2005). The cross-cultural comparison of communicative gestures in human infants during the transition to language. *Gesture, 5*, 201–217.

Blaker, N.M., Rompa, I., Dessing, I.H., Vriend, A.F., Herschberg, C. & van Vugt, M. (2013). The height leadership advantage in men and women: Testing evolutionary psychology predictions about the perceptions of tall leaders. *Group Processes and Intergroup Relations, 16*, 17–27.

Blaney, N.T., Stephan, C., Rosenfield, D., Aronson, E. & Sikes, J. (1977). Interdependence in the classroom: A field study. *Journal of Educational Psychology, 69*, 121–128.

Blanton, H. & Christie, C. (2003). Deviance regulations: A theory of action and identity. *Review of General Psychology, 7*, 115–149.

Blanton, H., Stuart, A.N. & VandenEijnden, R.J.M.M. (2001). An introduction to deviance-regulation theory: The effect of behavioural norms on message framing. *Personality and Social Psychology Bulletin, 27*, 848–858.

Blanton, H., VandenEijnden, R.J.J.M., Buunk, B.P., Gibbons, F.X., Gerrard, M. & Bakker, A. (2001). Accentuate the negative: Social images in the prediction and promotion of condom use. *Journal of Applied Psychology, 31*, 274–295.

Blass, T. (2012). A cross-cultural comparison of studies of obedience using the Milgram paradigm: A review. *Social & Personality Psychology Compass, 6*, 196–205.

Blaxter, M. (1990). *Health and lifestyles.* London: Tavistock/Routledge.

Bleske-Recheck, A.L. & Buss, D.M. (2001). Opposite sex friendship: Sex differences and similarities in initiation, selection and dissolution. *Personality and Social Psychology Bulletin, 27*, 1310–1323.

Bloom, B., Asher, S.J. & White, S.W. (1978). Marital disruption as a stressor: A review and analysis. *Psychological Bulletin, 85*, 867–894.

Bloom, M. (2007). *Dying to kill: The allure of suicide terror.* New York: Columbia University Press.

Blumenfeld, M., Levy, N.B. & Kaufman, D. (1979). The wish to be informed of a fatal illness. *Omega, 9*, 323–326.

Blumer, H. (1951). Social movements. In A.M. Lee (Ed.), *New outline of the principles of sociology* (2nd ed.). (pp. 199–220). New York: Barnes & Noble.

Blumer, H. (1969). *Symbolic interactionism.* Englewood Cliffs, NJ: Prentice-Hall.

Bocchiaro, P. & Zimbardo, P. (2010). Defying unjust authority: An exploratory study. *Current Psychology, 29*, 155–170.

Bodenhausen, G.V. (1988). Stereotype biases in social decision making and memory: Testing process models of stereotype use. *Journal of Personality and Social Psychology, 55*, 726–737.

Bogaert, A.F. (2005). Sibling sex ratio and sexual orientation in men and women: New tests in two national probability samples. *Archives of Sexual Behaviour, 34*, 111–116.

Bohner, G., Bless, H., Schwarz, N. & Strack, F. (1988). What triggers causal attributions? The impact of valence and subjective probability. *European Journal of Social Psychology, 18*, 335–345.

Bohner, G., Danner, U., Siebler, F. & Samson, G. B. (2002). Rape myth acceptance and judgments of vulnerability to sexual assault: An Internet experiment. *Experimental Psychology, 49*, 257–269.

Boker, S.M. & Rotondo, J.L. (2002). Symmetry building and symmetry breaking in synchronized movement. In M. Stamenov & V.P.V. Gallese (Eds), *Mirror neurons and the evolution of brain and language* (pp. 163–171). Amsterdam: John Benjamins.

Bolger, N., DeLongis, A., Kessler, R.C. & Schilling, E.A. (1989). Effects of daily stress on negative mood. *Journal of Personality and Social Psychology, 57*, 808–818.

Bonanno, G.A. (2004). Loss, trauma, and human resilience: Have we underestimated the human capacity to thrive after extremely aversive events? *American Psychologist, 59*, 20–28.

Bond, C.F., Jr. & Titus, L.J. (1983). Social facilitation: A meta-analysis of 241 studies. *Psychological Bulletin, 94*, 265–292.

Bond, C.F., Jr. (1982). Social facilitation: A self-presentational view. *Journal of Personality and Social Psychology, 42*, 1042–1050.

Bond, G.G., Aiken, L.S. & Somerville, S.C. (1992). The health beliefs model and adolescents with insulin-dependent diabetes mellitus. *Health Psychology, 11*, 190–198.

Bond, M.H. (1988). Finding universal dimensions of individual variation in multicultural studies of values: The Rokeach and Chinese value surveys. *Journal of Personality and Social Psychology, 55*, 1009–1015.

Bond, R. & Smith, P.B. (1996). Culture and conformity: a meta-analysis of studies using Asch's line judgement task. *Psychological Bulletin, 119*, 111–137.

Boninger, D.S., Krosnick, J.A., Berent, M.K. & Fabrigar, L.R. (1995). The causes and consequence of attitude importance. In R.E. Petty & J.A. Krosnick (Eds), *Attitude strength: Antecedents and consequences* (pp. 159–189). Mahwah, NJ: Erlbaum.

Boone, C., Declerck, C. & Kiyonari, T. (2010). Inducing cooperative behavior among Proselfs versus Prosocials: The moderating role of incentives and trust. *Journal of Conflict Resolution, 54*, 799–824.

Booth-Kewley, S. & Friedman, H.S. (1987). Psychological predictors of heart disease: A quantitative review. *Psychological Bulletin, 101*, 343–362.

Bornstein, B.H. & Greene, E. (2011). Jury decision-making: Implications for and from psychology. *Current Directions in Psychological Science, 20*, 63–67.

Boss LP. (1997). Epidemic hysteria: A review of the published literature. *Epidemiologic Reviews, 19*, 233–243.

Boucher, H.C. (2010). Understanding Western-East Asian differences and similarities in self-enhancement. *Social and Personality Psychology Compass, 4*, 304–317.

Boulding, K.E. (1980). Science: Our common heritage. *Science, 207*, 831–836.

Bourhis, R.Y. (1979). Language in ethnic interaction: A social psychological approach. In H. Giles & B. Saint-Jacques (Eds), *Language and ethnic relations*. Oxford: Pergamon.

Bourhis, R.Y. (1982). Language policies and language attitudes: Le monde de la francophonie. In E.R. Ryan & H. Giles (Eds), *Attitudes towards language variation* (pp. 34–62). London: Edward Arnold.

Bourhis, R.Y. (1990). Organizational communication in bilingual settings: The linguistic work environment survey. In H. Giles, N. Coupland & J. Coupland (Eds), *Contexts of accommodation: Developments in applied psycholinguistics*. Cambridge: Cambridge University Press.

Bourhis, R.Y. (1994). Ethnic and language attitudes in Quebec. In J.W. Berry & J.A. La Ponce (Eds), *Ethnicity and culture in Canada: The research landscape* (pp. 322–360). Toronto: University of Toronto Press.

Bourhis, R.Y., Roth, S. & MacQueen, G. (1989). Communication in the hospital setting: A survey of medical and everyday language use among patients, nurses and doctors. *Social Science and Medicine, 28*, 339–346.

Bowlby, J. (1969). *Attachment and loss: Vol. 1 Attachment.* New York: Basic Books.

Bradac, J.J., Davies, R.A., Courtright, J.A., Desmond, R.J. & Murdock, J.I. (1977). Richness of vocabulary: An attributional analysis. *Psychological Reports, 41*, 1131–1134.

Bradley, G.W. (1978). Self-serving bias in the attribution process: A re-examination of the fact-or-fiction question. *Journal of Personality and Social Psychology, 36*, 56–71.

Bradley, J.P., Nicol, A.A.M., Charbonneau, D. & Meyer, J.P. (2002). Personality correlates of leadership development in Canadian Forces officer candidates. *Canadian Journal of Behavioural Science, 34*, 92–103.

Bradley, J.R. & Cartwright, S. (2002). Social support, job stress, health and job satisfaction among nurses in the United Kingdom. *International Journal of Stress Management, 9*, 163–182.

Braithwaite, V.A. & Scott, W.A. (1991). Values. In J.P. Robinson, P.R. Shaver & L.S. Wrightsman (Eds), *Measures of personality and social psychological attitudes*. New York: Academic Press.

Brambilla, M., Ravenna, M. & Hewstone, M. (2012). Changing stereotype content through mental imagery: Imagining intergroup contact promotes stereotype change. *Group Processes & Intergroup Relations, 15*, 305–315.

Brann, P. & Foddy, M. (1987). Trust and the consumption of a deteriorating common resource. *Journal of Conflict Resolution, 31*, 615–630.

Brauer, M., Judd, C.M. & Gliner, M.D. (1995). The effects of repeated expressions on attitude polarization during group discussions. *Journal of Personality and Social Psychology, 68*, 1014–1029.

Braun, O.L. & Wicklund, R.A. (1989). When discounting fails. *Journal of Experimental Social Psychology, 25*, 450–461.

Braun-Courville, D.K & Rojas, M. (2009). Exposure to sexually explicit web sites and adolescent sexual attitudes and behaviors. *Adolescent Health, 45*, 156–162.

Bray, R.M. & Kerr, N.L. (1982). Methodological considerations in the study of the psychology of the courtroom. In N.L. Kerr & R.M. Bray (Eds), *The psychology of the courtroom* (pp. 287–323). Orlando, FL: Academic Press.

Breckler, S.J. (1984). Empirical validation of affect, behavior and cognition as distinct components of attitude. *Journal of Personality and Social Psychology, 47*, 1191–1205.

Brehm, J. W. (1966). *A theory of psychological reactance.* New York: Academic Press.

Brehm, J.W. & Cohen A.R. (1962). *Explorations in cognitive dissonance.* New York: Wiley.

Brehm, S.S. (1985). *Intimate relationships.* New York: Random House.

Brendgen, M., Vitaro, F., Boivin, M., Dionne, G. & Pérusse, D. (2006). Examining genetic and environmental effects on reactive versus proactive aggression. *Developmental Psychology, 42*, 1299–1312.

Brew, F.P., Tan, J., Booth, H. & Malik, I. (2011). The effects of cognitive appraisals of communication competence in conflict interactions: A study involving Western and Chinese cultures. *Journal of Cross-Cultural Psychology, 42*, 856–874.

Brewer, M.B., Dull, V. & Lui, L. (1981). Perception of the elderly: Stereotypes as prototypes. *Journal of Personality and Social Psychology, 41*, 656–670.

Brewer, M.B. & Kramer, R.M. (1985). The psychology of intergroup attitudes and behavior. *Annual Review of Psychology, 36*, 219–243.

Brewer, N. & Palmer, M.A. (2011). Eyewitness identification tests. *Legal and Criminological Psychology, 15*, 77–96.

Brigham, J.C. & Cairns, D.L. (1988). The effect of mugshot inspections on eyewitness identification accuracy. *Journal of Applied Social Psychology, 18*, 1394–1410.

Brigham, J.C. & Malpass, R.S. (1985). The role of experience and contact in the recognition of faces of own- and other-race persons. *Journal of Social Issues, 41*, 139–156.

Brigham, J.C. & Pfeifer, J.E. (1994). Evaluating the fairness of lineups. In D.F. Ross & M.P. Toglia (Eds), *Adult eyewitness testimony: Current trends and developments* (pp. 201–222). New York: Cambridge University Press.

Britt, T.W. & Bliese, P.D. (2003). Testing the stress-buffering effects of self-engagement among soldiers on a military operation. *Journal of Personality, 71*, 245–265.

Brodbeck, F.C., Frese, M., Akerblom, S., Audia, G., Bakacsi, G., Bendova, H. et al. (2000). Cultural variation of leadership prototypes across 22 European countries. *Journal of Occupational and Organizational Psychology, 73*, 1–29.

Brody, N., Davis, D.C., Drushel, B.E., Green-Hamann. S., Hall, J.A., Johnson, A., Johnson, B., Kuznekoff, J.H. & Cunningham, C. (Eds) (2012*). Social Networking and Impression Management: Self-Presentation in the Digital Age.* London: Rowman & Littlefield.

Bronfenbrenner, U. (1961). The mirror image in Soviet-American relations: A social psychologist's report. *The Journal of Social Issues, 17*, 45–56.

Broverman., I.K., Vogel, S.R., Broverman, D.M., Clarkson, F.E. & Rosenkrantz, P.S. (1972). Sexual stereotypes: A current appraisal. *Journal of Social Issues, 28*, 59–78.

Brown, J.D.,& Siegel,J.M. (1988). Exercise as a buffer of life stress: A prospective study of adolescent health. *Health Psychology, 7*,341–353.

Brown, R. (1986). *Social Psychology* (2nd ed.). London: Collier MacMillan.

Browning, C.R. (1992). *Ordinary Men. Reserve Police Battalion 101 and the Final Solution in Poland.* New York: HarperCollins.

Brubacher, M.R., Fondacaro, M.R., Brank, E.M., Brown, C.E. & Miller, S.A. (2009). Procedural justice in resolving family disputes: Implications for childhood bullying. *Psychology, Public Policy, and Law, 15*, 149–167.

Bruckmüller, S. & Branscombe, R. (2010). The glass cliff: When and why women are selected as leaders in crisis contexts. *British Journal of Social Psychology, 49*, 433–451.

Bruner, J.S. & Tagiuri, R. (1954). The perception of people. In G. Lindzey (Ed.), *Handbook of Social Psychology* (pp. 634–654). Reading, MA: Addison-Wesley.

Brunvand, J.H. (1981). *The vanishing hitchhiker: American urban legends and their meanings.* New York: Norton.

Brunvand, J.H. (1986). *The choking Doberman.* New York: Norton.

Buck, R. (2002), The genetics and biology of true love: Prosocial biological affects and the left hemisphere. *Psychological Review, 109*, 739–744.

Buckholtz, J.W. & Marois, R. (2012). The roots of modern justice: Cognitive and neural foundations of social norms and their enforcement. *Nature Neuroscience, 15*, 655–661.

Buckhout, R. (1980). Nearly 2000 witnesses can be wrong. *Bulletin of the Psychonomic Society, 16*, 307–310.

Buehler, D. & Griffin, D. (1994). Change of meaning effects in conformity and dissent: Observing construal process over time. *Journal of Personality and Social Psychology, 67*, 984–996.

Buehler, R., Griffin, D. & Ross, M. (1995). It's about time: Optimistic predictions in work and love. In W. Stroebe & M. Hewstone (Eds), *European Review of Social Psychology*, (Vol. 6). (pp. 1–32). London: Wiley.

Buehler, R. & Ross, M. (1993). How do individuals remember their past statements? *Journal of Personality and Social Psychology, 64*, 538–551.

Bugental, D.E., Kaswan, J.E. & Love, L.R. (1970). Perception of contradictory meanings conveyed by verbal and nonverbal channels. *Journal of Personality and Social Psychology, 16*, 647–655.

Buller, D.J. (2005), Adapting minds: Evolutionary psychology and the persistent quest for human nature. Cambridge, MA: MIT Press.

Bulman, R.J. & Wortman, C.B. (1977). Attributions of blame and coping in the 'real world': Severe accident victims react to their lot. *Journal of Personality and Social Psychology, 35*, 351–363.

Burger, J.M. (1981). Motivational biases in the attribution of responsibility for an accident: A meta-analysis of the defensive attribution hypothesis. *Psychological Bulletin, 90*, 496–513.

Burger, J.M. (1986). Increasing compliance by improving the deal: The that's-not-all technique.

Journal of Personality and Social Psychology, 51, 277–283.

Burger, J.M. (2009). Replicating Milgram: Would people still obey today? *American Psychologist, 64*, 1–11.

Burgess, E.W. & Huston, T.L. (Eds). (1979). *Social exchange in developing relationships.* New York: Academic Press.

Burgoon, J. K., Buller, D. B. & Woodall, W. G. (1989). *Nonverbal communication: The unspoken dialogue.* New York: Harper & Row.

Burke, T.M. & Freedman, J.L. (1996, August). *The effects of pretrial publicity on jurors' verdicts.* 104th Convention of the American Psychological Association, Toronto.

Burman, B. & Margolin, G. (1992). Analysis of the association between marital relationships and health problems: An interactional perspective. *Psychological Bulletin, 112*, 39–63.

Burr, V. (1995). *Social constructionism.* East Sussex: Routledge.

Burt, M.R. (1980). Cultural myths and support for rape. *Journal of Personality and Social Psychology, 38*, 217–230.

Burton, M. & Kagan, C. (2009). Towards a really social psychology: Liberation Psychology beyond Latin America. In M. Montero & C. Sonn (Eds), *The psychology of liberation. Theory and applications* (pp. 51–72). New York: Springer.

Busboom, A.L., Collins, D.N., Givertz, M.D. & Levin, L.A. (2002). Can't we still be friends? Resources and barriers to friendship quality after romantic relationship dissolution. *Personal Relationships, 9*, 215–223.

Busenitz, L.W. & Barney, J.B. (1997). Differences between entrepreneurs and managers in large organizational biases and heuristics in strategic decision-making. *Journal of Business Venturing, 12*, 9–31.

Bushman, B.J. (1988). The effects of apparel on compliance: A field experiment with a female authority figure. *Personality and Social Psychology Bulletin, 14*, 459–467.

Bushman, B.J. & Anderson, C.A. (2001). Media violence and the American public: Scientific facts versus media misinformation. *American Psychologist, 36*, 477–498.

Bushman, B.J. & Anderson, C.A. (2002). Violent video games and hostile expectations: A test of the General Aggression Model. *Personality and Social Psychology Bulletin, 28*, 1679–1686.

Bushman, B.J. & Baumeister, R.F. (1998). Threatened egotism, narcissism, self-esteem, and direct and displaced aggression: Does self-love or self-hate lead to violence? *Journal of Personality and Social Psychology*, 75, 219–229.

Bushman, B.J. & Baumeister, R.F. (2002). Does self-love or self-hate lead to violence? *Journal of Research in Personality*, 36, 543–545.

Bushman, B.J., Baumeister, R.F. & Stack, A.D. (1999). Catharsis, aggression, and persuasive influence: Self-fulfilling or self-defeating prophecies? *Journal of Personality and Social Psychology*, 76, 367–376.

Bushman, B.J. & Gibson, B. (2011). Violent video games cause an increase in aggression long after the game has been turned off. *Social Psychological and Personality Science*, 2, 29–32.

Buss, D.M. (1994). *The evolution of desire: Strategies of human mating.* New York: Basic Books.

Buss, D.M. & Shackelford, T.K. (1997). Human aggression in evolutionary psychological perspective. *Clinical Psychology Review*, 17, 605–619

Busseri, M.A. & Sadava, S.W. (2011). A review of the tripartite structure of subjective well-being: Implications for conceptualization, operationalization, analysis, and synthesis. *Personality and Social Psychology Review*, 15, 290–314.

Busseri, M.A., Sadava, S.W. & DeCourville, N. (2007). A hybrid model for research on subjective well-being: Examining common- and component-specific sources of variance in life satisfaction, positive affect, and negative affect. *Social Indicators Research*, 83, 413–445.

Butterfield, D.A. & Grinnell, J.P. (1999). Reviewing gender, leadership, and managerial behavior: Do three decades of research tell us anything? In G.N. Powell (Ed.), *Handbook of gender and work* (pp. 223–238). Thousand Oaks, CA: Sage Publications.

Buunk, A.P., Zurriaga, R. & Peiro, J.M. (2010). Social comparison as a predictor of changes in burnout among nurses. *Anxiety, Stress & Coping*, 23, 181–194.

Buunk, B.P., Collins, R.L., Taylor, S.E., Van Yperen, N.W. & Dakof, G.A. (1990). The affective consequences of social comparison: Either direction has its ups and downs. *Journal of Personality and Social Psychology*, 59, 1238–1249.

Buunk, B.P. & Mutsaers, W. (1999). Equity perceptions and marital satisfaction in former and current marriage: A study among the remarried. *Journal of Social and Personal Relationships*, 16, 123–132.

Bylund, E., Abrahamsson, N. & Hyltenstam, K. (2010). The role of language aptitude in first language attrition: The case of pre-pubescent attriters. *Applied Linguistics*, 31, 443–464.

Byrne, D. (1971). *The attraction paradigm.* New York: Academic Press.

Byrne, D. & Clore, G.L. (1970). A reinforcement model of evaluative responses. *Personality: An International Journal*, 1, 103–128.

Byrne, D., Clore, G.L. & Smeaton, G. (1986). The attraction hypothesis. Do similar attitudes affect anything? *Journal of Personality and Social Psychology*, 51, 1167–1170.

Byrne, D., Ervin, C. & Lamberth, J. (1970). Continuity between the experimental study of attraction and real-life computer dating. *Journal of Personality and Social Psychology*, 51, 157–165.

Cacioppo, J.T, Hawkley, L.C., Crawford, E., Ernst, J.M., Berleson, M.H., Kowalewski, R.B., Malarkey, W.B., Van Cauter, E. & Berntson, G.G. (2002). Loneliness and health: Potential mechanisms. *Psychosomatic Medicine*, 64, 407–417.

Cacioppo, J.T., Hawkley, L.C. & Thisted, R.A. (2010). Perceived social isolation makes me sad: 5-year cross-lagged analyses of loneliness and depressive symptomatology in the Chicago Health, Aging, and Social Relations Study. *Psychology and Aging*, 25, 453–463.

Cacioppo, J.T. & Patrick, W. (2008). *Loneliness: Human nature and the need for social connection.* New York: Norton.

Cacioppo, J.T., Petty, R.E., Kao, C. & Rodriguez, R. (1986). Central and peripheral routes to persuasion: An individual difference perspective. *Journal of Personality and Social Psychology*, 51, 1032–1043.

Calhoun, J.B. (1962). Population density and social pathology. *Scientific American*, 206, 139–148.

Calhoun, L.G., Selby, J.W. & King, H.E. (1976). *Dealing with crisis.* Englewood Cliffs, NJ: Prentice-Hall.

Cameron, D. (2007). *The myth of Mars and Venus: Do men and women really speak different languages?* New York: Oxford University Press.

Cameron, K.A., Jacks, J.Z. & O'Brien, M.E. (2002). An experimental examination of strategies for resisting persuasion. *Current Research in Social Psychology*, 7, 205–224.

Campbell A., Shirley L. & Caygill L. (2002). Sex-typed preferences in three domains: Do two-year-olds need cognitive variables? *British Journal of Psychology*, 93, 203–217.

Campbell, D.T. (1963). Social attitudes and other acquired behavioral dispositions. In S. Koch (Ed.), *Psychology: A study of a science* (Vol. 6). (pp. 94–172). New York: McGraw-Hill Campbell, D.T. (1986). Introduction to the Wesleyan edition. In Sherif, M., Harvey, O.J., White, B.J., Hood, W.R. & Sherif, C., *The Robbers Cave experiment: Intergroup conflict and cooperation.* Middletown, Conn; Wesleyan University Press. (pp. xiii–xxi).

Campbell, J.B. & Fairly, P.J. (1989). Informational and normative routes to conformity: The effect of faction size as function of norm extremity and attention to the stimulus. *Journal of Personality and Social Psychology*, 57, 457–468.

Campbell, J.D. (1986). Similarity and uniqueness: The effects of attribute type, relevance, and individual differences in self-esteem and depression. *Journal of Personality and Social Psychology*, 50, 281–293.

Campbell, J.D., Trapnell, P.D., Heine, S.J., Katz, I.M., Lavallee, L.F. & Lehman, D.R. (1996). Self-concept clarity: Measurement, personality correlates and cultural boundaries: Correction. *Journal of Personality and Social Psychology*, 70, 141–156.

Campbell, T.A. & Campbell, D.E. (1997). Faculty/student mentor program: Effects on academic performance and retention. *Research in Higher Education*, 38, 727–742.

Campbell, W.J. (2010). Getting it wrong: Ten of the greatest misreported stories in American Journalism. Berkeley: University of California Press.

Campion☐Vincent, V. (2005). From Evil Others to Evil Elites: A Dominant Pattern in Conspiracy Theories Today. In G.A. Fine, V. Campion☐ Vincent & C. Heath (Eds), *Rumor mills: The social impact of rumor and legend.* New Brunswick, NJ: Aldine Transaction. (pp. 103–122).

Cantor, N. & Mischel, W. (1979). Prototypes in person perception. In L. Berkowitz (Ed.), *Advances in experimental social psychology*, 3–52 (Vol. 12). New York: Academic Press.

Cantril, H. (1940). *The invasion from Mars.* Princeton, NJ: Princeton University Press.

Caplan, N.S. & Paige, J.M. (1968). A study of ghetto rioters. *Scientific American, 219,* 15–21.

Caporael, L.R. (1981). The paralanguage of care-giving: Baby talk to the institutionalized aged. *Journal of Personality and Social Psychology, 40,* 876–884

Caporael, L.R., Lukaszewski, M.P. & Culbertson, G.H. (1983). Secondary baby talk: Judgments by institutionalized elderly and their caregivers. *Journal of Personality and Social Psychology, 44,* 746–754.

Capozza, D., Andrighetto, L., Di Bernardo, G.A. & Falvo, R. (2012). Does status affect intergroup perceptions of humanity? *Group Processes & Intergroup Relations, 15,* 363– 377.

Capozza, D., Boccato, G., Andrighetto, L. & Falvo, R. (2009). Categorization of ambiguous human/ape faces: Protection of ingroup but not outgroup humanity. *Group Processes & Intergroup Relations, 12,* 777–787.

Carli, L.L. (1990). Gender, language, and influence. *Journal of Personality and Social Psychology, 59,* 941–951.

Carli, L.L. (1999). Gender, interpersonal power and social influence. *Journal of Social Issues, 55,* 81–99.

Carli, L.L., Ganley, R. & Pierce-Otay, A. (1991). Similarity and satisfaction in roommate relationships. *Personality and Social Psychology Bulletin, 17,* 419–426.

Carlson, M., Marcus-Newhall, A. & Miller, N. (1990). Effects of situational aggressive cues: A quantitative review. *Journal of Personality and Social Psychology, 58,* 622–633.

Carlston, D.E. & Skowronski, J.J. (1994). Savings in the relearning of trait information as evidence for spontaneous trait generation. *Journal of Personality and Social Psychology, 66,* 840–856.

Carnagey, N.L., Anderson, C.A. & Bushman, B.J. (2007). The effect of video game violence on physiological desensitization to real-life violence. *Journal of Experimental Social Psychology, 43,* 489–496.

Carnaghi, A. & Maass, A. (2007). In-group and out-group perspectives in the use of derogatory group labels. *Journal of Language and Social Psychology, 26,* 142–156.

Carnevale, P.J. & Pruitt, D.G. (1992). Negotiation and mediation. *Annual Review of Psychology, 43,* 531–582.

Carroll, J.M. & Russell, J.A. (1997). Facial characteristics in Hollywood's portrayal of emotion.

Journal of Personality and Social Psychology, 72, 164–176.

Carver, C.S., Lawrence, J.W. & Scheier, M.F. (1999). Self-discrepancies and affect: incorporating the role of feared selves. *Personality and Social Psychology Bulletin, 25,* 783–792.

Carver, C.S. & Scheier, M.F. (1981). The self-attention-induced feedback loop and social facilitation. *Journal of Experimental Social Psychology, 17,* 545–568.

Carver, C.S. & Scheier, M.F. (1998). *On the self-regulation of behavior.* New York: Cambridge University Press.

Carver, C.S. & Scheier, M.F. (2011). A model of behavioral self-regulation. In P.A. Van Lange, A. Kruglanski & E.T. Higgins (Eds). *Handbook of theories of social psychology, Vol. 1* (pp. 237–259). London: Sage.

Cash, T.F. & Derlega, V.J. (1978). The matching hypothesis: Physical attractiveness among same-sexed friends. *Personality and Social Psychology Bulletin, 4,* 240–243.

Caspi, A., Herbener, E.S. & Ozer, D.J. (1992). Shared experience and the similarity of personalities: A longitudinal study of married couples. *Journal of Personality and Social Psychology, 62,* 281–291.

Caspi, A., McClay, J., Moffitt, T.E., Mill, J., Martin, J., Craig, I.W., Taylor, A. & Poulton, R. (2002). Role of genotype in the cycle of violence in maltreated children. *Science, 297,* 851–854.

Catmur, C., Gillmeister, H., Bird, G., Liepelt, R., Brass, M. & Heyes, C. (2008). Through the looking glass: Counter-mirror activation following incompatible sensorimotor learning. *European Journal of Neuroscience, 28,* 1208–1215.

Catmur, C., Walsh, V. & Heyes, C. M. (2007). Sensorimotor learning configures the human mirror system. *Current Biology, 17,* 1527–1531.

Caudill, B.D. & Marlatt, G.A. (1975). Modelling influences in social drinking: An experimental analogue. *Journal of Consulting and Clinical Psychology, 43,* 405–415.

Cavior, N. & Dorecki, P.R. (1969, April). Physical attractiveness and popularity among fifth grade boys. Meetings of the Southwestern Psychology Association, Austin, TX.

Chaiken, A.L. & Derlega, V.J. (1974). *Self-disclosure.* Morristown, NJ: General Learning.

Chaiken, S. (1980). Heuristic versus systematic information processing and the use of source versus message

cues. *Journal of Personality and Social Psychology, 39,* 752–766.

Chaiken, S. (1987). The heuristic model of persuasion. In C.P. Herman, M.P. Zanna & E.T. Higgins (Eds), *Social Influence: The Ontario Symposium* (pp. 3–39). Hillsdale, NJ: Erlbaum.

Chaiken, S. & Eagly, A.H. (1976). Communication modality as a determinant of message persuasiveness and message comprehensibility. *Journal of Personality and Social Psychology, 34,* 605–614.

Chaiken, S. & Eagly, A.H. (1983). Communication modality as a determinant of persuasion: The role of communicator salience. *Journal of Personality and Social Psychology, 45,* 241–256.

Chaiken, S. & Stangor, C. (1987). Attitude and attitude change. *Annual Review of Psychology, 38,* 575–630.

Chandler, T.A., Shama, D.D., Wolf, F.M. & Planchard, S.K. (1981). Misattributional causality: A five cross-national samples study. *Journal of Cross-Cultural Psychology, 12,* 207–221.

Chapman, L.J. & Chapman, J.P. (1969). Illusory correlations as an obstacle to the use of valid psychodiagnostic signs. *Journal of Abnormal and Social Psychology, 74,* 271–280.

Chartrand, T., Pinckert, S. & Burger, J.M. (1999). When manipulation backfires: The effects of time delay and requester on the foot-in-the-door technique. *Journal of Applied Social Psychology, 29,* 211–221.

Chartrand, T.L. & Bargh, J.A. (1999). The chameleon effect: The perception–behavior link and social interaction. *Journal of Personality and Social Psychology, 76,* 893–910.

Chau, L.L, Johnson, R.C., Bowers, J.K. & Darvill, T.J. (1990). Intrinsic and extrinsic religiosity as related to conscience, adjustment, and altruism. *Personality and Individual Differences, 11,* 397–400.

Chau, P.Y.K. & Hui, K.L. (1998). Identifying early adopters of new IT products: A case of Windows 95. *Information & Management, 33,* 225–230.

Check, J.V.P. (1985). *The effects of violent and non-violent pornography.* Ottawa: Department of Justice.

Check, J.V.P. & Dyck, D.G. (1986). Hostile aggression and Type A behavior. *Personality and Individual Differences, 7,* 819–827.

Check, J.V.P. & Guloien, T.H. (1989). Reported proclivity for coercive sex following repeated exposure to sexually violent pornography, nonviolent dehumanizing pornography, and erotica. In D. Zillmann & J. Bryant (Eds), *Pornography: Research advances and policy considerations* (pp. 159–184). Hillsdale, NJ: Erlbaum.

Check, J.V.P., Perlman, D. & Malamuth, N.M. (1985). Loneliness and aggressive behavior. *Journal of Social and Personal Relationships, 2,* 243–252.

Chemers, M.M. (1983). Leadership theory and research: A systems-process integration. In P.B. Paulus (Ed.), *Basic group processes.* New York: Springer-Verlag.

Chen, S., Bond, M., Chan, B., Tang, D. & Buchtel, E.E. (2009). Behavioral manifestations of modesty. *Journal of Cross-Cultural Psychology, 40,* 603–626.

Cherry, F. (1995). *The 'stubborn particulars' of social psychology.* London: Routledge.

Cherry, F. & Byrne, D. (1977). Authoritarianism. In T. Blass (Ed.), *Personality variables in social behavior.* Hillsdale, NJ: Erlbaum.

Chertkoff, J.M. & Conley, M. (1967). Opening offer and frequency of concession as bargaining strategies. *Journal of Personality and Social Psychology, 7,* 181–185.

Chiang, S-Y. (2010). 'Well I'm a lot of things but I'm sure not a bigot': Positive self-presentation in confrontational discourse on racism. *Discourse and Society, 21,* 273–294.

Chiriboga, D., Roberts, J. & Stein, J.A. (1978). Psychological well-being during marital separation. *Journal of Divorce, 2,* 21–36.

Chiu, C., Gries, P., Torelli, C. J. & Cheng, S. Y. Y. (2011). Toward a social psychology of globalization. *Journal of Social Issues, 67,* 663–676.

Choi, I. & Nisbett, R.E. (1998). Situational salience and cultural differences in the correspondence bias and actor-observer bias. *Personality and Social Psychology Bulletin, 24,* 949–960.

Choi, I., Nisbett, R.E. & Norenzayan, A. (1999). Causal attribution across culture: Variation and universality. *Psychological Bulletin, 125,* 47–63.

Choma, B.L., Ashton, M.C. & Hafer, C.L. (2010). Conceptualizing political orientation in Canadian political candidates: A tale of two (correlated) dimensions. *Canadian Journal of Behavioural Science, 42,* 24–33.

Choma, B.L. Busseri, M.A. & Sadava, S.W. (2009). Liberal and conservative political ideologies: Different routes to happiness? *Journal of Research in Personality, 43,* 502–505.

Choma, B.L., Hodson, G. & Costello, K. (2012). Intergroup disgust sensitivity as a predictor of Islamophobia: The modulating effect of fear. *Journal of Experimental Social Psychology, 48,* 499–506.

Chomsky, N. & Herman, E. (1988). Manufacturing consent: The political economy of the mass media. New York: Pantheon Books.

Chopra, S.R., Dahl, L.M. & Wrightsman, L.S. (1996, August 9–13). *The sequestered juror syndrome.* 104th convention of the American Psychological Association, Toronto.

Christensen, A., Sullaway, M. & King, C.E. (1983). Systematic error in behavioural reports of dyadic interaction. *Behavioural Assessment, 5,* 129–140.

Christensen, L. (1988). Deception in psychological research: When is its use justified? *Personality and Social Psychology Bulletin, 14,* 664–675.

Christianson, S. (1992). Emotional stress and eye-witness memory: A critical review. *Psychological Bulletin, 112,* 284–309.

Christianson, S. & Loftus, E.F. (1991). Remembering emotional events: The fate of detailed information. *Cognition and Emotion, 5,* 81–108.

Christie, R. & Jahoda, M. (Eds). (1954). *Studies in the scope and method of 'The Authoritarian Personality'.* New York: Free Press.

Chung, L.C. (2011). Crossing boundaries: Cross-cultural communication. In K.D. Keith (Ed.), *Cross-cultural psychology: Contemporary themes and perspectives.* West Sussex, England: Blackwell Publishing Limited, (pp. 400–420).

Cialdini, R.B., Brown, S.L., Lewis, B.P., Luce, C. & Neuberg, S.L. (1997). Reinterpreting the empathy-altruism relationship: When one into one equals oneness. *Journal of Personality and Social Psychology, 73,* 481–494.

Cialdini, R.B., Cacioppo, J.T., Bassett, R. & Miller, J.A. (1978). Low-ball procedure for producing compliance: Commitment then cost. *Journal of Personality and Social Psychology, 36,* 463–476.

Cialdini, R.B., Demaine, L.J., Sagarin B.J., Barrett, D.W., Rhoads, K. & Winter, P.L. (2006). Managing social norms for persuasive impact. *Social Influence, 1,* 3–15.

Cialdini, R.B., Trost, M.R. & Newsom, J.T. (1995). Preference for consistency: The development of a valid measure and the discovery of surprising behavioral implications. *Journal of Personality and Social Psychology, 69,* 318–328.

Cialdini, R.B., Vincent, J.E., Lewis, S.K., Catalon, J., Wheeler, D. & Darby, B.L. (1975). Reciprocal concessions procedure for inducing compliance: The door-in-the-face technique. *Journal of Personality and Social Psychology*, *31*, 206–215.

Clabaugh, A. & Morling, B. (2004). Stereotype accuracy of ballet and modern dancers. *The Journal of Social Psychology*, *144*, 31–48.

Clark, M. & Mills, J. (1993). The difference between communal and exchange relationships. What it is and is not. *Personality and Social Psychology Bulletin*, *19*, 684–691.

Clément, R. (1987). Second language proficiency and acculturation: An investigation of the effects of language status and individual characteristics. *Journal of Language and Social Psychology*, *5*, 271–290.

Clément, R., Baker, S.C. & MacIntyre, P.D. (2003). Willingness to communicate in a second language: The effects of context, norms, and vitality. *Journal of Language and Social Psychology*, *22*, 190–209.

Clément, R., Gardner, R.C. & Smythe, P.C. (1977). Interethnic contact: Attitudinal consequences. *Canadian Journal of Behavioural Science*, *9*, 205–215.

Clifford, M. & Walster, E. (1973). The effects of physical attraction on teacher expectation. *Sociology of Education*, *46*, 248.

Clore, G.L., Wiggins, N.H. & Itkin, G. (1975). Gain and loss in attraction: Attributions from non-verbal behavior. *Journal of Personality and Social Psychology*, *31*, 706–712.

Cloutier, J., Heatherton, T.F., Whalen, P.J. & Kelley, W.M. (2008). Are attractive people rewarding? Sex differences in the neural substrates of facial attractiveness. *Journal of Cognitive Neuroscience*, *20*, 941–951.

Coates, J. (1993). *Women, men and language: A sociolinguistic account of gender differences in language*. (2nd ed.). London: Longman.

Cohen, A.B. (2009). Many forms of culture. *American Psychologist*, *64*, 194–204.

Cohen, S. (1988). Psychosocial models of the role of social support in the etiology of physical disease. *Health Psychology*, *7*, 269–297.

Cohen, S., Frank, E., Doyle, W.J., Skoner, D.P., Rabin, B.S. & Gwaltney, J.M. Jr. (1998). Types of stressors that increase susceptibility to the common cold in healthy adults. *Health Psychology*, *17*, 214–223.

Cohen, S. & Herbert, T.B. (1996). Health psychology: Psychological factors and physical disease from the perspective of human psychoimmunology. *Annual Review of Psychology*, *47*, 113–142.

Cohen, S. & Williamson, G.M. (1988). Perceived stress in a probability sample of the United States. In S. Spacapan & S. Oskamp (Eds), *The social psychology of health* (pp. 31–67). Beverly Hills, CA: Sage Publications.

Cohen, S., Tyrrell, D.A.J. & Smith, A.P. (1993). Negative life events, perceived stress, negative affect and susceptibility to the common cold. *Journal of Personality and Social Psychology*, *64*, 131–140.

Coie, J.D. & Dodge, K.A. (1997). Aggression and antisocial behavior. In W. Damon & N. Eisenberg (Eds), *Handbook of child psychology: Vol. 3 Social, emotional and personality development* (5th ed). New York: Wiley.

Coleman, J.S. (1990). *The foundations of social theory*. Cambridge, MA: Harvard University press.

Collaer, M.L. & Hines, M. (1995). Human behavioral sex differences: A role for gonadal hormones during early development? *Psychological Bulletin*, *118*, 55–107.

Collie, R.M., Vess, J. & Murdoch, S. (2007). Violence-related cognition: Current research. In T.A. Gannon, T. Ward, A.R. Beech & D. Fisher (Eds), *Aggressive offenders' cognition: Theory, research, and practice*. Chichester, England: John Wiley & Sons (pp. 179–198).

Collier, G., Minton, H.L. & Reynolds, G. (1991). *Currents of thought in American social psychology*. New York: Oxford.

Colligan, M.J., Pennebaker, J.W. & Murphy, L.R. (1982). *Mass psychogenic illness*. Hillsdale, NJ: Erlbaum.

Collins, R.L. (1996). For better or worse: The impact of upward social comparison on self-evaluations. *Psychological Bulletin*, *119*, 51–69.

Colman, A.M. (1991). Crowd psychology in South African murder trials. *American Psychologist*, *46*, 1071–1079.

Confer, J.C., Easton, J.A., Fleischman, C.D., Goetz, C.D., Lewis, D.M.G., Perilloux, C. & Buss, D.M. (2010). Evolutionary psychology: Controversies, questions, prospects and limitations. *American Psychologist*, *65*, 101–126.

Conger, J.A. & Kanungo, R.N. (1998). *Charismatic leadership in organizations*. Thousand Oaks, CA: Sage Publications.

Conger, J.A., Kanungo, R.N. & Menon, S.T. (2000). Charismatic leadership and follower effects. *Journal of Organizational Behavior*, *21*, 747–767.

Conlon, D.E., Moon, H. & Ng, K.Y. (2002). Putting the cart before the horse: The benefits of arbitrating before mediating. *Journal of Applied Psychology*, *87*, 978–984.

Conlon, S.E., Lind, E.A. & Lissak, R.I. (1989). Nonlinear and nonmonotonic effects of outcome on procedural and distributive fairness judgements. *Journal of Applied Social Psychology, 19*, 1085–1099.

Conway, L.G., Dodds, D.P., Towgood, K.H., McCure, S. & Olson, J.M. (2011). The biological roots of complex thinking. Are heritable attitudes more complex? *Journal of Personality, 79*, 101–134.

Conway, L.G., Suedfeld, P. & Tetlock, P.E. (2001). Integrative complexity and political decisions that lead to war or peace. In D.J. Christie & R.V. Wegner (Eds), *Peace, conflict and violence: Peace psychology for the 21st century* (pp. 66–75). Upper Saddle River, NJ: Prentice-Hall.

Conway, M., Pizzamiglio, M.T. & Mount, L. (1996). Status, communality, and agency: Implications for stereotypes of gender and other groups. *Journal of Personality and Social Psychology, 71*, 25–38.

Cook, I.A., Warren, C., Pajot, S.K., Schairer, D. & Leuchter, A.E. (2011). Regional brain activation with advertising images. *Journal of Neuroscience, Psychology and Economics, 4*, 147–160.

Cook, S.W. (1970). Motives in a conceptual analysis of attitude-related behavior. In W.J. Arnold & D. Levine (Eds), *Nebraska symposium on motivation, 1969* (pp. 179–235). Lincoln, NE: University of Nebraska Press.

Cook, S.W. (1984). *Experimenting on social issues: The case of school desegregation.* 92nd Annual Convention of the American Psychological Association, Toronto.

Cook, S.W. & Selltiz, C. (1964). A multiple-indicator approach to attitude measurement. *Psychological Bulletin, 62*, 36–55.

Cooley, C.H. (1902). *Human nature and the social order.* New York: Scribner.

Cooper, J. (2011). Cognitive dissonance theory. In P.A. Van Lange, A. Kruglanski & E.T. Higgins (Eds). *Handbook of theories of social psychology*, (Vol. 1). (pp. 377–397). London: Sage.

Cooper, J. & Fazio, R.H. (1984). A new look at dissonance theory. In L. Berkowitz (Ed.), *Advances in experimental social psychology* (Vol. 17). (pp. 229–266). New York: Academic Press.

Cooper, J. & Hogg, M.A. (2007). Feeling the anguish of others: A theory of vicarious dissonance. In M.P. Zanna (Ed.) *Advances in Experimental Social Psychology, 39*, 359–403. San Diego,CA. Academic Press.

Cooper, J. & Worchel, S. (1970). Role of undesired consequences in arousing cognitive dissonance. *Journal of Personality and Social Psychology, 16*, 199–206.

Cooper J., Zanna, M.P. & Goethals, G.R. (1974). Mistreatment of an esteemed other as a consequence affecting dissonance reduction. *Journal of Experimental Social Psychology, 10*, 224–233.

Cooper, J., Zanna, M.P. & Taves, P.A. (1978). Arousal as a necessary condition for attitude change following induced compliance. *Journal of Personality and Social Psychology, 36*, 1101–1106.

Cooper, M.L., Shaver, P.R. & Collins, N.L. (1998). Attachment style, emotion regulation and adjustment in adolescence. *Journal of Personality and Social Psychology, 74*, 1380–1397.

Corcoran, K. & Mussweller, T. (2010). The cognitive miser's perspective: Social comparison as a heuristic in self-judgments. *European Review of Social Psychology, 1*, 7–113.

Corenblum, B. & Annis, R.C. (1993). Development of racial identity in minority and majority children: An effect discrepancy model. *Canadian Journal of Behavioural Science, 25*, 499–521.

Cornwell, D. & Hobbs, S. (1992). Rumour and legend: Interactions between social psychology and folkloristics. *Canadian Psychology, 33*, 609–613.

Coser, L.A. (1967). *Continuities in the study of social conflict.* New York: Free Press.

Cota, A.A., Evans, C.R., Dion, K.L. & Longman, R.S. (1995). The structure of group cohesion. *Personality and Social Psychology Bulletin, 21*, 572–580.

Cottrell, N.B. (1972). Social facilitation. In C.G. McClintock (Ed.), *Experimental social psychology.* New York: Holt, Rinehart & Winston.

Cottrell, N.B., Wack, D.L., Sekerak, G.J. & Rittle, R.H. (1968). Social facilitation of dominant responses by the presence of an audience and the mere presence of others. *Journal of Personality and Social Psychology, 9*, 245–250.

Couch, A. & Keniston, K. (1960). Yeasayers and naysayers: Agreeing response set as a personality variable. *The Journal of Abnormal and Social Psychology*, *60*, 151–174. doi: 10.1037/h0040372

Couch, C.J. (1968). Collective behaviour: An examination of some stereotypes. *Social Problems*, *15*, 310–312.

Couzin, I.D., Krause, J., Franks, N.R. & Levin, S.A. (2005). Effective leadership and decision-making in animal groups on movement. *Nature*, *434*, 513–516.

Covell, K., Dion, K.L. & Dion, K.K. (1994). Gender differences. In evaluations of tobacco and alcohol advertisements. *Canadian Journal of Behavioural Science*, *26*, 404–420.

Cox, S.J.B. (1985). No tragedy of the commons. *Environmental Ethics*, 7, 49–61.

Cozby, P.C. (1973). Self-disclosure: A literature review. *Psychological Bulletin*, *79*, 73–91.

Craig, K.D. (1978). Social modelling influences on pain. In R.A. Sternbach (Ed.), *The psychology of pain* (pp. 73–110). New York: Raven Press.

Craig, W.M. & Pepler, D.J. (2007). Understanding bullying: From research to practice. *Canadian Psychology*, *48*, 86–93.

Cramer, K.M., Nickels, J.B. & Gural, D.M. (1997). Uncertainty of outcomes, prediction of failure, and lack of control as factors explaining perceived helplessness. *Journal of Social Behavior & Personality*, *12*, 611–630.

Crandall, C.S. (1988). Social contagion of binge eating. *Journal of Personality and Social Psychology*, *55*, 588–598.

Crandall, C.S. & Eshleman, A. (2003). A justification-suppression model of the expression and experience of prejudice. *Psychological Bulletin*, *129*, 414–446.

Crary, J. (2001). Suspensions of perception: Attention, spectacle, and modern culture. Cambridge, MA: MIT Press.

Crawford, C. & Krebs, D. (Eds). (1998). *Handbook of evolutionary psychology: Ideas, issues, and applications.* Mahwah, NJ: Lawrence Erlbaum Associates.

Crawford, M.P. (1939). The social psychology of the vertebrates. *Psychological Bulletin*, *36*, 407–466.

Crisp, R. J. (2010). Prejudice and perceiving multiple identities. In J. F. Dovidio, M. Hewstone, P. Glick, & V. M. Esses (Eds). *Sage handbook of prejudice, stereotyping, & discrimination* (pp. 508–525). Thousand Oakes: Sage.

Crisp, R.J. & Hewstone, M. (1999). Differential evaluation of crossed category groups: Patterns, processes, and reducing intergroup bias. *Group Processes and Intergroup Relations*, *2*, 307–333.

Crisp, R.J. & Turner, R.N. (2011). Cognitive adaptation to the experience of social and cultural diversity. *Psychological Bulletin*, *137*, 242–266.

Crittenden, K.S. (1983). Sociological aspects of attribution. *Annual Review of Sociology*, *9*, 425–446.

Crocker, J. (1999). Social stigma and self-esteem: situational construction of worth. *Journal of Experimental Social Psychology*, *35*, 89–107.

Crocker, J. & Lawrence, J.S. (1999). Social stigma and self-esteem: The role of contingencies of worth. In Prentice, D.A. & Miller, D.T. (Eds), *Cultural divides: Understanding and overcoming group conflict* (pp. 364–392). New York: Russell Sage Foundation.

Crocker, J. & Major, B. (1989). Social stigma and self-esteem: The self-protective properties of stigma. *Psychological Review*, *96*, 608–630.

Crocker, J., Major, B. & Steele, C. (1998). Social Stigma. In D.T. Gilbert, S.T. Fiske & G. Lindzey (Eds), *The handbook of social psychology, Vols. 1 and 2* (4th ed.). (pp. 504–553). New York: McGraw-Hill.

Crocker, J. & Quinn, D. (1998). Racism and self-esteem. In J.L. Eberhardt & S.T. Fiske (Eds), *Confronting racism: The problem and the response.* Thousand Oaks, CA: Sage Publications, Inc.

Cromwell, R.L., Butterfield, E.C., Brayfield, F.M. & Curry, J.L. (1977). *Acute myocardial infarction: Reaction and recovery.* St. Louis, MO: Mosby.

Croson, R. & Marks, M. (1998). Identifiability of individual contributions in a threshold public goods experiment. *Journal of Mathematical Psychology*, *42*, 167–190.

Cross, C.P. & Campbell, A. (2011). Women's aggression. *Aggression and Violent Behavior*, *16*, 390–398.

Cross, S. &. Vick, N. (2001). The interdependent self-construal and social support: The case of persistence in engineering. *Personality and Social Psychology Bulletin*, *27*, 820–832.

Cross, S.E. & Madson, L. (1997). Models of the self: Self-construals and gender. *Psychological Bulletin*, *122*, 5–37.

Crutchfield, R.A. (1955). Conformity and character. *American Psychologist*, *10*, 191–198.

Csikszentmihalyi, M. & Figurski T.J. (1982). Self-awareness and overside experience in everyday life. *Journal of Personality*, *50*, 15–28.

Csizér, K. & Kormos, J. (2009). Modelling the role of inter-cultural contact in the motivation of learning English as a foreign language. *Applied Linguistics*, *30*, 166–185.

Cuddy, A., Fiske, S.T., Kwan, V.S.Y., Glick, P. & 20 others (2009). Stereotype content model across cultures: Towards universal similarities and some differences. *British Journal of Social Psychology*, *48*, 1–33.

Cuddy, A., Fiske, S.T. & Glick, P. (2008). Warmth and competence as universal dimensions of social perception: The stereotype content model and the BIAS map. In M.P. Zanna (Ed.). *Advances in experimental social psychology*, (Vol. 40). (pp. 61–149). San Diego, CA, US: Elsevier Academic Press.

Cui, M., Durtschi, J.A., Donnellan, M.B., Lorenz, F.O. & Conger, R.D. (2010). Intergenerational transmission of relationship aggression: A prospective longitudinal study. *Journal of Family Psychology*, *24*, 688–697.

Curran, J.P. & Lippold, S. (1975). The effects of physical attraction and attitude similarity on attraction in dating dyads. *Journal of Personality*, *43*, 528–538.

Curtis, R.C. & Miller, K. (1986). Believing another likes or dislikes you; Behavior makes the beliefs come true. *Journal of Personality and Social Psychology*, *51*, 284–290.

Cutler, B.L. & Kovera, M.B. (2011). Expert psychological testimony. *Current Directions in Psychological Science*, *20*, 53–57.

Cutrona, C.E. (1982). Transition to college: Loneliness and the process of social adjustment. In L.A. Peplau & D. Perlman (Eds), *Loneliness: A sourcebook of current theory, research and therapy* (pp. 291–309). New York: Wiley.

Da Gloria, J. (1984). Frustration, aggression and the sense of justice. In A. Mummendey (Ed.), *Social psychology of aggression: From individual behavior to social interaction* (pp. 127–142). New York: Springer-Verlag.

Dalal, A.K. & Misra, G. (2002). Social psychology in India: Evolution and emerging trends. In A.K. Dalal & G. Misra (Eds), *New directions in Indian psychology*, (Vol. 1). (pp. 1–26). New Delhi: Sage.

Daly, M. & Wilson, M. (1988). *Homicide.* New York: Aldine De Gruyter.

Damian, S., Phelps, E. & Banaji, M. (2008). The neural basis of implicit attitudes. *Current Directions in Psychological Science*, *17*, 164–170.

Danziger, K. (1983). Origins and basic principles of Wundt's Volkerpsychologie. *British Journal of Social Psychology*, *22*, 303–313.

Danziger, K. (1997). The varieties of social construction. *Theory and Psychology*, *7*, 399–416.

Darley, J. (1999). Method for the study of evil-doing actions. *Personality and Social Psychology Review*, *3*, 269–275.

Darley, J.M. & Latané, B. (1968). Bystander intervention in emergencies: Diffusion of responsibility. *Journal of Personality and Social Psychology*, *8*, 377–383.

Darley, J.M. & Latané, B. (1970). Norms and normative behavior: Field studies of social interdependence. In J. Macaulay & L. Berkowitz (Eds), *Altruism and helping behavior* (pp. 83–101). New York: Academic Press.

Darley, J.M., Loeb, I. & Hunter, J. (1996). Community attitudes on the family of issues surrounding the death of terminal patients. *Journal of Social Issues*, *52*, 85–104.

Darlington, R.B. & Macker, D.F. (1966). Displacement of guilt-produced altruistic behavior. *Journal of Personality and Social Psychology*, *4*, 442–443.

Darwin, C. (1872). *Descent of man.* New York: D. Appleton & Company.

DasGupta, P. (2011). Literature review: e-leadership. *Emerging Leadership Journeys*, *4*, 1–36.

Dashiell, J.F. (1935). Experimental studies of the influence of social situations on the behavior of individual human adults. In C. Murchison (Ed.), *Handbook of social psychology* (pp. 1097–1158). Worcester, MA: Clark University.

Davidowicz, L.C. (1975). *The war against the Jews, 1933–1945.* Holt, Rinehart & Winston: New York.

Davidson, A.R. & Morrison, D.M. (1983). Predicting contraceptive behavior from attitudes: A comparison of within- versus across-subjects procedures. *Journal of Personality and Social Psychology*, *45*, 997–1009.

Davies, K., Tropp, L.R., Aron, A., Pettigrew, T.F. & Wright, S.C. (2011). Cross-group friendships and intergroup attitudes: A meta-analytic review. *Personality and Social Psychology Review*, *15*, 332–351.

Davila, J., Karney, B.R. & Bradbury, T.N. (1999). Attachment change processes in early marriage.

Journal of Personality and Social Psychology, 76, 783–802.

Dawes, R.M. (1980). Social dilemmas. *Annual Review of Psychology, 31,* 169–193.

De Cremer, D. (1999). Trust and fear of exploitation in a public goods dilemma. *Current Psychology, 18,* 153–163.

De Cremer, D. & Van Lange, P.A.M. (2011). Why prosocials exhibit greater cooperation than pro-selfs: The rules of social responsibility and reciprocity. *European Journal of Personality, 15,* S5–S18.

De Mooij, M. and Hofstede, G. (2010). The Hofstede model: Applications to global branding and advertising strategy and research. *International Journal of Advertising, 29,* 85–110.

DeNeve, J-E., Mikhaylov, S., Dawes, C.T., Christakis, N.A. & Fowler, J.H. (2013). Born to lead? A twin design and genetic association study of leadership role occupancy. *The Leadership Quarterly, 24,* 45.

Deary, I.J., Batty, G.D. & Gale, C.R. (2008). Bright children become enlightened adults. *Psychological Science, 19,* 1–6.

Deaux, K. (1984). From individual differences to social categories. *American Psychologist, 39,* 105–116.

Deaux, K. (1985). Sex and gender. *Annual Review of Psychology, 36,* 49–81.

Deaux, K. & Emswiller, T. (1974). Explanations of successful performance on sex-linked tasks: What is skill for the male is luck for the female. *Journal of Personality and Social Psychology, 29,* 80–85.

Decety, J., Jackson, P.L., Somerville, J.A., Chaminade, T. & Meltzoff, A.N. (2004). The neural basis of cooperation and competition: An fMRI investigation. *Neuroimage, 23,* 744–751.

DeCourville, N. & Sadava, S.W. (1997). The structure of problem drinking in adulthood: A confirmatory approach. *Journal of Studies on Alcohol, 58,* 146–154.

Dehghani, M., Atran, S., Iliev, R., Sachdeva, S. & Medin, D. (2010). Sacred values and conflict over Iran's nuclear programme. *Judgment and Decision Making, 5,* 540–546.

Dejong, W. (1979). An examination of self-perception mediation of the foot-in-the-door effect. *Journal of Personality and Social Psychology, 37,* 2221–2239.

DeLongis, A., Coyne, J.C., Kakof, G., Folkman, S. & Lazarus, R.S. (1982). Relationship of daily hassles, uplifts and major life events to health status. *Health Psychology, 1,* 119–136.

Demorest, S.M., Morrison, S.J., Beken, M., Richards, T.L. & Johnson, C. (2010). An fMRI investigation of the cultural specificity of music memory. *Social Cognition and Affective Neuroscience, 5,* 282–291.

Dempsey, M.A. & Mitchell, A.A. (2010). The influence of implicit attitudes on choice when consumers are confronted with conflicting attribute information. *Journal of Consumer Research, 37,* 614–625.

DePaulo, B.M. & Coleman, L.M. (1986). Talking to children, foreigners, and retarded adults. *Journal of Personality and Social Psychology, 51,* 945–959.

DePaulo, B.M., Lindsay, J.J., Malone, B.E., Muhlenbruck, L., Charlton, K. & Cooper, H. (2003). Cues to deception. *Psychological Bulletin, 129,* 74–118.

DePaulo, B.M. & Pfeifer, R.L. (1986). On-the-job experience and skill at detecting deception. *Journal of Applied Social Psychology, 16,* 249–267.

DePaulo, B.M. & Rosenthal, R. (1979). Telling lies. *Journal of Personality and Social Psychology, 37,* 1713–1722.

Derlega, M.J., Catanzaro, D. & Lewis, R.J. (2001). Perceptions about tactile intimacy in same-sex and opposite-sex pairs based on research participants' sexual orientation. *Psychology of Men and Masculinity, 2,* 124–132.

Dermer, M.L. & Jacobsen, E. (1986). Some potential negative social consequences of cigarette smoking: Marketing research in reverse. *Journal of Applied Social Psychology, 16,* 702–725.

Dermer, M.L. & Pyszczynski, T.A. (1978). Effects of erotica upon men's loving and liking responses for women they love. *Journal of Personality and Social Psychology, 36,* 1302–1309.

De Rosa, A.S. (1986). The social representation of mental illness in children and adults. In W. Doise & S. Moscovici (Eds), *Current issues in European social psychology* (pp. 47–138). New York: Cambridge.

DeSantis, M., Mohan, P.J. & Steinhorst, R.K. (2005). Smiling in photographs: Childhood similarities between sexes become differences constant in adulthood. *Psychological Reports, 97,* 651–665

DeSantis, M. & Sierra, N. (2000). Women smiled more often and openly than men when photographed for a pleasant, public occasion in 20th Century United States Society. *Psychology: A Journal of Human Behaviour, 37,* 21–31.

Deschamps, J.C. & Doise, W. (1978). Crossed category memberships in intergroup relations. In H. Tajfel (Ed.), *Differentiation between social groups: Studies in the social psychology of inter-group relations* (pp. 141–158). London: Academic Press.

Desjarlais, M. & Willoughby, T. (2010). A longitudinal study of the relation between adolescent boys' and girls' computer use with friends and friendship quality: Support for the social compensation or the rich-get-richer hypothesis: *Computers in Human Behavior, 26,* 896–905.

Deutsch, F.M. & Lamberti, D.M. (1986). Does social approval improve helping? *Personality and Social Psychology Bulletin, 12,* 149–158.

Deutsch, M. & Gerard, H.B. (1955). A study of normative and informational social influences upon individual judgment. *The Journal of Abnormal and Social Psychology, 51,* 629–636.

Deutsch, M. & Solomon, L. (1959). Reactions to evaluations by others as influenced by self-evaluations. *Sociometry, 22,* 92–113.

Devine, P.G. (1989). Stereotypes and prejudice: Their automatic and controlled components. *Journal of Personality and Social Psychology, 56,* 5–18.

Devine, P.G. & Elliot, A.J. (1995). Are racial stereotypes really fading? The Princeton trilogy revisited. *Personality and Social Psychology Bulletin, 21,* 1139–1150.

DeVos, G.A. & Hippler, A.E. (1969). Cultural psychology: Comparative studies of human behavior. In G. Lindzey & E. Aronson (Eds), *The handbook of social psychology* (2nd ed.). (Vol. 4). (pp. 322–417). Reading, MA: Addison-Wesley.

DeVries, D.L. & Edwards, K.J. (1974). Student teams and learning games: Their effects on cross-race and cross-sex interaction. *Journal of Educational Psychology, 66,* 741–749.

DeWall, C.N. & Anderson, C.A. (2011). The General Aggression Model. In M. Mikulincer & P.R. Shaver (Eds), *Understanding and reducing aggression, violence, and their consequences.* Washington, DC: American Psychological Association. (pp. 15–33).

DeWall, C.N., Anderson, C.A. & Bushman, B.J. (2011). The general aggression model: Theoretical extensions to violence. *Psychology of Violence, 1,* 245–258

Diamond, L.M. & Dickenson, J.A. (2012). The neuroimaging of love and desire: review and future directions. *Clinical Neuropsychiatry: Journal of Treatment Evaluation, 9,* 39–50.

DiBartolo, P.M. & Rendón, M.J. (2012). A critical examination of the construct of perfectionism and its relationship to mental health in Asian and African Americans using a cross-cultural framework. *Clinical Psychology Review, 32,* 139–152.

Dickerson, C., Thibodeau, R., Aronson, E. & Miller, D. (1992). Using cognitive dissonance to encourage water conservation. *Journal of Applied Social Psychology, 22,* 841–854.

Dickert, S., Sagara, N. & Slovic, P. (2011). Affective motivations to help others: A two-stage model of donation decisions. *Journal of Behavioral Decision Making, 24,* 361.

Diener, E. (1984). Subjective well-being. *Psychological Bulletin, 95,* 542–575.

Diener, E. & Lucas, R.E. (2003). Personality and subjective well-being. In D. Kahneman, E. Diener, & N. Schwarz (Eds). *Well-being: Foundations of hedonic psychology* (pp. 213–229). New York: Russell Sage Foundation.

Dijk, C., Koenig, B., Ketelaar, T. & de Jong, P.J. (2011). Saved by the blush: being trusted despite defecting. *Emotion, 11,* 313–319.

Dijker, A.J.M. (1987). Emotional reactions to ethnic minorities. *European Journal of Social Psychology, 17,* 305–325.

Dijltstra, P., Groothof, H.A.K., Poel, G.A., Laverman, T.T.G., Schrier, M. & Buunk, B.P. (2001). Sex differences in the events that elicit jealousy among homosexuals. *Personal Relationships, 8,* 1–54.

DiMatteo, M.R., Sherbourne, C.D., Hays, R.D., Ordway, L., Kravitz, R.L., McGlynn, E.A., Kaplan, S. & Rogers, W.H. (1993). Physicians' characteristics influence patients' adherence to medical treatment: Results from the medical outcomes study. *Health Psychology, 12,* 93–102.

Dindia, K. (2000). Sex differences in self-disclosure, reciprocity of self-disclosure, and self-disclosure and liking: Three meta-analyses reviewed. In K. Dindia & S. Duck, (Eds) *Communication and personal relationships* (pp. 147–162). New York: John Wiley.

DiNicola, D.D. & DiMatteo, M.R. (1984). Practitioners, patients and compliance with medical regimes: A social psychological perspective. In A. Baum, S.E. Taylor & J.E. Singer (Eds),

Handbook of psychology and health (Vol. 4). (pp. 55–64). Hillsdale, NJ: Erlbaum.

Dion, K.K. (1972). Physical attractiveness and evaluations of children's transgressions. *Journal of Personality and Social Psychology, 24,* 207–213.

Dion, K.K., Berscheid, E. & Walster, E. (1972). What is beautiful is good. *Journal of Personality and Social Psychology, 24,* 285–290.

Dion, K.K. & Dion, K.L. (1985). Personality, gender and the phenomenology of romantic love. *Review of Personality and Social Psychology, 6,* 209–20.

Dion, K.K. & Dion, K.L. (1996). Cultural perspectives on Romantic love. *Personal Relationships, 3,* 5–17.

Dion, K.K., Pak, A.W. & Dion, K.L. (1990). Stereotyping physical attractiveness: A perspective. *Journal of Cross-Cultural Psychology, 21,* 378–398.

Dion, K.L. (1987). What's in a title? The Ms. stereotype and images of women's titles of address. *Psychology of Women Quarterly, 11,* 21–36.

Dion, K.L. (1989). *Ethnicity and perceived discrimination: A comparative survey of six ethnic groups in Toronto.* 10th Annual Conference of the Canadian Ethnic Studies Association, Calgary.

Dion, K.L. (2002). The social psychology of perceived prejudice and discrimination. *Canadian Psychology, 43,* 1–10.

Dion, K.L. & Dion, K.K. (1976). The Ames phenomenon revisited: Factors underlying the resistance to perceptual distortion of one's partner. *Journal of Personality and Social Psychology, 33,* 170–177.

Dion, K.L. & Dion, K.K. (1987). Belief in a just world and physical attractiveness stereotyping. *Journal of Personality and Social Psychology, 52,* 775–780.

Dion, K.L., Dion, K.K., Coambs, R. & Kozlowski, L. (1990, June). *Smokers and drinkers: A tale of two stereotypes.* Annual Convention of the Canadian Psychological Association, Ottawa.

Dion, K.L. & Earn, B.M. (1975). The phenomenology of being a target of prejudice. *Journal of Personality and Social Psychology, 32,* 944–950.

Dion, K.L., Earn, B.M. & Yee, P.H. (1978). The experience of being a victim of prejudice: An experimental approach. *International Journal of Psychology, 13,* 197–214.

Dion, K.L. & Kawakami, K. (1996). Ethnicity and perceived discrimination in Toronto: Another look at the personal/group discrimination discrepancy. *Canadian Journal of Behavioural Science, 28,* 203–213.

Dion, K.L. & Schuller, R.A. (1991). The Ms. Stereotype: Its generality and its relation to managerial and marital status stereotypes. *Canadian Journal of Behaviour Science, 23,* 25–40.

Ditecco, D. & Schlegel, R.P. (1982). Alcohol use among young males: An application of problem-behavior theory. In J.R. Eiser (Ed.), *Social psychology and behavioral medicine.* (pp. 199–233). Chichester: J.R. Wiley.

Ditto, P.H. & Hilton, J.L. (1990). Expectancy processes in the health care interaction sequence. *Journal of Social Issues, 46* (2), 97–124.

Dixon, D., Cruess, S., Kilbourne, K., Klimas, N., Fletcher, M., Ironson, G., Baum, A., Schneiderman, N. & Antoni, M.H. (2001). Social support mediates loneliness and human herpesvirus Type 6 (HHV-6) antibody titers. *Journal of Applied Social Psychology, 31,* 1111–1132.

Doan, B.D. & Gray, R.E. (1992). The heroic cancer patient: A critical analysis of the relationship between illusion and mental health. *Canadian Journal of Behavioural Science, 24,* 253–266.

Doise, W., Deschamps, J-C. & Meyer, G. (1978). The accentuation of intra-category similarities. In H. Tajfel (Ed.), *Differentiation between social groups: Studies in the social psychology of intergroup relations* (pp. 159–168). London: Academic Press.

Dollard, J., Doob, L.W., Miller, N.E., Mowrer, O.H. & Sears, R.R. (1939). *Frustration and aggression.* New Haven: Yale University Press.

Dollinger, S. J., & Clancy, S. M. (1993). Identity, self, and personality: II. Glimpses through the autophotographic eye. *Journal of Personality & Social Psychology, 64,* 1064–1071.

Dollinger, S. J., Preston, L. A., O'Brien, S. P., & DiLalla, D. L. (1996). Individuality and relatedness of the self: An autophotographic study. *Journal of Personality and Social Psychology, 71,* 1268–1278.

Dompierre, S. & Lavellée, M. (1990). Degré de contact et stress acculturatif dans le procéssus d'adaptation des refugiés africains. *International Journal of Psychology, 25,* 417–437.

Donakowski, D.W. & Esses, V.M. (1996). Native Canadians, First Nations, or aboriginals: The effect of labels on attitudes toward native peoples.

Canadian Journal of Behavioural Science, 28, 86–91.

Donnerstein, E., Linz, D. & Penrod, S. (1987). *The question of pornography*. New York: Free Press.

Donohue, W. A. (2012).The identity trap: The language of genocide. *Journal of Language and Social Psychology, 31*, 13–29.

Donovan, J.E., Jessor, R. & Costa, F.M. (1993). Structure of health-enhancing behaviors in adolescence: A latent-variable approach. *Journal of Health and Social Behavior, 34*, 346–362.

Donovan, J.E., Jessor, R. & Jessor, L. (1983). Problem drinking in adolescence and young adulthood. A follow-up study. *Journal of Studies on Alcohol, 44*, 109–137.

Doob, L.W. (1950). Goebbels' principles of propaganda. *Public Opinion Quarterly, 14*, 419–322.

Doosje, B. & Branscombe, N. R. (2003). Attributions for the negative historical actions of a group. *European Journal of Social Psychology, 33*, 235–248.

Douglas, K.M. & McGarty, C. (2002). Internet identifiability and beyond: A model of the effects of identifiability on communicative behavior. *Group-Dynamics. 6*, 17–26.

Dovidio, J.F. & Ellyson, S.L. (1985). Patterns of visual dominance behavior in humans. In S.L. Ellyson & J.F. Dovidio (Eds), *Power, dominance, and nonverbal behavior* (pp. 129–149). New York: Springer-Verlag.

Dovidio, J.F., Gaertner, S.L. & Pearson, A.R. (2005). On the nature of prejudice: The psychological foundations of hate. In R. Sternberg (Ed.). *The psychology of hate* (pp. 211–234). Washington, DC: American Psychological Association.

Dovidio, J.F., Hewstone, M., Glick, P. & Esses, V.M. (Eds) (2010). *The SAGE handbook of prejudice, stereotyping and discrimination*. London: Sage Publications.

Dovidio, J.F., Kawakami, K., Smoak, N. & Gaertner, S.L (2008). The nature of contemporary racial prejudice: Insight from implicit and explicit measures of attitudes. In R. Petty & R. Fazio (Eds). *Attitudes: Insights from the new implicit measures* (pp. 165–192). New York: Psychology Press.

Dovidio, J.F., Piliavin, J.A, Gaertner, S.L., Schroeder, D.A. & Clark, R.D. (1991). The arousal: cost–reward model in the process of intervention: a review of the evidence. *Review of Personality and Social Psychology, 12*, 83–118.

Drager, K., Hay, J. & Walker, A. (2010). Pronounced rivalries: Attitudes and speech production. *Te Reo, 53*, 27–53.

Draguns, J.G. (1988). Personality and culture: Are they relevant for the enhancement of quality of mental life? In P.R. Dasen, J.W. Berry & N. Sartorius (Eds), *Health and Cross-cultural Psychology: Towards applications*. Newbury Park, CA: Sage.

Drewnowski, A., Henderson, S.A. & Barratt-Fornell, A. (2001). Genetic taste markers and food preferences. *Drug Metabolism and Disposition, 29*, 535–538.

Drigotas, S.M. & Rusbult, C.E. (1992). Should I stay or should I go? A dependence model of breakups. *Journal of Personality and Social Psychology, 62*, 62–87.

Drigotas, S.M., Rusbult, C.E., Wieselquist, J. & Whitton, S.W. (1999). Close partner as sculptor of the ideal self: Behavioral affirmation and the Michelangelo phenomenon. *Journal of Personality and Social Psychology, 77*, 293–323.

Driscoll, R., Davis, K.W. & Lipetz, M.E. (1972). Parental interference and romantic love. *Journal of Personality and Social Psychology, 24*, 1–10.

Drury, J. (2002). When mobs are looking for witches to burn, nobody's safe. *Discourse and Society, 13*, 41–73.

Drury, J. (2003). Adolescent communication with adults in authority. *Journal of Language and Social Psychology, 22,* 66–73.

Drury, J., Cocking, C. & Reicher, S. (2009). Everyone for themselves? A comparative study of crowd solidarity among emergency survivors. *British Journal of Social Psychology, 48*, 47–506.

Drury, J. & Reicher, S.D. (2010). Crowd control: How we avoid mass panic. *Scientific American Mind, 21*(5), 58–65.

Drury, J., Reicher, S.D. & Stott, C. (2003). Transforming the boundaries of collective identity: From the 'local' anti-road campaign to 'global' resistance? *Social Movement Studies, 2*, 191–212.

DuBois, D., Rucker, D.D. & Tormala, Z.L. (2011). From rumors to facts, and facts to rumors: The role of certainty decay in consumer communications. *Journal of Marketing Research, 48*, 1020–1032.

Duckitt, J. & Sibley, C.G. (2010). Personality, ideology, prejudice, and politics: A dual-process motivational model. *Journal of Personality, 78*, 1861–1893.

Duguid, M.M. & Goncalo, J.A. (2012). Living large: The powerful overestimate their own height. *Psychological Science, 23*, 36–40.

Dunham, Y., Chen, E. & Banaji, M.R. (2013). Two signatures of implicit intergroup bias: Developmental invariance and early enculturation. *Psychological Science.* Published online before print April 4, 2013. doi:10.1177/0956797612463081

Dunkel-Schetter, C., Feinstein, L.G., Taylor, S.E. & Falke, R.L. (1992). Patterns of coping with cancer. *Health Psychology, 11*, 79–87.

Dunkel-Schetter, C. & Wortman, C.B. (1982). The interpersonal dynamics of cancer: Problems in social relationships and their impact on the patient. In H.S. Friedman & M.R. DiMatteo (Eds), *Interpersonal issues in health care* (pp. 69–100). New York: Academic.

Durante, F., Volpato, C. & Fiske, S. (2010). Using the stereotype content model to examine group depictions in fascism: An archival approach. European Journal of Social Psychology, *40*, 465–483.

Dutton, D.G. (1971). Reactions of restaurateurs to blacks and whites violating restaurant dress requirements. *Canadian Journal of Behavioural Science, 3*, 298–331.

Dutton, D.G. (1973). The relationship of amount of perceived discrimination toward a minority group on behaviour of majority group members. *Canadian Journal of Behavioural Science, 5*, 34–45.

Dutton, D.G. & Aron, A.P. (1974). Some evidence for heightened sexual attraction under conditions of high anxiety. *Journal of Personality and Social Psychology, 30*, 510–517.

Dutton, D.G. & Lake, R. (1973). Threat of own prejudice and reverse discrimination in interracial situations. *Journal of Personality and Social Psychology, 28*, 94–100.

Dutton, D.G. & Lennox, V.I. (1974). The effect of prior 'token' compliance on subsequent interracial behaviour. *Journal of Personality and Social Psychology, 29*, 65–71.

Dutton, D.G., Starzomski, A.J., Saunders, K. & Bartholomew, K. (1994). Intimacy-anger and insecure attachment as precursors of abuse in intimate relationships. *Journal of Applied Social Psychology, 24*(15), 1367–1386.

Duval, S. & Wicklund, R.A. (1972). *A theory of objective self-awareness.* New York: Academic Press.

Dweck, C.S. (2012). Mind sets in human nature: Promoting change in the Middle East, the schoolyard, the racial divide, and willpower. *American Psychologist, 67*, 614–622.

Eagly, A.H. (1974). Comprehensibility of persuasive arguments as a determinant of opinion change. *Journal of Personality and Social Psychology, 29*, 758–773.

Eagly, A.H. (1978). Sex differences in influenceability. *Psychological Bulletin, 85*, 85–116.

Eagly, A.H. (1987). *Sex differences in social behavior: A social-role analysis.* Hillsdale, NJ: Erlbaum.

Eagly, A.H. (1996, August 16–21). *Attitudes and the processing of attitude-relevant information.* XXVI International Congress of Psychology, Montréal.

Eagly, A.H., Ashmore, R.D., Makhijani, M.G. & Longo, L.C. (1991). What is beautiful is good but ... A meta-analytic review of research on the physical attractiveness stereotype. *Psychological Bulletin, 110*, 109–128.

Eagly, A.H. & Carli, L.L. (1981). Sex of researcher and sex-typed communications as determinants of sex differences in influenceability: A meta-analysis of social influence studies. *Psychological Bulletin, 90*, 1–20.

Eagly, A.H., Chen, S., Chaiken, S. & Shaw-Barnes, K. (1999). The impact of attitudes on memory: An affair to remember. *Psychological Bulletin, 125*, 64–89.

Eagly, A. H., & Chaiken, S. (1984). Cognitive theories of persuasion. In L. Berkowitz (Ed.) *Advances in experimental social psychology* (Vol. 17, pp. 267-359). New York: Academic Press.

Eagly, A.H. & Chaiken, S. (1998). Attitude structure and function. In D.T. Gilbert, S.T. Fiske & G. Lindzey (Eds). *Handbook of social psychology* (4th ed.) (Vol. 1). (pp. 269–322). New York: McGraw-Hill.

Eagly, A.H. & Chaiken, S. (1992). *The psychology of attitudes.* Fort Worth, TX: Harcourt Brace Jovanovich.

Eagly, A.H. & Chaiken, S. (1998). Attitude structure and function. In D.T. Gilbert & S.T. Fiske (Eds), *The handbook of social psychology* (pp. 269–322). Boston, MA: McGraw-Hill.

Eagly, A.H. & Crowley, M. (1986). Gender and helping behavior: A meta-analytic review of the social psychological literature. *Psychological Bulletin, 100*, 283–308.

Eagly, A.H. & Karau, S.J. (1991). Gender and the emergence of leaders: A meta-analysis. *Journal of Personality and Social Psychology*, *60*, 685–710.

Eagly, A.H., Karau, S.J. & Makhijani, M.G. (1995). Gender and the effectiveness of leaders: A meta-analysis. *Psychological Bulletin*, *17*, 125–145.

Eagly, A.H., Makhijani, M.G. & Klonsky, B.G. (1992). Gender and the evaluation of leaders: A meta-analysis. *Psychological Bulletin*, *111*, 3–22.

Eagly, A.H. & Steffen, V.J. (1986). Gender and aggressive behavior: A meta-analytic review of the social psychological literature. *Psychological Bulletin*, *100*, 309–330.

Eagly, A.H. & Wood, W. (1982). Inferred sex differences in status as a determinant of gender stereotypes about social influence. *Journal of Personality and Social Psychology*, *43*, 915–928.

Eagly, A.H. & Wood, W. (1985). Gender and influenceability: Stereotype versus behavior. In V.E. O'Leary, R.K. Unger & B.S. Wallston (Eds), *Women, gender and social psychology* (pp. 225–256). Hillsdale, NJ: Erlbaum.

Eagly, A.H., Wood, W. & Chaiken, S. (1978). Causal inferences about communicators and their effects on opinion change. *Journal of Personality and Social Psychology*, *36*, 424–435.

Eagly, A.H., Wood, W. & Fishbaugh, L. (1981). Sex differences in conformity: Surveillance by the group as a determinant of male non-conformity. *Journal of Personality and Social Psychology*, *40*, 384–394.

Eaton, A.A., Visser, P.S., Krosnick, J.A. & Anand, S. (2009). Social power and attitude strength over the life course. *Personality and Social Psychology Bulletin*, *35*, 1646–1660.

Eaton, J. (2001). Management communication: The threat of groupthink. *Corporate Communications: An International Journal*, *6*, 183–192.

Eaves, L. & Hatemi, P.K (2008). Transmission of attitudes toward abortion and gay rights: Effects of genes, social learning and mate selection. *Behavior Genetics*, *38*, 247–256.

Eckert, P. (2003). Language and adolescent peer groups. *Journal of Language and Social Psychology*, *22*, 112–118.

Edwards, J. & Jacobsen, M. (1987). Standard and regional standard speech: Distinctions and similarities. *Language in Society*, *16*, 369–380.

Edwards, K. (1990). The interplay of affect and cognition in attitude formation and change. *Journal of Personality and Social Psychology*, *59*, 202–216.

Effran, M.G. (1974). The effect of physical appearance on the judgment of guilt, interpersonal attraction, and severity of recommended punishment in a simulated jury task. *Journal of Research in Personality*, *8*, 45–54.

Effran, M.G. & Patterson, E.W.J. (1974). Voters vote beautiful: The effect of physical appearance on a national election. *Canadian Journal of Behavioural Science*, *6*, 352–356.

Ehrlich, D., Guttman, I., Schonbach, P. & Mills, J. (1957). Post-decision exposure to relevant information. *Journal of Personality and Social Psychology*, *54*, 98–102.

Ehrlinger, J. & Dunning, D. (2003). How chronic self-views influence (and potentially mislead) estimates of performance. *Journal of Personality and Social Psychology*, *84*, 5–17.

Eibach, R.P. & Mock, S.E. (2011). Idealizing parenthood to rationalize parental investments. *Psychological Science*, *22*, 203–208.

Eidelson, R.J. & Eidelson, J.I. (2003). Dangerous ideas. Five beliefs that propel groups toward conflict. *American Psychologist*, *58*, 182–192.

Einav, S. & Hood, B.M. (2008). Tell-tale eyes: Children's attribution of gaze aversion as a lying cue. *Developmental Psychology*, *44*, 1655–1667.

Eisenberg, N. (2002). Empathy-related emotional responses, altruism, and their socialization. In R.J. Davidson, and A. Harrington (Eds). *Visions of compassion: Western scientists and Tibetan Buddhists examine human nature* (pp. 131–164). London, Oxford University Press.

Eisenberg, N. & Fabes, R.A. (1990). Empathy: Conceptualization, assessment, and relation to prosocial behavior. *Motivation and Emotion*, *14*, 131–149.

Eisenberg, N., Fabes, R.A., Murphy, B., Karbon, M., Smith, M., & Maszk, P. (1996). The relations of children's dispositional empathy-related responding to their emotionality, regulation, and social functioning. *Developmental Psychology, 32*, 195–209.

Eisenberg, N., Guthrie, I.K., Cumberland, A., Murphy, B.C., Shepard, S.A., Zhou, Q. & Carlo, G. (2002). Prosocial development in early adulthood: A longitudinal study. *Journal of Personality and Social Psychology*, *82*, 993–1006.

Eisenberg, N. & Lennon, R. (1983). Sex differences in empathy and related capacities. *Psychological Bulletin*, *94*, 100–131.

Eisenberg, N. & Mussen, P.H. (1997). *The roots of prosocial behavior in children*. Cambridge: Cambridge University Press.

Eiser, J.R. (1987). *The expression of attitude*. New York: Springer-Verlag.

Eiser, J.R. & Pancer, S.M. (1979). Attitudinal effects of the use of evaluatively biased language. *European Journal of Social Psychology*, *9*, 39–47.

Eiser, J.R. & Ross, M. (1977). Partisan language, immediacy and attitude change. *European Journal of Social Psychology*, *7*, 477–489.

Eiser, J.R. & Van Der Pligt, J. (1984). Attitudes and social factors in adolescent smoking: In search of peer group influences. *Journal of Applied Social Psychology*, *14*, 348–363.

Ekman, P. (1982). *Emotion in the human face*. New York: Cambridge.

Ekman, P. & Friesen, W.V. (1969). Nonverbal leakage and clues to deception. *Psychiatry*, *32*, 88–106.

Ekman, P. & Friesen, W.V. (1974). Detecting deception from the body or face. *Journal of Personality and Social Psychology*, *29*, 188–198.

Ekman, P. & Friesen, W.V. (1978). *Facial action coding system*. Palo Alto, CA: Consulting Psychologists Press.

Ekman, P., O'Sullivan, M. & Frank, M.G. (1999). A few can catch a liar. *Psychological Science*, *10*, 263–266.

Elfenbein, H.A. & Ambady, N. (2002). On the universality and cultural specificity of emotion recognition: A meta-analysis. *Psychological Bulletin. 128*, 203–235.

Ellard, J.H., Miller, C.D., Baumle, T. & Olson, J.M. (2002). Just world processes in demonizing. In M. Ross & D.T. Miller (Eds). *The justice motive in everyday life* (pp. 350–362). New York: Cambridge University Press, 2002.

Ellemers, N. & Boezeman, E.D. (2010). Empowering the volunteer organization. In S. Stürmer, S. & M. Snyder (Eds) *The psychology of prosocial behaviour*. Chichester, UK: Blackwell. (pp. 245–266).

Elliott, R., Newman, J.L., Longe, O.A. & Deakin, J.F.W. (2004). Instrumental responding for rewards is associated with enhanced neuronal response in subcortical reward systems. *Neuroimage*, *21*, 284–290.

Ellul, J. (2006). The characteristics of propaganda. In Jowett, G.S. & O'Donnell B. (Eds). *The characteristics of propaganda*. (pp. 176–197). Thousand Oaks, CA., USA: Sage.

Ellyson, S.L. & Dovidio, J.F. (Eds). (1985). *Power, dominance, and nonverbal behavior*. New York: Springer-Verlag.

Emery, C.R. (2010). Controlling for selection effects in the relationship between child behavior problems and exposure to intimate partner violence. *Journal of Interpersonal Violence*, *26*, 1541–1558.

Emery, R.E. (1989). Family abuse. *American Psychologist, 44*, 321–328.

Emonds, J., Declerck, C.H., Boone, C., Vandervliet, E.J.M. & Parizel, P.M. (2011). Comparing the neural basis of decision making in social dilemmas of people with different social value orientations, a fMRI study. *Journal of Neuroscience, Psychology and Economics*, *4*, 11–24.

Endler, N. & Speer, R.L. (1998). Personality psychology: Research trends for 1993–1995. *Journal of Personality*, *66*, 621–669.

Englehartd, C.R., Bartholow, B.D., Kerr, G.T. & Bushman, B.J. (2011). This is your brain on violent video games: Neural desensitization to violence predicts increased aggression following violent video game exposure. *Journal of Experimental Social Psychology*, *47*, 1033–1036.

Eron, L.D. (1980). Prescription for reduction of aggression. *American Psychologist, 35*, 244–252.

Eron, L.D., Huesmann, L.R., Dubow, E., Romanoff, R. & Yarmel, P.W. (1987). Aggression and its correlates over 22 years. In N.H. Crowell, R.J. Blanchard, I. Evans & C.R. O'Donnel (Eds), *Childhood aggression and violence: Sources of influence, prevention and control*. New York: Academic Press.

Escobar-Chaves, S.L., Tortolero, S.R., Markham, C.M., Low, B.J., Eitel, P. & Thickstun, P. (2005). Impact of the media on adolescent sexual attitudes and behaviors. *Pediatrics*, *116*, 303–326.

Esser, J.K. (1998). Alive and well after 25 years: A review of groupthink research. *Organizational Behavior and Human Decision Processes*, *73*, 116–141.

Esses, V.M. & Seligman, C. (1996). The individual-group distinction in assessments of strategies to reduce prejudice and discrimination: The case of affirmative action. In R.M. Sorrentino & E.T. Higgins (Eds), *Handbook of motivation and cognition: (Vol. 3) The interpersonal context*. New York: Guilford Press.

Esses, V.M., Dovidio, J.F. & Hodson, G. (2002). Public attitudes toward immigration in the United

States and Canada in response to the September 11, 2001 'Attack on America'. *Analyses of Social Issues and Public Policy*, *2*, 69–85.

Esses, V.M., Haddock, G. & Zanna, M.P. (1993). Values, stereotypes, and emotions as determinants of intergroup attitudes. In D.M. Mackie & D.C. Hamilton (Eds), *Affect, cognition and stereotyping: Interactive processes in group perception* (pp. 137–166). New York: Academic Press.

Esses, V.M., Jackson, L.M. & Armstrong, T.L. (1998). Intergroup competition and attitudes towards immigrants and immigration. *Journal of Social Issues*, *54*, 699–724.

Esses, V.M. & Zanna, M.P. (1995). Mood and the expression of ethnic stereotypes. *Journal of Personality and Social Psychology*, *69*, 1052–1068.

Etcoff, N. (1999). *Survival of the prettiest: The science of beauty.* New York: Doubleday.

Éthier, L.S., Palacio-Quintin, E. & Jourdan-Ionescu, C. (1992). Abuse and neglect: Two distinct forms of maltreatment? *Canada's Mental Health*, *40*, 13–18.

Evans, L.M. & Petty, R.E. (2003). Self-guide framing and persuasion: Responsibility increasing message processing to ideal levels. *Personality and Social Psychology Bulletin*, *29*, 313–324.

Evans. J. St. B.T. (2008). Dual-processing accounts of reasoning, judgment and social cognition. *Annual Review of Psychology 59*, 255–278.

Exline, J.J. & Baumeister, R.F. (2000). Expressing forgiveness and repentance: Benefits and barriers. In M.E. McCullough, K.I. Pargament & C.E. Thoresen (Eds), *Forgiveness: Theory, research, and practice* (pp. 133–155). New York: Guilford Press.

Fabrigar, L.R. & Petty, R.E. (1999). The role of the affective and cognitive bases of attitudes in susceptibility to affectively and cognitively based persuasion. *Personality and Social Psychology Bulletin*, *25*, 363–381.

Fagan, G.G. (2011). *The lure of the arena.* Cambridge: Cambridge University Press.

Fajnzylber, P., Lederman, D. & Loayza, N. (2002). Inequality and violent crime. *Journal of Law and Economics*, *45*, 1–40.

Falk, A. & Heckman, J.J. (2009). Lab experiments are a major source of knowledge in the social sciences. *Science*, *326*, 535–538.

Falk, E.B., Ramneson, L., Berkman, E.T., Liao, B. & Kang, Y. (2010). The neural correlates of persuasion: A common network across cultures and media. *Journal of Cognitive Neuroscience*, *22*, 2447–2459.

Farago, L. (1942). *German psychological warfare.* New York: G.P. Putnam's Sons.

Faye, C. (2007). Governing the grapevine: the study of rumour during World War II. *History of Psychology*, *10*, 1–21.

Fazio, R.H., Blascovich, J. & Driscoll, D.M. (1992). On the functional value of attitudes: The influence of accessible attitudes on the ease and quality of decision making. *Personality and Social Psychology Bulletin*, *18*, 388–401.

Fazio, R.H., Jackson, J., Dunton, B.C. & Williams, C.J. (1995). Variability in automatic activation as an unobtrusive measure of racial attitudes: A bona fide pipeline. *Journal of Personality and Social Psychology*, *69*, 1013–1027.

Fazio, R.H., Sanbonmatsu, D.M., Powell, M.C. & Kardes, F.R. (1986). On the automatic activation of attitudes. *Journal of Personality and Social Psychology*, *50*, 229–238.

Feather, N.T. (1999). *Values, achievement, and justice: Studies in the psychology of deservingness.* Dordrecht, Netherlands: Kluwer Academic Publishers.

Fehr, B. & Russell, J.A. (1991). The concept of love viewed from a prototype perspective. *Journal of Personality and Social Psychology*, *60*, 425–438.

Fehr, B. (1988). Prototype analysis of the concepts of love and commitment. *Journal of Personality and Social Psychology*, *4*, 557–579.

Fehr, B. (1993). How do I love thee? Let me consult my prototype. In S. Duck (Ed.), *Individuals in relationships* (Vol. 1). (pp. 87–120). Newbury Park, CA: Sage.

Fehr, B. (1996). *Friendship processes.* Thousand Oaks, CA: Sage.

Fehr, B. (2008). Friendship formation. In S. Sprecher, A. Wenzel & J. Harvey (Eds). *The handbook of relationship initiation* (pp. 29–54). Thousand Oaks, CA: Sage.

Fehr, R., Gelfand, M.J. & Nag, M. (2010). The road to forgiveness: A meta-analytic synthesis of its situational and dispositional correlates. *Psychological Bulletin*, *136*, 894–914.

Feinberg, T.E. & Keenan, J.P. (Eds). (2005). *The lost self. Pathologies of the brain and identities.* New York: Oxford University Press.

Feingold, A. (1988). Matching for attractiveness in romantic partners and same-sex friends:

A meta-analysis and theoretical critique. *Psychological Bulletin*, *104*, 226–235.

Feldman-Summers, S. & Lindner, K. (1976). Perceptions of victims and defendants in criminal assault cases. *Criminal Justice Behavior*, *3*, 135–149.

Felmlee, D.H. (1995). Fatal attractions: Affection and disaffection in intimate relationships. *Journal of Social and Personal Relationships*, *12*, 295–311.

Feltovich, N., Harbaugh, R. & To, T. (2002). Too cool for school? Signalling and countersignalling. *RAND Journal of Economics*, *33*, 630–649.

Féré, Charles (1897). Sensation et mouvement: Etudes experimentales de psycho-mecanique. Paris: Alcan.

Ferguson, C.A. (1977). Baby talk as a simplified register. In C.E. Snow & C.A. Ferguson (Eds), *Talking to children: Language input and acquisition.* New York: Cambridge University Press.

Ferguson, C.A. (2011). Baby talk in six languages. *American Anthropologist*, *66*, 103–114.

Ferguson, C.J. & Dyck, D. (2012). Paradigm change in aggression research: The time has come to retire the General Aggression Model. *Aggression and Violent Behavior*, *17*, 220–228.

Ferguson, C.J. (2012). Positive female role-models eliminate negative effects of sexually violent media. *Journal of Communication*, first published online: 27 August 2012. DOI: 10.1111/j.1460-2466.2012.01666

Ferguson, C.J. (2013). Violent video games and the Supreme Court: Lessons for the scientific community in the wake of Brown v. Entertainment Merchants Association. *American Psychologist*, *68*, 57–74.

Ferguson, C.J. & Hartley, R.D. (2009). Pleasure is momentary … The expense damnable? The influence of pornography on rape and sexual assault. *Aggression and Violent Behavior*, *14*, 323–329.

Ferguson, C.J. & Kilburn, J. (2009). The public health risks of media violence: A meta-analytic review. *Journal of Pediatrics*, *154*, 759–763.

Ferguson, C.J. & Kilburn, J. (2010). Much ado about nothing: The misestimation and overinterpretation of violent video game effects in Eastern and Western nations: Comment on Anderson et al. (2010). *Psychological Bulletin*, *136*, 174–178.

Fernández-Dols, J.-M. & Ruiz-Belda, M.-A. (1995). Are smiles a sign of happiness? Gold medal winners at the Olympic Games. *Journal of Personality & Social Psychology*, *69*, 1113–1119.

Ferriday, C., Vartanian, O. & Mandel, D.R. (2011). Public but not private ego threat triggers aggression and narcissists. *European Journal of Social Psychology*, *41*, 564–568.

Festinger, L. (1954). A theory of social comparison processes. *Human Relations*, *7*, 117–140.

Festinger, L. (1957). *A theory of cognitive dissonance.* Stanford, CA: Stanford University Press.

Festinger, L. (1964). *Conflict, decision and dissonance.* Stanford, CA: Stanford University Press.

Festinger, L. & Carlsmith, J.M. (1959). Cognitive consequences of forced compliance. *Journal of Abnormal and Social Psychology*, *58*, 203–210.

Festinger, L., Pepitone, A. & Newcomb, T. (1952). Some consequences of deindividuation in a group. *Journal of Personality and Social Psychology*, *47*, 382–389.

Festinger, L., Riecken, H.W. & Schachter, S. (1956). *When prophecy fails: A social and psychological study of a modern group that predicted the destruction of the world.* New York: Harper.

Festinger, L., Schachter, S. & Back, K.W. (1950). *Social pressures in informal groups: A study of human factors in housing.* New York: Harper & Brothers.

Fiedler, F.E. (1967). *A theory of leadership effectiveness.* New York: McGraw-Hill.

Fiedler, F.E. (1971). *Leadership.* Morristown, NJ: General Learning Press.

Fiedler, F.E. (1981). Leadership effectiveness. *American Behavioral Scientist*, *24*, 619–632.

Fiedler, K., Semin, G.R., Finkenauer, C. & Berkel, I. (1995). Actor–observer bias in close relationships: The role of self-knowledge and self-related language. *Personality and Social Psychology Bulletin*, *21*, 525–538.

Fields, J.M. & Schuman, H. (1976). Public beliefs about beliefs of the public. *Public Opinion Quarterly*, *40*, 427–448.

Fincham, F.D., Jackson, H. & Beach, S.R.H. (2005). Transgression severity and forgiveness: Different moderators for objective and subjective severity. *Journal of Social and Clinical Psychology*, *24*, 860–875.

Fine, G.A. & Ellis, B. (2010). *The global grapevine: Why rumors of terrorism, immigration and trade matter.* New York: Oxford University Press.

Finkel, E.J., Eastwick, P.W., Karney, B.R., Reis, H.T. & Sprecher, S. (2012). Online dating: A critical analysis from the perspective of psychological science. *Psychological Science in the Public Interest*, *13*, 3–66.

Finlay, W.M. (2007). The propaganda of extreme hostility: Denunciation and regulation of the group. *British Journal of Social Psychology*, *46*, 323–341.

Fischer, C.S. (1976). *The urban experience.* New York: Harcourt, Brace, Jovanovich.

Fischer, C.S. & Phillips, S.L. (1982). Who is alone? Social characteristics of people with small networks. In L.A. Peplau & D. Perlman (Eds), *Loneliness: A sourcebook of current theory, research and therapy* (pp. 21–39). New York: Wiley Interscience.

Fischer, K., Schoeneman, T.J. & Rubanowitz, D.E. (1987). Attributions in the advice columns: II. The dimensionality of actors' and observers' explanations for interpersonal problems. *Personality and Social Psychology Bulletin*, *13*, 458–466.

Fischer, P., Greitemeyer, T., Pollozek, F. & Frey, D. (2006). The unresponsive bystander: are bystanders more responsive in dangerous emergencies? *European Journal of Social Psychology*, *36*, 267–278.

Fischer, P., Krueger, J.I., Greitemeyer, T., Vogrincic, C., Kastenmüller, A., Frey, D., Heene, M., Wicher, M. & Kainbacher, M. (2011). The bystander-effect: A meta-analytic review on bystander intervention in dangerous and non-dangerous emergencies. *Psychological Bulletin*, *137*, 517–537.

Fischer, R. & Boer, D. (2011). What is more important for national well-being: Money or autonomy? A metal-analysis of well-being, burnout ad anxiety across 63 societies. *Journal of Personality and Social Psychology*, *101*, 164–184.

Fishbein, M. & Ajzen, I. (1975). *Belief, attitude, intention and behavior: An introduction to theory and research.* Reading, MA: Addison-Wesley.

Fisher, J.D., Bell, P.A. & Baum, A. (1984). *Environmental psychology* (2nd ed.). New York: Holt, Rinehart & Winston.

Fisher, J.D., Nadler, A. & DePaulo, B.M. (1983). *New directions in helping.* (Vol. 1). New York: Academic Press.

Fisher, J.D., Nadler, A. & Whitcher-Alagna, S. (1982). Recipient reactions to aid. *Psychological Bulletin*, *91*, 27–54.

Fisher, R.J. (1989). *The social psychology of inter-group conflict resolution.* New York: Springer-Verlag.

Fisher, R.J. (1998). Applying group processes to international conflict analysis and resolution. In R.S. Tindale & L. Heath (Eds), *Theory and research on small groups: Social psychological applications to social issues* (Vol. 4). (pp. 107–126). New York: Plenum Press.

Fiske, S.T. (1980). Attention and weight on person perception. *Journal of Personality and Social Psychology*, *38*, 889–906.

Fiske, S.T. (1993). Controlling other people: The impact of power on stereotyping. *American Psychologist*, *48*, 621–628.

Fiske, S.T. (2010). Envy up, scorn down: How comparisons divide us. *American Psychologist*, *65*, 698–706.

Fiske, S.T. (2011). *Envy up, scorn down.* New York: Russell Sage Foundation.

Fiske, S.T. (2011). *Envy up, scorn down: How status divides us.* New York: Russell Sage Foundation.

Fiske, S.T., Cuddy, A., Glick, P. & Xu, J. (2002). A model of (often mixed) stereotype content: Competence and warmth respectively follow from perceived status and competition. *Journal of Personality and Social Psychology*, *82*, 878–902.

Fletcher, G.J.O. & Kerr, P.S.G. (2010). Through the eyes of love: Reality and illusion in intimate relationships. *Psychological Bulletin*, *136*, 627–658.

Flett, G.L. & Hewitt, P.L. (Eds) (2002). *Perfectionism: Theory, research and treatment.* Washington, D.C.: American Psychological Association.

Flett, G.L., Hewitt, P.L., Blankenstein, K.R. & Mosher, S.W. (1991). Perfectionism, self-actualization and personal adjustment. In Jones, A. & Crandall, R. (Eds) *Handbook of self-actualization (Special Issue). Journal of Social Behavior and Personality*, *6*, 147–160.

Flett, G.L., Hewitt, P.L., Blankenstein, K.R. & O'Brien, S. (1991). Perfectionism and learned resourcefulness in depression and self-esteem. *Personality and Individual Differences*, *12*, 61–68.

Foa, U.G. (1971). Interpersonal and economic resources. *Science*, *171*, 345–351.

Fogel, J., Albert, S.M., Schnabel, F., Ditkoff, B. & Neugut, A.I. (2002). Internet use and social support in women with breast cancer. *Health Psychology*, *21*, 398–404.

Fogelman, E. (1994). *Conscience and courage: Rescuers of Jews during the Holocaust.* New York: Doubleday.

Fogelman, E. & Wiener, V.L. (1985). The few, the brave, the noble. *Psychology Today, 19,* 61–65.

Fontana, A.F., Kerns, R.D., Rosenberg, R.L. & Colonese, K.L. (1989). Support, stress and recovery from coronary heart disease: A longitudinal causal model. *Health Psychology, 8,* 175–193.

Forbes, C.E. & Grafman, J. (2013). Social neuroscience: The second phase. *Frontiers in Human Neuroscience, 7,* 20. Published online 2013 February 6. doi: 10.3389/fnhum.2013.00020

Ford, T.E. & Stangor, C. (1992). The role of diagnosticity in stereotype formation: Perceiving group means and variances. *Journal of Personality and Social Psychology, 63,* 356–367.

Forgas, J.P. (1998). Asking nicely? The effects on mood of responding to more or less polite requests. *Personality and Social Psychology Bulletin, 24,* 173–185.

Forrester, M.A. (2010). Doing qualitative research in psychology: A practical guide. London: Sage.

Fortman, J. (2003). Adolescent language and communication from an intergroup perspective. *Journal of Language and Social Psychology, 22,* 104–111.

Foster, M. & Matheson, K. (1999). Perceiving and responding to the person-group discrimination discrepancy. *Personality and Social Psychology Bulletin, 25,* 1319–1329.

Fox, A.B., Bukatko, D., Hallahan, M. & Crawford, M. (2007). The medium makes a difference: Gender similarities and differences in instant messaging. *Journal of Language and Social Psychology, 26,* 389–397.

Fox, D. & Prilleltensky, I. (1997). *Critical Psychology: An Introduction.* London: Sage.

Fox, D., Prilleltensky, I. & Austin, S. (Eds) (2009). Critical psychology: An introduction (2nd ed.). London: Sage.

Frable, D.E.S. & Bem, S.L. (1985). If you are gender schematic, all members of the opposite sex look alike. *Journal of Personality and Social Psychology, 49,* 459–468.

Fraley, R.C. (2002). Attachment stability from infancy to adulthood: meta-analysis and dynamic modelling of developmental mechanisms. *Personality and Social Psychology Review, 6,* 123–151.

Franco, Z.E., Blau, K. & Zimbardo, P.G. (2011). Heroism: A conceptual analysis and differentiation between heroic action and altruism. *Review of General Psychology, 15,* 99–113.

Frankel, A. & Prentice-Dunn, S. (1990). Loneliness and the processing of self-relevant information. *Journal of Social and Clinical Psychology, 9,* 303–315.

Frankl, V. (1963). *Man's search for meaning.* New York: Washington Square Press.

Franklin, S. (1977). *A time of heroes 1940/1950.* Toronto: Natural Science of Canada Ltd.

Frederickson, B.L. (2001). The role of positive emotions in positive psychology. *American Psychologist, 56,* 218–226.

Freedman, J.L. (1965). Long–term behavioral effects of cognitive dissonance. *Journal of Experimental Social Psychology, 1,* 145–155.

Freedman, J.L. (1975). *Crowding and behavior.* New York: Viking Press.

Freedman, J.L. (1982). Theories of contagion as they relate to mass psychogenic illness. In M.J. Colligan, J.W. Pennebaker & L.R. Murphy (Eds), *Mass psychogenic illness* (pp. 171–182). Hillsdale, NJ: Erlbaum.

Freedman, J.L. & Fraser, S.C. (1966). Compliance without pressure: The foot-in-the-door technique. *Journal of Personality and Social Psychology, 4,* 195–202.

Freedman, J.L., Wallington, S.A. & Bless, E. (1967). Compliance without pressure: The effect of guilt. *Journal of Personality and Social Psychology, 7,* 117–124.

French, J.R.P. (1944). Organized and unorganized groups under fear and frustration. *University of Iowa Studies of Child Welfare, 20,* 231–308.

Frenkel, O. & Doob, A. (1976). Post-decision dissonance at the polling booth. *Canadian Journal of Behavioural Science, 8,* 347–350.

Freud, S. (1933). *New introductory lectures on psycho-analysis.* New York: Norton.

Frey, D. (1986). Recent research on selective exposure to information. In L. Berkowitz (Ed.), *Advances in experimental social psychology* (Vol. 19). (pp. 41–80). New York: Academic Press.

Frey, S., Hirsbrunner, H.P., Florin, A., Daw, W. & Crawford, R. (1983). A unified approach to the investigation of nonverbal and verbal behavior in communication research. In W. Doise & S. Moscovici (Eds), *Current issues in European social psychology* (Vol. 1). (pp. 143–199). Cambridge: Cambridge University Press.

Frick, R.W. (1985). Communicating emotion: The role of prosodic features. *Psychological Bulletin, 97,* 412–429.

Fridlund, A.J. (1994). *Human facial expression: An evolutionary view.* San Diego, CA: Academic Press.

Fried, C. & Aronson, E. (1995). Hypocrisy, misattribution and dissonance reduction: A demonstration of dissonance in the absence of aversive consequences. *Personality and Social Psychology Bulletin, 21,* 925–933.

Friedman, H.S. (1982). Nonverbal communication in medical interaction. In H.S. Friedman & M.R. DiMatteo (Eds), *Interpersonal issues in health care* (pp. 51–68). New York: Academic Press.

Friedman, H.S., Prince, L., Riggio, R. & DiMatteo, M. (1980). Understanding and assessing nonverbal expressiveness. *Journal of Personality and Social Psychology, 14,* 351–364.

Friedman, M. & Booth-Kewley, S. (1987). The 'disease-prone personality': A meta-analytic view of the concept. *American Psychologist, 42,* 539–555.

Friedman, M., Rholes, S.W., Simpson, J., Bond, M., Diaz-Loving, R. & Chan, C. (2010). Attachment, avoidance and the cultural fit hypothesis: A cross-cultural investigation. *Personal Relationships, 17,* 107–126.

Fritz, C.E. & Marks, E.F. (1954). The NORC studies of human behavior in disaster. *Journal of Social Issues, 10,* 26–41.

Fromkin, V., Rodman, R. & Hyams, N.M. (2011). An introduction to language. Boston: Wadsworth/ Cengage Learning.

Frost, R.O., Marten, P., Lahart, C. (1990). The dimensions of perfectionism. *Cognitive Therapy and Research, 14.* 449–468.

Fuertes, F.C. & Jiménez, L. (2000). Motivation and burnout in volunteerism. *Psychology in Spain, 4,* 75–81.

Fugita, S.S., Hogrebe, M.C. & Wexley, K.N. (1980). Perception of deception: Perceived expertise in detecting deception, successfulness of deception and nonverbal cues. *Personality and Social Psychology Bulletin, 6,* 637–643.

Funk, J.B. (2005). Children's exposure to violent video games and desensitization to violence. *Child and Adolescent Psychiatry Clinics of North America, 14,* 387–404.

Furnham, A. (1985). Just world beliefs in an unjust society: A cross-cultural comparison. *European Journal of Social Psychology, 15,* 363–366.

Furnham, A., Richards, S.C. & Paulhus, D.L. (2013). The Dark Triad of personality: A 10 year review. *Social and Personality Psychology Compass, 7/3,* 199–216.

Gaertner, S.L. & Dovidio, J.F. (2009). A common ingroup identity: A categorization-based approach for reducing intergroup bias. In T.D. Nelson (Ed.). *Handbook of prejudice, stereotyping, and discrimination* (pp. 489–505). New York: Psychology Press.

Gagnon, A. & Bourhis, R.Y. (1996). Discrimination in the minimal group paradigm: Social identity or self-interest? *Personality and Social Psychology Bulletin, 22,* 1289–1301.

Gal, S. (1978). Peasant men can't get wives: Language change and sex roles in a bilingual community. *Language in Society, 7,* 1–16.

Gallace, A. & Spence, C. (2010). The science of interpersonal touch: an overview. *Neuroscience and biobehavioral reviews, 34,* 246–259.

Gallagher, H., Jack, A.I., Roepstorff, A. & Frith, C.D. (2002). Imaging the intentional stance in a competitive game. *Neuroimage, 16,* 814–821.

Gallese, V., Gernsbacher, M.A., Heyes, C., Kickok, G. & Iacoboni, M. (2011). Mirror neuron forum. *Perspectives on Psychological Science, 6,* 369–407.

Gallo, L.C. & Smith, T.W (2001). Attachment style in marriage: Adjustment and response to interaction. *Journal of Social and Personal Relationships, 8,* 263–289.

Gallois, C., Terry, D., Timmins, P., Kashima, Y. & McCamish, M. (1994). Safe sexual intentions and behavior among heterosexuals and homosexual men: Testing the theory of reasoned action. *Psychology & Health, 10,* 1–16.

Gangestad, S.W. & Thornhill, R. (1998). Menstrual cycle variation in women's preferences for the scent of symmetrical men. *Proceedings of the Royal Society of London, 265,* 927–933.

Gannon, L. (2002). A critique of evolutionary psychology. *Psychology, Evolution & Gender, 4,* 173–218.

Garbarino, J. (1999). *Lost boys: Why our sons turn violent and how we can save them.* New York: The Free Press.

Gardiner, M. & Tiggemann, M. (1999). Gender differences in leadership style, job stress and mental health in male- and female-dominated industries. *Journal of Occupational and Organizational Psychology, 72,* 301–315.

Gardner, R.C. (1984). *Social psychological aspects of second language learning.* London: Edward Arnold.

Gardner, R.C. (1985). *Social psychology and second language learning.* London: Edward Arnold.

Gardner, R.C. & Desrochers, A. (1981). Second language acquisition and bilingualism: Research in Canada (1970–1980). *Canadian Psychology, 22,* 146–162.

Gardner, R.C., Gliksman, L. & Smythe, P.C. (1978). Attitude and behaviour in second language acquisition: A social psychological interpretation. *Canadian Psychological Review, 19,* 173–186.

Gardner, R.C. & Lambert, W.E. (1959). Motivational variables in second language acquisition. *Canadian Journal of Psychology, 13,* 266–272.

Gartner, R. (1995). Homicide in Canada. In J.I. Ross (Ed.), *Violence in Canada* (pp. 186–222). Don Mills: Oxford University Press.

Gawronski, B. (2009). Ten frequently asked questions about implicit measures and their frequently supposed, but not entirely correct answers. *Canadian Psychology, 50,* 141–150.

Gelfand, M.J., Erez, M. & Aycan, Z. (2007). Cross-cultural organizational behavior. *Annual Review of Psychology, 58,* 479–514.

Gelfand, M.J.,Triandis, H. & Chan, D. (1996). Individualism versus collectivism or versus authoritarianism? *European Journal of Social Psychology, 26,* 397–410.

Gentile, D.A., Anderson, C.A., Yukawa, S., Ihori, N., Saleem, M., Ming, L.K., Shibuya, A.,Liau, A.K., Khoo, A., Bushman, B.J., Huesmann, L.R. & Sakamoto, A. (2009). The effects of prosocial video games on prosocial behaviour: International evidence from correlational, longitudinal and experimental studies. *Personality and Social Psychology Bulletin, 35,* 752–763.

Gerard, H. (1967). Choice difficulty, dissonance, and the decision sequence. *Journal of Personality, 35,* 91–108.

Gergen, K.J. (1985). The social constructionist movement in modern psychology. *American Psychologist, 40,* 266–275.

Gergen, K.J., Ellsworth, P., Maslach, P. & Seipel, M. (1975). Obligation, donor resources, and the reactions to aid in three nations. *Journal of Personality and Social Psychology, 31,* 390–400.

Gergen, K.J., Gergen, M.M. & Meter, K. (1972). Individual orientations to prosocial behavior. *Journal of Social Issues, 28,* 105–130.

Gerson, A.C. & Perlman, D. (1979). Loneliness and expressive communication. *Journal of Abnormal Psychology, 88,* 258–261.

Gianakos, I. & Subich, L. (1988). Student sex and sex role in relation to college major choice. *The Career Development Quarterly, 36,* 259–268.

Gibb, C.A. (1969). Leadership. In G. Lindzey & E. Aronson (Eds), *Handbook of social psychology* (2nd ed.). (Vol. 4). Reading, MA: Addison-Wesley.

Gibbins, K. & Coney, J.R. (1981). Meaning of physical dimensions of women's clothes. *Perceptual and Motor Skills, 53,* 720–722.

Gibbons, F.X. & Wicklund, R.A. (1976). Selective exposure to self. *Journal of Research in Personality, 10,* 98–106.

Gibbons, F.X., Kingsbury, J.H. & Gerrard, M. (2012). Social-psychological theories and adolescent health risk behavior. *Social and Personality Psychology Compass, 6,* 170–183.

Gibson, S. (2011), Milgram's obedience experiments: A rhetorical analysis. *British Journal of Social Psychology.* Published online: 18 OCT 2011. doi: 10.1111/j.2044-8309.2011.02070.x.

Gifford, R. & Price, J. (1979). Personal space in nursery school children. *Canadian Journal of Behavioural Science, 11,* 318–326.

Gigerenzer, G. (2010). Moral satisficing: Rethinking moral behavior as bounded rationality. *Topics in Cognitive Science, 2,* 528–554

Gigerenzer, G. & Brighton, H.J. (2008). Homo heuristicus: Why biased minds make better inference. *Topics in Cognitive Science, 1,* 107–143

Gigerenzer, G. & Gray, J.A.M. (Eds) (2011). Better doctors, better patients, better decisions: Envisioning healthcare in 2020. Cambridge, Mass: MIT Press.

Gilbert, D.T. & Hixon, J.G. (1991). The trouble of thinking: Activation and application of stereotypic beliefs. *Journal of Personality and Social Psychology, 60,* 509–517.

Gilbert, D.T. & Malone, P.D. (1995). The correspondence bias. *Psychological Bulletin, 117,* 21–38.

Gilbert, F. & Daffern, M. (2011). Illuminating the relationship between personality disorder and violence: Contributions of the General Aggression Model. *Psychology of Violence,1,* 230–244.

Gilbert, G.M. (1951). Stereotype persistence and change among college students. *Journal of Abnormal and Social Psychology, 46,* 245–254.

Giles, H. (1973). Accent mobility: A model and some data. *Anthropological Linguistics, 15,* 87–105.

Giles, H., Bourhis, R.Y. & Davies, A. (1977). Prestige speech styles: The imposed norm and inherent value hypotheses. In W.C. McCormack & S. Wurm (Eds), *Language and society: Anthropological issues*. The Hague: Mouton.

Giles, H., Bourhis, R.Y. & Taylor, D.M. (1977). Towards a theory of language in ethnic group relations. In H. Giles (Ed.), *Language, ethnicity and intergroup relations* (pp. 307–348). London: Academic Press.

Giles, H., Bourhis, R.Y., Trudgill, P. & Lewis, A. (1974). The imposed norm hypothesis: A validation. *The Quarterly Journal of Speech*, *60*, 405–410.

Giles, H. & LePoire, B.A. (2006). Introduction. The ubiquity and social meaningfulness of non-verbal communication. In V.L. Manusov & M.L. Atterson, *The Sage handbook of nonverbal communication*. London: Sage. (pp. xv–xviii).

Giles, H. & Powesland, P. (1975). *Speech style and social evaluation.* London: Academic Press.

Giles, H. & Smith, P.M. (1979). Accommodation theory: Optimal levels of convergence. In H. Giles & R. St. Clair (Eds), *Language and social psychology*. Oxford: Basil Blackwell.

Giles, H. & Wadleigh, P.M. (1999). Accommodating nonverbally. In H. Giles, P.M. Wadleigh, K. Floyd, A. Ramirez Jr., J.K. Burgoon, J.N. Cappella, P.A. Andersen, N. Miczo & L. Allspach (Eds), *The nonverbal communication reader: Classic and contemporary readings* (2nd ed.). Prospect Heights, IL: Waveland Press.

Gilligan, C. (1982). *In a different voice: Psychological theory and women's development.* Cambridge, MA: Harvard University Press.

Gilligan, F. (1977). Comments: Eyewitness identification. *Military Law Review*, *58*, 183–207.

Giorgi, G., Ando, M., Arenas, A., Shoss, M.K. & Leon-Perez, J.M. (2012). Exploring personal and organizational determinants of workplace bullying and its prevalence in a Japanese sample. *Psychology of Violence*, *3*, 185–197.

Girandola, F. (2002). Sequential requests and organ donation. *Journal of Social Psychology*, *142*, 171–178.

Glass, D.C. & Singer, J.E. (1973). Experimental studies of uncontrollable and unpredictable noise. *Representative Research in Social Psychology*, *4*, 165–183.

Glass, G.V., McGaw, B. & Smith, M.L. (1981). *Meta-analysis in Social Research*. Beverly Hills, CA: Sage.

Glasser, M., Campbell, D., Glasser, A., Leitch, I. & Farrelly, S. (2001). Cycle of child sexual abuse: Links between being a victim and becoming a perpetrator. *The British Journal of Psychiatry*, *179*, 482–494.

Glick, P. & Fiske, S.T. (2001). Ambivalent stereotypes as legitimizing ideologies: Differentiating paternalistic and envious prejudice. In J.T. Jost & B. Major (Eds). *The psychology of legitimacy: Emerging perspectives on ideology, justice, and intergroup relations* (pp. 278–). New York: Cambridge University Press, 2001.

Glick, P., Demorest, J.A. & Hotze, C.A. (1988). Self-monitoring and beliefs about partner compatiblity in romantic relationships. *Personality and Social Psychology Bulletin*, *14*, 485–494.

Glick, P., Fiske, S.T., Mladinic, A., Abrams, J.L. & 28 others (2000). Beyond prejudice as simple antipathy: Hostile and benevolent sexism across cultures. *Journal of Personality and Social Psychology*, *79*, 763–775.

Glick, P., Lameiras, M., Fiske, S.T., Eckes, T.M. & 11 others (2004). Bad but bold: Ambivalent attitudes toward men predict gender inequality in 16 nations. *Journal of Personality and Social Psychology*, *86*, 713–728.

Glick, P., Zion, C. & Nelson, C. (1988). What mediates sex discrimination in hiring decisions? *Journal of Personality and Social Psychology*, *55*, 178–186.

Goffman, E. (1955). On face-work: An analysis of ritual elements in social interaction. *Psychiatry*, *18*, 213–231.

Goffman, E. (1959). *The presentation of self in everyday life.* New York: Doubleday.

Gold, J.A., Ryckman, R.M. & Mosley, N.R. (1984). Romantic mood induction and attraction to a dissimilarly other: Is love blind? *Personality and Social Psychology Bulletin*, *10*, 358–368.

Goldberg, I. (2000). Compliance with the medical management of glaucoma. *Asian Journal of Ophthalmology*, *2*, 3–6.

Goldberg, M.E. & Gorn, G.J. (1979). Television's impact on preferences for non-white playmates: Canadian Sesame Street inserts. *Journal of Broadcasting*, *23*, 27–32.

Goldberg, P. (1968). Are some women prejudiced against women? *Trans-Action*, *5*, 28–30.

Goldstein, A.G. & Papageorge, J. (1980). Judgments of facial attractiveness in the absence of eye movements. *Bulletin of the Psychonomic Society*, *15*, 269–270.

Goldstein, N.E., Arnold, D.H., Rosenberg, J.L., Stowe, R.M. & Ortiz, C. (2001). Contagion of aggression in day care classrooms as a function of peer and teacher responses. *Journal of Educational Psychology*, *93*, 708–719.

Goldstein, N.J. & Cialdini, R.B. (2007). Using social norms as a lever of social influence. In A.R. Pratkanis (Ed.), *The science of social influence*. New York: Psychology Press (pp. 167–191).

Goldstein, N.J., Cialdini, R.B. & Griskevicius, V. (2008). A room with a viewpoint: Using social norms to motivate environmental conservation in hotels. *Journal of Consumer Research*, *35*, 472–482.

Golimbet, V.E. Alfimova, M.V. Gritsenko, I.K. Ebstein, R.P. (2007). Relationship between dopamine system genes and extraversion and novelty seeking. *Neuroscience and Behavioral Physiology*, *37*, 601–606.

Gonzales, G., Chronister, K.M., Linville, D. & Knoble, N.B. (2012). Experiencing parental violence: A qualitative examination of adult men's resilience. *Psychology of Violence*, *2*, 90–103.

Gonzales, R., Ellsworth, P.C. & Pembroke, M. (1993). Response biases in lineups and showups. *Journal of Personality and Social Psychology*, *64*, 525–537.

Goodwin, R., Cook, O. & Yung, Y. (2001). Loneliness and life satisfaction among three cultural groups. *Personal Relationships*, *8*, 225–230.

Gordon, A.M., Impett, E.A., Kogan, A., Oveis, C. & Keltner, D. (2012). To have and to hold: Gratitude promotes relationship maintenance in intimate bonds. *Journal of Personality and Social Psychology*, *103*, 257–274.

Gordon, E. (1997). Sex, speech and stereotypes: Why women use prestige speech forms more than men. *Language in Society*, *26*, 47–63.

Gosling, S.D., Sandy, C.J., John, O.P. & Potter, J. (2010). Wired but not WEIRD: The promise of the Internet in reaching more diverse samples. *Behavioral and Brain Sciences*, *33*, 94–95.

Gottfredson, L. (2004). Intelligence: Is it the epidemiologists' elusive 'fundamental cause' of social class inequities in health? *Journal of Personality and Social Psychology*, *86, 174–199.*

Gottlieb, B.H. (1985). Social networks and social support: An overview of research, practice and policy implications. *Health Education Quarterly*, *12*, 221–238.

Gottman, J.M. & Levenson, R.W. (1992). Marital processes predictive of later dissolution: Behavior, physiology and health. *Journal of Personality and Social Psychology*, *63*, 221–233.

Gottschall, J., Anderson, K., Burbank, C., Burch, J. & 27 others (2008). The 'beauty myth' is no myth. *Human Nature*, *19*, 174–188.

Gouldner, A.W. (1960). The norm of reciprocity: A preliminary statement. *American Sociological Review*, *25*, 161–179.

Graham, J., Haidt, J., Nosek & B.A. (2009). Liberals and conservatives rely on different sets of moral foundations. *Journal of Personality and Social Psychology*, *96*, 1029–1046

Graham, J.M. (2011). Measuring love in a romantic relationship: A meta-analysis. *Journal of Social and Personal Relationships*, *28*, 748–771.

Grammar, K. & Thornhill, R. (1994). Human (Homo sapiens) facial attractiveness and sexual selection: The role of symmetry and averageness. *Journal of Comparative Psychology*, *108*, 233–242.

Grant, A.M. & Gino, F. (2010). A little thanks goes a long way: Explaining why gratitude expressions motivate prosocial behavior. *Journal of Personality and Social Psychology*, *98*, 946–955.

Graumann, C.F. & Moscovici, S. (Eds). (1987). *Changing conceptions of conspiracy*. New York: Springer-Verlag.

Gray, J. (1992). *Men are from Mars, women are from Venus*. New York: HarperCollins.

Green, D.P., Glaser, J. & Rich, A. (1998). From lynching to gay bashing: The elusive connection between economic conditions and hate crime. *Journal of Personality and Social Psychology*, *75*, 82–92.

Greenberg, J. & Prszczynski, T. (1985). The effect of an overheard slur on evaluation of a target. *Journal of Experimental Social Psychology*, 21, 61–72.

Greenberg, J., Prszczynski, T. & Soloman, S. (1994). Role of consciousness and accessibility of death-related thoughts in mortality salience effects. *Journal of Personality and Social Psychology*, *67*, 627–637.

Greenglass, E.R. (1982). *A world of difference: Gender roles in perspective*. Toronto: Wiley.

Greenwald, A.G. & Banaji, M.R. (1995). Implicit social cognition: Attitudes, self-esteem, and stereotypes. *Psychological Review*, *102*, 4–27.

Greenwald, A.G., Banaji, M.R., Rudman, L., Farnham, S.D., Nosek, B.A. & Mellott, D.S. (2002). A unified theory of implicit attitudes, stereotypes, self-esteem and self-concept. *Psychological Review, 109,* 3–25.

Greenwald, A.G. & Ronis, D.L. (1978). Twenty years of cognitive dissonance: A case study of the evaluation of a theory. *Psychological Review, 85,* 53–57.

Greenwald, A.G., McGhee, D.E. & Schwartz, J.L.K. (1998). Measuring individual differences in implicit cognition: The implicit association test. *Journal of Personality and Social Psychology, 74,* 1464–1480.

Greenwald, A.G., Poehlman, T.A., Uhlmann, E. & Banaji, M.R. (2009). Understanding and using the Implicit Association Test: III. Meta-analysis of predictive validity. *Journal of Personality and Social Psychology, 97,* 17–41.

Greenwood, J.D. (2004). *The disappearance of the social in American social psychology.* New York: Cambridge University Press.

Greitemeyer, T., Osswald, S. & Brauer, M. (2010). Playing prosocial video games increases empathy and decreases schadenfreude. *Emotion, 10,* 796–802.

Griffin, D. & Buehler, R. (1993). Role of construal processes in conformity and dissent. *Journal of Personality and Social Psychology, 65,* 657–669.

Griffith, K.H. & Hebl., M.R. (2002). The disclosure dilemma for gay men and lesbians: 'Coming out' at work. *Journal of Applied Psychology, 87,* 1191–1199.

Griskevicius, V., Goldstein, N.J., Mortensen, C.R., Sundie, J.M. & Cialdini, R.B. (2009). Fear and loving in Las Vegas: Evolution, emotion and persuasion. *Journal of Marketing Research, 46,* 384–395.

Groh, D. (1987). The temptation of conspiracy theory, or: Why do bad things happen to good people. Part I: Preliminary draft.

Grondelaers, S., van Hout, R. & Steegs, M. (2010). Evaluating regional accent variation in standard Dutch. *Journal of Language and Social Psychology, 29,* 101–116.

Grove, J.R., Hanrahan, S.J. & McInman, A. (1991). Success/failure bias in attributions across involvement categories in sport. *Personality and Social Psychology Bulletin, 17,* 93–97.

Grube, J.W., Weir, I.L., Getzlaf, S. & Rokeach, M. (1984). Own value system, value images, and cigarette smoking. *Personality and Social Psychology Bulletin, 10,* 306–313.

Gruder, C.L. (1974). Cost and dependency as determinants of helping and exploitation. *Journal of Conflict Resolution, 18,* 473–485.

Gruenfeld, D.H., Inesi, M.E., Magee, J.C. & Galinsky, A.D. (2008). Power and the objectification of social targets. *Journal of Personality and Social Psychology, 95,* 111–127.

Guadagno, R.E., Asher, T., Demaine, L. & Cialdini, R.B. (2001). When saying yes leads to saying no: Preference for consistency and the reverse foot-in-the-door effect. *Personality and Social Psychology Bulletin, 27,* 859–867.

Guadagno, R.E. & Cialdini, R.B. (2010). Preference for consistency and social influence: A review of current research findings. *Social Influence, 5,* 152–163.

Guéguen, N. (2010). Smile and gender in students' yearbook: A cultural replication. *Research Journal of International Studies, 14,* 4–7.

Guéguen, N., Joule, R-V. & Marchand, M. (2013). La technique du leurre: Impact du délai, du solliciteur et de l'implication sur la soumission. *Canadian Journal of Behavioural Science/Revue Canadienne Des Sciences Du Comportement, 45,* 138–147.

Guimond, S., Bégin, G. & Palmer, D.L. (1989). Education and causal attributions: The development of 'person-blame' and 'system-blame' ideology. *Social Psychology Quarterly, 52,* 126–140.

Guimond, S. & Dubé, L. (1989). La représentation des causes de l'infériorité économique des québecois francophones. *Revue Canadienne des Sciences du comportement, 21,* 28–39.

Guimond, S. & Palmer, D.L. (1993). Developmental changes in ingroup favouritism among bilingual and unilingual francophone and anglophone students. *Journal of Language and Social Psychology, 12,* 318–351.

Guinote, A. & Phillips, A. (2010). Power can increase stereotyping: Evidence from managers and subordinates in the hotel industry. *Social Psychology, 41,* 3–9.

Gundlach, M.J., Douglas, S.C. & Martinko, M.J. (2003). The decision to blow the whistle: A social information processing framework. *Academy of Management Review, 28,* 107–123.

Gutchess, A.H., Welsh, R.C., Boduroğlu, A. & Park, D.C. (2006). Cultural differences in neural function associated with object processing. *Cognitive, Affective and Behavioral Neuroscience*, 6, 102–109.

Haddock, G. & Zanna, M.P. (1997). Impact of negative advertising on evaluation of political candidates: The 1993 Canadian Federal elections. *Basic and Applied Social Psychology*, 19, 205–223.

Haddock, G. & Zanna, M.P. (1998). Assessing the impact of affective and cognitive information in predicting attitudes toward capital punishment. *Law and Human Behavior*, 22, 325–339.

Hadjistavropoulos, T. & Genest, M. (1994). The underestimation of the role of physical attractiveness in dating preferences: Ignorance or taboo? *Canadian Journal of Behavioural Science*, 26, 298–318.

Hadjistavropoulos, T., McMurtry, B. & Craig, K.D. (1996). Beautiful faces in pain: biases and accuracy in the perception of pain. *Psychology and Health*, 11, 411–420.

Hafer, C.L. (2000). Do innocent victims threaten the belief in a just world? Evidence from a modified Stroop task. *Journal of Personality and Social Psychology*, 79, 165–173.

Hafer, C.L. & Bègue, L. (2005). Experimental research on just-world theory: Problems, developments and future challenges. *Psychological Bulletin*, 131, 126–167.

Hafer, C.L. & Olson, J.M. (1989). Beliefs in a just world and reactions to personal deprivation. *Journal of Personality*, 57, 799–823.

Hafer, C.L. & Olson, J.M. (1993). Beliefs in a just world, discontent, and assertive actions by working women. *Personality and Social Psychology Bulletin*, 19, 30–38.

Hafer, C.L. & Olson, J.M. (2003). Analysis of empirical research on the scope of justice. *Personality and Social Psychology Review*, 7, 311–323.

Hafer, C.L., Reynolds, K.L. & Obertynski, M.A. (1996). Message comprehensibility and persuasion: Effects of complex language in counterattitudinal appeals to laypersons. *Social Cognition*, 14, 317–337.

Hagestad, G.O. & Smyer, M.A. (1982). Dissolving long-term relationships: Patterns of divorcing in middle-age. In S. Duck (Ed.), *Personal relationships, 4: Dissolving relationships* (pp. 211–235). New York: Academic Press.

Haggard, L.M. & Williams, D.R. (1992). Identity affirmation through leisure activities: Leisure symbols of the self. *Journal of Leisure Research*, 24, 1–18.

Hagger, M.S., Chatzisarantis, N.L.D. & Biddle, S.J.H. (2002). A meta-analytic review of the theories of reasoned action and planned behavior in physical activity: Predictive validity and the contribution of additional variables. *Journal of Sport and Exercise Psychology*, 24, 3–32.

Hagger, M.S., Wood, C., Stiff, C. & Chatzisarantis, N.L.D. (2010). Ego depletion and the strength model of self-control: a meta-analysis. *Psychological Bulletin*, 136, 495–525.

Hains, S.C., Hogg, M.A. & Duck, J.M. (1997). Self-categorization and leadership: Effects of group prototypicality and leader stereotypicality. *Personality and Social Psychology Bulletin*, 23, 1087–1100.

Halabi, S. & Nadler, A. (2010). Receiving help: Consequences for the recipient. In S. Stürmer, S. & M. Snyder (Eds) (2010). *The psychology of prosocial behavior*. Chichester, UK: Blackwell. (pp. 121–138).

Halberstadt, J. & Rhodes, G. (2000). The attractiveness of nonface averages: Implications for an evolutionary explanation of the attractiveness of average faces. *Psychological Science*, 11, 285–289.

Halevy, N., Chou, E.Y. & Murnighan, J.K. (2012). Mind games: The mental representation of conflict. *Journal of Personality and Social Psychology*, 102, 132–148.

Hall, E.T. (1966). *The hidden dimension.* New York: Doubleday.

Hall, J.A., Epstein, A.M., Deciantis, M.L. & McNeil, B.J. (1993). Physicians' liking for their patients: More evidence for the role of affect in medical care. *Health Psychology*, 12, 140–146.

Hall, J.A., Irish, J.T., Roter, D.L., Ehrlich, C.M. & Miller, L.H. (1994). Gender in medical encounters: an analysis of physician and patient communication in a primary care setting. *Health Psychology*, 13, 384–392.

Hall, J.A. & Veccia, E.M. (1990). More 'touching' observations: New insights on men, women and interpersonal touching. *Journal of Personality and Social Psychology*, 59, 1159–1162.

Halperin, E. (2008). Group-based hatred in intractable conflict in Israel. *Journal of Conflict Resolution*, 52, 713–736.

Halperin, E., Russell, A.G., Trzesniewski, K.H., Gross, J.J. & Dweck, C.S. (2011). Promoting the

Middle East peace process by changing beliefs about group malleability. *Science, 333*, 1767–1769.

Hamamura, T. (2012). Are cultures becoming more individualistic? A cross-temporal comparison of individualism-collectivism in the United States and Japan. *Personality and Social Psychology Review, 16*, 3–24.

Hamamura, T. & Heine, S.T. (2008). Approach and avoidance motivation across cultures. In T. Hamamura & S.T. Heine (Eds). *Handbook of approach and avoidance motivation* (pp. 557–570). New York, N.Y., U.S: Psychology Press.

Hamblin, R.L. (1958). Leadership and crises. *Sociometry, 21*, 322–335.

Hamill, R., Wilson, T.D. & Nisbett, R.E. (1980). Insensitivity to sample bias: Generalizing from atypical cases. *Journal of Personality and Social Psychology, 39*, 578–589.

Hamilton, D.L. & Gifford, R.K. (2000). Illusory correlation in interpersonal perception: A cognitive basis of stereotypic judgments. In C. Stangor (Ed.), *Stereotypes and prejudice: Essential readings. Key readings in social psychology* (pp. 161–171). Philadelphia, PA: Psychology Press.

Hamilton, D.L. & Rose, T.L. (1980). Illusory correlation and the maintenance of stereotypes. *Journal of Personality and Social Psychology, 39*, 832–845.

Hamilton, D.L. & Sherman, S.J. (1989). Illusory correlations: Implications for stereotype theory and research. In D. Bar-Tal, C.F. Graumann, A.W. Kruglanski & W. Stroebe (Eds), *Stereotyping and prejudice: Changing conceptions* (pp. 59–82). New York: Springer-Verlag.

Hamilton, D.L. & Zanna, M.P. (1972). Differential weighting of favorable and unfavorable attributes in impressions of personality. *Journal of Experimental Research in Personality, 6*, 204–212.

Hamilton, M.A. & Tafoya, M.A. (2012). Toward a collective framework on verbal aggression: Hierarchical and antagonistic processes. *Journal of Language and Social Psychology, 31*, 112–130.

Haney, C., Banks, C. & Zimbardo, P. (1973). Interpersonal dynamics in a simulated prison. *International Journal of Criminology, 1*, 69–97.

Haney, C. & Manzolatti, J. (1981). Television criminology: Network illusions of criminal justice reality. In E. Aronson (Ed.), *Readings about the social animal* (3rd ed.). (pp. 125–136). San Francisco: W.H. Freeman.

Hanselmann, M. & Tanner, C. (2008). Taboos and conflicts in decision-making: Sacred values, decision difficulty and emotion. *Judgment and Decision Making, 3*, 51–63.

Hansen, E.M., Kimble, C.E. & Biers, D.W. (2001). Actors and observers; Divergent attributions of constrained unfriendly behavior. *Social Behavior and Personality, 29*, 87–104.

Hardie, E. A. (1997). PMS in the workplace: Dispelling the myth of cyclic dysfunction. *Journal of Occupational and Organizational Psychology, 70*, 97–102.

Hardin, G. (1968). The tragedy of the commons. *Science, 162*, 1243–1248.

Hardyck, J.A. & Braden, M. (1962). When prophecy fails again: A report of a failure to replicate. *Journal of Abnormal and Social Psychology, 65*, 136–141.

Hare, A.P. (1962). *Handbook of small group research.* Glencoe, NY: Free Press.

Hare, R.D. & McPherson, L.M. (1984). Violent and aggressive behavior by criminal psychopaths. *International Journal of Law and Psychiatry, 7*, 35–50.

Harkins, S.G. (1987). Social loafing and social facilitation. *Journal of Experimental Social Psychology, 23*, 1–18.

Harkins, S.G. & Petty, R.E. (1987). Information utility and the multiple sources effect. *Journal of Personality and Social Psychology, 52*, 260–268.

Harkins, S.G. & Szymanski, K. (1989). Social loafing and group evaluation. *Journal of Personality and Social Psychology, 56*, 934–941.

Harmon-Jones, E. (2000). Cognitive dissonance and experienced negative affect: Evidence that dissonance increases negative affect even in the absence of aversive consequences. *Personality and Social Psychology Bulletin, 26*, 1490–1501.

Harmon-Jones, E., Brehm, J.W., Greenberg, J., Simon, L. & Nelson, D.E. (1996). Evidence that the production of aversive consequences is not necessary to produce cognitive dissonance. *Journal of Personality and Social Psychology, 70*, 5–16.

Harrigan, J.A. & Rosenthal, R. (1983). Physicians' head and body positions as determinants of perceived rapport. *Journal of Applied Social Psychology, 13*, 496–509.

Harris, L.T. & Fiske, S. (2009). Social neuroscience evidence for dehumanized perception. *European Review of Social Psychology*, 20, 192–231.

Harris, R.N., Snyder, C.R., Higgins, R.L. & Schrag, J.L. (1986). Enhancing the predictability of self-handicapping. *Journal of Personality and Social Psychology*, 51, 1191–1199.

Harrison, J.A., Mullen, P.D. & Green, L.W. (1992). A meta-analysis of studies of the health beliefs model with adults. *Health Education Research*, 7, 107–116.

Hartmann, T., and Klimmt, C. (2006). Gender and computer games: Exploring females' dislikes. *Journal of Computer-Mediated Communication*, 11, 910–931

Harvey, J.H. & Omarzu, J. (1997). Minding the close relationship. *Personality and Social Psychology Review*, 1, 224–240.

Harwood, J. & Vincze, L. (2012). Ethnolinguistic identity and television. *Journal of Media Psychology*, 24, 135–142

Haslam, S.A. & Reicher, S.D. (2012). Contesting the 'nature' of conformity: What Milgram and Zimbardo's studies really show. *PLoS Biology*, 10(11): e1001426.

Haslam, S.A., Reicher, S.D. & Reynolds, K.J. (2012). Identity, influence, and change: Rediscovering John Turner's vision for social psychology. *British Journal of Social Psychology*, 51, 201–218,

Hass, R.G. & Grady, K. (1975). Temporal delay, type of forewarning, and resistance to influence. *Journal of Experimental Social Psychology*, 11, 459–469.

Hatemi, P.K., Funk, C., Medland, S.E., Maes, H., Silberg, J., Martin, N. & Eaves, L.J. (2009). Genetic and environmental transmission of political attitudes over a life time. *Journal of Politics*, 71, 1141–1156.

Hatemi, P.K., Hibbing, J.A., Alford, J., Martin, N. & Eaves, L. (2009). Is there a party in your genes? *Political Research Quarterly*, 62, 584–600.

Hatemi, P.K., Medland, K.I. Morley, A.C., Heath, A.C. & Martin, N.G. (2007). The genetics of voting an Australian twin study. *Behavior Genetics*, 37, 435–448.

Hatfield, E. & Rapson, R.L. (2009). Unmasking passionate love: The face and the brain. In Freitas-Magalhães, A. (Ed.). *Emotional expression: The brain and the face*. (pp. 194–220). Porto, Portugal: Edições Universidade Fernando Pessoa.

Hatfield, E., Bensman, L. & Rapson, R.L. (2012). A brief history of social scientists' attempts to measure passionate love. *Journal of Social and Personal Relationships*, 29, 143–164.

Hatfield, E., Cacioppo, J. & Rapson, R. (1994). *Emotional contagion*. New York: Cambridge Press.

Hatfield, E. & Sprecher, S. (1986). Measuring passionate love in intimate relations. *Journal of Adolescence*, 9, 383–410.

Haugtvedt, C.P. & Petty, R.E. (1992). Personality and persuasion: Need for cognition moderates the persistence and resistance of attitude changes. *Journal of Personality and Social Psychology*, 63, 308–319.

Hawkley, L.C. & Cacioppo, J.T. (2003). Loneliness and pathways to disease. *Brain, Behavior, and Immunity*, 17(Suppl.1), Special issue: Biological mechanisms of psychosocial effects on disease: Implications for cancer control, S98–S105.

Hawkley, L.C. & Cacioppo, J.T. (2010). Loneliness matters: A theoretical and empirical review of consequences and mechanisms. *Annals of Behavioral Medicine*, 4, 218–227.

Hawkley, L.C., Thisted, R.A. & Cacioppo, J.T (2009). Loneliness predicts reduced physical activity: Cross-sectional & longitudinal analyses. *Health Psychology*, 28, 354–363.

Hawkley, L.C., Thisted, R.A., Masi, C.M. & Cacioppo, J.T. (2010). Loneliness predicts increased blood pressure: 5-year cross-lagged analyses in middle-aged and older adults. *Psychology and Aging*, 25, 132–141.

Hayes-Smith, R.M., Levett L. (2011). Jury's still out: How television and crime show viewing influences jurors' evaluations of evidence. *Applied Psychology in Criminal Justice*, 7, 29–46.

Haynes, S.G., McGibbon, K.A. & Kanani, R. (1996). Systematic review of randomized trials of intervention to assist patients to follow prescriptions for medications. *Lancet*, 348, 336–348.

Hazan, C. & Shaver, P.R. (1987). Romantic love conceptualized as an attachment process. *Journal of Personality and Social Psychology*, 59, 270–280.

Health and Welfare Canada (1987). *The active health report: Perspectives on Canada's health promotion survey*, 1985. Catalogue No. H-39-109/1987 E. Ottawa: Supply and Services Canada.

Heatherton, T.F. (2011). Neuroscience of self and self-regulation. *Annual Review of Psychology*, 62, 363–390.

Heaven, P. & St. Quintin, D. (2003). Personality factors predict racial prejudice. *Personality and Individual Differences, 34*, 625–634.

Hebb, D.O. & Thompson, W.R. (1968). The social significance of animal studies. In G. Lindzey & E. Aronson (Eds), *The handbook of social psychology* (2nd ed.). (Vol. 1). (pp. 729–774). Reading, MA: Addison-Wesley.

Hefez, A. (1985). The role of the press and the medical community in the epidemic of 'mysterious gas poisoning' in the Jordan West Bank. *American Journal of Psychiatry, 142*, 833–837.

Hehman, E., Gaertner, S.L. & Dovidio, J.F. (2011). Evaluations of presidential performance: Race, prejudice, and perceptions of Americanism. *Journal of Experimental Social Psychology, 47*, 430–435.

Heider, F. (1958). *The psychology of interpersonal relations.* New York: Wiley.

Heine, S.J. & Lehman, D.R. (1995). Cultural variation in unrealistic optimism: Does the West feel more invulnerable than the East? *Journal of Personality and Social Psychology, 68*, 595–607.

Heine, S.J. & Lehman, D.R. (1999). Culture, self-discrepancies and self-satisfaction. *Personality and Social Psychology Bulletin, 25*, 915–925.

Heine, S.J. (2011). Evolutionary explanations need to account for cultural variations. *Behavioral and Brain Sciences, 34*, 26–27.

Heine, S.J., Lehman, D.R., Markus, H.R. & Kitayama, S. (1999). If there a universal need for positive self-regard? *Psychological Review, 106*, 766–794.

Heine, S.J., Takata,T. & Lehman, D. (2000). Beyond self-presentation: Evidence for self-criticism among Japanese. *Personality and Social Psychology Bulletin, 26*, 71–78.

Hejmadi, A., Davidson, R.J. & Rozin, P. (2000). Exploring Hindu Indian emotional expressions: Evidence for accurate recognition by Americans and Indians. *Psychological Science, 11*, 183–187.

Helmreich, R., Aronson, E. & LeFan, J. (1970). To err is humanizing sometimes: Effects of self-esteem, competence, and a pratfall on interpersonal attraction. *Journal of Personality and Social Psychology, 16*, 259–264.

Henderson-King, E.I. & Nisbett, R.E. (1996). Anti-black prejudice as a function of exposure to the negative behaviour of a single black person. *Journal of Personality and Social Psychology, 71*, 654–664.

Hendrick, C. & Hendrick, S. (1986). A theory and a method of love. *Journal of Personality and Social Psychology, 50*, 392–402.

Hendrick, S. & Hendrick, C. (2000). Romantic love. In C. Hendrick & Susan Hendrick (Eds), *Close relationships: A sourcebook* (pp. 203–215). Thousand Oaks, CA: Sage Publications.

Hendrick, S. & Hendrick, C. (2002). Linking romantic love with sex: Development of the perceptions of Love and Sex scale. *Journal of Social and Personal Relationships, 19*, 361–378.

Henein, C.M. & White, T. (2009). Front to back communication in a microscopic crowd model. In Klingsch, W.W.F., Rogsch, C., Schadschneider, A. & Schreckenberg, M. (Eds), *Pedestrian and evacuation dynamics 2008.* New York: Springer. (pp. 321–334).

Henley, M. (1973). Status and sex: Some touching observations. *Bulletin of the Psychonomic Society, 2*, 21–27.

Hennessy, D.A. & Wiesenthal, D.L. (1999). Traffic congestion, driver stress, and driver aggression. *Aggressive Behavior, 25*, 409–423.

Hennessy, D.A. & Wiesenthal, D.L. (2002). Aggression, violence, and vengeance among male and female drivers. *Transportation Quarterly, 56*, 65–75.

Hennessy, M. & Saltz, R.F. (1993). Modelling social influences on public drinking. *Journal of Studies on Alcohol, 54*, 139–145.

Henrich, J., Boyd, R., Bowles, S., Camerer, C., Fehr, E., Gintis, H., McElreath, R., Alvard, M., Barr, A., Ensminger, J., Hill, K., Gil-White, F., Gurven, M., Marlowe, F., Patton, J.O., Smith, N. & Tracer, D. (2005). 'Economic man' in cross-cultural perspective: Behavioral experiments in 15 small-scale societies. *Behavioural and Brain Sciences, 28*, 795–855.

Henrich, J., Heine, S. J., & Norenzayan, A. (2010a). Most people are not WEIRD. *Nature, 466*, 29.

Henrich, J., Heine, S.J. & Norenzayan, A. (2010b). The weirdest people in the world? *Behavioural and Brain Sciences, 33*, 61–83.

Henrich, N. & Henrich, J. (2007). *Why humans cooperate.* Oxford: Oxford University Press.

Henry, F. (1985/86). Heroes and helpers in Nazi Germany: Who aided Jews? *Humboldt Journal of Social Relations, 13*, 306–319.

Hepach, R., Vaish, A. & Tomasello, M. (2012). Young children are intrinsically motivated to see others helped. *Psychological Science, 23*, 967–972.

Herbert, T.B. & Cohen, S. (1993). Depression and immunity: A meta-analytical review. *Psychological Bulletin, 113*, 472–486.

Herd, J.A. & Weiss, S.M. (1984). Overview of hypertension: Its treatment and prevention. In J.D. Matarazzo, S.M. Weiss, J.A. Herd, N.E. Miller & S.M. Weiss (Eds), *Behavioral health* (pp. 789–804). New York: Wiley.

Herek, G.M. (2000). The social construction of attitudes: Functional consensus and divergence in the US public's reactions to AIDS. In G. Maio & J. Olson (Eds), *Why we evaluate: Functions of attitudes* (pp. 325–364). Mahwah, NJ: Lawrence Erlbaum.

Herek, G.M. (2009). Hate crimes and stigma-related experiences among sexual minority adults in the United States: Prevalence estimates from a national probability sample. *Journal of Interpersonal Violence, 24*, 54–74.

Herman, C.P., Roth, D.A. & Polivy, J. (2003). Effects of the presence of others on food intake: A normative interpretation. *Psychological Bulletin, 129*, 873–886.

Hermann, A. & Rammal, H.G. (2010). The grounding of the 'flying bank'. *Management Decision, 48*, 1051.

Hertel, P.T. & Navarez, A. (1986). Confusing memories for verbal and nonverbal communication. *Journal of Personality and Social Psychology, 50*, 474–481.

Hertenstein, M.J., Holmes, R., McCullough, M. & Keltner, D. (2009). The communication of emotion via touch. *Emotion, 9*, 566–579.

Hertwig, R. & Ortmann, A. (2008). Deception in social psychological experiments: Two misconceptions and a research agenda. *Social Psychology Quarterly, 71*, 222–227.

Hessing, D.J., Elffers, H. & Weigel, R. (1988). Exploring the limits of self-reports and reasoned action: An investigation of the psychology of tax-evasion behavior. *Journal of Personality and Social Psychology, 54*, 405–413.

Heuer, L. & Penrod, S. (1986). Procedural preference as a function of conflict intensity. *Journal of Personality and Social Psychology, 51*, 700–710.

Hewes, G.W. (1957). The anthropology of posture. *Scientific American, 196*, 123–132.

Hewitt, P.L., Flett, G.L. Sherry, S.B., Habke, M., Lam, R.W., McMurtry, B. Ediger, E.F., Stein, M.B. (2003). The interpersonal expression of perfection: Perfectionistic self-presentation and psychological distress. *Journal of Personality and Social Psychology, 84*, 1303–1325.

Hewlett, N. & Beck, J.M. (2006). *An introduction to the science of phonetics*. Mahweh, NJ: Lawrence Erlbaum.

Hewstone, M. (1989). Changing stereotypes with disconfirming information. In D. Bar-Tal, C.F. Graumann, A.W. Kruglanski & W. Straube (Eds), *Stereotyping and prejudice: Changing conceptions* (pp. 207–223). New York: Springer-Verlag.

Hewstone, M. & Jaspars, M.F. (1984). Social dimensions of attribution. In H.Tajfel (Ed.), *The social dimension* (pp. 379–404). Cambridge: Cambridge University Press.

Hewstone, M., Rubin, M. & Willis, H. (2002). Intergoup bias. *Annual Review of Psychology, 53*, 575–604.

Heyes, C. (2010). Where do mirror neurons come from? *Neuroscience and Biobehavioural Reviews, 34*, 575–583.

Heyes, C. (2011). Automatic imitation, *Psychological Bulletin, 137*, 463–483.

Higbee, K.L. (1969). Fifteen years of fear arousal: Research on threat appeals: 1953–1968. *Psychological Bulletin, 72*, 426–444.

Higgins, E.T. (1987). Self-discrepancy: A theory relating self and affect. *Psychological Review, 94*, 319–340.

Higgins, E.T. (1996). The 'self-digest': Self-knowledge serving self-regulatory functions. *Journal of Personality and Social Psychology, 71*, 1062–1083.

Higgins, E.T. (2011). Regulatory focus theory. In P.A. Van Lange, A. Kruglanski & E.T. Higgins (Eds). *Handbook of theories of social psychology*, (Vol. 1). (pp. 483–505). London: Sage.

Higgins, E.T. & Bryant, S.L. (1982). Consensus information and the fundamental attribution error: The role of development and in-group versus out-group knowledge. *Journal of Personality and Social Psychology, 43*, 889–900.

Higham, P.A. & Carment, D.W. (1992). The rise and fall of politicians: The judged heights of Broadbent, Mulroney and Turner before and after the 1988 Canadian federal election. *Canadian Journal of Behavioural Science, 24*, 404–409.

Hill, C.T., Rubin, Z. & Peplau, L.A. (1976). Breakups before marriage: The end of 103 affairs. *Journal of Social Issues, 32*, 147–168.

Hill, C.T. & Stull, D.E. (1981). Sex differences in the effects of social and value similarity in same-sex friendships. *Journal of Personality and Social Psychology, 41*, 488–502.

Hilton, J.L. & Von Hippel, W. (1996). Stereotypes. *Annual Review of Psychology, 47*, 237–271.

Hinduja, S. & Patchin, J.W. (2010). Bullying, cyberbullying, and suicide. *Archives of Suicide Research, 14*, 206–221.

Hinkin, T.R. & Schriesheim, C.A. (1989). Development and application of new scales to measure the French and Raven (1959) bases of social power. *Journal of Applied Social Psychology, 74*, 561–567.

Hirt, E.R., Deppe, R.K. & Gordon, L.J. (1991). Self-reported versus behavioral self-handicapping: Empirical evidence for a theoretical distinction. *Journal of Personality and Social Psychology, 61*, 981–991.

Ho, M.Y. & Fung, H.H. (2011). A dynamic process model of forgiveness: A cross-cultural perspective. *Review of General Psychology, 15*, 77–84.

Ho, R. & Penney, R.K. (1992). Euthanasia and abortion: Personality correlates for the decision to terminate life. *Journal of Social Psychology, 132*, 77–86.

Hodgins, D.C. & Kalin, R. (1985). Reducing sex bias in judgements of occupational suitability by provision of sex-typed personality information. *Canadian Journal of Behavioural Science, 17*, 346–358.

Hodson, G. (2011). Do ideologically intolerant people benefit from intergroup contact? *Current Directions in Psychological Science, 20*, 154–159.

Hodson, G. & Busseri, M. (2012). Bright minds and dark attitudes: Lower cognitive ability predicts greater prejudice through right-wing ideology and low intergroup contact. *Psychological Science, 23*, 187–195.

Hodson, G., Hooper, H., Dovidio, J. F. & Gaertner, S.L. (2005). Aversive racism in Britain: The use of inadmissible evidence in legal decisions. *European Journal of Social Psychology, 35*, 437–448.

Hoffman, C., Lau, I. & Johnson, D.R. (1986). The linguistic relativity of person cognition. An English-Chinese comparison. *Journal of Personality and Social Psychology, 51*, 1097–1105.

Hoffmann, M.L. (1981). Is altruism a part of human nature? *Journal of Personality and Social Psychology, 40*, 121–137.

Hofstede, G. (1983). Dimensions of national cultures in fifty countries and three regions. In J.B. Deregowski, S. Dziurawiec & R.C. Annis (Eds), *Explications in cross-cultural psychology* (pp. 335–355). Lisse: Svets & Zeitlinger B.V.

Hofstede, G. (2001*). Culture's consequences: comparing values, behaviors, institutions, and organizations across nations* (2nd ed.). Thousand Oaks, CA: Sage.

Hofstede, G. & Hofstede, G.J. (2005). *Cultures and organizations: Software of the mind* (2nd ed.). New York: McGraw-Hill.

Hogg, M.A. (2001). A social identity theory of leadership. *Personality and Social Psychology Review, 5*, 184–200.

Hogg, M.A. (2006). Social identity theory. In P.J. Burke (Ed.), *Contemporary social psychological theories* (pp. 111–136). Palo Alto, CA: Stanford University Press.

Hogg, M.A. & Williams, K.D. (2000). From I to we: Social identity and the collective self. *Group Dynamics: Theory, Research, and Practice, 4*, 81–97.

Holland, J., Silva, A.S. & Mace, R. (2012). Lost letter measure of variation in altruistic behaviour in 20 neighbourhoods. *PLoS One, 7(8):* e43294

Hollander, E.P. (1958). Conformity, status, and idiosyncrasy credit. *Psychological Review, 65*, 117–127.

Hollander, E.P. (1992). The essential interdependence of leadership and followership. *Current Directions in Psychological Science, 1*, 71–75.

Holler, J. & Stevens, R. (2007). The effect of common ground on how speakers use gesture and speech to represent size information. *Journal of Language and Social Psychology, 26*, 4–27.

Holmes, J. & Brown, D.F. (1977). Sociolinguistic competence and second language learning. *Topics in Culture Learning, 5*, 72–82.

Holmes, T.H. & Rahe, R.H. (1967). The social readjustment rating scale. *Journal of Psychosomatic Research, 11*, 213–218.

Holtgraves, T. (1986). Language structure in social interaction: Perceptions of direct and indirect speech acts and interactants who use them. *Journal of Personality and Social Psychology, 51*, 305–314.

Holtzworth-Munroe, A. & Jacobson, N.S. (1985). Causal attributions of married couples: When do they search for causes? What do they conclude when they do? *Journal of Personality and Social Psychology, 48,* 1398–1412.

Holzkamp, K. (1983). *Grundlegung der psychologie.* Frankfurt: Campus.

Homans, G.C. (1958). Social behavior and exchange. *American Journal of Sociology, 63,* 597–606.

Homans, G.C. (1961). *Social behavior: Its elementary forms.* New York: Harcourt, Brace and World.

Homans G.C. (1974). *Social behavior: Its elementary forms* (Revised ed.). New York: Harcourt Brace Jovanovich.

Homer, P.M. & Kahle, L. (1988). A structural equation test of the value-attitude-behavior hierarchy. *Journal of Personality and Social Psychology, 54,* 638–646.

Hong, J.S. & Espelage, D.L. (2012). A review of research on bullying and peer victimization in school: An ecological system analysis. *Aggression and Violent Behavior, 17,* 311–322.

Honts, C.R., Hodes, R.L. & Raskin, D.C. (1985). Effects of physical counter measures on the physiological detection of deception. *Journal of Applied Psychology, 70,* 177–187.

Hooghiemstra, P. (2000). Corporate communication and impression management: New perspectives on why companies engage in corporate social reporting. *Journal of Business Ethics, 27,* 55–68.

Hook, J.N., Worthington, E.L. Jr. & Utsey, S.O. (2009). Collectivism, forgiveness, and social harmony. *The Counseling Psychologist, 37,* 821–847.

Hooker, S. (1988, May 9). It's still a question of black and white. *The Globe and Mail.*

Horvath, F. (1977). Effect of selected variables on interpretation of polygraph records. *Journal of Applied Psychology, 62,* 127–136.

Horvath, F. (1984). Detecting deception in eyewitness cases: Problems and prospects in the use of the polygraph. In G.L. Wells & E.F. Loftus (Eds), *Eyewitness testimony: Psychological perspectives* (pp. 214–255). Cambridge: Cambridge University Press.

Hoshino-Browne, E. (2012). Cultural variations in motivations for cognitive consistency: Influence of self-systems on cognitive dissonance. *Social and Personality Psychology Compass, 6,* 126–141.

Hoshino-Browne, E., Zanna, M., Spencer, S.J., Zanna, M.P., Kitayama, S. & Lackenbauer, S. (2005). On the cultural guises of cognitive dissonance: The case of Easterners and Westerners.

Journal of Personality and Social Psychology, 89, 294–310.

Hotta, M. & Strickland, L.H. (1991). Social psychology in Japan. *Canadian Psychology, 32,* 596–611.

Houghton, D.P. (2008). Invading and occupying Iraq: Some insights from political psychology. *Peace and Conflict, 14,* 169–192.

Houlden, P., Latour, S., Walker, L. & Thibaut, J. (1978). Preference for modes of dispute resolution as a function of process and decision control. *Journal of Experimental Social Psychology, 14,* 13–30.

House, J.S., Landis, K.R. & Umberson, D. Social relationships and health. (1988). *Science, 241*(4865), 540–545.

House, J.S. & Wolf, S. (1978). Effects of urban residence on interpersonal trust and helping behavior. *Journal of Personality and Social Psychology, 36,* 1029–1043.

House, R. (1977). A 1976 theory of charismatic leadership. In J.G. Hunt & L. Larson (Eds), *Leadership: The cutting edge* (pp. 189–207). Carbondale: Southern Illinois University Press.

Hove, M.J. & Risen, J.L. (2009). It's all in the timing: Interpersonal synchrony increases affiliation. *Social Cognition, 27,* 949–960.

Hovland, C.I., Harvey, O.J. & Sherif, M. (1957). Assimilation and contrast effects in reactions to communications and attitude change. *Journal of Abnormal and Social Psychology, 55,* 244–252.

Hovland, C.I., Janis, I. & Kelley, H.H. (1953). *Communication and persuasion.* New Haven: Yale University Press.

Hovland, C.I., Lumsdaine, A.A. & Sheffield, F.D. (1949). *Experiments on mass communication.* Princeton, NJ: Princeton University Press.

Hovland, C.I. & Sears, R.R. (1940). Minor studies of aggression: VI. Correlation of lynchings with economic indices. Journal of Psychology: *Interdisciplinary and Applied, 9,* 301–310.

Howard, P.N., Duffy, A., Freelon, D., Hussain, M., Mari, W. & Mazaid, M. (2011). Opening closed regimes: What was the role of social media during the Arab Spring? *Working Paper 2011.1, project on Information Technology and Political Islam.* Downloaded on February 27, 2013 from http://pitpi.org/wp-content/uploads/2013/02/2011_Howard-Duffy-Freelon-Hussain-Mari-Mazaid_pITPI.pdf

Howell, J.M. & Frost, P.J. (1989). A laboratory study of charismatic leadership. *Organization Behavior and Human Decision Processes, 43*, 243–269.

Huba, G.J., Dent, C. & Bentler, P.M. (1980, September). *Causal models of peer-adult support and youthful alcohol use.* American Psychological Association, Montréal.

Huesmann, L.R. (1988). An information processing model for the development of aggression. *Aggressive Behavior, 14*, 13–24.

Huesmann, L.R. (2007). The impact of electronic media violence: Scientific theory and research. *Journal of Adolescent Health, 41*, S6–S13.

Huesmann, L.R., Eron, L.D., Lefkowitz, M.M. & Walder, L.O. (1984). Stability of aggression over time and generations. *Developmental Psychology, 20*, 1120–1134.

Huesmann, L.R., Eron, L.D. & Yarmel, P.W. (1987). Intellectual functioning and aggression. *Journal of Personality and Social Psychology, 52*, 232–240.

Huesmann, L.R. & Guerra, N.G. (1997). Children's normative beliefs about aggression and aggressive behavior. *Journal of Personality and Social Psychology, 72*, 408–419.

Huesmann, L.R., Lagerspetz, K. & Eron, L.D. (1984). Intervening variables in the TV violence–aggression relation: Evidence from two countries. *Developmental Psychology, 20*(5), 746–775.

Huesmann, L.R. & Kirwil, L. (2007). Why observing violence increases the risk of violent behavior by the observer. In D.J. Flannery, A.T. Vazsony & I. Waldman (Eds), *The Cambridge handbook of violent behavior and aggression* (pp. 545–570). Cambridge: Cambridge University Press.

Huesmann, L.R. & Rowell (2010). Nailing the coffin shut on doubts that violent video games stimulate aggression: Comment on Anderson et al. (2010). *Psychological Bulletin, 136*, 179–181.

Hughes, R. & Reed, B.S. (2011). Learning about speech by experiment: Issues in the investigation of spontaneous talk within the experimental research paradigm. *Applied Linguistics, 32*, 197–214.

Hunsberger, B. (1995). Religion and prejudice: The role of religious fundamentalism, quest, and right-wing authoritarianism. *Journal of Social Issues, 51*, 113–129.

Hunsberger, B. (1996). Religious fundamentalism, right-wing authoritarianism, and hostility toward homosexuals in non-Christian religious groups. *International Journal for the Psychology of Religion, 6*, 39–49.

Hunsberger, B., Lea, J., Pancer, S.M., Pratt, M. & McKenzie, B. (1992). Making life complicated: Prompting the use of integratively complex thinking. *Journal of Personality, 60*, 95–114.

Hunsberger, B., Pratt, M. & Pancer, S.M. (1994). Religious fundamentalism and integrative complexity of thought: A relationship for existential content only? *Journal for the Scientific Study of Religion, 33*, 335–346.

Hunt, W.A., Barnett, L.W. & Branch, L.G. (1971). Relapse rate in addiction programs. *Journal of Clinical Psychology, 27*, 455–456.

Hurt, S.W. & Schnurr, P.P. (1992). 'Using daily ratings to confirm premenstrual syndrome/late luteal phase dysphoric disorder: I. and II.': Comment. *Psychosomatic Medicine, 54*, 723–725.

Hurt, W., Schnurr, P.P., Severino, S.K., Freeman, E.W., Gise, L.H., Rivera-Tovar, A. & Steege, J.E. (1992). Late-luteal phase dysphoric disorders in 670 women evaluated for premenstrual complaints. *American Journal of Psychiatry, 149*, 525–530.

Huston, M. & Schwartz, P. (1995). The relationships of lesbians and of gay men. In J.T. Wood & S. Duck. (Eds). *Under-studied relationships: Off the beaten track.* (pp. 89–121). Thousand Oaks, CA: Sage Publications.

Hutton, D.G. & Baumeister, R.F. (1992). Self-awareness and attitude change: Seeing oneself on the central route to persuasion. *Personality and Social Psychology Bulletin, 18*, 68–75.

Iacoboni, M. (2009). Mirroring people: The science of empathy and how we connect with others. New York: Picador.

Iacono, W.G. & Lykken, D.T. (1997). Forensic 'lie detection': Procedures without scientific basis. *Journal of Applied Psychology, 82*, 426–433.

Ickes, W., Park, A. & Robinson, R. (2012). F#!%ing rudeness: predicting the propensity to verbally abuse strangers. *Journal of Language and Social Psychology, 31*, 75–94

Idler, E.L. & Binyamini, Y. (1997). Self-rated health and mortality: A review of 27 community studies. *Journal of Health and Social Behavior, 38*, 21–37.

Imada, T. & Kitayama, S. (2010). Social eyes and choice justification: Culture and dissonance revisited. *Social Cognition, 28*, 589–608.

Inglehart, R. (1987). Extremist political positions and perceptions of conspiracy: Even paranoids have real enemies. In C.F. Graumann & S. Moscovici (Eds), *Changing conceptions of conspiracy* (pp. 231–244). New York: Springer-Verlag.

Insko, C.A. (1964). Primacy versus recency in persuasion as a function of the timing of arguments and measures. *Journal of Abnormal and Social Psychology*, *69*, 381–391.

Ip, G.W. & Bond, M.H. (1995). Culture, values and the spontaneous self-concept. *Asian Journal of Psychology*, *1*, 29–35.

Isaacson, W. (2011). *Steve Jobs*. New York: Simon & Schuster.

Isen, A.M. (1970). Success, failure, attention and reaction to others. *Journal of Personality and Social Psychology, 15,* 294–301.

Isenberg, D.J. (1986). Group polarization: A critical review and meta-analysis. *Journal of Personality and Social Psychology*, *50*, 1141–1151.

Iverson, J.M. & Goldin-Meadow, S. (1998). Why people gesture as they speak. *Nature*, *396*, 228.

Izzett, R. & Fishman, L. (1976). Defendant sentences as a function of attractiveness and justification for actions. *Journal of Social Psychology*, *100*, 285–290.

Jacoby, L.L., Kelley, C., Brown, J. & Jasechko, J. (1989). Becoming famous overnight: Limits on the ability to avoid unconscious influences of the past. *Journal of Personality and Social Psychology*, *56*, 326–338.

Jaffe, P., Wolfe, D., Wilson, S. & Zak, L. (1986). Similarities in behavioural and social adjustment among child victims and witnesses to family violence. *American Journal of Orthopsychiatry*, *56*, 142–146.

Jamieson, D.W., Lydon, J.E. & Zanna, M.P. (1987). Attitude and activity preference similarity: Differential bases of interpersonal attraction for low and high self-monitors. *Journal of Personality and Social Psychology*, *53*, 1052–1060.

Jamous, H. & Lemaine, W. (1962). Compétition entre groupes d'inégales resources. Expérience dans un cadre naturel. *Psychologie française*, *7*, 216–222.

Janis, I.L. (1951). Air war and emotional stress: Psychological studies of bombing and civilian defense. New York: McGraw-Hill.

Janis, I.L. (1958). *Psychological stress*. New York: Wiley.

Janis, I.L. (1972). *Victims of groupthink*. Boston: Houghton Mifflin.

Janis, I.L. (1982). *Groupthink* (2nd ed.). Boston: Houghton Mifflin.

Janis, I.L. & Feshbach, S. (1953). Effects of fear-arousing communications. *Journal of Abnormal and Social Psychology*, *48*, 78–92.

Janis, I.L. & Hovland, C.I. (1959). An overview of persuasibility research. In C.I. Hovland & I.L. Janis (Eds), *Personality and persuasibility* (pp. 1–28). New Haven, CT: Yale University Press.

Jankowiak, W. (1995). *Romantic passion: A universal experience?* New York: Columbia University Press.

Janowski, C.L. & Malloy, T.E. (1992). Perceptions and misperceptions of leadership: Components, accuracy and dispositional correlates. *Personality and Social Psychology Bulletin*, *18*, 700–708.

Janz, N.K. & Becker, M.H. (1984). The health belief model: A decade later. *Health Education Quarterly*, *11*, 1–47.

Javidan, M. & House, R.J. (2001). Cultural acumen for the global manager: Lessons from Project GLOBE. *Organizational Dynamics*, *29*, 289–305.

Jaworski, A. (1999). The power of silence in communication. In L.K. Guerrero, J.A. DeVito & M.L. Hecht (Eds), *The nonverbal communication reader* (pp. 156–162). Prospect Heights, IL: Waveland Press.

Jenkins, A.C. & Mitchell, J.P. (2011). Medial prefrontal cortex subserves diverse forms of self-reflection. *Social Neuroscience*, *6*, 211–218.

Jessor, R. (1993). Successful adolescent development among youth in high-risk settings. *American Psychologist*, *48*, 117–126.

Jessor, R., Donovan, J.E. & Widmer, K. (1980). Psychosocial factors in adolescent alcohol and drug use: The 1978 national sample study and the 1974–78 panel study. Boulder, CO: Institute of Behavioral Science, University of Colorado. 1–161 (unpublished report).

Jessor, R. & Jessor, S.L. (1977). *Problem behavior and psychosocial development: A longitudinal study of youth.* New York: Academic Press.

Jha, P.K., Yadav, K.P. & Kumari, U. (1997). Gender difference and religio-cultural variation in altruistic behaviour. *Indian Journal of Psychometry and Education*, *28*, 105–108.

Jia, L., Hirt, E.R. & Karpen, S.C. (2009). Lessons from a faraway land: The effects of spatial distance on creative cognition. *Journal of Experimental Social Psychology*, *45*, 1127–1131.

Jin, S-A.A (2011). My avatar behaves well and this feels right. *Social Behavior and Personality*, *39*, 1175–1182.

Joad, C.E.M. (1957). *Guide to philosophy*. New York: Dover.

Johansson, G., Collins, A. & Collins, V.P. (1983). Male and female psychoneuroendocrine response to examination stress: A case report. *Motivation and Emotion*, *7*, 1–9.

Johnson, B.T. & Eagly, A.H. (1989). Effects of involvement on persuasion: A meta-analysis. *Psychological Bulletin*, *106*, 290–314.

Johnson, D.M. (1945). The 'Phantom Anesthetist' of Mattoon: A field study of mass hysteria. *The Journal of Abnormal and Social Psychology*, *40*, 175–186.

Johnson, J.E. & Leventhal, H. (1974). Effects of accurate expectations and behavioral instructions on reactions during a noxious medical examination. *Journal of Personality and Social Psychology*, *29*, 710–718.

Johnson, R.D. & Downing, L.L. (1979). Deindividuation and valence of cues: Effects on prosocial and antisocial behavior. *Journal of Personality and Social Psychology*, *37*, 1532–1538.

Johnson, R.D., Stone, D.L. & Nichole, P.T. (2008). Relations among ethnicity, gender beliefs, attitudes and intentions to pursue a career in information technology. *Journal of Applied Social Psychology*, *38*, 999–1022.

Johnson, R.N. (1972). *Aggression in man and animals*. Philadelphia: Saunders.

Johnson, R.W., Kelly, R.J. & Leblanc, B.A. (1995). Motivational basis of dissonance: Aversive consequences or inconsistency? *Personality and Social Psychology Bulletin*, *21*, 850–855.

Jonason, P.K., Webster, G.D., Schmitt, D.P., Li, N.P. & Crysel, L. (2012). The antihero in popular culture: Life history theory and the dark triad personality traits. *Review of General Psychology*, *16*, 192–199.

Jones, E.E. & Baumeister, R. (1976). The self-monitor looks at the ingratiator. *Journal of Personality*, *44*, 654–674.

Jones, E.E. & Davis, K.E. (1965). From acts to dispositions: The attribution process in person perception. In L. Berkowitz (Ed.), *Advances in experimental social psychology* (Vol. 2). (pp. 220–266). New York: Academic Press.

Jones, E.E., Davis, K.E. & Gergen, K. (1961). Role playing variations and their informational value for person perception. *Journal of Abnormal and Social Psychology*, *63*, 302–310.

Jones, R.A. (1990). Expectations and delay in seeking medical care. *Journal of Social Issues*, *46* (2), 81–95.

Jones, E.E. & Harris, V.A. (1976). The attribution of attitude. *Journal of Experimental Psychology*, *3*, 1–24.

Jones, E.E. & Pittman, T.S. (1982). Towards a general theory of strategic self-presentation. In J. Suls (Ed.), *Psychological perspectives on the self* (pp. 231–262). Hillsdale, NJ: Erlbaum.

Jong, J.T., Kao, T., Lee, L.Y., Huang, H.H., Lo, P.T. & Wang, H.C. (2010). Can temperament be understood at birth? The relationship between neonatal pain cry and their temperament: A preliminary study. *Infant Behavioral Development*, *33*, 266–272.

Josephson, W.L. (1987). Television violence and children's aggression: Testing the priming, social script, and disinhibition predictions. *Journal of Personality and Social Psychology*, *53*, 882–890.

Jost, J.T., Federico, C.M. & Napier, J.L. (2009). Political ideology: Its structure, functions, and elective affinities. *Annual Review of Psychology*, *60*, 307–337.

Jost, J.T., Glaser, J., Kruglanski, A.W. & Sulloway, F. (2003). Political conservatism as motivated social cognition. *Psychological Bulletin*, *129*, 339–375.

Jost, J.T., Kivetz, Y., Rubini, M., Guermandi, G. & Mosso, C. (2005). System-justifying functions of complementary regional and ethnic stereotypes: Cross-national evidence. *Social Justice Research*, *18*, 305–333.

Joule, R.V., Gouilloux, F., and Weber, F. (1989). The lure: A new compliance procedure. *Journal of Social Psychology*, *129*, 741–749.

Jowett, G.S. & O'Donnell, V. (1992). *Propaganda and persuasion, Second Edition*. London: Sage.

Jussim, L., Madon, S. & Chapman, C. (1994). Teacher expectations and student achievement: Self-fulfilling prophecies, biases and accuracy. In L. Heath, R.S., Tindale, J. Edwards, E. Posovac, F.B. Bryant, E. Henderson-King, Y. Suarez-Balcazar & J. Myers (Eds), *Applications of heuristics and biases to social issues* (pp. 303–333). New York: Plenum Press.

Jussim, L.J., McCauley, C.R. & Lee, Y. (1995). Why study stereotype accuracy and inaccuracy?

In Y. Lee & L.J. Jussim (Eds), *Stereotype accuracy: Toward appreciating group differences* (pp. 3–27). Washington, DC: American Psychological Association.

Kahneman, D. (2011). *Thinking fast and slow.* New York: Farrar, Straus and Giroux.

Kahneman, D., Knetsch, J.L. & Thaler, R.H. (1990). Experimental tests of the endowment effect and the Coase Theorem. *Journal of Political Economy, 98,* 1325–1348.

Kahneman, D. & Tversky, A. (1982). The simulation heuristic. In D. Kahneman, P. Slovic & A. Tversky (Eds), *Judgements under uncertainty: Heuristics and biases.* New York: Cambridge University Press.

Kaiser, F.G., Byrka, K. & Hartig, T. (2010). Reviving Campbell's paradigm for attitude research. *Personality and Social Psychology Review, 14,* 351–367.

Kaiser, R. B., McGinnis, J. & Overfield, D. V. (2012). The how and the what of leadership. *Consulting Psychology Journal: Practice and Research, 64,* 119–135.

Kalick, S.M. & Hamilton, T.E. (1988). A closer look at a matching simulation. *Journal of Personality and Social Psychology, 54,* 447–452.

Kalick, S.M., Zebrowitz, L.A., Langlois, J.H. & Johnson, R.M. (1996, August 9–13). *Does attractiveness advertise health or are we blinded by beauty?* American Psychological Association, Toronto.

Kalin, R. & Berry, J.W. (1982). The social ecology of ethnic attitudes in Canada. *Canadian Journal of Behavioural Science, 14,* 97–109.

Kalin, R. & Hodgins, D.C. (1984). Sex bias in judgements of occupational suitability. *Canadian Journal of Behavioural Science, 16,* 311–325.

Kalman, Y.M. & Rafaeli, S. (2011). Online pauses and silence: Chronemic expectancy violations in written computer-mediated communication. *Communication Research, 38,* 54–69.

Kamas, L. & Preston, A. (2012). The importance of being confident: Career choice and willingness to compete. *Journal of Economic Behavior and Organization, 83,* 82–97.

Kamin, L.J. (1974). *The science and politics of I.Q.* New York: Halsted Press.

Kandel, D.B. (1978a). Convergences in prospective longitudinal surveys of drug use in normal populations. In D.B. Kandel (Ed.), *Longitudinal research on drug use: Empirical findings and methodological issues.* Washington, DC: Hemisphere.

Kandel, D.B. (1978b). Similarity in real-life adolescent friendship pairs. *Journal of Personality and Social Psychology, 36,* 306–312.

Kanekar, S. (2001). Helping norms in relation to religious affiliation. *Journal of Social Psychology, 141,* 617–626.

Kanner, A.D., Coyne, J.C., Schaefer, C. & Lazarus, R.S. (1981). Comparison of two models of stress measurement: Daily hassles and uplifts versus major life events. *Journal of Behavioral Medicine, 4,* 1–29.

Kaplan, M.F. & Martin, A.N. (2006). Understanding world jury systems through social psychological research. New York: Psychology Press.

Karau, S.J. & Hart, J.W. (1998). Group cohesiveness and social loafing: Effects of a social interaction manipulation on individual motivation within groups. *Group Dynamics, 2,* 185–191.

Karau, S.J. & Williams, K.D. (1993). Social loafing: A meta-analytic review and theoretical integration. *Journal of Personality and Social Psychology, 65,* 681–706.

Karlins, M. & Abelson, H.I. (1970). *How opinions and attitudes are changed* (2nd ed.). New York: Springer.

Karlins, M., Coffman, T.L. & Walters, G. (1969). On the fading of social stereotypes: Studies in three generations of college students. *Journal of Personality and Social Psychology, 13,* 1–16.

Karpf, A. (2006). The human voice: The story of a remarkable talent. London: Bloomsbury Publishing.

Kärtner, J., Keller, H., & Chaudhary, N. (2010). Cognitive and social influences on early prosocial behavior in two socio-cultural contexts. *Developmental Psychology, 46,* 905–914.

Kassin, S.M. & Barndollar, K.A. (1992). The psychology of eyewitness testimony: A comparison of experts and prospective jurors. *Journal of Applied Social Psychology, 22,* 1241–1249.

Kassin, S.M., Reddy, M.E. & Tulloch, W.F. (1990). Juror interpretation of ambiguous evidence: The need for cognition, presentation order and persuasion. *Law and Human Behavior, 14,* 43–55.

Katz, D. & Braly, K. (1933). Racial stereotypes of one hundred college students. *Journal of Abnormal and Social Psychology, 28,* 280–290.

Katz, E. & Lazarsfeld, P.F. (1955). *Personal influence: The part played by people in the flow of mass communication.* Glencoe, IL: Free Press.

Katz, I. & Hass, R.G. (1988). Racial ambivalence and American value conflict: Correlational and priming studies of dual cognitive structures. *Journal of Personality and Social Psychology, 55,* 893–905.

Kawachi, I., Kennedy, B.P. & Wilkinson, R.G. (1999). Crime: Social disorganization and relative deprivation. *Social Science & Medicine, 48,* 719–731.

Kawamura S., Komori, M. & Miyamoto, Y. (2008). Smiling reduces masculinity: Principal component analysis applied to facial images. *Perception,* 37, 1637–1648.

Kawashima, R., Sugiura, M., Kato, T., Nakamura, A., Hatano, K., Ito, K., Fukuda, H., Kojima, S. & Nakamura, K. (1999). The human amygdala lays an important role in gaze monitoring: A PET study. *Brain, 122,* 779–783. Cited by McRae et al. (2002).

Kay, A.C., Jimenez, M. & Jost, J.T. (2002). Sour grapes, sweet lemons and the anticipatory rationalization of the status quo. *Personality and Social Psychology Bulletin, 28,* 1300–1312.

Kayser, D.K., Greitemeyer, T., Fischer, P. & Frey, D. (2010). Why mood affects help giving, but not moral courage: Comparing two types of prosocial behaviour. *European Journal of Social Psychology, 40,* 1136–1157.

Keashly, L. & Fisher, R.J. (1996). A contingency perspective on conflict interventions: Theoretical and practical considerations. In J. Bercovitch (Ed.), *Resolving international conflicts: The theory and practice of mediation* (pp. 235–261). Boulder, CO: Lynne Rienner Publishers.

Keashly, L., Fisher, R.J. & Grant, P.R. (1993). The comparative utility of third party consultation and mediation within a complex simulation of intergroup conflict. *Human Relations, 46,* 371–391.

Keating, J.P. & Loftus, E.F. (1981). The logic of fire escape. *Psychology Today, 15*(6), 14–18.

Keefe, J.M. & Fancey, P.J. (2002). Work and eldercare: Reciprocity between older mothers and their employed daughters. *Canadian Journal on Aging, 21,* 229–241.

Keelan, J.P.R., Dion, K.L. & Dion, K.K. (1994). Attachment style and heterosexual relationships among young adults: A short-term panel study. *Journal of Personal and Social Relationships, 11,* 201–214.

Keinan, G. & Hobfoll, S.E. (1989). Stress, dependency and social support: Who benefits from the husband's presence in delivery? *Journal of Social and Clinical Psychology, 8,* 32–44.

Kelley, H.H. (1950). The warm-cold variable in first impressions of persons. *Journal of Personality, 18,* 431–439.

Kelley, H.H. (1972). Attribution in social interaction. In E.E. Jones, D.E. Kanouse, H.H. Kelley, R.E. Nisbett, S. Valins & B. Weiner (Eds), *Attribution: Perceiving the causes of behavior* (pp. 1–26). Morristown, NJ: General Learning Press.

Kelly, L.E. & Conley, J.J. (1987). Personality and compatibility: A prospective analysis of marital stability and marital satisfaction. *Journal of Personality and Social Psychology, 52,* 27–40.

Kelley, H.H. & Stahelski, A.J. (1970). The social interaction basis of cooperators' and competitors' beliefs about others. *Journal of Personality and Social Psychology, 16,* 66–91.

Kelman, H.C. (1958). Compliance, identification, and internalization: Three processes of attitude change. *Journal of Conflict Resolution, 2,* 51–60.

Kelman, H.C. (1961). Processes of opinion change. *Public Opinion Quarterly, 25,* 57–78.

Kelman, H.C. (1967). Human use of human subjects: The problem of deception in social psychological experiments. *Psychological Bulletin, 67,* 1–11.

Kempf, D.S. (1999). Attitude formation from product trial: Distinct roles of cognition and affect for hedonic and functional products. *Psychology & Marketing, 16,* 35–50.

Kennedy, T.D. & Haygood, R.C. (1992). The discrediting effect in eyewitness testimony. *Journal of Applied Social Psychology, 22,* 70–82.

Kennedy-Kollar, D. & Charles, C.A.D. (2012). Hegemonic masculinity and mass murderers in the United States. *The Southwest Journal of Criminal Justice, 8,* 61–73.

Kenrick, D.T. & Cialdini, R.B. (1977). Romantic attraction: Misattribution versus reinforcement explanations. *Journal of Personality and Social Psychology, 35,* 381–391.

Kenrick, D.T., Li, N.P. & Butner, J. (2003). Dynamical evolutionary psychology: Individual decision rules and emergent social norms. *Psychological Review, 110,* 3–28.

Kenworthy, J.B., Miller, N., Collins, B.E., Read, S.J. & Earleywine, M. (2011). A trans-paradigm theoretical synthesis of cognitive dissonance theory:

Illuminating the nature of discomfort. *European Review of Social Psychology*, *22*, 36–113.

Kerckhoff, A.C. & Davis, K.E. (1962). Value consensus and need complementarity in mate selection. *American Sociological Review*, *27*, 295–303.

Kernis, M.H., Grannemann, B.D. & Barclay, L.C. (1989). Stability and level of self-esteem as predictors of anger arousal and hostility. *Journal of Personality and Social Psychology*, *56*, 1013–1022.

Kerr, N. L. & Hertel, G. (2011). The Köhler Group Motivation Gain: How to motivate the 'weak links' in groups. *Social and Personality Psychology Compass*, *5*, 43–55.

Kerr, N.L., Messé, D-H., Sambolec, R.B. & Park, E.S. (2007). Psychological mechanisms underlying the Köhler motivation gain. *Personality and Social Psychology Bulletin*, *33*, 828–841.

Kershaw, I. S (1998). *Hitler 1889–1936: Hubris*. New York: W.W. Norton.

Keyes, C.L.M., Shmotkin, D. & Ryff, C.D. (2002). Optimizing well-being: The empirical encounter of two traditions. *Journal of Personality and Social Psychology*, *82*, 1007–1022.

Keyes, R. (1980). *The height of your life*. Boston: Little, Brown.

Kidd, R.F. & Chayet, E.F. (1984). Why do victims fail to report? The psychology of criminal victimization. *Journal of Social Issues*, *40*, 39–50.

Kiecolt-Glaser, J.K., McGuire, L., Robles, T.F. & Glaser, R. (2002). Psychoneuroimmunology: Psychological influences on immune function and health. *Journal of Consulting and Clinical Psychology*, *70*, 537–547.

Kiecolt-Glaser, J.K. & Newton, T.L. (2001). Marriage and health: His and hers. *Psychological Bulletin*, *127*, 472–503.

Kiesler, C.A. (1968). Commitment. In R.P. Abelson, E. Aronson, W.J. McGuire, T.H. Newcomb, M.J. Rosenberg & P.H. Tannenbaum (Eds), *Theories of cognitive consistency: A sourcebook* (pp. 448–455). Skokie, IL: Rand-McNally.

Kiesler, C.A. & Pallak, M.S. (1976). Arousal properties of dissonance manipulations. *Psychological Bulletin*, *83*, 1014–1025.

Kihlstrom, J.F., Cantor, N., Albright, J.S., Chew, B.R., Klein, S.B. & Niedenthal, P.M. (1988). Information processing and the study of the self. In L. Berkowitz (Ed.), *Advances in experimental social psychology* (Vol. 21). (pp. 145–178). New York: Academic Press.

Kilham, W. & Mann, L. (1974). Level of destructive obedience as a function of transmitter and executant roles in the Milgram obedience paradigm. *Journal of Personality and Social Psychology*, *29*, 692–702.

Killian, L.M. (1952). The significance of multiple-group membership in a disaster. *American Journal of Sociology*, *57*, 309–314.

Kim, H.S., Sherman, D.K. & Taylor, S.E. (2009). The irony of cultural psychology research. *American Psychologist*, *64*, 564–565.

Kim, Y.H., Cohen, D. & Au, W. (2010). The jury and abjury of my peers. The self in face and dignity cultures. *Journal of Personality and Social Psychology*, *98*, 904–916.

Kim, Y.S., Barak, G. & Shelton, D.E. (2009). Examining the 'CSI-effect' in the cases of circumstantial evidence and eyewitness testimony: Multivariate and path analyses. *Journal of Criminal Justice*, *37*, 452–460.

Kimmell, A.J. (2011). Deception in psychological research – A necessary evil? *The Psychologist*, *24*, 580–585.

King, K.B., Reis, H.T., Porter, L.A. & Norsen, L.H. (1993). Social support and long-term recovery from coronary artery surgery: Effects on patients and spouses. *Health Psychology*, *12*, 56–63.

Kipnis, D. (1972). Does power corrupt? *Journal of Personality and Social Psychology*, *24*, 33–41.

Kitayama, S. & Markus, H.R. (1994). Culture and the self: How culture influences how we view ourselves. In D. Matsumoto (Ed.), *People: Psychology from a cultural perspective* (pp. 17–37). Pacific Grove, CA: Brooks/Cole.

Kitayama, S., Markus, H.R., Matsumoto, H. & Norasakkunkit, V. (1997). Individual and collective processes of self-esteem management: Self-enhancement in the United States and self-depreciation in Japan. *Journal of Personality and Social Psychology*, *72*, 1245–1267.

Kitterman, D.H. (1988). Those who said 'no': Germans refuse to execute civilians during World War II. *German Studies Review*, *11*, 241–254.

Kitterman, D.H. (1991). Those who said 'no' to the Holocaust. *Nonviolent Sanctions*, *2*(4), 3.

Kiyonari, T. & Barclay, P. (2008). Cooperation in social dilemmas: Free riding may be thwarted by second-order reward rather than by punishment.

Journal of Personality and Social Psychology, 95, 826–842.

Klama, J. (1988). *Aggression.* Burnt Hill: Longman.

Klapp, O.E. (1972). *Currents of unrest.* New York: Holt, Rinehart & Winston.

Klapwijk, A. & Van Lange, P.A.M. (2009). Promoting cooperation and trust in 'noisy' situations: The power of generosity. *Journal of Personality and Social Psychology, 96*, 83–103.

Klein, J.G. (1991). Negative effects in impression formation: A test in the political arena. *Personality and Social Psychology Bulletin, 17*, 412–418.

Klein, K.J. & House, R.J. (1998). On fire: Charismatic leadership and levels of analysis. In F. Dansereau & F.J. Yammarino (Eds), *Leadership: The multiple-level approaches: Contemporary and alternative. Monographs in organizational behavior and industrial relations, 24*, Part B. (pp. 3–52). Stamford, CT: JAI Press, Inc.

Kliger, D. & Kudryavtsev, A. (2010). The availability heuristic and investors' reaction to company-specific events. *Journal of Behavioral Finance, 11*, 50–65.

Klinesmith, J., Kasser, T. & McAndrew, F.T. (2006). Guns, testosterone, and aggression: an experimental test of a mediational hypothesis. *Psychological Science, 17*, 568–571.

Kling, K.C., Hyde, J.S., Showers, C.J. & Buswell, B.N. (1999). Gender differences in self-esteem: A meta-analysis. *Psychological Bulletin, 125*, 470–500.

Klohn, L.S. & Rogers, R.W. (1991). Dimensions of the severity of a health threat: The persuasive effects of visibility, time of onset and rate of onset on young women's intentions to prevent osteoporosis. *Health Psychology, 10*, 323–329.

Knafo, A., Israel, S. & Ebstein, R.P. (2011). Heritability of children's prosocial behaviour and differential susceptibility to parenting by variation in the dopamine receptor D4 gene. *Development and Psychopathology, 23*, 53–67.

Knafo, A., Schwartz, S. H. & Levine, R. V. (2009). Helping strangers is lower in embedded cultures. *Journal of Cross-Cultural Psychology, 40*, 875–879.

Knapp, M.L. & Hall, J.A. (1992). *Nonverbal communication in human interaction* (3rd ed.). Fort Worth, TX: Harcourt Brace.

Knox, R.E. & Inkster, J.A. (1968). Postdecision dissonance at post time. *Journal of Personality and Social Psychology, 8*, 319–323.

Koenig, A.M., Eagly, A.H., Mitchell, A.A. & Ristikari, T. (2011). Are leader stereotypes masculine? A meta-analysis of three research paradigms. *Psychological Bulletin, 137*, 616–642.

Koenig, K. (1985). *Rumor in the marketplace.* Dover, MA: Auburn House.

Kogan, N. & Wallach, M.A. (1967). Risk taking as a function of the situation, the person, and the group. In G. Mandler, P. Mussen, N. Kogan & M.A. Wallach (Eds), *New directions in psychology III.* New York: Holt, Rinehart & Winston.

Köhler, O. (1926). Kraftleistungen bei Einzel- und Gruppenabeit [Physical performance in individual and group situations]. *Industrielle Psychotechnik, 3*, 274–282.

Kohnken, G. & Maass, A. (1988). Eyewitness testimony: False alarms on biased instructions? *Journal of Applied Psychology, 73*, 363–370.

Kollmuss, A. & Agyeman, J. (2002). Mind the gap: Why do people act environmentally and what are the barriers to pro-environmental behavior? *Environmental Education Research, 8*, 239–260.

Komorita, S.S., Hilty, J.A. & Parks, C.D. (1991). Reciprocity and cooperation in social dilemmas. *Journal of Conflict Resolution, 35*, 494–518.

Komorita S.S. & Parks, C.D. (1995). Interpersonal relations: Mixed-motive interaction. *Annual Review of Psychology, 46*, 183–207.

Koole, S.L., Dijksterhuis, A. & van Knippenberg, A. (2001). What's in a name? Implicit self-esteem and the automatic self. *Journal of Personality and Social Psychology, 80*, 669–685.

Kormos, J., Kiddle, T. & Csizér, K. (2011). Systems of goals, attitudes, and self-elated beliefs in second-language-learning motivation. *Applied Linguistics, 32*, 495–516.

Korte, C. & Kerr, N. (1975). Response to altruistic opportunities in urban and non-urban settings. *The Journal of Social Psychology, 95*, 183–184.

Kosfeld, M., Heinrichs, M., Zak, P.J., Fischbacher, U. & Feh, E. (2005). Oxytocin increases trust in humans. *Nature, 435*, 673–676.

Kosson, D.S., Suchy, Y., Mayer, A.R. & Libby, J. (2002). Facial affect recognition in criminal psychopaths. *Emotion, 2*, 398–411.

Kouzakova, M., Ellemers, N., Harinck, F. & Scheepers, D. (2012). The implications of value conflict: How disagreement on values affects self-involvement and perceived common ground.

Personality and Social Psychology Bulletin, 38, 798–807.

Krahé, B., Busching, R. & Möller, I. (2012). Media violence use and aggression among German adolescents: Associations and trajectories of change in a three-wave longitudinal study. *Psychology of Popular Media Culture, 1,* 152–166.

Krahé, B., Möller, I., Huesmann, L., Kirwil, L., Felber, J. & Berger, A. (2011). Desensitization to media violence: Links with habitual media violence exposure, aggressive cognitions, and aggressive behavior. *Journal of Personality and Social Psychology,100,* 630–646.

Kramer, R.M. (1998). Revisiting the Bay of Pigs and Vietnam decisions 25 years later: How well has the groupthink hypothesis stood the test of time? *Organizational Behavior and Human Decision Processes, 73,* 236–271.

Krantz, M.J. & Johnson, L. (1978). Family members' perceptions of communications in late-stage cancer. *International Journal of Psychiatry in Medicine, 8,* 203–216.

Kraus, S.J. (1995). Attitudes and the prediction of behavior: A meta-analysis of the empirical literature. *Personality and Social Psychology Bulletin, 21,* 58–75.

Krauss, R.M., Freyberg, R. & Morsella, E. (2002). Inferring speakers' physical attributes from their voices. *Journal of Experimental Social Psychology, 38,* 618–625.

Krauss, R.M. & Pardo, J.S. (2006). Speaker perception and social behaviour: Bridging social psychology and speech science. In P.A.M. van Lange (Ed.), *Bridging Social Psychology: The Benefits of Transdisciplinary Approaches* (pp. 273–278). Hillsdale, NJ: Erlbaum.

Kraut, R.E. (1978). Verbal and non-verbal cues in the detection of lying. *Journal of Personality and Social Psychology, 36,* 380–391.

Kraut, R.E., Patterson, M., Lundmark, V., Kiesler, S., Mukopadhyay, T. & Scherlis, W. (1998). Internet paradox: A social technology that reduces social involvement and psychological well-being. *American Psychologist, 53,* 1017–1031.

Kraut, R.E. & Poe, D. (1980). Behavioral roots of person perceptions: The deception judgements of the customs inspectors and laymen. *Journal of Personality and Social Psychology, 39,* 784–798.

Krebs, D.L. (1970). Altruism: An examination of the concept and a review of the literature. *Psychological Bulletin, 73,* 258–302.

Krebs, D.L. & Adinolfi, A.H. (1975). Physical attractiveness, social relations and personality style. *Journal of Personality and Social Psychology, 31,* 245–253.

Krebs, D.L. & Miller, D.T. (1985). Altruism and aggression. In G. Lindzey & E. Aronson (Eds), *Handbook of social psychology* (3rd ed.). (Vol. 2). (pp. 1–71). New York: Random House.

Krefting, L.A., Berger, P.K. & Wallace, M.J. (1978). The contribution of sex distribution, job content, and occupational classification to job sex-typing: Two studies. *Journal of Vocational Behavior, 13,* 181–191.

Kreiner, D.S. (2011). Language and culture: Commonality, variation, and mistaken assumptions. In K.D. Keith (Ed.), *Cross-cultural psychology: Contemporary themes and perspectives.* West Sussex, England: Blackwell Publishing Limited, (pp. 383–399).

Kristiansen, C.M. (1986). A two-value model of preventive health behavior. *Basic and Applied Social Psychology, 7,* 173–183.

Kristiansen, C.M. & Matheson, K. (1990). Value conflict, value justification, and attitudes toward nuclear weapons. *Journal of Social Psychology, 130,* 665–675.

Kristiansen, C.M. & Zanna, M.P. (1988). Justifying attitudes by appealing to values: A functional perspective. *British Journal of Social Psychology, 27,* 247–256.

Kroger, R.O. & Wood, L.A. (1992). Whatever happened to language in social psychology? *Canadian Psychology, 33,* 584–594.

Krosnick, J.A. & Alwin, D.F. (1989). Aging and susceptibility to attitude change. *Journal of Personality and Social Psychology, 57,* 416–425.

Krosnick, J.A. & Petty, R.E. (1995). Attitude strength: An overview. In R.E. Petty & J.A. Krosnick (Eds), *Attitude strength: Antecedents and consequences; Ohio State University series on attitudes and persuasion.* (Vol. 4). (pp. 1–24). Mahwah, NJ: Lawrence Erlbaum Associates.

Krueger, J. (1998). Enhancement bias in descriptions of self and others. *Personality and Social Psychology Bulletin, 24,* 505–516.

Krug, K. (2007). The relationship between confidence and accuracy: Current thoughts of the literature and a new area of research. *Applied Psychology in Criminal Justice, 3,* 7.

Kruger, J., Eply, N., Parker, J. & Ng, Z-W, (2005). Egocentrism over e-mail: Can we communicate as well as we think? *Journal of Personality and Social Psychology, 89,* 925–936.

Kruglanski, A.W. (1987). Blame-placing schemata and attribution research. In C.F. Graumann & S. Moscovici (Eds), *Changing conceptions of conspiracy* (pp. 191–202). New York: Springer-Verlag.

Kruglanski, A.W. (2001). That 'vision thing': The state of theory in social and personality psychology at the edge of the new millennium. Journal of *Personality and Social Psychology, 80,* 871–875.

Krull, D.S. (2001). On partitioning the fundamental attribution error: Dispositionism and the correspondence bias. In G.B. Moscowitz (Ed.), *Cognitive social psychology. The Princeton Symposium on the Legacy and Future of Social Cognition* (pp. 211–227). Manwah, NJ: Erlbaum

Krull, D.S., Loy, M., Lin, J., Wang, C., Chen, S. & Zhao, X. (1999). The fundamental attribution error. Correspondence bias in individualistic and collectivist cultures. *Personality and Social Psychology Bulletin, 25,* 1208–1219.

Kugihara, N. (2001). Effects of aggressive behaviour and group size on collective escape in an emergency: A test between a social identity model and deindividuation theory. *British Journal of Social Psychology, 40,* 575–598.

Kuijer, R.G., Buunk, B.P., bema, J.F. & Wobbes, T. (2002). The relation between perceived inequity, marital satisfaction and emotions among couples facing cancer. *British Journal of Social Psychology, 41,* 39–56.

Kulbok, P.A. & Cox, C.L. (2002). Dimensions of adolescent health behavior. *Journal of Adolescent Health, 31,* 394–400.

Kulik, J.A. & Mahler, H.I.M. (1989a). Stress and affiliation in a hospital setting: Preoperative roommate preferences. *Personality and Social Psychology Bulletin, 15,* 183–193.

Kulik, J.A. & Mahler, H.I.M. (1989b). Social support and recovery from surgery. *Health Psychology, 8,* 221–238.

Kunda, Z. & Oleson, K.C. (1995). Maintaining stereotypes in the face of disconfirmation: Constructing grounds for subtyping deviants. *Journal of Personality and Social Psychology, 65,* 657–669.

Kunda, Z. & Spencer, S.J. (2003). When do stereotypes come to mind and when do they colour judgment? A goal-based theoretical framework for stereotype activation and application. *Psychological Bulletin, 129,* 522–544.

Kunstman, J.W. & Maner, J.K. (2011). Sexual overperception: Power, mating motives, and biases in social judgment. *Journal of Personality and Social Psychology, 100,* 282–294.

Kunstman, J.W. & Plant, E.A. (2008). Racing to help: Racial bias in high emergency helping situations. *Journal of Personality and Social Psychology, 95,* 1499–1510. doi: 10.1037/a0012822

Kurdek, L.A. (1993). Predicting marital dissolution: A five-year prospective longitudinal study of newlywed couples. *Journal of Personality and Social Psychology, 64,* 221–242.

Kurdek, L.A. (2000). Attractions and constraints as determinants of relationship commitment: Longitudinal evidence from gay, lesbian, and heterosexual couples. *Personal Relationships, 7,* 245–262.

Kutner, B., Wilkins, C. & Yarrow, P.R. (1952). Verbal attitudes and overt behavior involving social prejudice. *Journal of Abnormal and Social Psychology, 47,* 649–652.

Kwong, M.J., Bartholomew, K. & Dutton, D.G. (1999). Gender differences in patterns of relationship violence in Alberta. *Canadian Journal of Behavioural Science, 31,* 150–160.

Kyung, E.J., Menon, G. & Trope, Y. (2010). Reconstruction of things past: why do some memories feel so close and others so far away? *Journal of Experimental Social Psychology, 46,* 217–220.

Lachman, M.E. & Andreoletti, C. (2006). Strategy use mediates the relationship between control beliefs and memory performance for middle-aged and older adults. *The Journals of Gerontology: Series B: Psychological Sciences and Social Sciences, 61B(2),* 88–94.

Lai, J. & Linden, W. (1993). The smile of Asia: Acculturation effects on symptoms reporting. *Canadian Journal of Behavioural Science, 25,* 303–313.

Lakoff, R. (1975). *Language and the woman's place.* New York: Harper & Row.

Lalonde, R.N. (1992). The dynamics of group differentiation in the face of defeat. *Personality and Social Psychology Bulletin, 18,* 336–342.

Lalonde, R.N. & Cameron, J.E. (1993). An intergroup perspective on immigrant acculturation with a focus on collective strategies. *International Journal of Psychology*, *28*, 57–74.

Lalonde, R.N. & Gardner, R.C. (1984). Investigating a causal model of second language acquisition: Where does personality fit? *Canadian Journal of Behavioural Science*, *16*, 224–237.

Lamal, P.A. (1979). College student common beliefs about psychology. *Teaching of Psychology*, *6*, 336–342.

Lambert, G. (2012). The marketplace of perceptions. *Harvard Magazine*, *375*, 1–15.

Lambert, W.E. (1978). Some cognitive and sociocultural aspects of being bilingual. In J.P. Alatis (Ed.), *International dimensions of bilingual education*. Washington, DC: Georgetown University Press.

Lambert, W.E. (1981). Bilingualism and language acquisition. *Annals of the New York Academy of Sciences*, *379*, 9–22.

Lambert, W.E., Gardner, R.C., Barik, H.C. & Tunstall, K. (1963). Attitudinal and cognitive aspects of intensive study of a second language. *Journal of Abnormal and Social Psychology*, *66*, 358–368.

Lambert, W.E. & Taylor, D. (1984). Language and the education of ethnic minority children in Canada. In R.J. Samuda, J.W. Berry & M. Laferriere (Eds), *Multiculturalism in Canada*. Toronto: Allyn & Bacon.

Lambrecht, L., Kreifelts, B. & Wildgruber, D. (2012). Age-related decrease in recognition of emotional facial and prosodic expressions. *Emotion, 12*, 529–539.

Landsberg, M. (2009). *The tools of leadership: Vision, inspiration and momentum*. London: Profile Books.

Langer, E.J. (1975). The illusion of control. *Journal of Personality and Social Psychology*, *32*, 311–328.

Langer, E.J. (1989). *Mindfulness*. Reading, MA: Addison-Wesley.

Langer, E., Blank, A. & Chanowitz, B. (1978). The mindlessness of ostensibly thoughtful action: The role of 'placebic' information in interpersonal interaction. *Journal of Personality and Social Psychology*, *36*, 635–642.

Langer, E.J. & Rodin, J. (1976). The effects of choice and enhanced personal responsibility for the aged: A field experiment in an institutional setting. *Journal of Personality and Social Psychology*, *34*, 191–198.

Langfred, C.L. (1998). Is group cohesiveness a double-edged sword? An investigation of the effects of cohesiveness on performance. *Small Groups Research*, *29*, 124–143.

Langholtz, H.J. (Ed.) (1998). *The psychology of peacekeeping*. Westport, CT: Praeger.

Langlois, J.H., Kalakanis, L, Rubenstein, A.J., Larson, A., Hallam, M. & Smoot, M. (2000). Maxims or myths of beauty? A meta-analytic and theoretical review. *Psychological Bulletin*, *126*, 390–423.

Langlois, J.H. & Roggman, L.A. (1990). Attractive faces are only average. *Psychological Science*, *1*, 115–121.

Lansford, J.E., Skinner, A.T., Sorbring, E. & 15 Others (2012). Boys' and girls' relational and physical aggression in nine countries. *Aggressive Behavior*, *38*, 298–308.

LaPiere, R.T. (1934). Attitudes vs. actions. *Social Forces*, *13*, 230–237.

Larsen, K. (1974). Conformity in the Asch experiment. *Journal of Social Psychology*, *94*, 303–304.

Larson, R., Csikszentmihalyi, M. & Graef, R. (1982). Time alone in daily experience: Loneliness or renewal? In L.A. Peplau & D. Perlman (Eds). *Loneliness: A sourcebook of current theory, research and therapy* (pp. 40–53). New York: Wiley.

Lasch, C. (1979). *The culture of narcissism: American life in an age of diminishing expectations*. New York: Norton.

Lasswell, H. (1948). The structure and function of communication in society. In L. Bryson (Ed.), *The communication of ideas* (pp. 117–130). Urbana, IL: University of Illinois Press.

Latané, B. (1981). The psychology of social impact. *American Psychologist*, *36*, 343–356.

Latané, B. & Darley, J.M. (1968). Group inhibition of bystander intervention. *Journal of Personality and Social Psychology*, *10*, 215–221.

Latané, B. & Darley, J.M. (1969). Bystander 'apathy'. *American Scientist*, *57*, 244–268.

Latané, B. & Darley, J.M. (1970). *The unresponsive bystander: Why doesn't he help?* New York: Appleton-Century-Crofts.

Latané, B. & Rodin, J. (1969). A lady in distress: Inhibiting effects of friends and strangers on bystander intervention. *Journal of Experimental Social Psychology*, *5*, 187–202.

Latané, B., Williams, K. & Harkins, S. (1979). Many hands make light the work: The causes and consequences of social loafing. *Journal of Personality and Social Psychology, 37,* 822–832.

Latour, S., Houlden, P., Walker, L. & Thibaut, J.W. (1976). Some determinants of preferences for modes of conflict reduction. *Journal of Conflict Resolution, 20,* 319–356.

Latourette, T.R. & Meeks, S. (2000). Perceptions of patronizing speech by older women in nursing homes and in the community: Impact of cognitive ability and place of residence. *Journal of Language and Social Psychology, 19,* 463–473.

Lau, G.D.M., Tyson, G.A. & Bond, M.H. (2009). To punish or to rehabilitate: Sentencing goals as mediators between values, axioms and punitiveness towards offenders. *Journal of Psychology in Chinese Societies, 10,* 57–84.

Lau, R.R., Hartman, K.A. & Ware, J.E. (1986). Health as a value: Methodological and theoretical considerations. *Health Psychology, 5,* 25–43.

Lau, R.R. & Russell, D. (1980). Attribution in sports pages. *Journal of Personality and Social Psychology, 39,* 28–38.

Laursen, B. & Jensen-Campbell, L.A. (1999). The nature and functions of social exchange in adolescent romantic relationships. In W. Furman, B.B. Brown et al. (Eds), *The development of romantic relationships in adolescence: Cambridge studies in social and emotional development* (pp. 50–74). New York: Cambridge University Press.

Lavov, W., Ash, S. & Boberg, C. (2006). The atlas of North American English: Phonetics, phonology, and sound change. Berlin: Walter de Gruyter.

Le, B. & Agnew, C.R. (2003). Commitment and its theorized determinants: A meta-analysis of the investment model. *Personal Relationships, 10,* 37–57.

Lea, M. & Spears, R. (1995). Love at first byte? Building personal relationships over computer networks. In J.T. Wood & S. Duck (Eds), *Understudied relationships: Off the beaten track* (pp. 197–233). Thousand Oaks, CA: Sage.

Leach, M.M. & Harbin, J.J. (2009). Psychological ethics codes: A comparison of 24 countries. *Psychology: IUPsyS Global Resource.* http://e-book.lib.sjtu.edu.cn/iupsys/ethics/ethics_info.htm.

Leaper, C. & Robnett, R.D. (2011). Women are more likely than men to use tentative language, aren't they? A meta-analysis testing for gender differences and moderators. *Psychology of Women Quarterly,* 35, 129–142.

LeBon, G. (1895/1960). *The crowd: A study of the popular mind.* London: Ernest Benn.

Lee, J.A. (1973). Colours of love: an exploration of the ways to loving. Toronto: New Press.

Lee, K. & Ashton, M.C. (2005). Psychopathy, Machiavellianism, and Narcissism in the Five-Factor Model and the HEXACO model of personality structure. *Personality and Individual Differences, 38,* 1571–1582.

Lee, K., Ashton, M.C., Pozzebon, J.A., Visser, B.A. & Bourdage, J.S. (2009). Similarity and assumed similarity in personality reports of well-acquainted persons. *Journal of Personality and Social Psychology, 96,* 460–472.

Lee, S.W.S., Oyserman, D. & Bond, M. (2010). Am I doing better than you? That depends on whether you ask me in English or Chinese: Self-enhancement effects of language as a cultural mindset prime. *Journal of Experimental Social Psychology, 46,* 785–791.

Lefebvre, C.D., Marchand, Y., Smith, S.M. & Connolly, J.F. (2009). Use of event-related brain potentials (ERP's) to assess eyewitness accuracy and deception. *International Journal of Psychophysiology, 73, 218*–225.

Lefkovitz, M., Blake, B.R. & Mouton, M.J. (1955). Status factors in pedestrian violation of traffic signals. *Journal of Abnormal and Social Psychology, 51,* 704–706.

Leith, K.P. & Baumeister, R.F. (1996). Why do bad moods increase self-defeating behavior? Emotion, risk-taking and self-regulation. *Journal of Personality and Social Psychology, 71,* 1250–1267.

Lemaine, G. (1966). Inégalité, comparison et incomparabilité: Esquisse d'une théorie de l'originalité sociale. *Bulletin de Psychologie, 20,* 24–32.

Lemaine, G. (1974). Social differentiation and social originality. *European Journal of Social Psychology, 4,* 17–52.

Lemaine, G. & Kastersztein, J. (1972). Recherches sur l'originalité sociale, la différentiation et l'incomparabilité. *Bulletin de Psychologie, 25,* 673–693.

Lemaine, G., Kastersztein, J. & Personnaz, B. (1978). Social differentiation. In H. Tajfel (Ed.), *Differentiation between social groups: Studies in the social psychology of intergroup relations* (pp. 269–300). London: Academic Press.

550

Lennox, R.D. & Wolfe, R.N. (1984). Revision of the self-monitoring scale. *Journal of Personality and Social Psychology, 46*, 1349–1364.

Lepper, M.R., Zanna, M.P. & Abelson, R.P. (1970). Cognitive irreversibility in a dissonance reduction situation. *Journal of Personality and Social Psychology, 16*, 191–198.

Lerner, M.J. (1977). The justice motive: Some hypotheses as to its origins and forms. *Journal of Personality, 45*, 1–52.

Lerner, M.J. & Simmons, C.H. (1966). Observer's reaction to the 'innocent victim': Compassion or rejection? *Journal of Personality and Social Psychology, 4*, 203–210.

Leschied, A.W., Cummings, A.L., Van Brunschot, M., Cunningham, A. & Saunders, A. (2001). Aggression in adolescent girls: Implications for policy, prevention, and treatment. *Canadian Psychology, 42*, 200–215.

Lesthaeghe, R. & Meekers, D. (1986). Value changes and the dimensions of familism in the European Community. *European Journal of Population, 2*, 225–268.

Leung, K. (1997). Negotiation and reward allocations across cultures. In P.C. Earley & M. Erez (Eds), *New perspectives on international industrial organizational psychology.* San Francisco: New Lexington. (pp. 640–675).

Leung, K., Bond, M.H., Carment, D.W., Krishnan, L. & Liebrand, W.B.G. (1990). Effects of cultural femininity on preference for methods of conflict processing: A cross-cultural study. *Journal of Experimental Social Psychology, 26*, 373–388.

Leung, K., Brew, F.P., Zhang, Z-X & Zhang, Y. (2011). Harmony and conflict: A cross-cultural investigation in China and Australia. *Journal of Cross-Cultural Psychology, 42*, 795–816.

Leung, L. (2002). Loneliness, self-disclosure and ICQ ('I seek you') use. *CyberPsychology and Behavior, 5*, 241–251.

Levenson, R.W., Ekman, P. & Friesen, W.V. (1990). Voluntary facial action generates emotion-specific autonomic nervous system activity. *Psychophysiology, 27*,363–384.

Levenson, R.W., Ekman, P., Heider, K. & Friesen, W.V. (1992). Emotion and autonomic nervous system activity in the Minangkabau of West Sumatra. *Journal of Personality and Social Psychology, 62*, 972–988.

Levenson, R.W. & Ruef, A.M. (1992). *Journal of Personality and Social Psychology, 63*, 234–246.

Levenston, G.K., Patrick, C.J., Bradley, M.M. & Lang, P.J. (2000). The psychopath as observer: Emotion and attention in picture processing. *Journal of Abnormal Psychology, 109*, 373–385.

Leventhal, G.S. & Lane, D.W. (1970). Sex, age, and equity behavior. *Journal of Personality and Social Psychology, 15*, 312–316.

Leventhal, G.S., Weiss, T. & Long, G. (1969). Equity, reciprocity, and reallocating the rewards in the dyad. *Journal of Personality and Social Psychology, 13*, 300–315.

Leventhal, H. & Hirschman, R.S. (1982). Social psychology and prevention. In G.S. Sanders & J. Suls (Eds), *Social psychology of health and illness* (pp. 387–401). Hillsdale, NJ: Erlbaum.

Leventhal, H., Meyer, D.C. & Nerenz, D. (1980). The common sense representation of illness danger. In S. Rachman (Ed.), *Medical psychology* (Vol. 2). (pp. 184–211). New York: Pergamon.

Levesque, M.J. & Kenny, D.A. (1993). Accuracy of behavioral predictions at zero acquaintance: A social relations model. *Journal of Personality and Social Psychology, 65*, 1178–1187.

Levine, D. (2000). Virtual attraction: what rocks your boat. *CyberPsychology and Behavior, 3*, 565–573.

Levine, M. & Crowther, S. (2008). The responsive bystander: How social group membership and group size can encourage as well as inhibit bystander intervention. *Journal of Personality and Social Psychology, 95*, 1429–1439.

Levine, R., Sato, S., Hashimoto, T. & Verma, J. (1995). Love and marriage in eleven cultures. *Journal of Cross-Cultural Psychology, 26*, 554–571.

Levine, R.V., Martinez, T.S., Brase, G. & Sorenson, K. (1994). *Journal of Personality and Social Psychology, 67,* 69–82.

Levine, R.V., Norenzayan, A. & Philbrick, K. (2001). Cross-cultural differences in helping strangers. *Journal of Cross-cultural Psychology, 32*, 543–560.

Levinger, G.A. (1979). A social psychological perspective on marital dissolution. In G.A. Levinger & O.C. Moles (Eds). *Divorce and separation.* New York: Basic Books.

Levinger, G.A. & Snoek, J.D. (1972). *Attraction in relationships: A new look at interpersonal attraction.* Morristown, NJ: General Learning.

Levy, B. (1996). Improving memory in old age through implicit self-stereotypes. *Journal of Personality and Social Psychology, 71*, 1092–1107.

Levy, S.M. & Heiden, L.A. (1990). Personality and social factors in cancer outcome. In H.S. Friedman (Ed.), *Personality and disease* (pp. 254–279). New York: Wiley.

Lewin, K. (1948). *Resolving social conflicts.* New York: Harper & Row.

Lewin, K. (1951). *Field theory in social science.* New York: Harper.

Lewin, K., Lippitt, R. & White, R.K. (1939). Patterns of aggressive behavior in experimentally created social climates. *Journal of Social Psychology, 10,* 271–301.

Lewis, R.J., Derlegjt, V.J., Berndt, A., Morris, L.M. & Rose, S. (2001). An empirical analysis of stressors for gay men and lesbians. *Journal of Homosexuality, 42,* 63–88.

Loving, T.J., & Slatcher, R.B. (2013). Romantic relationships and health. In J. Simpson & L. Campbell (Eds), *The Oxford handbook of close relationships* (pp. 617–637). Oxford: New York.

Leyens, J. Ph., Rodriguez, A.P., Rodriguez, R.T., Gaunt, R., Paladino, M.P., Vaes, J. & Demoulin S. (2001). Psychological essentialism and the differential attribution of uniquely human emotions to ingroups and outgroups. *European Journal of Social Psychology, 31,* 395–411.

Lieberman, J.D. (2011). The utility of jury selection: Still murky after 30 years. *Current Directions in Psychological Science, 20,* 48–52.

Liew, J., Eisenberg, N., Losoya, S.H., Fabes, R.A., Guthrie, I.K. & Murphy, B.C. (2003). Children's physiological indices of empathy and their socioemotional adjustment: Does caregivers' expressivity matter? *Journal of Family Psychology, 17*(4), 584–597.

Lifton, R.J. (1986). *The Nazi doctors: Medical killing and the psychology of genocide.* New York: Basic Books.

Lind, E.A., Erickson, B.E., Friedland, N. & Dickenberger, M. (1978). Reactions to procedural models for adjudicative conflict resolution. *Journal of Conflict Resolution, 22,* 318–341.

Lind, E.A., Kurtz, S., Musante, L., Walker, L. & Thibaut, J. (1980). Procedure and outcome effects on reactions to adjudicated resolution of conflicts of interest. *Journal of Personality and Social Psychology, 39,* 643–653.

Linder, D.E., Cooper, J. & Jones, E.E. (1967). Decision freedom as a determinant of the role of incentive magnitude in attitude change. *Journal of Personality and Social Psychology, 6,* 245–254.

Lindsay, R.C.L. Wells, G.L. & O'Connor, F.J. (1989). Mock juror belief of accurate and inaccurate eye-witnesses: A replication and extension. *Law and Human Behavior, 13,* 333–339.

Lipp, R.F. (2001). Tragic, truly tragic: The Commons in modern life. In T.R. Machan (Ed.), *The Commons: Its tragedies and other follies.* (pp. 89–12). Stanford, CA: Hoover Press.

Lippmann, W. (1922). *Public opinion.* New York: The Free Press.

Lipton, J.A. & Marbach, J.J. (1984). Ethnicity and the pain experience. *Social Science & Medicine, 19,* 1279–1288.

Liska, A.E. (1984). A critical examination of the causal structure of the Fishbein/Ajzen attitude-behavior model. *Social Psychology Quarterly, 47,* 61–74.

Littlepage, G.E. & Pineault, M.A. (1979). Detection of deceptive factual statements from the body and the face. *Personality and Social Psychology Bulletin, 5,* 325–328.

Litvack-Miller, W., MacDougall, D. & Romney, D.M. (1997). The structure of empathy during middle childhood and its relationship to prosocial behaviour. *Genetic, Social and General Psychology Monographs, 123,* 303–324.

Lockwood, P. & Kunda, Z. (1997). Superstars and me. Predicting the impact of role models on the self. *Journal of Personality and Social Psychology, 73,* 91–103.

Lockwood, P. (2002). Could it happen to you? Predicting the impact of downward social comparison on the self. *Journal of Personality and Social Psychology, 82,* 343–358.

Lockwood, P. & Kunda, Z. (1999). Increasing salience of one's best selves can undermine inspiration by outstanding role models. *Journal of Personality and Social Psychology, 76,* 214–228.

Lockwood, P., Marshall, T.C. & Sadler, P. (2005). Promoting success or preventing failure: Cultural differences in motivation by positive and negative role models. *Personality and Social Psychology Bulletin, 31,* 379–392.

Loeber, R. & Hay, D.F. (1997). Key issues in the development of aggression and violence from childhood to early adulthood. *Annual Review of Psychology, 48,* 371–410.

Loftus, E.F. (1974). Reconstructing memory: The incredible eyewitness. *Psychology Today, 8,* 116–119.

Loftus, E.F. (1979). *Eyewitness testimony.* Cambridge, MA: Harvard University Press.

Loftus, E.F. (1983). Silence is not golden. *American Psychologist, 38*, 504–572.

Loftus, E.F. (1992). When a lie becomes memory's truth: Memory distortion after exposure to misinformation. *Current Directions in Psychological Science, 1*, 121–123.

Logel, C., Walton, G.M., Spencer, S.J., Iserman, E.C., Von Hippel, W. & Bell, A.E. (2009). Interacting with sexist men triggers social identity threat among female engineers. *Journal of Personality and Social Psychology, 96*, 1089–1103.

Lolliot, S., Schmid, K., Hewstone, M., Al Ramiah, A., Tausch, N. & Swart, H. (2013). Generalized effects of intergroup contact: The secondary transfer effect. In G. Hodson & M. Hewstone, (Eds). *Advances in intergroup contact* (pp. 81–112). New York: Psychology Press.

Lollis, C.M., Johnson, E.H. & Antoni, M.H. (1997), The efficacy of the health belief model for predicting condom usage and risky sexual practices in university students. *AIDS Education and Prevention, 9*, 551–563.

London, P. (1970). The rescuers: Motivational hypotheses about Christians who saved Jews from the Nazis. In J. Macaulay & L. Berkowitz (Eds), *Altruism and helping behavior* (pp. 241–250). New York: Academic Press.

Long, C.R. & Averill, J.R. (2003). Solitude: An exploration of benefits of being alone. *Journal of the Theory of Social Behavior, 33*, 21–44.

Lore, R.K. & Schultz, L.A. (1993). Control of human aggression. *American Psychologist, 48*, 16–25.

LoSchiavo, F.M. & Shatz, M.A. (2009). Reaching the neglected 95%. *American Psychologist, 64*, 571–574.

Lubek, I. (1990). Interactionist theory and disciplinary interactions: Psychology, sociology and social psychology in France. In W. Baker, R. Hezeuijk, B. Hyland & S. Terwee (Eds), *Recent trends in theoretical psychology, 2*, (pp. 347–350). New York: Springer-Verlag.

Luce, T.S. (1974). *The role of experience in inter-racial recognition.* Annual meeting of the American Psychological Association, New Orleans.

Luchins, A.S. (1957). Experimental attempts to minimize the impact of first impressions. In C.I. Hovland et al. (Eds), *The order of presentation in persuasion* (pp. 62–75). New Haven: Yale University Press.

Lund, F.H. (1925). The psychology of belief: IV. The law of primacy in persuasion. *Journal of Abnormal and Social Psychology, 20*, 183–191.

Lussier, Y. & Alain, M. (1986). Attribution et vécu émotionnel post-divorce. *Canadian Journal of Behavioural Science, 18*, 248–256.

Lydon, J.E. (1999). Commitment and adversity: A reciprocal relation. In A. Jeffrey & J. Warren (Eds). *Handbook of interpersonal commitment and relationship stability* (pp. 193–203). New York: Plenum Press.

Lydon, J.E., Fitzsimons, G.M. & Naidoo, L. (2003). Devaluation versus enhancement of attractive alternatives: A critical test using the calibration paradigm. *Personality & Social Psychology Bulletin, 29*, 349–359.

Lydon, J.E., Meana, M., Sepinwall, D., Richards, N. & Mayman, S. (1999). The commitment calibration hypothesis: When do people devalue attractive partners? *Personality and Social Psychology Bulletin, 25*, 152–161.

Lykken, D. (1974). Psychology and the lie detector industry. *American Psychologist, 29*, 725–739.

Lynch, J. (1977). *The broken heart: The medical consequences of loneliness.* New York: Basic Books.

Maass, A. (2009). Cultures two routes to embodiment. *European Journal of Social Psychology, 39*, 1290–1293.

Maass, A., Brigham, J.C. & West, S.G. (1985). Testifying on eyewitness reliability: Expert advice is not always persuasive. *Journal of Applied Social Psychology, 15*, 207–229.

Maass, A. & Clarke, R.D. III. (1984). Hidden impact of minorities: Fifteen years of minority influence research. *Psychological Bulletin, 95*, 428–450.

Maccoby, E.E. (1992). The role of parents in the socialization of children: An historical overview. *Developmental Psychology, 28*, 1006–1017.

MacCoun, R.J. & Kerr, N.L. (1988). Asymmetric influence in mock jury deliberation: Juror's bias for leniency. *Journal of Personality and Social Psychology, 54*, 21–33.

MacDonald, D., Jr. & Majunder, R.K. (1973). On the resolution and tolerance of cognitive inconsistency in another naturally occurring event: Attitudes and beliefs following the Senator Eagleton incident. *Journal of Applied Social Psychology, 3*, 132–143.

MacDonald, T.K. & Zanna, M.P. (1998). Cross-dimension ambivalence toward social groups: Can ambivalence affect intentions to hire feminists? *Personality and Social Psychology Bulletin, 24*, 427–441.

Machery, E. & Barrett, H.C. (2006). Essay review: Debunking adapting minds. *Philosophy of Science, 73*, 232–246.

Macionis, J.J., Clarke, J.M. & Gerber, L.M. (1994). *Sociology.* Scarborough: Prentice Hall Canada.

Macionis, J.J. & Gerber, L.M. (2011). *Sociology (7th Canadian Edition).* Toronto: Pearson.

Mackie, D.M. (1986). Social identification effects in group polarization. *Journal of Personality and Social Psychology, 50*, 720–728.

Maclean, H. & Kalin, R. (1994). Congruence between self-image and occupational stereotypes in students entering gender-dominated occupations. *Canadian Journal of Behavioural Science, 26*, 142–162.

Macrae, N., Alnwick, K.A., Milne, A.B. & Schloerscheidt, A.M. (2002). Person perception across the menstrual cycle: Hormonal influences on social-cognitive functioning. *Psychological Science, 13*, 532–536.

Macrae, C.N., Milne, A.B. & Bodenhausen, G.V. (1994). Stereotypes as energy-saving devices: A peek inside the cognitive toolbox. *Journal of Personality and Social Psychology, 66*, 37–47.

Maday, B.C. & Szalay, L.B. (1976). Psychological correlates of family socialization in the United States and Korea. In T. Williams (Ed.), *Psychological anthropology* (pp. 276–324). The Hague: Mouton.

Madden, T.J., Ellen, P.S. & Ajzen, I. (1992). A comparison of the theory of planned behavior and the theory of reasoned action. *Personality and Social Psychology Bulletin, 18*, 3–9.

Maddux, W.W., Yang, H., Falk, C., Adam, H., Adair, W., Endo, Y., Carmon, Z. & Heine, S.J. (2010). For whom is parting with possessions more painful? Cultural differences in the endowment effect. *Psychological Science, 21*, 1910–1917.

Madill, A. & Gough, B. (2008). Qualitative research and its place in psychological science. *Psychological Methods, 13*, 254–271.

Madon, S., Guyll, M., Aboufadel, K., Montiel, E., Smith, A., Palumbo, P. & Jussim, L. (2001). Ethnic and national stereotypes: The Princeton trilogy revisited and revised. *Personality and Social Psychology Bulletin, 27*, 996–1010.

Mahajan, N., Martinez, M.A., Gutierrez, N.L., Diesendruck, G., Banaji, M.R. & Santos, L.R. (2011). The evolution of intergroup bias: Perceptions and attitudes in rhesus macaques. *Journal of Personality and Social Psychology, 100*, 387–405.

Mahler, H.I.M. & Kulik, J.A. (1991). Health care involvement preferences and social-emotional recovery of male coronary-artery bypass patients. *Health Psychology, 10*, 399–408.

Major, B. & Deaux, K. (1982). Individual differences in justice behavior. In J. Greenberg & R. Cohen (Eds), *Equity and justice in social behavior* (pp. 43–76). New York: Academic Press.

Major, B., Kaiser, C.R. & McCoy, S.K. (2003). It's not my fault; When and why attributions to prejudice protect self-esteem. *Personality and Social Psychology Bulletin, 29*, 772–781.

Malamuth, N.M., Linz, D., Heavey, C.L., Barnes, G. & Acker, M. (1995). Using the confluence model of sexual aggressiveness to predict men's conflict with women: A 10-year follow-up study. *Journal of Personality and Social Psychology, 69*, 353–369.

Malkawi, A.H. (2011). Males' and females' language in Jordanian society. *Journal of Language Teaching and Research, 2*, 424–427.

Maloney, E.K., Lapinski, M.K. & Witte, K. (2011). Fear appeals and persuasion: A review and update of the Extended Parallel Process Model. *Social and Personality Psychology Compass, 5*, 206–219.

Mandela, N. (1994). Long walk to freedom: The autobiography of Nelson Mandela. New York: Back Bay Books.

Mann, J.W. (1963). Rivals of different rank. *Journal of Social Psychology, 61*, 11–27.

Mann, L. (1981). The baiting crowd in episodes of threatened suicide. *Journal of Personality and Social Psychology, 41*, 703–709.

Manne, S. & Badr, H. (2010). Intimacy processes and psychological distress among couples coping with head and neck or lung cancers. *Psycho-Oncology, 19*, 941–954.

Manning, R., Levine, M. & Collins, A. (2007). The Kitty Genovese murder and the social psychology of helping: The parable of the 38 witnesses. *American Psychologist, 62*, 555–562.

Mannino, C.A., Snyder, M. & Omoto, A.M. (2011). Why do people get involved? Motivations for volunteerism and other forms of social action. In D. Dunning (Ed.), *Social motivations* (pp. 127–146). New York: Psychology Press.

Mantell, D.M. (1971). The potential for violence in Germany. *Journal of Social Issues, 27*, 101–12.

Mantler, J., Schellenberg, E.G. & Page, J. (2003). *Canadian Journal of Behavioural Science 35*, 142–152.

Marecek, J. (2001). After the facts: Psychology and the study of gender. *Canadian Psychology*, *42*, 254–267.

Mares, M-L. & Woodard, E. (2005). Positive effects of television on children's social interactions: A meta-analysis, *Media Psychology*, *7*, 301–22.

Marini, Z., Fairbairn, L. & Zuber, R. (2001). Peer harassment in individuals with developmental disabilities: Towards the development of a multi-dimensional bullying identification model. *Developmental Disabilities Bulletin*, *29*, 170–195.

Markus, H. (1977). Self-schemata and processing information about the self. *Journal of Personality and Social Psychology*, *35*, 63–78.

Markus, H., Hamill, R. & Sentis, K. (1987). Thinking fat: Self-schemas for body weight and processing of weight-relevant information. *Journal of Applied Social Psychology*, *17*, 50–71.

Markus, H. & Kitayama, S. (1991). Culture and the self: Implications for cognition, emotion and motivation. *Psychological Review*, *98*, 224–253.

Markus, H. & Nurius, P. (1986). Possible selves. *American Psychologist*, *41*, 63–78.

Markus, H., Smith, J. & Moreland, R. (1985). Role of the self-concept in the perception of others. *Journal of Personality and Social Psychology*, *49*, 1494–1512.

Marlatt, G.A. & Gordon, J.R. (1979). Determinants of relapse: Implications for the maintenance of behavior change. In P. Davidson (Ed.), *Behavioral medicines: Changing health lifestyles* (pp. 410–452). New York: Brunner/Mazel.

Marmot, M., Ryff, C.D., Bumpass, L.L., Shipley, M. & Marks, N.F. (1997). Social inequalities: Next questions and converging evidence. *Social Science and Medicine*, *44*, 901–910.

Marquis, K.H., Marshall, J. & Oskamp, S. (1972). Testimony validity as a function of question form, atmosphere and item difficulty. *Journal of Applied Social Psychology*, *2*, 167–186.

Marsden, P.V (1987). Core discussion networks of Americans. *American Sociological Review*, *52*, 122–131.

Marsh, A.A., Kozak, M.N. & Ambady, N. (2007). Accurate identification of fear facial expressions predicts prosocial behaviour. *Emotion*, *7*, 239–251.

Marsh, H. W., & Alexander, S. Y. (1999). The lability of psychological ratings: The chameleon effect in global self-esteem. *Personality and Social Psychology Bulletin, 25*, 49–64.

Martin, C.L. (1986). A ratio measure of sex stereotyping. *Journal of Personality and Social Psychology*, *52*, 489–499.

Martin, R. & Hewstone, M. (1999). Minority influence and optimal problem solving. *European Journal of Social Psychology*, *29*, 825–832.

Martinie, M., Olive, T. & Millard, L. (2010). Cognitive dissonance induced by writing a counter-attitudinal essay facilitates performance on simple tasks but not on complex tasks that involve working memory. *Journal of Experimental Social Psychology*, *46*, 587–594.

Mashek, D., Aron, A. & Fisher, H. (2000). Identifying, evoking and measuring intense feelings of romantic love. *Representative Research in Social Psychology*, *24*, 48–55.

Mashek, D., Le, B., Israel, K. & Aron, A. (2011). Wanting less closeness in romantic relationships. *Basic and Applied Social Psychology*, *33*, 333–345.

Maslach, C. & Jackson. S.E. (1982). Burn-out in health professions. A social psychological analysis. In G.S. Sanders & J. Suls (Eds) *Social psychology of health and illness* (pp. 227–252). Hillsdale: Lawrence Erlbaum.

Masuda, T., Ellsworth, P.C.,Mesquita, B.,Leu, J.,Tanida, S. & Van de Veerdonk, E. (2008). Placing the face in context: Cultural differences in the expression of facial emotion. *Journal of Personality and Social Psychology*, *94*, 365–381.

Matlin, M. & Stang, D. (1978). *The Pollyanna principle: Selectivity of language, memory and thought.* Cambridge, MA: Schenkman.

Matsumoto, D. (2006). Culture and nonverbal behaviour. In V.L. Manusov & M.L. Atterson, *The Sage handbook of nonverbal communication*. London: Sage. (pp. 219–236).

Matsumoto, D. Hwang, H.S. & Yamada, H. (2012). Cultural differences in the relative contributions of face and context to judgments of emotion. *Journal of Cross-Cultural Psychology*, *43*, 198–218.

Matsumoto, D., Yoo, S. H., Fontaine, J. & 56 others. (2008). Mapping expressive differences around the world. The relationship between emotional display rules and individualism versus collectivism. *Journal of Cross-Cultural Psychology, 39*, 55–74.

Matthews, J.L. & Matlock, T. (2011). Understanding the link between spatial distance and social distance. *Social psychology, 42*, 185–192.

Matthews, K.A. & Gallo, L. (2011). Psychological perspectives on pathways linking socioeconomic status and physical health. *Annual Review of Psychology, 62*, 501–530.

Matthews, K.A., Glass, D.C., Rosenman, R.H. & Bortner, R.W. (1977). Competitive drive, Pattern A and coronary heart disease: A further analysis of some data from the Western Collaborative Study. *Journal of Chronic Disease, 30*, 489–498.

Maunder, R.G. & Hunter, J.J. (2001). Attachment and psychosomatic medicine: Developmental contributions to stress and disease. *Psychosomatic Medicine, 63*, 556–567.

Mayberry, R.I. & Nicoladis, E. (2000). Gesture reflects language development: Evidence from bilingual children. *Current Directions in Psychological Science, 9*, 192–196.

Maynard, D.W. & Peräkylä, A. (2003). Language and social interaction. In J. Delamater (Ed.), *Handbook of Social Psychology.* New York: Kluwer Academic.

McAndrew, S.T. (2009). The interacting roles of testosterone and challenges to status in human male aggression. *Aggression and Violent Behaviour, 14*, 330–335.

McCaul, K.D., Ployart, R.E., Hinsz, V.B. & McCaul, H.S. (1995). Appraisal of a consistent versus a similar politician: Voter preferences and intuitive judgments. *Journal of Personality and Social Psychology, 68*, 292–299.

McCauley, C. (1989). The nature of social influence in group-think: Compliance and internalization. *Journal of Personality and Social Psychology, 57*, 250–260.

McClelland, D.C. (1967). *The achieving society.* New York: Free Press.

McClelland, D.C., Alexander, C. & Marks, E. (1982). The need for power, stress, immune function and illness among male prisoners. *Journal of Abnormal Psychology, 91*, 61–70.

McClintock, C.G. & Hunt, R.G. (1975). Nonverbal indicators of affect and deception in an interview setting. *Journal of Applied Social Psychology, 5*, 54–67.

McClintock, C.G. & Nuttin, J.M., Jr. (1969). Development of competitive game behavior in children across two cultures. *Journal of Experimental Social Psychology, 5*, 203–218.

McCloskey, M. & Egeth, H.E. (1983). Eyewitness identification: What can a psychologist tell a jury? *American Psychologist, 38*, 550–563.

McCreary, D.R. (1990). Multidimensionality and the measurement of gender role attributes: A comment on Archer. *British Journal of Social Psychology, 29*, 265–272.

McCreary, D.R. & Korabik, K. (1994). Examining the relationship between socially desirable and undesirable aspects of agency and communion. *Sex Roles, 31*, 637–651.

McCreary, D.R. & Sadava, S.W. (1995). Mediating the relationship between masculine gender role stress and work satisfaction: The influence of coping strategies. *Journal of Men's Studies, 4*, 141–152.

McCreary, D.R. & Sadava, S.W. (2000). Stress, alcohol use and alcohol problems: The mediating role of negative and positive affect in two cohorts of young adults. *Journal of Studies on Alcohol, 61*, 466–474.

McCullough, M.E. (2001). Forgiveness: Who does it and how do they do it? *Current Directions in Psychological Science, 10*, 194–197.

McCullough, M.E., Emmons, R.A. & Tsang, J. (2002). The grateful disposition: A conceptual and empirical topography. *Journal of Personality and Social Psychology, 82*, 112–127.

McCullough, M.E., Kilpatrick, S.D., Emmons, R.A. & Larson, D.B. (2001). Is gratitude a moral affect? *Psychological Bulletin, 127*, 249–266.

McCullough, M.E., Worthington, E.L., Jr. & Rachal, K.C. (1997). Interpersonal forgiving in close relationships. *Journal of Personality and Social Psychology, 73*, 321–336.

McFarland, C. & Buehler, R. (1998). The impact of negative affect on autobiographical memory: The role of self-focussed attention to moods. *Journal of Personality and Social Psychology, 75*, 1424–1440.

McFarland, C., Ross, M. & Giltrow, M. (1992). Biased recall of older adults: The role of implicit theories in aging. *Journal of Personality and Social Psychology, 62*, 837–850.

McGee, B.J., Hewitt, P.L., Sherry, S.B., Parkin, M. & Flett, G.L. (2005). Perfectionistic self-presentation, body image and eating disorder symptoms. *Body Image, 2*, 29–40.

556

McGrath, J. (1984). *Groups: Interaction and performance.* Englewood Cliffs, NJ: Prentice-Hall.

McGregor, I., Newby-Clark, I.R. & Zanna, M.P. (1999). Epistemic discomforts as moderated by simultaneous accessibility of inconsistent elements. In E. Harmon-Jones & J. Mills (Eds), *Cognitive dissonance theory 40 years later: A revival with revisions and controversies* (pp. 166–192). Washington, DC: American Psychological Association.

McGuire, W.J. (1968). Personality and susceptibility to social influence. In E.F. Borgatta & W.W. Lambert (Eds), *Handbook of personality: Theory and research* (pp. 1130–1187). Chicago: Rand-McNally.

McGuire, W.J. (1969). The nature of attitudes and attitude change. In G. Lindzey & E. Aronson (Eds), *The handbook of social psychology* (2nd ed.). (Vol. 3). (pp. 136–314). New York: Addison-Wesley.

McGuire, W.J. & McGuire, C.V. (1988). Content and process in the experience of self. In L. Berkowitz (Ed.), *Advances in experimental social psychology* (Vol. 21). (pp. 97–144). New York: Academic Press.

McGuire, W.J. & Papageorgis, D. (1961). The relative efficacy of various types of prior belief-defense in producing immunity against persuasion. *Journal of Abnormal & Social Psychology*, 62, 327–337.

McGuire, W.J. & Papageorgis, D. (1962). Effectiveness of forewarning in developing resistance to persuasion. *Public Opinion Quarterly*, 26, 24–32.

McIntosh, D.N. (1996). Facial feedback hypotheses: Evidence, implications, and directions. *Motivation and Emotion*, 20, 121–147.

McKee, I.R. & Feather, N.T. (2008). Revenge, retribution and values: Social attitudes and punitive sentencing. *Social Justice Research, 21*, 138–163.

McKelvie, S. (2000). Quantifying the availability heuristic with famous names. *North American Journal of Psychology*, 2, 347–356.

McKenna, K.Y.A. (2002). Relationship formation on the Internet. What's the big attraction? *Journal of Social Issues, 58* (1), 9–31.

McKenna, K.Y.A. & Bargh, J.A (2000). Plan 9 from cyberspace: The implications of the Internet for personality and social psychology. *Personality and Social Psychology Review*, 4, 57–75.

McKinnon, S. (2005). Marriage: A critique of the genetic and gender calculus of evolutionary psychology. In S. McKinnon & S. Silverman (Eds), *Complexities: Beyond nature & nurture.* Chicago, IL: University of Chicago Press (pp. 106–131).

McLaren, L. (2007). Socioeconomic status and obesity. *Epidemiological Review*, 29, 29–48.

McLuhan, M. (1972). *Culture is our business.* New York: Ballantine Books.

McLuhan, M. & Powers, B.R. (1989). The global village: Transformations in world life and media in the 21st century. New York: Oxford University Press.

McPhail, C. (1991). *The myth of the madding crowd.* New York: Aldine De Gruyter.

Meadon, M. & Spurrett, D. (2010). It's not just the subjects – there are too many WEIRD researchers. *Behavioural and Brain Sciences*, 33, 104–105. doi:10.1017/S0140525X10000208

Medvec, V.H., Madey, S.F. & Gilovich, T. (2002). When less is more: Counterfactual thinking and satisfaction among Olympic medalists. In T. Gilovich, D. Griffin & D. Kahneman (Eds) *Heuristics and biases: The psychology of intuitive judgment.* (pp. 211–222). Cambridge, UK: Cambridge University Press.

Medvene, L.J., Teal, C.R. & Slavich, S. (2000). Including the other in the self: Implications for judgments of equity and satisfaction in close relationships. *Journal of Social and Personal Relationships*, 19, 396–419.

Meeker, R.J. & Shure, G.H. (1969). Pacifist bargaining tactics: Some 'outsider' influences. *Journal of Conflict Resolution*, 13, 487–493.

Meeus, W. & Raaijmakers, Q. (1986). Administrative obedience as a social phenomenon. In W. Doise & S. Moscovici (Eds), *Current issues in European social psychology.* (Vol. 2). (pp. 19–52). Cambridge, UK: Cambridge, University Press.

Megargee, E.I. (1966). Undercontrolled and overcontrolled personality types in extreme antisocial aggression. *Psychological Monographs*, 80, whole issue.

Mehrabian, A. (1971). Nonverbal betrayal of feeling. *Journal of Experimental Research in Personality*, 5, 64–73.

Meier, N.C., Mennenga, G.H. & Stoltz, H.J. (1941). An experimental approach to the study of mob behavior. *Journal of Abnormal Psychology*, 36, 506–524.

Melamed, S., Rabinowitz, S., Feiner, M., Weisberg, E. & Ribak, J. (1996). Usefulness of the protection motivation theory in explaining hearing protection device use among male industrial workers. *Health Psychology*, *15*, 209–215.

Melo, L., Colin, J, Delahunty, C., Forde, C. & Cox, D.N. (2010). Lifetime wine drinking, changing attitudes and associations with current wine consumption: A pilot study indicating how experience may drive current behavior. *Food Quality and Preference*, *21*, 784–790.

Meloy, J.R. Hempel, A.G., Gray, B.T., Mohandie, K., Shiva, A.A. & Richards, T.C. (2004). A comparative analysis of North American adolescent and adult mass murderers. *Behavioral Sciences and the Law*, *22*, 291–309.

Meloy, J.R. Hempel, A.G., Mohandie, K., Shiva, A.A. & Gray, B.T. (2001). Offender and offense characteristics of a nonrandom sample of adolescent mass murderers. *Journal of the American Academy of Child & Adolescent Psychiatry*, *40*, 719–728.

Meltzoff, A.N. & Moore, M.K. (1977). Imitations of facial and manual gestures by human neonates. *Science*, *198*, 75–78.

Menon, T., Morris, M., Chiu, C. & Hong, Y. (1999). Culture and the construal of agency: attribution to individual versus group dispositions. *Journal of Personality and Social Psychology*, *76*, 701–717.

Merari, A. (2010). *Driven to death*. Oxford: Oxford University Press.

Merrens, M.R. (1973). Nonemergency helping behavior in various sized communities. *Journal of Social Psychology*, *90*, 327–328.

Metropolitan Area Child Study Research Group (2007). Changing the way children 'think' about aggression: Social-cognitive effects of a preventive intervention. *Journal of Consulting and Clinical Psychology*, *75*, 160–167.

Meumann, E. (1904). Haus-und schularbeit: Experimente an kindern der volksschule. *Die Deutsche Schule*, *8*, 278–303, 337–359, 416–431.

Meyer, I.H. (2003). Prejudice, social stress and mental health in lesbian, gay and bisexual populations: Conceptual issues and research evidence. *Psychological Bulletin*, *129*, 674–697.

Mezulis, A.H., Abramson, L.Y., Hyde, J.S. & Hankin, B.L. (2004). Is there a universal positive bias in attributions? A meta-analytic review of individual, developmental and cultural differences in the self-serving bias. *Psychological Bulletin*, *130*, 711–747.

Middlebrook, P.N. (1974). *Social psychology and modern life*. New York: Alfred A. Knopf.

Midlarsky, E. & Bryan, J.H. (1972). Affect expressions and children's imitative altruism. *Journal of Experimental Research in Personality*, *6*, 195–203.

Miettinen, T. & Suetens, S. (2008). Communication and guilt in a Prisoner's Dilemma. *Journal of Conflict Resolution*, *52*, 945–960.

Mikula, G. (1994). Perspective-related differences in interpretations of injustice by victims and victimizers: A test with close relationships. In M.J. Lerner & G. Mikula (Eds), *Entitlement and the affectional bond: Justice in close relationships. Critical issues in social justice* (pp. 175–203). New York: Plenum Press.

Mikulincer, M. & Shaver, P.R. (2007). *Attachment in adulthood: Structure, dynamics and change*. New York: Guilford Press.

Miles, D. R. & Carey, G. (1997). Genetic and environmental architecture on human aggression. *Journal of Personality and Social Psychology*, *72*, 207–217.

Milgram, S. (1963). Behavioral study of obedience. *Journal of Applied Social Psychology*, *67*, 371–378.

Milgram, S. (1964). Issues in the study of obedience: A reply to Baumrind. *American Psychologist*, *19*, 848–852.

Milgram, S. (1965). Some conditions of obedience and disobedience to authority. *Human Relations*, *18*, 57–76.

Milgram, S. (1970). The experience of living in cities. *Science*, *167*, 1461–1468.

Milgram, S. (1974). *Obedience to authority*. New York: Harper & Row.

Miller, A.G. (2009). Reflections on 'replicating Milgram' (Burger, 2009). *American Psychologist*, *64*, 20–27.

Miller, D.T. & Porter, C.A. (1983). Self-blame in victims of violence. *Journal of Social Issues*, *39*, 139–152.

Milgram, S. & Toch, H. (1969). Collective behavior: Crowds and social movements. In G. Lindzey & E. Aronson (Eds), *The handbook of social psychology* (2nd ed.). (Vol. 4). (pp. 507–610). Reading, MA: Addison-Wesley.

Miller, G.E., Dopp, J.M., Myers, H.F., Stevens, S.Y. & Fahey, J.L. (1999). Psychosocial predictors of natural killer cell mobilization during marital conflict. *Health Psychology*, *18*, 262–271.

Miller, G.R. & Burgoon, J.K. (1982). Factors influencing judgments of witness credibility and truthfulness. In N.L. Kerr & R.M. Bray (Eds), *The psychology of the courtroom* (pp. 169–194). New York: Academic Press.

Miller, J.G. (1984). Culture and the development of everyday social explanation. *Journal of Personality and Social Psychology*, *46*, 961–978.

Miller, J.G. & Bersoff, D.M. (1992). Culture and moral judgment: How are conflicts between justice and interpersonal responsibilities resolved? *Journal of Personality and Social Psychology, 62,* 541–554.

Miller, L.E., Grabell, A., Thomas, A., Bermann, E. & Graham-Bermann, S.A. (2012). The associations between community violence, television violence, intimate partner violence, parent–child aggression, and aggression in sibling relationships of a sample of preschoolers. *Psychology of Violence*, *2*, 165–178.

Miller, N. & Campbell, D.T. (1959). Recency and primacy in persuasion as a function of the timing of speeches and measurement. *Journal of Abnormal and Social Psychology*, *59*, 1–9.

Miller, R.M. & Rivenbark, W. (1970). Sexual differences in physical attractiveness as a determinant of heterosexual liking. *Psychological Reports*, *27*, 701–702.

Miller, S.M. & Mangan, C.E. (1983). Interacting effects of information and coping style in adapting to gynecologic stress. Should the doctor tell all? *Journal of Personality and Social Psychology*, *45*, 223–236.

Mills, J. & Harvey, J. (1972). Opinion change as a function of when information about the communicator is received and whether he is attractive or expert. *Journal of Personality and Social Psychology*, *21*, 52–55.

Milroy, James, and Lesley Milroy (1999), *Authority in Language: Investigating Standard English*, (3rd ed.), Routledge: New York.

Minton, H.L. (1992). Root metaphors and the evolution of American social psychology. *Canadian Psychology*, *33*, 547–553.

Miranda, F., Caballero, B., Gomez & Zamorano M. (1981). 'Obediencia a la autoridad [Obedience to Authority]'. *Psiquis* 2: 212–221.

Mitchell, J., McCrae, C. & Banaji, M. (2004). Encoding-specific effects of social cognition on the neural correlates of subsequent memory. *Journal of Neuroscience*, *24*, 4912–4917.

Moghaddam, F.M. (1987). Psychology in the three worlds, as reflected by the crisis in social psychology and the move toward indigenous third-world psychology. *American Psychologist*, *42*, 912–920.

Moghaddam, F.M. (1990). Modulative and generative orientations in psychology: Implications for psychology in the three worlds. *Journal of Social Issues*, *46*, 21–41.

Molnar, D.S., Sadava, S.W., Flett, G.L. & Colautti, J. (2012). Perfectionism and health: A mediational analysis of the roles of stress, social support and health-related behaviours. *Psychology & Health*, *27*, 846–864.

Mongrain, M. & Vettese, L.C. (2003). Conflict over emotional expression: Implications for interpersonal communication. *Personality and Social Psychology Bulletin*, *29*, 545–555.

Monks, C.P., Smith, P.K., Naylor, P., Barter, C., Ireland, J.L. & Coyne, I. (2009). Bullying in different contexts: Commonalities, differences and the role of theory. *Aggression and Violence*, *14*, 146–156.

Monson, T.C. & Hesley, J.W. (1982). Causal attributions for behaviors consistent or inconsistent with an actor's personality traits: Differences between those offered by actors and observers. *Journal of Personality and Social Psychology*, *18*, 416–432.

Monsour, M. (1992). Meanings of intimacy in cross- and same-sex friendships. *Journal of Social and Personal Relationships*, *9*, 277–295.

Montepare, J.M. & Vega, C. (1988). Women's vocal reactions to intimate and casual male friends. *Personality and Social Psychology Bulletin, 14,* 103–113.

Moody, E.J. (2001). Internet use and its relationship to loneliness. *CyberPsychology and Behavior*, *4*, 393–401.

Moody, E.J., McIntosh, D.N., Mann, L.J. & Weisser, K.R. (2007). More than mere mimicry? The influence of emotion on rapid facial reactions to faces. *Emotion*, *7*, 447–457.

Moore, T. E., Copeland, P., & Schuller, R. (2009). Deceit, betrayal and the search for truth: Legal and psychological perspectives on the 'Mr Big' strategy. *Criminal Law Quarterly, 55,* 349– 405

Moore, T.E. & Fitzsimmons, C.L. (2011). Justice Imperiled: False Confessions & the Reid technique. *Criminal Law Quarterly*, *57*, 509–542.

Moore, T.E., Pepler, D., Mae, R. & Kates, M. (1989). Child witnesses to family violence: New directions for research and intervention. In B. Pressman, G. Cameron & M. Rothery (Eds), *Intervening with assaulted women: Current theory, research, and practice* (pp. 75–91). Hillsdale, NJ: Lawrence Erlbaum Assoc.

Moore, T.M., Elkins, S.R., McNulty, J.K., Kivisto, A.J. & Handsel, V.A. (2011). Alcohol use and intimate partner violence perpetration among college students: assessing the temporal association using electronic diary technology. *Psychology of Violence, 1*, 315–328.

Moorhead, G., Ference, R. & Neck, C.P. (1991). Group decision fiascos continue: Space shuttle Challenger and a revised groupthink framework, *Human Relations, 44*, 539–550.

Moos, R.H. (1982). Coping with acute health crises. In T. Millon, C. Green & R. Meagher (Eds), *Handbook of clinical health psychology* (pp. 129–151). New York: Plenum.

Moradian, A. (2009). Domestic violence against single and married women in Iranian society. *Tolerancy International*. http://en.tolerancy.org/index.php?option=com_content&view=article&id=176:2009-09-15-08-37-55&catid=43:events-a-reports&Itemid=90. Retrieved September 29, 2012.

Morales, A.C., Scott, M.L. & Yorkston, E.A. (2012). The role of accent standardness in message preference and recall. *Journal of Advertising, 41*, 33–45.

Moreland, R.L. & Levine, J.M. (1982). Socialization in small groups: Temporal Changes in individual-group relations. In L. Berkowitz (Ed.), *Advances in Experimental Social Psychology*, (Vol. 15). (pp. 137–193). London: Academic Press.

Moreland, R.L. & Zajonc, R.B (1982). Exposure effects in person perception: Familiarity, similarity and attraction. *Journal of Experimental Social Psychology, 18*, 395–415.

Morris, M. & Peng, K. (1994). Culture and cause: American and Chinese attributions for social and physical events. *Journal of Personality and Social Psychology, 67*, 949–971.

Morris, W.N. & Miller, R.S. (1975). The effects of consensus-breaking and consensus preempting partners on reduction of conformity. *Journal of Experimental Social Psychology, 11*, 215–223.

Morrison, E.R., Gralewski, L., Campbell, N. & Penton-Voak, I.S. (2007). Facial movement varies by sex and is related to attractiveness. *Evolution and Human Behavior, 28*, 186–192.

Morrison, M., Tay, L. & Diener, E. (2011). Subjective well-being and national satisfaction: Findings from a worldwide survey. *Psychological Science, 22*, 166–171.

Morry, M.M., Kito, M. & Ortiz, L. (2011). The attraction-similarity mode and dating couples: Projection, perceived similarity and psychological benefits. *Personal Relationships, 18*, 125–143.

Morse, D.S., Paldi, Y., Egbarya, S.S. & Clark, C.J. (2012). 'An effect that is deeper than beating': Family violence in Jordanian women. *Families, Systems & Health, 30*, 19–31.

Moscovici, S. (1980). Toward a theory of conversion behavior. In L. Berkowitz (Ed.), *Advances in experimental social psychology* (Vol. 13). (pp. 202–239). New York: Academic Press.

Moscovici, S. (1981). On social representations. In J.P. Forgas (Ed.), *Social cognition: Perspectives on everyday understanding* (pp. 211–254). London: Academic Press.

Moscovici, S. & Hewstone, M. (1983). Social representation and social explanation: From the naive to the amateur scientist. In M. Hewstone (Ed.), *Attribution theory: Social and functional explanations* (pp. 145–189). Oxford: Basil Blackwell.

Moscovici, S., Mugny, G. & Van Avermaet, E. (1985). (Eds). *Perspectives on minority influence.* Cambridge: Cambridge University Press.

Moss, E.M.A. (2012). Voices silenced, tweets heard. *Foreign Service Journal, 89*, 11.

Moyer-Gusé, E. & Nabi, R.L. (2010). Explaining the effects of narrative in an entertainment television programme: Overcoming resistance to persuasion. *Human Communications Research, 36*, 26–52.

Muczyk, J.P. & Holt, D.T. (2008). Toward a cultural contingency model of leadership. *Journal of Leadership & Organizational Studies, 14*, 277–286.

Mullen, B. & Copper, C. (1994). The relation between group cohesiveness and performance: An integration. *Psychological Bulletin, 115*, 210–227.

Mullen, B., Salas, E. & Driskell, J.E. (1989). Salience, motivation, and artifact as contributions to the relation between participation rate and leadership. *Journal of Experimental Social Psychology, 25*, 545–559.

Muller, D. & Butera, F. (2007). The focusing effect of self-evaluation threat in coaction and social comparison. *Journal of Personality and Social Psychology, 93*, 194–211.

Muller, R.T. & Diamond, T. (1999). Father and mother physical abuse and child aggressive behaviour in two generations. *Canadian Journal of Behavioural Science, 31*, 221–228.

Mullin, C.R. & Linz, D. (1995). Desensitization and resensitization to violence against women: Effects of exposure to sexually violent films on judgments of domestic violence victims. *Journal of Personality and Social Psychology, 69*, 449–459.

Munhall, K.G. & Buchan, J.N. (2004). Something in the way she moves. *Trends in Cognitive Sciences, 8*, 51–53.

Munsterberg, H. (1908). *On the witness stand: Essays on psychology and crime.* New York: Doubleday Page.

Muraven, M. & Baumeister, R.F. (2000). Self-regulation and the depletion of limited resource. Does self-control resemble a muscle? *Psychological Bulletin, 126*, 247–259.

Murphy, P.L. & Miller, C.T. (1997). Post-decisional dissonance and the commodified self-concept: A cross-cultural examination. *Personality and Social Psychology Bulletin, 23*, 50–62.

Murphy, S.M., Wayne, S.J., Liden, R.C. & Erdogan, B. (2003). Understanding social loafing: The role of justice perceptions and exchange relationships. *Human Relations, 56*, 61–84.

Murray, S.L., Bellavia, G.M., Rose, P. & Griffin, D.W. (2003). Once hurt, twice hurtful. How perceived regard regulates daily marital interactions. *Journal of Personality and Social Psychology, 84*, 126–147.

Murray, S.L., Holmes, J.G. & Griffin, D.W. (1996). The benefits of positive illusions: Idealization and the construction of satisfaction in close relationships. *Journal of Personality and Social Psychology, 70*, 79–98.

Murray, S.L., Rose, P., Bellavia, G., Holmes, J.G. & Kusche, A. (2002). When rejection stings: How self-esteem constrains relationship-enhancement processes. *Journal of Personality and Social Psychology, 83*, 556–573.

Murstein, B.I. (1972). Physical attractiveness and marital choice. *Journal of Personality and Social Psychology, 22*, 8–12.

Myers, D.G. (2012). Reflections on religious belief and prosociality: Comment on Galen (2012). *Psychological Bulletin, 138*, 913–917. doi: 10.1037/a0029009

Myers, S.A. & Anderson, C.M. (2008). *The fundamentals of small group communication.* London: Sage.

Myrtek, M. (2001). Meta-analyses of prospective studies on coronary heart disease, type A personality, and hostility. *International Journal of Cardiology, 79*, 245–251.

Nabi, R.L. (2003). 'Feeling' resistance: Exploring the role of emotionally evocative visuals in inducing inoculation. *Media Psychology, 5*, 199–223.

Nadler, A. & Fisher, J.D. (1984). Effects of donor-recipient relationship on recipient's reactions to aid. In E. Staub, D. Bar-Tal, J. Karylowski & J. Reykowski (Eds), *Development and maintenance of prosocial behavior* (pp. 397–418). New York: Plenum Press.

Nagin, D. & Tremblay, R.E. (1999). Trajectories of boys' physical aggression, opposition, and hyperactivity on the path to physically violent and non-violent juvenile delinquency. *Child Development, 70*, 1181–1196.

Napier, J. & Tyler T. (2008). Does moral conviction really override concerns about procedural justice? A reexamination of the value protection model. *Social Justice Research 21*, 509–528.

Nathanson, A.I. (2003). The effects of mediation content and form on children's responses to violent television. *Human Communication Research, 29*, 111–134.

Navarette, C.D., Fessler, D.M.T. & Eng, S.J. (2009). Elevated ethnocentrism in the first trimester of pregnancy. *Evolution and Human Behavior, 28*, 60–65.

Neal, T.M.S., Christiansen, A., Bornstein, B.H. & Robicheaux, T.R. (2012). The effects of mock jurors' beliefs about eyewitness performance on trial judgments. *Psychology Crime and Law 18*, 49–64.

Neighbors, C., Vietor, N.A. & Knee, C.R. (2002). A motivational model of driving anger and aggression. *Personality and Social Psychology Bulletin (PSPB), 28*, 324–335.

Nel, E., Helmreich, R. & Aronson, E. (1969). Opinion change in the advocate as a function of the persuasibility of his audience. *Journal of Personality and Social Psychology, 12*, 117–124.

Nelly, A-K, Goldstein, R.Z., Tomasi, D., Woicik, P.A., Moeller, S.J. et al. (2009). Neural mechanisms of anger regulation as a function of genetic risk for violence. *Emotion, 9*, 385–396.

Nelson, C. & McLemore, T. (1988). *National Centre for Health Statistics. The National Ambulatory Medical Care survey: U.S. 1975–1981 and 1985 trends.* Vital and Health Statistics, series 13, no. 93, DHHS pub. no. (PHS) 88–1754. Washington, DC: US Government Printing Office.

Nelson, T. E., Biernat, M. R., Manis, M. (1990). Everyday base rates (sex stereotypes): Potent and resilient. *Journal of Personality and Social Psychology*, *59*, 664–675.

Nemati, A. & Bayer, J.M. (2007). Gender differences in the use of linguistic forms in the speech of men and women: a comparative study of Persian and English. *Language in India*, *7*, 2–12.

Nemeth, C. (1981). Jury trials: Psychology and law. *Advances in Experimental Social Psychology*, *14*, 309–367.

Nemeth, C. (1986). Differential contributions of majority and minority influence. *Psychological Review*, *93*, 23–32.

Nemeth, C.J. & Chiles, C. (1988). Modelling courage: The role of dissent in fostering independence. *European Journal of Social Psychology*, *18*, 275–280.

Nemeth, C.J. & Kwan, J.L. (1987). Minority influence, divergent thinking and detection of correct solutions. *Journal of Applied Psychology*, *17*, 788–799.

Neuberg, S.L., Cialdini, R.B., Brown, S.L., Luce, C., Sagarin, B.D. & Lewis, B.P. (1997). Does empathy lead to anything more than superficial helping? Comment on Batson et al. (1997*). Journal of Personality & Social Psychology*, *73*, 510–516.

Neumann, R. & Strack, F. (2000). 'Mood contagion': The automatic transfer of mood between persons. *Journal of Personality and Social Psychology*, *79*, 211–223.

Newby-Clark, I.R., McGregor, I. & Zanna, M.P. (2002). Thinking and caring about cognitive inconsistency: When and for whom does attitudinal ambivalence feel uncomfortable? *Journal of Personality and Social Psychology*, *82*, 157–166.

Newcomb, M.D. & Bentler, E.M. (1980). Cohabitation before marriage: A comparison of married couples who did and did not cohabit. *Alternative Life Styles*, *3*, 65–85.

Newcomb, M.D., Huba, G.J. & Bentler, E.M. (1986). Determinants of sexual and dating behavior among adolescents. *Journal of Personality and Social Psychology*, *50*, 428–438.

Newcomb, T.M. (1943). *Personality and social change: Attitude formation in a student community.* New York: Dryden.

Newcomb, T.M. (1961). *The acquaintance process.* New York: Holt, Rinehart & Winston.

Newcomb, T.M., Koenig, L.E., Flacks, R. & Warwick, D.P. (1967). *Persistence and change: Bennington College and its students after twenty-five years.* New York: Wiley.

Newell, A. & Simon, H.A. (1972). *Human problem solving.* Englewood Cliffs, NJ: Prentice-Hall.

Newman, L.S. & Erber, R. (Eds) (2002). *Understanding genocide. The social psychology of the Holocaust.* New York: Oxford University Press.

Newton, A.W. & Vandeven, A.M. (2010). Child abuse and neglect: A worldwide concern. *Current Opinion in Pediatrics*, *22*, 226–233.

Ng, S.H. (2007). Language-based discrimination: Blatant and subtle forms. *Journal of Language and Social Psychology*, *26*, 106–122.

Nicks, S.D., Korn, J.H. & Mainieri, T. (1997). The rise and fall of deception in social psychology and personality research, 1921 to 1994. *Ethics and Behavior*, *7*, 69–77.

Niedzielski, Nancy A., and Dennis R. Preston (2000). *Folk Linguistics*, Berlin: Mouton de Gruyter. Cited by Morales et al. (2012).

Nielson, W.R. & Neufeld, R.W.J. (1986). Utility of the uncontrollability construct in relation to the Type A behaviour pattern: A multidimensional investigation. *Canadian Journal of Behavioural Science*, *18*, 224–237.

Nisbett, R.E. & Borgida, E. (1975). Attribution and the psychology of prediction. *Journal of Personality and Social Psychology*, *32*, 932–943.

Nisbett, R.E. (2003). The geography of thought: How Asians and Westerners think differently... and why. New York: Free Press.

Nisbett, R.E., Caputo, C., Legant, P. & Maracek, J. (1973). Behavior as seen by the actor and as seen by the observer. *Journal of Personality and Social Psychology*, *27*, 154–164.

Nisbett, R.E. & Gordon, A. (1967). Self-esteem and susceptibility to social influence. *Journal of Personality and Social Psychology*, *5*, 268–276.

Nisbett, R.E. & Wilson, T.D. (1977). Telling more than we can know: Verbal reports on mental processes. *Psychological Review*, *84*, 231–259.

Norenzayan, A. & Heine, S.J. (2005). Psychological universals: What are they and how can we know? *Psychological Bulletin*, *135*, 763–784.

Norenzayan, A. & Nisbett, R. (2000). Culture and causal cognition. *Current Directions in Psychological Science, 9,* 132–135.

Norman, R. (1976). When what is said is important: A comparison of expert and attractive sources. *Journal of Experimental Social Psychology, 12,* 294–300.

Norman, R.N.G. (1985). *The nature and correlates of health behaviour.* Ottawa: Health Promotion Directorate.

Northoff, G. & Panskepp, J. (2008). The trans-species concept of self and subcortical-cortical midline system. *Trends in Cognitive Sciences 12,* 259–264.

Norton, M.I., Monin, B., Cooper, J. & Hogg, M.A. (2003). Vicarious dissonance: Attitude change from the inconsistency of others. *Journal of Personality and Social Psychology, 85,* 47–62.

Nosek, B., Banaji, M.R., Greenwald, A.G. (2002). Math = male, me = female, therefore math not = me. *Journal of Personality & Social Psychology, 83,* 44–59.

Notani, A.S. (1998). Moderators of perceived behavioral control's predictiveness in the theory of planned behavior: A meta-analysis. *Journal of Consumer Psychology, 7,* 247–271.

Notz, W.W. & Starke, F.A. (1987). Arbitration and distributive justice: Equity or equality? *Journal of Applied Psychology, 72,* 359–365.

Novak, D. & Lerner, M.J. (1968). Rejection as a consequence of perceived similarity. *Journal of Personality and Social Psychology, 9,* 147–152.

Nuttin, J.M. (1987). Affective consequence of mere ownership: The name letter effect in twelve European languages. *European Journal of Social Psychology, 17,* 381–402.

Nyquist, L.V. & Spence, J.T. (1986). Effects of dispositional dominance and sex role expectations on leadership behaviors. *Journal of Personality and Social Psychology, 50,* 87–93.

O'Boyle, E.H., Forsyth, D.R., Banks, G.C. & McDaniel, M.A. (2012). A meta-analysis of the Dark Triad and work behavior: A social exchange perspective. *Journal of Applied Psychology, 97,* 557–579.

O'Meara, J.D. (1989). Cross-sex friendship; four basic challenges of an ignored relationship. *Sex Roles, 21,* 525–543.

O'Meara, J.D. (1994). Cross-sex friendships opportunity challenge: Uncharted terrain for exploration. *Personal Relationships Issues, 2,* 4–7.

Oldridge, N.B. & Streiner, D.L. (1990). The health belief model: Predicting compliance and dropout in cardiac rehabilitation. *Medicine & Science in Sports & Exercise, 22,* 678–683.

Oliner, S.P. & Oliner, P. (1992). *The altruistic personality: Rescuers of Jews in Nazi Europe.* San Francisco: Free Press.

Olson, J.M. (1990). Self-inference processes in emotion. In J.M. Olson & M.P. Zanna (Eds), *Self-inference processes: The Ontario symposium* (Vol. 6). (pp. 17–42). Hillsdale, NJ: Erlbaum.

Olson, J.M. & Hafer, C.L. (1990). In Olson, J. & Zanna, M.P. (Eds), *Self-inference processes: The Ontario Symposium* (Vol. 6). (pp. 293–320). Hillsdale, N.J.: Erlbaum.

Olson, J.M. & Hafer, C.L. (1996). Affect, motivation and cognition in relative deprivation research. In R.M. Sorrentino & E.T. Higgins (Eds), *Handbook of motivation and cognition* (pp. 85–117). New York: Guilford.

Olson, J.M. & Hafer, C.L. (2001). Tolerance of personal deprivation. In J. Jost & B. Major (Eds), *The psychology of legitimacy: Emerging perspectives on ideology, justice, and intergroup relations* (pp. 157–175). New York: Cambridge University Press, 2001.

Olson, J.M., Hafer, C.L., Couzens, A., Kramins, I. & Taylor, L. (1997). *Resentment about deprivation: A self-presentation perspective.* Unpublished manuscript, University of Western Ontario.

Olson, J.M., Vernon, P.A., Harris, J.A. & Jang, K.L. (2001). The heritability of attitudes: A study of twins. *Journal of Personality and Social Psychology, 80,* 845–860.

Olson, J.M. & Zanna, M.P. (1993). Attitude and attitude change. *Annual Review of Psychology, 44,* 117–154.

Olweus, D. (1972). *Personality and aggression. In Nebraska symposium on motivation, 1972* (pp. 261–323). Lincoln, NB: University of Nebraska Press.

Omato, A. & Snyder, M. (1995). Sustained helping without obligation: Motivation, longevity of service, and perceived attitude change among AIDS volunteers. *Journal or Personality and Social Psychology, 68,* 671–687.

Orbell, J.M., Van-De-Kragt, A.J. & Davies, R.M. (1989). Explaining discussion-induced cooperation. *Journal of Personality and Social Psychology, 54,* 811–819.

Orne, M.T. (1962). On the social psychology of the psychology experiment: With particular reference to demand characteristics and their implications. *American Psychologist*, *17*, 776–783.

Ortega, R., Elipe, P., Mora-Mercha, J.A., Genta, L., Brighi, A., Guarini, A., Smith, P.K., Thompson, F. & Tippett, N. (2012). The emotional impact of bullying and cyberbullying on victims: A European cross-national study. *Aggressive Behaviour*, *38*, 342–356.

Osborn, K.A., Irwin, D.C., Skogsberg, N.J. & Feltz, D.L. (2012). The Köhler effect: Motivation gains and losses in real sports groups. *Sport, Exercise, and Performance Psychology*, *1*, 242–253.

Osgood, C.E., Suci, D.J. & Tannenbaum, P.H. (1957). *The measurement of meaning*. Urbana, IL: University of Illinois Press.

Oshi, S. & Schimmack, U. (2010). Culture and well-being: A new inquiry into the psychological wealth of nations. *Perspective on Psychological Science*, *5*, 463–471.

Osterman, L.L. & Brown, R.P. (2011). Culture of honour and violence against itself. *Personality and Social Psychology Bulletin*, *37*, 1611–1623.

Ostrowsky, M.K. (2010). Are violent people more likely to have low self-esteem or high self-esteem? *Aggression and Violent Behavior*, *15*, 69–75.

Owen, I.R. (1995). Social constructionism and the theory, practice and research of psychotherapy: A phenomenological psychology manifesto. *Boletin de Psicologia*, *46*, 161–186.

Oyserman, D., Coon, H. M. & Kemmelmeier, M. (2002). Rethinking individualism and collectivism: Evaluation of theoretical assumptions and meta-analyses. *Psychological Bulletin*, *128*, 3–72.

Oyserman, D.L. & Lee, S.W.S. (2008). Does culture influence what and how we think? Effects of priming individualism and collectivism. *Psychological Bulletin*, *134*, 311–342.

Packer, D.J. (2008). Identifying systematic disobedience in Milgram's obedience experiments: A meta-analytic review. *Perspectives on Psychological Science*, *3*, 301–304.

Pae, T-I. (2008). Second language orientation and self-determination theory: A structural analysis of the factors affecting second language achievement. *Journal of Language and Social Psychology, 27*, 5–27.

Paladino, M-P & Vaes, J. (2009). Ours is human: On the pervasiveness of infra-humanization intergroup relations. *British Journal Of Social Psychology*, *48*, 237–251.

Palmer, D.L. (1996). Determinants of Canadian attitudes toward immigration: More than just racism. *Canadian Journal of Behavioural Science*, *28*, 180–192.

Paluck, E. & Green, D. P. (2009). Prejudice reduction: What works? A review and assessment of research and practice. *Annual Review of Psychology*, *60*, 339–367.

Pampel, F.C., Krueger, P.M. & Denney, J.T. (2010). Socioeconomic disparities in health behaviors. *Annual Review of Sociology*, *16*, 149–170.

Pancer, S.M., Brown, S.D., Gregor, P. & Claxton-Oldfield, S.P. (1992). Causal attributions and the perception of political figures. *Canadian Journal of Behavioural Science*, *24*, 371–381.

Pancer, S.M., Jackson, L.M., Hunsberger, B., Pratt, M.W. & Lea, J. (1995). Religious orthodoxy and the complexity of thought about religious and nonreligious issues. *Journal of Personality*, *63*, 213–232.

Panksepp, J. & Panksepp, J.B. (2000). The seven sins of evolutionary psychology. *Evolution and Cognition*, *6*, 108–131.

Panksepp, J. & Panksepp, J.B. (2001). A continuing critique of evolutionary psychology: seven sins for seven sinners, plus or minus two. *Evolution and Cognition*, *7*, 56–80.

Papastamou, S. & Mugny, G. (1985). Rigidity and minority influence: The influence of the social in social influence. In S. Moscovici, G. Mugny & E. Van Avermaet (Eds). *Perspectives on minority influence* (pp. 113–136). Cambridge: Cambridge University Press.

Papastamou, S. (1983). Strategies of minority and majority influence. In W. Doise & S. Moscovici (Eds). *Current Issues in European Social Psychology* (Vol. 1). (pp. 33–83). Cambridge: Cambridge University Press.

Pape, R.A. (2006). *Dying to win*. New York: Random House.

Park, K. (2011). Estimating juror accuracy, juror ability and the relationship between them. *Law and Human Behavior*, *35*, 288–305.

Park, N., Peterson, C. & Seligman, M.E.P. (2004). Strengths of character and well-being. *Journal of Social and Clinical Psychology*, *23*, 603–610.

Parker, I. (1999). Critical Psychology: Critical Links, *Radical Psychology* also *Annual Review of Critical Psychology*, *1*, 3–18.

Parker, P.A., Middleton, M.S. & Kulik, J.A. (2002). Counterfactual thinking and quality of life among women with silicone breast implants. *Journal of Behavioral Medicine, 25*, 317–335.

Parkinson, B. (2005). Do facial movements express emotions or communicate motives? *Personality and Social Psychology Review, 9*, 278–311.

Parkovnick, S. (1992). The implications of social influence research for a conceptual framework for psychological social psychology. *Canadian Psychology, 33*, 619–622.

Parks, C.D. & Stone, A.B. (2010). The desire to expel unselfish members from the group. *Journal of Personality and Social Psychology, 99*, 303–310.

Parliamentary Assembly of the Council of Europe (2000), http://assembly.coe.int/Main.asp?link=http%3A%2F%2Fassembly.coe.int%2FDocuments%2F-WorkingDocs%2Fdoc00%2FEDOC8667.HTM. Downloaded September 29, 2012.

Pastel, R.H. (2001). Collective behaviors: Mass panic and outbreaks of multiple unexplained symptoms. *Military Medicine, 166*, 44–46.

Patterson, A.C. & Veenstra, G. (2010). Loneliness and risk of mortality: A longitudinal investigation in Alameda County, California. *Social Science and Medicine, 71*, 181–186.

Patterson, G.R. (1982). *Coercive family processes.* Eugene, OR: Castilia Press.

Patterson, M.L. (1982). A sequential functional model of nonverbal exchange. *Psychological Review, 89*, 231–249.

Patterson, M.L. (1983). *Nonverbal behaviour: A functional perspective.* New York: Springer.

Paulhus, D.L. (1990). Measurement and control of response bias. In J.P. Robinson, P.R. Shaver & L.S. Wrightsman (Eds), *Measures of personality and social psychological attitudes* (pp. 17–59). San Diego, CA: Academic Press.

Paulhus, D.L. & Bruce, M.N. (1992). The effects of acquaintanceship on the validity of personality impressions: A longitudinal study. *Journal of Personality and Social Psychology, 63*, 816–824.

Paulus, P.B., Ozindolet, M.T., Poletes, G. & Camacho, L.M. (1993). Perception of performance in group brainstorming: The illusion of group productivity. *Personality and Social Psychology Bulletin, 19*, 78–89.

Paulhus, D.L. & Reid, D.B. (1991). Enhancement and denial in socially desirable responding. *Journal of Personality and Social Psychology, 60*, 307–317.

Paulhus, D.L. & Williams, K.M. (2002). The dark triad of personality: Narcissism, Machiavellianism and psychopathy. *Journal of Research in Personality, 36*, 556–563.

Payne, D.L., Lonsway, K.A. & Fitzgerald, L.F. (1999). Rape myth acceptance: Exploration of its structure and its measurement using the Illinois rape myth acceptance scale. *Journal of Research in Personality, 33*, 27–68.

Peacock, S. & Patel, S. (2008). Cultural influences on pain. *Reviews in Pain, 1*, 6–9.

Pedersen, P. & Thomas, C.D. (1992). Prevalence and correlates of dating violence in a Canadian university sample. *Canadian Journal of Behavioural Science, 24*, 490–501.

Pei, M. (1965). *The story of language* (2nd ed.). Philadelphia: Lippincott.

Pelham, B.W., Mirenberg, M.C. & Jones, J.T. (2002). Why Susie sells seashells by the seashore: Implicit egoism and major life decisions. *Journal of Personality and Social Psychology, 82*, 469–487.

Pellegrini, E., Scandura, T. & Jayaraman, V. (2010). Cross-cultural generalizability of paternalistic leadership: An expansion of leader-member exchange theory (LMX). *Group and Organization Management, 35*, 391–420.

Pemberton, C., McCormack, P. & Russell, A. (1998). Have women's voices lowered across time? A cross-sectional study of Australian women's voices. *Journal of Voice, 12*, 208–213.

Pendleton, M.G. & Batson, C.D. (1979). Self-presentation and the door-in-the-face technique for inducing compliance. *Journal of Personality and Social Psychology, 5*, 77–81.

Pennebaker, J.W. & King, L.A. (1999). Linguistic styles: Language use as an individual difference. *Journal of Personality and Social Psychology, 77*, 1296–1312.

Penner, L.A. & Finkelstein, M.A. (1998). Dispositional and structural determinants of volunteerism. *Journal or Personality and Social Psychology, 74*, 525–537.

Pennington, N. & Hastie, R. (1992). Explaining the evidence: Tests of the story model for juror decision making. *Journal of Personality and Social Psychology, 62*, 189–206.

Pentian, I., Taylor, D.G. & Voelker, T.A. (2009). The role of self-discrepancy and social support in young females' decision to undergo cosmetic procedures. *Journal of Consumer Behavior*, *8*, 149–165.

Peplau, L.A. (2003). Human Sexuality: How do men and women differ? *Current Directions in Psychological Sciences, 12*, 37–40.

Peplau, L.A., Bikson, F.K., Rook, K.S. & Goodchilds, J.D. (1982). Being old and living alone. In L.A. Peplau & D. Perlman (Eds), *Loneliness: A sourcebook of current theory, research, and therapy* (pp. 327–349). New York: Wiley Interscience.

Peplau, L.A. & Gordon, S.L. (1985). Women and men in love: Gender differences in close heterosexual relationships. In V.E. O'Leary, R.K. Unger & B.S. Wallston (Eds), *Women, gender, and social psychology* (pp. 257–291). Hillsdale, NJ: Erlbaum.

Peplau, L.A. & Perlman, D. (1982). Perspectives on loneliness. In L.A. Peplau & D. Perlman (Eds), *Loneliness: A sourcebook of current theory, research and therapy* (pp. 1–20). New York: Wiley.

Peplau, L.A., Russell, D. & Heim, M. (1979). The experience of loneliness. In I.H. Frieze, D. Bar-Tal & J.S. Carroll (Eds), *New approaches to social problems: Applications of attribution theory*. San Francisco: Jossey-Bass.

Pepler, D.J. & Craig, W.M. (1995). A peek behind the fence: Naturalistic observations of aggressive children with remote audiovisual recording. *Developmental Psychology, 31*, 548–553.

Pepler, D.J., Craig, W.M., Connolly, J. & Henderson, K. (2002). Bullying, sexual harassment, dating violence, and substance use among adolescents. In C. Wekerle & A-M. Wall (Eds), *The violence and addiction equation: Theoretical and clinical issues in substance abuse and relationship violence* (pp. 153–168). New York: Brunner-Routledge.

Perlini, A.H. & Ward, C. (2000). HIV prevention interventions: The effects of role-play and behavioural commitment on knowledge and attitudes. *Canadian Journal of Behavioural Science, 32*, 133–143.

Perlman, D. & Oskamp, S. (1971). The effects of picture content and exposure frequency on evaluations of Negroes and Whites. *Journal of Experimental Social Psychology, 7*, 503–514.

Perlman, D. & Peplau, L.A. (1981). Toward a social psychology of loneliness. In S. Duck & R. Gilmour (Eds), *Personal relationships 3: Personal relationships in disorder*. London: Academic Press.

Perrin, S. & Spencer, C. (1981). Independence or conformity in the Asch experiment as a reflection of cultural and situational factors. *British Journal of Social Psychology, 20*, 205–209.

Persico, N., Postlewaite, A. & Silverman, D. (2004). The effect of adolescent experience on labor market outcomes: The case of height. *Journal of Political Economy, 112*, 1019–1053.

Personnaz, M. & Personnaz, B. (1994). Perception and conversion. In S. Moscovici, F. Mucchi & A. Maass, (Eds), *Minority influence* (pp. 165–183). Chicago: Nelson-Hall.

Peters, J.H., Hock, M. & Krohne, H.W. (2012). Sensitive maintenance. A cognitive process underlying individual differences in memory for threatening information. *Journal of Personality and Social Psychology, 102*, 200–213.

Peters, L.H., Hartke, D.D. & Pohlmann, J.T. (1985). Fiedler's contingency theory of leadership: An application of the meta-analytic procedure of Schmidt and Hunter. *Psychological Bulletin, 97*, 274–285.

Peterson, C. (2006). Strengths of character and happiness: Introduction to special issue. *Journal of Happiness Studies, 7*, 289–291.

Peterson, C. & Seligman, M.E.P. (2003). Character strengths before and after September 11. *Psychological Science, 14*, 381–384.

Pettigrew, T.F. (1997). Generalized intergroup contact effects on prejudice. *Personality and Social Psychology Bulletin, 23*, 173–185.

Pettigrew, T.F. (1998). Intergroup contact theory. *Annual Review of Psychology, 49*, 65–85.

Pettigrew, T.F. (2001). Personality and sociocultural factors in intergroup attitudes: A cross-national comparison. In M. Hogg & D. Abrams (Eds), *Intergroup relations: Essential readings* (pp. 18–29). New York: Psychology Press.

Pettigrew, T.F. & Tropp, L.R. (2011). *When groups meet: The dynamics of intergroup contact.* New York: Psychology Press.

Petty, R.E. & Briñol, P. (2012). A multiprocess approach to social influence. In Kenrick, D.T., Goldstein, N.J. & Braver, S.L. (Eds), *Six degrees of social influence: Science, application, and the psychology of Robert Cialdini*, (pp. 49–58). Oxford, UK: Oxford University Press.

Petty, R.E., Briñol, P. & Tormala, Z.L. (2002). Thought confidence as a determinant of persuasion: The self-validation hypothesis. *Journal of Personality and Social Psychology, 82*, 722–741.

Petty, R.E. & Cacioppo, J.T. (1977). Forewarning, cognitive responding, and resistance to persuasion. *Journal of Personality and Social Psychology, 35,* 645–655.

Petty, R.E. & Cacioppo, J.T. (1981). *Attitude and persuasion: Classic and contemporary approaches.* Dubuque, IO: W.C. Brown.

Petty, R.E., Cacioppo, J.T. & Goldman, R. (1981). Personal involvement as a determinant of argument-based persuasion. *Journal of Personality and Social Psychology, 41,* 847–855.

Petty, R.E., Ostrom, T.M. & Brock, T.C. (1981). *Cognitive responses in persuasive communication: A text in attitude change.* Hillsdale, NJ: Erlbaum.

Petty, R.E., Schumann, D.W., Richman, S.A. & Strathman, A.J. (1993). Positive mood and persuasion – different roles for affect under high- and low-elaboration conditions. *Journal of Personality and Social Psychology, 64,* 5–20.

Petty, R.E., Wegener, D.T. & Fabrigar, L.R (1997). Attitude and attitude change. *Annual Review of Psychology, 48,* 609–647.

Petty, R.E., Wells, G.L. & Brock, T.C. (1976). Distraction can enhance or reduce yielding to propaganda: Thought disruption versus effort justification. *Journal of Personality and Social Psychology, 34,* 874–884.

Pfau, M., Semmler, S.M., Deatrick, L.,Lane, L., Mason, A., Nisbett, G., Craig, E., Cornelius, J. & Banas, J.A. (2009). Nuances about the role and impact of affect and enhanced threat in inoculation. *Communication Monographs, 76,* 73–98.

Pfeifer, J.E. (1992). The psychological framing of cults: Schematic representations and cult evaluations. *Journal of Applied Social Psychology, 22,* 531–544.

Pfeifer, J.E. (1999). Perceptual biases and mock juror decision making: Minority religions in court. *Social Justice Research, 12,* 409–419.

Pfeiffer, U.J., Timmermans, B., Vogeley, K., Frith, C.D. & Schilbach, L. (2013). Towards a neuroscience of social interaction. *Frontiers of Human Neuroscience, 7:* 22. Published online 1 February, 2013. doi: 10.3389/fnhum.2013.00022

Pheterson, G.I., Kiesler, S.B. & Goldberg, P.A. (1971). Evaluation of the performance of women as a function of their success, achievements, and personal history. *Journal of Personality and Social Psychology, 19,* 114–118.

Phoenix, A., Frosh, S. & Pattman, R. (2003). Producing contradictory masculine subject positions: Narratives of threat, homophobia and bullying in 11–14-year-old boys. *Journal of Social Issues, 9,* 179–195.

Piliavin, I.M. & Piliavin, J.A. (1972). The effect of blood on reactions to a victim. *Journal of Personality and Social Psychology, 23,* 253–261.

Piliavin, I.M., Rodin, J. & Piliavin, J.A. (1969). Good Samaritanism: An underground phenomenon? *Journal of Personality and Social Psychology, 13,* 289–299.

Piliavin, J.A., Dovidio, J.F., Gaertner, S.L. & Clark, R.D. (1981). *Emergency intervention.* New York: Academic Press.

Pilisuk, M. & Minkler, M. (1985). Supportive ties: A political economy perspective. *Health Education Quarterly, 12,* 93–106.

Pinker, S. (1994). *The language instinct: How the mind creates language.* New York: William Morrow and Company.

Pinker, S. (2011a). Representations and decision rules in the theory of self-deception. *Behavioral and Brain Science, 34,* 35–37.

Pinker, S. (2011b). The better angels of our nature: The decline of violence in history and its causes. London: Allen Lane.

Pinquart, M. & Sorensen, S. (2001). Influences on loneliness in older adults: A meta-analysis. *Basic and Applied Social Psychology, 23,* 245–266.

Plant, E. & Devine, P.G. (2003). The antecedents and implications of interracial anxiety. *Personality and Social Psychology Bulletin, 29,* 780–792.

Platania, J. & Moran, G.P. (2001). Social facilitation as a function of the mere presence of others. *The Journal of Social Psychology, 141,* 190–197.

Platek, S. & Krill, A. (2009). Self-face resemblance attenuates other-race face effect in the amygdala. *Brain Research, 1284,* 155–160.

Platow, M., van Knippenberg, D., Haslam, S. et al. (2006), 'A special gift we bestow on you for being representative of us: Considering leader charisma from a self-categorization perspective'. *British Journal of Social Psychology, 45,* 303–320.

Platt, J. (1973). Social Traps, *American Psychologist, 28,* 641–651.

Polivy, J., Hackett, R. & Bycio, P. (1979). The effect of perceived smoking status on attractiveness. *Personality and Social Psychology Bulletin, 5,* 401–404.

Polivy, J. & Herman, C.P. (2000). The false-hope syndrome: Unfulfilled expectations of self-change. *Current Directions in Psychological Science, 9,* 128–131.

Polivy, J. & Herman, C.P. (2002). If at first you don't succeed. False hopes of self-change. *American Psychologist, 57,* 677–689.

Pollard, W.E. & Mitchell, T.R. (1972). Decision theory analysis of social power. *Psychological Bulletin, 78,* 433–446.

Polster, M.F. (1992). *Eve's daughters: The forbidden heroism of women.* New York: Jossey-Bass.

Pomerantz, E.M., Chaiken, S. & Tordesillas, R.S. (1995). Attitude strength and resistance processes. *Journal of Personality and Social Psychology, 69,* 408–419.

Porier, G.W. & Lott, A.J. (1967). Galvanic skin responses and prejudice. *Journal of Personality and Social Psychology, 5,* 253–259.

Porter, S., Spencer, L. & Birt, A R. (2003). Blinded by emotion? Effect of the emotionality of a scene on susceptibility to false memories. *Canadian Journal of Behavioural Science, 35,* 165–175.

Postmes, T. & Spears, R. (1998). Deindividuation and antinormative behavior: A meta-analysis. *Psychological Bulletin, 123,* 238–259.

Potter, J. (1996). Discourse analysis and constructionist approaches: theoretical background. In J.T.E. Richardson (Ed.) *Handbook of qualitative research handbook of qualitative research methods,* (pp. 125–140). Leicester: B.P.S. Publications.

Potter, J. (2012). Discourse analysis and discursive psychology. In H. Cooper, (Ed.). *APA handbook of research methods in psychology: Vol. 2. Quantitative, qualitative, neuropsychological, and biological,* (pp. 111–130). Washington: American Psychological Association Press.

Potter, J. & Wetherell, M. (1987). *Discourse and social psychology: Beyond attitudes and behaviour.* London: Sage.

Poulin, F. & Boivin, M. (2000). The role of proactive and reactive aggression in the formation and development of boys' friendships. *Developmental Psychology, 36,* 233–240. doi: 10.1037/0012-1649.36.2.233

Powers, T.A., Koestner, R, Zuroff, D.C., Milyavskaya, M. & Gorin, A.A. (2011). The effects of self-criticism and self-oriented perfectionism on goal pursuit. *Personality and Social Psychology Bulletin, 37,* 964–975.

Pratkanis, A.R. & Aronson, E. (1991*). Age of propaganda. The everyday use and abuse of persuasion.* New York: Freeman.

Pratkanis, A.R., Greenwald, A.G., Leippe, M.R. & Baumgardner, M.H. (1988). In search of reliable persuasion effects. III. The sleeper effect is dead. Long live the sleeper effect. *Journal of Personality and Social Psychology, 54,* 203–218.

Pratt, M.W., Pancer, M., Hunsberger, B. & Manchester, J. (1990). Reasoning about the self and relationships in maturity: An integrative complexity analysis of individual differences. *Journal of Personality and Social Psychology, 59,* 575–581.

Praxmarer, S. (2011). How a presenter's perceived attractiveness affects persuasion for attractiveness-unrelated products. *Quarterly Review of Marketing Communications, 30,* 839–865.

Pressman, S.D. & Cohen, S. (2005). Does positive affect influence health? *Psychological Bulletin, 131,* 905–971.

Princz, M. (1992). Dating violence: Not an isolated phenomenon. *Vis-à-vis, 9,* 1–4.

Pronk, T.M., Karremans, J.C., Overbeek G., Vermulst, A.A., Wigboldus, D.H. (2010). What it takes to forgive: When and why executive functioning facilitates forgiveness. *Journal of Personality and Social Psychology, 98,* 119–131.

Provine, R.R., Spencer, R.J. & Mandell, D.L. (2007). Emoticons punctuate website text messages. *Journal of Language and Social Psychology, 26,* 299–307.

Pruitt, D.G. (1976). Power and bargaining. In B. Seidenberg & A. Snadowsky (Eds), *Social psychology: An introduction.* (pp. 343–376). New York: Free Press.

Pruitt, D.G. (2012). A history of social conflict and negotiation research. In A.W. Kruglanski & W. Stroebe (Eds), *Handbook of the history of social psychology.* New York: Psychology Press. (pp. 431–452).

Puente, S. & Cohen, D. (2003). Jealousy and the meaning (or nonmeaning) of violence. *Personality and Social Psychology Bulletin, 29,* 449–460.

Pyke, S. (2001). Feminist psychology in Canada: Early days. *Canadian Psychology, 42,* 268–275.

Quarantelli, E.L. (1957). The behavior of panic participants. *Sociology and Social Research, 41,* 187–194.

Quarantelli, E.L. (2001). Sociology of panic. In N.J. Smelser & P.B. Baltes (Eds), *International*

Encyclopedia of the Social and Behavioral Sciences (pp. 11020–11023). New York: Pergamon Press.

Quine, L., Rutter, D.R. & Arnold, L. (2000). Comparing the Theory of Planned Behavior and the Health Beliefs Model: The example of helmet use among schoolboy cyclists. In P. Norman & C. Abraham (Eds), *Understanding and changing health behavior: From health beliefs to self-regulation* (pp. 73–98). Amsterdam: Harwood Academic Publishers.

Quist, R.M. & Wiegand, D.M. (2002). Attributions of hate: The media's causal attributions of a homophobic murder. *American Behavioral Scientist*, *46*, 93–107.

Radke-Yarrow, M. & Zahn-Waxler, C. (1984). Roots, motives, and patterns in children's prosocial behavior. In E. Staub, D. Bar-Tal, J. Karylowski & J. Reykowski (Eds), *Development and maintenance of prosocial behavior* (pp. 81–99). New York: Plenum Press.

Radsch, C.C. (2012). Unveiling the revolutionaries: Cyberactivism and the role of women in the Arab uprisings. James A. Baker III Institute for Public Policy, Rice University. Downloaded February 27, 2013 from http://www.scribd.com/doc/98088364/Unvieling-the-Revolutionaries-Cyberactivism-and-the-Role-of-Women-in-the-Arab-Uprisings.

Ragins, B.R. & Sundstrom, E. (1989). Gender and power in organizations: A longitudinal perspective. *Psychological Bulletin*, *105*, 51–88.

Rahim-Williams, W.B., Riley, J.L.,Williams, S.K. & Fillingim, R.B. (2012). A quantitative review of ethnic group differences in experimental pain response: Do biology, psychology and culture matter? *Pain Medicine*, *13*, 522–540.

Rai, T.S. & Fiske, A. (2010). ODD (observation- and description-deprived) psychological research. *Behavioural and Brain Sciences*, *33*, 107–108. doi:10.1017/S0140525X10000221

Raikkonen, K., Matthews, K.A., Flory, J.D. & Owens, J.F. (1999). Effects of hostility on ambulatory blood pressure and mood during daily living in healthy adults. *Health Psychology 18*, 44–53.

Ramsden, E. (2009). The urban animal: Population density and social pathology in rodents and humans. *Bulletin of the World Health Organization*, *87*, 82. doi: 10.2471/BLT.09.062836

Rand, M. & Levinger, G. (1979). Implicit theories of relationships: An intergenerational study.

Journal of Personality and Social Psychology, *37*, 645–661.

Rappoport, L. & Kren, G. (1993). Amoral rescuers: The ambiguities of altruism. *Creativity Research Journal*, *6*, 129–136.

Raubolt, R.R. (2003). Attack on the self and authoritarian group supervision. *Group*, *27*, 65–77.

Raven, B.H., Schwarzwald, J. & Koslowsky, M. (1998). Conceptualizing and measuring a power/interaction model of interpersonal influence. *Journal of Applied Social Psychology*, *28*, 307–332.

Regan, D.T. & Totten, J. (1975). Empathy and attribution: Turning observers into actors. *Journal of Personality and Social Psychology*, *32*, 850–856.

Regan, D.T., Williams, M. & Sparling, S. (1972). Voluntary expiation of guilt: A field experiment. *Journal of Personality and Social Psychology*, *24*, 42–45.

Reicher, S. (1996). 'The crowd' century: Reconciling practical success with theoretical failure. *British Journal of Social Psychology*, *35*, 535–553.

Reicher, S. & Haslam, S.A. (2006). Rethinking the psychology of tyranny: The BBC Prison Study. *British Journal of Social Psychology*, *45*, 1–40.

Reicher, S. & Haslam, S. A. (2011a). After shock? Towards a social identity explanation of the Milgram 'obedience' studies. *British Journal of Social Psychology*, *50*, 163–169.

Reicher, S. & Haslam, S.A. (2011b). Stanley Milgram taught us we have more to fear from zealots than zombies. Http://www.guardian.co.uk/science/blog/2011/sep/01/stanley-milgram-research-zealots-zombies. Downloaded December 1, 2012.

Reicher, S. & Haslam, S.A. (2012). Obedience: Revisiting Milgram's shock experiments. In J.R. Smith & S.A. Haslam (Eds), *Social psychology: Revisiting the classic studies*. London: Sage. (pp. 106–125).

Reicher, S. Haslam, S.A. & Smith, J.R. (2012). Working towards the experimenter: Reconceptualizing obedience within the Milgram paradigm as identification-based followership. *Perspectives on Psychological Science*, *7*, 315–324.

Reicher, S., Spears, R. & Postmes, T. (1995). A social identity model of deindividuation phenomena. *European Review of Social Psychology*, *6*, 161–198.

Reid, J.B. (1978). Study of drinking in natural settings. In G.A. Marlatt & P. Nathan (Eds),

Behavioral approaches to alcoholism (pp. 58–75). New Brunswick, NJ: Rutgers Center of Alcohol Studies.

Reis, H.T. & Aron, A. (2008). What is it, why does it matter, and how does it operate? *Perspectives on Psychological Science*, *3*, 80–86.

Reisenzein, R. (1986). A structural equation analysis of Weiner's attribution-affect model of helping behavior. *Journal of Personality and Social Psychology*, *50*, 1123–1133.

Remland, M. S., Jones, T. S. & Brinkman, H. (1991). Proxemic and haptic behaviour in three European countries. *Journal of Nonverbal Behaviour*, *15*, 215–232.

Rennie, D. (2002). Qualitative research: History, theory and practice. Special Issue, *Canadian Psychology*, *43*, 179–189.

Rentsch, J.R. & Heffner, T.S. (1994). Assessing self-concept: Analysis of Gordon's coding scheme using 'Who am I?' responses. *Journal of Social Behavior and Personality*, *9*, 283–300.

Renz, B.B. (2010). *Our own worst enemy as protector of ourselves*. Lanhan, MD: University Press of America.

Repacholi, B.M. & Meltzoff, A.N. (2007). Emotional eavesdropping: infants selectively respond to indirect emotional signals. *Child Development*, *78*, 503–521.

Repacholi, B.M., Meltzoff, A.N. & Olsen, B. (2008). Infants' understanding of the link between visual perception and emotion: 'If she can't see me doing it, she won't get angry'. *Developmental Psychology*, *44*, 561–574.

Report of the Media Violence Commission (2012). *Aggressive Behavior*, *28*, 335–341.

Reykowski, J. (2002). The justice motive and altruistic helping: Rescuers of Jews in Nazi-occupied Europe. In M. Ross & D.T. Miller (Eds), *The justice motive in everyday life* (pp. 251–270). New York: Cambridge University Press.

Reynaud, M., Karila, L., Blecha, L. & Benyamina, A. (2010). Is love passion an addiction? *American Journal of Alcohol and Drug Abuse*, *36*, 261–267.

Rhodes, N. & Wood, N. (1992). Self-esteem and intelligence affect influenceability: The mediating role of message reception. *Psychological Bulletin*, *111*, 156–171.

Rice, M.E. (1997). Violent offender research and implications for the criminal justice system. *American Psychologist*, *52*, 414–423.

Richerson, P.J. & Boyd, R. (2005). Not by genes alone: How culture transforms human evolution. Chicago: University of Chicago Press.

Richetin, J. & Richardson, D.S. (2008). Automatic processes and individual differences in aggressive behavior. *Aggression and Violent Behavior*, *13*, 423–430.

Riess, M., Rosenfeld, R., Melburg, V. & Tedeschi, J.T. (1981). Self-serving attributions: Biased private perceptions and distorted public descriptions. *Journal of Personality and Social Psychology*, *41*, 224–231.

Rilling, J.R. & Sanfey, A.G. (2011). The neuroscience of social decision-making. *Annual Review of Psychology*, *62*, 23–48.

Rimé, B. (1983). Nonverbal communication or nonverbal behavior? In W. Doise & S. Moscovici (Eds), *Current issues in European social psychology* (Vol. 1). (pp. 85–141). Cambridge: Cambridge University Press.

Ringelmann, M. (1913). Recherches sur les moteurs animés: Travail de l'homme. *Annales de l'Institut National Agronomique, 2e Série-tome XII*, 1–40.

Rink, F., Ryan, M.K., Stoker, J.I. (2012). Influence in times of crisis: how social and financial resources affect men's and women's evaluations of glass-cliff positions. *Psychological Science*, *23*, 1306–1313.

Ritter, J.M., Casey, R.J. & Langlois, J.H. (1991). Adults' responses to infants varying in appearance of age and attractiveness. *Child Development*, *62*, 68–82.

Rivers, I. (2001). The bullying of sexual minorities' at school: Its nature and long-term correlates. *Educational and Child Psychology*, *18*, 33–46.

Rivis, A., Sheeran, P. & Armitage, C.J. (2009). Expanding the affective and normative components of the theory of planned behavior: A Meta-analysis of anticipated affect and moral norms. *Journal of Applied Social Psychology*, *39*, 2985–3019.

Roberts, W.L. (1999). The socialization of emotional expression: Relations with prosocial behaviour and competence in five samples. *Canadian Journal of Behavioural Science*, *31*, 72–85.

Robins, L.N., Helzer, J.E. & Davis, D.H. (1975). Narcotic use in Southeast Asia and afterward: An interview study of 898 Vietnam returnees. *Archives of General Psychiatry*, *32*(8), 955–961.

Robinson, M.D. & Ryff, C.D. (1999). The role of self-deception in perceptions of past, present and future happiness. *Personality and Social Psychology Bulletin, 25,* 595–606.

Robinson, R.J., Keltner, D., Ward, A. & Ross, L. (1995). Actual versus assumed differences in construal: Naive realism in intergroup perception and conflict. *Journal of Personality and Social Psychology, 68,* 404–417.

Robinson, W.P. & Giles, H. (2001). *The new handbook of language and social psychology.* West Sussex, England: John Wiley and Sons.

Roddy, D.B. (2003, March 16). Bush is playing 'chicken' not only with Saddam, but with the U.N. and allies, as well *Pittsburg Post-Gazette.* Downloaded on September 24, 2003 from http://www.post-gazette.com/nation/20030316brinkmanship0316p3.asp.

Rodin, J. (1992). The social construction of premenstrual syndrome. *Social Science and Medicine, 35,* 49–56

Rodin, J. & Janis, I.L. (1979). The social power of health care practitioners as agents of change. *Journal of Social Issues, 35,* 60–81.

Rodin, J. & Langer, E.J. (1977). Long-term effects of a control-relevant intervention with the institutionalized aged. *Journal of Personality and Social Psychology, 35,* 897–902.

Roese, N.J. (1997). Counterfactual thinking. *Psychological Bulletin, 121,* 133–148.

Roese, N.J. & Olson, J.M. (1997). Counterfactual thinking: The intersection of affect and function. In M.P. Zanna (Ed.). *Advances in experimental social psychology* (pp. 1–59). San Diego, USA: Academic Press.

Roese, N.J. & Sande, G.N. (1993). Backlash effects in attack politics. *Journal of Applied Social Psychology, 23,* 632–653.

Rogers, E.M. (2003/1962). *Diffusion of innovations.* New York: Free Press.

Rogers, R.W. (1975). A protection motivation theory of fear appeals and attitude change. *Journal of Psychology, 91,* 93–114.

Rogers, R.W. (1983). Cognitive and physiological processes in fear appeals and attitude change: A revised theory of protection motivation. In J.T. Cacioppo & R.E. Petty (Eds), *Social psychophysiology: A sourcebook* (pp. 153–176). New York: Guilford.

Rogers, T.B., Kuiper, N.A. & Kirker, W.S. (1977). Self-reference and the encoding of personal information. *Journal of Personality and Social Psychology, 35,* 677–688.

Rohan, M.J. (2000). A rose by any name? The values construct. *Personality and Social Psychology Review, 4,* 255–277.

Rohlinger, D.A. & Snow, D.A. (2003). Social psychological perspectives on crowds and social movements. In Delamater, J. (Ed.), Handbook of Social Psychology. New York: Kluwer Academic. (pp. 503–527).

Rokeach, M. (1968). *Beliefs, attitudes, and values.* San Francisco: Jossey-Bass.

Rokeach, M. (1979). *Understanding human values: Individual and societal.* New York: Free Press.

Romaine, S. (2000). *Language in society: An introduction to sociolinguistics* (2nd ed.). Cary, NC, USA: Oxford University Press.

Ronis, D.L. (1992). Conditional health threats: Health beliefs, decisions and behaviors among adults. *Health Psychology, 11,* 127–134.

Rorum, R., Fein, R. & Vossekuil, B. (2012). A dimensional approach to analyzing lone offender terrorism. *Aggression and Violent Behavior, 17,* 389–396.

Rosen, S., Tomarelli, M.M., Kidda, M.L., Jr. & Medvin, N. (1986). Effects of motive for helping recipient's inability to reciprocate, and sex on devaluation of the recipient's competence. *Journal of Personality and Social Psychology, 50,* 729–736.

Rosenbaum, L.L. & Rosenbaum, W.B. (1971). Morale and productivity consequences of group leadership style, stress and type of task. *Journal of Applied Psychology, 55,* 343–348.

Rosenberg, M. (1957). *Occupations and values.* Glencoe, IL: Free Press.

Rosenbaum, M.E. (1986). The repulsion hypothesis: On the nondevelopment of relationships. *Journal of Personality and Social Psychology, 51,* 1156–1166.

Rosenberg, M.J. (1965). When dissonance fails: On eliminating evaluation apprehension from attitude measurement. *Journal of Personality and Social Psychology, 1,* 28–42.

Rosenhan, D. (1970). The natural socialization of altruistic autonomy. In J. Macaulay & L. Berkowitz (Eds), *Altruism and helping behavior.* New York: Academic Press.

Rosenhan, D. (1972). Learning theory and prosocial behavior. *Journal of Social Issues, 28,* 151–164.

Rosenman, R.H., Brand, R.J., Jenkins, C.D., Friedman, M., Straus, R. & Wurm, M.

(1975). Coronary heart disease in the Western Collaborative Group Study: Final follow-up experience of 8 years. *Journal of the American Medical Association, 233*, 872–877.

Rosenthal, R. (1966). *Experimenter effects in behavioral research.* New York: Appleton-Century-Crofts.

Rosenthal, R, & Jacobsen, L. (1968). *Pygmalion in the classroom: Teacher expectation and pupils' intellectual development.* New York: Holt, Rinehart and Winston.

Rosenzweig, J.M. & Daley, D.M. (1989). Dyadic adjustment/sexual satisfaction in women and men as a function of psychological sex-role self-perception. *Journal of Sex and Marital Therapy, 15*, 42–56.

Roskos-Ewoldsen, D.R. & Fazio, R.H. (1992a). On the orienting value of attitudes: Attitude accessibility as a determinant of an object's attraction of visual attention. *Journal of Personality and Social Psychology, 63*, 198–211.

Roskos-Ewoldsen, D.R. & Fazio, R.H. (1992b). The accessibility of source likeability as a determinant of persuasion. *Personality and Social Psychology Bulletin, 18*, 19–25.

Rosnow, R.L. (1991). Inside rumor. *American Psychologist, 46*, 484–496.

Rosnow, R.L. & Fine, G.A. (1976). *Rumor and gossip: The social psychology of hearsay.* New York: Elsevier.

Rosnow, R.L., Yost, J.H. & Esposito, J.L. (1986). Belief in rumor and likelihood of rumor transmission. *Language and Communication, 6*, 189–194.

Ross, A.S. & Braband, J. (1973). Effect of increased responsibility on bystander intervention II: The cue value of a blind person. *Journal of Personality and Social Psychology, 25*, 254–258.

Ross, L. (1977). The intuitive psychologist and his shortcomings: Distortions in the attribution process. In L. Berkowitz (Ed.), *Advances in experimental social psychology* (Vol. 10). New York: Academic Press.

Ross, L., Amabile, T.M. & Steinmetz, J.L. (1977). Social roles, social control and biases in social perception processes. *Journal of Personality and Social Psychology, 35*, 485–494.

Ross, L., Greene, D. & House, P. (1977). The 'false consensus effect': An egocentric bias in social perception and attribution processes. *Journal of Experimental Social Psychology, 13*, 279–301.

Ross, M. (1989). Relation of implicit theories to the construction of personal histories. *Psychological Review, 96*, 341–357.

Ross, M. & Conway, M. (1985). Remembering one's own past: The construction of personal histories. In R. Sorrentino & E.T. Higgins (Eds), *Handbook of motivation and cognition* (pp. 122–144). New York: Guilford.

Ross, M., McFarland, C., Conway, M. & Zanna, M.P. (1983). Reciprocal relation between attitude and behavior recall: Committing people to newly formed attitudes. *Journal of Personality and Social Psychology, 45*, 257–267.

Ross, M. & Sicoly, F. (1979). Egocentric biases in availability and attribution. *Journal of Personality and Social Psychology, 37*, 322–336.

Ross, M. & Wilson, A.E. (2002). It feels like yesterday. Self-esteem valence of personal past experiences and judgments of subjective distance. *Journal of Personality and Social Psychology 82*, 792–803.

Ross, W.H. & Conlon, D.E. (2000). Hybrid forms of third-party dispute resolution: Theoretical implications of combining mediation and arbitration. *Academy of Management Review, 25*, 416–427.

Roter, D.L. & Hall, J.A. (1992). *Doctors talking with patients/Patients talking with doctors.* Westport, CT: Auburn House.

Roter, D.L., Hall, J.A., Merisca, R. & Nordstrom, B. (1998). Effectiveness of interventions to improve patient compliance: A meta-analysis. *Medical Care, 36*, 1138–1161.

Rothbart, M.K., Ahadi, S.A. & Evans, D.E. (2000). Temperament and personality: Origins and outcomes. *Journal of Personality and Social Psychology, 78*, 122–135.

Rotton, J. & Cohn, E.G. (2000). Violence is a curvilinear function of temperature in Dallas. *Journal of Personality and Social Psychology (JPSP), 78*, 1074–1081.

Roy, M.P., Steptoe, A. & Kirschbaum, C. (1998). Life events and social support as moderators of individual differences in cardiovascular and cortisol reactivity. *Journal of Personality and Social Psychology, 75*, 1273–1281.

Ruback, R.B. & Dabbs, J.M. (1988). Group vocal patterns and leadership in India: Effects of task, language, and sex of subjects. *Journal of Cross-Cultural Psychology, 19*, 446–464.

Ruben, D.H. (1998). Social exchange theory: Dynamics of a system governing the dysfunctional family and guide to assessment. *Journal of Contemporary Psychotherapy, 28*, 307–325.

Rubenfeld, S., Clément, R., Vinograd, J., Lussier, D., Amireault, V., Auger, R. & Lebrun, M. (2007). Becoming a cultural intermediary: A further social corollary of second-language learning. *Journal of Language and Social Psychology, 26*, 182–203.

Rubenstein, C.M. & Shaver, P. (1982). The experience of loneliness. In L. Peplau & D. Perlman (Eds), *Loneliness: A sourcebook of current theory, research and therapy*. New York: Wiley.

Rubin, J. (1976). How to tell when someone is saying no. *Topics in Culture Learning, 4*, 61–65.

Rubin, Z. (1973). *Liking and loving: An invitation to social psychology*. New York: Holt, Rinehart & Winston.

Rubin, Z. (1974). Lovers and other strangers: The development of intimacy in encounters and relationships. *American Scientist, 62*, 182–190.

Rubin, Z. (1975). Disclosing oneself to a stranger: Reciprocity and its limits. *Journal of Experimental Social Psychology, 11*, 233–260.

Ruby, C.L. & Brigham, J.C. (1996). A criminal schema: Role of chronicity, race and SES in law enforcement officials' perception of others. *Journal of Applied Social Psychology, 26*, 95–111.

Rudman, L.A. & Glick, P. (1999). Feminized management and backlash toward agentic women: The hidden costs to women of a kinder, gentler image of middle-managers. *Journal of Personality and Social Psychology, 77*, 1004–1010.

Rudman, L.A. & Glick, P. (2001). Prescriptive gender stereotypes and backlash toward agentic women. *Journal of Social Issues, 57*, 743–762.

Rudmin, F.W. (1985). William McDougall in the history of social psychology. *British Journal of Social Psychology, 24*, 75–76.

Rudmin, F.W. (1989). The pleasure of serendipity in histological research: On finding 'stereotype' in Morier's (1824) Hajji Baba. *Cross-Cultural Psychology Bulletin, 23*, 8–11.

Ruggiero, K.M. & Taylor, D.M. (1995). Coping with discrimination. How disadvantaged group members perceive the discrimination that confronts them. *Journal of Personality and Social Psychology, 68*, 826–838.

Ruggiero, K.M. & Taylor, D.M. (1997). Why minority group members perceive or do not perceive the discrimination that confronts them. Role of

self-esteem and perceived control. *Journal of Personality and Social Psychology, 72*, 373–389.

Rule, B.G. & Adair, J. (1984). Contributions of psychology as a social science to Canadian society. *Canadian Psychology, 25*, 52–58.

Rule, B.G. & Nesdale, A.R. (1974). Differing functions of aggression. *Journal of Personality, 42*, 467–481.

Rule, N.O., Ambady, N, Adams, R.B., Ozono, H., Nakashima, S., Yoshikawam, S. & Watabe, M. (2010). Polling the face: Prediction and consensus across cultures. *Journal of Personality and Social Psychology, 98*, 1–15.

Rusbult, C.E. (1983). A longitudinal test of the investment model: The development (and deterioration) of satisfaction and commitment in heterosexual involvement. *Journal of Personality and Social Psychology, 45*, 101–117.

Rusbult, C.E., Finkel, E.J. & Kumashiro, M. (2009). The Michelangelo phenomenon. *Current Directions in Psychological Science, 18*, 305–309.

Rusbult, C.E., Kubacka, K.E., Kumashiro, M. & Finkel, E.J. (2009). 'The part of me that you bring out'. Ideal similarity and the Michelangelo phenomenon, *Journal of Personality and Social Psychology, 96*, 61–82.

Rusbult, C.E. & Martz, J.M. (1995). Remaining in an abusive relationship: An model analysis of nonvoluntary dependence. *Personality and Social Psychology Bulletin, 21*, 558–571.

Rusbult, C.E., Kubacka, K.E., Kumashiro, M. & Finkel, E.J. (2009). 'The part of me that you bring out'. Ideal similarity and the Michelangelo phenomenon, *Journal of Personality and Social Psychology, 96*, 61–82.

Rusbult, C.E., Kumashiro, M., Wolf, S.L. & Scott T. (2005). The Michelangelo Phenomenon in Close Relationships. In A. Tesser, J.V. Wood. & D.A. Stapel (Eds), *On building, defending and regulating the self: A psychological perspective* (1–29). New York: Psychology Press.

Russell, D., Peplau, L.A. & Cutrona, C.E. (1980). The revised UCLA loneliness scale: Concurrent and discriminant validity evidence. *Journal of Personality and Social Psychology, 39*, 472–480.

Russell, J.A. & Mehrabian, A. (1978). Approach-avoidance and affiliation as functions of the emotion-eliciting quality of an environment. *Environment and Behavior, 10*, 355–388.

Russell, N.J.C. (2011). Milgram's obedience to authority experiments: Origins and early evolution. *British Journal of Social Psychology, 50,* 140–162.

Rutter, M. (1987). Psychological resilience and protective mechanisms. *American Journal of Orthopsychiatry, 57,* 316–331.

Ryan, E.B., Bartolucci, G., Giles, H. & Henwood, K. (1986). Psycholinguistics and social psychological components of communication by and with older adults. *Language and Communication, 6,* 1–22.

Ryan, M.K. & Haslam, S.A. (2005). The glass cliff: Evidence that women are over-represented in precarious leadership positions. *British Journal of Management, 16,* 81–90.

Ryff, C.D. (1989). Happiness is everything, or is it? Explorations on the meaning of psychological well-being. *Journal of Personality and Social Psychology, 57,* 1069–1081.

Ryff, C.D., Singer, B.H. & Love, G.D. (2004). Positive health: connecting well-being with biology. *Philosophical Transactions of the Royal Society, London, 359,* 1383–1394.

Ryff, C.D., Singer, B., Wing, E., & Love, G.D. (2001). Elective affinities and uninvited agonies: Mapping emotion with significant others onto health. In C.D. Ryff & B. Singer (Eds), *Emotion, social relationships and health (*pp. 133–175). New York: Oxford University Press.

Sabbaugh, C. & Golden, D. (2007). Reflecting upon etic and emic perspectives on distributive justice. *Social Justice Research, 20,* 372–387.

Sabini, J., Siepman, M. & Stein, J. (2001). The really fundamental attribution error in social psychological research. *Psychological Inquiry, 12,* 1–15.

Sachdev, I. (2007). Communication, language and discrimination: A prologue. *Journal of Language and Social Psychology, 26,* 101–105.

Sachs-Ericsson, N., Medley, A.N., Kendall–Tackett, K. & Taylor, J. (2011). Childhood abuse and current health problems among older adults: The mediating effects of self-efficacy. *Psychology of Violence, 1,* 106–120.

Sachweh, S. (1998). Granny darling's nappies: Secondary babytalk in German nursing homes for the aged. *Journal of Applied Communication Research, 26,* 52–65.

Sadava, S.W. (1985). Problem behavior theory and consumption and consequences of alcohol use. *Journal of Studies on Alcohol, 46,* 392–397.

Sadava, S.W., Busseri, M., Molnar, D.S., Perrier, C. & DeCourville, N. (2011). Adult attachment orientation and health: Investigating a four-pathway model in university undergraduate and adult clinical sample. *Journal of Social and Personal Relationships, 26,* 604–633.

Sadava, S.W., DeCourville, N. & McCreary, D. (1996). Depression and health: Linkages to health-protective behaviours. Canadian Psychological Association: Hamilton, Ontario.

Sadava, S.W. & Forsyth, R. (1977a). Person-environment interaction and college student drug use: A multivariate longitudinal study. *Genetic Psychology Monographs, 96,* 211–245.

Sadava, S.W. & Forsyth, R. (1977b). Turning on, turning off and relapse: Social psychological determinants of status change in cannabis use. *International Journal of the Addictions, 12,* 509–528.

Sadava, S.W. & Matejcic, C. (1987). Generalized and specific loneliness in early marriage. *Canadian Journal of Behavioural Science, 19,* 56–66.

Sadava, S.W., O'Connor, R. & McCreary, D.R. (2000). Employment status and health in young adults: Economic and behavioural mediators? *Journal of Health Psychology, 5,* 549–560.

Sadava, S.W. & Thompson, M.M. (1986). Loneliness, social drinking and vulnerability to alcohol problems. *Canadian Journal of Behavioural Science, 18,* 133–139.

Safdar, S., Friedlmeier, W., Matsumoto, D., Yoo, S.H., Kwantes, C.T., Kakai, H. & Shigemasu, E. (2009). Variations of emotional display rules within and across cultures: A comparison between Canada, US and Japan. *Canadian Journal of Behavioural Science, 41,* 1–10.

Sagarin, B.J., Cialdini, R.B., Rice, W.E. & Serna, S.B. (2002). Dispelling the illusion of invulnerability: The motivations and mechanisms of resistance to persuasion. *Journal of Personality and Social Psychology, 83,* 526–541.

Salmivalli,C. (2010). Bullying and the peer group: A review. *Aggression and Violent Behavior, 15,* 112–120.

Salmon, S. & Crawford, C. (2008). Evolutionary psychology: The historical context. In C. Crawford & D. Krebs (Eds), *Foundations of evolutionary psychology.* New York: Taylor & Francis. (pp. 1–21).

Sampson, E.E. (1975). On justice as equality. *Journal of Social Issues, 31,* 45–64.

Sampson, E.E. (1977). Psychology and the American ideal. *Journal of Personality and Social Psychology*, *35*, 767–782.

Samuelson, C.D., Messick, D.M., Rutte, C.G. & Wilke, H. (1984). Individual and structural solutions to resource dilemmas in two cultures. *Journal of Personality and Social Psychology*, *47*, 94–104.

Sande, G.N. (1990). The multifaceted self. In J.M. Olson & M.P. Zanna (Eds), *Self-inference processes: The Ontario symposium* (Vol. 6). (pp. 1–16). Hillsdale, NJ: Erlbaum.

Sanders, G.S. (1983). An attentional process model of social facilitation. In A. Hare, H. Blumberg, V. Kent & M. Davies (Eds), *Small Groups*. London: Wiley.

Sanders, G.S., Baron, R.S. & Moore, D.L. (1978). Distraction and social comparison as mediators of social facilitation effects. *Journal of Experimental Social Psychology*, *14*, 291–303.

San Jose-Cabezudo, R., Gutierrez-Arranz, A.M. & Gutierrez-Cillán, J. (2009). The combined influence of central and peripheral routes in the online persuasion process. *CyberPsychology & Behavior*, *12*, 299–308.

Sappington, A.A. & Baker, J. (1995). Refining religious belief–behavior relations. *International Journal for the Psychology of Religion*, *5*, 38–48.

Sashkin, M. (1977). The structure of charismatic leadership. In J.G. Hunt & L.L. Larson (Eds), *Leadership: The cutting edge* (pp. 212–218). Carbondale: Southern Illinois University Press.

Sastry, J. & Ross, C.E. (1998). Asian ethnicity and the sense of personal control. *Social Psychology Quarterly*, *61*, 101–120.

Saucier, D.A. & Webster, R.J. (2010). Social vigilantism: Measuring individual differences in belief superiority and resistance to persuasion. *Personality and Social Psychology Bulletin*, *36*, 19–32.

Saul, E.V. & Kass, T.S. (1969). Study of anticipated anxiety in a medical school setting. *Journal of Medical Education*, *44*, 526.

Saulnier, K. & Perlman, D. (1981). The actor-observer bias is alive and well in prison: A sequel to Wells. *Personality and Social Psychology Bulletin*, *7*, 559–564.

Savage, S.A. & Clarke, V.S. (1996). Factors associated with screening mammography and breast self-examination intentions. *Health Education Research*, *11*, 409–421.

Sawada, Y. (2003). Blood pressure and heart rate responses to an intrusion on personal space. *Japanese Psychological Research*, *45*, 115–121.

Sawrey, J.M. & Telford, C.W. (1975). *Adjustment and personality* (5th ed.). Boston: Allyn & Bacon.

Sbisà, M. (2009). Speech act theory. In J. Verschueren & J.- O. Östman (Eds), *Key notions for pragmatics*. Amsterdam: John Benjamins Publishing Company. (pp. 229–245).

Schachter, S. (1951). Deviation, rejection and communication. *Journal of Abnormal Social Psychology*, *46*, 190–207.

Schachter, S. (1959). *The psychology of affiliation.* Stanford, CA: Stanford University Press.

Schachter, S. (1964). The interaction of cognitive and physiological determinants of emotional state. In L. Berkowitz (Ed.), *Advances in experimental social psychology*, (Vol. 1). (pp. 48–81). New York: Academic Press.

Schachter, S. & Burdeck, H. (1955). A field experiment on rumour transmission and distortion. *Journal of Abnormal and Social Psychology*, *50*, 363–371.

Scheier, M.F. & Bridges, M.W. (1995). Person variables and health: Personality predispositions and acute psychological states as shared determinants for disease. *Psychosomatic Medicine*, *57*, 255–268.

Scher, S.J. & Cooper, J. (1989). Motivational basis of dissonance: The singular role of behavioral consequences. *Journal of Personality and Social Psychology*, *56*, 899–906.

Schlegel, R.P., D'Avernas, J.R., Zanna, M.P., De Courville, N.H. & Manske, S.R. (1992). Problem drinking: A problem for the theory of reasoned action. *Journal of Applied Social Psychology*, *22*, 358–385.

Schlegel, R.P., Manske, S.R. & D'Avernas, J.R. (1985). Alcohol and drug use in young adults. Selected findings in a longitudinal study. *Bulletin of the Society of Psychologists in Addictive Behavior*, *4*, 213–225.

Schmader, T., Johns, M. & Forbes, C. (2008). An integrated process model of stereotype threat effects on performance. *Psychological Review*, *115*, 336–356.

Schmidt, D.E. & Keating, J.P. (1979). Human crowding and personal control. *Psychological Bulletin*, *86*, 680–700.

Schmidt, M.F.H. & Tomasello, M. (2012). Young children enforce social norms. *Current Directions in Psychological Science*, *21*, 232.

Schmitt, B.H., Gilovich, T., Goore, N. & Joseph, L. (1986). Mere presence and social facilitation: One more time. *Journal of Experimental Psychology, 22*, 242–248.

Schmitt, D.P., Alcalay & 128 others (2004). Patterns and universals of adult romantic attachment across 62 cultural regions: Are models of self and others pancultural constructs? *Journal of Cross-Cultural Psychology, 35*, 367–402.

Schmitt, D.P., Youn, G., Bond, B., Brooks, S., Frye, H., Johnson, S., Klesman, J., Peplinski, C., Sampias, J., Sherrill, M. & Stoka, C. (2009). When will I feel love? The effects of personality, culture, and gender on the psychological tendency to love. *Journal of Research in Personality, 43*, 830–846.

Schneier, B. (2012). Lance Armstrong and the Prisoners' Dilemma of doping in professional sports. *Wired.com.* Retrieved 2012.11.01

Schoeneman, T.J. & Rubanowitz, D.E. (1985). Attributions in the advice columns: I. Actors, observers, causes and reasons. *Personality and Social Psychology Bulletin, 11*, 315–325.

Schuller, R.A. (1992). The impact of battered woman syndrome evidence on jury decision processes. *Law and Human Behavior, 16*, 597–620.

Schuller, R.A. (1994). Application of battered woman syndrome evidence in the courtroom. In M. Costanzo & S. Oskamp (Eds), *Violence and the law. The Claremont Symposium on Applied Social Psychology* (pp. 113–134). Thousand Oaks, CA: Sage.

Schuller, R.A. & Hastings, P.A. (1996). Trials of battered women who kill: The impact of alternative forms of expert evidence. *Law and Human Behavior, 20*, 167–187.

Schuller, R. A. & Hastings, P. A. (2002). Complainant sexual history evidence: It impact on mock jurors' decisions. *Psychology of Women Quarterly, 26*, 252–261.

Schuller, R.A. & Rzepa, S. (2002). Expert testimony pertaining to battered woman syndrome: Its impact on jurors' decisions. *Law and Human Behavior, 26*, 655–673.

Schuller, R.A., Smith, V.L. & Olson, J.M. (1994). Jurors' decisions in trials of battered women who kill: The role of prior beliefs and expert testimony. *Journal of Applied Social Psychology, 24*, 316–337.

Schuller, R.A. & Vidmar, N. (1992). Battered woman syndrome evidence in the courtroom: A review of the literature. *Law and Human Behavior, 16*, 273–291.

Schultz, T.R. & Lepper, M.R. (1996). Cognitive dissonance as constraint satisfaction. *Psychological Review, 103*, 219–240.

Schultz, T.R., Léveillé, E. & Lepper, M.R. (1999). Free choice and cognitive dissonance revisited: Choosing the 'lesser evils' versus 'greater goods'. *Personality & Social Psychology Bulletin, 25*, 40–48.

Schultz, W. (2000). Multiple reward signals in the brain. *Nature Reviews Neuroscience, 1*, 199–207.

Schut, C., Linder, D., Brosig, B., Niemeier, V., Ermler, C., Madejski, K., Saad, S., Gieler, U. & Kupfer, J. (2011). Appraisal of touching behavior, shame and disgust: A cross-cultural-study. *International Journal of Culture and Mental Health, 6*, 1–15.

Schwartz, S. (1994). Heuristics and biases in medical judgement and decision making. In L. Heath, R.S. Tindale, J. Edwards, E.J. Posavac, F.B. Bryant, E. Henderson-King, Y. Suarez-Balcazar & J. Myers (Eds) *Applications of heuristics and biases to social issues*. New York: Plenum Press. (pp. 45–72).

Schwartz, S. (1996). Value priorities and behavior: Applying a theory of integrated value systems. In C. Seligman, J.M. Olson & M.P. Zanna (Eds), *The Psychology of values: The Ontario symposium* (Vol. 8). (pp. 1–24). Hillsdale, NJ: Lawrence Erlbaum Associates.

Schwartz, S.H. (1992). Universals in the content and structure of values: Theoretical advances and empirical tests in 20 countries. In M. Zanna (Ed.), *Advances in experimental social psychology* (Vol. 25). (pp.1–65). New York: Academic Press.

Schwartz, S.H. (1994). Are there universals in the content and structure of values? *Journal of Social Issues, 50*, 19–45.

Schweingruber, D. &. Wohlstein, R.T. (2005). The madding crowd goes to school: Myths about crowds in introductory sociology. *Teaching Sociology, 33*, 136–153.

Scrimshaw, E.W. (2002). Social support, conflict and integration among women living with HIV/AIDS. *Journal of Applied Social Psychology, 32*, 2022–2042.

Searle, J.R. (1969). *Speech acts.* Cambridge: Cambridge University Press.

Searle, J.R. (1975). Indirect speech acts. In P. Cole & J.L. Morgan (Eds), *Syntax and semantics*

3: Speech acts (pp. 283–298). Hillsdale, NJ: Erlbaum.

Sears, D.O. (1983). The person-positivity bias. *Journal of Personality and Social Psychology*, *44*, 233–250.

Seaton, M., Marsh, H.W. & Craven, R.G. (2009). Earning its place as a pan-human theory: Universality of the big-fish-little-pond effect across 41 culturally and economically diverse countries. *Journal of Educational Psychology*, *101*, 403–419.

Sedikides, C. & Anderson, C.A. (1994). Causal perception of intertrait relations: The glue that holds person types together. *Personality and Social Psychology Bulletin*, *21*, 294–302.

Seligman, C., Fazio, R.H. & Zanna, M.P. (1980). Effects of salience of extrinsic rewards on liking and loving. *Journal of Personality and Social Psychology*, *38*, 453–460.

Seligman, C., Tucker, G.R. & Lambert, W.E. (1972). The effects of speech style and other attributes on teachers' attitudes towards pupils. *Language in Society*, *1*, 131–142.

Selye, H. (1956). *The stress of life.* New York: McGraw-Hill.

Seo, D., Patrick, C.J. & Kennealy, P.J. (2008). Role of serotonin and dopamine system interactions in the neurobiology of impulsive aggression and its comorbidity with other clinical disorders. *Aggression and Violent Behaviour*, *13*, 383–395.

Sermat, V. (1978). Sources of loneliness. *Essence*, *2*, 271–276.

Seto, M.C. & Lalumière, M.L. (2010). What is so special about male adolescent sexual offending? A review and test of explanations using meta-analysis. *Psychological Bulletin*, *136*, 526–575.

Settle, J.E., Dawes, C.T., Christakis, N.S. & Fowler, J.H. (2010). Friendships moderate an association between dopamine gene variant and political ideology. *Journal of Politics*, *72*, 1189–1198.

Ševčíková, A. & Šmahel, D. (2009). Online harassment and cyberbullying in the Czech Republic: Comparison across age groups. *Zeitschrift fur Psychologie /Journal of Psychology*, *217*, 227–229.

Seydel, E., Taal, E. & Wiegman, O. (1990). Risk-appraisal, outcome and efficacy expectancies: Cognitive factors in preventive behavior related to cancer. *Psychology and Health*, *4*, 99–109.

Shanab, M.E. & Yahya, K.A. (1977). A behavioral study of obedience in children. *Journal of Personality and*

Social Psychology, *35*(7), 530–536. doi:http://dx.doi.org/10.1037/0022-3514.35.7.530

Shannon, C. & Weaver, W. (1949). *The mathematical theory of communication.* Urbana, IL: University of Illinois Press.

Shanteau, J. & Nagy, G.F. (1979). Probability of acceptance in dating choice. *Journal of Personality and Social Psychology*, *37*, 522–533.

Shapiro, D.E., Boggs, S.R., Melamed, B.G. & Graham-Pole, J. (1992). The effects of varied physician affect on recall anxiety and perceptions in women at risk for breast cancer: An analogue study. *Health Psychology*, *11*, 61–66.

Shapiro, D.M. & Stelcner, M. (1987). Earning disparities among linguistic groups in Québec, 1970–1980. *Analyse de politique*, *13*, 97–104.

Shapiro, P.N. & Penrod, S. (1986). Meta-analysis of facial identification studies. *Psychological Bulletin*, *100*, 139–156.

Shaw, L.H. & Gant, L.M. (2002). In defence of the Internet. The relationship between Internet communication and depression, loneliness, self-esteem and perceived social support. *CyberPsychology and Behavior*, *5*, 157–171.

Shaw, M.E. (1981). *Group dynamics: The psychology of small group behavior* (3rd ed.). New York: McGraw-Hill.

Shen, H., Wan, F. & Wyer, R.S. (2011). Cross-cultural differences in the refusal to accept a small gift: The differential influence of reciprocity norms on Asians and North Americans. *Journal of Personality and Social Psychology*, *100*, 271–281. doi: 10.1037/a0021201

Shepherd, J.W., Deregowski, J.B. & Ellis, H.D. (1974). A cross-cultural study of recognition memory for faces. *International Journal of Psychology*, *9*, 205–211.

Sheppard, B.H. & Vidmar, N. (1980). Adversary pre-trial procedure and testimonial evidence: Effects of lawyer's role and Machiavellianism. *Journal of Personality and Social Psychology*, *39*, 320–332.

Sherif, M. (1936). *The psychology of social norms.* New York: Harper & Row.

Sherif, M. (1937). An experimental approach to the study of attitudes. *Sociometry*, *1*, 90–98.

Sherif, M. (1958). Superordinate goals in the reduction of intergroup conflict. *American Journal of Sociology*, 349–356.

Sherif, M. & Cantril, H. (1947). *The psychology of ego involvement: Social attitudes and identification.* New York: Wiley.

Sherif, M., Harvey, O.J., White, B.J., Hood, W.R. & Sherif, C. (1961). *Intergroup conflict and cooperation: The Robbers Cave experiment.* Norman, OK: University of Oklahoma Press.

Sherman, M. (1997). *Why people believe weird things.* New York: Freeman.

Sherman, S.J., Chassin, L., Presson, C.L. & Agostinelli, G. (1984). The role of evaluation and similarity principles in the false consensus effect. *Journal of Personality and Social Psychology, 47,* 1244–1262.

Sherrod, D.R. (1974). Crowding, perceived control and behavioral after effects. *Journal of Applied Social Psychology, 4,* 171–186.

Shestowsky, D., Wegener, D.T. & Fabrigar, L.R. (1992). Need for cognition and interpersonal influence: Individual differences in dyadic decisions. *Journal of Personality and Social Psychology, 74,* 1317–1328.

Shibutani, T. (1966). *Improvised news: A sociological study of rumor.* Indianapolis, IL: Bobbs-Merrill.

Shniderman, A.B. (2013). Ripped from the headlines. Juror perceptions in the 'Law and Order' era. *Law and Psychology Review,* 38 in press.

Shoemaker, D.J., South, D.R. & Lowe, J. (1973). Facial stereotypes of deviants and judgments of guilt or innocence. *Social Forces, 51,* 427–433.

Shotland, R.L. & Goodstein, L. (1992). Sexual precedence reduces the perceived legitimacy of sexual refusal: An examination of attributions concerning date rape and consensual sex. *Personality and Social Psychology Bulletin, 18,* 756–764.

Shteynberg, G. (2010). A silent emergence of culture. The social tuning effect, *Journal of Personality and Social Psychology, 99,* 683–689.

Shuang-shuang, L. (2010). A tentative study of the impoliteness phenomenon in computer-mediated communication. *Cross-cultural communication, 6,* 92–107.

Sibley, C. G. & Duckitt, J. (2008). Personality and prejudice: A meta-analysis and theoretical review. *Personality and Social Psychology Review, 12,* 248–279

Sibley, C.G. & Duckitt, J. (2008). Personality and prejudice: A meta-analysis and theoretical review. *Personality and Social Psychology Review, 12,* 248–279.

Sidanius, J., Levin, S., Federico, C.M. & Pratto, F. (2001). Legitimizing ideologies: The social dominance approach. In J.T. Jost & B. Majors (Eds), *The psychology of legitimacy: Emerging perspectives on ideology, justice, and intergroup relations* (307–331). New York: Cambridge University Press.

Siem, F.M. & Spence, J.T. (1986). Gender-related traits and helping behaviors. *Journal of Personality and Social Psychology, 51,* 615–621.

Sigall, H. & Ostrove, N. (1975). Beautiful but dangerous: Effects of offender attractiveness and nature of the crime on juridic judgement. *Journal of Personality and Social Psychology, 31,* 410–414.

Sigall, H. & Page, R. (1971). Current stereotypes: A little fading, a little faking. *Journal of Personality and Social Psychology, 18,* 247–255.

Silver, R.L., Boon, C. & Stones, M.H. (1983). Searching for meaning in misfortune: Making sense of incest. *Journal of Social Issues, 39,* 81–100.

Silverman, I. (1971). On the resolution and tolerance of cognitive consistency in a natural occurring event: Attitudes and beliefs following the Senator Edward M. Kennedy incident. *Journal of Personality and Social Psychology, 17,* 171–178.

Silverstein, B. (1987). Toward a science of propaganda. *Political Psychology, 8,* 49–59.

Simon, B. (1992). The perception of ingroup and outgroup homogeneity: Reintroducing the intergroup context. *European Review of Social Psychology, 3,* 1–30.

Simon, B., Loewy, M., Stürmer, S., Weber, U., Freytag, P., Habig, C., Kampmeier, C. & Spahlinger, P. (1998). Collective identification and social movement participation. *Journal of Personality and Social Psychology, 74,* 646–658.

Simon, R.J. & Mahan, L. (1971). Quantifying burdens of proof: A view from the bench, the jury and the classroom. *Law and Society Review, 5,* 319–330.

Simons, R.L., Lei, M.K., Stuart, E.A., Beach, S.R.H., Brody, G.H., Philibert, R.A. & Gibbons, F.X. (2012). Social adversity, genetic variation, street code, and aggression: A genetically informed model of violent behaviour. *Youth Violence and Juvenile Justice, 10,* 3–24.

Simpson, J.A. (1987). The dissolution of romantic relationships: Factors involved in relationship stability and emotional distress. *Journal of Personality and Social Psychology, 53,* 683–692.

Simpson, J.A., Rholes, W.S. & Nelligan, J.S. (1992). Support seeking and support giving within

578

couples in an anxiety-provoking situation: The role of attachment styles. *Journal of Personality and Social Psychology, 62,* 434–446.

Simpson, S., McCarry, M. & Edwards, H.P. (1987). Relationship of supervisors' sex role stereotypes to performance evaluation of male and female subordinates in non-traditional jobs. *Canadian Journal of Administrative Science, 4,* 15–30.

Sims, H.P. & Manz, C.C. (1984). Observing leader verbal behavior: Toward reciprocal determinism in leadership theory. *Journal of Applied Psychology, 69,* 222–232.

Sinaceur, M, Van Kleef, G.A., Neale, M.A., Adam, H. &, Haag, C. (2011). Hot or cold: Is communicating anger or threats more effective in negotiation? *Journal of Applied Psychology, 96,* 1018–1032.

Sinclair, C. (1993). Codes of ethics and standards of practice. In K.S. Dobson & D.J.G. Dobson (Eds), *Professional psychology in Canada.* Germany: Hogrefe and Huber.

Sinclair, C. (2002). A brief history of ethical principles in professional codes of ethics. Retrieved on May 28, 2013 from http://e-book.lib.sjtu.edu.cn/iupsys/ethics/eth3_sin.html.

Sinclair, C., Poizner, S., Gilmour-Barrett, K. & Randall, D. (1987). The development of a code of ethics for Canadian psychologists. *Canadian Psychology, 28,* 1–8.

Sinclair, L. & Kunda, Z. (2000). Motivated stereotyping of women. She's fine if she praised me but incompetent if she criticized me. *Personality & Social Psychology Bulletin, 26,* 1329–1342.

Sinclair, R.C., Lee, T. & Johnson, T.E. (1995). The effect of social-comparison feedback on aggressive responses to erotic and aggressive films. *Journal of Applied Social Psychology, 25,* 818–837.

Sinclair, R.C. & Mark, M.M. (1992). The influence of mood state on judgement and action: Effects on persuasion, categorization, social justice, person perception and judgmental accuracy. In L.L. Martin & A. Tesser (Eds), *The construction of social judgements* (pp. 165–193). Hillsdale, NJ: Erlbaum.

Sinclair, R.C., Mark, M.M. & Clore, G.L. (1994). Mood-related persuasion depends on (mis)attributions. *Social Cognition, 12,* 309–326.

Singer, J.L. & Singer, D.G. (1986). Family experiences and television viewing as predictors of children's imagination, restlessness and aggression. *Journal of Social Issues, 42,* 107–124.

Singh, D. & Young, R.K. (1995). Bodyweight, hip-to-waist ratio, breasts and hips: Role in judgments of female attractiveness and desirability for relationship. *Ethology and Sociobiology, 16,* 483–507.

Singh, R. & Ho, S.Y. (2000). Attitudes and attraction: A new test of the attraction, repulsion and similarity-dissimilarity asymmetry hypothesis. *British Journal of Social Psychology, 39,* 197–211.

Sistrunk, F. & McDavid, V.W. (1971). Sex variable in conformity behavior. *Journal of Personality and Social Psychology, 17,* 200–207.

Six, U. (1989). The functions of stereotypes and prejudices in the process of cross-cultural understanding: A social psychological approach. In P. Funckle (Ed.), *Understanding the U.S.A.: A cross-cultural perspective.* Tubingen: Narr.

Skowronski, J.J. & Carlston, D.E. (1989). Negativity and extremity biases in impression formation: A review of explanations. *Psychological Bulletin, 105,* 131–142.

Slatcher, R.B. (2010). Marital functioning and physical health: Implications for social and personality psychology. *Social and Personality Psychology Compass, 4,* 455–469.

Slater, M., Antley, A., Davison, A., Swapp, D., Guger, C., Barker, C., Pistrang, N. & Sanchez-Vives, M.V. (2006). A virtual reprise of the Stanley Milgram obedience experiments. *PLoS One, 1,* e39.

Slovic, P. (2007). 'If I look *at* the mass I will never act': Psychic numbing and genocide. *Judgment and Decision Making, 2,* 179–95.

Sluka, J. (1992). The anthropology of conflict. In C. Nordstrom & J. Martin (Eds), *The paths to domination, resistance, and terror.* Berkeley: University of California Press. (pp. 18–36).

Small, D.A., Loewenstein, G. & Slovic, P. (2007). Sympathy and callousness: The impact of deliberative thought on donations to identifiable and statistical victims. *Organizational Behavior and Human Decision Processes, 102,* 143–153.

Smeaton, G., Byrne, D. & Murnen, S.K. (1989). The repulsion hypothesis revisited: Similarity irrelevance or dissimilarity bias? *Journal of Personality and Social Psychology, 56,* 54–59.

Smith, C.P. (1983). Ethical issues: Research on deception, informed consent, and debriefing. In L. Wheeler & P. Shaver (Eds), *Review of personality and social psychology* (Vol. 4). (pp. 297–328). Beverly Hills, CA: Sage.

Smith, E.R. & DeCoster, J. (2000). Dual-process models in social and cognitive psychology: Conceptual integration and links to underlying memory system. *Personality and Social Psychology Review*, *4*, 108–131.

Smith, J.L. (2004). Understanding the process of stereotype threat: A review of mediational variables and new performance goal directions. *Educational Psychology Review*, *16*, 177–206.

Smith, K.B., Oxley, R., Hibbing, M.V., Alford, J.R. & Hibbing, J.R. (2011). Reconceptualizing political ideology. *Political Psychology*, *32*, 369–397.

Smith, P.B. (2005). Is there an indigenous European social psychology? *International Journal of Psychology*, *40*, 254–262.

Smith, P.B., Dugan, S. & Trompenaars, F. (1996). National culture and the values of organizational employees. *Journal of Cross-Cultural Psychology*, *27*, 231–264.

Smith, S.M., & Petty, R.E. (1996). Message framing and persuasion: A message processing analysis. *Personality and Social Psychology Bulletin*, *22*, 257–268.

Snethen, G. & Van Puymbroeck, M. (2008). Girls and physical aggression: Causes, trends and intervention guided by Social Learning Theory. *Aggression and Violent Behavior*, *13*, 346–354.

Snow, C.P. (1961) Either-or. *Progressive*, 25 (2), 24.

Snyder, M. (1979). Self-monitoring processes. In L. Berkowitz (Ed.), *Advances in experimental social psychology* (Vol. 12). (pp. 85–128). New York: Academic Press.

Snyder, M. & DeBono, K.G. (1985). Appeals to image and claims about quality: Understanding the psychology of advertising. *Journal of Personality and Social Psychology*, *49*, 586–597.

Snyder, M. & Omoto, A.M. (2008). Volunteerism: Social issues perspectives and social policy implications. *Social Issues and Policy Review*, *2*, 1–36.

Soenens, B., Vansteenkiste, M., Lens, W., Luyckx, K., Goossens, L., Beyers, W., et al. (2007). Conceptualizing parental autonomy support: Adolescent perceptions of promotion of independence versus promotion of volitional functioning. *Developmental Psychology*, *43*, 633–646.

Soifer, E. (1996). Euthanasia and persistent vegetative state individuals: The role and moral status of autonomy. *Journal of Social Issues*, *52*(2), 31–50.

Solano, C.H., Batten, P.G. & Parish, E.A. (1982). Loneliness and patterns of self-disclosure. *Journal of Personality and Social Psychology*, *43*, 524–531.

Solano, C.H. & Koester, N.H. (1989). Loneliness and communication problems: Subjective anxiety or objective skills? *Personality and Social Psychology Bulletin*, *15*, 126–133.

Solari, C.D. & Mare, R.D. (2012). Housing crowding effects on children's well-being. *Social Science Research*, *41*, 464–476.

Sole, K., Marton, J. & Hornstein, H.A. (1975). Opinion similarity and helping: Three field experiments investigating the bases of promotive tension. *Journal of Experimental Social Psychology*, *11*, 1–13.

Solomon, D. & Yaeger, J. (1969). Effect of content and intonation on perceptions of verbal reinforcers. *Perceptual and Motor Skills*, *28*, 319–327.

Solomon, L. (1960). The influence of some types of power relationships and game strategies upon the development of interpersonal trust. *Journal of Abnormal and Social Psychology*, *61*, 223–230.

Solomon, M.R. (1986). Dress for effect. *Psychology Today*, *20*(4), 20–28.

Sommer, B. (1992). Cognitive performance and the menstrual cycle. In J.T. Richardson (Ed.), *Cognition and the menstrual cycle: Research, theory and culture* (pp. 249–277). New York: Springer-Verlag.

Sommer, R. (1969). *Personal space: The behavioral basis of design*, Prentice-Hall, Englewood Cliffs.

Song, Z. & Chon, K. (2012). General self-efficacy's effect on career choice goals via vocational interests and person–job fit: A mediation model. *International Journal of Hospitality Management*, *31*, 798–808.

Sontag, S. (1978). *Illness as metaphor*. New York: Farrar, Straus & Giroux.

Sorokowski, P. (2010). Did Venus have long legs? Beauty standards from various historical periods reflected in works of art. *Perception*, *39*, 1427–1430.

Soussignan, R. (2002). Duchenne smile, emotional experience, and autonomic reactivity: A test of the facial feedback hypothesis. *Emotion*, *2*, 52–54.

Spence, J.T. (1985). Gender identity and its implications for the concepts of masculinity and femininity. In T.B. Sonderegger (Ed.), *Nebraska symposium on motivation: Psychology and gender* (pp. 59–95). Lincoln, NE: University of Nebraska Press.

Spence, J.T. & Helmreich, R.L. (1979). Comparison of masculine and feminine personality attributes and sex-role attitudes across age groups. *Developmental Psychology, 15*, 583–594.

Spencer, S.J., Steele, C.M. & Quinn, D.M. (1999). Stereotype threat and women's math performance. *Journal of Experimental Social Psychology, 35*, 4–28.

Spiegel, D., Bloom, J.R., Kraemer, H.C. & Gottheil, E. (1989). Psychological support for cancer patients. *Lancet, 2*, 1447.

Sporer, S.L., Penrod, S., Read, D. & Cutler, B. (1995). Choosing, confidence and accuracy: A meta-analysis of the confidence-accuracy relation in eyewitness identification studies. *Psychological Bulletin, 118*, 315–327.

Sprafkin, J.N., Liebert, R.M. & Poulos, R.W. (1975). Effects of a prosocial televised example on children's helping. *Journal of Experimental Child Psychology, 20*, 119–126.

Sprecher, S. (2001a). Equity and social exchange in dating couples; Associations with satisfaction, commitment and stability. *Journal of Marriage and the Family, 63*, 599–613.

Sprecher, S. (2001b). A comparison of emotional consequences of and changes in equity over time using global and domain-specific measures of equity. *Journal of Social and Personal Relationships, 18*, 477–501.

Sprecher, S., Felmlee, D., Metts, S., Fehr, B. & Vanni, D. (1998). Factors associated with distress following breakup of a close relationship. *Journal of Social and Personal Relationships, 15*, 791–809.

Srull, T.K. & Wyer, R.J. (1980). Category accessibility and social perception: Some implications for the study of personal memory and interpersonal judgements. *Journal of Personality and Social Psychology, 38*, 841–856.

Srull, T.K. & Wyer, R.J. (1989). Person memory and judgement. *Psychological Review, 96*, 58–83.

Stahelski, A.J. & Frost, D.E. (1989). Use of socially dependent bases of power: French and Raven's theory applied to workgroup leadership. *Journal of Applied Social Psychology, 19*, 283–297.

Stalde, D.R. (2012). The role of dissonance, social comparison and marital status in thinking about divorce. *Journal of Social and Personal Relationships, 29*, 302–323.

Stallen, M., De Dreu, C.K.W., Shalvi, S., Smidts, A. & Sanfey, A.G. (2012). The herding hormone: Oxytocin stimulates in-group conformity. *Psychological Science, 23*, 1288–1292.

Stark, C. (2001). Psychological climate changes for women in academic psychology: Forecasts, sources, and implications. *Canadian Psychology, 42*, 286–300.

Statistics Canada (1989). *Homicide in Canada 1988: A statistical perspective.* Ottawa: Ministry of Supply and Services.

Statistics Canada (2002). Sexual and physical assault. http://www. statcan.ca/english/freepub/85–224–XIE/85–224–XIE00002.pdf

Statistics Canada (2011). *Family Violence in Canada: A Statistical Profile.* Ottawa: Canadian Centre for Justice Statistics.

Statistics Canada (2012). *Police-reported crime statistics in Canada, 2011.* Ottawa: http://www.statcan.gc.ca/pub/85-002-x/2012001/article/11692-eng.htm#a16. Downloaded October 1, 2012.

Staub, E. (1974). Helping a distressed person: Social, personality and stimulus determinants. In L. Berkowitz (Ed.), *Advances in experimental social psychology* (Vol. 7). (pp. 294–341). New York: Academic Press.

Staub, E. (2005). The origins and evolution of hate, with notes on prevention. In R.J. Sternberg (Ed.), *The psychology of hate* (pp. 51–66). Washington, DC: American Psychological Association.

Staub, E. & Baer, R.S. (1974). Stimulus characteristics of a sufferer and difficulty of escape as determinants of helping. *Journal of Personality and Social Psychology, 30*, 279–285.

Steblay, N.M. (1987). Helping behavior in rural and urban environments: A meta-analysis. *Psychological Bulletin, 102*, 346–356.

Steele, C.M. (1997). A threat in the air. How stereotypes shape intellectual identity and performance. *American Psychologist, 52*, 613–629.

Steele, C.M. & Aronson, J. (1995). Stereotype threat and the intellectual test performance of African Americans. *Journal of Personality and Social Psychology, 69*, 797–811.

Steele, C.M. & Liu, T.J. (1983). Dissonance process as self-affirmation. *Journal of Personality and Social Psychology, 45*, 5–19.

Steele, C.M., Southwick, L.C. & Critchlow, B. (1981). Dissonance and alcohol: Drinking your troubles away. *Journal of Personality and Social Psychology, 41*, 831–846.

Steg, L. & de Groot, J. (2010). Explaining prosocial intentions: Testing causal relationships in the norm activation model.

British Journal of Social Psychology, *49*, 725–743

Stel, M. & Harinck, F. (2011). Being mimicked makes you a prosocial voter. *Experimental Psychology*, *58*, 79–84.

Stel, M., Rispens, S., Leliveld, M. & Lokhorst, A.M. (2011). The consequences of mimicry for prosocials and proselfs: Effects of social value orientation on the mimicry-liking link. *European Journal of Social Psychology*, *41*, 269–274

Stel, M., Van Baaren, R.B. & Vonk, R. (2007). Effects of mimicking: Acting pro-socially by being emotionally moved. *European Journal of Social Psychology*, *38*, 965–976.

Stephan, W.G. & Stephan, C.W. (1985). *Intergroup anxiety. Journal of Social Issues*, *41*, 157–175.

Sternberg, R.J. (1986). A triangular theory of love. *Psychological Review*, *93*, 119–135.

Sternberg, R.J., Conway, B.E., Ketron, J.L. & Bernstein, M. (1981). People's conception of intelligence. *Journal of Personality and Social Psychology*, *41*, 37–55.

Sternberg, R.J. & Grajek, S. (1984). The nature of love. *Journal of Personality and Social Psychology*, *47*, 312–329.

Sternberg, R.J. & Sternberg, K. (2008). *The nature of hate*. New York: Cambridge University Press.

Stewart, M., Ryan, E. & Giles, H. (1985). Accent and social class effects on status and solidarity evaluations. *Personality and Social Psychology Bulletin*, *11*, 98–105.

Stirling, G. & Reid, D.W. (1992). The application of participatory control to facilitate patient well-being: An experimental study of nursing impact on geriatric patients. *Canadian Journal of Behavioural Science*, *24*, 204–219.

Stogdill, R. (1974). *Handbook of leadership*. New York: Free Press.

Stone, A. & Neale, J.M. (1982). Development of a methodology for assessing daily experiences. In A. Baum & J.E. Singer (Eds), *Advances in environmental psychology* (Vol. 4). (pp. 49–83). Hillsdale: Erlbaum.

Stone, J. (2003). Self-consistency for low self-esteem in dissonance processes: The role of self-standards. *Personality and Social Psychology Bulletin*, *29*, 846–858,

Stone, J., Aronson, E., Crain, A.L., Winslow, M.P. & Fried, C. (1994). Inducing hypocrisy as a means of encouraging young adults to use condoms. *Personality and Consumer Research*, *28*, 636–649.

Storms, M.D. (1973). Videotape and the attribution process: Reversing actor's and observer's points of view. *Journal of Personality and Social Psychology*, *27*, 165–175.

Stover, E. & Nightingale, E.O. (1985). *The breaking of bodies and minds. Torture, psychiatric abuse, and the health professions*. New York: W.H. Freeman.

Strauman, T.J. (1996). Stability within the self: A longitudinal study of the structural implications of self-discrepancy theory. *Journal of Personality and Social Psychology*, *71*, 1142–1153.

Strecher, V.J., Champion, V.L. & Rosenstock, I.M. (1997). The health beliefs model and health behaviour. In D.S. Gochman et al. (Eds), *Handbook of health behaviour research: 1. Personal and social determinants* (pp. 71–91). New York: Plenum Press.

Strenziok, M., Krueger, F., Deshpande, G., Lenroot, K., van der Meer, E. & Grafman, J. (2011). Fronto-parietal regulation of media violence exposure in adolescents: A multi-method study. *Social Cognitive and Affective Neuroscience*, *6*, 537–547.

Strickland, L.H. (1958). Surveillance and trust. *Journal of Personality*, *26*, 200–215.

Strickland, L.H. (1991). Russian and Soviet social psychology. *Canadian Psychology*, *32*, 580–595.

Stroebe, M.S. & Stroebe, W. (1983). Who suffers more? Sex differences in health risks of the widowed. *Psychological Bulletin*, *93*, 279–301.

Stroebe, W. (2012). The truth about Triplett (1898), but nobody seems to care. *Perspectives on Psychological Science*, 7, 54–57. doi: 10.1177/1745691611427306

Stroebe, W., Diehl, M. & Abakoumkin, G. (1992). The illusion of group effectivity. *Personality and Social Psychology Bulletin*, *18*, 643–650.

Strube, M.J. (2005). What did Triplett really find? A contemporary analysis of the first experiment in social psychology. *American Journal of Psychology*, *118*, 271–286.

Strube, M.J. & Garcia, J.E. (1981). A meta-analytic investigation of Fiedler's contingency model of leadership effectiveness. *Psychological Bulletin*, *90*, 307–321.

Stulp, G., Buunk, A.P., Verhulst, S & Pollet, T.V. (2013). Tall claims? Sense and nonsense about the importance of height of US presidents. *The Leadership Quarterly, 24*, 159–171.

Sturges, J.W. & Rogers, R.W. (1996). Preventive health psychology from a developmental perspective: An extension of protection motivation theory. *Health Psychology, 15*, 158–166.

Suedfeld, P. (2000). Reverberations of the Holocaust fifty years later: Psychology's contributions to understanding persecution and genocide. *Canadian Psychology, 41*, 1–9.

Suedfeld, P. (2003). Canadian space psychology: The future may be almost here. *Canadian Psychology, 44*, 85–92.

Suedfeld, P. & Bluck, S. (1993). Changes in integrative complexity accompanying significant life events: Historical evidence. *Journal of Personality and Social Psychology, 64*, 124–130.

Suedfeld, P. & Piedrahita, L.E. (1984). Intimations of mortality: Integrative simplification as a precursor of death. *Journal of Personality and Social Psychology, 47*, 848–852.

Suedfeld, P. & Rank, A.D. (1976). Revolutionary leaders: Long-term success as a function of changes in conceptual complexity. *Journal of Personality and Social Psychology, 34*, 169–176.

Suedfeld, P., Rank, A.D. & Borrie, R. (1975). Frequency of exposure and evaluation of candidates and campaign speeches. *Journal of Applied Psychology, 5*, 118–126.

Sullivan, M.J.L., Bishop, S.R. & Pivik, J. (1995). The Pain Catastrophizing Scale: Development and validation. *Psychological Assessment, 7*, 524–532.

Sullivan, M.J.L., Rodgers, W.M. & Kirsch, I. (2001). Catastrophizing, depression and expectancies for pain and emotional distress. *Pain, 91*, 147–154.

Suls, J., Wan, C.K. & Sanders, D.S. (1988). False consensus and false uniqueness in estimating the prevalence of health-protective behaviors. *Journal of Applied Social Psychology, 18*, 66–79.

Sumi, K. & Kanda, K. (2002). Relationships between neurotic perfectionism, depression, anxiety and psychosomatic symptoms: a prospective study among Japanese men. *Personality and Individual Differences, 32*, 817–826.

Super, D.E. (1980). A life-span life-space approach to career development. *Journal of Vocational Behaviour, 16*, 282–298.

Surette, R. (2002). Self-reported copycat crime among a population of serious and violent juvenile offenders. *Crime and Delinquency, 48*, 46–49.

Sussman, N.M. & Rosenfeld, H.M. (1982). Influence of culture, language and sex on conversational distance. *Journal of Personality and Social Psychology, 42*, 66–74.

Sutton, S. (1998). Predicting and explaining intentions and behaviour. *Journal of Applied Social Psychology, 28*, 1317–1338.

Sutton, S.R. (1982). Fear-arousing communications: A critical examination of theory and research. In J.R. Eiser (Ed.), *Social psychology and behavioral medicine* (pp. 303–338). New York: Wiley.

Swann, W. (1990). To be adored or to be known? The interplay of self-enhancement and self-verification. In R.M. Sorrentino & E.T. Higgins (Eds), *Motivation and cognition* (pp. 414–448). New York: Guilford Press.

Swann, W. (1992). Seeking 'truth', finding despair: Some unhappy consequences of a negative self-concept. *Current Directions in Psychological Science, 1*, 15–18.

Swann, W., Jetten, J., Gómez, A., Whitehouse, H. & Bastian, B. (2012). When group membership gets personal: A theory of identity fusion. *Psychological Review, 119*, 441–456.

Swann, W., Stein-Seroussi, A. & Giesler, R.B. (1992). Why people self-verify. *Journal of Personality and Social Psychology, 62*, 392–401.

Swart, H., Hewstone, M., Christ, O. & Voci, A. (2011). Affective mediators of intergroup contact: A three-wave longitudinal study in South Africa. *Journal of Personality and Social Psychology, 101*, 1221–1238.

Sweeney, P.D., Anderson, K. & Bailey, S. (1986). Attribution style in depression: A meta-analytic review. *Journal of Personality and Social Psychology, 50*, 974–991.

Swim, J., Borgida, E. & Maruyama, G. (1989). Joan McKay versus John McKay: Do gender stereotypes bias evaluation? *Psychological Bulletin, 105*, 409–429.

Swim, J. & Hyers, L.L. (2009). Sexism. In T.D. Nelson (Ed.), *Handbook of prejudice, stereotyping, and discrimination* (pp. 407–430). New York: Psychology Press.

Swim, J. & Sanna, L.J. (1996). He's skilled, she's lucky: A meta-analysis of observers' attributions for women's and men's successes and failures. *Personality and Social Psychology Bulletin, 22*, 507–519.

Sykes, R.E., Rowley, R.D. & Schaeffer, J.M. (1993). The influence of time, gender and group size on heavy drinking in public bars. *Journal of Studies on Alcohol, 54,* 133–138.

Szymanski, K. & Harkins, S. (1987). Social loafing and self-evaluation with a social standard. *Journal of Personality and Social Psychology, 53,* 891–897.

Tabibnia, G. & Lieberman, M.D. (2007). Fairness and cooperation are rewarding: Evidence from social cognitive neuroscience. *Annals of the New York Academy of Science, 1118,* 90–101.

Tafalla, R.J. (2007). Gender differences in cardiovascular reactivity and game performance related to sensory modality in violent videogame play. *Journal of Applied Social Psychology, 37,* 2008–2023.

Tagliamonte, S.A. (2006). *Analyzing sociolinguistic variation.* Cambridge: Cambridge University Press.

Tait, R.C. & Chibnall, J.T. (2005). Racial and ethnic disparities in the evaluation and treatment of pain. Psychological Perspectives. *Professional Psychology: Research and Practice, 36,* 595–601.

Tajfel, H. (1970). Experiments in intergroup discrimination. *Scientific American, 223*(5), 96–102.

Tajfel, H. (1972). La catégorization sociale [Social categorization]. In S. Moscovici (Ed.), *Introduction à la psychologie sociale,* (Vol. 1), Paris: Larousse.

Tajfel, H. (1974). Social identity and intergroup behaviour. *Social Science Information, 13,* 65–93.

Tajfel, H. (Ed.) (1978). *Differentiation between social groups: Studies in the social psychology of inter-group relations.* London: Academic Press.

Tajfel, H. (1982). Social psychology of intergroup relations. *Annual Review of Psychology, 33,* 1–39.

Tajfel, H. & Turner, J.C. (1979). An integrative theory of intergroup conflict. In W.G. Austin & S. Worchel (Eds), *The social psychology of inter-group relations* (pp. 33–47). Monterey, CA: Brooks/Cole.

Tajfel, H. & Turner, J.C. (1986). The social identity theory of intergroup relations. In S. Worchel & W.G. Austin (Eds) *The social psychology of intergroup relations* (pp. 7–24). Monterey, CA: Brooks/Cole.

Takemura, K. & Yuki, M. (2007). Are Japanese groups more competitive than Japanese individuals? A cross-cultural validation of the interindividual-intergroup discontinuity effect. *International Journal of Psychology, 42*(1), 27–35.

Tallman, I., Burke, P.J. & Gecas, V. (1998). Socialization into marital roles: Testing a contextual,

developmental model of marital functioning. In T.N. Bradbury et al. (Eds), *The developmental course of marital dysfunction* (pp. 312–342). New York: Cambridge University Press.

Tan, D.T.Y. & Singh, R. (1995). Attitudes and attraction: A developmental study of the similarity-attraction and dissimilarity-repulsion hypotheses. *Personality and Social Psychology Bulletin, 21,* 975–986.

Tanford, S. & Penrod, S. (1984). Social influence processes in juror judgements of multiple offence trials. *Journal of Personality and Social Psychology, 95,* 189–225.

Tang, C. S.-K. & Lai, B. P-Y. (2008). A review of empirical literature on the prevalence and risk markers of male-on-female intimate partner violence in contemporary China, 1987–2006. *Aggression and Violent Behavior, 13,* 10–28.

Tannen, D. (1990). *You just don't understand: Women and men in conversation.* New York: Morrow.

Taylor, D.M. (1981). Stereotypes and intergroup relations. In R.C. Gardner & R. Kalin (Eds), *A Canadian social psychology of ethnic relations* (pp. 151–171). Toronto: Methuen.

Taylor, D.M. (2011). Where it all began: A tribute to Wallace E. Lambert. *Journal of Language and Social Psychology, 20,* 259–263.

Taylor, D.M. & Lalonde, R.N. (1987). Ethnic stereotypes: A psychological analysis. In L. Driedger (Ed.), *Ethnic Canada: Identities and inequalities.* Toronto: Copp Clark Pittman.

Taylor, D.M. & Moghaddam, F.M. (1987). *Theories of intergroup relations: International social psychological perspective.* New York: Praeger.

Taylor, D.M. & Simard, L. (1975). Social interaction in a bilingual setting. *Canadian Psychological Review, 16,* 240–254.

Taylor, D.M. & Usborne, E. (2007). Is the social psychology of language a genuine field of study? *Journal of Language and Social Psychology, 16,* 204–211.

Taylor, D.M., Wright, S.C. & Porter, L.E. (1994). Dimensions of perceived discrimination: The personal/group discrimination discrepancy. In M.P. Zanna & J.M. Olson (Eds), *The Ontario symposium. Vol. 7: The psychology of prejudice* (pp. 233–255). Hillsdale, NJ: Erlbaum.

Taylor, D.M., Wright, S.C., Moghaddam, F.M. & Lalonde, R.N. (1990). The personal/group discrimination discrepancy: Perceiving my group but not myself to be a target of discrimination. *Personality and Social Psychology Bulletin, 16,* 254–262.

Taylor, J. & Macdonald, J. (2002). The effects of asynchronous computer-mediated group interaction on group processes. *Social Science Computer Review, 20,* 260–274.

Taylor, J. & Riess, M. (1989). Self-serving attributions to valenced causal factors. *Personality and Social Psychology Bulletin, 15,* 337–348.

Taylor, S.E. (1979). Hospital patient behavior: Reactance, helplessness or control? *Journal of Social Issues, 35,* 156–184.

Taylor, S.E. & Brown, J.D. (1988). Illusion and well-being: A social-psychological perspective on mental health. *Psychological Bulletin, 103,* 193–210.

Taylor, S.E., Falke, R.L., Shoptaw, S.J. & Lichtman, R.R. (1986). Social support, support groups and the cancer patient. *Journal of Consulting and Clinical Psychology, 54,* 608–615.

Taylor, S.E., Welch, W.T., Kim, H.S. & Sherman, D.K. (2007). Cultural differences in the impact of social support on psychological and biological stress responses. *Psychological Science, 18,* 831–837.

Taynor, J. & Deaux, K. (1973). Equity and perceived sex differences: Role behavior as defined by the task, the mode, and the actor. *Journal of Personality and Social Psychology, 32,* 381–390.

Tedeschi, J.T. (1983). Social influence theory and aggression. In R.G. Geen & E.I. Donnerstein (Eds), Aggression—Theoretical and methodological reviews (Vol. 1, pp. 135–162). New York: Academic Press.

Tennen, H., Affleck, G., Urrows, S., Higgins, P. & Mendola, R. (1992). Perceiving control, construing benefits and daily processes in rheumatoid arthritis. *Canadian Journal of Behavioural Science, 24,* 186–203.

Tennov, D. (1979). *Love and limerance: The experience of being in love.* New York: Stein and Day.

Terrance, C.A., Matheson, K. & Spanos, N.P. (2000). Effect of judicial instructions and case characteristics in a mock jury trial of battered women who kill. *Law and Human Behavior, 24,* 207–228.

Tessari, T., Rubaltelli, E., Tomelleri, S., Zorzi, C. & Pietroni, D. (2011). €1 ≠ €1.: Coins versus banknotes and people's spending behavior. *European Psychologist, 16,* 238–246.

Tesser, A. (1978). Self-generated attitude change. In L. Berkowitz (Ed.), *Advances in experimental social psychology* (Vol. 11). (pp. 288–338). New York: Academic Press.

Tesser, A. (1988). Toward a self-evaluation maintenance model of social behavior. In L. Berkowitz (Ed.), *Advances in experimental social psychology* (Vol. 21). (pp. 181–227). New York: Academic Press.

Tesser, A. & Paulhus, D.L. (1976). Toward a causal model of love. *Journal of Personality and Social Psychology, 34,* 1095–1105.

Tesser, A. & Rosen, S. (1975). *Why subjects say they would or would not communicate affectively-toned messages.* Annual Meeting of Southeastern Psychological Association, Atlanta, GA.

Tetlock, P.E. (1979). Identifying victims of groupthink from public statements of decision makers. *Journal of Personality and Social Psychology, 37,* 1314–1324.

Tetlock, P. E. (1984). Cognitive style and political belief systems in the British House of Commons. *Journal of Personality and Social Psychology, 46,* 365–375.

Tetlock, P.E. (1986). A value pluralism model of ideological reasoning. *Journal of Personality and Social Psychology, 50,* 819–827.

Tetlock, P.E. (2000). Cognitive biases and organizational correctives: Do both disease and cure depend on the politics of the beholder? *Administrative Science Quarterly, 45,* 293–326.

Tetlock, P.E. (2003). Thinking the unthinkable: Sacred values and taboo cognitions. *Trends on Cognitive Science, 7,* 320–324.

Tetlock, P.E., Armor, D. & Peterson, R.S. (1994). The slavery debate in antebellum America: Cognitive style, values conflict and the limits of compromise. *Journal of Personality and Social Psychology, 66,* 115–126.

Thayer, S. & Saarni, C. (1975). Demand characteristics are everywhere (anyway): A comment on the Stanford prison experiment. *American Psychologist, 30,* 1015–1016.

Thebaud, S. (2010). Gender and entrepreneurship as a career choice: Do self-assessments of ability matter? *Social Psychology Quarterly, 73,* 288–304.

Thibaut, J.W. & Kelley, H.H. (1959). *The social psychology of groups.* New York: Wiley.

Thibodeau, R. & Aronson, E. (1992). Taking a closer look: Reasserting the role of the self-concept in dissonance theory. *Personality and Social Psychology Bulletin, 18*, 591–602.

Thibaut J.W. & Walker L. (1975). *Procedural justice: A psychological analysis*. Hillsdale, New Jersey: Erlbaum,

Thompson, B. & Borrello, G.M. (1992). Different views of love: Deductive and inductive lines of inquiry. *Current Directions in Psychological Science, 1*, 154–156.

Thompson, K.S. & Oskamp, S. (1974). Difficulties in replicating the proselytizing effect in doomsday groups. *Psychological Reports, 35*, 971–978.

Thompson, L.F., Sebastianelli, J.D. & Murray, N.P. (2009). Monitoring online training behaviors: Awareness of electronic surveillance hinders e-learners. *Journal of Applied Social Psychology, 39*, 2191–2212

Thompson, L.L., Wang, J. & Gunia, B.C. (2010). Negotiation. *Annual Review of Psychology, 61*, 491–515.

Thompson, M.M. & Zanna, M.P. (1995). The conflict individual: Personality-based and domain-specific antecedents of ambivalent social attitudes. *Journal of Personality, 63*, 259–288.

Thompson, M.M., Zanna, M.P. & Griffin, D.W. (1995). Let's not be indifferent about (attitudinal) ambivalence. In Petty, R.E. & Krosnick, J.A. (Eds) *Attitude strength: Antecedents and consequences* (pp. 361–386). Hillsdale, NJ: Erlbaum.

Thompson, S.C. (1999). Illusions of control: How we overestimate our personal influence. *Current Directions in Psychological Science, 8*, 187–190.

Thompson, S.C., Armstrong, W. & Thomas, C. (1998). Illusion of control, underestimations and accuracy: a control heuristic explanation. *Psychological Bulletin, 123*, 143–161.

Thornhill, R. & Gangestad, S.W. (1993). Human facial beauty: Averageness, symmetry and parasite resistance. *Human Nature, 4*, 237–269.

Tice, D.M., Butler, J.L., Muravan, M.B. & Stillwell, A.M. (1995). When modesty prevails: Differential favorability of self-presentation to friends and strangers. *Journal of Personality and Social Psychology, 69*, 1120–1138.

Ting Kin, N.G. & Cheng, C.H.K. (2010). The effects of intimacy passion and commitment on satisfaction in romantic relationships among Hong Kong Chinese people. *Journal of Psychology in Chinese Societies, 11*, 123–146.

Tinker, J. E., & Tucker, J. A. (1997). Motivations for weight loss and behavior change strategies associated with natural recovery from obesity. *Psychology of Addictive Behaviors, 11*(2), 98–106.

Toch, H. (1965). *The social psychology of social movements*. Indianapolis, IL: Bobbs-Merrill.

Todorov, A., Fiske, S. &. Prentice, D. (Eds) (2011). *Social neuroscience: Toward understanding the underpinnings of the social mind*. Oxford, England: Oxford University Press.

Todorov, A., Mandisodza, A.N., Goren, A. & Hall, C. (2005). Inferences of competence from faces predict election outcomes. *Science, 308*, 1623–1626. http://psych.princeton.edu/psychology/research/todorov/pdf/Todorov_Science2005.pdf.

Tolan, P., Gorman-Smith, D. & Henry, D. (2006). Family violence. *Annual Review of Psychology, 57*, 557–583.

Tolstedt, B.E. & Stokes, J.P. (1984). Self-disclosure, intimacy and the depenetration process. *Journal of Personality and Social Psychology, 46*, 84–90.

Torelli, C.J. & Cheng, S.Y.Y. (2011). Cultural meanings of brands and consumption: A window into the cultural psychology of globalization. *Social and Personality Psychology Compass, 5*, 251–262.

Tormala, Z.L. & Petty, R.E. (2002). What doesn't kill me makes me stronger: The effects of resisting persuasion on attitude certainty. *Journal of Personality and Social Psychology, 83*, 1298–1313.

Tormala, Z.L. & Rucker, D.D. (2007). Attitude certainty: A review of past findings and emerging perspectives. *Social and Personality Psychology Compass, 1*, 469–492.

Totterdall, P., Kellett, S., Teuchmann, K. & Briner, R.B. (1998). Evidence of mood linkage in work groups. *Journal of Personality and Social Psychology, 74*, 1504–1515.

Tougas, F., Brown, R., Beaton, A.M. & Joly, S. (1995). Neosexism: Plus ça change, plus c'est pareil. *Personality and Social Psychology Bulletin, 21*, 842–849.

Tourangeau, R. & Rasinski, K.A. (1988). Cognitive processes underlying context effects in attitude measurement. *Psychological Bulletin, 103*, 299–314.

Toussaint, L.L., Owen, A.D. & Cheadle, A. (2012). Forgive to live: Forgiveness, health and longevity. *Journal of Behavioral Medicine, 35*, 375–386.

Tovée, M.J., Swami, V., Furnham, A. & Mangalparsad, R. (2006). Changing perceptions of attractiveness as observers are exposed to a different culture. *Evolution and Behavior*, *27*, 443–456.

Townsend, P. & Davidson, N. (1982). *Inequalities in health*. Harmondsworth, UK: Penguin.

Trafimow, D. (2009). The theory of reasoned action. A case study of falsification in psychology. *Theory and Psychology*, *19*, 501–518.

Trafimow, D. & Finlay, K.A. (2001). Evidence for improved sensitivity of within-participants analyses in tests of the theory of reasoned action. *The Social Science Journal, 38*, 629–635.

Traupmann, J. & Hatfield, E. (1981). Love and its effect on mental and physical health. In R. Fogel, E. Hatfield, S. Kiesler & E. Shanas (Eds), *Aging: Stability and change in the family* (pp. 253–274). New York: Academic Press.

Travis, L.E. (1925). The effect of a small audience upon eye–hand coordination. *Journal of Abnormal and Social Psychology*, *20*, 142–146.

Trawalter, S., Adam, E., Chase-Lansdale, P.L. & Richeson, J.A. (2012). Concerns about appearing prejudiced get under the skin: Stress responses to interracial contact in the moment and across time. *Journal of Experimental Social Psychology*, *48*, 682–693.

Triandis, H.C. (1972). *The analysis of subjective culture*. New York: John Wiley & Sons.

Triandis, H.C. (1987). The self and social behavior in differing cultural contexts. *Psychological Review, 96,* 506–520.

Triandis, H.C. (1989). The Self and Social Behavior in differing cultural contexts. *Psychological Review*, *96*, 506–520.

Triplett, N. (1898). The dynamogenic factors in pacemaking and competition. *American Journal of Psychology*, *9*, 507–533.

Trochim, W.M.K. (1999). Research methods knowledge base (2nd ed.) [Online]. Retrieved from the World Wide Web: www. trochim.human.cornell. edu/kb/qual.htm.

Trope, Y. & Liberman, N, (2010). Construal-level theory of psychological distance. *Psychological Review*, *117*, 440–463.

Trudgill, P. (1974). *The Social Differentiation of English in Norwich*. Cambridge: Cambridge University Press.

Truman-Schram, D.M., Cann, A., Calhoun, L. & Vanwallendael, L. (2000). Leaving an abusive dating relationship: An investment model comparison of women who stay versus women who

leave. *Journal of Social & Clinical Psychology*, *19*, 161–183.

Trumpeter, N., Watson, P.J. & O'Leary, B.J. (2006). Factors within the multidimensional perfectionism scales: Complexity of relationships with self-esteem, narcissism, self-control and self-criticism. *Personality and Individual Differences*, *41*, 849–860.

Tseloni, A., Mailley, J., Farrell, G. & Tilley, M. (2010). Exploring the international decline in crime rates. *European Journal of Criminology*, *7*, 375–394.

Tseng, W., Kan-Ming, M., Hsu, J., Li-Shuen, L., Li-Wah, O., Guo-Qian, C. & Da-Wei, J. (1988). A sociocultural study of koro epidemics in Guangdong, China. *American Journal of Psychiatry*, *145*, 1538–1543.

Tucker, G.R. (1981). Social policy and second language teaching. In R.C. Gardner & R. Kalin (Eds), *A Canadian social psychology of ethnic relations* (pp. 77–92). Toronto: Metheun.

Turkel, S. (2011). Alone together: *Why we expect more from technology and less from each other*. New York: Basic Books.

Turner, J.C. (1982). Toward a cognitive redefinition of the social group. In H. Tajfel (Ed.), *Social identity and intergroup relations* (pp. 15–40). Cambridge: Cambridge University Press.

Turner, J.C. (1985). Social categorization and the self-concept: A social-cognitive theory of group behaviour. In J.E. Lawler (Ed.), *Advances in group processes* (Vol. 2). (pp. 77–122). Greenwich: JAI Press.

Turner, J.C. & Oakes, P. (1986). The significance of the social identity concept for social psychology with reference to individualism, interactionism and social influence. *British Journal of Social Psychology, 25,* 237–252.

Turner, J.C., Wetherell, M.S. & Hogg, M.A. (1989). Referent informational influence and group polarization. *British Journal of Social Psychology*, *18*, 135–147.

Turner, M.E., Pratkanis, A.R. & Struckman, C.K. (2007). In In A.R. Pratkanis (Ed.), *The science of social influence*. New York: Psychology Press. pp. 223–246.

Turner, R.N., Crisp, R.J. & Lambert, E. (2007). Imagining intergroup contact can improve intergroup attitudes. *Group Processes & Intergroup Relations*, *10*, 427–441.

Turner, R.N., Hewstone, M., Voci, A., Paolini, S. & Christ, O. (2007). Reducing prejudice via direct and extended cross-group friendship. *European Review of Social Psychology*, *18*, 212–255.

Tutaj, K. & van Reijmersdal, E. (2012). Effects of online advertising format and persuasion knowledge on audience reactions. *Journal of Marketing Communications*, *18*, 2–18.

Tversky, A. & Kahneman, D. (1973). Availability: A heuristic for judging frequency and probability. *Cognitive Psychology*, *5*, 207–232.

Tversky, A. & Kahneman, D. (1974). Judgement under uncertainty: Heuristics and biases. *Science*, *185*, 1124–1131.

Tversky, A. & Kahneman, D. (1982). Judgment under uncertainty: Heuristics and biases. In D. Kahneman, P. Slovic & A. Tversky (Eds), *Judgment under uncertainty: Heuristics and biases* (pp. 3–20). Cambridge: Cambridge University Press.

Twenge, J.M. (2009). Change over time and obedience: The jury's still out, but it might be decreasing. *American Psychologist*, *64*, 28–31.

Twenge, J.M. & Campbell, W.K. (2003). 'Isn't it fun to get the respect that we're going to deserve?' Narcissism, social rejection and aggression. *PSPB*, *29*, 261–272.

Twenge, J.M., Campbell, W.K. & Gentile, B. (2012). Changes in Pronoun Use in American Books and the Rise of Individualism, 1960–2008. *Journal of Cross-Cultural Psychology*, *44*, 406–415.

Twenge, J.M. & Foster, J.D. (2010). Birth cohort increases in narcissistic personality traits among American college students, 1982–2009. *Social Psychological and Personality Science*, *1*, 99–106.

Tykocinski, O.E. & Pittman, T.S. (1998). The consequences of doing nothing: Inaction inertia as avoidance of anticipated counterfactual regret. *Journal of Personality and Social Psychology*, *73*, 607–616.

Tyler, T.R. & Caine, A. (1981). The influence of outcomes and procedures on satisfaction with formal leaders. *Journal of Personality and Social Psychology*, *41*, 642–655.

Tyler, T.R. & Degoey, P. (1995). Collective restraint in social dilemmas: Procedural justice and social identification effects on support for authorities. *Journal of Personality and Social Psychology*, *69*, 482–494.

Tyler, T.R. & Lind, E.A. (2001). Procedural justice. In J. Sanders & V.L. Hamilton (Eds), *Handbook of justice research in law*, (pp. 65–92). Dordrecht, Netherlands: Kluwer Academic Publishers.

Tyler, T.R., Rasinski, K.A. & McGraw, K.M. (1985). The influence of perceived injustice on the endorsement of political leaders. *Journal of Applied Social Psychology*, *15*, 700–725.

Tzeng, J. (2010). College students self-discrepancy on the Internet from the perspective of desktop practices, self-control and academic training. *Cyberpsychology, Behavior and Social Networking*, *13*, 495–502.

Ubbink, E.M. & Sadava, S.W. (1974). Rotter's generalized expectancies as predictors of helping behavior. *Psychological Reports*, *35*, 865–866.

Underwood, B., Froming, W.J. & Moore, B.S. (1977). Mood, attention, and altruism: A search for mediating variables. *Developmental Psychology*, *13*, 541–542.

Unger, D.G. & Wandersman, L.P. (1985). Social support and adolescent mothers: Action research contributions to theory and applications. *Journal of Social Issues*, *41*, 29–46.

United Nations Office on Drugs and Crime (2004). International Homicide Statistics Downloaded from http://www.unodc.org/documents/data-and-analysis/IHS-rates-05012009.pdf on May 21, 2013.

United Nations Office on Drugs and Crime (2011). *2011 global study on homicide*. Geneva: United Nations Office on Drugs and Crime.

United States Department of Justice (2010). *Crime in the United States, 2009*. Washington, DC: United States Department of Justice.

VaidVaid, J., Paivio, A., Gardner, R.C. & Genesee, F. (2010). Obituary: Wallace E. Lambert (1922–2009). *American Psychologist*, *65*, 290–291.

Vailláncourt, R. (2010). *Gender differences in police-reported violent crime in Canada, 2008*. Ottawa: Statistics Canada. http://www.statcan.gc.ca/pub/85f0033m/85f0033m2010024-eng.pdf.

Vaillancourt, T. (2005). Indirect aggression among humans: Social construct or evolutionary adaptation? In R.E. Tremblay, W.W. Hartup & J. Archer (Eds). (2005). *Developmental origins of aggression*. New York: Guilford Press, (pp. 158–177).

Valins, S. (1966). Cognitive effects of false heartrate feedback. *Journal of Personality and Social Psychology*, *4*, 400–408.

Van Baaren, R.B., Holland, R.W., Kawakami, K. & van Knippenberg, A. (2004). Mimicry and prosocial behavior. *Psychological Science*, *15*, 71–74.

Van Bavel, J.J. & Cunningham, W.A. (2010). A social neuroscience approach to self and social categorisation: A new look at an old issue. *European Review of Social Psychology*, *21*, 237–284.

Van den Bos, K., Bruins, J., Wilke, H.A.M. & Dronkert, E. (1999). Sometimes unfair procedures have nice aspects: On the psychology of the fair process effect. *Journal of Personality and Social Psychology*, *77*, 324–336.

Van den Bos, G.R. & Bulatao, E.Q. (2000). Observations on entrepreneurial psychologists. *Psychologist-Manager Journal*, *4*, 97–102.

van der Weiden, A., Veling, H. & Aarts, H. (2010). When observing gaze shifts of others enhances object desirability. *Emotion*, *10*, 939–943.

Van Dijk, E. & van Knippenberg, D. (1998). Trading wine: On the endowment effect, loss aversion, and the comparability of consumer goods. *Journal of Economic Psychology*, *19*, 485–495.

Van Dijk, W.W., Ouwerkerk, J.W., Wesselong, Y.M. & Van Koningsbruggen, G.M. (2011). Towards understanding pleasure at the misfortune of others: The impact of self-evaluation threat on schadenfreude. *Cognition and Emotion*, *15*, 360–368.

Van Dulmen, S., Siuijs, E., van Dilk, L., Heerdink, R. & Benzing, J. (2007). Patient adherence to medical treatment. *Journal of Negative Results in Biomedicine*, *7*, 55. doi.10.1186/1472-6963-7-55

Van Gelder, L. (1996). The strange case of the electronic lover. In Kling, R (Ed.) Computerization and controversy: Value conflicts and social choices (2nd Edition) (pp. 533–546). New York: Academic Press.

Van Koppen, P. & Penrod, S. (Eds). (2003). *Adversarial versus inquisitorial justice: Psychological perspectives on criminal justice systems*. New York: Kluwer Academic/Plenum Publishers.

Van Lange, P.A.M. & Visser, K. (1999). Locomotion in social dilemmas: How people adapt to cooperative, tit-for-tat, and non-cooperative partners. *Journal of Personality and Social Psychology*, *77*, 762–773.

Van Overwalle, F. (1997). Causal explanation as constraint satisfaction: A critique and feedforward connectionist alternative. *Journal of Personality and Social Psychology*, *74*, 312–328.

Van Swol, Lyn M. (2009). 'Extreme members and group polarization'. *Social Influence*, *4* (3), 185–199.

Van Veen, V., Krug, M.K., Schooler, J.W. & Carter, C.S. (2009). Neural activity predicts attitude change in cognitive dissonance. *Nature Neuroscience*, *12*, 1469–1474.

Van Vugt, M., Hogan, R. & Kaiser, R.B. (2008). Leadership, followership, and evolution. *American Psychologist*, *63*, 182–196.

Van Vugt, M. & Van Lange, P.A.M. (2006). The altruism puzzle: Psychological adaptations for prosocial behavior. In M. Schaller, J.A. Simpson & D.T. Kenrick (Eds), *Evolution and social psychology*. New York: Psychology Press. (pp. 237–261).

Vantress, F.E. & Williams, C.B. (1972). The effect of the presence of the provocator and the opportunity to counteraggress on systolic blood pressure. *Journal of General Psychology*, *86*, 63–68.

Vasiljevic, M. & Crisp, R.J. (2013). Tolerance by surprise: Evidence for a generalized reduction in prejudice and increased egalitarianism through novel category combination. *PLoS ONE*, *8*(3), e57106. doi:10.1371/journal.pone.0057106.

Vaughn, L.A. & Weary, G. (2002). Roles of the availability of explanations, feelings of ease, and dysphoria in judgments about the future. *Journal of Social & Clinical Psychology*, *21*, 686–704.

Venis, S. & Horton, R. (2002). Violence against women: A global burden. *The Lancet*, *359*, 9313.

Verona, E. & Sullivan, E.A. (2008). Emotional catharsis and aggression revisited: Heart rate reduction following aggressive responding. *Emotion*, *8*, 331–340.

Verplanken, B. (1991). Persuasive communication of risk information: A test of cue versus message processing effects in a field experiment. *Personality and Social Psychology Bulletin*, *17*, 188–193.

Vescio, T.K., Sechrist, G.B. & Paolucci, M.P. (2003). Perspective taking and prejudice reduction: The mediational role of empathy arousal and situational attributions. *European Journal of Social Psychology*, *33*, 455–472.

Vidmar, N. & Schuller, R.A. (2001). The jury: Selecting twelve impartial peers. In R.A. Schuller & J. Ogloff (Eds). *Introduction to psychology and law: Canadian perspectives (*pp. 126–156). Toronto: University of Toronto Press.

Villagran, M., Hajek, C., Zhao, X., Peterson, E. & Wittenberg-Lyles, E. (2011). Communication and culture: Predictors of treatment adherence among Mexican immigrant patient. *Journal of Health Psychology*, *17*, 443–452.

Vinacke, W.E. (1969). Variables in experimental games: Toward a field theory. *Psychological Bulletin, 71*, 293–318.

Vinacke, W.E. & Gullickson, G.R. (1964). Age and sex differences in the formation of coalitions. *Child Development, 35*, 1217–1231.

Virkler, H.A. (1995). *Hermeneutics: Principles and processes of biblical interpretation*. Grand Rapids, MI: Baker Publishing.

Visser, P.S. & Krosnick, J.A. (1999). Development of attitude strength over the life cycle: Surge and decline. *Journal of Personality and Social Pychology, 75*, 1389–1410.

Von Hippel, W. & Trivers, R. (2011). The evolution and psychology of self-deception. *Behavioral and Brain Sciences, 34*, 1–56.

Vorauer, J., Cameron, J.J., Holmes, J.G. & Pearce, D.G. (2003). Invisible overtures: Fear of rejection and the signal amplification bias. *Journal of Personality and Social Psychology, 84*, 793–812.

Vorauer, J.D., Main, K.J. & O'Connell, G. (1998). How do individuals expect to be viewed by members of lower status groups? Content and implications of meta-stereotypes. *Journal of Personality and Social Psychology, 75*, 917–937.

Vroom, V.H. (1964). *Work and motivation*. New York: Wiley.

Vrugt, A. & Van Eechoud, M. (2002). Smiling and self-presentation of men and women for job photographs. *European Journal of Social Psychology, 32*, 419–431.

Vul, E., Harris, C., Winkielman, P. & Pashier, H. (2009). Puzzlingly high correlations in fMRI studies of emotion, personality and social cognition. *Perspectives on Psychological Science, 4*, 274–290.

Wagner, H.L., Macdonald, C.J. & Manstead, A.S.R. (1986). Communication of individual emotions by spontaneous facial expression. *Journal of Personality and Social Psychology, 50*, 737–743.

Wagner, U., Hewstone, M. & Machleit, U. (1989). Contact and prejudice between Germans and Turks: A correlational study. *Human Relations, 42*, 561–574.

Walchli, S. & Landman, J. (2003). Effects of counterfactual thought on postpurchase consumer affect. *Psychology & Marketing, 20*, 23–46.

Walker, C.J. & Beckerle, C.A. (1987). The effect of state anxiety on rumor transmission. *Journal of Social Behavior and Personality, 2*, 353–360.

Walker, I. & Smith, H.J. (2002). Fifty years of relative deprivation research. In I. Walker & H.J. Smith (Eds), *Relative deprivation: Specification, development, and integration.* (pp. 1–90). New York: Cambridge University Press, 2002.

Wall, A-M. & Schuller, R.A. (2000). Alcohol and rape: The impact of alcohol on jurors' decisions in trials of sexual assault. *Journal of Applied Social Psychology, 30*, 253–274.

Wallach, M.A. & Wallach, L. (1983). *Psychology's sanction for selfishness.* San Francisco: WH Freeman.

Waller, J. (2002). *Becoming evil. How ordinary people commit genocide and mass killing.* New York: Oxford University Press.

Walster, E. (1964). The temporal sequence of post-decision processes. In L. Festinger (Ed.), *Conflict, decision and dissonance* (pp. 112–128). Stanford, CA: Stanford University Press.

Walster, E. (1966). Assignment of responsibility for an accident. *Journal of Personality and Social Psychology, 3*, 73–79.

Walster, E. & Walster, G.W. (1978). *A new look at love.* Reading, MA: Addison-Wesley.

Walster, E., Walster, G.W. & Berscheid, E. (1978). *Equity theory and research.* Boston: Allyn & Bacon.

Walters, G.C. & Grusec, J.E. (1977). *Punishment.* San Francisco: W.H. Freeman.

Walters, V., Lenton, R., French, S., Eyles, J., Mayr, J. & Newbold, B. (1996). Paid work, unpaid work and social support: a study of the health of male and female nurses. *Social Science Medical, 43*, 1627–1636.

Walther, J.B., Loh, T. & Granka, L. (2005). Interchange of verbal and nonverbal cues in computer-mediated and face-to-face affinity. *Journal of Language and Social Psychology, 24*, 36–65. doi: 10.1177/0261927X04273036

Walton, G.M. & Cohen, G.L. (2003). Stereotype lift. *Journal of Experimental Social Psychology, 39*, 456–467.

Wan, C. & Chiou, W. (2010). Inducing attitude change toward online gambling among adolescent players based on dissonance theory: The role of threats and justification of effort. *Computers and Education, 54*, 162–168.

Wandner, L.D., Scipio, C.D., Hirsh, A.T., Torres, C.A. & Robinson, M,E. (2012). The perception of pain in others: How gender, race and age influence pain expectations. *Journal of Pain, 13,* 220–227.

Wang, L. & Ladegaard, H.J. (2008). Language attitudes and gender in China: Perceptions and reported use of Putonghua and Cantonese in the southern province of Guangdong. *Language Awareness, 17,* 57–77. doi:10.2167/la425.0

Ware, J.E. & Young, J. (1979). Issues in the conceptualization and measurements of the value placed on health. In S.J. Mushkin & D.W. Dunlop (Eds), *Health: What is it worth?* (pp. 141–156). New York: Pergamon.

Warneken, F. & Tomasello, M. (2009). The roots of human altruism. *British Journal of Psychology, 100,* 455–471.

Watkins, D., Adair, J., Akande, A., Gerong, A., McInerney, D., Sunar, D., Watson, S., Wen, Q. & Wondimu, H. (1998). Individualism/collectivism, gender and the self-concept: A nine-culture investigation. *Psychologia: An International Journal of Psychology in the Orient, 41,* 259–271.

Watkins, D., Akande, A., Fleming, J., Ismail, M., Lefner, K., Regmi, M., Watons, S., Yu, J., Adair, J., Cheng, C., Gerong, A., McInerney, D., Mpofu, E., Singh-Sengupta, S. & Wondimu, H. (1998). Cultural dimensions, gender and the nature of self-concept: A fourteen country study. *International Journal of Psychology, 33,* 17–31.

Watson, B. & Gallois, C. (2002). Patients' interactions with health providers: A linguistic category model approach. *Journal of Language and Social Psychology, 21,* 32–52.

Watson, D. & Pennebaker, J.W. (1989). Health complaints, stress and distress: Exploring the central role of negative affectivity. *Psychological Review, 96,* 234–254.

Watson, N., Bryan, B.C, & Thrash, T.M. (2010). Self-discrepancy: Comparisons of the psychometric properties of three instruments. *Psychological Assessment, 22,* 878–892.

Watts, C. & Zimmerman, C. (2002). Violence against women: Global scope and magnitude. *Lancet, 359,* 1232–1237.

Weber, J.M. & Murnighan, J.K. (2008).Suckers or saviors? Consistent contributors in social dilemmas. *Journal of Personality and Social Psychology, 95,* 1340–1353.

Weber, M. (1947). *The theory of social and economic organization.* Glencoe, IL: Free Press.

Wegner, D.M. & Wheatley, T. (1999). Apparent mental causation. Sources of the experience of will. *American Psychologist, 54,* 480–492.

Weidner, G., Istvan, J. & McKnight, J.D. (1989). Clusters of behavioral coronary risk factors in employed men and women. *Journal of Applied Social Psychology, 19,* 468–480.

Weigel, R.H. & Newman, L.S. (1976). Increasing attitude–behavior correspondence by broadening the scope of the behavioral measure. *Journal of Personality and Social Psychology, 33,* 793–802.

Weigel, R.H., Wiser, P.L. & Cook, S.W. (1975). The impact of cooperative learning experience on cross-ethnic relations and attitudes. *Journal of Social Issues, 31,* 219–244.

Weimann, G. & Winn, C. (1986). *Hate on trial: The Zundel affair, the media, and public opinion in Canada.* Oakville: Mosaic Press.

Weiner, B. (1974). *Achievement motivation and attribution theory.* Morristown, NJ: General Learning Press.

Weiner, B. (1980). A cognitive (attribution)–emotion–action model of motivated behavior: An analysis of judgements of help giving. *Journal of Personality and Social Psychology, 39,* 186–200.

Weiner, B. (1985). 'Spontaneous' causal thinking. *Psychological Bulletin, 97,* 74–84.

Weiner, B., Figueroa-Muñoz, A. & Kakihara, C. (1991). The goals of excuses and communication strategies related to causal perceptions. *Personality and Social Psychology Bulletin, 17,* 4–13.

Weinstein, E.A., DeVaughan, W.L. & Wiley, M.G. (1969). Obligation and the flow of deference. *Sociometry, 32,* 1–12.

Weinstein, M.D., Smith, M.E. & Wiesenthal. D.L. (1995). Masculinity and hockey violence. *Sex Roles, 33,* 831–847.

Weir E. (2005). Mass sociogenic illness. *Canadian medical Association Journal, 172,* 36.

Weisbuch, M. & Ambady, N. (2009). Unspoken cultural influence: Exposure to and influence of nonverbal bias. *Journal of Personality and Social Psychology, 96,* 1104–1119.

Weiss, D.J. (2001). Deception by researchers is necessary and not necessarily evil. *Behavioral and Brain Sciences, 24,* 431–432.

Weiss, R. (1973). *Loneliness: The experiences of emotional and social isolation.* Cambridge, MA: MIT Press.

Weiss, R. (1975). *Marital separation.* New York: Basic Books.

Weldon, E. & Gargano, G.M. (1988). Cognitive loafing: The effects of accountability and shared responsibility on cognitive effort. *Personality and Social Psychology Bulletin, 14*, 159–171.

Wellman, B. (1992). Men in networks; Private communities, domestic friendships. In P.M. Nardi (Ed.), *Men's friendships* (pp. 74–114). Newbury Park: Sage.

Wellman, R.J. & Sugarman, D.B. (1996). Social perceptions of termination of medical treatment: Suicide or rational decision. *Journal of Social Psychology, 26*, 1378–1399.

Wells, G.L. (1978). Applied eyewitness-testimony research: System variables and estimator variables. *Journal of Personality and Social Psychology, 36*, 1546–1557.

Wells, G.L. (1984). The psychology of lineup identifications. *Journal of Applied Psychology, 14*, 89–103.

Wells, G.L. (1992). Naked statistical evidence of liability: Is subjective probability enough? *Journal of Personality and Social Psychology, 62*, 739–752.

Wells, G.L. & Hasel, L.E. (2008). Eyewitness identification: Issues in common knowledge and generalization In E. Borgida & S.T. Fiske (Eds), *Beyond common sense: Psychological science in the courtroom* (pp. 159–176). Malden: Blackwell Publishing.

Wells, G.L. & Luus, C.A.E. (1990). Police lineups as experiments: Social methodology as a framework for properly conducted lineups. *Personality and Social Psychology Bulletin, 16*, 106–117.

Wells, G.L., Memon, A. & Penrod, S.D. (2006). Eyewitness evidence: Improving its probative value. *Psychological Science in the Public Interest, 7*, 45–75.

Wells, G.L. & Murray, B.M. (1983). What can psychology say about the Neil vs. Biggers criteria for judging eyewitness accuracy? *Journal of Applied Psychology, 68*, 347–362.

Wells, G.L. & Olson, E.A. (2002). Eyewitness identification: Information gain from incriminating and exonerating behaviors. *Journal of Experimental Psychology: Applied, 8*, 155–167.

Wells, G.L., Olson, E.A. & Charman, S.D. (2002). The confidence of eyewitnesses in their identifications from lineups. *Current Directions in Psychological Science, 11*, 151–154.

Wells, G.L., Small, M., Penrod, S., Malpass, R.S. Fulero, S.M. & Brimacombe, C.A.E. (1998). Eyewitness identification procedures: Recommendations for lineups and photospreads. *Law and Human Behavior, 22*, 603–647.

Wells, G.L. & Turtle, J.W. (1986). Eye-witness identification: The importance of lineup models. *Psychological Bulletin, 29*, 320–329.Wenzel, M., Woodyatt, L. & Hendrick, K. (2012). No genuine self-forgiveness without accepting responsibility: Value affirmation as a key to maintaining positive self-regard. *European Journal of Social Psychology, 42*, 617–627.

Werner, E.E. (1989). High-risk children in young adulthood: A longitudinal study from birth to 32 years. *American Journal of Orthopsychiatry, 59*, 69–78.

Werthemier, A.J. & Santella, T.M. (2009). Medication compliance research. Still so far to go. *Journal of Applied Research in Clinical and Experimental Therapeutics, 9*, 254–261.

Wertz, F.J., Charmaz, K., McMullen, L.M.,Josselson, R.A. & McSpadden, E. (2011). *Five ways of doing qualitative analysis.* New York: Guilford Press.

Wessely, S. (1987). Mass hysteria: two syndromes? *Psychological Medicine, 17*, 109–120.

Wessely, S. (2002). Protean nature of mass sociogenic illness: From possessed nuns to chemical and biological terrorism fears. *British Journal of Psychiatry, 180*, 300–306.

West, S.G. & Brown, T.J. (1975). Physical attractiveness, the severity of the emergency and helping: a field experiment and interpersonal simulation. *Journal of Experimental Social Psychology, 11*, 531–538.

Wetherell, M. & Potter, J. (1992). *Mapping the language of racism. Discourse and the legitimation of exploitation.* New York: Columbia University Press.

Whalen, J.M. & Pexman, P.M. (2009). 'Should be fun – not!' Incidence and marking of nonliteral language in e-mail. *Journal of Language and Social Psychology, 28*, 263–280.

Wheeler, A. & Petty, R. (2001). The effects of stereotype activation on behavior: A review of possible mechanisms, *127*, 792–826.

White, K. & Lehman, D.R. (2005). Culture and social comparison seeking: The role of self motives. *Personality and Social Psychology Bulletin, 31*, 232–242.

White, R. (2002). Indigenous young Australians, criminal justice and offensive language. *Journal of Youth Studies*, *5*, 21–34.

White, S. (1989). Backchannels across cultures: A study of Americans and Japanese. *Language and Society*, *18*, 59–76.

Whyte, G. (1989). Group-think reconsidered. *Academy of Management Review*, *14*, 40–56.

Whyte, G. (1998). Recasting Janis's groupthink model: The key role of collective efficacy in decision fiascos. *Organizational Behavior and Human Decision Processes*, *73*, 185–209.

Wicker, A.W. (1969). Attitudes versus actions: The relationship of verbal and overt behavioral responses to attitude objects. *Journal of Social Issues*, *25*, 41–78.

Wicklund, R. A., & Brehm, J. W. (1976). *Perspectives on cognitive dissonance*. Hillsdale, NJ: Erlbaum.

Widom, C.S. (1989). Does violence beget violence? A critical examination of the literature. *Psychological Bulletin*, *106*, 3–28.

Wiegman, O. (1985). Two politicians in a realistic experiment: Attraction, discrepancy, intensity of delivery, and attitude change. *Journal of Applied Social Psychology*, *15*, 673–686.

Wiemann, J.M. & Giles, H. (1988). Interpersonal communication. In M. Hewstone, W. Stroebe, J-P. Codol & G.M. Stephenson (Eds), *Introduction to social psychology* (pp. 199–221). Oxford: Basil Blackwell.

Wiener, M., Carpenter, J.T. & Carpenter, B. (1957). Some determinants of conformity behavior. *Journal of Social Psychology*, *45*, 289–297.

Wieselquist, J. (2009). Interpersonal forgiveness, trust and the investment model of commitment. *Journal of Social and Personal Relationships*, *26*, 531–54.

Wiik, K.A., Bernhardt, E. & Noack, T. (2009). A study of commitment and relationship quality in Sweden and Norway. *Journal of Marriage and the Family*, *71*, 465–477.

Wild, B., Erb, M., Bartels, M. (2001). Are emotions contagious? Evoked emotions while viewing emotionally expressive faces: quality, quantity, time course and gender differences. *Psychiatry Research*, *102*, 109–124.

Wilder, D.A. (1977). Perception of group size of opposition and social influence. *Journal of Experimental Social Psychology*, *13*, 253–268.

Wilder, D.H. & Shapiro, P.N. (1989). Role of competition-induced anxiety in limiting the beneficial impact of positive behaviour by an out group member. *Journal of Personality and Social Psychology*, *56*, 60–69.

Wildschut, T. & Insko, C.A. (2007). Explanations of inter-individual-intergroup discontinuity: A review of the evidence. *European Review of Social Psychology*, *18*, 175–211.

Wildschut, T., Insko, C.A. & Pinter, B. (2007). Interindividual-intergroup discontinuity as a joint function of acting in a group and interacting with a group. *The European Journal of Social Psychology*, *37*(2), 390–399.

Williams, E. (1975). Medium or message: Communications medium as a determinant of interpersonal evaluations. *Sociometry*, *38*, 119–130.

Williams, P. & Aaker, J.L. (2002). Can mixed emotions peacefully coexist? *Journal of Consumer Research*, *28*, 636–649.

Williamson, S., Hare, R.D. & Wong, S. (1987). Violence: Criminal psychopaths and their victims. *Canadian Journal of Behavioural Science*, *19*, 454–462.

Willis, J., & Todorov, A. (2006). First impressions: Making up your mind after 100 ms exposure to a face. *Psychological Science, 17*, 592–598.

Willoughby, T., Chalmers, H. & Busseri, M. (2003). Where is the syndrome? Where is the risk? Examining co-occurrence among problem behaviors in adolescence. Submitted for publication.

Wills, T.A. (1981). Downward comparison principles in social psychology. *Psychological Bulletin*, *90*, 245–271.

Wilsnack, S. (1982). *Prevention of alcohol problems in women*. In N.I.A.A.A. alcohol and health monograph #4. Special population issues (77–110). D.H.H.S. Publication No. (ADM) 82–1193. Washington: US Government Printing Office.

Wilson, D.W. & Donnerstein, E. (1976). Legal and ethical aspects of nonreactive social research: An excursion into the public mind. *American Psychologist*, *36*, 765–773.

Wilson, G. T. (1984). Weight control treatments. In J. D. Matarazzo, S. M. Weiss, J. A. Herd, N. E. Miller, & S. M. Weiss (Eds), *Behavioral health: A handbook of health maintenance and disease prevention* (pp. 657–670). New York: Wiley.

Wilson, R.E., Gosling, S.D. & Graham, L.T. (2012). A review of Facebook research in the social sciences. *Perspectives on Psychological Science*, *7*, 203–220.

Wilson, T.D. & Aronson, E. & Carlsmith, K. (2010). The art of laboratory experimentation. In S. Fiske, D. Gilbert & G. Lindzey (Eds), *The handbook of social psychology* (5th ed.), (pp. 49–79). New York: Wiley.

Wilson, T.D., Lindsey, S. & Schooler, T.Y. (2000). A model of dual attitudes. *Psychological Review, 107*, 101–126.

Wilson, W. & Miller, H. (1968). Repetition, order of presentation, and timing of arguments and measures as determinants of opinion change. *Journal of Personality and Social Psychology, 9*, 184–188.

Winch, R.F. (1954). The theory of complementary needs in mate selection: An analytic and descriptive study. *Annual Social Review, 19*, 241–249.

Winch, R.F. (1958). *Mate selection: A study of complementary needs.* New York: Harper & Row.

Wing-Tung, A. & Komorita, S.S. (2002). Effects of initial choices in the prisoner's dilemma. *Journal of Behavioral Decision-Making, 15*, 343–359.

Wit, A.P. & Kerr, N.L. (2002). 'Me versus just us versus us all' categorization and cooperation in nested social dilemmas. *Journal of Personality and Social Psychology, 83*, 616–637.

Witte, K. (1994). Fear control and danger control: A test of the extended parallel process model. *Communication Monographs, 61*(2), 113–134.

Wohl, M.J.A., Branscombe, N.R. & Klar, Y. (2006). Collective guilt: Emotional reactions when one's group has done wrong or been wronged. *European Review of Social Psychology, 17*, 1–37.

Wolf, N. (1991). *The beauty myth.* Toronto: Vintage Books.

Wolf, S.T., Insko, C.A., Kirchner, J.L. & Wildschut, T. (2008). Interindividual–intergroup discontinuity in the domain of correspondent outcomes: The roles of relativistic concern, perceived categorization, and the doctrine of mutual assured destruction. *Journal of Personality and Social Psychology, 94*, 479–494.

Wolfram, W. (2004). Social varieties of American English. In E. Finegan & J.R. Rickford (Eds), *Language in the USA: Themes for the twenty-first century.* New York: Cambridge Univ. Press. (pp. 58–75).

Wollin, D.D. & Montagne, M. (1981). The college classroom environment. *Environment and Behavior, 13*, 707–716.

Wood, J.V. (1989). Theory and research concerning social comparisons of personal attributes. *Psychological Bulletin, 106*, 231–248.

Wood, M.L. (2007). Rethinking the inoculation analogy: Effects on subjects with differing preexisting attitudes. *Human Communication Research, 33*, 357–378.

Wood, W. & Eagly, A.H. (2002). A cross-cultural analysis of the behavior of women and men: Implications for the origins of sex differences. *Psychological Bulletin, 128*, 699–727.

Wood, W. & Vanderzee, K. (1997). Social comparisons among cancer patients: Under what conditions are comparisons upward and downward? In B.P. Buunk & F.X. Gibbons (Eds), *Health, coping and well-being: Perspectives from social comparison theory.* Manwah, NJ: Erlbaum.

Woods, J.V., Taylor, S.E. & Lichtman, R.R. (1985). Social comparison in adjustment to breast cancer. *Journal of Personality and Social Psychology, 49*, 1169–1183.

Worchel, S. (1984). The darker side of helping. In E. Staub, D. Bar-Tal, J. Karylowski & J. Reykowski (Eds), *Development and maintenance of prosocial behavior* (pp. 375–395). New York: Plenum Press.

Worchel, S., Andreoli, V. & Eason, J. (1975). Is the medium the message? A study of the effects of media, communicator and message characteristics on attitude change. *Journal of Applied Social Psychology, 5*, 157–172.

Worchel, S. & Teddlie, C. (1976). The experience of crowding: A two-factor theory. *Journal of Personality and Social Psychology, 34*, 36–40.

World Health Organization (2005). *Summary report, WHO multi-country study on women's health and domestic violence against women.* Geneva: WHO Press.

World Health Organization (2007). The cycles of violence: The relationship between childhood maltreatment and the risk of later becoming a victim or perpetrator of violence. Rome: Violence and Injury Prevention Programme, WHO European Centre for Environment and Health.

Wortman, C.B. (1975). Some determinants of perceived control. *Journal of Personality and Social Psychology, 31*, 282–294.

Wright, E.F., Rule, B.G., Ferguson, T.J., McGuire, G.R. & Wells, G.L. (1992). Misattribution of dissonance and behaviour-consistent attitude change. *Canadian Journal of Behavioural Science, 24*, 456–464.

Wright, M.J. (1982). Psychology at Manitoba. In M.J. Wright & C.R. Myers (Eds), *History of academic psychology in Canada* (pp. 170–177). Toronto: Hogrefe.

Wright, M.J. (1990). Personal communication.

Wright, M.W. (1982). Psychology at Manitoba. In M.J. Wright & C.R. Myers (Eds), *History of academic psychology in Canada.* (pp. 170–177). Toronto: Hogrefe.

Wright, S. (1978). *Crowds and riots.* Beverly Hills, CA: Sage.

Wulfert, E. & Wan, C.K. (1993). Condom use: A self-efficacy model. *Health Psychology, 12,* 346–354.

Xie, D., Leong, F.T.L. & Feng, S. (2008). Culture-specific personality correlates of anxiety among Chinese and Caucasian college students. *Asian Journal of Social Psychology, 11,* 163–174.

Yang, D.Y-J., Chiu, C., Chen, X., Cheng, S.Y.Y., Kwan, L.Y-Y., Kim-Pong Tam, Kuang-Hui Yeh (2011). Lay psychology of globalization and its social impact. *Journal of Social Issues, 67,* 677–695.

Yang, Y., Glenn, A.L. & Raine, A. (2008). Brain abnormalities in antisocial individuals: implications for the law. *Behavioral Sciences & the Law, 28,* 65–83.

Yang, Y. & Raine, A. (2009). Prefrontal structural and functional brain imaging findings in antisocial, violent, and psychopathic individuals: A meta-analysis. *Psychiatry Research, 174,* 81–88.

Yardi, S. & Boyd, D. (2010). 'Dynamic Debates: An analysis of group polarization over time on Twitter'. *Bulletin of Science, Technology and Society, 30,* 316–327.

Yarmey, A.D. (1979). *The psychology of eyewitness testimony.* New York: Free Press.

Yarmey, A.D. & Jones, H.P. (1983a). Accuracy of memory of male and female eyewitnesses to a criminal assault and rape. *Bulletin of the Psychonomic Society, 21,* 89–92.

Yarmey, A.D. & Jones, H.P. (1983b). Is the psychology of eyewitness identification a matter of common sense? In S. Lloyd-Bostock & B.R. Clifford (Eds), *Evaluating witness evidence* (pp.13–40). Chichester, England: Wiley.

Ybarra, M.L., Mitchell, K.J., Hamburger, M., Diener-West, M. & Leaf, P.J. (2011). X-rated material and perpetration of sexually aggressive behavior among children and adolescents: Is there a link? *Aggressive Behavior, 37,* 1–18.

Yelland, L.M. & Stone, W.F. (1996). Belief in the Holocaust: Effects of personality and propaganda. *Political Psychology, 17,* 551–561.

Young, L.J. (2009). Love: Neuroscience reveals all: poetry it is not. Nor is it particularly romantic. But reducing love to its component parts helps us to understand human sexuality and may lead to drugs that enhance or diminish our love for another. *Nature, 457,* 7226–7228.

Young, M.Y. & Gardner, R.C. (1990). Modes of acculturation and second language proficiency. *Canadian Journal of Behavioural Science, 22,* 59–71.

Younger, J.C., Walker, L. & Arrowood, A.J. (1977). Post decision dissonance at the fair. *Personality and Social Psychology Bulletin, 3,* 284–287.

Yurchesyn, K.A., Keith, A. &. Renner, K.E. (1992). Contrasting perspectives on the nature of sexual assault provided by a service for sexual assault victims and by the law courts. *Canadian Journal of Behavioural Science, 24,* 71–85.

Zagefka, H., Noor, M., Brown, R., De Moura, G.R. & Hopthrow, T. (2011). Donating to disaster victims: Responses to natural and humanely caused events. *European Journal of Social Psychology, 41,* 353–363.

Zajonc, R.B. (1965). Social facilitation. *Science, 149,* 269–274.

Zajonc, R.B. (1968). Attitudinal effects of mere exposure. *Journal of Personality and Social Psychology, Monograph Supplement, 9,* 1–27.

Zajonc, R.B. (1970). Brainwashing: Familiarity breeds comfort. *Psychology Today (February),* 32–35, 60–62.

Zajonc, R.B. & Markus, H. (1982). Affective and cognitive factors in preferences. *Journal of Consumer Research, 9,* 123–131.

Zak, P.J., Stanton, A.A. & Ahmadi, A. (2007). Oxytocin increases generosity in humans. *PLoS ONE, 2*(11), e1128.

Zanna, M.P. & Rempel, J.K. (1988). Attitudes: A new look at an old concept. In Bar-Tal, D. & Kruglanski, A.W. (Eds). *The social psychology of knowledge* (pp. 315–334). New York: Cambridge University Press.

Zaragoza, M.S. & Mitchell, J.J. (1996). Repeated exposure to suggestion and the creation of false memories. *Psychological Science, 7,* 294–300.

Zborowski, M. (1969). *People in pain.* San Francisco: Jossey-Bass.

Zebrowitz, L.A. (2003). Aging stereotypes – Internalization or inoculation? A commentary. *The Journals of Gerontology: Series B: Psychological*

Sciences and Social Sciences, 58B(4), P214–P215.

Zeigler-Hill, V. & Terry, C. (2007). Perfectionism and explicit self-esteem: the moderating role of implicit self-esteem. *Self and Identity, 6*, 137–153.

Zentall R. (2010). Justification of effort by humans and pigeons: Cognitive dissonance or contrast? *Current Directions in Psychological Science, 19*, 296–300.

Zick, A., Pettigrew, T.F. & Wagner, U. (2008). Ethnic prejudice and discrimination in Europe. *Journal of Social Issues, 64*(2), 233–251.

Ziegler, R., Diehl, M. & Ruther, A. (2002). Multiple source characteristics and persuasion: Source inconsistency as a determinant of message scrutiny. *Personality and Social Psychology Bulletin, 28*, 496–508.

Zillmann, D. (1984). Transfer of excitation in emotional behavior. In J.T. Cacioppo & R.E. Petty (Eds), *Social psychophysiology: A sourcebook* (pp. 215–240). New York: Guilford Press.

Zillmer, E.A., Harrower, M., Ritzler, B.A. & Archer, R.P. (1995). *The quest for the Nazi personality: A psychological investigation of Nazi war criminals*. Hillsdale: Erlbaum.

Zimbardo, P.G. (1969). The human choice: Individuation, reason, and order versus deindividuation, impulse, and chaos. *Nebraska Symposium on Motivation, 17*, 237–307.

Zimbardo, P.G. (1970). The human choice: Individuation, reason, and order versus deindividuation, impulse, and chaos. In W.J. Arnold & D. Levine (Eds), *Nebraska symposium on motivation* (Vol. 17). (pp. 237–307). Lincoln: University of Nebraska Press.

Zimbardo, P.G. (2007). *The Lucifer Effect: How good people turn evil*. London: Random House.

Zimbardo, P.G., Haney, C., Banks, W.C. & Jaffe, D. (1982). The psychology of imprisonment. In J.C. Brigham & L.Wrightsman (Eds), *Contemporary issues in social psychology* (4th ed.). (pp. 230–235). Monterey, CA: Brooks/Cole.

Zuber, J.A., Crott, H.W. & Werner, J. (1992). Choice shift and group polarization: An analysis of the status of arguments and social decision schemes. *Journal of Personality and Social Psychology, 62*, 50–61.

Zuckerman, M., DePaulo, B.M. & Rosenthal, R. (1981). Verbal and non-verbal communication of deception. In L. Berkowitz (Ed.). *Advances in Experimental Social Psychology* (pp. 1–59). New York: Academic Press.

Zuckerman, M., Koestner, R. & Alton, A.O. (1984). Learning to detect deception. *Journal of Personality and Social Psychology, 46*, 519–528.

Zuroff, D.C. (1989). Judgements of the frequency of social stimuli: How schematic is personal memory? *Journal of Personality and Social Psychology, 56*, 890–898.

Zuwerink, J.R. & Devine, P.G. (1996). Attitude importance and resistance to persuasion: It's not just the thought that counts. *Journal of Personality and Social Psychology, 70*, 931–944.

GLOSSARY

abstinence violation effect (15) If people recovering from substance abuse slip backwards, they may attribute the slip to themselves, and experience the slip as dissonant, after which they tend to relapse.

accent (7) How consonants and vowels are pronounced.

acculturation (13) The process that occurs when groups come into contact with one another, resulting in changes in the original cultural patterns.

action research (Introduction) Studies in which the data are fed back into a system in order to influence change.

actor/observer bias (2) The tendency to attribute our own behaviour to situations and the behaviour of others to dispositions.

additive bilingualism (7) Bilingualism of members of a majority language group for whom bilingualism represents the acquisition of a socially useful skill.

adversary procedure (15) A trial system in which both sides are responsible for gathering their own evidence and presenting their own case to a neutral judge and/or jury.

affect regulation hypothesis (8) Securely attached people can deal with strong emotions such as fear or anger through their attachment to another person even in that person's absence.

affiliation (8) Being with others.

agency (3) A concern with achieving goals and being active in the world.

agentic state (6) Acting on behalf of authority rather than one's own values and desires.

aggression (11) Behaviour that is intended to harm or destroy another person.

altruism (9) Actions that are carried out voluntarily to help someone without expectations of reward from external sources. Sometimes used to mean such behaviour without expectation of internal self-reward either (see *prosocial behaviour*).

altruistic personality (9) Associated with higher internalized standards of justice and responsibility and with greater empathy, self-control and integrity.

anchoring (2) Integrating an unfamiliar cognition into an existing social cognitive structure.

androgens (11) Male sex hormones.

anxious/ambivalent attachment (8) Feeling that others are not as close as one would wish, sometimes clinging to partners.

arbitration (10) A process by which the intervener in a conflict reaches a decision about what is a fair resolution to the conflict; the decision is usually binding.

archival approach (1) Approach in which the researcher uses data that have already been collected and tabulated for some other purpose by someone else.

arousal: cost–reward model of helping (9) As physiological arousal increases the probability of helping increases, determined by the rewards and costs of various possible actions.

aschematic (3) Without schema; when a characteristic is not included in self-schema.

attachment (8) A state of intense emotional bonding with someone.

attempt-suppressing signals (7) Non-verbal cues used by a speaker in a conversation to prevent interruption.

attitude (4) A relatively stable pattern of beliefs, feelings and behavioural tendencies towards some object.

attitude congeniality (5) Attitudes bias memory in favour of attitudinally agreeable information – so that we tend to remember information consistent with our attitudes and forget about the information that conflicts with our attitudes.

attribution (2) An inference of the reason for, or cause of, a person's behaviour.

attributional model of loneliness (8) The experience of loneliness depends on a person believing a stable personal explanation for being alone or isolated.

attributional model of romantic love (8) A person experiences a state of physiological arousal where cues lead the person to attribute the arousal to romantic love.

attributional theory of crowding (14) Postulates that people who feel crowded first experience arousal because of violations of personal space and then attribute this arousal to the crowded situation.

audience effects (6) The effect of passive observers on performance.

authoritarianism (11, 14) A personality syndrome characterized by cognitive rigidity, prejudice and an excessive concern with power.

autokinetic effect (6) An illusion in which a stationary spot of light in a dark environment appears to be moving.

availability heuristic (2) A strategy of making judgements in terms of information that readily comes to mind.

averaging model (2) The hypothesis that our overall impression of someone is the sum of our evaluations of the person with regard to various traits, divided by the number of traits evaluated.

avoidant attachment (8) Feeling uncomfortable when too close or intimate with someone.

baby talk (7) The manner in which adults talk to two- to five-year-olds.

back-channel communication (7) Non-verbal signals from listeners indicating attention and interest in a conversation.

bandwagon effect (6) Conformity with an assumption that if everybody is doing it, it must be right.

behavioural mimicry (6, 7, 9, 14) Automatic and *non-conscious* imitation of another person's movements and gestures.

behaviourism (1) A psychological theory based on the premise that behaviour is governed by external reinforcement.

belief in a just world (2,15) The belief that good outcomes only happen to good people and bad outcomes only happen to bad people; you get what you deserve.

blind (of an experimental participant) (1) Unaware of which experimental group one is in, e.g., unaware of whether one is receiving an intervention or a placebo.

bogus pipeline (4) An attitude measurement technique in which the respondents are led to believe that some electrodes attached to them will reveal their real attitudes, thereby inducing them to self-report attitudes accurately.

brainstorming (6) The uncritical and uninhibited expression of ideas, usually in a group setting.

Byrne's law (8) Attraction to a stranger is a function of the proportion of similar attitudes.

bystander effect (9) When people witness an emergency, the probability of any particular person helping decreases with the number of other people present.

case study (1) An in-depth investigation and analysis of a single instance of a phenomenon of interest.

catharsis (11) Reduction in arousal, e.g., anger, as a result of acting out or observing the actions of someone else.

causal inference (1) A conclusion about cause and effect.

central route persuasion (5) Attitude change that follows logical argumentation and thought about the issue.

central trait (2) A characteristic of people that determines how we evaluate them on other characteristics.

character strengths (4) A set of self-described values representing keys to living a life that is, at once, personally fulfilling and morally sound.

charisma (12) Exceptional personal qualities in some leaders that enable them to attract many committed followers.

charismatic leader (12) Also *transformational leader*. A leader with an exceptional quality that enables him or her to gather a large number of disciples by appearing to possess extraordinary capabilities.

Chicken game (10) A game in which the payoff matrix is such that mutual competitive response are disastrous.

chronemics (7) The use of pauses and silences in communication.

coaction effects (6) A situation in which people work or perform in a similar way at the same time and place without interacting.

code of honour (11) Related to aggression, a set of cultural beliefs that insist on violent retribution for actions perceived to bring dishonour to the individual or the family.

cognitive dissonance (1, 5) A state of uncomfortable arousal that occurs when one cognition is logically opposed to another.

cognitive neo-associationist model of aggression (11) A revision of the frustration–aggression hypothesis in which an aversive stimulus triggers a fight or flight response depending on whether the thoughts triggered are related to anger or fear.

cognitive response analysis (5) A contrast is drawn between instances that involve thought (elaboration) and instances that do not involve thought (invoking a rule of thumb).

cognitive scripts (11) Event schemata that tell us what is likely to occur in a given situation, how we should respond, and what is the likely outcome.

cohesiveness (12) Extent to which members are attracted to a group.

collective behaviour (14) Relatively unorganized and unplanned actions that emerge spontaneously among a collectivity of people as a result of inter-stimulation among them. These actions are not governed by social norms.

collective dilemma (10) A situation in which the individually rational actions of a number of people produce an outcome that is undesirable for all involved.

collectivism (3,4) A set of norms and values that stress the group or community rather than the individual.

commitment calibration (8) People act to save the relationship when adversity and commitment are more-or-less equivalent.

commons problem (10) A situation in which a response which would be rational for one person (adding one cow to the herd) would be disastrous when everyone does it.

communal relationships (8, 13) Relationships built not on maximizing one's own rewards, but on providing a benefit for the other and continuing the relationship.

communication accommodation theory (7) The modification of personal speech style to a speech style that is like the person being spoken to.

communicative competence (7) Learning to recognize when and how the intent of a communication in the second language is different from the meaning of the words spoken.

comparison level (10) In exchange theory, the difference between the current outcome and what one considers that one should receive.

comparison level for alternatives (10) In exchange theory, availability of another relationship with more benefits/fewer costs.

compensatory justice (15) When someone has been harmed by the actions of another, restitution is offered.

competition (10) A form of social exchange in which individuals act to maximize their gains in relation to others.

compliance (6) Acquiescent behaviour in response to a direct request.

conflict (10) Discord between two or more parties.

conflict spiral schema (10) A series of escalating threats and counter-threats.

conformity (6) Behaviour that adheres to group norms and yields to perceived group pressures.

conspiracy theory (14) An irrational set of beliefs, or a 'theory' about a supposed group of conspirators. These beliefs are held in common by a group of people, and then applied with a very rational and stubborn logic.

construal level (2) A perception along a continuum from psychologically distant to psychologically close.

constructive reality (6) A view of the world, especially of its ambiguities, that is provided by the group.

contact hypothesis (13) The notion that if members of different groups can get together under certain circumstances, prejudice will be reduced.

contagion (14) The rapid spreading of emotions, attitudes and behaviour throughout a crowd or population.

contagion of anxiety (14) The rapid dissemination of exaggerated fears throughout a populace, often resulting in unrestrained emotionalism.

contagion of enthusiasm (14) The spread of an extraordinary hope or delusion, usually about becoming wealthy.

content analysis (1,3) The systematic study of verbal or written materials to determine underlying trends.

contingency theory (12) A theory attributing leadership effectiveness to a good match between leadership style and aspects of the group situation.

control group post-test design (1) A type of quasi-experiment in which samples from two different groups are measured only once, after the event of interest has taken place.

convergence (7) One's manner of speaking becomes more similar to the other speaker during a conversation.

conversation control (7) Use of non-verbal communication to regulate the form and pace of a conversation.

cooperation (10) A form of social exchange in which two or more parties act together to achieve a shared goal.

copycat aggression (11) Imitative repetition by adults of spectacular crimes of violence recounted in newspapers.

correlational approach (1) An approach to the study of social behaviour based on trying to find which variables 'go together'.

correspondence bias (2) Assuming that an act matches a disposition.

correspondent inference (2) Attribution of an act to a stable disposition.

counterfactual thinking (2) Thoughts about the past in which it is imagined how the outcome of events might have been different.

covariation principle (2) A principle stating that if two events are perceived as occurring together and never separately, one will be interpreted as the cause of the other.

cross-categorization (12) A situation in which a person is similar to others on one dimension but different from them on another.

cross-cultural research (Introduction) Studies in which subjects from more than one society or ethnic group are compared.

cross-lagged procedure (11) Method of comparing correlations between two variables over two points in time in order to infer which is more likely to be a cause of the other.

crowd (14) A relatively large collection of people physically close enough to influence each other's behaviour although there is no particular relationship among them.

crowding (14) A subjective state of discomfort arising from the perception that there are too many people present.

cultural display rules (7) Rules about non-verbal communication such as appropriate facial expressions, postures, gaze, distance to keep between oneself and others, how to orient one's body during interactions and when to engage in touch.

dangerous game (10) A mixed-motive conflict in which, if neither side backs down, both may suffer catastrophic losses.

Dark Triad (personality traits) (11) A combination of narcissism, psychopathy, and Machiavellianism.

debriefing (1) Following an experiment, discussing with the subjects the true nature of the experiment and exposing any deception.

deception cues (15) Behaviour that suggests an individual is lying.

de-hoaxing (1) As part of debriefing, informing subjects that they have been deceived and explaining the purpose of the experiment.

deindividuation (14) A complex process in which individuals come to see themselves more as members of a group than as individuals, leading to a lowered threshold for normally restrained behaviour.

demand characteristics (1) Characteristics of an experimental situation that seem to cry out for a certain response, thus biasing results.

density–intensity hypothesis (14) The hypothesis that high-density situations magnify our usual reactions so that they tend to seem either extremely unpleasant, or quite pleasant and exciting.

density–social pathology hypothesis (14) The hypothesis that population density itself produces or is in some way related to high rates of crime and mental illness.

dependent variable (1) A variable that is being measured and that is hypothesized to relate to some other variable (the independent variable).

depersonalization (12) We come to see ourselves not as unique individuals, but as prototypical members of the groups and categories to which we belong.

desensitization (debriefing) (1) Part of debriefing; intended to help the subjects accept the new information they have about themselves, and to put it into context and respond to questions and anxieties that might arise.

desensitization (to violence) (11) Decrease in reactivity to violence as a result of having witnessed violence on television or elsewhere.

deterrence schema (10) The assumption that a realistic threat can prevent war or other hostile acts.

dialect (7) A form of a language spoken by people in a particular geographic region or social class.

differential susceptibility model (11) Suggests that as a result of genetic variation, some brains are more 'plastic' than others, and the greater the plasticity, the more the development of the brain will be affected by environmental factors as the person is growing up.

diffusion of responsibility (9) A tendency for the individual to feel less of a sense of personal duty to act in a prosocial manner when others are present.

dignity culture (3) A culture in which your self-evaluation and your self-respect are derived from your value as a unique person.

direct speech (7) The meaning of the sentence is consistent with the speaker's meaning.

discounting cue hypothesis (5) An hypothesis stating that when the source of a communication is not trusted, the message tends to be disregarded.

discounting principle (2) In attributions, the principle that the role of one factor is perceived as less important if other plausible causes are present.

discrimination (13) Negative actions directed to members of a specific group.

discursive method (1) A research approach based on studying how people use language to construct reality and memory.

dispositional loneliness (8) Unpleasant emotional state arising out of perceived deficiencies in relationships due to the perceiver's innate disposition.

distraction-conflict theory (6) The theory that when people are in the presence of others, information overload causes them to concentrate on the task.

distributive justice (15) The conditions under which the allocation of a resource or the outcome of an event would be judged as just or unjust.

divergence (7) Individuals deliberately emphasize the differences between their speech style and that of another person.

door-in-the-face (6) When a first request is so extreme that the person is likely not to comply, compliance is more likely to a second, smaller request.

double-blind (1) A control in research whereby neither the subject nor the experimenter who interacts with the subject knows which condition the subject has been assigned to.

double-coded speech (7) Meaning is conferred both by the grammar and by the way in which the words are said.

downward comparison (3) A tendency to evaluate ourselves with reference to people who are lower in status or advantage.

dual-processing model (6) Conforming because of informational and normative influences.

dual-systems model (2) A theory of two modes of thinking: rapid, automatic, unconscious, and slow, deliberate, conscious.

egocentric bias (8) People tend to overestimate their own contributions, e.g., in self-disclosure.

ego-defensive functions (4) The ability of certain attitudes to protect or enhance the self-esteem of the person who holds them.

ego depletion (3) One's capacity for self-regulation is impaired for some time after exhibiting self-control.

elaboration likelihood model (5) A theory that central and peripheral routes of attitude change are differentiated by the amount of cognitive activity involved.

emotion-expression model (7) Hypothesis that facial displays, including smiles, are innately linked to emotion and are therefore universal.

emotional loneliness (8) Loneliness due to a lack of intimate relationships.

empathy (9) A vicarious emotional response (a feeling) elicited by and congruent with the perceived emotional state of another person.

empathy–altruism hypothesis (9) Pure altruism is elicited as a result of a vicarious emotional response induced by witnessing a person in distress.

equity theory (8,15) A relationship is adversely affected if one or both partners feel that they receive less than they give relative to the other person.

Eros (11) The life instinct, according to Freud.

estrogens (11) Female sex hormones.

ethnocentrism (13) A belief in the superiority of one's own ethnic or cultural groups.

ethnolinguistic vitality (7) The relative status and strength of a language in a particular social structure, reflecting the proportion of the population that speaks the language.

eudaimonic well-being (15) Defines well-being in terms of living a life that is personally meaningful.

evaluation apprehension (1, 6) A concern about the assessment of one's behaviour.

event schema (2) A set of interconnected cognitions about a specific occurrence or type of occurrence.

exchange relationships (8) Relationships built on an economic model, in which people seek to maximize benefits and minimize costs.

excitation transfer theory (11) Intensification of an emotional reaction to a new stimulus brought about by residues of nervous system arousal from an earlier emotional reaction.

experimental method (1) A research approach in which subjects are randomly assigned to two or more groups and an independent variable is varied, in order to assess its effect on a dependent variable.

experimental realism (1) The extent to which the experimental situation 'grabs' subjects and involves them so that they react naturally to the situation rather than as they might think appropriate to the laboratory situation.

experimenter effects (1) Biases in an experiment due to the influence of the experimenter, who, knowing the hypothesis under study, can unintentionally influence the subjects to act in a way that confirms the hypothesis.

external validity (1) The degree to which the behaviour observed in the laboratory corresponds to 'real' behaviour in the outside world.

extraneous variable (1) A variable that might interfere with the outcome of the research.

extrinsically oriented religiosity (9) Views being religious as a way of achieving other goals, such as gaining power and influence.

face culture (3) Your self-respect is derived from your position in society and how others perceive you.

facial feedback hypothesis (14) Emotional experience is directly affected by the feedback our brains receive about our facial expressions.

fad (14) A short-lived, extreme and frivolous, collective behaviour.

false consensus effect (2) The tendency to overestimate the extent to which others act or think as we do.

false hope syndrome (3) A pattern of unrealistic expectations about eventual success after repeated failures.

fashion (14) A widespread collective preference that is relatively short-lived.

feared self (3) The kind of person you would not want to become.

field experiment (1) The use of the experimental method in a natural setting, in which the subjects are not aware that they are subjects.

field study (1) Direct observation of people in a natural setting.

file-drawer problem (1) A study with non-significant findings that is never presented to the public.

final-offer arbitration (10) In a conflict, each side presents the arbitrator with its final position and the arbitrator then selects one or the other, so that there is no compromise.

fMRI (1, 3) Functional magnetic resonance imagery, a means of measuring activity in a specific brain area through blood flow to that area.

foot-in-the-door (6) If you can induce someone to agree to a small request, that person is subsequently more likely to agree to carry out a larger request.

forgiveness (9) A prosocial response in which the recipient of malice or harm excuses or absolves the transgressor.

free rider (10) Someone who benefits from a public good without contributing.

front-to-back communications failure (14) A situation in which people at the front of a crowd trying to escape from danger are trampled because those at the back, unaware that people at the front are unable to move more quickly, continue to push ahead.

frustration–aggression hypothesis (11) The hypothesis that aggression follows frustration and frustration precedes aggression.

fundamental attribution error (2) Tendency of people to exaggerate the importance of personal dispositions as the causes of behaviour.

gain/loss effect (8) In a social interaction, the tendency for a person to be more attracted to someone who expresses increasing liking or praise for him or her than to someone who expresses constant liking or praise.

game theory (10) A model of social conflict in which people are assumed to act rationally in order to maximize their gains and minimize their losses.

gender schematic (11) A characteristic of individuals who tend generally to view males and females in terms of sex-typed dimensions.

General Aggression Model (11) A comprehensive theory of aggression including the effects of biological factors, personality, social processes, basic cognitive processes and decision-making processes.

general uncertainty (14) Widely held doubt and apprehension within a collectivity of people that is likely to give rise to rumours.

gene-culture co-evolution theory (9) As ideas, knowledge, and skills are transmitted via social learning across generations within a society, some aspects of this cultural heritage are more likely to promote survival of the group than others and therefore will be subject to the pressures of natural selection.

generic norm of out-group discrimination (12) Disposition to reject or discriminate against members of all out-groups, regardless of the group or context.

genocide neglect (9) While we can relatively easily process information about a single individual in need and feel empathy for that person, it is difficult to experience an empathic response to large numbers of unidentifiable people.

glass ceiling (12) Barriers that prevent women from rising up to the top of an organizational structure.

glass cliff (12) Women are more likely to be made leaders during times of crisis in an organization.

gratitude (9) A prosocial response in which the recipient of others' good deeds is appreciative.

great person approach to leadership (12) Leadership emerges from personal characteristics, including inherited characteristics of the leader.

group (12) (a) Small group research: A collection of people distinguished by common goals and stable relationships rather than superficial similarities. (b) Social Identity Theory and Self-Categorization Theory: A category to which people belong, such as religion, nationality, ethnic group or gender.

groupthink (6) Tendency of a highly cohesive and elitist group to achieve a rapid consensus without dissent or outside influences.

group-induced polarization effect (12) Group decisions are more risky or more cautious than the average of the individual decisions.

group socialization (12) Process of becoming part of the group, being accepted by it and learning to adapt to its norms and rules.

haptics (7) The use of touch as communication.

hate (13) An enduring, relatively intense negative emotion toward some person or group.

health beliefs model (15) A theory that accounts for health-related behaviour in terms of recognizing a personally relevant threat and a choice of actions.

hedonic well-being (15) Defined in terms of one's emotional states, positive and negative, and satisfaction with life.

heroism (9) Prosocial intervention in the face of extraordinary risk.

heterosexuality subschema (11) A schema that, when primed, leads to viewing interactions with people of the opposite sex in sexual terms.

heuristics (2) Assumptions and biases that guide our decisions about uncertain events.

hostile aggression (11) Aggression that expresses anger or some other negative emotion (contrast with *instrumental aggression*).

hostile masculinity (11) An insecure, distrustful, defensive and hypersensitive orientation towards others, especially women, as well as gratification from dominating and controlling women.

hypertension (15) High blood pressure.

hypothesis (1) A testable proposition derived from theory.

hypothetical construct (1) A concept which does not have a physical existence but is used to represent a reality.

hysterical contagion (14) The spread of a strong emotional reaction, sometimes accompanied by apparent physical symptoms that in reality have no physical cause.

ideal self (3) A self-guide embodying one's hopes and aspirations: 'myself as I wish I were'.

identifiable victim effect (9) Greater willingness to provide assistance to a single sufferer.

identity fusion (12) A 'visceral feeling of oneness' with the group.

ideology (4) A more or less integrated or coherent set of attitudes, often political.

idiosyncrasy credit (6, 12) Tolerance for nonconformity to group norms by a high-status member who is perceived to have contributed much to the group.

imposed norm hypothesis (7) The non-standard form of a language is viewed negatively because of social norms that are biased against it.

individualism (3, 4) A cultural value which emphasizes the individual person as opposed to the group.

inherent value hypothesis (7) Standard dialect becomes the prestige form of the language because it is the aesthetically ideal form of that language.

illusion of control (2) A commonly held and exaggerated belief that people can determine their lives and the events around them.

illusory correlation (2, 13) Perception that two variables are related to one another when they are not.

image-repair hypothesis (9) The idea that a person who is embarrassed by his or her behaviour may help others in order to improve a damaged image.

immersion programme (7) A form of second-language education in which the second language is used for instruction and interaction rather than being treated as a separate subject.

implicit attitude (4) Attitudes not fully in consciousness.

implicit personality theory (2) The assumptions of people about which traits go together and about human nature.

impression management (3) Actions taken by individuals to control or influence how others evaluate them.

in-group (12) A social category to which a person belongs.

independent variable (1) The variable manipulated (varied) by the experimenter in a psychological experiment.

indirect speech (7) The meaning of the sentence is not consistent with the speaker's meaning.

individualistic bias (4) A North American ideal of the self-contained person, which has influenced the definition of concepts and problems in social psychology.

individualistic culture (3) A set of norms and values that stress the individual rather than the group or community.

informational social influence (6) The matching of our own ideas to the group in order to determine whether they are 'correct'.

informed consent (1) Agreement of subjects to participate in an experiment after being told what will happen to them.

infrahumanization (12) People tend to attribute fewer uniquely human traits to members of an out-group.

ingratiation (3) Strategies of enhancing our attractiveness to others in order to create a positive impression.

inoculation effect (5) An effect by which exposure to relatively weak arguments against our own position strengthens our later resistance to persuasion.

inquisitorial procedure (15) A courtroom approach in which the judge is assigned a role in collecting evidence and questioning witnesses.

instinct (11) Supposed inborn behavioural tendencies that motivate certain actions.

instrumental aggression (11) Behaviour intended to harm as a means to some desired end (contrast to *hostile aggression*).

instrumental function (4) A function served by an attitude that brings rewards or lessens costs.

instrumental values (4) Preferred modes of conduct, such as honesty or thrift.

integrative complexity (2) Extent to which people can use several schemata and standards in a flexible way when processing information.

interactionist approach (12) Research that takes into account both individual and group influences.

intergroup anxiety (13) Negative feelings regarding anticipated adverse consequences of contact between groups.

interindividual–intergroup discontinuity effect (10) As individuals yield to group pressures about excessive competitiveness, the group as a whole typically becomes much more competitive and less cooperative than one would expect on the basis of the motivations of the particular individuals involved.

interpersonal balance model (8) Liking someone tends to be accompanied by perceived similarity in attitudes.

interpersonal–intergroup continuum (12) At the interpersonal end, interactions between people are the result of their personal relationships with each other and their individual characteristics, while at the intergroup extreme, their social group membership determines their behaviour toward one another.

internal validity (1) Degree to which changes in behaviour were brought about by experimental manipulations rather than extraneous factors.

intrinsically oriented religiosity (9) A view of religion as an end in itself.

investment model (8) A model of intimate relationships that considers commitment to a relationship in terms of the investment put into the relationship.

jealousy (8) An unpleasant reaction to a perceived rival, arising out of social comparison or a desire for exclusivity.

kernel-of-truth hypothesis (13) The idea that social stereotypes are necessarily based on some supportable evidence.

kinesics (7) All bodily movements except those that involve contact with someone else; the 'body language' of popular literature.

kin selection (9) A putative process in which helping relatives survive long enough to reproduce improves the chances of being able to pass our genes on to the next generation.

kinship principle (9) Hypothesized motivation to provide help primarily to close relatives.

Kohler motivation gain effect (6) When less capable members of a group perform better when performing with others, relative to performing the same task on their own.

knowledge function (4) A function served by an attitude that helps one make sense of the world.

laboratory experiment (1) The use of the experimental method in a laboratory setting.

language (7) A system of vocal sounds, writing or formal gestures embodying symbols that have meaning in communication.

leader (12) An individual in a group who has the greatest influence over other members.

leakage (15) Behaviour that unintentionally reveals the truth when a person is lying.

legitimate power (12) Our capacity to influence others based on their acceptance of our authority.

Likert summated ratings (4) A method of attitude self-report in which the respondent is asked to indicate agreement or disagreement with a series of statements.

locus of control (9) The extent to which people believe that the events in their lives are caused by their own actions (internal), or by luck, higher forces, or other powerful people (external).

loneliness (8) Unpleasant emotional state arising out of perceived deficiencies in relationships.

longitudinal study (1) Research in which two or more variables are studied in the same subjects at several different points over a span of time.

looking-glass self (3) A self-concept constructed from the way we appear to others, which is then reflected back to us.

loss effect (8) In a social interaction, the tendency for a person to be less attracted to someone who expresses decreasing liking or praise than to someone who expresses constant dislike or criticism.

loss of control (14) A sense of not being in control in a high-density situation, leading to feelings of helplessness and vulnerability.

lost letter technique (9) Dropping on the sidewalk a sealed and stamped letter addressed to the researcher and comparing rates of return in various conditions.

low-ball technique (6) A means of inducing someone to carry out a requested act by first requesting him or her to carry out the act, and only then increasing the cost of fulfilling the request.

marginality (7) A feeling experienced by immigrants or people learning a new language of being estranged from their own group, yet not part of the new group.

mass emergency behaviour (14) Includes all possible crowd behaviours, both mass panic and rational escape activity, that can occur in a mass emergency event.

mass emergency event (14) When panic flight does occur, it is because an avenue of escape is available but is closing quickly.

mass panic (14) A contagion of fear, when people in a crowd are frightened and in danger; it is not surprising that they try to escape the danger in a great hurry.

mass psychogenic illness (14) Symptoms of physical illness, without any physical basis, that spread through a collectivity of people.

mediation (10) Third-party intervention in a conflict that assists in the negotiation process but does not impose solutions.

mediating variable (1) A variable which explains a relationship between other variables.

mere exposure effect (8) Familiarity with a novel stimulus usually leads to more positive ratings and greater attraction.

meta-analysis (1) A method of statistically combining the results of many different studies on the same topic in order to identify consistent patterns in these results.

meta-contrast principle (12) We accentuate similarities within the category and exaggerate differences between groups.

Michelangelo phenomenon (8) Intimate partners in long-term relationships influence each other's personality characteristics, interests and aspirations.

mind guards (12) Members of a decision-making group who filter information from outside so that the group remains largely unaware of external, dissenting opinions.

mirror neurons (6, 9, 14) When we passively observe another person's bodily movements, particular motor neurons in our brains respond selectively to activate muscles in our bodies corresponding to those that are involved in the observed behaviour.

mixed motive game (10) A conflict in which there are rewards for both competition and cooperation.

M'Naghten Rule (15) A principle of law in which a person is not held legally responsible for an action if he or she did not know the nature and quality of the act or did not know that the action was wrong.

MODE model (4) Motivation and opportunity as determinants of whether deliberate or spontaneous actions are taken between attitudes and behaviour.

model (1) A mini-theory, or set of propositions and assumptions, about a specific phenomenon.

moderating variable (1) A variable that influences the strength of a relationship between other variables.

modern racism (13) People are ambivalent, they want to see themselves as unprejudiced but still harbour feelings of discomfort or worse towards certain groups.

moral development (9) The process by which the capacity for moral judgements matures throughout childhood.

morpheme (7) Unit of meaning in language.

motive-communication model (7) Posits that facial displays are deliberately used to communicate particular social motives to the individuals being addressed.

multiculturalism hypothesis (13) The contention that positive feelings towards members of other groups vary with how secure and comfortable people feel about their own cultural identity and background.

mundane realism (1) Extent to which a situation encountered in an experiment is perceived as naturalistic or corresponding to some real-life situation.

mutuality (8) A relationship characterized by some degree of involvement, commitment and intimacy between two people.

narcissism (3) Complete self-absorption, living for yourself and for the moment, with no concern for the community, the past or the future.

need for approval (9) People with this need court the admiration of others.

need for cognition (5) A propensity to analyse the situation, search for clues and information and work on solving difficult problems.

negative-state relief hypothesis (9) The hypothesis that an observer's empathic response to a sufferer's distress produces personal sadness, and that the individual acts to help the sufferer because of the egoistic motivation to relieve his or her own sadness (negative-state).

negativity effect (2) Tendency for overall impressions of people to be more influenced by negative than by positive traits.

neosexism (13) A form of gender attitudes defined as a manifestation of a conflict between egalitarian values and residual negative feelings towards women.

non-reactive measure (1) A measurement that cannot influence the behaviour being considered.

non-verbal communication (7) The sending of information to another person (or persons) without the use of words.

non-zero-sum game (10, 12) A conflict situation in which some outcomes are mutually preferable – a mixed-motive game.

norm activation model (9) That prosocial behaviour flows from *personal* norms that involve moral obligations to act, triggered by a sense of personal responsibility for possible consequences and a capacity to act.

norm of equity (9) The generally shared belief that fairness should serve as a criterion for the way that we treat others.

norm of reciprocity (9) The generally shared belief that people should help those who have helped them. In self-disclosure, a tendency for people to respond in kind to self-disclosure.

norm of social responsibility (9) The generally shared belief that people should help those who need help.

normative influence (6) Influence that leads to actions consistent with the norms of the group, even when contrary to personal beliefs.

obedience (6) Acquiescent behaviour in response to a direct order.

objectification (2) A process by which an abstract idea becomes part of concrete experience.

observational learning (6) The experience of modelling influence through which a novel behaviour is acquired.

oculesics (7) Eye movement and gaze.

operational definition (1) A definition of a construct in terms of how it is measured.

opinion leaders (6) Highly influential people who transmit new attitudes to many others.

ostracism (6) Rejection by the group.

ought self (3) A self-guide reflecting the obligations we place on ourselves, our own sense of duty and responsibility: myself as I should be.

out-group (12) A social category to which an individual does not belong.

out-group homogeneity effect (12) The effect by which members of another group are perceived to be more similar to one another than are the members of one's own group to each other.

paralanguage (7) Non-verbal aspects of speech that convey information.

paralinguistic drawl (7) The practice of speaking the final syllable in an utterance in a slow, drawn-out fashion.

parallel response model (5) People respond to a fear-arousing message, both to avert the danger mentioned in the message and to cope with the unpleasant feelings engendered by the message.

participant observer (1) A researcher who participates in the group being studied.

particularism (8) In social exchange, the extent to which the value of a resource is influenced by the person who provides it.

perceived norm (4) An expectation of how significantly other people would react to a particular action by a person.

perfectionism (3) Tendency to hold unrealistically high self-guides, unrealistic standards for the self.

peripheral route persuasion (5) Attitude change not accompanying deliberate thought about the issue, usually occurring in association with distractors.

person-oriented leader (12) Leader with focus on social-emotional concerns; gives high rating to least-preferred co-worker.

person schema (2) A set of interconnected cognitions about a specific individual.

personal anxiety (14) Anxiety produced by apprehension about an imminent and disappointing outcome; contributes to development of rumours.

personal space (7) The comfortable physical distance that we maintain between ourselves and others.

persuasibility (5) The extent to which a person can be readily persuaded.

phenomenological approach (1) A research approach based on the experience of the participants.

phonemes (7) The system of short, meaningless sounds.

positive illusions (8) A somewhat unrealistic optimism about oneself, the world and the future is beneficial to mental and physical well-being.

positivity bias (2) A tendency to perceive others in a favourable light.

post-decision dissonance (5) A state of psychological discomfort that occurs after a difficult choice has been made.

prejudice (13) Illogical, inaccurate and unjustifiable attitudes about members of a group.

primacy effect (5) Tendency for information presented early in a sequence to have a greater impact than information presented later.

priming (2) Activation of a particular category or schema by a specific cue.

Prisoner's Dilemma Game (10) A special type of non-zero-sum game where the optimal solution is mutual cooperation.

proactive aggression (11) Intentional harm which is a premeditated means to some desired end and not accompanied by anger.

problem behaviour theory (15) A model of adolescent behaviour based on a syndrome of personal, environmental and behavioural nonconventionality linked with consequences.

procedural justice (15) Relationship between the methods used to arrive at a decision and the perception that the decision was just.

promiscuous-impersonal sex (11) A tendency to avoid commitment and to be unfaithful in sexual relationships.

promise (10) A communication that the other person or group will experience positive consequences if a demand is complied with.

propaganda (5) A type of persuasion, in which important information is withheld, facts are presented selectively and invoking heuristic strategies to elicit 'rapid thinking'.

propinquity effect (8) The principle that when people are in close physical proximity, the probability of interaction and attraction increases.

prosocial behaviour (9) Actions voluntarily carried out for the sole purpose of helping others, without expectation of reward from external sources.

prosodic features of language (7) Non-verbal aspects of speech, such as timing, pitch and loudness.

protection motivation model (15) A model of fear-arousing communication that states that people respond to danger if they believe the danger to be severe and personally relevant.

prototype (2) A typical example of a category.

provision of public goods dilemma (10) Relates to contributions by individuals to the collective or public good that benefit everyone, contributors and non-contributors alike.

proxemics (7) The study of how we use space to regulate our social interactions.

psychological androgyny (3) High scores in both masculine and feminine traits.

psychological realism (1) Extent to which processes occurring in the lab correspond to those in reality.

psychopathic personality (11) A particular cluster of personality traits that has a strong connection with antisocial behaviour (synonymous with *antisocial personality* or *sociopathy*).

public goods dilemma (10) A collective dilemma in which individuals must decide how much to contribute to a public good, knowing that their own contribution will have little or no effect on what they receive in return.

qualitative method (1) A method of studying behaviours that cannot be quantified.

quantitative method (1) Variables are defined by measures and data are aggregated across participants.

quasi-experiment (1) A research method, using a pre-post comparison or a comparison of two groups, that examines the effects of some real-life event or change over which the experimenter has no control.

random assignment (1) Assigning subjects by chance to generate two or more groups that are presumed to be the same with regard to the characteristic being measured, so that the researcher can later judge whether an independent variable led to changes in a dependent variable.

reactive aggression (11) Harmful behaviour which is accompanied by anger.

reactive measure (1) A measurement that may influence the behaviour being considered.

realistic conflict theory (13) In cases where there are limited resources, groups may find themselves in conflict and prejudice can increase.

reciprocal determinism (6) People determine their own environment, which influences behaviour.

reform movement (14) A social movement that accepts the basic structure of a society but seeks to modify a part of it.

regression analysis (1) An extension of basic co-relational analysis that involves more than two predictor variables.

regulatory focus (3) The extent to which people focus on attaining desired outcome or avoiding undesired outcomes.

reinforcement-affect model of attraction (1, 8) The idea that through a process of conditioning, people become attracted to others with whom they associate stimuli or events that arouse positive feelings.

relative deprivation (3, 14, 15) When people compare themselves to other appropriate groups and find that the others are better off, this leads to frustration and discontent, and becomes the basis for social unrest.

reliability (1) The degree to which a measure yields the same results when used more than once to measure some unchanging object, trait or behaviour.

reparative altruism (9) Helping or other prosocial acts performed by someone after having done something harmful in order to compensate for the harm done (not necessarily to the person harmed).

replication (1) Reproducing the results of a scientific study.

representativeness heuristic (2) A cognitive shortcut for making judgements in conditions of uncertainty, whereby we estimate the likelihood that a person or object belongs to a particular category on the basis of how much resemblance there is to members of that category.

reproductive fitness (8) A perception of a prospective partner based on attractiveness, symmetry etc.

repulsion hypothesis (8) Dissimilarity in attitudes produces rejection between people.

resource dilemma (10) A decision faced by individuals about how much of a public resource they should take for their own good, in circumstances where the rational individual choices produce an irrational collective outcome (also known as the 'problem of the commons').

response facilitation (6) Increase in the likelihood that a behaviour will occur in a given situation as a result of modelling influence.

retributive justice (15) Ensuring that the punishment fits the crime.

reverse discrimination (13) Excessively positive actions towards members of a specific group, which may not reflect positive attitudes.

revolutionary movement (14) Social movement that seeks to overthrow the existing social order and replace it with something else.

'rich get richer' hypothesis (8) People who have strong social skills can use them in the context of social media.

right-wing authoritarianism (13) A cluster of personality characteristics involving a high degree of submissiveness to authorities (who are perceived as having legitimate power), strong adherence to conventional social values, and hostility and punitiveness towards people who deviate from those values.

risky shift effect (12) Tendency for some group decisions to involve higher levels of risk than the average individual decision (see *polarization effect*).

role-play (1) A method in which subjects are given a description of a situation by the experimenter and then asked to behave as they think other people would in such a situation.

role schema (2) An organized mental structure about a social category.

Romeo and Juliet effect (8) Romantic love increases as parental interference increases.

rumour (14) A specific proposition or belief, passed along from person to person, usually by word-of-mouth, without secure standards of evidence being present.

sacred values (4) Involves fundamental religious beliefs, national and ethnic identities or moral norms.

sample (1) A relatively small group of subjects taken to be representative of a larger, defined population of interest.

scapegoating (13) A response to frustration whereby the individual displaces aggression onto a socially disapproved out-group.

schema (2) An organized system of cognitions about something such as an event, a role, a type of person or ourselves.

scope of justice (15) The range of situations in which an individual takes into account issues of right and wrong or fairness.

secondary baby talk (7) Speech register similar to that used to talk to babies but used to speak to certain categories of adults, such as the elderly and infirm.

selective exposure to information (4) People will seek out information that decreases cognitive dissonance and avoid information that increases it.

self-concept (3) The sum of feelings, beliefs and impressions that individuals have of themselves.

self-disclosure (8) Revealing information about oneself to another person.

self-discrepancy theory (3) A theory based on the premise that the gaps between actual and possible selves (ideal ought) can lead to emotional difficulty.

self-effacement (3) Tendency to include the negative in how people view themselves.

self-enhancement bias (3, 12) The extent to which individuals seek to maintain or improve their evaluation of themselves.

self-esteem (3) People's evaluation of themselves.

self-fulfilling prophecy (8, 13) A phenomenon whereby people's expectations lead them to behave in a way that causes the expectations to come true.

self-guides (3) The standards to which individuals strive, represented by themselves as they would wish to be and ought to be.

self-handicapping (3) Acting in a way that will interfere with the successful performance of a subsequent task in order to protect one's self-esteem from the effects of failure.

self-monitors (3) People who are unusually sensitive to the subtle responses of others in evaluating their own behaviour.

self–other overlap (9) The extent to which a potential helper feels a sense of oneness with the person to be helped.

self-presentation (3) Acting in ways that create or maintain a positive image of ourselves.

self-promotion (3) A technique of impression management based on an attempt to be seen as unusually competent.

self-reference effect (3) People's tendency to remember information better when they can relate it to themselves.

self-schema (3) An organized set of cognitions, impressions and memories about ourselves.

self-serving bias (2) Attributions motivated by a desire to protect or enhance our own self-esteem.

self-verification (3) Seeking feedback from others that is consistent with our actual self-concept.

semantic differential (4) The rating of a concept along a set of polar adjective scales.

sensory overload (14) The hypothesis that when people are exposed to too much stimulation, sensory inputs are received too fast to be processed. People react by screening out much of the stimulation, paying attention only to what seems important or unusual.

sexism (13) Prejudice towards women.

signal amplification bias (8) A person assumes that the other person can and should take into account their anxieties and recognize how they really feel.

simulation (1) A study using an artificially created situation made to resemble a real-life situation, in which subjects are observed as they act and react to each other and to the situation.

simulation heuristic (2) A cognitive shortcut by which we estimate the likelihood of an event by the ease with which we can imagine it occurring.

single group pre-test/post-test design (1) Quasi-experiment in which subjects are measured before and after some event.

situational approach to leadership (12) The idea that different circumstances call for different kinds of leaders and that the person who happens to have those traits and abilities needed at a particular time will emerge as leader.

sleeper effect (5) Tendency for a communication to increase in persuasiveness over time when emanating from a low-credibility source.

social capital (11) Aspects of community involvement that lead to cooperation among residents.

social categorization (12) Automatically classifying people into categories, or schemata, that we already know something about.

social cognitive neuroscience (1) An interdisciplinary approach that examines interactions among social and neurological factors.

social comparison (1, 3, 8, 12) A tendency for people to evaluate themselves in relation to other people, especially when a situation is ambiguous or uncertain.

social compensation hypothesis (8) People who lack the social skills to find friends and lovers in person tend to use social media for that purpose.

social differentiation (12) Tendency to overestimate the similarities among members of the same category and to overestimate the differences among members of different categories.

social dominance orientation (13) The extent to which people desire to see their own in-groups as dominant over other groups in society and are willing to endorse values and actions that suppress the other groups.

social exchange theory (1, 8, 10) A view of social interaction based on the rewards and costs that people provide for each other.

social impact theory (6) People are affected by social impact that is strong, immediate and emanates from larger group size.

social identification (12) The process whereby individuals define themselves with respect to other people.

social identity theory (12) A theory that posits that the groups to which we belong provide us with a feeling of belonging to the social world, a social identity.

Social Identity Model of Deindividuation Effects (SIDE) (14) In the absence of formal organization and leadership, people in the crowd look to other people close by for cues as to what is the salient social group.

social learning theory (1, 11) A learning experience through the observation of others' actions and the consequences of those actions.

social loafing (6) A decrease in individual effort when co-acting with others.

social loneliness (8) Loneliness reflecting a lack of a network of friends.

social modelling (6) Social influence experienced as a result of observing the behaviour of someone else.

social movement (14) A spontaneous, large collectivity constituted in support of a set of purposes shared by the members.

social pathology hypothesis (14) Suggests that significant overcrowding leads to high rates of crime and mental illness.

social power (12) The capacity to influence another person or group to act in a desired way.

social psychology (Introduction) The discipline that sets out to understand how the thoughts, feelings and behaviours of individuals are influenced by the actual, imagined or implied presence of others.

social representation (2) A schema about persons, roles and events not based solely on personal experience but developed by a group or society and communicated or taught to its members.

social support (5, 15) Relationships with others that provide encouragement, acceptance and assistance.

social value orientation (10) A person's predisposition to act in a cooperative (prosocial) or competitive (proself) manner.

sociobiology (9) An evolutionary theory which states that behaviours are subject to the same evolutionary processes that affect physical characteristics.

sociolinguistic competence (7) Skill at using a language in a social context.

sociometric test (8) Each person in a sample identifies their closest friends.

speech act theory (7) The study of correspondence (or lack thereof) between what the speaker says.

speech register (7) Combination of intonation and pitch within a given speech style that is used in speaking to a particular type of person or in a particular situation.

speech style (7) Manner of speaking a language that is particular to a specific geographic location, social class or educational level.

standard speech style (7) A style of speaking socially defined as desirable or preferable.

statistical significance (1) Refers to results that are unlikely to have occurred by chance.

status marking (14) Actions taken by people to distinguish themselves from people of a different social status.

stereotype (2, 13) A rigid set of cognitions about a group that are applied indiscriminately to all members of the group.

stereotype content model (13) Stereotypes vary along two dimensions: perceived warmth and perceived competence.

stereotype threat (13) Stereotyped individuals are at a disadvantage in a performance situation if they have internalized the stereotype.

stimulus pairing (11) An effect whereby a situational cue (e.g., a gun) elicits an aggressive response because of its past classically conditioned association with violence.

strategy (10) A plan that contains instructions about what to do in every imaginable contingency.

stress (15) A system of challenges to health which includes a stressor and a stress response.

stress-buffering effect (15) People are clearly better able to avoid illness when under stress and to recover from any illness that might develop if they have social support.

structured interview (1) A series of carefully constructed questions.

subtractive bilingualism (7) Bilingualism of members of a minority language group for whom bilingualism is a threat to the continued importance or existence of their first language in that society.

superordinate goal (10) An outcome desired and shared by parties who must cooperate in order to achieve it.

survey method (1) A research technique involving going out and asking questions about the phenomenon of interest, usually using a structured interview or a questionnaire.

symbolic beliefs (13) Beliefs that a particular group threatens or supports social values and norms.

sympathy (9) A heightened awareness of another person's suffering and a desire to eliminate it.

task-oriented leader (12) Person who rates least-preferred co-worker low and focuses on the goals of the group.

temperament (11) How excitable a person is, combined with the ability to calm down.

terminal values (4) Preferences for certain end-states of life, such as freedom or equality.

terror management theory (13) A means of coping with awareness of our own eventual death.

terrorism (10) A violent action meant to bring intense fear to a population by directly and randomly attacking civilian targets.

thanatos (11) According to Freud, a death instinct that at an unconscious level promotes a return to an inanimate state.

'that's-not-all' technique (6) Compliance by offering a product to a person at a high price, preventing the person from responding for a few seconds, and then enhancing the deal either by adding another product or decreasing the price.

theory (1) A set of statements and assumptions that link concepts and hypotheses to observations.

threat (10) A communication that the other person or group will suffer negative consequences unless a demand is complied with.

threat–counter-threat spiral (10) A series of escalating threats by both sides in a conflict.

trade-off reasoning (4) In conditions of value pluralism, a flexible way of thinking in which all sides of an issue are considered, leading to the selection of one value over another.

triangular model of hate (13) A model that defines hate in terms of negation of intimacy, passion (negative) and commitment.

triangular model of love (8) A model that defines love in terms of intimacy, passion and commitment.

tit-for-tat strategy (10) In a series of interactions, each time a participant is cooperative, the confederate produces a cooperative response the next time.

two-step flow of communication (6) Information becomes disseminated first to opinion leaders, then to others.

type-A personality (15) A pattern of competitiveness, impatience and unexpressed anger.

upward comparison (3) A tendency to evaluate ourselves with reference to people who are higher in status or advantage.

utilitarian functions of attitudes (4) Those attitudes serving to maximize rewards and minimize costs to the individual.

utility (10) The importance or value of an outcome to the recipient.

validity (1) Extent to which a measure corresponds to the characteristic that it is intended to measure.

value (4) Central, higher-order set of preferences for goals in life and ways of living that are felt to be ideal and important.

value-expressive function (4) An aspect of an attitude that serves to demonstrate a uniqueness and that reflects one's values.

value justification effect (4) Justifying a particular attitude by relating it to a specific value.

value pluralism (4) Competing values associated with a particular issue.

vicarious reinforcement (6) A positive feeling of reward in response to observing someone else being rewarded.

violence (11) The intentional use of physical force or power, threatened or actual, against oneself, another person, or against a group or community, that either results in or has a high likelihood of resulting in injury, death, psychological harm or deprivation.

virtual group (12) Groups that exist only in that particular electronic environment of the Internet.

volunteerism (9) Use of volunteers to perform charitable or educational work.

volunteer process model (9) While dispositional factors such as personal motives and current circumstances influence the initial decision to volunteer, the person's evaluation of the experience determines whether that individual will continue to volunteer.

warm glow of success (9) An increased tendency to engage in prosocial behaviour under the influence of a good mood induced by success.

weapons effect (11) Cues associated with aggression can promote aggression from an individual in a state of autonomic arousal.

weighted averaging model (2) A model of impression formation in which our overall evaluation of a person consists of the average of how we rate a person on various characteristics, influenced more by those characteristics judged to be more important.

zero-sum game (10) A conflict situation in which one party's gains match exactly the losses of the other.

AUTHOR INDEX

SUBJECT INDEX